The
SECRETS
of BAKING

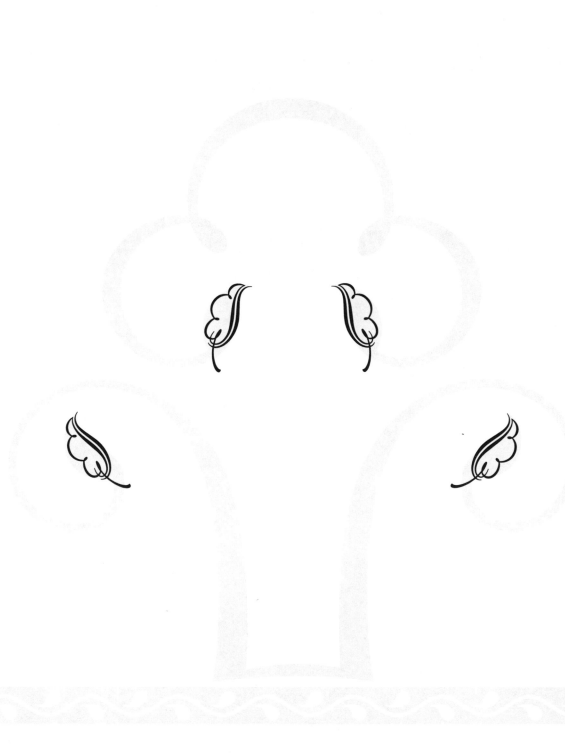

SHERRY YARD

The Secrets of Baking

SIMPLE TECHNIQUES for

SOPHISTICATED DESSERTS

HOUGHTON MIFFLIN COMPANY   BOSTON   NEW YORK

For information about permission to reproduce
selections from this book, write to Permissions,
Houghton Mifflin Company,
215 Park Avenue South,
New York, New York 10003.

Visit our Web site: www.houghtonmifflinbooks.com.

Library of Congress Cataloging-in-Publication Data

Yard, Sherry.
    The secrets of baking / Sherry Yard.
        p.   cm.
    ISBN 0-618-13892-7
    1. Baking. 2. Desserts. I. Title.

    TX765.Y37 2003
    641.8'15—dc21   2003051144

Book design by Anne Chalmers
Cover photographs by Ron Manville
Food styling by Rori Trovato
Prop styling by Yolande Yorke Edgell

PRINTED IN THE UNITED STATES OF AMERICA

RRD 10 9 8 7 6 5 4 3 2

In memory of

"H O O T E R"

(Ann Cartwright–Jest),

My Grandmother

Who taught me to taste

and to dance in marabou pumps

ACKNOWLEDGMENTS

COLLABORATION, INSPIRATION, AND LOVE ARE THE KEYS TO MY EVOLVING life and to this book.

I am truly blessed to have an amazing array of people in my life who teach me on a daily basis that the more I know, the more I should hunger to know.

For their unconditional love, I would like to thank my family: Mom and Dad (Ann and Bill Yard); my sisters, Terry, Laurie, and Lynne; my godson, Blake Andrew Panten; and my fairy godparents, Uncle Peter and Aunt Irene, cousins, nieces, and nephews.

My friends for their support and love through this process: Stephanie, who started this long culinary journey with me at the Coney Island McDonald's, and Martha Forstner, my first friend to get a job in the big city. Jackie and Ted Goldstein, who keep it real for me. Joan, for our midnight walks. Debbie Doodles, for listening. Heidi White, controller and pastry chef, who put up with my bad computer karma. Johnny Romoglia, the best-dressed "gal" in the dining room. Many thanks to Maggie Boone and Jannis Swerman, for their support and organizational skills. Shelly Balloon, for being Shelly Balloon.

My Spago family, Barbara Lazaroff and Wolfgang Puck: Mom and Pop at the local Beverly Hills eating establishment. Lee Hefter, "the general," Matt Bencievenga, and all the chefs who keep the fires rolling in the most dynamic kitchen I have ever experienced. It has been quite a ride.

The cookie monsters of Spago: Tracy, Jenne, Maria, Michael B., Kevin, Ricky, and Jamie.

The runners, Alberto, Flaco, Ricky, Reyes, Efrain, May, Fermin, and Chico, for years have delivered desserts in the speediest manner.

The guests who lick their plates clean every night!

To Janis Donnaud, my agent, who believed in me, pushed me, and guided this project from dream to fruition.

To the *Secrets of Baking* relay team, who helped me turn an idea into a book. Leadoff position, Teri Gelber, for the proposal that came to be. Leslie Bilderbach, for getting it down on paper and adding life to the project. Third leg, Simone Heymann and Suzanne Griswold, for recipe testing. Finally, anchor position, Martha Rose Shulman, the savior, for the amazing polishing up.

Thanks to my mentor Jacques Pépin, for a foreword that made me cry.

To Rux Martin, who saw my vision and believed, and the gang at Houghton Mifflin. Thanks to Anne Chalmers for her beautiful design.

To Ron Manville, for the beautiful photography, and to Rori Trovato and Yolanda Yorke Edgell, who survived the rain.

To the people I have learned from along the way: my instructor/professors at New York City Technical College, Patricia Bartholomew and Julia Jordan. At the Culinary Institute of America, the late Jean-Pierre Le Masson, Joseph McKenna, and Nobel Masse. Susan Notter and Ewald Notter. Donald Wressell, who let me borrow a cup of sugar when I needed it. David Blom, who taught me plated desserts.

A good pastry chef would be nothing without great farmers: the Chino family; Kim and Clarence Blaine; Fitz Kelly; Harry Nichols; Mike Cirrune; Romeo, Bill, and the Coleman Gang; Art Lang; Phil and Arturo at McGraths; Bob Polito; the Pudwills; Frank, Anne, and John Tennerelli: to you, I give my utmost respect and admiration. To Laura, who brings the Santa Monica market together.

A team is like a chain. With one broken link, it does not function. With my whole heart, I would like to thank past and present staff for the lessons that they have taught me. Like pastry angels, they have come into my life, creating the most special desserts with love and dedication. They make me so proud. Sixto Pocasangre, Suzanne Griswold, Elizabeth Gottfried, Xuan Ngo,

Ian Flores, Johnny Ventura, Artemio Sanchez, Jackie Goldstein, Jorgie Lopez, Fredy Garcia, Ana Pelen, Gustavo Escalante, Juan Pocasangre, Julian Saldana, Raul Gutierrez, Giovanni Oajaca, Leta Nichols, Helen Arsen, Steven Peungraksa, Dale Gresch, Annie Miler, Kim Boyce, Anna Delaforice, Gabriella, Leslie Cotterman, Denise Kordan, Miho Haramaki, Richard Carmona, Ashley Morris, Daysi Hernandez, Tara, Tess McDonough.

And, of course, my chocolate Labrador, Chunk, who teaches me to live in the moment.

CONTENTS

FOREWORD

BY JACQUES PÉPIN

I FIRST MET SHERRY YARD IN THE EARLY 1990S WHEN I WAS STAYING AT THE Campton Place Hotel in San Francisco. I couldn't believe that this young woman, who looked like an ebullient first-year cooking student, was in charge of pastry in the prestigious kitchen. Furthermore, she had previously worked in some of the greatest restaurants in New York, from the Rainbow Room to Montrachet to Tribeca Grill. We became friends and still go out for dinner occasionally when I'm in Los Angeles and she has a night off from her duties as pastry chef at Spago Beverly Hills.

Sherry's youthful enthusiasm for anything that has to do with baking and cooking is contagious, and happily for us, she has a profound desire to teach what she knows. The fun side of Sherry belies her serious nature; she is knowledgeable, is thoroughly trained in classical baking, and has the gift of making things clear and comprehensible.

In this bold and masterly book, Sherry shows how to acquire the necessary baking techniques and expand on that general base to create a much larger repertoire. Her structured and organized mind has compiled the great classic desserts and broken them down into traditional categories. Twelve "mother recipes" are the foundation of her book, and each of these fundamental recipes introduces a chapter containing a series of recipes emanating from it. I have always favored this approach in my own teaching, and this logical progression satisfies my Cartesian mind.

Most of the foundations of cooking—and even more so baking, since it is more structured —can and should be taught from mother recipes: custard cream can become ice cream, crème brûlée, or buttercream, or it can be transformed into pastry cream, a base for a soufflé, or a crème chiboust. This process of learning was the classic approach in Paris when I was a child in the 1950s. It teaches not just recipes but how to bake and cook, so that at some point, using that basic knowledge, pastry chefs or cooks can do variations of their own, creating very personal new recipes from old techniques.

The Secrets of Baking is a very serious book, fascinating and easy to learn from. It is a stunning first work by this young author, who I hope will continue with her indomitable spirit to create new recipes and to astonish us again with the quality of her work.

—JACQUES PÉPIN

The
SECRETS
of BAKING

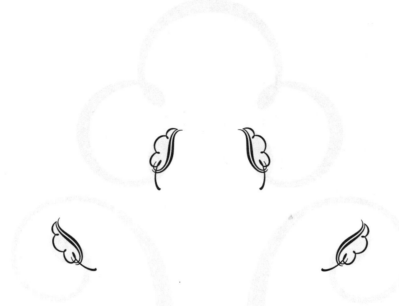

INTRODUCTION

DESSERTS ARE MY LIFE—MAKING THEM, EATING THEM, AND teaching others how to prepare them perfectly. As an executive pastry chef, first at the original Spago in Hollywood and now at Spago Beverly Hills, I have created hundreds of fancy and delicious desserts. But sophisticated though they may be, they are all based on simple ingredients and basic pastry techniques—techniques that I never stop trying to perfect.

Over the years I've noticed that most of the questions I get from aspiring bakers concern the fundamentals. What makes pie dough flaky? Why are some batches of cookies crisp and some chewy, even when you use the same recipe? Why are pound cakes dense and génoise cakes airy and light? What causes vanilla sauce to thicken, and why does it sometimes curdle? Can you substitute powdered sugar for granulated sugar and get the same results?

When I was a cooking student, I felt overwhelmed by the vast amounts of information I was expected to absorb from huge textbooks and grueling classes. I was often frustrated when I tried to find out the answers to simple questions like these. I'd search through tome after tome, only to find that I had to piece things together for myself.

In writing this book, my goal is to take the fear, mystery, and guesswork out of baking by providing answers to many ordinary questions as well as ones you may not think about asking. Besides giving you the recipes for my most requested desserts, I show you how the ingredients interact with one another, so you'll know the reasons behind the steps you're following.

I BEGAN THIS PROJECT MORE THAN FIVE YEARS AGO, AND my first task was to bring order to my bulging file of recipes. Follow-

> In writing this book, my goal is to take the fear, mystery, and guesswork out of baking.

ing the example of the pastry cookbooks on my shelves, I started to organize the pages into the usual categories: cakes and cookies, pies and tarts, soufflés, breads, and so forth. But as I divided them into piles, I grew dissatisfied.

According to tradition, truffles, chocolate mousse, chocolate icing, and chocolate torte should be in different chapters. But these desserts are all variations on a single recipe: a combination of chocolate and cream called *ganache*. Crème brûlée, pastry cream, and the Italian frozen dessert semifreddo are usually separated by hundreds of pages in cookbooks, although they all descend from a simple vanilla sauce. Similarly, the thin, crisp cookies known as *tuiles* would normally appear with the other cookies. But in the kitchens at Spago, I discovered that they're best when made from a batter with proportions similar to those in pound cake, and I wanted to underline the connections between the two by putting them in the same chapter.

Moreover, basics such as ganache, caramel, génoise, vanilla sauce, and puff pastry, the cornerstones of every pastry-making course, are usually relegated to the back of the cookbook. I asked myself how I could put the most important recipes where my readers would look first. So I began again, this time placing the fundamental recipes first and grouping related recipes around them.

Learn one technique, and you'll have many different possibilities at your fingertips.

IN THIS BOOK, EACH CHAPTER CENTERS ON A "MASTER" RECIPE, which offers the secret to a whole group of desserts. A family tree shows how each recipe is related to the next. Learn one technique, and you'll have many different possibilities at your fingertips.

Once you've mastered pâte à choux, a simple dough of butter, flour, and eggs, for example, you can make more than a dozen desserts, not to mention variations. Fill the choux puff with pastry cream and cover it with chocolate glaze and it becomes an éclair. Put a scoop of ice cream inside, and you have a profiterole. Dip the same little puffs in caramel and pile them into a pyramid, and you've created the festive croquembouche. Mix Gruyère cheese into the batter and the result is the savory appetizer gougère. Add cocoa instead, dip sliced bananas into the dough, and deep-fry, and you get crisp, light Chocolate Banana Beignets. Or you can form small dumplings from the batter and poach them in Blackberry-Merlot Sauce. If you know how to make brioche dough, you can make bread, coffeecake, sticky buns, and doughnuts. Learn laminated dough, and you can turn out irresistible French cookies known as *palmiers,* napoleons, and even your own croissants.

IN THE INTRODUCTIONS TO EACH CHAPTER, I SHOW YOU HOW ingredients like butter, sugar, eggs, and flour work together and how they play new roles in different recipes. A cake made by beating butter and granulated sugar together, for instance, isn't anything like one made with powdered sugar and melted butter. Milk chocolate and dark chocolate don't behave the same way in baked goods. Adding just a few drops of lemon juice to a caramel can change its chemistry. Even the question of whether an ingredient is liquid or solid isn't always clear-cut, because some ingredients that look solid actually behave like liquids in the oven.

Similarly, different techniques applied to the same ingredients will result in completely different pastries. That's why one kind of pie crust is flaky and another, also made with butter, sugar, and flour, is crumbly, and why pound cake is dense and sponge cake is light.

When you understand the science behind the recipes, you'll become a more confident baker and a more skillful one too, because you can improve your techniques based on your knowledge of ingredients. You can use *The Secrets of Baking* to take a short course in pastry making or dip into it and make single desserts as you please.

Rather than following recipes by rote, you'll be able to create your own signature desserts by moving around the basic building blocks and combining them with one another (you'll find my favorite combinations on page 306). Fill a flavored pie crust with crème brûlée and driz-

When you understand the science behind the recipes, you'll become a more confident baker and a more skillful one.

zle a favorite fruit sauce on the plate. Choose from different curds, pastry creams, whipped creams, and mousses to fill cakes, cream puffs, and puff pastry. Finish off a fruit tart with apple caramel glaze. Transform the ganache or lemon curd in your refrigerator into a breathtaking soufflé. Only you need know how fundamentally simple the most imaginative of these desserts really are.

MY BAKESHOP RULES

Environment

To manage pastry, you have to control the environment in which you work. A key factor is temperature. Your room should optimally be at 68° to 70°F. If your kitchen is terribly warm (80°F or more), keep your flour in the refrigerator. If your kitchen is very cold, you may need to place the eggs in warm water for a few minutes. Remember, you control your area; your area should not control you.

Work Area

If you find yourself constantly crossing over and doing the two-step to reach for things, stop! Think about reorganizing your kitchen. Create a designated pastry work area, complete with equipment, tools, and ingredients. Your flour and baking ingredients such as spices and salt can be on an upper shelf (move your plates to another cabinet), your mixer directly below. The drawer underneath can store your basic tools—whisk, spatulas, scraper. Always keep them in the same "home" drawer. Nearby should be the sink, and below, your garbage pail. Your work surface needn't be longer than four feet or so (a bit less than your arm span). It should be two feet deep and stand just below your waist. If you have a tiny apartment kitchen, remember that the kitchens of sophisticated restaurants often have limited space too. Your sink can be a work

Remember, you control your area; your area should not control you.

surface and a tool as well. Cover it with a baking sheet or a cutting board, and you've got another counter. Fill it with ice cubes and water, and it becomes an ice bath. The top of your garbage pail can also serve as a surface.

Organization

Organization will save you time in the kitchen and make your baking effortless. Efficiency is key to a successful kitchen. For that reason, do as pastry chefs do: set out everything before beginning. This advance preparation is called *mise en place* in French, meaning "put in place." Begin a recipe by setting the oven temperature and collecting the equipment and tools required to complete the job. Place all tools like whisks and spatulas in a canister on your work surface. Keep them at arm's length. Clean your station as you go. A great chef is a ballet dancer in motion.

Make yourself aerodynamic.

Personal Management

Sleeves up and hair back. Make yourself aerodynamic. Sleeves get in the way, fall into batter, and catch on pot handles. Roll them up above your elbows. If you're worried about burns, use oven mitts that cover your forearms. Hair is not only distracting but can get into the food. When your date arrives, you can pull your hair back down.

To avoid a sore back and undue fatigue, stand up straight with your shoulders down and back. It's amazing how much difference good posture can make when it comes to your stamina in the bakeshop. Pastrymaking may be hard work, but bad posture is what will make that work hard on your body.

Brush your teeth often. Remember, you are working with sugar and flour. Sugar can not only ruin your teeth but coat and dull your palate. All of my pastry assistants keep a toothbrush in their lockers, and I urge them to brush (and rinse very thoroughly) before their shift, during each break, and at the end of the shift.

Care for Tools

Wash delicate tools by hand and dry them immediately. One way to prevent rust is to place heatproof tools in the oven with just the pilot light on for a few minutes. This will dry any excess moisture.

Ingredients

Buy the best!

Taste your ingredients as you go. Make sure milk and butter are fresh. Flavors such as sweetness can be adjusted to taste. Educate your palate; listen to your tongue.

Chop butter before melting. It will melt faster and more evenly.

Chop it before mixing, too. This is especially important for doughs. If the butter needs to be at room temperature, it should be pliable and yield easily to a knife, but it should not collapse when you press on it with your finger.

Don't overwhip cream. Perfectly whipped cream is sensual. It has a smooth, satiny, even look and texture. Overwhipped cream breaks down into globules of fat and water; it looks rough and craggy, and eventually you'll have butter. Overwhipped cream has less volume than perfectly whipped cream, which should have soft peaks. If you are using the cream for garnish, it should be slightly stiffer; for decoration, a little stiffer again, so that it holds its shape.

Measuring

Precision is essential to consistent pastry work. When measuring, it's important to use the proper tool and method.

Don't use liquid and dry measures interchangeably. For dry ingredients, use stainless-steel flat-edge graduated cup measures. For liquid ingredients, clear plastic or Pyrex cups work best.

When measuring flour, use the dip-and-sweep method. With a metal spatula, fluff up the flour, then dip the measuring cup into the fluffed flour, filling it gently above the top. Use the spatula to sweep

Precision is essential to consistent pastry work.

off the excess. The same goes for powdered sugar. Some cooks spoon the flour or sugar in, which is OK as long as you stir it first, pile it above the top of the cup, and then level it off. For brown sugar, pack it in tightly and press down using the back of a slightly smaller cup measure.

For liquid measures, be sure to place the measuring cup on a flat surface and pour in your ingredients. Holding it in your hand and pouring in the liquid will not guarantee a correct measure. Bring your eye down to the measure, not the measure up to your eye. Don't measure 2 ounces of liquid in a 32-ounce container; it isn't calibrated for such small amounts.

With butter and other ingredients that come in blocks, such as cream cheese, don't use the wrapper to measure, since it is not always fitted correctly. If the butter is divided into sticks, remove it from the wrapper and cut the stick in half, then in half again. That will equal 2 tablespoons. Measure ingredients in advance if possible and store airtight in a cool environment until ready to use.

Don't use liquid and dry measures interchangeably.

Sifting

Sifting removes lumps and distributes ingredients. I measure ingredients first, then sift. BEFORE SIFTING, TOSS THE DRY INGREDIENTS WITH A SPOON OR YOUR HANDS TO ENSURE EVEN DISTRIBUTION. For best results, use a triple sifter, a very fine sifter with more than one mesh. Beginning with the largest-quantity ingredient called for (such as flour), place the ingredient in the sifter. Top with the smaller quantities of ingredients (baking powder, baking soda, salt). First stir together and then sift. If you do not own a triple sifter, sift a minimum of two times.

Baking

The times given in this book are estimates and guidelines and should be used as such. It's more important to exercise your sense of smell, sight, and touch to ascertain when a baked good is ready to be removed from the oven.

Have your oven rack in the right place. Heat is different in the lower, middle, and top parts of your oven. Prebaking pie crusts, baking cookies and soufflés, and roasting fruit should all be done in the lower third of the oven for quick, even browning. All other baked products except palmiers (page 274), including filled prebaked pie crusts, are baked in the middle. Palmiers should be baked in the top part of the oven to achieve the caramelization of the sugar. See the chart below for quick reference.

Test Your Oven

The recipes in this book were all made in a conventional (not convection) gas oven. All ovens differ slightly. You can have the same model as your mother, yet the two will not necessarily bake at the same rate. Keep a thermometer in your oven to check the temperature. Compare the temperature on the oven dial against the temperature on the thermometer. You can also use this method to discover hot spots in the oven.

Keep an eye on all baked items, especially after the halfway point. Make notes of your results (right on the page of the book) and adjust the cooking times accordingly. You may need to move your racks up or

	LOWER THIRD	CENTER RACK	UPPER RACK
Vanilla Sauce (custards)	x		
Cakes		x	
Financier		x	
Pâte à Choux		x	
Cookies	x		
Pie Dough	x		
Sweet Dough	x		
Brioche		x	
Laminated Dough		x	
Palmiers			x
Fruit (roasted)	x		
Soufflés	x		

down. You may need to place an empty baking sheet above your baked item if your oven is particularly hot on top or set your baking sheet inside another one for high bottom heat. Throw out the rule that you should never open the oven door when something is baking. It's more important to check on the item, and if you open the oven door gently and don't slam it shut or jostle the item, then your cake or cookies won't fall. It's best to wait 20 to 25 minutes before opening the door for cakes, 30 minutes for breads, but the main thing is not to worry about it.

Timers are mandatory. Please set timers for pastry precision. Do not answer the phone if the timer is going off. Check your pastries and, if necessary, let your answering machine pick up.

Test your thermometer. Plunge it into boiling water. Water boils at 212°F (100°C) at sea level. Make adjustments for your altitude as necessary. If your thermometer reads 220°F, for example, when the water boils, add 8°F to the thermometer when you use it.

The Value of Experience

Experience is bouncing back from a mistake and trying your best not to repeat it. In *The Simple Art of Perfect Baking,* Flo Braker says, "Serve less than perfect desserts in a dimly lit room." To that I would add, "Sprinkle them with lots of powdered sugar."

Finally, cook with love. Love is by far the most important ingredient.

All ovens differ slightly. You can have the same model as your mother, yet the two will not necessarily bake at the same rate. Keep a thermometer in your oven to check the temperature.

GANACHE

Ganache Recipes

When i was in cooking school, i loved showing off my newly acquired culinary skills in front of my sisters. One winter break, my sister Laurie was baking a birthday cake for a friend in my mother's wood-paneled Brooklyn kitchen. Being a typical culinary student, I was appalled to see her reach for a can of ready-made frosting.

"Why don't you just make ganache?" I asked in my best I-know-something-that-you-don't-know tone.

"What's that?" she asked.

Seizing the opportunity to impress my sister with a basic pastry technique, I looked around the kitchen for chocolate and cream. I heated the cream in the microwave and poured it over the chocolate. From those humble ingredients emerged a luxurious, decadent frosting. She was amazed. What sounded exotic and mysterious was so easy that even her sister could do it!

While it does sound exotic, basic ganache is made with just two ingredients: chocolate and cream. By varying techniques and tweaking ingredients, you can turn basic ganache into a truffle, a glaze, a frosting, a mousse, a tart, a warm drink, or a frozen pop.

Adjusting the proportion of chocolate and cream changes the density of the finished product. More cream makes it thinner and lighter and more chocolate makes it thicker and denser. You can also manipulate ganache by changing its temperature. It becomes thinner as it heats and thicker as it cools.

The idea of mixing two ingredients seems simple. But mixing chocolate and cream is equivalent to mixing oil and water, which can't normally be done. This process of mixing two unmixable ingredients is called *emulsification*.

Remember the school science fair? Wasn't there always a kid with an oil and water display? He'd plop some oil into the water, but instead of dissolving, it would float to the top. What that kid didn't know is that oil and water actually can be mixed, with a little help from heat and agitation.

The emulsification that results in ganache combines the fat in chocolate (cocoa butter) with the water in cream. To accomplish this, you must first liquefy the fat. Hot cream is combined with the chocolate, melting the fat into liquid form. Stirring breaks down the fat into microscopic droplets, small enough to be suspended within the water. Whipping and heavy cream may be used interchangeably to make ganache. They differ in the amount of butterfat they contain. As a general rule, the higher the fat content of the cream, the richer the finished ganache will be.

While it sounds exotic, basic ganache is made with just two ingredients: chocolate and cream.

TEMPERATURE IS AN IMPORTANT FACTOR IN THE EMULSIFICATION of ganache. If the temperature is not controlled carefully, the result will not be smooth. The optimal emulsification temperature for ganache is 90° to 110°F. If the temperature rises above 110°F, the cocoa butter gets too hot. Droplets of fat will pool together and rise to the surface, separating from the mixture. When this occurs, the ganache is referred to as "broken."

Ganache can also be lumpy if the chocolate is not chopped into very fine pieces before being combined with the hot cream. If the chocolate pieces are larger than ¼ inch, they will not melt completely and the resulting ganache will have lumps. Lumpy ganache can be repaired by being reheated. Reheating, however, can easily cause the fat to overheat, pool together, and break the ganache.

After the cream is poured over the chocolate to melt the cocoa butter, the mixture is set aside to warm undisturbed for a minute and then stirred in a slow, circular motion. Steady agitation is essential in reducing the fat to tiny droplets. Care must be taken to resist excessive beating, which can bring the temperature of the fat below 90°F too quickly, producing ganache with a grainy texture.

REPAIRING A BROKEN OR GRAINY GANACHE

If your ganache looks broken or feels grainy, there is still hope for it. To repair a broken ganache, divide it in half. Warm one half over a double boiler to a temperature of 130°F. The fat will melt and pool at this temperature, making the mixture thinner. Cool the remaining ganache to 60°F by stirring it over a bowl of ice. The fat in this portion will begin to solidify, causing the ganache to thicken.

When both halves have reached the desired temperatures, slowly stream the hot ganache into the cold and stir to combine. You can use a food processor for this step by placing the cool ganache into the bowl of the food processor, turning on the machine, and streaming in the warm ganache. The mixture will not fall below 90°F during this procedure, so there is no risk of creating a grainy texture. Combining the two portions of ganache in this way averages the temperature into the optimal working range, and the fat droplets will be suspended evenly in the water.

If your ganache looks broken or grainy, there is still hope for it.

CHOCOLATE CHOICES

The most common chocolate used for ganache is dark chocolate. *Dark* refers to the color and includes sweet, semisweet, bittersweet, and unsweetened chocolates. Chocolate is made from cocoa beans that have been roasted and pulverized. The result is chocolate liquor, also known as *cocoa mass*.

As the beans are ground, they exude cocoa butter. Different amounts of cocoa butter are added back into the mixture, depending on which type of chocolate is being made. Dark chocolate contains less cocoa butter than milk chocolate. White chocolate is comprised of nearly all cocoa butter and no chocolate liquor. (Due to the lack of chocolate liquor, white chocolate is not technically chocolate. However, it can be used in the same manner as types containing chocolate liquor, with certain modifications.)

Chocolates also differ in the amount of sugar they contain. Bittersweet has less sugar than semisweet. Unsweetened chocolate has no added sugar, and I often used it in conjunction with bittersweet for an extra dark, intense flavor.

Milk solids, which contain milk fat, are used to make milk and white chocolate. The added fat and the increased cocoa butter content make the lighter chocolates softer and more susceptible to damage from heat. You can certainly make ganache from milk or white chocolate, using the traditional technique, but you'll have to adjust the proportion of cream downward to compensate for the increased fat content.

Chocolates differ in the amount of sugar they contain.

ALL THE RECIPES IN THIS CHAPTER BEGIN WITH THE SAME ingredients and techniques. The Master Ganache is made with an equal ratio of chocolate to cream. This is considered a ganache of medium consistency. Recipes categorized as firm are made with more than 50 percent chocolate. Soft ganaches have more than 50 percent cream. The recipes are not mysterious, nor are they difficult. If, however, you want to impress your sister, keep this information to yourself.

Ganache
FAMILY TREE

MEDIUM

1 part chocolate : 1 part cream

MASTER GANACHE

Truffles

Fudge Fondue

Milk Chocolate Ganache

White Chocolate Ganache

Caramel Ganache

Frozen Chocolate Parfait

Chocolate Soufflé

Ganache Glaze

Chocolate Sabayon

FIRM

2 parts chocolate : 1 part cream

Raspberry Ganache

Banana Ganache

John Do Ya Ganache Candy Bars

Baked Whiskey Tortes

Chocolate Frosting

SOFT

1 part chocolate : 2 or more parts cream

Chocolate Whipped Cream

Campton Place Hot Chocolate

Chocolate Sauce

Chocolate Mousse Trio

Deep, Dark Chocolate Tart

MEDIUM-TEXTURED GANACHE is the MASTER GANACHE, and all the recipes that are derived from it begin with a **1 : 1 ratio** of chocolate to cream. (Adjustments have been made to the Milk and White Chocolate Ganache recipes to achieve a medium texture.)

FIRM-TEXTURED GANACHE is made with **2 : 1 ratio** of chocolate to cream and is suitable for icings, fillings, and baking.

SOFT-TEXTURED GANACHE uses a **1 : 2 ratio** of chocolate to cream or even more cream.

All the recipes are related to the Master Ganache. They all begin with the same ingredients and techniques. Note that the ratio is based on weight, not volume.

YIELD: 2 cups

SPECIAL TOOLS:

Food processor (optional)

Candy thermometer

8 ounces bittersweet
chocolate

1 cup heavy cream

Master Ganache

CAN DEEP, DARK, INTENSE, RICH, VELVETY SMOOTH CHOCOLATE *be a spiritual experience? It certainly is heavenly when mixed with cream. Praise the pastry angels and pass the bonbons!*

This is the basic ganache recipe. Use it for truffles, tarts, fillings . . . you name it. Follow the same technique when adjusting the recipe for firm and soft ganache. An alternative food processor method is given, which can be applied to any ganache recipe in this chapter.

I want to introduce you to ganache and persuade you to make it a staple in your refrigerator. As long as you don't eat it all as a midnight snack, it can be available to help you throw together dessert at a moment's notice.

1. Using a serrated knife, finely chop the chocolate into ¼-inch pieces. Don't be lazy here. Big chunks will not melt.

TRADITIONAL METHOD

2. Place the chocolate in a medium heatproof bowl. Bring the cream to a boil in a small saucepan over medium heat. Boiling means the cream will actually rise up in the pan and threaten to boil over.

3. Immediately pour the boiling cream over the chopped chocolate. Tap the bowl on the counter to settle the chocolate into the cream, then let it sit for 1 minute. Using a rubber spatula, slowly stir in a circular motion, starting from the center of the bowl and working out to the sides. Be careful not to add too much air to the ganache. Stir until all the chocolate is melted, about 2 minutes. It may look done after 1 minute of stirring, but keep going to be sure it's emulsified.

FOOD PROCESSOR METHOD

2. Place the chopped chocolate in a food processor fitted with the steel blade. Bring the cream to a boil in a small saucepan over medium heat (or bring to a boil in the microwave).

3. Immediately pour the hot cream into the food processor, on top of the chocolate. Let sit for 1 minute, then pulse the machine three times. Scrape down the sides with a rubber spatula and pulse three more times, until all the chocolate is melted. This smooth, silky chocolate is now ganache. Transfer the ganache to a bowl.

4. Let the ganache sit at room temperature until it cools to 70°F. In a 65°F room, this will take only 15 minutes. You can speed up the process by pouring the ganache out onto a clean baking sheet (thinner layers cool faster). Once the ganache reaches 70°F, it is ready to be used. At this point it can also be covered and stored in the refrigerator for up to 2 weeks.

NOTE
I prefer using a serrated knife for chopping chocolate. It's safer because the blade doesn't slip off the hard surface of the chocolate. And I find that it's easier to get small chunks.

Variations

❧ TANGY GANACHE: Replace all or part of the cream with crème fraîche.

❧ EARL GREY GANACHE: Place 1 bag of Earl Grey tea in the cream and bring it to a boil. Cover and let it steep for 10 minutes. Remove the tea bag and squeeze over the cream. Rewarm the tea-infused cream and continue with the recipe.

❧ LAVENDER GANACHE: Place 1 to 2 tablespoons lavender flowers in the cream and bring it to a boil. Remove from the heat, cover, and let it steep for 10 minutes. Strain and rewarm the lavender-infused cream, then continue with the recipe.

❧ ORANGE GANACHE: Add 1 tablespoon finely grated orange zest to the cream and bring to a boil; strain into the chocolate. When the ganache is complete, add 1 tablespoon Grand Marnier.

Ganache
MEDIUM

SPECIAL TOOLS:

Candy thermometer

Piping bag with a large
(#6) plain tip (optional)

Parchment paper

1 recipe Master Ganache
(page 16), with the
addition of:

2 tablespoons (¼ stick)
unsalted butter, softened

1 tablespoon light corn syrup

2 tablespoons liquor, such as
Grand Marnier, kirsch,
bourbon, or rum

FOR THE COATING

2 cups sifted unsweetened
cocoa powder

8 ounces bittersweet
chocolate

Truffles

THE ORIGINAL CHOCOLATE TRUFFLE WAS A FRENCH *confection meant to simulate the much-sought-after truffle fungus. It was rolled rough like the real fungus, not round, and covered in cocoa powder to replicate the dirt it grows in. (Whose idea was it to make people think they were eating dirt?) Chocolate truffles are a rich, decadent treat with a special elegance all their own. Don't be intimidated! Truffles are easy to make and always appreciated.*

The choice of alcohol to use is yours. It can be a liqueur, such as Chambord or Grand Marnier, or another spirit like bourbon or rum. The alcohol can also be left out entirely. Substitutions for it could include brewed coffee, orange juice, or fruit puree.

1. Follow the method for Master Ganache, adding the butter to the chocolate and the corn syrup to the cream before bringing the cream to a boil.

2. Pour the hot cream and corn syrup over the chopped chocolate and butter. Tap the bowl on the counter to settle the chocolate into the cream, then let it sit for 1 minute. Using a rubber spatula, stir slowly in a circular motion, starting from the center of the bowl and working out to the sides. Be careful not to add too much air to the ganache. Stir until the chocolate is completely melted, about 2 minutes.

3. Add the liquor and stir to combine. Allow the ganache to cool at room temperature until it is firm. This should take at least 4 hours in a 65°F room or 2 hours in the refrigerator.

4. Once the ganache is firm, it can be formed into truffle balls. Using a piping bag, a mini ice cream scoop, or a tablespoon, make 1-inch-diameter blobs. Then roll the blobs into somewhat uniform balls by hand. This is messy, no doubt about it. If they begin to warm up and become soft, refrigerate for 10 to 15 minutes. If you have hot hands or it is a hot day, it may feel as though you can't get a grip on the truffle. Work near a sink with cold running water. When the ganache feels like it's melting, cool your hands under the running water, then dry them and dust with a little of the cocoa powder. Be careful not to get too much cocoa powder on the truffles, or they will taste like cocoa powder.

COATING

After the truffles are rolled, they can be finished in a variety of ways. The original cocoa powder coating is the easiest, and quite good.

1. Line a baking sheet with parchment paper.

2. Using a serrated knife, finely chop the chocolate into ¼ inch-pieces and place it in a medium heatproof bowl. Fill a medium saucepan half full of water, bring it to a simmer, then turn off the heat. Create a double boiler by placing the bowl on top of the saucepan. Stir the chocolate occasionally with a rubber spatula until it melts, about 2 minutes.

3. When the chocolate has melted, take it off the heat. Stir it slowly with a rubber spatula until the temperature drops to 90°F, about 5 minutes. Place the remaining cocoa powder in a small bowl.

4. Drop one rolled ganache ball into the melted chocolate. Remove it with a fork, tap off the excess chocolate, and toss it into the cocoa powder. Roll the truffle around in the cocoa until it is well coated. Transfer the truffle to the prepared baking sheet and let it harden. Repeat with each truffle, coating one at a time.

Truffles should be stored in an airtight container at 60° to 65°F. Refrigerating them is OK too. If condensation forms when they come out of the refrigerator, simply toss them in more cocoa powder before serving.

Variations

- Other delightful coatings include finely chopped toasted nuts (see page 366), toasted unsweetened coconut, grated milk chocolate, and powdered sugar. Match the coating of the truffles to the liquor used in the ganache, such as Frangelico truffles with hazelnut crunch coating. This will create an interesting depth of flavor.

- Steep 1 black currant tea bag in the cream and add 2 tablespoons Chambord as the liquor.

- Add 1 tablespoon instant espresso powder to the cream and use 2 tablespoons Kahlúa as the liquor.

- Add 1 tablespoon finely chopped orange zest and ½ teaspoon orange oil to the cream. Let sit for 10 minutes. Strain out the zest. Use 2 tablespoons Grand Marnier as the liquor.

- Add 2 tablespoons strained blackberry puree (or the puree of another fruit) instead of the liquor.

- Peel and grate fresh ginger and squeeze from it 2 tablespoons ginger juice. Add this and ½ teaspoon fresh lemon juice instead of the liquor.

- Combine ½ cup raisins and ½ cup Champagne or brandy in a small saucepan. Bring to a boil over high heat, then turn off the heat and let the raisins cool and absorb the liquor. Drain off any remaining liquid, chop the raisins, and stir the raisins into the warm ganache.

Ganache
MEDIUM

YIELD: 1²/₃ cups, serving 6

SPECIAL TOOLS:

Candy thermometer

Fondue pot or serving dish

Skewers

8 ounces bittersweet
chocolate

½ cup sweetened condensed
milk

½ cup whole milk

½ teaspoon finely chopped
orange zest

NOTE

Some of my favorite fruits to dip
include:

Crisp fresh apple wedges

Dehydrated apple chips

Juicy pear wedges

Bananas

Fresh cherries

Dried cherries: Combine ¼ cup
dried cherries, ¼ cup port, and
¼ teaspoon freshly ground black
pepper in a small saucepan. Bring
to a boil, then turn off the heat.
Cool and let the cherries absorb
the liquor. Spear them with
skewers.

Raisins: Combine ¼ cup raisins
with ¼ cup verjuice or white
wine and 1 teaspoon fresh lemon
juice in a small saucepan and
bring to a boil. Turn off the heat
and let the raisins cool. Spear
them with skewers.

Fudge Fondue

*FONDUE IS BACK! THIS WILL BE GOOD NEWS TO THOSE OF
you who didn't get your fill in the 1970s. Traditional fondue is melted
cheese into which you dip hunks of bread. My chocolatey version is
perfect for dipping pieces of fruit, cubes of cake, or cookies. Though
it's really no more than a glorified chocolate sauce, fondue is a great
excuse to cover everything in chocolate.*

*This dish always appears on my Valentine's Day menu. It's a
great way to get a romantic conversation going. If you don't have an
old fondue set in the garage, any dish will do. No skewers? Go ahead
and use your fingers.*

1. Using a serrated knife, finely chop the chocolate into ¼-inch
pieces and place it in a medium heatproof bowl.

2. Bring the milks to a boil in a small saucepan over medium
heat. Pour over the chopped chocolate. Tap the bowl on the counter
to settle the chocolate into the cream, then let it sit for 1 minute.
Using a rubber spatula, slowly stir in a circular motion, starting from
the center of the bowl and working out to the sides. Stir until all the
chocolate is melted, about 2 minutes.

3. When the chocolate has melted, insert a thermometer. When
the temperature reaches 98°F, add the orange zest and stir to incorporate. Serve the fondue immediately or let it cool, cover it with plastic wrap, and store it at room temperature overnight. To reheat, place
a bowl of fondue over a saucepan half full of simmering water, creating a double boiler, and stir continuously until melted, about 5 minutes. Do not let the temperature exceed 100°F when reheating, or the
ganache can break. The fondue will also keep for up to 2 weeks in the
refrigerator.

Variations

❧ Infuse the milk with your favorite spice, then strain. My
favorite combination is a star anise pod, a 2-inch cinnamon stick, and ¼ teaspoon ground cinnamon.

❧ Spike the milk with 2 tablespoons rum, Grand Marnier,
or Poire William.

Milk Chocolate Ganache

YIELD: 1⅓ cups

SPECIAL TOOL:

Candy thermometer

8 ounces milk chocolate

½ cup plus 2 tablespoons heavy cream

1 tablespoon light corn syrup

SOME PEOPLE (INCLUDING MOST IN MY FAMILY) LOVE MILK *chocolate and even prefer it to bittersweet. Because it's sweeter and creamier than dark chocolate, milk chocolate lends itself to chocolate-caramel combinations like the caramel truffles on page 23, where I prefer it to bittersweet.*

Working with milk chocolate is different from working with dark chocolate. Milk chocolate has a higher cocoa butter content as well as added fat from the milk solids. The extra fat makes milk chocolate softer and gives it a lower melting point. For this reason, the same ratio of ingredients in Master Ganache cannot be used for Milk Chocolate Ganache. The ganache would never become firm enough to roll.

To create a workable Milk Chocolate Ganache, I add less liquid and a touch of corn syrup for elasticity. The finished product is a bit softer than the dark chocolate version, but it can still be used for truffles, fondues, and fillings, just like the Master Ganache.

1. Using a serrated knife, finely chop the chocolate into ¼-inch pieces and place it in a medium heatproof bowl.

2. Bring the cream and corn syrup to a boil in a small saucepan over medium heat. Immediately pour it over the chopped chocolate. Tap the bowl on the counter to settle the chocolate into the cream, then let it sit for 1 minute. Using a rubber spatula, slowly stir in a circular motion, starting from the center of the bowl and working out to the sides. Be careful not to add too much air to the ganache. Stir until all the chocolate is melted, about 2 minutes.

3. Allow the temperature of the ganache to drop to 70°F. At 70°F, the ganache will be firm enough to roll, pipe, or spread. If the ganache is not going to be used right away, it can be stored in the refrigerator for up to 2 weeks.

White Chocolate Ganache

YIELD: 1½ cups

SPECIAL TOOL:

Candy thermometer

8 ounces white chocolate

4 tablespoons (½ stick)
unsalted butter, softened

¼ cup heavy cream

1 tablespoon light corn syrup

1 tablespoon dark rum

LIKE THE MILK CHOCOLATE GANACHE, THIS WILL BE SOFTER *than the dark version, and like the Master Ganache, it can be used as a filling, sauce, or glaze. White chocolate pairs well with acidic fruits, especially the floral essence of tropical fruits.*

1. Using a serrated knife, finely chop the white chocolate into ¼-inch pieces and place it in a medium heatproof bowl with the butter.

2. Bring the cream and corn syrup to a boil in a small saucepan over medium heat. Immediately pour the hot cream over the chocolate. Tap the bowl on the counter to settle the chocolate into the cream, then let it sit for 1 minute. Using a rubber spatula, slowly stir in a circular motion, starting from the center of the bowl and working out to the sides. Be careful not to add too much air to the ganache. Stir until all the chocolate is melted, about 2 minutes. When the mixture is smooth, stir in the rum.

3. Allow the temperature of the ganache to drop to 70°F. If the ganache is not going to be used right away, it can be stored in the refrigerator for up to 2 weeks. Use this ganache as a filling for tarts or cakes, thin it to make a sauce, or roll and coat it for truffles (page 18).

Variations

 Infuse the cream with 1 tablespoon lavender flowers, 1 tablespoon honey, 1 tablespoon sliced fresh ginger, or 1 tea bag, then strain.

 Use framboise and Grand Marnier or other liquors in place of the rum.

Caramel Ganache

4 ounces bittersweet
chocolate

4 ounces milk chocolate

½ cup sugar

2 tablespoons water

1 tablespoon light corn syrup

1 cup heavy cream

I LOVE THIS GANACHE ROLLED INTO A TRUFFLE AND COATED *in chopped toasted almonds (see page 366) and pulverized Croquante (page 55). When I serve truffles, I always combine several different types on a plate. I use a different coating for each type to give the presentation a more interesting look and so I can tell them apart without biting into each one.*

This method includes making a caramel sauce. If you've never made it before, it's a good idea to read about it (page 58) before you begin. In addition to truffles, this ganache makes a great tart or cake filling, and it's incredible swirled into caramel gelato. To form truffles, see the method on page 18.

1. Using a serrated knife, finely chop the dark and milk chocolates into ¼-inch pieces and place them in a medium heatproof bowl. Set aside.

2. Combine the sugar, water, and corn syrup in a medium saucepan and stir them together. Cover and cook undisturbed over medium heat for 4 minutes. Uncover and continue to cook until the mixture reaches 350°F, about 6 minutes. It will be deep amber in color. When the caramel is ready, remove it from the heat and let it sit for 30 seconds, or until all the bubbles disperse.

3. Meanwhile, bring the cream to a boil in a small saucepan over medium heat. Pour the cream into the caramel, stirring carefully to combine (careful, it will bubble up). This is now caramel sauce.

4. Pour the hot caramel sauce over the chopped chocolate. Tap the bowl on the counter to settle the chocolate into the caramel, then let it sit for 1 minute. Using a rubber spatula, slowly stir in a circular motion, starting from the center of the bowl and working out to the sides. Be careful not to add too much air to the ganache. Stir until all the chocolate is melted, about 2 minutes.

5. Allow the temperature of the ganache to drop to 70°F. At 70°F the ganache will be firm enough to roll, pipe, or spread. If the ganache is not going to be used right away, it can be stored in the refrigerator for up to 2 weeks.

YIELD: Six 6-ounce servings

SPECIAL TOOLS:

Decorative mold(s) or six 6-ounce ramekins

Candy thermometer

Standing electric mixer fitted with a whisk attachment (optional)

4 ounces bittersweet chocolate

½ cup heavy cream

½ teaspoon vanilla extract

2 tablespoons instant espresso powder

3 large eggs

2 tablespoons sugar

Frozen Chocolate Parfait

PARFAIT, A FRENCH WORD MEANING "PERFECT," IS A confusing term in the pastry world. In the United States we think of it as a layered dessert in a tall, thin glass. In France, however, parfait is a molded frozen custard, and that's what this one is. Typically made from a base of eggs and cream, it is frozen into a brick or mold and then sliced for serving.

Parfait can be scooped like ice cream. It can be layered with cake or cookies, studded with fruit and nuts, or swirled with a sauce. To make sure that my parfaits will unmold easily, I first coat the inside of my mold pan with spray, then line it with plastic wrap. The spray helps the wrap stick, and the wrap provides a handle to help pull out the parfait. Parfait takes about 6 hours to freeze completely, so plan ahead.

1. Coat the desired mold or molds or ramekins with pan spray and then line with plastic film. This will make unmolding easier.

2. Using a serrated knife, finely chop the chocolate into ¼-inch pieces and place it in a medium heatproof bowl.

3. Bring the cream, vanilla, and espresso powder to a boil in a small saucepan over medium heat. Immediately pour the mixture over the chopped chocolate. Tap the bowl on the counter to settle the chocolate into the cream, then let it sit for 1 minute. Using a rubber spatula, slowly stir in a circular motion, starting from the center of the bowl and working out to the sides. Stir until all the chocolate is melted, about 2 minutes. Set aside.

4. Combine the eggs and sugar in the bowl of your standing mixer or in a medium heatproof bowl and briefly whisk them together.

5. Fill a medium saucepan halfway with water and bring to a simmer over medium heat. Create a double boiler by placing the bowl of eggs and sugar over the simmering water, making sure the bowl doesn't touch the water. Whisk continuously for 2 to 3 minutes, or until the sugar has dissolved and the eggs have warmed to 110°F. (To see if the sugar is dissolved into the eggs, touch them. If they feel grainy, continue to warm and stir for 1 to 2 minutes.) Watch carefully so the eggs don't scramble.

6. Using the standing mixer fitted with a whisk attachment or a hand mixer at high speed, whip the eggs until they are a light yellow color and have tripled in volume, about 4 minutes.

7. Stir one third of the whipped eggs into the chocolate mixture with a rubber spatula to lighten the batter and make it easier to add the remaining eggs. Gently fold the remaining eggs into the batter so the eggs do not deflate.

8. Pour the mixture into the prepared mold or dish, cover with plastic wrap, and freeze for at least 6 hours or overnight. To release the parfait, invert the mold and use the plastic wrap lining to ease the parfait out of the mold. It can also be scooped out like ice cream. Parfait will last about 1 week before it starts to taste like a freezer. For the best texture, let sit at room temperature for 10 minutes before serving.

Variations

- ❧ TOFFEE: Before the parfait is frozen, fold in 1 cup toffee bits or smashed toffee candy bars.

- ❧ CHOCOLATE: Before the parfait is frozen, fold in 1 cup chocolate shavings or chips.

- ❧ SWIRL: Layer the parfait in the mold with 1 cup Creamy Caramel Sauce (page 58) or Chocolate Sauce (page 39). Before freezing, stir it once with a spoon to swirl the layers together.

Chocolate Soufflé

I ALMOST ALWAYS HAVE A SOUFFLÉ ON MY MENU. DESPITE *what you may have heard, they are really quite easy. The French word* soufflé *means "puffed" or "puffy," which explains what happens to a soufflé in the oven. Air trapped within the foam of the egg whites expands with the heat of the oven, making the soufflé rise. The ingredient list calls for potato flour, which is also known as potato starch. Besides strengthening the eggs, potato flour helps retain moisture throughout the baking process. If you can't find it, you can leave it out. The soufflé will be more delicate.*

YIELD: Six 8-ounce servings or one large (1½-quart) soufflé

SPECIAL TOOLS:

One 1½-quart soufflé dish or six 8-ounce ramekins

Candy thermometer

Standing electric mixer with a whisk attachment (optional)

FOR COATING THE DISHES

2 tablespoons (¼ stick) unsalted butter, melted

¼ cup sugar

FOR THE SOUFFLÉ

4 ounces bittersweet chocolate

½ cup heavy cream

3 large egg yolks, at room temperature

2 tablespoons potato flour (potato starch)

8 large egg whites, at room temperature

Pinch of cream of tartar (less than ⅛ teaspoon)

¼ cup sugar

Powdered sugar for dusting

Preheat the oven to 425°F. Adjust a rack to the center of the oven. Lightly brush six 8-ounce ramekins or a 1½-quart soufflé dish with melted butter and then lightly but thoroughly coat them with sugar.

SOUFFLÉ(S)

1. Using a serrated knife, finely chop the chocolate into ¼-inch pieces and place it in a medium heatproof bowl.

2. Bring the cream to a boil in a small saucepan over medium heat. Immediately pour the hot cream over the chopped chocolate. Tap the bowl on the counter to settle the chocolate into the cream, then let it sit for 1 minute. Using a rubber spatula, slowly stir in a circular motion, starting from the center of the bowl and working out to the sides. Stir until all the chocolate reaches 100°F and is melted, about 2 minutes. Set aside.

3. In a small bowl, whisk together the egg yolks and the potato flour. Set aside.

4. Using a standing mixer fitted with a whisk attachment or a hand mixer at medium speed, whip the egg whites. When large bubbles appear, add the cream of tartar. Continue whipping until they reach the soft-peak stage, about 1 minute. Then slowly sprinkle in the sugar, taking about 1 minute to get it all in. Stop whipping when the egg whites are at the medium-peak stage. This is a meringue.

5. Using a rubber spatula, stir the room-temperature egg yolk mixture into the warm chocolate ganache. Stir until the mixture is just combined.

6. Fold one third of the egg whites into the ganache mixture to lighten the batter and make it easier to add the remaining whites. Carefully fold in the remaining whites, trying not to deflate them.

7. Spoon the soufflé into the prepared dish or dishes, filling them to the rim, and flatten them off with an offset spatula. Gently run a paring knife around the inside wall of the soufflé dish or dishes. This creates an inner wall of air between the soufflé and the ramekin, which helps the soufflé rise up straight.

8. Place the soufflés on a baking sheet and bake for 15 to 20 minutes, or until they are tall and dry on the sides (bake a large single soufflé for 40 to 45 minutes). They should be dry on the outside and creamy in the center. Serve immediately with a light dusting of powdered sugar.

BEATING EGG WHITES

- Always have your egg whites at room temperature; they will achieve the best volume. They should be free of yolk, fats, and water.

- Your bowl, whisk, and any other utensils involved should be dry and immaculate. I like to wipe my bowl with a clean towel that I have barely dampened with lemon juice.

- Copper bowls are great for beating egg whites because of a chemical reaction that occurs between the copper and the egg whites.

- Always begin beating whites on low speed, then move up to medium speed. When the whites begin to foam, you can add cream of tartar and 1 tablespoon of the sugar (if called for). When I see the mixture becoming shiny, I begin to slowly stream in the remaining sugar, 1 tablespoon at a time.

- I prefer to finish beating whites by hand. I can get to the pool at the bottom of the bowl that electric beaters in a standing mixer can't reach. Also, I have more control over the final consistency. It takes only about 10 more beats before whites reach a medium peak, and if you do it by hand you can avoid overbeating the whites. See "Baking Terms" (page 326) for a description of *soft peaks, medium peaks,* and *stiff peaks.* Overbeaten egg whites lose their sheen and separate into chunks. They will not be able to aerate your dessert.

Ganache Glaze

YIELD: 2 cups, enough for
two 9-inch cakes

SPECIAL TOOL:

Candy thermometer

8 ounces bittersweet
chocolate

4 tablespoons apricot jelly

½ cup heavy cream

¼ cup milk

2 tablespoons light corn syrup

THIS IS A SEXY GLAZE FOR TOPPING ANY TYPE OF CAKE.
*It has a beautiful, velvety shine. It's based on the firm ganache varia-
tion, with corn syrup added for gloss and a touch of apricot jelly to
balance the overall flavor. For the most glistening glaze, be sure to
use a smooth, clear apricot jelly and not a chunky jam.*

*The key to successful glazing is to keep the ganache at 90ºF
so it stays thin and viscous. It should flow easily over the cake without much prompting from a spatula. Covering a cake with ganache
is not hard, but it can be messy. (Don't wear white if it's your first
time.)*

1. Using a serrated knife, finely chop the chocolate into ¼-inch
pieces and place it in a medium heatproof bowl.

2. Warm the apricot jelly in a small saucepan over low heat for 2
to 3 minutes, stirring until it is melted. Whisk in the cream, milk,
and corn syrup. Increase the heat to medium and bring the mixture
to a boil.

3. Pour the hot cream mixture over the chopped chocolate. Tap
the bowl on the counter to settle the chocolate into the cream, then
let it sit for 1 minute. Using a rubber spatula, slowly stir in a circular
motion, starting from the center of the bowl and working out to the
sides. Be careful not to add too much air to the ganache. Stir until all
the chocolate is melted, about 2 minutes.

4. When all the chocolate has melted, insert a thermometer.
The temperature should be 90°F for the best glazing results. If the
temperature is too low, place the bowl over a saucepan half full of
simmering water, creating a double boiler, and gently stir until the
thermometer reads 90°F. If the temperature is too high, occasionally
stir the ganache off the heat until it is ready to be poured. Glazing
should be done as soon as the ganache reaches 90°F for maximum
viscosity. The glaze can be chilled for later use, then reheated slowly
over simmering water. If the reheated glaze seems too thick, add 1 tablespoon water.

GLAZING A CAKE

1. Line a baking sheet with parchment or wax paper and place a
cooling rack on top. Position the cake on the cooling rack. The
ganache will flow over the cake, through the cooling rack, and onto
the baking sheet below.

2. Warm the ganache to 90°F. Pour all of the warm ganache onto the top of the cake, directly in the center. The speed and weight of the pouring ganache will push itself over the edges, coating the sides of the cake. If some spots are left uncoated, carefully lift the cooling rack and swirl the cake gently to coax the ganache into place. Give the rack a couple of gentle taps on the counter to send any remaining ganache over the edge. Let the cake sit for 5 minutes at room temperature to settle.

3. Before the cake is chilled, transfer it to a cardboard circle or serving platter so that it doesn't stick to the rack. Chill the cake until the ganache is set, about 30 minutes. After chilling, the cake is ready to be decorated or cut and served. To cut the cake, use a warm, moist knife and wipe it with a towel after each cut.

YIELD: 2 to 3 cups

SPECIAL TOOLS:

    Food processor (optional)

    Candy thermometer

½ cup Master Ganache
    (page 16)

3 large egg yolks

½ cup Banyuls wine (see
    headnote, right)

2 tablespoons sugar

½ cup heavy cream, whipped
    to soft peaks

Chocolate Sabayon

SABAYON IS THE FRENCH WORD FOR THE ITALIAN DESSERT *zabaglione. It is an airy custard, made on the stovetop by whisking egg yolks, sugar, and Marsala wine over simmering water until light and fluffy. Traditional zabaglione is cooked tableside by handsome Italian waiters using a special copper double boiler.*

My version breaks from tradition and is much more French in style than Italian. Besides the addition of chocolate, I use Banyuls in place of the Marsala. Banyuls is a French fortified red wine from the Languedoc-Roussillon region, made mainly from the Grenache grape. It has a sweet, grapey-berry flavor. It is classically paired with chocolate and works wonderfully here. If you cannot find Banyuls, substitute equal amounts of a fruity red wine such as Syrah or port.

I like to spoon this sabayon over fresh raspberries, slices of cake, or warm tarts or serve it alone in a parfait glass. I have also baked it inside a tart shell. The result is like a soft soufflé. Because sabayon is thickened by air, it has a fairly short life span. I generally make it as close to serving time as I can.

1. Warm the ganache in a small heatproof bowl set over a saucepan half full of simmering water, creating a double boiler, or in the microwave at 50 percent power, stirring often, until it reaches 90°F, about 2 minutes. Set it aside at room temperature.

2. Fill a medium saucepan halfway with water. Bring the water to a boil, then turn the heat down to low. Combine the egg yolks, wine, and sugar in a medium bowl. Place it on top of the saucepan, creating a double boiler and making sure the bottom doesn't touch the water, and immediately begin to whip, using a wire balloon whisk. Continue whisking, lifting the whisk out of the eggs with each pass to incorporate as much air as possible. Whip until the egg yolks have thickened and are light yellow, about 3½ minutes.

3. Fold the whipped yolks into the warmed ganache, one third at a time. Fold in the whipped cream. The sabayon is now ready to serve.

Variation

❧ Replace the Banyuls wine with ¼ cup Chambord and ¼ cup water.

8 ounces bittersweet
chocolate

4 tablespoons (½ stick)
unsalted butter

1 cup raspberries (about
3 ounces), pureed and
strained, at room
temperature (½ cup
puree)

Raspberry Ganache

GANACHE DOES NOT ALWAYS HAVE TO INCLUDE HEAVY *cream. Here pureed raspberries take the place of the liquid and butter is added. The aromatic sweetness of the raspberries has enough oomph to counter the bittersweet chocolate. Use this ganache for Chocolate Financier with Raspberry Ganache on page 322 or fill a tart with raspberries, then top with piped raspberry ganache. It makes a luscious ending to a meal.*

1. Using a serrated knife, finely chop the chocolate into ¼-inch pieces and place in a medium heatproof bowl. Place over a saucepan of simmering water, creating a double boiler, and melt the chocolate. Cool to 100°F.

2. In the microwave or in a small saucepan, melt the butter and allow it to cool to 100°F. When both the chocolate and the butter reach 100°F, pour the butter into the chocolate. Using a rubber spatula, stir in a circular motion, starting from the center of the bowl and working out to the sides.

3. Stir in the raspberry puree with the same circular motion.

4. Allow the temperature of the ganache to drop to 70°F. At 70°F the ganache will be firm enough to roll, pipe, or spread. If not using it right away, store the ganache, tightly covered, in the freezer for up to 2 weeks.

Banana Ganache

YIELD: 2 to 2½ cups

SPECIAL TOOLS:

    Food processor (optional)

    Candy thermometer

4 ounces bittersweet
    chocolate

4 ounces milk chocolate

2 ripe bananas

½ cup heavy cream

2 tablespoons light corn syrup

THE COMBINATION OF BANANAS AND CHOCOLATE IS ALWAYS *a hot seller. There is something wonderfully reminiscent of childhood about the pair, perhaps because it reminds me of frozen chocolate-covered bananas. For those of you who are sick of making banana bread, it's a great way to use up those overripe bananas.*

This recipe was developed as a filling for Chocolate Banana Beignets (page 134).

Food processors do an excellent job of mashing bananas, making a very smooth puree. In fact, the entire recipe can be done in the food processor (see page 338), which means less cleanup. However, you can also use a fork or a potato masher. The bananas will be a little chunkier, but I like the texture they add.

1. Using a serrated knife, finely chop the chocolates into ¼-inch pieces and place it in a medium heatproof bowl.

2. Puree the bananas in a food processor or with a fork or potato masher and set aside.

3. Bring the cream and corn syrup to a boil in a small saucepan over medium heat. Immediately pour the cream over the chopped chocolate. Tap the bowl on the counter to settle the chocolate into the cream, then let it sit for 1 minute. Using a rubber spatula, stir in a circular motion, starting from the center of the bowl and working out to the sides. Stir until all the chocolate is melted, about 2 minutes. Stir in the pureed bananas.

4. Allow the temperature of the ganache to drop to 70°F. At 70°F, the ganache will be firm enough to roll, pipe, or spread. If not used right away, the ganache should be stored, tightly covered, in the freezer for up to 2 weeks.

YIELD: 2 dozen small bars

SPECIAL TOOLS:

    Food processor

    Parchment paper (for storing)

8 ounces bittersweet gianduja or milk chocolate

8 ounces bittersweet chocolate

1 cup heavy cream

½ cup Homemade Hazelnut Paste (page 34) or Nutella

½ cup sliced almonds, toasted (see page 366)

John Do Ya Ganache Candy Bars

GIANDUJA IS AN INCREDIBLE HAZELNUT-FLAVORED chocolate. It is also difficult for people to pronounce. When I realized that it took my staff longer to say "gianduja" than it took them to make this recipe, I began spelling it phonetically.

A similar product called Nutella can be used in this recipe. Nutella was created in 1940 in response to chocolate rationing. Cocoa was mixed with ground hazelnuts and vegetable oils to produce an economical spread. Nutella is a European pantry staple and outsells all the peanut butter brands combined. Gianduja can be found in specialty markets and comes in both milk and bittersweet varieties.

1. Line a baking sheet with plastic film, so that the bottom and all four edges are covered. Using a serrated knife, finely chop the gianduja and chocolate into ¼-inch pieces and place them in a medium heatproof bowl.

2. Bring the cream to a boil in a small saucepan over medium heat. Immediately pour the hot cream over the chopped chocolate. Tap the bowl on the counter to settle the chocolate into the cream, then let it sit for 1 minute. Using a rubber spatula, slowly stir in a circular motion, starting from the center of the bowl and working out to the sides. Stir until all the chocolate is melted, about 2 minutes. Fold in the hazelnut paste or Nutella and the almonds.

3. Pour onto the prepared baking sheet. Using an offset spatula, spread it out evenly, about ½ inch thick. Allow the ganache to cool at room temperature until it is set, about 2 hours.

4. When the ganache is set, invert the pan and use the plastic wrap to help ease it out of the baking sheet. Remove the plastic film and cut the candy bars into the desired shape and serve. The ganache candy bars can be stored in the refrigerator for up to 2 weeks. Layer them between pieces of parchment in an airtight container.

1 cup hazelnuts (filberts),
preferably skinless

1 tablespoon hazelnut oil
or vegetable oil

Homemade Hazelnut Paste

1. Preheat the oven to 350°F.

2. Place the nuts on a baking sheet and toast until they are dark golden brown, about 12 minutes. They should fill the room with a toasty nut smell. If the nuts have skins, remove them by wrapping the nuts in a towel and rubbing them.

3. Immediately transfer the hot nuts to a food processor and puree them to a fine paste by pulsing the machine on and off, about 2 minutes.

4. Turn on the processor and slowly drizzle in the oil. When all the oil is in, stop the machine and scrape any stray nuts back into the mix. Start the machine again and run it for 15 seconds more. The nut paste is ready to use, or it can be stored, covered, for up to 2 weeks in the refrigerator.

YIELD: Four 6-ounce servings

SPECIAL TOOL:

Candy thermometer

1 tablespoon unsalted butter,
melted

8 ounces bittersweet
chocolate

3/4 cup heavy cream

5 tablespoons sugar

3 tablespoons whiskey

2 large eggs, at room
temperature

Whipped crème fraîche, for
serving

Baked Whiskey Tortes

BY SIMPLY ADDING EGGS TO GANACHE YOU CAN CREATE *this cool, superfudgy cake. The recipe starts with a ganache, in which a small portion of the cream has been replaced by whiskey. I love the over-the-top combination of chocolate and whiskey. I usually serve these tortes warm in ramekins, with a dollop of cold crème fraîche on top. Cool cream with hot chocolate lingers on the tongue, and as it goes down, the heat of the whiskey kicks in. It's a knockout!*

The word whiskey comes from a Gaelic phrase meaning "water of life." I usually use American Jack Daniel's, my favorite, for this, or a nonalcoholic alternative, such as coffee or raspberry puree.

1. Preheat the oven to 325°F. Adjust the rack to the center of the oven. Brush the inside of four 6-ounce ramekins with melted butter.

2. Using a serrated knife, finely chop the chocolate into 1/4-inch pieces and place it in a medium heatproof bowl.

3. Bring the cream and sugar to a boil in a small saucepan over medium heat. Stir to dissolve the sugar. Immediately pour the cream over the chopped chocolate. Tap the bowl on the counter to settle the chocolate into the cream, then let it sit for 1 minute. Using a rubber spatula, stir in a circular motion, starting from the center of the bowl and working out to the sides. Stir until all the chocolate is melted, about 2 minutes.

4. Combine the whiskey and eggs in a large bowl. Whisk them together and then gently stir them into the ganache. When the eggs are thoroughly incorporated, pour the mixture into the ramekins, filling them three-quarters full.

5. Place the filled ramekins in a large baking pan. Carefully pour hot water into the large pan until it comes halfway up the ramekins. Bake the tortes for 20 to 25 minutes, or until they feel firm to the touch. Allow the tortes to cool slightly before serving. The tortes can be made up to 1 day in advance and rewarmed before serving in a 325°F oven for 8 to 10 minutes. Serve with a small dollop of whipped crème fraîche.

Chocolate Frosting

YIELD: 2 cups, enough for a
2-layer 9-inch cake

SPECIAL TOOL:
Standing electric mixer with a
paddle attachment (optional)

8 ounces bittersweet
chocolate

4 ounces (1 stick) unsalted
butter, softened

½ cup powdered sugar

THIS THICKER VARIATION OF GANACHE IS GREAT FOR *frosting cakes. The cream used in the firm ganache is replaced with butter. The ganache is transformed to frosting consistency by the addition of powdered sugar.*

This frosting is best used immediately after being made, so it's best to have your cake baked and cooled before you start. However, you can refrigerate the frosting for later use. To make chilled frosting manageable, place it in the bowl of a standing mixer fitted with the paddle attachment and beat for 3 to 4 minutes or use a hand mixer and a large bowl. If the frosting is too thick for your purpose, the consistency can be adjusted with a drop or two of hot water. If it is too thin, add a little more powdered sugar. Don't lick your fingers too much or you'll get a tummy ache.

1. Using a serrated knife, finely chop the chocolate into ¼-inch pieces and place it in a medium heatproof bowl with the butter.

2. Create a double boiler by placing the bowl of chocolate over a medium pot of simmering water. Stir the chocolate occasionally until it is melted, about 2 minutes. When it is melted, remove the bowl from the heat.

3. Sift the powdered sugar into the melted chocolate and slowly stir it in, using a rubber spatula. Stir for 3 or 4 minutes, until all the powdered sugar is absorbed. It will look like cottage cheese at first, but as more sugar is stirred in, it will smooth out.

4. The frosting should be used immediately for easy spreadability. If you need to store it for later use, wrap it tightly and refrigerate it for up to 2 days. To use, beat for 3 to 4 minutes in a standing mixer fitted with a paddle attachment or a hand mixer.

YIELD: 2 to 3 cups

- 8 ounces bittersweet chocolate
- 2 cups heavy cream
- 1 tablespoon sugar (optional)

Chocolate Whipped Cream

WHILE NOT A TRADITIONAL CHOCOLATE MOUSSE, *Chocolate Whipped Cream is an excellent filling for cakes, tarts, and cream puffs. It's also a great substitute for standard whipped cream when you're feeling indulgent. If you have a sweet tooth, add the optional sugar to the cream before it is heated.*

This recipe is the Master Ganache plus an extra cup of cream. Be careful. Don't overwhip the cream. It will take less than a minute for the cream to reach the desired consistency if you use a mixer.

1. Using a serrated knife, finely chop the chocolate into ¼-inch pieces and place it in a medium heatproof bowl.

2. Bring the cream and the sugar, if using, to a boil in a small saucepan over medium heat. Immediately pour the hot cream over the chopped chocolate. Tap the bowl on the counter to settle the chocolate into the cream, then let it sit for 1 minute. Using a rubber spatula, slowly stir in a circular motion, starting from the center of the bowl and working out to the sides. Stir until all the chocolate is melted, about 2 minutes.

3. Pour the ganache into a medium container, cover it, and refrigerate it for 4 hours or overnight. It should be the consistency of peanut butter.

4. Once the ganache has chilled, transfer it to a large bowl. Using a balloon whisk, whip the ganache by hand until it just reaches soft peaks, about 2 minutes. Be sure to lift the whisk out of the cream with each pass to bring in as much air as possible. Do not overwhip. Don't worry if the cream doesn't seem firm enough. It will have the consistency of mustard but will solidify a little more after it sets in the refrigerator. You can also use a hand mixer.

5. Use this cream immediately to fill pastries, tarts, and cakes. After the dessert is filled, refrigerate it for about 1 hour to set the Chocolate Whipped Cream. Store Chocolate Whipped Cream in the refrigerator for up to 2 days.

Variation

~ Substitute 1 cup crème fraîche for 1 cup of the heavy cream. It adds an interesting bite.

Campton Place Hot Chocolate

YIELD: Five 8-ounce cups or mugs

2 cups whole milk

½ cup cream

2 tablespoons unsweetened cocoa powder

1 recipe Master Ganache (page 16)

½ teaspoon Tía Maria or vanilla extract

½ recipe Chocolate Whipped Cream (page 37) and chocolate shavings for serving (optional)

BEFORE I CAME TO SPAGO, I LIVED AND WORKED IN SAN Francisco. Critics hailed my Hot Chocolate Elixir at Campton Place as the "best hot chocolate anywhere." It was totally decadent topped with Chocolate Whipped Cream.

Enhance this hot chocolate with peppermint or cinnamon or add another liquor, such as rum or Grand Marnier. You can vary not only the flavor but the form as well. Check out the variations following the recipe.

1. Bring the milk and cream to a boil in a small saucepan over medium heat. Add the cocoa powder and whisk or blend with an immersion blender to dissolve. Remove from the heat and add the ganache. Let sit for 1 minute, then stir until well combined, about 4 minutes. Stir in the Tía Maria or vanilla.

2. Serve the hot chocolate right away as is or store it covered in the refrigerator for up to 2 weeks. It can be reheated easily on the stovetop or in the microwave. If you wish, top with Chocolate Whipped Cream and chocolate shavings.

Variations

~ FUDGE ICED POPS: Cool the hot chocolate and pour it into small paper cups. Cover the cups with plastic wrap and insert a Popsicle stick. Freeze overnight, or until it is completely solid. Remove the ice pops by rubbing the cup with warm hands. If they don't pop right out, tear the cups away. To serve, put on your bathing suit and take the ice pop out to the backyard.

~ FRAPPÉ: Freeze the hot chocolate in ice cube trays. When solid, throw them in a blender and blend until smooth. Add cold coffee for a mocha frappé.

Chocolate Sauce

THIS SAUCE IS GLOSSY AND SMOOTH, LOOKS GREAT ON A *white plate, and has a really well-balanced flavor. It's based on the Master Ganache, with half the cream replaced by crème fraîche. The alcohol can be varied according to your taste and the dessert with which the sauce is to be served. For a nonalcoholic sauce, use espresso to create a deeper chocolate flavor.*

This sauce should be served warm. All sauces are thicker when cold and thinner when hot. If you want a cold chocolate sauce, use the cold variation following the recipe. Wrap a container of the sauce in a heating pad to keep it warm until you need it.

My sauce uses simple syrup, which is a standard pantry item in professional kitchens. To make it, combine equal amounts of sugar and water and bring to a boil. (See why they call it simple?) Simple syrup keeps for weeks in the refrigerator.

YIELD: 1¾ cups

SPECIAL TOOL:

Candy thermometer

¼ cup sugar

¼ cup water

2 ounces unsweetened chocolate

6 ounces bittersweet chocolate

¼ cup heavy cream

¼ cup crème fraîche

2 tablespoons (¼ stick) unsalted butter

2 tablespoons Tía Maria

1. Make a simple syrup by combining the sugar and water in a small saucepan over high heat. Stir to moisten the sugar and insert a thermometer. Cook until the temperature reaches 220°F, about 5 minutes. Immediately remove from the heat and allow to cool. Measure out ¼ cup; discard the rest.

2. Using a serrated knife, finely chop the chocolates into ¼-inch pieces and place in a medium heatproof bowl.

3. Bring the cream, crème fraîche, and butter to a boil in a small saucepan over medium heat. Immediately pour the cream over the chopped chocolate. Tap the bowl on the counter to settle the chocolate into the cream, then let it sit for 1 minute. Using a rubber spatula, slowly stir in a circular motion, starting from the center of the bowl and working out to the sides. Stir until all the chocolate is melted, about 2 minutes.

4. Add the Tía Maria and simple syrup and stir for 1 minute, or until smooth and thoroughly combined. Cover the sauce and keep it warm near the stove until it is served.

Variation

❧ COLD CHOCOLATE SAUCE: Add 1 additional cup liquid. It can be milk, water, or coffee. Simple syrup would be a bad choice here, since it would make the sauce too sweet.

Chocolate Mousse Trio

HERE ARE THREE VARIATIONS ON THE CLASSIC CHOCOLATE *mousse. The method is the same in each variation. The French word* mousse *means "foam" or "lather," and indeed, the recipe includes whipped egg whites. They add air, and the protein they contain adds stability.*

Choose your favorite flavor of mousse or make all three and serve them together, layered in a cute mold or pretty glasses. At Spago, I layer all three in a pyramid-shaped mold — a martini glass works just fine — with bittersweet at the bottom, milk chocolate in the middle, and white chocolate on the top. When combining the three, cut the recipes into thirds or you'll have enough mousse to feed a moose!

This recipe requires the separate whipping of two elements, egg whites and cream. When using a standing mixer with only one bowl, I always whip the egg whites first. They need a clean, fat-free environment to whip up nice and high. Cream, however, doesn't care if it's whipped in a dirty bowl, so I add it right after transferring the whites out and save myself a little cleanup.

YIELD: Six 6-ounce servings

SPECIAL TOOLS:

Candy thermometer

Standing electric mixer with a whisk attachment (optional)

FOR BITTERSWEET CHOCOLATE MOUSSE

1 cup Master Ganache (page 16)

3 large eggs, separated, at room temperature

Pinch of cream of tartar (less than 1/8 teaspoon)

2 tablespoons sugar

1 cup heavy cream

FOR MILK CHOCOLATE MOUSSE

1 cup Milk Chocolate Ganache (page 21)

3 large eggs, separated, at room temperature

Pinch of cream of tartar (less than 1/8 teaspoon)

1 tablespoon sugar

1 cup heavy cream

FOR WHITE CHOCOLATE MOUSSE

1 cup White Chocolate Ganache (page 22)

3 large eggs, separated, at room temperature

Pinch of cream of tartar (less than 1/8 teaspoon)

1 tablespoon sugar

1 cup heavy cream

1. Melt the ganache in a medium heatproof bowl over a saucepan half full of simmering water, creating a double boiler, or in the microwave for 30-second intervals on medium power. When melted, remove from the heat. Don't worry if the ganache separates when reheated. It will come back together when the eggs are added. Set aside.

2. Using a standing mixer fitted with a whisk attachment or a hand mixer, whip the egg whites on medium speed. When large bubbles appear, add the cream of tartar. Continue to whip until they reach the soft peak stage, about 1 minute. Slowly sprinkle in the sugar, taking about 1 minute to get it all in. Stop whipping the egg whites when they reach the medium peak stage, about 4 minutes. Transfer to a clean bowl and set aside.

3. Using the same bowl, whip the cream on medium speed until it reaches soft peaks, about 2 minutes. Set aside in the refrigerator.

4. Whisk the egg yolks in a small bowl. Pour them into the warm ganache and quickly stir together using a rubber spatula.

5. Gently fold in the egg whites. Any lumps of egg white that remain after folding will be smoothed out by the addition of the cream. (If the egg whites deflated a little as they sat, whip them up by hand for 10 to 15 seconds.) Carefully fold in the whipped cream.

6. Pour the mousse into a serving dish or mold. If your plan is to layer several glasses or molds with the trio of mousses, use a ladle or cup measure to measure out the same amount of mousse into each glass.

7. Cover and chill the mousse for at least 1 hour before serving. If you are going to layer the mousse, chill each layer completely before adding the next layer. Chocolate mousse will keep well in the refrigerator for 2 days.

Deep, Dark Chocolate Tart

YIELD: One 12-inch tart
or four 3-inch tartlets

SPECIAL TOOLS:

Candy thermometer

Standing electric mixer with a
paddle attachment (optional)

Pie weights (optional)

1 12-inch or four 3-inch
prebaked Chocolate Short
Dough shells (page 221)

8 ounces bittersweet
chocolate

2 tablespoons (¼ stick)
unsalted butter, softened

1½ cups heavy cream

2 tablespoons brewed coffee
or espresso

COFFEE IS A COMMON INGREDIENT IN MANY CHOCOLATE recipes. While it may not make the dish taste like coffee, it does intensify the bitterness, making the chocolate taste darker. This is the principle behind the tart filling, which uses the soft variation of ganache. While I prefer to use Chocolate Short Dough, any type of prebaked pie shell will work here.

This tart is beyond decadent, so serve it in small pieces. I suggest you balance the richness with orange segments or crème fraîche.

1. Place the prebaked tart shell, still in its pan, on a baking sheet.

2. Using a serrated knife, finely chop the chocolate into ¼-inch pieces and place it in a medium heatproof bowl along with the butter.

3. Bring the cream to a boil in a small saucepan over medium heat. Immediately pour the cream over the chopped chocolate. Tap the bowl on the counter to settle the chocolate into the cream, then let it sit for 1 minute. Using a rubber spatula, slowly stir in a circular motion, starting from the center of the bowl and working out to the sides. Stir until the temperature of the chocolate and butter reaches 90°F, about 2 minutes. The mixture should be completely melted.

4. Add the coffee and stir until well incorporated. Immediately pour the ganache into the tart shell. Carefully place the tart in the refrigerator to set, which will take approximately 1 hour before slicing and serving. Once completed, this tart will stay crisp for up to 3 days if stored in the refrigerator.

Variations

❧ FRUIT FILLING: Spread the bottom of the tart with mandarin oranges, raspberries, jam, or marmalade before pouring in the ganache.

❧ DOUBLE GANACHE: Fill the shell halfway with White Chocolate Ganache (page 22), Milk Chocolate Ganache (page 21), or Banana Ganache (page 32). Once that layer is set, pour on the deep, dark ganache.

❧ SPICED: Infuse flavors into the cream before adding it to the chocolate, then strain. I like to use Chinese five-spice powder, cinnamon sticks, Earl Grey tea, or fresh ginger juice.

CARAMEL

WHEN I WAS A KID, A TYPICAL HALLOWEEN NIGHT ENDED WITH my sisters and me barely making it home by our eight o'clock curfew. Mom would hose off the shaving cream and eggs that neighborhood pranksters inevitably coated us with, then let us camp out at opposite ends of the living room to sort our loot. As the bargaining began, my sisters went for the mini chocolate bars, rare treasures among the candy corn and lollipops. My favorites, though, were the cellophane-wrapped caramel squares, which far outnumbered the candy bars. I learned to negotiate, getting up to twelve caramels for one Snickers bar. Lucky me!

I may have gotten hooked on this soft, chewy, buttery, and mysterious candy watching our neighbor, Mrs. Friscatti, prepare the candy apples that she would treat us to every year at her Halloween parties. I sometimes helped her and will never forget watching her heat the caramels with milk, turning them into a warm dipping sauce for green apples.

Whether I have actually grown up since those days is open to debate, but my understanding of caramel has definitely matured. No longer merely my favorite candy, caramel is a key ingredient and an indispensable flavoring in many of my best desserts. The slightly bitter taste of caramelized sugar adds a unique dimension to the most basic recipe. I like to combine it with ingredients like crème fraîche, fruit juices, spices, herbs, and teas; their flavors fuse with the distinctive flavor of the caramel, adding another taste dimension.

ALL CARAMELS BEGIN WITH THE MELTING AND HEATING of ordinary table sugar. Caramelization is the process that transforms this simple granular white sugar into liquid brown sugar. Sugar melts into a syrup when it is heated, and as the temperature rises, the syrup becomes thicker and more concentrated and gradually the color gets darker. As it goes from light yellow to dark brown, the flavor deepens as a result of the myriad chemical reactions that occur when the broken-down sugar molecules are heated.

All types of sugar will caramelize — indeed, it is the caramelization of the sugars in meats and vegetables that results in browning when they are cooked at high heat and that are responsible for bread's dark brown, slightly bitter crust. But granulated sugar is the one used for desserts.

The chemical name for this sugar is *sucrose.* Sucrose is a disaccharide, which means it is made up of two simple sugar molecules, glucose and fructose, joined together in a particular form that we identify as a sugar crystal. When the sugar is heated, these molecules break apart, forming a solution that will concentrate and darken the hotter it gets.

TO CARAMELIZE SUGAR, YOU COMBINE SUGAR, WATER, AND corn syrup in a saucepan, cover it, and set it over high heat. As the mixture heats, it releases steam, which the lid traps. Condensation forms and runs down the inside of the pot, washing away any stray sugar crystals. After 4 minutes, you can remove the lid. The sugar will be boiling and noticeably thicker. Set a thermometer in the pot to monitor the temperature, which at this point should read between 230° and 240°F.

As the water heats up, it evaporates. The sugar begins to thicken, and the bubbles get bigger. As the temperature increases, the color deepens and the flavor intensifies. These changes occur more quickly as the temperature rises. At 310°F, the sugar begins to turn a pale golden color and the caramel should be watched closely. At 310° to 325°F, the color is golden brown. Above 375°F, the caramel becomes quite bitter. Because the caramelization process is irreversible, this stage should be avoided. In a heavy pot on high heat, the entire process should take

No longer merely my favorite candy, caramel is an indispensable flavoring in many of my best desserts.

about 10 minutes. I like my caramel dark, and I often cook it just to the point of being bitter. However, there's a fine line between bitter and burned, so I advise you to take it off the heat at 325°F for golden caramel and 350°F for dark caramel.

THE MAIN CHALLENGE TO THE CARAMEL MAKER IS TO PREVENT the sugar molecules from rejoining to form crystals, a process that is irreversible once it begins and that will turn your caramel into a grainy, useless mass. When a foreign particle such as a bit of food from dirty equipment, lint from towels, or a stray grain of sugar gets into the pot, it can act as a "seed" to which sugar molecules are attracted. They attach themselves, and as they accumulate, they form into large, irregular, solid crystals. Soon the pot of liquid sugar will become solid again.

To prevent crystallization, open a new bag of sugar and use fresh, clean water and clean equipment. Stirring and sloshing the sugar as it cooks can also cause crystallization by pushing the sugar molecules together. Avoid any unnecessary movement of the syrup. If a candy recipe does call for stirring, use a metal spoon. Small particles can hide in the pores of a wooden spoon.

As the sugar boils, popping bubbles on the surface will deposit sugar particles on the side of the pot. These stray particles can also become seeds for crystallization and should be washed down as necessary with a moist pastry brush. (The pastry brush should be of good quality, because cheaper brushes often lose their bristles, causing crystallization.) It's best to dedicate one pastry brush to sugar cooking and keep it very clean.

Adding acid to the pot, such as a few drops of lemon juice or vinegar, can also discourage crystallization. Acid will cause some of the sugar molecules to split into smaller glucose and fructose molecules. These

The main challenge to the caramel maker is to prevent the sugar molecules from rejoining to form crystals.

smaller molecules form chains that get in the way of the crystallization process. Using a sweetener whose makeup is similar but not identical to sugar will also prevent the formation of crystals. In my basic caramel recipe, I use corn syrup, which is made up primarily of glucose with some maltose.

EXPERIENCED CARAMEL MAKERS CAN RELY ON THEIR EYES and nose to determine when the caramel is perfect. Novices should use an accurate candy thermometer. A digital thermometer will give you the fastest, most accurate reading when it comes to making caramel. Buy a good-quality digital thermometer (see page 346 for recommendations) and test its accuracy in boiling water. An accurate thermometer should read 212°F (100°C) in boiling water at sea level. While you are cooking, store the thermometer in a container of warm water when not in use. This will discourage sugar crystals from forming on the thermometer, which could be introduced into the pot the next time it is used.

Fast, even heat is also important. Most confectioners use copper pots for cooking sugar because they are heavy and distribute heat more evenly. Heavy-gauge stainless steel with a copper core is a good substitute. If you don't have a pot like this, use the sturdiest one on hand. Never use a pot with a nonstick surface or a plastic handle, which can be damaged by the intense heat.

DON'T BE AFRAID OF MAKING CARAMEL. IT REALLY IS EASY, and with this master recipe you won't have to worry about crystallization. The only special tool you'll need is a candy thermometer, preferably a digital one, and the only precaution you need to take is to keep a bowl of

A digital thermometer will give you the fastest, most accurate reading when it comes to making caramel.

CARAMEL STAGES

TEMPERATURE

°F	SUGAR STAGE	DESCRIPTION
400	Burned Caramel	Too bitter, no good — do over
375	Very Dark Caramel	Dark and bittersweet
350	Dark Caramel	Dark and intense
345	Amber Caramel	Rich and sweet
325	Light Caramel	Brittle/Lollipops/Spun Sugar
320		
285–315	Hard Crack	Caramel stage begins at 310°F
275–280	Crack	
270–275	Soft Crack	Taffy
260–265	Hard Ball	Divinity/Nougat
245–255	Firm Ball	Firmer Caramel Candies
240–245	Soft Ball	Fondant/Fudge/Soft Caramel Candies
230–235	Thread	Italian Meringue
225	Clear	Syrup
223		Syrup
215		Syrup
213		Syrup
212	Boiling	

Sugar stage refers to the form and color hot sugar syrup takes when it is cool. When a spoonful of 235°F syrup cools, it will be a pliable, "soft ball." When a syrup that has been cooked to 280°F cools down, it will become brittle and shatter or "crack" very easily. Test the stage by dipping a spoonful of hot sugar into ice water.

ice water on hand for emergencies. Because of the high temperature, a sugar burn can be very painful. If you should get hot caramel on you, apply ice water immediately.

If sugar is caramelized and then cooled, it will harden completely. In this form, caramel is used to make decorative shapes or flat sheets. If broken, these shapes will shatter like glass. Other ingredients added when the caramel is still hot will alter the form that caramel takes when it is cooled. Ingredients such as juice or cream will dilute the caramel, giving it the consistency of a sauce. Additions like these are the basis from which the entire family of caramel confections is created.

BUTTERMILK
BIRTHDAY
CUPCAKES
(page 156)

CAMPTON PLACE
HOT CHOCOLATE
(page 38)

FUDGE FONDUE
(page 20)

Opposite:
LEMON PUDDING CAKES *(page 82)*
(Inset) MASTER LEMON CURD *(page 75)*

CARAMEL–BLACK CHERRY GELÉE

(*page 69*)

CROQUEMBOUCHE
(page 124)

CARAMEL
POACHED APPLES
(*page 66*)

BLACKBERRY SORBET
(page 297)

Opposite:
MINI LEMON SOUFFLÉ TART
WITH BLACKBERRY GRANITA
(page 320)

CLASSIC CROISSANT
(page 279)

Opposite:
APRICOT MASCARPONE CANNOLI
(page 130)

LEMON POUND CAKE

(page 142)

BLACKBERRY JELLIES

(page 299)

Caramel
FAMILY TREE

CRUNCHY
MASTER CARAMEL
Golden Spun Sugar
Caramel Sticks
Croquante
Hazelnut Brittle
Pecan Pralines

CREAMY
Creamy Caramel Sauce
Whipped Caramel Cream
Caramel Soufflé
Caramel Crème Fraîche Candy
Caramel Custard Tart
Caramel Gelato

CLEAR
Apple Caramel Glaze
Caramel Poached Apples
Caramel Semifreddo
Caramel–Cranberry Granita
Caramel–Black Cherry Gelée
Oven-Roasted Caramel Anjou Pears

All recipes in the caramel family tree begin with the technique of the master.
Additional ingredients transform the caramel into either clear or creamy.

crunchy
+
heavy cream
=
CREAMY

crunchy
+
water or juicy liquid
=
CLEAR

YIELD: ¾ cup

SPECIAL TOOL:

    Candy thermometer

¼ cup water

1 cup sugar

2 tablespoons light corn syrup

Master Caramel

THE MASTER CARAMEL IS THE FIRST STEP TOWARD CREATING *creamy, crunchy, or clear caramel confections. Hot liquid caramel can be manipulated into decorative shapes that harden when cool. Add nuts and the master caramel turns into brittle. Poured into a ramekin, it becomes the base for crème caramel. Add cream, and it becomes caramel sauce. Add juice, and it becomes a glaze.*

    It's vital to remember that caramel is hot. Always keep a bowl of ice water at your side when working with hot sugar. If a finger should touch the hot caramel, immediately plunge it into the ice water.

    Cleanup tip: After the cooking is complete, your pot and utensils will be coated in hardened caramel. The easiest way to clean a sugar pot is to fill it with water and bring it to a boil. Tools with hardened sugar can be placed inside and boiled clean as well. It helps to keep a pot of water at a simmer for quick cleanup of utensils.

1. Wash and dry your hands thoroughly. Combine the water, sugar, and corn syrup in a medium saucepan. Stir them together with very clean fingers, making sure no lumps of dry sugar remain. Brush down the inside of the pan with a little water, using your hand to feel for any stray granules of sugar.

2. Cover the saucepan and place it over medium heat for 4 minutes. After 4 minutes, remove the lid, increase the heat to high, and bring to a boil. Do not stir from this point on. Keep an eye on the pan. It will be very bubbly. When stray sugar crystals appear on the side of the pan, brush them down with a clean, wet pastry brush.

3. As the sugar cooks, the bubbles will get larger. Insert a candy thermometer, and when the temperature reaches 300°F, lower the heat to medium, which will slow the cooking. Continue to cook the sugar until it reaches 325°F; this will happen quickly. It will be golden brown. At 325°F, remove the pot from the heat and let it sit for 1 minute, or until the bubbles subside.

NOTE

When making caramel, keep in mind that the sugar will continue to cook from the heat of the saucepan even after it is removed from the stove. If you find the sugar is getting too dark too fast, dip the bottom of the saucepan in ice water to stop the cooking process.

4. The caramel can be used immediately or stored for later use. To store, pour the hot caramel no more than 1 inch deep into disposable aluminum cups or a clean or new aluminum pie pan (use the pie pan if you'll be smashing up the caramel later). Cool it for 1 hour and then cover it so it is airtight. It will last for up to 2 weeks in a cool, dry place.

TO REHEAT CARAMEL

Break up the caramel and place in a clean, heavy pot. Reheat over low heat, stirring, until just melted. Remove from the heat.

Variation

  CHOCOLATE CARAMEL: When the caramel has reached 325°F, remove it from the heat and let the bubbles subside. Add 2 tablespoons finely chopped bittersweet chocolate and stir to combine. The chocolate variation can be used in place of any standard caramel. It makes great lollipops.

Caramel
CRUNCHY

YIELD: 30 to 40 nests

SPECIAL TOOLS:

Candy thermometer

Parchment paper (optional)

Silica gel (optional)

1 recipe Master Caramel
(page 50), prepared
through step 3

Golden Spun Sugar

SPUN SUGAR IS CARAMELIZED SUGAR MANIPULATED INTO *fine, hairlike strands. This classic garnish is traditionally used around a croquembouche, atop oeufs à la neige (floating islands), and as "moss" on top of a bûche de Noël. It adds a special touch to any dessert: wrap it around a cake, fashion it into a nest, or loosely gather it into balls.*

Nothing is added to the Master Caramel recipe, but it must be cooled to just the right temperature. Pastry chefs use several different methods to spin sugar, including custom-made spinning tools. I prefer a stainless-steel fork.

Finished spun sugar has a short life span. Caramel attracts moisture, so moisture must be kept to a minimum if caramel pieces are to remain crisp when stored. Any humidity will cause it to melt into a sticky puddle. To prevent this, place a dehumidifying agent in the container with the caramel to attract any moisture. Silica gel is the most commonly used dehumidifying agent. Silica gel is used to dehydrate flowers and can be found at craft supply stores. If you don't want to worry about the effects of humidity, save the spinning until just before serving.

1. Let the Master Caramel cool to 300°F, 5 to 8 minutes. It should be thick but still liquid, like molasses. Scoop up a forkful of the caramel and let it fall back into the pot. If it flows in a smooth, steady stream, it is ready to use. If the sugar drips as it pours, it is still too hot.

2. While the caramel is cooling, prepare the spinning area. Position two medium saucepans with metal handles at the edge of a counter, 12 inches apart, letting the handles extend out over the floor parallel to one another. The sugar will be spun over the pot handles. Directly under the handles, place some parchment paper or newspaper on the floor to catch any drips. If you're not using the spun sugar right away, prepare a storage container with a lining of parchment paper and a small sachet of silica gel to absorb moisture.

3. Dip a fork into the caramel and carefully scoop some out. Position the fork 12 inches above the two extended pot handles, and

let the caramel flow off the fork, quickly wiggling the fork and draping the caramel back and forth over the handles. After two or three forkfuls, stop and gather up the spun-sugar threads, set aside on a piece of parchment paper, then begin again. If the caramel becomes too cool, reheat it over medium heat for 3 to 4 minutes, stirring. Do not let the temperature exceed 300°F.

4. Use immediately or store the spun sugar in the prepared container with sheets of parchment between the layers. Spun sugar can be stored for only a few hours in an airtight container (less if the environment is humid).

NOTE
You can thicken the caramel by whisking it vigorously with a fork. Thicker caramel is easier to control. Whisking will also lighten the color.

Caramel
CRUNCHY

YIELD: One hundred 6-inch sticks

SPECIAL TOOLS:

   Silicone mat or parchment paper

   Candy thermometer

1 recipe Master Caramel
(page 50), prepared
through step 3

Caramel Sticks

CARAMEL STICKS ARE PENCIL-THIN STRIPS OF CARAMEL THAT *harden like glass and look like swizzle sticks. They're a fun and easy dessert garnish that adds crunch, height, and sweetness, turning an ordinary dessert into an unforgettable one.*

Once you get the hang of these caramel sticks, try making other shapes. Squiggles and zigzags of caramel look great tucked into a dollop of whipped cream or crowning a scoop of ice cream. You can even use the liquid caramel to write the initials of someone special.

1. Line a baking sheet with a silicone mat or parchment paper coated with butter or pan spray.

2. Let the Master Caramel cool to 300°F, 5 to 8 minutes. It should be thick but still liquid, like molasses. Scoop up a spoonful of the caramel and let it fall back into the pot. If it flows in a smooth, steady stream, it is ready to use. If the sugar drips as it pours, it is still too hot.

3. Carefully scoop out 1 teaspoon of the caramel and position it 6 inches above the prepared baking sheet. Pour the caramel off the spoon across the baking sheet, forming a line of caramel the length of the baking sheet. The caramel stick will harden immediately. Repeat with the remaining caramel. The sticks can be left long or broken into different lengths by tapping them with a knife.

4. If the caramel becomes too cool to work with before you finish making all of the sticks, reheat it. If it has hardened completely, smash it up and place the pan over medium heat. Cook, stirring for 3 to 4 minutes. The temperature should not exceed 300°F.

5. Store the caramel sticks in an airtight container. To prevent any air from getting in, wrap the container in several layers of plastic wrap. The sticks can be stored this way for up to 24 hours. Do not refrigerate, because any additional moisture will make the sugar sticky. For prolonged storage, caramel sticks can be frozen, as long as they are wrapped airtight. Use them immediately after removing them from the freezer.

Caramel
CRUNCHY

Croquante

YIELD: Twenty-four 2-inch squares

SPECIAL TOOLS:

    Silicone mat or parchment paper

    Candy thermometer

1 cup almonds, sliced or chopped

1 cup sugar

¼ cup light corn syrup

¼ cup water

    Tempered chocolate (see below)

CROQUANTE, ALSO KNOWN BY THE GERMAN KROKANT, IS A cousin to American-style brittle. It is traditionally thinner and is used in more elegant applications than the Yankee version. It can be cut into squares and served as a confection, pulverized and sprinkled over ice cream, or molded into elaborate centerpieces. The French croquembouche, a towering pyramid of cream puffs, is traditionally mounted on an intricate base made of croquante. I like to dip small squares of croquante in chocolate and serve them at the end of a meal. The croquante must be stirred to prevent the nuts from sinking to the bottom and burning.

1. Line a baking sheet with a silicone mat or parchment paper coated with butter or pan spray. Preheat the oven to 350°F in case you need to reliquefy the caramel.

2. Combine the almonds, sugar, corn syrup, and water in a medium saucepan. Heat over high heat, stirring occasionally to prevent the almonds from sinking to the bottom and burning, until the temperature reaches 325°F, about 12 minutes. If sugar crystals appear on the side of the pan, wash them down with a clean, wet pastry brush. As the sugar darkens, stir continuously.

3. At 325°F, the mixture will be a golden color. Remove it from the heat and immediately pour it onto the prepared baking sheet. Using an oiled metal spatula or an oiled rolling pin, flatten the mixture to a thickness of ¼ inch. If the croquante hardens and is too thick, reliquefy it by placing it on a baking sheet lined with a silicone mat and baking it for 1 minute. The heat will cause the croquante to melt and spread.

4. Quickly, while the croquante is still hot and pliable, score it into 2-inch squares with an oiled chef's knife. When the croquante cools, the squares will snap apart easily. Dip them partially into tempered chocolate and let them cool at room temperature. Croquante can be stored in an airtight container at room temperature for up to 2 weeks.

TEMPERED CHOCOLATE

Place ½ cup finely chopped bittersweet chocolate in a medium heatproof bowl over a saucepan of water that has been brought to a boil and turned off. Stir until melted. Remove from the heat and cool to 80° to 85°F. Place the bowl back over the hot water and bring the temperature back up to 90°F. The chocolate is now ready for dipping. Maintain at 88°F.

Hazelnut Brittle

YIELD: Ten 2-inch pieces

SPECIAL TOOLS:

> Silicone mat or parchment paper
>
> Candy thermometer

½ cup hazelnuts, toasted (page 362), skinned, and roughly chopped

Double recipe (1½ cups) Master Caramel (page 50), prepared through step 3

¼ teaspoon finely chopped orange zest

CULTIVATED HAZELNUTS, ALSO MARKETED AS *FILBERTS*, HAVE *been grown extensively in the Pacific Northwest since 1940. The thin brown skin found on the nut after it has been removed from the shell has a slightly bitter flavor. To remove the skins, see page 362.*

Hazelnut brittle is great to use as a crunchy garnish or a topping for ice cream, or simply to satisfy a sweet tooth. You'll be tempted to experiment with other nuts after you've made this recipe. Go ahead. Make it with macadamia nuts, peanuts, Brazil nuts, or your favorite nut.

1. Warm the hazelnuts in a low oven. Line a baking sheet with a silicone mat or parchment paper coated with butter or pan spray. Heat a saucepan of water and place a large metal spoon in it. Preheat the oven to 350°F in case you need to reliquefy the caramel.

2. When the bubbles have subsided in the prepared caramel, add the hazelnuts and zest, stirring with the warmed metal spoon to incorporate evenly. Pour the mixture onto the prepared baking sheet. Spread it with an oiled offset spatula to a thickness of ½ inch. If the brittle cools and is too thick, reliquefy it by placing it on a baking sheet and baking it for 1 to 2 minutes. The heat will cause it to melt and spread. Let the brittle cool completely at room temperature.

3. When the brittle is hard, break it into large pieces. Use it right away or store it in an airtight container at room temperature for up to 2 weeks.

Variation

❧ FAIRY DUST: To create a garnish with a more delicate crunch, break up the cooled brittle and place in a food processor. Pulse the processor on and off until the brittle is pulverized, about 1 minute. Freeze the dust in an airtight container for up to 1 month. It will last only 1 to 2 hours at room temperature. Use the dust to coat a scoop of ice cream, press it onto the sides of a cake, or sprinkle it over a dessert before serving.

Caramel

CRUNCHY

Pecan Pralines

YIELD: 12 to 15 pralines

SPECIAL TOOLS:

   Silicone mat or parchment paper

   Candy thermometer

1 cup sugar

2 tablespoons light corn syrup

¼ cup water

1 tablespoon honey

½ cup light brown sugar

2 tablespoons unsalted butter

¼ teaspoon finely grated
   orange zest

¼ teaspoon salt

⅛ teaspoon freshly ground
   black pepper

1 cup pecan halves

IN CLASSICAL CUISINE, THE TERM *PRALINE* REFERS TO HARD *caramel brittle with nuts (like Hazelnut Brittle, page 56). In New Orleans, however, pralines are completely different. These candies (pronounced PRAW-leens) have a soft, crumbly texture that is the result of crystallization. By adding ingredients and stirring vigorously, you force the caramel to crystallize as it cools. This is one of the few times that crystallization is actually desirable. I like to spice up my pralines by adding a pinch of black pepper or grated orange zest. They're nutty, supersweet, and addictive.*

1. Line a baking sheet with a silicone mat or parchment paper coated with butter or pan spray. Heat a saucepan of water and place a whisk and two soupspoons in it.

2. Combine the sugar, corn syrup, and water in a medium saucepan. Cover and place over medium heat for 4 minutes. Remove the lid, increase the heat to high, and bring to a boil. Do not stir from this point on. Keep an eye on the pan. If stray sugar crystals appear on the side, brush them down with a clean wet pastry brush.

3. As the sugar cooks, the bubbles will get larger. Insert a candy thermometer. After about 8 minutes, the sugar will turn light golden brown. When the temperature reaches 335°F, remove the sugar from the heat. Allow the bubbles to subside, about 1 minute.

4. Add the honey, brown sugar, butter, orange zest, salt, and pepper. Stir well to distribute the ingredients evenly. Stir in the pecans.

5. Using one soupspoon, scoop up tablespoon-size pieces of the mixture and transfer to the prepared baking sheet, spacing them 1 inch apart. (Use the other soupspoon to ease the caramel off the spoon.) If the mixture begins to harden before it is all spooned out, warm over low heat until it reliquefies. Let cool completely at room temperature before serving. As the pralines cool, they will lose their shine and become opaque. This is the crystallization process in action, and it is perfectly fine here. Cooled pralines can be stored in an airtight container at room temperature for up to 2 weeks or frozen for 1 month.

Creamy Caramel Sauce

YIELD: 1¼ cups

SPECIAL TOOL:

Candy thermometer

1 recipe Master Caramel (page 50), prepared through step 3 but heated to 350°F

½ cup heavy cream, warmed to 100°F

¼ cup crème fraîche

1 tablespoon sugar

½ teaspoon fresh lemon juice

Pinch of salt (less than ⅛ teaspoon)

CARAMEL SAUCE IS PERHAPS THE MOST VERSATILE *incarnation of caramel. Besides being both a hot and cold sauce, it makes a great filling for tarts and other pastries. It is also a major ingredient in some of my other recipes, such as truffles that I make with Caramel Ganache (page 23), and Caramel Soufflé (page 61). I always keep a variety of caramel blends refrigerated in my bakeshop. They last for weeks and are ready at a moment's notice to fulfill the inevitable special request.*

When I make creamy and clear caramels that have liquid added to them, I take the caramel to a higher temperature, because I want a more intense flavor that won't be diluted when the caramel is stretched. For example, you'll be heating the sugar to 350°F in this recipe, and you'll want to watch it carefully so that it doesn't burn.

Adding any liquid to hot caramel will cause it to bubble up like an eruption of molten lava. Using a pot that is at least twice the volume of the ingredients will prevent boil-over. Heating the liquid first reduces the volatility of this reaction but does not eliminate it, so be prepared. Oven mitts and a long-handled whisk are helpful, and don't stick your head or arms directly over the pot. It is important to remember that the steam rising out of a pot of hot caramel is as hot as the caramel inside, and nothing is as painful as a steam burn.

Crème fraîche adds the perfect balance to this sauce, taming the sweetness with a touch of acidity. If you can't find it and don't have time to make it (see page 358), sour cream is a good substitute. I also balance the flavor of this sauce with a second addition of sugar and a little lemon juice at the very end. This adds another subtle dimension of flavor.

1. Heat a saucepan of water and place a whisk in it. When you remove the prepared caramel from the heat, it should be dark instead of golden brown. Let it rest for 1 minute, or until all the bubbles have subsided. Add the cream to the caramel. It will bubble up vigorously, so be careful.

2. Vigorously whisk in the crème fraîche, sugar, lemon juice, and salt. This sauce is now ready to be served warm or cooled to room temperature. It will keep stored airtight in the refrigerator for up to 1 month. When cold, it has the consistency of peanut butter.

Variations

- ❧ PENUCHE CARAMEL SAUCE: Replace the crème fraîche with an equal amount of condensed milk.

- ❧ BUTTERSCOTCH SAUCE: Replace the 1 tablespoon sugar with 2 tablespoons light brown sugar.

- ❧ HONEY OR MAPLE CARAMEL SAUCE: Replace the 1 tablespoon sugar with 2 tablespoons maple syrup or honey.

- ❧ CHOCOLATE-CARAMEL SAUCE: Stir in 2 ounces finely chopped bittersweet chocolate along with the crème fraîche. Stir until the chocolate is melted.

- ❧ SALTY PEANUT-CARAMEL SAUCE: Add ½ cup toasted chopped salted peanuts along with the crème fraîche.

- ❧ BANANA-CARAMEL SAUCE: Add 1 mashed banana along with the crème fraîche.

- ❧ TANGY CARAMEL SAUCE: Add 2 tablespoons raspberry vinegar or Champagne vinegar after the finished sauce has cooled. The added acid gives an extra zing to the sweet caramel.

Whipped Caramel Cream

YIELD: 3 cups

SPECIAL TOOLS:

Candy thermometer

Standing electric mixer with a
whisk attachment (optional)

1 recipe Creamy Caramel
Sauce (page 58)

1 cup heavy cream

½ cup crème fraîche

2 tablespoons sugar

THIS DELICIOUS CREAM ENHANCES MANY OF MY DESSERTS. *It's great served with fresh berries or citrus fruits and a good nutty cookie. I also use it as a filling between layers of moist pound cake and as the surprise center of my Halsey Tart (page 324). My all-time favorite way to serve this cream, however, is layered into a napoleon with crunchy, freshly baked puff pastry and strawberries. The contrasting textures in this classic are what makes napoleons among the best pastries.*

1. Allow the Creamy Caramel Sauce to chill completely in the refrigerator, at least 2 hours. It should have the consistency of peanut butter.

2. Using a standing or hand mixer, whip the cream, crème fraîche, and sugar for about 3 minutes, or until medium-stiff peaks form.

3. Using a rubber spatula, carefully fold the cream mixture into the caramel sauce. Use the cream immediately or store it covered in the refrigerator for up to 5 hours.

Caramel Soufflé

SOUFFLÉS ARE ELEGANT AND EASY. AS SOON AS YOU HAVE *made one flavor, you'll be ready to try another. Don't be intimidated by their mystique. Just be sure to serve them when they come out of the oven.*

Traditionally, the waiter brings the soufflé to the table, splits it open magically with two spoons held in one hand, and fills it with sauce. I often serve sauce on the side of a soufflé in a small cream pitcher. With this caramel soufflé, I serve fresh peaches and more caramel sauce.

YIELD: 1 large soufflé or 6 individual soufflés

SPECIAL TOOLS:

Candy thermometer

1 large (1½-quart) soufflé dish or six 6- to 8-ounce ramekins

Standing electric mixer with a whisk attachment (optional)

FOR THE DISH(ES)

2 tablespoons (¼ stick) unsalted butter, melted

¼ cup sugar

FOR THE SOUFFLÉ

1 cup Creamy Caramel Sauce (page 58), at room temperature

3 large egg yolks, at room temperature

9 large egg whites, at room temperature

Pinch of cream of tartar (less than ⅛ teaspoon)

⅓ cup sugar

Preheat the oven to 425°F. Adjust the rack to the lower third of the oven. Brush the inside of six 6- to 8-ounce ramekins or 1 large soufflé dish with melted butter and then lightly but completely dust the inside with sugar.

SOUFFLÉ(S)

1. Whisk together the caramel sauce and egg yolks in a medium bowl. This mixture is the soufflé base.

2. Using a standing mixer fitted with a whisk attachment or a hand mixer, whip the egg whites for about 30 seconds, or until soft foam appears. Add the cream of tartar and continue to whip the whites for 2 minutes. Add the sugar and beat until the egg whites reach the medium-peak stage.

3. Using a rubber spatula, fold one third of the egg whites into the caramel mixture to lighten the base. Fold in the remaining whites carefully so that the mixture is not deflated. The most efficient way to fold is to rotate the bowl and spatula simultaneously in opposite directions, one clockwise and the other counterclockwise.

4. Spoon the soufflé into the dish or ramekins, filling them to the rim. Flatten the top with a metal spatula. Gently run a paring knife around the inner wall of the ramekin. This creates a small wall of air between the soufflé and the ramekin, which helps the soufflé rise up straight. Place the soufflés on a baking sheet. Bake for 15 to 20 minutes for individual soufflés or 30 to 40 minutes for a large soufflé. When finished, the soufflés should be tall, golden brown, dry on the edges, and creamy in the center. Serve immediately.

Caramel Crème Fraîche Candy

YIELD: One hundred 1-inch candies

SPECIAL TOOLS:

    Silicone mat (optional)

    Candy thermometer

    Cellophane candy wrappers
    (optional)

1 cup sugar

¼ cup plus 2 tablespoons
    light corn syrup

¼ cup water

1 cup crème fraîche

4 tablespoons (½ stick)
    unsalted butter

½ vanilla bean, split
    and scraped

1 teaspoon vanilla extract

THESE CANDIES MAKE A TERRIFIC GIFT. THE BUTTER MAKES *them rich and smooth and adds another layer of flavor. They are unbeatable as is but can also be dipped in chocolate or mixed with nuts.*

This recipe begins with a variation on Master Caramel, using an increased amount of corn syrup, which contributes to the final chewy texture of the candy. After the caramel is dark golden, the remaining ingredients are added. To keep the temperature even throughout the mixture and to prevent ingredients from scorching, the caramel must be stirred from that point on.

1. Line a baking sheet with a silicone mat or lightly buttered aluminum foil.

2. Combine the sugar, corn syrup, and water in a large saucepan over high heat. Follow the method for Master Caramel (page 50), but heat to 350°F. Let cool for 1 minute as directed.

3. When the bubbles have subsided, add the crème fraîche, butter, vanilla seeds (save the pod for another use), and vanilla extract. The mixture will bubble up vigorously, so be careful. Place the pan back over high heat and continue to cook, stirring occasionally, for about 5 minutes, or until the caramel reaches 245°F. Test the consistency of the caramel at this point by dropping a small amount into ice water. It should be at the firm-ball stage, which means it holds its shape but is chewy. If the texture is not correct, continue to cook, testing with ice water every minute until the firm-ball stage is reached.

4. At the firm-ball stage, pour the caramel out onto the prepared baking sheet and allow it to cool completely at room temperature, about 1 hour.

5. When the caramel is cool and firm, turn it out onto a cutting board. With a sharp buttered chef's knife, cut the caramel into 1-inch cubes. Serve the candies as is or wrap them in pretty cellophane candy wrappers (available at fine stationers and party supply stores). They can be stored in an airtight container at room temperature for up to 2 weeks.

YIELD: One 9-inch tart

SPECIAL TOOLS:

> 9-inch tart pan
>
> Standing electric mixer with a paddle attachment (optional)
>
> Pie weights (optional)
>
> Candy thermometer

1 9-inch prebaked Sweet Dough tart shell (page 216)

1 cup Creamy Caramel Sauce (page 58)

½ cup whole milk

½ cup heavy cream

½ cup crème fraîche

2 large egg yolks

1 large egg

Caramel Custard Tart

THIS CARAMEL FILLING, A VARIATION OF CRÈME BRÛLÉE, *which is normally baked in ramekins and topped with a layer of caramelized sugar, also fits into the family of baked custards. Here the caramel and custard are combined, poured into a prebaked tart shell, and baked until firm. The tart can be baked as is. Or you can add fresh berries, citrus sections, figs, or spices. Even though the caramel is already in the custard, the tart can be topped with a layer of caramelized sugar, just like crème brûlée (for an explanation of how to use a blowtorch to caramelize the sugar, see Crème Brûlée (page 112).*

I like to use Sweet Dough (page 216) for this tart shell, but any dough will work, including Short Dough (page 220) or Rugelach Dough (page 215). The shell must be blind-baked, which means it is baked empty with a filling of beans, rice, or pie weights. For an explanation of blind baking, see the "Pie and Tart Dough" chapter, page 205.

1. Preheat the oven to 325°F. Adjust the rack to the center of the oven. Place the prebaked tart shell, still in its pan, in the center of a baking sheet.

2. Combine the Creamy Caramel Sauce, milk, cream, and crème fraîche in a medium saucepan over medium heat. Stir continuously for 2 to 3 minutes, or until the ingredients are well combined. Do not bring to a boil.

3. Combine the egg yolks and egg in a large bowl and whisk them together well. Continue to whisk while slowly pouring the warm caramel mixture into the egg mixture. When it is well combined, pour it through a fine-mesh strainer to remove any stray bits of egg. This is a custard base.

4. Pour the custard carefully into the tart shell, filling it to the rim. Place the baking sheet with the tart shell in the oven. Bake for about 35 minutes, or until just set.

5. Cool the tart to room temperature and then chill it in the refrigerator for 1 hour, or until firm, before slicing and serving. Do not try to cut the tart at room temperature, or the filling will run out. The refrigerated tart will last for about 3 days.

Caramel Gelato

GELATO IS THE ITALIAN EQUIVALENT OF ICE CREAM. IT IS *slightly denser, because Italian gelato machines churn less air into the mixture than ice cream machines do. Thankfully, you don't have to buy a gelato machine to make this recipe; an ice cream machine works fine.*

Dress up this gelato by folding in crushed Hazelnut Brittle (page 56), chopped chocolate, or pieces of your favorite candy bar. Better yet, try it with a swirl of cold caramel sauce.

YIELD: 1 quart

SPECIAL TOOLS:

Candy thermometer

Ice cream machine

1 recipe Master Caramel (page 50), prepared through step 3 but heated to 360°F

3 cups whole milk

1 cup heavy cream

6 large egg yolks

¼ cup sugar

2 tablespoons amaretto

1 tablespoon fresh lemon juice

1. Heat a saucepan of water and place a metal spoon in it for stirring the caramel. Prepare an ice bath, using a large bowl to hold the ice.

2. Remove the caramel from the heat, and while waiting for the bubbles to subside, bring the milk and cream to a simmer in a large saucepan over medium heat. Carefully pour half of the mixture into the hot caramel. (Watch out; it will bubble up.) Stir with the warm spoon to combine thoroughly, then pour back into the pot with the remaining milk mixture and combine well. Bring to a boil over medium-low heat. Remove from the heat.

3. Whisk together the egg yolks and sugar in a large bowl. Pour 1 cup of the hot caramel mixture into the yolks, whisking quickly to incorporate it. (This is called *tempering,* and it is a way to slowly heat eggs without scrambling them.) Pour the yolk mixture back into the pot of caramel, turn the heat down to medium, and stir continuously until the mixture thickens, about 3 minutes. Watch carefully! It should have the texture of eggnog. When the mixture reaches 170°F, remove it from the heat. This is the gelato base.

4. Immediately strain your gelato base into a medium bowl. Place the bowl on the ice bath and stir it occasionally for 20 to 30 minutes, or until the temperature drops to 40°F. When cool, add the amaretto and lemon juice.

5. When the base is cool, it is ready to be churned. Follow the operating instructions that came with the ice cream machine. When churned, the gelato will have a soft-serve consistency, which means it is too soft to scoop. Transfer it to a cold freezer container and allow it to firm up in the freezer for about 4 hours before serving. (This is called *packing.*) After the gelato has been packed, it will be thick enough to scoop. The gelato will keep tightly covered in the freezer for about 2 weeks.

YIELD: 1¼ cups

SPECIAL TOOL:

Candy thermometer

1 recipe Master Caramel
(page 50), prepared
through step 3 but
heated to 350°F

½ cup apple juice

¼ cup water

2 tablespoons sugar

1 tablespoon sliced peeled
fresh ginger

1 3-inch cinnamon stick

1 star anise pod

SMASHING CARAMEL

Cool the Master Caramel in a
clean or new aluminum pie pan.
When ready to smash, tap the
pie pan on top of the work surface, tapping the north side,
then the south side, the east
side, and the west side. Large
leftover pieces can be cut with
an offset serrated knife. Be
careful. The caramel shards will
be very sharp.

Apple Caramel Glaze

ADDING A CLEAR, FAT-FREE LIQUID TO THE MASTER CARAMEL
creates a beautiful, clear caramel sauce. Its uses are infinite. I love it
as a sauce because it looks like liquid gold on a white plate. And
since it is clear, it is the perfect medium in which to suspend spices,
specks of vanilla bean, or even lavender buds. I use this glaze as a
poaching liquid, a dipping sauce for fruit, and a glaze for tarts and
pastries. It also gets incorporated into other recipes, such as gelées
and granitas.

I call this recipe Caramel Apple Glaze because it is made with
apple juice. Many different glazes can be created just as easily
using other juices, such as cranberry, grapefruit, or orange.

If you have some premade Master Caramel, use it in this
recipe. Smash it into pieces and place it in a small saucepan over
very low heat, stirring continuously until it is liquefied.

1. Heat a saucepan of water and place a whisk in it.

2. Meanwhile, bring the apple juice, water, sugar, and spices to
a boil in a medium saucepan over high heat. Immediately remove the
syrup from the heat and carefully add it to the caramel. (Be careful; it
will bubble up.) Stir with the warm whisk to incorporate completely.

3. Cover the pan and let it cool at room temperature for 20 minutes, then remove the spices with a slotted spoon or strainer. The glaze
can be used immediately or refrigerated for later use. Caramel glaze
will keep stored airtight in the refrigerator for up to 1 month. When
cold, the glaze will be thicker. Be sure to warm it gently over low heat. It
can also be heated in a microwave. Use medium power in 30-second
intervals, stirring in between, until the desired consistency is reached.

Uses and Variations

- ❧ BREAD GLAZE: Use warm caramel glaze to give breads and
  pastries a glossy crust. Brush a light coat on top as soon as
  they come out of the oven.

- ❧ TART GLAZE: Give fruit tarts extra shine and flavor by
  lightly brushing warm caramel glaze on the top before serving.

- ❧ SPICED GLAZE: Replace the ginger and star anise with a
  scraped vanilla bean or juniper berries.

Caramel Poached Apples

YIELD: 4 servings

SPECIAL TOOLS:

Candy thermometer

Parchment paper or cheesecloth

Double recipe (2½ cups)
Apple Caramel Glaze
(page 65)

1 cup apple cider

1 cup white verjuice
or dry white wine

¼ cup sugar

2 tablespoons fresh
lemon juice

1 vanilla bean, split
and scraped

4 apples, peeled and cored

POACHING IS AN EASY AND ELEGANT WAY TO FEATURE *seasonal fruit in a dessert. I like to poach apples—Fujis, Braeburns, and, when I can get them, Black Jonathans—and serve them warm in a pool of the poaching liquid with a scoop of Caramel Gelato (page 64). Although this recipe calls for apples, I usually let the market determine which fruit I use. The recipe works just as nicely with pears, peaches, or oranges. I also poach raisins and other dried fruits before adding them to cookies, muffins, or cakes.*

This recipe features verjuice, which is an acidic, nonalcoholic juice pressed from young grapes. Gourmet shops often sell it, but if you can't find it, dry white wine is a suitable replacement.

1. Bring the Apple Caramel Glaze, apple cider, verjuice or white wine, sugar, lemon juice, and vanilla bean and the scraped seeds to a boil in a large saucepan over high heat.

2. Add the apples and poach over low heat for 20 to 25 minutes, turning them over halfway through, until the apples are tender. To keep the apples submerged, place a round of parchment paper or cheesecloth, cut just smaller than the circumference of your pot, directly on top of the poaching liquid and fruit. Test for doneness by inserting a knife into the center of an apple. It should feel soft all the way through. Serve immediately. The apples can be refrigerated for up to 3 days. Remove them from the liquid and cool completely on a plate. Then place them back in the cooled liquid and refrigerate.

Variations

☙ ALTERNATIVE JUICE: Replace the apple juice with an equal amount of any other fruit juice, such as cranberry or orange.

☙ WINE POACHING LIQUID: Replace the verjuice with an equal amount of a light, fruity red wine such as Beaujolais.

☙ ALTERNATIVE FRUIT: Use any other firm-fleshed fruit. Try pears, oranges, or peaches.

☙ SIMPLE FLAVOR: Replace the three liquids with any one liquid, such as all apple juice.

Caramel Semifreddo

YIELD: 6 servings

SPECIAL TOOLS:

Standing electric mixer with a whisk attachment (optional)

Candy thermometer

1 cup heavy cream

1½ teaspoons vanilla extract or ¼ vanilla bean, split and scraped

2 large eggs

2 tablespoons sugar

2 tablespoons water

½ cup Apple Caramel Glaze (page 65), cooled

THIS "HALF-COLD" ITALIAN DESSERT IS PARTIALLY FROZEN, *with a texture softer than that of ice cream. Semifreddo is made without an ice cream machine. The purpose of an ice cream machine is to add air to the base; for a semifreddo, air is added in the form of egg foam and whipped cream. The result is fluffier than typical ice cream but no less refreshing.*

Semifreddo can be frozen in a container and scooped out like ice cream, or it can be frozen in decorative glasses or cups and spooned out or layered like a parfait with fruit, sauce, or cream.

1. Using a standing mixer fitted with a whisk attachment or a hand mixer, whip the cream and vanilla extract or seeds (save the pod for another use) on medium speed for about 3 minutes, or until it reaches the medium-peak stage. (The mixture should stand up in peaks, but then the peaks will double over.) Set aside in the refrigerator. Clean and dry the beaters.

2. In a separate bowl, whip the eggs on medium speed for 5 minutes, until thick and pale yellow in color. (This is referred to as the *ribbon stage.* When a spoonful is lifted out and drizzled back in, the trail it leaves looks like a ribbon for a moment before it sinks back in.)

3. Meanwhile, bring the sugar and water to a boil in a small saucepan over medium heat. Remove from the heat. This is the simple syrup.

4. As soon as the eggs reach the ribbon stage, drizzle in the simple syrup very slowly, still whipping at medium speed. This will prevent the eggs from scrambling. Take about 2 minutes to add all the syrup. Continue whipping for 5 minutes, or until the eggs have tripled in volume and are cool to the touch.

5. Transfer the whipped eggs to a large bowl. (A large bowl will ensure proper folding.) Add the glaze and, using a rubber spatula, fold the egg foam and glaze together. Next, fold in the reserved whipped cream. This is the semifreddo base. Pour the base into a freezer container, cups, or glasses, and freeze until firm, about 3 hours, before serving.

Variation

↬ CARAMEL BAVARIAN CREAM: The semifreddo recipe can also be used to create a caramel Bavarian cream by adding 1 envelope powdered gelatin. Dissolve the gelatin by sprinkling it over ¼ cup cold water and letting it sit for 5 minutes. Stir the gelatin into the syrup, add the mixture to the eggs in step 4, and continue with the recipe. Refrigerate until set, about 1 hour, before serving.

Caramel–Cranberry Granita

YIELD: 2½ cups

SPECIAL TOOL:

    Candy thermometer

½ batch (¼ cup plus
    2 tablespoons) Master
    Caramel (page 50),
    prepared through step
    3 but heated to 340°F
    (make the entire batch and
    save the rest for another
    purpose)

1 cup cranberry juice

1 cup water

2 tablespoons sugar

2 tablespoons fresh
    lemon juice

GRANITA IS AN ITALIAN ICE. UNLIKE SNOW CONES OR *shaved ice, which are coarser, granita is made up of small ice crystals formed by frequently stirring a liquid while it freezes. The crunchy, light frozen texture is refreshing on its own, but pairing it with another dessert of contrasting texture is even better. I like to serve granita with whipped cream, ice cream, or even gelées.*

Espresso granita is typical in Italy. The French version, granité, is commonly made with good Bordeaux wine. Any juicy liquid can be made into granita, but excessive alcohol will inhibit freezing. Sweet wines, such as Sauternes or Gewürztraminer, will freeze nicely because of their high sugar content. Vodka, on the other hand, will not freeze unless extra sugar is added.

As soon as granita is scooped onto a plate, it begins to melt. To minimize this effect, serve granita on chilled plates or glasses and scoop it out at the very last minute.

1. Prepare an ice bath, using a large bowl to hold the ice and a medium bowl to hold the granita base after it is made.

2. Bring the cranberry juice, water, and sugar to a boil in a small saucepan over high heat. Cook until the sugar is dissolved, about 3 minutes.

3. After the caramel has rested for 2 minutes, carefully pour the cranberry mixture into the caramel. (Be careful; it will bubble up.) This is the granita base. Transfer to the medium bowl.

4. Nest the bowl in the ice bath and cool the granita, stirring occasionally, for 20 minutes. Stir in the lemon juice. When the base is completely cool, pour it into a 9-x-13-inch baking pan and place it in the freezer.

5. Fluff the granita with a fork every 20 minutes. Bring the frozen crystals that form around the edge of the pan into the center. This forces the unfrozen liquid to the edges to freeze. The crystals are delicate, so don't overstir. Set a timer for 20-minute intervals. If forgotten, the mixture will freeze into a solid block. If this should happen, place chunks of the frozen granita in a food processor and quickly pulse until icy.

6. The granita is ready when all the liquid is frozen into small ice crystals, about 2 hours. Once the ice crystals are formed, the granita can be stored airtight in the freezer for up to 1 week. Serve it directly from the freezer, because it melts fast.

YIELD: 2½ cups

SPECIAL TOOLS:

    Candy thermometer

    Decorative mold (optional)

    Cherry pitter (optional)

1 ¼-ounce envelope
    powdered gelatin
    (2 teaspoons)

½ cup cold water

1½ cups water

1½ cups black cherry
    concentrate

1 tablespoon fresh lemon juice

½ cup Master Caramel (page
    50), prepared through step
    3 but heated to 340°F

    Fresh Bing cherries, pitted
    (optional)

Caramel—Black Cherry Gelée

GELATIN DESSERTS ARE ENJOYING A COMEBACK *(everything retro is). You loved Jell-O as a kid, so why not enjoy a more adult version of it now? My gelée is simply the granita base with gelatin added. For a more grown-up version, you can replace the cranberry juice in the granita recipe with Champagne or coffee. Almost any liquid can be gelled, except fresh pineapple juice. Pineapples contain a meat-tenderizing enzyme called bromelain, which prevents gelatin from setting. (Bromelain is the same enzyme that causes your mouth to hurt after you've eaten too much pineapple.) The enzyme is neutralized by heat, which is why canned pineapple juice, which is heated in the canning process, is always called for instead of fresh in recipes involving gelatin. Black cherry concentrate can be found at whole foods stores. It is bottled and is sometimes shelved with sweeteners.*

1. Soften the powdered gelatin by sprinkling it over the ½ cup cold water and letting it sit for 10 minutes.

2. Meanwhile, bring the 1½ cups water, black cherry concentrate, and lemon juice to a boil in a medium saucepan over medium heat.

3. Let the bubbling caramel, which should be a golden brown, rest for 2 minutes, then carefully pour in the black cherry mixture. (Be careful; it will bubble up.) This is the gelée base.

4. Add the softened gelatin and stir until it is completely dissolved. Pour it into a chilled decorative mold, bowl, baking dish, glasses, or ice cube trays. If using fresh cherries, fill the mold with the gelée, then pour out one quarter to one third of the gelée into a small bowl and set aside at room temperature. Turn the mold to coat with the gelée. Chill in the refrigerator until set. Pour in the remaining gelée and chill for 15 minutes. Just before the top layer sets, add the cherries. Poke with a skewer where desired and press them into the gelée.

5. Chill the gelée in the refrigerator for about 2 hours, or until completely set, then serve from the molds, spooning out into individual dishes. The gelée will last for about 3 days, covered, in the refrigerator.

YIELD: 4 servings

TIME: 25 to 40 minutes

SPECIAL TOOLS:

Melon baller (optional)

Candy thermometer

4 ripe Anjou pears

2 tablespoons (¼ stick)
unsalted butter

2 fresh thyme sprigs

2 tablespoons honey

1 cup Apple Caramel Glaze
(page 65)

2 tablespoons water

Oven-Roasted Caramel Anjou Pears

ANJOU IS A REGION OF THE LOIRE VALLEY IN FRANCE WHERE *many varieties of pears are grown. Anjou pears are also called beurre d'Anjou or "butter of Anjou" pears, which isn't surprising, since ripe Anjou pears are soft and creamy like butter. Cooking this fruit requires a gentle touch so that it retains its shape. Boiling or sautéing would be much too vigorous, but roasting is perfect. If you cannot find Anjou pears, ripe Bartletts or Comices are the next best choice. Any one of these pears will be sweet and smooth. The Bosc pear is commonly used in desserts, mainly because of its exaggerated pear shape. It may look better, but its flavor is not nearly as good.*

This recipe can also be made with other firm fruits, such as apples or peaches. When I use pears, I serve them warm, topped with Maytag blue cheese and toasted walnuts.

1. Preheat the oven to 375°F.

2. Peel and halve the pears and scoop out the core using a melon baller or a small paring knife. Place a single layer of pears in a baking dish, core side down.

3. Melt the butter in a small saucepan over low heat and cook until the solids sink to the bottom and begin to brown, 3 to 4 minutes. Add the thyme and honey and cook for 1 minute more. Add the caramel glaze and water and stir to combine. This is the roasting liquid.

4. Pour the liquid over the pears. Roast for 25 to 30 minutes, basting every 10 minutes. The pears are done when they are tender and caramelized. Test for doneness by inserting a knife into the center. It should feel soft all the way through. To appreciate the pears' full depth of flavor and texture, serve them warm or at room temperature. They can be refrigerated for up to 24 hours, then rewarmed in a 350°F oven for 10 minutes before serving.

CURD

ALSO KNOWN AS LEMON BUTTER, LEMON CREAM, ENGLISH lemon curd, and lemon filling, lemon curd is wonderfully versatile. You can transform it at a moment's notice into cake, ice cream, soufflés, and sauces. It is the filling in lemon meringue pie, and it can be spread on warm scones for afternoon tea. Sweet and tart, creamy and bright, lemon curd can set firm or flow smoothly. It doesn't even have to be lemon. Curd can be made in many fantastic flavors with different fruits.

The techniques for making curd are some of the easiest in baking: lemon juice, sugar, eggs, and butter are measured, combined, and cooked on top of the stove. But even in the simplest of recipes, it's a good idea to understand what lies behind the process, especially if you plan to vary the original recipe.

CURD IS NOT THE MOST ROMANTIC OF TERMS, BUT IT IS descriptive. This dessert is actually a stovetop custard, which means the ingredients are cooked together until they thicken. The effects of acid, heat, and agitation act simultaneously on the protein in the eggs to produce a smooth, creamy mixture that sets firm when cooled.

Proteins are actually strings of amino acids that are held in place by additional side chains. When the eggs are heated, the side chains loosen and the protein unfolds. This process is known as *denaturing*.

After the protein is denatured, the side chains are free to form other bonds, producing a new network, which bunches up the protein into a tighter mass: what we recognize as cooked food. As the proteins denature, reconnect, and tighten, coagulation occurs.

ALTHOUGH HEATING IS THE MOST COMMON WAY TO DENATURE a protein, the addition of acid or salt and agitation (in the form of whisking) have the same effect. The combination of the heat and the acid gives the curd its unique texture. The ingredients are usually heated only to 160°F so fewer of the protein side chains will be loosened and less coagulation will occur, which keeps the curd creamy and smooth. At the same time, the acid ensures that enough protein chains are sufficiently loosened to keep the mixture from being too thin. The acid must have a pH level that does not exceed 2.5 to create a firm curd. Lemon juice has a pH of 2.3. Orange juice, on the other hand, has a pH higher than 3. For this reason, orange curd requires a combination of lemon and orange juices, which will lower the overall pH, producing the requisite silky texture and stability and also protecting against the growth of microorganisms like salmonella.

Curd is not the most romantic of terms, but it is descriptive.

CHEMISTRY LESSON: THE pH SCALE

The pH scale measures how acidic or alkaline a substance is. Just as *hot* and *cold* describe the two extremes of temperature, *acid* and *alkaline* (or *basic*) describe two extremes of chemicals. Pure water is neutral, with a pH of 7.0. A pH less than 7 is acidic. A pH greater than 7 is alkaline or basic.

	ACID						NEUTRAL						ALKALINE		
	0	1	2	3	4	5	6	7	8	9	10	11	12	13	14
Battery Acid	x														
Stomach Acid		x													
Lemon Juice			x												
Orange Juice				x											
Grapefruit Juice				x											
Tomato					x										
Coffee						x									
Milk							x								
Pure Water								x							
Sea Water									x						
Baking Soda										x					
Ammonia													x		
Drain Cleaner															x

As for the other agent of the denaturing process, agitation, I love using a food processor, but if no food processor is handy, you can simply use a whisk and a little elbow grease. To avoid discoloration and a metallic flavor, stay away from aluminum tools. Use stainless-steel pans, stainless or pyrex bowls, and stainless-steel or heatproof plastic utensils.

My favorite time to make lemon curd is the middle of winter.

EVEN THOUGH LEMONS ARE ALWAYS AVAILABLE, MY FAVORITE time to make lemon curd is the middle of winter, when the California Meyer lemon season is at its peak. At other times of year, I enjoy making curd with blackberries, passion fruit, or grapefruit. Try some of the recipe variations for a change of pace. You'll never look at a lemon meringue pie the same way again.

Curd
FAMILY TREE

STOVETOP
MASTER LEMON CURD
Blackberry–Lime Curd
Passion Fruit Curd

BAKED
Lemon Soufflé
Lemon Bars
Lemon Pudding Cakes

AUGMENTED
Lime Fondue
Passion Fruit Bavarois
Ginger–Lemon Curd Ice Cream

MASTER LEMON CURD is the basic recipe. Replacing the lemon juice with another juice or juices creates new flavors. These variations are all made with the traditional stovetop method. Ingredients like flour or egg foam can be added to the Master Lemon Curd to create completely different baked desserts. The recipes that include curd but are not baked are referred to as AUGMENTED.

Master Lemon Curd

2/3 cup sugar

2 tablespoons finely chopped or grated lemon zest

3 large eggs

4 large egg yolks

1/2 cup fresh lemon juice

1/4 cup fresh lime juice

4 tablespoons (1/2 stick) unsalted butter chilled and cut into 1/2-inch cubes

LEMON CURD WHISKS ME AWAY TO THE TIME I SPENT STUDYING *in London. The flavor reminds me of afternoon tea and the grocery shelves at Harrods.*

Here is the basic version of lemon curd. Use it as a filling for pies, tarts, cakes, and cookies. Thin it to make a sauce or whip it with cream for a topping. I use a small amount of lime juice in this recipe to bring out the citrus dimension, but you can use all lemon juice if you wish.

Citrus zest is a vital ingredient in lemon curd. It contains the essential oils that give the fruit its flavor. I use a Microplane (see page 347) to grate citrus zest. It creates the finest zest imaginable. If you don't have a Microplane, use the finest holes on a standard box grater. Room-temperature citrus yields more juice, but cold citrus is easier to zest. Zest the lemons straight out of the refrigerator, then pop them into the microwave for 10 to 15 seconds before juicing.

Be sure to choose lemons that are completely yellow. Patches of green mean that the fruit is not yet ripe. The fruit should also feel heavy with juice. Use any type of juicer to get the juice out of the fruit. A good one will yield 1 cup of juice from 5 or 6 medium lemons.

1. Prepare an ice bath, using a large bowl to hold the ice. Fill a medium saucepan three-quarters full of water and bring to a simmer over medium heat.

2. Combine the sugar and lemon zest in a food processor and pulse until the sugar is yellow and very fragrant, about 1 minute. The friction of the machine heats up the zest, releasing its oils into the sugar. (Alternatively, use a mortar and pestle or a small bowl and a fork to blend the two together.)

3. Combine the lemon sugar, eggs, and egg yolks in a medium heatproof bowl and whisk together for 30 seconds, to distribute the sugar evenly, which prevents premature coagulation. Place the bowl over the simmering water and immediately begin whisking. Whisk continuously for 15 seconds, or until the sugar is dissolved. To see if the sugar has dissolved, place a finger in the mixture. If you feel grains, continue to whisk.

4. Add the lemon and lime juices and cook, whisking continuously, for about 5 minutes. Use a rubber spatula to scrape the sides and bottom of the bowl from time to time. Insert a thermometer and check the curd's temperature. The curd is done when it has the con-

sistency of sour cream and a temperature of 160°F. Rinse and dry the food processor, if using.

5. Transfer the curd to the food processor or a large bowl. Pulse while you add the butter, piece by piece, or whisk it in by hand. Once all of the butter has been added, pulse or whisk for 10 seconds, or until the texture is homogenous. Rinse and dry the heatproof bowl.

6. Strain the curd through a fine-mesh strainer back into the bowl and set in the ice bath to cool. Cover with plastic film, pressing it directly onto the surface of the curd to prevent a skin from forming. Stir the curd occasionally until it has cooled completely. At this point, the curd can be used or refrigerated in an airtight container for up to 1 week.

Variations

- For a richer curd, you can increase the butter to ¼ pound (1 stick).

- CURD TARTS: Pour the finished curd into a prebaked tart crust. Bake for 15 to 25 minutes in a 350°F oven, until the top is set. Cool on a rack.

- LEMON SAUCE: Use ¼ to ½ cup Simple Syrup (page 333) to thin the curd to the desired consistency.

- LEMON-CHAMOMILE SAUCE: Make the Lemon Sauce variation, adding 1 tablespoon fresh chamomile flowers (from the farmers' market) or 1 chamomile tea bag to the simple syrup just after the water and sugar have come to a boil. Let steep for 10 minutes, then strain. Use to thin the curd to the desired consistency and serve with ice cream.

- YUZU CURD: Substitute yuzu juice (see page 374) for the lime juice.

- CITRUS CURD: Use 2 tablespoons lemon zest, 1 tablespoon orange zest, and 1 tablespoon grapefruit zest. Substitute 2 tablespoons each orange, grapefruit, and fresh lemon juice for the lemon and lime juice.

- GRAPEFRUIT-VANILLA CURD: Substitute ½ cup grapefruit juice and ¼ cup fresh lemon juice for the lemon and lime juice and add ¼ vanilla bean, split and scraped. Bring the curd to 170°F.

- TANGERINE OR BLOOD ORANGE CURD: Use tangerine or blood orange zest instead of lemon zest. Substitute ½ cup tangerine or blood orange juice and ¼ cup fresh lemon juice for the lemon and lime juice.

- LEMON-LIME CURD: Use 1 tablespoon lemon zest and 1 tablespoon lime zest. Use ½ cup fresh lime juice and ¼ cup fresh lemon juice.

Blackberry–Lime Curd

YIELD: About 2½ cups

SPECIAL TOOLS:

> Food processor or blender
> Candy thermometer

> 2 pints (4 cups) fresh
>   blackberries
> ¼ pound (1 stick) unsalted
>   butter, cut into ½-inch
>   cubes
> ½ cup sugar
> ¼ cup fresh lime juice
> 3 large eggs
> 4 large egg yolks

Variation

↜ HUCKLEBERRY:
> Substitute huckleberry
> puree for the blackberry
> puree.

THIS BLACKBERRY-LIME CURD HAS A FANTASTIC COLOR. *I use it as a filling for tarts, breakfast pastries, and doughnuts. With its creamy tartness, it contrasts with crisp, buttery pastry.*

1. Prepare an ice bath, using a large bowl to hold the ice. Fill a medium saucepan three-quarters full of water and bring to a simmer over medium heat.

2. Puree the berries in a food processor or blender, then pass the puree through a fine-mesh strainer into a small bowl. Measure 1 cup of puree and reserve any remaining puree for another use.

3. Melt the butter and blackberry puree together in a small saucepan over low heat, stirring occasionally, for about 1 minute. Stir in the sugar and lime juice and stir until the sugar is dissolved.

4. Combine the eggs and egg yolks in a medium heatproof bowl and whisk briefly to combine. Slowly drizzle the hot blackberry mixture into the eggs, whisking continuously. (Place the bowl on top of a damp towel shaped into a doughnut to prevent it from spinning as you whisk.)

5. When all the mixture has been added to the eggs, place the bowl over the saucepan of simmering water. Cook, whisking continuously, for about 5 minutes. Use a rubber spatula to scrape the sides and bottom of the bowl from time to time. Insert a thermometer and check the temperature. The curd is done when it has the consistency of sour cream and a temperature of 160°F.

6. Strain the curd through a fine-mesh strainer into another medium bowl and set in the ice bath to cool. Stir the curd occasionally until it has cooled completely. At this point, the curd can be used or refrigerated in an airtight container for up to 1 week.

DO YOU KNOW HOW MANY TYPES OF BLACKBERRIES THERE ARE?

Blackberries come in many varieties and colors. The loganberry, from Santa Cruz, California, is a hybrid of the blackberry and raspberry. The boysenberry was an attempt by Rudolf Boysen to cross the loganberry with red raspberry and blackberry. He failed, but Walter Knott (of Knott's Berry Farm fame) had better luck with it. The youngberry, named after its Louisiana grower, is a cross between a blackberry and the smaller, fatter dewberry. The long, juicy olallieberry is a combination of the youngberry and the loganberry. The delicious marionberry is a hybrid of the chehalemberry and olallieberry, grown exclusivly in Marion County, Oregon, in the beautiful Willamette Valley.

To tell a blackberry from a raspberry, examine the part that once connected to the stem. If there is a hollow cavity where the core of the berry once was, it's a raspberry. If the core is still inside, it's a blackberry.

YIELD: About 2 cups

SPECIAL TOOL:

> Candy thermometer

¾ cup sugar

½ cup plus 2 tablespoons
> strained pureed
> passion fruit

3 tablespoons fresh
> lemon juice

4 large eggs

3 large egg yolks

6 tablespoons (¾ stick)
> unsalted butter, cut
> into ½-inch cubes

Passion Fruit Curd

IF YOU'VE NEVER SEEN A FRESH PASSION FRUIT, YOU MAY *be shocked when you do. It looks like a fat prune when ripe, but the skin is as hard as leather. The passion lies within. The flavor of passion fruit is beautifully floral, wildly exotic, and highly acidic, which makes it perfect for curd. It takes approximately 30 fruits to yield 1 cup of juice, so an expedition to find frozen passion fruit puree is worth the time. If you use fresh fruit, select the most wrinkled ones, because they yield the most juice. Their thick, juicy pulp is full of edible seeds; I usually strain them out, but reserve a few for decoration if you wish. You can find passion fruit at gourmet markets and some supermarkets.*

I. Prepare an ice bath, using a large bowl to hold the ice. Fill a medium saucepan three-quarters full of water and bring to a simmer over medium heat.

2. Combine the sugar, passion fruit puree, and lemon juice in a small saucepan over low heat. Heat, stirring occasionally, until the sugar is dissolved, about 2 minutes. Remove from the heat.

3. Combine the eggs and egg yolks in a medium heatproof bowl and whisk briefly to combine. Slowly drizzle the hot passion fruit mixture into the eggs, whisking continuously. (Place the bowl on top of a damp towel shaped into a doughnut to prevent it from spinning as you whisk.)

4. When all of the passion fruit mixture has been added to the eggs, place the bowl over the simmering water and add the butter. Cook, whisking continuously, for about 5 minutes. Use a rubber spatula to scrape the sides and bottom of the bowl from time to time. Insert a thermometer and check the curd's temperature. The curd is done when it has the consistency of sour cream and a temperature of 160°F.

5. Strain the curd through a fine-mesh strainer into another medium bowl and set in the ice bath. Stir the curd occasionally until it has cooled completely. At this point, the curd can be used or refrigerated in an airtight container for up to 1 week.

Lemon Soufflé

AT SPAGO, I PILE THE BATTER FOR THIS EASY SOUFFLÉ high in the ramekin. When it cooks, it puffs up like fluffy cotton candy. I have to be careful when I make it, because it's Wolfgang Puck's favorite! Like a kid, he is always trying to sneak a taste. Serve the soufflés as soon as they come out of the oven, dusted with powdered sugar and drizzled with Blackberry-Merlot Sauce (page 295). The proper way to serve a dessert baked in a ramekin like this is on another plate lined with a doily or napkin. Besides being pretty, the lining keeps the ramekin from sliding around on the plate.

YIELD: Six 4- to 6-ounce ramekins or one large (1½-quart) soufflé dish

SPECIAL TOOLS:

    Candy thermometer

    Food processor (optional)

    Standing electric mixer with a whisk attachment (optional)

    Six 4- to 6-ounce ramekins or a 1½-quart soufflé dish

FOR THE RAMEKINS

    2 tablespoons (¼ stick) unsalted butter, melted

    ¼ cup sugar

FOR THE SOUFFLÉ(S)

    1 cup Master Lemon Curd (page 75)

    2 tablespoons fresh lemon juice

    6 large egg whites

    Pinch of cream of tartar (less than ⅛ teaspoon)

    ¼ cup sugar

Preheat the oven to 425°F. Adjust the rack to the lower third of the oven. Using an upward motion, brush six 4- to 6-ounce ramekins or 1 large soufflé dish with melted butter and lightly but completely coat them with sugar.

SOUFFLÉ(S)

1. Combine the lemon curd and lemon juice in a large bowl.

2. Using a standing electric mixer fitted with the whisk attachment or a hand mixer, whip the egg whites on medium speed until a soft foam appears, about 30 seconds. Stop the machine and add the cream of tartar. Continue to whip to the soft-peak stage, about 1 minute. Gradually sprinkle in the sugar while beating. Whip for 2 minutes more, or until the whites are at the stiff-peak stage.

3. Using a rubber spatula, carefully fold the whipped egg whites into the lemon curd, one third at a time. To fold efficiently, rotate the bowl and fold with the spatula in opposite directions, one clockwise, the other counterclockwise.

4. Spoon the soufflé into the prepared dishes. Pile it up, no more than 3 inches above the rim, and create a swirling, conical dome. Place the soufflés on a baking sheet. Bake the soufflés for about 12 minutes, or until they are tall and golden brown. They should be pudding-like and a little creamy in the center. Serve immediately.

Lemon Bars

YIELD: Twenty-five 2-inch bars

SPECIAL TOOLS:

Standing electric mixer with a
paddle attachment (optional)

Pie weights

Parchment paper

Food processor (optional)

Candy thermometer

½ recipe Short Dough
(page 220)

¾ cup sugar

1 tablespoon finely grated
or chopped lemon zest

4 large eggs

¾ cup fresh lemon juice

¼ cup fresh lime juice

¼ cup whole milk

2 tablespoons all-purpose
flour

⅛ teaspoon salt

Powdered sugar

LEMON BARS ARE BY FAR THE MOST POPULAR BAR COOKIE
*and are perfect for lunchboxes. This version uses the curd technique
with the addition of milk and flour. It is a stiffer curd, and when it
bakes, it becomes firm and will hold its shape when cut. Traditionally, Short Dough is used as a crust for lemon bars. To make a lemon
bar that's a little more sophisticated than usual, you can add unexpected flavor with ingredients like citrus zest, lavender flowers, or
even pink peppercorns to the basic short crust recipe.*

1. Preheat the oven to 350°F. Adjust the rack to the center of
the oven. Coat a 9-x-13-inch baking pan with pan spray. Cut a piece
of parchment paper to fit the bottom and lay it in the pan. Coat the
parchment lightly with pan spray.

2. Press out the Short Dough to a ¼-inch thickness in the pan.
Chill the dough for 30 minutes. Pierce, or "dock," the dough with a
fork to prevent bubbling. Line it with parchment paper and fill it
with pie weights. Blind-bake the crust for 20 minutes, or until light
golden. Remove the pie weights and parchment and bake for another
10 minutes, or until deep golden brown. Set the baking dish aside at
room temperature.

3. Reduce the oven temperature to 325°F. Fill a medium
saucepan three-quarters full of water and bring to a simmer over
medium heat.

4. Combine the sugar and lemon zest in a food processor and
pulse until the sugar is yellow and very fragrant, about 1 minute. (Alternatively, use a mortar and pestle or a small bowl and a fork to
blend the two together.)

5. Whisk together the lemon sugar and eggs in a medium heatproof bowl. Place the bowl over the simmering water and whisk continuously until the sugar is dissolved, 30 seconds to 1 minute. To see
if the sugar has dissolved, place a finger in the mixture. If you feel
grains of sugar, continue to whisk.

6. When the sugar has dissolved, slowly whisk in the lemon
juice, lime juice, and milk. Cook, whisking continuously, for about 7
minutes. Use a rubber spatula to scrape the sides and bottom of the
bowl from time to time. Insert a thermometer and check the curd's
temperature. The curd is done when it has the consistency of sour
cream and a temperature of 160°F.

7. Remove the curd from the heat and whisk in the flour and salt. Pour into the baked crust and spread evenly. Bake for 15 to 20 minutes, or until just set and firm to the touch. Cool the bars to room temperature and then place in the refrigerator to chill for 1 hour before cutting into bars.

8. Cut the cooled bars into 2-inch diamonds: Using a ruler as a straight edge, cut diagonally from the top right corner (A) to the bottom left corner (B). The rectangle is now two right triangles. Continue to make parallel cuts above and below the first cut at 2-inch intervals, using the ruler to keep the cuts parallel. Repeat in the opposite direction, cutting from the top left corner (C) to the bottom right corner (D). Make cuts above and below the center cut in 2-inch, parallel intervals, creating 2-inch diamonds. Once the diamonds are cut, the bars can be removed from the pan using a metal offset spatula. To finish, dust the top of each bar with sifted powdered sugar and serve. Store lemon bars, tightly wrapped, at room temperature for 2 days or in the freezer for 1 week.

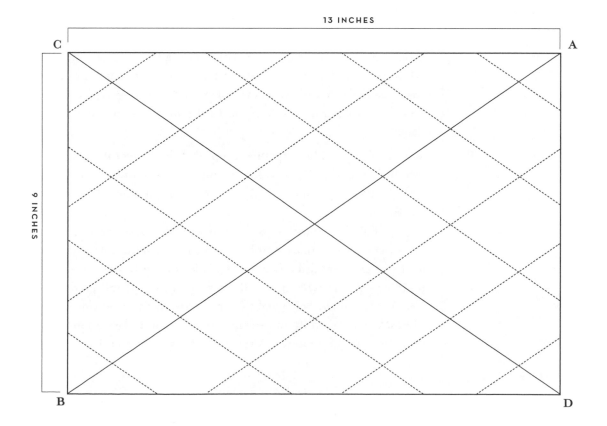

13 INCHES

9 INCHES

C   A

B   D

Lemon Pudding Cakes

YIELD: Eight 4- to 6-ounce ramekins

SPECIAL TOOLS:

Candy thermometer

Standing electric mixer with a
whisk attachment (optional)

Eight 4- to 6-ounce ramekins

FOR THE RAMEKINS

2 tablespoons (¼ stick)
unsalted butter, melted

¼ cup sugar

FOR THE CAKES

1 recipe Master Lemon Curd
(page 75)

2 tablespoons all-purpose
flour

½ cup whole milk

3 large egg whites

Pinch of cream of tartar
(less than ⅛ teaspoon)

5 tablespoons sugar

WHEN THIS BAKES, THE BATTER BECOMES BOTH CAKE AND
pudding, dessert and garnish in one dish.

*I usually serve the cakes warm from the oven, topped with a
few just-picked juicy boysenberries. The cakes need no frosting, and
I can prepare them up to 2 days ahead. I simply rewarm them in the
oven and bring them hot to the table.*

*I like to use Meyer lemons for this dessert, but it's wonderful
with regular lemons as well.*

Preheat the oven to 325°F. Adjust the rack to the center of the oven.
Brush eight 4- to 6-ounce ramekins with melted butter and then
lightly but completely coat them with sugar. Fill a medium saucepan
three-quarters full of water and bring to a simmer over medium heat.

CAKES

1. Remove the prepared lemon curd from the heat and sift in
the flour, then whisk in the milk. Stir to combine, then set aside at
room temperature.

2. Using a standing mixer fitted with the whisk attachment or a
hand mixer, whip the egg whites at high speed until soft foam appears,
about 30 seconds. Stop the machine and add the cream of tartar.
Whip to the soft-peak stage, about 1 minute. At the soft-peak stage,
continue to whip while you gradually pour in the sugar. Continue to
whip for 1 to 2 minutes more, until the whites reach the stiff-peak
stage.

3. Using a rubber spatula, carefully fold the whipped egg whites
into the lemon curd, one third at a time. As you fold, move the bowl
and spatula in opposite directions, one clockwise, the other counterclockwise.

4. Fill the ramekins to the top with the pudding cake batter.
Place the ramekins in a larger baking dish and fill the baking dish with
warm water to reach halfway up the sides of the ramekins. Bake the
pudding cakes for 20 to 30 minutes, or until just set, golden, and
firm to the touch. Serve right from the oven, inverted onto serving
dishes. Or wrap tightly and refrigerate for up to 2 days, then warm at
350° for 4 to 5 minutes, invert onto serving dishes, and serve.

Lime Fondue

YIELD: 4 cups, serving 8 to 10

SPECIAL TOOLS:

Food processor (optional)

Candy thermometer

Skewers

1 cup sugar

2 tablespoons finely grated
   lime zest

4 large eggs

2 large egg yolks

1 cup fresh lime juice

¼ cup fresh lemon juice

1 cup sweetened
   condensed milk

THIS IS A FUN TWIST ON TRADITIONAL CURD. I'VE REPLACED *the butter in the master recipe with condensed milk to create a flavor reminiscent of Key lime pie. The mixture is pulsed in a food processor, and the resulting texture is very creamy and smooth. We serve the fondue as a dip for tropical fruits such as mango, papaya, roasted pineapple, and caramelized banana. The idea can easily be applied to any of the other curds in this chapter. Try making cranberry fondue as a dip for spicy nut bread, dip crispy coconut meringues into passion fruit fondue, or dip fresh summer berries into blackberry fondue. If you can find Key limes, by all means use them in this recipe. The fondue makes a great dip for cookies as well as fruit.*

1. Fill a medium saucepan three-quarters full of water and bring to a simmer over medium heat.

2. Combine the sugar and lime zest in a food processor and pulse until the sugar is light green and very fragrant, about 1 minute. (Alternatively, use a mortar and pestle or a small bowl and a fork to blend the two together.)

3. Whisk together the lime sugar, eggs, and egg yolks in a medium heatproof bowl. Place the bowl over the simmering water and whisk for 1 to 2 minutes, or until the sugar is dissolved. To see if the sugar has dissolved, place a finger in the mixture. If you can feel grains of sugar, continue to whisk.

4. When the sugar has dissolved, whisk in the lime and lemon juices. Cook, whisking continuously, for about 5 minutes. Use a rubber spatula to scrape the sides and bottom of the bowl from time to time. Insert a thermometer and check the curd's temperature. The curd is done when it has the consistency of sour cream and a temperature of 160°F. Rinse and dry the food processor, if using.

5. Transfer the curd to the food processor or a large bowl. Add the condensed milk and pulse or whisk until the texture is homogenous, about 1 minute. Rinse and dry the heatproof bowl. Strain through a fine-mesh strainer back into the bowl. At this point, the fondue can be served or chilled and stored for later use. If not using it right away, place the bowl over an ice bath and stir occasionally until cool. Store in an airtight container in the refrigerator for up to 1 week.

KEY LIMES

When ripe, Key limes
have a yellow tint to
their skin.

Passion Fruit Bavarois

YIELD: 8 servings

SPECIAL TOOLS:

    Candy thermometer

    Standing electric mixer with a
      whisk attachment (optional)

    Decorative 2-quart mold
      (optional)

½ cup cold water

1 ¼-ounce envelope
  powdered gelatin
  (2 teaspoons)

1¼ cups sugar

3 large eggs

4 large egg yolks

¾ cup strained pureed passion
  fruit (see page 78)

2 tablespoons fresh
  lemon juice

1 cup heavy cream

4 large egg whites

BAVAROIS, OR BAVARIAN CREAM, IS TRADITIONALLY MADE from vanilla sauce, whipped cream, and meringue, stabilized with gelatin. Using curd gives this classic recipe a refreshing twist. I use this bavarois as a mousse filling for cakes, tarts, and charlottes. I also set it in dainty fluted 4-ounce molds and serve it with tropical fruits and cream.

1. Pour ¼ cup of the water into a small bowl and sprinkle the gelatin over it. Set it aside to soften. Prepare an ice bath, using a large bowl to hold the ice. Fill a medium saucepan three-quarters full of water and bring to a simmer over medium heat.

2. Whisk together ¾ cup of the sugar, the eggs, and egg yolks in a medium heatproof bowl. Place the bowl over the simmering water and whisk until the sugar is dissolved, about 1 minute. To see if the sugar has dissolved, place a finger in the mixture. If you feel grains of sugar, continue to whisk.

3. When the sugar has dissolved, slowly whisk in the passion fruit puree and lemon juice. Cook, whisking continuously, for about 5 minutes. Use a rubber spatula to scrape the sides and bottom of the bowl from time to time. Insert a thermometer and check the curd's temperature. The curd is done when it has the consistency of sour cream and a temperature of 160°F.

4. Strain the curd through a fine-mesh strainer into another medium bowl and set in the ice bath. Stir the curd occasionally until it has cooled to 70°F.

5. Using a standing mixer fitted with a whisk attachment or a hand mixer, whip the cream on high speed for about 3 minutes, or until it reaches the medium-peak stage. Set aside in the refrigerator. Clean the whisk or beaters.

6. In a clean bowl, whip the egg whites with the mixer for 1 minute, to the soft-peak stage. Turn off the mixer while you make the sugar syrup.

7. Combine the remaining ½ cup sugar and the remaining ¼ cup water in a small saucepan over high heat. Stir to moisten the sugar and insert a thermometer. Cook until the temperature reaches 235°F, about 5 minutes. Immediately remove the syrup from the heat. Add the softened gelatin to the syrup and stir it to dissolve.

8. Begin whipping the egg whites again and slowly drizzle the

sugar syrup into the whipping whites. (Be sure to drizzle the syrup between the moving whisk and the bowl. If it hits the whisk, it can harden there or be spun up onto the sides of the bowl.) When all the syrup has been added, stop the machine and scrape down the bowl with a rubber spatula. Turn the machine back on and continue to whip the whites until they are stiff and shiny, about 3 minutes. This is the meringue.

9. When the curd reaches 70°F, remove it from the ice bath, transfer it to a large bowl, and fold in the meringue using a rubber spatula. To fold efficiently, rotate the bowl and spatula in opposite directions, one clockwise, the other counterclockwise. When the meringue is partially incorporated, fold in the whipped cream.

10. Immediately pour the bavarois into a decorative mold, or use it as a filling for cakes or charlottes. Place it in the refrigerator until set, about 2 hours. To remove the bavarois from a mold, invert the mold onto a serving dish. Rub the outside with a warm damp towel and tap the mold onto the plate to loosen the gelatin. The bavarois will stay fresh, tightly covered, in the refrigerator for up to 3 days.

Ginger—Lemon Curd Ice Cream

GINGER HAS BEEN POPULAR SINCE ANCIENT TIMES, WHEN *only pepper outranked it in popularity. I love the way its slightly hot flavor balances with sugar in pastries. In this ice cream, cold, hot, and sweet sensations hit the tongue all at once.*

If you don't have any fresh ginger in the fridge, you can use dried, but beware: it is hotter and spicier than fresh. Substitute 1 teaspoon dried ginger for 2 tablespoons ginger juice.

YIELD: 1½ quarts

SPECIAL TOOLS:

Candy thermometer

Food processor (optional)

Ice cream machine

1 recipe Master Lemon Curd (page 75), cooled

2 tablespoons fresh ginger juice (see page 370)

1½ cups whole milk

1 cup heavy cream

2 tablespoons fresh lemon juice

Pinch of salt (less than ⅛ teaspoon)

I. Whisk together the lemon curd and ginger juice in a large bowl. Whisk in the milk, cream, lemon juice, and salt. This is the ice cream base.

2. Transfer the ice cream base to an ice cream machine and churn, following the manufacturer's instructions.

3. After the ice cream has been churned, it will have a soft-serve consistency and will probably be too soft to scoop. Transfer it to a freezer container and place in the freezer to firm up for about 4 hours. (This is called *packing.*) After it is packed, the ice cream will be thick enough to scoop. Homemade ice cream will last for about 3 days, tightly covered, in the freezer.

Variation

CANDIED GINGER: Before packing the ice cream, fold in ¼ cup finely chopped candied ginger.

VANILLA SAUCE

When somebody mentions vanilla, I can't help thinking about a television commercial that I used to see. A beautiful girl gliding on a swing in a white chiffon dress is asked, "If you could be any flavor, what flavor would you be?" I immediately knew that I would pick my favorite, vanilla. The girl in the commercial says, "If I were a flavor, I would most definitely *not* be vanilla." I was crushed. How dare she insinuate that vanilla was plain?

To my horror, vanilla has become ordinary. It has somehow turned into the opposite of chocolate. Poor vanilla! How can you compete in this world of extracrunchy, sticky, chewy, chunky-monkey, action-packed flavors? If only the world knew how special you are.

My favorite use for the TV world's most underestimated ingredient is vanilla sauce, a.k.a. crème anglaise, meaning "English cream." It's a white custard sauce made from egg yolks, sugar, and milk and flavored with vanilla bean. Variations on vanilla sauce lead to different types of custards, soufflés, frozen creations, and molded desserts. The addition of flour or cornstarch produces a filling for tarts and pastries called *pastry cream*. With flavorings such as chocolate or coconut, it becomes a delicious cream pie filling. Pastry cream can also serve as a base for cookies and soufflés. Folding whipped cream or meringue into pastry cream transforms it into silky, light crème chiboust, which is handy for filling pastries. Adding gelatin creates classic Bavarian cream and the heavenly chiffon pie. Much of pastry, in fact, involves vanilla sauce.

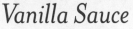

Vanilla Sauce
FAMILY TREE

MASTER VANILLA SAUCE
Vanilla Ice Cream
Strawberry Semifreddo
Banana Bavarois

OVEN-BAKED CUSTARD
Vanilla Pots de Crème
Crème Caramel
Crème Brûlée

WITH ADDED STARCH
STOVETOP CUSTARD
Pastry Cream
Crème Chiboust

SECONDARY COOKING PROCEDURE
BAKED STOVETOP CUSTARD
Baked Vanilla Chiboust Soufflé
Cappuccino Soufflé
Pastry Cream Cookies

All recipes in the vanilla sauce family tree begin by tempering
eggs and sugar with milk. When starch is added in the initial
tempering, the result is classic pastry cream. Pastry cream
can be incorporated into other recipes and baked.

VANILLA SAUCE IS ACTUALLY A STOVETOP CUSTARD, SINCE it is cooked from start to finish in a saucepan. As with curd, the key to its smooth, rich consistency is the egg—or, rather, the egg yolk—which thickens the sauce. During cooking, the proteins in the egg coagulate, or solidify, providing texture and structure.

To achieve the desired eggnog-like texture, you have to monitor the temperature of the sauce carefully to prevent the eggs from exceeding their maximum coagulation temperature. When eggs are diluted with ingredients such as milk or sugar, the temperature of coagulation rises. Slow, even heat ensures that all the proteins are completely coagulated. If the temperature rises above 170°F, their proteins squeeze together and harden like scrambled eggs. Egg yolks coagulate at a temperature between 149° and 158°F. Above 158°F, the yolks will clump.

For that reason, constant stirring is a must to maintain a consistent temperature throughout the sauce as it cooks. If you stop stirring, the proteins closest to the heat source at the bottom of the pot will coagulate and overcook.

As in all pastry, the way in which you combine your ingredients will increase the chances of success. You start by adding simmering milk to a mixture of eggs and sugar. This step is called *tempering.* The term refers to temperature, and it is a way to ease two ingredients of extremely different temperatures together to prevent premature coagulation. To temper, you whisk a small portion of heated milk into the egg and sugar mixture. The eggs begin to warm. Then you whisk the prewarmed egg mixture back into the pot.

If the doorbell rings and you leave your post at the stove, the vanilla sauce will look like scrambled egg soup. It is possible to save a scrambled sauce, however, with the help of a trusty blender or food processor (see page 93).

Constant stirring is a must to maintain a consistent temperature throughout the sauce as it cooks.

ONE BRANCH OF THE VANILLA SAUCE FAMILY TREE INCLUDES custards baked in the oven rather than on the stove. Warm milk or cream is tempered into eggs and sugar, just as in vanilla sauce, but unlike vanilla sauce, custards are often made from whole eggs. Both stovetop and baked custards follow this general ratio:

1 quart whole milk : 6–8 large egg yolks : 6–8 ounces sugar

Any component of the recipe can be varied. Cream, condensed milk, buttermilk, or coconut milk can replace part of the milk. All or some of the eggs can be replaced with yolks. (As a rule, 2 yolks or 2 whites equal 1 whole egg.) Any other natural sweetener can replace the sugar, though not always in the same proportion. Honey, for instance, is twice as sweet as sugar. Brown sugar, maple syrup, and cane sugar have distinctly different flavors, which should be taken into account before substituting them.

THE THREE MOST POPULAR DESSERT CUSTARDS ARE VARIATIONS on the standard formula.

Crème caramel (also known as *crème renversée* in France and *flan* in Spain and Central America) is made with whole eggs and milk. Whole eggs are used, and the albumin protein in the egg whites holds the custard together when it's unmolded. The thin layer of caramel lining the baking dish is transformed into a sauce when the finished custard is inverted. Although it has a jelly-like consistency, it should be creamy and smooth, not rubbery or dry.

Pots de crème are made with whole eggs, egg yolks, milk, and cream. These "pots of cream" taste like pudding but better. The method is the same as for crème caramel, but without the caramel, and the cus-

Tempering is a way to ease two ingredients of extremely different temperatures together to prevent premature coagulation.

tard is not inverted. Pots de crème are traditionally baked and served in little covered pots created specifically for this dessert.

Crème brûlée, or "burned cream," is the richest of the baked custards. It's made with egg yolks and cream, which yield a dense, velvety texture. Crème brûlée is finished with a thin layer of caramelized sugar on top. Traditionally an iron disk called a *brûlée iron* was heated over a flame and then pressed onto the sugar coating to caramelize it, but most chefs today use a propane torch.

The key to the baked custards, as for the stovetop variety, is gentleness. Cook the eggs slowly at a low temperature. Use a water bath to slow the conduction of heat, and cover the custards to avoid overcooking the tops. The finished custards should be pale and smooth, with no trace of browning, and not lumpy, bubbly, or souffléd. When they look as they did when they went into the oven but are set, with a gentle jiggle, you have reached perfection.

The key to baked custards is gentleness.

✑

VANILLA IS THE CLASSIC CUSTARD FLAVOR, AND IT'S STILL the best. If you think vanilla is ordinary, you may want to infuse flavors such as coffee, tea, nuts, spices, citrus zest, or chocolate into the warmed milk and cream.

YIELD: 2½ cups

SPECIAL TOOL:

  Candy thermometer

1 cup whole milk

1 cup heavy cream

½ vanilla bean, split and scraped

4 large egg yolks, chilled

⅓ cup sugar

  Pinch of salt (less than ⅛ teaspoon)

Master Vanilla Sauce

THIS IS MY VERSION OF THE CLASSIC CRÈME ANGLAISE. *True crème anglaise is made with milk only, but many chefs substitute cream. The more cream that is used, the thicker and richer the sauce will be. Do not use an aluminum saucepan. Excessive stirring in an aluminum pot scrapes aluminum into the sauce, turning it gray.*

Using a real vanilla bean is the best way to get good vanilla flavor. The long bean, or pod, is technically a seed capsule that holds thousands of teeny-tiny seeds. To get all the lusciousness out of the bean, slice it in half lengthwise with a paring knife. Use the knife to press one of the halves open and scrape out the inside of the bean. The black paste inside the pod is actually the seeds. When they are mixed into a recipe, they dissipate into visible black specks, which carry the vanilla flavor.

Vanilla seed has a very strong flavor. I often use only half of a bean at a time, so one bean can last through several recipes. Once all the seeds are out of a bean, the pod itself still has a lot of vanilla oil. I never waste any bit of these precious beans. First I steep the empty pod in a liquid, such as the milk for vanilla sauce. For maximum flavor, it should steep for at least 20 minutes. After the pod is strained out, I rinse it off and dry it for 1 week. Then I combine the dried, spent pod with granulated sugar in a food processor and pulverize it into vanilla sugar. The remaining vanilla oil is absorbed, creating wonderfully aromatic sugar that is great to use in any recipe for an extra kick of vanilla flavor.

1. Prepare an ice bath, using a large bowl to hold the ice.

2. Bring the milk, cream, and vanilla bean and scraped seeds to a simmer in a medium nonreactive saucepan over medium heat. Do not bring to a rolling boil. Immediately remove the pan from the heat, cover with plastic film, and let steep for 15 minutes.

3. Meanwhile, quickly whisk together the egg yolks, sugar, and salt in a medium bowl. It is important not to let the sugar sit in a clump on the eggs for any period of time. This will result in grainy eggs, often referred to as *cooked*. (The acid in the sugar can coagulate the yolks.)

4. Remove the plastic film and bring the milk mixture back to a simmer over medium heat. Remove the pan from the heat and ladle out ½ cup of the hot milk. Drizzle it slowly into the eggs while whisking. This is tempering. Once the ½ cup milk is incorporated into the

eggs, pour the mixture back into the hot milk, whisking constantly. Be sure to scrape all the eggs into the pot with a rubber spatula.

5. Place the pan over low heat and insert a thermometer. Immediately begin to stir the sauce. A heat-resistant rubber spatula is the best tool for this job because it can scrape the entire bottom surface of the pot, preventing spots of coagulation. Stir constantly in figure eights around the edge of the pan and into the center. Watch the wake of the spatula. After about 2 minutes, the waves will begin to thicken. The sauce is ready when it has the consistency of thick cream and a temperature of 170°F. Dip the spatula into the sauce, pull it out, and run your finger across the back of the spatula. It should leave a clear trail, with the rest of the spatula remaining coated with sauce. If the sauce runs, cook for 1 minute more, or until the consistency is right. Rinse and dry the medium bowl.

6. Immediately strain the sauce through a fine-mesh strainer back into the bowl and set in the ice bath to cool. Stir the sauce occasionally for 5 to 10 minutes, or until the temperature drops to 40°F. The sauce will become thicker as it cools. Once it is completely cool, cover and refrigerate for up to 2 days.

BROKEN VANILLA SAUCE

A broken vanilla sauce can be saved. The lumps indicate that the eggs were too hot, so they scrambled in the milk. To remove the lumps, blend the sauce in a blender or food processor or with a hand-held immersion blender. The blending will chop up the egg. Once it is strained, it can be used.

Variations

🐦 **BLACK CURRANT TEA:** Place 1 black currant tea bag into the simmered milk and cream. Remove from the heat and cover with plastic film. Let steep for 10 minutes, remove the tea bag, and continue as directed.

🐦 **ALMOND:** Substitute almond milk (see page 349) for the milk. When the sauce is complete, add 1 teaspoon almond extract or amaretto to intensify the flavor.

🐦 **CHOCOLATE:** Add 2 ounces finely chopped bittersweet chocolate to the simmered milk and cream. Stir until melted and well combined.

🐦 **SPICED:** Toast one 3-inch cinnamon stick, 6 cardamom pods, ¼ teaspoon anise seeds, 1 clove, ½ teaspoon freshly grated nutmeg, and 1 teaspoon pink peppercorns in a small saucepan over low heat, stirring, for 1 minute, or until aromatic. Add the milk and cream, bring to a simmer, and let steep for 10 minutes. Strain the mixture and continue as directed.

🐦 **LAVENDER:** Place 1 tablespoon lavender flowers in the milk and cream. When it reaches a simmer, remove from the heat and cover with plastic film. Let steep for 15 minutes. Strain, and continue as directed.

YIELD: 6 cups (about twelve ½-cup servings)

SPECIAL TOOLS:
Candy thermometer
Ice cream machine

3 cups heavy cream
1 cup whole milk
1 vanilla bean, split and scraped
8 large egg yolks, chilled
1 cup sugar
Pinch of salt (less than ⅛ teaspoon)

Vanilla Ice Cream

THIS IS BY FAR MY FAVORITE VARIATION ON VANILLA *sauce. In fact, it's my favorite dessert. There is nothing better than cold vanilla ice cream melting over a slice of hot apple pie, unless it's vanilla ice cream dripping with hot fudge. The method is identical to that of vanilla sauce, but this recipe is richer because most of the liquid is heavy cream.*

There are many ice cream machines on the market, and they can all be used successfully with this recipe. Some automatically chill the ice cream base as it churns. Some have an insert that must be frozen before the ice cream can be made. The old-fashioned machines use a combination of ice and salt, packed around a cylindrical canister that holds the ice cream base. The salt melts the ice, chilling the ice cream base. As the canister is turned (by motor or by hand), air is incorporated into the base by a paddle in the center of the canister. The simultaneous action of adding air and freezing is what gives ice cream its texture.

A great way to showcase fresh seasonal fruit is to fold chunks in after the ice cream comes out of the machine. I also like to swirl in toasted nuts, chocolate shavings, toffee bits, or crushed cookies.

1. Prepare an ice bath, using a large bowl to hold the ice.

2. Bring the cream, milk, and vanilla bean and scraped seeds to a simmer in a medium nonreactive saucepan over medium heat. Do not bring to a rolling boil. Immediately remove the pan from the heat, cover with plastic film, and let steep for 15 minutes.

3. Meanwhile, quickly whisk together the egg yolks, sugar, and salt in a medium bowl. (Don't let the sugar sit in a clump on the eggs, or the acid in the sugar may coagulate the yolks.)

4. Remove the plastic film and bring the cream mixture back to a simmer over medium heat. Remove the pan from the heat and ladle out ½ cup of the cream mixture. Drizzle it slowly into the eggs while whisking. Once the ½ cup of cream mixture is incorporated into the eggs, pour the mixture back into the hot cream, whisking constantly. Be sure to scrape all the eggs into the pot with a rubber spatula.

5. Place the pan over low heat and insert a thermometer. Immediately begin to stir the sauce with a heat-resistant rubber spatula. Stir constantly in figure eights around the edge of the pan and into the center. The sauce is ready when it has the consistency of thick

cream and a temperature of 170°F. Dip the spatula into the sauce, pull it out, and run your finger across the back of the spatula. It should leave a clear trail, with the rest of the spatula remaining coated with sauce. If the sauce runs, cook for 1 minute more, or until the consistency is right. Rinse and dry the medium bowl.

6. Immediately strain the sauce through a fine-mesh strainer back into the bowl and set in the ice bath to cool. Stir the sauce occasionally for 5 to 10 minutes, or until the temperature drops to 40°F.

7. When the base has cooled to 40°F, it is ready to be churned. Follow the instructions that came with the ice cream machine. When churned, the ice cream will have a soft-serve consistency and will be too soft to scoop. Transfer it to a freezer container and allow it to firm up in the freezer for about 4 hours. (This is called *packing*.) After the ice cream has been packed, it will be thick enough to scoop. Homemade ice cream will last for about 2 weeks, tightly covered, in the freezer. ,

Variations

- ❧ DEEP DARK CHOCOLATE: Add 1 cup Master Ganache (page 16) to the warm, strained, completed base in step 6.

- ❧ PISTACHIO: Add 1 cup lightly toasted finely chopped pistachios to the cream and steep overnight in the refrigerator. Strain and proceed as directed.

- ❧ MASCARPONE: Replace 2 cups of the cream with 1 cup milk and 1 cup mascarpone cheese, whisked together. Add the vanilla bean and seeds and proceed as directed.

- ❧ LEMON VERBENA: Use 1 cup heavy cream and 3 cups milk. Substitute 6 whole lemon verbena leaves for the vanilla bean. Once the base has cooled in step 6, add ½ teaspoon fresh lemon juice before freezing the ice cream.

Vanilla Sauce
STOVETOP CUSTARD

YIELD: 8 cups, serving 12

SPECIAL TOOLS:

  Blender or food processor

  Candy thermometer

  Standing electric mixer with a whisk attachment (optional)

FOR THE STRAWBERRIES

  2 pints strawberries, rinsed, stemmed, and halved

  2 tablespoons sugar

  2 tablespoons Grand Marnier

  2 tablespoons fresh lemon juice

FOR THE SEMIFREDDO BASE

  1 cup whole milk

  4 large egg yolks, chilled

  ½ cup sugar

  Pinch of salt (less than ⅛ teaspoon)

FOR THE FINAL ENRICHMENT

  2 large egg whites

  Pinch of cream of tartar (less than ⅛ teaspoon)

  2 tablespoons sugar

  ½ cup mascarpone

  1 cup heavy cream

Strawberry Semifreddo

THE METHOD FOR THIS RECIPE IS IDENTICAL TO THAT FOR *vanilla sauce,* with additional whipped cream and egg whites folded in at the end. The added air gives a delightful texture that is similar to ice cream but lighter. My recipe calls for mascarpone, a rich Italian double-cream cheese. If you can't find it, use heavy cream instead.

    My favorite trick for keeping the bowl of eggs from spinning during this maneuver involves a wet kitchen towel. Wrap the towel into a doughnut shape and set the bowl in the middle.

STRAWBERRIES

Toss together the strawberries, sugar, Grand Marnier, and lemon juice in a large bowl. Set them aside at room temperature to macerate for at least 20 minutes. Puree in a blender or food processor.

SEMIFREDDO BASE

1. Prepare an ice bath, using a large bowl to hold the ice.

2. Bring the milk to a simmer in a medium nonreactive saucepan over medium heat.

3. Meanwhile, quickly whisk together the egg yolks, sugar, and salt in a large bowl.

4. When the milk comes to a simmer, remove it from the heat and ladle out ½ cup of the hot milk. Drizzle it slowly into the eggs while whisking. Once the ½ cup milk is incorporated into the eggs, pour the mixture back into the milk, whisking constantly. Be sure to scrape all the eggs into the pan with a rubber spatula.

5. Place the pan over low heat and insert a thermometer. Immediately begin to stir the sauce with a heat-resistant rubber spatula. Stir constantly in figure eights around the edge of the pan and into the center. The sauce is ready when it has the consistency of thick cream and a temperature of 170°F. Dip the spatula into the sauce, pull it out, and run your finger across the back of the spatula. It should leave a clear trail, with the rest of the spatula remaining coated with sauce. If the sauce runs, cook for 1 minute more, or until the consistency is right. Rinse and dry the large bowl.

6. Remove the pan from the heat and stir in the pureed strawberries. Pour the mixture back into the bowl and set in the ice bath. Stir occasionally for 5 to 10 minutes, or until the temperature drops to 40°F.

FINAL ENRICHMENT AND FREEZING

1. While the base is cooling, using a standing mixer fitted with a whisk attachment or a hand mixer, whisk the egg whites for 30 seconds on medium speed, until they begin to foam. Add the cream of tartar and whip for 30 seconds more, or until the whites reach the soft-peak stage. Slowly add the sugar and whip for 1 or 2 minutes more, or until they reach the medium-peak stage. Transfer the whipped whites to a clean bowl and set aside at room temperature.

2. Combine the mascarpone and heavy cream in the same bowl used to whip the whites. Using the electric mixer, whip them together on medium speed until they reach the very-soft-peak stage, about 30 seconds. Set aside in the refrigerator.

3. Using a balloon whisk, fold the whipped egg whites into the strawberry-vanilla sauce, turning the bowl and lifting the whisk after each pass. When they are partially combined, add the mascarpone mixture and finish folding. Pour the semifreddo base into a large freezer container, cover, and freeze until solid, about 4 hours. When the semifreddo is firm, it is ready to be served, or it may be stored in the freezer, wrapped airtight, for up to 2 weeks.

Variations

- Any fruit that can be pureed can replace the strawberries.

- Macerate the fruit in other liquors, such as rum, framboise, or Sauternes.

YIELD: 8 cups, serving 8

SPECIAL TOOLS:

Candy thermometer

Standing electric mixer with a
whisk attachment (optional)

Decorative 2-quart mold
(optional)

FOR THE GELATIN

1 ¼-ounce envelope
powdered gelatin
(2 teaspoons)

¼ cup cold water

FOR THE VANILLA SAUCE

1 cup whole milk

1 vanilla bean, split
and scraped

6 large egg yolks, chilled

¼ cup sugar

Pinch of salt (less than
⅛ teaspoon)

2 tablespoons dark rum

1 cup pureed banana

FOR THE WHIPPED CREAM

2 cups heavy cream

FOR THE ITALIAN MERINGUE

4 large egg whites

¼ cup sugar

¼ cup water

Banana Bavarois

BAVAROIS (BAV-AR-WAH), OR "BAVARIAN CREAM," IS A
*gelatin-based dessert that can be served on its own or used as a fil-
ling for other desserts, such as charlottes.*

*There are four components to a Bavarian cream: vanilla sauce,
gelatin, whipped cream, and Italian meringue. Like common meringue, Italian meringue is made with egg whites and sugar, but in
this case the sugar is liquefied, cooked to the soft-ball stage, then
added hot to the whipping whites. The heat of the sugar cooks and
stabilizes the whites, creating a strong, long-lasting meringue.*

GELATIN

Soften the gelatin by sprinkling it over the water in a small bowl. Set it
aside to soften for 10 minutes.

VANILLA SAUCE

1. Prepare an ice bath, using a large bowl to hold the ice.

2. Bring the milk and vanilla bean and scraped seeds to a simmer in a medium nonreactive saucepan over medium heat.

3. Meanwhile, quickly whisk together the egg yolks, sugar, and
salt in a large bowl.

4. When the milk comes to a simmer, remove from the heat and
ladle out ½ cup of the hot milk. Drizzle it slowly into the eggs while
whisking. Once the ½ cup milk is incorporated into the eggs, pour
the mixture back into the milk, whisking constantly. Be sure to scrape
all the eggs into the pan with a rubber spatula.

5. Place the pan over low heat and insert a thermometer. Immediately begin to stir the sauce with a heat-resistant rubber spatula.
Stir constantly in figure eights around the edge of the pan and into
the center. The sauce is ready when it has the consistency of thick
cream and a temperature of 170°F. Dip the spatula into the sauce,
pull it out, and run your finger across the back of the spatula. It
should leave a clear trail, with the rest of the spatula remaining coated
with sauce. If the sauce runs, cook for 1 minute more, or until the
consistency is right. Rinse and dry the large bowl.

6. Immediately strain the sauce through a fine-mesh strainer
back into the bowl and set in the ice bath. Stir the sauce occasionally
for 1 to 2 minutes, or until it cools to 70°F. Stir in the rum and
pureed banana.

WHIPPED CREAM

Using a standing mixer fitted with a whisk attachment or a hand mixer, whip the cream on medium speed to the soft-peak stage, about 1 minute. Transfer it to a clean container and set it aside in the refrigerator. Clean and dry your bowl and whisk.

ITALIAN MERINGUE

1. Whip the egg whites on low speed to the soft-peak stage. Set aside.

2. In a small saucepan, combine the sugar and water. Stir to moisten the sugar, and then insert a thermometer. Place the pan over high heat and cook until the temperature reaches 235°F, about 3 minutes.

3. At 235°F, immediately remove the syrup from the heat. Add the softened gelatin to the syrup and stir to dissolve. Turn the mixer to medium speed and continue whipping the egg whites while slowly drizzling in the syrup, being careful not to hit the moving whisk with the syrup. If it hits the whisk, it can harden there or be spun up onto the sides of the bowl. When all the syrup has been added, stop the machine and scrape down the inside of the bowl with a rubber spatula. Turn the machine back on and continue to whip the whites until they are stiff and shiny, about 2 minutes.

ASSEMBLY

1. Immediately whip one third of the Italian meringue into the cooled vanilla sauce, then fold in the rest, turning the bowl with each pass. Fold in the whipped cream.

2. Pour the bavarois into a mold (or use it as a filling for cakes or charlottes). Place it in the refrigerator until set, about 2 hours. The bavarois will stay fresh, tightly covered, in the refrigerator for up to 3 days.

YIELD: 2 to 2 ¼ cups, enough for
two 9-inch tarts

SPECIAL TOOLS:

Parchment paper

Food processor (if necessary)

2 cups milk

½ cup sugar

1½ teaspoons finely chopped
orange zest

½ vanilla bean, split and
scraped, or 2 teaspoons
vanilla extract

3 tablespoons all-purpose
flour or cornstarch

Pinch of salt (less than
⅛ teaspoon)

5 large egg yolks or 3 large
eggs, chilled

1 tablespoon unsalted butter,
softened

Pastry Cream

THE FRENCH NAME FOR THIS RECIPE IS *CRÈME PÂTISSIÈRE*, *or "pastry chef's cream." It uses the same method as vanilla sauce, but the ingredients are a little different. The liquid is all milk, and there is added starch. This binds the milk, producing a thick, silky cream with the consistency of pudding. I prefer to use flour as my starch, but other chefs use cornstarch, tapioca, or even agar agar, a gelatin derived from seaweed.*

Pastry cream has dozens of applications. It is creamy but firm, so it makes the perfect filling for fresh fruit tarts. Add chocolate, coconut, or bananas, and it becomes an incredible cream pie filling. Classic cream puffs, éclairs, and napoleons are filled with it as well. I also use pastry cream as a base for soufflés and cookies.

Do not use an aluminum pot for this recipe: constant stirring will scrape aluminum into the cream and turn it gray. When I'm in a hurry, I strain the finished pastry cream onto a baking sheet lined with plastic film. The thin layer cools quickly, and the plastic keeps the cream and the tray clean. This recipe works equally well using yolks or whole eggs. Egg yolks only will yield a richer, yellower pastry cream.

1. If you will need to cool this quickly, line a baking sheet with plastic film and set aside.

2. Bring the milk, ¼ cup of the sugar, the orange zest, and the vanilla bean and seeds to a simmer in a medium nonreactive saucepan over medium heat.

3. Meanwhile, sift together the remaining ¼ cup sugar, the flour or cornstarch, and salt onto a piece of parchment paper. Whisk the egg yolks or eggs in a large bowl. Add the sifted dry ingredients and whisk until fluffy.

4. When the milk comes to a simmer, remove from the heat and ladle out ½ cup of the hot milk. Drizzle it slowly into the eggs while whisking. Once the ½ cup milk is incorporated into the eggs, pour the mixture back into the hot milk, whisking constantly. Be sure to scrape all the eggs into the pan with a rubber spatula.

5. Immediately begin to rapidly whisk the pastry cream. In less than 1 minute, it will boil and begin to thicken. Continue to whisk for about 3 minutes, or until it has the consistency of pudding. To test the cream for doneness, tilt the saucepan to one side. The cream should pull away from the pan completely. Rinse and dry the large bowl.

6. Strain the pastry cream through a fine-mesh strainer back into the bowl. Add the butter and stir until it is melted and incorporated. If the cream seems grainy, pulse it in a food processor until smooth. The cream is now ready to use, or it can be cooled to room temperature and refrigerated for up to 3 days. To cool the pastry cream quickly, spread it out on a baking sheet lined with plastic film. To prevent a skin from forming as it cools, place a sheet of plastic film directly on the surface.

Variations

Almost any flavor can be infused into the milk to produce dozens of different pastry creams. Examples include:

- CHOCOLATE: Add 3 ounces finely chopped bittersweet chocolate to the pastry cream when you add the butter. Stir it until it is melted and incorporated.

- MOCHA: Substitute ¼ cup brewed espresso or strong regular coffee for ¼ cup of the milk. Add 3 ounces finely chopped bittersweet chocolate to the pastry cream when you add the butter. Stir it until it is melted and incorporated.

- PRALINE: Fold ½ cup Nutella or Homemade Hazelnut Paste into the finished pastry cream (page 34).

- COCONUT: Replace 1 cup of the milk with 1 cup canned unsweetened coconut milk.

- CRÈME BAUMANIÈRE: Thin ½ recipe of chilled pastry cream by stirring in 2 tablespoons Grand Marnier, then fold in 1 cup stiffly whipped heavy cream.

- FRIED: Pipe or spoon the pastry cream onto a sheet of plastic film. Roll the film around the cream, making a log or sausage, and chill it completely, about 2 hours. Line up three bowls on the counter. Fill one with ½ cup milk, one with ½ cup all-purpose flour, and one with ½ cup plain bread crumbs. Slice the chilled pastry cream into 1-inch disks. Dredge them in milk, flour, milk again, and then bread crumbs. Fry the disks in 350°F canola oil for 2 minutes, or until golden brown. Drain on paper towels, sprinkle with powdered sugar, and serve.

YIELD: 4½ cups, serving 6

SPECIAL TOOLS:

Parchment paper

Food processor (if necessary)

Standing electric mixer with a
whisk attachment (optional)

Candy thermometer

1 ¼-ounce envelope
powdered gelatin
(2 teaspoons)

¾ cup cold water

1 recipe Pastry Cream
(page 100), still warm

4 large egg whites, at
room temperature

¾ cup sugar

Crème Chiboust

CHIBOUST WAS A NINETEENTH-CENTURY FRENCH PASTRY *chef. His namesake cream combines pastry cream, Italian meringue, and gelatin. The entire concoction is a test of skill, often used to judge young pastry apprentices and culinary students.*

The pastry cream for chiboust can be made ahead. If using chilled pastry cream, measure it into a bowl, allow it to warm to room temperature, then whisk it by hand until it is smooth. It should be the same temperature as the meringue when they are folded together.

1. Soften the gelatin by sprinkling it over ¼ cup of the water in a small bowl. Set it aside to soften for 10 minutes.

2. Whisk the warm Pastry Cream in a large bowl until smooth. Place a sheet of plastic film directly on the surface to prevent a skin from forming. Set aside.

3. Using a standing mixer fitted with a whisk attachment or a hand mixer, whip the egg whites for 1 minute, or until they reach the soft-peak stage.

4. Combine the sugar and the remaining ½ cup water in a small saucepan. Stir to moisten the sugar, then insert a thermometer. Place the pan over high heat and cook until the temperature reaches 235°F, about 5 minutes.

5. At 235°F, immediately remove the syrup from the heat. Add the softened gelatin to the syrup and stir to dissolve. Turn the mixer on again to medium speed and whip the egg whites while slowly drizzling in the syrup, being careful not to hit the moving whisk with the syrup. If it hits the whisk, it can harden there or be spun up onto the sides of the bowl. When all the syrup has been added, stop the machine and scrape down the bowl with a rubber spatula. Turn the machine back on high speed and whip the whites until stiff and shiny, about 3 minutes. This is the meringue.

6. Immediately fold the meringue into the Pastry Cream. Use a balloon whisk for the most efficient folding and turn the bowl in the opposite direction of the whisk as you fold. As soon as the meringue is incorporated, the chiboust is finished and must be used. Pour it immediately into a tart shell, use it as the filling of a cake, or freeze it in individual molds or tart shells to be baked.

Variation

- CHOCOLATE CHIBOUST: Add 3 ounces finely chopped bittersweet chocolate to the pastry cream while it is still hot. Whisk to combine thoroughly before folding in the Italian meringue.

Baked Vanilla Chiboust Soufflé

CHIBOUST IS TYPICALLY USED AS A FILLING FOR CAKES and tarts. It is light because of the air whipped into the meringue but strong because of the gelatin. My favorite way to use this cream, however, is to bake it. First, I freeze chiboust in individual tart shells. These tarts go straight from the freezer to the oven, where they bake until they puff up like golden brown mushrooms. They have a delightful texture: soft, light, creamy, and hot.

Rather than use premade pastry cream here, I make it fresh, with the addition of crème fraîche. The gentle tang offsets the rich, sweet meringue. I also use cornstarch rather than flour, since the cream needs a little more stability when baked. For fun, pop a chocolate truffle in the bottom of each tartlet. It is important to use Sweet Dough, not flaky, so that the dough stays crisp.

YIELD: Eight 4-inch tartlets

SPECIAL TOOLS:

Standing electric mixer with a whisk attachment (optional)

Pie weights (optional)

Candy thermometer

1 ¼-ounce envelope powdered gelatin (2 teaspoons)

2 tablespoons cold water

8 4-inch prebaked Sweet Dough tartlet shells (page 216)

FOR THE PASTRY CREAM

½ cup plus 2 tablespoons whole milk

½ cup plus 2 tablespoons crème fraîche

½ vanilla bean, split and scraped

4 large egg yolks, chilled

3 tablespoons cornstarch

1 tablespoon sugar

Pinch of salt (less than ⅛ teaspoon)

FOR THE SOUFFLÉ BASE

4 large egg whites

½ cup sugar

¼ cup water

Soften the gelatin by sprinkling it over the water in a small bowl. Set it aside to soften for 10 minutes. Place the prebaked tartlet shells on a baking sheet, still in their pans, and set aside.

PASTRY CREAM

1. Bring the milk, crème fraîche, and vanilla bean and seeds to a simmer in a medium nonreactive saucepan over medium heat.

2. Meanwhile, whisk together the egg yolks, cornstarch, sugar, and salt in a large bowl.

3. When the milk mixture comes to a simmer, remove from the heat and ladle out ½ cup of the hot milk mixture. Drizzle it slowly into the eggs while whisking. Once the ½ cup milk is incorporated into the eggs, pour the mixture back into the hot milk, whisking constantly. Be sure to scrape all the eggs into the pan with a rubber spatula.

4. Immediately begin to rapidly whisk the pastry cream. In less than 1 minute, it will boil and begin to thicken. Continue to whisk for about 3 minutes, or until it has the consistency of pudding. To test the cream for doneness, tilt the saucepan to one side. The cream should pull away from the pan completely. Rinse and dry the large bowl.

5. Strain the pastry cream through a fine-mesh strainer back into the bowl. Add the gelatin and stir until it is melted and incorporated. Set aside at room temperature, with a sheet of plastic film directly on the surface to prevent a skin from forming.

SOUFFLÉ BASE

1. Using a standing mixer fitted with the whisk attachment or a hand mixer, whip the egg whites on low speed for 1 minute, or until they reach the soft-peak stage.

2. In a small saucepan, combine the ½ cup sugar and ¼ cup water. Stir to moisten the sugar and then insert a thermometer. Place the pan over high heat and cook until the temperature reaches 235°F, about 5 minutes.

3. At 235°F, immediately remove the syrup from the heat. Turn the mixer on again to medium speed and whip the egg whites while slowly drizzling in the syrup, being careful not to hit the moving whisk with the syrup. If it hits the whisk, it can harden there or be spun up onto the sides of the bowl. When all the syrup has been added, stop the machine and scrape down the bowl with a rubber spatula. Turn the machine back on high speed and whip the whites until they are stiff and shiny, about 3 minutes.

4. Immediately fold the egg-white mixture into the warm pastry cream. Use a balloon whisk for the most efficient folding and turn the bowl in the opposite direction to the whisk as you fold. Just as soon as the whites have been incorporated, the soufflé must be poured into the tart shells. Smooth the surface of the tarts with an offset metal spatula, then place them in the freezer on the baking sheet until firm, about 3 hours.

BAKING

1. Preheat the oven to 350°F and adjust the rack to the center of the oven.

2. Remove the tarts from the freezer and bake for 12 to 15 minutes, or until golden brown. Serve immediately, while hot. Unbaked tarts can be kept in the freezer, tightly wrapped, for up to 1 week.

YIELD: Six 6- to 8-ounce ramekins

SPECIAL TOOLS:

Six 6- to 8-ounce ramekins

Standing electric mixer with a
whisk attachment (optional)

Candy thermometer

FOR THE RAMEKINS

2 tablespoons (¼ stick)
unsalted butter, melted

¼ cup sugar

FOR THE SOUFFLÉ BASE

2 cups milk

½ cup coarsely ground
espresso beans or
2 tablespoons instant
coffee

4 large egg yolks, chilled

½ cup sugar

3 tablespoons all-purpose
flour

Pinch of salt (less than
⅛ teaspoon)

FOR THE EGG-WHITE FOAM

9 egg whites, at room
temperature

Pinch of cream of tartar
(less than ⅛ teaspoon)

⅓ cup sugar

Powdered sugar

Chocolate Sauce (page 39)

Cappuccino Soufflé

IN THIS CAPPUCCINO SOUFFLÉ, THE COFFEE FLAVOR IS *mellowed by a thick, slow-cooked pastry cream. The name could just as easily be café au lait, café latte, or cup o' joe with cream.*

Soufflés are always made the same way. Two elements, a base and an egg-white foam, are folded together. The base is always more dense than the foam, and it carries the flavor. In this case, my base is coffee-flavored pastry cream. The same method can be used to create any number of soufflés, simply by flavoring the pastry cream first.

Preheat the oven to 425°F and adjust the rack to the lower third of the oven. Brush six 6- to 8-ounce ramekins with a light coat of melted butter and then lightly but completely coat them with sugar. Set aside.

SOUFFLÉ BASE

1. Bring the milk and espresso beans or instant coffee to a simmer in a large nonreactive saucepan over medium heat. Remove from the heat, cover, and let steep for 10 minutes. After 10 minutes, strain the milk into a medium bowl.

2. Meanwhile, whisk together the egg yolks, sugar, flour, and salt in a large bowl.

3. Return the milk to the saucepan and bring to a simmer over medium heat. Remove from the heat and ladle out ½ cup of the hot milk. Drizzle it slowly into the egg yolks while whisking. Once the ½ cup milk is incorporated into the eggs, pour the mixture back into the hot milk, whisking constantly. Be sure to scrape all the eggs into the pan with a rubber spatula.

4. Return to the heat and immediately begin to rapidly whisk the pastry cream. In less than 1 minute, it will boil and begin to thicken. Continue to whisk for about 3 minutes, or until it has the consistency of pudding. To test the cream for doneness, tilt the saucepan to one side. The cream should pull away from the pan completely. This mixture is the soufflé base. Rinse and dry the large bowl.

5. Strain it back into the large bowl. To prevent a skin from forming, place a sheet of plastic film directly on the surface. Set the base aside to cool at room temperature.

EGG-WHITE FOAM

Using a standing mixer fitted with the whisk attachment or a hand mixer, whip the egg whites on medium speed until they begin to foam, about 30 seconds. Add the cream of tartar and a bit of the sugar and whip for 1 minute more, or until the whites reach the soft-peak stage. Gradually pour in the remaining sugar while whipping. Whip for 2 minutes more, or until the whites reach the medium-peak stage.

FINAL MIXING AND BAKING

1. Transfer the room-temperature soufflé base to a large bowl and whisk until smooth. Fold one third of the stiff egg whites into the base with a rubber spatula to lighten the batter. The most efficient way to fold is to rotate the bowl and spatula simultaneously in opposite directions, one clockwise, the other counterclockwise. Fold in the remaining whites carefully so the air you just whipped in is not deflated.

2. Spoon the soufflé into the prepared ramekins, filling them to the rim. Smooth them with a metal spatula. Gently run a paring knife around the inside of the soufflé dish between the ramekin and the soufflé. This creates an inner wall of air that helps the soufflé rise up straight.

3. Place the soufflés on a baking sheet. Bake for 15 to 20 minutes, or until they are tall and golden brown. They should be pudding-like and creamy in the center. Serve the soufflés immediately with a light dusting of powdered sugar and the Chocolate Sauce.

Pastry Cream Cookies

THIS RECIPE WAS ONE OF MY BEST-KEPT SECRETS UNTIL *now, and displays the creative use of leftovers. Because pastry cream is always on hand at the restaurant, I began using it whenever I needed to whip up a batch of cookies at the last minute. By throwing in whatever nuts or spices I had around and stale cake crumbs, I could create dozens of different cookies at a moment's notice. As luck would have it, the pastry cream cookies became very popular. They're moist, cakey, and nutty and taste as though they were made with almond paste. In fact, now we have to prepare pastry cream specifically for them. So much for spur of the moment!*

YIELD: 4 dozen 3-inch cookies

SPECIAL TOOLS:

    Parchment paper

    Food processor (if necessary)

    Standing electric mixer with a paddle attachment (optional)

½ cup Pastry Cream (page 100), cooled

¼ cup hazelnuts, toasted (see page 362), skinned, and chopped

¼ cup almonds, toasted (see page 366) and chopped

1 cup cake crumbs from Master Pound Cake (page 140) or other stale cake crumbs

2 tablespoons powdered sugar, plus more for dusting

1 teaspoon dark rum

1. Preheat the oven to 350°F. Adjust the rack to the lower third of the oven. Line a baking sheet with parchment paper.

2. Combine the Pastry Cream, hazelnuts, and almonds in a large bowl. Slowly add the cake crumbs, powdered sugar, and rum, and stir until well incorporated.

3. Using two soupspoons, spoon tablespoon-size portions of dough 1 inch apart on the prepared baking sheet and flatten slightly with the back of the spoon. Bake for 12 to 15 minutes, or until the edges are golden brown. Slide the parchment off the sheets and cool the cookies on the parchment. Dust with powdered sugar and serve. The cookies will keep in an airtight container for 2 days.

Vanilla Sauce
BAKED CUSTARD

YIELD: Six 4-ounce ramekins (3 cups)

SPECIAL TOOL:

Six 4-ounce ramekins

1½ cups whole milk

½ cup heavy cream

½ cup sugar

½ vanilla bean, split and scraped

2 large eggs, chilled

2 large egg yolks, chilled

Pinch of salt (less than ⅛ teaspoon)

Variation

➤ CHOCOLATE: Add 3 ounces finely chopped bittersweet chocolate to the hot cream mixture.

Vanilla Pots de Crème

POTS DE CRÈME PETITS ARE SLIGHTLY RICHER THAN CRÈME caramel and a little less rich than crème brûlée. This is the easiest of the three custards because it requires no extra step of caramelizing sugar. I usually serve pots de crème with a dollop of whipped cream and a crisp cookie on the side.

Traditionally, pots de crème are baked and served in small china cups, or pots. Made of fine porcelain, these pots hold only about 3 ounces of custard. They have one small handle and a tight-fitting lid, usually with a decorative finial. The cups came with either a saucer, like a teacup, or a matching porcelain tray. They are hard to find but worth the hunt. If you don't have them, don't worry. Ramekins or ovenproof coffee cups work just fine.

1. Preheat the oven to 325°F. Place a rack in the center of the oven. Place the ramekins in a larger baking pan, making sure the larger pan is at least ½ inch deeper than the ramekins.

2. Bring the milk, cream, sugar, and vanilla bean and scraped seeds to a simmer in a large nonreactive saucepan over medium heat. Remove from the heat, cover the pan with plastic film, and let steep for 15 minutes.

3. Meanwhile, whisk together the eggs, egg yolks, and salt in a medium bowl.

4. After steeping, bring the milk mixture back to a simmer over medium heat. Remove from the heat and ladle out ½ cup of the hot milk. Drizzle it slowly into the eggs while whisking. When the milk mixture is incorporated into the eggs, pour the mixture back into the hot milk, whisking constantly. Be sure to scrape all the eggs into the pan with a rubber spatula. This is the custard base.

5. Strain through a fine-mesh strainer into the bowl or into a large heatproof glass measuring cup. Fill each ramekin to the rim with the custard. Fill the larger baking pan with hot water until the water rises two thirds of the way up the ramekins.

6. Cover the baking dish loosely with aluminum foil and bake for 40 to 45 minutes. The custards are done when they are set but have a uniform jiggle. They should not be brown, nor should they have risen.

7. Chill the custards for at least 2 hours before serving. Place each ramekin on a plate lined with a doily or napkin. Finished pots de crème will keep, tightly covered, in the refrigerator for up to 2 days.

Vanilla Sauce
BAKED CUSTARD

YIELD: Six ½-cup servings

SPECIAL TOOLS:

Six 4-ounce ramekins

Candy thermometer

1 recipe Master Caramel (page 50)

2 cups whole milk

⅓ cup sugar

1 teaspoon vanilla extract

3 large eggs, at room temperature

Pinch of salt (less than ⅛ teaspoon)

Crème Caramel

THIS RECIPE IS THE SAME AS FOR SPANISH FLAN AND FRENCH crème renversée. *I like to cook the custards in individual ramekins because they bake faster and more evenly than in a larger pan, but a 9-inch cake pan can be used instead. Ceramic ramekins work well, as do small aluminum cups.*

The first step is caramelizing sugar, which is explained in the caramel chapter (page 43). If you already have Master Caramel on hand, smash it into bits, place it in a small saucepan, and warm it over very low heat. Once it is liquefied, use it to coat the ramekins.

Good crème caramel should be perfectly smooth and creamy. Don't overwhisk the sauce, or you'll incorporate too much air into it, and when you pour the sauce through a strainer, do it gently from just above the strainer. Watch it carefully as it bakes. Set a timer in case the phone rings.

1. Preheat the oven to 325°F. Adjust the rack to the center of the oven.

2. Carefully and quickly pour about 2 tablespoons of the hot caramel into each of six 4-ounce ramekins. Carefully lift each ramekin and swirl the caramel to coat the bottom evenly. Set the coated ramekins in a large baking pan, making sure the baking pan is at least ½ inch deeper than the ramekins.

3. Whisk together the milk, sugar, and vanilla in a medium bowl.

4. Whisk together the eggs and salt in a large bowl. Pour in the milk mixture. This is the custard base.

5. Fill each ramekin to the rim with custard. Fill the larger baking pan with hot water until the water rises two thirds of the way up the ramekins. Cover the baking dish loosely with aluminum foil and bake for 40 to 45 minutes. The custards are finished when they are set but have a uniform jiggle. They should not be brown, nor should they have risen.

6. Chill the custards completely before serving, at least 4 hours or preferably overnight. (The longer the custards sit, the more sauce will be created by the breakdown of the caramel.) To serve, release the custard from the ramekins with a small paring knife and then invert them onto serving plates. The caramel will have liquefied overnight and will spill out onto the plate as a sauce. Crème caramel will keep for up to 2 days in the refrigerator if kept in the ramekins and covered airtight.

Variations

- ALMOND: Replace the milk with almond milk, available at health food stores.

- ESPRESSO: Heat the milk, cool, and steep ¼ cup coarsely ground espresso beans in it for 30 minutes. Strain out the beans and proceed with step 3 of the recipe.

- GINGER: Heat the milk, cool, and steep 2 tablespoons chopped peeled fresh ginger in it for 30 minutes. Strain out the ginger and proceed with step 3 of the recipe.

- SPICED: Heat the milk, cool, and steep any spice in it for 30 minutes. Strain out the spice and proceed with step 3 of the recipe. My favorite combination is 2 cinnamon sticks and 2 star anise pods.

Crème Brûlée

THIS IS BY FAR THE MOST POPULAR OF THE BAKED CUSTARDS. *The smooth texture of the custard contrasts nicely with the crisp sheet of caramelized sugar on top.*

Most pastry chefs have a sugar preference when it comes to the topping for crème brûlée (and most will insist that their way is the best). Brown sugar, white sugar, powdered sugar, crystal sugar, and turbinado sugar all work. Although I prefer white sugar because it's much easier to work with, I am a firm believer in individualism.

Propane torches for caramelizing the top are inexpensive and easy to find at most hardware stores. You can caramelize the sugar under a broiler, but watch carefully, because the direct high heat can overcook the top portion of the custard.

YIELD: Six 6-ounce servings

SPECIAL TOOLS:

Six 6-ounce ramekins

Candy thermometer

Propane or butane blowtorch (optional; see headnote)

3 cups heavy cream

1 cup sugar

1 vanilla bean, split and scraped

6 large egg yolks, chilled

1. Preheat the oven to 300°F. Adjust the rack to the center of the oven. Place six 6-ounce ramekins in a larger baking pan, making sure the larger pan is at least ½ inch deeper than the ramekins.

2. Bring the cream, ½ cup of the sugar, and the vanilla bean and scraped seeds to a simmer in a large nonreactive saucepan over medium heat. Remove from the heat, cover the pan with plastic film, and let steep for 15 minutes.

3. Meanwhile, gently whisk the egg yolks in a large bowl.

4. After steeping, the cream mixture should be at 165°F. Gently whisk it into the egg yolks. When the cream is incorporated into the egg yolks, strain the mixture through a fine-mesh strainer into a medium bowl or large heatproof glass measuring cup. This is the custard base.

5. Fill each ramekin to the rim with custard. Fill the larger baking pan with hot water until the water rises two thirds of the way up the ramekins. Cover the baking dish loosely with aluminum foil and bake for 40 to 45 minutes. The custards are done when they are set but have a uniform jiggle. They should not be brown, nor should they have risen.

6. Chill the custards for at least 2 hours before caramelizing and serving. Crème brûlée will keep tightly covered in the refrigerator for up to 2 days.

7. To serve, you will be coating the top in two thin layers of caramelized sugar. Coat the top of the custards with some of the remaining ½ cup sugar in a thin, even layer. Wipe off any sugar that

sticks to the rim of the ramekin. Melt the sugar by moving the flame from a propane or butane torch back and forth across the top of the custard from a height of not less than 8 inches. As soon as it melts and starts to color, dust lightly with a second coating of sugar and continue to melt and caramelize the sugar. Circulate the torch for even coloring. Within 1 minute, the sugar will begin to melt, bubble, and then turn into golden caramel. Even though the name of this custard is French for "burned cream," try not to burn the sugar on top. Remove the torch when the sugar is a dark golden color. Allow the caramel to cool and harden for 2 minutes before serving. Place the ramekin on a plate lined with a napkin or doily. Do not caramelize the top until just before serving. The caramelized top will begin to melt after 1 hour.

Variations

- EGGNOG: To the cream in step 2, add ¼ teaspoon ground cinnamon, 1 tablespoon ground ginger, 2 tablespoons Jack Daniel's whiskey, and 2 tablespoons brandy. Omit the vanilla bean.

- GINGER: To the cream in step 2, add 1 inch of fresh ginger, peeled and sliced. Omit the vanilla bean.

- PASSION FRUIT: Replace 2 cups of the cream with 2 cups milk. Add to the cream-milk mixture in step 2 1 cup passion fruit puree, 2 tablespoons fresh orange juice, and 1 tablespoon fresh lemon juice. Omit the vanilla bean. Add 2 additional egg yolks.

- PUMPKIN: Add to the cream in step 2 2 tablespoons honey, 2 teaspoons ground ginger, 1 teaspoon ground cinnamon, a pinch of ground cloves (less than ⅛ teaspoon), and 1 teaspoon vanilla extract. Omit the vanilla bean. Proceed with the recipe, and when the custard base is complete, add 1 cup pumpkin puree (canned solid-pack pumpkin), 1 teaspoon fresh lemon juice, and a pinch of salt. Bake for an additional 5 to 7 minutes.

PÂTE À CHOUX

WHEN I WAS GROWING UP IN BROOKLYN, OUR FAMILY always shopped at Leon's Bakery on Knapp Street. Whenever we went to the bakery (on my dad's fireman budget), the four of us kids had to agree on one large cake or pastry that my mother would buy for the group. I'll never forget the day I went to the bakery without my sisters. Mom decided to surprise me and said I could pick out whatever pastry I wanted from the case. I chose the biggest éclair I could find. Biting through that shiny chocolate-glazed pastry and finding the cool surprise of vanilla custard inside was magical.

Éclairs are made from an unusual dough called *pâte à choux* (we sometimes call it "choux pastry" or "choux puffs"). In French, the word *pâte* (pronounced "pat") means "dough" or "paste." The word *choux* (pronounced "shoe") means "cabbages," but *mon petit chou* (literally "my little cabbage") is also an endearment—"darling" or "dear." Many people believe *pâte à choux* means "pastry cabbage," presumably because the dough puffs up into a cabbagelike shape, but I prefer the translation "darling pastry," because I have so much affection for it.

PÂTE À CHOUX IS UNIQUE IN THE WORLD OF PASTRY because of the way it's made. A dough, or batter, is first made on top of the stove, then spooned onto a baking sheet. As it bakes, pâte à choux puffs into golden, light pastries that are airy and moist on the inside and nearly hollow. When cool, the space inside can be filled with any number of fillings, such as whipped cream, pastry cream, ice cream, or even savory salads and cheese. Every time I pull the magical little puffs out of the oven, I tingle with excitement and awe for their perfect hollow centers and golden brown sheen.

Whenever I make a batch of pâte à choux, I can't help wondering who the heck thought this up. It's an old recipe, with versions appearing as early as the eighteenth century. Unlike the culinary marvels of cheese (milk coagulation) and wine (yeast fermentation), which likely happened by accident, pâte à choux must have been created by a chef who had a thorough understanding of dough and the properties of flour and eggs.

It's a truly amazing process: water is heated with butter, a little sugar, and salt. Flour is added, and as it's mixed, the mixture transforms from a lumpy, pasty mass to a smooth, mashed-potato-like dough. Off the heat, eggs are added, one at a time. They provide moisture that along with the moisture in the butter will convert to steam when the dough heats up in the hot oven. As more steam accumulates within the dough, the choux expands to three times its original size.

Properly baked, the puffs will retain their size and shape as they cool. If underbaked, they will deflate into flat little pancakes. To be sure the puffs have been in the oven long enough, let them cook to a dark nutty brown color. This stage of baking ensures that the protein in the crust of the puffs has solidified fully and can support its own weight.

I like to use bread flour for my pâte à choux. The resulting pastry is hearty and substantial, almost breadlike. You can also use all-purpose flour, which will give you a lighter puff.

THOUGH MY INFATUATION WITH PÂTE À CHOUX BEGAN IN the early days of my training, it wasn't until years later when I was on my own as a pastry chef that I really understood the virtues of this amazing dough. I continuously experimented and discovered many uses the instructors had never taught us in school. The dough can be deep-fried

Whenever I make a batch of pâte à choux, I can't help wondering who the heck thought this up.

into a fritter or poached into a dumpling and flavored in countless ways.

Many cookbooks warn you to be cautious when making pâte à choux. They tell you that it's fragile and temperamental, not to let it sit too long, and not to refrigerate it. I disagree. Despite its reputation, pâte à choux is one of the easiest doughs to make and store. It doesn't have to be used right away (it's easier to pipe if it sits for an hour), and it can be stored in the refrigerator for up to 2 days. The pastries can also be baked ahead and frozen. The puffs defrost into perfectly fresh treats, ready to be filled at a moment's notice.

Pâte à choux is one of the easiest doughs to make and store.

Pâte à Choux
FAMILY TREE

MASTER PÂTE À CHOUX

BAKED AND AUGMENTED

Chocolate Cream Puffs

Profiteroles

Religieuses

Croquembouche

Éclairs

Plum and Ginger Carolines

Gougères

Hazelnut Paris-Brest

POACHED OR FRIED
AND AUGMENTED

Apricot Mascarpone Cannoli

Blackberry-Merlot Dumplings

Chocolate Banana Beignets

Cherry Almond Fritters

The pâte à choux family tree shows the versatility of choux paste. All the recipes begin with choux paste. On its own, choux can be piped into small bites or large round puffs and baked, then filled. Choux can be cooked in other ways, such as poached or fried. With the addition of ingredients such as cheese or folded-in egg whites, the choux takes on new forms and flavors.

YIELD: 1½ pounds dough, enough for approximately 24 large, 36 medium, or 48 small cream puffs

SPECIAL TOOLS:

Standing electric mixer with a paddle attachment (optional)

Candy thermometer

Parchment paper

Piping bag with a large (#6) plain tip (optional; see headnote)

1 cup bread flour
   or all-purpose flour

1 teaspoon sugar

¼ teaspoon salt

½ cup water

½ cup whole milk

6 tablespoons (¾ stick) unsalted butter

4–5 large eggs

FOR EGG WASH

1 large egg, plus 1 egg yolk

Master Pâte à Choux

THIS SIMPLE PÂTE À CHOUX IS THE BASIS FOR COUNTLESS *dessert and savory items. The classic cream puff starts with a medium or large puff and is filled with whipped cream or pastry cream. Medium puffs can be filled with ice cream for profiteroles or stacked high in a pyramid for croquembouche. Small puffs make terrific cheese puffs or canapés stuffed with savory fillings.*

Professional chefs use a pastry bag to form puffs because it's the fastest, easiest way. Old-fashioned canvas pastry bags should be washed and dried immediately after use. For easy cleanup, I prefer using disposable plastic pastry bags. A small ice cream scoop works well for making uniform puffs. Dip it into cold water after each scoop to prevent the pastry from sticking to the spoon. You can also dollop spoonfuls onto the baking sheets, although the result is a little less uniform. This dough will yield more or fewer pastries, depending on the size tip you use for piping.

For crispy, golden crusts, I put a cup of hot water in a pan on the floor of the oven, which circulates more steam in the oven. Added moisture allows the crust to stay soft longer, enabling it to stretch a little thinner. The moisture also promotes browning by converting more starch to sugar for caramelization. I prefer the center of my choux to be slightly moist, but some chefs like to dry out the center.

You may use all-purpose flour instead of bread flour, but the puffs will be less substantial.

1. Sift together the flour, sugar, and salt in a large bowl. Set aside.

2. Bring the water, milk, and butter to a boil in a large saucepan over medium heat. At the boil, remove the pan from the heat and add the flour mixture all at once. Using a sturdy spoon, stir vigorously to combine.

3. Return the mixture to medium heat and stir constantly in figure eights. Cook for at least 4 minutes, or until the mixture has a smooth, mashed-potato-like appearance. This helps to break down the starch and develop the gluten. Remove it from the heat.

MIXER METHOD

4. Transfer the hot mixture to the bowl of a standing mixer fitted with a paddle attachment or use a hand mixer. Mix on low speed for 1 to 2 minutes, or until the dough cools to 180°F. Add 4 of the eggs, one at a time. Be sure to let the batter absorb each egg and scrape down the sides of the bowl with a rubber spatula before adding the next. Before adding the last egg, test for consistency. Pinch off about 1 teaspoon of dough with your thumb and index finger, then pull your fingers apart. The dough should stretch rather than break. If it breaks, add the last egg. Mix on low speed until thoroughly incorporated, about 2 minutes. Do the finger test for consistency again. The dough should be shiny and smooth. It is now ready to be piped. To store for later use, cover the surface with plastic wrap and refrigerate for up to 2 days.

SAUCEPAN METHOD

4. If you don't have a standing mixer or you want to avoid dirtying an extra bowl, you can do everything in the saucepan. Once you've removed the pan from the heat, stir by hand with a sturdy spoon to cool the dough down to 180°F. Add 4 of the eggs, one at a time, mixing until thoroughly incorporated. Pinch off about 1 teaspoon of dough with your thumb and index finger, then pull your fingers apart. The dough should stretch rather than break. If it breaks, add the last egg.

SHAPING

Fit a large (#6) plain tip into a large plastic piping bag. Make a big cuff at the top of the bag and fill the bag halfway with choux paste. Uncuff and twist the top of the bag to push the contents toward the tip. For large cream puffs, pipe mounds of pâte à choux 2 inches in diameter and 1 inch high onto the first baking sheet, 2 inches apart. For medium puffs, the mounds should be 1½ inches in diameter and 1 inch high. Small puffs should be ½ inch in diameter and ½ inch high. At this stage, the unbaked cream puffs can be frozen. Cover with plastic film and freeze for up to 2 weeks. Defrost at room temperature for about 30 minutes before baking.

EGG WASH AND BAKING

1. Preheat the oven to 425°F. Adjust the rack to the center of the oven and place a heatproof baking dish or pan on the floor of the oven.

Prepare a baking sheet by lining it with parchment paper. Glue each corner of the parchment to the sheet with a dab of choux paste. This keeps the paper in place during piping and baking. Line a second baking sheet with parchment paper and place a rack on it.

2. Make the egg wash by whisking the egg and yolk in a small bowl. Brush lightly but evenly over the puffs.

3. Place the puffs in the oven and pour the hot water into the pan on the oven floor. Quickly close the door to keep all the steam in the oven. Bake for 10 minutes, or until the puffs begin to rise, then turn the oven down to 350°F and rotate the baking sheet. Prop the oven door open slightly with a wooden spoon and bake for 18 to 20 minutes more for large puffs, or until the puffs turn nutty brown. (For medium puffs, bake for 15 to 18 minutes more; for small puffs, bake for 10 to 12 minutes more.) Remove from the oven and cool completely on a rack, about 15 minutes, before filling and serving. At this stage, the cream puffs can be frozen for later use. Place the cooled puffs in an airtight plastic bag and freeze for up to 2 weeks. They will also keep for 24 hours at room temperature before being filled.

Chocolate Cream Puffs

THIS DEPARTURE FROM THE TRADITIONAL CREAM PUFF IS *filled with a rich, creamy ganache, which is incredibly easy to whip up. It may be more spectacular and decadent than the traditional version, and it's also quicker to make. This recipe calls for the puffs to be medium size, but of course you can vary the size.*

YIELD: About 36 medium cream puffs

SPECIAL TOOLS:

Standing electric mixer with a paddle attachment (optional)

Candy thermometer

Parchment paper

Paper cupcake liners

Piping bag with large (#6) plain and medium (#4) star tips

1 recipe Master Pâte à Choux (page 118), made into medium puffs and baked

1 recipe Ganache Glaze (page 28; you won't use it all)

1 recipe Chocolate Whipped Cream (page 37)

1. When the baked choux puffs are completely cool, cut the top half off each one, using an offset serrated knife, and set them on the rack over the second baking sheet. Drizzle some of the Ganache Glaze over each puff top, letting the excess run onto the baking sheet below. Place the puff tops in the refrigerator to set, about 15 minutes.

2. Fill the puffs. Fit a medium star tip into a large plastic piping bag and fill the bag halfway with the Chocolate Whipped Cream. Pipe the cream into the bottom halves of the puffs, mounding it up at least 1 inch above the cut edge. (The cream can also be dolloped in with a spoon.) Place the puff bottoms on a serving plate or in paper cupcake liners. Replace the ganache-glazed puff tops, and serve. Filled cream puffs will last for 3 to 4 hours in the refrigerator.

Variations

- ❧ CARAMEL CREAM PUFFS: Replace the Chocolate Whipped Cream with Whipped Caramel Cream (page 60).

- ❧ VANILLA CREAM PUFFS: Replace the Chocolate Whipped Cream with standard crème chantilly (whipped cream sweetened with sugar and flavored with vanilla).

- ❧ CREAM PUFF SURPRISE: Before piping cream into the bottom half of the puff, place a tablespoon of raspberry preserves, ganache, caramel sauce, or a few pieces of fresh fruit into the bottom of each.

Profiteroles

SO NAMED BECAUSE THEY COST LITTLE TO MAKE BUT *yielded high profits, these choux puffs are filled with vanilla ice cream and slathered in rich, dark chocolate sauce. But I can't help going off on my own tangents. Depending on the season, I fill the choux puffs with a variety of ice creams and sorbets.*

YIELD: About 36 medium puffs

SPECIAL TOOLS:

Standing electric mixer with a paddle attachment (optional)

Candy thermometer

Piping bag with a large (#6) plain tip (optional)

Parchment paper

1 recipe Master Pâte à Choux (page 118), made into medium puffs and baked

1 quart Vanilla Ice Cream (page 94 or store-bought; you won't use it all)

1 recipe Chocolate Sauce (page 39; you won't use it all)

1. Allow the baked choux puffs to cool completely, then cut off the top half of each one.

2. Using a small ice cream scoop or melon baller, scoop up a perfectly round ball of ice cream for each puff. Place a scoop of ice cream on the bottom half of each puff, and put the top half back over the ice cream.

3. Place 3 profiteroles on each plate and top each puff with a generous amount of Chocolate Sauce. Serve immediately.

Religieuses

COMMON IN FRENCH PÂTISSERIES, THESE DELECTABLE *puffs are rarely seen in the United States. Their shape is meant to represent a nun, with one large and one small cream puff filled with coffee-flavored pastry cream, joined together with caramel like a snowman. Mocha glaze is then drizzled on top to look like a nun's habit. While usually seen in the smaller version, a religieuse can also be made like croquembouche, with the mocha-filled puffs stacked into a pyramid.*

1. Using a paring knife, make a small hole in the bottom of each cooled medium and small puff. Using a plastic piping bag fitted with a medium plain tip, inject the Mocha Pastry Cream into the center of each puff. Set them aside in the refrigerator.

2. When the hot caramel has stopped bubbling, carefully dip the bottom of each small puff into it and then press a small puff onto the top of each medium puff. Set aside at room temperature to harden. Place the stacked puffs on a rack set over a baking sheet.

3. Combine the powdered sugar, espresso, and milk in a small bowl and whisk vigorously to combine. Adjust the consistency of the glaze with additional powdered sugar as needed. Spoon a generous amount of the mocha glaze over the top of each stacked puff. Refrigerate until ready to serve. Religieuses will keep for 3 to 4 hours in the refrigerator.

YIELD: 24 nuns

SPECIAL TOOLS:

Standing electric mixer with a paddle attachment (optional)

Candy thermometer

Piping bag with large (#6) and medium (#4) plain tips

Parchment paper

Food processor (if necessary)

1 recipe Master Pâte à Choux (page 118), made into 24 medium and 24 small puffs and baked

1 recipe Mocha Pastry Cream (page 101)

1 recipe Master Caramel (page 50; you won't use it all)

1 cup powdered sugar, sifted, plus more if needed

2 tablespoons brewed espresso

1 tablespoon milk

YIELD: 1 pyramid of 36 puffs

SPECIAL TOOLS:

Standing electric mixer with a paddle attachment (optional)

Candy thermometer

Silica gel (optional)

Food processor (if necessary)

Piping bag with large (#6) and medium (#4) plain tips

Silicone mat or parchment paper

½ batch Master Pâte à Choux (page 118), made into thirty-six ¾-inch puffs and baked (make the entire recipe and use half for another purpose)

1 recipe Pastry Cream (page 100)

1 recipe Master Caramel (page 50)

1 recipe Croquante (page 55), cut into a 12-inch circle to be used as a base for the completed croquembouche (optional)

1 recipe Golden Spun Sugar (page 52)

Croquembouche

THIS STUNNING DESSERT IS TRADITIONALLY RESERVED IN *France for weddings, although it pops up at many celebratory occasions in the United States. Croquembouche is a common sight at Christmas because of its conical tree shape. Pronounced croak-em BOOSH, the name translates from the French as "crackle in the mouth." And it does, because each puff is generously coated with caramel, which hardens into a brittle golden shell. Traditionally the puffs are filled with vanilla pastry cream, but I rarely stick to tradition. (See the variations for some of my favorite fillings and garnishes.) Making croquembouche is not complicated, but it does take time and patience. Be sure to have plenty of both before you start. (Keep a bowl of ice water on hand; sugar burns are painful.) After you've completed your first one, you may wish to try to top the world's record, a croquembouche that stands at 13½ feet tall. .*

1. With a paring knife, make a small hole in the bottom of each cooled puff. Using a piping bag fitted with a medium plain tip, inject the Pastry Cream into the center of each puff. Set them aside in the refrigerator.

2. Draw an 8-inch circle on a piece of parchment paper and place it on a baking sheet. This will serve as your template as you begin to build the croquembouche.

3. When the hot caramel has stopped bubbling, using a pair of tongs, dip 1 filled puff halfway into the hot caramel. Remove it, carefully shake off the excess caramel, and place it on the parchment paper template, on the line you drew. Use a fork to help ease the puff off the tongs. Repeat with another 8 to 10 puffs, placing them side by side along the line, until a complete circle is formed. The caramel coating will act as glue, sticking the puffs together as it cools.

4. Repeat the process, making another ring of dipped puffs on top of the first ring. Make the second ring slightly smaller, so that as the croquembouche is built up it will take on a conical shape.

5. Continue making smaller and smaller rings of caramel-dipped puffs until the cone is complete. (If the caramel cools and becomes too thick, reheat it. Place it over low heat without stirring for 5 minutes, or until it liquefies.)

6. When the last layer of caramel has hardened, about 10 minutes, the croquembouche may be transferred to the serving platter. Carefully slide a metal offset spatula between the paper and the croquembouche to release any hardened caramel. Then, holding the top of the cone, carefully lift the croquembouche with the spatula onto a serving platter, on top of the croquante, if using. Wrap the spun sugar around the croquembouche just before serving.

Variations

❧ MINI CROQUEMBOUCHE: Smaller versions of this classic centerpiece can be made by starting with a smaller circle of puffs. Even individual croquembouches can be made. Place three puffs together in a triangle and one more on top.

❧ LAVENDER CROQUEMBOUCHE: When making the Pastry Cream, add I tablespoon lavender flowers to the milk at the beginning of the recipe. Garnish the croquembouche with sugared lavender flowers. Dip lavender sprigs in soft-peak egg whites, roll them in sugar, and dry for I hour on a parchment-lined baking sheet.

❧ CHOCOLATE CROQUEMBOUCHE: Fill the puffs with Chocolate Mousse (page 40). Decorate with shaved dark chocolate, milk chocolate, and white chocolate.

Pâte à Choux
BAKED AND AUGMENTED

YIELD: 24 éclairs

SPECIAL TOOLS:

Standing electric mixer with a paddle attachment (optional)

Candy thermometer

Food processor (if necessary)

Piping bag with a large (#6) plain piping tip

Parchment paper (optional)

Decorative paper cups (optional)

1 recipe Master Pâte à Choux (page 118), prepared through step 4

1 recipe Ganache Glaze (page 28)

1 recipe Pastry Cream (page 100)

Éclairs

PIPED INTO FINGER-LENGTH BATONS, THESE CHOCOLATE-*glazed puffs are filled with pastry cream that can be made in a variety of flavors. The name means "flash," as in a flash of light or lightning, which is fitting, because that's how quickly they disappear.*

Éclairs are made by piping choux paste through a pastry bag fitted with a medium plain or starred tip (the starred tip makes a very pretty éclair). To pipe straight, draw a line on the underside of the parchment paper as a guide. Be sure to draw the line on the underside, or the mark will transfer to the éclair during baking.

1. Fit a large (#6) plain tip into a large piping bag and fill the bag halfway with Pâte à Choux dough as directed in the master recipe. Pipe twenty-four 4-inch strips. Stagger the rows on the diagonal and space them 1 inch apart. Brush the éclairs with the egg wash as directed on page 120, but before baking, run a fork down the length of each puff. These score marks will help the éclair expand evenly. Bake the éclairs in the same manner as the puffs, then allow them to cool completely. Wash and dry the pastry bag and tip.

2. When the éclairs are completely cool, cut the top half off each one and set the tops on the rack over a second baking sheet. Spoon the Ganache Glaze over each éclair top, letting the excess run off onto the baking sheet below. Place the tops in the refrigerator to set, about 15 minutes.

3. Fill the éclairs. Fit the large tip into the piping bag and fill the bag halfway with the Pastry Cream. Fill the entire length of the éclair by piping a slow, steady strip. (The pastry cream can also be dolloped in with a spoon.) When all of the éclairs are filled, place them in decorative paper cups or on a serving platter. Replace the chocolate-glazed tops. The éclairs are ready to be served, or they can be refrigerated for up to 4 hours.

Variations

- CHOCOLATE ÉCLAIRS: Replace the Pastry Cream with the chocolate variation (page 101).

- LEMON CURD ÉCLAIRS: Replace the Pastry Cream with Master Lemon Curd (page 75).

YIELD: Thirty-two 2-inch pastries

SPECIAL TOOLS:

Standing electric mixer with a paddle attachment (optional)

Candy thermometer

Piping bag with a small (#2) plain tip (optional)

Coffee grinder (optional)

FOR THE PUFFS

½ batch Master Pâte à Choux (page 118), prepared through step 4 (make the entire recipe and use half for another purpose)

FOR THE FILLING

2 cups 1-inch pieces red-fleshed plums

¼ cup sugar

⅛ teaspoon ground cinnamon

⅛ teaspoon ground star anise (ground in a coffee grinder or with a Microplane)

3 tablespoons fresh orange juice

FOR THE GLAZE

1 cup powdered sugar

1 tablespoon fresh ginger juice (from an 8-inch piece of fresh ginger; see page 370)

1 tablespoon water

½ teaspoon fresh lemon juice

Plum and Ginger Carolines

CAROLINES (PRONOUNCED CA-RO-LEEN) ARE MINIATURE *éclairs. Inspired by the Asian flavors of Bella Lantsman and Wolf-gang Puck's award-winning Chinois restaurant, in Santa Monica, California, these mini-éclairs, filled with plum compote and brushed with a spicy ginger glaze, make a perfectly sweet, bite-size ending to any meal. In the California summer, I prefer to use Elephant Heart or Santa Rosa plums, but any sweet, juicy red-fleshed plum will do.*

PUFFS

Fit a small (#2) plain tip into a piping bag and fill the bag with Pâte à Choux dough. Pipe thirty-two 2-inch strips. Stagger the rows on the diagonal and space them 1 inch apart. Brush the mini-éclairs with egg wash as directed on page 120, but before baking, score the éclairs down their length with a fork. (The score marks will help them expand evenly.) Bake the éclairs in the same manner as the puffs, then allow them to cool completely.

FILLING

Combine the plums, sugar, cinnamon, star anise, and orange juice in a medium saucepan over medium heat. Cook for 5 to 7 minutes, stirring occasionally, until the plums begin to soften. Remove from the heat and set aside to cool.

GLAZE

Combine the powdered sugar, ginger juice, water, and lemon juice in a small bowl. Whisk until smooth, then set aside at room temperature.

FINISHING THE CAROLINES

Cut each éclair in half crosswise. Spoon 2 to 3 teaspoons of plum compote into each bottom half and replace the top. Brush the top with the ginger glaze. Serve immediately or refrigerate for 2 to 3 hours.

PETITS FOURS

Miniature pastries such as these are technically referred to as *petits fours*. The name means "little ovens." Traditionally in France, after large cakes were baked, small portions of leftover batter were put into the oven to bake as the oven cooled down. Although petits fours are commonly thought of as tiny cakes with elaborate decorations, any small baked goods, including cookies, are considered part of this category. French formal dinners often will include a final serving of petits fours, referred to as the *mignardise*.

YIELD: 36 gougères

SPECIAL TOOLS:

Standing electric mixer with a
paddle attachment (optional)

Candy thermometer

Parchment paper

Piping bag with a large (#6) plain
tip (optional)

¼ cup firmly packed grated
Gruyère cheese

¼ cup firmly packed grated
sharp Cheddar cheese,
preferably Vermont

¼ cup firmly packed grated
Parmigiano-Reggiano
cheese

⅛–½ teaspoon cayenne pepper
(optional)

1 recipe Master Pâte à Choux
(page 118), prepared
through step 4

Gougères

RECENTLY BROUGHT BACK TO LIFE BY MY DEAR FRIEND,
*pastry chef Nicole Plue, these cheesy snacks are having a revival all
over the country. The delicate savories make an excellent hors
d'oeuvre for a party. Or delight your guests by serving them in the
breadbasket.*

*From the Burgundy region in France, gougères are typically
made with Gruyère, a Swiss firm cheese with a sharp, nutty flavor. I
prefer a blend of Parmigiano-Reggiano, Vermont Cheddar, and
Gruyère, but feel free to mix and match your favorite cheeses.*

1. Preheat the oven to 425°F. Adjust the rack to the center of
the oven.

2. Combine the cheeses with the cayenne pepper in a medium
bowl. While the Pâte à Choux dough is still warm, stir in three quarters of the cheese mixture.

3. Line a baking sheet with parchment paper and glue it in place
with a dab of dough in each corner. Fit a large (#6) plain tip into a
large piping bag and fill the bag halfway with the dough. Pipe the
dough onto the baking sheet into 1½-inch circles, spaced 1 inch apart
as directed in the master recipe. (You can also spoon out the dough.)
Brush with egg wash as directed on page 120. Sprinkle the remaining
cheese mixture over the tops, distributing it evenly.

4. Bake for 10 minutes. Turn the oven down to 350°F and rotate the baking sheet. Prop the oven door open slightly with a wooden
spoon and bake for 5 to 10 minutes more, or until the gougères turn
nutty brown. Remove from the oven and serve warm or at room temperature. The gougères can be stored in airtight plastic bags and
frozen for up to 2 weeks. Defrost at room temperature for 30 minutes, then refresh in a 350°F oven for 10 minutes.

Variations

☙ HERB GOUGÈRES: Add 2 tablespoons chopped chives,
chervil, tarragon, or a combination along with the first addition of cheese. A tablespoon of premixed fines herbes or
herbes de Provence will work nicely too.

YIELD: Nine 3-inch pastries

SPECIAL TOOLS:

    Standing electric mixer with a
    paddle attachment (optional)

    Candy thermometer

    Piping bag with a medium (#4)
    plain tip

½ batch Master Pâte à Choux
    (page 118), prepared
    through step 4 (make the
    entire recipe and use half
    for another purpose)

1 cup finely chopped skinned
    hazelnuts (page 362)

1 recipe Pastry Cream
    (page 100; you will not
    need all of it)

Powdered sugar

Hazelnut Paris-Brest

THE PARIS-BREST-PARIS, OR PBP, A GRUELING 1,200-kilometer bicycle race from the capital of France to the port city of Brest and back again, has been held since the late nineteenth century. It is more a test of endurance than a race, and today many amateur cyclists participate in it. In the early years of the race, a French baker was inspired to create a pastry to honor the brave athletes. His wheel-shaped éclair can now be found in French bakeries all over the world, but especially in Paris and Brest.

    Serge, one of our regular customers at Spago, used to complain about Americans who thought they knew how to make "real French pastry." Finally, after he teased me too many times, I decided to prove him wrong. I knew it wasn't difficult to turn out a great Paris-Brest. After his first bite, I could tell by his expression that he would never rant about Americans again.

1. Fit a medium (#4) plain tip into a piping bag and fill the bag with the Pâte à Choux dough. Pipe 3-inch rings (leaving the centers open) and space the rings 1 inch apart on the baking sheets. After brushing the rings lightly but thoroughly with the egg wash as directed on page 120, sprinkle the tops generously with the chopped hazelnuts. Bake as directed, then allow them to cool completely. Wash and dry the pastry bag and tip.

2. Slice the cooled rings in half horizontally. With the medium tip, pipe 3 to 4 tablespoons of the Pastry Cream onto the bottom half of each ring, then replace the top. Sift a fine layer of powdered sugar over the tops and serve immediately.

Variations

🍃 HAZELNUT PASTRY CREAM: Stir ¼ cup Nutella or Homemade Hazelnut Paste (page 34) into the Pastry Cream before filling the choux rings.

🍃 PRALINE WHIPPED CREAM: Whip 1 cup heavy cream to stiff peaks, then fold in ¼ cup Nutella or Homemade Hazelnut Paste (page 34). Use in place of the Pastry Cream.

🍃 LARGE PARIS-BREST: To make a stunning dessert centerpiece, pipe the pâte à choux into 3 concentric circles, starting with an 8-inch circle, then working inward. Bake the choux ring at 400°F for 15 minutes, or until the ring begins to rise, then turn the oven down to 350°F and rotate the baking sheet. Prop the oven door open slightly with a wooden spoon and bake for 30 to 40 minutes more. Fill in the same manner as the smaller rings.

Apricot Mascarpone Cannoli

HAVE YOU EVER NOTICED HOW HARD IT IS TO FIND A GREAT *cannoli? Often the shell is tough and hard or soggy and stale, the filling bland and tasteless. Desperate for a good cannoli, my cravings led me to develop my own. Tender and delicate, these are filled with mascarpone cream studded with fresh apricots and pistachios.*

Traditional cannoli dough is a variation on pie dough, with butter or lard cut into a base of flour and sugar. After trying several variations, I still could not find a dough that was tender yet crisp. Then, after frying some pâte à choux fritters, it dawned on me. My hero, pâte à choux, to the rescue again!

YIELD: 12 cannoli

SPECIAL TOOLS:

Candy thermometer

Standing electric mixer with a paddle attachment (optional)

Rolling pastry cutter (optional)

Cannoli tubes or 4-inch dowels

Deep fryer (optional)

Piping bag with a medium (#4) plain tip

FOR THE PASTRY

½ batch Master Pâte à Choux (page 118), prepared through step 4 (make the entire recipe and use half for another purpose)

1 cup all-purpose flour

1 teaspoon instant espresso or instant coffee powder

2 teaspoons unsweetened cocoa powder

FOR THE FILLING

2 cups mascarpone cheese

3 tablespoons sugar

2 tablespoons Frangelico (hazelnut liqueur)

1 cup chopped pitted apricots

¼ cup finely chopped pistachios

FOR FRYING AND ASSEMBLY

1 quart safflower or sunflower oil

1 cup powdered sugar, sifted

PASTRY

1. Put the Pâte à Choux dough in a medium bowl, cover with plastic film, and chill for 4 hours.

2. Sift together the flour, coffee powder, and cocoa into a small bowl. On a lightly floured surface, gently knead the flour mixture into the chilled choux paste, ¼ cup at a time. Knead until completely incorporated. Divide the dough into 4 equal pieces, wrap in plastic film, and chill for 30 minutes.

3. With a rolling pin, roll one portion of dough out on a well-floured work surface to a thickness of ⅛ inch. Flour the surface as necessary. Using a chef's knife or a rolling pastry cutter, cut each portion into three 4-inch squares. Place one point of a square of dough in the center of a metal cannoli tube or dowel and wrap the square around the tube. Pinch the edges together. Repeat with the remaining squares. Chill the wrapped tubes while you make the filling. (If you run out of tubes, chill the 4-inch squares of dough and work in batches.)

FILLING

Using a standing mixer fitted with the paddle attachment or a hand mixer, mix the mascarpone, sugar, and Frangelico. By hand, fold in the apricots and pistachios. Set aside in the refrigerator.

FRYING AND ASSEMBLY

1. In a deep fryer or heavy skillet, heat the oil over medium heat. When it reaches 375°F, carefully place 2 or 3 cannoli at a time in the oil, using tongs. Deep-fry for 1 to 2 minutes, turning, until golden brown. Drain on paper towels. When the metal tubes have cooled, pull them out from the shells. Continue frying until all the dough is used. At this point, the shells can be frozen for up to 2 weeks.

2. Pipe or spoon the filling into each shell, filling the tube to about ½ inch from each end. Dust a light layer of powdered sugar over the tops and serve immediately.

Blackberry–Merlot Dumplings

YIELD: 20 to 24 dumplings, serving 6

SPECIAL TOOLS:

Standing electric mixer with paddle and whisk attachments (optional)

Candy thermometer

Blender or immersion blender

Parchment paper

FOR THE COMPOTE

3 pints blackberries

½ cup sugar

½ small orange, peeled and thinly sliced

½ lemon, peeled and thinly sliced

1 3-inch cinnamon stick

¼ vanilla bean, split and scraped

½ cup full-bodied red wine, such as Merlot

½ cup fresh orange juice

½ cup water

FOR THE DUMPLINGS

½ batch Master Pâte à Choux (page 118), prepared through step 4 (make the entire recipe and use half for another purpose)

Finely grated zest of 1 orange

2 large egg whites, at room temperature

Pinch of cream of tartar (less than ⅛ teaspoon)

2 tablespoons sugar

¾ cup crème fraîche or sour cream

I CREATED THIS DESSERT ONE HOT SUMMER AT CATAHOULA Restaurant in California's Napa Valley after a neighbor bestowed several cases of juicy, perfectly ripe blackberries on me.

I found some extra pâte à choux, lightened it with some whipped egg whites, and dropped teaspoons into the bubbling pot of the berry compote. In minutes, the little balls turned into delicate, tasty dumplings, and I served them in their own cooking liquid with a dollop of crème fraîche.

To enhance the flavor of the pâte à choux, I have added orange zest, but lime or lemon zest is just as nice. I have also had success with fresh herbs, such as rosemary and lemon thyme.

COMPOTE

1. Bring 2 pints of the berries, the sugar, orange, lemon, cinnamon stick, vanilla bean and scraped seeds, wine, orange juice, and water to a boil in a medium saucepan over medium heat. Cook, stirring occasionally, until the berries have softened, about 3 minutes. Remove from the heat, cover with plastic film, and set aside for 20 minutes to allow the flavors to infuse.

2. Remove the orange, lemon, cinnamon stick, and vanilla bean from the compote. Using a blender or a hand-held immersion blender, puree the compote for 1 minute, or until smooth and thick. Strain through a medium strainer. Set aside at room temperature.

DUMPLINGS

1. While the Pâte à Choux dough is still warm, fold in the orange zest and set aside at room temperature.

2. Using a standing mixer fitted with a whisk attachment or a hand mixer, whip the egg whites on medium speed. When large bubbles appear, add the cream of tartar. Continue whipping until they reach the soft-peak stage, about 1 minute. Begin slowly sprinkling in the sugar, taking about 1 minute to get it all in. Stop whipping when the egg whites are at the medium-peak stage. Gently fold one third of the egg whites into the pâte à choux to lighten the mixture, then fold in the rest.

3. Pour the berry puree back into the saucepan, if necessary, and return it to medium heat. Add the remaining 1 pint berries and bring to a boil over medium heat.

4. Spoon the pâte à choux by the scant tablespoonful, in batches, into the boiling compote and cook for 3 minutes, stirring gently. Be careful not to overcrowd or break the dumplings. Cook, keeping the compote at a boil, and transfer them to a large bowl as they are done. (Cover the bowl with the dumplings as you work.) When all of the dumplings have been poached, keep them at room temperature, covered, until ready to serve.

5. To serve, divide the compote and dumplings evenly among 6 bowls. Using a standing electric mixer fitted with a whisk attachment or a hand mixer, whip the crème fraîche to soft peaks, about 1 minute. Add a generous dollop to each bowl and serve.

Chocolate Banana Beignets

NOBODY CAN RESIST THIS TASTY COMBINATION. FRESH *banana wedges are dipped into a chocolate choux paste and fried to a perfect crispness. When I put these on the menu at Spago, they are always the first item that sells out. The ripeness of the bananas is crucial. If they are underripe, they won't taste luscious, but if they are overripe, they will be too mushy to hold their shape. If I can't find bananas at the perfect ripeness, I substitute chunks of frozen Banana Ganache (page 32). It can easily be made with overripe bananas.*

YIELD: 24 beignets

SPECIAL TOOLS:

    Standing electric mixer with a paddle attachment (optional)

    Candy thermometer

    Deep fryer (optional)

1 recipe Master Pâte à Choux (page 118), prepared through step 2

2 tablespoons unsweetened cocoa powder, sifted

2 tablespoons sugar

1 ounce bittersweet chocolate, chopped

1 large egg white, beaten to soft-peak stage

1 quart safflower or sunflower oil

2–3 ripe but firm bananas

½ cup powdered sugar, sifted

1 recipe Chocolate Sauce (page 39), warm

1. Stir the cocoa powder, sugar, and chocolate into the flour-milk mixture and stir until melted. Continue with steps 3 and 4 of the master recipe, using all 5 eggs. Cover with plastic film and chill for at least 2 hours. At this stage, the pâte à choux can be stored in the refrigerator for up to 5 days or frozen for up to 2 months.

2. In a deep heavy skillet, wide saucepan, or deep fryer, heat the oil to 375°F over medium heat.

3. Meanwhile, remove the chocolate choux paste from the refrigerator and stir until smooth. Stir in the beaten egg white. Peel the bananas and cut them into 1-inch chunks. Using a fork, dip the banana chunks into the chocolate paste, stirring to coat completely.

4. When the oil reaches 375°F, carefully drop the coated bananas into the oil and fry in batches until golden brown, about 1 minute per side. Do not overcrowd the pan. Remove with a slotted spoon and place on a paper towel–lined platter. Repeat with the remaining banana slices.

5. To serve, dust the top of the beignets with powdered sugar and place them in pools of warm Chocolate Sauce on plates.

YIELD: 36 fritters, serving 6

SPECIAL TOOLS:

  Standing electric mixer with a
    paddle attachment (optional)

  Candy thermometer

  Cherry pitter (optional)

  Deep fryer (optional)

FOR THE FRITTERS

  1 recipe Master Pâte à Choux
    (page 118), prepared
    through step 4, made with 5
    eggs

  2 tablespoons sugar

  ½ teaspoon ground cardamom

  ½ teaspoon freshly grated
    nutmeg

  1 teaspoon almond extract

FOR THE SAUCE

  2 cups tawny port

  2 teaspoons fresh orange juice

  2 teaspoons fresh lemon juice

  ½ cup sugar

  Finely chopped zest of
    1 orange

  ½ vanilla bean, split and
    scraped

FOR FRYING AND SERVING

  1 quart safflower or sunflower
    oil

  1½ cups sliced almonds

  3 cups Bing or Burlat cherries,
    pitted

  ½ cup powdered sugar, sifted

Cherry Almond Fritters

WHEN CHERRIES FIRST COME INTO SEASON IN THE EARLY *summer, I go a bit mad. After waiting almost an entire year for them to return to the farmers' market, I come back to the restaurant with cases of cherries piled into the back seat of my car. These sublime fritters came about after one of those early-season shopping sprees. The cherries are dipped in almond-flavored choux paste, fried to a golden crispness, and drizzled with port sauce. Add a scoop of Vanilla Ice Cream (page 94) if you like. Burlats are an early beginning-of-the-season cherry. Feel free to use Bings instead.*

FRITTERS

While the Pâte à Choux dough is still warm, stir in the sugar, cardamom, nutmeg, and almond extract. Cover the bowl with plastic film and chill for at least 2 hours.

SAUCE

Bring the port, orange juice, lemon juice, sugar, orange zest, and vanilla bean and scraped seeds to a boil in a medium saucepan over medium heat. Cook until the liquid is reduced by half, 10 to 15 minutes, then remove the vanilla bean, cover with plastic film, and set the sauce aside at room temperature.

FRYING AND SERVING

1. In a deep fryer or heavy skillet, heat the oil to 375°F over medium heat. Insert a deep-frying thermometer.

2. Meanwhile, place the almonds in a shallow bowl. Remove the choux paste from the refrigerator and stir until smooth. Using a fork, dip a cherry into the choux paste, stirring to coat completely. Release the cherry from the fork into the bowl of sliced almonds and toss to coat.

3. When the oil reaches 375°F, place each coated cherry on a slotted spoon and carefully drop it into the oil. Fry the cherries, in batches, until golden brown, about 1 minute per side. Do not overcrowd the skillet. Remove with a slotted spoon and place on a paper towel–lined platter. Repeat with the remaining cherries.

4. To serve, dust the top of the fritters with powdered sugar, then place 6 fritters on a pool of port sauce on each plate.

POUND CAKE & GÉNOISE

WHEN I FIRST BEGAN BAKING PROFESSIONALLY, I SPENT A lot of time trying to perfect pound cake. In so doing, I learned a lot about the science of baking and revised the way I thought about what constitutes a liquid and a solid.

That issue is key to understanding pound cakes, which are made from half liquid ingredients and half solid ingredients. This sounds straightforward. But not all liquid ingredients are liquid to begin with, nor are all solids firm. Butter and sugar, for example, are solid until they are heated; when they are baked as part of a batter, they melt and become absorbed by the solid ingredients around them. Liquids, then, are best defined as ingredients that can be absorbed at any stage during the baking process, and the liquid ingredients in pound cake are sugar and butter.

Solids, too, can be deceiving. Raw eggs are wet, but they solidify when heated. Therefore, eggs should be classified as a solid; they are packed with protein and provide structure in a cake. Flour, the last ingredient in pound cake, is also a solid. It absorbs the liquid added to it, binding all the ingredients together and giving the cake structural stability.

TRADITIONALLY, FOUR EQUAL QUANTITIES OF BUTTER, SUGAR, flour, and eggs are called for in pound cake. For that reason, this cake is known as *quatre quarts,* or "four quarters," in France. It's *pound cake* in English because the recipe usually calls for a pound of each of the four quarters. Pound cake recipes are begun by creaming the butter and sugar together. Beating the sugar into the butter pushes the sugar crystals through the fat to create tiny tunnels of air. As the sugar works through the butter, it breaks down and gradually dissolves. Creaming simultaneously adds air and softens the butter so that the rest of the ingredients can be added more easily.

The creaming method produces cakes that can rise without the addition of a chemical leavener. Leavening is simply the process of introducing gas to a batter or dough. Chemical leaveners provide lift by releasing bubbles of carbon dioxide. In pound cake, the gas is usually nothing more than air, which is trapped in the butter through the process of creaming.

Before baking powder and baking soda were invented, Colonial women made all their cakes this way, and I can only imagine their forearms from all the beating and creaming of the butter.

USING THE SAME INGREDIENTS FOUND IN POUND CAKE BUT changing their method of preparation produces a completely different cake called *génoise*. The French adopted this cake from Italian bakers in Genoa. The method used for making it is called *foaming*. The term *foam* refers to the appearance of the eggs after they have been whipped. Foams are made possible by the egg protein called *albumin*. It is unusual in the world of protein because it is quite viscous yet sturdy. Whipping loosens the albumin and incorporates bubbles of air. The more the egg is whipped, the more air bubbles are introduced. The albumin stretches into a web strong enough to hold the air bubbles captive. Bubbles in the foam expand with heat, just like the air in the creamed butter of a pound cake.

You begin the foam for a génoise by warming eggs and sugar over a hot water bath. Warm albumin accepts more air than cold albumin. When the temperature reaches 110°F, you whip the eggs until they become a light lemony yellow foam and their volume triples.

Liquids are best defined as ingredients that can be absorbed at any stage during the baking process.

Before adding it to the foam, you triple-sift the flour to aerate it and lighten it. After sifting, you carefully fold the flour into the foam to bind it and provide structure. If you baked the batter at this point, the result would be a standard sponge cake. Sponge cakes, known in French as *biscuits,* are typically used as a base for creams and mousses, because on their own they are quite dry.

Génoise, however, has one more element: butter. It is added in its liquid form, while still warm, to provide moisture and so that it can be distributed more evenly around the foam. If the butter is too cool, it will form streaks in the batter, so be sure to add it right after melting. Once baked, this batter becomes a spongy, airy cake with a rich, buttery flavor.

The key to successful génoise is in the folding. You must incorporate the ingredients carefully to maintain the foam. Folding too vigorously will deflate the foam and prevent the cake from rising fully. You want to minimize the number of times the foam is disturbed while still incorporating the ingredients thoroughly, covering as much territory in as few strokes as possible. The right tool—the wire balloon whisk—makes this possible. A balloon whisk drawn through foam in one motion cuts about twenty tunnels through the foam, dragging a portion of the dry ingredients through each tunnel.

The principles of creaming and foaming, so critical to cake baking, appear in nearly all other baked desserts as well. This chapter contains many examples of these methods, often with very different results.

The key to successful génoise is in the folding.

Pound Cake and Génoise
FAMILY TREE

liquid: 2 pounds : solid: 2 pounds

1 pound butter   1 pound eggs

1 pound sugar   1 pound flour

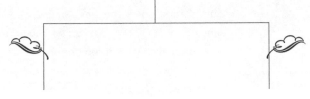

CREAMING

MASTER POUND CAKE
Lemon Pound Cake
Marble Cake
Tuiles
Blondies
Banana Pound Cake
Orange Blossom Honey Madeleines

FOAMING

MASTER GÉNOISE
Chocolate Génoise
Buttermilk Birthday Cupcakes
Torta Sabiosa
Brown Butter Baumkuchen

All the recipes in this chapter are based on the master ratio of half liquid, half solid. The Master Pound Cake and Master Génoise are equal parts butter, sugar, flour, and eggs. CREAMING produces denser products like pound cakes and cookies. FOAMED products like génoise are lighter and airier. Note that the ratio is based on weight, not volume.

Master Pound Cake

YIELD: One 9-inch loaf cake

SPECIAL TOOLS:

    Parchment paper

    Standing electric mixer with a
    paddle attachment (optional)

½ pound (2 sticks) unsalted
    butter, softened if using a
    hand mixer

1 cup plus 2 tablespoons
    sugar

4 large eggs

2 teaspoons vanilla extract

1¾ cups all-purpose or cake
    flour (or half each), sifted
    3 times

    Pinch of salt

THIS IS A TRADITIONAL POUND CAKE. WHILE AT FIRST GLANCE *the recipe may not look like the classic formula of four equal parts, it is (1 cup plus 2 tablespoons sugar = 8 ounces; 4 large eggs = approximately 8 ounces; 1¾ cups flour = 8 ounces).*

The entire leavening process is a result of incorporating lots of air. To add such a large amount of air efficiently, I recommend using a standing electric mixer. However, a hand mixer and the old-fashioned elbow-grease methods work too. Believe me, after making just one pound cake by hand, you will have a new appreciation of your ancestors. (That, or you'll go buy a standing mixer!) No matter how you cream the batter, it is essential to stop mixing every few minutes and scrape down the sides of the bowl with a rubber spatula. This ensures even incorporation of the ingredients, which in turn produces an evenly textured crumb.

I always add flavorings to a cake at the very beginning of a recipe, with the butter. Fat is an excellent flavor carrier. Even if the flavor is in a dry form, like cinnamon, the butter is still the best place to put it. When it's creamed, the friction will create heat, releasing the oils into the dry ingredients.

Although this recipe uses vanilla, there are several other possibilities. Try adding orange zest, ginger, and spices, or toasted chopped nuts (see Variations). Using cake flour will produce a somewhat lighter cake.

1. Preheat the oven to 350°F. Adjust the rack to the center of the oven. Spray a 9-x-5-x-3-inch loaf pan with pan spray and line it with a strip of parchment paper, running along the length of the pan. Spray the paper.

2. Using a standing electric mixer fitted with a paddle attachment or a hand mixer, beat the butter on high speed until soft and creamy, about 1 minute. Slowly add the sugar, beating continuously on high speed. It should take 5 to 6 minutes to add the sugar. Don't cheat and add it too quickly. Scrape down the sides of the bowl with a rubber spatula. All this beating is very important, because it is adding air, which is the only leavener. The mixture should be fluffy, light, and a creamy white color.

3. Add the eggs, one at a time. Be sure that each egg is completely incorporated and scrape down the sides of the bowl before adding the next one. (The mixture may take on a broken appearance, which is fine, because when the flour goes in the batter will come together.) Add the vanilla. Slowly add the flour, ½ cup at a time, and the salt.

4. Pour the batter into the prepared pan. Bake the cake for 50 to 70 minutes, or until a toothpick inserted in the center comes out clean. Let cool in the pan on a rack for 5 to 10 minutes, then remove it from the pan and set it on the rack to cool. (This prevents condensation from collecting at the bottom of the pan.) Serve warm or at room temperature. The pound cake will last for up to 2 days at room temperature or 3 weeks in the freezer if wrapped airtight.

Variations

- For a lighter-textured cake, sift 2 teaspoons baking powder with the flour. Cakes with chemical leavening rise faster and will often split down the middle as they grow.

- ORANGE POUND CAKE: Add 2 tablespoons finely grated orange zest and 2 tablespoons orange flower water with the sugar in addition to the vanilla.

- GINGER AND SPICE POUND CAKE: Substitute 2 tablespoons ground ginger, 1 teaspoon ground cinnamon, and ½ teaspoon freshly grated nutmeg for the vanilla.

- NUTTY POUND CAKE: Add 1 cup toasted chopped nuts with the flour and omit the vanilla if desired.

- VICTORIAN POUND CAKE: Substitute 2 tablespoons rose water for the vanilla.

YIELD: Two 9-inch loaf cakes

SPECIAL TOOLS:

Parchment paper (for loaf cakes)

Standing electric mixer with a paddle attachment (optional)

FOR THE CAKE

1½ cups all-purpose flour

1½ cups cake flour

1 teaspoon baking powder

¼ teaspoon salt

1 cup buttermilk

2 tablespoons fresh lemon juice

1 pound (4 sticks) unsalted butter, softened if using a hand mixer

2 cups sugar

¼ cup finely grated or chopped lemon zest

4 large eggs

FOR THE LEMON SYRUP

½ cup plus 1 tablespoon fresh lemon juice

¾ cup sugar

Lemon Pound Cake

LEMON POUND CAKE WAS THE FIRST POUND CAKE I FELL IN *love with. My mother used to bring them back from the half-price store, and I would eat the top, leaving the drier cake underneath for my sisters. It took me a while to figure out how to make a cake like the one I was served on Thanksgiving at the home of my chef friend Jean-Paul de Sourdie. It was tart, moist, and delicate in texture, exactly what I had been trying in vain to create.*

After many attempts to duplicate that cake, I learned that the secret to Jean-Paul's success was lemon syrup poured over the cake while it was still hot. Soaking a cake with flavored syrup is a time-honored foolproof way of adding moisture and flavor.

This variation of pound cake uses chemical leavening (baking powder) in addition to air incorporated by creaming. The result is a slightly lighter crumb than pound cake made in the traditional manner. The ingredients are slightly different as well, but it is still a basic pound cake. The liquids here are butter, sugar, buttermilk, and lemon juice, and when combined they equal 4 cups. The solids are lemon zest, eggs, flour, baking powder, and salt, and they also equal 4 cups.

CAKE

1. Preheat the oven to 350°F. Adjust the rack to the center of the oven. Prepare two 9-x-5-x-3-inch loaf pans as directed in step 1 of Master Pound Cake (page 140).

2. Triple-sift the flours, baking powder, and salt into a medium bowl and set aside. Combine the buttermilk and lemon juice in a small bowl and set aside.

3. Using a standing mixer fitted with a paddle attachment or a hand mixer, beat the butter on high speed until it is soft and creamy, about 1 minute. Slowly add the sugar and lemon zest and beat on high speed until fully incorporated and the mixture is fluffy, light, and a creamy white color, about 10 minutes. Stop the mixer and scrape down the sides of the bowl with a rubber spatula.

4. Add the eggs, one at a time. Be sure each egg is completely incorporated and scrape down the sides of the bowl before adding the next.

5. Add one third of the sifted dry ingredients to the batter and mix on low speed until just incorporated. Add one third of the buttermilk mixture and mix until just incorporated. Repeat with the remaining two thirds of the dry and wet ingredients, in two additions. Be sure each addition is completely absorbed before adding the next.

6. Pour the batter into the prepared pans. Bake for 1 hour and 20 minutes, or until a toothpick inserted in the center comes out clean. Let cool in the pans on a rack for 5 to 10 minutes, then carefully remove them from the pans and set on the rack to cool.

SYRUP

1. Meanwhile, bring the lemon juice and sugar to a boil in a small saucepan over medium heat, stirring. Cook until the sugar has dissolved, about 3 minutes.

2. While the cakes are still warm, poke holes all over the tops with a skewer or fork. Use a pastry brush to apply the lemon syrup. The holes help the syrup penetrate into the center of the cake. Serve warm or at room temperature. The pound cake will last for up to 2 days at room temperature or 3 weeks in the freezer if wrapped airtight.

YIELD: One 10-inch bundt or
tube cake

SPECIAL TOOLS:

Standing electric mixer with a
paddle attachment (optional)

2¼ cups cake flour

1 tablespoon plus 1 teaspoon
baking powder

½ teaspoon baking soda

¼ teaspoon salt

2 ounces bittersweet
chocolate

1 tablespoon brewed
espresso or strong regular
coffee

¼ pound (1 stick) unsalted
butter, softened if using a
hand mixer

½ teaspoon ground cinnamon

1¼ cups sugar

2 large eggs

¾ cup sour cream

1½ teaspoons vanilla extract

⅓ cup milk

Marble Cake

EVERYONE THINKS THE SWIRLS OF CHOCOLATE AND
*vanilla blended perfectly into a rich, moist marble cake are pure
magic. This cake is actually quite simple. All you do is add chocolate
to half the batter. Many chocolate cakes contain cocoa powder.
Somehow, though, they never taste chocolatey enough for me. I prefer melted bittersweet chocolate. To further intensify the chocolate
flavor, I always add brewed espresso, which accentuates the bitterness, giving the cake a richer and darker taste.*

1. Preheat the oven to 350°F. Adjust the rack to the center of
the oven. Spray a bundt or tube pan with pan spray.

2. Triple-sift the flour, baking powder, baking soda, and salt
into a medium bowl and set aside.

3. Fill a medium saucepan half full of water and bring it to a
simmer over medium heat. Combine the chocolate and coffee in a
small bowl. Create a double boiler by placing the bowl over the simmering water. Stir occasionally until the chocolate melts, 2 to 3 minutes. Remove from the heat and set aside.

4. Using a standing mixer fitted with a paddle attachment or a
hand mixer, beat the butter and cinnamon on high speed until soft
and creamy, about 1 minute. Slowly add the sugar and beat on high
speed until fully incorporated and the mixture is light, fluffy, and a
creamy white color, 5 to 6 minutes. Stop the mixer and scrape down
the sides of the bowl with a rubber spatula.

5. Add the eggs, one at a time. Be sure each egg is completely
incorporated and scrape down the sides of the bowl before adding the
next. Add the sour cream and the vanilla.

6. On low speed, add the sifted dry ingredients and the milk in
thirds, alternating dry and wet ingredients, mixing until just incorporated, and scraping down the sides of the bowl after each addition.

7. Divide the batter equally between two medium bowls. Add the
melted chocolate mixture to one of the bowls and stir to combine.

8. Fill the prepared pan with alternating spoonfuls of each batter. Insert a knife into the batter and make two or three figure eights to create a marbled effect. Don't mix the batter more than that, or the cake will be tan rather than marbled. The spoonfuls of batter will settle when they begin to warm.

9. Bake for 1 hour to 1 hour and 15 minutes, or until a toothpick inserted in the center comes out clean. Let cool in the pan on a rack for 5 to 10 minutes, then remove from the pan and set on the rack to cool. Serve warm or at room temperature. It will keep for up to 2 days at room temperature or 3 weeks in the freezer if wrapped airtight.

Tuiles

YIELD: 25 to 30 tuiles

SPECIAL TOOLS:

Silicone mat or parchment paper
(optional)

Standing electric mixer with a
paddle attachment (optional)

¼ pound (1 stick) unsalted
butter, softened if using a
hand mixer

1 cup powdered sugar

4 large egg whites

2 teaspoons vanilla extract

¾ cup cake flour, sifted 3 times
Pinch of salt

TUILES, ALSO KNOWN AS *HIPPENMASSE* IN GERMAN, ARE *very thin, waferlike cookies that can easily be shaped into anything while hot. Tuile is the French word for "tile," and the traditional tuiles were curved into a Pringle shape to replicate the tile roofs seen all along the Côte d'Azur. Today they are more often seen shaped like a bowl. I have included lots of ideas for other interesting tuile shapes.*

You may wonder why a cookie recipe is in the pound cake chapter. In fact, with the exception of the powdered sugar and the use of egg whites instead of whole eggs, the ingredients are identical. I discovered this at Spago after struggling with various tuile batters for years. Traditional tuiles are prone to breaking if the ingredients are not combined at the right temperature. After fooling around with several ratios, I tried equal amounts of each ingredient, and — voilà! — my foolproof tuile batter was born.

1. Preheat the oven to 350°F. Adjust the rack to the center of the oven. Line a baking sheet with a silicone mat or parchment paper, spray it with pan spray, or brush it with melted butter.

2. Using a standing mixer fitted with a paddle attachment or a hand mixer, beat the butter on high speed until it is soft and creamy, about 1 minute. Slowly add the powdered sugar and beat on high speed until fully incorporated, 5 to 7 minutes. Stop the mixer and scrape down the sides of the bowl with a rubber spatula.

3. Add the egg whites, one at a time. Be sure each egg white is completely incorporated and scrape down the sides of the bowl before adding the next. Add the vanilla.

4. Slowly add the flour and salt, beating on low speed. Occasionally stop the machine to scrape down the sides of the bowl.

5. To form paper-thin 3-inch round cookies, place about six 1-tablespoon mounds of batter on the baking sheet 3 inches apart. Using an offset metal spatula like a windshield wiper, smear each mound in a half circle. Rotate the baking sheet and smear the other side of the rounds using the same motion to complete the circle.

6. Bake for 5 minutes. Rotate the baking sheet and bake for 4 to 5 minutes more, or until golden brown.

7. Let the tuiles cool for just 15 seconds, then gently lift one off the sheet with an offset metal spatula and shape it (see below). Work quickly, because they become rigid as they cool. If that happens, warm the tuiles again in the oven for a few seconds to soften them. Finished tuiles can be stored in an airtight container for up to 24 hours. After that, they will lose their crispness.

COOKIE SHAPES

TRADITIONAL TILE-SHAPED TUILES: As soon as you lift the tuiles off the baking sheet, drape them over a rolling pin and allow to cool.

STICKS: Pipe the batter through a pastry bag fitted with a #2 tip or a squeeze bottle into straight lines, 3 to 4 inches long, about 12 sticks per sheet.

CORKSCREWS: Pipe 6-inch lines, about 6 to a sheet, and curl the stick, while hot, around a wooden spoon.

STENCILED: Use an old plastic lid and cut a stencil with an X-Acto knife and use to make leaves, spoons, letters, anything.

BOWL: Spread the batter into two 6-inch circles. Shape the tuiles by placing them on top of an overturned small bowl while hot.

Variations

- CHOCOLATE: Add 2 tablespoons unsweetened cocoa powder to the batter with the flour.

- HONEY-GINGER: Add ½ cup honey and 2 tablespoons ground ginger to the butter while creaming.

- NUT GARNISH: Sprinkle chopped or sliced nuts, coconut, or grated chocolate on top of the cookie shapes before baking them. In the oven, they will fuse to the batter for a speckled cookie. I like sliced almonds.

Blondies

   2 cups all-purpose flour
   1 teaspoon baking powder
   ½ teaspoon salt
   6 ounces (1½ sticks) unsalted
      butter, softened
   ⅓ cup sugar
   1 cup packed light brown
      sugar
   4 large eggs
   1 tablespoon plus 1 teaspoon
      light corn syrup
   1 tablespoon vanilla extract
   1 cup Creamy Caramel Sauce
      (page 58)

BLONDIES, SOMETIMES CALLED BUTTERSCOTCH BROWNIES, first became popular during the Depression and were dubbed Blondies after Chick Young's comic-strip heroine. Chewy and golden, they're often studded with chocolate chips, butterscotch chips, or nuts. I have added a swirl of Creamy Caramel Sauce to the traditional recipe. Serve them with a big glass of milk and schedule time for a nap afterward.

I. Preheat the oven to 350°F. Adjust the rack to the center of the oven. Spray a 9-x-13-inch baking pan with pan spray and line it with a strip of parchment paper, running the length of the pan. Spray the paper.

2. Triple-sift the flour, baking powder, and salt into a medium bowl and set aside.

3. Using a standing mixer fitted with a paddle attachment or a hand mixer, beat the butter on high speed until soft and creamy, about 1 minute. Slowly add the sugars and beat on high speed until fully incorporated and the mixture is light and fluffy, about 10 minutes. Stop the mixer and scrape down the sides of the bowl with a rubber spatula.

4. Add the eggs, one at a time. Be sure each egg is completely incorporated and scrape down the sides of the bowl before adding the next one. Add the corn syrup and vanilla.

5. Slowly add the dry ingredients and mix on low speed until just combined.

6. Pour the batter into the prepared pan. Bake for 25 to 30 minutes, or until a toothpick inserted in the center comes out clean.

7. Poke holes in the surface of the cake with a skewer or fork. Using a squeeze bottle or a piping bag fitted with a #3 tip, fill the holes with the caramel sauce. Let cool in the pan on a rack, then cut into 2-inch squares before serving. If wrapped airtight, Blondies keep well for 3 days at room temperature or up to 3 weeks in the freezer.

Banana Pound Cake

YIELD: One 9-inch loaf cake

SPECIAL TOOLS:

  Parchment paper

  Food processor

  Standing electric mixer with a
  paddle attachment (optional)

2¼ cups all-purpose flour

1 tablespoon baking powder

1 teaspoon baking soda

¼ teaspoon salt

½ cup sour cream

½ cup mascarpone

6 ounces (1½ sticks) unsalted
  butter, softened

½ teaspoon ground cinnamon

1 cup sugar

2 large eggs

2 fully ripe bananas, pureed

¾ cup chocolate chips

THIS RICH BANANA POUND CAKE IS EXTREMELY MOIST *and delicious. The chocolate chips give it just the right amount of kid appeal. While I usually bake it in a standard loaf pan, this batter also makes great cupcakes. Glaze them with Banana Ganache (page 32) and watch your little monkeys go ape.*

The recipe includes mascarpone, which is a thick Italian cream, used most frequently in the dessert tiramisù. If you can't find mascarpone, replace it with the same amount of sour cream, using 1 cup in all.

1. Preheat the oven to 350°F. Adjust the rack to the center of the oven. Spray a 9-x-5-x-3-inch loaf pan with pan spray and line it with a strip of parchment paper, running the length of the pan. Spray the paper.

2. Triple-sift the flour, baking powder, baking soda, and salt into a medium bowl and set aside. Combine the sour cream and mascarpone in a small bowl and set aside.

3. Using a standing mixer fitted with a paddle attachment or a hand mixer, beat the butter with the cinnamon on high speed until soft and creamy, about 1 minute. Slowly add the sugar, 1 tablespoon at a time, beating continuously on high speed. It should take 5 to 10 minutes to add the sugar. The mixture should be light, fluffy, and a creamy white color. Stop the mixer and scrape down the sides of the bowl with a rubber spatula.

4. Add the eggs, one at a time. Be sure each egg is completely incorporated and scrape down the sides of the bowl before adding the next.

5. Add one third of the flour mixture to the batter and beat until it is just incorporated. Add one third of the mascarpone mixture and mix until it is just incorporated. Add the flour and mascarpone mixture in two more additions, mixing until each addition is incorporated before adding the next. Fold in the bananas and chocolate chips.

6. Pour the batter into the prepared pan. Bake for 1 hour to 1 hour 15 minutes, or until a toothpick inserted in the center comes out clean. Cool in the pan on a rack for 5 to 10 minutes, then remove from the pan and set on the rack to cool. Serve warm or at room temperature. It will keep for a week in the refrigerator or 3 weeks in the freezer if wrapped airtight.

Orange Blossom Honey Madeleines

YIELD: About 8 dozen tiny cookies
(1 inch) or 4 dozen standard-size
cookies

SPECIAL TOOLS:

Mini or standard madeleine pan(s)

Standing electric mixer with a
paddle attachment (optional)

½ cup all-purpose flour

½ cup cake flour

½ cup almond flour

½ teaspoon baking powder

¼ teaspoon salt

¼ pound (1 stick) unsalted
butter, softened

¾ cup sugar

¼ cup orange blossom honey

1 tablespoon vanilla extract

2 teaspoons orange flower
water

2 tablespoons chopped
kumquats or 1 tablespoon
minced orange zest

4 large eggs

MADELEINES ARE BEST KNOWN AS THE CAKE MARCEL PROUST
nibbled, sending him reeling into nostalgia in Remembrance of
Things Past. *These lovely little cakes, shaped like scallop shells, were
created in the French town of Commercy in the Lorraine region. It is
believed that the nuns of Commercy sold the recipe to a baker for a
great deal of money.*

*A true madeleine has a knob on its back, a slightly crispy
crust, and a huge buttery flavor. I serve them fresh from the oven,
which is easy to do because everything can be prepared in advance
and held for up to 4 hours. Almond flour (see page 348) adds flavor
and lightness to this madeleine.*

1. Triple-sift the flours, baking powder, and salt into a medium
bowl and set aside.

2. Using a standing electric mixer fitted with a paddle attachment or a hand mixer, beat the butter on high speed until soft and
creamy, about 1 minute. Slowly add the sugar, 1 tablespoon at a time,
beating continuously on high speed. It should take 5 to 10 minutes to
add the sugar. The mixture should be light, fluffy, and a creamy white
color. Stop the mixer and scrape down the sides of the bowl with a
rubber spatula. Beat in the honey, vanilla, orange flower water, and
kumquats or orange zest. Scrape down the sides of the bowl with a
rubber spatula.

3. Add the eggs, one at a time. Be sure each egg is completely
incorporated and scrape down the sides of the bowl before adding the
next one.

4. Add the flour mixture to the batter in thirds, beating on low
speed until just incorporated. Cover the batter and chill it for at least
2 hours and up to 4 hours.

5. Preheat the oven to 375°F. Adjust the rack to the center of
the oven. Brush the mini or standard madeleine molds with melted
butter, then dust them lightly with flour.

6. Carefully spoon the chilled batter into the madeleine pan, filling each shell three-quarters full. Bake for 10 minutes for mini madeleines or for about 15 minutes for standard-size, or until they are golden brown and firm to the touch. Repeat until all the batter has been used, brushing the pans with butter if needed. The madeleines are best served warm from the oven but can be stored, wrapped airtight, at room temperature for up to 3 days and in the freezer for up to 3 weeks.

Variations

- **LEMON:** Replace the kumquats or orange zest with finely chopped lemon zest. If desired, add a drop of yellow food color.

- **PISTACHIO:** Replace ¼ cup of the cake flour with ¼ cup pistachio flour. (Pistachio flour can be made by finely grinding pistachios.)

- **CHOCOLATE:** Replace ¼ cup of the cake flour with ¼ cup unsweetened cocoa powder.

Génoise

YIELD: Two 9-inch round cakes

SPECIAL TOOLS:

Parchment paper

Candy thermometer

Standing electric mixer with a
whisk attachment (optional)

6 large eggs

1 cup sugar

2–8 ounces (½–2 sticks) butter,
melted (it should remain
warm and liquid)

1 cup cake flour, sifted 3 times

Master Génoise

I USE GÉNOISE AS A BASE FOR WEDDING CAKES, BIRTHDAY *cakes, jellyrolls, and petits fours. The crumb is strong but tender (like the perfect man), and it can hold every filling imaginable. The absorbent crumb is also capable of holding liquid without getting soggy, so génoise is commonly soaked in flavored syrup to add moisture and another layer of flavor. Soaking syrups are based on simple syrup, typically flavored with some kind of alcohol, extract, or infusion.*

All pastry chefs know the basic technique for génoise. It's a common test of skill, used in culinary schools, competitions, and job auditions. The method is not difficult for the home cook so long as the instructions are followed exactly. The key to success is in the folding. It must be done with a gentle hand. After tons of air has been whipped into the eggs, it's important to keep it there. Génoise can be very light, with only 2 ounces of butter, or incredibly rich, with ½ pound. The more butter you use, the denser the cake will be.

1. Preheat the oven to 350°F. Adjust the rack to the center of the oven. Spray the bottoms only of two 9-x-2-inch round cake pans with pan spray. Line each with a circle of parchment paper and spray the paper.

2. Fill a medium saucepan halfway with water and bring it to a simmer over medium heat. Combine the eggs and sugar in the bowl of your standing mixer (or another bowl) and place it over the simmering water, creating a double boiler, being careful that the bottom of the bowl does not touch the water. Insert a thermometer. Whisk continuously until the temperature reaches 110°F, 3 to 4 minutes.

3. Remove from the heat and transfer the bowl to a standing mixer fitted with a whisk attachment, or use a hand mixer. Whip on high speed for 5 to 8 minutes, or until the eggs are three times their

HOW TO FOLD

An easy way to fold properly is to think of the bowl as a clock. Start the whisk at twelve o'clock. Drag the whisk through the foam to six o'clock. Lift the whisk out of the bowl and turn the bowl counterclockwise one quarter turn. Repeat the pattern by starting back at twelve o'clock and dragging it to six. The whisk will go through a fresh area of foam because twelve o'clock is in a new spot. Continue to repeat the pattern, twelve to six, quarter turn, twelve to six, quarter turn, until all the ingredients are mixed. It should take five or six passes to incorporate all the ingredients. Properly folded, the foam should maintain its fluffiness and body. If it becomes runny, it has been overfolded.

original volume, are thick and pale yellow in color, and form a ribbon when drizzled from a spatula. Turn down the mixer to medium speed and whip for 2 minutes more. This stabilizes the foam. On low speed, stream the warm melted butter into the batter and mix for 15 seconds until incorporated.

4. Add the flour to the foam all at once and fold it in carefully with a balloon whisk just until incorporated, maintaining as much of the foam as possible.

5. Pour the batter into the prepared pans, filling them two-thirds full. Tap each pan lightly on the table three times to eliminate air bubbles. Then, using the same jerking wrist action you would use to throw a Frisbee, swing each pan around on the table so that the batter is forced up the sides of the pan. This will prevent a dome from forming in the middle of the cake.

6. Bake for 15 minutes. Switch the pans front to back and rotate them, then bake for 10 to 12 minutes more. Test the cake for doneness by lightly touching the top of it with a finger. The finger indentation should spring right back into place. If it doesn't, bake for 5 to 10 minutes more. The cake is also done when it begins to pull away slightly from the sides of the pan.

7. Let cool in the pans on a rack for 15 minutes, then invert onto the rack, remove the pans and parchment, and cool for at least 2 hours before using. Génoise may also be kept at room temperature for up to 2 days or frozen for up to 2 weeks, wrapped airtight.

Variation

❧ GÉNOISE BAKED IN A SHEET PAN: This cake is extremely versatile and can be baked in any type of pan. My favorite is a sheet pan. In a shallow pan like this, the cake bakes and cools in half the time. But remember that the shallower the pan, the shorter the baking time. Spray a 12½-x-17½-inch baking sheet tray with pan spray and line with parchment. Spray the parchment. Bake for 10 minutes and rotate the pan. Bake for 5 to 7 minutes more, or until the cake is golden brown and springs back when pressed. Remove from the oven and immediately run a knife around the edge of the pan. Invert onto a tabletop. With a metal spatula, flip the cake upright and place on a rack to cool completely.

Chocolate Génoise

CHOCOLATE GÉNOISE HAS A LIGHT, DELICATE CHOCOLATE *flavor and color. It is not meant to be deep, dark, and moist like devil's food cake or decadent and gooey. On the contrary, the purpose of génoise is to support other elements and flavors. Traditionally, desserts built on a foundation of génoise are delicate and refined.*

YIELD: Two 9-inch round cakes

SPECIAL TOOLS:

Parchment paper

Candy thermometer

Standing electric mixer with a whisk attachment (optional)

6 large eggs

1 cup sugar

4 tablespoons (½ stick) unsalted butter, melted (it should remain warm and liquid)

⅓ cup unsweetened cocoa powder

⅓ cup hot water

1 teaspoon vanilla extract

¾ cup cake flour, sifted 3 times

1. Preheat the oven to 350°F. Adjust the rack to the center of the oven. Prepare two 9-x-2-inch round cake pans as directed in step 1 of Master Génoise (page 152).

2. Fill a medium saucepan halfway with water and bring it to a simmer over medium heat. Combine the eggs and sugar in the bowl of your standing mixer (or another bowl) and place it over the simmering water, creating a double boiler, being careful that the bottom of the bowl does not touch the water. Insert a thermometer. Whisk continuously until the temperature reaches 110°F, 2 to 3 minutes.

3. Remove from the heat and transfer the bowl to a standing mixer fitted with a whisk attachment, or use a hand mixer. Whip on high speed for 5 to 8 minutes, or until the eggs are three times their original volume, are thick and pale yellow in color, and form a ribbon when drizzled from a spatula. Turn down the mixer to medium speed and whip for 2 minutes more. This stabilizes the foam. On low speed, stream the warm melted butter into the batter and mix it in until incorporated.

4. Combine the cocoa powder, hot water, and vanilla in a small bowl, stirring well to eliminate any lumps and create a smooth mixture. Fold the cocoa mixture into the foam with a balloon whisk.

5. Add the flour to the foam all at once and fold it in carefully with the whisk, just until it is incorporated, maintaining as much of the foam as possible.

6. Pour the batter into the prepared pans, filling them two-thirds full. Tap each pan lightly on the table three times to eliminate air bubbles. Then, using the same jerking wrist action you would use to throw a Frisbee, swing each pan around on the table so that the batter is forced up the sides of the pan. This will prevent a dome from forming in the middle of the cake. Bake for about 25 minutes,

switching the pans and rotating them after the first 15 minutes. Test the cake for doneness by lightly touching the top of it with a finger. The finger indentation should spring right back into place. If it doesn't, bake for 5 to 10 minutes more. The cake is also done when it begins to pull away slightly from the sides of the pan.

7. Let cool in the pans on a rack for 15 minutes, then invert onto the rack, remove the pans and parchment, and cool for at least 2 hours before using. The cakes may also be kept at room temperature for up to 2 days or frozen for up to 2 weeks, wrapped airtight.

Variation

⤷ CHOCOLATE CHIFFON CAKE: Replace the butter with ⅓ cup vegetable oil and add ½ teaspoon baking powder to the flour before sifting.

Buttermilk Birthday Cupcakes

YIELD: About 2 dozen 2-inch cupcakes

FROSTING TIME: 20 minutes

SPECIAL TOOLS:

Paper cupcake liners

Candy thermometer

Standing electric mixer with a
whisk attachment (optional)

1 cup all-purpose flour

1 teaspoon baking powder

1/2 teaspoon salt

1 cup sugar

4 large eggs

6 ounces (1½ sticks) unsalted
butter, melted (it should
remain warm and liquid)

1/2 cup buttermilk

2 teaspoons vanilla extract

I SERVE INDIVIDUAL DESSERTS AT SPAGO FAR MORE THAN *slices off larger items. They are elegant and make the guest feel a little more special. Cupcakes are the original individual dessert. Since a cupcake is so reminiscent of childhood, it is perfect for birthday celebrations. What better time to feel young again?*

Though evocative of childhood, cupcakes can step up to more adult dining simply by the way they are presented. They can have frosting with sprinkles or silky ganache glaze and spun sugar. They can be towered like a pyramid with fresh flowers and silver dragées (a French candy with a hard coating) or packed into a lunchbox. These cupcakes have a dense texture.

1. Preheat the oven to 350°F. Adjust the rack to the center of the oven. Prepare a muffin pan by coating it with pan spray and inserting paper cupcake liners.

2. Triple-sift the flour, baking powder, and salt into a medium bowl and set aside.

3. Fill a medium saucepan halfway with water and bring it to a simmer over medium heat. Combine the sugar and eggs in the bowl of your standing mixer (or another large bowl) and place it over the simmering water, creating a double boiler, being careful that the bottom of the bowl does not touch the water. Insert a thermometer. Whisk continuously until the temperature reaches 110°F, 2 to 3 minutes.

4. Remove from the heat and transfer the bowl to a standing mixer fitted with a whisk attachment, or use a hand mixer. Whip on high speed for 5 to 8 minutes, or until the eggs are three times their original volume, are thick and pale yellow in color, and form a ribbon when drizzled from a spatula. Turn down the mixer to medium speed and whip for 2 minutes more. This stabilizes the foam. On low speed, stream the warm melted butter into the batter and mix it in until incorporated.

5. Fold in one third of the dry ingredients using a balloon whisk. Be careful not to deflate the foam. Add one third of the buttermilk and continue to fold carefully. Continue adding the dry ingredients and buttermilk alternately in thirds, until all ingredients are incorporated. Add the vanilla.

6. Pour the batter into the prepared muffin cups, leaving ¼ inch of space at the top of each cup. Bake for 20 minutes, or until the tops are golden brown and spring back from the touch of a finger. Let cool in the pan on a rack for 5 minutes, then remove the cupcakes from the pan and set on the rack to cool. The cupcakes are ready to be glazed, decorated, and served when cooled, or they may be stored, unfinished, at room temperature for up to 2 days or in the freezer for up to 2 weeks if wrapped airtight.

Variations

- CHOCOLATE: Replace ¼ cup of the flour with ¼ cup unsweetened cocoa powder.

- "COCO-NUT": Fold in ½ cup toasted shredded coconut and ½ cup toasted (see page 366) chopped pecans into the batter just before baking.

- WHITE CHOCOLATE: Fold 1 cup white chocolate chunks or chips into the batter just before baking.

YIELD: Two 9-inch round cakes

SPECIAL TOOLS:

    Parchment paper

    Candy thermometer

    Standing electric mixer with a
    whisk attachment (optional)

1¾ cups potato flour
    (potato starch)

  1 tablespoon baking powder

  4 large eggs

  1 cup sugar

¼ cup brandy

¼ cup water

  6 ounces (1½ sticks) unsalted
    butter, melted and cooled
    (it should remain warm
    and liquid)

  2 teaspoons vanilla extract

  2 tablespoons finely chopped
    lemon zest

Torta Sabiosa

I ADAPTED THIS ITALIAN RECIPE FROM A DESSERT I WAS *served at the beautiful Tra Vigne restaurant in Napa Valley. The name means "sand cake" in Italian, and it refers to the superlight texture of the cake's crumb. It isn't gritty, as the name might suggest, but moist and crumbly. The unique texture of Torta Sabiosa comes from the use of potato flour. This ingredient allows cakes to hold in more moisture than those made with only wheat flour. You can buy potato flour at specialty groceries.*

I usually serve Torta Sabiosa with sweetened mascarpone, which is an Italian double- or triple-cream cheese, thicker than sour cream but not quite as thick as butter. Its smooth, rich texture contrasts beautifully with the crumb of this cake.

1. Preheat the oven to 350°F. Adjust the rack to the center of the oven. Spray the bottoms only of two 9-x-2-inch round cake pans with pan spray. Line each with a circle of parchment paper and spray the paper.

2. Triple-sift the potato flour and baking powder into a medium bowl and set aside.

3. Fill a medium saucepan halfway with water and bring it to a simmer over medium heat. Combine the eggs, sugar, brandy, and water in the bowl of your standing mixer (or in another bowl) and place it over the simmering water, creating a double boiler, being careful that the bottom of the bowl does not touch the water. Insert a thermometer. Whisk continuously until the temperature reaches 110°F, 2 to 3 minutes.

4. Remove from the heat and transfer the bowl to a standing mixer fitted with a whisk attachment, or use a hand mixer. Whip on high speed for 5 to 8 minutes, or until the eggs are three times their original volume, are thick and pale yellow in color, and form a ribbon when drizzled from a spatula. Turn down the mixer to medium speed and whip for 2 minutes more. This stabilizes the foam. On low speed, stream in the melted butter along with the vanilla and lemon zest and mix until incorporated.

5. Fold in the sifted dry ingredients using a balloon whisk.

6. Pour the batter into the prepared pans, filling them two-thirds full. Tap each pan lightly on the table three times to eliminate air bubbles. Then, using the same jerking wrist action you would use to throw a Frisbee, swing each pan around on the table so that the batter is forced up the sides of the pan. This will prevent a dome from forming in the middle of the cake. Bake for 30 minutes, switching the pans and rotating them halfway through, until a toothpick inserted in the center comes out clean. If it does not, bake for 5 to 10 minutes more.

7. Let cool in the pans on a rack for 30 minutes, then invert onto the rack and remove the pans and parchment. The cake may now be served, or it will keep at room temperature for up to 2 days, or in the freezer for up to 2 weeks if wrapped airtight.

YIELD: One 10-inch round cake

SPECIAL TOOLS:

Parchment paper

Candy thermometer

Standing electric mixer with a whisk attachment (optional)

FOR THE CAKE

7 ounces (1¾ sticks) unsalted butter

1½ cups sugar

9 large eggs

¼ cup water

1 teaspoon freshly grated nutmeg

2 tablespoons dark rum

1¼ cups cake flour, sifted 3 times

2 tablespoons heavy cream

FOR THE APRICOT GLAZE

1 cup apricot jelly

½ cup water

Ganache Glaze (page 28)

Brown Butter Baumkuchen

I LEARNED THIS FASCINATING VERSION OF GERMAN POUND *cake on a visit to Austria. The name means "tree cake," because its many layers are reminiscent of a tree's rings. Traditionally a spit is coated lightly in batter and baked over an open fire. Once cooked, another layer of batter is brushed on. The process continues until the spit is coated in up to twenty-five layers of cake. When removed from the spit, the cake stands tall like a tree and slices reveal rings of caramelized batter that look like the rings of a tree.*

Since I do not have the traditional spit, I began baking the thin layers horizontally. I use a standard cake pan in a standard oven, and I have found that it works well. It is a time-consuming process but totally worth the effort. The finished cake has a unique flavor, with beautiful caramelized layers. Baumkuchen can be served with only a light shiny coat of apricot jelly, or coated in Ganache Glaze, or coated with both. Any way, it's the best-tasting tree I've ever had.

CAKE

1. Preheat the oven to 425°F. Adjust the rack to the upper part of the oven. Spray the bottom only of a 10-x-3-inch round cake pan or two 9-x-2-inch pans with pan spray. Line each with a circle of parchment and spray the paper. Place the prepared pans inside empty cake pans if you have enough cake pans. This prevents the outside of the cake from browning too much.

2. Melt the butter in a medium saucepan over medium heat. Cook until the solids separate and begin to brown on the bottom of the pan, about 7 minutes. When this happens, turn off the heat and set the butter aside to cool slightly. It should remain liquid.

3. Fill a medium saucepan halfway with water and bring it to a simmer over medium heat. Combine the sugar, eggs, water, nutmeg, and rum in the bowl of your standing mixer (or another bowl) and place it over the simmering water, creating a double boiler, being careful that the bottom of the bowl does not touch the water. Insert a thermometer. Whisk continuously until the temperature reaches 110°F, 2 to 3 minutes.

4. Remove from the heat and transfer the bowl to a standing mixer fitted with a whisk attachment, or use a hand mixer. Whip on high speed for 5 to 8 minutes, or until the eggs are three times their original volume, are thick and pale yellow in color, and form a ribbon when drizzled from a spatula. Turn down the mixer to medium

speed and whip for 2 minutes more. This stabilizes the foam. Fold in the cream and browned butter. Be sure to scrape all the browned butter bits in. Carefully scrape the batter into a large, wide bowl.

5. Fold in the flour using a balloon whisk, being careful not to deflate the foam.

6. Pour 1½ cups of the batter into the prepared pan or pans, enough to coat the pan(s) in a thin layer. Keep the remaining batter away from the stove's heat so that it doesn't deflate. Bake for 7 minutes, or until the top is golden brown. Remove it from the oven and pour another 1 to 1½ cups of batter on top. Return the cake pan to the oven and bake for 5 minutes more, or until the top is golden brown. Repeat until all the batter has been used. Once the final layer has been baked, remove the cake from the oven and immediately turn it out of the pan onto a rack set over a sheet of aluminum foil. Stack one cake on top of the other.

GLAZE
Combine the apricot jelly and water in a small saucepan and warm over low heat until the jelly is liquefied. While the cake is still hot, brush the top and sides with the apricot glaze. Cool the cake completely, about 1 hour. If using the Ganache Glaze, apply it now. When the glaze has set, serve. The cake will keep at room temperature for up to 2 days or in the freezer for up to 2 weeks if wrapped airtight.

FINANCIER

THE FRENCH WORD *FINANCIER* (PRONOUNCED "FEE-nan-ci-AY") is an English word as well, and it's an apt name for a cake that provides rich underpinnings to a number of desserts. Moist and extremely versatile, it is relatively unknown in the United States, and for that reason I consider it my little secret.

This cake has many virtues. The batter can be refrigerated and held for up to two weeks — in fact it's best made a day in advance. The cake stays fresh for days after it is baked. It lends itself to dozens of variations. Spice, nuts, fruits, leftover chocolate, vanilla, or caramel sauce can be added to the batter. The cooled cake can be layered with fillings like curd and ganache. At Spago, I keep at least one and as many as five variations of financier batter in the fridge at any given time. Like a rich benefactor, it comes to my rescue whenever I need to make a special dessert on the spot.

THE MOST OUTSTANDING ATTRIBUTE OF FINANCIER IS ITS moistness, and both the ingredients and the method are designed to enhance that feature. Only egg whites are used. They have the same amount of stabilizing protein as the yolk but much more water. And while most cake recipes call for whipping air into the whites, creating a foam, in financier the whites remain liquid.

Butter also adds to the moist texture of this cake. While in typical cakes solid butter is creamed at the beginning of a recipe, here it is melted and added to the batter last.

Omitting the foaming and creaming steps maximizes the cake's shelf life. Both procedures add air to cake batter. Less air means less risk of oxidation since the introduction of oxygen causes batters to discolor and fats to become rancid.

UNLIKE OTHER CAKES, FINANCIER USES POWDERED SUGAR. The finely ground sugar can dissolve easily and mix more thoroughly into a batter, important for a cake made without creaming or whipping. The amount of sugar, too, is calculated to increase the cake's moisture levels. Financier has a higher percentage of sugar than any other cake, nearly twice the amount of any other ingredient. Sugar is hydroscopic, which means it attracts moisture and holds it within the crumb.

The most outstanding attribute of financier is its moistness.

ANY TYPE OF FLOUR MAY BE USED SUCCESSFULLY IN FINANCIER, as long as at least a quarter of the flour is wheat flour. Wheat is the only grain that contains enough gluten protein to maintain the structure of leavened baked goods. This gluten protein has an elastic structure capable of stretching as a cake rises and holding in excessive moisture and fat. Other flours include nut flours, potato flour, cornmeal, semolina, whole wheat, and oatmeal.

Almond flour appears in the classic financier. It is made by finely grinding the nutmeat that is left over when oil is pressed out of the nut. (Almond meal, which is ground from the whole nut, is coarser and oilier than almond flour. While it can be substituted, it will not produce as delicate a texture.)

FINANCIER CAN BE BAKED SUCCESSFULLY IN NEARLY ANYTHING — in a decorative tin, or in ramekins, or in a muffin pan. I have also spread financier onto a baking sheet and baked it jellyroll style. But perhaps my favorite way to bake it is in savarin molds. These ring molds come in many sizes. I like to use miniature savarin molds and serve the financiers as cookies, topped with fruit and cream. These little gems are a touch of luxury. No one but you needs to know how easy they are to make.

Like a rich benefactor, financier comes to my rescue whenever I need to make a special dessert.

Financier
FAMILY TREE

MASTER FINANCIER
Chocolate Financier
Gingerbread Financier
Pumpkin Financier
Carrot Cake

FLOUR VARIATION
Cornmeal Financier

The financier family tree demonstrates a straight lineage. The master recipe begins with an almond batter. It can be varied with myriad ingredients to create individual desserts and other cakes.

Master Financier

½ pound (2 sticks) unsalted
    butter

1¼ cups almond flour or almond
    meal (see page 348)

¾ cup cake flour

2½ cups powdered sugar

8 large egg whites, at room
    temperature

ONCE YOU MAKE THIS CAKE, YOU'LL SEE WHY I LOVE IT *so much. It's very nice served on its own, or with fruit.*

If you are baking it in a standard pan, coat the pan lightly with pan spray and line it with parchment, cut to fit the bottom of the pan exactly. A final, light coat of pan spray on the paper helps to keep it from sticking to the finished cake. If you are using an intricately shaped pan, such as a fluted mold, a layer of parchment paper is not possible. In that case, a light dusting of flour over the pan spray will do the trick. Place a tablespoon or two of flour in the sprayed mold, swirl it around to coat the entire surface, then tap out the excess.

It's important that the butter not be too hot when you add it to the batter. It needs to cool at room temperature, but it must remain liquid. If it's hot, your cake will be gooey or clumpy. Melt and brown it about 30 minutes before you begin, so that it will cool sufficiently.

1. Melt the butter in a medium saucepan over medium heat. Cook until the solids separate and brown to a dark golden color, 7 to 10 minutes. Remove from the heat and let cool at room temperature until it reaches 70°F, about 30 minutes. Don't chill it. It needs to remain in liquid form — but it also can't be hot when you add it to the other ingredients. Set aside.

2. Preheat the oven to 350°F. Adjust the rack to the center of the oven. Spray a 10-x-2-inch round cake pan with pan spray, line it with a piece of parchment paper, then coat the paper lightly with pan spray.

3. Toast ½ cup plus 2 tablespoons of the almond flour in a small baking dish in the oven for 5 to 10 minutes, or until golden brown. Sift together the toasted and untoasted almond flour, cake flour, and powdered sugar into the bowl of a standing mixer fitted with a paddle attachment, or use a large bowl and a hand mixer. Turn the machine on low and mix the dry ingredients for 30 seconds. Add the egg whites all at once and mix on medium speed for 3 minutes.

4. Add the melted butter all at once. Be sure to scrape in all the browned bits from the bottom of the pan. Mix for 3 minutes on medium speed, scraping down the sides of the bowl well (the butter tends to sink to the bottom). Financier batter will keep in the refrig-

erator for up to 2 weeks. When using refrigerated batter, be sure to bring it back to room temperature, then stir the entire mixture from the bottom up to the top to reincorporate any butter that might have separated and sunk to the bottom. Beat the batter by hand or with a mixer to warm it up and mix it well.

5. Pour the batter into the prepared pan. Bake for 15 minutes. Rotate the cake for even browning and bake for 15 minutes more, or until a toothpick inserted in the center comes out clean. Let cool in the pan on a rack for 5 minutes, then invert it onto the rack, remove the cake pan and parchment, and cool completely before serving. Wrapped airtight, financier will keep at room temperature for up to 2 days or in the freezer for up to 2 weeks.

Chocolate Financier

YIELD: One 10-inch round cake

SPECIAL TOOLS:

Parchment paper

Standing electric mixer with a
paddle attachment (optional)

4 tablespoons (½ stick)
unsalted butter

10 ounces bittersweet
chocolate, finely chopped

1¼ cups heavy cream

2½ cups almond flour or almond
meal (see page 348)

1 cup all-purpose flour

1 cup powdered sugar

½ teaspoon baking powder

¼ teaspoon salt

7 large egg whites, at room
temperature

1 teaspoon vanilla extract

THE ADDITION OF GANACHE MAKES THIS CAKE A DEEP, DARK
*chocolate experience. I have included the recipe for ganache here,
but if you already have ganache on hand, you can use that in place
of step 3. It's important to use a high-quality chocolate for this, like
Valrhona 70 percent.*

1. Preheat the oven to 350°F. Adjust the rack to the center of
the oven. Spray a 10-x-2-inch round cake pan with pan spray, line it
with a piece of parchment paper, then coat the paper lightly with pan
spray.

2. Melt the butter in a medium saucepan over medium heat.
Cook until the solids separate and brown to a dark golden color, 7 to
10 minutes. Remove from the heat and let cool at room temperature
until it reaches 70°F, about 30 minutes. Don't chill it. It needs to remain in liquid form. Set aside.

3. Place the chopped chocolate in a medium bowl. Bring the
cream to a boil in a small saucepan over medium heat. At the boil,
immediately pour the hot cream over the chopped chocolate. Tap the
bowl on the counter to settle the chocolate into the cream, then let it
sit for 30 seconds. Using a rubber spatula, slowly stir in a circular
motion, starting from the center of the bowl and working out to the
sides. Stir until all the chocolate is melted, about 2 minutes. This
mixture is the ganache. Set aside at room temperature to cool to
70°F.

4. Sift together the almond flour, flour, powdered sugar, baking powder, and salt into the bowl of a standing mixer fitted with a
paddle attachment or use a large bowl and a hand mixer. Turn the
machine on low and mix the dry ingredients for 30 seconds. Add the
egg whites all at once and mix on medium speed for 3 minutes. Add
the ganache and vanilla and mix for 30 seconds.

5. Add the melted butter all at once. Be sure to scrape in all the
browned bits from the bottom of the pan. Mix for 30 seconds on
medium speed, then turn the mixer to high speed and mix for 3 minutes more, scraping down the sides of the bowl well. Financier batter
will keep in the refrigerator for up to 2 weeks. (To mix refrigerated
batter, see pages 166–167.)

6. Pour the batter into the prepared pan. Bake for 15 minutes. Rotate the cake for even browning and bake for 15 minutes more, or until a toothpick inserted in the center comes out clean. Let cool in the pan on a rack for 5 minutes, then invert it onto the rack, remove the cake pan and parchment, and cool completely before serving. Wrapped airtight, financier will keep at room temperature for up to 2 days or in the freezer for up to 2 weeks.

Gingerbread Financier

YIELD: One 10-inch round cake

SPECIAL TOOLS:

    Parchment paper

    Standing electric mixer with a
    paddle attachment (optional)

6 ounces (1½ sticks) unsalted
  butter

1 cup almond flour or almond
  meal (see page 348)

¾ cup cake flour

1 cup powdered sugar

⅓ cup sugar

⅓ cup packed light brown
  sugar

2 teaspoons ground ginger

½ teaspoon ground cinnamon

¼ teaspoon freshly grated
  nutmeg

¼ teaspoon ground white
  pepper

⅛ teaspoon ground cloves

8 large egg whites, at room
  temperature

¼ cup unsulfured blackstrap
  molasses

1 teaspoon finely chopped
  orange zest

I THINK OF THIS CAKE AS A HIGH-CLASS GINGERBREAD. THE addition of white pepper sets it apart. Its unique flavor and heat give the cake an Old World flavor, quite unlike most gingerbread. I prefer unsulfured blackstrap molasses, which has the best kick. You can find it at whole foods stores. For an added twist, I like to bake the cakes in 1-inch savarin molds and stud them with dried cranberries or finely diced apples.

1. Melt the butter in a medium saucepan over medium heat. Cook until the solids separate and brown to a dark golden color, 7 to 10 minutes. Remove from the heat and let cool at room temperature until it reaches 70°F, about 30 minutes. Don't chill it. It needs to remain in liquid form. Set aside.

2. Preheat the oven to 350°F. Adjust the rack to the center of the oven. Spray a 10-x-2-inch round cake pan with pan spray, line it with a piece of parchment paper, then coat the paper lightly with pan spray.

3. Sift together the almond flour, cake flour, and powdered sugar into the bowl of a standing mixer fitted with a paddle attachment or use a large bowl and a hand mixer. Add the sugar, brown sugar, and spices. Turn the machine on low and mix the dry ingredients for 30 seconds. Add the egg whites all at once and mix on medium speed for 3 minutes. Add the molasses and orange zest and mix for 30 seconds.

4. Add the melted butter all at once. Be sure to scrape in all the browned bits from the bottom of the pan. Mix for 30 seconds on medium speed, then turn the mixer to high speed and mix for 3 minutes more, scraping down the sides of the bowl. Financier batter will keep in the refrigerator for up to 2 weeks. (To mix refrigerated batter, see page 169.)

5. Pour the batter into the prepared pan. Bake for 15 minutes. Rotate the cake for even browning and bake for 15 minutes more, or until a toothpick inserted in the center comes out clean. Let cool in the pan on a rack for 5 minutes, then invert it onto the rack, remove the cake pan and parchment, and cool completely before serving. Wrapped airtight, financier will keep at room temperature for up to 2 days or in the freezer for up to 2 weeks.

Pumpkin Financier

YIELD: One 10-inch round cake

SPECIAL TOOLS:

    Parchment paper

    Standing electric mixer with a
    paddle attachment (optional)

½ pound (2 sticks) unsalted
   butter

1¼ cups almond flour or almond
   meal (see page 348)

1¼ cups all-purpose flour

1½ cups powdered sugar

1 teaspoon baking powder

½ teaspoon baking soda

¼ teaspoon salt

½ teaspoon ground cinnamon

½ teaspoon ground ginger

¼ teaspoon freshly grated
   nutmeg

2 tablespoons tightly packed
   light brown sugar

8 large egg whites, at room
   temperature

½ cup pumpkin puree (canned
   solid-pack pumpkin)

½ teaspoon finely chopped
   orange zest

WHO SAYS PUMPKINS ARE JUST FOR FALL? YOU CAN BUY *solid-pack pumpkin year-round. My favorite way to serve this cake is with fresh figs — the perfect marriage of summer and fall.*

This cake pairs nicely with many other flavors: chocolate, caramel, or vanilla in the form of sauce, ice cream, or frosting. Golden raisins, cranberries, apricots, and currants, warmed in rum or apple juice, make a great compote to spoon on top. Nuts or pumpkin seeds can be toasted and folded into the batter. Or top a slice with whipped cream and sprinkle it with nut brittle (see page 56).

1. Melt the butter in a medium saucepan over medium heat. Cook until the solids separate and begin to brown to a dark golden color, 7 to 10 minutes. Remove from the heat and let cool at room temperature until it reaches 70°F. Don't chill it. It needs to remain in liquid form. Set aside.

2. Preheat the oven to 350°F. Adjust the rack to the center of the oven. Spray a 10-x-2-inch round cake pan with pan spray, line it with a piece of parchment paper, then coat the paper lightly with pan spray.

3. Sift together the almond flour, flour, powdered sugar, baking powder, baking soda, and salt into the bowl of a standing mixer fitted with a paddle attachment or use a large bowl and a hand mixer. Add the spices and brown sugar. Turn the machine on low and mix the dry ingredients for 30 seconds. Add the egg whites all at once and mix on medium speed for 3 minutes. Add the pumpkin puree and orange zest and mix for 30 seconds.

4. Add the melted butter all at once. Be sure to scrape in all the browned bits from the bottom of the pan. Mix for 30 seconds on medium speed, then turn the mixer to high speed and mix for 3 minutes more, scraping down the sides of the bowl. Financier batter will keep in the refrigerator for up to 2 weeks. (To mix refrigerated batter, see pages 166–167.)

5. Pour the batter into the prepared pan. Bake for 15 minutes. Rotate the cake for even browning and bake for 20 to 25 minutes more, or until a toothpick inserted in the center comes out clean. Let cool in the pan on a rack for 5 minutes, then invert it onto the rack, remove the cake pan and parchment, and cool completely before serving. Wrapped airtight, financier will keep at room temperature for up to 2 days or in the freezer for up to 2 weeks.

Carrot Cake

YIELD: Two 10-inch round cakes

SPECIAL TOOLS:

> Parchment paper
>
> Standing electric mixer with a paddle attachment (optional)

½ pound (2 sticks) unsalted butter

1 cup all-purpose flour, sifted 3 times

½ cup almond flour or almond meal (see page 348)

1 teaspoon baking powder

1 teaspoon baking soda

½ cup sugar

1 teaspoon ground cinnamon

½ cup powdered sugar

½ cup packed light brown sugar

3 large eggs, at room temperature

1 tablespoon vanilla extract

1¾ cups grated carrots (about 2 medium carrots)

1 cup grated unsweetened coconut

1 cup crushed pineapple, well drained

Luscious Cream Cheese Frosting (page 174)

THIS IS AN AMERICAN FAVORITE. THE IDEA OF GRATING *carrots into a cake batter could have come only from a mother with vegetable-phobic kids. Even if the kids were wise to the carrots, how could they resist the luscious cream cheese frosting?*

> *The best carrot cakes are dense and moist, and this version doesn't disappoint. It is done in the financier method but uses whole eggs instead of just whites. I also add coconut and pineapple. Many people prefer only nuts, or raisins, or even chocolate chips. Replace the pineapple and coconut with 2 cups of your favorite garnish.*

1. Melt the butter in a medium saucepan over medium heat. Cook until the solids separate and brown to a dark golden color, 7 to 10 minutes. Remove it from the heat and let cool at room temperature until it reaches 70°F, about 30 minutes. Don't chill it. It needs to remain in liquid form. Set aside.

2. Preheat the oven to 350°F. Adjust the rack to the center of the oven. Spray two 10-x-2-inch round cake pans with pan spray, line them with a piece of parchment paper, then coat the paper lightly with pan spray.

3. Sift together the flour, almond flour, baking powder, and baking soda into the bowl of a standing mixer fitted with a paddle attachment or use a large bowl and a hand mixer. Turn the machine on low and mix for 30 seconds. Set aside.

4. Combine the granulated sugar and cinnamon in a medium bowl and stir to blend. Add the powdered sugar and stir to blend, then add the brown sugar and stir again to blend. In another medium bowl, whisk the eggs lightly. Add the sugar mixture and the vanilla, and whisk together quickly to combine well.

5. Turn the mixer on low and stream the sugar mixture into the dry ingredients. Once lightly incorporated, increase the speed to medium and whip for 2 minutes.

6. Reduce the speed to low and slowly stream in the melted butter. Be sure to scrape in all the browned bits from the bottom of the pan. Mix for 30 seconds on medium speed, then turn the mixer to high speed and mix for 3 minutes more, scraping down the sides of the bowl well.

7. Using a balloon whisk, gently fold in the carrots, coconut, and pineapple. Carrot cake batter will keep in the refrigerator for up to 2 weeks. (To mix refrigerated batter, see pages 166–167.)

8. Pour the batter into the prepared pans. Bake for 45 minutes or until a toothpick inserted in the center comes out clean. Let cool in the pans on a rack for 5 minutes, then invert onto the rack, remove the pans and parchment, and cool completely before serving. Wrapped airtight, carrot cake will keep at room temperature for up to 2 days or in the freezer for up to 2 weeks.

9. When the cake is completely cool, top with the frosting and spread evenly to coat. The frosted cake can be stored for 1 day at room temperature or refrigerated for up to 3 days.

Variation

~❧ Add nuts instead of, or in addition to, the pineapple and coconut.

YIELD: Enough to frost two 10-inch
round cakes

SPECIAL TOOL:

Standing electric mixer with a
paddle attachment (optional)

1 pound (two 8-ounce
packages) cream cheese,
softened

¼ pound (1 stick) unsalted
butter, softened

2½ cups powdered sugar, sifted

2 teaspoons finely grated
lemon zest

2 tablespoons fresh lemon
juice

2 tablespoons rum

1 teaspoon vanilla extract

Luscious Cream Cheese Frosting

THE BEST CARROT CAKE IN LOS ANGELES CAN BE FOUND AT
*Nicks, a hole-in-the-wall diner downtown. After baking the cake, the
cooks slather on the frosting and serve it right out of the pan. None
of that sissy layering!*

*Be sure to cream the butter and cream cheese slowly in this
recipe. Overworking cream cheese can alter its consistency, making
it too runny to spread.*

1. Using a standing mixer fitted with a paddle attachment or a
hand mixer, cream the cream cheese and butter together on the lowest speed. Stop the machine and scrape down the sides after 2 minutes.

2. When the cream cheese mixture is completely smooth and
lump free, about 4 minutes, slowly add the powdered sugar. When it
is fully incorporated, about 2 minutes, add the lemon zest, lemon
juice, rum, and vanilla. Mix to combine. Cream cheese frosting can
be used right away or stored in the refrigerator for up to 3 days.

YIELD: One 10-inch round cake

SPECIAL TOOLS:

Parchment paper

Standing electric mixer fitted with a paddle attachment (optional)

½ pound (2 sticks) unsalted butter

2 cups powdered sugar

1 cup cake flour

¾ cup almond flour or almond meal (see page 348)

½ cup yellow cornmeal

8 large egg whites, at room temperature

Variation

⟋SOUTHWESTERN CORNSTICKS: Reduce the powdered sugar to 1 cup and add 2 teaspoons baking powder and ½ teaspoon salt to the dry ingredients. Fold in up to 1¼ cups fresh corn kernels, ¼ cup grated Cheddar or Monterey Jack cheese, and ¼ cup finely chopped red bell pepper. Bake in a cast-iron cornstick pan or in a 9-x-6-inch or 8-inch square baking pan. Serve the cornsticks with sour cream and jalapeño or prickly pear jelly.

Cornmeal Financier

CORNMEAL GIVES THIS VARIATION A SWEET, SLIGHTLY *crunchy texture. Served with a compote of dried fruits marinated in cognac, and toasted nuts and mascarpone, the cake becomes Mediterranean in flavor. Layered with papaya, pineapple, mango, guava, and coconut cream, it becomes a tropical dessert. For a more American cake, fold in blueberries or layer it with blackberry curd.*

This recipe can also be turned into a southwestern "cornstick." See the variation following the recipe.

1. Melt the butter in a medium saucepan over medium heat. Cook until the solids separate and brown to a dark golden color, 7 to 10 minutes. Remove from the heat and let cool at room temperature until it reaches 70°F, about 30 minutes. Don't chill it. It needs to remain in liquid form. Set aside.

2. Preheat the oven to 350°F. Adjust the rack to the center of the oven. Spray a 10-x-2-inch round cake pan with pan spray, line it with a piece of parchment paper, then coat the paper lightly with pan spray.

3. Sift together the powdered sugar, cake flour, almond flour, and cornmeal into the bowl of a standing mixer fitted with a paddle attachment or use a large bowl and a hand mixer. Turn the machine on low and mix the dry ingredients for 30 seconds. Add the egg whites all at once and mix on medium speed for 3 minutes.

4. Add the melted butter all at once. Be sure to scrape in all the browned bits from the bottom of the pan. Mix for 30 seconds on medium speed, then turn the mixer to high speed and mix for 3 minutes more, scraping down the sides of the bowl well. Financier batter will keep in the refrigerator for up to 2 weeks. (To mix refrigerated batter, see pages 166–167.)

5. Pour the batter into the prepared pan. Bake for 15 minutes. Rotate the cake for even browning and bake for 15 minutes more, or until a toothpick inserted in the center comes out clean. Let cool in the pan on a rack for 5 minutes, then invert it onto the rack, remove the pan and parchment, and cool completely before serving. Wrapped airtight, financier will keep at room temperature for up to 2 days or in the freezer for up to 2 weeks.

COOKIES

I ALWAYS SOLD MORE COOKIES THAN ANY OTHER GIRL Scout in my troop. I'm sure it was overcompensation for never being allowed to bake them at home. That activity belonged to my older sister Terry. What's worse, everything she made was peanut flavored, and she knew I despised peanuts.

My quintessential cookie is a bittersweet chocolate chunk cookie, served straight from the oven. It has a crisp exterior and a slightly soft, buttery center with bitter chocolate that oozes onto the tongue. Chocolate chip cookies are just one of the hundreds of different types emanating from a master dough whose fundamental ingredients are butter, sugar, flour, and eggs, with butter playing the pivotal role. Over the centuries, cooks in many cultures have altered one or more of the ingredients in the basic formula and shaped, rolled, piped, or simply dropped dough onto the baking sheet in spoonfuls to produce a wealth of possibilities.

THIS CHAPTER FOCUSES ON COOKIES MADE BY CREAMING, the traditional method for combining butter and sugar. It's similar to the method used to make cakes, except that the butter is usually cold when you begin. As you beat the butter and sugar together, the sugar crystals are pushed through the fat, adding air and softening the butter. The lumps are beaten out, and the mixture becomes light and more absorbent. The only other parts of the equation are egg, which lightens and leavens a bit more and provides structure, and flour, which provides more structure.

The cookie's personality is shaped by the way the basic ingredients are used and by the flavorings added. Increase the sugar and re-

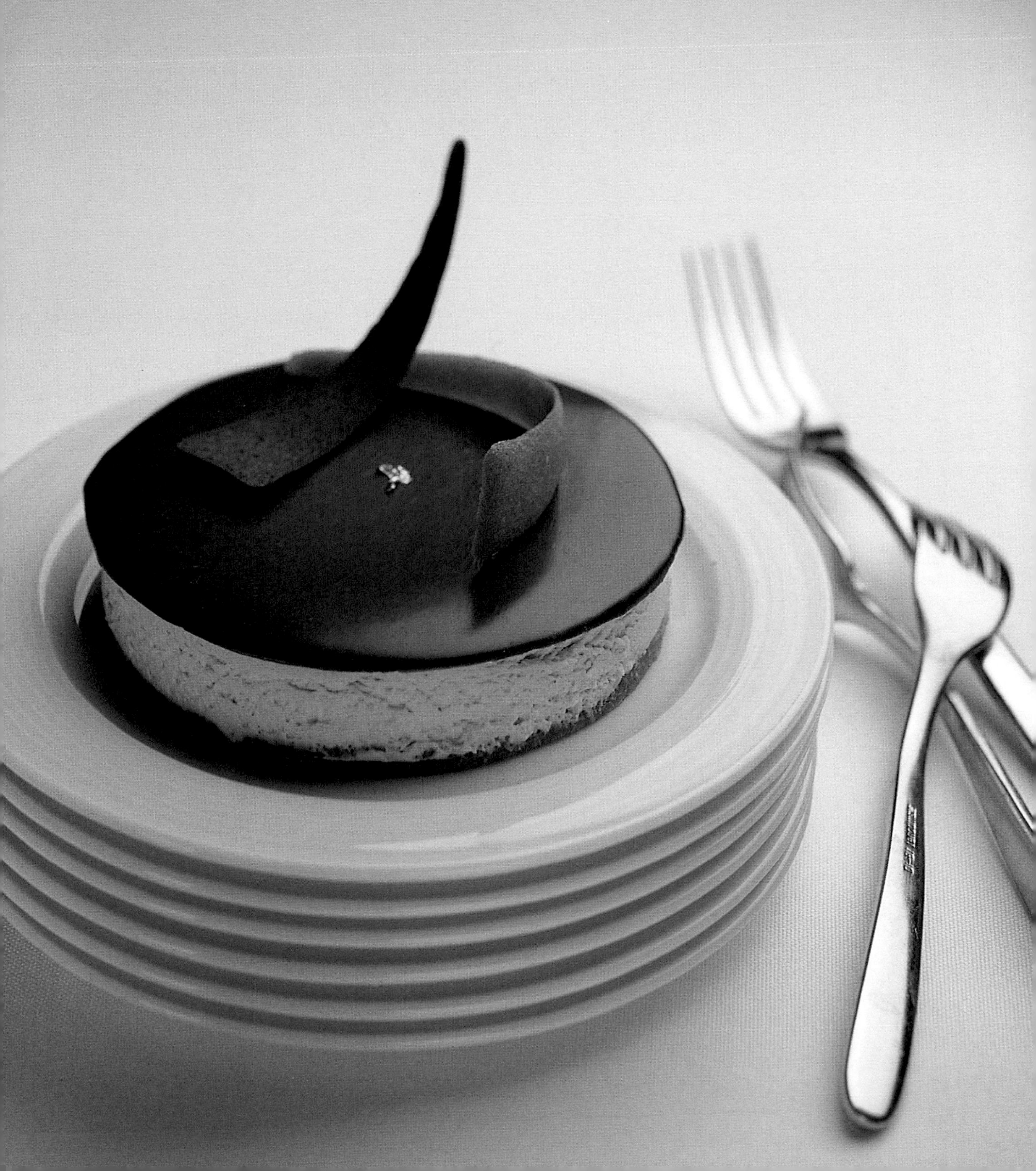

HALSEY TART

(*page 324*)

PAIN AU CHOCOLATE

(*page 282*)

NECTARINE TARTE TATIN

(*page 313*)

ORANGE BLOSSOM HONEY MADELEINES
(page 150)

Opposite:
TOASTED LEMON POUND CAKE
WITH GRAPEFRUIT-VANILLA
CURD AND GRAPEFRUIT
(page 315)

CHOCOLATE
POTS DE CRÈME
(page 109)
with TUILES
(page 146)

CRÈME BRÛLÉE

(page 112)

CHALLAH
(*page 254*)

Opposite:
MASTER BRIOCHE
(*page 230*)

CHOCOLATE SOUFFLÉS
(page 26)

DANISH BRAID

(page 287)

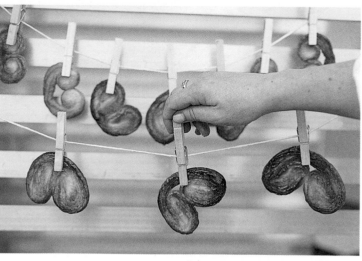

ROASTED PINEAPPLE
RUGELACH ENVELOPES
WITH SOUR CREAM-
PINEAPPLE GLACÉ
(page 314)

PALMIERS
(page 274)

Opposite:
CINNAMON TWISTS
(page 290)

BOYSENBERRY BRIOCHE PUDDING
À LA HEATHER HO

(page 310)

Opposite:
MINIATURE GINGERBREAD FINANCIERS
BAKED IN SAVARIN MOLDS

(page 170)

DEEP, DARK CHOCOLATE TART
(page 42)

duce the butter in the master recipe and you get soft, chewy Snicker-doodles. At the opposite end of the spectrum sits the Orange Vanilla Anise Shortbread, with half a stick more butter, no egg, and a very short, buttery texture. Compare this to the sandy-textured, cakey Brown Butter Meltaways, in which powdered sugar is substituted for granulated. Many cookies, like Chocolate Chip Cookies, are further leavened with a chemical agent—baking powder or baking soda.

There are countless variations on the basic sugar cookie recipe: adding lemon zest or ginger, for example, or replacing some of the flour with cocoa powder. (See page 181 for more ideas.)

THE KEY TO SUCCESSFUL COOKIE BAKING IS THE WAY THE butter is handled. I classify butter and sugar as liquids, because they become liquid when heated. During the creaming method, butter and sugar are mixed quickly, creating friction, which imparts heat. If you overcream, the butter will break down and begin to melt. The dough will be soft and runny, and when baked, the fat, which is already melted, will spread quickly. On the other hand, if you add an egg that is too cold to the creamed butter, the temperature of the egg will cause the butter to lump, resulting in a batter with a broken appearance. (If this happens, just proceed with the recipe. The dough will come together when the flour is added.)

The temperature of the butter is crucial to the success of your recipe. Butter that is too soft produces greasy cookies. Use it right from the refrigerator, cut it into ½-inch bits, and beat it in a bowl for a few minutes before continuing. Of course there are always exceptions to the rule. Room-temperature or softened butter is preferred when making

The temperature of the butter is crucial to the success of your recipe.

powdered sugar–based cookies, since powdered sugar lacks the crystals that help the butter soften during the creaming process. The cookies will have a soft, melt-in-your-mouth texture.

Sooner or later, every baker is faced with what I call "the Toll-House conundrum." Even though the same recipe appears on the back of every bag of morsels, the cookies do not always come out of the oven the same. Sometimes they are very thin and crisp, while at other times they are thick and chewy. One recipe: two cookies. I'm often asked to explain this mystery. Again, the different textures are the result of your handling of the butter: its temperature and how long and how vigorously you beat it. Beating butter for a long time and/or using room-temperature butter causes it to become more liquid, which makes the cookies spread. If you like thin, crisp cookies, increase the beating time of the butter or start with softened butter.

When you understand the role of butter and its friends sugar, eggs, and flour, you can experiment.

BE CAREFUL NOT TO OVERMIX THE DOUGH AFTER YOU ADD the flour. If a completed batter is overworked, the dough will be tough, because the beating develops the gluten in the flour. Toughened dough does not spread well, and the finished cookies will be denser than normal. Once the dry ingredients are added and incorporated, it's important to mix the dough just until it comes together.

Every baker has a favorite cookie. When you understand the role of butter and its friends sugar, eggs, and flour, you can experiment. Analyzing a recipe is the first step toward customizing your perfect cookie.

Cookie
FAMILY TREE

WITH GRANULATED SUGAR
MASTER SUGAR COOKIES
Brooklyn Baci
Butterscotch Cookies
Graham Cookies

WITH POWDERED SUGAR
Brown Butter Meltaways
Rose Water Almond Tea Cookies

WITH CHEMICAL LEAVENING
Chocolate Chip Cookies
Triple Chocolate Fudge Cookies
Gingersnaps
Gingerbread People
Chinese Almond Cookies
Snickerdoodles
Orange Vanilla Anise Shortbread
Lemon Ginger Cookies

All the cookies in this family tree are made with the creaming method. The master recipe and its derivatives use granulated sugar. Powdered sugar–based cookies have a softer, more delicate texture. Cookies with baking powder, baking soda, or cream of tartar have a lighter, chewier consistency.

YIELD: About 3 dozen 3-inch round cookies

SPECIAL TOOLS:

Standing electric mixer with a paddle attachment (optional)

Parchment paper

6 ounces (1½ sticks) cold unsalted butter, cut into ½-inch pieces

½ cup plus 1 tablespoon sugar, plus ¼ cup for rolling

¼ teaspoon salt

1 teaspoon vanilla extract

1 large egg, at room temperature

1¾ cups all-purpose flour, sifted

NOTE

If you plan on freezing these cookies after they are baked, underbake them slightly, thaw, and crisp the cookies in a 350°F oven for 5 minutes before serving.

Master Sugar Cookies

THIS BASIC COOKIE CAN BE FLAVORED IN LOTS OF WAYS. *Because it holds its shape in the oven, it makes a great cookie-cutter cookie. It's also good as a classic refrigerator cookie — rolled into a log, chilled, then cut into disks. At the restaurant, I use a sheet of parchment paper in three ways: to transfer dry ingredients, to roll the dough, and finally to line the baking sheet. A refrigerator log can also be rolled in sugar before it is cut, creating a crisp, crystal cookie "frame" when baked.*

Most cookie recipes, including this one, will result in two different styles of cookie if you alter the temperature and baking time. Baking at a lower temperature (325°F) for a longer period of time results in a crisp cookie. Baking at a higher temperature (350°F) for a shorter time creates a softer, chewier center. Regardless of the style, cookies should always be spaced evenly on the baking sheet for even browning. If I am baking in a standard oven, I like to bake the cookies in the bottom third of the oven. Because heat rises, they tend to brown better when they have more headroom. Every oven is different, however. Most brown unevenly, with different hot spots from an uneven heat source. For that reason, you should rotate the baking sheet halfway through the baking process.

1. Using a standing mixer fitted with a paddle attachment or a hand mixer, cream the butter on medium speed until pale yellow, about 2 minutes. Scrape down the sides of the bowl and the paddle or beaters. Add the sugar, salt, and vanilla. Cream on medium speed until it is smooth, about 1 minute. Stop the mixer and scrape down the sides of the bowl and the paddle.

2. Add the egg and beat on low speed for 15 seconds, or until fully incorporated. Do not overbeat. Scrape down the sides of the bowl and the paddle.

3. On low speed, add the flour. Beat until all of the flour is incorporated. Scrape down the sides of the bowl, then mix on low speed for 15 to 30 seconds, or until you have an even-textured dough.

4. Remove small handfuls of dough from the mixer and plop them down the middle of a sheet of parchment paper, creating a log about 1½ inches wide and 12 inches long. Fold the parchment over, creating a sausage. Chill for at least 1 hour. At this point, the dough will keep nicely, tightly wrapped, in the refrigerator for up to 1 week or in the freezer for up to 1 month. (Thaw frozen dough at room temperature for about 30 minutes, or until you can slice it.)

5. Preheat the oven to 350°F. Adjust the rack to the lower third of the oven. Line two baking sheets with parchment paper.

6. When the dough has chilled, remove it from the parchment, pour the remaining ¼ cup sugar onto your work surface, and roll the log in the sugar. Using a chef's knife, slice ⅓-inch-thick rounds off the log. Place the cookies 1 inch apart on the prepared baking sheets. Alternate the rows, checkerboard fashion.

7. Bake one sheet at a time for 12 to 15 minutes, or until golden brown around the edges, turning the baking sheet front to back halfway through the baking. Remove from the oven and carefully slide the parchment onto a work surface. Wait at least 5 minutes before serving or 20 minutes before storing in an airtight container for up to 3 days at room temperature. The cookies can also be frozen for up to 1 month.

Royal Icing

1 large egg white
1 teaspoon fresh lemon juice
1½ cups powdered sugar

Combine the egg white and lemon juice in the bowl of a standing electric mixer or with a hand mixer. Sift the sugar in and beat on low speed until combined and smooth.

Variations

- CUT-OUT COOKIES: Place the dough between two sheets of parchment, roll it out ¼ inch thick, and freeze for at least 1 hour. Carefully peel off the parchment and place the dough on a work surface dusted lightly with flour. Dip the cookie cutter in flour as needed. Once on the baking sheet, the cookies can be decorated with colored sugars or candy sprinkles or dusted with granulated sugar. Cut-out cookies can also be iced after baking. Use Master Ganache (page 16), Chocolate Frosting (page 36), or Royal Icing (see above).

- LEMON-POPPY SEED: Add 3 tablespoons poppy seeds and 3 tablespoons finely chopped or grated lemon zest to the butter while creaming.

- CHOCOLATE: Replace ¼ cup of the all-purpose flour with ¼ cup cocoa powder. To up the ante, you can add 1½ ounces melted bittersweet chocolate to the butter while creaming.

- SWIRLS: Roll together equal portions of Master Sugar Cookie dough and the chocolate variation. Do this by rolling the dough out flat, layering one dough on top of the other, pressing the two pieces together, and rolling into a sausage. Chill for at least 60 minutes, then roll in sugar, slice, and bake.

- SPICED: Add 1½ teaspoons ground ginger, 1 teaspoon ground cinnamon, ¼ teaspoon freshly ground nutmeg, and a pinch of ground cloves to the butter while creaming.

- PEANUT BUTTER: Add ½ to 1 cup creamy peanut butter to the butter while creaming. You can also add ½ cup coarsely chopped toasted nuts (salted or unsalted—your pleasure).

- FANCY EDGES: The dough log can also be rolled in cinnamon sugar, clear or colored crystal sugar, turbinado sugar, chopped nuts, or shredded unsweetened coconut before being cut.

Brooklyn Baci

THIS IS THE SAME RECIPE AS THE MASTER COOKIE, WITH A *few additions. Baci means "kisses" in Italian. These cookies are dusted with powdered sugar before they go into the oven, which gives them a sweet, crunchy outer crust. Though you can bake the cookies in advance and freeze them, it's best not to freeze the dough.*

YIELD: About 4 dozen 1-inch cookies

SPECIAL TOOLS:

    Parchment paper

    Standing electric mixer with a paddle attachment (optional)

    Pastry bag and medium (#4) plain tip

1½ cups all-purpose flour

½ cup unsweetened cocoa powder

2 ounces finely chopped bittersweet chocolate

6 ounces (1½ sticks) cold unsalted butter, cut into ½-inch pieces

½ cup sugar

2 tablespoons honey

1 teaspoon instant espresso powder

1 teaspoon vanilla extract

¼ teaspoon salt

1 large egg, at room temperature

2 tablespoons heavy cream

1 cup powdered sugar, sifted

NOTE

If you plan on freezing these cookies after they are baked, underbake them slightly, thaw, and crisp the cookies in a 350°F oven for 5 minutes before serving.

1. Preheat the oven to 350°F. Adjust the rack to the lower third of the oven. Line two baking sheets with parchment paper.

2. Sift together the flour and cocoa powder into a medium bowl and set aside.

3. Fill a small saucepan three-quarters full of water and bring to a simmer over medium heat. Place the chocolate in a small bowl and place over the simmering water, creating a double boiler. Stir occasionally until it is melted, about 5 minutes. Remove the bowl from the heat and set aside.

4. Using a standing mixer fitted with a paddle attachment or a hand mixer, cream the butter on medium speed until pale yellow, about 2 minutes. Scrape down the sides of the bowl and the paddle. Add the sugar, honey, instant espresso powder, vanilla, and salt. Cream on medium speed until it is smooth and lump free, about 1 minute. Stop the mixer and scrape down the sides of the bowl and the paddle.

5. Add the chocolate and beat on medium speed for 30 seconds. Add the egg and beat until fully incorporated, about 15 seconds.

6. On low speed, add the flour mixture. Beat until all the dry ingredients are incorporated. Scrape down the sides of the bowl. Add the cream and mix it in, about 30 seconds.

7. Transfer the dough to a large piping bag fitted with a medium (#4) plain tip. Pipe the dough onto the prepared baking sheet in kiss shapes. To achieve a kiss, touch the pastry tip to the tray and squeeze the bag, pulling straight up as you squeeze. Stop squeezing when the cookie is 1 inch in diameter and quickly lift the bag straight up. Sift powdered sugar over the kisses.

8. Bake one sheet at a time for 12 to 15 minutes, or until firm and dry to the touch, turning the baking sheet front to back halfway through the baking. Cool on a rack before serving. Store in an airtight container for 3 days at room temperature. The cookies can also be frozen for up to 1 month.

Butterscotch Cookies

YIELD: About 3 dozen 3-inch
round cookies

SPECIAL TOOLS:

Standing electric mixer with a
paddle attachment (optional)

Parchment paper

6 ounces (1½ sticks) cold
unsalted butter, cut into ½-
inch pieces

¾ cup tightly packed dark
brown sugar

2 tablespoons sugar

¼ teaspoon salt

2 large eggs, at room
temperature

1 teaspoon vanilla extract

1½ cups all-purpose flour, sifted

¼ cup Demerara sugar or other
granulated brown sugar,
for dusting

THE RICH BUTTERSCOTCH FLAVOR OF THESE COOKIES COMES *from dark brown sugar, which I prefer over light brown because the flavor is more intense. Brown sugar is white sugar with molasses, a byproduct of sugar refinement, added back in. Demerara sugar, which I use for dusting these cookies, is one type of raw brown sugar. You can find it at supermarkets and whole foods stores. This dough is somewhat gooey. Don't worry if it doesn't slice neatly.*

1. Using a standing mixer fitted with a paddle attachment or a hand mixer, cream the butter on medium speed until pale yellow, about 2 minutes. Scrape down the sides of the bowl and the paddle. Add the brown sugar, sugar, and salt. Cream on medium speed until it is smooth and lump free, about 1 minute. Stop the mixer and scrape down the sides of the bowl and the paddle.

2. Add the eggs, one at a time, and the vanilla, beating on low speed for 15 seconds after each addition, or until fully incorporated. Do not overbeat. Stop the machine and scrape down the sides of the bowl and the paddle.

3. On low speed, add the flour. Beat until all of the flour is incorporated. Scrape down the sides of the bowl, then mix on low speed until the dough is smooth and uniform.

4. Remove small handfuls of dough from the mixer and plop them down the middle of a sheet of parchment paper, creating a log about 1½ inches wide and 12 inches long. Fold the parchment over, creating a sausage. Chill for at least 1 hour. At this point, the dough will keep nicely, tightly wrapped, in the refrigerator for up to 1 week or in the freezer for up to 1 month. (Thaw frozen dough at room temperature for about 30 minutes, or until you can slice it.)

5. Preheat the oven to 350°F. Adjust the rack to the lower third of the oven. Line two baking sheets with parchment paper.

6. When the dough has chilled, using a chef's knife, slice ⅓-inch-thick rounds off the log. Place the cookies 1 inch apart on the prepared baking sheets. Sprinkle evenly with the Demerara sugar.

7. Bake one sheet at a time for 12 to 15 minutes, or until golden brown around the edges, turning the baking sheet front to back halfway through the baking. Remove from the oven and carefully slide the parchment directly onto a work surface. Wait at least 5 minutes before serving or 20 minutes before storing in an airtight container for up to 3 days at room temperature.

Graham Cookies

YIELD: About 2 dozen 2-inch square cookies

COOKING TIME: 15 minutes

SPECIAL TOOLS:

Standing electric mixer with a paddle attachment (optional)

Rolling pastry wheel (optional)

Parchment paper

2 cups graham flour or whole wheat flour

1 cup cake flour

1 teaspoon baking powder

½ teaspoon baking soda

¼ teaspoon salt

6 tablespoons (¾ stick) cold unsalted butter, cut into ½-inch pieces

½ teaspoon ground cinnamon

½ cup sugar

¼ cup tightly packed brown sugar

⅓ cup honey

1 large egg, at room temperature

¼ cup milk

1 tablespoon fresh lemon juice

1 teaspoon vanilla extract

GRAHAM FLOUR WAS MADE POPULAR IN THE MID–NINETEENTH *century by Sylvester Graham. He was a vegetarian and nutrition guru who advocated a healthy diet and consumption of homemade bread and crackers made from a coarsely ground whole wheat flour and abstinence from white bread, alcohol, tobacco, red meat, and salt. He was nutritionally ahead of his time, although many people thought he was a nut. You can find graham flour at whole foods stores; if you can't find it, substitute stone-ground whole wheat flour. This is a cakey cookie, and for that reason I use cake flour. All-purpose will also work. If you want a crisp, less cakey cookie, divide the dough in half and roll it out thin, about ⅛ inch thick. Bake for only 12 to 15 minutes.*

1. Sift together the graham flour, cake flour, baking powder, baking soda, and salt into a medium bowl. Dump the bran remaining in the sifter into the sifted ingredients. Set aside.

2. Using a standing mixer fitted with a paddle attachment or a hand mixer, cream the butter and cinnamon on medium speed until pale yellow, about 2 minutes. Scrape down the sides of the bowl and the paddle. Add the sugar, brown sugar, and honey. Cream on medium speed until it is smooth and lump free, about 1 minute. Stop the mixer and scrape down the sides of the bowl and the paddle.

3. Add the egg, milk, lemon juice, and vanilla and beat until incorporated. The mixture will look broken, but don't worry; it will come together in the end.

4. On low speed, add the flour mixture. Beat until it is incorporated. Scrape down the sides of the bowl.

5. Press the dough into a disk ½ to 1 inch thick, wrap it in plastic film, and chill for at least 30 minutes. At this point, the dough will keep nicely, tightly wrapped, in the refrigerator for up to 1 week or in the freezer for up to 1 month. (Thaw frozen dough at room temperature for about 30 minutes before rolling.)

6. Place the chilled dough on a sheet of parchment paper and, using a rolling pin, roll it out ¼ inch thick. Chill the dough for at least 1 hour.

7. Preheat the oven to 350°F. Adjust the rack to the lower third of the oven.

8. Use a fork to poke holes evenly all over the surface of the dough. (This is called *docking,* and it prevents steam from accumulating under the dough, which causes bumps and bubbles.) Cut evenly spaced horizontal, then vertical lines using a pastry wheel or a knife. Leave the dough in place. Slide the parchment paper and docked and scored cookie dough onto a baking sheet.

9. Bake for 15 to 20 minutes, or until light golden brown around the edges, turning the sheet front to back halfway through the baking. Cool on a rack before serving. Once the cookies have cooled, they can be snapped apart. Store graham cookies in an airtight container for up to 3 days at room temperature.

Brown Butter Meltaways

YIELD: About 2 dozen 1-inch
round cookies

SPECIAL TOOLS:

Standing electric mixer with a
paddle attachment (optional)

Parchment paper

½ pound (2 sticks) unsalted
butter

1½ cups plus 2 tablespoons
powdered sugar, plus up
to 1 cup for dusting, as
needed

¼ teaspoon salt

1½ cups all-purpose flour, sifted

I CALL THESE COOKIES *MELTAWAYS* BECAUSE THE POWDERED
sugar in the dough creates a texture that melts in your mouth. In
fact, the cookie is known by many names. In the Midwest, it is a
snowball. Add pecans and masa, and it's transformed into a Mexican
wedding cookie. Switch to walnuts, and it's a Russian tea cake, and
the Greek version calls for almonds and olive oil. Whatever the variation, it's important to coat them thoroughly with the powdered
sugar while still hot.

The dough is a simple variation of the master recipe. Powdered sugar stands in for granulated. There's no egg, which results in
a denser, drier crumb. Brown butter replaces regular butter, con-
tributing a rich depth of flavor. Brown and chill the butter several
hours before you make the cookies or up to several days in advance.

1. A few hours before you wish to make the cookies, make the
brown butter. Melt the butter in a medium saucepan over medium
heat. Cook until the solids separate and brown to a dark golden
color, 7 to 10 minutes. Remove from the heat and let cool at room
temperature, and then chill it in the refrigerator until it is solid.

2. Using a standing mixer fitted with a paddle attachment or a
hand mixer, cream the brown butter on medium speed until cream-
colored, about 2 minutes. Scrape down the sides of the bowl and the
paddle. Add the 1½ cups plus 2 tablespoons powdered sugar and the
salt. Cream on medium speed until it is smooth and lump free, about
1 minute. Stop the mixer and scrape down the sides of the bowl and
the paddle.

3. On low speed, add the flour. Beat until just incorporated.
Do not overbeat. Scrape down the sides of the bowl and the paddle.
Remove the dough from the mixer, wrap it in plastic film, and chill
for at least 30 minutes. At this point, the dough will keep nicely,
tightly wrapped, in the refrigerator for up to 1 week or in the freezer
for up to 1 month. (Thaw frozen dough at room temperature for
about 30 minutes, or until you can pinch off pieces.)

4. Preheat the oven to 350°F. Adjust the rack to the lower third
of the oven. Line two baking sheets with parchment paper.

5. Flour your hands. Pinch off pieces of dough and roll them
into 1-inch balls. Place the balls 1 inch apart on the prepared baking
sheets. Continue to flour your hands as needed to prevent the dough
from sticking.

6. Bake one sheet at a time for 12 to 15 minutes, or until light golden brown around the edges, turning the sheet front to back halfway through the baking. Do not overbake, or your cookies will be too dry and crisp.

7. As soon as you remove the cookies from the oven, cover them completely with powdered sugar. The best way to do this is to place the powdered sugar in a strainer and tap it over the cookies on the baking sheet. I like the image of snow in Austria to guide how much sugar to use. Let the cookies cool completely before removing them from the sheets and serving. Store the meltaways in an airtight container for up to 3 days at room temperature. The cookies can also be frozen for up to 2 weeks.

Variations

- MEXICAN WEDDING COOKIES: Substitute ¼ cup masa harina for ¼ cup of the all-purpose flour. Masa harina is available at many supermarkets and specialty stores; do not confuse it with cornmeal. Add 1 cup coarsely chopped, toasted pecans (cooled) to the butter while creaming. (To toast, see page 366.) My friend Elizabeth Faulkner of Citizen Cake recommends rolling the cookies first in granulated sugar and then in the powdered sugar before baking for a wonderful texture. When cooled, coat them again in powdered sugar.

- LEMON, LIME, OR ORANGE: Add 3 tablespoons finely chopped or grated citrus zest and 2 tablespoons citrus juice to the butter while creaming.

- RUSSIAN TEA CAKES: Add 1 cup coarsely chopped, toasted walnuts (cooled) to the butter while creaming. (To toast, see page 366.)

- GREEK POWDER COOKIES (*KOURABIEDES*): Substitute ½ cup very fresh extra-virgin olive oil for the butter and add 1 cup coarsely chopped, toasted almonds (cooled) to the butter while creaming. (To toast, see page 366.) These cookies have a lovely floral flavor from the olive oil, so use the very best you can find.

Rose Water Almond Tea Cookies

YIELD: About 3 dozen 3-inch
round cookies

SPECIAL TOOLS:

Standing electric mixer with a
paddle attachment (optional)

Parchment paper

1½ cups all-purpose flour

½ cup almond meal (see
headnote)

6 ounces (1½ sticks) cold
unsalted butter, cut into
½-inch pieces

1½ cups powdered sugar, plus
up to ½ cup, sifted, for
dusting, as needed

½ teaspoon salt

1 teaspoon vanilla extract

2 tablespoons rose water

2 large eggs, at room
temperature

THESE DELICATE, SANDY-TEXTURED COOKIES HAVE A *subtle floral flavor that comes from rose water. A distillation of tea made from rose petals, rose water was a popular household ingredient in the Victorian era, used for both baking and toiletries. It was easy for women to make, because in those days most well-to-do families owned a small spirit distillery. If you don't have a still in the cellar, the best place to find rose water today is at an Indian or Middle Eastern market. Almond meal, ground from whole almonds, can be made in your food processor or spice mill or bought at a specialty market.*

1. Sift together the flour and almond meal into a medium bowl and set aside.

2. Using a standing mixer fitted with a paddle attachment or a hand mixer, cream the butter on medium speed until pale yellow, about 2 minutes. Scrape down the sides of the bowl and the paddle. Add the 1½ cups powdered sugar, the salt, vanilla, and rose water. Cream on medium speed until it is smooth and lump free, about 1 minute. Stop the mixer and scrape down the sides of the bowl and the paddle.

3. Add the eggs, one at a time, scraping down the bowl after each addition, and beat on low speed for 15 seconds, or until fully incorporated. Do not overbeat. Stop the machine and scrape down the sides of the bowl and the paddle.

4. On low speed, add the flour mixture. Beat until just incorporated. Scrape down the sides of the bowl. Remove the dough from the mixer, wrap it in plastic film, and refrigerate for at least 30 minutes. At this point, the dough will keep nicely, tightly wrapped, in the refrigerator for up to 1 week or in the freezer for up to 1 month. (Thaw frozen dough at room temperature for about 30 minutes, or until you can pinch off pieces.)

5. Preheat the oven to 350°F. Adjust the rack to the lower third of the oven. Line two baking sheets with parchment paper.

6. Flour your hands. Pinch off pieces of dough and roll them into 1-inch balls. Place the balls 1 inch apart on the prepared baking sheets. Continue to flour your hands as needed to prevent the dough from sticking.

7. Bake one sheet at a time for 12 to 15 minutes, or until light golden brown around the edges, turning the sheet front to back halfway through the baking.

8. As soon as you remove the cookies from the oven, cover them completely with sifted powdered sugar. Let the cookies cool completely before removing them from the sheets and serving. Store the tea cookies in an airtight container for up to 3 days at room temperature.

Variation

꙳ VIENNESE GOLDEN CRESCENTS: Replace the eggs with 4 egg yolks. Increase the powdered sugar to 2 cups. Omit the rose water and almond meal. After chilling, form the dough into 2-inch crescents before baking. Coat with powdered sugar while hot.

Chocolate Chip Cookies

YIELD: About 3 dozen 3-inch
round cookies

SPECIAL TOOLS:

Standing electric mixer with a
paddle attachment (optional)

Parchment paper

1½ cups all-purpose flour

½ teaspoon baking soda

¼ pound (1 stick) cold unsalted
butter, cut into ½-inch
pieces

½ cup plus 2 tablespoons
sugar

½ cup plus 2 tablespoons
tightly packed light brown
sugar

¼ teaspoon salt

1 teaspoon vanilla extract

1 large egg, at room
temperature

7 ounces bittersweet
chocolate, cut into
½-inch chunks

THESE CHOCOLATE CHIP COOKIES ARE RICH AND CREAMY. *I once had a customer who complained that my chocolate chip cookies were too puffy. To make flatter cookies, you had to overcream the butter or add liquid to the dough. It was a busy night, and no one had time to make a new batch of dough, so I half-baked cookies, then pulled the baking sheet out, slapped it twice on the counter, and put it back to finish baking. Voilà: instant flat cookies.*

What I did was counteract the leavening. Chemical leaveners like baking soda and baking powder create carbon dioxide when they're activated, which is how they raise baked goods. Baking powder is activated by moisture and heat, baking soda by an acid. The gas expands in the heat of the oven, and the cookies rise. By slapping the tray on the workbench, I forced the carbon dioxide out, causing the cookies to fall and my customer to return the next day for more.

1. Sift together the flour and baking soda into a medium bowl and set aside.

2. Using a standing mixer fitted with a paddle attachment or a hand mixer, cream the butter on medium speed until pale yellow, about 2 minutes. Scrape down the sides of the bowl and the paddle. Add the sugar, brown sugar, salt, and vanilla. Cream on medium speed until it is smooth and lump free, about 2 minutes. Stop the mixer and scrape down the sides of the bowl and the paddle.

3. Add the egg and beat on low speed for 15 seconds, or until fully incorporated. Do not overbeat. Stop the machine and scrape down the sides of the bowl and the paddle.

4. On low speed, add the flour mixture. Beat until just incorporated. Scrape down the sides of the bowl. Add the chocolate chunks and mix until they are just incorporated. If using a hand mixer, use a wooden spoon to stir them in.

5. If you want to bake these right away, preheat the oven to 350°F. Adjust the rack to the lower third of the oven. Line two baking sheets with parchment paper. Spoon the dough by heaped teaspoons 2 inches apart onto the prepared baking sheets.

If not baking right away, remove small handfuls of dough from the mixer and plop them down the middle of a sheet of parchment paper, creating a log about 2 inches wide and 12 inches long.

Fold the parchment over, creating a sausage. Chill for at least I hour. At this point, the dough will keep nicely, tightly wrapped, in the refrigerator for I week, or in the freezer for up to I month. (Thaw frozen dough at room temperature for about 30 minutes, or until you can slice it.)

6. When the dough has chilled, remove it from the parchment. Using a serrated knife, slice ⅓-inch-thick rounds off the log. Place the cookies 2 inches apart on the prepared baking sheets.

7. Bake one sheet at a time for 12 to 15 minutes, or until golden brown around the edges, turning the sheet front to back halfway through the baking. Remove the sheet from the oven and carefully slide the parchment directly onto a work surface. Wait at least 5 minutes before serving or 20 minutes before storing in an airtight container for up to 3 days at room temperature.

Variations

- WHITE CHOCOLATE-CHERRY: Replace the bittersweet chocolate chunks with ½ cup white chocolate chunks and ½ cup dried sour cherries.

- MOIST AND CAKEY: If you want a moister, cakelike cookie, add I more egg and bake for I to 2 minutes longer.

YIELD: About 3 dozen 3-inch round cookies

SPECIAL TOOLS:

Standing electric mixer with a paddle attachment (optional)

Parchment paper

1½ cups all-purpose flour

2 tablespoons unsweetened cocoa powder

½ teaspoon baking soda

¼ pound (1 stick) cold unsalted butter, cut into ½-inch pieces

½ cup plus 2 tablespoons sugar

½ cup plus 2 tablespoons tightly packed light brown sugar

¼ teaspoon salt

1 teaspoon vanilla extract

1 large egg, at room temperature

½ cup ½-inch chunks white chocolate

½ cup ½-inch chunks bittersweet chocolate

Triple Chocolate Fudge Cookies

THIS COOKIE HAS THE SAME TEXTURE AS A CHOCOLATE *chip cookie, but it's much more chocolatey. The three chocolates are cocoa powder and bittersweet and white chocolate chunks. The white chocolate chunks look striking against the dark brown dough.*

Take extra care when baking these cookies. It's hard to judge when a dark chocolate cookie is golden brown. When a cookie bakes, several things take place: gases expand, fats melt, proteins coagulate, and moisture evaporates. The evaporation of moisture is what will help you determine when these cookies are done. Open the oven door and take a look. If the cookies look wet and shiny, there is still some moisture that needs to evaporate. If they look dry, touch a top with your finger. The cookie should be firm, and the fingerprint should bounce back. Be careful not to overbake the cookies, because cooking chocolate reduces its flavor. To quote Christopher Kimball's Dessert Bible, *"Always err on the side of too little oven time when making chocolate cookies."*

1. Sift together the flour, cocoa powder, and baking soda into a medium bowl and set aside.

2. Using a standing mixer fitted with a paddle attachment or a hand mixer, cream the butter on medium speed until pale yellow, about 2 minutes. Scrape down the sides of the bowl and the paddle. Add the sugar, brown sugar, salt, and vanilla. Cream on medium speed until it is smooth and lump free, about 1 minute. Stop the mixer and scrape down the sides of the bowl and the paddle.

3. Add the egg and beat on low speed for 15 seconds, or until fully incorporated. Do not overbeat. Scrape down the sides of the bowl and the paddle.

4. On low speed, add the flour mixture. Beat until all the dry ingredients are incorporated, 15 to 30 seconds. Scrape down the sides of the bowl. Add the white and bittersweet chocolate chunks and mix until they are just incorporated. If using a hand mixer, use a wooden spoon to stir them in.

5. If you want to bake these right away, preheat the oven to 350°F. Adjust the rack to the lower third of the oven. Line two baking sheets with parchment paper. Spoon the dough by heaped teaspoons 2 inches apart onto the prepared baking sheets.

If not baking right away, remove small handfuls of dough from the mixer and plop them down the middle of a sheet of parchment paper, creating a log about 2 inches wide and 12 inches long. Fold the parchment over, creating a sausage. Chill for at least 1 hour. At this point the dough will keep nicely, tightly wrapped, in the refrigerator for up to 1 week, or in the freezer for up to 1 month. (Thaw frozen dough at room temperature for about 30 minutes, or until you can slice it.)

6. When the dough has chilled, remove it from the parchment. Using a serrated knife, slice ⅓-inch-thick rounds off the log. Place the cookies 2 inches apart on the prepared baking sheets.

7. Bake one sheet at a time for 12 to 15 minutes, or until the cookies look dry and feel firm, turning the sheet front to back halfway through the baking. Remove the sheet from the oven and carefully slide the parchment directly onto a work surface. Wait at least 5 minutes before serving or 20 minutes before storing in an airtight container for up to 3 days at room temperature.

YIELD: About 3 dozen 3-inch cookies

SPECIAL TOOLS:

Standing electric mixer with a paddle attachment (optional)

Parchment paper

2½ cups all-purpose flour

½ teaspoon baking soda

½ pound (2 sticks) cold unsalted butter, cut into ½-inch pieces

½ cup sugar, plus 1 cup for coating

½ cup packed light brown sugar

1 tablespoon ground ginger

½ teaspoon ground allspice

½ teaspoon ground cinnamon

¼ teaspoon ground white pepper

¼ teaspoon salt

1 large egg, at room temperature

¼ cup unsulfured blackstrap molasses

Gingersnaps

THIS GINGERSNAP IS A SLIGHTLY CHEWY COOKIE, ROLLED IN *granulated sugar before it is baked. Crispy and gooey variations are at the end of the recipe. Ginger-flavored pastries are ancient, with variations appearing in nearly every European country. Germany has flat, fancifully iced lebkuchen. France has pain d'épices.*

I love gingersnaps because I love spice, and I want the spiciness to take center stage in this recipe. Spices and flavorings are typically added to a recipe with the dry ingredients. But when they are added to the butter during the creaming process, their flavors will permeate the dough.

1. Sift together the flour and baking soda into a medium bowl and set aside.

2. Using a standing mixer fitted with a paddle attachment or a hand mixer, cream the butter on medium speed until pale yellow, about 2 minutes. Scrape down the sides of the bowl and the paddle. Add the ½ cup sugar, the brown sugar, spices, and salt. Cream on medium speed until it is smooth and lump free, about 1 minute. Stop the mixer and scrape down the sides of the bowl and the paddle.

3. Add the egg and molasses and beat on low speed for 15 seconds, or until fully incorporated. Do not overbeat. Scrape down the sides of the bowl and the paddle.

4. On low speed, add the flour mixture. Beat until all the dry ingredients are incorporated, 15 to 30 seconds. Scrape down the sides of the bowl. Remove the dough from the mixer, wrap it in plastic film, and chill for at least 30 minutes. At this point, the dough will keep nicely, tightly wrapped, in the refrigerator for up to 1 week or in the freezer for up to 1 month. (Thaw frozen dough at room temperature for about 30 minutes, or until you can pinch off pieces.)

5. Preheat the oven to 350°F. Adjust the rack to the lower third of the oven. Line two baking sheets with parchment paper.

6. Place the remaining 1 cup sugar in a medium bowl. When the dough is chilled, pinch off pieces of it and roll into 1-inch balls. Drop the balls into the sugar, coat them thoroughly, and then place them 1 inch apart on the prepared baking sheets.

7. Bake one sheet at a time for 12 to 15 minutes, or until the cookies look dry and feel firm, turning the sheet front to back halfway through the baking. Remove the sheet from the oven and carefully slide the parchment directly onto a work surface. Wait at least 5 minutes before serving or 20 minutes before storing in an airtight container for up to 3 days at room temperature.

Variations

∽ GOOEY: Add an extra ¼ cup molasses and replace the granulated sugar with brown sugar. This version is spicier. Feel free to decrease the molasses if it is too much for you.

∽ CRISP: Bake the cookies at 325°F for 15 to 20 minutes.

YIELD: About 2 dozen

SPECIAL TOOLS:

Standing electric mixer with a paddle attachment (optional)

Cookie cutter(s) in the shape of gingerbread people

1¾ cups all-purpose flour

1 teaspoon baking soda

6 ounces (1½ sticks) cold unsalted butter, cut into ½-inch pieces

¾ cup packed light brown sugar

2 tablespoons ground ginger

1½ teaspoons ground cinnamon

1 teaspoon ground allspice

½ teaspoon ground cloves

¼ teaspoon salt

1 large egg, at room temperature

¼ cup unsulfured blackstrap molasses

Gingerbread People

IN OLD ENGLAND, WHEN A YOUNG WOMAN WAS LOOKING *for a mate she would eat a gingerbread "husband" for luck. After the Brothers Grimm published their book of fairy tales,* Kinder- und Hausmärchen, *in 1812, gingerbread houses became popular. This dough is perfect for making husbands, houses, or any other gingerbread shape. It is crisper than gingersnaps and holds its shape better when baked. Because the dough is quite wet, it is essential to chill it properly before rolling it out and to freeze the rolled-out dough before attempting to cut out shapes.*

1. Sift together the flour and baking soda into a medium bowl and set aside.

2. Using a standing mixer fitted with a paddle attachment or a hand mixer, cream the butter on medium speed until pale yellow, about 2 minutes. Scrape down the sides of the bowl and the paddle. Add the brown sugar, spices, and salt. Cream on medium speed until it is smooth and lump free, about 1 minute. Stop the mixer and scrape down the sides of the bowl and the paddle.

3. Add the egg and molasses and beat on low speed for 30 seconds, or until fully incorporated. Do not overbeat. Scrape down the sides of the bowl and the paddle.

4. On low speed, add the flour mixture. Beat until all the dry ingredients are incorporated, about 30 seconds. Scrape down the sides of the bowl. Remove the dough from the mixer, press it into a ½- to 1-inch-thick disk, wrap it in plastic film, and chill for at least 30 minutes. At this point, the dough will keep nicely, tightly wrapped, in the refrigerator for up to 1 week or in the freezer for up to 1 month. (Thaw frozen dough at room temperature for about 30 minutes before rolling out.)

5. Dust a work surface lightly with flour. Place the dough between two sheets of lightly floured parchment paper, roll it out ¼ inch thick, and freeze it for at least 1 hour.

6. Preheat the oven to 350°F. Adjust the rack to the lower third of the oven. Line two baking sheets with parchment paper.

7. When the dough has frozen, carefully peel off the parchment and place the dough on a work surface dusted lightly with flour. Dip the cookie cutter in flour as needed so the dough comes out of the cutter more easily, then cut out the gingerbread people. Place the cookies 1 inch apart on the prepared baking sheet. Gather the scraps together and roll out again.

8. Bake one sheet at a time for 12 to 15 minutes, or until the cookies look dry and feel firm, turning the sheet front to back halfway through the baking. Remove the sheet from the oven and carefully slide the parchment directly onto a work surface. Wait at least 5 minutes before serving or 30 minutes before storing in an airtight container for up to 3 days at room temperature.

Chinese Almond Cookies

YIELD: About 3 dozen 3-inch
round cookies

SPECIAL TOOLS:

Standing electric mixer with a
paddle attachment (optional)
Parchment paper

2½ cups all-purpose flour

1½ teaspoons baking powder

6 ounces (1½ sticks) cold
unsalted butter, cut into
½-inch pieces

¾ cup sugar, plus up to ¼ cup
for rolling as needed

½ cup almond paste

1 tablespoon grated
orange zest

¼ teaspoon salt

2 teaspoons amaretto

1 large egg, at room
temperature

1 large egg white, lightly
beaten

1 cup almonds

TEAHOUSES ALL OVER THE WORLD SERVE A VARIATION OF *this cookie. I use amaretto to flavor these cookies even though it's Italian and not Chinese. Amaretto is an Italian liqueur made from bitter almonds and apricot pits. Apricots are in the same family as almonds. Their pits are often marketed as "Chinese almond," and are used in many traditional Chinese dishes. If amaretto is unavailable, use ½ teaspoon almond extract. The recipe also calls for almond paste, which you can find in well-stocked supermarkets. It has less sugar than marzipan.*

I. Sift together the flour and baking powder into a medium bowl and set aside.

2. Using a standing mixer fitted with a paddle attachment or a hand mixer, cream the butter until pale yellow, about 2 minutes. Scrape down the sides of the bowl and the paddle. Add the ¾ cup sugar, almond paste, orange zest, salt, and amaretto. Cream on medium speed until it is smooth and lump free, about I minute. Stop the mixer and scrape down the sides of the bowl and the paddle.

3. Add the egg and beat on low speed for 30 seconds, or until fully incorporated. Do not overbeat. Scrape down the sides of the bowl and the paddle.

4. On low speed, add the flour mixture. Beat until the dry ingredients are incorporated, about 30 seconds. Scrape down the sides of the bowl. Remove small handfuls of the dough from the mixer and plop them down the middle of a sheet of parchment paper, creating a log about 2 inches wide and 12 inches long. Fold the parchment over, creating a sausage. Chill for at least I hour. At this point, the dough will keep nicely, tightly wrapped, in the refrigerator for up to I week or in the freezer for up to I month. (Thaw frozen dough at room temperature for about 30 minutes, or until you can slice it.)

5. Preheat the oven to 350°F. Adjust the rack to the lower third of the oven. Line two baking sheets with parchment paper.

6. When the dough has chilled, remove it from the parchment, pour the remaining ¼ cup sugar onto your work surface, and roll the log in the sugar. Using a chef's knife, slice ⅓-inch-thick rounds off the log. Place the cookies 2 inches apart on the prepared baking sheets. Brush each cookie lightly with the beaten egg white, then press a whole almond into the center of each.

7. Bake one sheet at a time for 12 to 15 minutes, or until golden brown around the edges, turning the sheet front to back halfway through the baking. Remove the sheet from the oven and carefully slide the parchment directly onto a work surface. Wait at least 5 minutes before serving or 20 minutes before storing in an airtight container for up to 3 days at room temperature.

Variation

⮞ Add ½ cup sliced toasted (see page 366) almonds to the dough to give the cookies more texture.

YIELD: About 3½ dozen 3-inch round cookies

SPECIAL TOOLS:

Standing electric mixer with a paddle attachment (optional)

Parchment paper

1½ cups all-purpose flour

½ teaspoon baking soda

½ teaspoon cream of tartar

¼ pound (1 stick) cold unsalted butter, cut into ½-inch pieces

¾ cup sugar, plus ¼ cup for dusting

1½ teaspoons ground cinnamon, plus 1 tablespoon for dusting

⅛ teaspoon salt

1½ teaspoons vanilla extract

1 large egg, at room temperature

Snickerdoodles

THE SNICKERDOODLE IS A CLASSIC AMERICAN COOKIE *named after a series of twentieth-century children's adventure stories. Snickerdoodle was a miniature hero who drove a peanut car and cut giant problems down to size. The pintsize champ was the nephew of Yankee Doodle and the cousin of Polly Wolly Doodle. In the tradition of Paul Bunyan and Johnny Appleseed, Snickerdoodle adventures were spread by storytellers and weren't written down until the 1960s.*

You can tell this is an old recipe by its leavening. Before baking powder was available, bakers made their own by mixing baking soda and cream of tartar. Baking soda needs an acid to activate, and cream of tartar is powdered tartaric acid. Combined, the two create carbon dioxide, just like baking powder. You can substitute 1 tablespoon baking powder, but it won't have the same old-fashioned flavor. Whatever you use, be sure to serve the cookies with a big glass of milk.

1. Sift together the flour, baking soda, and cream of tartar into a medium bowl and set aside.

2. Using a standing mixer fitted with a paddle attachment or a hand mixer, cream the butter on medium speed until pale yellow, about 2 minutes. Scrape down the sides of the bowl and the paddle. Add the ¾ cup sugar, the 1½ teaspoons cinnamon, the salt, and the vanilla. Cream on medium speed until it is smooth and lump free, about 1 minute. Stop the mixer and scrape down the sides of the bowl and the paddle.

3. Add the egg and beat on low speed for 30 seconds, or until fully incorporated. Do not overbeat. Scrape down the sides of the bowl.

4. On low speed, add the flour mixture. Beat until all the dry ingredients are incorporated, about 30 seconds. Scrape down the sides of the bowl. Remove the dough from the mixer, wrap it in plastic film, and chill for at least 30 minutes. At this point, the dough will keep nicely, tightly wrapped, in the refrigerator for up to 1 week or in the freezer for up to 1 month. (Thaw frozen dough at room temperature for about 30 minutes, or until you can pinch off pieces.)

5. Preheat the oven to 350°F. Adjust the rack to the lower third of the oven. Line two baking sheets with parchment paper.

6. Combine the remaining ¼ cup sugar and the remaining 1 tablespoon cinnamon in a medium bowl. When the dough has chilled, pinch off pieces of it and roll into 1-inch balls. Drop the balls into the cinnamon sugar, coat them thoroughly, and then place them 2 inches apart on the prepared baking sheets. Alternate the rows like a checkerboard.

7. Bake one sheet at a time for 12 to 15 minutes, or until the cookies look dry and feel firm, turning the sheet front to back halfway through the baking. Remove from the oven and carefully slide the parchment directly onto a work surface. Wait at least 5 minutes before serving or 30 minutes before storing in an airtight container for up to 3 days at room temperature.

Orange Vanilla Anise Shortbread

THE ADDITION OF POTATO FLOUR GIVES THESE DELICATELY *flavored cookies a traditional, crumbly shortbread texture. They can be rolled out and cut into pretty shapes or pressed into a baking sheet and cut into bars. The dough is also suitable for baking in a traditional decorative shortbread mold.*

Anise and citrus are a classic combination. Vanilla adds distinction to the mix. The anise seeds should be toasted lightly to release their flavorful oil and then pulverized to a fine powder in a coffee grinder.

1½ cups all-purpose flour

½ cup potato flour (potato starch; see page 367)

½ teaspoon baking soda

½ pound (2 sticks) cold unsalted butter, cut into ½-inch pieces

½ cup plus 2 tablespoons sugar

2 tablespoons vanilla extract

½ vanilla bean, split and scraped

2 tablespoons anise seeds, toasted (see page 369) and ground

2 tablespoons finely grated orange zest

⅛ teaspoon salt

1 tablespoon orange flower water

1 large egg, at room temperature

1. Sift together the flour, potato flour, and baking soda in a medium bowl and set aside.

2. Using a standing mixer fitted with a paddle attachment or a hand mixer, cream the butter on medium speed until pale yellow, about 2 minutes. Scrape down the sides of the bowl and the paddle. Add the sugar, vanilla extract and scraped seeds from the bean, anise seeds, orange zest, salt, and orange flower water. Cream on medium speed until it is smooth and lump free, about 1 minute. Stop the mixer and scrape down the sides of the bowl and the paddle.

3. Add the egg and beat on low speed for 30 seconds, or until fully incorporated. Do not overbeat. Scrape down the sides of the bowl.

4. On low speed, add the flour mixture. Beat until all the dry ingredients are incorporated, about 30 seconds. Scrape down the sides of the bowl. The dough will be gooey. Remove the dough from the mixer, scrape it onto a sheet of plastic film, press it into a ½- to 1-inch-thick disk, wrap tightly, and chill for at least 1 hour. At this point, the dough will keep nicely, tightly wrapped, in the refrigerator for up to 1 week or in the freezer for up to 1 month. (Thaw frozen dough at room temperature for about 30 minutes, or until you can slice it.)

5. Dust a work surface lightly with flour. Place the dough between 2 sheets of lightly floured parchment paper, roll it out ¼ inch thick, and freeze it for at least 1 hour.

6. Preheat the oven to 350°F. Adjust the rack to the lower third of the oven. Line two baking sheets with parchment paper.

7. When the dough has frozen, carefully peel off the parchment and place the dough on a work surface dusted lightly with flour. Dip a 3-inch round cookie cutter in flour, then cut out the cookies. Place the cookies 1 inch apart on the prepared baking sheets, alternating the rows like a checkerboard. Return the dough to the freezer for 15 minutes or more whenever it becomes too sticky to cut.

8. Bake one sheet at a time for 12 to 15 minutes, or until golden brown around the edges, turning the sheet front to back halfway through the baking. Remove from the oven and carefully slide the parchment directly onto a work surface. Wait at least 5 minutes before serving or 30 minutes before storing the cookies in an airtight container for up to 3 days at room temperature.

Lemon Ginger Cookies

THESE COOKIES ARE MUCH LIKE THE MASTER SUGAR *cookies, but a bit cakier due to the chemical leavening. Lemon and ginger are a refreshing, summery combination.*

YIELD: About 3 dozen 3-inch round cookies

SPECIAL TOOLS:

Standing electric mixer with a paddle attachment

Parchment paper

1½ cups all-purpose flour

½ teaspoon baking soda

¼ pound (1 stick) cold unsalted butter, cut into ½-inch pieces

¾ cup sugar, plus ¼ cup for rolling

1 tablespoon finely grated lemon zest

1 teaspoon ground ginger

¼ teaspoon salt

1 large egg, at room temperature

¼ cup finely diced crystallized ginger

CRYSTALLIZED GINGER

Crystallized ginger can be found at any Asian market, or it can be made at home. It's an ancient method of preservation. Cook peeled and sliced ginger in simmering simple syrup (half sugar, half water) for 1 hour. Strain out the ginger and dredge it in sugar. Reserve the simple syrup, now flavored with ginger, for poaching fruit, sweetening sauces, or moistening cakes.

1. Sift together the flour and baking soda into a medium bowl and set aside.

2. Using a standing mixer fitted with a paddle attachment or a hand mixer, cream the butter on medium speed until pale yellow, about 2 minutes. Scrape down the sides of the bowl and the paddle. Add the ¾ cup sugar, lemon zest, ginger, and salt. Cream on medium speed until it is smooth, about 1 minute. Stop the mixer and scrape down the sides of the bowl and the paddle.

3. Add the egg and beat on low speed for 30 seconds, or until fully incorporated. Do not overbeat. Scrape down the sides of the bowl.

4. On low speed, add the flour mixture. Beat until all the dry ingredients are incorporated, about 30 seconds. Scrape down the sides of the bowl. Add the crystallized ginger and mix until just incorporated.

5. Remove small handfuls of the dough from the mixer and plop them down the middle of a sheet of parchment paper, creating a log about 2 inches wide and 12 inches long. Fold the parchment over, creating a sausage. Chill for at least 1 hour. At this point, the dough will keep nicely, tightly wrapped, in the refrigerator for up to 1 week or in the freezer for up to 1 month. (Thaw frozen dough at room temperature for about 30 minutes, or until you can slice it.)

6. Preheat the oven to 350°F. Adjust the rack to the lower third of the oven. Line two baking sheets with parchment paper.

7. When the dough has chilled, remove it from the parchment, pour the remaining ¼ cup sugar onto your work surface, and roll the log in the sugar. Using a chef's knife, slice ⅓-inch-thick rounds off the log. Place the cookies 2 inches apart on the prepared baking sheets. Alternate the rows checkerboard fashion.

8. Bake one sheet at a time for 12 to 15 minutes, or until brown around the edges, turning the sheet front to back halfway through the baking. Remove from the oven and carefully slide the parchment directly onto a work surface. Wait at least 5 minutes before serving or 30 minutes before storing in an airtight container for up to 3 days at room temperature.

PIE & TART DOUGH

IN MY QUEST TO UNDERSTAND THE HOWS AND WHYS OF baking, I'm reminded time and again that the one thing all recipes have in common is the combining of liquids and solids and that their relationship to each other determines the nature of the pastry. Many recipes call for equal parts of liquid to solid, and "3-2-1" flaky pie dough is a great example of this. It consists of three parts flour, two parts fat, and one part water. Flour is a solid that gives structure to the dough. Butter, which is more or less 20 percent water, will melt when heated and is therefore a solid that becomes a liquid. Water, which binds the dough, is a liquid, making 3 parts liquid in all, thus approximately equal to the flour. (Each cup of flour weighs 5 ounces, for approximately 12 ounces in the master recipe on page 209, a measure proportionate to 8 ounces butter + 4 ounces water.)

THE SECRET TO FLAKY PASTRY IS TO MAKE THE BUTTER believe it is solid. The small pieces of cold butter must be left whole and flattened within the dough. They must not be allowed to combine with the flour but should remain intact. Later, when the dough is baked, the butter will melt and the water in the butter will let off steam. The steam rises, pushing up the surrounding dough, leaving behind tiny buttery pockets of air. Voilà! Flaky pastry.

To ensure that the small pieces of butter remain solid, a method called *cutting in* is used to incorporate fat and dry ingredients. Cutting in will succeed only if you use very cold butter. When pressed, it will break up into flattened broken walnut-meat-size pieces, which are perfect for pie dough.

To keep the butter cold, it's very important to limit the amount of contact warm hands have with the dough. Standing mixers, wire pastry cutters, forks, or butter knives are often used to break down, or shatter, the butter, because they can keep it cold longer than fingers can.

After you cut the butter into the flour, you add water to bind the mixture all together, using ice water to maintain a low dough temperature. An acidic ingredient such as vinegar is added to the ice water to balance flavor and help inhibit the gluten proteins, which makes rolling a bit easier.

The key to flaky pastry is to make the butter believe it is solid.

Temperature is still important after the dough is complete. You have to chill the finished dough before you can handle it successfully. The butter needs to stay cold, and the flour needs time to fully absorb the water. The flaky dough is ready to roll out after an hour or so in the refrigerator.

WHEN SUGAR IS SUBSTITUTED FOR THE WATER IN PIE DOUGH, an entirely new kind of dough is created. Sweet dough, known as *pâte sucrée* in French, is a crisp yet tender dough. The ratio is still 3-2-1, but the water is replaced by the liquid of sugar. Sugar is considered a liquid because it will melt when heated.

A different ingredient calls for a different method. I use the blending method for combining ingredients in sweet dough, rather than the cutting-in method used for flaky pastry. With this kind of dough, you don't want lumps of butter, so you cream it to soften it and eliminate the lumps, making the further incorporation of ingredients easier. Then you quickly blend in the sugar. The best way to blend the butter is to beat it on low speed with a standing mixer fitted with the paddle attachment, or with a hand mixer. You cream the butter without sugar so that air is not introduced (as it is in cookie dough and pound cake, for example). When the butter is soft and lump free, 2 to 3 minutes, you add and blend in the sugar. This results in a dough that has a firm texture with some crunch and a melt-in-your-mouth feel.

3-2-1 Pie and Tart Dough

FAMILY TREE

3	:	2	:	1
SOLID		**SOLID**		**LIQUID**
Flour		*Butter*		*Water*
				or
				Sugar/Eggs

CUT-IN METHOD	BLENDING METHOD
FLAKY	CRISPY
(PIE DOUGH)	(SWEET DOUGH)
3 flour : 2 butter : 1 water	*3 flour : 2 butter : 1 sugar/eggs*

MASTER 3-2-1	SWEET DOUGH
FLAKY PIE DOUGH	(PÂTE SUCRÉE)

Almond Pie Dough	Sweet Pine Nut Dough
Cornmeal Pie Dough	Chocolate Sucrée
Orange-Spice Pâte Brisée	Short Dough (Pâte Sablée)
Rugelach Dough	Chocolate Short Dough
	Rice Short Dough

Both flaky and sweet pastry have the same proportions of solids and liquids, but they are made using different techniques, resulting in two different types of dough. Flaky pastry is flaky because the butter is cut in and remains in relatively large pieces, so that when the dough is baked, it melts quickly, creating steam and causing the dough to puff. The butter in sweet dough is blended with the flour, resulting in a more crumbly, cookielike pastry.

Both flaky and crispy dough are handled in the same way. Limit the amount of dough you roll out at any one time to just enough to line one 9- or 10-inch pan. If you try to roll out the entire batch at once, the dough will be difficult to manage. Keep the remaining dough covered and chilled until needed.

Egg yolks go in next, adding moisture, color, richness, and structure from their protein; they are solids and coagulate when heated. Then you add the flour, salt, and a small amount of cream. Excessive beating at this stage will activate the gluten protein in the flour, creating an overworked dough and making it tough.

Unlike the flaky dough, sweet dough must be chilled for a minimum of 4 hours before it can be handled easily. The butter must resolidify, and the flour must absorb all the liquid. Once it's solid, you must soften the dough to roll it out. Cut it up into eight or more pieces and either place it in a standing mixer fitted with the dough hook and knead on low speed for 1 minute or gently knead the pieces by hand. Gather the dough together and roll it out.

WHICHEVER PIE CRUST YOU CHOOSE TO MAKE, IT SHOULDN'T be a mere bland vessel to hold a filling, but an element that people remember. Once you've mastered the basic flaky and sweet pie crusts here, you can go on to make memorable crusts like Chocolate Short Dough and Almond Pie Dough.

Whichever pie crust you choose, it shouldn't be a mere bland vessel to hold a filling, but an element that people remember.

BRIOCHE DOUGHNUTS
(page 260)

CREAMY
CARAMEL SAUCE
(page 58)
on
VANILLA ICE CREAM
(page 94)

BROWN BUTTER
BAUMKUCHEN
(*page 160*)

PASSION FRUIT
PINWHEEL ROULADE
WITH ROASTED
PINEAPPLE SALAD
(page 318)

PUFF PASTRY DOUGH: CHOCOLATE, PISTACHIO, AND MASTER

(pages 270–72)

CLASSIC MILLE-FEUILLE NAPOLEON
WITH CRÈME BAUMANIÈRE
(page 312)

BEIGNETS
(page 262)

Opposite:
MILE-HIGH APPLE PIE
(page 316)

CRÈME BRÛLÉE APRICOT TART
WITH LAVENDER-VANILLA SAUCE
(page 308)

Opposite: The Candy Shop

CARAMEL LOLLIPOPS *and* CARAMEL STICKS *(page 54)*
PECAN PRALINES *(page 57)*
HAZELNUT BRITTLE *(page 56)*
CARAMEL CRÈME FRAÎCHE CANDIES *(page 62)*

THUMBPRINT LIME MELTAWAYS
(page 321)

Opposite:
ÉCLAIRS
(page 126)

PASSION FRUIT BAVAROIS
(page 84)

CHOCOLATE MOUSSE TRIO
(page 40)

TRUFFLES
(page 18)

Opposite:
STRAWBERRY SEMIFREDDO
(page 96)

PECAN PRALINE
(page 57)

YIELD: Enough for two 9- or 10-inch single-crusted pies or one 9- or 10-inch double-crusted pie

SPECIAL TOOLS:

Standing electric mixer with a paddle attachment (optional)

Pie weights (optional)

½ pound (2 sticks) cold unsalted butter

2½ cups all-purpose flour

2 tablespoons sugar

1 teaspoon salt

½ cup ice water (see note)

½ teaspoon white wine vinegar or Champagne vinegar

NOTE

The amount of water is variable. It is better to have a slightly wet, tacky dough than one that is too dry. Add a little more water if your dough seems dry.

Master *3-2-1 Flaky Pie Dough*

THIS IS THE PERFECT PIE DOUGH. IT'S SO GOOD THAT I HAVE *tricked other chefs into thinking it was puff pastry. Because the butter pieces are kept large and flat, the pie crust is extremely flaky.*

The small amount of sugar in this recipe adds a subtle sweetness, and because sugar caramelizes in heat, it gives the dough a lovely golden brown color when baked. If you plan to use it for a savory recipe, such as quiche or turkey potpie, reduce the sugar from 2 tablespoons to 2 teaspoons. The resulting dough will not be sweet, but it will still be golden brown.

1. Cut the butter into 1-inch pieces and place it in the freezer to chill for 15 minutes.

2. Sift together the flour and sugar into the bowl of a standing mixer fitted with a paddle attachment. (To mix the dough by hand, see page 211.) Sifting eliminates lumps and aerates the mixture, making the dough tenderer and lighter. Add the partially frozen butter and the salt. Mix on low speed for 2 minutes, or until the butter is reduced to the size of broken walnut meats. Stop the machine and by hand pinch flat any large pieces of butter that remain.

3. Combine the ice water and vinegar in a small bowl. Turn the mixer on low speed and add the liquid all at once. Mix just until the dough comes together, about 15 seconds. The dough should be tacky but not sticky.

4. Remove the dough from the bowl and wrap it in plastic film. Do not squeeze the dough together or overwork it. Chill for at least 1 hour. At this point, the dough will keep in the refrigerator for up to 3 days or in the freezer for up to 3 weeks. For freezing, however, I prefer to roll it out into sheets and wrap them airtight in plastic film first.

ROLLING OUT THE DOUGH

Using the proper rolling pin is essential. There are two basic rolling pin styles, one with handles and one without. For tart or pie shells, a pin without handles is best. It is called a *dowel* or *French rolling pin* and can be tapered at the ends or completely cylindrical. A small piece of pie dough does not need the power and leverage that a handled pin provides. The maneuverability of the dowel pin is ideal.

1. To begin rolling, shape the dough into a flat disk, 1 inch thick. If the dough is round when the rolling starts, it is more likely to be round when the rolling is complete. Knead the dough briefly to make it more pliable, but be careful not to overwork it, or it will become tough.

2. Dust the work surface and the dough lightly with all-purpose flour to keep the dough from sticking. Place the rolling pin firmly on the dough and rock it back and forth a few times to soften it. Dust frequently and lightly with all-purpose flour when necessary. Roll over the dough three times with the pin and then use your hands to give the dough a quarter turn clockwise; this will prevent the dough from sticking to the surface. Repeat the three passes with the pin and then turn the dough clockwise again.

3. By rotating the dough frequently you make the finished dough more or less round, and you will immediately know if the dough sticks to the surface. Continue the rolling pattern until the dough is ¼ inch thick and 2 to 3 inches larger than the pan it's going to bake in. If the dough begins to stick, scrape it from underneath with an offset metal spatula. Pull the dough back and dust the work surface with all-purpose flour.

4. After rolling, the dough should still be cool. Wind the circle of dough around the rolling pin and lift it over the pan, then place it loosely inside. Holding the edge of the dough up, ease the dough into the pan. (If the dough has warmed up a bit, gently fold the dough in half, then into quarters. Lift it into the pan and unfold the dough. Cover with plastic film and refrigerate for at least 15 minutes.) Gently press the dough into the corners. This step prevents the sides of the dough from shrinking when a filling is added. Gently press off the excess dough by hand or cut it away using scissors. Do *not* roll the pin over the sharp edges of a tart pan, because it will put nicks in the pin.

5. To flute or crimp the edges of a tart or pie, use scissors to cut the excess dough off ½ inch from the edge of the pan. Fold the ½ inch of dough under and pinch it together. Then go around the edge again, decoratively fluting it with your fingers or pressing it with a fork or spoon. After crimping, chill the shell for at least 15 minutes to help maintain the decorative shape when filling and baking. (It can also be wrapped airtight and frozen.)

PREBAKING

For most pies that do not have a double crust, the tart shell must be pre-baked. This is necessary when the intended filling is precooked, like lemon curd, uncooked, like fresh strawberries, or cooks very briefly, like a quiche. This method is called *blind baking*. The shell is filled with a faux filling, which weighs down the dough during baking, allowing it to maintain its shape in the pan. Typical blind-bake fillings include dry beans, uncooked rice, or store-bought aluminum pie weights. The shell is first lined with parchment paper or wax paper. Heavy-gauge aluminum foil works too, as does a second pie pan nested on top. But my all-time favorite is a wide round coffee filter, the kind that fits an electric coffee maker, sprayed with pan spray. The filters are porous and soft and can't cut through the dough, as foil or parchment can. A 9- to 12-inch flaky dough bakes in 30 to 35 minutes with the oven set first at 425°F, then turned down to 350°F. High heat creates the best flaky dough because it forces the steam out of the butter. Lower temperatures will simply melt the butter, which causes the dough to sag.

1. To blind-bake, preheat the oven to 425°F. Adjust the rack to the lower third of the oven. Prick the bottom of the pastry a few times with a fork. Line the pastry shell with parchment paper, aluminum foil, plastic film (no, it doesn't melt), or a pan-sprayed coffee filter. Fill the lined shell a quarter of the way up with the faux filling and gently press the filling into the corners. Bake for 10 minutes, then turn the heat down to 350°F and bake for 10 minutes more.

2. Remove from the oven and remove the faux filling and the lining. Bake for 10 minutes more, or until the center turns golden and looks dry. There should be no sign of moisture. Remove from the oven and cool in the pan on a rack.

These methods for rolling and blind baking can be used with any dough in this chapter, but check recipes for time and temperature variations. Practice makes perfect, so make tarts and pies often. Your family and neighbors will love you, and you'll become an expert in no time.

TO MIX FLAKY PIE DOUGH BY HAND

Sift the dry ingredients into a large bowl. Add the partially frozen butter and, using a wire pastry cutter, incorporate it into the flour as directed in the recipe. Or use your fingers, pressing the butter and flour between your thumb and index finger to create flattened broken walnut-meat-size pieces. Add the liquid all at once, mixing it in lightly with a fork until the dough just comes together.

Almond Pie Dough

YIELD: Enough for two 9- or 10-inch
single-crusted pies or one 9- or
10-inch double-crusted pie

SPECIAL TOOLS:

Standing electric mixer with a
paddle attachment (optional)

Pie weights (optional)

6 ounces (1½ sticks) cold
unsalted butter

1 cup sugar

1¼ cups cake flour

1 cup all-purpose flour

½ cup almond flour (see
headnote)

1 large egg

⅛ teaspoon salt

FLAVORING TART DOUGH IS AN EASY AND EFFECTIVE WAY to add another dimension to a dish. Almonds complement many foods, and this dough is particularly versatile. It pairs nicely with apricots, cherries, pears, chocolate, coffee, caramel, and vanilla, to name just a few. This recipe calls for almond flour, which is ground from the nutmeat remaining after the almonds have been pressed to extract their oil. You can find it in specialty food markets. Almond meal or home-ground nuts will work just as well. The grind will not be as fine, though, so the dough will have a little more texture. Because of the fat content of the almond flour, this dough requires a lower prebaking temperature (350°, then 325°F) than the master recipe.

1. Cut the butter into 1-inch pieces and place it in the freezer to chill for 15 minutes.

2. Sift together the sugar, cake flour, all-purpose flour, and almond flour into the bowl of a standing mixer fitted with a paddle attachment. (To mix the dough by hand, see page 211.) Add the partially frozen butter. Mix on low speed for 2 minutes, or until the butter is reduced to the size of broken walnut meats. Stop the machine and by hand pinch flat any large pieces of butter that remain.

3. Combine the egg and salt in a small bowl and mix until the salt dissolves. Turn the mixer on low speed and add the egg all at once. Mix just until the dough comes together, about 15 seconds. The dough should be tacky but not sticky.

4. Remove the dough from the bowl and wrap it in plastic film. Do not squeeze the dough together or overwork it. Chill for at least 1 hour. At this point, the dough will keep in the refrigerator for up to 3 days or in the freezer for up to 3 weeks.

5. Roll out the dough as directed in Master 3-2-1 Flaky Pie Dough (see page 209). It has a tendency to crumble; patch it together if it breaks.

6. To prebake, preheat the oven to 350°F. Adjust the rack to the lower third of the oven. Prick the bottom of the pastry shell a few times with a fork. Line the dough with a faux filling as directed in the master recipe (see page 211). Bake for 10 minutes, then turn the heat down to 325°F and bake for 10 minutes more. Remove the faux filling and liner and bake for 10 minutes more, or until golden brown. Cool on a rack before using.

Cornmeal Pie Dough

THE ADDITION OF CORNMEAL TO THIS DOUGH PROVIDES A *subtle sweetness, a little crunch, and a lovely yellow color. Although this recipe calls for yellow cornmeal, you can also use white, blue, or red. (Be careful not to confuse cornmeal with corn flour. In the United States, corn flour is a superfine grind of cornmeal.) The dough is slightly tacky and extremely easy to roll out. Cornmeal pie dough is a great choice for fruit tarts with pastry cream. Use it also for blueberry pies.*

Pastry flour is available in whole foods stores and specialty markets and by mail order.

YIELD: Enough for two 9- or 10-inch single-crusted pies or one 9- or 10-inch double-crusted pie

SPECIAL TOOLS:

Standing electric mixer with a paddle attachment (optional)

Pie weights (optional)

½ pound (2 sticks) cold unsalted butter

2 cups pastry flour (see headnote)

1 cup medium-grind yellow cornmeal

⅓ cup sugar

2 teaspoons finely chopped lemon zest

4 large egg yolks

¼ cup heavy cream

1 teaspoon salt

1. Cut the butter into 1-inch pieces and place it in the freezer to chill for 15 minutes.

2. Sift together the pastry flour, cornmeal, and sugar into the bowl of a standing mixer fitted with a paddle attachment. (To mix the dough by hand, see page 211.) Add the partially frozen butter and lemon zest. Mix on low speed for 2 minutes, or until the butter is reduced to the size of broken walnut meats. Stop the machine and by hand pinch flat any large pieces of butter that remain.

3. Combine the egg yolks, cream, and salt in a small bowl and mix until the salt dissolves. Turn the mixer on low speed and add the egg-yolk mixture all at once. Mix just until the dough comes together, about 15 seconds. The dough should be tacky but not sticky.

4. Remove the dough from the bowl and wrap it in plastic film. Do not squeeze the dough together or overwork it. Chill for at least 1 hour. At this point, the dough will keep in the refrigerator for up to 3 days or in the freezer for up to 3 weeks.

5. This dough is slightly sticky and is easier to roll out if you place it between pieces of lightly floured parchment. Roll out as directed in Master 3-2-1 Flaky Pie Dough (see page 209).

6. To prebake, preheat the oven to 400°F. Adjust the rack to the lower third of the oven. Prick the bottom of the pastry shell a few times with a fork. Line the dough with a faux filling as directed in the master recipe (see page 211). Bake for 10 minutes, then turn the heat down to 350°F and bake for 10 minutes more. Remove the faux filling and lining and bake for 10 minutes more, or until golden brown. Cool on a rack before using.

Orange–Spice Pâte Brisée

THIS DOUGH IS TENDER BUT VERY STURDY. IT ALSO CARRIES *a lot of flavor. The cinnamon, ginger, and orange juice combine perfectly to offset a rich custard filling. It pairs nicely with pastry cream, mousse, Bavarian creams, and fresh fruits.*

YIELD: Enough for two 9- or 10-inch single-crusted pies or one 9- or 10-inch double-crusted pie

SPECIAL TOOLS:

Standing electric mixer with a paddle attachment (optional)

Pie weights (optional)

½ pound (2 sticks) cold unsalted butter

2½ cups all-purpose flour

¼ cup sugar

2 teaspoons ground cinnamon

2 teaspoons ground ginger

¼ teaspoon salt

¼ cup cold water

3 tablespoons fresh orange juice

1 large egg, at room temperature

1. Cut the butter into 1-inch pieces and place it in the freezer to chill for 15 minutes.

2. Sift together the flour, sugar, spices, and salt into the bowl of a standing mixer fitted with a paddle attachment. (To mix the dough by hand, see page 211.) Add the partially frozen butter. Mix on low speed for 2 minutes, or until the butter is reduced to the size of broken walnut meats. Stop the machine and by hand pinch flat any large pieces of butter that remain.

3. Whisk together the water, orange juice, and egg in a small bowl. Turn the mixer on low speed and add the liquid all at once. Mix just until the dough comes together, about 15 seconds. The dough should be tacky but not sticky.

4. Remove the dough from the bowl and wrap it in plastic film. Do not squeeze the dough together or overwork it. Chill for at least 1 hour. At this point, the dough will keep in the refrigerator for up to 3 days or in the freezer for up to 1 month.

5. Roll out the dough as directed in Master 3-2-1 Flaky Pie Dough (see page 209).

6. To prebake, preheat the oven to 400°F. Adjust the rack to the lower third of the oven. Prick the bottom of the pastry shell a few times with a fork. Line the dough with a faux filling as directed in the master recipe (see page 211). Bake for 10 minutes, then turn the heat down to 350°F and bake for 10 minutes more. Remove the faux filling and liner and bake for 10 minutes more, or until golden brown. Cool on a rack before using.

YIELD: Enough for two 9- or 10-inch
single-crusted pies or one
9- or 10-inch double-crusted pie

SPECIAL TOOLS:

Standing electric mixer with a
paddle attachment (optional)

Pie weights (optional)

½ pound (2 sticks) cold
unsalted butter

1½ cups all-purpose flour

1 cup pastry flour

3 tablespoons sugar

1 teaspoon baking powder

¼ teaspoon salt

½ pound cream cheese

1 large egg

1 teaspoon vanilla extract

Variation

☙ RUGELACH COOKIES: Make
the dough as directed, but roll out
into rectangles. Cut into triangles
about 4 inches long and
2 inches across. Sprinkle with
finely chopped chocolate chips or
bittersweet chocolate, with
chopped nuts, or with poppy
seeds. Starting at the bottom
edge, roll up tightly. Brush with
beaten egg and sprinkle with
sugar. Place on baking sheets and
bake at 350°F for 8 to 12 minutes,
or until brown.

Rugelach Dough

THIS IS MY FAVORITE FLAKY DOUGH, ADAPTED FROM THE
*traditional Hanukkah cookie. Rolled into a crescent, the cookie is
usually filled with dried fruits, nuts, jam, or poppy seeds.*

*I have always loved the creamy quality that cream cheese
adds to this dough. I often pair its richness with acidic fruits, such as
cranberries or pineapple. Whenever I create a dessert, I find that
flavors, textures, and temperatures are far more interesting when
they are combined with their opposites.*

*Note that this crust is prebaked at a lower temperature than
the master recipe.*

1. Cut the butter into 1-inch pieces and place it in the freezer
to chill for 15 minutes.

2. Sift together the all-purpose flour, pastry flour, sugar, baking powder, and salt into the bowl of a standing mixer fitted with a
paddle attachment. (To mix the dough by hand, see page 211.) Add
the partially frozen butter. Mix on low for 2 minutes, or until the
butter is reduced to the size of broken walnut meats. Stop the machine and by hand pinch flat any large pieces of butter that remain.

3. Break the cream cheese into small pieces, add them to the
bowl, and mix on low speed for 1 minute.

4. Combine the egg and vanilla in a small bowl. Turn the mixer
on low speed and add the egg mixture all at once. Mix just until the
dough comes together, about 15 seconds. The dough should be
slightly sticky but will be less so after chilling.

5. Remove the dough from the bowl and wrap it in plastic film.
Do not squeeze the dough together or overwork it. Chill for at least
1 hour. At this point, the dough will keep in the refrigerator for up to
3 days or in the freezer for up to 3 weeks.

6. Roll out the dough as directed in Master 3-2-1 Flaky Pie
Dough (see page 209).

7. To prebake, preheat the oven to 350°F. Adjust the rack to
the lower third of the oven. Prick the bottom of the pastry shell a few
times with a fork. Line the dough with a faux filling as directed in the
master recipe (see page 211). Bake for 20 minutes. Remove the faux
filling and liner and bake for 10 minutes more, or until golden.
Cool on a rack before using.

Sweet Dough (Pâte Sucrée)

YIELD: Enough for two 9- or 10-inch tarts

SPECIAL TOOLS:

    Standing electric mixer with a paddle attachment (optional)

    Pie weights (optional)

½ pound (2 sticks) unsalted butter, softened but still cool

½ cup sugar

½ teaspoon salt

2 large egg yolks, at room temperature

3 cups pastry flour, sifted

2 tablespoons heavy cream

ONE OF MY FAVORITE PLACES IN THE WORLD IS THE SIDEWALK *in front of the Fauchon pastry shop in Paris. The windows are filled with incredible pastries, including beautiful fresh fruit tarts. Sweet dough, or pâte sucrée as the French call it, is the base of those tarts. It is a sweet silky dough that bakes up crisp and tender. Sweet dough does not require a high oven temperature and blind-bakes in 20 to 25 minutes.*

To create fresh fruit tarts like the ones at Fauchon, blind-bake a sweet dough tart shell, fill it with Pastry Cream (page 100), and top it with your favorite fruit. Then put on some accordion music and prepare to be swept away.

1. Place the butter in the bowl of a standing mixer fitted with a paddle attachment. (To mix the dough with a hand mixer, see the opposite page.) Beat on low speed for 2 to 3 minutes, or until lightly creamed. Stop the mixer and scrape down the sides of the bowl. Add the sugar and mix for 30 seconds.

2. Add the salt and egg yolks, one at a time, scraping down the sides of the bowl after each addition.

3. Add the flour and mix until the dough just about comes together, about 30 seconds. Add the cream, then pulse the mixer on low speed for 15 to 30 seconds, or until the dough is smooth.

4. Remove the dough from the bowl and wrap it in plastic film. Chill for at least 4 hours. At this point, the dough will keep in the refrigerator for up to 3 days or may be rolled out and frozen for up to 1 month.

5. When you remove the dough from the refrigerator, it will be very hard, because of the butter and sugar. To make it pliable enough to roll out, you must soften it without warming it up too much. There are a number of ways to do this:

- Cut the dough into 8 or more pieces and gently knead each piece, then gather back together into 2 equal-size balls.

- Cut the dough into 8 or more pieces and place in a standing electric mixer fitted with a dough hook. Knead on low speed for 1 minute. Gather the dough up into 2 equal-size balls.

❧ Cut the dough into 8 or more pieces and gently pound each piece with a rolling pin until pliable. Gather the dough up into 2 equal-size balls.

6. Roll out the dough as directed in Master 3-2-1 Flaky Pie Dough (see page 209).

7. To prebake, preheat the oven to 350°F. Adjust the rack to the lower third of the oven. Prick the bottom of the pastry shell a few times with a fork. Line the dough with a faux filling as directed in the master recipe (see page 211). Bake for 15 to 18 minutes. Remove the faux filling and bake for 6 to 10 minutes more, or until deep golden brown. Cool on a rack before using.

TO MIX SWEET DOUGH USING A HAND MIXER

Place the butter in a large bowl and beat on low speed until lightly creamed. Mix in the remaining ingredients as directed, turning the mixer off and on to pulse it while you add the flour and the liquid ingredients.

Variation

❧ ORANGE-ALMOND SUCRÉE: Replace the pastry flour with 2 cups all-purpose flour and 1 cup almond flour (available at specialty markets, or substitute almond meal or home-ground nuts) and add 2 tablespoons finely chopped orange zest.

Sweet Pine Nut Dough

YIELD: Enough for two 10- or 12-inch
single-crusted pies

SPECIAL TOOLS:

   Food processor

   Standing mixer with a paddle
   attachment (optional)

   Pie weights (optional)

  3 cups all-purpose flour

  2 cups pine nuts, toasted
     and cooled (see below)

  1 teaspoon salt

½ pound (2 sticks) unsalted
     butter, softened but
     still cool

½ cup sugar

  1 large egg, at room
     temperature

  1 large egg yolk, at room
     temperature

TOASTING PINE NUTS

Toast the pine nuts in a medium skillet over low heat, shaking the pan so they toast evenly, until lightly browned, about 5 minutes. Immediately transfer to a bowl and let cool.

ALSO CALLED PIÑON AND PIGNOLI, PINE NUTS ARE THE seeds of a pine tree, found inside the pinecone. They are used in the cuisines of many regions, including Italy, China, India, Mexico, and the Middle East. The distinctive, pungent flavor pairs nicely with dried fruits and cheeses. This crust is a good one to use with nutty fillings. Try lining the bottom with chopped almonds or hazelnuts and topping with Master Ganache (page 16).

1. Combine half the flour, half the pine nuts, and half the salt in a food processor and grind to a fine meal, about 30 seconds. Transfer to a small bowl. Repeat with the remaining flour, nuts, and salt, add to the bowl, and set aside.

2. Place the butter in the bowl of a standing mixer fitted with a paddle attachment. (To mix the dough with a hand mixer, see page 217.) Beat on low speed for 2 to 3 minutes, or until lightly creamed. Stop the mixer and scrape down the sides of the bowl. Add the sugar and mix for 30 seconds.

3. On low speed, add the egg and egg yolk and mix until incorporated, about 1 minute. Scrape down the sides of the bowl.

4. Add the flour mixture and mix on low speed just until the dough comes together, about 30 seconds. The dough should be tacky but not sticky.

5. Remove the dough from the bowl and wrap it in plastic film. Chill for at least 4 hours. At this point, the dough will keep in the refrigerator for up to 3 days or may be rolled out and frozen for up to 1 month.

6. Roll out and prebake the dough as directed in Sweet Dough (page 216). Cool on a rack before using.

Chocolate Sucrée

IT'S ALMOST IMPOSSIBLE TO RESIST CHOCOLATE IN ANY form, but especially when it appears in unexpected places — like tart crust. This dough is rich with chocolate and butter and has a crisp, crunchy texture. I use it for chocolate fillings, tangy fruits, and creamy custards.

YIELD: Enough for two thin 9-inch single-crusted pies or one 9-inch double-crusted pie

SPECIAL TOOLS:

Standing electric mixer with a paddle attachment (optional)

Pie weights (optional)

1½ cups pastry flour

2 tablespoons almond meal (see page 348)

2 tablespoons unsweetened cocoa powder

½ teaspoon salt

¼ pound (1 stick) unsalted butter, softened but still cool

1 cup powdered sugar

1 large egg, at room temperature

1. Sift together the flour, almond meal, cocoa powder, and salt into a medium bowl and set aside.

2. Place the butter in the bowl of a standing electric mixer fitted with a paddle attachment. (To mix the dough with a hand mixer, see page 217.) Beat on low speed for 2 to 3 minutes, or until lightly creamed. Stop the mixer and scrape down the sides of the bowl. Add the powdered sugar and mix for 30 seconds. Scrape down the sides of the bowl.

3. Add the egg and mix on low speed until incorporated. Scrape down the sides of the bowl.

4. Add the flour mixture and mix on low speed just until the dough comes together, about 15 seconds.

5. Remove the dough from the bowl and wrap it in plastic film. Chill for at least 4 hours. At this point, the dough will keep in the refrigerator for up to 3 days or may be rolled out and frozen for up to 1 month.

6. Roll out and prebake the dough as directed in Sweet Dough (page 216). Cool on a rack before using.

Short Dough (Pâte Sablée)

YIELD: Enough for two 9- or 10-inch
single-crusted pies

SPECIAL TOOLS:
Standing electric mixer with a
paddle attachment (optional)
Pie weights (optional)

3 cups pastry flour

1 teaspoon salt

¾ pound (3 sticks) unsalted
butter, softened but
still cool

2 cups powdered sugar

2 teaspoons vanilla extract

2 large eggs, at room
temperature, beaten

THE TERM *SHORT* REFERS TO SHORTENING, OR FAT. SHORT *dough is named for the high ratio of butter it contains, which makes it very tender and crumbly. The French name for this dough is* pâte sablée, *which means "sandy dough" and refers to its crumbly texture. Because of this texture, it's easier to press this dough into a tart or pie pan than to roll it out.*

I use short dough as a prebaked base for pastries such as Lemon Bars (page 80) and on its own as shortbread cookies. Chopped nuts, grated citrus zest, or ground spices can be added to jazz up this dough, but there's nothing quite like the tender, buttery original.

1. Sift together the pastry flour and salt into a medium bowl and set aside.

2. Place the butter in the bowl of a standing mixer fitted with a paddle attachment. (To mix the dough with a hand mixer, see page 217.) Beat on low speed until smooth, about 1 minute. Stop the mixer and scrape down the sides of the bowl. Add the powdered sugar and mix on low speed for 30 seconds. Scrape down the sides of the bowl.

3. On low speed, add the vanilla and then the eggs. Scrape down the sides of the bowl.

4. Add the flour mixture and mix on low speed just until the dough comes together, about 15 seconds.

5. Remove the dough from the bowl and wrap it in plastic film. Chill for at least 4 hours. At this point, the dough will keep in the refrigerator for up to 3 days or may be rolled out and frozen for up to 1 month.

6. When ready to use the dough, press it into the pans rather than attempting to roll it out.

7. Prebake the dough as directed in Sweet Dough (page 217). Cool on a rack before using.

Variations

⤙ CHOCOLATE SHORTBREAD: Replace ½ cup of the pastry flour with ½ cup unsweetened cocoa powder.

⤙ CARDAMOM-BROWN BUTTER SHORTBREAD: Melt the butter in a medium saucepan over medium heat. Cook until the solids separate and brown to a dark golden color, 7 to 10 minutes. Chill the browned butter until it solidifies, then follow step 2 of the recipe. Add ½ teaspoon ground cardamom along with the powdered sugar.

Chocolate Short Dough

YIELD: Enough for one 9- or 10-inch
single-crusted pie

SPECIAL TOOLS:

Standing electric mixer with a
paddle attachment (optional)

Pie weights (optional)

1½ cups all-purpose flour

½ cup unsweetened cocoa
powder

½ pound (2 sticks) unsalted
butter, softened but
still cool

½ cup powdered sugar

CHOCOLATE TART DOUGH IS ALWAYS A HIT. THIS DOUGH IS *easy to make, and the result is extremely light and delicate. It is perfect for ganache tarts, fruit tarts, and bar cookies. It's a classic French sablée, or "sand dough," which means that only the butter binds the dry ingredients together. The dough is easiest to work with when it is well chilled, but it can be rolled out or pressed into the pan.*

1. Sift together the flour and cocoa powder into a medium bowl and set aside.

2. Place the butter in the bowl of a standing mixer fitted with a paddle attachment. (To mix the dough with a hand mixer, see page 217.) Beat on low speed for 2 to 3 minutes, or until lightly creamed. Stop the mixer and scrape down the sides of the bowl. Add the powdered sugar and mix for 30 seconds. Scrape down the sides of the bowl.

3. Add the flour mixture and mix on low speed just until the dough comes together, about 30 seconds.

4. Remove the dough from the bowl and wrap it in plastic film. Chill for at least 4 hours. At this point, the dough will keep in the refrigerator for up to 3 days or may be rolled out and frozen for up to 1 month.

5. Roll or press out and prebake the dough as directed in Sweet Dough (page 216). Cool on a rack before using.

YIELD: Enough for two 9- or 10-inch
single-crusted pies

SPECIAL TOOLS:

Coffee grinder

Standing electric mixer with a
paddle attachment (optional)

½ cup long-grain white rice

2 cups all-purpose flour

1 teaspoon baking powder

¼ teaspoon salt

½ pound (2 sticks) unsalted
butter, softened but
still cool

¾ cup sugar

2 large egg yolks, at room
temperature

Rice Short Dough

ADDING PULVERIZED RICE TO THIS BASIC SHORT DOUGH IS
*an ingenious way to increase crispness. I use it as a base for my
Halsey Tart (page 324), named after Mr. Halsey, the inventor of the
Twix candy bar.*

*You could use commercial rice flour for this, but I find that it is
ground too fine; I like the unique texture that ground rice gives the
dough. The easiest way to pulverize the rice is in an electric coffee
grinder. Once ground, the rice should resemble ground espresso. Sift
out the larger bits and repulverize to fine powder; you may have to
grind the rice a few times.*

1. Using a coffee grinder, pulverize the rice to a fine powder.
Sift it together with the flour, baking powder, and salt into a medium
bowl. If any large bits of rice remain in the sifter, pulverize them and
sift again. Set aside.

2. Place the butter in the bowl of a standing mixer fitted with a
paddle attachment. (To mix the dough with a hand mixer, see page
217.) Beat on low speed for 2 to 3 minutes, or until lightly creamed.
Stop the mixer and scrape down the sides of the bowl. Add the sugar
and mix on low speed for 1 minute. Scrape down the sides of the
bowl.

3. Add the egg yolks and mix on low speed until incorporated.
Scrape down the sides of the bowl.

4. Add the flour mixture and mix on low speed just until the
dough comes together, about 15 seconds.

5. Remove the dough from the bowl and wrap it in plastic film.
Chill for at least 4 hours. At this point, the dough will keep in the refrigerator for up to 3 days or may be rolled out and frozen for up to 1
month.

6. Roll out and prebake the dough as directed in Sweet Dough
(page 216). Cool on a rack before using.

BRIOCHE

BRIOCHE IS A SLIGHTLY SWEET YEASTED DOUGH, ENRICHED with butter and eggs. I love watching it evolve from a sticky, gooey mess to a silky, strong, beautiful dough. This metamorphosis occurs through kneading, which creates elasticity. After all these years, the process still amazes me.

The classic brioche roll is called *brioche à tête*, or "brioche with a head." It has a topknot and is baked in a little fluted mold. *Brioche à tête* can be found at breakfast tables all over France. Because the richness of this dough lends itself well to both sweet and savory dishes, a pastry department will often be asked to make brioche for the chef's savory dishes. It's commonly used as an accompaniment to foie gras, wrapped around salmon in a coulibiac, or used to cover a *pâté en croûte*. Brioche is also baked in loaves and thinly sliced for tea sandwiches and canapés.

BRIOCHE IS MADE FROM A RICH DOUGH, SO CALLED BECAUSE of its high fat content. Rich doughs like brioche are found in many cuisines. Italian panettone, German stollen, and Jewish challah are a few examples. The shape and flavor of these breads vary. They can be tall, short, long, round, oblong, or ring shaped. They can be studded with fruits, citrus peel, chocolate, nuts, or herbs and spices. Whatever their history or significance, however, these breads are all rich, and they all begin the same way: with water, yeast, flour, and salt.

Bread, which requires a more complex structure than cookies or cakes, needs a flour with a higher protein content. I use mostly bread flour, which is made from high-protein hard wheat and yields a highly elastic dough with excellent structure. All-purpose flour, a blended flour made from hard wheat and lower-gluten soft wheat, can also be used in breadmaking.

The gluten, the elastic component of wheat flour that is crucial for breadmaking, is created from the endosperm, the principal component of the grain, from which the flour is milled. The endosperm is composed of protein and starch. When the proteins are moistened and kneaded, a tight, strong, elastic structure is created. This elasticity allows the dough to stretch without breaking, which is important when the dough rises. The higher the percentage of protein in the flour, the more elasticity created.

ALL THIS ELASTICITY IS NECESSARY WHEN YEAST IS ADDED to the equation. Yeast is a living microscopic fungus. Like you and me, yeast needs oxygen, food, and a warm environment to grow. And like you and me, yeast exhales carbon dioxide. A well-developed gluten structure will trap that carbon dioxide and hold it in the dough. As the yeast continues to feed, it produces more and more carbon dioxide, and the dough, still holding it in, stretches and stretches. This is what happens when dough rises, by a process called *fermentation.*

Fermentation occurs several times in breadmaking. The first time, the liquid, yeast, sugar, and a small amount of flour are mixed together to create a little batter called a *sponge.* It is also known as a *biga* in Italian, a *poolish* in French, a *predough,* or a *preferment.* This step gives the fermentation a head start, which in turn gives the finished bread a more pronounced flavor.

The second fermentation comes after the dough is kneaded and is usually referred to as *rising,* or *doubling.* The longer this process takes, the more flavor develops in the dough. To prolong this fermentation, the

Like you and me, yeast needs oxygen, food, and a warm environment to grow.

dough is often punched. Punching, which is actually a brief knead or fold, deflates the dough, expelling carbon dioxide that has built up and letting fresh oxygen in to feed the yeast, prolonging the fermentation. The dough then doubles again, usually in the refrigerator.

The final fermentation is called the *proof.* This fermentation is quick and takes place when the dough is in the shape of the loaf, just before it gets baked. This one last poof of carbon dioxide from the yeast lightens the texture of the crumb and gives the loaf a fuller, prettier shape. Professional bakers use a proof box, in which the heat and humidity can be controlled. At home, you can create a similar environment by simply covering the loaf with oiled plastic wrap. With regular bread, you can bake the loaf after 20 to 60 minutes, depending on the size of the loaf and the temperature of the dough and the room. Brioche is refrigerated for the second rise, so the final proof takes longer, 1 to 2 hours. If the brioche hasn't been refrigerated, then the final proof will be short, about 20 minutes.

BAKERS CAN CONTROL THE FERMENTATION OF DOUGH IN several ways, including temperature. Because yeast likes to be warm, a cool environment will slow down fermentation. If I am in a hurry, I can speed fermentation by placing the dough near a warm oven. I refrigerate the dough to slow the process down. If the dough is frozen, the yeast goes dormant. When it defrosts, the yeast continues where it left off. If I plan ahead, I prefer to ferment as slowly as possible, because slower fermentation creates bread with more flavor. But for all of these recipes, know that you can always speed up the process by allowing the dough to rise outside the refrigerator. The exception is the rich brioches, which need the long refrigerated rise because they contain so much butter.

Brioche is the king of the fatty breads.

THE PERFECT PROOFING ENVIRONMENT

Professional kitchens use a proof box for rising dough. As with an oven, its temperature can be adjusted and maintained. A heating unit with a reservoir of water controls the humidity. Over the top of this reservoir are holes that can be adjusted to regulate the amount of steam entering the proof box, where the dough rises.

A controlled environment is important for a perfectly baked and consistent product, especially if there's a lot of butter in it. Regulating humidity is crucial because it keeps the dough soft and moist, so a crust cannot form and prevent the dough from rising properly. The ideal humidity level for proofing is 80 percent.

If the temperature is too hot, the perfectly encapsulated butter will seep out instead of staying in the dough. If the dough rises too quickly, it will tear your layers if you're making laminated dough (see page 264). If the dough proofs for too long in an overly warm environment, it will exhaust the yeast's food source and the dough will collapse. Too cold and the yeast can die. All of these situations can cause over-fermentation. The ideal temperature for proofing is 85° to 90°F, but kitchen temperatures can vary from 60° to 90°F. Above all, use your eyes and touch to gauge readiness.

You can make successful bread without a proof box, as most home bakers do. But if you want to try one out, you can create your own. Find the warmest area in your kitchen. Be sure it is cleared off and large enough to place a baking sheet. Heat rises, so the top of your fridge would be a good spot (and good for keeping hungry dogs at bay). Place your bowl or pans inside a large garbage bag with a cup of hot tap water. Gather up the bag and blow into it, as you would a balloon. Tie it up and check halfway through the projected proofing time. Clear bags work great here, since you do not have to open them (releasing humidity) to see how your dough is doing.

Another alternative is to run your dishwasher without detergent, turning it into a steam cabinet. Place the bowl or pans of dough inside the machine on the bottom after the rinse cycle has completed. This is the express (and energy-inefficient) way of proofing.

Brioche

FAMILY TREE

MEDIUM
MASTER BRIOCHE
(25% butter)

Pumpkin Brioche
Bee Schnitten
Coffeecake
Sticky Buns
Stollen

RICH
(40–50% butter)

Panettone
Rich Brioche
Gingerbread Brioche

LEAN
(10–15% butter)

Lean Brioche
Challah
Pâte Savarin
Chocolate Brioche

FRIED
Brioche Doughnuts
Beignets

Variations on the master recipe swap ingredients and vary in shape. Additional fat, mainly butter, creates a richer variation of brioche, while a reduction in fat creates the lean variation. The same dough can be embellished with flavors, fillings, or toppings, baked in small or large forms, or even fried in oil.

The addition of fat can inhibit the fermentation of bread dough. While butter does add tenderness and flavor, it is slippery. Slippery, greased-up gluten has to work extra hard to stretch. Because of this, dough with added fat will rise more slowly and less fully than those without. Brioche is the king of fatty breads.

Fat comes in many forms, many of which are found in brioche. Butter, milk, and eggs all add fat and contribute to the bread's rich texture, flavor, and appearance. Quality ingredients are essential. Unsalted butter should be softened but still cool to the touch. Large fresh eggs work best if used straight from the fridge. These cooler temperatures make handling a rich dough much easier.

Professional bakers prefer to use fresh yeast, also known as *compressed* or *moist* or *cake* yeast, because it is easier to weigh and has a superior flavor. Fresh yeast does not need warm liquid to be activated. It dissolves and blends easily in cold water, which makes the initial mixing quicker but allows a longer fermentation. Fresh yeast can be found in the refrigerated section of many markets. However, if you can't find it, the granulated yeast alternative has been included in each recipe.

WHEN A LOAF OF BREAD BAKES, SEVERAL THINGS OCCUR IN the oven: the proteins solidify, the gas expands, and the moisture evaporates. Understanding the evaporation of moisture is a good way to determine whether a loaf has finished baking. Water is contained in many ingredients: eggs, milk, even butter. When the dough hits the oven, all this moisture begins to evaporate. When the moisture leaves, only air is left in its place. This is why when a finished loaf is thumped, it makes a hollow sound. The finished loaf should also be lighter than the dough was, because it has lost all that heavy water. If the loaf feels heavy, it is

If a loaf feels heavy, it is probably not cooked inside.

probably not cooked inside. To be sure, use an instant-read thermometer. The internal temperature should be 180°F.

LIKE ALL OF THE RECIPES I LOVE, BRIOCHE IS EXTREMELY versatile. By changing the cooking method and handling techniques, I can create hundreds of variations. The recipes in this chapter are not just for bread but also for yeasted cakes, fried doughnuts, fritters, and traditional holiday treats. In fact, I once made a three-tiered brioche wedding cake for a couple. It was baked in wedding cake pans and layered with smoked salmon, onions, capers, and dill. To make it look like a traditional wedding cake, I iced the entire thing in crème fraîche. The guests were surprised, to say the least.

I once made a three-tiered brioche wedding cake for a couple, layered with smoked salmon, onions, capers, and dill.

YIELD: 2½ pounds dough
(see chart, page 233)

SPECIAL TOOLS:

Standing electric mixer with a
paddle attachment or a food
processor

Brioche molds
(*brioche à tête;* optional)

Instant-read thermometer

FOR THE SPONGE

¾ ounce (1 cake) fresh yeast or
2½ teaspoons (1
envelope) active dry yeast

½ cup whole milk, at room
temperature

¼ cup sugar

½ cup bread flour or
all-purpose flour

FOR THE DOUGH

3 cups bread flour or
all-purpose flour

1¼ teaspoons salt

4 large eggs, lightly beaten

½ pound (2 sticks) unsalted
butter, softened but still
cool (see opposite page)

FOR THE EGG WASH

1 large egg, plus 1 large egg
yolk

Master Brioche

BRIOCHE IS THE GATEWAY TO THE LAND OF BREAD. ONCE *you master it, everything else seems easy. It is a very difficult dough to make by hand, and for this reason I recommend using a heavy-duty standing mixer or a food processor. If you use a food processor, you will be able to make only half the quantity, for one very nice brioche. If you use a standing mixer, use the paddle attachment rather than the dough hook, which will just spin and will not adequately work the dough. Once all of the ingredients have been added and you're kneading, if using the paddle attachment seems to strain your machine, switch to the dough hook. Make no mistake: this is a time-consuming project. Make the full recipe that yields two loaves, baking one today and one tomorrow.*

This recipe makes 2½ pounds of dough, which is enough for two standard 9-x-5-inch loaves. All of the recipes in this chapter can also be baked in fluted brioche à tête molds or large coffee cans. The yields tell you how much dough — by weight — the recipe makes. How many loaves that produces depends on how you decide to shape the dough. Refer to the chart on page 233.

When making any dough with a high fat content, the most important factor is temperature. The friction of kneading, which generates heat, the temperature of the room, and the temperature of your ingredients should all be taken into consideration.

Proper kneading is another important element of breadmaking. Stay by the mixer and watch the transformation while the machine kneads the dough. It's a lumpy mass at first, but after 2 minutes it becomes smooth and satiny. Continue mixing for 3 minutes more, and the dough will begin to pull up into a ball. From then on, the dough almost relaxes, reaching and stretching out with elastic fingers. This elasticity is the gluten protein essential for the dough's development and rise. This is the point at which you will add softened butter, a little at a time. When the dough is baked, those strands of elastic protein expand and solidify, creating the crumb of the bread. Breads with a high fat content, like brioche, have a small crumb because the fat makes it hard for the gluten to stretch. Lean loaves, like French bread, have a larger crumb.

I use bread flour for most of these breads, because its high gluten content provides good structure. However, all of the recipes will work well with all-purpose flour, substituted cup for cup.

SPONGE

Combine the yeast and milk in the bowl of a standing mixer fitted with a paddle attachment and whisk until the yeast is dissolved. (To make brioche in a food processor, see page 232.) Stir in the sugar and flour, forming a thick batter. Cover with plastic film and let rest in a warm environment for 30 to 45 minutes. As fermentation begins, bubbles will form.

DOUGH

1. Add the bread flour and salt to the sponge, then add the eggs. Mix on low speed for 2 minutes, or until the eggs are absorbed. Increase the speed to medium and knead the dough for 5 minutes. The dough will eventually begin to slap around and pull away from the sides of the bowl. Then it will form a ball on the paddle. Finally it will relax and reach back out to the sides of the bowl. At this point, it will be a shiny, satiny dough. While all of this is going on, don't walk away. Watch the transformation and hold on to the mixer when necessary, since it may jump around.

2. On medium speed, add the butter, 2 tablespoons at a time. Stop the mixer and scrape down the sides of the bowl occasionally. Knead until the dough is shiny and smooth, about 5 minutes. Scrape out the dough, wash and dry the bowl, and coat it lightly with oil.

3. Place the dough in the oiled bowl and turn it so that the top is coated with oil. Cover with plastic film and let rise at room temperature until doubled in volume, about 2 hours.

4. After the dough has doubled in volume, press down to deflate, folding one half into the other. Fold two or three times, either in the bowl or on a lightly floured surface. (This step is called *punching*.) Cover with plastic film and place in the refrigerator for at least 4 hours or overnight. (If you don't have that much time, you can let the dough rise for the second time at room temperature. It will take 45 to 60 minutes. This applies to all of the medium and lean brioche recipes, but not to the rich brioche.) This is the second rise.

5. Spray two 9-x-5-x-3-inch loaf pans or three 7- or 8-inch *brioche à tête* pans with pan spray.

6. Remove the dough from the refrigerator. Turn it out onto a lightly floured work surface. Divide the dough evenly in half. Cover one

Butter that is softened but still cool — about 65°F — should be firm yet supple. It should yield easily to a knife but should not collapse when pressed gently by a fingertip. It is neither cold nor warm but cool to the touch — room temperature — and shiny but not greasy or mushy.

There are two ways to bring refrigerated butter to room temperature:

- Let stand at room temperature for 1 hour.
- Cream in a standing mixer fitted with the paddle attachment for 2 to 3 minutes.

piece with plastic film while you shape the other. Dust the top of the dough lightly with all-purpose flour. With a rolling pin, roll the dough into a rectangle equal to the length of the pan and double its width. Starting from a short side, roll up the dough like a jellyroll. Pinch the seam together. Place the dough seam side down in the prepared pan. Gently work the dough into the pan with your fingers so that it touches all sides. The dough should fill the pan halfway. Repeat with the remaining dough.

7. Cover the dough with plastic film coated with pan spray and let rise at room temperature until it has doubled in size and filled the pans completely. This step is called *proofing*, and is the final fermentation before the dough is baked. It should take 1½ to 2 hours, depending on the temperature of your room. (If the dough has risen at room temperature the second time, the final proof will be only 15 to 20 minutes. This applies to all of the medium and lean brioche recipes, but not to the rich brioche.)

8. Toward the end of the proofing, preheat the oven to 400°F. Adjust the rack to the center of the oven.

EGG WASH

Most bakers use 1 whole egg, 1 tablespoon water, and a pinch of salt for their egg wash. To get a darker, richer coat on my brioche, I beat together a whole egg with 1 egg yolk, rather than with water.

Whisk together the egg and egg yolk in a small bowl. This will give the finished bread a dark golden brown crust. Gently brush the surface of the dough with the egg wash.

FOOD PROCESSOR BRIOCHE

A food processor works well for mixing small quantities of brioche. If you have a commercial-size machine, you can use the full recipe. If you have a household machine, halve the ingredients. (Your manual should tell you how much dough your processor can handle.)

In a medium bowl, mix the ingredients for the sponge.

After 30 minutes, place the sponge in your food processor. To make the dough, add the flour, salt, and eggs. Pulse for 30 seconds, or until the mixture is smooth and shiny. Add the butter, 2 tablespoons at a time, and pulse for 5 seconds after each addition, or until incorporated. Scrape down the sides of the bowl after each addition. After all of the butter is incorporated into the dough, pulse the machine for 5 seconds more. Scrape out the dough and place in an oiled bowl as directed in step 3 of the master recipe. Since pulsing the dough warms it quite a bit, the dough will probably double more quickly than in the master recipe. Proceed as directed in the master recipe, but check the dough at 30-minute intervals to see if it has doubled.

BAKING

1. Bake for 10 minutes. Turn down the oven temperature to 350°F and bake for 30 minutes more, or until the brioche has a dark golden crust, has an internal temperature of 180°F (stick an instant-read thermometer into the bottom of a loaf so you won't see a hole), and makes a hollow sound when thumped on the bottom.

2. Remove the brioche from the pans as soon as they come out of the oven and cool on a rack before serving. When cool, the loaves can be wrapped tightly in plastic and frozen for up to 2 weeks. To use a frozen loaf, defrost at room temperature, wrap in aluminum foil, and refresh in a 350°F oven for 10 minutes. Tightly wrapped loaves will stay fresh at room temperature for up to 2 days.

BRIOCHE YIELDS

	2 POUNDS DOUGH	2½ POUNDS DOUGH	3 POUNDS DOUGH
	Lean Brioche Chocolate Brioche	Master Brioche	Pumpkin Brioche Rich Brioche Gingerbread Brioche Panettone Stollen
PAN SIZE			
# 10 coffee can	-	-	1
9-x-5-inch loaf pan	2	2	3
BRIOCHE À TÊTE MOLDS			
8 inch	2	2	3
7 inch	3	3	4
6.5 inch	4	5	6
5.5 inch	8	10	12
4 inch	11	13	16
3.5 inch	16	20	24
3 inch	21	27	32
ROUND PANETTONE MOLDS			
9½ inch x 3 inch	-	-	2
8¼ inch x 3 inch	-	-	3
7 inch x 5 inch	-	-	1
5½ inch x 4 inch	-	-	2
3 inch x 2 inch	-	-	6

Variations

❧ *Brioche à Tête:* This is the classic fluted loaf with a topknot. You can prepare 2 large (8-inch) *brioches à tête* or several small ones (pans come in different sizes). Spray fluted brioche pans (or an 8- or 9-inch cake pan) with pan spray and divide the dough into the desired number of portions as instructed in step 6. Instead of flattening the dough and forming it into a jellyroll, shape each piece of dough into a smooth, tight ball. Cover with plastic film coated with pan spray and let sit for 10 minutes. Turn the ball onto its seam, roll it into a fat log, and pinch off the top third of the dough. Shape the large and small balls into rounds. Place the large ball in the center of a prepared pan. Hold the smaller ball in the palm of one hand and, with the other hand positioned at a 45-degree angle, pat the ball out so that it is cone shaped, sort of like the top of a bowling pin. Set aside. Dip your index and middle finger into all-purpose flour and make an indentation in the center of the large ball, pushing your fingers straight down and out to create a hole for the smaller ball of dough. Place the conical piece of dough, smaller end down, in the hole. Push it down so that it's well tucked in, with the topknot sticking out. Cover with plastic film coated with pan spray and proof in a warm environment for 1 hour, or until doubled in size. Brush with egg wash and bake as directed in the master recipe.

❧ *Cinnamon Swirl:* After the dough has been rolled out into a rectangle in step 6, sprinkle the surface with ½ cup sugar mixed with 2 table-spoons ground cinnamon. Roll it up, place it in the prepared loaf pan seam side down, and continue as directed in the master recipe. Once baked, the slices will show a cinnamon swirl.

❧ *Pilgrim Brioche:* Just before removing the completed dough from the mixer, add 2 tablespoons honey, 1 cup rolled oats, ½ cup toasted chopped pecans (to toast, see page 366), and ½ cup raisins.

❧ *Whole Wheat-Honey:* Replace ½ cup of the flour with whole wheat flour. Add ⅓ cup honey along with the eggs. You may need an extra ½ cup of flour.

❧ *Walnut-Beer:* Replace the milk with dark beer. Just before removing the dough from the mixer, add 2 cups diced onion, sautéed and cooled to room temperature (1 cup sautéed). Replace 4 tablespoons of the butter with ¼ cup walnut oil.

Brioche
MEDIUM

YIELD: 3 pounds dough
    (see chart, page 233)

SPECIAL TOOLS:
    Standing electric mixer with
      a paddle attachment or
      a food processor
    Brioche molds
      (*brioche à tête;* optional)
    Instant-read thermometer

FOR THE SPONGE
¾ cup whole milk, at room
    temperature
¾ ounce (1 cake) fresh yeast or
    2½ teaspoons (1 envelope)
    active dry yeast
1 cup pumpkin puree
⅓ cup sugar
1 cup bread flour or
    all-purpose flour

FOR THE DOUGH
5 cups bread flour or
    all-purpose flour
2 teaspoons salt
6 large eggs, lightly beaten
½ pound (2 sticks) unsalted
    butter, softened

FOR THE EGG WASH
1 large egg, plus 1 large
    egg yolk

Pumpkin Brioche

THIS RECIPE MAKES LOVELY ROLLS, AND THE BREAD MAKES *super turkey sandwiches. Rather than cook and puree a fresh pumpkin, I often use canned solid-pack pumpkin. I have also made this with pureed butternut squash, sweet potatoes, red yams, or carrots.*

To puree fresh vegetables, begin by cooking them. Sweet potatoes and yams can be punctured and baked in the oven or microwaved whole, with the skin on. When cool, scoop out the tender center. I prefer to steam carrots, squash, and pumpkin. Peel the vegetable and cut it into large chunks. Place in a steamer basket over simmering water, cover, and cook until tender. Once the vegetables are cooked, puree them in a food processor or put through a potato ricer or food mill fitted with the fine or medium blade.

SPONGE

Combine the milk and yeast in the bowl of a standing mixer fitted with a paddle attachment and whisk until the yeast is dissolved. (To make brioche in a food processor, see page 232.) Let stand for 5 minutes, then stir in the pumpkin puree, sugar, and flour, forming a thick batter. Cover with plastic film and let rest in a warm environment until bubbles form, 30 to 45 minutes.

DOUGH

1. Add the flour and salt to the sponge, then add the eggs. Mix on low speed for 2 minutes, or until the eggs are absorbed. Increase the speed to medium and knead the dough for 5 minutes. The dough will begin to slap around. Hold on to the mixer when necessary.

2. On medium-low speed, add the butter, 2 tablespoons at a time. Stop the mixer and scrape down the sides of the bowl occasionally. Knead until the dough is shiny and smooth, about 5 minutes. Scrape out the dough, wash and dry the bowl, and coat it lightly with oil.

3. Place the dough in the oiled bowl and turn it so that the top is coated with oil. Cover with plastic film and let rise at room temperature until doubled in volume, about 2 hours.

4. After the dough has doubled in volume, press down to deflate, folding one half into the other. Cover with plastic film and place in the refrigerator for at least 4 hours or overnight. This is the second rise.

5. Spray three 9-x-5-x-3-inch loaf pans with pan spray.

6. Remove the dough from the refrigerator. Turn it out onto a lightly floured work surface. Divide the dough evenly into thirds. Cover two pieces with plastic film while you shape the other. Dust the top of the dough lightly with all-purpose flour. With a rolling pin, roll the dough into a rectangle equal to the length of the pan and double its width. Starting from a short side, roll up the dough like a jellyroll. Pinch the seam together. Place the dough seam side down in the prepared pan. Gently work the dough into the pan with your fingers so that it touches all sides. The dough should fill the pan halfway. Repeat with the remaining dough.

7. Cover the dough with plastic film coated with pan spray and let rise at room temperature until it has doubled in size and filled the pans completely, 1½ to 2 hours.

8. Toward the end of the proofing, preheat the oven to 400°F. Adjust the rack to the center of the oven.

EGG WASH

Whisk together the egg and yolk in a small bowl. Gently brush the surface of the dough with the egg wash.

BAKING

1. Bake for 10 minutes. Turn down the oven temperature to 350°F and bake for 30 minutes more, or until the brioche has a dark golden crust, has an internal temperature of 180°F, and makes a hollow sound when thumped on the bottom.

2. Remove the brioche from the pans as soon as they come out of the oven and cool it on a rack before serving. When cool, the loaves can be wrapped tightly in plastic and frozen for up to 2 weeks. Tightly wrapped loaves will stay fresh at room temperature for up to 2 days.

Variation

❧ PUMPKIN ROLLS: Divide the dough into 2-ounce (golf-ball-size) pieces and roll into smooth, tight balls. Proof in pan-sprayed paper-lined muffin cups for easy baking. Brush with egg wash. Just before baking, cut a cross in the tops with scissors. Bake at 350°F for 20 to 25 minutes, or until golden brown.

Bee Schnitten

SCHNITTEN MEANS "CUT" IN GERMAN, AND THIS TRADITIONAL *rich Austrian loaf, whiuch is more like a cake than a bread, is cut in half and filled with sweet pastry cream. It's named* bee *because honey is brushed on top of the loaf before baking, giving each bite a pronounced honey flavor. Warm rum syrup is soaked into the crust of the finished bread for an added layer of flavor.*

YIELD: One 8-x-3-inch round loaf

SPECIAL TOOLS:

Standing electric mixer with a paddle attachment or a food processor

Springform pan (optional)

Parchment paper

Instant-read thermometer

½ recipe Master Brioche (page 230), prepared through step 4, the second rise of dough)

½ cup honey

½ cup blanched almonds, finely chopped

¼ cup sugar

⅓ cup water

3 tablespoons dark rum

1 recipe Pastry Cream (page 100)

1. Coat a 9-x-3-inch round cake pan or a springform pan with pan spray, line with a circle of parchment paper, and spray the paper.

2. Turn the brioche dough out onto a lightly floured work surface. Flatten it gently by hand and form it into a ball by folding the edges into the center. Turn the dough so that the smooth side is up and place it in the prepared pan. Press down on the dough until it fills the pan.

3. Cover the dough with plastic film and let rise for 1½ to 2 hours (15 to 20 minutes if the second rise was at room temperature), or until doubled in size. Toward the end of the proofing, preheat the oven to 400°F. Adjust the rack to the center of the oven, with a baking sheet on the lower rack to catch drips.

4. Heat the honey until just warm in a small saucepan over very low heat. Brush the honey all over the surface of the dough. Sprinkle the top with the almonds.

5. Bake for 10 minutes. Turn down the oven temperature to 350°F and bake for 30 minutes more, or until the *schnitten* has a dark golden crust, has an internal temperature of 180°F, and makes a hollow sound when thumped on the bottom.

6. Cool in the pan on a rack set over a sheet of parchment for 10 minutes, then remove the loaf from the pan and cool on the rack.

7. Bring the sugar, water, and rum to a boil in a small saucepan over medium heat. Remove from the heat. Using a pastry brush, lightly paint the crust of the warm *schnitten* with the syrup. Let the syrup soak in for 5 minutes, then repeat, until all the syrup has been applied.

8. When the loaf has cooled completely, use a serrated knife to slice it in half horizontally. Cover with the Pastry Cream, then replace the top and serve. The tightly wrapped loaf will stay fresh if refrigerated for up to 2 days. Unfilled, the loaf can be wrapped tightly in plastic film and frozen for up to 2 weeks. Defrost slowly in the refrigerator, wrap in aluminum foil, and refresh in a 350°F oven for 10 minutes.

YIELD: One 9-inch round coffeecake

SPECIAL TOOLS:

Standing electric mixer with
a paddle attachment or a
food processor

Parchment paper

Instant-read thermometer

½ recipe Master Brioche
(page 230), prepared
through step 4, the second
rise)

FOR THE FILLING

1 cup golden raisins

1 cup pecans, toasted
(see page 366) and
chopped

⅓ cup sugar

⅓ cup packed light brown
sugar

1 teaspoon ground cinnamon

½ teaspoon freshly grated
nutmeg

FOR THE EGG WASH

1 large egg, plus 1 large egg
yolk

FOR THE ICING

1¼ cups powdered sugar

2 tablespoons milk

½ teaspoon vanilla extract

¼ teaspoon fresh lemon juice

Coffeecake

IN THIS RECIPE, THE DOUGH IS FORMED INTO A RING, THEN *cut and fanned out like a blooming flower. It can just as easily be left in a smooth ring or baked in a loaf pan.*

The filling for this cake calls for golden raisins, my favorite. If you prefer standard dark raisins, dried currants, or any other dried fruit, feel free to substitute. Taste them before adding to the filling. If they seem a bit dry or leathery, plump them in hot water for 30 minutes before adding them.

FILLING

While the brioche dough is rising, combine the raisins, pecans, sugar, brown sugar, cinnamon, and nutmeg in a medium bowl. Set aside.

COFFEECAKE

1. Line a baking sheet with parchment paper.

2. Turn the dough out onto a lightly floured work surface. Using a rolling pin, roll it into a rectangle approximately 12 x 16 inches. Sprinkle the filling evenly over the surface of the dough, leaving a 1-inch margin at the top edge. Starting from the long side closest to you, roll up the dough like a jellyroll. Place the rolled dough seam side down on the prepared baking sheet and form it into a ring.

3. Using a bench scraper or chef's knife, make cuts every 1½ inches around the outside edge of the ring. The cuts should extend three quarters of the way through the roll, making a thick fringe around the outside, as if cinnamon buns were being cut off the roll, but not quite. Take each partially cut section and twist it to the right so that the cut edge is facing up. When all the sections are turned, the coffeecake will look like a blooming flower.

4. Cover the dough with plastic film and let rise at room temperature to proof for 1½ hours (10 to 20 minutes if the earlier second rise was at room temperature), or until the dough feels slightly poofed.

5. Toward the end of the proofing, preheat the oven to 400°F. Adjust the rack to the center of the oven.

EGG WASH

Whisk together the egg and egg yolk in a small bowl. Gently brush the surface of the dough with the egg wash.

BAKING

Bake for 10 minutes. Turn down the oven temperature to 350°F and bake for 25 to 30 minutes more, or until the coffeecake has a dark golden crust and an internal temperature of 180°F. Cool on a rack set over a piece of parchment paper.

ICING

Whisk the powdered sugar, milk, vanilla, and lemon juice in a small bowl until smooth. Drizzle the icing over the top of the warm coffeecake. Serve immediately or let cool to room temperature. Store the coffeecake airtight at room temperature for up to 1 day. An unfrosted cake can be frozen, wrapped airtight, for up to 2 weeks. Reheat in a 200°F oven if desired.

YIELD: 12 large buns

SPECIAL TOOLS:

Standing electric mixer with a paddle attachment or a food processor

Parchment paper

½ recipe Master Brioche (page 230), prepared through step 4, the second rise)

FOR THE TOPPING

¼ pound (1 stick) unsalted butter, softened

¾ cup packed light brown sugar

¼ cup honey

2 tablespoons sugar

½ cup pecans or walnuts, coarsely chopped (optional)

FOR THE FILLING

1 tablespoon ground cinnamon

½ cup sugar

¼ cup raisins (optional)

2 tablespoons milk, at room temperature

Sticky Buns

THERE IS NOTHING QUITE LIKE STICKY BUNS. THIS INDULGENT *bread is merely a cinnamon roll baked on top of a gooey mixture of sugar, butter, and honey. In the oven, the mixture melts and turns into an incredible caramel.*

These buns can be baked individually in special sticky bun pans, muffin pans, or even coffee cups. I have also baked five or six buns together in a cake pan. The buns grow together in the pan for a beautiful, pull-apart cake. Line the pan with parchment and space the buns at least 1 inch apart.

Turn the buns out of the pan as soon as they come out of the oven, or the caramel will harden and make removal very difficult. Try to resist eating them, though, until they have cooled. Hot caramel will burn your tongue and fingers!

While the brioche dough is rising, generously spray a large muffin pan with pan spray, both the cups and on top. Or spray a 9- or 10-inch cake pan and line with parchment paper, then spray the paper.

TOPPING

In the bowl of a standing mixer fitted with a paddle attachment or with a hand mixer, combine the butter, brown sugar, honey, and sugar on medium speed until smooth. Place 1 heaped tablespoon of the topping in the bottom of each muffin cup. If using nuts, divide them evenly among the cups and sprinkle the topping over them.

FILLING AND BUNS

1. Combine the cinnamon, sugar, and raisins (if using) in a small bowl.

2. Turn the dough out onto a lightly floured work surface. Using a rolling pin, roll it into a rectangle approximately 12 x 16 inches. Use a pastry brush to coat the entire surface of the dough with the milk. Sprinkle the filling evenly over the surface of the dough, leaving a 1-inch margin at the top edge. Starting from the long side closest to you, roll up the dough like a jellyroll. Transfer the log to a baking sheet, cover with plastic film, and freeze for 10 minutes. This will make cutting the buns clean and even.

3. Using a bench scraper or chef's knife, cut the log crosswise into 12 pieces, about 1½ inches thick. Place a bun in each muffin cup, cut side up, or arrange them 1 inch apart in the cake pan.

4. Cover the dough with plastic film and let rise for 1½ to 2 hours (10 to 20 minutes if the second rise was at room temperature), or until the buns have doubled in size. At this point, the sticky buns can be wrapped tightly in plastic film and frozen for up to 1 week. Defrost slowly in the refrigerator before baking.

5. Toward the end of the proofing, preheat the oven to 400°F. Adjust the rack to the center of the oven, with a baking sheet on the lower rack to catch drips.

6. Bake for 10 minutes. Turn down the oven temperature to 350°F and bake for 15 to 20 minutes more, or until the crust is golden and the topping is bubbly. Immediately invert them onto a serving platter. If they are not removed immediately, the topping will harden, making them impossible to remove nicely. Do not touch the topping; it's hot! Let the buns cool before serving. Wrapped airtight, sticky buns will stay fresh for up to 2 days at room temperature or frozen for up to 1 week.

YIELD: 3 pounds dough
(see chart, page 233)

SPECIAL TOOLS:

Standing electric mixer with a
paddle attachment

Parchment paper

Instant-read thermometer

FOR THE FRUIT

1 cup finely chopped
dried apricots

½ cup finely chopped
dried cherries

½ cup finely chopped
dried Mission figs

½ cup golden raisins

¾ cup dark rum

FOR THE SPONGE

½ cup whole milk, at room
temperature

1½ ounces (2 cakes) fresh yeast
or 1 tablespoon plus
2 teaspoons (2 envelopes)
active dry yeast

¼ cup sugar

½ cup bread flour or all-
purpose flour

Stollen

HERE IS GERMANY'S ENTRY INTO THE CHRISTMAS BREAD
*hall of fame. A specialty of Dresden, it is properly pronounced
"shtollen." Here the shape is meant to represent the baby Jesus
wrapped in swaddling clothes. The dough is folded to create a ridge,
which, if you squint and stare for a few minutes, looks like a baby.
Stollen calls for almond paste, which you can find at supermarkets.
Almond paste is not as sweet as marzipan.*

*The flavor of the stollen must have time to develop and ma-
ture. If you have the willpower, set the baked bread aside for two
weeks before serving it.*

*When I add almonds to bread, I typically prefer to use whole,
skin-on nuts and coarsely chop them myself. I think the nut skin adds
a nice variation of color. The final butter and sugar coating will
harden into a thick layer, which helps preserve the bread.*

FRUIT

Bring the apricots, cherries, figs, raisins, and rum to a simmer in a
small saucepan over low heat. Cook for 2 minutes, taking care that
the mixture does not ignite. Remove from the heat and set aside at
room temperature to plump until cool, about 1 hour. All of the rum
will be absorbed by the fruit.

SPONGE

Combine the milk and yeast in the bowl of a standing mixer fitted
with the paddle attachment. Let stand for 5 minutes, then stir in the
sugar and flour, forming a thick batter. Cover with plastic film and
let rest at room temperature for about 30 minutes, or until bubbles
form.

FOR THE DOUGH

- 3 cups bread flour or all-purpose flour, plus more if needed
- 2 tablespoons almond paste
- 2 teaspoons finely chopped lemon zest
- 2 teaspoons finely chopped orange zest
- 1 teaspoon salt
- ½ teaspoon ground cardamom
- ½ teaspoon freshly grated nutmeg
- 2 large egg yolks, at room temperature, lightly beaten
- 2 tablespoons cognac or vanilla extract
- ½ pound (2 sticks) unsalted butter, softened
- ½ cup sliced almonds

FOR THE EGG WASH

- 1 large egg, plus 1 large egg yolk

FOR THE COATING

- 1 cup sugar
- ½ cup powdered sugar
- ¼ pound (1 stick) unsalted butter, melted
- 1 tablespoon vanilla extract

FOR DUSTING

- ¼ cup powdered sugar

DOUGH

1. Add the flour, almond paste, lemon zest, orange zest, salt, cardamom, nutmeg, egg yolks, and cognac or vanilla to the sponge. Mix at low speed for 2 minutes, or until the egg yolks are absorbed.

2. On low speed, add the butter, 2 tablespoons at a time. Increase the speed to medium and knead the dough for 5 minutes, or until moist, silky, and slightly sticky. Scrape down the sides of the bowl and the paddle. Cover with plastic film and let rest for 10 minutes.

3. On low speed, add the plumped dried fruits and the sliced almonds and mix until fully incorporated. Alternatively, mix in the fruit by hand, folding the dough over onto itself in sweeping strokes to incorporate all of the fruit evenly. If the dough is very sticky, add up to ¼ cup more flour as you are folding in the fruit. Scrape out the dough, wash and dry the bowl, and coat it lightly with oil.

4. Form the dough into a large round, place it in the oiled bowl, and turn it so that the top is coated with oil. Cover with plastic film and let rise at room temperature for 1 hour, or until doubled in volume.

5. When the dough has doubled in volume, punch it down by folding it two or three times. Cover with plastic film and let rise at room temperature for 30 minutes, or until doubled in volume.

6. Line a baking sheet with a piece of parchment paper. Turn the dough out onto a lightly floured work surface. Flatten it slightly into a 4-x-8-inch rectangle. Dust the dough lightly with flour. Lightly press a rolling pin or the side of your hand down the middle of the length of the rectangle to create a flattened center channel. Your rectangle should expand a little, to measure about 6 x 12 inches, with a fat edge on either side of the channel.

7. Fold the fat bottom part of the dough up so that it lies over the entire channel. Fold the top part of the dough over this, leaving ½ inch of the bottom part showing. Place on the prepared baking sheet. Cover the dough with plastic film coated with pan spray and let it proof for 1 hour.

8. Toward the end of the proofing, preheat the oven to 350°F. Adjust the rack to the center of the oven.

EGG WASH

Whisk together the egg and yolk in a small bowl. Thoroughly brush the loaf with the egg wash.

BAKING

1. Bake for 50 to 60 minutes, or until the stollen has a dark brown crust, an internal temperature of 180°F, and makes a hollow sound when tapped on the bottom. (Test with an instant-read thermometer.)

2. Set the bread on a rack over a sheet of parchment paper.

COATING

1. Whisk the sugar, powdered sugar, melted butter, and vanilla in a small bowl until smooth.

2. Immediately brush the entire loaf with the coating. When it has cooled and hardened, brush with another layer, until all of the coating has been used. When the last layer has been absorbed, dust with the powdered sugar.

3. When the loaf is completely cool, you can serve it, but its flavor will be best if you wrap it tightly in plastic film and set it aside at room temperature to mature for 2 weeks. The loaf can be frozen for up to 2 months. Defrost at room temperature.

Variation

❧ BRAID OR LOAF: This bread can easily be formed into other, more common shapes.

Panettone

THIS FRUIT-PACKED ITALIAN BREAD IS TRADITIONALLY *served at Christmas and on other special occasions. It is sweet, yeasty, light, and perfect with coffee or tea. It also makes great French toast.*

The recipe differs from the other breads in this chapter in that it involves a two-day process. The sponge is held overnight, developing more flavor than standard brioche. With the long fermentation, the butter develops an almost cheeselike flavor. The fruits, too, must macerate for as long as possible, preferably overnight, to hydrate fully and soften. These drunken fruits and the slow fermentation are the key to this rich, flavorful bread.

The traditional panettone pan, made out of tin, glass, or paper, is tall and cylindrical and can be fluted or straight. A springform pan works just as well, as do coffee cans lined with pan spray and parchment paper or buttered brown paper lunch bags.

YIELD: 3 pounds dough
(see chart, page 233)

SPECIAL TOOLS:

Standing electric mixer with paddle and dough hook attachments

Panettone molds (optional)

Parchment paper (optional)

Instant-read thermometer

FOR THE FRUIT

½ cup golden raisins

¼ cup finely chopped candied orange peel

1 vanilla bean, split and scraped

½ cup white wine or verjuice plus ½ cup dark rum, or 1 cup cognac

FOR THE SPONGE

½ cup whole milk, at room temperature

¼ ounce fresh yeast or ½ teaspoon active dry yeast

½ cup bread flour or all-purpose flour

FRUIT

Combine the raisins, orange peel, vanilla bean plus scraped seeds, white wine or verjuice plus rum, or the cognac in a small bowl. Cover with plastic film and set aside to plump overnight at room temperature. Drain off any excess liquid and discard the vanilla bean.

SPONGE

Combine the milk and yeast in the bowl of a standing mixer fitted with a paddle attachment and whisk until the yeast is dissolved. Let stand for 5 minutes, then stir in the flour, forming a thick batter. Cover with plastic film and let rest at room temperature for 4 hours, then transfer to the refrigerator to ferment overnight.

(Recipe continues on page 246.)

FOR THE DOUGH

½ cup water

¾ ounce (1 cake) fresh yeast or 2½ teaspoons (1 envelope) active dry yeast

⅓ cup sugar

1 tablespoon light brown sugar

3½ cups bread flour or all-purpose flour, plus more if needed

¼ cup finely chopped lemon zest

1 teaspoon salt

2 large eggs, chilled, lightly beaten

4 large egg yolks, chilled, lightly beaten

¼ cup amaretto

10 ounces (2½ sticks) unsalted butter, softened but still cool

FOR THE EGG WASH

1 large egg, plus 1 large egg yolk

2 tablespoons unsalted butter, melted

DOUGH

1. Add the water, yeast, sugar, and brown sugar to the sponge. Mix on low speed until incorporated. Add the flour, lemon zest, salt, eggs, egg yolks, and amaretto. Beat on low speed for 2 minutes, or until the eggs are absorbed. Increase the speed to medium and knead the dough for 5 minutes, or until the dough looks smooth and shiny. Cover the dough with plastic film and let it rest at room temperature for 20 minutes.

2. On low speed, add the butter, 2 tablespoons at a time. If the dough seems sticky, add more flour, a little at a time. Turn off the mixer and switch from the paddle to the dough hook. Knead the dough for 8 to 10 minutes, or until firm and satiny. Add the drained fruit and knead until evenly incorporated. Scrape out the dough, wash and dry the bowl, and coat it lightly with oil.

3. Roll the dough into a large round, place it in the oiled bowl, and turn it so that the top is coated with oil. Cover with plastic film and let rise at room temperature for 2 hours, or until doubled in volume.

4. Spray molds or a 10-inch springform pan and line with parchment, or line a baking sheet with parchment.

5. When the dough has doubled in volume, divide it into 6 pieces and roll each piece into a tight ball. Place the balls into the prepared molds or springform pan or 4 inches apart on the baking sheet. Cover them with plastic film coated with pan spray and let rise again at room temperature until doubled in volume, 2 to 3 hours.

6. Toward the end of the proofing, preheat the oven to 350°F. Adjust the rack to the center of the oven.

EGG WASH

Whisk together the egg and yolk in a small bowl. Gently brush the surface of the dough with the egg wash. Using a razor blade or a sharp serrated knife, slice an X in the top of each loaf. Lightly brush the melted butter in the center of each X.

BAKING

Bake for 50 to 60 minutes, or until the loaves are dark golden brown, with an internal temperature of 180°F. Cool in the molds or on the baking sheet on a rack for 10 minutes, then remove and cool completely on the rack before serving. When completely cool, the loaves can be wrapped tightly in plastic film and frozen for up to 2 weeks. Defrost in the refrigerator overnight, wrap in aluminum foil, and refresh in a 350°F oven for 10 minutes. Tightly wrapped loaves will stay fresh at room temperature for up to 2 days.

Rich Brioche

THIS IS NOT YOUR EVERYDAY BREAD, AND ALTHOUGH IT would make a superb peanut butter and jelly sandwich, I do not recommend it as a staple. I save it for special occasions, when I really want to indulge someone.

The large amount of butter in this dough — 1 pound — makes it more sensitive to warm temperatures than the Master Brioche, so refrigeration is critical to this recipe. It also needs a longer rising and proofing time than the Master Brioche and must rise and proof the second time in the refrigerator, again because of all the butter.

YIELD: 3 pounds dough
   (see chart, page 233)

SPECIAL TOOLS:

   Standing electric mixer with a paddle attachment or a food processor

   Brioche molds
   (*brioche à tête*; optional)

   Parchment paper

FOR THE SPONGE

   2 tablespoons water

   1 ounce fresh yeast or 1 tablespoon active dry yeast

   1/3 cup milk

   1/4 cup sugar

   1/2 cup bread flour or all-purpose flour

FOR THE DOUGH

   3 1/2 cups bread flour or all-purpose flour

   2 teaspoons salt

   6 large eggs, chilled, lightly beaten

   2 large egg yolks, chilled

   1 pound (4 sticks) unsalted butter, softened but still cool

FOR THE EGG WASH

   1 large egg, plus 1 large egg yolk

SPONGE

Combine the water and yeast in the bowl of a standing mixer fitted with a paddle attachment and whisk until the yeast is dissolved. (To make brioche in a food processor, see page 232.) Let stand for 5 minutes, then stir in the milk, sugar, and flour, forming a thick batter. Cover with plastic film and let rest at room temperature for 30 to 45 minutes, or until bubbles form.

DOUGH

1. Add the flour and salt to the sponge, then add the whole eggs. Mix on low speed for 2 minutes, or until the eggs are absorbed. Increase the speed to medium and knead the dough for 5 minutes. The dough will begin to slap around. Hold on to the mixer when necessary. Add the 2 egg yolks and knead until absorbed.

2. On medium-low speed, add the butter, 2 tablespoons at a time. Stop the mixer and scrape down the sides of the bowl occasionally. Knead for 5 minutes, or until the dough is shiny; it will be more like a batter than a dough. Scrape out the dough, wash and dry the bowl, and coat it lightly with oil.

3. Place the dough in the oiled bowl and turn it so that the top is coated with oil. Cover with plastic film and let rise at room temperature until doubled in volume, about 2 hours.

4. When the dough has doubled in volume, punch it down by folding it two or three times. Cover with plastic film and refrigerate for at least 4 hours or overnight. This is the second rise.

5. Remove the dough from the refrigerator. Line a baking sheet with parchment paper or spray three 7- or 8-inch *brioche à tête* molds or large muffin pans with pan spray. Divide the dough into 24 golf-ball-size pieces, about 2 ounces each. Roll each piece into a tight ball

and place the balls on the prepared baking sheet or in the muffin cups. Cover with plastic film coated with pan spray. Let rise at room temperature until doubled, 1 to 2 hours.

6. Toward the end of proofing, preheat the oven to 400°F. Adjust the rack to the center of the oven.

EGG WASH

Whisk together the egg and egg yolk. Gently brush each roll with the egg wash. If using muffin cups, just before baking, cut a cross in the tops with scissors.

BAKING

1. Bake for 10 minutes. Turn down the oven temperature to 350°F and bake for 10 minutes more, or until the rolls are golden brown.

2. Transfer the rolls to a rack to cool before serving. Cooled rolls can be wrapped tightly in plastic and frozen for up to 2 weeks. Defrost at room temperature, then refresh in a 350°F oven for 10 minutes. Tightly wrapped rolls will stay fresh at room temperature for up to 2 days.

Variations

⌁ LARGE RICH BRIOCHE LOAVES: In step 5, divide the dough into 2 equal pieces, flatten them, and form into tight rounds by folding the edges to the center. Place seam side down in large brioche pans or cake pans that have been sprayed with pan spray and lined with parchment. Bake as for the rolls, but for a longer period at 350°F, about 40 minutes.

⌁ BRIOCHE MOUSSELINE: When Rich Brioche is baked in a tall, cylindrical mold, it is referred to as *brioche mousseline.* If you look into the window of the Fauchon pastry shop in Paris, you will see this bread standing impressively tall, like a chef's toque, and wrapped in cellophane. Shape the dough into 3 tight balls. In the absence of a mousseline pan, a large coffee can works just fine. Spray and line with parchment. To make removal of the finished loaf easy, be sure to cut three or four holes in the bottom of the can with a can opener and line the sides with a sheet of parchment paper. Bake for 10 minutes at 400°F, then for 30 minutes at 350°F.

Brioche
RICH

YIELD: 2½ pounds dough
(see chart, page 233)

SPECIAL TOOLS:

Standing electric mixer with
a paddle attachment or a
food processor

Brioche molds
(*brioche à tête; optional*)

Instant-read thermometer

FOR THE SPONGE

½ cup whole milk, at
room temperature

1 ounce fresh yeast or
1 tablespoon active
dry yeast

2 tablespoons sugar

½ cup bread flour or
all-purpose flour

FOR THE DOUGH

⅓ cup unsulfured blackstrap
molasses

3 tablespoons packed light
brown sugar

2 tablespoons ground ginger

1 tablespoon ground
cinnamon

1 teaspoon freshly grated
nutmeg

¼ teaspoon ground allspice

¼ teaspoon ground cloves

3½–4 cups bread flour or all-
purpose flour

2 teaspoons salt

6 large eggs, slightly beaten

9 ounces (2 sticks plus
2 tablespoons) unsalted
butter, softened but
still cool

FOR THE EGG WASH

1 large egg, plus 1 large egg
yolk

Gingerbread Brioche

THIS BREAD IS GREAT ON ITS OWN, BUT I MAKE IT
*specifically for French toast and serve it with orange butter (see the
opposite page) and walnut-maple syrup. Be sure to use dark blackstrap molasses, such as Plantation brand, for this. The dough is very
moist.*

SPONGE

Combine the milk and yeast in the bowl of a standing mixer and whisk
until the yeast is dissolved. (To make brioche in a food processor, see
page 232.) Let stand for 5 minutes, then stir in the sugar and flour,
forming a thick batter. Cover with plastic film and let rest at room
temperature for 30 to 45 minutes, until bubbles form.

DOUGH

1. Add the molasses, brown sugar, spices, flour, and salt to the
sponge. Add the eggs. Beat with the paddle attachment on low speed
for 2 minutes, until the eggs are absorbed. Increase the speed to
medium and knead the dough for 5 minutes; it will still be sticky.
Hold on to the mixer when necessary.

2. Turn the machine down to medium-low speed and add the
butter, 2 tablespoons at a time. Knead for another 5 minutes, until
the dough is shiny. Scrape out the dough and clean and lightly oil the
bowl. Don't worry if the dough is difficult to handle.

3. Place the dough in the bowl, then turn it over so that the top
is oiled. Cover with plastic film and let rise at room temperature for
2 hours, until doubled.

4. When the dough has doubled in volume, punch it down by
folding it two or three times. Cover and refrigerate for 4 hours or
overnight.

5. After the second rise, the dough is ready to be shaped. Spray
two 9-x-5-x-3-inch loaf pans with pan spray. Turn the dough out
onto a lightly floured work surface and divide it into 2 equal portions. Using a rolling pin, roll each portion into a rectangle with a
width equal to the length of the pan. Starting from a short side, roll
the dough up jellyroll style. Place the rolled dough into the prepared
loaf pan, seam side down. Cover the dough with pan-sprayed plastic
film. Proof until the dough fills the pans, 1½ to 2 hours.

6. Toward the end of proofing, preheat the oven to 400°F. Adjust the rack to the center of the oven.

EGG WASH

Whisk together the egg and egg yolk in a small bowl. Brush a light coating of egg wash over the surface of the dough.

BAKING

1. Bake for 10 minutes, then turn down the oven temperature to 350°F and bake for at least 30 more minutes, or until the loaves have a dark golden crust, have an internal temperature of 180°F, and make a hollow sound when thumped on the bottom.

2. Immediately remove the loaves from the pans so that condensation does not form on the bottom. Cool on a rack before serving. When cool, the loaves can be wrapped tightly in plastic film and frozen for up to 2 weeks. Defrost in the refrigerator overnight, wrap in aluminum foil, and refresh in a 350°F oven for 10 minutes. Tightly wrapped loaves will stay fresh at room temperature for up to 2 days.

Variation

➤ After you add the butter to the dough, fold in 1 cup chocolate chips, toasted nuts (see page 366), candied citrus, or dried fruits.

Lean Brioche

YIELD: 2 pounds dough
(see chart, page 233)

SPECIAL TOOLS:

Standing electric mixer with a
paddle attachment or a food
processor

Instant-read thermometer

FOR THE SPONGE

2/3 cup whole milk, at room
temperature

1/2 ounce fresh yeast or
2 teaspoons active
dry yeast

1/2 cup bread flour or
all-purpose flour

1/4 cup sugar

FOR THE DOUGH

3 cups bread flour or
all-purpose flour

1 1/2 teaspoons salt

4 large eggs, lightly beaten

1/4 pound (1 stick) unsalted
butter, at room
temperature

FOR THE EGG WASH

1 large egg, plus 1 egg yolk

I USE THIS BRIOCHE WHEN I NEED SLICED BREAD FOR *sandwiches, canapés, or any rich dish. The crumb is tight, with no holes for the sandwich filling or spread to fall through.*

This is the dough for pain de mie, *the French sandwich bread used to create such classics as croque monsieur (grilled ham and cheese) and croque madame (grilled ham and cheese with a fried egg). The bread is baked in a rectangular pan with a tight-fitting lid. When the dough expands in the oven, it is forced into the corners of the pan, which makes for very square slices of bread. Interestingly, the French think of* pain de mie *as an American-style bread.*

Because lean brioche doughs do not have as much fat as the medium and rich brioches, they don't require refrigeration (although it's always an option if you need the time). The second rise can be accomplished at room temperature in 45 minutes to an hour. If the dough rises at room temperature, the final proof will also be much shorter, 15 to 20 minutes.

SPONGE

Combine the milk and yeast in the bowl of a standing mixer fitted with the paddle attachment and whisk until the yeast is dissolved. (To make brioche in a food processor, see page 232.) Stir in the flour and sugar, forming a thick batter. Cover with plastic film and let rest in a warm environment for 30 to 45 minutes, or until bubbles form.

DOUGH

1. Add the flour and salt to the sponge, then add the eggs. Mix on low speed for 2 minutes, or until the eggs are absorbed. Increase the speed to medium and knead the dough for 5 minutes. The dough will begin to slap around. Hold on to the mixer when necessary. If the machine seems strained, switch to the dough hook.

2. On medium-low speed, add the butter, 2 tablespoons at a time. Stop the mixer and scrape down the sides of the bowl occasionally. Knead until the dough is shiny and smooth, about 5 minutes. Scrape out the dough, wash and dry the bowl, and coat it lightly with oil.

3. Place the dough in the oiled bowl and turn it so that the top is coated with oil. Cover with plastic film and let rise at room temperature until doubled in volume, about 2 hours.

4. When the dough doubles in volume, punch it down by folding it two or three times. Cover with plastic film and let rise until doubled in volume, 45 to 60 minutes at room temperature or 4 hours in the refrigerator.

5. Preheat the oven to 400°F. Adjust the rack to the center of the oven. Spray two 9-x-5-x-3-inch loaf pans or other pans with pan spray.

6. Turn the dough out onto a lightly floured work surface and divide into two equal pieces. Using a rolling pin, roll each piece into a rectangle with a width equal to the length of the pan. Starting from a short side, roll up each piece of dough like a jellyroll. Place the rolled dough seam side down in the prepared pans.

7. Cover the dough with plastic film coated with pan spray. Let rise until the dough fills the pan, 10 to 20 minutes if the second rise was at room temperature, 1 to 2 hours if it was refrigerated.

EGG WASH

Whisk the egg and yolk together in a small bowl. Gently brush the surface of the dough with the egg wash.

BAKING

1. Bake for 10 minutes. Turn down the oven temperature to 350°F and bake for 30 minutes more, or until the brioche has a dark golden crust, has an internal temperature of 180°F, and sounds hollow when thumped on the bottom.

2. Cool in the pans on a rack for 10 minutes, then remove the loaves from the pans and cool completely on the rack. When cool, the loaves can be wrapped tightly in plastic film and frozen for up to 2 weeks. Defrost in the refrigerator overnight, wrap in aluminum foil, and refresh in a 350°F oven for 10 minutes. Tightly wrapped loaves will stay fresh at room temperature for up to 2 days.

Brioche
LEAN

YIELD: 1 large braided loaf
or 2 smaller braided loaves

SPECIAL TOOLS:

Standing electric mixer with
paddle and dough hook
attachments or a food
processor

Parchment paper

Instant-read thermometer

FOR THE SPONGE

½ ounce fresh yeast or
2 teaspoons active
dry yeast

1 cup cold water

2 tablespoons honey

1 cup bread flour or all-
purpose flour

FOR THE DOUGH

2½ cups bread flour or
all-purpose flour

1½ teaspoons salt

2 large eggs, lightly beaten

2 large egg yolks, lightly
beaten

2 tablespoons vegetable oil

FOR THE EGG WASH

1 large egg, plus 1 egg yolk

Challah

CHALLAH IS THE TRADITIONAL JEWISH EGG BREAD, SERVED *on the Sabbath and at holidays. Challah cannot contain dairy products, which, according to kosher laws, should not be consumed with meat. Oil is used instead of butter and water instead of milk. Otherwise the ingredients and method are the same. Challah is usually braided but may take other forms on specific holidays. I have given instructions for the typical three-strand braid, but more intricate braids could be made as well.*

SPONGE

Combine the yeast and water in the bowl of a standing mixer fitted with a paddle attachment and whisk until the yeast is dissolved. (To make challah in a food processor, see page 232.) Stir in the honey and flour, forming a thick batter. Cover with plastic film and let rest in a warm environment for 20 to 30 minutes, or until bubbles just begin to form.

DOUGH

1. Add the flour and salt to the sponge, then add the eggs, egg yolks, and oil. Mix on low speed for 2 minutes, or until the eggs are absorbed. Switch to the dough hook, increase the speed to medium, and knead the dough for 8 to 10 minutes, or until it forms a smooth, tight ball. The dough will begin to slap around. Hold on to the mixer when necessary. Scrape out the dough, wash and dry the bowl, and coat it lightly with oil.

2. Place the dough in the oiled bowl and turn it so that the top is coated with oil. Cover with plastic film and let rise at room temperature for 1 hour, or until not quite doubled. On a lightly floured work surface, knead the dough for 1 minute. Return the dough to the oiled bowl, cover, and let rise for 1 hour more, or until doubled.

3. Line a baking sheet with parchment paper. Turn the dough out onto a lightly floured work surface and divide it into 3 equal portions (or 6 for smaller loaves). Roll each piece of dough into a tight ball, then cover with plastic film and let rest for 10 minutes.

4. Form each round of dough into a thick 12-inch rope with tapered ends. Roll up and down with lightly oiled hands, pressing and stretching outward with each roll. Transfer the 3 ropes to the prepared sheet pan. Join them together at one end and braid them all the way down to the end of the ropes, then pinch the ends together. Repeat with the remaining dough if making 2 challahs.

EGG WASH

Whisk together the egg and yolk in a small bowl. Gently brush the surface of the dough with the egg wash.

BAKING

1. Cover the dough with plastic film and proof at room temperature until the dough is 1½ times its original size, 1 to 1½ hours.

2. Toward the end of proofing, preheat the oven to 350°F. Adjust the rack to the center of the oven.

3. Bake for 40 minutes, or until the crust is golden brown and the internal temperature reaches 180°F. Transfer to a rack to cool before serving. When the loaf is completely cool, it can be wrapped tightly in plastic and frozen for up to 2 weeks. Defrost in the refrigerator overnight, in aluminum foil, and refresh in a 350°F oven for 10 minutes. Tightly wrapped loaves will stay fresh at room temperature for up to 2 days.

Variations

- SESAME OR POPPY SEED CHALLAH: After the dough has been braided, proofed, and egg-washed, sprinkle it with sesame or poppy seeds.

- RAISIN CHALLAH: Add 1½ cups plumped raisins to the dough in the last 2 minutes of kneading.

Pâte Savarin

SAVARIN IS A CAKE MADE FROM A VERY SOFT YEASTED dough, baked in a ring mold, then soaked with a spiked sugar syrup. The hole in the center of the savarin is generally filled with whipped cream and garnished with seasonal fruits. The dough is also used for the yeasted cake baba au rhum. Babas are similar to the savarin but generally contain currants and don't have the ring shape.

YIELD: 2 dozen 3-inch savarins

SPECIAL TOOLS:

Standing electric mixer with a paddle attachment or a food processor

2 dozen 3-inch savarin molds

Parchment paper

FOR THE SPONGE

½ ounce fresh yeast or 2 teaspoons active dry yeast

½ cup whole milk, at room temperature

½ cup bread flour or all-purpose flour

¼ cup sugar

FOR THE DOUGH

1½ cups bread flour or all-purpose flour

½ teaspoon salt

4 large eggs, lightly beaten

6 tablespoons (¾ stick) unsalted butter, softened

FOR THE SYRUP

2 cups sugar

1 quart water

¼ cup dark rum

FOR THE GLAZE

½ cup apricot jam

2 tablespoons water

SPONGE

Combine the yeast and milk in the bowl of a standing mixer fitted with a paddle attachment and whisk until the yeast is dissolved. (To make pâte savarin in a food processor, see page 232.) Let stand for 5 minutes, then stir in the flour and sugar, forming a thick batter. Cover with plastic film and let rest at room temperature for 30 to 45 minutes, or until bubbles form.

DOUGH

1. Add the flour and salt to the sponge, then add the eggs. Mix on low speed for 2 minutes, or until the eggs are absorbed. Increase the speed to medium, and knead the dough for 5 minutes. Hold on to the mixer when necessary.

2. On medium-low speed, add the butter, 2 tablespoons at a time. Stop the mixer and scrape down the sides of the bowl occasionally. Mix until the dough is shiny and smooth, about 5 minutes.

3. Cover the bowl with plastic film and let rise at room temperature until doubled in volume, about 2 hours.

4. Preheat the oven to 400°F. Adjust the rack to the center of the oven. Spray the savarin molds lightly with pan spray.

5. Spoon the dough into the prepared molds until they are half full. Use your fingertips to spread it evenly. Cover them with plastic film coated with pan spray and let rise at room temperature until they double in volume, about 30 minutes.

6. Bake for 12 to 15 minutes, or until golden brown. Let cool in the molds on a rack for 10 minutes, then remove from the molds and cool on the rack. At this point, the savarins can be stored, tightly wrapped, in the freezer for up to 2 weeks or at room temperature overnight.

I. Bring the sugar, water, and rum to a boil in a small saucepan over medium heat. Cook until the sugar is dissolved, about 2 minutes.

2. Transfer the syrup to a wide bowl. Dip each savarin into the hot syrup, one at a time. Turn the savarin over to coat both sides (it should be saturated with syrup), then place on a rack set over a piece of parchment paper. Be careful, since the savarins are delicate.

GLAZE

Combine the apricot jam and water in a small saucepan over medium heat. Stir until the jam is liquefied and thin. Using a pastry brush, coat the top of each savarin with hot glaze. Serve the savarins warm or at room temperature.

Variation

    LARGE SAVARIN: Bake in a large (9-inch) savarin mold for 10 minutes at 400°F. Turn the oven down to 350°F and bake for 15 to 30 minutes more, or until golden.

YIELD: 2 pounds dough
(see chart, page 233)

SPECIAL TOOLS:
Standing electric mixer with paddle and dough hook attachments

Instant-read thermometer

FOR THE CHOCOLATE BUTTER
2 ounces bittersweet chocolate, finely chopped

¼ pound (1 stick) unsalted butter, softened

¼ cup unsweetened cocoa powder

FOR THE SPONGE
¾ ounce (1 cake) fresh yeast or 2½ teaspoons (1 envelope) active dry yeast

¼ cup warm water

¾ cup lukewarm (80ºF) brewed coffee

½ cup bread flour or all-purpose flour

⅓ cup sugar

FOR THE DOUGH
3 cups bread flour or all-purpose flour

1¾ teaspoons salt

4 large egg yolks, lightly beaten

4 ounces bittersweet chocolate, finely chopped

FOR THE EGG WASH
1 large egg yolk

1 tablespoon heavy cream

Chocolate Brioche

THIS IS AS DECADENT AS BREAD GETS. IT IS GOOD ON ITS *own, but it also makes great French toast and incredible bread pudding. Or try making tea sandwiches. Thinly slice the bread and fill it with ganache (see page 10), peanut butter and banana, raspberry jam, or toasted marshmallows.*

CHOCOLATE BUTTER

Place the chocolate in a small heatproof bowl. Fill a small saucepan three-quarters full of water and bring it to a simmer over medium heat. Place the bowl of chocolate over the simmering water, creating a double boiler, and stir until melted, about 2 minutes. Set the chocolate aside at room temperature. In the bowl of a standing mixer fitted with a paddle attachment, cream the butter until soft and lump free, about 1 minute. Add the cocoa powder and the cooled melted chocolate and beat until well incorporated. Set the chocolate butter aside at room temperature.

SPONGE

Combine the yeast and water in the bowl of a standing mixer fitted with the paddle attachment and whisk until the yeast is dissolved. Let stand for 5 minutes, then stir in the coffee, flour, and sugar, forming a thin batter. Cover with plastic film and let rest at room temperature for about 30 minutes, or until bubbles form.

DOUGH

1. Sift together the flour and salt into the sponge, then add the egg yolks. Mix on low speed for 2 minutes, or until the egg yolks are absorbed. Increase the speed to medium and knead the dough for 5 minutes, or until smooth and satiny.

2. On medium-low speed, add the chocolate butter, 1 tablespoon at a time. Stop the mixer and occasionally scrape down the sides of the bowl. Switch to the dough hook. Mix until the dough is shiny and smooth, about 5 minutes. Add the chocolate and knead until incorporated. Scrape out the dough, wash and dry the bowl, and coat it lightly with oil.

3. Shape the dough into a large round, place it in the oiled bowl, and turn it so that the top is coated with oil. Cover with plastic film and let rise at room temperature until doubled in volume, about 2 hours.

4. When the dough doubles in volume, punch it down by folding it two or three times. Cover with plastic film and let rise until doubled in volume, in the refrigerator for 4 hours or overnight, or at room temperature for 45 to 60 minutes.

5. Spray two 9-x-5-x-3-inch pans with pan spray. Turn the dough out onto a lightly floured work surface and divide it in half. Cover one half loosely with plastic wrap while you shape the first loaf. Using a rolling pin, roll it into a rectangle with a width equal to the length of the pan. Starting from a short side, roll up the dough like a jellyroll. Place the rolled dough seam side down into the prepared pan. Repeat with the remaining dough.

6. Cover with plastic film coated with pan spray and proof until the dough fills the pans, 15 to 20 minutes if the dough is at room temperature, 1½ to 2 hours if it's cold.

7. Toward the end of proofing, preheat the oven to 350°F. Adjust the rack to the center of the oven.

EGG WASH

Whisk the egg yolk and cream together in a small bowl. Gently brush the surface of the dough with the egg wash.

BAKING

1. Bake for 40 to 45 minutes, or until the loaves have an internal temperature of 180°F and sound hollow when thumped on the bottom.

2. Remove the finished loaves from the pans and cool on a rack before serving. When cool, the loaves can be wrapped tightly in plastic and frozen for up to 2 weeks. Defrost in the refrigerator overnight, wrap in aluminum foil, and refresh in a 350°F oven for 10 minutes. Tightly wrapped loaves will stay fresh at room temperature for up to 2 days.

Brioche Doughnuts

HOW CAN YOU LOSE WITH THE COMBINATION OF DOUGH, *sugar, and deep frying? These doughnuts are incredibly indulgent.*

I like to use a neutral oil, such as safflower, so the doughnuts won't pick up an oil flavor. It is very important to use a candy or deep-frying thermometer to monitor the temperature. Frying below 360°F will cause the oil to be absorbed, resulting in greasy dough-nuts. Oil above 375°F will form a crust too quickly, which results in a smaller doughnut that is raw inside. It is important to note that most oils ignite at 500°F. Keep water away from frying oil. If flames should erupt, cover the pan to suffocate the fire.

YIELD: 2 dozen 2½-inch doughnuts

SPECIAL TOOLS:

Standing electric mixer with paddle and dough hook attachments or a food processor

Doughnut cutter or two round cutters of graduated size

Deep fryer (optional)

Candy thermometer

FOR THE SPONGE

¾ ounce (1 cake) fresh yeast or 2½ teaspoons (1 envelope) active dry yeast

½ cup whole milk, at room temperature

½ cup all-purpose flour

1 tablespoon light brown sugar

FOR THE DOUGH

3 cups all-purpose flour

1 teaspoon salt

½ teaspoon ground cardamom

¼ teaspoon ground cinnamon

4 large eggs, lightly beaten

¼ pound (1 stick) unsalted butter, softened

1 quart safflower or sunflower oil for frying

1 cup sugar for coating, or more to taste

SPONGE

Combine the yeast and milk in the bowl of a standing mixer fitted with the paddle attachment and whisk until the yeast is dissolved. (To make brioche doughnuts in a food processor, see page 232.) Let stand for 5 minutes, then stir in the flour and brown sugar, forming a thick batter. Cover with plastic film and let rest at room tempera-ture for 30 to 45 minutes, or until bubbles form.

DOUGH

1. Add the flour, salt, cardamom, and cinnamon to the sponge, then add the eggs. Mix on low speed for 2 minutes, or until the eggs are absorbed. Switch to the dough hook, increase the speed to medium, and knead the dough for 5 minutes, or until the dough be-gins to slap around.

2. On medium-low speed, add the butter, 2 tablespoons at a time. Stop the mixer and occasionally scrape down the sides of the bowl. Knead until the dough is shiny and smooth, about 5 minutes. Scrape out the dough, wash and dry the bowl, and coat it lightly with oil.

3. Place the dough in the oiled bowl and turn it so that the top is coated with oil. Cover with plastic film and let rise at room tempera-ture until doubled in volume, about 2 hours.

4. When the dough has doubled in volume, punch it down by folding it two or three times. Cover with plastic film and let rise at room temperature until doubled in volume, about 45 minutes.

5. Turn the dough out onto a lightly floured work surface. Using a rolling pin, roll it out to a thickness of ½ inch. If the dough

is difficult to handle after rolling, place it in the freezer for 20 minutes. Cut the dough using a doughnut cutter or two round cutters of graduated size. Dip the cutters in flour each time to make it easier. Once cut, the dough can be stored in the freezer for up to 1 week. Defrost in the refrigerator and let sit at room temperature for 10 to 15 minutes before frying.

6. Heat the oil in a heavy skillet, wide, heavy saucepan, or deep fryer over medium heat. Insert a candy thermometer. When the oil reaches 350° to 360°F, carefully place 4 or 5 doughnuts in the oil. Fry for 1 minute, then use a slotted spoon to flip them over carefully. Fry the other sides for 1 minute, then flip the doughnuts again and fry for 30 seconds more, or until dark golden brown. Remove the doughnuts from the oil and drain them on paper towels for 30 seconds before coating them with the sugar. Repeat with the remaining doughnuts. Serve immediately. Fried doughnuts stay fresh for only about 2 hours.

Variations

- CINNAMON-SUGAR: Combine 1 cup sugar with 2 tablespoons ground cinnamon. Coat the top of the doughnuts with the mixture while they are still hot and wet with oil. If they cool down and dry, the sugar will not stick.

- POWDERED SUGAR: When the doughnuts have cooled and the oil has dried, sift powdered sugar generously on top. If the powdered sugar goes on when the doughnuts are hot and wet, the oil will soak it all up.

- GLAZED: Combine 2 cups powdered sugar, ¼ cup milk, and 1 teaspoon vanilla extract in a small bowl. Drizzle the mixture over the hot doughnuts and let dry.

- CHOCOLATE-GLAZED: Combine 4 ounces bittersweet chocolate and ¼ pound (1 stick) unsalted butter in a small bowl. Place the bowl over a pot of simmering water and stir until melted. Or combine the chocolate and butter in a microwave-safe bowl and melt in the microwave at 50 percent power. Dip the top of each doughnut into the chocolate. Before the glaze sets, top each doughnut with candy sprinkles, jimmies, chopped nuts, or coconut.

YIELD: 4 dozen fritters

SPECIAL TOOLS:

Standing electric mixer with paddle and dough hook attachments or a food processor

Deep fryer (optional)

Candy thermometer

FOR THE SPONGE

½ cup water, at room temperature

¾ cup evaporated milk, at room temperature

½ ounce yeast or 2 teaspoons active dry yeast

½ cup bread flour or all-purpose flour

FOR THE DOUGH

¼ cup water

3 cups bread flour or all-purpose flour

1 teaspoon salt

1 large egg, lightly beaten

2 tablespoons unsalted butter, softened

1 quart safflower or sunflower oil for frying

2 tablespoons powdered sugar for dusting

Beignets

HERE IS ANOTHER CONFUSING CULINARY TERM. LIKE *pralines and parfait,* beignet *has multiple meanings. In France, anything fried in batter can be called a beignet. Apples, bananas, peaches, and plums are commonly dipped in batter and fried this way, as are savory foods, such as cheese, squash blossoms, green beans, and even crab.*

But in New Orleans beignets can mean only one thing: square doughnuts doused in powdered sugar and served with chicory coffee au lait. You cannot leave the city without trying at least one beignet at the Café du Monde. It has been in the French Quarter, serving the same menu with little variation, since 1862.

SPONGE

Combine the water, evaporated milk, and yeast in the bowl of a standing mixer fitted with the paddle attachment and whisk until the yeast is dissolved. (To make beignets in a food processor, see page 232.) Let stand for 5 minutes, then stir in the bread flour, forming a thin batter. Cover with plastic film and let rest at room temperature for 30 to 45 minutes, or until bubbles form.

DOUGH

1. Add the water, flour, and salt to the sponge, then add the egg. Mix on low speed for 2 minutes, or until the egg is absorbed. Add the butter. Switch to the dough hook. Increase the speed to medium and knead the dough for 8 to 10 minutes, or until smooth and satiny. Scrape out the dough, wash and dry the bowl, and coat it lightly with oil.

2. Place the dough in the oiled bowl and turn it so that the top is coated with oil. Cover with plastic film and let rise at room temperature until doubled in volume, about 2 hours.

3. Turn the dough out onto a lightly floured work surface. Using a rolling pin, roll it out to a thickness of ¼ inch. Using a chef's knife or rolling pastry wheel, cut the dough into 2-inch squares. Cover the squares with plastic film and let rest for 10 minutes. Keep them covered with plastic film until they are fried.

4. Heat the oil in a heavy skillet, wide, heavy saucepan, or deep fryer over medium heat. Insert a candy thermometer. When the oil reaches 350° to 360°F, carefully place 4 or 5 beignets in the oil. Fry for 1 minute, then use a slotted spoon to flip them over carefully. Fry for 1 to 2 minutes more, or until golden brown. Carefully remove the beignets from the oil and drain them on paper towels. Repeat with the remaining beignets. Sift powdered sugar over the tops, and serve immediately. Fried beignets stay fresh for only about 2 hours.

Variation

✎ JELLY-FILLED: Roll out the dough to ⅛ inch thick and cut it into squares. Place a dollop of raspberry jam in the center of one square, then moisten the edges with a little water. Place another square on top and press to seal. Fry as directed.

LAMINATED DOUGH

LAMINATED DOUGH, OR ROLL-IN, AS IT IS SOMETIMES called, consists of many alternating layers of dough laminated with thin sheets of butter. Puff pastry is the most recognizable of these doughs. A tradition that has been handed down over many generations of bakers, it is nothing short of magic.

What begins as simple dough wrapped around butter, then rolled and folded in a layering process, results in an endlessly versatile product that is easily transformed into hundreds of different desserts. Once baked to perfection, it yields a deep, nutty, and flaky pastry like no other, which can puff up miraculously to eight times its original height. Sure, it takes a long time, and it's tricky, but laminated dough is the quintessential mark of a great pastry chef. And yes, you can buy puff pastry in the freezer section (many chefs do), but if you have the patience, precision, and care to make it by hand, you may get hooked. The laminated dough you make yourself will be crisper, more delicate, and airier than commercial dough. It will not be greasy, and it will taste better, because you will have given the flavors a longer time to develop.

LAMINATED DOUGH IS MADE UP OF TWO COMPONENTS: a ball of dough, known in French as the *détrempe,* and a butter block, known in French as the *beurrage,* or *beurre de tourage.* The two are sandwiched together (in French this is called the *paton*), then rolled out and folded many times. Each fold and roll of a laminated dough is called a *turn,* and each turn results in several thin layers of dough alternating with thin layers of butter. When the dough hits the heat of the oven, the water contained within each layer of butter evaporates into steam. The steam rises and pushes up the layers of *détrempe.* The end product is a pastry with many flaky layers.

The *détrempe* is a lean, rustic-looking, nonelastic dough made of flour, salt, butter, and water. It will have the best texture and a more even rise if it has plenty of time to rest. Laminated doughs have varying types of *détrempe,* some with leavening, some without. Puff pastry contains no yeast and relies on a high percentage of butter and an elaborate rolling method to create the steam that will raise the dough. The other laminated doughs in this chapter—croissant dough, Danish dough, and laminated brioche—are yeasted. In croissant dough, water is replaced by milk. In Danish dough, milk, eggs, and sugar are used. This makes Danish rich, tender, and elastic. Laminated brioche is the richest of these doughs, containing the highest amount of butter and eggs. Try them all and choose your favorite. Because all of these doughs contain a considerable amount of butter, it is difficult to make them without a standing mixer.

The butter block can be simply butter or butter mixed with flour. The flour assists in breaking down the butter, which makes rolling in easier, but too much flour will inhibit the dough from puffing. The butter block should be neither too small nor too big. If there's too little butter in the *beurrage,* your layers will be too thin; the butter will tear when you roll out the dough, and thin layers won't have the rise that defines puff pastry. If the butter layer is too thick, it will melt out of the dough. The more butter you use in the *beurrage,* the more layers your finished dough will require.

Laminated dough is one that contains many alternating layers of dough laminated with thin sheets of butter.

TEMPERATURE IS A KEY ELEMENT IN SUCCESSFUL ROLLING. The *détrempe* and *beurrage* should have the same feel (somewhat like firm clay) and temperature—about 40°F. If the butter block is significantly softer and warmer than the *détrempe,* there is a good chance it will squirt out when you roll out the dough. Soft butter is fluid and will find its way

Laminated Dough
FAMILY TREE

MASTER PUFF PASTRY
Palmiers

Apple Turnovers

PLUS YEAST

Croissant Dough
Classic Croissants
Pain au Chocolat

Danish Dough
Danish Envelopes
Danish Braid

Laminated Brioche
Cinnamon Twists
Cinnamon-Raisin Snails

The laminated family tree begins with puff pastry. More voluptuous doughs are created by adding combinations of yeast and enriching ingredients, such as more butter, milk, and eggs. Croissant dough has added yeast, milk, and extra butter; Danish has yeast, milk, and eggs. Laminated brioche is the richest by far, with yeast, milk, eggs, and a full pound of butter, extending the family to new heights. The richer the dough, the more soft and tender the result.

through weak portions of the dough. If the butter oozes, pinch off the butter that has oozed out. Dip your fingers in flour and pinch the dough back together. Refrigerate the pinched-off butter and the dough for 15 minutes. Roll out the dough as instructed, and before folding smear the ooze evenly onto the center of the dough. Continue the folding process and refrigerate until the next turn.

If the butter block is chilled too solidly and is colder and harder than the dough, rolling can be equally problematic. When butter is cold, spreading it is difficult. Instead of spreading, cold butter cracks and shatters. The cracked, shattered butter will be visible through the *détrempe* and could possibly tear it. The resulting dough will rise unevenly. If you find yourself in this situation, lightly dust the butter with flour and bang it several times with a rolling pin to soften it.

EACH FOLD OF A LAMINATED DOUGH IS CALLED A *TURN*. THIS term is something of a misnomer, because the dough is really being folded. The word actually refers to the three-step process of rolling out, folding, then refrigerating the dough. There are two types of turns, and they work equally well. The simplest turn is the single turn. It is a three-fold one, done exactly like a business letter. The rectangular sheet of dough is marked into three equal columns. One side is folded over the center third, and the opposite side is folded on top. Each time a turn is made, the dough triples its layers. Dough made using this method requires six turns, resulting in more than 1,400 layers.

The second type of turn is called a *double turn,* or *book turn.* The dough is marked into four columns. The two edges are folded to meet in the center, and then the left edge is folded over, as if closing a book. Each time a double turn is made, the dough quadruples its layers. Dough made using double turns requires only four turns, resulting in

What begins as a simple dough wrapped around butter, then rolled and folded in a layering process, results in an endlessly versatile product.

more than 750 layers. The double turn is not used in these recipes but could easily be applied to any of them. The benefit of using double turns is that the dough will be ready to bake sooner, since there are only four turns. You can determine which is best for you.

A rolling pin with handles is the best choice for rolling out laminated dough. It provides crucial leverage and can be rolled in longer, more continuous strokes than a dowel pin. Long, continuous passes are more effective than short, jerky rolls for spreading the butter evenly. Try to roll the pin over the entire piece of dough, switching directions each time. Turn the dough to make this easier and dust it with flour.

With each turn, brush excess flour off the surface of the dough with a dry pastry brush. Pockets of flour rolled into the layers inhibit the rise. When making each fold, line the edges up as flush as possible. If the corners are rounded, ease them into a square angle.

Each laminated dough recipe calls for a 30-minute resting period between turns. This is vitally important. The chilled rest serves two purposes: after excessive rolling, the butter needs to resolidify, and the gluten needs to relax. Warm butter and tight gluten are difficult to roll out effectively. Don't cheat on this step. It is also essential that you complete the first four turns back to back. The remaining turns can be accomplished hours later. By the fourth turn, the butter and dough have been distributed into even layers.

In baking, color generally equals flavor.

❧

WHEN SHAPING LAMINATED DOUGH INTO PASTRIES, KEEPING it cool is crucial. Well-chilled dough has a smooth, silky, but strong texture and is easier to handle and shape. For this reason, once the dough is completed and rolled out to the desired thickness, I recommend that you place it on a baking sheet in the freezer. When the dough is very cold, it must be cut and shaped as efficiently as possible. Unlike with cookie dough, scraps cannot simply be wadded together and rerolled. They will lose their layers and will not rise nearly as well as fresh dough. Layer excess scraps, wrap in plastic film, and refrigerate for 20 minutes. Roll them out and use for sacristains (page 273), which do not require a high rise.

Laminated dough must be baked at a high temperature. If the dough is heated too slowly, the fat will melt before the water evaporates. The pastries will come out of the oven in small puddles of melted butter, with little rise from steam.

Americans seem to prefer their pastries blonder than Europeans do. But in baking, color generally equals flavor. The dark color comes from the caramelization of the sugars present in the flour. I prefer deep brown pastries.

Each laminated dough recipe calls for a 30-minute resting period between turns. This is vitally important.

PASTRY MYSTERY

I once had two assistants, Tess, a dainty 5-foot, 2-inch girl, and Ken, a burly 6-foot, 4-inch guy. Both were responsible for making croissant and puff pastry during their shift. She made beautiful puff pastry but had difficulty with croissant dough. He made great croissant dough but horrible pastry.

I eventually decided to walk through the recipes with them so that I could figure out what they were doing wrong. I watched Tess work gently with the rolling pin, perfect for the many thin layers of puff pastry. Hard rolling with a pin can quickly bruise and smoosh the many layers, resulting in a poor rise once the pastry is baked. When she made the tight, glutinous yeasted croissant dough, however, she did not have the muscle needed to roll it out evenly.

When I watched the brawny giant, I discovered the opposite problem. He worked the puff pastry to death, pounding down on the dough with tremendous strength. When he applied the same force to his croissant, the result was an even and controlled dough.

The elements in pastry determine how you work with it — in this case how you roll in the layers of puff pastry and yeasted croissant dough.

Master Puff Pastry

SPECIAL TOOLS:

> Standing electric mixer with
> a paddle attachment (optional)
>
> Parchment paper

FOR THE DOUGH (*Détrempe*)

> 2 cups bread flour (see
> headnote)
>
> 1 cup all-purpose flour
>
> 2 teaspoons salt
>
> ¼ pound (1 stick) cold unsalted
> butter, cut into ½-inch
> pieces
>
> 1 cup ice water, ice strained
> out
>
> 1½ teaspoons white wine
> vinegar or Champagne
> vinegar

FOR THE BUTTER BLOCK (*Beurrage*)

> ¾ pound (3 sticks) cold
> unsalted butter
>
> ¼ cup all-purpose flour

THE FRENCH NAME FOR PUFF PASTRY IS *PÂTE FEUILLETÉE*, which means "pastry leaves." It refers to the flaky layers of dough created by multiple turns. Napoleons (see page 312) are my favorite dessert to create with puff pastry.

The détrempe for puff pastry should be a bit rustic-looking. Since there's no sugar in puff pastry, it's great for both sweet and savory preparations.

Six single turns are required for this dough. For best results, roll the last two turns the next day. After the last turn, allow 30 minutes before rolling out the dough.

Once the dough is rolled out, if you don't plan to bake it right away, the sheets are best wrapped airtight in plastic film and frozen uncooked. Vinegar reduces the leavening power of puff pastry, so omit if storing the dough in the freezer.

I always use some bread flour in my laminated doughs, because it lends structure to the dough. But you may substitute all-purpose if bread flour is not available.

DOUGH

1. Combine the bread flour, all-purpose flour, and salt in the bowl of a standing mixer fitted with the paddle attachment. Add the butter and mix for 30 seconds on low speed. Stop the mixer and flatten any fat pieces of butter with your fingers. Scrape down the sides of the bowl. Mix for 30 seconds more, or until the butter is barely visible. (To mix by hand, use a large bowl and cut the butter in with a wire pastry cutter or your fingers.)

2. On low speed, stream the ice water and vinegar into the bowl. Stop the mixer, scrape down the sides of the bowl, and pull up flour from the bottom. Mix on low speed until a rustic dough forms, about 1 minute.

3. Transfer the dough to a floured work surface. Roll the dough into a ball. Using a sharp knife, cut an X extending halfway through the dough. This will expand as the dough relaxes and will aid in rolling later.

4. Cover the dough with plastic film and let rest in the refrigerator for at least 2 hours or overnight.

BUTTER BLOCK

Cut each butter stick in half lengthwise. Place on a piece of lightly floured parchment paper and dust the top with flour. Using a rolling pin, gently bang the butter to tenderize it. Four taps should do it. Form the butter into a 6-inch square, about 1 inch thick.

LAMINATING

1. Remove the dough from the refrigerator and unwrap it. Lightly dust your work surface with all-purpose flour. The dough should be 40°F and feel like firm clay. Place the dough on your work surface and dust the top of the dough with flour.

2. Using a rolling pin, roll the dough out from the center to each corner, following the X shape. Roll three times in one direction, then stop and turn the dough 180 degrees. Dust with flour as necessary and roll out, turning it after every three rolls, to a 12-inch square about ½ inch thick.

3. Place the square butter block like a diamond into the center of the dough X. Fold each corner of dough up and over the butter block like an envelope, leaving no air pockets. Press and pinch the edges together with your fingers to complete the seal. Be sure that the butter is completely concealed by the dough.

4. Lightly flour the work surface and dough. Using a rolling pin, tap the top of the dough, working toward you to seal the butter in. Turn a quarter turn and dust with flour if necessary. Tap again until the dough is flat enough to roll, about 1 inch thick. Now begin to roll the dough, repeating the X rolling technique as you move from the center to the corners. Keep moving the dough, dusting with flour when necessary and always rolling away from you. Roll the dough first to a 12-inch square, then vertically until you have a rectangle, about 10 x 18 inches and ½ inch thick. Roll in long, continuous strokes, passing over the entire surface of the dough each time. Do not roll over the ends of the dough.

5. Turn the dough so that it is horizontal, with a longer edge nearest to you. With a dry pastry brush, dust any excess flour off the surface. Mark the rectangle into 3 equal columns. Fold the right third of the rectangle over the center third. Fold the left third over the center third, like a business letter. The first turn has now been completed.

Now it is time to lock in this turn. Place the rolling pin on an unsealed edge of the dough, gently press down to keep it in place, and repeat with the remaining two sides. Now roll over the dough with four even strokes, two up, two down. Lock in the corners again (you will be so happy when you pull the dough out to roll the next turn, because the locking in assists in creating a perfect, more manageable rectangle). Dust off any excess flour. Wrap airtight in plastic film, place on a baking sheet, and refrigerate for 30 minutes. Using a marker, gently create a line for each turn. This will help you keep track.

6. After 30 minutes, place the rectangular dough lengthwise on a lightly floured work surface. The open ends should be to your right and left. Using a rolling pin, roll the dough out into another horizontal rectangle ½ inch thick. Fold the right third over the center third and the left third over that. The second turn has now been completed. Wrap airtight, mark the turn number, and refrigerate for 30 minutes.

Variations

  ❧ HEAVY CREAM PUFF PASTRY: Substitute heavy cream for half or all of the water. This is an easy dough to roll out.

  ❧ CHOCOLATE PUFF PASTRY: Use 2 cups butter for the butter block. Add to it ½ cup unsweetened cocoa powder or 2 ounces bittersweet chocolate, melted and cooled. Mix on low speed for 30 seconds and scrape down the sides of the bowl. Remove from the mixer and scrape onto a sheet of plastic. Form a 6-inch square about 1 inch thick, cover with plastic film, and refrigerate for 20 minutes, then proceed with laminating.

  ❧ PISTACHIO PUFF PASTRY: In the bowl of an electric mixer fitted with a paddle attachment or a food processor, cream the butter for 30 seconds. Scrape down the sides of the bowl and add 3 ounces pistachio paste (you can find this at gourmet food stores). Cream for 30 seconds more, then scrape down the sides of the bowl. Scoop out onto plastic film and form a 6-inch square about 1 inch thick. Cover with plastic film and refrigerate for 20 minutes. Proceed with laminating. On the last two turns, dust the rolled-out dough with ¼ cup sugar before folding.

7. In all, there will be six turns, each with a 30-minute refrigerated resting period. This 30-minute rest is very important. Don't try to rush it. It is essential to complete the first four turns in one day. The fifth and sixth can be completed up to four hours later or on the following day.

8. Once the turns are complete, chill the dough for 30 minutes. At this point, the dough is ready to use or store. Freeze the dough if you will not be using it within 24 hours. To freeze, cut the dough into 4 equal pieces and roll it out with a rolling pin into ½- to 1-inch thick sheets (pastry chefs call this *sheeting*). Wrap it tightly with plastic film and freeze. The thinner the dough is, the easier it will be to defrost. Defrost the dough slowly in the refrigerator for easiest handling. Puff pastry will keep in the freezer for up to 1 month.

TO PREBAKE A SHEET OF PUFF PASTRY

Preheat the oven to 425°F. Adjust the rack to the center of the oven. Line a baking sheet with parchment paper. Roll out the puff pastry dough to a ¼-inch-thick rectangle and place on the prepared baking sheet. Top the dough with another sheet of parchment, and place a cooling rack, preferably one that fits right into the baking pan, over the parchment to prevent the dough from puffing up too much. Bake for 15 minutes. Reduce the heat to 350°F, rotate the pan from back to front, and bake for 15 minutes more, or until golden. Cool on a rack.

To reuse puff pastry scraps

SACRISTAINS

Roll out about ¼ inch thick any excess puff pastry and dust with sugar. Fold the dough in half, then cut 1-inch strips and roll them in sugar. Twist the strips like a barber pole, and place in the freezer for 1 hour. Bake at 350°F for 15 minutes, or until golden brown.

Laminated Dough

Palmiers

YIELD: 3 dozen palmiers

SPECIAL TOOLS:

    Standing electric mixer with
      a paddle attachment (optional)

    Silicone mat or parchment paper

½ recipe Master Puff Pastry
    (page 270)

1–1½ cups sugar, to taste

THIS IS ONE OF THE WORLD'S EASIEST AND MOST BEAUTIFUL *cookies. Some people call them elephant ears, and in Mexico they are known as orejas ("ears"). They are simply rolled and sliced puff pastry with sugar added between the layers. In the oven, the sugar melts and caramelizes into a beautiful, crisp coating. As the puff pastry cooks, it grows sideways, opening up the cookie.*

I prefer the classic palmier, but many chefs embellish the recipe with flavored sugar. Cinnamon, citrus zest, vanilla, and even lavender make lovely sugars that can be used in place of plain sugar in this recipe.

To form palmier dough, you make a double, or book, turn with one extra fold. Try to keep your folds even; palmiers look much more professional when they are uniform.

1. On a lightly floured work surface, use a rolling pin to roll the Puff Pastry to an 18-x-12-inch rectangle, ¼ inch thick.

2. Cover the entire surface of the dough with a generous layer of sugar. With your finger, draw a vertical line through the sugar down the center of the rectangle, so that you see two 9-x-12-inch rectangles. Divide each of those sections into thirds by drawing four more vertical lines through the sugar. At the end, you should have six sections, each a 3-x-12-inch rectangle.

3. To form the palmier, fold each outside edge toward the center, until it touches the second line. Next fold the outside edges toward the middle again, so both edges meet at the centerline. Coat the exposed surface with more sugar. Using the rolling pin, press the sugar into the dough and lightly crease the folded edges. Now fold the dough in half, as if closing a book. Freeze the log of dough for 30 to 60 minutes to ensure crisp, clean cuts. At this point, the dough can be frozen, wrapped airtight, for up to 1 week.

4. Preheat the oven to 350°F. Adjust the rack to the top of the oven. Line two baking sheets with silicone mats or parchment paper.

5. When the dough has firmed up, using a chef's knife, slice off ¼-inch-thick cookies. The cookies will be heart shaped. Sprinkle each cookie with more sugar before placing them 1 inch apart on the prepared baking sheet. Open up the heart slightly to help ease expansion.

6. Bake the cookies one sheet at a time for 10 minutes, or until they look as though they are starting to set and have colored only slightly around the edges. Quickly remove the sheet from the oven and flip each cookie with a metal offset spatula. Bake for 8 to 12 minutes more, or until golden brown. Cool completely on a rack before serving. Palmiers will keep at room temperature for up to 2 days in an airtight container. They can be frozen for 1 month.

Apple Turnovers

YIELD: 8 turnovers

SPECIAL TOOLS:

Standing electric mixer with
a paddle attachment (optional)

Parchment paper

Rolling pastry wheel (optional)

FOR THE APPLE FILLING

4 Fuji or other apples, peeled,
cored, and cut into ¼-inch
pieces

½ cup sugar

1 teaspoon ground cinnamon

½ vanilla bean, split and
scraped

¼ cup fresh lemon juice

4 tablespoons (½ stick)
unsalted butter

½ recipe Master Puff Pastry
(page 270)

FOR THE EGG WASH

1 large egg

Pinch of salt (less than
⅛ teaspoon)

1 tablespoon water

½ cup sugar

TURNOVERS CAN BE MADE WITH ANY SWEET DOUGH, BUT *they are really special when made with Puff Pastry. The stuffed triangle of dough puffs up like a giant clam, revealing hundreds of flaky layers.*

Apples are commonly used to fill these turnovers, but hundreds of other foods can be used in their place. Preserves, fresh fruit of any kind, pastry cream, ganache, or even savory fillings like cheese or caramelized onions make super turnovers. The size can vary as well. This large version makes a great breakfast. A mini turnover is nice for dessert, with a scoop of vanilla ice cream and a squirt of caramel sauce.

I prefer to use Fuji apples for the filling because they have a nice balance of tart and sweet, but any apple works. Choose the one that tastes best to you.

FILLING

Toss together the apples, sugar, cinnamon, vanilla seeds (reserve the bean for another use), and lemon juice in a large bowl. Melt the butter in a large sauté pan over medium heat until it turns a light nutty color, 6 to 8 minutes. Add the apple mixture and sauté until the apples are softened and caramelized, 10 to 15 minutes. Transfer the cooked apples to a baking sheet to cool completely before forming the turnovers (they will cool faster when spread in a thin layer over the surface of the sheet). After they have cooled, the filling can be stored in the refrigerator for up to 3 days.

PASTRY

On a lightly floured surface, use a rolling pin to roll the Puff Pastry out to a 10-x-20-inch rectangle, ¼ inch thick. Using a ruler and a chef's knife or rolling pastry wheel, cut the dough in half horizontally, then into fourths vertically, creating eight 5-inch squares.

EGG WASH

Whisk together the egg, salt, and water in a small bowl. Using a pastry brush, lightly brush all four edges of each pastry square with the egg wash.

SHAPING

1. Place ¼ to ½ cup of the filling on the center of each pastry square. Fold one corner over the filling to meet flush with the opposite corner, forming a perfect right triangle. Press the edges together with a fork and repeat with the remaining squares. At this point, the turnovers can be frozen, wrapped tightly, for up to 1 week.

2. Preheat the oven to 400°F. Place a rack in the center of the oven. Line a baking sheet with parchment paper.

3. Carefully transfer the turnovers to the prepared baking sheet, placing them 1 inch apart. Brush a light coat of egg wash onto each turnover, then sprinkle each with a pinch of sugar.

4. Bake the turnovers for 10 minutes. Rotate the pan from back to front, turn the oven temperature down to 350°F, and bake for 10 to 15 minutes more, or until puffed and golden brown. Serve the turnovers warm or cool and store in an airtight container for up to 24 hours.

YIELD: 2 pounds dough, enough for 14 croissants and 4 mini croissants

SPECIAL TOOL:

Standing electric mixer with a dough hook

FOR THE DOUGH (*Détrempe*)

1 cup whole milk, chilled

1 ounce fresh yeast or 1 tablespoon active dry yeast

2 cups bread flour

1 cup all-purpose flour

2 tablespoons sugar

2¼ teaspoons salt

¼ pound (1 stick) cold unsalted butter

FOR THE BUTTER BLOCK (*Beurrage*)

¾ pound (3 sticks) cold unsalted butter

¼ cup all-purpose flour

Croissant Dough

BECAUSE THE *DÉTREMPE* FOR CROISSANTS IS YEASTED, IT *has a lot more flavor than Puff Pastry. For this reason, I often use it for pastries, and I also like it for tarts.*

The original croissant dough was ordinary bread dough and was later refined by the French into the laminated version we know today. The crescent shape of the pastry was adopted by Viennese bakers from the symbol on the Turkish flag, in celebration of the Austrian defeat of the Turks in 1686.

DOUGH

1. Combine the milk and yeast in the bowl of a standing mixer fitted with the dough hook and whisk until the yeast is dissolved. Combine the bread flour, all-purpose flour, sugar, and salt in a separate mixing bowl. Add the butter and work the butter into the flour with your fingers until barely visible.

2. Add the flour mixture to the yeast mixture. Knead on low speed for 1 minute. Mix on medium speed for 3 to 5 minutes more, or until smooth and warm (70° to 75°F). If the dough seems too dry, add 1 tablespoon water. Do not work the dough too much; it's best not to have too much elasticity in croissant dough.

3. Transfer the dough to a floured work surface. Roll the dough into a ball. Using a sharp knife, cut an X extending halfway through the dough. This will expand as the dough relaxes and will aid in rolling later. Cover airtight with plastic film, place on a baking sheet, and refrigerate for at least 4 hours or overnight.

BUTTER BLOCK

1. Make the butter block as directed in Master Puff Pastry (pages 270–71).

2. Laminate the dough as directed in Master Puff Pastry (page 271). The laminated dough rectangle should measure only 8 x 18 inches, and you need to do only three turns.

3. After the third turn, wrap the dough in plastic film and refrigerate for at least 5 hours or overnight. If you will not be using the dough within 24 hours, freeze it. To freeze, roll the dough out until it is ½ to 1 inch thick and wrap tightly in plastic film. The thinner it is, the more quickly it will defrost. The dough should be defrosted slowly in the refrigerator for easiest handling. Croissant dough will keep in the freezer for up to 1 month.

4. To shape and bake, see pages 279–83.

Classic Croissants

YIELD: **14 croissants and 4 mini croissants**

SPECIAL TOOLS:

Standing electric mixer with a dough hook attachment

Rolling pastry wheel (optional)

Parchment paper

1 recipe Croissant Dough (page 278)

FOR THE EGG WASH

1 large egg, plus 1 large egg yolk

YOU CAN MAKE THE CROISSANTS AHEAD OF TIME, FORMING *them and freezing them until needed. Then defrost slowly in the refrigerator before baking.*

When working with croissant dough, or any laminated dough for that matter, it is important to keep the temperature of the room in mind. As the dough warms up, it becomes harder to handle. Don't hesitate to stop working and throw the dough into the fridge for 15 minutes. It will make the whole task much easier.

Although the instructions for cutting the croissants may seem daunting, they create triangles with as little waste as possible. If the word isosceles *sends you into shivers of math anxiety, you can avoid the entire process with the purchase of a croissant cutter. This tool is a rolling pin of triangular cutters that is dusted with flour and rolled once over the dough to create perfect triangles, ready to be rolled up.*

1. On a lightly floured work surface, use a rolling pin to roll the croissant dough into a 20-x-18-inch rectangle, ¼ inch thick. (See the diagram on page 280.) If the dough seems very elastic and springs back when you roll it, let it rest for 5 minutes, then roll again.

2. Using a ruler and a chef's knife or rolling pastry wheel, cut the rectangle in half horizontally, making two smaller rectangles, one on top of the other, each measuring 20 x 9 inches.

3. Using a ruler and a paring knife, make very tiny score marks every 5 inches along the top and bottom edges of the large rectangle.

Variation

❧ ALMOND CROISSANTS: After the egg wash is applied, sprinkle each croissant with sliced almonds. Bake as directed. When the croissants are removed from the oven, brush each one lightly with simple syrup (page 333).

Using the straight edge of a ruler, connect the bottom left corner (A) of the large rectangle with the first top score mark (B). Cut diagonally along this line. Next, move the straight edge one mark to the right and connect the first bottom score mark (C) to the second top score mark (D) and cut along this line. Repeat this diagonal cut from the second bottom score mark (E) to the third top (F) and the third bottom (G) to the right top corner (H). When complete, you will have 6 perfect parallelograms and 4 partial ones .

4. Next, reverse the diagonal cut pattern from the top left corner (I) to the first bottom score mark (C). Repeat the lines, moving across, from left to right (B to E, D to G, and F to J). This step cuts the parallelograms in half, leaving 14 isosceles triangles and 4 right triangles.

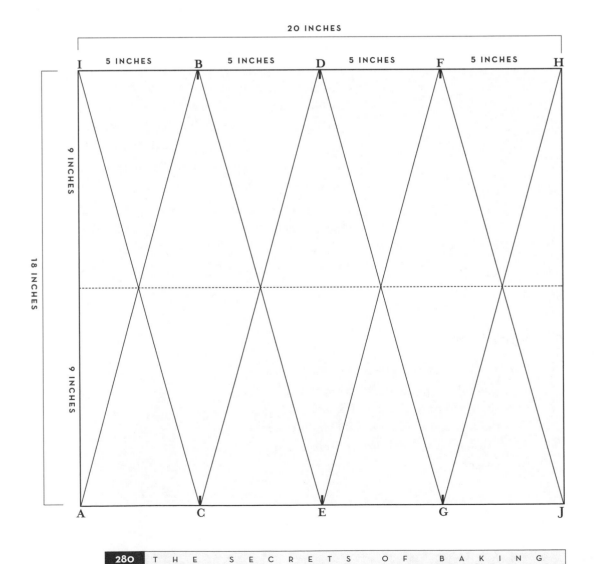

5. Line two baking sheets with parchment. To form each croissant, take a triangle of dough and make a short slit in the middle of the short side. Stretch that short side a bit, then begin to roll the triangle up toward the point. Be sure the tip is tucked under, then place the croissants 2 inches apart on the prepared pan. Repeat until the pan is full, then cover with pan-sprayed plastic film. Roll up the partial triangles to make mini croissants.

6. When you are ready to proceed, proof the dough, following the chart below, until poofy and light to the touch.

PROOFING TEMPERATURE	FOR FRESH DOUGH (ROOM-TEMPERATURE)	FOR REFRIGERATED DOUGH
70°F	1½–2 hours	2½–3 hours
75°F	1¼–1½ hours	2–2½ hours
80°F	1–1¼ hours	1½–2 hours
85°F	45 minutes–1 hour	1–1½ hours
90°F	45 minutes	1 hour

7. Toward the end of the proofing, preheat the oven to 400°F. Place a rack in the center of the oven.

EGG WASH
Whisk together the egg and yolk in a small bowl. Brush each croissant lightly with the egg wash.

BAKING
Bake for 12 minutes. Turn the oven temperature down to 350°F, rotate the pan from back to front, and bake for 10 to 12 minutes more, or until crispy and amber brown. Cool and serve. Store cooled croissants in a brown bag at room temperature for up to 2 days. They can also be frozen for a month.

YIELD: 12 pastries

SPECIAL TOOLS:

Standing electric mixer with a dough hook attachment

Silicone mats or parchment paper

Rolling pastry wheel (optional)

1 recipe Croissant Dough (page 278)

FOR THE EGG WASH

1 large egg, plus 1 large egg yolk

6 ounces bittersweet chocolate, cut into twenty-four ¼-ounce batons (see headnote) or finely chopped

Pain au Chocolat

CHOCOLATE CROISSANTS ARE THE EPITOME OF DECADENCE *or the breakfast of champions. I have very little self-control when faced with this luscious pastry. Hot from the oven, the flakes of buttery, yeasty dough crumble between my teeth as the hot, creamy chocolate seeps through.*

When making pain au chocolat, professional chefs typically wrap the croissant dough around a thin bar of chocolate known as a baton. Batons are not commonly found in the grocery store, but you can make them using a bar of chocolate. Place a block of chocolate in the microwave and zap it three times on high power for 5 seconds, then cut the block into ¼-x-2-inch bars. The warmed chocolate will not shatter when you cut it, and the small bars will stay in the dough perfectly. You could also use finely chopped chocolate to fill the pain au chocolat.

1. Line two baking sheets with silicone mats or parchment paper. On a lightly floured work surface, use a rolling pin to roll the croissant dough into an 18-x-20-inch rectangle, ¼ inch thick. If the dough seems very elastic and springs back when you roll it, let it rest for 5 minutes, then roll again.

2. Using a ruler and a chef's knife or rolling pastry wheel, cut the rectangle into 3 horizontal rectangles, each measuring 6 x 20 inches. Next, make vertical cuts through all three strips every 5 inches. The result will be 12 small rectangles, each measuring 6 x 4 inches.

EGG WASH

Whisk together the egg and yolk in a small bowl. Using a pastry brush, paint the top edge of each rectangle with the egg wash.

PASTRIES

1. Place 2 batons (or ½ ounce finely chopped chocolate) at opposite edges of each rectangle. Starting at the chocolate end, roll up each croissant like a jellyroll. Tuck the edges under, then put the croissant on the prepared baking sheet. Repeat with the remaining dough and chocolate. Place the croissants 2 inches apart on the baking sheet.

2. Proof at room temperature or, if possible, in a controlled 90°F environment (see page 281), for about 2 hours, or until doubled in volume and light to the touch.

3. Toward the end of the proofing, preheat the oven to 400°F. Place a rack in the center of the oven.

4. Brush each croissant lightly with the egg wash. Bake for 12 minutes. Rotate the pan from back to front, turn the oven temperature down to 350°F, and bake for 10 to 12 minutes more, or until crispy and amber brown. Cool and serve. Store cooled croissants in an airtight container at room temperature for up to 2 days.

Danish Dough

YIELD: 2½ pounds dough, enough for 18 pastries

SPECIAL TOOL:

Standing electric mixer with paddle and dough hook attachments

FOR THE DOUGH (*Détrempe*)

1 ounce fresh yeast or 1 tablespoon active dry yeast

½ cup whole milk

⅓ cup sugar

Zest of 1 orange, finely grated

¾ teaspoon ground cardamom

1½ teaspoons vanilla extract

½ vanilla bean, split and scraped

2 large eggs, chilled

¼ cup fresh orange juice

3¼ cups all-purpose flour

1 teaspoon salt

FOR THE BUTTER BLOCK (*Beurrage*)

½ pound (2 sticks) cold unsalted butter

¼ cup all-purpose flour

DANISH IS CALLED *DANISH* EVERYWHERE EXCEPT DENMARK, *where it is called* wienerbröd, *or "Vienna bread." It was introduced to Denmark by Viennese bakers, who were brought in to replace striking Danish bakers. Classically used for breakfast pastries of all kinds, Danish is a sweet, flavorful version of laminated dough. The Danish* détrempe *is richer and sweeter than that of croissant and puff pastry, with more sugar and eggs but no butter. As a result, the* détrempe *is much softer than the others, and must be kneaded longer.*

Danish dough recipes vary from chef to chef but almost always include cardamom. Native to India, where it grows wild, cardamom was first used in the preparation of curries, drinks, and medicines. The Vikings discovered cardamom in Constantinople and carried it back to Scandinavia, where it is used mainly as a spice for sweets and baked goods.

DOUGH

Combine the yeast and milk in the bowl of a standing mixer fitted with the paddle attachment. Mix on low speed. Slowly add the sugar, orange zest, cardamom, vanilla extract, vanilla seeds (reserve the bean for another use), eggs, and orange juice and mix well. Change to the dough hook. Combine the flour and salt and add 1 cup at a time, increasing the speed to medium as it is incorporated. Knead the dough for 5 minutes, or until smooth. Add a little more flour if it is sticky. Transfer the dough to a floured baking sheet. Cover with plastic film and refrigerate for 30 minutes.

BUTTER BLOCK

1. Meanwhile, combine the butter and flour in the bowl of a standing electric mixer fitted with a paddle attachment. Cream on medium speed for 1 minute. Stop the mixer and scrape down the sides of the bowl and the paddle. Cream for 1 minute more, or until smooth and lump free. Set aside at room temperature.

2. When the *détrempe* has chilled for 30 minutes, transfer it to a lightly floured work surface. Using a rolling pin, roll the dough out to a rectangle approximately 18 x 13 inches and ¼ inch thick. The dough may be sticky. Keep dusting it with flour. Spread the butter evenly over the center and right thirds of the dough. Fold the left edge

of the *détrempe* to the right, covering half of the butter block. Fold the right third of the rectangle over the center third. The first turn has now been completed. Place the dough on a baking sheet, wrap it in plastic film, and refrigerate for 30 minutes.

3. Place the dough lengthwise on a floured work surface. The open ends should be to your right and left. Using a rolling pin, roll the dough into another approximately 13-x-18-inch, ¼-inch-thick rectangle. Again, fold the left third of the rectangle over the center third and the right third over the center third. (No butter is placed on the *détrempe* this time. It is already in the dough.) The second turn has now been completed. Refrigerate the dough for 30 minutes.

4. Roll out, turn, and refrigerate the dough two more times, for a total of four single turns. Refrigerate the dough after the final turn for at least 5 hours or overnight. The Danish dough is now ready to be used. If you will not be using the dough within 24 hours, freeze it. To do this, roll the dough out 1 inch thick, wrap tightly in plastic film, and freeze. The thinner the dough is, the easier it will be to defrost. Defrost the dough slowly in the refrigerator for easiest handling. Danish dough will keep in the freezer for up to 1 month.

YIELD: 18 pastries

SPECIAL TOOLS:

Standing electric mixer with paddle and dough hook attachments

Rolling pastry wheel (optional)

Silicone mats or parchment paper

1 recipe Danish Dough (page 284)

2 cups filling: jam, Pastry Cream (page 100), Master Lemon Curd (page 75), cream cheese (see headnote), or Master Ganache (page 16)

FOR THE EGG WASH

1 large egg, plus 1 large egg yolk

Danish Envelopes

THIS IS THE EASIEST DANISH SHAPE TO FORM. IT CAN BE *filled with many different things, including pastry cream, lemon curd, fruit preserves, almond cream, or ganache. My personal favorite is cream cheese filling: ¾ pound cream cheese, ½ cup sugar, 1 large egg, and 1 teaspoon vanilla extract, creamed together until smooth. When spooned onto the Danish and baked, it tastes just like a cheesecake.*

1. Cut the Danish dough into 2 equal pieces. On a lightly floured work surface, use a rolling pin to roll each half into a 12-inch square, ¼ inch thick. If the dough seems very elastic and springs back when you roll it, let it rest for 5 minutes, then roll again.

2. Using a ruler and a chef's knife or a rolling pastry wheel, cut the square into 3 horizontal rectangles, each measuring 4 x 12 inches. Next, make vertical cuts through all three strips every 4 inches. The result will be nine 4-inch squares.

3. Line two baking sheets with silicone mats or parchment paper.

EGG WASH

Whisk together the egg and egg yolk in a small bowl. Gently brush each square with some of the egg wash.

ENVELOPES

1. Place a heaped tablespoon of filling in the center of each square. Fold two opposite corners into the center of the square and press down firmly to seal. Place the Danish 2 inches apart on the prepared pans. Repeat with the remaining dough and filling. Cover with plastic film.

2. Proof at room temperature or, if possible, in a controlled 90°F environment (see page 281) for about 2 hours, or until doubled in volume and light to the touch.

3. Meanwhile, preheat the oven to 400°F. Place a rack in the center of the oven.

4. Brush each envelope lightly with the remaining egg wash. Bake for 10 minutes. Rotate the pan from back to front, turn the oven down to 350°F, and bake for 10 to 15 minutes more, or until golden brown. Cool and serve. Store cooled Danish in an airtight container at room temperature for up to 2 days.

Laminated Dough

PLUS YEAST

Danish Braid

YIELD: **2 coffeecakes**

SPECIAL TOOLS:

Standing electric mixer with paddle and dough hook attachments

Silicone mat or parchment paper

Rolling pastry wheel (optional)

1 recipe Danish Dough (page 284)

2 cups apple filling (see page 276), jam, or preserves

FOR THE EGG WASH

1 large egg, plus 1 large egg yolk

THIS IS AN ELEGANT-LOOKING COFFEECAKE. THE EFFECT IS *more of a herringbone pattern than a braid, but I hesitate to use the word* herring *when naming any pastry! This pastry looks best when it is filled with a fruit filling that is not too juicy. The apple filling I use for turnovers (see page 276) works wonderfully, as does any thick fruit preserve.*

1. Line a baking sheet with a silicone mat or parchment paper. On a lightly floured work surface, use a rolling pin to roll the Danish dough into a 15-x-20-inch rectangle, ¼ inch thick. If the dough seems very elastic and springs back when you roll it, let it rest for 5 minutes, then roll again. Transfer the rectangle of dough to the prepared baking sheet.

2. Create a fringe down one long side of the pastry by making parallel, 5-inch-long cuts with a chef's knife or rolling pastry wheel, spacing them 1 inch apart. Repeat on the opposite long side.

3. Spoon the filling down the center of the rectangle. Starting at one end, fold the strips of fringe over the filling, alternating one by one, left, right, left, right, and so on. When the last strips have been folded over, trim the ends neatly.

EGG WASH

Whisk together the egg and yolk in a small bowl. Using a pastry brush, lightly coat the braid with the egg wash.

PROOFING AND BAKING

1. Cover with pan-sprayed plastic film, and proof at room temperature or, if possible, in a controlled 90°F environment (see page 281) for about 2 hours, or until doubled in volume and light to the touch.

2. Meanwhile, preheat the oven to 400°F. Place a rack in the center of the oven.

3. Bake for 10 minutes. Rotate the pan from back to front, turn the oven temperature down to 350°F, and bake for 15 to 20 minutes more, or until golden brown. Cool and serve the braid. The cooled braid can be wrapped airtight and stored in the refrigerator for up to 2 days, or freeze for 1 month.

Laminated Dough

PLUS YEAST

Laminated Brioche

YIELD: 3¼ pounds dough

SPECIAL TOOL:

Standing electric mixer with paddle and dough hook attachments or a food processor

FOR THE SPONGE

⅓ cup whole milk

½ ounce fresh yeast or 2 teaspoons active dry yeast

2 tablespoons plus 1 teaspoon sugar

⅓ cup bread flour or all-purpose flour

FOR THE DOUGH (*Détrempe*)

3 cups bread flour or all-purpose flour

1½ teaspoons salt

4 large eggs, chilled

6 ounces (1½ sticks) cold unsalted butter

FOR THE BUTTER BLOCK (*Beurrage*)

1 pound (4 sticks) cold unsalted butter

THIS IS INCREDIBLE DOUGH AND ONE NOT COMMONLY SEEN *in the United States. Similar to the dough for Danish Braid in feel, this one is moistened mostly by eggs. It is the richest of all laminated doughs. The first portion of this recipe involves making a yeasted brioche dough (before beginning, it's a good idea to familiarize yourself with brioche; see page 223), which is well kneaded and chilled in the refrigerator. The cold relaxed dough is then laminated in two single turns.*

I use laminated brioche to create very rich breakfast pastries. Although I am providing instructions for cinnamon twists and snails, this dough can be used interchangeably with all of the laminated doughs in this chapter.

SPONGE

Combine the milk and yeast in the bowl of a standing mixer fitted with the paddle attachment and whisk until the yeast is dissolved. Add the sugar and flour, forming a thick batter. Cover with plastic film and let rest at room temperature for about 1 hour, or until bubbles form.

DOUGH

1. Add the flour and salt to the sponge. Mix on low speed using the dough hook attachment. Add the eggs and mix on low speed for 2 minutes, or until incorporated. Increase the speed to medium and knead the dough for 5 minutes, or until the dough begins to slap around. Hold on to the mixer when necessary.

2. On medium-low speed, add the butter, 2 tablespoons at a time. Stop the mixer and scrape down the sides of the bowl occasionally. Knead on medium speed until the dough is shiny and smooth, about 5 minutes. Scrape out the dough, wash and dry the bowl, and coat it lightly with oil.

3. Place the dough in the oiled bowl and turn it so that the top is coated with oil. Cover with plastic film and let rise at room temperature until doubled in volume, about 2 hours.

4. When the dough doubles in volume, punch it down by folding it over two or three times. Let rise until doubled in volume again, about 45 minutes at room temperature or 4 hours in the refrigerator.

5. Transfer the dough to a lightly floured work surface. Using a rolling pin, roll the dough into an 18-x-13-inch rectangle, ¼ inch thick. Spread the butter over the center and right thirds of the rectangle in an even layer.

6. Fold the left edge of the dough to the right, covering half of the butter. Fold the right third of the rectangle over the center third, like a business letter. The first turn has now been completed. Place the dough on a baking sheet, wrap it in plastic film, and refrigerate for 30 minutes.

7. After 30 minutes, place the dough lengthwise on a floured work surface. The open ends should be to your right and left. Using a rolling pin, roll the dough into another 18-x-13-inch rectangle, ¼ inch thick. Again, fold the left third of the rectangle over the center third and the right third over the center, like a business letter. (Note that no butter is placed on the dough this time. It is already in the dough.) The second turn has now been completed. Wrap and refrigerate the dough again for 30 minutes.

8. After 30 minutes, roll out, turn, and refrigerate the dough one last time, for a total of three single turns. Wrap in plastic film and refrigerate for 5 hours or overnight. The laminated brioche is now ready to be used. If you will not be using the dough within 24 hours, freeze it. To do this, roll the dough out 1 inch thick, wrap it tightly in plastic film, and freeze. The thinner the dough is, the easier it will be to defrost. Defrost the dough slowly in the refrigerator for easiest handling. Laminated brioche dough will keep in the freezer for up to 1 month.

YIELD: 20 pastries

SPECIAL TOOLS:

 Standing electric mixer with paddle and dough hook attachments

 Silicone mats or parchment paper

 Rolling pastry wheel (optional)

 1 recipe Laminated Brioche (page 288)

 ¾ cup sugar

 2 tablespoons ground cinnamon

FOR THE EGG WASH

 1 large egg, plus 1 large egg yolk

Cinnamon Twists

THIS IS A VERY EASY BREAKFAST PASTRY TO FORM. *Cinnamon twists are usually made plain, but if you shape them into spirals, you can add a filling. Place a dollop of fruit, jam, pastry cream, or cream cheese on top just before baking.*

1. On a lightly floured work surface, use a rolling pin to roll the Laminated Brioche dough into a 10-x-20-inch rectangle, ¼ inch thick. If the dough seems very elastic and springs back when you roll it, let it rest for 5 minutes, then roll it again.

2. Combine the sugar and cinnamon in a small bowl. Spread the mixture over the entire surface of the dough. Using the rolling pin, lightly press the sugar into the dough. Fold the rectangle in half lengthwise, creating a 5-x-20-inch rectangle. Refrigerate for 15 minutes.

3. Line two baking sheets with silicone mats or parchment paper. When the dough has chilled, return it to the lightly floured work surface with the folded edge to the right. Using a ruler and a chef's knife or rolling pastry wheel, cut the rectangle horizontally into twenty 1-inch-wide strips. Each strip should have a folded edge at one end.

4. Twist each strip several times so that it resembles a tight barbershop pole. Fold the twisted strip in half again and give it one more twist, as if you were closing a wire twist tie. Place the pastries 2 inches apart on the prepared baking sheets.

EGG WASH

Whisk the egg and yolk together in a small bowl. Lightly brush the twists with the egg wash.

PROOFING AND BAKING

1. Cover with plastic film and proof at room temperature or, if possible, in a 90°F environment (see page 281) for 30 to 40 minutes, or until they are slightly poofy.

2. Meanwhile, preheat the oven to 400°F. Place a rack in the center of the oven.

3. Bake for 10 minutes. Rotate the pans from back to front, turn the oven down to 350°F, and bake for 10 to 15 minutes more, or until golden brown. Cool and serve. Store the cooled baked twists in an airtight container at room temperature for up to 2 days.

YIELD: 12 pastries

SPECIAL TOOLS:

> Standing electric mixer with paddle and dough hook attachments
>
> Silicone mats or parchment paper

1 cup golden raisins

1 cup cognac

2 tablespoons (½ stick) unsalted butter

¾ cup sugar

2 tablespoons ground cinnamon

1 recipe Laminated Brioche (page 288)

FOR THE EGG WASH

> 1 large egg, plus 1 large egg yolk

Cinnamon-Raisin Snails

THESE ARE VERY RICH CINNAMON BUNS. THE LAYERS OF *rich, flaky dough are rolled into a spiral, like a snail shell. I like to add plumped raisins, but they can easily be omitted or replaced by other dried fruits, such as cherries, apricots, or figs. If plumping them in cognac seems a bit too much for a breakfast pastry, use orange or apple juice instead.*

I. Combine the raisins and cognac in a small bowl and set aside at room temperature to plump for at least I hour, or overnight if time allows.

2. Line two baking sheets with silicone mats or parchment paper. Melt the butter in a small saucepan over low heat, then set aside at room temperature. Combine the sugar and cinnamon in a small bowl and set aside.

3. On a lightly floured work surface, use a rolling pin to roll the Laminated Brioche dough into an 18-x-13-inch rectangle, ¼ inch thick. If the dough seems very elastic and springs back when you roll it, let it rest for 5 minutes, then roll it again. Position the dough so that the short edges are to your right and left.

4. Using a pastry brush, paint a light, even coat of melted butter over the surface of the dough. Sprinkle the cinnamon sugar over the dough, covering all but I inch at the top edge of the rectangle. Squeeze the excess liquid from the raisins and sprinkle them on top of the cinnamon sugar.

5. Starting at the long edge closest to you, begin to roll up the rectangle like a jellyroll. Roll tightly at first, then ease up and push the dough into a log.

6. Using a metal bench scraper or a chef's knife, cut the log crosswise every 1½ inches, creating 12 spiraled buns. Place the buns 2 inches apart, cut side up, on the prepared baking sheets. Cover loosely with plastic film.

7. Proof at room temperature or, if possible, in a 90°F environment (see page 281) for 30 to 40 minutes, or until they are slightly poofy.

8. Meanwhile, preheat the oven to 400°F. Place a rack in the center of the oven.

EGG WASH

Whisk together the egg and yolk in a small bowl. Using a pastry brush, lightly coat each snail with egg wash.

BAKING

Bake for 10 minutes. Rotate the pans from back to front, turn the oven temperature down to 350°F, and bake for 10 to 15 minutes more, or until the snails are golden brown. Store the baked snails in an airtight container at room temperature for up to 2 days.

FRUIT

FRUIT RECIPES

A RIPE, JUICY PIECE OF FRESH FRUIT CAN BE A DESSERT in itself, requiring nothing more than a napkin. But cooked fruit makes a terrific accompaniment to pastry, cakes, chocolate, and caramel. It can be a filling or a sauce, a garnish or a focal point. Cooking fruit helps soften its flesh and fibers so that more natural juices can be released. I use three different cooking methods: boiling, sautéing, and roasting. Each one gives the fruit a distinctly different flavor.

For fruit sauces, I use the boiling method. Some chefs make sauce out of fruit by pureeing the raw fruit with a little sugar in a blender. Cooking the fruit has benefits, however. Sauces made from cooked fruit and sugar are less likely to separate and have more intense color and flavor. When I use the boiling method for berries, I skip the blender step and pass the cooked fruit through a chinois (a fine-mesh strainer can be used as well), producing a jewel-like sauce. Once the sauce is made, it can be used as is or transformed into something else. Sorbet, granita, and gelée all begin life as fruit sauce.

FOR A MORE CARAMELIZED TASTE, I SAUTÉ FRUIT IN BUTTER and sugar. Bananas and apples lend themselves to this approach. Sautéed fruit is great with ice cream, or it can be pureed while still hot and spread over the bottom of a tart shell for extra flavor. Folding the sautéed fruit mixture into egg whites and baking transforms it into a soufflé.

Roasted fruit—pineapple is my favorite—also has a caramelized flavor, but it is slightly more intense. Sliced roasted fruits make wonderful toppings for tarts and upside-down cakes, or they can be left on their own and served with a drizzle of honey, a sprinkle of crunchy nuts, and a scoop of your favorite sorbet.

Fruit
FAMILY TREE

FRESH FRUIT

BOILED
Blackberry-Merlot Sauce
Blackberry Granita
Blackberry Sorbet
Blackberry Soufflé
Blackberry Jellies

SAUTÉED
Banana Schmutz
Banana–Chocolate
Chip Soufflé
Banana Sorbet

ROASTED
Roasted Voodoo
Vanilla Pineapple
Roasted Pineapple
Granita
Sour Cream–Pineapple
Glacé

These three fruit preparations can be made with more than one type of fruit.

Blackberry–Merlot Sauce

1½ pounds fresh or two 10-
   ounce bags frozen
   blackberries

1 orange, peeled and sliced

1 lemon, peeled and sliced

½ cup plus 2 tablespoons sugar
   (½ cup if using frozen)

½ vanilla bean, split
   and scraped

2 cups Merlot

½ cup water

1 3-inch cinnamon stick

3 tablespoons Chambord
   Pinch of salt (less than
   ⅛ teaspoon)

THIS IS A BASIC RECIPE THAT I USE EVERY DAY. THE SUGAR, *lemon juice, and salt brighten the natural flavors of the fruit. The overtones of berry, plum, and cherry in the Merlot make it the perfect wine to use in this sauce.*

Be sure to taste the fruit before you begin the recipe. A single variety can taste completely different from one day to the next and from one basket to the next. Increasing or reducing the amount of sugar is fine if the fruit is overly tart or sweet.

1. Prepare an ice bath by filling a large bowl with ice.

2. Bring the blackberries, orange, lemon, sugar, vanilla bean and seeds, Merlot, and water to a boil in a large saucepan over medium heat. Microwave the cinnamon stick on high for 10 seconds to release the oils or heat in a small, dry skillet over medium heat until fragrant. Carefully remove it and add it to the sauce. Reduce the heat to low and simmer for 10 minutes.

3. Remove from the heat, cover with plastic film, and let the flavors infuse for 30 minutes.

4. Pour the mixture through a fine-mesh strainer into a medium bowl and firmly press out the juices (do not puree, or the sauce will turn cloudy). Place the bowl over the ice bath and cool completely. Add the Chambord and salt. The sauce can be used immediately, refrigerated in an airtight container for up to 3 days, or frozen for up to 3 months.

Variation

❧ This sauce makes a great poaching liquid for peeled Adriatic, Fiori, or Black Mission figs. Reduce the sauce by one third, until it is thick but still runny. Add 2 tablespoons sugar and up to 6 large figs. Simmer over low heat for 5 to 7 minutes. Remove from the heat and serve.

Blackberry Granita

YIELD: 8 generous ½-cup servings

3 cups Blackberry-Merlot
    Sauce (page 295)
1½ cups sparkling mineral water

THIS IS BY FAR ONE OF THE EASIEST DESSERTS TO CREATE. *It is also one of the most appreciated, especially in hot weather. My recipe calls for sparkling water. Bubbly water has a perkier flavor than tap water, all the more so if it has a high sodium content like San Pellegrino. The resulting granita is bright, cool, and slightly extravagant.*

1. Place a baking pan in the freezer for at least 10 minutes, or until icy cold.

2. Whisk together the Blackberry-Merlot Sauce and the water in a large bowl,

3. Pour the mixture in the chilled roasting pan and put in the freezer. Fluff the granita with a fork every 20 minutes. Bring the frozen crystals that form around the edge of the pan into the center. This forces the unfrozen liquid to the edges to freeze. Set a timer for 20-minute intervals. If forgotten, the mixture will freeze into a solid block and the freezing process must be started over. If this should happen, place chunks of the frozen granita in a food processor and quickly pulse until icy.

4. The granita is ready when all the liquid is frozen into small ice crystals, about 2 hours. Once the ice crystals have formed, the granita can be stored airtight in the freezer for up to 1 week. Serve it directly from the freezer, because it melts fast.

Variation

↝ GELÉE: Soften 2 tablespoons powdered gelatin in ¼ cup cold water. Bring the sauce to a boil. Remove from the heat. Add the gelatin and stir to dissolve. Add the sparkling water, then chill until set. (See Caramel–Black Cherry Gelée, page 69.)

Blackberry Sorbet

YIELD: 8 generous ½-cup portions

SPECIAL TOOL:

Ice cream machine

2 cups warm Blackberry-
  Merlot Sauce (page 295)

2 tablespoons fresh
  orange juice

2 tablespoons light corn syrup

1 tablespoon fresh lime juice

2 tablespoons sugar

Pinch of salt (less than
  ⅛ teaspoon)

THIS LIGHT, REFRESHING SORBET NOT ONLY IS DELIGHTFUL *after a rich meal but also makes a perfect afternoon sweet. I like to serve it with berries. Since home ice cream machines do not typically incorporate as much air into the mixture as professional models, sorbet needs to be packed after churning, or it will be soft and difficult to scoop. Be sure to plan for an extra 2 to 4 hours in the freezer to firm it up.*

1. Whisk together the blackberry sauce, orange juice, corn syrup, lime juice, sugar, and salt in a large bowl. This is the sorbet base.

2. Pour the sorbet base into an ice cream machine and churn according to the manufacturer's instructions. When finished, the sorbet will have a soft-serve consistency and usually will be too soft to scoop. Pack it into a freezer container and let it firm up in the freezer for about 4 hours before serving. It will keep in the freezer for 3 months.

Variation

❧ SORBET SWIRL: Pack two or more complementary flavors of sorbet together in one container. As you scoop out the sorbet, the flavors will swirl together.

Blackberry Soufflé

LIGHT, AIRY, AND EXTRAVAGANT, THIS SOUFFLÉ IS LIKE A *magical purple cloud. I serve it with more blackberry sauce and a few fresh berries.*

YIELD: Eight 1-cup servings

SPECIAL TOOL:

 Standing electric mixer with a whisk attachment (optional)

FOR THE RAMEKINS

 2 tablespoons (¼ stick) unsalted butter, melted

 ¼ cup sugar

FOR THE SOUFFLÉS

 1 cup Blackberry-Merlot Sauce (page 295)

 1 teaspoon fresh lemon juice

 8 large egg whites

 Pinch of cream of tartar (less than ⅛ teaspoon)

 ½ cup sugar

Preheat the oven to 375°F. Adjust the rack to the lower third of the oven. Lightly coat eight 8-ounce ramekins with the melted butter and then lightly but completely dust them with sugar. Place the ramekins on a baking sheet.

SOUFFLÉS

1. Combine the blackberry sauce and lemon juice in a medium mixing bowl and set aside at room temperature.

2. Using a standing mixer fitted with the whisk attachment or a hand mixer, whip the egg whites for about 30 seconds on medium speed, or until soft foam appears. Add the cream of tartar. As the whites are whipping, slowly sprinkle in the sugar. Whip the whites for 1 or 2 minutes more, until they reach the medium-peak stage. Do not overbeat.

3. Using a rubber spatula, fold one third of the egg whites into the blackberry mixture. Carefully fold in the remaining whites to avoid deflating the mixture. The most efficient way to fold is to rotate the bowl and spatula simultaneously in opposite directions, one clockwise, the other counterclockwise.

4. Spoon the soufflé into the prepared ramekins, filling them to the rim. Smooth the tops with a metal spatula. Gently run a paring knife around the inside edge of each ramekin. This creates a wall of air that helps the soufflé rise up straight. Place the ramekins on a baking sheet.

5. Bake for 15 to 20 minutes, or until tall, golden brown, dry on the edges, and creamy in the center. Serve immediately.

Blackberry Jellies

YIELD: Eighty 1-inch square jellies

SPECIAL TOOL:

    Candy thermometer

FOR THE PECTIN MIXTURE

½ cup sugar

  2 tablespoons plus 1 teaspoon
    apple pectin (see
    headnote)

FOR THE JELLIES

  2 cups Blackberry-Merlot
    Sauce (page 295)

1½ cups sugar

  1 cup light corn syrup

¼ teaspoon citric acid,
    dissolved in ¼ teaspoon
    water

¾ cup sugar for coating

THESE GUMMY CANDIES ARE A SLIGHTLY MORE REFINED *version of gumdrops. The fruit sauce is solidified with pectin, a natural jelling fiber found in many fruits and vegetables. (It can be found in specialty stores; do not substitute supermarket pectin.) For an extra zing, I like to add citric acid, an additive made from fermented citrus juice that is used to create the sour flavor in sour candies. It can be found at specialty supermarkets, at baking supply stores, or in the kosher aisle under the name sour salt.*

    When making candy, precision and cleanliness are essential. Use a candy thermometer and measure your ingredients precisely.

Line a 9-x-13-inch baking sheet with aluminum foil and lightly spray the foil with pan spray.

PECTIN MIXTURE

Combine the sugar and pectin in a small bowl and set aside.

JELLIES

    1. Bring the Blackberry-Merlot Sauce, sugar, and corn syrup to a simmer in a large saucepan over medium heat. Whisk in the pectin mixture and stir until dissolved. Insert a candy thermometer and cook, whisking constantly, until the temperature reaches 220°F, 4 to 6 minutes.

    2. Remove from the heat and whisk in the dissolved citric acid. Pour onto the prepared baking sheet. Let cool to room temperature, about 4 hours or overnight.

    3. When set, cut the jellies into 1-inch squares and toss with the sugar. Serve or store in an airtight container at room temperature (65° to 68°F) for up to 2 weeks.

Banana Schmutz

I NAMED THIS BASIC SAUTÉED SAUCE *SCHMUTZ* (THE GERMAN word for "dirt") because that is exactly what it looks like. It's thick and brown, like mud. It may look unappetizing, but its flavor is extraordinary, and you will quickly be seduced by it when you use it in ice cream, Banana-Chocolate Chip Soufflé (page 301), or Banana Sorbet (page 302).

The subtle caramel flavor that is created in the sauté pan enhances the natural flavor of the bananas. The verb *sauter* means "to jump" in French, which is exactly what the bananas must do if they are to caramelize properly. A sauté pan is designed with slanted sides so that food may be tossed easily with a jiggle and a flip of the wrist. Constant stirring with a spoon works just as well.

YIELD: About 2 cups

SPECIAL TOOL:

Food processor

2 tablespoons (¼ stick) unsalted butter

½ cup sugar

½ cup packed light brown sugar

3 large very ripe bananas, peeled and cut into ½-inch pieces

¼ cup dark rum

1 tablespoon fresh lemon juice

Pinch of salt (less than ⅛ teaspoon)

1. In a large sauté pan, melt the butter over medium heat until the solids separate, sink to the bottom, and begin to brown, 3 to 5 minutes. When the butter is a dark golden color, add the sugar and brown sugar and stir until dissolved, 5 to 8 minutes.

2. Add the bananas and sauté, stirring constantly, for about 2 minutes, or until the bananas are softened and caramelized. Remove from the heat and carefully add the rum, lemon juice, and salt. Place the pan back over low heat and cook for 1 minute more.

3. Remove from the heat and immediately spoon half of the banana mixture into a food processor. (Be careful: the mixture is molten!) Pulse until the mixture becomes a smooth paste. Remove and repeat with the remaining banana mixture. Use the warm schmutz immediately or cool and refrigerate in an airtight container for up to 3 days.

Variations

- ✥ ADDITIONAL FLAVORING: Add one of the following flavors to the schmutz at the beginning of the recipe: 1 3-inch cinnamon stick, heated for a few minutes in a dry skillet to release the oils, or ½ teaspoon ground allspice or ½ vanilla bean, split and scraped. Remove the whole spices before pureeing.

- ✥ BANANA-CARAMEL SAUCE: Add 1 recipe Creamy Caramel Sauce (page 58) to the bananas in the food processor and puree them together.

- ✥ BANANA ICE CREAM: Combine 1 recipe Banana Schmutz with 1 recipe Vanilla Ice Cream (page 94) and churn as usual.

Banana—Chocolate Chip Soufflé

BANANA AND CHOCOLATE IS A MATCH MADE IN HEAVEN. *I usually chop bittersweet chocolate into chip-size pieces for this dish, but store-bought chips work fine. Additional garnishes could be added as well, including toasted nuts, coconut, caramel, or even banana chunks.*

YIELD: Eight 6- to 8-ounce servings

SPECIAL TOOLS:

    Food processor

    Standing electric mixer with a whisk attachment (optional)

FOR THE RAMEKINS

  2 tablespoons (¼ stick) unsalted butter, melted

  ¼ cup sugar

FOR THE SOUFFLÉS

  1 cup Banana Schmutz (previous page), at room temperature

  ½ cup finely chopped bittersweet chocolate

  8 large egg whites

    Pinch of cream of tartar (less than ⅛ teaspoon)

  ½ cup sugar

    Chocolate Sauce (page 39), for serving

Preheat the oven to 375°F. Adjust the rack to the lower third of the oven. Lightly coat eight 6- to 8-ounce ramekins with the melted butter and then lightly but completely dust them with sugar. Place the ramekins on a baking sheet.

SOUFFLÉS

1. Combine the Banana Schmutz and chocolate in a medium bowl and set aside at room temperature.

2. Using a standing mixer fitted with the whisk attachment or a hand mixer, whip the egg whites for about 30 seconds, or until soft foam appears. Add the cream of tartar. As the whites are whipping, slowly sprinkle in the sugar. Whip the whites for 1 to 2 minutes more, or until they reach the medium-peak stage.

3. Using a rubber spatula, fold one third of the egg whites into the banana mixture. Carefully fold in the remaining whites to avoid deflating the mixture.

4. Spoon the soufflé into the prepared ramekins, filling them to the rim. Smooth the tops with a metal spatula. Gently run a paring knife around the inside edge of each ramekin. This creates a wall of air that helps the soufflé rise up straight. Place the ramekins on a baking sheet.

5. Bake for 15 to 20 minutes, or until tall, golden brown, dry on the edges, and creamy in the center. Serve immediately with Chocolate Sauce.

Banana Sorbet

YIELD: About 4 cups

SPECIAL TOOLS:

Food processor

Ice cream machine

2 cups water

¼ cup sugar

2 cups Banana Schmutz (page 300), heated

2 tablespoons dark rum

2 tablespoons fresh lemon juice

Pinch of salt (less than ⅛ teaspoon)

SCHMUTZ MAKES INCREDIBLE SORBET. IT'S DELICIOUS SERVED *with toasted Banana Pound Cake (page 149) and hot Chocolate Sauce (page 39). The trick to this sorbet is to use hot schmutz. Stream in warm sugar syrup to thin the schmutz and create an amazing emulsified sorbet base.*

1. Bring the water and sugar to a boil in a small saucepan over medium heat, stirring occasionally. Immediately remove from the heat.

2. Using a hand-held mixer on medium speed, stream the hot syrup into the hot Banana Schmutz. Let cool, then add the rum, lemon juice, and salt. This is the sorbet base.

3. Pour the sorbet base into an ice cream machine and churn according to the manufacturer's instructions. When finished, the sorbet will have a soft-serve consistency and will usually be too soft to scoop. Transfer it to a freezer container and let it firm up in the freezer for about 4 hours before serving. The sorbet will keep for 3 months.

Roasted Voodoo Vanilla Pineapple

YIELD: 8 servings

1 large pineapple, peeled, quartered, and cored

4 dried vanilla bean halves or 1 vanilla bean, split and quartered

2 cups water

1 cup dark rum

½ cup Banana Schmutz (page 300)

1 cup sugar

6 ¼-inch-thick slices peeled fresh ginger

Pinch of Thai chile flakes (available at Asian markets) or hot red pepper flakes

Variation

❧ For summer cooking, place the entire pan on the dying embers of your barbecue and proceed as directed.

REMEMBER WHEN I TOLD YOU TO SAVE AND DRY OUT YOUR scraped vanilla beans? (See page 92.) Here's another great use for them: Poke the dried vanilla beans into the sides of a peeled and cored whole pineapple, then roast the pineapple, basting it with sugars and spices. The result is a terrific stand-alone dessert. You can also use the pineapple for tarts, fruit skewers, and gratins. Or create a sauce by pureeing the roasted pineapple in a food processor and passing it through a strainer to remove any large fibers. You can make the sauce into sorbet, ice cream, or granita.

1. Preheat the oven to 375°F. Adjust the rack to the center of the oven.

2. Peel and core the pineapple and place it in a large baking dish. Poke or push the vanilla bean pieces into the flesh of the pineapple. The dried ones will be stiff enough to go in on their own, but for a fresh bean, you may need to poke the holes with a paring knife.

3. Whisk together the water, rum, Banana Schmutz, sugar, ginger, and chile flakes in a medium bowl. Pour this mixture over the pineapple.

4. Bake for 35 to 45 minutes, basting every 15 minutes, until the juices are bubbly and the outside of the pineapple is lightly caramelized. Remove from the oven and cool to room temperature. The whole pineapple may be sliced and served immediately or stored in the refrigerator, wrapped airtight, for up to 3 days.

PINEAPPLES

Portuguese traders helped spread the pineapple from its native Brazil to Europe in the seventeenth century. There cultivation began in hothouses. The effort spent in growing this delicious tropical fruit made it extremely fashionable. The pineapple can be seen as a symbol of hospitality in art and architecture from the seventeenth to the twentieth century.

Pineapple is what is known as a *composite fruit*, actually formed from 100 to 200 separate fruitlets, or "eyes," that grow together into one. The eyes of a pineapple are always arranged in the same pattern. Because of this regularity, they are often removed by slicing a decorative, spiraled pattern of grooves.

Although you can buy pineapple peeled and cored, I prefer skin-on whole fruits so I can take advantage of all their juice. Using an offset serrated knife, slice off the top and bottom of the fruit so it stands steady on the table, then slice the skin off in a downward motion. Remove the core by cutting the pineapple into quarters lengthwise, then slicing the core out on an angle.

Roasted Pineapple Granita

YIELD: Eight ½-cup servings

SPECIAL TOOL:

Blender or food processor

½ Roasted Voodoo Vanilla
     Pineapple (page 303)

2 cups sparkling mineral water

3 tablespoons fresh lime juice

1 teaspoon fresh lemon juice

Pinch of salt (less than
     ⅛ teaspoon)

¼ cup sugar

THERE ARE FEW FRUITS AS REFRESHING AS THE PINEAPPLE, *so it's a natural for granita. Granita is a terrific solution when you feel like ice cream but don't have an ice cream machine. Just puree leftover roasted pineapple, add sparkling water, and freeze. Serve it after a spicy summer meal.*

1. Place a 9-x-13-inch baking pan in the freezer for 10 minutes, or until icy cold.

2. Cut the roasted pineapple into 1-inch cubes and place in a blender or food processor. Pulse on and off until the pineapple is pureed. Pour the pineapple puree through a fine-mesh strainer into a large bowl. Add the sparkling water, lime juice, lemon juice, salt, and sugar and stir to combine. This is the granita base.

3. Pour the granita base into the chilled baking pan and put in the freezer. Fluff the granita with a fork every 20 minutes. Bring the frozen crystals that form around the edge of the pan into the center. This forces the unfrozen liquid to the edges to freeze. Set a timer for 20-minute intervals. If forgotten, the mixture will freeze into a solid block and the freezing process must be started over. If this should happen, put chunks of the frozen granita into a food processor and quickly pulse until icy.

4. The granita is ready when all the liquid is frozen into small ice crystals, about 2 hours. Once the ice crystals have formed, the granita can be stored airtight in the freezer for up to 1 week. Serve it directly from the freezer, because it melts fast.

Sour Cream—Pineapple Glacé

¼ Roasted Voodoo Vanilla
    Pineapple (page 303)
2 cups sour cream
1 cup simple syrup (see page
    333)
1 tablespoon plus 2 teaspoons
    fresh lemon juice
Pinch of salt (less than
    ⅛ teaspoon)

AT FIRST, THE THOUGHT OF PAIRING TART PINEAPPLE AND sour cream sounds mouth-puckering. But actually the result is creamy and rich, due in part to the addition of simple syrup. In the pink peppercorn variation, the hot pungent spice complements the cold, sweet pineapple wonderfully.

1. Cut the pineapple into 1-inch cubes and place in a blender or food processor. Pulse on and off until the pineapple is pureed. Pour the pineapple puree through a fine-mesh strainer into a large bowl. Add the sour cream, syrup, lemon juice, and salt and stir to combine. This is the sorbet base.

2. Pour the sorbet base into an ice cream machine and churn according to the manufacturer's instructions. When finished, the sorbet will have a soft-serve consistency and will usually be too soft to scoop. Pack it into a freezable container and let it firm up in the freezer for about 4 hours before serving. Homemade sorbet will last for about 3 months, packed airtight, in the freezer.

Variation

꙳ Macerate 1 tablespoon pink peppercorns in the hot simple syrup for 30 minutes, then strain and proceed with the recipe.

MASTER COMBINATIONS

ONCE YOU'VE MASTERED THE BASICS, YOU CAN MAKE restaurant-style desserts with ease by adding to and combining basic recipes. It's like ordering Chinese food: pick one dish from column A and another from column B.

The desserts in this chapter come from my imagination or are inspired by those of other pastry chefs. Many are based on the plentiful fruit available in southern California. Feel free to twist and tweak them. By experimenting with combinations of flavors, textures, and temperatures, you can create your own signature desserts. For me, this is where the fun begins.

Master Combinations

Crème Brûlée Apricot Tart with Lavender-Vanilla Sauce

Pumpkin Crème Brûlée
and Gingerbread Financier Jack-o'-Lanterns

Boysenberry Brioche Pudding à la Heather Ho

Classic Mille-Feuille Napoleon with Crème Baumanière

Nectarine Tarte Tatin with Verbena Ice Cream

Roasted Pineapple Rugelach Envelopes
with Sour Cream–Pineapple Glacé

Toasted Lemon Pound Cake
with Grapefruit-Vanilla Curd and Grapefruit

Mile-High Apple Pie à la Mode

Passion Fruit Pinwheel Roulade with Roasted Pineapple Salad

Blackberry-Lime Curd–Filled Doughnuts
with Blackberry Sorbet and Berries

Mini Lemon Soufflé Tart with Blackberry Granita

Thumbprint Lime Meltaways

Chocolate Financier with Raspberry Ganache

Frozen Hot Chocolate Tower

Halsey Tart

YIELD: Eight 3-inch tarts

SPECIAL TOOLS:

    Candy thermometer

    Propane or butane blowtorch

    Parchment paper

    3-inch round cookie cutter

    Pie weights (optional)

    Eight 3-inch tart pans

    Standing electric mixer with a
      paddle attachment (optional)

1 recipe Crème Brûlée (page
   112), prepared through step
   5, but baked in a 9-x-13-
   inch baking pan and frozen

8 prebaked 3-inch Almond Pie
   Dough tart shells
   (page 212)

6 medium apricots, preferably
   Royal Blenheims, cut
   into eighths, pits discarded

1 cup lavender-infused Vanilla
   Sauce (see page 93)

Crème Brûlée Apricot Tart
with Lavender–Vanilla Sauce

BY BAKING CRÈME BRÛLÉE IN SHEETS AND FREEZING IT, *I can cut it into any shape and caramelize it at a moment's notice. Royal Blenheims, with their incredible depth of sweet-tangy flavor, are the aristocrats of the apricot family. But other fresh, ripe sweet apricots can be substituted. The season begins the second week of June in southern California and passes quickly.*

1. Preheat the oven to 350°F. Adjust the rack to the lower third of the oven.

2. Remove the roasting pan with the frozen crème brûlée from the freezer. Run the edge of a paring knife dipped in hot water around the crème brulée. Lay a piece of parchment paper on your work surface. Flip the crème brûlée out onto the parchment. Cut out circles using a 3-inch cookie cutter. Immediately place the brûlée circles back in the freezer. Reserve the remaining brûlée for another tart later on. It can be stored in the freezer or the refrigerator.

3. Line the tart shells with the apricots. Remove the crème brûlée circles from the freezer. Place one circle on top of the apricots in each tart shell.

4. Caramelize the top of each tart as directed in Crème Brûlée (page 112).

5. Place the tarts on a baking sheet. Bake for 5 minutes, or until the custard is defrosted and the tart is slightly warm. Serve immediately, placing the tarts on individual plates and spooning a little Vanilla Sauce around them.

COMPONENTS

Financier

+

Caramel

+

Crème Brûlée

YIELD: 8 servings

SPECIAL TOOLS:

Candy thermometer

Parchment paper

Standing electric mixer with a paddle attachment (optional)

Propane or butane blowtorch

X-Acto knife

¼ cup Apple Caramel Glaze (page 65)

¼ cup water

8 mini (3–4 inches wide) pumpkins

1 recipe Gingerbread Financier (page 170)

1 recipe Pumpkin Crème Brûlée (see page 113), prepared through step 5, but baked in a 9-x-13-inch baking pan

½ cup Croquante dust (see page 55; optional)

1 pomegranate, seeded (optional)

Pumpkin Crème Brûlée and Gingerbread Financier Jack-o'-Lanterns

WHEN MINI PUMPKINS ARRIVE JUST BEFORE HALLOWEEN, *I hollow them out and use them as decorative bowls, filling them with cake and topping them with a rich crème brûlée filling. The tops of the custard can be caramelized with a torch or at the last moment sprinkled with Croquante dust. Croquante dust will have the same caramel flavor but a different texture and look.*

You can also make these in 6-ounce ramekins, if you can't find little pumpkins.

1. Bring the glaze and water to a boil in a small saucepan. Remove from the heat and set aside.

2. With an X-Acto knife (this tool works best and will prevent you from cutting yourself), carefully cut a circle around the top of each mini pumpkin to create a lid. With a chef's knife, cut off excess bits from the inside of the lid to create a smooth, neat surface. Spoon out the seeds and fiber from the pumpkins and discard, leaving hollow shells.

3. Cut 1-inch-thick, 3-inch-wide circles of financier to fit perfectly into your pumpkins. Press into the pumpkins and spoon the caramel syrup over the financier. Top with the crème brûlée, spooning in enough to fill the pumpkins to the top. Using an offset metal spatula, smooth over the tops. Refrigerate until ready to serve.

4. Before serving, caramelize the tops as directed in Crème Brûlée (page 112) or dust liberally with Croquante pulverized into dust. Sprinkle with the pomegranate seeds. Lean the pumpkin tops against the pumpkins and serve.

COMPONENTS

Brioche

+

Vanilla Sauce

+

Fruit Sauce

+

Caramel

YIELD: 8 servings

SPECIAL TOOLS:

Standing electric mixer with a paddle attachment or a food processor

Instant-read thermometer

Silicone mat or parchment paper

Candy thermometer

½ loaf Master Brioche (page 230), cut into 1-inch cubes

1 recipe Spiced Vanilla Sauce (see page 93)

2 cups boysenberries, blackberries, or raspberries

¼ cup sugar

½ cup Blackberry-Merlot Sauce (page 295)

½ cup Apple Caramel Glaze (page 65)

Boysenberry Brioche Pudding à la Heather Ho

THIS DESSERT SPRANG FROM A NEED TO USE EVERY SCRAP *of food in the house. Stale bread makes a perfect sponge to soak up custard. The late pastry chef Heather Ho invented a brilliant nouveau version of bread pudding by baking it in a thin layer, then chilling it and layering it. The result is incredible, like a bread pudding napoleon. It can be made in advance, cut into individual portions, covered, and served warm in a matter of minutes. Serve with your choice of ice cream. If you can't find boysenberries, substitute blackberries or raspberries.*

1. Preheat the oven to 325°F. Adjust the rack to the center of the oven. Line a 9-x-13-inch baking pan with a silicone mat or parchment paper.

2. Place the cubed brioche in a medium bowl. Pour the vanilla sauce over the brioche and let sit for 10 to 15 minutes, or until the sauce is absorbed.

3. Pour the bread and custard mixture into the prepared baking pan. Spread evenly with an offset spatula. Cover with aluminum foil. Bake for 15 to 18 minutes. Remove the aluminum foil to check the custard. It should be set with a slight jiggle. If not set, continue to bake, checking every 5 minutes. Remove from the oven and place in the refrigerator to cool completely. This should take 30 to 60 minutes.

4. While the custard is cooling, place the boysenberries, sugar, and Blackberry-Merlot Sauce in a medium saucepan over medium heat and bring to a boil. Cook, stirring constantly and mashing the berries with a whisk, for 6 to 8 minutes, or until it has a jamlike consistency. Remove from the heat and let cool to room temperature.

5. Remove the bread pudding sheet from the refrigerator. Place a piece of parchment paper on your work surface. Flip the pudding out onto the work surface and remove the mat or the parchment. Cut the bread pudding sheet lengthwise into 4 strips. Place a 12-inch-square piece of aluminum foil on your work surface. Place one strip of the pudding in the center of the aluminum foil. Spread with

⅓ cup of the berry mixture. Place the next strip on top. Spread with the berry mixture. Continue with the remaining 2 pieces, alternating pudding and berries and ending with a strip of pudding. Tightly wrap in the aluminum foil. At this point the pudding can be refrigerated for 1 day until ready to use.

6. Preheat the oven to 350°F. Adjust the rack to the center of the oven.

7. Transfer the foil-wrapped bread pudding to a baking sheet. Bake for 10 to 12 minutes (15 to 20 minutes if the bread pudding has been chilled for a day), or until warmed through. Remove from the oven, unwrap, and slice off each portion. Top with Apple Caramel Glaze and serve immediately.

YIELD: 8 servings

SPECIAL TOOLS:

Standing electric mixer with a paddle attachment (optional)

Candy thermometer

Parchment paper

1 prebaked 9-x-15-inch sheet **Master Puff Pastry** (page 270)

¼ cup powdered sugar

1 recipe **Crème Baumanière** (see page 101)

2 cups strawberries, hulled and quartered

Classic Mille-Feuille Napoleon with Crème Baumanière

THE CONTRASTING TEXTURES OF PERFECTLY BAKED, CRISP, *nutty puff pastry and soft cream in this dessert are sublime. To make the cutting of the napoleons easier and neater, I cut the puff pastry into pieces before adding the final caramelized strip of pastry. My inspiration for this dish came from Wolfgang Puck and L'Oustau de Baumanière, a restaurant in Provence. Use small wild strawberries if you are lucky enough to have them or fresh local berries from your farmers' market.*

1. Preheat the broiler. Adjust the rack to 3 inches away from the broiler.

2. Using a serrated bread knife, gently cut the puff pastry into three 3-x-12-inch rectangles. Saw back and forth without leaning on the pastry so that it doesn't break. Place 1 layer on a baking sheet. Generously dust with powdered sugar, being sure to cover the top completely so that there are no exposed areas. Carefully place under the broiler. This process will take only a minute or two. Watch carefully as the sugar begins to caramelize and adjust the sheet for even broiling. Broil until completely caramelized. Remove from the broiler and set aside. This will be the top layer of your napoleon.

3. Place one of the remaining strips of puff pastry on a parchment-lined cutting board, upside-down baking sheet, or platter. Spread ½ cup of the Crème Baumanière evenly over the strip of pastry. Stud the cream with 1 cup of the strawberries, pressing the berries down gently. Gently spread ½ cup of the cream over the berries. Top with the second strip of puff pastry.

4. Cut into 8 even slices, using a serrated or offset knife to cut through both layers of pastry. Use a gentle sawing motion, allowing the knife to do the cutting. Realign the layers if necessary. Finish the napoleon by spreading ½ cup of the remaining cream onto the puff pastry and gently pressing in the remaining 1 cup berries. Spread evenly with the remaining cream, then top with the caramelized pastry strip.

5. Just before serving, using a serrated or offset knife, carefully cut the completed napoleon into 8 pieces. It will not be difficult, because the bottom layers are already cut. The napoleon will hold for a couple of hours, but it's best if you serve it at once.

COMPONENTS

Croissant Dough

+

Caramel

+

Ice Cream

YIELD: One 9-inch tart, serving 8 to 10

SPECIAL TOOLS:

Standing electric mixer with a dough hook attachment

Parchment paper

Candy thermometer

Ice cream machine

½ recipe Croissant Dough (page 278)

1 large egg

1 large egg yolk

2 tablespoons sugar

½ cup Apple Caramel Glaze (page 65)

8 medium nectarines, pitted and thinly sliced

1 recipe Lemon Verbena Ice Cream (see page 95) or whipped crème fraîche

Nectarine Tarte Tatin with Verbena Ice Cream

TRADITIONALLY TARTE TATIN IS MADE WITH APPLES, COOKED *slowly with sugar and butter until a rich, thick caramel emerges. In this variation, sliced nectarines are fanned on top of a caramel glaze, then inverted onto the crisp pastry. My version uses croissant dough instead of puff pastry. Puff pastry may be substituted.*

1. Roll the croissant dough out into a ¼-inch-thick round, 12 inches in diameter. Place on a parchment paper–lined baking sheet. Fold 1 inch of the dough in all the way around, pleating it over itself and pinching as you go, to make a rustic tart shell. Prick the center of the shell with a fork, cover with plastic film, and leave in a warm environment to proof for 1 hour.

2. Preheat the oven to 375°F. Adjust the rack to the center of the oven. Butter a 9-inch round cake pan.

3. Beat together the egg and yolk in a small bowl and brush the folded edge of the crust with this egg wash. Sprinkle the edge of the crust with the sugar. Bake for 20 to 25 minutes, or until amber brown. Remove from the oven and set aside.

4. Pour the Apple Caramel Glaze into the prepared cake pan and swirl to coat the pan. If it is hot, allow to cool.

5. Fan the sliced nectarines over the glaze, packing them in tight. Distribute any extra slices evenly over the pan.

6. Bake the nectarines for 20 minutes, or until tender, then place the prebaked pastry round on a baking sheet in the oven and rewarm it.

7. Place the round of pastry on top of the cake pan and invert the serving dish over the pastry. Then, holding one hand against the serving dish and the other, protected by an oven mitt or towel, under the cake pan, invert the cake pan onto the round and remove. Cut the tarte into wedges, top with a scoop of Lemon Verbena Ice Cream or whipped crème fraîche, and serve immediately.

COMPONENTS

Pie Dough

+

Fruit

+

Sorbet

YIELD: 16 envelopes, serving 8

SPECIAL TOOLS:

Standing electric mixer with a
  paddle attachment (optional)

Pie weights (optional)

Food processor

Ice cream machine

Parchment paper

FOR THE EGG WASH

1 large egg, plus 1 large
  egg yolk

Pinch of salt (less than
  1/8 teaspoon)

1 recipe Rugelach Dough
  (page 215), rolled out into
  a 16-inch square

3/4 cup Banana Schmutz
  (page 300)

1 Roasted Voodoo Vanilla
  Pineapple (page 303),
  chopped

1/4 cup sugar

1 recipe Sour Cream–
  Pineapple Glacé (page
  305)

Roasted Pineapple
Rugelach Envelopes with
Sour Cream—Pineapple Glacé

THIS IS A WONDERFUL COMBINATION OF FLAVORS AND
*textures: the mellow sweetness of roasted pineapple enveloped by a
tangy cream-cheese pastry, topped with ice cream.*

Preheat the oven to 375°F. Adjust the rack to the center of the oven.
Line a baking sheet with parchment paper.

EGG WASH

1. Whisk the egg, yolk, and salt together in a small bowl.

2. Lightly brush the sheet of dough with some of the egg wash.
Cut the dough into sixteen 4-inch squares. Place 2 teaspoons Banana
Schmutz in the middle of each square. Place 2 tablespoons of the
pineapple over each mound of banana.

ENVELOPES

1. Bring the four corners up to meet in the middle and gently
press together, sealing at the center. At this point the envelopes may
be chilled for several hours, or until ready to serve.

2. Place the envelopes on the prepared baking sheet. Lightly
brush the tops with egg wash, then dust lightly with sugar. Bake for 20
to 25 minutes, or until golden brown. Place 2 envelopes on each
plate and top with a scoop of glacé.

COMPONENTS
Pound Cake

+

Curd

+

Caramel

YIELD: 8 servings

SPECIAL TOOLS:

Parchment paper

Standing electric mixer with
paddle attachment (optional)

2½-inch round cookie cutter

¾-inch or 1-inch round cookie
cutter

Toaster oven (optional)

Food processor (optional)

Candy thermometer

8 1-inch-thick slices Lemon
Pound Cake (page 142)

1 cup Grapefruit-Vanilla Curd
(page 76)

1 white grapefruit, preferably
Oro Blanco, peeled and
segmented

1 red grapefruit, preferably
Ruby Red, peeled and
segmented

½ cup Apple Caramel Glaze
(page 65), at room
temperature

Toasted Lemon Pound Cake with Grapefruit–Vanilla Curd and Grapefruit

TOASTED POUND CAKE HAS A WONDERFUL TEXTURE. I LOVE *biting through the crisp outer crust into the warm, tender crumb. Pairing vanilla curd and grapefruit mellows the tanginess of the fruit. Hidden in the center of the cake, the curd adds a melt-in-your-mouth surprise. Oro Blanco grapefruits are a white variety that is softer and sweeter than many other varieties. The Texas Ruby Reds, however, are sweet, sweet, sweet.*

1. Using a 2½- or 3-inch round cookie cutter, cut each slice of cake into a circle. Using a ¾- or 1-inch cookie cutter, cut a hole in the center of each round to produce a doughnut shape. Reserve the cake scraps for another use. You can also use a doughtnut cutter.

2. Toast the cake "doughnuts" in a toaster oven or under the broiler on medium heat for 2 minutes, or until golden brown. Transfer to individual serving plates and spoon the grapefruit–vanilla curd into the holes. Spoon a small amount of the curd onto the cake, then arrange the grapefruit segments over the cake, fanning them from the center in alternate colors.

3. Just before serving, brush with the caramel glaze, then serve immediately.

COMPONENTS

Pie Dough

+

Caramel

+

Caramel Sauce

+

Vanilla Sauce

YIELD: One 9-inch pie, serving 8

SPECIAL TOOLS:

 Parchment paper

 Standing electric mixer with a
  paddle attachment (optional)

 Pie weights (optional)

 Candy thermometer

 Ice cream machine

6 Braeburn apples, peeled,
 cored, and cut into eighths

6 Fuji apples, peeled, cored,
 and cut into eighths

1 cup fresh lemon juice

1 recipe Master 3-2-1 Flaky Pie
 Dough (page 209)

4 tablespoons (½ stick)
 unsalted butter

½ cup sugar

1 cup Apple Caramel Glaze
 (page 65)

1 cup Creamy Caramel Sauce
 (page 58)

½ cup heavy cream

FOR THE EGG WASH

1 large egg

1 tablespoon water

 Pinch of salt (less than
  ⅛ teaspoon)

1 recipe Vanilla Ice Cream
 (page 94)

Mile-High Apple Pie à la Mode

THIS PIE IS PACKED WITH APPLES AND CARAMEL. BECAUSE *the apples are cooked before you put them into the pie, you don't have to worry about the fruit shrinking away from the crust or not being fully cooked. I love to combine several apples of varying tartness: Fuji, Braeburn, and Royal Gala or Granny Smith and Black Jonathan. Use whatever you can get.*

1. Line two baking sheets with parchment paper.

2. Place the apple slices in a large bowl. Add the lemon juice and toss to coat the apples evenly. Set aside.

3. Roll out half of the dough into a 12-inch round. Fold it in half and then in half again and position it over a 9-inch pie pan. Unfold and ease the dough into the pan, releasing any air pockets, until it fits perfectly along the bottom. Do not stretch the dough. Using scissors, cut off the excess dough from the rim, leaving a ½-inch overhang. Reserve the excess. Refrigerate for at least 30 minutes.

4. Add the excess trimmings to the remaining half of the dough. Dust lightly with flour and roll into a 13-inch round. Place on one of the prepared baking sheets, cover with plastic film, and refrigerate for at least 30 minutes.

5. Cook the apples in batches (otherwise it will be difficult to get a good caramelization). Heat 2 tablespoons of the butter and ¼ cup of the sugar in a very large sauté pan over high heat. Cook until medium-dark brown, 2 to 3 minutes. Add ½ cup of the Apple Caramel Glaze and ½ cup of the Creamy Caramel Sauce and bring to a boil. Add half of the apples with half of the liquid in the bowl. Cook over high heat, tossing occasionally, until the apples are caramelized evenly, 4 to 5 minutes. Add ¼ cup of the heavy cream and cook for 30 seconds more. Remove from the heat. Using a slotted spoon, transfer the apples to the second prepared baking sheet to cool and carefully pour the liquid into a bowl. Set aside. Repeat with remaining butter, sugar, caramel sauce and glaze, apples and their liquid, and cream. Transfer the apples to the baking sheet. Return the liquid from the first batch to the pan. Bring to a boil over high heat. Boil for 7 to 8 minutes, or until reduced by half and thickened. Pour into a bowl and allow to cool.

6. Preheat the oven to 425°F. Adjust the rack to the lower third of the oven.

Whisk together the egg, water, and salt in a small bowl.

ASSEMBLING THE PIE

1. Fill the pie shell with the prepared apples and cooled reduced liquid. Lightly brush the rim of the shell with some of the egg wash. Place the remaining circle of dough over the top and tuck the edge of the overhanging dough under the edge of the bottom dough. Press together to form a seal with your fingers. Crimp the edges together, pinching with thumb to finger, finger to thumb, to make an attractive fluted edge. Lightly brush the crust with egg wash. With scissors or a sharp knife, make a few slashes in the top crust. Place on a baking sheet.

2. Bake for 10 minutes. Turn the oven down to 350°F and bake for 30 to 35 minutes more, or until the crust is dark golden brown. Cool the pie on a rack until ready to serve. Top with Vanilla Ice Cream.

YIELD: 8 servings

SPECIAL TOOLS:

  Parchment paper

  Standing electric mixer with a
    whisk attachment (optional)

  Candy thermometer

  Food processor

½ cup water

½ cup sugar

1 jasmine tea bag

1 recipe Master Génoise,
   baked in a 12½-x-17½-inch
   baking sheet, made with
   4 tablespoons (½ stick)
   butter (see Variation,
   page 153)

2 cups Passion Fruit Curd
   (page 78)

½ Roasted Voodoo Vanilla
   Pineapple (page 303),
   cut into ½-inch cubes

½ mango, peeled, pitted, and
   cut into ½-inch cubes

4 strawberries, cut into
   ¼-inch cubes

2 fresh mint leaves, finely
   julienned

Powdered sugar

Passion Fruit Pinwheel Roulade with Roasted Pineapple Salad

TURNING AN ORDINARY CAKE INTO A ROULADE (ROLLED-UP *cake*) *is no more trouble than filling it in the traditional way. In fact, I think it's a little easier. The presentation, however, is much more special. The ingredients here are exotic. This dessert is great after a spicy meal.*

1. Bring the water, sugar, and tea bag to a boil in a small saucepan over high heat. Remove from the heat and let steep for 5 minutes. Squeeze out the tea bag before discarding it.

2. Place the cake on a sheet of parchment paper and brush it with all of the jasmine syrup. Top with the Passion Fruit Curd, spreading it over all but 1 inch of one long side of the génoise with an offset spatula.

3. Using the parchment to help, roll the cake up into a jellyroll. Place in the refrigerator for at least 1 hour.

4. Meanwhile, toss together the pineapple, mango, strawberries, and mint in a small bowl.

5. Remove the cake from the refrigerator and slice off the two ends. Then cut into 8 even slices, each about 2 inches thick. An easy way to do this is to cut the roulade in half, then cut each half in half, and cut the quarters in half again. Place each wheel on a plate. Dust with powdered sugar, garnish with the pineapple salad, and serve.

COMPONENTS

Brioche

+

Curd

+

Fruit Sauce

+

Sorbet

YIELD: 12 doughnuts, serving 6

SPECIAL TOOLS:

 Deep fryer (optional)

 Candy thermometer

 Food processor or blender

 Pastry bag with a small or medium
 (#2 or #4) plain tip

 Standing electric mixer with
 paddle and dough hook
 attachments or a food
 processor

 2-inch cookie cutter

 Ice cream machine

 2 quarts vegetable oil

1¼ cups Blackberry-Lime Curd
 (page 77)

½ batch Brioche Doughnut
 dough (page 260),
 prepared through step 4
 (make the entire batch and
 use the rest for another
 purpose)

 2 tablespoons powdered
 sugar

1½ cups Blackberry-Merlot
 Sauce (page 295)

 1 recipe Blackberry Sorbet
 (page 297)

 2 cups berries, such as
 blackberries, raspberries,
 or blueberries

Blackberry–Lime Curd–Filled Doughnuts with Blackberry Sorbet and Berries

WARM DOUGHNUTS ARE TRULY COMFORT FOOD. AT SPAGO, *I serve the doughnuts with sorbet and fresh ollalieberries, which are fatter and a touch more acidic than boysenberries.*

1. Heat the oil to 350°F in a 4-quart pot or deep fryer.

2. Fill a pastry bag fitted with a plain tip half full of Blackberry-Lime Curd. Set aside.

3. Roll the doughnut dough out into a ½-inch-thick rectangle, about 9½ x 12½ inches. Cut into circles using a 2-inch cookie cutter.

4. Carefully place the circles, in batches, in the oil. Deep-fry on the first side for 1 minute, then flip the doughnuts over with a slotted spoon and fry for 1 minute more, or until brown. Drain on a rack set over paper towels.

5. When the doughnuts are cool enough to handle, make a small incision in the side of each one with a paring knife. Insert the pastry-bag tip into the incision and fill with a squirt of Blackberry-Lime Curd. Repeat with the remaining doughnuts and curd. Place a pool of Blackberry-Merlot Sauce on each of six dessert plates or in wide dessert bowls. To serve, dust the doughnuts with powdered sugar and set 2 on each plate on top of the sauce. Finish with a scoop of Blackberry Sorbet and berries on the side, and serve immediately.

YIELD: 8 servings

SPECIAL TOOLS:

8 martini glasses

Standing electric mixer with paddle and whisk attachments (optional)

2-inch mini tart pans

Pie weights (optional)

Food processor (optional)

Candy thermometer

4 cups Blackberry Granita (page 296)

16 Sweet Dough 2-inch mini tart shells, blind-baked (page 216)

½ cup Master Lemon Curd (page 75)

½ recipe Lemon Soufflé (page 79), but made with the full amount (¼ cup) of sugar

Mini Lemon Soufflé Tarts with Blackberry Granita

I CREATED THESE TINY TARTS FOR OUR TASTING MENU AT *Spago. They're great when you need a light dessert. The tartlets are placed right on top of the granita and eaten with a spoon.*

1. Preheat the oven to 425°F. Adjust the rack to the center of the oven. Place the martini glasses in the freezer for 15 minutes.

2. Scrape the granita with a fork and spoon it into the chilled glasses. Return to the freezer.

3. Place the prebaked mini tart shells on a baking sheet and fill them with the lemon curd. Set aside.

4. Make the soufflé base. Top each mini tart with 3 tablespoons of the soufflé base, creating a cotton candy–like swirl.

5. Bake for 7 to 8 minutes, or until golden brown.

6. Just before removing the tarts from the oven, remove the martini glasses from the freezer. Carefully remove the tarts from the oven and place one directly on the granita and the other on the plate. Serve immediately.

COMPONENTS
Cookie Dough

+

Curd

YIELD: About 2 dozen cookies

SPECIAL TOOLS:

Standing electric mixer with a paddle attachment (optional)

Silicone mats or parchment paper

Food processor (optional)

Candy thermometer

Pastry bag with small (#2) piping tip

1 recipe Lime Meltaways, rolled but not baked (see page 187)

½ cup powdered sugar for dusting

1½ cups Master Lemon Curd (page 75)

Thumbprint Lime Meltaways

THESE MAKE A COOL AND REFRESHING COMBINATION. SERVE *them on a sunny afternoon with iced mint tea or a mojito cocktail.*

1. Preheat the oven to 350°F. Adjust the rack to the lower third of the oven. Line two baking sheets with silicone mats or parchment paper.

2. Place the rolled cookies on the prepared baking sheets. Press your thumb into each ball, creating a concave center.

3. Bake the cookies for 8 to 10 minutes, or until light golden brown. Remove from the oven and immediately dust with a generous amount of powdered sugar.

4. Let the cookies cool, then fill the indentations with the Lemon Curd, using a pastry bag, and serve.

COMPONENTS

Financier

+

Ganache

YIELD: 8 servings

SPECIAL TOOLS:

Eight 8-inch savarin molds

Standing electric mixer with a paddle attachment (optional)

Candy thermometer

Piping bag with a medium (#4) star tip

2¾ cups Chocolate Financier batter (page 168) (make the entire recipe and save the rest for another purpose)

1 recipe Raspberry Ganache (page 31)

2 cups raspberries

Chocolate Financier with Raspberry Ganache

THESE ELEGANT LITTLE DESSERTS ARE INCREDIBLY *chocolatey. I fill regular or mini savarin molds with chocolate financier batter and bake. Once the cakes have cooled, I pipe soft ganache into the center. You could also fill the center with warm chocolate sauce, jam, or berries.*

1. Preheat the oven to 350°F. Adjust the rack to the center of the oven. Spray the savarin mold(s) with pan spray.

2. Fill the molds with the Chocolate Financier batter. Bake for 15 to 20 minutes, or until a toothpick comes out clean. Cool to room temperature.

3. Fill a piping bag with the Raspberry Ganache and swirl 2 to 3 tablespoons into the center hole of each cake.

4. Serve with raspberries on the side.

COMPONENTS

Génoise

+

Ganache

YIELD: 6 servings

SPECIAL TOOLS:

Standing electric mixer with a whisk attachment

Parchment paper

Candy thermometer

1 recipe Bittersweet Chocolate Mousse (page 40), prepared through step 5

1 9-inch round Chocolate Génoise (page 154)

2 ounces milk chocolate, shaved with a Microplane (1½ cups shaved chocolate)

Frozen Hot Chocolate Tower

THIS DESSERT IS AN HOMAGE TO DESSERT PASTRY CHEF *and genius Pierre Hermé and is the only challenging one in this book. A mentor to all pastry chefs, Hermé has taken traditional French pastry to new heights. This is a version of his wonderful chocolate tower.*

1. Spray a 9-x-5-x-3-inch loaf pan with pan spray. Line the pan with a large piece of plastic film. Press well into the edges, leaving no wrinkles, to create a perfect lining.

2. Spoon the mousse into the center and, using an offset spatula, smooth the surface evenly. Drape the excess plastic wrap over the top to cover and freeze for 4 hours, or until frozen solid.

3. Cut the génoise into twelve 1-inch squares, ½ inch thick (if the bottom is too thick, the tower will wobble). This will serve to anchor your towers.

4. Line a cutting board with parchment paper. Working quickly in a cool environment, remove the mousse loaf from the pan. Using a chef's knife, trim the sides so that all the edges are straight and the corners are square. Cut the loaf into thirds lengthwise to make 3 strips. Turn each strip over on its side and cut each in half lengthwise again, to give you six 9-inch strips. Cut each strip in half across the middle, yielding twelve 4½-x-1¼-inch rectangles. Make sure the bottoms are level, and trim if necessary. Stand the rectangles upright atop the génoise squares and very gently press them down onto the génoise, being careful not to make indentations on the sides with your fingers. Freeze for 30 minutes, or until frozen solid. If you are worried about the mousse melting while you are making the towers, freeze the pieces you're not working with. The towers will keep, well wrapped, in the freezer for 2 weeks.

5. Remove the towers from the freezer just before serving and roll them in the chocolate shavings until completely coated. Place 2 towers on each plate and serve.

COMPONENTS

Short Dough

+

Ganache

+

Caramel

YIELD: 8 individual tarts

SPECIAL TOOLS:

Standing electric mixer with paddle and whisk attachments (optional)

Pie weights (optional)

Candy thermometer

Pastry bag with a large (#6) plain tip

1 recipe Chocolate Short Dough (page 221)

2 cups Whipped Caramel Cream (page 60)

½ cup Creamy Caramel Sauce (page 58)

½ cup Ganache Glaze (page 28), warmed

Halsey Tart

I HAD THE HONOR OF WORKING IN LONDON WITH A RETIRED *candy maker for Mars, Mr. Halsey, who taught me the original recipe for the Twix bar. This is my restaurant rendition.*

1. Roll out the dough into 8 individual 3-inch tart shells. Preheat the oven to 350°F. Adjust the rack to the lower third of the oven. Prick the dough and line with a faux filling as directed on page 211. Place on a baking sheet and set aside.

2. Fit a pastry bag with a large (#6) plain tip and fill it half full of Whipped Caramel Cream. Pipe a ring of cream around the inside edge of each tart, like a doughnut. The cream should be higher than the edges of the crust. Fill the "doughnut holes" to just below the top of the cream with a heaped tablespoon of Creamy Caramel Sauce. Cover with the remaining Whipped Caramel Cream. Using an offset spatula, carefully smooth the tops, creating a flat surface.

3. Place in the freezer for at least 20 minutes.

4. Remove the tarts from the freezer and spoon 1 tablespoon warm Ganache Glaze over the top of a tart. Pick it up and quickly swirl the topping over the cream to coat evenly. Repeat with the remaining tarts. Refrigerate for 15 minutes, then serve.

NOTE

The tarts can be frozen before glazing (step 4) for up to 2 weeks in an airtight container. Remove from the freezer, glaze as directed, then refrigerate for 2 hours to thaw the frozen tarts.

BAKING TERMS

Baba au rhum [ba-ba o ROOM] A sponge cake baked in a tall cylindrical mold, studded with dried fruits and soaked in rum syrup. A cousin to **savarin**.

Bain-marie [ban-mah-REE] French term for **water bath**.

Ball, soft and hard Descriptions of stages of sugar syrup at different temperatures. When a small amount of boiling sugar syrup is dropped into water, it forms a pliable ball. At the soft-ball stage, it remains pliable and will collapse when removed from the water. The temperature ranges from 240° to 245°F. At the hard-ball stage, the ball is pliable but will retain its shape. This stage ranges from 260° to 265°F.

Bavarian cream or bavarois [bah-vah-RWAH] A cold cream composed mainly of an egg custard, whipped cream, various flavorings, and gelatin.

Beignet [ben-YAY] French term for a small, light, batter-coated, deep-fried item similar to a fritter. In English, the term refers to a deep-fried **pâte à choux** pastry or, in New Orleans, a deep-fried yeasted pastry served hot with a dusting of powdered sugar.

Bench flour Flour kept in a separate bowl, used for lightly dusting the work surface and dough. Always use all-purpose flour, since the other types of flour are too high either in starch or in gluten.

Beurrage [burr-RAJ] French term for the butter once it has been made ready for laminated dough. Also called **beurre de tourage** or **butter block**.

Beurre French word for butter.

Beurre de tourage [BURR de toor-AHJ] French term meaning "butter for turning," this butter is used in the laminating process. It is a room-temperature block of butter that is spread over dough in an even layer and, through a series of folds and turns, transformed into many layers of butter sandwiched between layers of dough.

Beurre noisette/noir Butter that has been melted and cooked until the salts and solids separate, sink to the bottom, and begin to color. When the solids become golden brown, the butter is referred to as *beurre noisette*, or "hazelnut butter." When the solids become dark brown, it is *beurre noir*, or "black butter."

Biga [BEE-gah] A wet **sponge** consisting of water, flour, and yeast mixed together, used in dough making to assist in a preliminary fermentation process. During this process, spongelike bubbles form.

Blind baking The prebaking of a tart or pie shell. A faux filling, such as pie weights or small dried beans, is used to hold the dough in shape during baking, thus preventing the sides from melting and the bottom from bubbling.

Bloom 1. (noun) Grayish film that appears on chocolate. This discoloration is caused by fluctuating temperatures. Chocolate that has bloomed is perfectly good for melting and baking and should never be discarded.
2. (verb) To "bloom" gelatin means to add cold water, which allows the gelatin to soften before it is dissolved.

Bûche de Noël [BOOSH duh noh-EHL] French term for Yule log. Traditionally a Christmas cake made of chocolate **génoise** baked in a sheet, spread with chocolate or mocha buttercream, and rolled up and roughly frosted to resemble a log. It is often decorated with **meringue** "mushrooms" and pistachio "moss."

Butter block See **beurrage**.

Brioche [BREE-ohsh] French term for a rich yeasted bread dating back to medieval times, from the word *brier (broyer)*, meaning "to break apart."

Brittle A confection of cooked sugar, usually containing nuts, that becomes brittle when cooled

Cannoli [can-NO-lee] A traditional Sicilian pastry made from a thinly rolled dough that is cut into rounds, wrapped around metal tubes, and deep-fried. Once cooled, the dough is filled with sweetened ricotta cheese and often chocolate chips, candied orange peel, and nuts.

Caramelizing The complex process that occurs when sugar, either granulated sugar or the natural sugar present in ingredients such as vegetables or milk, is heated and begins to cook, liquefying and darkening in color from golden to very dark brown.

Chemical leavening Baking powder or baking soda, which aids in the process of leavening.

Chiboust [chi-BOOST] French term for a pastry cream lightened with **meringue** (preferably Italian).

Confiture	French term for preserved fruits.
Crack, soft and hard	Descriptions of stages of sugar syrup when heated. When a small bit of boiling sugar syrup is dropped into water, it forms strands. At the soft-crack stage, the strands remain pliable. This stage ranges in temperature from 270° to 275°F. At the hard-crack stage, the sugar syrup will separate into thin, brittle strands. This stage ranges from 285° to 315°F.
Creaming	The process of beating, usually fat or fat and sugar, until the texture is softened and lumps are eliminated. The texture becomes nearly liquid, which makes it easy to add more ingredients.
Crème	[krehm] French word for cream.
Crème anglaise/English cream	[KREHM ahn-GLAZE] French term for rich, pourable custard. AKA vanilla sauce.
Crème brûlée	[krehm broo-LAY] French term for a delicate baked cream custard with a hard caramelized sugar topping.
Crème caramel	[KREHM kah-rah-MEHL] French term for a custard that is baked in a caramel-coated mold. When chilled and unmolded, the cooked caramel runs out onto the plate as a sauce.
Crème chantilly	[KREHM shan-tee-YEE] French term for lightly sweetened whipped cream, often flavored with vanilla or liqueur.
Crème pâtissière	[KREHM pah-tis-si-AYRE] French term for pastry cream.
Crimp	To pinch or press pastry, either to seal it or to form decorative edges or ridges.
Croissant	[kwah-SAHN] French term for crescent. This buttery, rich pastry is made from yeasted **laminated** dough.
Croquante	[kroh-KAWNT] This French term meaning "crispy" or "crunchy" refers to a confection made of nut brittle.
Croquembouche	[kroh-kuhm-BOOSH] French term meaning "crunch in the mouth." It refers to a whole array of elaborate pastries traditionally served at weddings, baptisms, and other religious celebrations. The modern versions are architectural masterpieces made of cream puffs coated with caramel and stacked into a pyramid shape.
Crumb	The inside of a baked product.
Crumb coat	A thin layer of frosting applied to a cake as a base coat to seal in the crumb of the cake. Additional frosting is then applied lavishly over it.
Curd	A smooth custardlike mixture made from juice (traditionally citrus), sugar, butter, and egg yolks. Once cooked and cooled, the yolks congeal and form a thick, spreadable mixture.

Cutting in	The process of combining a quantity of fat (butter, lard, shortening) into a quantity of dry ingredients (flour, sugar, leavening). The two are rubbed together until the fat is broken down to the desired size (usually walnut, pea, or cornmeal size). Care must be taken to keep the ingredients cold, which prevents the fat and dry ingredients from actually mixing together and creates flakiness.
Denaturing	Literally, the shaking loose or unfolding of protein structures as a result of heating, agitating, or acidifying, which opens them up to realignment. This is what happens when you make **curd** and vanilla sauce. Egg proteins break down and realign, resulting in a thicker mixture.
Détrempe	[DAY-tromp] French term for the dough used in the preparation of **puff pastry** and other **laminated** doughs in which a dough and a block of butter, through a series of folds and turns, form many layers.
Dock	To prick holes all over the surface of a dough (pie, tart, bread, crackers) before baking to prevent uneven bubbling or rising. The holes allow the steam that accumulates under a dough to escape as it bakes.
Dredge	To sprinkle or coat with a powdered substance, usually flour.
Dulce de leche	[DUL-chay duh LAY-chay] Spanish for "sweet cream," this caramel is made by heating and reducing sweetened condensed milk. You can find it in Mexican markets or specialty food stores.
Dumpling	A rounded mass of steamed or boiled dough, sometimes flavored and often filled or stuffed.
Dutch process	Adding alkali to cocoa powder, which darkens the powder and reduces acidity and clumping.
Éclair	[ay-KLEHR] Meaning "flash of light" or "lightning," this traditional French pastry is a custard-filled **pâte à choux** tube that is glazed with chocolate.
Egg wash	A glaze made up of beaten egg(s), sometimes with the addition of water and a pinch of salt, that is brushed over pastries before baking.
Emulsify	To suspend small globules of one liquid in a second liquid in such a way that the two substances, which are normally incapable of mixing, blend together. Ice cream, mayonnaise, and ganache are all emulsions.
Faux filling	See **pie weights**.
Fermentation	A chemical reaction in which microorganisms (yeast) eat up sugar and other carbohydrates, giving off gas (carbon dioxide) and alcohol, which gives lift to dough and converts sweet foods to alcohol.
Financier	[fee-nahn-see-AY] A simple yet highly versatile batter that can be baked into cookies and cakes. The word comes from the French word for

banker. Traditionally the loaves were baked in rectangular pans resembling gold bricks.

Flute	See **crimp** or **scallop**.
Foaming	Whipping ingredients to incorporate air, resulting in a mass of bubbles.
Folding	To gently incorporate two or more ingredients, such as egg whites and batter, in as few strokes as possible, maintaining the integrity of the ingredients while combining fully.
Fondue	From the French word for "melted," fondue has several meanings, but all refer to dishes in which something is dipped into a hot melted substance.
Ganache	[gahn-AHSH] French term for a rich, versatile mixture made up of equal parts pasteurized cream and chocolate.
Gelato	[jeh-LAH-toh] Italian version of ice cream, which is churned with less air than ordinary ice cream, resulting in a denser texture.
Génoise	[jayn-WHAHZ] French term for a sponge cake in which eggs and sugar are heated together over hot water before being whisked. This recipe was taken to France from Genoa, Italy.
Gluten	The protein found in wheat, which, when developed properly, lends its elastic strength to bread dough, enabling the dough to capture gas and rise. Different flours have different levels of gluten. The more gluten, the tougher the dough and the better for things like yeasted breads. The less gluten, the less elastic and more tender the dough, and the better for cakes.
Gougère	[goo-ZHEHR] A choux/cream puff pastry flavored with gruyère cheese.
Granita/granité	[grah-nee-TAY] Italian or French term for a sweet, flavored frozen ice mixture, which is stirred frequently during the freezing time to create a fine grainy texture.
High ratio	Term referring to specific cakes that contain more sugar than flour.
Homogenous	Refers to a product mixed to the point at which all of the separate particles are the same size and the whole is stabilized.
Ice bath	A container filled halfway with ice and cold water, into which another container will be set.
Laminated	From the Latin word *laminae* (layers). Refers to the process of creating hundreds of thin layers of dough by rolling in butter and folding the dough over onto itself many times. Puff pastry, croissants, Danish, and pain au chocolat are all made with laminated doughs.
Lean	Refers to dough that does not have a high content of butter and eggs compared to other, richer doughs.

Leavening	From the Latin meaning "to lift," or "lighten," a raising agent for baked goods, such as yeast, baking soda, or baking powder.
Lightening the batter	The process of blending a quarter or third of the lighter ingredient into a batter (for example, whipped eggs) before folding in the rest.
Liquefiers	Also known as *tenderizers,* these can moisten, color, lubricate, and aid in the **creaming** process. Examples are sugar, butter, or liquids such as water, milk, and cream.
Macerate	To infuse with flavor or soften food by soaking in a liquid.
Madeleine	A small buttery cake baked in a traditional scallop-shell mold and served as a cookie.
Meringue	An airy, crisp confection made with beaten egg whites, sugar, and sometimes flavoring. There are three basic types of meringue. For Italian meringue, the sugar is dissolved into a 240°F syrup, which is then drizzled slowly into the egg whites as they are being beaten. For Swiss meringue, the egg whites and sugar are heated together and then beaten to their desired peak. For common or French meringue, the sugar is gradually sprinkled over the egg whites as they are being beaten.
Mocha	The common name for the flavor combination of chocolate and coffee, named for Arabian coffee beans shipped from the port of Mocha, Yemen.
Mousse	French term for foam or lather.
Noisette	[nwah-ZETT] French word for hazelnut. It can refer to something made from hazelnuts or something with a dark and nutty flavor.
Oeufs à la neige	[EUHFS ah lah NEHZH] French term for floating islands, sweetened meringue mounds poached in milk and then placed over a thin custard or other type of sauce.
Oven spring	Rapid rise of yeasted dough in the oven in the first 10 minutes of baking.
Oxidation	Loss of freshness as a result of prolonged exposure to air.
Packing	The process of packing freshly made ice cream into containers and freezing to give it a firmer consistency.
Paddle	A flat, spade-shaped attachment for a standing electric mixer, designed to beat or cream ingredients with a minimum of air incorporation.
Pain au chocolat	[PAN o shock-o-LAH] French term for bread with chocolate, traditionally made with **croissant** dough wrapped around a strip of chocolate. The dough is rolled up into a small, square package resembling a croissant.
Palmiers	[palm-YAYS] Puff pastry cookies traditionally made in the shape of elephant ears.

Parfait	[pahr-FAY] From the French word meaning "perfect," a parfait is a frozen custard dessert.
Pâte à choux	[paht ah SHOO] Cream puff dough, from the French words meaning "pastry cabbage."
Pâte brisée	[paht bree-ZAY] French term for short pastry.
Pâte feuilletée	[paht foy-yuh-TAY] French term for pastry leaves or puff pastry, referring to the flaky layers of dough created by multiple turns.
Pâte sablée	[paht sab-LAY] French term for dough with a high proportion of butter and thus having a sandy, crumbly texture.
Pâte sucrée	[paht soo-KRAY] French term for a rich sweetened pastry with a high butter content, often used for tarts.
Paton	[pa-TON] French term for a block of laminated dough after the butter is folded into the **détrempe**, as in **puff pastry** or **croissants**.
Pie weights	Small bean-size weights of ceramic or metal used to weigh down the bottom of a pie shell that is being blind-baked.
Poach	To cook food in barely simmering (not boiling) liquid.
Poolish	[poo-LISH] French term for a Polish technique of creating a wet **sponge** to assist in a preliminary fermentation process. See **biga**.
Pot de crème	[poh duh KREHM] French term meaning "pot of cream," a traditional creamy custard cooked and served in small ramekins.
Praline	A candy made with almonds or other nuts and caramelized sugar. It can be eaten as is or ground to create a paste for fillings. In New Orleans, pralines are made with brown sugar and pecans.
Profiterole	A small **pâte à choux** pastry filled with ice cream, much like a cream puff.
Proof	To ferment yeast or a yeasted product. Technically the term refers to the last **fermentation** before a product is baked, when it is already in the shape of the loaf or pastry. Also used to describe the "proving" of granular yeast, in which it is combined with warm water and sugar as a test for freshness. Fresh yeast should bubble and foam within several minutes.
Puff pastry	Flaky layered pastry made with unyeasted dough laminated with many layers of butter. Also called **pâte feuilleté**.
Punch down	To agitate a fermented dough to expel stale carbon dioxide and incorporate fresh oxygen. This allows the dough to ferment, or rise again, improving the texture and flavor of the finished bread.
Religieuse	[ruh-li-je-EUZ] Stacked choux/cream puff pastries named in French for their resemblance to nuns wearing habits.

Ribbon	The stage at which a whipped mixture (usually including eggs) forms a pattern reminiscent of a ribbon when it is scooped up and allowed to fall off the spoon back into the bowl.
Roll in	To incorporate a block of butter (butter block or **beurre de tourage**) into the dough (**détrempe**) when making **laminated** dough.
Room temperature	A temperature between 65° and 75°F. Not chilled and not warmed. Ingredients at room temperature are usually easier to stir, spread, cream, and fold than those that are chilled.
Rotate	To turn a pan or baking sheet 180° halfway through baking to ensure even color and baking. Also refers to moving ingredients periodically through the refrigerator, freezer, and pantry so that the oldest is in front and therefore used first. Professionals refer to the rotation of products as FIFO—"first in, first out." This ensures that products are at their freshest and reduces spoilage.
Roulade	[roo-LAHD] French term for something that has been rolled up like a jellyroll, usually with a sweet or savory filling.
Rugelach	[RUHG-uh-lahkh] A dough made with cream cheese that is rolled into a crescent shape and filled with jam, nuts, or dried fruits. Traditionally served during Hanukkah.
Sabayon	[sah-bah-YAWN] French term for a frothy sauce made of beaten egg yolks, wine, and sugar (*zabaglione* in Italian).
Sacristains	[SAC-ris-tans] French corkscrew-shaped cookies made of puff pastry, often rolled in nuts and crystal sugar. Named for a wand, which the cookie resembles, used by priests in the Roman Catholic Church.
Savarin	A cake made from a soft yeasted dough. It is baked in a doughnut-shaped mold and soaked in syrup.
Scallop	Refers to a fluted-edge pastry or cutter.
Score	To make indentations on the surface of food as decoration or to assist in the cutting of foods once they have been cooked. See **dock**.
Semifreddo	From the Italian word for half-cold, the term refers to a variety of partially frozen desserts, including cakes and custards.
Short	Having a high fat content, which makes cookies and pastries tender.
Short dough	Dough that has a high amount/ratio of butter.
Sift	To aerate a quantity of dry ingredients before combining into a batter or dough by passing through a fine wire mesh. Sifting removes lumps and adds air.
Simple syrup	A liquid ingredient, made by boiling sugar and water until the sugar is

dissolved. Standard simple syrup is equal parts sugar and water. It is used for sweetening, glazing, soaking cakes, and poaching. To make syrup, stir together equal parts of sugar and water in a saucepan, bring to a boil over medium-high heat, stirring occasionally, and boil until the sugar is dissolved, about 1 minute. Cover immediately with plastic film or a lid and allow to cool.

Soft-serve Refers to the texture of ice cream or piped ganache when silky and smooth.

Sorbet [sore-BAY] French term for a frozen dessert made by combining fruit (usually) and syrup and processing the mixture in an ice cream machine.

Soufflé [soo-FLAY] From the French word *souffler,* meaning "to blow or puff." Egg whites are beaten to medium-peak stage and folded into a base. When baked, the mixture puffs into a wonderful dessert.

Sponge A thin batter of flour, water, yeast, and sometimes sugar, made at the beginning of a bread recipe. It gives the dough a head start toward fermentation and adds flavor and texture to the finished bread.

Stabilizers Also known as *solidifiers,* stabilizers give structure to and strengthen, thicken, and solidify baked products. Examples are flour and eggs.

Streaming Adding an ingredient in a steady flow.

Temper To adjust the temperature of a product.

- **EGGS** are tempered before being added to a hot ingredient to prevent them from scrambling. A small amount of the hot ingredient is stirred into the egg to warm it, then the egg is added to the hot ingredient.

- **CHOCOLATE** is tempered to stabilize the fat crystals, which results in a shiny, hard chocolate that snaps when broken. Tempering chocolate requires several stages of cooling and reheating. Chocolate in block or bar form is in the tempered state. Once it is melted, the temper is lost and must be reinstituted by the cook if a shiny, crisp finish is desired. Chocolate that has lost its temper is subject to a hazy film called **bloom**.

- **ICE CREAM OR SORBET** can be tempered if it is too hard to scoop. Leave it at room temperature until it begins to soften, then return it to the freezer for 10 minutes. Repeat until the desired consistency is reached.

Truffle Named after the much-sought-after and rare fungus it resembles, this is a rich ganache confection made of chocolate, cream, and/or butter with various flavorings such as liqueurs and spices.

Turns Single and double, or "book," turns refer to the process of folding **laminated** dough to create many flaky layers.

Warming	Heating very slightly. Keeping in mind that your body temperature is 98.6°F, warm is only a moderate degree of heat.
Water bath	Used to diffuse the heat when melting chocolate and cooking custards. The chocolate or custard is placed in a separate vessel above or within a pot or pan of boiling water, so that it cooks or melts without reaching the boiling point. Also known by the French term *bain-marie*.
Whip	To incorporate air into a mixture of ingredients, most often egg whites, eggs, or cream, by stirring with a wire whisk. Stages of whipped ingredients are measured in terms of "peaks" (soft, medium, or stiff).

- **SUPERSOFT PEAK** will barely cling to the beater; it has body, yet if you run your finger through the center of the egg whites, it barely forms a line. The slightly thickened consistency is perfect for mousses or bavarians.

- **SOFT PEAK**: The egg whites or cream just cling to the beater. If you run your finger through, it will form a line, which will then come back together. Best used for topping off a dessert.

- **MEDIUM PEAK** stands up, then the end of the peak falls over ever so gently. Best for covering/icing cakes and for soufflés.

- **FIRM PEAK** stands at attention; the egg whites have expanded to their fullest volume. Firm whipped cream peaks are good for piping decorations.

BASIC TOOLS

More than any other kind of cooking, baking requires the right tools for the right job. This doesn't mean that it's always necessary to buy the newest gadgets (I still cherish my grandmother's pastry wheels), but there are times to make investments in your kitchen arsenal. Equipment like standing mixers and food processors are dear in cost, yet they are well worth the money because they simplify the job and with care will last for years and sometimes generations. Paper-thin pots, pans, and baking sheets result in uneven and overbaked products; heavy ones can make the difference between a restaurant-quality dessert and an amateur one.

Apple corer I like the kind with teeth. It helps me get a grip on the fruit and seems to last longer than its circular counterparts.

Baking sheets These also go by the name of *cookie sheets*, *sheet pans*, or *sheet trays* (that's what we call them in the restaurant trade), *half-sheets*, and *jellyroll pans*. They're rectangular flat pans with a lip, usually ½ inch high. The standard 12½-x-17½-inch tray is technically called a *half-sheet*. That's the size you will use at home. I recommend heavy-gauge baking sheets with a ½-inch rim; they won't warp in the oven, and they conduct heat evenly. Buy sheet trays directly from kitchen-supply stores. While Teflon pans prevent sticking, the material has a tendency to produce overbaked and unevenly baked pastries. Pans with dark coating create a dark product.

Bench scraper/dough scraper Also known as a *bench knife*, a slightly flexible rectangular metal blade with a wood, plastic, or metal handle. Bench scrapers are great for dividing and lifting dough and make cleanup easy. I use one all day to scrape off my work surface. Turn your bench scraper on its side and you have a great edge that is perfect for finishing iced cakes. It's an invaluable tool at little cost.

Bowls see **mixing bowls**.

Brush see **pastry brush**.

Cake pans and pie pans see **pans**.

Cannoli tubes	These metal tubes are used for shaping and frying cannoli. Dowels or even 4-inch sawed-off broom handles may be substituted.
Cheesecloth	Found in houseware stores, cheesecloth has myriad uses, from straining to clarifying sauces. I also use it to dust cakes with confectioners' sugar by creating a sachet package and tying the four corners with butcher's twine or a twist tie.
Cherry pitter	A hand-held spring-loaded tool, great when preparing pies. Nonetheless, I prefer to split the cherry in half with a paring knife, then remove the pit. The fruit retains its integrity, and the odds of ending up with a pit in your pie are reduced.
Chinois	See **strainers**.
Clothespins	Great for sealing the end of a resting piping bag. If you need to refill your bag, pinch the bottom of the bag with a clothespin, right above the tip. Fill the bag with the remaining batter. Grab the bag, twisting the top, and batter will not run out from the tip onto your hand. Jumbo paper clips will also do the job.
Coffee grinder or spice mill	I use a Braun electric coffee grinder, which I devote exclusively to grinding fresh spices such as star anise and cardamom pods, small amounts of nuts, and rice for rice flour. The machine will retain flavors if not cleaned out properly. To clean out, pulse a few chunks of bread and then discard the bread. Keep a separate mill for coffee grinding; otherwise the coffee beans will pick up other flavors.
Colander	Useful for rinsing fruit.
Cooling racks	I recommend rectangular or square racks that will fit inside your **baking sheet**, so that you can use them for other purposes, such as icing cakes. Heavy-duty tight-weave racks are best. Special round cake-cooling racks are unnecessary since you can always use the rectangular ones.
Corrugated cardboard and cake rounds	Available at baking supply shops, these come in all different sizes and are great for frosting and transporting cakes. You can make use of old boxes by cutting out circles and desired shapes. I pipe elaborate chocolate designs on plain white plates, then stack them between cardboard rounds, using the rounds to protect my artwork and save table space. Foam core, from art supply stores, makes a great substitute.
Cutters	These come in metal and in plastic, in all sorts of shapes and sizes—round, fluted, or scalloped. I prefer metal cutters, which are heat resistant. To care for them properly, always wipe dry after washing and place in the oven to dry completely. This will prevent rust from forming and keep them in good condition for years. In a pinch, you can substitute a cup, glass, or bowl for a cookie cutter.

Cutting board	Plastic boards are great for pastry, terrific for cutting fruits and chocolate, and can be washed in the dishwasher. I use a yellow plastic cutting board designated "pastry only." This prevents cross-contamination from raw savory food. When you are cutting strongly flavored fruit like pineapple, wipe off and flip the board after cutting the fruit; the scent will marry with other flavors in an instant.
Docker/pastry pricker	A tool used to puncture puff pastry dough before baking to ensure even cooking. It looks like a small paint roller with spikes; I prefer the metal to the plastic version. A fork can be substituted. Hold the tines downward and tap the pastry in a uniform line.
Double boiler	A set of two pots, one set atop and slightly into the other, so that food can be cooked in the top pot or bowl, above a pot of boiling water, without fear of scalding. Rather than buy a fancy double-boiling pot, I prefer to create my own double boilers, using different size pots and matching stainless-steel bowls, depending on the recipe. The bowl is set in the pot, which is filled partway with water. Make sure that the bowl does not touch the surface of the water.
Food processor	This is a great asset to the modern pastry kitchen. I use mine to chop chocolate into fine pieces, mix curd, create pie dough, smooth out ganache, even make small batches of brioche. Opt for the largest model (6-cup unit).
Graters	These come in several different sizes and shapes. Buy a stainless-steel grater, since they are heavy duty and with care will not rust. Box graters are great because they have four different perforations. A gadget called the *Microplane* is my favorite toy. A long rasplike wand with holes of varying degrees of fineness, it makes grating much more consistent. I keep one for zesting citrus and a larger model for grating chocolate and cheeses. See **zester**.
Hands/fingers	Use your hands and fingers to feel dough, see if sugar has dissolved, or ascertain whether your crème anglaise has thickened. Your sense of touch is an invaluable tool. Stop the machine and break down the butter in pie dough with your fingers to get a feel for the flattening. Run your finger through the spoon of vanilla sauce. Play with your food.
Ice cream machine	The recipes in this book have been tested with the Cuisinart double-batch freezing unit, which comes complete with two one-quart freezing drums. The extra capacity is well worth the extra money.
Ice cream scoops	Useful for muffin batter or just-made cookie dough. I prefer to scoop ice cream with a concave spoon dipped in hot water. This technique creates an egg-shaped scoop called a *quenelle* in French.

Jellyroll pans/cookie sheets	See **baking sheets**.
Knives	Good carbon-steel knives come in a variety of sizes and with different handles, either wooden or plastic, and will last a lifetime. Ask for assistance when purchasing knives; hold them in your hand and get a feel for them. I prefer wooden handles with a stainless-steel blade that runs completely through the handle (full tang). Take time to learn how to sharpen a knife. Dull knives give terrible cuts. Wash all knives by hand: dishwashers can put unnecessary wear and tear on knives. Here are my four knife recommendations:

- OFFSET SERRATED-EDGE KNIFE: I couldn't go a day in the bakeshop without this all-purpose knife, which has a blade that is slightly lower than the handle. It's perfect for slicing apples, getting an edge on cumbersome chocolate, and cutting frozen cookie dough rolls/tubes. I use this in place of a bread knife and sometimes in place of a chef's knife.

- PARING KNIFE: A 3-inch blade works well for peeling, segmenting, trimming, and cutting fruits, as well as releasing cake from molds. It should fit perfectly in your hand for the best control.

- CHEF'S OR FRENCH KNIFE: An 8- or 10-inch chef's knife is perfect for chopping fruits and vegetables and slicing cakes. I use this knife when cutting glazed cakes. I first heat the knife with a torch, running it through the flame twice, then wipe with a wet cloth between cuts.

- X-ACTO KNIFE: I find this a great tool for cutting out templates and stencils for unique tuile cookie work.

Ladles	I recommend buying stainless-steel ladles with exact measurements embossed on the side. They are great for glazing cakes and serving sauces. A 4-ounce ladle is an all-purpose ladle, while the 2-ounce is perfect for straining sauce through a chinois. Spun-sugar baskets are made by turning a ladle upside down and gliding threads of caramel sugar over the top.
Measuring cups and spoons	You'll need two sets of measuring cups, one plastic or glass with a spout for liquid and the other metal with handles for dry ingredients. For convenience, keep two sets of measuring spoons, one for dry and one for wet ingredients.

- LIQUID MEASURES: Buy an 8-ounce and a 16-ounce clear plastic or glass measure with graduated measures.

- DRY MEASURES: Metal cups with handles enable you to dip, fluff, scoop, and level the measured ingredient.

Melon baller	A small half ball–shaped tool used to create 1-inch balls out of melon or

other fruits and vegetables. Buy one made of stainless steel, with the metal running through the handle. It's a great garnishing tool.

Metal or ceramic pie weights or baking beans These are used to prebake or blind-bake pies and tarts. They hold the pastry in place, prevent rising, and promote even baking. Kidney beans or rice placed in a coffee filter sprayed with pan spray or a foil liner are less expensive and work well. Use them over and over again. Metal or ceramic beans are expensive, but they ensure even baking. Be warned: make sure no beans have slipped through your pastry liner, or somebody will end up needing to make an emergency trip to the dentist.

Mixers

- HAND-HELD ELECTRIC MIXERS are great for pureeing fruits, whipping cream, beating eggs and egg whites, and incorporating butter into sauces. They are relatively inexpensive.

- STANDING ELECTRIC MIXER: This is the most important and expensive piece of equipment in your pastry arsenal. Make the investment, and your pastry-making life will be easier. For all-around baking, nothing beats a KitchenAid mixer. Buy the model with the highest capacity and an adjustable handle. It can handle tough dough and delicate whipped cream like a charm.

Mixing bowls Mixing bowls come in many sizes and materials. The most versatile all-purpose bowls, the ones I use for everything (except melting chocolate in the microwave), are stainless steel. They are inexpensive and fit all kinds of needs: they're perfect for fitting into a saucepan to create a double boiler, for melting chocolate, or for making lemon curd or sabayon sauce. Heating these bowls up and cooling them down is a snap because stainless steel does not retain heat well. Keep at least one set of small (1-quart), medium (2-quart), large (4-quart), and extra-large (6-quart) bowls on hand. Other types of bowls include:

- CERAMIC: Ceramic bowls are bulky, but they're great for proofing dough.

- COPPER: Copper bowls are the best for whipping egg whites; the copper creates a stable environment and high volume.

- PLASTIC: These are great for melting chocolate in the microwave. Butter and fat will leave a film on plastic, so wash them very well. It's best not to use plastic when whipping egg whites, because invisible fat residue may cling to the surface, which inhibits the egg whites from foaming.

- GLASS: These look great, but they are more apt to chip and break.

Molds

❧ **BRIOCHE MOLDS**, also called *brioche à tête*, look like sophisticated cupcake molds with a slanted, fluted edge. The nonstick molds work best, allowing the bread to slide out easily. They can be used for many baked goods besides brioche: I have put everything from panna cotta to financier in these molds. Just flip the cake out and top with berries and cream. They come in many sizes, from 3 to 8 inches in diameter.

❧ **MADELEINE MOLDS** create the spongy cookie/cake known in France as a madeleine. The shape resembles that of a seashell. They come in two different sizes, with 12 standard or 24 minis on a tray. I prefer the standard aluminum to the nonstick. Remember to butter and lightly dust your pan with flour.

❧ **SAVARIN MOLDS** are ring molds with a center hole cut out, traditionally used for the baked yeasted dough that is then soaked in syrup and served with seasonal fruit and cream. Savarin molds come in several sizes. Three-inch molds are useful for individual desserts, whereas a classic large savarin will be baked in an 8- to 10-inch mold.

Ovens

All of the recipes in this book have been tested in both electric and gas ovens, with little difference in the results. Check your oven with a thermometer for hot spots and precise temperatures. Keep an oven thermometer in your oven at all times.

❧ **CONVECTION: When baking the recipes in this book in a convection oven, reduce the oven temperature by 25°F and cut back the baking time by 5 to 10 minutes, depending on the baked item**. Baked custards are not recommended for baking in a convection oven with the fan on. Turn the fan off.

❧ **MICROWAVE:** For years, I didn't have a microwave. Then I heard Julia Child say: "If Escoffier had had a microwave, he would have used it." The microwave is now a permanent fixture in my kitchen. I use it to melt chocolate and butter, defrost frozen fruit purees, and reheat chocolate sauce. Every microwave varies. Watch your ingredients as you cook them. It takes only a minute to turn chocolate into charcoal in some microwaves.

Pans

❧ **BRIOCHE:** See **molds**.

❧ **BUNDT:** These are also known as *tube* or *kugelhopf* pans. The best are made of cast iron, which conducts heat incredibly. Because the pans heat up so well, **when using bundt pans, I reduce the baking temperature by 25°F**. The recipes in this book that call for bundt pans have taken this into account.

- **CAKE:** I have bought many sizes over the years. I recommend buying cake pans that are at least 3 inches deep. Anything from cheesecakes to delicate tortes can be baked in them, eliminating the need for several shallower pans. Choose heavy-duty aluminum.

- **LOAF:** These pans can double as bread and pound cake pans. I prefer aluminum. Darker cast-iron pans create a very dark cake, but they can be great for breads.

- **MUFFIN:** These metal pans aren't just for muffins. You can line them with paper cups for birthday cupcakes or use them for tart shells or freezer pop molds. I line them with plastic film and pour in panna cotta or mousse. I love to use the mini-muffin pans for bite-size desserts. If you are baking only 10 muffins in a pan that holds 12, fill the remaining empty tins two thirds of the way up with warm water. This ensures even baking.

- **PIE PANS:** The standard pie pan size is 9 or 10 inches wide and 1 1/2 inches deep; tart pans come in many different sizes. Deep-dish pans have a depth of 2 inches or more and are best for double-crusted pies. Opinions about the best pie pan to use vary widely. If you're taking the pie someplace, there's nothing better than aluminum disposable pie pans: first, because they're good conductors of heat; second, because you can cut into the pie without any worry of destroying the pan lining; and last, because when you visit a friend, there's no pan to wash or remember to take home. That said, you do have to watch and adjust the baking time downward, because your pies will bake faster.

  CERAMIC: These are not great heat conductors, so they don't work as well for flaky pastry. They do work well for sweet dough.

  METAL: These are best for single-crusted pies because they brown a crust very quickly. They are difficult to break and perfect for transporting.

  PYREX: Great for viewing the crust as it bakes. Glass is a good conductor of heat, resulting in a crisp crust.

  TEFLON: Don't use them. Teflon does not conduct heat well, and what's more, once you cut into the pie, you can damage the lining and get Teflon into your slice.

  SPRINGFORM PANS: The all-purpose 9-x-3-inch spring-loaded, hinged pan is great for cheesecakes and other delicate cakes that are difficult to remove from ordinary cake pans. Buy the heavy-duty pans. I have a tendency to lose the bottoms. It's a good idea to transfer the cake to a serving plate when you're taking it to a friend. Springform pans have lots of crevices, so for best care, wash well and place in an oven with the pilot light on so that the pan dries out quickly and doesn't rust.

TUBE PANS: Otherwise known as *angel food cake pans,* these are round with a long tube in the center. The best have removable bottoms. The worst are tube pans with a nonstick coating. Angel food cakes sag and are limp when baked in this pan.

Parchment paper
A versatile nonstick baking paper that is used to line baking sheets and other baking pans. Parchment prevents baked goods from sticking and burning and makes cleanup easier. Removing freshly baked cookies from baking sheets is a breeze—just hold the baking sheet with an oven mitt and with the other hand carefully release the parchment paper and slide the cookies onto your table. I use parchment paper to line ring molds for mousses and to line the bottom of cake pans for easy release. I also line my work surface with it and sift the dry ingredients directly on top. Then I can just grab either end and gently add the ingredients to creamed butter. Parchment can be cut into a triangle to create paper piping bags or cones for decorating cakes or other desserts with chocolate or sugar icing. If you buy parchment paper boxed in sheets, cut the sheets to fit your baking sheets and store them together. See also **silicone mat**.

Pastry bags
Although disposable plastic pastry bags are not friendly to the environment, they are terrific for sanitation and cleanup. A good substitute is a heavy-duty plastic storage bag; cut a corner off one side of the bottom. If you use a linen piping bag, always wash and dry it well before putting it away.

Pastry brush
I have several sizes and special designated pastry brushes in my arsenal. Choose one with a plastic handle rather than a metal-based one with nails, because the metal rusts and the nails fall out. I buy paintbrushes at paint or hardware stores.

Pastry wheel/crimper
This creates a decorative fluted cut in pastry dough.

Peeler
I prefer a Swiss, or U-shaped, peeler with the blade set across the end to the old-fashioned type.

Piping bags
See **pastry bags**.

Pizza wheel
Great for cutting out pie dough circles and lattices.

Plastic containers
Leftover yogurt containers make excellent storage containers.

Pots and pans
Good-quality heavy-duty pots and pans will last a lifetime. Heavy stainless-steel pots with a copper core and, most important, a heavy metal bottom will ensure even cooking of crème anglaise and puddings. Enameled cast-iron pots and pans are also nonreactive and heavy. Heavy nonstick frying pans are great for quick cleanup and cooking foods like bananas and apples, but they won't stand up to the heat of caramel.

Keep in mind that when reducing a sauce you should use a shallow wide pot. For custards and fillings, a saucepan is best.

🖎 Copper pots are the most expensive and the best conductors of heat. I have one copper pot dedicated to caramel and candy making. I clean the pot by boiling water to remove leftover caramel, then scrubbing any impurities away with the scrubby side of a sponge and 2 tablespoons of lemon juice and rinsing with water. If I am not going to use the pot right away, I cover it securely with plastic wrap so dust won't get in.

🖎 Aluminum may react with cooked acid products like citrus and brown sugar.

Propane torch   Nothing caramelizes crème brûlée and lemon curd custard as easily and professionally as a propane or butane blowtorch. Pick one up at your local hardware store. I prefer the model with a gun shape and safety clicker. It locks in place and, with a flick of the index finger, releases and shuts off the flame. For safety's sake, leave the top separate from the propane until ready to use. Small torches, made specifically for caramelizing crème brûlée, are also available. They are a little slower but less intimidating to the novice.

Rolling pin   A necessary tool for any baker. I like the straight pin with ball bearings and no handles. A narrow straight pin enables you to feel the dough better as you are rolling it out and ensures a lighter touch, which is important. Rolling pins can also be used to shape tuiles and to tap the air out of chocolate molds. A good sturdy rolling pin will last a lifetime.

Ruler   Good for cutting out dough accurately and creating straight lines.

Scale   I recommend using a digital scale for accuracy. You can increase and decrease amounts easily.

Scissors   This is one tool I could not be without. I use it for such tasks as cutting dough around the edge of pies and cutting parchment.

Scrapers   Plastic scrapers are very handy in the kitchen. They are multipurpose and very inexpensive. Buy the firmest ones you can find, but they should still be flexible. My favorite is the Matfer, available through Chef's Toys. You can improvise by cutting out a 4-x-3-inch square from a plastic lid or container; it will get the job done. If you want to get fancy, round off the edges. For a tool that both scrapes and cuts, a metal bench scraper is best (see **bench scraper/dough scraper**).

Sheet pans   See **baking sheets.**

Sifters/tamis   The finer the sifter, the finer the product. The finest sifters are called *triple sifters,* but any sifter will do if you use it properly.

Silicone mats	Nonstick silicone baking sheets. Used by professionals for years, these sheets may seem pricey, but they last a long time. They can be bought at gourmet shops and by mail order. They come in different sizes and fit directly into a baking sheet. They can withstand temperatures of up to 500°F and can be used endlessly.
Skewers	Available at houseware stores, these bamboo items can be used in endless ways—testing cakes for doneness; skewering and barbecuing (soak first in water); lighting a burner; and even cleaning difficult spots like fluted knobs and corners. I wouldn't go a day without them.

Spatulas

- Flexible metal spatulas are great for perfect cake icing. The blade creates a clean edge.

- Offset metal spatulas are excellent for smearing cake batter into a pan to create a level cake for icing.

- Rubber spatulas come in both large and small sizes. They are great for folding in batters and stirring sauces. Be sure to buy heat-resistant ones. I like Rubbermaid, with the red handle. A cheap spatula may melt in your hot pan.

Spoons

- Heavy-duty plastic spoons are great for stirring chocolate, since they do not affect the temperature of the chocolate.

- Slotted spoons are terrific for frying. The holes allow the hot oil to escape back into the pot.

- Wooden spoons: Great for stovetop use because they do not conduct heat. Take care to smell the spoon before using: a garlic smell will contaminate your sweet creation.

Spray bottles	A great way to spritz ingredients like chocolate onto baked items, which saves time and controls the flow. If the bottle gets clogged, pop it into the microwave for 5-second intervals.
Squeeze bottles	Plastic squeeze bottles can be used to create fun decorations on plates. New hair-dye bottles work best because they are small and have a very fine tip. You can find them at beauty supply houses.
Strainers	A medium-size fine strainer or a conical metal *chinois* is essential for making fruit purees and straining sauces like vanilla sauce.
Thermometers	These are essential for consistent professional-quality pastry. A controlled environment is often the key to success with baked goods. Be aware of the temperature of your room, refrigerator, and oven (some

ovens are not calibrated properly and have hot spots). My recipes often instruct you to take the temperature of the food you are working with. If you are deep-frying, you need a candy thermometer. Once these factors are taken out of the equation, the guesswork can be put to rest.

- CANDY/INSTANT-READ THERMOMETER: Buy a digital one. I love the Polder instant-read thermometer. Taylor also makes a good one. Get the one that not only measures temperature but also serves as a timer. This is great for sugar and caramel work. Set the timer for the advised recipe time and also for the designated temperature. I set it a few degrees below the given temperature to ensure accuracy. I cannot overemphasize the importance of a good digital thermometer.

- OVEN THERMOMETER: This is a must. Do *not* put anything into your oven without being sure of the temperature.

- REFRIGERATOR AND FREEZER THERMOMETER: A refrigerator thermometer will ensure that the internal temperature is 40°F or below. For freezing, 0°F is the best temperature.

- ROOM THERMOMETER: The temperature of your room affects the end result of the pastry. If you know your room temperature, you can control the outcome of your baking endeavors by doing simple things like refrigerating flour.

Timers　I'm not a fan of decorative dial timers. They look great but are inaccurate. Instead, buy a multipurpose digital thermometer/timer, which is fairly inexpensive and a great asset. I keep two on hand. The best kind allows you to count down the seconds, and then it counts up again, just in case you were on the phone when the timer went off. When you do get to the timer, it will tell you how much time has elapsed.

Tongue　This is the most important culinary tool—and luckily, it's free. Taste everything and develop your own "taste memory" and style.

Toolbox　Not a bad thing to have: it locks, which is great for keeping your knives out of harm's way. It has separate compartments and drawers, so all of your precious tools have a home. When asked what my favorite tool is after my tongue, I always answer the toolbox. My bakeshops would not be complete without it.

Towels　Do as cooks in professional kitchens do. Always keep two towels at the ready, one wet and ready for cleaning as you go, the other *always* dry for handling hot items. Remember that wet and hot are a bad combination. Buy absorbent heavy-duty kitchen towels, not decorative lightweight towels. They are available at kitchen supply stores.

Turntables	These are handy for icing cakes. A heavy cast-iron stand topped with a revolving 12-inch plate is best. Get one with a plastic twist screw that keeps the plate from moving. Oil the base to ensure smooth spinning. The top of your lazy Susan works well, too.
Whisk/whip	A stirring tool used to incorporate air, made from several bent wires. Whisks come in several gauges. Heavy or stiff whisks are used for thick batters. Light and pliable whisks are used for foams and creams. Use wire whisks, not plastic. Store them properly, either hung from a rack or in a crock. If you store them in a drawer, the wires will be flattened and your whisk will be damaged.

- WIRE WHISK: A good stiff medium-size whisk is essential for all sorts of tasks.

- WIRE BALLOON WHISK: The perfect whip for beating a batch of cream or egg whites. Use it as well for folding in ingredients in cake, soufflé, or mousse recipes.

Zester	When zesting a citrus fruit, the object is to remove only the colored outer surface and leave all the bitter white pith behind. I prefer to use a grater to remove zest. Many chefs, however, use a classic tool called a *zester*. The zester removes zest in long, thin strands, which are too often left long. Too-long strips create an unpleasant texture in pastries. When I have to use a zester, I always chop the strands very finely with a chef's knife or in a coffee grinder. Not long ago, an ingenious chef discovered that a standard sanding tool called a *rasp* is also perfect for grating zest. A rasp with the addition of holes and a fancy handle, the *Microplane* has taken kitchens by storm. It grates zest finer than any standard grater and can also be used to grate cheese. It can be found at cookware stores.

INGREDIENTS

Almonds   Closely related to the apricot, almonds come in both sweet and bitter varieties. Sweet almonds are used in most recipes, while bitter almonds are used to make liqueurs and extracts. Almonds can be toasted, in or out of their skins, at 350°F for 5 to 10 minutes, or until they smell toasty. Store almonds in the freezer so they don't become rancid.

MARKET FORMS   In the shell, whole blanched, whole skin-on, whole salted, sliced blanched (skins removed), sliced skin-on, slivered blanched.

USES   Chopped and toasted, almonds can be folded into batters and doughs, adding crunch. Sliced almonds are often used to garnish the outside of desserts or pressed onto the side of tortes.

Almond extract   A clear flavoring made from the bitter almond. The flavor is very strong and distinct, and it should be used sparingly.

MARKET FORMS   Available in small bottles for the home cook and in larger quantities for the professional. Do not mistake almond oil for almond extract. Almond oil is pressed out of sweet almonds, while the extract is an infusion of bitter almonds and alcohol. (Avoid imitation almond extract, which is manufactured by scientists and doesn't taste as good.)

USES   Flavoring.

Almond flour/meal   Almond flour is a fine powder ground from the cake of almond that remains after the nuts have been pressed for their oil. It can be used interchangeably with almond meal, which is ground from the whole nut and is therefore slightly oilier and grittier. Store in the freezer.

MARKET FORMS   Specialty stores and Middle Eastern markets carry almond flour. Grinding almonds in a food processor is easy. To avoid making almond butter, chill the nuts before pulverizing them with a metal blade.

USES   Ground almonds can be used to flavor breads, pastry, cookies, cakes, and fillings, as well as to replace flour for wheat-free baking.

Almond milk A liquid produced by adding water to whole almonds, which are then cooked. The mixture is blended and strained, producing a milky, lactose-free liquid. Store in the refrigerator once the carton is opened.

MARKET FORMS Specialty stores, some supermarkets, and whole foods stores sell almond milk in cartons.

USES Substitute for milk in ice cream recipes and sauces.

Almond paste A mixture of ground blanched almonds, sugar, and glucose, thicker than peanut butter and coarser than marzipan. It can be stored wrapped in plastic film in an airtight container in the refrigerator for up to 6 months.

MARKET FORMS Produced by California almond companies or imported, it is packaged in small tins or sausage-shaped tubes in most supermarkets and specialty stores. It's available in bulk, from 7-pound cans to 25-pound boxes.

USES Almond paste is creamed into batters, fillings, and creams. It can be used to replace a percentage of fat in a recipe or added as a garnish.

Amaretto An Italian liqueur flavored with bitter almonds and the pit of the closely related apricot. Originally produced in Saronno, Italy.

MARKET FORMS Both the original Amaretto di Saronno and several domestic brands of amaretto are widely available. Do not confuse it with amaretto extract or amaretto-flavored oil, both of which are highly concentrated.

USES Amaretto can be used to enhance the flavor of almonds in many recipes, including sauces, creams, or syrups.

Apple pectin A strong fruit pectin used in candy making.

MARKET FORMS Specialty pastry supply stores.

USES Used to make solid fruit jellies.

Arrowroot A thickening agent made from a West Indian tuber. It is more expensive than cornstarch and unlike cornstarch does not have a chalky taste when undercooked.

MARKET FORMS Arrowroot is found in the spice section at supermarkets and can be bought from mail-order merchants like Penzeys (see page 375).

USES Use it interchangeably with cornstarch.

Baking powder A chemical leavening agent that contains baking soda (bicarbonate of soda), cream of tartar (acidic salts), and an ingredient to absorb moisture, such as cornstarch. When the powder is activated by moisture and heat, it releases carbon dioxide, causing the baked product to rise. The most commonly used type is double-acting baking powder, which reacts twice, first with moisture and then with heat. The original baking powder was single-acting and reacted quickly to moisture.

MARKET FORMS Home cooks can find 10-ounce cans of baking powder at any supermarket. Baking powder loses its potency, so replace it every six months. Check for freshness by combining ½ teaspoon baking powder with ¼ cup hot water. If it bubbles up, it's good to go.

USES Leavening for cookies, cakes.

Baking soda A chemical leavening agent made from soda ash (sodium carbonate), which can be either manufactured or mined. When the soda ash is dissolved and introduced to carbon dioxide, pure baking soda (sodium bicarbonate) is created. When baking soda is combined with a moist acidic ingredient, carbon dioxide is released. The gas accumulates, causing the product to rise. Recipes that call for baking soda always have some type of acidic ingredient as well, such as lemon juice, vinegar, buttermilk, sour cream, molasses, or honey. Unlike double-acting baking powder, baking soda reacts as soon as it is added to most ingredients. For this reason, batter or dough containing baking soda should be put into the oven quickly after being mixed.

MARKET FORMS Purchase it in small quantities, since it loses its potency after three months. It can be used if it bubbles up when combined with vinegar (test by adding ½ teaspoon of baking soda to ¼ cup of vinegar).

USES Leavening for cookies, cakes, breads.

Banyuls [ban-YOOLS] A fortified wine from the Languedoc Roussillon region of France, made with mostly Grenache grapes. One of France's most prestigious sweet wines, it has a rich, berry-grapey flavor and is paired with chocolate in many traditional desserts. In a pinch, you can substitute port, using three parts port mixed with one part water.

MARKET FORMS Available where better wines and spirits are sold.

USES Flavoring, poaching, sauces.

Brandy Liquor made from distilled wine or fruit juice. Fine brandies, such as cognac, are aged in oak barrels.

MARKET FORMS You don't have to spend a fortune, but don't choose the cheapest brand.

USES Flavoring.

Brown sugar See **sugar**.

Butter According to USDA standards, butter must contain 80 percent milk fat. Unsalted butter (80 percent fat, 15 percent water) is best for baking. It has a sweet flavor and allows the cook to be sure about the amount of salt in a recipe. All recipes in this book and in most baking books call for unsalted butter. Salted butter contains a higher percentage of water, which increases the amount of water in a recipe, as well as the amount of salt. Fat absorbs odor easily, so store butter airtight and refrigerated.

Clarified butter is pure fat, with the solids removed through melting and skimming. It can be heated to higher temperatures than ordinary butter without burning.

MARKET FORMS Butter is sold in 4-ounce sticks for home use and 1-pound bricks for professionals. European butter tends to have less water than domestically produced butter and produces richer pastries. Plugrá is an American-made European-style butter.

USES Tenderizing and enriching baked products, carrying flavor, adding color.

Buttermilk See **milk**.

Calvados Apple brandy from the Normandy region of France.

MARKET FORMS Available where fine wines and spirits are sold.

USES Flavoring.

Cassis The French name for the black currant, a small berry used mainly for preserves and the French cordial crème de cassis. These berries are completely unrelated to the dried currant, a mini raisin made from dried small zante grapes.

MARKET FORMS The fresh fruit is a seasonal item at gourmet produce markets. The cordial can be found at specialty stores and finer liquor stores.

USES Flavoring.

Cayenne pepper A hot spice made from tropical chiles.

MARKET FORMS Dried in a jar.

USES Flavoring.

Chambord Black raspberry–flavored liqueur from France.

MARKET FORMS Can be found at specialty stores and finer liquor stores; it is even sold in very small bottles.

USES Flavoring.

Champagne	Sparkling wine from the Champagne region of France.
MARKET FORMS	Widely available where wine is sold. For recipes, Perrier-Jouët works well. Other dry French, Italian, Spanish, and California sparkling wines may be substituted. Never substitute Cold Duck.
USES	Flavoring, poaching, sauces.
Chinese five-spice powder	A spice blend, used extensively in Asian cooking, that contains cinnamon, cloves, star anise, fennel seeds, and Sichuan peppercorns.
MARKET FORMS	Available at most supermarkets and specialty stores. Five-spice powder can also be made at home by toasting an equal amount of each spice, then grinding them in a mortar or electric coffee grinder.
USES	Infuse into cream for ganache, ice cream, custards, or sauces, or add to poaching liquids.
Chocolate	Real chocolate comes from the cocoa bean, which is found inside the large, papaya-size pod that grows along the trunk and branches of the cacao tree. The beans are first roasted to develop their flavor and determine the color. Once they are cooled, the beans are cracked open, separating the hard cocoa bean shell from the interior meat of the bean, called the *nib*. The nibs are then ground. The friction of grinding causes the cocoa butter held within the bean to liquefy, turning the ground nibs into a smooth shiny paste called *chocolate liquor*. Chocolate liquor is the main ingredient in all chocolate-based products. In making chocolate, the cooled chocolate liquor is ground to a fine powder and supplemented with additional cocoa butter, sugar, cream or milk, nuts, and/or spices, according to the manufacturer's own recipe. The friction from continuous kneading, known as *conching,* turns the mixture into smooth, creamy liquid chocolate.
	Store chocolate well wrapped and airtight in a cool dry place (60° to 65°F, but not the refrigerator). Chocolate contains fat, which absorbs odors easily, so keep it away from other foods with strong odors.
MARKET FORMS	Each brand of chocolate has a distinct flavor, color, and texture. All brands are interchangeable for cake baking, as long as they are real chocolate. I use many different types of chocolate, but my favorite is Valrhona, a superb chocolate produced in France. It is smooth and dark, and when it's melted, it has a nice viscosity, perfect for piping.

TYPES OF CHOCOLATE AND CHOCOLATE PRODUCTS

❧ UNSWEETENED/BAKING/BITTER CHOCOLATE has approximately 99 percent chocolate liquor, of which 50 percent is cocoa butter and the remaining amount is cocoa solids. It has no sugar added. If I want to pump up the bitter-chocolate flavor in a recipe or if the recipe is very sweet, I replace 10 percent of the chocolate called for with this kind.

- **BITTERSWEET CHOCOLATE** has a relatively high percentage of chocolate liquor, up to 75 percent. This is one of my favorites because of its intense bitter flavor, with a hint of sugar. It can be an acquired taste. My all-purpose chocolate is a 64 percent bittersweet chocolate.

- **SEMISWEET CHOCOLATE** has a minimum of 35 percent chocolate liquor. I find it to be somewhat wimpy and use it rarely, except in conjunction with bitter chocolate, which kicks up the flavor.

- **MILK CHOCOLATE** is very sweet, with 10 to 15 percent chocolate liquor and approximately 15 percent milk solids. I love to pair milk chocolate with dark, bitter caramel. The milk chocolate balances the integrity of the caramel flavor, without masking it, as bittersweet chocolate would do.

- **CHOCOLATE MORSELS** are usually made with palm and coconut oils and are not good-quality baking chocolate. Do not confuse these with palets and pistoles, chocolate coins produced by many international manufacturers that can be purchased with the same chocolate liquor percentages as bitter, bittersweet, milk, and white chocolates.

- **WHITE CHOCOLATE** does not contain any chocolate liquor, and so, according to the USDA, it cannot legally be called chocolate. Because white chocolate is made from cocoa butter (plus sugar, milk solids, and vanilla), it is used and categorized as chocolate. The brand I prefer (even insist on) is Valrhona Ivoire. Another good choice is Callebaut.

- **GIANDUJA [john-DO-ya]** is chocolate that has been flavored with hazelnuts.

  MARKET FORMS: Available at specialty stores.

  USES: Any recipes that call for milk or white chocolate will work with the soft, fatty gianduja.

- **COCOA BUTTER:** The natural vegetable fat contained in cocoa beans, extracted during the chocolate-making process. Cocoa butter is what gives chocolate its smooth, satiny, crisp texture and its melt-on-your-tongue quality. Cocoa butter is pressed into blocks and used to create chocolate and other confections, as well as cosmetics, suntan oils, and soaps. Store airtight in a cool environment.

  MARKET FORMS: Available in block form at specialty stores and by mail order.

  USES: Addition of cocoa butter to melted chocolate thins it for dipping and enhances the texture of chocolate confections.

- **COCOA POWDER** is made from the chocolate liquor paste that is produced during the chocolate-making process (see page 352). The chocolate liquor that results from the grinding of the cocoa bean nibs is heated to release more cocoa butter. The remaining chocolate liquor is pressed into a hard cake, dried again, then pulverized into unsweetened cocoa powder. Although it is widely believed to be fat free, cocoa powder does retain a small percentage of cocoa butter. A technique known as the **Dutch process** adds alkali to the cocoa powder, neutralizing the naturally occurring acid. The alkali makes the cocoa powder darker in color and increases its solubility.

MARKET FORMS: Readily available at supermarkets and specialty stores. There are different brands of cocoa powder with varying amounts of fat and in various shades of brown, including the nearly black "ebony" or "extra brut." Do not substitute cocoa mix, which contains sugar.

USES: Adds chocolate flavor to recipes as a dry ingredient.

≈ COUVERTURE [koo-vehr-TYOOR] is a high-quality chocolate with a cocoa butter content of at least 30 percent. The word *couverture* comes from the French term *couvrir,* which means "to coat or cover." This type of chocolate was first used exclusively for coating confections. The higher fat content provides greater viscosity and smoother texture. Store as you would chocolate, well wrapped and in a cool, dry place but not the refrigerator.

MARKET FORMS: Available from specialty purveyors and fine food stores. Comes in all levels of sweetness, as well as milk and white varieties.

USES: For fine chocolate work.

Cider vinegar	See **vinegar**.

Cinnamon sugar	Sugar mixed with ground cinnamon.
MARKET FORMS	Make your own with 1 cup sugar and 2 to 3 tablespoons ground cinnamon.
USES	Flavoring.

Citric acid	A granular food additive, designed to increase the tart, sour flavor of food, made from fermented citrus juices.
MARKET FORMS	Available by mail order and at specialty stores and pharmacies.
USES	Any recipe in which sourness needs to be enhanced, such as candies and sour apple–flavored dishes.

Clabbered cream	Unpasteurized milk that has soured and thickened naturally. An American version of crème fraîche.

| MARKET FORMS | Available at specialty cheese stores and gourmet grocers, and through mail order. |

| USES | An accompaniment to tart or sour fruits and desserts or any dish in which whipped cream or crème fraîche would be used. |

Clotted cream   Cream, thickened by heat, traditionally spooned over fruit or spread on scones. A specialty of Devonshire, England.

| MARKET FORMS | Available at specialty cheese stores and gourmet grocers, and through mail order. |

| USES | An accompaniment to tart or sour fruits and desserts in which whipped cream would be used. |

Cocoa butter   See **chocolate**.

Cocoa powder   See **chocolate**.

Coconut milk   A thick liquid, rich in coconut fat and flavor, not to be confused with the clear liquid in the interior of the coconut. Coconut milk is made by shredding or desiccating the white coconut meat, simmering it in water, then straining and squeezing it.

| MARKET FORMS | Coconut milk can be purchased in 14-ounce cans. It's found at many supermarkets with the Asian products. Do not substitute cream of coconut, such as Coco López (shelved with cocktail mixes in many supermarkets), which has added sugar. |

| USES | Can be used in place of milk in many recipes. |

Coffee   There are two main varieties of shrub grown to produce coffee beans. *Coffea robusta* thrives at lower altitudes, while *C. arabica* does better at three to six thousand feet. Arabica beans are widely thought to be less harsh and more complex than robusta. Once the coffee beans are harvested and dried, the coffee producer will roast and blend them to meet specific standards.

| MARKET FORMS | Coffee is available in numerous forms, including whole bean, ground (coarse or fine), instant, and liquid extract. For baking, the more potent forms are preferred. To add as a dry ingredient, use instant espresso powder, made in Italy and available at finer grocers. For adding as a liquid ingredient, a thick, intense coffee extract from France called Trablit is available at specialty stores. |

| USES | Flavoring and stimulant. |

Cognac A fine brandy, double-distilled from grapes grown in the Cognac region of France and aged for three to seven years in oak barrels.

MARKET FORMS Available where fine wines and spirits are sold. Avoid the cheapest brands.

USES Flavoring.

Cointreau A liqueur made from brandy and scented with sweet and bitter orange peels.

MARKET FORMS Available where fine wines and spirits are sold.

USES Flavoring.

Condensed milk Also known as *sweetened condensed milk,* this is evaporated milk, with 60 percent of the water removed, to which sugar has been added. Do not substitute evaporated milk for condensed milk.

MARKET FORMS Available in supermarkets in 12- or 14-ounce cans that can be stored at room temperature until opened.

USES A substitute for sweetened milk used to enrich recipes.

Confectioners' sugar See **sugar**.

Conserve A thick fruit jam, traditionally made to preserve or conserve the bounty of summer fruit for the winter months. Sometimes made with nuts.

MARKET FORMS Found at better markets. Look for brands with the least amount of sugar (40 to 50 percent). The color should be bright. The darker the conserve, the longer the fruit has been cooked, which dulls the flavor.

USES A spread and filling for breads, pastries, cakes.

Cornmeal Coarse flour, ground from whole dried corn kernels.

MARKET FORMS Available in yellow, white, blue, and red. It is ground fine, medium, or coarse.

USES A replacement for flour to add flavor and texture to baked goods.

Cornstarch A thickening agent made from the endosperm (interior) of corn. To thicken hot liquids and prevent lumps, dissolve cornstarch first in a small amount of cold liquid. Excessive, prolonged heat will reverse the thickening properties.

MARKET FORMS Cornstarch is widely available in 1-pound boxes.

USES Thickener.

Corn syrup A form of glucose, made from cornstarch treated with acid.

MARKET FORMS Light corn syrup is clear. Dark corn syrup has had caramel added to it to intensify the color and flavor. If color is not a factor, the two can be used interchangeably.

USES Inhibits crystallization of sugar while it is cooking and prevents ice crystals from forming in ice cream and sorbet.

Couverture See **chocolate**.

Cream Creams vary in the amount of milk fat they contain.

- HALF-AND-HALF is equal parts of milk and cream, with a milk fat content of 10 to 18 percent.

- LIGHT CREAM has between 18 and 30 percent milk fat. Neither half-and-half nor light cream will whip.

- LIGHT WHIPPING CREAM contains 30 to 36 percent milk fat.

- HEAVY CREAM/WHIPPING CREAM contains 36 to 40 percent milk fat.

  MARKET FORMS: Heavy whipping cream is available at most supermarkets. Do not buy "whipped cream," sold in pressurized cans, which contains sugar and stabilizers.

  USES: Liquid ingredient that enriches any pastry it goes into; whipped topping. See page 335 for the stages of whipped cream.

Cream cheese A soft, mild spreadable cheese made from cow's milk.

MARKET FORMS Available in full-fat (at least 33 percent milk fat), light, low-fat, fat-free, and whipped forms.

USES Use the full-fat variety for cheesecakes and icings.

Cream of tartar An acidic salt that is a byproduct of winemaking. White crystals of tartaric acid form inside wine barrels as the grape juice ferments and precipitates.

MARKET FORMS Powdered cream of tartar is available in the spice section of most supermarkets. Tartaric acid can be bought in its crystalline form at specialty shops.

USES A major ingredient in baking powder, acidic cream of tartar is used to soften and stabilize egg white foams. Tartaric acid in crystalline form is used to invert boiling sugar for decorative pulled and blown sugar and in cheesemaking to thicken curds.

Crème	The French word for **cream**.
Crème fraîche	[KREHM FRESH] A thickened, matured cream with a tangy, nutty flavor, somewhat similar to sour cream but richer tasting and less sour. It is made in France with unpasteurized cream, which contains the essential bacteria to thicken it into a sharp, sour cream–like product. Because cream is pasteurized in the United States, a coagulating agent, usually buttermilk, is added to create the same effect. To make your own crème fraîche, combine ½ cup buttermilk or 2 tablespoons lemon juice with 1½ cups heavy cream. Stir them together and leave the mixture covered at room temperature for 48 hours, then refrigerate it overnight.
MARKET FORMS	Crème fraîche can be found in the refrigerated dairy section of gourmet supermarkets, sold in small containers or by the pint. Or make your own (see above).
USES	Crème fraîche can be whipped like cream and used to accompany dishes that would benefit from its slight acidity. It can be used in recipes in place of sour cream.
Dairy	See **milk, butter, cream,** and **eggs**. All dairy products absorb the smells from other refrigerated foods. Keep well sealed to protect from unwanted odors. All dairy products are perishable and should display an expiration date.
Dried fruits	I prefer to use the unsulfured variety; while the color isn't as intense, the flavor is. I keep many varieties reconstituted in liquid in my refrigerator (reconstituted dried fruits are referred to as "fatty" because they are plumped).
MARKET FORMS	Purchase by the pound.
USES	An accompaniment to bread puddings and many pastries.
Eggs	The color of the shell is determined by the breed of chicken and has nothing to do with the egg's flavor. The white becomes thinner as the egg ages. The fresher the egg whites, the more volume they will have when whipped. Eggs are porous and should be stored in their containers in the refrigerator (not in the door of the refrigerator), or they will absorb odors. Bring them to room temperature only if a recipe says to do so. To avoid contamination by salmonella, make sure the eggs stay below 40°F when raw and reach a temperature over 165°F when used in cooking. They can be stored in the refrigerator for up to 1 month, deteriorating slowly. Whites can easily be frozen. Yolks must be mixed with a pinch of salt or 1½ teaspoons corn syrup before freezing.

MARKET FORMS Eggs are available in a variety of sizes. Most recipe books, including this one, call for large eggs.

USES Act as a leavening and thickening agent in baked products.

Espresso Properly brewed espresso must be made with an espresso machine, which can range from a small aluminum stovetop model to a multi-spigot computerized machine made of hand-hammered copper and decorated with gold leaf. For baking, powdered espresso, available in specialty stores and gourmet stores, is often used.

MARKET FORMS You can use any bean to make espresso coffee, simply by grinding it to the proper size and brewing it in the proper machine. Traditionally, though, the darkest, oiliest beans are preferred. Beans or ground coffee labeled *espresso* can also be brewed in a standard coffeepot if ground to the proper coarseness.

USES Flavoring.

Farmer cheese A fresh cheese similar to small-curd cottage cheese. It is pressed, releasing most of the whey, which yields a sliceable, crumbly cheese.

MARKET FORMS Look for it in specialty cheese stores and fine food markets.

USES A substitute for ricotta or cottage cheese.

Fat An integral part of cooking and baking, fat can take many forms, but the one used most often in baking is **butter**, which has an amazing ability to carry flavors and to give wonderful, melt-in-your-mouth and/or flaky texture to pastry. A saturated animal fat, meaning that it is solid at room temperature, butter must be kept refrigerated; when wrapped tightly, it will last for up to two weeks. It can be frozen for several months. Other fats used in baking are lard and vegetable oil, which also should be refrigerated.

MARKET FORMS Available at all supermarkets.

USES Both saturated and unsaturated fats are used to carry flavor and nutrients, tenderize, add color, and help maintain moisture in baked goods.

Filberts See **hazelnuts.**

Flour White flour is milled from the endosperm, or center, of the wheat kernel. The endosperm contains starch and protein, the percentages of which determine the type of flour it will become. All-purpose flour is available bleached or unbleached. Avoid bleached flour, which has a chemical flavor. High-gluten, hard-wheat flours are used for breads; lower-gluten, soft-wheat flours are used for cakes and pastries.

- ALL-PURPOSE FLOUR: A blend of hard-wheat and soft-wheat flours. It has an average protein content of 5 to 7 percent and a fine texture.

- BREAD FLOUR: Made of hard wheat, which is rich in protein, bread flour is often referred to as a *high-gluten flour* at 12 percent protein and above. Used in breads and puff pastry, it's good for structure. All-purpose flour can be substituted one to one, but for the best texture, seek out bread flour. It's available at health food markets and many supermarkets.

- CAKE FLOUR: A fine white flour made from soft wheat, with a protein content of 3 to 5 percent. It's best used for delicate cakes, such as angel food. Do not use it to roll out dough; it contains too much starch, which will stick to the dough.

- GRAHAM FLOUR: Coarse whole-wheat flour. Graham flour and whole wheat flour can be used interchangeably in most recipes.

- PASTRY FLOUR: One step above cake flour in protein content (4 to 6 percent), pastry flour is also ground from soft wheat. It is used to make tender cakes and cookies and some pie crusts.

- WHOLE WHEAT FLOUR: Whole wheat flour still contains the bran (fibrous cellulose) and vitamin-rich, oil-containing germ of the wheat berry. Because it contains oil from the germ, whole wheat flour has a shorter shelf life and should be refrigerated if left unused for more than two weeks. Flour without the germ is enriched with niacin, riboflavin, thiamine, iron, and often vitamins A and D.

MARKET FORMS All-purpose flour is widely available. Bread flour and cake flour are available at better supermarkets. Stone-ground flours, graham flour, pastry flour, and flour from other grains are available at specialty stores and whole food or health food stores, and through mail order.

USES Flour provides protein, starch, and structure in baked goods.

Fondant
Cooked and aerated sugar that can be poured over cinnamon buns or petits fours, rolled like dough to cover cakes, or dipped into chocolate for creamy bonbons. Store in the refrigerator tightly wrapped in plastic.

MARKET FORMS Premade poured and rolled fondant is available at specialty shops. Fondant can also be made from scratch.

USES Decorative coatings and candy fillings.

Framboise	French for "raspberry" and the name of a French raspberry liqueur.
MARKET FORMS	Clear distilled raspberry eau de vie is available at better stores selling fine spirits. Red- or pink-colored raspberry brandies are also available but are not nearly as good.
USES	Flavoring creams, cakes, custards, mousses, sauces.
Frangelico	A hazelnut-flavored liqueur made in the Piedmont region of northern Italy. It was first made in the seventeenth century by the Christian monk Fra Angelico, who distilled it from roasted local hazelnuts and berries. It still bears his name, and the bottle is shaped like his robe.
MARKET FORMS	Available where spirits are sold.
USES	Flavoring.
Gelatin	A thickening agent derived from collagen found in the cartilage and connective tissue of animal bones.
MARKET FORMS	Powdered gelatin is widely available in supermarkets. Do not mistake fruit-flavored gelatin desserts for plain gelatin. Powdered gelatin must be sprinkled over cold water to soften. After about 10 minutes, the gelatin will have absorbed the water, and the mixture is then added to a warm portion of a recipe, so that it can dissolve.
USES	Gelées, Bavarian creams, mousses.
Gianduja	See **chocolate**.
Glucose	A form of sugar found in corn, honey, and grapes. It is less sweet than table sugar (sucrose), and it resists crystallization.
MARKET FORMS	Professionals can order glucose in large tubs from confectionery suppliers. For the home cook, corn syrup is the most common form of glucose.
USES	See **corn syrup.**
Grand Marnier	French cognac flavored with orange peel and aged in oak barrels.
MARKET FORMS	Available where fine spirits are sold. Triple Sec has a less distinguished flavor but can be substituted in a pinch.
USES	Flavoring for creams custards, sauces.
Granulated sugar	See **sugar.**

Gruyère	A nutty cheese from Switzerland, made from cow's milk. Aged for up to one year.
MARKET FORMS	Widely available by the wedge at cheese shops and better supermarkets.
USES	Gruyère pairs nicely with fruit as an after-dinner course. It is the basis for the French cheese puffs called Gougères.
Hazelnuts	Also known as *filberts,* these nuts are grown widely throughout Europe, as well as the Pacific Northwest. Their flavor shows up in many sweet and savory dishes. Like all nuts, they should be stored in the freezer. Hazelnuts have a thin brown skin, which is bitter. To skin, toast the shelled nuts at 300°F for 15 to 20 minutes and then place up to 12 nuts at a time in a towel. Fold the towel over the nuts and rub. This will remove nearly all of the skins. For toasted hazelnuts, turn heat up to 350°F after skinning, and toast for 5 to 10 minutes more, or until brown.
MARKET FORMS	Hazelnuts can be purchased in their hard shell, whole or in pieces, blanched with the thin, dark brown skin removed, or raw. Hazelnut paste, also known as *praline paste,* is a pastry shop staple. It has the consistency of peanut butter and, like Nutella, is sweetened.
USES	Hazelnuts add flavor and texture to many bakery items. Hazelnut paste can be folded into creams, butters, sauces, and custards.
Heavy cream	See **cream.**
Herbs	Dried herbs are a bit stronger in flavor than fresh, and sometimes more bitter, but they lose their potency if stored too long. They will last for up to six months at room temperature, sealed tightly. Once cut, fresh herbs will last for several days if refrigerated, wrapped in damp paper towels or upright in a jar of water.
USES	Flavoring.
Honey	Sweet, liquid sugar made by bees from flower nectar. It is a complex sugar, twice as sweet as table sugar, containing levulose, dextrose, maltose, and sucrose. Often referred to as "the world's most perfect food," honey will never spoil. As it ages, honey becomes darker and slightly stronger tasting. It may also crystallize but can easily be brought back to its liquid state by being heated. The names *clover, orange blossom,* and *sage* refer to the flowers from which the pollen was collected; each type of honey has a distinctive flavor. Most honey is pasteurized to inhibit crystallization.

MARKET FORMS	Honey is widely available at supermarkets, whole foods stores, gourmet markets, and farmers' markets. Wildflower honey is a good all-purpose honey; I use orange-blossom honey for a light and delicate taste and buckwheat honey for robust flavor, especially in candy making.
USES	Flavoring, sweetening.
Icing sugar	See **sugar**.
Juniper berries	A pungent spice, these berries come from an evergreen shrub. They give gin its distinctive flavor.
MARKET FORMS	Available in the spice section of many supermarkets.
USES	Their distinctive flavor pairs nicely with ginger and cloves.
Kahlúa	A liqueur from Mexico that is flavored with roasted coffee, chocolate, and vanilla.
MARKET FORMS	Widely available where fine spirits are sold. There are also many domestic brands of coffee liqueur, but most are thicker and sweeter than Kahlúa.
USES	Flavoring.
Key limes	AKA *Mexican limes* and *West Indian limes*. Small limes with a flavor that is slightly sweeter and less abrasive than that of the larger, standard Persian limes. When ripe, their skin has a yellow tint.
MARKET FORMS	Available at Mexican markets and some gourmet supermarkets.
USES	Flavoring.
Kirsch	A German brandy distilled from the juice and pits of cherries. Also known as *kirschwasser* ("cherry water").
MARKET FORMS	Available where fine spirits are sold.
USES	Flavoring.
Kosher salt	See **salt**.
Lavender	A flowering herb with a perfumy flavor and aroma. Related to mint, it is a common flavor in the cuisine of Provence.
MARKET FORMS	Dried lavender flowers can be found at specialty and ethnic grocers or through mail order. Store in a cool, dry place, as you would other herbs.
USES	Flavoring.

Lemon verbena	See **verbena**.
Macadamia nut	A large, round, pale nut, extremely high in fat, native to Australia but now grown mainly in Hawaii.
MARKET FORMS	Available roasted and salted at most supermarkets and raw at specialty food stores. Store in the freezer.
USES	Flavoring and garnish for cookies, cakes, breads, ice creams.
Maple syrup	I use grade A, the lightest.
MARKET FORMS	Available at grocery stores and gourmet shops. Do not substitute pancake syrup, which is flat tasting and overly sweet, without the lively flavor of maple.
USES	Flavoring.
Marsala	A Sicilian fortified wine.
MARKET FORMS	Available at most stores that carry spirits.
USES	Flavoring.
Marzipan	Sweetened almond paste, used to create edible decorations, like fruit, flowers, and animals. Store unopened at room temperature, then wrap in plastic film and store in the refrigerator once opened.
MARKET FORMS	Available at gourmet markets.
USES	Filling; decorative modeling medium.
Masa harina	Dried, processed flour made from lime-soaked dried field corn. Much finer than cornmeal, with a different flavor. Maseca is one common brand.
MARKET FORMS	Widely available at supermarkets and Mexican markets.
USES	Used for corn tortillas and in this book in a sandy-textured cookie called Mexican Wedding Cookies (see page 187).
Mascarpone	A delicate double-cream cheese from Italy.
MARKET FORMS	Available at better markets (always in the cheese section) and cheese stores.
USES	Use in place of cream cheese or sour cream to enrich and accompany baked goods.

Merlot A wine grape, traditionally blended in the great wines of Bordeaux and enjoying popularity today as a red wine varietal, particularly in California. It has a straightforward fruit flavor and lends itself well to fruit sauces.

MARKET FORMS Available at most stores that carry spirits.

USES Flavoring.

Meyer lemons A southern California lemon, first taken there from China in the early twentieth century. Meyer lemons are low in acid, with soft, thin, orange-lemon skin. They are in season from late November through May.

MARKET FORMS Available at specialty markets and through mail order, and at California farmers' markets.

USES Flavoring.

Milk Most recipes assume the use of whole milk. Substitutions of skim milk (0.5 percent fat) and low-fat milk (1 percent fat) produce slightly less rich products. Low-fat has more flavor than skim and is preferable if you are making substitutions. Buttermilk was traditionally the liquid left over after butter was churned. Today manufacturers add bacteria to low-fat milk, giving it a tangy flavor. Powdered or dry milk is a common ingredient in bread baking.

MARKET FORMS Widely available.

USES A liquid dairy ingredient, used in place of water to add richness, sweetness, and nutrition.

Mint The most commonly used fresh mint is spearmint, but also available are several forms of peppermint, which is much stronger and slightly sweet. Keep refrigerated, wrapped in damp paper towels, or upright in a glass of water. Available in dry form as well as in oils and extracts.

MARKET FORMS Available at some supermarkets and at farmers' markets.

USES Flavoring.

Molasses The byproduct of sugar refinement. It's a thick, dark, sticky syrup that adds a spicy flavor to baked goods.

MARKET FORMS Light, dark, and blackstrap are available at supermarkets and whole foods stores. I prefer to use unsulfured Plantation Blackstrap, which has the most flavor.

USES Flavoring.

Nutella   A hazelnut and chocolate spread. Store in a cool place.

MARKET FORMS   Available at most supermarkets.

USES   See *gianduja* under **chocolate**.

Nuts   Most are high in fat and should be used quickly or refrigerated to prevent rancidity. For superior flavor, toast nuts to a dark color to release the oils. **To toast nuts:** Place on a baking sheet in a 350°F oven for 5 to 10 minutes, or until they smell toasty and have turned a darker shade of brown. Nuts that I use include almonds, Brazil nuts, cashews, chestnuts, hazelnuts, macadamia nuts, pecans, pistachios, pine nuts, and walnuts.

MARKET FORMS   Most nuts are available shelled and skinned as well as whole.

USES   A flavoring and garnish in all sorts of pastry and bread.

Oats   A grain that is processed in many different ways. Rolled oats or old-fashioned oats are flattened with industrial rollers and steamed. They cook in 15 minutes. Quick oats are cut before steaming and rolling. They cook in 5 minutes. Instant oats are completely precooked and dried and are not good for baking because they soften as soon as they are combined with a liquid. In a cake batter, they turn to mushy lumps. Old-fashioned rolled oats are my favorite baking oats, because of their chewy texture. I use equal parts of old-fashioned and instant in my oatmeal cookies. The blend gives texture and structure.

MARKET FORMS   Available at supermarkets and whole foods stores.

USES   Cookies, breads, toppings.

Oils   Vegetable oil is best used in challah bread. Nut oil blends and seed oils like safflower and sunflower oil are great for frying, because they have a higher smoke point, 440°F and above. They are more stable and less likely to foam.

Orange flower water   Distilled orange blossoms.

MARKET FORMS   Look for small bottles at Middle Eastern groceries and stores that sell liquor.

USES   Flavoring, Middle Eastern pastries.

Parmigiano-Reggiano (Parmesan)   A hard, dried cheese made from skimmed cow's milk that has been aged a minimum of 2 years and up to 4 years.

MARKET FORMS   Sold by the ounce, at cheese stores and better markets.

USES   Great for Gougères.

Pectin See **apple pectin.**

Pepper Whole peppercorns have a superior shelf life and more intense flavor than preground pepper. White pepper marries well with honey, ginger, and mixed spices as in lebkuchen. Black pepper pairs well with assertive herbs like rosemary and basil.

USES Flavoring.

Pink peppercorns Despite the name, pink peppercorns come from a type of rose plant and not from a pepper plant. A syrup infused with pink peppercorns pairs beautifully with pineapple.

MARKET FORMS Available at finer supermarkets and gourmet stores.

USES Flavoring.

Pistachio flour Finely ground pistachios.

MARKET FORMS Found at gourmet groceries and baking supply stores.

USES Flavoring.

Port A fortified wine from the northern region of Portugal. Ruby ports are bright red in color and very fruity. They are aged approximately two years and are very inexpensive. Tawny ports are brown in color and deep in mellow fruity flavor because they are aged in wood for as long as forty years.

MARKET FORMS Found where spirits are sold.

USES Great for sauces and syrups.

Potato flour (also called potato starch) A flour made from cooked and dried ground potatoes.

MARKET FORMS Found at Middle Eastern stores, kosher and Italian delis, and some whole foods stores.

USES In this book, Torta Sabiosa (page 158).

Rice I use ground long-grain rice for my Rice Short Dough.

MARKET FORMS Available at all supermarkets. Basmati and Thai are available at Asian markets, and Arborio is available at Italian and gourmet markets.

USES In this book, Rice Short Dough (page 222).

Ricotta Some Italian delis sell fresh ricotta, which is superior.

MARKET FORMS	Available at supermarkets, Italian markets, and gourmet markets as whole, low-fat, and nonfat.
USES	Cannoli fillings, cheesecakes.

Rolled oats See **oats**.

Rose water A distillate made from rose petals. It has a sweet perfume flavor.

MARKET FORMS	Available in bottles from Middle Eastern markets.
USES	Flavoring.

Royal icing A simple frosting or glaze made from powdered sugar and egg whites.

MARKET FORMS	Typically made from scratch but also available as an instant powder from specialty stores.
USES	Decorative piping for cakes and cookies and a quick icing for yeasted buns and muffins.

Rum I prefer to make desserts with good dark rum, which has a deep, intense flavor.

MARKET FORMS	Available where spirits are sold. Look for a good dark rum like Myers's.
USES	Flavoring.

Saffron The stigma of a purple crocus flower. Each flower has only three stigmas, which must be harvested by hand, making saffron very expensive. Store in a cool dry environment for up to six months. Crush before using.

MARKET FORMS	Found at specialty stores, gourmet groceries, and some supermarkets.
USES	Flavoring, for color, and baked in bread.

Salt A natural preservative from salt mines and the sea.

- SEA SALT is made by evaporating seawater. It comes in both coarse and fine grains, and each kind of sea salt has a very distinct flavor. I prefer to use finely ground sea salt in my baking. It dissolves beautifully and adds very nice flavor to pastries. It costs a bit more, but it is worth every penny. The finest sea salt from France is called *fleur de sel.*

- KOSHER SALT has a coarse grain and is made without additives. Many chefs cook with kosher salt exclusively, but I use it only to top pretzels and bread because I find that it does not dissolve properly in batter and dough.

- ROCK SALT is grayish and is used to make ice cream in old-fashioned ice cream machines.

> **TABLE/IODIZED SALT** is small grained, with additives to keep it dry and to prevent hypothyroidism. It dissolves well but is harsh tasting.

USES To enhance and round out the natural flavor of food.

Sauternes A highly regarded sweet white wine from the Sauternes region of France. Sauternes is quite expensive due to the labor-intensive harvest.

MARKET FORMS Available at stores that sell fine wines and spirits.

USES Flavoring, poaching.

Sour cream Pasteurized cream with at least 18 percent milk fat that has been cultured with bacteria that cause the production of tangy lactic acid. I use full-fat sour cream.

MARKET FORMS Whole, low-fat, and nonfat.

USES As a soured, liquid dairy ingredient and condiment.

Spices It's essential to keep fresh spices on hand so that they will have vivid flavors. I purchase all my spices from Penzeys (see page 375). They are very fresh and always a good buy. After six months, spices will lose their flavor. Store in a cool dry place, preferably the freezer. Do not expose to sunlight. I recommend storing rarely used spices in small zipper plastic bags, airtight in the freezer. When using spices, take care not to go overboard, since they can overpower subtle flavors of other ingredients. Always add dry spices with the fats when creaming; this will bring out the natural oils present in the spice. **TO TOAST SPICES:** Heat in a small, dry skillet over medium-high heat, stirring or shaking the pan, until they begin to change color and smell toasty. Immediately transfer to a small bowl. The spices I use most in baking are:

> **ALLSPICE:** Native to North and South America, allspice is a round, dried unripe berry of the evergreen pimiento tree. It is given its name because of its complex smell, which resembles that of cinnamon, nutmeg, and clove.

> **ANISE** and **ANISE SEED:** Native to Greece, a member of the parsley family. Its flavor is sweet licorice.

> **CARAWAY SEEDS:** Seeds from an herb in the parsley family. The flavor is widely associated with rye bread.

> **CARDAMOM:** A spice, related to ginger, contained in white, green, or black pods. I recommend the green, which are the most delicate. Inside each pod are several small seeds that must be ground before being used. Look for whole cardamom pods rather than ground, in specialty and ethnic grocers, especially Indian.

- **CHINESE FIVE-SPICE POWDER**: See **Chinese five-spice powder**.

- **CINNAMON**: Made from the inner bark of either the Ceylon cinnamon (soft stick) or cassia (hard stick) tree. Ceylon cinnamon is milder. Cassia is the strong, spicy-sweet cinnamon familiar to most Americans. I prefer Vietnamese cassia cinnamon for its assertive yet floral flavor. Cinnamon is sold ground or in sticks.

- **CLOVES**: The dried unopened buds of the tropical evergreen clove tree. Can be purchased in dried and whole form. Be careful not to add too much, since this spice packs a whopping punch.

- **GINGER**: A rhizome that can be found fresh, dried ground, candied, or juiced. When I want to add the flavor of ginger to a recipe, I add it in the form of ginger juice, which I make by grating fresh ginger into a fine-mesh strainer, then pressing out the juice.

- **MACE**: The outer membrane of the nutmeg seed. When dried it is orange in color. It has the flavor of a heady nutmeg.

- **NUTMEG**: The hard seed from the center of an apricotlike fruit. It has a warm spicy flavor. I use it in custard and gingerbread cake to balance the sweetness of cinnamon. I prefer using freshly grated whole nutmeg. Ground nutmeg becomes less pungent with age.

- **STAR ANISE**: Native to China, star anise has a licorice flavor that is bitter and almost tannic compared to anise seeds.

Sugar An ingredient used to sweeten foods. Sugar is hydroscopic, which means it attracts and holds moisture, improving the shelf life of baked goods.

- **BROWN SUGAR**: White sugar mixed with molasses. Light (or golden) brown has a mild molasses flavor, while dark is more intense. I prefer to use light as my all-purpose brown sugar. Store brown sugar in an airtight container to retain the moisture and keep it soft. If it dries out and gets hard, soften it by placing it in the microwave with a piece of fresh bread for 30 seconds.

- **DEMERARA SUGAR**: Raw, coarse-textured, golden-colored dry sugar. It has an assertive molasses flavor because it is less refined. Light brown sugar may be substituted one to one.

- **GRANULATED SUGAR**: All-purpose table sugar. Granulated sugar (sucrose) is refined from sugar cane or sugar beets. It is the most common form of sugar because it combines well with other flavors and dilutes easily in liquid.

- **HONEY**: See **honey**.

- **MOLASSES:** See **molasses**.

- **MUSCOVADO** or **BARBADOS SUGAR:** A dark brown raw sugar with slightly coarser crystals and a stronger flavor than regular brown sugar. It can be substituted one to one for dark brown sugar.

- **SUPERFINE SUGAR:** Fine granulated sugar. It's excellent for baking because it breaks down easily. It can be substituted one to one for granulated sugar.

- **TURBINADO SUGAR:** Coarse raw sugar with a light molasses color and flavor. It can be substituted one to one for light brown sugar.

- **POWDERED, CONFECTIONERS', ICING, OR 10X SUGAR:** Granulated sugar that has been refined into a fine powder and mixed with a small amount of cornstarch (3 percent) to prevent clumping. It comes in several grades from 14x to 4x, the most common of which is 10x sugar. The x factor tells the baker how many times the sugar was ground, 14x being the finest and 4x being the coarsest. Powdered sugar dissolves instantly with moisture. Although the cornstarch helps to prevent clumping and crystallization, powdered sugar is still lumpy. Sift it before adding it. The volume of powdered sugar is 25 percent greater than that of granulated. When heated, granulated sugar breaks down and becomes a liquid more quickly than does powdered sugar.

USES   When cooked, sugar caramelizes and imparts color and more flavor. Coarse granulated sugar assists in the creaming process. Used in bread-making as a food for yeast.

Tea   The style of tea is determined by climate, soil, harvest, and processing. Green tea is steamed and dried, black tea leaves are fermented, and oolong uses a combined method. These basic teas are blended and mixed with aromatic ingredients to create hundreds of tea varieties. The black tea I use most often in baking is Earl Grey, which has distinctive flavors, including the essence of bergamot, a small orange, often candied, whose oil is used in candies and perfumes. I also use black currant tea. Herb tea (technically called a *tisane* [tee-SAHN], the French word for "herb tea") is simply an infusion of flowers or herbs and is not a true tea. The herb teas I use most in desserts are verbena (also known as lemon verbena) and chamomile.

MARKET FORMS   For baking, tea bags are most practical for infusions.

USES   Poaching liquids, custards, sauces.

Tía Maria	A liqueur made with Blue Mountain coffee and rum.
MARKET FORMS	Available wherever spirits are sold.
USES	Flavoring.
Vanilla	One of my favorite flavorings, essential for a baker's pantry.

- **VANILLA BEAN:** A long, black shriveled pod, the dried fruit of the only type of orchid that bears fruit. Its flowers open only once a year and must be hand-pollinated. After a year, the mature green pods are picked by hand and then dried in the sun for up to six months. Inside each pod are thousands of tiny seeds, which carry the vanilla flavor into your desserts. Because they have a very strong flavor, only a half or quarter of a bean is needed for most recipes. The scraped vanilla pod can also be used to flavor liquids for vanilla sauce and granulated sugar, since it contains a good amount of vanilla oil.

  There are three types of vanilla beans. The most common variety, from which most extract is made, is the bourbon Madagascar bean, from the island off the coast of Africa. The rare Mexican vanilla bean has a very distinctive flavor. The fattest and most aromatic beans come from Tahiti. They have a subtle flavor and a rich aroma. I use Madagascar and Tahitian vanilla beans. I maximize their flavor by buying beans at least one month before using and storing the beans in jars containing vanilla extract. To use, split the bean lengthwise, scoop out the seeds with the point of a knife into the dessert, use the pod as directed in the recipe, then fish it out. After using the vanilla bean, wash and dry it, then pulverize the bean with granulated sugar and use in cookies and other pastries that would benefit from vanilla-flavored sugar.

- **VANILLA EXTRACTS:** Extracts are made by infusing and aging the beans in alcohol. Avoid imitation vanilla, which is made with chemicals instead of beans and does not have a sweet, pure vanilla flavor.

Verbena (or lemon verbena)	[ver-BEE-nuh] A plant with long, slender leaves that has a lemony scent and flavor.
MARKET FORMS	Fresh verbena can be found at some farmers' markets and is easy to grow. Dried verbena is found wherever herb teas are sold.
USES	Infusing teas and syrups.
Verjuice	An acidic, nonalcoholic juice pressed from young grapes. It is less acidic than vinegar or lemon juice but slightly more acidic than wine, and this in-between quality adds complexity to any dish. Verjuice was commonly

used in medieval cookery and is still called for in many Middle Eastern recipes. It's popular in restaurants, and some wineries are producing it from varietal grapes, such as Chardonnay and Pinot Noir.

MARKET FORMS   Bottled by independent wineries, available at specialty stores or through mail order.

USES   Replaces wine, lemon juice, or vinegar to brighten the flavor of sauce, poaching liquid, or sorbet.

Vinegar

I use vinegar in small amounts to add a little acid to a recipe, either to brighten the flavor and balance the sweetness of a sauce, poaching liquid, or sorbet, or for a tenderizing effect. Most often I use Champagne vinegar or white wine vinegar. Apple cider vinegar can also be used.

MARKET FORMS   Champagne vinegar can be found at gourmet shops and many supermarkets.

USES   Used to brighten flavor and balance sweetness.

Water

I am a stickler for good water and usually use bottled water in my baking and particularly in my sorbets. Tap water often has a strong chemical flavor and will affect the flavor of your dessert. Since water is a main ingredient in so many recipes, the quality of its flavor should not be overlooked.

MARKET FORMS   Water bottled with and without bubbles is available at most supermarkets, as are pitchers with built-in water filters.

USES   Breads, pastries, sorbets, sauces, poaching.

Whiskey

My favorite is Jack Daniel's, which has a sweetness and heat that hold up to baking.

MARKET FORMS   Available wherever spirits are sold.

USES   Flavoring.

Yeast

Yeast feeds on carbohydrates such as sugar, producing carbon dioxide and alcohol, which assist in the leavening and flavoring of bread. Different strains of yeast can produce more carbon dioxide (for bakers) or more alcohol (for winemakers and brewers).

MARKET FORMS   Professional bakers prefer to use fresh yeast, also known as *compressed* or *moist yeast,* because it is easier to weigh and has a superior flavor. Fresh yeast does not need warm liquid to be activated. It dissolves and blends easily in cold water. It is harder to find than granulated dried yeast (look in the refrigerated section). Granulated or dry yeast and rapid-rise yeast are available at most supermarkets. Three quarters of an ounce of fresh compressed yeast is equivalent to 2½ teaspoons dry yeast.

USES   Breadmaking.

Yuzu   A Japanese variety of yellow-skinned citrus with a distinctive, soft lemon-lime-orange flavor. Be careful not to get the salted variety.

MARKET FORMS   Yuzu juice is sold bottled at Japanese specialty stores.

USES   Can substitute for all or part of lemon or lime juice in some recipes.

Zest   The brightly colored outer layer of the skin of citrus fruit. Much of the flavor of a lemon, or any citrus fruit, comes from the oil of the peel. It is stored in the zest, which is on the surface of the fruit, in the beautifully colored skin. Just below the zest is the bitter white pith. Be sure not to include the pith with your zest.

MARKET FORMS   Widely available on a citrus fruit near you. Also available in pure oil form from specialty food stores.

USES   Removed by grating or peeling, the zest is used to flavor all types of foods. Zest can be removed from the fruit and frozen for later use.

SUPPLIERS

Chef's Toys
16540A Aston Street
Irvine, CA 92606
(800) 755-8634
www.cheftoys.net
Professional kitchen supply
store with a mobile unit that
serves southern California,
driving tools right to your door.
Tell them Sherry sent you!

Chocosphere.com
(800) 992-4626
Chocolate from 21 world-class
chocolatiers.

Cooking.com
(800) 663-8810
Cooking equipment and supplies.

Dean & DeLuca
560 Broadway
New York, New York 10012
(800) 999-0306
www.deandeluca.com
Great for tools, as well as specialty items such as chocolate,
spices, and even produce.

Home Depot
Find your local Home Depot
on its Web site
or call (800) 553-3199
www.homedepot.com
Great for tools like paint
brushes, scrapers, and tool
boxes.

J. B. Prince
36 East 31st Street
New York, NY 10016
(800) 473-0577
Fax: (212) 683-4488
www.jbprince.com
High-quality chef's equipment
and tools.

King Arthur Flour
Baker's Catalogue
P.O. Box 876
Norwich, VT 05055
(800) 827-6836
Fax: (800) 343-3002
www.kingarthurflour.com
All your baking needs, from
great flour to equipment and
tools.

Penzeys, Ltd.
19300 West Janacek Court
Brookfield, WI 53008
(800) 741-7787
Fax: (262) 785-7678
www.penzeys.com
Great spices and vanilla.

Sur la Table
1765 Sixth Avenue South
Seattle, WA 98134
(800) 243-0852
www.surlatable.com
Well-made baking equipment
and utensils.

Surfas Suppliers
8825 National Boulevard
Culver City, CA 90232
(310) 559-4770
Fax: (310) 559-4983
www.surfasonline.com
Restaurant equipment, cooking
equipment, and specialty foods.

Williams–Sonoma, Inc.
Mail Order Department
P.O. Box 379900
Las Vegas, NV 89137
(800) 541-2233
www.williams-sonoma.com
Well-made baking equipment
and utensils.

Wilton Industries
2240 West 75th Street
Woodbridge, IL 60517
(800) 794-5866;
www.wilton.com
Complete online bakeware store
for home cooks and professionals.

BIBLIOGRAPHY

Amendola, Joseph. *The Baker's Manual*. Rochelle Park, NJ: Hayden Book Company, 1978.

Amendola, Joseph, and Donald Lundberg. *Understanding Baking*. New York: Van Nostrand Reinhold, 1992.

Baggett, Nancy. *The All-American Cookie Book*. Boston: Houghton Mifflin, 2001.

Braker, Flo. *The Simple Art of Perfect Baking*. Boston: Houghton Mifflin, 1998.

Child, Julia. *Baking with Julia*. New York: William Morrow, 1996.

Corriher, Shirley O. *CookWise*. New York: William Morrow, 1997.

Cunningham, Marion. *The Fannie Farmer Baking Book*. Avenel, NJ: Random House Value Publishing, 1984.

Davidson, Alan. *The Oxford Companion to Food*. Oxford: Oxford University Press, 1999.

Fance, Wilfred J. *The Student's Technology of Breadbaking and Flour Confectionery*. London: Routledge and Kegan Paul, 1982.

Frieberg, Bo. *The Professional Pastry Chef*. New York: Van Nostrand Reinhold, 1996.

Grausman, Richard. *At Home with French Classics*. New York: Workman Publishing, 1988.

Hillman, Howard. *Kitchen Science*. Boston: Houghton Mifflin, 2003.

Kamman, Madeleine. *The New Making of a Cook*. New York: William Morrow, 1997.

Kimball, Christopher. *The Dessert Bible*. Boston: Little, Brown, 2000.

McGee, Harold. *On Food and Cooking: The Science and Lore of the Kitchen*. New York: Charles Scribner's Sons, 1984.

Neal, Bill. *Biscuits, Spoonbread, and Sweet Potato Pie*. New York: Alfred A. Knopf, 1996.

Pépin, Jacques. *Jacques Pépin's Complete Techniques*. New York: Times Black Dog & Leventhal, 2001.

Purdy, Susan G. *The Family Baker*. New York: Broadway Books, 1999.

—— *The Perfect Pie*. New York: Broadway Books, 2000.

Rombauer, Irma S., and Marion Rombauer Becker. *The Joy of Cooking*. New York: Scribner, 1975.

Roux, Michel. *Michel Roux's Finest Desserts*. Translated by Kate Whiteman. Toronto: Stoddart Publishing Co., 1995.

Sax, Richard. *Classic Home Desserts*. Boston: Houghton Mifflin, 2000.

Schunemann, Claus, and Gunter Treu. *Baking: The Art and Science*. Calgary, Alberta: Baker Tech Inc., Publications Division, 1986.

Tyler Herbst, Sharon. *Food Lover's Companion*. 2nd edition. New York: Barron's Educational Series, 2001.

Willan, Anne. *Anne Willan's Look and Cook: Perfect Pies and Tarts*. New York: Dorling Kindersley, 1994.

INDEX

The Greenwood
Encyclopedia of Daily Life

3 15th AND 16th
CENTURIES

The Greenwood
Encyclopedia of Daily Life

A Tour through History from Ancient Times to the Present

Joyce E. Salisbury
GENERAL EDITOR

Lawrence Morris
VOLUME EDITOR

GREENWOOD PRESS
Westport, Connecticut • London

Library of Congress Cataloging-in-Publication Data

The Greenwood encyclopedia of daily life : a tour through history from ancient times to the
present / Joyce E. Salisbury, general editor.
  p. cm.
  Includes bibliographical references and index.
  Contents: v. 1. The ancient world / Gregory S. Aldrete, volume editor; v. 2. The medieval
world / Joyce E. Salisbury, volume editor; v. 3. 15th and 16th centuries / Lawrence Morris,
volume editor; v. 4. 17th and 18th centuries / Peter Seelig, volume editor; v. 5. 19th
century / Andrew E. Kersten, volume editor; v. 6. The modern world / Andrew E. Kersten,
volume editor.
  ISBN 0–313–32541–3 (set: alk. paper) — ISBN 0–313–32542–1 (v. 1: alk. paper)
— ISBN 0–313–32543–X (v. 2: alk. paper) — ISBN 0–313–32544–8 (v. 3: alk. paper)
— ISBN 0–313–32545–6 (v. 4: alk. paper) — ISBN 0–313–32546–4 (v. 5: alk. paper)
— ISBN 0–313–32547–2 (v. 6: alk. paper)
  1. Manners and customs—History—Encyclopedias. I. Salisbury, Joyce E.
GT31.G74   2004
390—dc21   2003054724

British Library Cataloguing in Publication Data is available.

An online version of *The Greenwood Encyclopedia of Daily Life* is available from
Greenwood Press, an imprint of Greenwood Publishing Group, Inc. at:
http://dailylife.greenwood.com (ISBN 0–313–01311–X).

Library of Congress Catalog Card Number: 2003054724
ISBN: 0–313–32541–3 (set)
    0–313–32542–1 (vol. 1)
    0–313–32543–X (vol. 2)
    0–313–32544–8 (vol. 3)
    0–313–32545–6 (vol. 4)
    0–313–32546–4 (vol. 5)
    0–313–32547–2 (vol. 6)

First published in 2004

Greenwood Press, 88 Post Road West, Westport, CT 06881
An imprint of Greenwood Publishing Group, Inc.
www.greenwood.com

Printed in the United States of America

The paper used in this book complies with the
Permanent Paper Standard issued by the National
Information Standards Organization (Z39.48–1984).

10 9 8 7 6 5 4 3 2 1

Everyday life consists of the little things one hardly notices in time and space. . . . Through the details, a society stands revealed. The ways people eat, dress, or lodge at the different levels of that society are never a matter of indifference.

~Fernand Braudel, *The Structures of Everyday Life*
(New York: Harper and Row, 1979), 29.

CONTENTS

Contents

CONTENTS

Contents

TOUR GUIDE: A PREFACE FOR USERS

What did people, from the most ancient times to the most recent, eat, wear, and use? What did they hope, invent, and sing? What did they love, fear, or hate? These are the kinds of questions that anyone interested in history has to ask. We spend our lives preoccupied with food, shelter, families, neighbors, work, and play. Our activities rarely make the headlines. But it is by looking at people's everyday lives that we can truly understand history and how people lived. *The Greenwood Encyclopedia of Daily Life* brings into focus the vast majority of human beings whose existence is neglected by the standard reference works. Here you will meet the anonymous men and women of the past going about their everyday tasks and in the process creating the world that we know.

Organization and Content

The Greenwood Encyclopedia of Daily Life is designed for general readers without a background in the subject. Articles are accessible, engaging, and filled with information yet short enough to be read at one sitting. Each volume provides a general historical introduction and a chronology to give background to the articles. This is a reference work for the 21st century. Rather than taking a mechanical alphabetical approach, the encyclopedia tries something rather more elegant: it arranges material thematically, cascading from broad surveys down to narrower slices of information. Users are guided through this enormous amount of information not just by running heads on every page but also by "concept compasses" that appear in the margins: these are adapted from "concept mapping," a technique borrowed from online research methods. Readers can focus on a subject in depth, study it comparatively through time or across the globe, or find it synthesized in a way that provides an overarching viewpoint that draws connections among related areas—and they can do so in any order they choose. School curricula have been organizing research materials in this fashion for some time, so this encyclopedia will fit neatly into a modern pedagogical framework. We believe that this approach breaks new ground in the structuring of reference material. Here's how it works.

Level 1. The six volumes of the encyclopedia are, naturally, arranged by time period: the ancient world, the medieval world, 15th and 16th centuries, 17th and 18th centuries, the 19th century, and the modern world.

Level 2. Within each volume, information is arranged in seven broad categories, as shown in this concept compass:

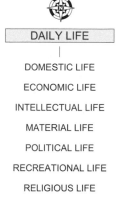

DAILY LIFE

DOMESTIC LIFE

ECONOMIC LIFE

INTELLECTUAL LIFE

MATERIAL LIFE

POLITICAL LIFE

RECREATIONAL LIFE

RELIGIOUS LIFE

Level 3. Each of the introductory essays is followed by shorter articles on components of the subject. For example, "Material Life" includes sections on everything from the food we eat to the clothes we wear to the homes in which we live. Once again, each category is mapped conceptually so that readers can see the full range of items that make up "Material Life" and choose which ones they want to explore at any time. Each volume has slightly different categories at this level to reflect the period under discussion. For example, "eunuchs" appear under "Domestic Life" in volume 2 because they served a central role in many cultures at that time, but they disappear in subsequent volumes as they no longer served an important role in some households. Here is one example of the arrangement of the concepts at this level (drawn from the "Domestic Life" section of volume 1):

DOMESTIC LIFE

FAMILY LIFE

WOMEN

MARRIAGE

CHILDREN

SEXUALITY

Level 4. These conceptual categories are further subdivided into articles focusing on a variety of representative cultures around the world. For example, here users can read about "Children" in Egypt, Greece, medieval Europe, and 16th-century Latin America. Here is an example of a concept compass representing the entry on money in Ancient India:

ECONOMIC LIFE

|

MONEY

|

Mesopotamia

Egypt

Greece

Rome

India

The articles at each level can stand alone, but they all also offer integrated information. For example, readers interested in food in ancient Rome can focus right in on that information. If curious, they can look at the next conceptual level and learn how Roman food compares with that of other cultures at the same time, or they can see how food fits into material life in general by looking at the highest conceptual level. Readers may also decide to compare ancient Roman food with menus in Italy during the Renaissance; they need only follow the same process in another volume. Readers can begin at any of the levels and follow their interests in all directions: knowledge is linked conceptually in these volumes, as it is in life. The idea is to make it easy and fun to travel through time and across cultures.

This organization offers a number of advantages. Many reference works provide disparate bits of information, leaving it to the reader to make connections among them. More advanced reference tools assume that readers already have the details and include articles only on larger conceptual issues. *The Greenwood Encyclopedia of Daily Life* assumes no previous knowledge but recognizes that readers at all stages benefit from integrated analysis. The concept-mapping organization allows users to see both the details of the trees and the overall shape of the forest. To make finding information even easier, a cumulative subject index to the entire encyclopedia appears at the end of each volume. With the help of detailed running heads, concept compasses, and an index, anyone taking this "Tour through History" will find it almost impossible to get lost.

This encyclopedia is the work of many contributors. With the help of advisory boards, specialists in daily life around the world wrote the detailed articles in the "level 4" concept category. Many of these experts have published books in Greenwood's award-winning "Daily Life through History" series, and their contributions were crafted from those books. Each volume's editor wrote all of the many higher-level conceptual articles that draw connections across the topics, thus providing a consistent voice and analysis throughout the volume.

Coverage

The chronological coverage of this encyclopedia is consistent with the traditional organization of history as it is taught: the six volumes each take on one of the standard periods. But in reality, history is messy, and any strictly chronological organization has flaws. Some societies span centuries with little change, whereas others change rapidly (usually because of cross-cultural interactions). We have addressed these questions of change and continuity in two ways. Sometimes, we introduce cultures in one volume, such as the Australian Aborigines in volume 1, and then we do not mention them again until they were transformed by colonial contact in volume 4. In these entries, readers are led by cross-references to follow the story of the Australian indigenous peoples from one volume to another. At other times, cultures have experienced enough change for us to introduce many new entries. For example, volume 5, devoted to the 19th century, includes many entries on Muslim lands. But some aspects of the 19th-century Muslim world (e.g., education) had long remained largely unchanged, and in these instances readers are led by cross-references to entries in earlier volumes. This network of cross-references highlights connections and introduces users to the complexities of change and continuity that form the pattern of the social fabric.

We also depart from the chronological constraints of each volume when describing cultures that left few written records. Borrowing from anthropological methods, we sometimes (cautiously) use evidence from later periods to fill in our understanding of earlier lives. For example, colonial observers have at times informed our description of earlier indigenous cultures in many parts of the world.

The geographic scope of this encyclopedia reflects the relatively recent recognition that culture has always operated in a global context. In the Stone Age, bloodstone from Rhum, an inaccessible island off the stormy coast of Scotland, was traded throughout Europe. Domesticated plants and animals from Mesopotamia spread to Africa through Nubia in the third millennium B.C.E., and throughout the ancient world the trade between China and the Mediterranean was an essential part of life. Global history is woven throughout these volumes.

We do not attempt to document every one of the thousands of societies that have arisen throughout history and around the world. Our aim—to provide a general reference source on everyday life—has led to a careful focus on the most studied and representative cultures of each period. For example, ancient India is introduced in volume 1 and then reappears in the complexities of a global society in volumes 5 and 6. Nubia, the path from Egypt to sub-Saharan Africa, is introduced in volume 1, but the range of African cultures is addressed in depth in volume 4 and again in volume 6. Muslim cultures are introduced in volume 2 with the birth of the Prophet, reappearing in volume 3 with the invigorated society of the Turks and then again in volumes 5 and 6 with modern Muslim states. This approach draws from archaeological methods: we are taking deep samples of cultures at various points in time. The overall picture derived from these samples offers a global perspective that is rich and comprehensive. We have covered every area of the world from Australia and the South Pacific to Viking Scandinavia, from indigenous cultures to colonial ones, from age-old Chinese civilization to the modern United States.

Another issue is that of diversity within some dizzyingly complex regions. Africa, China, Polynesia, and India, for example, all contain many cultures and peoples whose daily life is strikingly diverse. Rather than attempt exhaustiveness, we indicate the range of diversity within each entry itself. For instance, the many entries on Africa in volume 4 recognize that each society—Yoruba, Swahili, Shona, and all the others—is unique, and each entry focuses on the cultures that best represent trends in the region as a whole.

The United States is yet another complex region. It grew from its inception with a mingling of European, Native American, African, and other cultural groups. Instead of treating each individually, we combine them all within the entries on the United States. For example, as volume 4 discusses Colonial New England, it weaves a description of Native American life within the entries showing the full range of social interaction between native peoples and colonists. This organization recognizes the reality that all these groups grew together to become the United States.

Features

This work has been designed by educators, and pedagogical tools help readers get the most out of the material. In addition to the reader-friendly organization already described, we have added the following special features:

- *Concept compasses*. Each section of each volume contains a concept compass that visually details the contents of that section. Readers are immediately able to see what topics are covered and can decide which ones they want to explore.
- *Illustrations*. The illustrations drawn from primary sources are in themselves historical evidence and are not mere ornament. Each shows some aspect of daily life discussed in the text, and the captions tell what the picture illuminates and what readers can see in it.
- *Maps*. Maps give readers the necessary geographic orientation for the text. They have been chosen to reinforce the global perspective of the encyclopedia, and readers are consistently offered the view of the parts of the world under discussion.
- *Chronologies*. In addition to geography, students can quickly lose track of the chronology of events. Each volume offers a list of the major events of the periods and of the cultures covered in the volumes. These chronologies serve as a quick reference that supplements the historical introduction.
- *Snapshots*. The fascinating details of the past engage our curiosity. Each volume is scattered with boxed features that highlight such evidence of past life as a recipe, a song, a prayer, an anecdote, or a statistic. These bits of information enhance the main entries; readers can begin with the snapshot and move to more in-depth knowledge or end with the details that are often designed to bring a smile or a shocked insight.
- *Cross-references*. Traditional brief references point readers to related entries in other volumes, highlighting the changes in daily life over time. Other "See" references replace entries and show readers where to find the information they seek within the volume.
- *Primary documents*. The encyclopedia entries are written to engage readers, but nothing brings the past to life like a primary source. Each volume offers a selection of documents that illustrate the kinds of information that historians use to re-create daily life. Sources range widely, from the unforgettable description of Vikings blowing their noses in a water basin before they wash their faces in it to a ration book issued by the United States government during World War II.

- *Bibliography*. Most entries are followed by a section called "For More Information." These sections include recommended readings, as one might expect in a bibliographic attachment, but they often provide much more. For this media age, the authors recommend Web sites, films, educational videos, and other resources.
- *Index*. Even in the 21st century, a comprehensive index is essential. Concept compasses lead readers from one topic to the next, but an index draws connections among more disparate entries: for example, the history of the use of wine or cotton can be traced across many volumes and cultures. A cumulative index appears in each volume to allow fast and easy navigation.

The Greenwood Encyclopedia of Daily Life: A Tour through History from Ancient Times to the Present has been a labor of love. At the end of the day, we hope that readers will be informed and entertained. But we also hope that they will come to a renewed appreciation of an often-spoken but seldom-felt reality: at the most basic level all humans, across time and space, share concerns, pleasures, and aspirations, but the ways these are expressed are infinite in their range. The six volumes of this encyclopedia reveal both the deep similarities and the fascinating differences among people all over the world. We can participate in our global village more intelligently the more we understand each other's lives. We have also learned that people are shown at their best (and sometimes their worst) in the day-to-day activities that reveal our humanity. We hope readers enjoy taking this tour of people's lives as much as we have enjoyed presenting it.

~Joyce E. Salisbury

Acknowledgments

I would like to express my thanks to all who helped me in completing this project, including Brian Ulrich and Paula Rentmeester. Particular thanks go to Professor Joyce E. Salisbury for inviting me to contribute to this project. The staff of Greenwood Publishing and their associates also have my heartfelt appreciation for their skills in proofreading, illustrations, and cartography. I hope that all who use this volume find it as interesting to read as I did to compile.

~Lawrence Morris

1

HISTORICAL OVERVIEW

At the start of the 15th century, a person in Castile (a region now in modern-day Spain) lived in a small province in a peninsula that was fractured into many small states that were frequently at war with each other. By the end of the 16th century, a person in Castile was a member of a nation that controlled not only the Iberian peninsula (modern-day Spain and Portugal), but territories that stretched all the way around the globe, including much of South, Central, and North America, and territories in the Pacific, such as the Philippines. For Europe and the Middle East, the course of the 15th and 16th centuries saw the transformation of several countries from small, feudal, medieval societies to world-spanning bureaucratic empires that would endure until the 19th century and beyond. This volume will focus on several of these nations, namely England, Spain, Italy, and the Ottoman Empire.

While these centuries witnessed the rise of empires in Europe and the Middle East, they witnessed the destruction of empires in the Americas. In 1500, shortly after Columbus had landed in the Americas for the first time, the Aztecs, Maya, and Incas (the Native American peoples examined in this volume) all had well-developed societies that occupied vast amounts of territory and demanded large amounts of political savvy in order to be run properly. These societies were complete with large temples, palaces, and government buildings. These Native American empires had full-time armies, craftsmen, and politicians, in addition to many farmers. Their skill in building, astronomy, and especially farming was tremendous. By 1600, these empires had all been destroyed, over 90 percent of the population had disappeared due to disease and warfare, and those people that remained were under the political control of the Spanish, and were often forced to labor against their will.

Clearly, the years 1400–1600 were of immense importance, and it is worth examining briefly some of the major historical events of the period. To understand the situation of the world in 1400, it is useful to be familiar with some of the events that had shaped that situation. While other volumes of this encyclopedia have sketched the earlier history of Europe and the Middle East, the Mesoamerican and South American peoples appear for the first time in this volume, and it is worthwhile to sketch their earlier history before turning to the 15th and 16th centuries.

Early History of Mesoamerica and South America through the 15th Century

Sometime between forty thousand and twenty thousand years ago, the first human beings entered the Americas. These people seem to have crossed over from Russia on the Bering land bridge, a wide strip of land connecting northeast Russia to Alaska. The Bering land bridge was not under water then, as it is now, because the water level of the world's oceans was lower, due to the Ice Age. These first immigrants were most likely following herds of animals that they hunted for food. Once in the Americas, they dispersed all over North, Central, and South America.

During what is known as the Archaic Age (6000–1500 b.c.e.), these wandering groups of people, who had been living mostly as hunter-gatherers, started making permanent settlements. This shift into permanent settlements went hand in hand with the domestication of various plants and animals. The settlers would no longer have to follow the food because they were able to produce the food at home. In Mesoamerica, the earliest settlements appeared along the Pacific coast around 1700–1500 b.c.e., and their inhabitants were most likely living in a mixed economy: they derived part of their food from farming, part of their food from domesticated animals, and part of their food from wildlife resources, especially fish.

In Peru, the first stage of cultural development is called the Preceramic Period (up to 1800 b.c.e.). Its most notable event was the development of settled communities with domesticated plants and animals. By 3000 b.c.e., highland communities had domesticated llama and alpaca and were growing corn, beans, squash, potatoes, and other foods. Settlement along the coast did not take place until much later, around 2000 b.c.e. Perhaps the time difference was due to the environment. While the highland peoples needed to domesticate plants and animals to ensure a stable food supply in the harsh conditions of the Andes Mountains, those people living on the seacoast had a more abundant wild food supply surrounding them in the lakes and fields. Highland and coastal peoples built several large buildings during this period. These buildings were much larger than average homes, up to 33 feet in height, and were probably temples.

In Mesoamerica the settled communities started to build capital cities, featuring some of the largest temples ever built in Mesoamerica, around the year 400 b.c.e. These large-scale projects were made possible by the large populations that had arisen due to improved farming techniques. Also important was the increase in trade throughout the Mesoamerican area. Highland communities produced obsidian, jade, and other minerals that they traded with communities along the seacoast. These communities in turn traded with other peoples living up and down the coast. This political and social arrangement is now known as Early Maya Civilization (1500 b.c.e.–250 c.e.).

At around the same time, the Olmec Civilization (1500–400 B.C.E.) sprang up around the humid lowlands of the Gulf coast of Mexico, north of the Maya. Two key Olmec sites are the village cities of La Venta and San Lorenzo. La Venta is located on an island surrounded by a swamp. Archaeological evidence indicates that the Olmec had developed a sophisticated means of farming such swampy regions, and that they supplemented their harvests with fishing, hunting, and gathering. The Olmec also appear to have developed their own writing system, though few carvings remain. Those carvings that survive are impressive. The Olmec are now famous for their carvings of kings. These carvings were made on basalt stones weighing several tons. Because such stone is not found at La Venta, these large basalt slabs must have been transported to the Olmec site from many miles away, perhaps on huge log rafts. The stones demonstrate that the Olmec had a complex society capable of organizing labor to accomplish difficult tasks. The carvings also demonstrate that the civilization had strong rulers who may have been worshipped as gods.

Another culture that flourished at this time was the Oaxacan Civilization (1500–400 B.C.E.). This civilization developed in the Valley of Oaxaca in southern Mexico. The archaeological evidence suggests that the civilization consisted of independent cities, each dominated by a ruler and his associated temple. The Oaxacans, like the Olmec, carved monumental stelae (standing stone slabs), but the images they carved focused on warriors and war captives more than on kings. On their pottery, the Oaxacans favored images of fire-serpents and jaguar-men, which were symbols associated with ruling families throughout Mesoamerica.

In South America around this time there were two cultural stages: the Initial Period (1800–900 B.C.E.) and the Early Horizon (900–200 B.C.E.). The Initial Period began with the appearance of pottery and baked-clay vessels. Another advancement was irrigation, which could bring water to fields further away from a water source. This advancement seems to have caused a population shift inland away from the sea. Around 900 B.C.E., a new artistic style, called Chavin, swept the Peruvian area. The style is named after the site of Chavin de Huántar, in the central highlands, that is dominated by this style. The city itself was a true urban center with the resulting trade specialization, featuring potters, builders, carpenters, farmers, and others.

In Mesoamerica, the Maya achieved their peak of importance during the period called Middle Maya Civilization (250–900 C.E.), which is frequently divided up into subperiods called Early Classic (250–600 C.E.), Late Classic (600–800 C.E.), and Terminal Classic (800–900 C.E.). The population of the Maya swelled during this period, and two great cities arose in the southern lowlands: Tikal and Calakmul. For some reason, however, large numbers of people fled the lowlands between 800 and 900 C.E. and moved to the highlands and to the northern lowlands.

Peruvian culture went through the Early Intermediate Period (200 B.C.E.—600 C.E.) and Middle Horizon (600–1000 C.E.) at this time. The Early Intermediate Period witnessed the disappearance of Chavin influence and the rise of the Moche, or Mochica, along the northern coast of Peru. The decorated pottery left by the Moche suggests that their society was dominated by a warrior caste that ritually drank the blood of their enemies. The Moche are most famous for their burial sites.

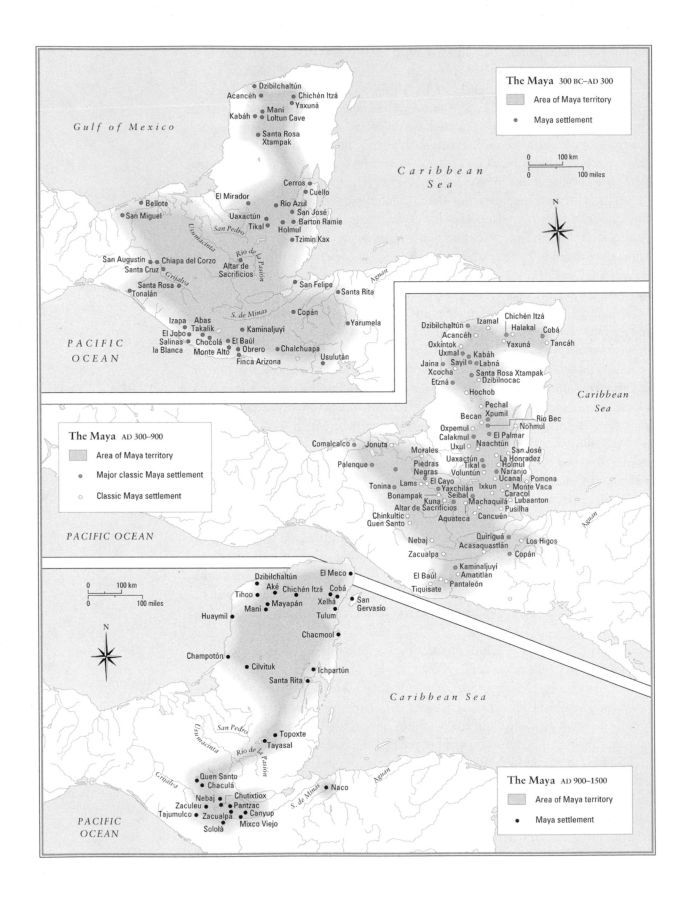

The Maya 300 BC–AD 300

Area of Maya territory

Maya settlement

Gulf of Mexico

Dzibilchaltún
Acancéh
Chichén Itzá
Maní Yaxuná
Kabáh Loltun Cave
Santa Rosa Xtampak

Caribbean Sea

0   100 km
0   100 miles

N

Cerros
Cuello
El Mirador
Río Azul
Bellote
San José
Uaxactún San Felipe Barton Ramie
San Miguel
Tikal Holmul
Tzimin Kax

Usumacinta
San Pedro
Río de la Pasión

San Augustín Chiapa del Corzo
Santa Cruz *Grijalva* Altar de
Sacrificios
Santa Rosa
Tonalán San Felipe
Santa Rita

S. de Minas Copán
Yarumela

Izapa Abas
Takalik
El Jobo Kaminaljuyí
Salinas Chocolá El Baúl
la Blanca Monte Alto Obrero Chalchuapa
Finca Arizona Usulután

PACIFIC OCEAN

The Maya AD 300–900

Area of Maya territory

● Major classic Maya settlement

○ Classic Maya settlement

PACIFIC OCEAN

Dzibilchaltún Izamal Chichén Itzá
Acancéh Halakal Cobá
Oxkintok Yaxuná Tancáh
Uxmal Kabáh
Jaina Sayil Labná
Xcocha Santa Rosa Xtampak
Etzná Dzibilnocac

Caribbean Sea

Hochob
Pechal
Becan Xpumil
Río Bec
Oxpemul Nohmul
Comalcalco Jonuta Calakmul El Palmar
Uxul Naachtún San José
Morales La Honradez
Palenque Piedras Uaxactún Holmul
Negras Tikal Naranjo
Voluntún Ucanal Pomona
Tonina Lams El Cayo Ixkun Monte Vaca
Bonampak Yaxchilán Seibal Caracol
Kuna Machaquilá Lubaanton
Chinkultic Altar de Sacrificios Pusilha
Quen Santo Aquateca Cancuén
Nebaj Quiriguá Los Higos
Zacualpa Acasaquastlán Copán
Kaminaljuyí
El Baúl Amatitlán
Tiquisate Pantaleón

Aguan

The Maya AD 900–1500

Area of Maya territory

● Maya settlement

Dzibilchaltún El Meco
Aké Chichén Itzá Cobá
Tihoo Xelhá
Maní Mayapán San Gervasio
Huaymil Tulum
Chacmool
Champotón Cilvituk Ichpartún
Santa Rita

San Pedro
Usumacinta
Río de la Pasión
Grijalva

Topoxte
Tayasal

Quen Santo Naco
Chaculá
Nebaj Chutixtiox *S. de Minas*
Zaculeu Pantzac
Tajumulco Zacualpa Canyup
Sololá Mixco Viejo

Caribbean Sea

PACIFIC OCEAN

0   100 km
0   100 miles

N

Aguan

They were one of the first societies to bury their dead in pyramid mounds. Along with the corpse, the Moche interred many material possessions, including huge amounts of gold, silver, shells, feathers, and precious stones. The Nasca culture also developed in the Early Intermediate Period. While not as complex a society as the Moche, the Nasca created many geoglyphs (figures many kilometers long created by scraping the ground surface). The images are only clearly visible from the air, and tremendous amounts of planning and precise measurement must have been involved in their production. It is not clear what purpose these geoglyphs, sometimes called Nazca Lines, served.

The Middle Horizon Period of Peruvian civilization saw the rise and fall of two powerful societies: the Tiahuanaco and the Huari. The Tiahuanaco lived around Lake Titicaca in the highland region and devised a system to grow crops effectively despite the extreme altitude. Their agricultural and resulting economic success caused their expansion. The Huari, although they lived at a lower altitude, also needed to overcome agricultural difficulties. In their case, most of the land consisted of mountainsides and was not flat. To compensate, the Huari designed a series of terraces that they built into the sides of the mountains. Both these societies waned before the end of the Middle Horizon Period, for reasons that are not fully known.

While the Huari and Tiahuanaco cultures were beginning their decline in Peru, the Toltec empire (950–1150 C.E.) was beginning its rise in Mesoamerica, around the Basin of Mexico. The Toltecs are particularly important for the study of the Aztecs because the Aztecs viewed the Toltecs as genius inventors of all the important crafts and claimed descent from them. The Toltecs did indeed have an advanced society, as can be seen from the large ritual buildings at Tollan. According to myth, a great priest-king named Topiltzin Quetzalcoatl (which means Our Young Prince, the Feathered Serpent) ushered in a golden era of political stability and agricultural abundance. Invasions from the north and the development of rival factions within Tollan itself, however, precipitated the collapse of the Toltec empire in the 12th century. Toltec refugees drifted toward the center of the Basin area and settled in the area surrounding Lake Tezcoco. These groups of refugees, such as the Acolhuas, Tepanecs, and Otomies, eventually formed separate identities, but all shared a common heritage as descendants from the Toltecs, whom they glorified in song and art. When the Aztecs arrived in the Basin area, they quickly adopted the customs, myths, and even claims of Toltec descent from their new neighbors.

The Aztecs or Mexica, as they are often called, arrived in the Basin of Mexico around the year 1300 C.E. Where they had come from is not entirely clear, but the Aztec origin legends claim that the people emerged from seven caves somewhere far to the north of the Basin of Mexico. According to this legend, a leader of the people was instructed in a dream by their god, Huitzilpochtli, to travel south to a better land that the god would show them. The Mexica set off, traveling for over a century, before they came upon the sign the god had told them about: an eagle standing on a cactus with a snake in his mouth. The grateful people built their capital city, Tenochtitlan, on that spot and laid the beginnings of an expansive empire. The image of the eagle with the snake in its mouth is found on the flag of Mexico (which is named after the Mexica) in recognition of this fateful event.

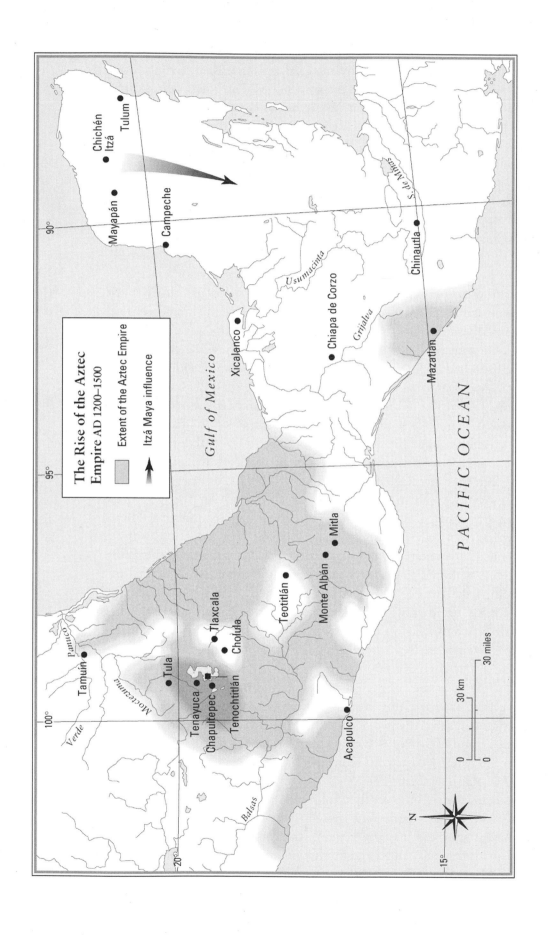

The Rise of the Aztec
Empire AD 1200–1500

☐ Extent of the Aztec Empire

➤ Itzâ Maya influence

PACIFIC OCEAN

Gulf of Mexico

Tulum

Chichén
Itzá

Mayapán

Campeche

Xicalanco

Chiapa de Corzo

Chinautla

Mazatlán

Usumacinta

Grijalva

S. de Minas

Tamuín

Tula

Tenayuca

Chapultepec

Tenochtitlán

Tlaxcala

Cholula

Teotitlán

Monte Albán

Mitla

Acapulco

Pánuco

Verde

Moctezuma

Balsas

90°

95°

100°

20°

15°

N

0   30 km

0   30 miles

With regard to the Maya culture, the final era of precontact (i.e., before the arrival of the Spanish) culture is called Late Maya Civilization (900–1500 C.E.). This period is marked by repeated shifts in power. At the start of the period, the northern Yucatán peninsula flourished, and the city Chichen Itza dominated the political landscape. This city was founded by the Putun Maya, also called the Itza Maya, who were originally from the southwest of the Maya area but had migrated north. Chichen Itza rose in prominence at least in part because of its location. Situated almost in the middle of the Yucatán peninsula, the city was able to dominate both the overland trade network and the seaport of Isla Cerritos. Wall murals from the city also suggest that it had a strong army. The government of Cichen Itza may also have given it an advantage. Instead of relying upon one person, the king, Chichen Itza was governed by a *multepal* (*mul* "group," *tepal* "govern"), a kind of council formed by nobles from leading families. Chichen Itza, nevertheless, was eventually overthrown and replaced as the dominant power by another city, called Mayapan, which eventually disintegrated into a collection of squabbling states. The highlands were dominated by two powerful but disunited groups: the Quiche Maya and the Cakchiquel Maya. When the Spaniards arrived and ended Late Maya civilization, the Maya regions were occupied by small independent and often mutually hostile states.

While the 15th century witnessed the full flowering of the Aztec empire and the gradual decline in Maya society, as noted above, it also witnessed the tremendous growth of the Inca empire. In the Late Intermediate Period (1000–1438 C.E.) of Peruvian history, the Inca were one of many small groups of people living in the highlands and valleys of the Andes mountains. In the year 1438, however, all that changed. In that year, the Inca made the first of many conquests in their rise to empire by defeating the neighboring Chanca people. The rise and empire of the Incas is known as the Late Horizon Period (1438–1532 C.E.). The Inca leaders Pachacuti, Topa Inca, and Huayna Capac each gradually extended the limits of the Inca realm until a large part of the Andes mountains and Peruvian coastland lay under their control. The Incas appear to have been particularly skilled in the bureaucracy necessary to run a vast empire occupying many different environmental and cultural areas.

The 15th Century: Europe and the Ottoman Empire

For all practical purposes, much of Europe was still living in the Middle Ages at the start of the 15th century. Great change was underway, however, because the Renaissance was taking firm hold in the Italian peninsula. The term Renaissance, which means rebirth, refers to the renewed interest in the classical literature and art of the ancient Greeks and Romans. Society had disapproved of much of this literature during the Middle Ages due to its explicitly pagan nature. It also depicted scenes of immorality, which were offensive to early Christian sensibilities. Ovid's *Metamorphoses* for example, written in the 1st century B.C.E., depicts many scenes of stylized rape. Italian scholars and authors such as Petrarch (1304–74 C.E.), however, began taking a renewed interest in this literature during the course of the 14th century and attempted to imitate the style of this literature in their own writings.

While the term Renaissance thus refers specifically to a renewed interest in pagan antiquity, it is also used to refer to an increasing willingness to question authority. Petrarch, for example, went against established opinion. Other authors went much further. Giovanni Pico della Mirandola (1463–94), for example, argued that human beings were capable of achieving divinity. Although versions of this theological idea were well established, Mirandola's emphasis on humankind as the center of the universe, and of study, marked a significant departure from medieval philosophy and theology, which focused mostly on the nature of God, not the nature of human beings. This emphasis on human beings as the main focus of study and scholarly investigation started the tradition called Humanism.

Politically, the 14th century and early 15th witnessed the flourishing of the Italian *signorie* (singular *signoria*). The *signorie* were city-states that were dominated by one particular family, who frequently styled themselves *principi* (princes). Most of these *signorie* had risen to power during the 13th century, replacing the *commune* form of government, which was run by the leading citizens and businessmen of the city. Among the great families were the Este at Ferrara, the Scaligeri in Verona, the Malatesta at Rimini, the Visconti in Milan, and the very powerful Medici family in Florence. The economies of the various city-states varied considerably. Venice and Genoa had strong shipping fleets and controlled the trade of spices and other eastern goods, while inland cities such as Florence and Milan specialized in wool and the manufacture of textiles.

The various city-states in Italy frequently squabbled and attempted to extend their influence and control through economic, political, and military means. In the first part of the 15th century, Venice in particular expanded in northern Italy at the expense of the Duchy of Milan. Another major political coup happened in 1442 when Alfonso d'Aragona, king of Sicily, seized the throne of Naples as well. The Visconti family, which had gone into decline in Milan, was replaced by the Sforza family in 1448. To stem the ongoing strife, the states of Milan, Florence, Venice, Rome, and Naples agreed in the Peace of Lodi (1454) to maintain the peace for 40 years through the *Lega Italica*, a kind of United Nations for the Italian peninsula.

Much like the United Nations, the Lega Italica and the Peace of Lodi had only limited success. Within 10 years, the Sforza family, based in Milan, had succeeded in taking control of Genoa. In the Kingdom of Naples, moreover, various barons were involved in seditious plots. Another serious problem was the failure of several powerful banking families, such as the Bardi and Peruzzi. As a result of these difficulties, the kingdoms of France and Spain attempted to expand into Italy. Charles VII of France claimed the throne of Naples in 1494, and his successor Louix XII hoped to get the Duchy of Milan. Meanwhile Spain was hoping to control southern Italy.

Geneva

DUCHY OF SAVOY

Turin

SALUZZO

ASTI

MONTFERRATO

DUCHY OF MILAN

Milan

Po

REPUBLIC OF GENOA

Genoa

Mantua
MANTUA

DUCHY OF MODENA

Ferrara
DUCHY OF FERRARA

REPUBLIC OF VENICE

Venice

ISTRIA
(Venetian)

HOLY ROMAN EMPIRE

KINGDOM OF HUNGARY

OTTOMAN EMPIRE

REPUBLIC OF LUCCA

Lucca

Pisa

Florence

REPUBLIC OF FLORENCE

Arno

San Marino

Siena

REPUBLIC OF SIENA

Urbino

PAPAL STATES

Tiber

Apennines

Adriatic Sea

DALMATIA
(Venetian)

REPUBLIC OF RAGUSA

FRANCE

SARDINIA
(Spanish)

Rome

Naples

Amalfi

Bari

KINGDOM OF NAPLES
(Spanish)

Taranto

Tyrrhenian Sea

N

Palermo

KINGDOM OF SICILY
(Spanish)

Mediterranean Sea

8°   12°   16°

46°

42°

38°

Renaissance Italy
c. 1500

Border of the Holy
Roman Empire

0   100 km

0   100 miles

While Italy was divided into small city-states during the 15th century, the Spanish mainland, though fragmented, featured somewhat larger kingdoms. The most important of these were Aragón, in the northeast; Castile, which controlled most of the center of the peninsula and also the northwest; and Granada, a largely Muslim kingdom in the south. Along the far west coast was the kingdom of Portugal. The major event of the century was the unification of the peninsula. This unification began with the union of the crowns of Aragón and Castile, which was brought about by marriage. In 1469, Isabella, princess of Castile, married her cousin Ferdinand, prince of Aragón. Isabella gained the throne of Castile in 1474, upon the death of her brother Henry IV, and Ferdinand ascended the throne of Aragón upon the death of his father in 1479. While the two kingdoms technically remained independent, they were practically united in policy and goals. The first major undertaking was the reconquest of Granada, the last remaining Muslim-run state on the peninsula. War commenced in 1482 and ended in 1492 when Christian forces captured the city of Granada itself. Immediately after the capture, Isabella and Ferdinand attempted to impose a unity of faith on the peninsula by giving believers in Judaism a few months to either leave the country or convert to Christianity.

The same year that Granada fell, 1492, an even more momentous event occurred: Columbus landed in the so-called New World. While the full effects of this discovery would not be clear until the 16th century and later, other more immediate political happenings that would increase the Spanish empire were under way. In 1496, prince Philip, son of Maximilian I, the ruler of the Holy Roman Empire (sometimes called the Habsburg empire after the ruling family), which controlled lands throughout Germany and central Europe, married Juana, the daughter of Ferdinand and Isabella of Spain. Queen Isabella died in 1504, and Juana and Philip arrived in Spain in 1506 to claim the throne of Castile. Philip died soon after, however, and Juana went insane, apparently due to heartbreak. Ferdinand ruled both the kingdoms of Castile and Aragón until his death in 1516, whereupon Charles, the son of Juana and Philip, inherited the united Spanish possessions.

While Spain was thus becoming an empire, so were the Ottoman Turks. The Ottoman kingdom had been started by Osman (from whom the name Ottoman was derived) in the late 13th century as a small kingdom in northwest Anatolia (modern-day Turkey), which had been carved out from Byzantine lands by bands of Turkish Muslim warriors. By the year 1400, the Ottomans had succeeded in taking over most of the Balkan peninsula as well, so that what can already be called the Ottoman Empire stretched from northwest Turkey through modern-day Greece. When the king, Bayezit I, attempted to expand eastward across the rest of Anatolia, however, the Ottomans were defeated at the Battle of Ankara, and Bayezit himself died in captivity in 1403. A civil war between Bayezit's sons followed, from which Mehmet I eventually emerged the victor.

Mehmet I, called the Restorer, concentrated on consolidating the Ottoman possessions in Europe and Anatolia, while avoiding unnecessary conflicts. His

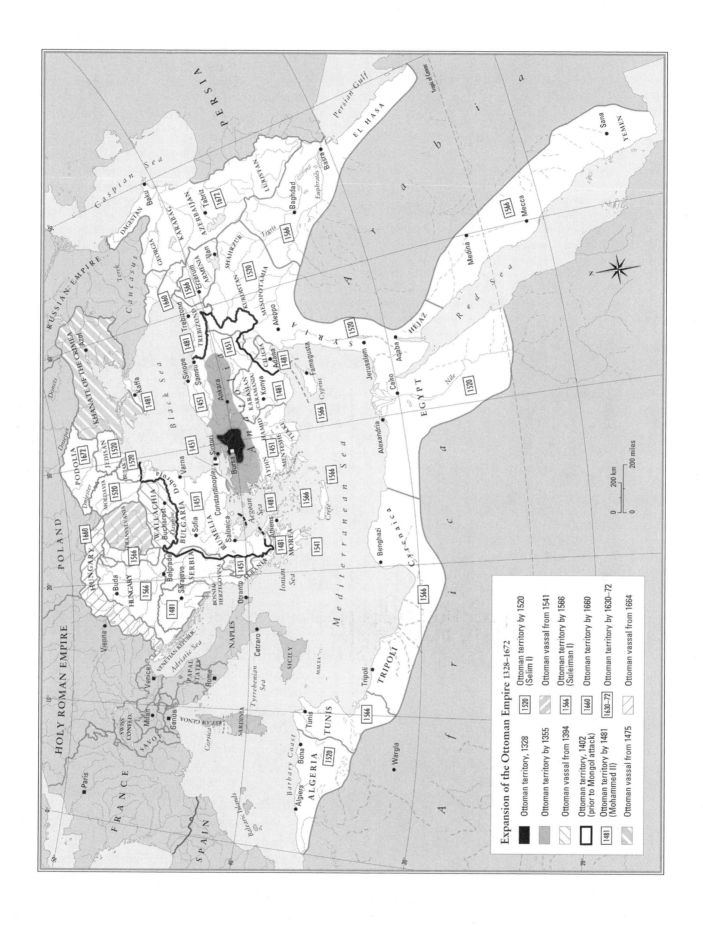

Expansion of the Ottoman Empire 1328–1672

⬛	Ottoman territory, 1328	▨	Ottoman territory by 1520 (Selim I)
▩	Ottoman territory by 1355	⬜	Ottoman vassal from 1541
▨	Ottoman vassal from 1394	▧	Ottoman territory by 1566 (Suleiman I)
⬜	Ottoman territory, 1402 (prior to Mongol attack)	⬜	Ottoman territory by 1660
⬜	Ottoman territory by 1481 (Mohammed II)	▤	Ottoman territory by 1630–72
1481		▧	Ottoman vassal from 1664
	Ottoman vassal from 1475		

successor, Murat II, who came to the throne in 1421, resumed the empire's expansion into Europe. He waged war against the Venetian sea empire and succeeded in capturing Salonika. His gains in Albania caused war with Hungary, who led an army of allies that included Hungary, Poland, Bosnia, Wallachia, and Serbia against Murat II. The Hungarians, under John Hunyadi, won a pitched battle, and Murat signed a 10-year truce at Szegedin in 1444. After this truce, he abdicated in favor of his 14-year-old son, Mehmet, and retreated to a life of religious study and contemplation. When the Hungarians broke the truce however, Murat came out of seclusion and defeated the Hungarians decisively in the second Battle of Kosovo.

The reign of Mehmet II (1451–81), however, saw the most dramatic event in Ottoman 15th-century history: the fall of Constantinople. This city, the capital and last city of the once vast and wealthy Byzantine Empire, fell to Ottoman troops in 1453. The city itself had been an isolated outpost surrounded by Ottoman territory for several decades, but its fall represented the end of the last officially Christian kingdom in the eastern half of the old Roman Empire. Constantinople, also known as Byzantium, was renamed Istanbul and now became the capital of the Ottoman Empire. This event is sometimes viewed as the start of the classical age of the Ottoman Empire. Ottoman expansion still continued further west, and Serbia, Bosnia, and Albania were consolidated within the empire. Several of these regions, such as Bosnia and Serbia, voluntarily entered the Ottoman Empire since they trusted the sultan more than they trusted the western European nations who were vying for control of their governments. In 1480, an Ottoman army took Otranto in southern Italy, causing great fear throughout western Europe that the Ottoman Empire, now that it had taken over much of eastern Europe, would also take over the west. The reign of Bayezit II (1481–1512) concluded the 15th century. Like Mehmet I, Bayezit II was most concerned with consolidating the recent territorial acquisitions, though he significantly defeated the Venetians once more, thereby maintaining control of much of the Mediterranean.

The situation in England in the late 14th and 15th centuries can best be called chaotic. While England was recognized as a united geopolitical entity, unlike Spain and Italy at the start of the 15th century, the kings of England laid claim to much of France, and the country itself was repeatedly wracked by civil war. The claim to France derived in part from the descent of the English kings from William the Conqueror, who had come from Normandy (a western region of France) and conquered England in 1066 C.E. The control of the English monarchy over western France diminished over time but was reasserted strongly in the 14th century by Edward III, who started the Hundred Years War, which was England's attempt to gain more territorial possessions in France. Despite initial success, by 1399 England had once again lost its French lands.

The year 1399 witnessed one of the many overthrows of English monarchs, when Henry IV, who had been exiled by Richard II, overthrew the domestically unpopular Richard and seized the throne. Henry's main accomplishment was withstanding a series of revolts, the most powerful led by Owen Glendower, who proclaimed himself King of Wales. On his death in 1413, Henry bequeathed a secure realm to his son Henry V. Henry V had a flair for military tactics and successfully regained England's French positions. The famous battle of Agincourt (1415), which the English won despite being outnumbered 50,000 to 6,000, gave the English army a tremendous morale boost and is stirringly portrayed in Shakespeare's play *Henry V*. Henry sought to secure the lands won militarily by forming a political alliance. He therefore married Katherine of Valois, the daughter of Charles VI, King of France, in 1420. Theoretically, the thrones of England and France were now united and the son of Henry and Katherine, also called Henry, was set to inherit the rule of both kingdoms.

However, Henry V died in 1422, when his son, now Henry VI, was just a year old. Opposition to English rule grew in France during this early period, and by 1429 a young French peasant girl, Joan of Arc, inspired by a series of visions she believed to be sent by God, was leading a French army and retaking towns and cities. The Dauphin (as the son of the French king was traditionally called), who had been disinherited by the 1420 treaty between his father and Henry V, was popularly proclaimed king of France with the name Charles VII. The English attempted to stem the tide by having Henry VI hastily crowned in Paris, but by 1453 England had lost all its French possessions except for the city of Calais. Also in 1453, King Henry VI went mad.

The illness prompted what is known as the War of the Roses, in which the House of Lancaster (led by Henry and his wife Margaret) fought against the House of York (led by Richard, Duke of York, the king's cousin). When Henry VI became incapacitated due to his insanity, a group of nobles elected York to govern the country while Henry was ill. When Henry's sanity suddenly returned in 1455, Richard refused to return power, and both sides raised large armies. The war lasted several years, with first one side victorious, and then the other side. Queen Margaret, the French wife of Henry VI, was particularly active in the campaigning; nobles loyal to her defeated and killed York at the Battle of Wakefield in 1460. York's son, Edward, took up his father's cause and was proclaimed king as Edward IV in London in March 1461. Edward decisively defeated the Lancastrian forces at the Battle of Towton three weeks later. Margaret fled to France, but briefly regained the throne for Henry VI in 1470. However, by May 1471, Edward had again defeated the Lancastrians, whose direct male line ended with the murder of Henry VI in the Tower of London and the death of his son, Prince Edward, in battle.

While Henry VI was a pious man, pardoning criminals and avoiding unnecessary bloodshed, Edward IV was a wastrel, given up to lust and gluttony. He died in 1483, allegedly as a result of excessive eating and drinking. Edward's 12-year-old son, Edward V, was never crowned. On his way to London, Edward, along with his younger brother, was captured by his uncle Richard (brother of Edward IV) and imprisoned. They eventually disappeared, presumably murdered, and Richard took the throne, ruling from 1483–85 as Richard III.

In 1485, Richard was overthrown at the Battle of Bosworth Field by Henry VII, who was supported by many of the old supporters of the Lancastrian side in the war of the Roses. Henry was the grandson of Owen Tudor and Katherine of Valois, the wife of Henry V who secretly remarried after Henry's death. He was also related on his mother's side to John of Gaunt, who was the progenitor of the Lancastrian line of kings. While his claim to the throne was weak, it proved strong enough to gain Henry the Lancastrian support. Once Henry VII took power, he solidified his claim to the throne by uniting both the Lancastrian and Yorkist factions from the War of the Roses. He did this by marrying Elizabeth of York, daughter of Edward IV. Henry VII was a capable ruler, and, on his death in 1509, he left a secure kingdom to his son, Henry VIII.

The 16th Century: Europe, the Ottoman Empire, and the Americas

Henry VIII dramatically changed the future and nature of England by separating England from union with the Pope as the head of the Catholic Church. This change separated England fundamentally from the Catholic countries, such as Italy and especially Spain, and created new alliances with the small nation-states in northern Europe, such as northern Germany and the Netherlands. The enmity with Spain, the rising power in Europe, created particular tension in foreign affairs for the rest of the 16th century and into the 17th. Henry VIII's decision to separate from Rome was largely due to marital affairs. His first wife, Katherine of Aragón, had not borne him a son that lived, despite several years of marriage. In addition to this, Henry was concerned that Katherine had previously been married to his older brother, who had died. According to some theologians, a person could not marry his brother's wife. While this scruple of conscious may have bothered Henry, it should be noted that the king was remarkably unfaithful—he was evidently sleeping with Anne Boleyn while still married to Katherine, and he later entered a relationship with Jane Seymour while Anne was still alive.

As a result of Katherine's failure to produce a male heir for the throne, Henry was anxious to be rid of her. This desire became even more urgent when Anne became pregnant. The Pope, however, refused to declare that Henry's marriage to Katherine was invalid. Without the Pope's consent, Henry would not be able to be rid of Katherine and free to marry Anne. In part, the Pope's refusal of consent was due to threats from the Spanish Emperor Charles I (V), who was related to Katherine. In 1531, the English parliament decreed that Henry was the supreme head of the Church in England, in 1532 Henry secretly married the pregnant Anne, and in 1533 the Acts of Appeal declared that theological disputes were to be directed to the Archbishop of Canterbury and not to the Pope. Thomas Cranmer, Archbishop of Canterbury, duly decreed after a show trial in 1533 that Henry's marriage to Kath-

Sixteenth-Century England and Wales

● Towns with populations of over 5000 by 1603

0   50 km
0   50 miles

N

SCOTLAND

IRELAND

Irish Sea

ISLE OF MAN

North Sea

Berwick

NORTHUMBERLAND
NEWCASTLE
UPON TYNE
Carlisle   Durham
CUMBERLAND   COUNTY PALATINE
OF DURHAM
Keswick

WESTMORLAND
Kendal
Kirkby
Lonsdale   YORKSHIRE
Ripon
LANCASHIRE   York
Halifax   Leeds   Hull
Wakefield
Manchester   Sheffield
Liverpool

ANGLESEY   FLINT   Buxton
CHESTER   NOTT-
CAERNARVON   DENBIGH   CHESHIRE   INGHAM-
Nantwich   DERBY-   SHIRE   Lincoln
MERIONETH   SHIRE   LINCOLNSHIRE
STAFFORD-   Newark
SHIRE
Oswestry   Stafford   Nottingham
MONTGOMERY   SHROPSHIRE   Lichfield   LEICESTER-   Stamford
SHREWSBURY   SHIRE   LYNN   NORWICH   YARMOUTH
Wolverhampton   WARWICK   Leicester   RUT-
CARDIGAN   Ludlow   Birmingham   SHIRE   LAND   NORFOLK
WORCESTER-   COVENTRY   HUNT-   Dunwich
RADNOR   SHIRE   Northampton   INGDON-   CAMBS   SUFFOLK
Cardigan   Bewdley   Warwick   SHIRE   Lavenham
CARMARTHEN-   HEREFORD-   WORCESTER   Stratford   CAMBRIDGE   IPSWICH
SHIRE   Brecon   SHIRE   NORTHAMPTONSHIRE   BEDFORD-   Saffron
PEMBROKE-   BRECKNOCK   Tewkesbury   SHIRE   Royston   Walden   COLCHESTER
SHIRE   Carmarthen   Banbury   OXFORD-   HERTFORD-
MONMOUTH-   Gloucester   SHIRE   SHIRE   Chelmsford
GLAMORGAN-   SHIRE   GLOUCESTER-   Burford   St Albans   ESSEX
SHIRE   SHIRE   Cirencester   BUCKINGHAMSHIRE
Cardiff   BRISTOL   OXFORD   MIDDLESEX
BERK-   Henley   LONDON   CANTERBURY
Bristol Channel   Malmesbury   SHIRE   Reading   Windsor   Maidstone   Sandwich
Bath   Newbury   SURREY   KENT
WILTSHIRE   HAMPSHIRE   Calais
Glastonbury   SALISBURY   Winchester   SUSSEX   Rye   (English
Barnstaple   SOMERSET   Southampton   1347–1558)
DEVONSHIRE   DORSET   Chichester   Boulogne
EXETER   Poole   Portsmouth   (English
Totnes   ISLE OF WIGHT   1544–49)
CORNWALL   PLYMOUTH

English Channel

F R A N C E

erine was null and void, and that his marriage to Anne was valid. In 1534, the Act of Supremacy stated that the Pope no longer had authority over the English Church, and that the King was the church's supreme head.

Unfortunately for Henry, Anne's child was a girl. When no more children came, Henry ordered Anne decapitated on trumped-up charges of infidelity; Henry himself had already entered into an adulterous relationship with Jane Seymour, whom he married shortly after Anne's death in 1536. Jane bore the long-awaited male heir, Edward, in 1537, but she died 12 days later due to medical complications. The next wife, Anne of Cleves, was not to Henry's liking and parliament quickly annulled the marriage. Catherine Howard, the next wife, was not as lucky and was beheaded in 1542. Catherine Parr, the last wife, managed to outlive Henry, who died in 1547. By this time, Henry had become a sour man, with a probably syphilitic ulcer on his leg that left him howling in pain, and so grossly overweight that he needed a special device to carry him up stairs.

On Henry's death, Edward was only nine years old, and it was uncertain who should rule. Henry had established a council of ministers to rule till Edward came of age. First the Duke of Somerset and then the Duke of Northumberland dominated the council. When Edward died at the young age of 15, Northumberland attempted to install Jane Grey, a great-granddaughter of Henry VII, as a puppet king, but Mary, the daughter of Henry VIII and Katherine of Aragón, raised an army, was recognized as the rightful ruler by the people, and defeated Northumberland. Mary was very interested in reestablishing Catholicism in England and avidly sought to root out Protestants from the realm. Three hundred people were burned for heresy during her reign. This avid persecution, as well as her marriage to Philip, son of Charles I (V) of Spain, alienated some of the people from her, but she died of natural causes in 1558.

On Mary's death, Elizabeth, the daughter of Henry VIII and Anne Boleyn, ascended the throne. Elizabeth was an exceedingly competent statesman and was particularly skillful at handling budgets, particularly in the early part of her reign. While Elizabeth was not Catholic and separated the Church of England permanently from the Pope, she was restrained in punishing those who dissented, usually imposing fines instead of death sentences. With such qualities, Elizabeth guided the country to political stability once more, and England started its rise to Empire. English explorers and pirates, such as Francis Drake, started by plundering the Spanish ships carrying treasure back from the Americas to Spain. The English navy scored a tremendous victory in 1588, when they defeated the Spanish Armada, a large fleet sent by Philip of Spain to conquer England. While the Spanish fleet was large, the English vessels were more agile, and, perhaps most importantly, a fierce storm dispersed and drove off a large part of the Spanish fleet. The stability brought to the kingdom by Elizabeth's long reign, which lasted until her death in 1603, also encouraged the arts scene in England. William Shakespeare was the most influential artist to emerge from the Elizabethan era, or any era of English literature thus far.

In Italy, the 16th century witnessed a period of increasing foreign domination. Francis I of the French Valois dynasty seized Milan in 1515 and was still interested in the Kingdom of Naples. In the Peace of Noyon in 1516, however, the French king Francis I agreed with the Spanish ruler and Holy Roman Emperor Charles I (V) to divide Italy into two halves. The French were to have control of the northern half, while the Spanish were to have control of the southern half and of the islands. Disagreement between the French and Spanish continued, however, until the Peace of Bateu-Cambrésis (1559), in which the dominance of Spain over most of Italy was recognized. By this time, most of the city-states had in effect become puppet governments of the Spanish; the only truly independent states left were the Republic of Venice and the Papal States, but even these were under constant military threat, as seen by the sacking of Rome in 1527 by forces loyal to Charles I (V). Spain's influence can also be seen in the pope's refusal to annul the king of England's (Henry VIII) marriage with the Spanish noblewoman Katherine of Aragón. As a result of this foreign domination, Italy lost out on the exploration of the Americas. While Spain, and then England, reaped wealth from the newly discovered lands, Italy was left almost like an isolated province.

With regard to Spain, it was a perilous empire that Charles I inherited in 1516. Charles had been educated in Flanders (modern-day Belgium) and arrived in Spain with Flemish councilors who controlled the top government positions. Upon the death of his grandfather Maximilian I in 1519, Charles inherited the title of Holy Roman Emperor and the vast lands that went with it in modern-day Germany, Czech Republic, Slovakia, and Hungary. He was Charles V with regard to the Holy Roman Empire, but was Charles I with regard to Spain. Shortly after gaining the title of emperor, Charles returned to the Netherlands in 1520 after first extracting a good deal of money from the Cortes (parliaments) of Castile and Aragón. Seething with anger, Castile rose in revolt. Aristocrats loyal to Charles rallied and succeeded in putting down the rebellion in 1520. During the following years, Charles concentrated his efforts on wars on a variety of fronts: against Protestant forces in Europe, against the Ottoman Turks in the Balkans, against the pirates of the Barbary coast, and against the French Valois dynasty. He also expanded the empire overseas.

When Charles I (V) abdicated in 1556, he granted his possessions in Spain, the Netherlands, Italy, and the Americas to his son Philip II. Philip pursued an aggressive foreign policy, building substantial Atlantic and Mediterranean fleets. To finance this military expansion, Philip relied largely upon treasure from the Americas, as well as European lenders, but the expense and debt took investment away from industry and agriculture, and the economy suffered as a result. In 1575, Philip arbitrarily canceled his foreign debts and imposed a heavy tax that left many people homeless and begging in the streets.

While Philip's domestic economic policy was disastrous, his foreign policy was more successful. Together with Austria, Venice, and the Papal States of Italy, the Spanish fleet met the Turks in the naval Battle of Lepanto, which turned the tide in the war with the Turks, who had been threatening to occupy more of Europe, particularly southern Italy. In 1580, Philip inherited the Portuguese throne, along with its extensive overseas possessions. Philip pressed his luck by preparing an invasion of England in 1587. Philip had been married to Mary, Queen of England, who was succeeded by Elizabeth. When Elizabeth put a Catholic rival to the throne (Mary of Scotland) to death, Philip decided to act. The English and Spanish had

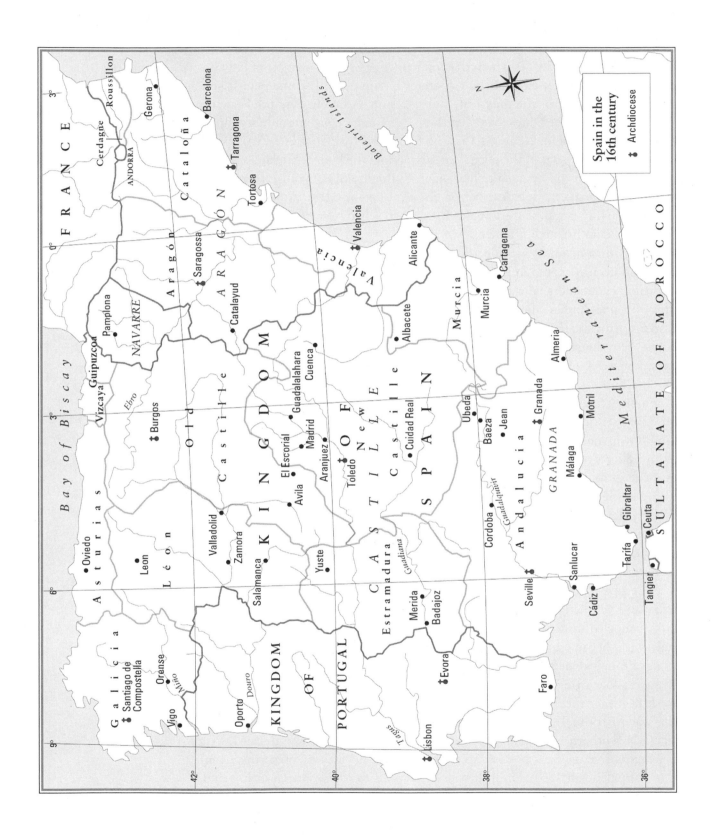

Spain in the 16th century
✝ Archdiocese

FRANCE

Roussillon
Cerdagne
ANDORRA
Cataloña

Gerona
Barcelona
Tarragona
Tortosa

ARAGÓN

A r a g ó n
✝ Saragossa
Catalayud

NAVARRE
Pamplona

Bay of Biscay

Guipuzcoa
Vizcaya
Ebro

Asturias
Oviedo

León
Leon

Galicia
Santiago de Compostella
Orense
Vigo
Miño
Douro
Oporto

KINGDOM
OF
PORTUGAL

Valladolid
Zamora
Salamanca
Yuste
Avila

Old Castille
✝ Burgos

KINGDOM

Guadalalahara
Cuenca
El Escorial
Madrid
Aranjuez
✝ Toledo

New Castille

Estramadura
Merida
Badajoz
Guadiana
✝ Evora

Lisbon
Tagus
Faro

OF

Valencia
✝ Valencia
Alicante

Balearic Islands

Mediterranean Sea

Murcia
Murcia
Cartagena

Albacete

CASTILLE

SPAIN

Cuidad Real
Ubeda
Baeza
Jean
Cordoba
Guadalquivir

Andalucia

GRANADA
✝ Granada
Almeria
Motril
Málaga

Sanlucar
Seville
Cádiz
Tarifa
Gibraltar
Ceuta
Tangier

SULTANATE OF MOROCCO

N

3°
0°
3°
6°
9°

42°
40°
38°
36°

been skirmishing for several years already in the Netherlands. His huge fleet attacked in 1588 but met incredibly bad weather and was driven back by the English and nature at great loss. On his death in 1598, Philip II left his son, Philip III, with a bankrupt country that was also waning in foreign influence.

In Europe generally, there were two important religious developments during this century: the Reformation and the Spanish Inquisition. The Reformation was a movement that sought to purify the Church of certain practices and beliefs that the Reformers thought were heretical. Martin Luther and John Calvin were the two most important figures in the Reformation movement, and both flourished in the 16th century. Luther is particularly famous for posting the 95 Theses on a castle door in Wittenberg in 1517. These Theses objected principally to a variety of abuses in the Catholic Church, particularly the selling of indulgences (special pardons from sin). Luther would express more controversial ideas later on and would break with the Catholic Church three years later. Calvin, who lived in the generation after Luther, would depart even more radically from the Catholic teachings, most strikingly perhaps in his emphasis on predestination. Calvin also did not share Catholic beliefs in sacraments (rituals that were supposed to impart spiritual benefits). See the section on Religious Life for more information.

In part as a response to the Reformation, the Spanish Inquisition was very prominent during the 16th century. The Inquisition was an attempt by the Catholic Church to root out heresy and false teachings by arresting and trying people suspected of heresy. Most nations, whether Catholic or Protestant, had legislative bodies that punished heresy with death, but Spain was particularly vigorous both in seeking out culprits and in applying the penalties. As was the case with regular criminal trials, suspects and even witnesses were frequently tortured during the investigation in an attempt to discover the truth. Of course, many people, exhausted by the physical pain, would agree to anything. Others, stronger perhaps, or fortunate to have a less severe inquisitor, were tortured but found innocent. Those who confessed or were convicted by the testimony of witnesses or other evidence were usually given the chance to repent and to give up their false beliefs. If the convict refused to give up these beliefs, or had been repeatedly convicted of heresy, he or she would be executed, usually by burning. When the Spanish started to settle the Americas, they brought the Inquisition with them.

Another Catholic movement, the Counter-Reformation, played a large role in religious affairs in the later 16th century. This movement began with the Council of Trent and clarified Catholic teaching concerning a variety of contested topics. In addition to providing doctrinal clarity, the Council also sought to improve the preaching and teaching of the people. Many great artists, most particularly perhaps El Greco, sought to incorporate these ideals into their artwork.

While the Ottoman Empire, unlike Spain, did not have any overseas possessions, its empire did expand tremendously during the 16th century. Bayezit II was forced to abdicate in 1512 by Selim I after Selim had won a civil war among Bayezit's sons, all of whom were seeking to gain control of the kingdom. While previous rulers of the Ottoman Empire had focused mostly on expansion into Europe, Selim I focused successfully on expanding the Ottoman Empire into the Middle East. Selim subdued eastern Anatolia and Kurdistan in 1515, and gained some small territory from the Safavi kingdom in Persia (modern-day Iraq and Iran), before turning southward, and taking Damascus and then Egypt from the Mamluk rulers. Cairo itself fell in 1517. With these gains, the Ottomans controlled the entire coastline of the eastern Mediterranean, and while they did not take over the Arabian peninsula itself, they did take responsibility for the holy city of Mecca and became the protectors of the pilgrimage routes.

Suleyman I, the Lawgiver or the Magnificent, who reigned from 1520–66, is given credit for steering the Ottoman Empire to its zenith of power and culture. Under Suleyman, whose name is a version of Solomon, the famous wise man from the Hebrew scriptures, the Ottoman Empire expanded to control Baghdad, North Africa up to Morocco, and Hungary. Suleyman even formed an alliance with Francis I of France against the Holy Roman Empire and laid siege to Vienna in 1529. The Ottoman navy, meanwhile, dominated the Mediterranean, but also operated in the Indian Ocean. Suleyman himself was a diligent ruler and oversaw the reform and regularization of the legal and governing systems. When Suleyman died while on campaign in Hungary in 1566, however, the prosperity of the Ottoman Empire began a slow decline.

Selim II became the head of the empire upon Suleyman's death, but he did not take as active a role in government as Suleyman had and instead allowed the Grand Vezir (Chancellor) Mehmet Sokollu to run the empire. Militarily, the Ottoman Empire had mixed success. While the Ottomans gained Cyprus from the Venetians, they suffered a major setback in the Battle of Lepanto in 1571. This battle effectively ended the geographic expansion of the Ottoman Empire. During the reign of the next sultan, Murat III (1574–95), the Ottoman Empire began to face increasing destabilizing pressures, especially after the death of Mehmet Sokollu. Wars with the Habsburgs, who controlled the Holy Roman Empire, and with the Persians stretched the Ottoman's military forces, while the influx of wealth from the Americas and the shifting trade patterns caused rapid inflation. The following centuries would see the slow decentralization and breakup of the Ottoman Empire.

While the Ottoman Empire was reaching its zenith in the 16th century, the American empires collapsed as a result of the Spanish invasion. In the Aztec kingdom, Motecuhzoma, often called Montezuma in English, was the Aztec ruler in charge when the Spanish came. Motecuhzoma, whose name means Angry Lord, had ascended the throne in 1502 and had successfully led the Mexica in many battles. The king was held in great reverence and respect by his own people and was regarded with great fear and hatred by the peoples he and his ancestors had subjugated. The Spanish would use that fear to gain powerful allies against the Aztecs when they arrived.

In 1519, Hernando Cortés, a Spanish explorer, met a Spaniard, Gerónimo de Aguilar, who had been shipwrecked in the Yucatán in 1511 and now spoke the Mayan language fluently. Among the Maya, Cortés also met Doña Marina, who was an Aztec that had been sold into slavery amongst the Maya and therefore spoke both Nahuatl and Maya. In addition to becoming Cortés's mistress, Doña Marina also became an important translator during Cortés's Aztec campaign: she would translate from Nahuatl into Maya, and Aguilar would translate from Maya into Spanish.

Armed with these translators and a large number of Spanish soldiers, Cortés moved north in 1519. When he landed, Motecuhzoma was informed, and the Aztec ruler sent him several fine gifts—it may be the case, as a later story reported, that Motecuhzoma thought Cortés was the returning divine hero Topiltzin Quetzalcoatl, especially since Cortés landed on the day called Topiltzin Quetzalcoatl in the Aztec calendar. Cortés proceeded to make alliances both with enemies of the Aztec, such as Tlaxcala and Cempoala, and with Motecuhzoma, who invited Cortés into Tenochtitlan in an attempt to woo the Spanish over to his side. While Motecuhzoma showed them the courtesy of lavish guest quarters, Cortés took Motecuhzoma captive. The city became restless. When Cortés left the city to forestall a newly arrived Spanish force from halting his campaign, Cortés's second-in-command, Pedro de Alvarado, massacred unarmed warriors and priests during a holy festival. The city rose up in revolt and drove the Spaniards from the city with much loss of life to all sides. This battle is called La Noche Triste (The Sad Night) in Mexico. During the uprising, Motecuhzoma was killed, though it is not clear whether the Spanish or the Aztecs, disgruntled with Motecuhzoma's handling of the situation, were the culprits. Cuitlahuac took control of the city, and was followed after his death from smallpox two months later by Cuauhtemoc.

The Spanish recuperated and then returned with their Native American allies to besiege Tenochtitlan. They cut off the food supplies to the disease-ravaged city and attacked at every opportunity, using their cannon to weaken the walls of the city. After various attacks, counterattacks, and the sacrifice of some of the Spanish men and horses captured by the Aztecs, the Spanish captured most of the city and Cuauhtemoc attempted to flee across the lake but was captured. Tenochtitlan itself was systematically plundered, with robbery and rape. The Mexica were forced into servitude. The Aztec empire had come to an end. The year was 1521 C.E.

The Inca empire lasted longer than the Aztec, primarily due to their distance from the Spanish base in Cuba, but internal conflict threatened to destroy the kingdom even without the Spanish. In 1527 C.E., the Inca ruler Huayna Capac died suddenly, perhaps due to smallpox that had spread to South America from Central America, where it had been brought by the Spanish. Huayna Capac's heir also died, before he could name his own heir. Huascar, another son of Huayna Capac, was proclaimed king in Cuzco; but yet another son, Atahuallpa, claimed that he had been given the rule of the northern provinces by Huayna Capac. A civil war ensued, and Atahuallpa eventually killed Huascar and all the nobles loyal to Huascar, thus securing the throne for himself.

Atahuallpa's rule was short-lived, however. In fact, it ended before it even began. The Spanish explorer Pizarro landed in northern Peru in 1532 C.E. Atahuallpa, who was on his way to Cuzco to be invested as king, arranged to meet with the Spaniards. The Spaniards launched a surprise attack, however, and took Atahuallpa captive. They held the king for ransom, but after they had received much of the gold to be found in Cuzco, Pizarro had Atahuallpa strangled and set up a puppet ruler in his place. The Spanish then commenced the dismantling of the Inca empire.

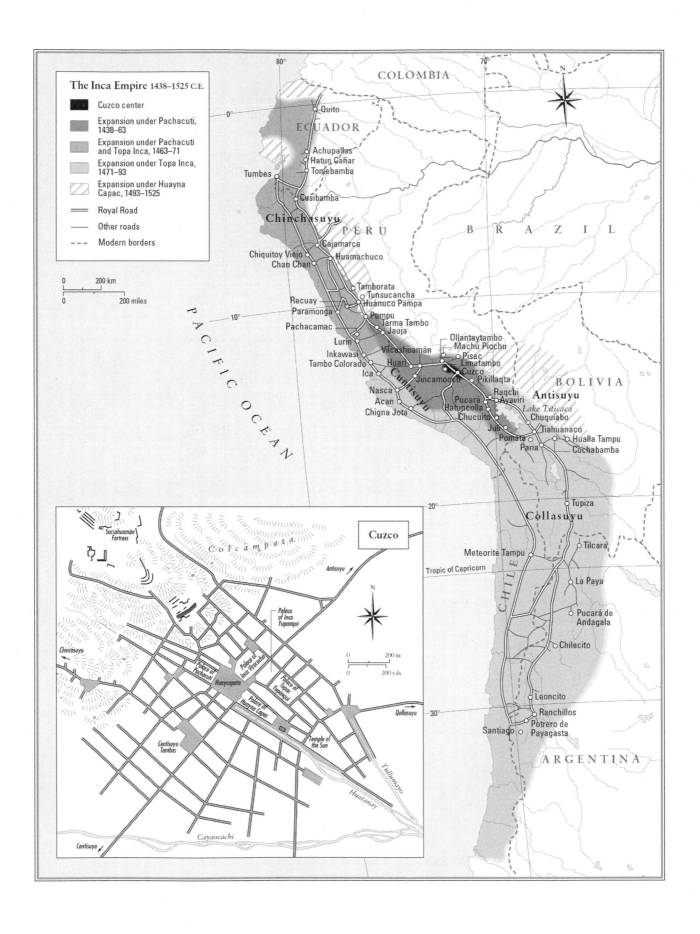

The Inca Empire 1438–1525 C.E.

- Cuzco center
- Expansion under Pachacuti, 1438–63
- Expansion under Pachacuti and Topa Inca, 1463–71
- Expansion under Topa Inca, 1471–93
- Expansion under Huayna Capac, 1493–1525
- Royal Road
- Other roads
- Modern borders

200 km
200 miles

COLOMBIA

Quito

ECUADOR

Achupallas
Hatun Cañar
Tomebamba

Tumbes

Cusibamba

Chinchasuyu

PERU

BRAZIL

Cajamarca
Chiquitoy Viejo
Chan Chan
Huamachuco

Tamborata
Tunsucancha
Recuay
Huánuco Pampa
Paramonga
Pumpu
Pachacamac
Tarma Tambo
Lurín
Jauja
Inkawasi
Vilcashuamán
Ollantaytambo
Machu Picchu
Tambo Colorado
Huari
Pisac
Limatambo
Ica
Jincamocco
Cuzco
Cuntisuyu
Pikillaqta
Nasca
Raqchi
Antisuyu
Acan
Pucará
Ayaviri
Chigna Jota
Hatuncolla
Lake Titicaca
Chucuito
Chuquiabo
Juli
Tiahuanaco
Pomata
Hualla Tampu
Paria
Cochabamba

BOLIVIA

Tupiza

Collasuyu

Meteorite Tampu

Tropic of Capricorn

Tilcara

CHILE

La Paya

Pucará de Andagala

Chilecito

Leoncito

Ranchillos

Santiago
Potrero de Payagasta

ARGENTINA

PACIFIC OCEAN

Cuzco

Sacsahuamán Fortress

Colcampata

Antisuyu

Chinchasuyu

Palace of Inca Yupanqui
Palace of Pachacuti
Palace of Inca Viracocha
Huaycapata
Palace of Tupac Yupanqui
Palace of Huayna Capac
Qollasuyu
Temple of the Sun
Centisuyu Tambos
Tullumayo
Centisuyu
Cayaocachi
Huatanay

200 m
200 yds

The rest of the 16th century was mainly filled with disappointment and suffering for the native population. Many of the peoples subjugated by the Aztecs and Incas were initially happy to have their old task masters removed from power, but the Spaniards soon assumed the role of repressor and put many Native Americans into forced labor. The Spaniards, meanwhile, sparred violently amongst themselves in an attempt to acquire the most land possible, particularly in Peru, where Francisco Pizarro himself was assassinated in 1541. There were some bright points, however. Many of the Spanish Catholic priests, who went to the Americas in order to spread Christianity, were shocked at the cruelties practiced by many of the Spanish adventurers and attempted to protect the Native Americans through exercising their influence as church officials. At least in part due to this pressure, the Spanish crown abolished the practice of forced labor in 1549, although many Spanish landlords, especially those further away from central authority, ignored this decree. The Native Americans took quickly to the new religion; one of the most famous events in the spread of Christianity was the appearance of the Blessed Virgin Mary in Guadalupe to a Mexican named Juan Diego. An image of Mary was left on Diego's coat and this image is still honored today by many Catholics, especially in Latin America. While the first missionaries were enthusiastic at the progress made, by the end of the century it had become apparent that many Native Americans were still practicing some pre-Christian rituals in addition to Christianity. As a result, some priests became more wary of the Native Americans. This more-distanced approach suited many of the conquistadors, who did not want to admit that the Native Americans were on a spiritual and intellectual par with the Europeans. Nevertheless, the schools established for the Native Americans by Franciscan priests, in particular, gave ample evidence that the Native Americans were the equals of the European settlers.

The demography of Meso- and South America had also changed dramatically by the close of the 16th century. While many millions of Native Americans, over 90 percent of the population, were killed off by European diseases such as smallpox, the number of Europeans that settled in the Americas, drawn by the prospects of adventure, wealth, and a fresh start, increased steadily. There were already over one hundred thousand Spaniards in the Spanish lands in America by the mid-16th century. These new settlers also brought large numbers of African slaves with them. Since the Spanish were no longer able to force the Native Americans to work, due to the 1549 decree (but also due to the plummeting numbers of Native Americans), they turned to the burgeoning African slave trade to supply the needs of their work force. The Native Americans were becoming one of a large variety of peoples living in the Americas.

Nevertheless, there was some organized Native American resistance to the Spanish conquest. In Peru, one of Huayna Capac's sons, Manco Inca, escaped to the mountains of Vilcabamba to the north of Cuzco. There, he continued to control a large mountainous region where he maintained Inca ways and denounced the Spanish and Christianity. This kingdom was continued by his sons Sayri Tupac, and then Titu Cusi. Titu Cusi, in turn, planned a massive uprising, which never occurred, in conjunction with the Taqui Ongo movement. This movement, rooted in Native American religion, claimed that the gods would soon overthrow the Spanish and the temporarily victorious Christian god. Vigorous investigation by the Spanish authorities uncovered the leaders of Taqui Ongo, and the movement largely disappeared by the 1570s. Tupac Amaru took control of the Inca mountain refuge upon the death of Titu Cusi in 1571, but his reign was short, for the Spanish viceroy Francisco de Toledo captured the Inca ruler and executed him in the public square in Cuzco in 1571.

Other groups, such as the Chiriguanos, originally from Paraguay, fought the Spanish along their borders in Peru throughout the later part of the 16th century. Another group, the Araucanians in Chile, adapted quickly to Spanish fighting techniques and developed efficient countermeasures, including double rows of pikes and their own cavalry. By the 1560s, the Araucanian cavalry was as skillful as that of the Spanish. While the Araucanians were eventually brought under Spanish control in later centuries, they had notable victories in their wars. In 1598, for example, a general revolt by Araucanians in captured territory led to the capture and execution of Martin Garcia de Loyola, who had led the military expedition that had captured the Inca Tupac Amaru.

By 1600, Europe and the Americas had met, empires had risen and fallen, and the seeds of the modern world had been planted.

~Lawrence Morris

Chronology of the 15th and 16th Centuries

In addition to events in the 15th and 16th centuries, earlier events in the development of the native cultures of Meso- and South America have been given. For the earlier development of European cultures, see volumes 1 and 2 of this encyclopedia. Central Mexico refers to the area occupied by the Aztecs at the time of the Spanish conquest.

ca. 30,000 B.C.E.	First human beings cross over the Bering land bridge into the Americas
6000–1500 B.C.E.	Archaic Age in Mesoamerica: domestication of agricultural plants, such as corn and beans, occurs in Central Mexico
1500–400 B.C.E.	Olmec and Oaxacan civilizations flourish in Central Mexico
1500–250 B.C.E.	Early Maya Civilization flourishes
900–200 B.C.E.	Early Horizon Period in Peru: Chavin artistic style popular
400–200 B.C.E.	Earliest carved monuments appear among the Maya
150 B.C.E.–750 C.E.	Teotihuacan civilization flourishes in Central Mexico
200–600	Early Intermediate Period in Peru: Moche and Nasca cultures flourish

200–900	Classic Period in Mesoamerica
250–900	Middle Maya Civilization: population increases and cities of Tikal and Calakmul are prominent
583–604	Lady Kanal Ikal (Maya queen) rules Palenque
600–1000	Middle Horizon Period in Peru: Tiahuanaco and Huari civilizations flourish
900–1524	Late Maya Civilization
950–1150	Toltec civilization flourishes in Central Mexico
1200	Manufacture of earliest surviving Inca artifacts
late 1200s	Osman wins lands in northwest Anatolia from Byzantine Empire, and founds Ottoman Empire
1300	Mexica (Aztec) groups migrate to Basin of Mexico
1304–74	Life of Petrarch, the first great Renaissance thinker
1325	Tenochtitlan (future Aztec capital) is founded
mid-1300s	Italian *signorie* flourish
1375–96	Acamapichtli reigns as first *tlatoani* (ruler) of the Aztecs
1399	Henry IV overthrows Richard II in England
1403	Bayezit I of Ottoman Empire defeated at Battle of Ankara
1413	Henry V ascends the English throne
1415	Heavily outnumbered English defeat the French at the Battle of Agincourt
1417	Council of Constance ends papal schism—the pope moves back to Rome from Avignon, France
1420	Henry V marries Katherine of Valois, theoretically uniting the French and English thrones
1421	Mehmet I of Ottoman Empire ascends the throne and begins expanding the empire
1422	Death of Henry V of England: England ruled by councilors while Henry VI is too young
1425–30	Venice fights Turks for control of eastern Mediterranean
1429	Joan of Arc emerges as leader of the French army resisting the English
1438	Chanca tribe attacks Inca at Cuzco—King Inca Urcon flees, but Inca Yupanqui saves city, claims kingship, and takes name Pachacuti
1438–63	King Pachacuti leads expansion of Inca empire, taking Lake Titicaca and Lake Junín
1442	King Alfonso d'Aragona of Sicily seizes the throne of the Kingdom of Naples
1451	Mehmet I ascends the Ottoman throne
1453	Henry VI of England goes mad; Ottoman Empire captures Constantinople/Byzantium
1454	Peace of Lodi establishes the *Lega italica*
1455	War of the Roses begins in England with the first battle at St. Albans

1461	Edward IV of York wins the English throne from Henry VI at the Battle of Towton
1463	Topa Inca, son of Pachacuti, extends empire to include northern and central Peru and western Ecuador
1470	Henry VI of Lancaster is restored to the English throne
1471	Topa Inca becomes king and captures much of Chile, Bolivia, and northwestern Argentina; Edward IV secures the English throne for the Yorkists
1479	Isabella of Castile and Ferdinand of Aragón begin joint rule of Spain
1480	Spanish Inquisition is established; Ottoman Empire captures Otranto in southern Italy
1481	Bayezit II ascends the Ottoman throne
1482–92	Isabella and Ferdinand of Spain capture Muslim kingdom of Granada
1483	Richard III deposes his nephew Edward V and assumes the English Crown; Edward and his younger brother are presumed murdered by their uncle
1485	Henry Tudor, Earl of Richmond, defeats and kills Richard III at Bosworth Field and ascends English throne as Henry VII, first monarch of the Tudor dynasty
1492	Christopher Columbus sets sail from Spain; Ferdinand and Isabella expel the Jews from Spain
1493	Huayna Capac becomes king and extends Inca empire to its greatest size
1494	Charles VIII of France invades northern Italy
1500	First Maya contact with Spaniards
1502–20	Motecuhzoma Xocooyotzin reigns as ninth *tlatoani* of the Aztec
1504	Spanish rule established over Naples and southern Italy
1509	Henry VIII ascends the English throne
1512	Selim I comes to power in Ottoman Empire and expands the empire to the south and east
1513	Michelangelo finishes painting the ceiling of the Sistine Chapel in Rome
1516	Peace of Noyon: Spain and France divide Italy into two spheres of influence; Sir Thomas More publishes *Utopia*
1517	Charles I ascends the Spanish throne; Ottoman Empire captures Cairo; Martin Luther nails his 95 Theses to a castle door in Wittenberg in Germany
1519	Hernan Cortés arrives in Mexico
1520–66	Reign of Suleyman the Magnificent of the Ottoman Empire
1521	Spanish conquer Tenochtitlan, the Aztec capital
1524–27	Pedro de Alvarado conquers the Southern Maya
1527	Huayna Capac dies; civil war starts between two rivals for the Incan kingship: Huascar and Atahuallpa; forces of the Holy Roman Empire sack Rome

1527–46	Elder and Younger Montejos conquer the Northern Maya
1530	Medici family members are installed as hereditary rulers of the Italian city-state of Florence
1530–39	Henry VIII breaks with the Catholic Church, dissolves the English monasteries, and confiscates monastic lands to the Crown
1531	Virgin of Guadalupe appears to Juan Diego, a Mexican Indian
1532	Atahuallpa defeats Huascar to be Inca ruler; Spaniards arrive, kill Atahuallpa, and install puppet ruler as Inca king
1536	Anne Boleyn, second wife of Henry VIII of England and mother of Elizabeth I, is executed for adultery
1537	Manco Inca leads revolt against Spanish: his defeat marks the end of large-scale resistance to Spanish rule
1545–63	Council of Trent begins the Catholic Counter Reformation
1547	Edward VI ascends the English throne
1549	Forced labor of Native Americans banned by the Spanish Crown
1553	Mary I becomes queen of England and restores the English Church to papal obedience
1556	Charles I (Charles V of the Holy Roman Empire) abdicates the Spanish throne and is succeeded by his son Philip II
1558	Elizabeth I, last monarch of the House of Tudor, becomes queen of England
1559	Peace of Cateu-Cambrésis ends Franco-Spanish war and assures Spanish dominance in Italy
1561	Madrid is established as official capital of Spain
1566	Selim II ascends throne of Ottoman Empire
1570	Pope Pius V excommunicates Elizabeth I
1571	Battle of Lepanto: European allies defeat Ottoman fleet and halt Turkish threat to Italy; Tupac Amaru, last independent Inca king, executed in Cuzco
1574	Murat III ascends the Ottoman throne, while the empire begins its decline
1577–80	Sir Francis Drake, an English privateer, raids the coasts of Spanish America and circumnavigates the globe
1580	Philip II of Spain seizes the throne of Portugal
1582	Pope Gregory XIII introduces modern calendar, which is quickly adopted by most of Catholic Europe
1585	War erupts between England and Spain: English troops are sent to fight the Spanish in the Netherlands
late 1580s	William Shakespeare's first plays are produced; Sir Walter Raleigh tries unsuccessfully to found an English colony in Virginia
1588	Spanish Armada is defeated by bad weather and the English fleet
1596	Irish lord Hugh O'Neill revolts against Elizabeth I of England
1598	Philip III ascends the Spanish throne; Araucanians revolt against Spanish rule in South America

1600	Robert Devereaux, Earl of Essex, unsuccessfully rebels against Elizabeth I of England
1603	Death of Elizabeth I of England: accession of James VI of Scotland to the English throne (as James I)
1697	Martin de Ursua conquers Tayasal, the last independent Maya state

HISTORICAL OVERVIEW: WEB SITES

http://www.wsu.edu/~dee/CIVAMRCA/AZTECS.HTM
http://www.learner.org/exhibits/renaissance/
http://www.museo.org/inca-history.html
http://www.class.uidaho.edu/arch499/nonwest/mayan/history.htm
http://www.didyouknow.cd/history/16thcentury.htm
http://www.anthro.mankato.msus.edu/prehistory/latinamerica/south/cultures/inca.html
http://www.mesoweb.com/encyc/encyc/index.html
http://www.mediahistory.umn.edu/time/1400s.html
http://www.lepg.org/sixteen.htm

2

DOMESTIC LIFE

DOMESTIC LIFE
|
LIFE CYCLES
WOMEN'S ROLES
CHILDREN

The center of daily life is the home and, more important, the people who inhabit our domestic space. Domestic life here is defined as the humans who share our private spaces rather than our friends and acquaintances with whom we interact in the public worlds of work, politics, and sometimes recreation. However, even this definition of domestic life is a little slippery, because we include family members within our private sphere even if they live in separate homes and join us for the holidays and celebrations that mark our domestic life. Over time the definitions of those who are our intimates has changed. Who are the people who might share our domestic life?

The first ties are between a married couple and their children. But even these relationships defy clear definition: throughout history children have often depended upon the kindness of strangers to raise them, whether they were orphaned or fostered or fed by wet nurses. All these people shared the domestic intimacy of home life. Furthermore, households included others outside the nuclear family, from relatives to servants to slaves. In ancient Rome, the head of the family (the paterfamilias) was responsible for family, relatives, slaves, and freed slaves, and he also cared for clients who put themselves in his charge. Families might also include unmarried partners or even roommates who combine living space for convenience or necessity or concubines who shared the private lives of rulers. The relationships that make up domestic life are impossible to define perfectly, but (like art) we recognize them when we see them.

A study of domestic life not only includes the people who create a private sphere but also encompasses the roles they play—including at times the emotional functions they fill. Fathers of 19th-century families were to be distant and angry, while mothers were to be accessible and nurturing. Mothers in ancient Rome, by contrast, were stern disciplinarians and teachers of values, while the nursemaids handled the nurturing. Here in the domestic life, societies define the roles of men, women, children, and everyone else who shares this space. It is here that we learn early on who we are and how we are to act and feel.

In the entries that follow, we will examine three areas of domestic life: life cycles, women's lives, and childhood. Life cycles are the events that mark the passage of life from birth to the grave. They trace the varying roles, in the home and in society, that a human being assumes as he or she grows older. Domestic spaces were associated with women in particular during the 15th and 16th centuries, both in Europe and in the Americas, so particular attention is paid to the roles women played. Special attention is also due women because they frequently do not appear in traditional political histories of the Renaissance. Since women were rarely politicians, business leaders, or university lecturers, they did not directly engage in political activity in the same way as men. As a result, political and diplomatic history books sometimes forget about the indispensable roles played by women in all societies. Of course, there are notable exceptions to women's noninvolvement in politics, Queen Elizabeth I of England being the most memorable. A separate entry on men's roles has not been included in this section because they appear frequently in the rest of the volume, such as in the section on economic life. Finally, the entry on children examines in depth the processes involved in becoming a functioning adult in various societies. Childhood, a time of rapid growth and change, was marked by severe discipline and a plethora of rites of passage, but it was still often a time of play and wonderment.

~*Joyce E. Salisbury and Lawrence Morris*

FOR MORE INFORMATION

Veyne, P., ed. *A History of Private Life*. Vols. 1 and 2. Cambridge, Mass.: Harvard University Press, 1987.

DOMESTIC LIFE
|
LIFE CYCLES
|
England

Spain

Italy

Ottoman Empire

Maya

Aztec

Inca

Life Cycles

In every civilization people are born, grow up, work, and die. Anthropologists and others use the term *life cycle* to refer to the series of socially recognized changes that mark an individual's passage from the womb to the grave. Certain changes, such as birth, puberty, marriage, and death, are recognized by most societies around the world, from London, England, to Lima, Peru. These major changes are usually marked by rituals—complex prescribed actions designed to sanctify (make holy) the individual entering a new stage of life. While European and Native American rituals differed in content during the 15th and 16th centuries, they nevertheless celebrated many of the same changes.

As a result of the common Christian inheritance, the life-cycle rituals in different European countries tended to resemble each other. An Italian traveler in Spain, for example, would instantly be able to recognize many of the customs surrounding the Spanish life cycle. While such similarities could create unity among nations, they could also create isolation and even strife. Members of minority religious communities, such as Jews or Muslims, could not, and did not want to, participate in many of the life-cycle rituals due to the rituals' explicitly Christian content. While the rest of the community was celebrating a baptism or marriage, a Jew or Muslim would be excluded from the rites and often the festivities. Even among Christians the meaning of rituals and questions about their proper practice could become bones of contention. Some Christians, for example, believed that only adults, and not children, should be baptized. These people, called Anabaptists, were frequently persecuted, sometimes driven from their homes and even killed. Later on, when Anabaptists rose to political power in some regions, they persecuted pedobaptists (people who believed it was good to baptize children). While ritual could thus become a form of exclusion for some parts of society, for most members of society ritual served as a way of unifying the community and celebrating together the changes and stages of life.

In Europe, the major rituals of the life cycle were baptism, confirmation, marriage, and burial. In baptism, a priest or minister sprinkled or immersed briefly an infant (except in the case of Anabaptists or adult converts) with water in the name of God. Baptism was meant to recall Christ's death and resurrection, to remove mankind's collective guilt from the child, and to bring the child into communion with the Holy Spirit. After baptism, the child was an official member of the Christian Church. Confirmation was frequently given at an early age, for example, at six or seven in England. At confirmation, the participants confirmed their desire to remain in the church into which they had been baptized. Confirmation marked the end of early childhood, and from then on the child would begin to study or to do chores. Curiously, Renaissance Christianity did not have a standard ceremony marking puberty, unlike many other religions. However, secular firsts, such as a person's first full-time job, did tend to happen around 14.

Marriage marked the beginning of independent adulthood for many. The Catholic Church viewed marriage as a sacred bond between two people whom God had joined together. As a result, the promises the couple made to support each other for better or for worse were taken very seriously and divorce was prohibited. In Protestant countries, however, divorce was allowed in exceptional circumstances. With marriage generally came a degree of independence—the man and woman were now the head of a new household of children and property for which they were ultimately responsible.

Except in times of plague and other crises, all people were buried. At funerals, the community gathered to support the bereaved. Funerals were also an occasion to contemplate the meaning of life and the Christian hope of salvation. In Catholic countries, the seriously ill, especially those wealthy enough to have private chaplains or those living in church accommodation (such as hospitals or almshouses), would receive extreme unction, sometimes called last rites. In this ritual, the priest anointed the sick person with oil and forgave the believer's sins in the name of Christ and on behalf of the church community. The ritual was also believed to impart some health benefits.

Native American religion was very different from Christianity and also varied from area to area. The rituals naturally differed as well, yet there are some interesting similarities between European and Mesoamerican and South American customs, especially Aztec customs. For example, Aztec children underwent a purifying ritual in which the midwife gave the child a ritual bath, touching water to the child's head and chest while invoking a goddess to cleanse the child and make it good. The elements of water and the need for purification parallel the themes and symbols in Christian baptism. Similarly, the Aztecs, like the Europeans, took only one wife and valued fidelity to the marriage partner. Other Native American rituals and customs were very different from European ones. Inca kings, for example, married their sisters, and men who were part of the Inca aristocracy generally had many wives. The Maya *hetzmek*, which initiated a new child into the community, focused on carrying the child on the hip and did not use water, unlike baptism and the Aztec rituals. Also unlike European practice, the Maya and particularly the Inca had complex and important rituals marking puberty.

Thus when the European and American worlds met, they had much in common. They all celebrated and sanctified birth, marriage, and death. The differences, though, could be much more striking. As in Europe, rituals could be a source of both understanding and conflict.

The Ottoman Empire, meanwhile, had different rituals from those of Europe and the Americas. Predominantly Muslim, the Ottoman life cycle reflected Islamic practice, but it was heavily influenced by indigenous Turkish customs. Nevertheless, like Europe and the Americas, the Ottomans used ritual to mark many of the same stages of life, particularly birth, marriage, and death.

~*Lawrence Morris*

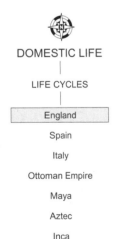

DOMESTIC LIFE

LIFE CYCLES

England

Spain

Italy

Ottoman Empire

Maya

Aztec

Inca

ENGLAND

Life began at home quite literally in 15th- and 16th-century England, since most children were born at home with the aid of a midwife and the neighboring women. The first major ritual in the child's life, baptism, took place on a Sunday within a week or two after birth. The ritual of baptism involved dipping the baby in a font of holy water in the parish church. Theologically, baptism purified the child for entry into the church community, but the ceremony also marked the child's entry into the broader social community. The child received his or her name at the christening, and the baptismal record, instead of a birth certificate, served as the legal verification of a person's age and origin. At the baptism, the child also received several godparents. Godparents were adults charged with ensuring that the child was instructed in the Christian life, but godparents were considered to be genuine relatives and could be used as contacts later in life. Poorer families would thus sometimes attempt to find godparents from more well-to-do families.

For the first six years, children remained mostly at home, but at the age of six they began their preparation for adult life. Boys of wealthier families would attend a petty school, where they were taught to read and write in English, while boys of the less well-off would start helping out with small chores in the fields. Young girls, by contrast, learned the skills of spinning, dyeing, cooking, and basic medicine. At the age of 14, the academically talented members of the petty schools, or the very wealthy, went on to grammar school, where they were taught the Latin language and literature and perhaps some French or Greek. The emphasis was mostly on Latin, however, for Latin was still the language of learning and international communication. Those not going on to grammar schools entered trades as apprentices and were considered to be part of the working public. In the countryside, too, by 14 the children were considered to be full members of the economy and would be expected to work full time.

While most people worked from the age of 14, it was only upon marriage that they achieved full individual status in society. Before that time, they were considered, for the most part, to be under the authority of their parents. The average age of marriage was relatively late, despite the impression given by plays such as *Romeo and Juliet* with its 14-year-old Juliet. The average age was 27 for a man and 24 for a woman, though the ages were somewhat lower among the upper classes: 24 and 19 among the aristocracy. This difference reflects, at least in part, the need to have sufficient wealth to be self-sufficient, and it naturally took the laboring classes longer to gain the requisite wealth.

Betrothal was taken very seriously. It had to be conducted before witnesses and was considered a legally binding contract—those who reneged on a promise to marry could be prosecuted in the church courts. Often a symbolic exchange of gifts marked the occasion, or the man would give the woman a gift—rings were a common choice, but gloves and bracelets were sometimes chosen. The wedding itself was celebrated in the church and was marked by the man's placing a wedding ring on the woman's ring finger. It was also the practice for a woman to take her husband's surname. The marriage was recorded in the parish register, which served the legal role of the modern marriage certificate. The married couple was legally required to live together. Separation was only permitted by court order, and only in such extreme circumstances as cruelty or adultery. In these cases the separated couple were to remain celibate, and the wife might receive alimony.

While the high overall mortality rate dictated that the population of England was relatively young, a 40-year-old was not thought to be elderly. In fact, the forties and fifties were considered the prime of a man's life. If any age marked the beginning of old age, it was 60: laboring people were no longer required by law to work after that age or liable for military service. It has been estimated that nearly 10 percent of the population were age 60 or older. Nonetheless, the prevalence of disease and the primitive level of medicine meant that illness could easily end a life long before its prime. Life expectancy at birth was only about 48 years, although anyone who made it through the first 30 years was likely to live for another 30. Life expectancy varied from place to place—it was particularly low in the cities, where crowded conditions and poor sanitation increased the dangers of disease.

As death approached, a person would be called upon to make a will, if this had not yet been done (estates under £5 did not require a will). The will related principally to moveable property, since most landholdings had to be passed on according to the custom of the holding. Among the upper classes and in open-field areas, land was passed on by primogeniture: the eldest son inherited all the land; this would prevent the landholding from being broken up into pieces too small to

A Deathbed Scene. The costly four-poster bed and spacious bedroom clearly show that the dying man was wealthy. The priest reading prayers may have been a private chaplain employed by the household. At such scenes, it was common for the dying man to pass on words of wisdom, and some people wrote their last words well in advance of the event. From Charles Hindley, *The Roxburghe Ballads,* 1837–74.

support the landholder's needs. Woodland areas were more likely to follow partible inheritance, whereby each of the sons was given a share of the land.

When a person was on the deathbed, the parish bell would toll. This was called the passing bell, and it was a signal for all hearers to pray for the dying person. After the death, there would be one short peal; from its sound the hearers could tell whether the deceased was male or female. The deceased would be laid out at home; indeed, since hospitals were not used for acute medical treatment, death like birth typically happened at home. The corpse was then brought to the churchyard, where the priest met it at the gate to begin the religious ceremony of burial. Church bells would ring just before and after the burial ceremony. The privileged would be buried in coffins, often within the church under elaborate wood, brass, or stone markers bearing the effigies of the deceased. Ordinary folk were buried in the churchyard in a simple woolen shroud in unmarked graves. The funeral of an important person was often an occasion for almsgiving and a public feast. As baptism and marriage were recorded in the parish register, so too was burial, the ceremony of the third great passage of life (Singman, 35–54).

FOR MORE INFORMATION

Byrne, M. St. Clare. *Elizabethan Life in Town and Country*. London: Methuen, 1950.

Emmison, F. G. *Elizabethan Life: Morals and the Church Courts*. Clemsford: Essex County Council, 1973.

Singman, J. L. *Daily Life in Elizabethan England*. Westport, Conn.: Greenwood, 1995.

DOMESTIC LIFE
|
LIFE CYCLES
|
England

Spain

Italy

Ottoman Empire

Maya

Aztec

Inca

SPAIN

The birth of a child was generally an occasion of great ceremony. When a woman was in labor, friends, relatives, and neighbors gathered in her home to offer encouragement and assistance, and the new baby was the center of attention for everyone. Baptism followed as soon as possible after birth to ensure the child its place in heaven if it should not survive. During the baptismal ceremony a Christian name was given, often that of a favorite saint or the name of the saint on whose day the child was born. In the more affluent families it was common to have a little party after the baptismal event, at which time the parents and baby usually received a few small gifts.

Until the age of six or seven, the daily life of the child revolved around sleep, food, and play. Then the sacrament of confirmation marking the child's official admission to the church was given, and around this age girls and boys began to be steered by parents and society into their own differentiated spheres.

In the country it was customary for the sons of peasant farmers at a young age to be moved away from the guidance of female members of the household into male company. In the vast majority of cases, this meant that the children were placed into an orbit of farmwork where they learned the tasks of herding animals, and, as they grew stronger, plowing, planting, and harvesting; milking and sheering sheep;

and snaring rabbits and birds for the table. Girls, in contrast, would begin to learn the skills necessary to cook and make clothing and to perform the other household duties.

City boys from reasonably well-off families of the bourgeoisie generally received two or three years of schooling learning to read and write and some arithmetic. Then it was common for them to learn a trade. Sometimes this happened at home with the boy following in his father's footsteps; otherwise, he was sent to learn and not uncommonly to live in the home of someone else skilled in a trade. An apprenticeship was a desirable option, and room and board were provided even if little or no pay was forthcoming. Sometimes the father had to pay the master to take on his son. The master had the right to treat the boy as his own, even to punish him if he was not always up to standard. Conflicts naturally arose between them, and often enough the apprentice ran away from the job.

Marriage was a serious economic as well as personal enterprise. Marriage negotiations were often a delicate affair conducted by intermediaries. The economic aspects were settled beforehand between the partners, stipulating the assets to be brought by the wife into the marriage and the property contributed by the groom. Marriages were often arranged within a circle of friends or business associates with the view to committing the family networks to continuing cooperation and prosperity.

Women generally married at about age 23 and men at about 25. The number of women who never married at all also varied by region, but overall the rate was about 10 percent during the Early Modern period. When a girl was old enough to marry, she went from the confinement by her parents to that by her husband. Most houses had windows that overlooked a patio or garden and not the street, so women of this elite group had little contact with the outside world except, perhaps, through the servants.

With few exceptions, marriage was for life. The couple was required to cohabit, and neither was permitted to enter a monastery or convent or become celibate without the consent of the other. Divorce was not sanctioned. On occasion a marriage could be annulled if it had been invalid in the first place—for example, on the basis of bigamy or close kinship—or if it was never consummated. An official separation, releasing the couple from the requirement of cohabitation, was also allowed in matters of cruelty or adultery. Remarriage was permitted on the death of one of the partners.

In the 16th century, one major life-choice a Spaniard, particularly a man, could make was to emigrate. Since its discovery, America irresistibly attracted many Spaniards to its distant shores, seeking fame, fortune, or land and escape from the class-bound restrictions at home. Stories circulated, often much exaggerated, about the wealth and opportunities of the New World, but there were abundant examples of men who had returned home rich after an exciting life of adventure. Cases of the many who died of disease or shipwreck deterred few. Families were often split up as many individuals saved their money or sold their property to purchase passage to the new land. Young people saw in the prospect of emigration a future far from the drudgery, hunger, and toil of everyday life in the villages or cities of Spain.

However a person managed it, if he or she was fortunate enough to reach the age of about 25 or 30 with no major disabilities from disease or accidents, he or she was well on the way to reaching old age eventually. At the time, old age was considered to begin about 60, and retirement, at least for those with family backing or wealth, became a possibility. Society made no provisions for a man or woman's golden age, and individuals either provided it themselves or continued working until they dropped dead. Aristocrats with land and rentals, well-heeled bourgeois, and some members of guilds had little problem securing a pension for their declining years. Wealthy peasants or even those not so wealthy might exchange property holdings for financial support and a house to live in. Even a faithful steward or cook on a baronial estate might be looked after in old age by his employer. Similarly, monasteries sometimes took in the aged and gave them a room and meals in exchange for property, cash, or something else of value.

The many hundreds of thousands without family connections or with negligible ones—itinerant workers, lowly paid clerks or municipal employees, service staff, small entrepreneurs, landless peasants, poor writers, soldiers and sailors—were all vulnerable to an unmemorable old age of begging on the streets and dying in a gutter or in a charity hospital. Uneducated peasant women, who at the time of marriage were generally younger than their husbands, could often expect to spend long years in lonely widowhood and extreme poverty.

At all levels of society, on the death of someone, friends and neighbors immediately rallied to the side of the bereaved. Dramatic funerals, characterized by an emotional gathering of friends and family with women weeping and wailing, were common. They were affairs with large congregations of people parading through the streets of the city. Gatherings of the clan would take place to show solidarity and support long after the corpse was buried. The rallies were so large that the Church and the state tried to curb them by stipulating the number of people who could hold candles in the funerary procession, restricting mourning dress to only members of the household, and ordering that no food be served at the gatherings. With these limitations fewer people would be involved, lessening the threat of vendettas and civil disobedience that might come with a large crowd. These restrictions were not very successful, did not apply uniformly to all areas, and applied not at all to the region of Aragón.

Lineage and class were nowhere more evident than in the burial site. Commoners were interred in the churchyard with neither coffin nor commemorative marker. For people of noble background, or those wealthy enough to afford a substantial donation to the church and a stone coffin, a niche inside the church would be found.

Members of the same noble family tended to be interred in a communal vault, but each time a particular branch of the family came to an end, or when one branch superseded the others in wealth and power, a new vault would be constructed. Sometimes this took the form of a new chapel in the church where the bones of the deceased would rest. The burial site was then to remain as a testimony to the family that established it. Neither burial chambers nor carved stone figures and marble sarcophagi were cheap, so their use was restricted to the wealthy. The practice generally gave way to a simple inscribed slab of marble over the grave site (Anderson, 160–67).

FOR MORE INFORMATION

Alcalá-Zamora, J. *La vida cotidiana en la España de Velázquez*. Madrid: Temas de Hoy, 1989.
Anderson, J. *Daily Life during the Spanish Inquisition*. Westport, Conn.: Greenwood, 2002.
Casey, J. *Early Modern Spain: A Social History*. London: Routledge, 1999.

ITALY

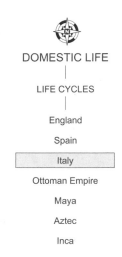

Renaissance Italian theorists divided the life of humans into various stages. Due to the tendency to count in sevens (compare the modern tendency to count by tens or fives), many of the ages referenced are multiples of seven. The first stage of life, from years 1–7, was infancy, which etymologically means "without speech." Of course, babies learned to talk long before the age of 7, where the numerical conventions fixed the end of this first phase. Childhood, the second step, continued until the youngster achieved, supposedly around age 14, discretion, that is, the capacity to make decisions, to tell good from bad. Next, adolescence extended from the mid-teens to the mid-twenties, to age 28 if one was multiplying sevens. Only in the next age, virility, did a man attain his full powers, which he could expect to enjoy for a full four sevens, until age 56. Thereafter, decline set in, though gradually, first old age until 70 years and then a collapse into final decrepitude.

For all Christians, several of the seven sacraments provided important rites of passage that marked life stages. Baptism signaled birth and extreme unction signaled death. Between them, marriage was another turning point that was experienced by most people, although the church's role in it became very central only as the period went on. Other moments of lesser resonance, some ritualized and many others not, punctuated the process of growing up. For some men, by birth or choice, there were entry ceremonies such as the ordaining of priests, the dubbing of knights, or the receiving of masters into guilds. But even where formal recognition of such transitions was lacking, we can trace the general shape of a sequence of life stages for men and women.

Baptism was a ceremonial acknowledgment of the new arrival through which a baby or convert acquired a social identity and a Christian soul. Normally the baby was carried by the midwife and accompanied by a few friends and neighbors to the church or baptistery. There was enacted what anthropologists call a rite of passage, in which a person moves from one life stage into another through a ceremonial sequence of steps: first, a separation from the past, then an intermediary limbo, and finally an incorporation into a new social state. Thus baptism began in front of the building, where a priest first exorcised the child to banish the spirits of evil into which, as a descendant of Adam, it had been born. Then the assemblage moved with the newcomer, now without sin but still without identity, into the sacred space. Immersed in or sprinkled with water at the baptismal font, the baby received a name and acceptance into the Christian community—a membership necessary for salvation and heaven.

Children before the age of 6 were generally looked after by women. At around 6, though, fathers began to participate more directly, guiding their children toward their adult roles. They assumed responsibility for the education of sons, overseeing training where they did not themselves teach. For girls of this same age, in Florence, fathers started paying into an account with the civic dowry fund, the "Monte delle Doti," so that 10 years later the daughter would be able to marry. As these paternal activities suggest, at this stage gender differentiation intensified. Earlier, although parental expectations for girls and boys were clearly distinct, their care and experiences had a lot in common. They wore similar clothes and played similar games. But at 6 or 7 years, gender differences began to sharpen.

Child in a Wooden Walker. Note how the picture portrays the realm of children as belonging to the world of women, who are busy at work spinning, sewing, and embroidering. The male child's struggling to the door, however, symbolically represents his future role in the outside world, apart from the domestic space of women. Civica Raccolta delle Stampe Achille Bertarelli–Milano.

For many children, introduction to work occurred between ages 6 and 12. In the city and the country, in homes and workshops and on farms, youngsters learned the elementary practices of adult work. Girls observed the mixed tasks of housekeeping—including preparing foods, sweeping, fetching water, washing and drying clothes, feeding and minding small animals—and began to perform the simpler ones. Boys too gradually acquired basic skills, while their orbit of activity expanded beyond the domestic compass to streets and hillsides where they ran errands and watched over grazing animals. For some number of boys and a few girls, education in reading, writing, and arithmetic might also begin in these years.

There were also religious clubs for young boys. Aimed originally at boys of 12 to 15 years, they came to admit ones as young as 8 or even 6. Meeting regularly on Sundays, these clubs, called confraternities, sought to give constructive shape to youths' leisure time, leavening the dose of religion and organizational life with ball games and virtuous play. Catechism classes, multiplying across Italy especially during the 16th century, offered preparation for first communion to children between 6 and 12 years old. These lessons aimed to teach basic Christian belief and practice to those of modest means. In Bologna these schools reached more than half the boys.

Somewhere in the years between ages 12 and 15 childhood merged into adolescence with neither a sharp break nor a major rite of passage. In becoming adolescent, older children gradually took on a range of new physical, sexual, moral, and intellectual capacities that translated into greater social and legal responsibilities. Young girls from wealthier families tended to be restricted to the home to protect their chastity from unscrupulous men, but male adolescents started to play roles in the public sphere.

In several forms, ritualized behavior by groups of young people, almost exclusively males, served as a kind of collective conscience for society as a whole. The conventional notion of the innocence of the young could be played on for the general benefit. Processions of children and adolescents invoking God and true religion were a familiar sight in Renaissance cities. Occasionally, apparently spontaneous congregations coalesced in times of crisis.

Although circumstances and timing varied with social class, for females marriage provided a fairly clear moment of transition. Within the values of her culture, the status of wife, although subordinate to husband, earned a woman recognition and honor. To a wife came the full range of responsibilities that society imposed on females. At the same time, a few women—for example, nuns and the dowryless poor—never married yet still left childhood behind. As for men, marriage also served to mark adulthood. It meant dominance over a wife and children. In other zones of life, adulthood brought new roles but an autonomy that was often only partial. Economically, much depended on the longevity of a man's father and on the structure of the family enterprise. Although an adult male had the physical abilities and technical skills to earn a living, more senior men often exploited or controlled his labor.

For the Catholic Church of the Renaissance, marriage was a sacrament, the sign of a divine intervention that sanctified its participants. Yet before the mid-16th century, a man and a woman could—and often did—contract a religiously binding alliance without the presence of a priest. By Church law, the core of a marriage was the free consent of the two parties in "words in the present tense." These are reciprocal vows in the form—"I, Caterina, take you, Pietro, to be my husband"—that remain at the crux of the Christian ritual to the present day. This exchange of commitments, once sealed by sexual consummation, created an unbreakable bond. Earlier public statements of the intention to marry "in the future tense," witnesses to such vows, and a priestly benediction were all desirable. Still, even without publicity and blessing, a secret marriage was legal and binding. From the medieval Church's point of view, the couple and their obligations to one another were the center. The purposes of marriage were to procreate and to aid one another, especially toward salvation. In particular, marriage avoided sin by providing sexual appetite a legitimate outlet. Sex was a marital right; husbands owed it to their wives, not only vice versa.

Regarding matrimony, social traditions had concerns that were quite different from those of religion. The dominant model, reflecting elite views and practices, saw marriage as linking not merely two individuals but two families. Exchanging economic and political resources and cementing social alliances, marriage benefited not only the bridal pair but also wider networks of kin and associates. Dowries, paid by the father of the bride to the bridegroom, played a major role in the marriage negotiations of the wealthy. When there was tight competition for prospective grooms, dowries could even outstrip the son's inheritance. While the dowry was a major expense, the groom's family was expected to provide a kind of counter-dowry that was worth from one-third to half of the bride's dowry. It should also be noted that the wife was technically entitled to the return of her dowry after the death of her husband—it could form a kind of insurance policy for the young wife. Due to the delicate nature of these negotiations and the many diverse interested parties, marriages were usually negotiated by third parties. Marriages due to love were rare among the wealthy, most especially because young men and young women were not frequently allowed in each other's company.

The ritual of the wedding itself had three phases. These might bunch together over a few days but could also stretch over weeks or months. The solemnities had no single crowning moment; thus when trouble intervened before all the steps had been completed, there might be disputes over whether the couple was in fact married. The first formality was the signing of the contract. At this all-male assembly in front of the notary, supporters from both parties witnessed the groom and the bride's father put their names to a legal document detailing the agreement. Exchanging handshakes or kisses, the men made public their mutual commitments. Only at another gathering did the bride herself appear. This second stage of the wedding took place at her house. With a small party, the groom came and, before a company of her kin and friends and a notary, exchanged consent with the bride, marking the event by giving her a ring. He also bestowed other gifts that made up the counter-dowry. The bride's family then sponsored a banquet and festivities for their guests. The ring ceremony initiated the symbolic transfer of the woman out of her natal family and her incorporation into her marital one. This transition was completed only during the third phase of the nuptial rite of passage with the physical movement of her person and goods to the home of her new husband. In a highly visible procession, the bride, clothed in her finery and accompanied by her trousseau, went to her new residence. There the man's family offered further celebrations and gifts. As part of the display, wealthy families liked to have chests and even walls lavishly painted with nuptial themes. The consummation of the marriage, which definitively displayed the bride's honor and placed it in her husband's hands, traditionally occurred that night; guests might make much ado of bedding the new couple. The wedding night and the morning after often featured playful, noisy, and bawdy revelry.

Old age was hard to define in practice. While some were considered old at 40 if they became ill, many continued in active life for much longer. The average age of the pope at election in the 16th century was 61, the famed artist Michelangelo started on the *Last Judgment* in the Sistine Chapel when he was 65, and the lord Bartolomeo Colleone led his last battle at the age of 67. Old age, however, could be much harder on women, who were deprived of many of the employment opportunities available to men. A widow generally hoped to live either with her children or else on her reclaimed dowry.

Death was, of course, the final ritual. In the Italian mindset, you should live well, fearing death. You should die well too. There was a clear picture of what to do with the last hours. The scene at the deathbed was a sacred and a social drama. It became a moment of gathering for family, associates, a notary, and a priest. While some people prepared their wills in advance, many did not. Some used their last breaths to make or remake the arrangements; the possible beneficiaries hung about grieving and offering solace, while vying with rivals to protect their interests. The death of a wealthy paterfamilias (head of the family) with many dependents to provide for was a particularly intense occasion. Wills settled worldly matters, often parceling out major assets among the heirs and showering gifts in cash and kind specified at length—clothing, jewelry, weapons, art—on kin, friends, and faithful dependents.

Testaments also typically attended to the fate of their makers in the life beyond. Donations to charity and the church to rectify specific sins such as usury were intended to unburden the soul of part of its weight of transgression. In the later Renaissance, dying penitents made fewer such designated bequests, but left more and more funds to religious institutions to pray and say masses for their souls and for those of deceased family members. With the future of the testator and his or her kin provided for as best as could be, the dying person then confessed and received the sacrament of extreme unction.

Whenever the family could afford it, funerals were elaborate affairs. The first stage was a vigil around the corpse in the family house. Family members and neighbors burned candles and kept watch. Tradition called for women to mourn dramatically—crying out, unbinding their hair, and tearing their skin and clothing. Women also had the practical role of washing the body and dressing it for burial, usually in its best apparel. After the domestic vigil came the public stages of the funeral: the procession, requiem, and burial. The procession, in particular, was often marked by great pomp. The body was accompanied by troops of clergy, crowds of mourners, family members in rich but somber garb, caparisoned horses, banners and drapery, and many candles and torches. These all proclaimed the prestige of the deceased as well as of the family or the corporate bodies to which he or she had belonged. For ordinary people, death rituals were less grand affairs. Nevertheless, the commoner's desire for a decent funeral, on the part of both the dying and survivors, reflected similar attitudes. Belonging to guilds or, especially, confraternities allowed men and women with fewer assets to enjoy some funeral splendor. A major function of these corporations was as burial societies; they provided mourners, regalia, and sometimes even funds to see their members conveyed to the grave with due honor (Cohen and Cohen, 177–214).

FOR MORE INFORMATION

Cohen, E. S., and T. V. Cohen. *Daily Life in Renaissance Italy.* Westport, Conn.: Greenwood, 2001.

Herlihy, D., and C. Klapisch-Zuber. *Tuscans and Their Families.* New Haven: Yale University Press, 1985.

Muir, E. *Ritual in Early Modern Europe.* Cambridge: Cambridge University Press, 1997.

OTTOMAN EMPIRE

In the Ottoman Empire, people went through a number of different rituals marking different developments in life. These rituals varied based on an individual's culture and religion. To Turkish Muslims in Anatolia, birth, circumcision, marriage, and death represented important stages in life as people strove to live according to God's word and law. Each event's celebration mixed elements of both Islamic and Turkish practices. Frequently the role of men and women remained distinct, and women often found themselves excluded from such fundamental activities as the

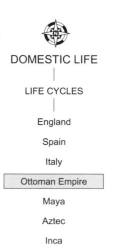

celebration of weddings and the burial of the dead. Yet even death could become a chance for celebration and togetherness within the family and larger community.

Births represented a chance for celebration. Families, especially in rural areas, gained labor and prestige from their offspring, and the father of a family gave a feast for each new child, while people scattered confetti and presented the newborn with gifts. Ideally, women gave birth in special walnut chairs that featured a solid rim as a seat and strong arms for the mother to clutch while in labor. The process was assisted by a midwife, a position in the Ottoman Empire for which one earned great respect and that was sometimes hereditary. Once the baby was born, the midwife cried "God is great" three times, then the father or an imam (Muslim cleric) made the call to prayer, also three times. To ward off the evil eye, a Qur'an (Koran), a blue bead, and a clove of garlic could be hung over the newborn's bed.

Children in the Turkish Ottoman lands were named in two stages. At the time of the cutting of the umbilical cord, the midwife would give the child a name. All girls were named Havva, the Islamic equivalent of Eve, while all boys received the names of great heroes of the past. (Eve, in Islam, is not seen as a negative figure, as both she and Adam equally bore the blame for the expulsion from paradise.) The father then gave the child the real name that he or she would bear throughout his or her life. Often this name would reflect something of the time the child was born. Hence, a child born at the time a cloth merchant arrived might have the name "Kumas Han," meaning "Cloth Khan."

As children grew up, they passed through many different milestones and rites of passage. For example, during the first week, the child would sleep alone in its cradle for the first time, which marked its separation from its mother. After 40 days, the infant would accompany his or her mother to the baths for a purification ceremony. The emergence of the child's first tooth was celebrated with singing, dancing, and presents, and boiled wheat was sprinkled onto the child's head. The most important rite of passage for boys, circumcision, was especially elaborate. The circumcision celebration for two sons of Sultan Mehmed II lasted three days and featured Qur'an readings, lectures, poetry, and much food and drink.

Marriage represented another important event in the lives of most Ottoman citizens. This took place during the teenage years with the match usually arranged by the parents, though the children, especially the prospective groom, could voice their opinions. Unless one had maturity problems, boys tended to marry in order of seniority, with cousins representing the preferred marriage partners. In rural areas, the bride and groom usually knew each other prior to the engagement, as they would have played and worked the fields together while growing up. While economic concerns sometimes entered into marriage decisions, especially for the wealthy, most parents also showed genuine concern for the happiness and well-being of their offspring.

Once concluded, families usually kept an engagement secret to defend against black magic. The bride and groom were separated from each other, although the groom sent presents to the bride and her family. Then, four days prior to the wedding, the groom's family announced the wedding, and he gave a party featuring dancing, wrestling, and men dressed as dancing girls, while the girl entertained her friends

Funeral Procession. As this picture shows, Ottoman graveyards resembled their western European counterparts. © Leonard de Selva/CORBIS.

in private. The next day, the girl remained at home surrounded by female relations, while the women of the groom's family began the wedding preparations.

The wedding ceremony itself usually took place on a Thursday or Saturday. The bride wore a red veil and remained apart from the main celebration, which included feasting, dancing, and continual drumming. After the celebration the groom went home to await his bride, who was escorted by a wedding procession, ideally led by a local religious leader. The bride always sent ahead two presents: a mirror and a copy of the Qur'an. Once they were alone, the groom officially saw his new wife's face for the first time, and they presumably copulated. Elite weddings in the cities were even more elaborate, though the basic pattern remained the same.

Muslims in the Ottoman Empire believed death was the most important part of life, and it was celebrated by those who remained behind. With the approach of death, family members filled the room and began wailing after the dying person drew his or her last breath. After death, the body was washed and balls of cotton wool soaked in warm water and covered in calico were placed in the body's orifices. The shroud was an all-white sleeveless garment—preferably brought from the hajj (pilgrimage to Mecca). Burial took place the next day according to Islamic law. Women remained behind during the funeral, ostensibly so that their cries did not disturb the dead. After the mourners had left, a religious leader remained behind to ensure that the soul safely made it into the custody of the angels who would escort it to the afterlife. Ceremonies of commemoration took place after a week, 40 days, or sometimes 52 days.

In the Ottoman Empire, ceremonies that marked an individual's passage through life and beyond were events that the whole community came together to celebrate. Despite differences in the scale and specifics of the celebrations, both rich and poor, as well as people from urban and rural areas, followed similar rituals and marked the same events. Islam played a crucial role in the way things were done, but many aspects of these celebrations were derived from ancient Turkish customs as well. Such ceremonies as these formed an important part of the people's identity that stayed with them from generation to generation.

To read about life cycles in Medieval Islam, see the Islam entries in the sections "Kinship" and "Marriage" in chapter 2 ("Domestic Life") in volume 2 of this series; for Islam in the 19th century, see the Islamic World entry in the section "Family Life" in chapter 2 ("Domestic Life") in volume 5 of this series.

~*Brian Ulrich*

FOR MORE INFORMATION

Cicek, K., ed. *The Great Ottoman-Turkish Civilisation 2: Economy and Society.* Ankara: Yeni Turkiye, 2000.

Goodwin, G. *The Private World of Ottoman Women.* London: Saqi, 1997.

DOMESTIC LIFE
|
LIFE CYCLES
|
England

Spain

Italy

Ottoman Empire

Maya

Aztec

Inca

MAYA

As in other cultures, the birth of a child was an important event for the Maya. The Maya still perform ceremonies marking a child's acceptance into society. In Yucatán this ceremony is the *hetzmek*, performed when the baby is carried astride the mother's hip for the first time. For girls the *hetzmek* is held at three months; for boys, at four months. The girl's age of three months symbolizes the three stones of the Maya hearth, an important focus of a woman's life. The boy's age of four months symbolizes the four sides of the maize field, an important focus of a man's life. Participants in the ceremony, besides the infant, are the parents and another husband and wife who act as sponsors. The child is given nine objects symbolic of his or her life and is carried on the hip nine times by both sponsoring parents. The ceremony closes with offerings and a ritual feast.

In colonial Yucatán, as today, children were raised by their mothers until the age of three or four. At about age four, girls were given a red shell that was tied to a string around their waists. At the same age, boys received a small white bead that was fastened to their hair. Both symbols of childhood were worn until puberty when another ceremony marked the transition to adulthood.

In all Maya communities the girls learned women's roles from their mothers throughout childhood—doing household chores, buying and selling in the market, and assisting with specialized activities such as making pottery or weaving textiles. Boys were taught the skills of farming, hunting, fishing, and other male tasks by their fathers.

In colonial Yucatán the 260-day almanac was consulted to select an auspicious day for the community puberty ceremony marking the end of childhood and the beginning of adulthood. It was held every few years for all children deemed ready to take this step. The ceremony was conducted by a shaman; four assistant shamans, or *chacs* (after the Maya rain god); and a respected elder of the community. The parents, children, and their sponsors assembled in the patio of the community elder's house, which was purified by a ritual conducted by the shaman. The patio was swept and covered by fresh leaves and mats.

After the *chacs* placed pieces of white cloth on the children's heads, the shaman said a prayer for the children and gave a bone to the elder, who used it to tap each child nine times on the forehead. The shaman used a scepter decorated with rattle-snake rattles to anoint the children with sacred water, after which he removed the white cloths from their heads. The children then presented offerings of feathers and cacao beans to the *chacs*. The shaman cut the white beads from the boys' hair, and the mothers removed the red shells from their daughters' waists. Pipes of tobacco were smoked, and a ritual feast of food and drink closed the ceremony. After this both the girls and boys were considered adults and eligible to marry.

Until they married, young women continued to live with their parents and were expected to follow the customs of modesty. When unmarried women met a man, they turned their backs and stepped aside to allow him to pass. When giving a man food or drink, they were to lower their eyes. In colonial times the young unmarried men of the community lived in a house set apart for them; this was probably an ancient custom. They painted themselves black until they were married but did not tattoo themselves until after marriage.

In colonial times marriages were often arranged between families while the boy and girl were still very young. The wedding took place when they came of age, usually when the couple was around 20 years old. Today in most Maya communities the average age of men at marriage is about the same, and the average age of women at marriage is 16 or 17 years.

In colonial Yucatán it was customary for a father to approve of the prospective spouse for his son, being careful that the young woman was of the same social class and of the same village. According to marriage taboos, it was incestuous to marry a girl who had the same surname or for a widower to marry the sister of his deceased wife or the widow of his brother. However, because they would always have different surnames, cross-cousin marriages were fairly common (marriage between the children of a brother and sister). A professional matchmaker (*ah atanzahob*) was often hired to make the arrangements, plan the ceremony, and negotiate the amount of the dowry, a custom that survives in some Maya communities today.

For the dowry the groom's father usually provided dresses and household articles for the bride, and the groom's mother made clothing for both her son and prospective daughter-in-law. Today in Yucatán, the groom or his family usually covers the expenses of the wedding, including the bride's trousseau.

The wedding ceremony was traditionally held at the house of the bride's father. It was performed by a shaman, who began the ceremony by explaining the details of the marriage agreement. After this he burned incense and blessed the new couple. Everyone enjoyed a special feast that concluded the ceremony.

Monogamy was and remains the most common form of marriage, but in pre-Columbian times (i.e., before 1492) polygyny (multiple wives) was permitted. Because of its greater economic demands, it was probably much more widespread among the elite than the nonelite. Divorce was uncomplicated, consisting of a simple repudiation by either party. By custom, widowers and widows remained single for at least a year after the death of their spouses. They could then remarry without ceremony; the man simply went to the house of the woman of his choice; and if she accepted him and gave him something to eat, they were considered married.

After the marriage the groom lived and worked in the house of his wife's parents (uxorilocal residence). His mother-in-law ensured that her daughter gave her husband food and drink as a token of the parental recognition of the marriage; but if the young man failed to work, he could be put out of the house. After a period of no more than six or seven years, the husband would build a new house adjacent to that of his father and move his new family there (patrilocal residence). According to ethnohistorical sources, the family slept in one room on mats set on low platforms of poles. Today in the highlands, mats are still used, although hammocks are often favored in the hotter lowland regions.

After marriage and full entry into independent adulthood, the next major rituals centered on death. The Maya believed the dead went to Xibalba, the underworld beneath the earth, just as the sun did when it died at sunset before being reborn each dawn. Xibalba was a place of rest, but it was not a paradise. There is evidence that Maya kings promoted special rituals to grant divine status to their dead predecessors. Several examples of this ritual apotheosis are recorded in early texts. Once deified, it was believed that the dead kings escaped Xibalba to dwell in the sky thereafter.

Common people did not have the luxury of deification. According to Bishop Landa, the Maya expressed deep and enduring grief over the death of a loved one: "During the daytime they wept silently for them, but during the nighttime they wept with loud and sorrow-filled cries, so that it was pitiful to hear them. They stayed in this great sorrow for many days, and they performed fasts and abstinences for the dead one, especially if it was a husband or wife."

The body was wrapped in a shroud and the mouth was filled with ground maize and one or more jadeite beads. Commoners were buried under the floors or behind their houses. Into the grave were placed idols of clay, wood, or stone and objects indicating the profession or trade of the deceased. Archaeologically excavated Maya burials usually contain offerings that vary according to the sex and status of the deceased but almost always include a jade bead in the mouth.

Burials of the elite were the most elaborate. Bishop Landa reports that in colonial-era Yucatán the bodies of high-status individuals were burned and their ashes were placed in urns beneath temples. The construction of funerary shrines over tombs is well documented by archaeology. But, although evidence of cremation is not often found, there is evidence of burial ritual involving fire. At Copan, for example, one elaborate tomb was reentered on several occasions for rituals that included fire and smoke and the painting of the bones with red cinnabar.

During Late Maya Civilization, the ruling lineage of Mayapan, the Cocom, reduced their dead to bones by boiling. The front of the skull was used as the base for a face modeled from resin, and this effigy was kept in the household shrines. These effigies were held in great veneration, and on feast days offerings of food were made to them so they would remain well fed. When the Cenote of Sacrifice at Chichen Itza was dredged, a skull was recovered that had the crown cut away. The eye sockets were filled with wooden plugs, and there were remains of painted plaster on the face (Sharer, *Daily Life*, 117–29).

To read about life cycles in 20th-century Latin America, see the Latin America entry in the section "Family Life" in chapter 2 ("Domestic Life") in volume 6 of this series.

FOR MORE INFORMATION

Chase, A. F., and D. Z. Chase, eds. *Mesoamerican Elites: An Archaeological Assessment.* Norman, Okla.: University of Oklahoma Press, 1992.

Sharer, R. J. *The Ancient Maya.* 5th ed. Stanford: Stanford University Press, 1994.

———. *Daily Life in Maya Civilization.* Westport, Conn.: Greenwood, 1996.

AZTEC

From the moment of childbirth, Aztec parents were greatly concerned that their children avoid becoming "fruitless trees" and instead become productive citizens. They believed that infants were exposed to the greatest dangers and that a child could be invaded by either natural or supernatural sources. In fact, very young children who had not yet eaten corn were considered pure, able to communicate with the gods in direct ways. After children had eaten corn, which meant that they had begun to internalize the fruits of the earth and the cultivation of nature by human effort (and also to internalize the forces of death because something of the earth had been killed to feed them), education became the key to gaining strength and knowledge to one day become part of the economic and social community.

The direction this education would take was determined early in the child's life, in fact, twenty days after birth. At this time, the parents chose what kind of education they wanted their child to have and then took the infant to the appropriate temple or school. The parents of a child destined for the priesthood took gifts of cloaks, loincloths, and food to the priests at the *calmecac* (school for priests), where they presented the infant. The following prayer was said:

Our Lord, Lord of the Near and Close, [this child] is your property, he is your venerable child, your venerable child. We place him under your power, your protection with other venerable children; because you will teach him, educate him, because you will make eagles, make ocelots of them because you educate him for our mother, our father, Tlaltecuhtli, Tonatiuh. Now we dedicate him to Yohualli, to Ehecatl, Tlacatl, Telpochtli, Yaotzin, Titlacahuan, to Tezcatlipoca. (Carrasco, 94)

The pact between the family, the gods, and the temple was sealed by incisions made in the body of the child. These physical marks were visible signs of a spiritual change. The lower lips of boys were cut open and a jewel was inserted. Girls were initiated when small cuts were made with obsidian blades in their breasts and hips. These

DOMESTIC LIFE

LIFE CYCLES

England

Spain

Italy

Ottoman Empire

Maya

Aztec

Inca

incisions signified that they had been initiated into the lifelong educational process upon which their lives depended.

The first ritual of a person's life came soon after birth. In a scene from the *Codex Mendoza* of how a child was treated and named soon after birth, a mother who has recently given birth is seated next to a cradle where her infant lies with four flower symbols above it. Four days after birth, the midwife, who played a major role in Aztec culture, took the naked child to the courtyard of the house, where a ritual cleansing took place. The midwife had prepared a mat of rushes or reeds with a small earthen tub of water, and she bathed the infant. She breathed upon the water, made the child taste it, touched the baby's chest and head with the water and said, "My youngest one, my beloved youth. . . . Enter, descend into the blue water, the yellow water. . . . Approach thy mother Chalchiuhtlicue, Chalchiuhtlatonac! May she receive thee. . . . May she cleanse thy heart; may she make it fine, good. May she give thee fine, good conduct!"

When Aztec infants were taken for their first bath, the appropriate symbols were placed in their hands. If the child were a boy, a shield would be placed in his left hand and an arrow in his right hand. After the bath, the midwife would tell the three boys who assisted her to call out loudly the new name of the baby who had just been cleaned. Then the umbilical cord was taken and buried with the symbols the child had carried to the bath. For boys, the umbilical cord and the little shield and arrows were carried to a battlefield and buried in the ground. For girls, the umbilical cord and a female symbol would be buried at home under the metate, or stone for grinding corn.

When a child was four years old, his or her parents became more specific in the tasks they wanted their child to carry out, and girls and boys began wearing different clothes appropriate to their gender. This was the year that children underwent a special growth ritual that was repeated every four years in the month of Izcalli (Growth). Children of both sexes born during the previous four years were purified by fire and had their earlobes pierced and earrings inserted. The ceremony was called Quinquechanaya (they stretch their necks), in which the children were lifted by their foreheads and had their limbs stretched. Another ceremony held every 260 days, on the day 4 Movement, saw the children's noses, necks, ears, fingers, and legs pulled to encourage proper growth during the next 260-day cycle.

At the age of four, mothers began to teach girls the fundamentals of weaving, and fathers guided boys beyond the confines of the home and had them assist in water carrying. At five, boys helped in toting light loads of firewood and carrying light bundles of goods to the *tianquiztli*, or neighborhood marketplace. This allowed them to greet people, watch the process of exchanges in the market, and meet other children. Girls began to spin with their mothers, learning how to sit, use their hands, and manipulate the cotton.

Between the ages of 7 and 10, boys were given nets to fish with, while girls continued to learn how to spin and cook. Young girls were already proficient in their labor and art by this age and were supervised rather than instructed by their mothers. Children got well into line by their 13th and 14th years. Boys were responsible for carrying firewood from the hills and are depicted transporting sedges, bulrushes, and other grasses for the household and fishing successfully in their canoes. Girls would grind maize and make tortillas for their parents and are shown weaving, cooking, and effectively handling the different foods, utensils, and life of the kitchen. In fact, a girl who could grind corn and make the *atole* drink was considered a maiden of marriageable age.

When Aztec children reached the age of 15, they embarked on an important period of transition in their lives: a transition of space, activity, and religious and social responsibility. At this time, parents were required to bring their teenager to a neighborhood school (which they had selected shortly after the child's birth) and initiate the next stage of his or her educational process. From this moment on, children would grow into a new identity that required intense discipline, the strength to face physical and spiritual ordeals, and the capacity to acquire the trusted knowledge of the society.

One of the most meaningful transitions for Aztec youth was the marriage ceremony, which involved families, friends, matchmakers, feasts, soothsayers, and, of course, speeches. Marriages typically occurred when young women reached the age of 15, though the young men were usually older, around 20, when they had finished their formal education. As with all rites of passage, the ritual of marriage involved days and acts of preparation, a special space for the ceremony, elders who imparted sacred teachings and moments, and symbols of the profound change taking place.

One of the most important preparations involved the family consultation with a soothsayer, who helped pick a favorable day for a wedding. Good days for weddings included the day signs Reed, Monkey, Alligator, Eagle, and House. Prior to this choice, the prospective bride and groom both had received instructions from their parents on how to prepare themselves for marriage by remaining chaste so that they would have their full sexual potency when the knot was tied.

 Snapshot

An Aztec Father's Advice to His Son on Marriage

Take heed, O my son. . . . For the lord of the near, of the nigh, hath said, thou art ordained one woman for one man . . . thou art not to devour, to gulp down the carnal life as if thou wert a dog. . . . Then, thereby, thou wilt become strong in the union, in the marriage . . . in thy carnal life thou wilt be rugged, strong, swift, diligent. (Carrasco, 117)

In the process of arranging marriages, as with most things, Aztec society favored males and gave them more power in making their wishes and choices known. For instance, when it was time for a young man to marry, as determined by his parents, who deemed him mature, the family of the youth consulted with him as to which woman they would request. When the choice was determined, a matchmaker, usually an elder woman, was sent to the young woman's home to discuss the possibility with her family. To explore the possibility fully, the matchmaker traditionally visited the family for five days. We know that the parents of young women gave careful thought to their daughters' futures and traditionally asked, "Will she move the humble one, the unembittered one, the unseasoned one? And if at times they will be poor, if her heart will suffer pain and affliction, how will he regard the maiden?" In other words, when difficult days came, how would their daughter be treated? If the match was pleasing to both families, then the wedding day was set and formal preparations began.

Strenuous efforts went into the preparation of a feast that included tamales, corn, cacao (chocolate), sauces, pulque (also known as *octli*, the fermented juice of the maguey plant), turkeys, tobacco, and many gifts. Most important, perhaps, a wedding space was chosen and laid out around the sacred hearth without which a wedding could not take place. All homes and temples had hearths where Xiuhtecuhtli (the fire god) lived, ensuring warmth, cooked food, and the vital soul force of *tonalli*, which emanated throughout the building. Prior to the feast, libations and morsels of food were offered to the fire god. Formal invitations were sent to friends and family on the day before the wedding feast, and by noon the next day the guests assembled and placed their gifts before the hearth. Elders were permitted to drink pulque in generous quantities; they would inevitably get drunk by sundown, when the wedding ceremony began.

The Wedding Ceremony. This drawing has two different scenes. In one, the bride-to-be is carried to the groom's house, surrounded by torch-bearers. In the other, the capes of the bride and groom are tied together. Note the elders, drunk on the pulque liquor, depicted as speaking divine utterances. From the *Codex Mendoza*, courtesy of Frances F. Berdan and Patricia Reiff Anawait.

As sunset approached, the bride was bathed by the women in her family. Filled with emotion, they washed her with soap, perfumed her, decorated her with red feathers, and sprinkled her face with red or yellow colors. She was covered with a *huipilli* (a kind of cape) and a head cloth. Following instructions from her elders, she was lifted on the back of a woman who carried her, amid a procession of two rows of people carrying torches, to the groom's house. "And all the woman's kinsmen went in concourse about her; they went surrounding her; it was as if the earth rumbled behind her. And as they accompanied her, it was as if all eyes were fixed upon her; all the people looked at her."

The young woman, who had undergone a steady ritual transformation—she had a new appearance and was moved to a new social place—then entered into the heart of the ceremony that would give her a new identity. She was placed on a large woven reed mat, facing her husband-to-be, in front of the burning hearth. The mother of the groom placed a new *huipilli* on the bride and gave a similar gift to her mother. The bride's mother tied a cape on the groom and placed a new loincloth in front of him. Then, the matchmakers came forward and actually "tied the knot" by tying a corner of the groom's cape and the bride's new *huipilli* together. The mother of the groom washed the bride's mouth, set out tamales and sauce in bowls, and fed her four mouthfuls. The bride then fed the groom four mouthfuls. The matchmakers then led the young couple to a bedchamber, closed the door for four days, and stood watch outside. On the fifth day, the young married couple came out, and feasting, dancing, and exchanges of gifts by in-laws took place as the newlyweds heard more speeches about their new duties to one another and their responsibilities as adults. The wedding feast ended as the families returned to their homes "content . . . feeling good in their hearts."

Death is one part of life that all must go through. Every aspect of the passage from life to death and the destiny of an individual's souls (for the Aztecs believed that each human being had not one but three souls) was marked by rites that assisted in the dangerous and powerful passage. In simple terms, death was a part of life in that (1) it accompanied humans every day of their earthly existence (in a partial way), (2) it was one of the stages of the existence of the human soul, and (3) the states of death and life were parts of the cycle of regeneration.

The three souls controlled different aspects of a person. The *tonalli*, located in the head, was the soul of will and intelligence; the *teyolia*, located in the heart, was the soul of fondness and vitality; and the *ihiyotl*, located in the liver, was the soul of passion, luminous gas, and aggression. All three were gifts from the gods deposited in the human body, but they were also found in animals, plants, and objects. At the time of death, these three souls in the human body dispersed into different regions of the universe. Although the texts about this separation of souls are not always consistent, it appears that they could go to one of four places: (1) Mictlan, which was in the underworld, for those who died an ordinary death; (2) the Sky of the Sun, for warriors who died in combat, people sacrificed to the sun, and women who died while giving birth for the first time; (3) Tlalocan, the rain god's mountain paradise, for those whose death was caused by water or water-related forces like frost or cold sicknesses; or (4) Chichihualcuauhco, which was exclusively reserved for infants who died while still nursing from their mothers, that is, who had not yet eaten from the earth.

After the death of the body, it took extended periods of time for the souls to reach their destination. It took 4 years to reach Mictlan, which was the lowest of the 9 levels, but only 80 days to reach the Sky of the Sun, where the souls of warriors accompanied the solar god on his daily journey. During this time, the mourners carried out ritual offerings to assist the souls. Once the warrior's soul arrived in the Sky of the Sun, or Tonatiuh Ilhuicatl, the mourners could bathe and groom themselves for the first time in 80 days.

Still another funerary ritual was designed to keep some of the souls of the deceased near the living family. Before cremation, locks of hair were cut from the top of the head of the deceased and placed (along with hair cut during the first days of the deceased's life) with an effigy of the person in a box or earthen vessel, which was kept in the home or in the temple of the *calpulli*. This refers specifically to the *tonalli* soul (which resided in the head), which would continue to give vitality and strength to the family for years (Carrasco, 92–126).

To read about life cycles in 20th-century Latin America, see the Latin America entry in the section "Family Life" in chapter 2 ("Domestic Life") in volume 6 of this series.

FOR MORE INFORMATION

Berdan, F. F., and P. Rieff Anawalt, eds. *The Codex Mendoza*. 4 vols. Berkeley: University of California Press, 1992.

Carrasco, D., with S. Sessions. *Daily Life of the Aztecs: People of the Sun and Earth.* Westport, Conn.: Greenwood, 1998.

Soustelle, J. *Daily Life of the Aztecs: On the Eve of the Spanish Conquest.* Trans. Patrick O'Brien. Stanford: Stanford University Press, 1970.

INCA

For the Incas, the most significant developments in life were the child's first haircut, puberty, marriage, and death. All marked important transitions in the individual's life, and the Incas celebrated them with important rituals.

No special event marked the birth of a child. A woman simply went to the nearest stream and bathed herself and the newborn. She then resumed her duties around the household. After four days the baby was placed in a cradle, where it spent most of its time until it could walk.

It was an interesting custom of the Incas not to name a child until it was weaned from its mother's breast, around one year of age. This important event was associated with the child's first haircut. A great party was given for friends and relatives of the child's parents, with much drinking and dancing. At the end of the party the oldest male relative cut a small piece of the child's hair and its nails, and gave it a name. Then other relatives cut off a lock of hair and each gave the child a gift. The nails and hair were carefully kept. The name given to the child at this ceremony was not his or her permanent name; he or she received a new one upon reaching maturity.

Childhood was spent learning the activities of the household. When boys were old enough and strong enough, they would help in the fields and with tending animals. Girls would help with the many household tasks of cooking, cleaning, making clothing, and probably taking care of younger brothers and sisters.

The end of childhood and the beginning of adulthood were marked differently for boys and girls. A girl became a woman at her first menstruation, and a ceremony was held to mark this notable transition. The girl was restricted to her house for three days, eating virtually nothing except a little raw corn on the third day. On the fourth day relatives assembled at her house, and she was bathed by her mother, who also braided her hair. She then put on new clothes and went out to serve her relatives food and drink. The most important uncle then gave her a permanent name and she received gifts from all involved.

A common puberty ritual was held for all boys reaching the age of 14, although the event only roughly coincided with the onset of puberty for the participants. For boys of the royal class living in the capital of Cuzco, the ritual took place in December at the same time as the Capac Raymi festival. The ceremony actually was a series of activities spread out over three weeks, with preparations lasting a good deal longer. Mothers had to prepare fine new garments to be worn at the different activities, a task that must have begun months in advance.

In November the boys made a pilgrimage to the sacred mountain of Huanacauri, located outside Cuzco. The purpose of the trip was to ask the spirit of the mountain for permission to perform the puberty ceremony. Each boy brought along a llama, which was sacrificed by slitting its throat. The llama's blood was smeared on the boy's face by a priest. Then each participant was given a sling to signify his new status as a warrior. Much dancing followed; and the boys had to do certain chores, such as collecting straw for their relatives to sit on and chewing the corn for preparing the *chicha* (maize beer) for the ceremonies to come.

During the puberty ceremony the boys again made a pilgrimage to Huanacauri to make more sacrifices of llamas. The boys were whipped on their legs by relatives on the return home, as a means of making them strong and brave. The participants then performed a sacred dance, after which they drank some of the *chicha* they had helped to prepare previously. A week of rest was followed by another series of sacrifices, beatings, and dancing at the hill of Anahuarque, located near Huanacauri. The boys then participated in a race from the top of the hill to the bottom (the race often resulted in falls, some of them serious). At the end, each boy was given *chicha* by girls from the same royal class.

The final part of the puberty ceremony involved a trip to other hills near Cuzco where the boys were given loincloths, formally marking them as men. Then the boys traveled to a sacred spring called Callispuquio, where relatives gave them their weapons: the most important uncle gave a shield, a sling, and a mace. Other relatives gave gifts and advice on how to act as a man and as a proper Inca. The final activity was the piercing of the boys' ears for wearing the earplugs that were the hallmark of Inca nobility. This marked the participant as a warrior.

Inca nobles and other privileged individuals could have more than one wife, although it is uncertain how many nobles other than the king actually had multiple wives. There was always a distinction between the principal wife and secondary ones. The principal wife was married in a ceremony, whereas the secondary ones were simply taken into the household. A secondary wife could not become a principal wife even if the original principal wife died. This custom prevented jealousy and perhaps even murder of a principal wife by secondary wives.

The Incas believed that all their kings were directly descended from Inti, the Sun, the principal god of the Incas. Therefore the kings were considered to be divine. For this reason it was important to keep the bloodline of the kings as pure as possible. To ensure this, among the later Inca kings the principal wife, or *coya*, always had to be a full sister of the king. However, the king could also have as many other wives as he wished, and it was from those wives that the members of the *panacas* (royal houses) were conceived. For nonroyal *ayllus* (families), marriage to a sister was not necessary because the founding members were not divine.

Apparently, marriages were arranged either by the couple themselves or by parents. Women married between the ages of 16 and 20; men married around age 25. The marriage ceremony itself was relatively simple. The groom and his family traveled to the home of the bride, whose family formally presented her to them. The groom's family accepted her by placing a sandal on her foot; it was made of wool if the bride was a virgin or of grass if she wasn't. (The Spanish writers are silent about how this was known. It *is* known that virginity

Mummy of an Inca King. Since kings were thought to be divine, their bodies were preserved and brought out to participate in major rituals. Note how the clothing and the upright sitting position make the mummy seem alive. The circular headdress links the king with the sun and moon shown in the picture. Picture by Guaman Poma.

was not a requirement of marriage.) Then the families proceeded to the home of the groom. There the bride presented him with gifts, and their families lectured them on the duties and responsibilities of family life. As with other ceremonies, the marriage ended with a feast and presentation of gifts to the newlyweds.

The final ritual of the life cycle was the funeral for the dead. Upon dying, an individual was wrapped in a shroud. Part of the person's belongings were burned and the rest were buried with the body. Mourners did a slow dance around the body before burial took place. Afterward, women relatives cut their hair and wore their cloaks over their heads as a symbol of mourning, and other relatives wore black. The period of mourning for nobles lasted one year. Nobles' funerals were more elaborate versions of the simple one.

Funerals of the kings were especially elaborate, including special treatment of the body and particular ceremonies. At death, the king's body was preserved—probably with herbs. The cold, dry air of the mountains also helped to naturally mummify the body. The eyes were replaced with replicas made of shell. Because the king was thought to be divine, he could not really be considered dead. Therefore the mummified body was kept in his palace, attended by his servants and family members, and brought out to participate in major festivals. The period of mourning lasted one year, during which special songs and poems were written about the king's deeds. These were performed by professional mourners, both men and women. To officially close the period, at the end of the year a special ceremony was held in which people washed away the pain of grief with sooty ashes.

In contrast to modern societies, there were a variety of burial practices in the Andes. No tomb of a noble person has been found; all were probably destroyed by treasure hunters during the time after the Spanish Conquest. Thus we do not know how the nobility buried their dead. In other areas of the Andes, funerary chambers called *chullpas* were built. These were round or rectangular free-standing structures. The bodies were placed in the *chullpas*, which could be used for several individuals (Malpass, 75–93).

To read about life cycles in 20th-century Latin America, see the Latin America entry in the section "Family Life" in chapter 2 ("Domestic Life") in volume 6 of this series.

FOR MORE INFORMATION

Kendall, A. *Everyday Life of the Incas*. New York: Putnam, 1973.

Malpass, M. *Daily Life in the Inca Empire*. Westport, Conn.: Greenwood, 1996.

Rowe, J. "Inca Culture at the Time of the Spanish Conquest." In *Handbook of South American Indians*. Vol. 2, *The Andean Civilizations*, ed. Julian Steward, 183–330. Washington, D.C.: Bureau of American Ethnology Bulletin 143, 1946.

DOMESTIC LIFE

WOMEN'S ROLES

England

Spain

Italy

Ottoman Empire

Maya

Aztec

Inca

Women's Roles

In all of the societies examined here, gender played a major role in determining an individual's activities and expectations. Generally, the woman was expected to be engaged in domestic activities, such as cooking, weaving, and child care, while the man was expected to be engaged with the outside world, through business, labor, and even relaxation. These gender associations therefore not only determined an individual's activities but also the spaces that he or she could occupy. For example, an Italian man might wander unaccompanied into the local inn for a drink and conversation with friends, but it would be scandalous for a well-bred Italian woman to wander in by herself. Instead, she would entertain friends at home. Pictures of parades and other such events often show men marching in the street, while the windows of the houses are crowded with the faces of women. In all of these societies, a man, be it husband or father, was considered the head of the household.

Before laying down hard and fast rules about the opportunities for women, it is important to remember that there were many exceptions to the trends sketched above. Thus, while one might say that women were generally thought of as inferior to men, upper-class women were definitely thought to be superior to lower-class men. It was a common sight for the lady of the house to order male servants about. Some of the most notable exceptions to traditional gender roles are queens, such as Elizabeth I in England or the Maya ruler Lady Kanal Ikal. These women ruled their countries single-handedly. Indeed, Elizabeth was perhaps the most powerful monarch that England had during the 15th and 16th centuries. Priestesses are another example of powerful women. While Christian Europe and the Muslim Ottoman Empire did not have priestesses, female priests were in charge of several important cults in the Americas, such as the cult of the Moon among the Incas, and had considerable influence and prestige as a result. While Europe did not have priestesses, it did have many female mystics and holy people who influenced their local communities and sometimes even kings and popes, as Catherine of Siena had done in the 14th century.

Most women, however, did not rule nations and occupied their time with the usual domestic tasks. These tasks included cooking, cleaning, looking after children, and weaving. Weaving was a particularly important chore in both Europe and the Americas. In the rural households of England, for example, selling spun cloth earned significant amounts of money and was one of the chief ways that many rural families survived. Likewise, among the Incas, the Chosen Women played a large role in the economy through their weaving. Weaving was also important in regular Inca households, and each family was expected to offer one cloth garment per year as tribute to the Inca state.

While wealthy women did many of the same chores as less well-off women, they tended to be more involved in managing the work than in doing the work themselves. Thus a wealthy woman might set the menus for the household and oversee the kitchen staff, but she would not do the actual cooking herself. Wealthy women frequently turned over even the breast-feeding of their own infants to professional wet nurses. Nevertheless, many wealthy women sewed or wove as a means of usefully passing the time. These wealthy women did have more time for leisure, however, and were well known to enjoy literature in the vernacular, at least in Europe. Many of the romantic tales of love and adventure were written especially with a female audience in mind. The ability to read was not essential for enjoying these tales: those who could not read would group around a literate person who would read the story out loud. Such reading could take place even while the women were working, giving their minds something to think about while their hands were busy.

Finally, some mention should be made of the sexual mores expected of women. In both Europe and the Americas, chastity and virginity were particularly prized in women. A woman was expected to refrain from sexual relations until marriage and to remain faithful to her husband after marriage. Theoretically, men were also expected to adhere to this same code of behavior, but society sometimes cast a blind eye on male misbehavior. In part, more attention was paid to female chastity since unchastity could become very noticeable in a woman: a woman could become pregnant while the man could still pretend not to have done anything wrong. A family might attempt to rectify this situation by getting the name of the man from a pregnant daughter and forcing the man to marry her. In general, however, society determined that preventive action was the best method, and nubile women from well-off backgrounds were closely chaperoned and usually sequestered indoors away from the gazes of any possible seducers. Such measures reinforced the general idea that the woman's place, for her own safety, was in the home.

~*Lawrence Morris*

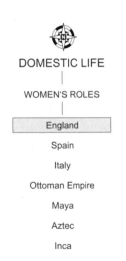

DOMESTIC LIFE

WOMEN'S ROLES

England

Spain

Italy

Ottoman Empire

Maya

Aztec

Inca

ENGLAND

The status of every Renaissance English person was governed by gender even more than by social class. In fact, gender was a clearer factor: social class can be vague and flexible, but gender is obvious and permanent.

According to a proverb that was current during the Renaissance, England was "the hell of horses, the purgatory of servants, and the paradise of women." The phrase is highly revealing. On the one hand, it confirms the observations of contemporary visitors from the Continent who remarked that English women were particularly free and had substantial control over their own households. At the same time, it reminds us that women, like horses and servants, were expected to be in a position of subordination. The Renaissance political theorist Sir Thomas Smith, in his *De Republica Anglorum* (On the English State), offered this view of a woman's role in society:

Women . . . nature hath made to keep home and to nourish their family and children, and not to meddle with matters abroad, nor to bear office in a city or commonwealth no more than children or infants.

Whereas a male child might have some expectation of moving to a position of relative social and economic independence at some point in his life, a girl would exchange subordination to her father for subordination to an employer or to a husband. Only in widowhood was a woman legally recognized as an independent individual. A widow took over as head of her husband's household; if he left her sufficient means to live on, she might do quite well, perhaps taking over his trade, and she would be free to remarry or not as she chose.

Yet the theory was rather harsher than the practice. Women played a very important role in the Elizabethan economy, a fact that must have enhanced their real status. They sometimes even served as churchwardens or manorial officials. Even if husbands believed that God had placed them in authority over their wives, husbands' power could not be exercised through sheer force, as recognized in Nicholas Breton's advice on how a husband should treat a wife:

Cherish all good humors in her: let her lack no silk, crewel, thread, nor flax, to work on at her pleasure, force her to nothing, rather prettily chide her from her labor, but in any wise commend what she doeth: if she be learned and studious, persuade her to translation, it will keep her from idleness, and it is a cunning kind task: if she be unlearned, commend her to housewifery, and make much of her carefulness, and bid her servants take example at their mistress. . . . At table be merry to her, abroad be kind to her, always be loving to her, and never be bitter to her, for patient Griselda [a legendary figure famous for obedience to her husband] is dead long ago, and women are flesh and blood. (Singman, 18)

Although the economy was organized around men, women played a crucial role in the economic life of the country. In fact, both husband and wife were expected to work, although she was normally engaged in labor that could be done at home. One of her primary responsibilities was tending the family livestock. People often owned cattle; perhaps three-quarters of agricultural laborers had at least one cow, and even townsfolk would keep one on the town fields. Other common domestic animals were pigs, goats, sheep, chicken, ducks, geese, and pigeons. The woman's responsibility for the animals meant that she was also in charge of making cheese and butter, as well as collecting eggs from the poultry.

The woman also had the care of the garden, a common feature of both rural and urban households. During harvest and haymaking time, a country woman might assist in the fields, since the pressures of time required as many hands as possible. She would also be involved in winnowing the grain after it was harvested. In addition, the woman was responsible for such domestic tasks as cooking, brewing, mending, and cleaning, and she often had some basic medical skills as well. Already in this period, women were often involved in elementary teaching. Women also engaged in various home industries, especially the spinning of wool thread. Knitting was another means by which a woman might earn extra money. As men had to work in the fields, the task of traveling to the market to buy and sell goods often fell to the woman. In towns, women engaged in a wide variety of work: they were especially likely to be employed as seamstresses, laundresses, and street vendors. The wife of a craftsman or tradesman often helped her husband in his work; and if he died, she might carry on the business herself. There were even a few instances of women plying crafts or trades in their own right in the city, but these were quite rare.

The wool industry was particularly important in Renaissance England, and very many women were involved daily in preparing wool. This work was time intensive and involved several steps. Once the sheep were shorn and the wool had been washed, it had to be carded. This involved stroking the wool between a pair of special brushes so that all the strands were running parallel, free of knots and tangles.

The carded wool was then spun into thread. Spinning involved drawing out wool from the carded mass and spinning it so that it was tightly twisted. (Wool fibers are covered with microscopic scales; when twisted in this way, the scaly strands cling to each other, making it possible for them to form thread.) Woolen thread could be spun with a drop spindle, essentially a disk with a stick passing through the center. The spindle was suspended from the wool fibers and set spinning, which caused the fibers to twist into thread. Alternatively, wool might be spun with a hand-cranked spinning wheel—the treadle wheel was used only for spinning flax into linen thread.

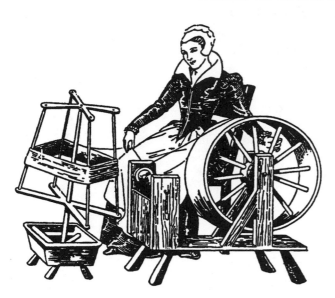

A Woman at Work. Note the hand-turned spinning wheel; spinning and weaving were perhaps the most common and the most economically important female activities. Picture by Herbert Norris, *Costume and Fashion*, 1924.

After spinning, the thread was woven into cloth on a horizontal loom. The cloth then had to be *fulled*, or washed, to shrink and felt it. This made the fibers join more tightly with each other, so that the fabric was both stronger and more dense, and therefore better at keeping out the English cold and rain. In fact, Elizabethan wools were so heavily felted that it was unnecessary even to hem them—they did not normally unravel. Sometimes the wool would be left its natural color, but often it would be dyed. This might happen as the very last stage, but sometimes it was done before the wool was even spun—hence the expression "dyed in the wool."

Not all time was spent on work, however. According to the Swiss tourist Thomas Platter, women were as likely to frequent taverns and alehouses as men: one might even invite another man's wife to such an establishment, in which case she would bring several other female friends and the husband would thank the other man for his courtesy afterward.

Games were often segregated by gender. Women did not engage in martial, dangerous, or extremely vigorous sports such as fencing, football, or tennis. However, they might take part in lighter physical games such as blindman's buff or barley break. Games with minimal physical activity such as bowls and card games were especially common pastimes for women; and they often participated as spectators at sports that they did not play themselves, even violent sports like bearbaiting (Singman, 17–18, 29–31, 141, 160).

To read about women's roles in Chaucer's England, see the Europe entry in the section "Women" in chapter 2 ("Domestic Life") in volume 2 of this series; for 18th-century England, see the entry on England in the section "Men and Women" in chapter 2 ("Domestic Life") in volume 4 of this series; for Victorian England, see the Victorian England entry in the section "Women" in chapter 2 ("Domestic Life") in volume 5 of this series.

FOR MORE INFORMATION

Bradford, G. *Elizabethan Women*. Cambridge, Mass.: Houghton Mifflin, 1936.
Camden, C. C. *The Elizabethan Woman*. Houston: Elsevier, 1952.
Singman, J. L. *Daily Life in Elizabethan England*. Westport, Conn.: Greenwood, 1995.

SPAIN

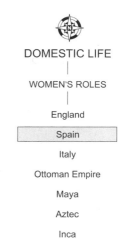

Gender did not play an important role in the first few years of life in Spain. Young children, regardless of gender, lived fairly similar lives. Until six or seven, a child's daily life revolved around sleep, food, and play. At this age, the sacrament of confirmation marking the child's official admission to the church as a full member was given, and around this age girls and boys began to be steered by parents and society into their own differentiated spheres. While boys would go off to help out their fathers around the farm or as apprentices in the towns, young girls would learn how to look after the house and domestic responsibilities. Girls were also admitted to some trades, however, such as the makers of lace, veils, and silk ribbons.

Urban girls, between the ages of 12 and 20 from well-off, socially oriented families, referred to as *doncellas* (maidens or virgins), were expected to be chaste, obedient, modest, and retiring and to maintain a serene countenance, downcast eyes, and a serious demeanor. Enclosed behind the bricks and mortar of the house and locked doors, they were protected from all possible dangers that might impugn family honor. Some of these girls spent their young lives indoors, even hidden from view when visitors called at the house, but others were allowed to attend church, their faces covered with a mantilla (a long veil), where they might be afforded a small opportunity to socialize with the opposite sex under the watchful eye of an escort, sometimes rented for the occasion. A note might be surreptitiously passed between admiring couples and coquettish glances exchanged.

Processions, religious festivals, and pilgrimages afforded other opportunities to escape the house, and girls with lenient fathers were sometimes allowed to visit the homes of girlfriends, where they could chat, eat fruit, and drink chocolate. Moral critics and the church frowned upon even this activity, which gave females too much freedom, claiming it was offensive to God.

When a girl was old enough to marry, she went from the confinement of her parents' home to that of her husband. Most houses had windows that overlooked a patio or garden and not the street, so women of this elite group had little contact with the outside world except, perhaps, through the servants.

With few exceptions, marriage was for life. The couple was required to cohabit, and neither was permitted to enter a monastery or convent or become celibate without the consent of the other. Divorce was not sanctioned. On occasion a marriage could be annulled if it had been invalid in the first place—for example, on the basis of bigamy or close kinship—or if it was never consummated. An official separation, releasing the couple from the requirement of cohabitation, was also allowed in matters of cruelty or adultery. Remarriage was permitted on the death of one of the partners. The purpose of marriage in the view of the church was procreation; abortion, contraception, or sexual acts that would not lead to conception were, therefore, prohibited.

In practice the woman in the marriage was a subordinate member. The husband could use corporal punishment to discipline her, just as he might do to a servant, with no fear of communal or ecclesiastical disapproval. The wife's relatives, however, might not be so tolerant.

Women remained at home looking after the children, tending to the requirements of the house, sewing or embroidering, or sometimes, if they were sufficiently educated, reading some romantic or devout book. This tiresome existence would at times be lightened by female neighbors calling in for a visit and a chat about the newest fashions or scandal. Kneeling on the carpet or pillows, they could exchange the latest news while sipping chocolate or chewing pieces of *búcaro*, a kind of clay imported from the Indies for making pots but with an aromatic flavor and medicinal attributes. *Búcaro* was so popular among Spanish women that their confessors sometimes imposed upon them the penance of abstinence from

Women Working. The kitchen was one of the main rooms for women's work. This picture contrasts strikingly the worlds of women and men. In the dark foreground, a woman instructs a servant; in the bright rear, a seated male instructs two junior members of the family. The contrasting use of colors and positions makes an emotional and political statement. Velaquez, *Kitchen Scene*. © National Gallery Collection. By kind permission of the Trustees of the National Gallery, London/CORBIS.

it for a day or two. A man's social life, for the most part, was spent outside the family circle and the home with male companions and acquaintances, gossiping in the open air or playing cards in the taverns.

As already mentioned, the upbringing of infants fell to the mother and other females in the household such as sisters or aunts, and until the child was about six years old, it was seldom outside the circle of the women. Breast-feeding the baby was considered the only safe means of ensuring a healthy child since animal milk was thought to be potentially hazardous for a delicate digestive system. If the mother was not capable of this method of nourishment or preferred not to perform it for whatever reason, the baby was given over to a wet nurse if the family could afford it. She either lived in, or the infant was sent to her domicile. Generally, she would be a woman who had lost her own infant. With the high rate of mortality among babies, there were always more women in a position to nurse a child than there were children to be nursed.

When the husband died, a widow could count at least on the return of her dowry (if it had not been squandered), along with whatever else had been promised her in the original contract or the will. Widows made up about 10 percent of the population in any given community and were the most disadvantaged of all the poor, especially when they had small children.

In rural hamlets and villages, widows whose husbands had been killed in war, in accidents, or by disease were numerous and their options were few, and those left with little assets apart from the cottage they lived in often subsisted on charity from the parish church and neighbors or from grown-up sons and daughters. They collected what leftover food they could after the harvest and gathered wild fruit. They had the option to remarry if the opportunity arose, but like most country widows, they often appeared old and haggard from heavy toil by age 30. A last resort was to move to the large cities and join the ranks of urban widows begging on the street corners (Anderson, 160–64).

FOR MORE INFORMATION

Anderson, J. *Daily Life during the Spanish Inquisition*. Westport, Conn.: Greenwood, 2002.
Casey, J. *Early Modern Spain: A Social History*. London: Routledge, 1999.

ITALY

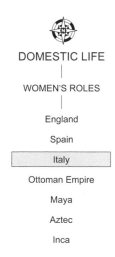

Maleness and femaleness, traits inborn and fixed, were crucial to status. Although class was even stronger, gender was a powerful discriminant. Males were destined to rule and to lord over females. Men had formal authority, electoral franchise, and full legal capacity to bear witness, to guarantee, and to contract. Females did have legal rights, but everywhere they were lesser. In church and state, males ruled and manned all offices. Female power was also real but more often informal: social, familial, and emotional. Women made their presence felt by influencing persons, and sometimes, through them, institutions over which, as females, they lacked statutory authority. In social dealings, women, though outranking class inferiors, were expected to defer to males of their own social class. It is true that courtiers at their games and lovers paying court played at putting ladies on a pedestal; nevertheless, everyone recognized the transparent artificiality of such an inversion of the proper order of the world.

While infants, the lives of boys and girls were not much different: they ate, slept, and played. As time passed, however, the boys would be expected to help their fathers in the fields or to take a trade, while girls would learn the many skills needed to run a household smoothly. Sexual maturity marked a major change for girls. For them, the acquisition of adult physical capacities led not to an expansion of their social range but to risk and restriction. From the heritage of the ancient Romans, 12 was the official age of female puberty, and so it remained in the 14th century. In the 15th century, experts, perhaps observing girls of their era more closely, tended to expect the onset of menstruation later, at age 13 or 14. The church nonetheless retained the traditional age of 12 as the minimal canonical age for a girl to marry.

The notion that women as young as 12 could legally consent to marriage meant at the same time that they could consent to sex. Their sexual potential, coupled with general recognition of women as creatures of desire and poor self-control, made it credible that even a young adolescent who lost her virginity or got pregnant might have done so willingly. In a law court, an adolescent girl was no longer presumed innocent; she had to convince the judges that she was not complicit. The specter of illicit sex alarmed a young female's keepers; protecting her from abusers, other seducers, and her own weakness required keeping her as far from trouble as possible. Guardians, be they fathers, mothers, brothers, masters, or mistresses, were supposed to restrict her public movements and supervise her contact with men. The application of these principles varied with social status. The elite could afford to seclude its nubile daughters, but working families had no such luxury. The story writer Bandello conjured a tragic tale of a poor girl who was raped because she had to work alone in the fields to help support her family; afterward, all she could do to save their honor was drown herself in the river. Though the story was perhaps fiction, the dangers were real, as were the consequent restraints on young women's freedom. Yet we should not exaggerate their degree; adolescent girls were not routinely locked up and shut away.

For women especially, and often for children and dependent young men as well, honor, as virtue, often hinged less on what one did than on what one refrained from. Self-restraint garnered praise. This self-checking looked like a kind of voluntary shame, a self-imposed sensitivity to the judgment of others. Its serene effect reversed that of *vergogna*, the involuntary shame imposed by disapproval. Italians called this good shame *pudore*, just what the impudent lacked. In women and subordinate males, the marks of good shame were a quiet bearing, modestly downcast eyes, and a self-conscious, virtuous blush.

Although voluntary shame was important to female honor, the truly crucial quality, closely related to it, was chastity. In a sense, chastity was a passive virtue, quite unlike the active virtues of generosity and fortitude so central for males. At first glance, chastity was what one did not do—that is, anything the least bit sexual outside marriage or in public. But hitched to *pudore*, chastity was also active in that an honorable woman was expected to express her self-control in countless words and gestures. She was, for instance, to cast down her eyes, rein in her movements, bridle her tongue, curb her laughter, hide her chest and limbs, and shun suggestive talk. Especially in the upper classes where this issue was most felt, every social exchange made a woman calibrate assertion and self-checking.

Female and male honor intersected in the collective reputation of the house and family. Nothing so distilled the honor of males as their capacity to keep their women chaste. The task fell first to fathers and husbands. Brothers and other kinsmen might also shoulder it. By general agreement, a strong man, because he could drive seducers off, could guard a house's chastity. Thus a daughter's seduction or a wife's adultery brought unspeakable shame, for both acts proved a man's weakness. By the code, a man of honor should marry off virgin daughters. Nevertheless, if, to his misfortune and hers, a nubile girl lost her virginity, there were remedies. If the father could take steps, he need not languish in lifelong infamy nor was the daughter doomed to prostitution. Though it might cost a larger dowry, a husband often could be found. A compromised woman without a dowry was in a rougher fix. In some cities, she might spend some time mending her honor in a monastery-like house of reform before being married off on charity or placed in service. Either destination respectably absolved the father of his responsibility and placed the girl under suitable discipline. Everyone assumed that a woman with no male keeper, given weak female will and strong female appetite, easily succumbed to seduction, bringing calamity on herself and her family.

When a woman did do wrong and brought disaster home, according to honor's notions, her protector could make the damage good. He had several options, which depended on the facts at hand. The harshest solution was to kill both lovers. Fathers sometimes did this drastic deed; it is hard to say how often. When such murders do surface in the records of the courts, the family's grief and its enduring sense of vindication, the community's grim yet sorrowful condonement of the slaughter, and the law's leniency all are patent. Murder aside, the adultery of a wife was a calamity not easily resolved. Nevertheless, honor notwithstanding, Italy was not littered with the corpses of unchaste women. Men often found ways of compromising with what might seem the iron laws of a retributive ethic. The neatest solution, if an unmarried daughter erred, was to force a marriage on her seducer. Second best, but still passable, was to compel the guilty man, in expiation, to cough up a generous dowry, making good the lost virginity, to help the young woman wed another despite her depreciated purity.

Gender also determined where women and men could go. Women claimed some places, at certain times, as their own; men dominated other locations where women usually felt out of place. In the Mediterranean region, these gendered differences, though most marked in Muslim countries, were felt in many Christian zones. In general, domestic space, especially the kitchen, was female, while public places—the street, the square, and the inn—were male. But the well and the collective wash tubs (or river bank), though out in the open, were places frequented largely by the women, and the market often had its female sellers. Certainly these general patterns held for Renaissance Italy. That is why so often in paintings of great processions, resolutely male, the windows are full of female faces; the sill was their habitual boundary. In general, the higher the woman's status, the less freely she moved about, and, when she sallied forth, the more she needed a chaperon. In Venice, elite women seldom left the narrow boundaries of their parishes. Village women, on the other hand, roamed widely, picking fruits and olives, fetching water, carrying washing, running errands; they were too useful to coop up at home. Similarly, for need and pleasure, lower-status urban women moved about the streets alone.

The house and domestic space in general was a prime site for play. The basic pleasures of eating, drinking, sleeping, and keeping company often took place at home. Occasionally there would be parties celebrating Carnival or a wedding. But recreation, especially for women, also reached out from domestic space with the eyes, ears, and voice. Women idled at their windows, watching and commenting on the passing theater of street life. For processions, races, and other spectacles, they dressed up to be seen at their sills; they were part of the show. The doorstep was another woman's place; there are countless tales of conversations in the street and of children playing out front under female eyes. Another pleasure was just to soak up a view. In the late 15th century, the Renaissance invented a high porch or gallery called a belvedere: the name means "Nice view!" In general, women's movement was restricted, but they seem to have made the most of it (Cohen and Cohen, 74–75, 91–92, 158, 193–94, 280).

Washing Day. While most women's work took place in the home, some activities, such as washing or harvesting, took place outside. Washing day was an opportunity to meet other women from the area and chat about recent events. Picture by Antonio Tempesta. Roma—Instituto Nazionale della Grafica. By gracious concession of the Ministero per i Beni e le Attività Culturali.

FOR MORE INFORMATION

Cohen, E. S., and T. V. Cohen. *Daily Life in Renaissance Italy.* Wesport, Conn.: Greenwood, 2001.

Gilmore, D., ed. *Honor and Shame and the Unity of the Mediterranean.* Washington, D.C.: American Anthropological Association, 1987.

Ruggiero, G. *The Boundaries of Eros: Sex Crime and Sexuality in Renaissance Venice.* New York: Oxford University Press, 1985.

DOMESTIC LIFE
|
WOMEN'S ROLES
|
England

Spain

Italy

Ottoman Empire

Maya

Aztec

Inca

OTTOMAN EMPIRE

Under the influence of Islam, Ottoman society sought to maintain a strict separation of the sexes in all areas of life. The women's sphere involved maintaining the home and family, while men engaged in economic and other public activities. However, people recognized women's roles as important, and the courts generally respected their rights both in terms of family relationships and in their ability to manage their property without interference. In addition, women's roles could vary based on their social class, as lower-class women worked to support themselves while those of elite households could even play a role in running the state.

In Middle Eastern societies, men and women have historically been separated both physically and legally, trends that continued under Islamic law as interpreted by Ottoman legal scholars. The physical signs of this were the ideal of seclusion, in reality practiced mainly by the upper classes, and the custom of women veiling in public to protect their modesty, which became a regular part of the Ottoman social landscape during the 16th century. Legally, Islamic law made women legal entities but frequently prescribed rights and responsibilities different from those of men, leading to inequality in some areas of life.

Agriculture was the primary occupation of the vast majority of Ottoman citizens, and in rural areas women's labor was considered both necessary and valuable. Land was assigned on the assumption that women would take part in planting and harvesting crops. If the husband of a family died without sons, however, the land was frequently confiscated by the landlords rather than assigned to the widow. In cities, some women worked as entertainers or prostitutes, neither of which was a respected position in society. More commonly, they acted as domestic servants to wealthier households or worked in the textile industry. Those who became servants worked for a fixed term of several years, at the end of which they could either advance within the household or be given a settlement and marry, sometimes far above their station.

Women of the urban artisan class performed the same types of household chores as servant women. The only difference was that they performed these chores in their own family's home instead of someone else's. These middle-class families tended to consist only of a single husband and wife and a few children; hence women had no option other than to do such things themselves. Many, however, took pride in this role, going so far as to have it depicted on their tombstones.

Women of the upper classes supervised their servants, while engaging in the types of leisure activities only they had the time and wealth to enjoy. Women of the upper classes tended to spend much money on mirrors and jewelry, while reading books primarily for pleasure. They also enjoyed going to the baths and having picnics in the countryside. Women in the ruling elite could even play a role in state policy through their influence within the family. In this respect, mothers of the reigning sultan became particularly important.

Women conducted business in much the same way as men did, though they invested more in domestic affairs. Studies show that during the Ottoman period women endowed 35 percent of all Muslim religious foundations, though only rarely did they manage these institutions. Under Islamic law, women retained the rights to their dowries after marriage, and because men were required to support them financially, they were often free to do with it what they wished. When transacting business, women would often go to court with a male guardian or send a male agent in their place to preserve their modesty. For example, when a Jewish ophthalmologist named Lifa sold her house in Jerusalem, she sent a man named Ubayd b. Muhammad as her representative when the matter was verified before the judge.

Women's domestic relations were governed almost entirely by Islamic law. Although all four schools of Islamic law—Hanbali, Maliki, Shafi'i, and Hanafi—were found throughout the empire, the Hanafi was the most influential, and although in many areas it represented the most liberal, with regard to women's rights it was the most restrictive. Marriage in the Ottoman Empire represented a legally binding contract between two people—the husband and the wife—and hence required the consent of both. Fathers could arrange marriage for daughters before they reached puberty, however, under the assumption that they would want what was best for their offspring. Marriage also had to be a joining of equals, which in social terms meant marriage outside of one's class was highly problematic. However, when it did occur, women became of the same social status as their husbands. Men could theoretically marry up to four wives, though in practice only a few could afford to support more than one.

Turkish Woman. The white head scarf indicated that she was unmarried; married women wore black head scarves. © Historical Picture Archive/CORBIS.

In marriage, men were heads of the household, and women had to obey them. However, under the Hanbali school practiced mainly in the Arabian peninsula, women could at the time of marriage add to the contract-binding conditions to ensure certain freedoms as long as they did not violate other aspects of Islamic law. Men were also required to provide their wives with adequate food, clothing, shelter, and opportunities to produce children. In Hanafi law, a woman's right to a divorce was extremely limited and essentially required her to prove the marriage was illegal in the first place. Men, on the other hand, could divorce their wives without cause simply by verbally stating the intent three times. An odd twist was that the divorce was binding even if done in jest or while intoxicated. During the Ottoman period, women who wished a divorce would go before a judge and declare that their husband had done this, thus obtaining the desired result.

Women in the Ottoman Empire thus played an important social and economic role that was respected as such under the law and in social perception. In many areas, such as family law, it remained unequal to that of men; however, women retained control of their property and could even become wealthy and independent with the proper combination of luck and financial skill. In addition, they performed a number of vital tasks in both the rural and urban economy. A number of Islamic religious foundations testify to their wealth and generosity.

To read about women's roles in Medieval Islam, see the Islam entry in the section "Women" in chapter 2 ("Domestic Life") in volume 2 of this series.

~Brian Ulrich

FOR MORE INFORMATION

Cicek, K., ed. *The Great Ottoman-Turkish Civilisation 2: Economy and Society.* Ankara: Yeni Turkiye, 2000.

Dengler, I. C. "Turkish Women in the Ottoman Empire: The Classical Age." In *Women in the Muslim World,* ed. Lois Beck and Nikki Keddie, 229–44. Cambridge: Harvard University Press, 1978.

Esposito, J. L., and N. J. DeLong-Bas. *Women in Muslim Family Law.* 2nd ed. Syracuse, N.Y.: Syracuse University Press, 2001.

Roded, R., ed. *Women in Islam and the Middle East: A Reader.* London: Tauris, 1999.

DOMESTIC LIFE

WOMEN'S ROLES

England

Spain

Italy

Ottoman Empire

Maya

Aztec

Inca

MAYA

Although archaeological evidence for gender roles in the Maya past is sparse, we can reconstruct some role differences on the basis of present-day society. We can assume that in the past, as today, girls were trained to take on the traditional roles associated with wife and mother in the Maya family. Before marriage, young women lived at home with their parents and were expected to follow the customs of modesty. When unmarried women met a man, they turned their backs and stepped aside to allow him to pass. When giving a man food or drink, they were to lower their eyes. In nonelite families women undoubtedly played an essential part in subsistence by collecting firewood, wild foods, and condiments. As they do today, Maya women most likely also tended to household gardens, growing fruits and vegetables. We can also assume that the processing and preparation of food was the responsibility of women. In addition, nonelite women probably engaged in a variety of household crafts, weaving textiles for clothing and making containers of clay, gourds, and other materials. Women probably took surplus food and goods to local markets where they exchanged them for other products. It can also be assumed that women undertook several community-level specializations, such as being midwives and matchmakers. We can assume that many nonelite women served as cooks and servants for the noble and royal families within each kingdom.

Beyond this we do not know how many occupations were open to women in the past. But at the elite level of society we know from both the texts and portraits of Middle Maya Civilization that the wives and mothers of royalty played essential roles in the rituals and other duties of Maya kings. Mothers of kings were vital to the ceremonies held for the designation of the heir to the throne and at the inauguration of the new ruler. The royal histories of Palenque record that two royal daughters assumed the throne in the absence of a male heir and held the position of ruler until their sons were old enough to become kings.

According to Palenque texts, Lady Kanal Ikal ascended the throne in 583 C.E. because her father had no sons. She went on to rule for 20 years, until her death in 604, at which time her son, Ac Kan, took the throne. Ac Kan also died without an heir in 612, however, and the throne passed to his niece, Lady Zac Kuk, who ruled for 3 years until her son Pacal ascended the throne at the age of 12. While these female rulers appear to be exceptional and exist only in the mists of verifiable history, their presence is important for establishing the theoretical possibility of female rule. It should be noted that, according to the creation myth, the patron gods of the Palenque kings had received their power from their mother, the First Mother, who was the origin of all creation. The theoretical female origin of

Weaving. As in today's society, weaving was an important part of a Maya woman's life. This woman uses a belt loom similar to the looms used in the 16th century. © Larry Towell/Magnum Photos.

dynastic rule may also be noted in the Maya glyphs used to note the start of a king's reign. These figures featured a male figure seated in an elevated niche, overseen by the figure of a woman, possibly representing his mother, or even the First Mother. Most women were not kings, however, and life for both Maya men and women meant hard work in cooperation with each other (Sharer, 67, 119–21, 183–84).

To read about women's roles in 19th-century Latin America, see the Latin America entry in the section "Women" in chapter 2 ("Domestic Life") in volume 5 of this series; for 20th-century Latin America, see the Latin America entry in the section "Women" in chapter 2 ("Domestic Life") in volume 6 of this series.

FOR MORE INFORMATION

Sharer, R. J. *Daily Life in Maya Civilization*. Westport, Conn.: Greenwood, 1996.

AZTEC

Differences in gender roles were made early on in an Aztec child's life. Four days after birth, the child would be brought to a ritual bath. Depending on the sex of the child, certain symbolic items would be laid out near the bath. The female symbols were a distaff with a spindle, a basket, and a broom. These objects signified the girl's future role as the keeper of the home: she would be educated into the labor and art of weaving, which was an invaluable part of Aztec life. The act of sweeping, to purify and to contribute to good health, was both a practical and a ritual activity associated with women. Aztec homes were extremely clean, as were the temples, where ritual sweeping was done in service to the gods. The spindle was also a fertility symbol

associated with the capacity of females to bear children. For instance, two spindles attached to cotton fillets were part of the headdress of a fertility goddess. One Aztec riddle went, "What is that which becomes pregnant in only one day? The spindle." After the bath, the female child's umbilical cord would be buried "by the hearth, signifying that the woman was to go nowhere. Her role was to be at home by the fire, by the grinding stone," as Sahagún noted in his 16th-century ethnography of the Aztecs.

The bathing ritual itself was designed to place the girl under the protection of a goddess. The soothsayers selected a positive day, and the family prepared a little skirt, plus the equipment of the little red basket, the spinning whorl, and the batten. The girl was bathed and raised as an offering in the four directions of the cosmos and then raised up and offered to the gods who resided in the celestial realms. She was given water to drink. Each time she was given water, the water was touched to the girl's head, chest, and hands, and when she was placed in the cradle for the first time, a short prayer was said: "Here is the coolness, the tenderness of Chalchiuhtlicue, who is eternally awake. . . . May she go with thee, may she embrace thee, may she take thee in her lap, in her arms, that thou mayest continue watchfully on earth."

> One Aztec riddle went, "What is that which becomes pregnant in only one day?"

Mothers provided instruction for their daughters in the domestic skills. When girls were four years old, their mothers began to teach them the fundamentals of weaving. At five, girls began to spin with their mothers, learning how to sit, use their hands, and manipulate the cotton. By the age of eight, young girls were already proficient in their labor and art and were supervised rather than instructed by their mothers.

When young women reached puberty, known as "the age of discretion," their mothers and fathers spoke to them about how to survive and maintain a life of balance in the critical years immediately ahead. The speeches are eloquent and formal and show the profound concerns and care that parents felt for their offspring. The daughter was addressed as "my precious necklace, my precious feather . . . my creation . . . my blood, my color, my image." The precious image was told to "grasp" why she was alive, why the gods had given her life. First, she was told that life would be a mixture of struggle, hardship, joy, and laughter. The world was difficult and always included weeping and torment. "This is the way things are . . . the earth is not a good place. It is not a place of contentment." But the gods gave humans laughter, sleep, food, strength, force, and also carnal knowledge so that "there would be peopling."

She was told that people must struggle to become responsible adults, workers, rulers, warriors, and home builders and raise families. Good marriages were crucial to this development. The girl was reminded that she was chipped from her mother's womb and that she had to be ever mindful of her family's well-being: "Know that thou comest from someone, thou art descended from someone, that thou wert born by someone's grace." The task of the girl was to be devout, to sleep well but rise early to pray to the gods in the proper fashion. "Seize the broom, be diligent with the sweeping." Here began the art of the woman's life, which was care of the home. "The art of good drink, the art of good food, which is called one's birthright," meant get to work sewing, grinding cornmeal, and cooking; but, as with everything else, do it in Aztec style. This style included a pronounced emphasis on artistic sensitivity. Young women were encouraged to observe and take in the arts of feather working, embroidering, and color-working, or, the creation of art.

The crucial message, however, was sexual abstinence. The young woman was a "precious green stone, yet a precious turquoise," who was to be kept clean, pure, and without sexual experience until a husband was chosen. Concerning her heart, she was told to let "nothing defile it, since it is still untouched, virgin, completely un-twisted, pure and undefiled." In fact, to covet carnal things before marriage was to lead one into a realm of excrement and self-destruction. However, when the right young man came along, the one sent by one of the divinities, meaning a match made in heaven, the young woman must not reject him. The message could not be made any clearer than in this admonition:

But meanwhile present yourself well, look well to your enemy that no one will mock you. Give yourself not to the wanderer, to the restless one who is given to pleasure, to the evil youth. Nor are two, three to know your face, your head. When you have seen the one who together with you he will endure to the end, do not abandon him. Seize him, hang onto him even though he be a poor person, even though he be a poor eagle warrior, a poor ocelot warrior. . . . Our lord, the wise one, the maker, the creator, will dispose for you, will array you. (Carrasco, 108)

The message was plain: wait and plan to marry once, knowing that the gods will reward you if you follow this straight and narrow path.

Marriage was not the only path in life open to women, however. Women also played a significant role in the priesthood. In some cases, an infant girl was taken to the temple by her mother a month or so after birth and dedicated to the priest-hood. The mother would give the priest a censer and copal incense as a sign that the family hoped she would enter a religious vocation when she was older. When she was a mature teenager, she would become a *cihuatlamacazqui*, or woman priest. Priestesses had to be celibate and concentrate intensely on their temple duties and the yearly round of ceremonies they ministered. Some accounts of the sacrificial festivals make it clear that priestesses were essential to the rites. For instance, Och-paniztli, the feast dedicated to the mother goddess Toci ("Our Grandmother"), was directed by a woman priest, while an assistant called Iztaccihuatl ("White Woman"—because she was painted white) was responsible for the decorations, the preparation of the ritual areas, the sweeping of the sacred sites, and the lighting and extinguishing of the ritual fires.

We are fortunate to have some vivid descriptions of these priestesses dressing, dancing, and giving spirit, beauty, and power to the ceremonies. One example comes from the feast of Huey tecuilhuitl, the "Great Feast of the Lords," where we are told,

the women were indeed adorned; they were indeed carefully dressed. All good were their skirts, their shifts which they had put on. Some of their skirts had designs of hearts; some had a mat design like birds' gizzards; some were ornamented like coverlets; some had designs like spirals or like leaves. . . . All had borders, all had fringes; all the women had fringed skirts. And some of their shifts had tawny streamers hanging, some had smoke symbols, some had dark green streamers hanging, some had house designs. . . . And when they danced, they unbound their hair; their hair just covered each one of them like a garment. But they brought braids of their hair across their foreheads. (Sahagún, vol. 2, 102)

During the sacred ceremony of Quecholli, the young priestesses dedicated to the goddess of maize carried seven ears of corn wrapped in cloth throughout parts of the procession. They were transformed into images of the goddess and wore feathers on their arms and legs and had their faces painted with fertility colors. They sang and processed through the streets until sundown, when they tossed handfuls of colored maize kernels and pumpkinseeds in front of the crowds. The people scrambled to get these seeds because they were signs that the coming year would have a good harvest.

Women Defending Their City. Note the scornful gesture of displaying the breasts. This symbol appears in other cultures also; amongst the early Irish, for example, displaying a woman's breast was thought to calm a warrior's fury. From Diego Durán, *Códice Durán*. Mexico City: Arrendadora International, 1990 (facsimile edition).

It was possible for a woman to leave the priesthood to be married. But it was necessary that the suitor make the proper approaches to the family, the temple, and the young woman. The details of this possibility reflect what we are beginning to see throughout our study, namely, that the life of women was very much under the control of male authorities and their families. One text tells us that a priestess could get married "if she were asked in marriage, if the words were said correctly, and if the fathers, the mothers, and all the notables agreed."

Women even took part in war occasionally. When the Spanish were laying siege to Tenochtitlan, the *tlatoani* (chieftain) Cuauhtémoc realized that he did not have enough men to defend the city, so he ordered the women to go up on the rooftops as a sign of strength and to make gestures of scorn to the Spanish. At first the Spanish were afraid due to the great force that appeared before them, but once the Spanish and their allies realized that the force was composed of women, they pressed their attack and vanquished the city. More usually, however, war impacted women by leaving them widowed. Other times, women might be captured in war. Women were often part of the immediate and long-term tribute that a conquered city-state would have to pay to the victorious city-state (Carrasco, 95–108, 142–45).

To read about women's roles in 19th-century Latin America, see the Latin America entry in the section "Women" in chapter 2 "Domestic Life" in volume 5 of this series; for 20th-century Latin America, see the Latin America entry in the section "Women" in chapter 2 ("Domestic Life") in volume 6 of this series.

FOR MORE INFORMATION

Carrasco, D., with S. Sessions. *Daily Life of the Aztecs: People of the Sun and Earth*. Westport, Conn.: Greenwood, 1998.

Sahagún, B. de. *Florentine Codex: General History of the Things of New Spain*. Ed. and trans. A. Anderson and C. Dibble. 13 vols. Santa Fe: School of American Research and University of Utah, 1950–82.

INCA

Less is known about the roles women played in everyday life of the Inca empire than about the roles of men, but it is clear that they were fundamentally important to most aspects of life. The Chosen Women, who will be described below, had important economic, social, and religious roles. The lives of noble women were no doubt easier than those of commoners: they had *yanaconas* (personal servants) to tend to many of the duties assigned to women. Yet fundamental activities such as spinning and weaving were conducted by all women, of high class or low. Principal wives were in charge of running the household and delegating duties to the secondary wives. The principal wives' tasks were more managerial: making sure that the household ran smoothly and that food and drink were prepared to high standards when important individuals were entertained. It probably fell to the secondary wives to do the preparations, especially in households that did not have *yanaconas*.

Women were in charge of other household activities as well, such as preparing meals, cleaning, washing, and making clothing for the family. They also cared for the children until they were old enough to contribute to household activities themselves. This is one reason why infants were strapped to their cradles for so long: to keep the mother's hands free for the other tasks she had to perform.

Although most Spanish chroniclers discuss the significant roles that men had in Inca society, recent interpretations of some of the reports suggest that women had important roles also. Women could own land and herds because inheritance was through both the mother's and the father's side of the family. Thus they controlled certain economic resources, although to what extent is uncertain. Women certainly played key roles in religious activities, as many of the main Inca gods—such as the Moon—were female. The principal leaders for these cults, therefore, were women.

The most famous women, however, were the *acllyaconas*, or Chosen Women. Selected from among conquered peoples in the provinces and from among noble families in Cuzco, they did a series of important jobs for the empire. They were selected for their physical attractiveness at around age 10 then were sent to schools where they learned spinning and weaving, cooking, *chicha* (maize beer) making, and other domestic activities. In the provinces there was a hierarchy of these women based on their physical perfection and social rank. The most perfect were sacrificed to the Inca gods. Next were women, also of high beauty, who might have been daughters of

Weaving. Weaving was a major and important task. Here a woman uses the common backstrap loom. Note the batten, the long piece of wood that is used to push the thread together to achieve a tight weft. Picture by Guaman Poma.

Planting Time. Note the cooperation of the man (with the foot plow) and the women (one placing the seed potato, the other ready to rake over the soil). Picture by Guaman Poma.

local *curacas* (government officials). They were taken to Cuzco and made attendants at the most important temples or became secondary wives of the Inca king. Many served as attendants to lesser Inca gods or were given as wives to lower-ranking *curacas*. Some became *mamaconas*, or teachers of other Chosen Women at Inca centers. Most Chosen Women probably remained in the provincial centers near their homelands. Daughters of the Cuzco nobility could also become Chosen Women and serve the same purposes: they became wives, priestesses in the temples, or *mamaconas*.

The Chosen Women apparently served a very important economic role, being in charge of producing the large quantities of cloth used by officials of the empire. They also prepared the food and *chicha* used at government installations for serving the *m'ita* (forced labor) workers, and perhaps they even provided entertainment. As a luxury commodity they were also given as favors by nobles to others, including conquered leaders, as a way of cementing alliances and social relationships. For these reasons the Chosen Women were very strictly controlled by the government. They were like slaves in the sense of having no personal freedom, but they were more highly regarded and their services were respected by the Incas.

Even though the Chosen Women were more important to the Inca empire's economic activities, the common women were important as well. Women were officially free from paying tribute, but they were part of a household that was obligated to do so. Thus when a husband or son was away fulfilling his *m'ita* obligation, women helped fulfill the other household obligations such as working the fields. In addition, any weaving or cloth production required by the empire fell to the women, because most weaving was a woman's occupation. In fact, all households were expected to make one cloth garment for the state each year; this would have been done by the women of the house.

Like their noble counterparts, conquered women were in charge of their household's food preparation, cleaning, and child care. A daily—and probably fairly strenuous—task was collecting fuel for the fire. In forested areas, such as the eastern foothills, this might have been a relatively simple task; but in other areas, finding wood or llama dung to burn might take a few hours. It is likely that by Inca times much of the native forest of the highland region had been cut. In addition, a woman returning from a long fuel-collecting trip might be carrying a child or two who were too tired to walk, as well as a heavy load of wood. There is little doubt that the woman was tired at the end of the day (Malpass, 52–4, 76–81, 91).

To read about women's roles in 19th-century Latin America, see the Latin America entry in the section "Women" in chapter 2 ("Domestic Life") in volume 5 of this series; for 20th-century Latin America, see the Latin America entry in the section "Women" in chapter 2 ("Domestic Life") in volume 6 of this series.

FOR MORE INFORMATION

Malpass, M. *Daily Life in the Inca Empire*. Westport, Conn.: Greenwood, 1996.
Silverblatt, I. *Moon, Sun, and Witches*. Princeton: Princeton University Press, 1987.

Children

DOMESTIC LIFE

CHILDREN

England

Spain

Italy

Maya

Aztec

Inca

When children around the world are born, they resemble each other immensely. They all cry, get hungry, and need their diapers changed. From this point of essential similarity onward, however, they will be molded in different ways by the various cultures into which they have been born: the baby will become English or Maya as a result of the upbringing the child receives. That said, the stages of life through which children passed in Europe and Mesoamerica and South America were very similar.

The cultures in Europe and in America were all affectionate toward their children. Parents in all the cultures spoke fondly of their offspring and desired their well-being. Nevertheless, parental discipline was generally more severe in the 15th and 16th centuries than it is today. The parents were not strict out of cruelty, however, but rather because they felt that discipline was necessary for a child to develop into a healthy and productive adult. Tough love was the order of the day. In Europe, this discipline could take the form of beating or depriving the child of dinner. Some Mesoamerican societies used a greater variety and more regimented system of correction. The *Codex Mendoza* describes a variety of aspects of Aztec social life and describes some of the punishments that the 16th-century inhabitants of Mexico used. These punishments included sticking thorns from the maguey plant in a 9-year old, while a 10-year old would be beaten with a stick, and an 11-year old would be subjected to chili smoke. While these methods of correction seem harsh by the standards of Western society today, they were widely accepted in their day and clearly succeeded in forming successful members of their society.

Most children in the 15th and 16th centuries started to work at a much earlier age than children today. At the age of six, for example, most children in the United States are in school, while in the 16th century, most children were doing small chores in the fields or in the house. While some children, especially in Europe, received formal education from a young age, most children received little or no schooling and simply started learning the chores appropriate to their gender according to their society. Young girls in both Europe and the Americas, for example, learned how to spin and weave, how to clean the house, how to cook, and how to help care for the garden, while young boys learned the basics of agriculture, carried pails of water from the well, hauled firewood, or even went off chasing rabbits.

While working life thus began at an early age, these children were not exactly miniature adults, as has sometimes been thought. Society recognized that young children were not able to do the same kinds of work as adults and the tasks given to children were generally lighter and less intensive. As the children grew older, though, they began to receive more hefty tasks, until they were eventually doing the same work as the adults, sometime in their teen years.

Major rituals marked the important stages in a child's life. After birth, most cultures had a naming and/or cleansing ritual. In England, Spain, and Italy, a newborn child soon received baptism, which cleansed the child from inherited sin, gave the child an official name, and marked the child's entry into the church and formal society. The different Native American cultures had various practices that served a similar function. The Maya *hetzmek,* for example, involved naming the child and also provided the child with a second set of adult parents, not unlike the godparent system in European countries.

The Mesoamerican and South American cultures often placed particular emphasis on the puberty rituals. The Inca had particularly elaborate ceremonies for noble boys that had come of age. The young men made several trips to the mountain Huanacari, sacrificed llamas, and were ritually beaten and whipped to encourage bravery. Toward the end of the puberty rituals, which were spread out over several weeks, the boys were given loincloths—the symbol of manhood—and a set of weapons, in addition to oral instruction on how to live as a good Inca. At the very end of the ceremony, the boys' ears were pierced and the distinctively large earplugs that symbolized the status of a noble Inca warrior were inserted. In Europe, by contrast, becoming an official apprentice might be the only marker of a change in status around puberty, though in some countries, confirmation, which marked a person's decisive entry into the church, was given around the age of 14.

Childhood, then, was a time of learning about the world and preparing for the tasks of adult life. It certainly was not all work, though, and children generally had more leisure and fewer cares than their adult guardians. Childhood was also a time of great change and development, frequently marked with elaborate rituals that strove to ensure the child's continued growth physically and spiritually. Given the strict discipline, moreover, most children must have tried hard to follow the roles society laid out for them.

~Lawrence Morris

DOMESTIC LIFE
|
CHILDREN
|

England

Spain

Italy

Maya

Aztec

Inca

ENGLAND

Children were normally born at home in Renaissance England. Renaissance hospitals were designed only for the long-term care of the poor and disabled, not for routine or emergency medicine. Rather than a doctor, midwives with knowledge based upon considerable experience helped with the births. Soon after the birth, the baby would be taken to the parish church for baptism, commonly called christening: this was supposed to happen on a Sunday or a holy day within a week or two of birth. The ritual of baptism involved dipping the baby in a font of holy water in the parish church. At the ceremony the child was sponsored by three godparents, two of the same sex and one of the opposite. These godparents were considered genuine relatives; children would ask their godparents' blessing whenever meeting them, much as they did of their parents every morning and evening. A christening was a major social occasion and might be followed by a feast.

At the core of the baptismal ceremony was the assigning of a name. The surname was inherited from the child's father. Given names in Renaissance England were mostly drawn from traditional stock, but they were much more varied and original than had been the case in the Middle Ages. Perhaps the most common were French names imported during the Middle Ages, such as William, Robert, and Richard for boys and Alice, Joan, and Jane for girls. Also popular were saints' names, such as John, Thomas, James, Catherine, Elizabeth, and Anne. Another religious source of names was the Old Testament, which provided such names as Judith, Adam, and Daniel. A few names came from Greek or Latin, such as Dorothy and Julius.

Childhood was a dangerous time in Elizabethan England. The infant mortality rate may have been about 135 out of 1,000, and in some places as high as 200 out of 1,000. By comparison, a child mortality rate of 125 out of 1,000 is exceptionally high in the modern Third World; the rate in the United States is around 10 out of 1,000. Between the ages of 1 and 4, the mortality rate was around 60 out of 1,000, and about 30 out of 1,000 between the ages of 5 and 9. This means that out of every 10 live births, only 7 or 8 children lived to 10 years of age. The high mortality rate was primarily due to disease. Young children have relatively weak immune systems, so the diseases that plagued 16th-century Europe took an especially high toll on children. It is sometimes supposed that because of the high mortality rate, parents were reluctant to invest emotion in their children, but evidence suggests that love was considered a normal and necessary part of the parent-child relationship.

Parents were expected to be strict, but this was seen as a sign of love. Children who were not disciplined properly would not learn how to interact with the rest of society: in the words of one Elizabethan proverb, "Better unfed than untaught." Undoubtedly there were cruel parents who abused their power, but there is no evidence to indicate that abusiveness was any more common then than now.

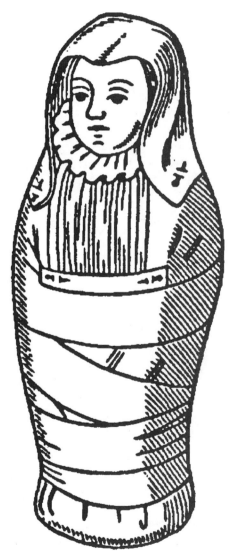

For the first six years or so, the Renaissance child would be at home and principally under female care. Most children were cared for by their own mothers, although privileged children might be in the keeping of a nurse. Young babies were kept in rocking cribs and dressed in baby caps and swaddling, bands of linen wrapped around their bodies to keep them warm and immobile so their limbs would grow straight. Elizabethan babies in wealthy families were often given pieces of coral attached to silver handles with bells on them: the bells provided amusement, and the child could suck or chew on the coral much as modern babies use pacifiers and teething rings. Babies were breast-fed and might be nursed in this way for about two years; aristocratic children often received their milk from a wet nurse. After coming out of swaddling clothes, both boys and girls were dressed in gowns and petticoats; only after age six or so were boys put into breeches. For Elizabethan children, like children today, the early years were primarily a time for exploration, play, and learning. During this time children would explore their world and begin to learn some of the basic tools of social interaction.

An Infant in Swaddling Clothes. Swaddling clothes are strips of cloth wrapped tightly around an infant; they were supposed to keep the child safe and some people thought they helped the limbs to grow straight. From George Clinch, *English Costume,* 1910.

Around six years old, the lives of girls and boys began to diverge. Boys from well-off families would go to school, while the rest would start learning to work. Initially, children's work would be centered on the home and family. Young boys and girls performed light tasks about the house or helped out by minding younger brothers and sisters. In the country, children were expected to work in the fields at harvest time when the demand for labor was at its highest, binding and stacking the grain after the harvesters had cut it down. At this age, girls began to learn the skills needed for running a household: spinning, dyeing, cooking, and basic medical skills. Boys in the country often helped with the lighter sorts of fieldwork, such as chasing or shooting birds at sowing time to keep them from eating the seeds, or clearing stones from the fallow fields. Children also helped their mothers by carding wool to be spun into thread, and they might be taught to knit to bring extra revenue into the home.

As children grew in age and strength, they were given more and heavier work and were increasingly likely to be sent to work outside the home, especially if they were boys whose families did not hold their own land. By the age of 12 or 14, a boy may not have been ready for the heaviest sorts of labor, but he was still expected to be fully integrated into the working economy: the Statute of Artificers declared that any boy aged 12 or older could be compelled to work.

During the teenage years, several points of passage marked a young man's or woman's integration into the adult world. By age 14, those children not of the privileged classes or under apprenticeship were expected to be full working participants in the economy. Fourteen was also the youngest age at which children could go through the ceremony of confirmation, which allowed them to receive communion at church; however, the ceremony was often put off until age 16 or even 18. Boys were subject to military service at age 16. The official age of majority was 21 (Singman, 36–40, 49).

To read about children in Chaucer's England, see the Europe entry in the section "Children" in chapter 2 ("Domestic Life") in volume 2 of this series; for 18th-century England, see the entry on England in the section "Children" in chapter 2 ("Domestic Life") in volume 4 of this series; for Victorian England, see the Victorian England entry in the section "Children" in chapter 2 ("Domestic Life") in volume 5 of this series.

FOR MORE INFORMATION

Palliser, D. M. *The Age of Elizabeth.* New York: Longman, 1992.
Pearson, L. *The Elizabethans at Home.* Stanford: Stanford University Press, 1957.
Singman, J. L. *Daily Life in Elizabethan England.* Westport, Conn.: Greenwood, 1995.

DOMESTIC LIFE
|
CHILDREN
|
England
Spain
Italy
Maya
Aztec
Inca

SPAIN

The birth of a child was generally an occasion of great ceremony. When a woman was in labor, friends, relatives, and neighbors gathered around to offer encouragement and assistance, and the new baby was the center of attention for everyone. Baptism followed as soon as possible after birth to ensure the child its place in heaven if it should not survive. During the baptismal ceremony a Christian name was given, often that of a favorite saint or the name of the saint on whose day the child was born. Names of relatives or of godparents might also be used. In the more affluent families it was common to have a little party after the baptismal event, at which time the parents and baby usually received a few small gifts.

The upbringing of the infant fell to the mother and other females in the household such as sisters or aunts, and until the child was about six years old, it was seldom outside the circle of the women. Breast-feeding the baby was considered the only safe means of ensuring a healthy child since animal milk was thought to be potentially hazardous for a delicate digestive system. If the mother was not capable of this method of nourishment or preferred not to perform it for whatever reason, the baby was given over to a wet nurse if the family could afford it. She either lived in, or the infant was sent to her domicile. Generally, she would be a woman who had lost her own infant. With the high rate of mortality among babies, there were always more women in a position to nurse a child than there were children to be nursed.

After a few months the infant's swaddling clothes were exchanged for a more sanitary shirt and gown, and as it learned to walk a protective padded bonnet cushioned the head from the inevitable falls.

For amusement, the baby was given a rattle to play with, which gave way as it grew to an assortment of toys such as dolls, whistles, tops, blocks, and hobbyhorses, plus the usual natural items of sand, wood, and stones from which the child built miniature castles, churches, and houses as well as dams, boats, and mills if water was close at hand.

Until the age of six or seven, the daily life of the child revolved around sleep, food, and play. Then the sacrament of confirmation marking the child's official admission to the church was given, and around this age girls and boys began to be steered by parents and society into their own differentiated spheres.

In the country it was customary for the sons of peasant farmers at a young age to be moved away from the guidance of female members of the household into male company. In the vast majority of cases, this meant into an orbit of farm work where they learned the tasks of herding animals, plowing, planting and harvesting, milking and sheering sheep, and snaring rabbits and birds for the table.

Most children never had the opportunity to go to school and remained illiterate. A little instruction from the parish priest was about all they received. For the majority, reading and writing were unobtainable goals, and instead they might learn to memorize the *Ave Maria*, the Creed, and the Lord's Prayer, all in Latin. Responsibility for a child's education lay with the parent, as did the actions of the child, who was considered too young to know the difference between good and bad behavior.

City boys from reasonably well-off families of the bourgeoisie generally received two or three years of schooling learning to read and write and some arithmetic. Then it was common for them to learn a trade. Sometimes this happened at home, with the boy following in his father's footsteps; otherwise, he was sent to learn and not uncommonly to live in the home of someone else skilled in a trade. An apprenticeship was a desirable option, and room and board were provided even if little or no pay was forthcoming. Sometimes the father had to pay the master to take on his son. The master had the right to treat the boy as his own, even to punish him if he was not always up to standard. Conflicts naturally arose between them, and often enough the apprentice ran away from the job.

Although these apprentices were mostly boys, it was also possible for girls to gain acceptance into one of the trades that admitted them such as lace and veil makers or producers of silk ribbons. Alternatively, domestic service was one of the few respectable options.

Urban girls, between the ages of 12 and 20, from well-off, socially oriented families, referred to as *doncellas* (maidens or virgins), were expected to be chaste, obedient, modest, and retiring and to maintain a serene countenance, downcast eyes, and a serious demeanor. Enclosed behind the bricks and mortar of the house and locked doors, they were protected from all possible dangers that might impugn family honor. Some of these girls spent their young lives indoors, even hidden from view when visitors called at the house, but others were allowed to attend church, their faces covered with a mantilla (long veil), where socializing with the opposite sex might afford a small opportunity for flirting under the watchful eye of an escort, sometimes rented for the occasion. A note might be surreptitiously passed between admiring couples and coquettish glances exchanged.

Processions, religious festivals, and pilgrimages afforded other opportunities to escape the house, and girls with lenient fathers were sometimes allowed to visit the homes of girlfriends, where they could chat, eat fruit, and drink chocolate. Moral critics and the church frowned upon even this activity, claiming it gave females too much freedom and was offensive to God.

The urban poor, both boys and girls, received little or no schooling and no vocational training and worked as unskilled laborers or servants, going to work as soon as they had the physical stamina for the job. Aware that girls reached physical maturity earlier than boys, the church set the age of girls at 12 and boys at 14 for the first confession. Teenagers were considered to be adults with corresponding responsibilities. At 14 or 15, they were considered eligible to labor in the fields and serve in the militia. Women generally married at about age 23 and men at about 25 (Anderson, 160–62).

FOR MORE INFORMATION

Anderson, J. *Daily Life during the Spanish Inquisition*. Westport, Conn.: Greenwood, 2002.

Casey, J. *Early Modern Spain: A Social History*. London: Routledge, 1999.

DOMESTIC LIFE
|
CHILDREN
|
England

Spain

Italy

Maya

Aztec

Inca

ITALY

Birth was a time of both joy and fear. While most children were born without incident, the possibility of an infant or mother dying was real. While families embraced the arrival of both boys and girls, males were especially welcome. High-ranking couples marked the arrival of firstborn sons with special parties. A ruling dynasty funded rejoicing throughout its domain when an heir was born. The fragile infant embodied the future of the lineage name and the promise of its economic and political security. Daughters, especially one or two whose marriages would build useful alliances, were a boon, but also a worry and a burden. Their chastity risked the family honor, and their dowries threatened to deplete its fortune.

Baptism was the next major event in a young child's life. In Italy, this sacrament was usually conferred within a day or two of birth. Several major things happened at baptism. First of all, the baby was cleansed from the sin of Adam and Eve and became a member of the church. Secondly, the baby acquired godparents, adults charged with looking after the spiritual welfare of the child. These adults could become valuable contacts and resources for the child and the family later in life. Finally, the child received a name.

The name a baby received at baptism might come from several sources. The repertoire of likely names varied from place to place. Regional heroes, rulers, and saints supplied possibilities, as did particular family traditions. Infants were named after ancestors, and especially after recently dead relatives, including siblings; fathers then spoke of "remaking" a member of the lineage. Unusual names often came from such local sources. Another colorful though uncommon sort of tag invoked blessings or good fortune: Benvenuto, for example, meant "welcome." Naming practices also followed larger policy or fashion. By the 15th century, the number of commonly given names had contracted sharply. In Tuscany, for example, nearly half the male population bore one of only some 15 or so names. Most names honored prominent saints, including Antonio, Francesco, Giovanni, and Bartolomeo. Similarly, many women bore female versions of these same names, but the favorite was Caterina, after the Sienese mystic. A birth close to the feast day of the saint, a parent's special devotion, or even a vow made in hopes of a safe arrival might govern the choice of a name.

Infants belonged in the domain of women. Women nonetheless bore a heavy load of diverse responsibilities. Mothering was just one, and not necessarily the most crucial for the family's well-being. Although their particular tasks varied between city and country and up and down the social scale, few mothers had the luxury to devote lots of time to direct care of their babies. Consequently, infants and older children had to share maternal attention not only with siblings but also with other people and activities. Frequently their care fell in some or substantial part into the hands of other women—grandmothers, older sisters, or servants.

The customs and techniques of handling the very young passed by word and example from woman to woman and from one generation to the next. During the Renaissance, however, male experts also began to pronounce on pregnancy, infant care, and raising families. Though sermons might be given in Italian, much of this literature was in Latin.

The central and most worrisome part of infant care was feeding. All babies, with a few unfortunate exceptions, were fed at the breast. The experts expressed grave distrust of other sources of nutrition, and with good reason. Animal milk, even where available, was unsafe; other liquids, such as almond water, or more solid foods, such as boiled wheat porridge, did not provide what the new baby needed and often troubled its digestion. Such food, people thought, might even addle the child's mind.

While the doctors warned against overfeeding infants, the much more common problem was lack of breast milk. Because many women's supply failed for one reason or another, emergencies cropped up in which an alternative had to be found quickly. An informal sharing among nursing women was the best solution; one would offer her breast to another's baby, hoping that someone would do the same for her another time. At other times, when no woman with milk could or would step in, infants were no doubt offered risky substitutes.

Wealthier women, instead of nursing their own children, often sought the assistance of a *balia* (wet nurse). The difficulties of finding and keeping a suitable wet nurse preoccupied parents and the medical experts who sought to advise them. While in general women handled infants' needs, the selection and payment of wet nurses was one responsibility in which fathers took part. Wet nurses were typically lower-status women who needed income. Their socially superior employers harbored chronic doubts about the physical health and moral character of these women on whose milk their infants would depend for their lives and even their personalities. The guides for parents offered detailed counsel on how to pick a good wet nurse. One contemporary authority, Michele de Savonarola, recommended a woman in her thirties, sturdy of body but not fat, with skin unblemished and milk a good white, not pale and watery.

Some parents could afford to keep a wet nurse at home. For many parents, however, to use a wet nurse meant sending the child away to live in her home, usually in the country. Thus only a few hours or days after birth, a city-born infant departed from its natal family and spent many months—even one, two, or more years—in a modest rural household. The distance caused stress. While some parents may have given little day-to-day thought to their absent offspring, others clearly worried, seeking reports on their child's health and arranging visits.

Besides nursing and the web of arrangements around it, the defining feature of the earliest period of life was swaddling. Freshly delivered from the mother, the newborn's body was washed and dressed in loose garments and diapers. Then the baby's limbs were carefully straightened, and strips of fabric were wound around from toe to head, often leaving only the face exposed. Experts claimed that swaddling kept the baby warm and secure from drafts and discouraged any movement that might invite danger. The wrapping was supposed to be done carefully to prevent too much pressure on fragile organs.

A good regime of care also called for unbound times for hygiene, stimulation, and exercise. Diaper cloths were to be changed several times a day, and experts recommended frequent baths. It was good to wash babies more often than adults washed themselves. Besides cleanliness and comfort, bathing provided an occasion for the child to move and stretch, free of tight swaddling. Caregivers could seize these moments to cuddle and play with the little ones.

Children, having left the breast and capable of speech and independent movement, entered a new phase of life. Their parents were responsible for beginning to teach them the values, attitudes, and skills that would enable them to function as adults. Some of this knowledge, such as fundamental religious and lay moralities, was nearly universal. Many other lessons were specific to the particular social niches to which gender and rank destined each child.

Until the age of six or seven, children remained largely in the turf of women. Fathers sometimes showed great interest in their offspring, but in early childhood it generally took the form of visits with them in domestic spaces.

About the age of six, as children became ready to take their first steps toward future adult roles, fathers began to participate more directly. They assumed responsibility for the education of sons, overseeing training where they did not themselves teach. For girls of this same age, in Florence, fathers started paying into an account with the civic dowry fund, the "Monte delle Doti," so that ten years later the daughter would be able to marry. As these paternal activities suggest, at this stage gender differentiation intensified. Earlier, although parental expectations for girls and boys were clearly distinct, their care and experiences had a lot in common. They wore similar clothes and played similar games. But at six or seven years, gender differences began to sharpen.

For many children, introduction to work occurred between ages 6 and 12. In the city and country, in homes and workshops and on farms, youngsters learned the elementary practices of adult work. Girls observed the mixed tasks of housekeeping—including preparing foods, sweeping, fetching water, washing and drying clothes, feeding and minding small animals—and began to perform the simpler ones. Boys too gradually acquired basic skills, while their orbit of activity expanded beyond the domestic compass to streets and hillsides where they ran errands and watched over grazing animals. For some number of boys and a few girls, education in reading, writing, and arithmetic might also begin in these years. While scions of the elite were sometimes tutored at home, a variety of schools trained city children.

For many children, introduction to work occurred between ages 6 and 12.

Somewhere in the years between the ages of 12 and 15, childhood merged into adolescence, with neither a sharp break nor a major rite of passage. In becoming adolescent, older children gradually took on a range of new physical, sexual, moral, and intellectual capacities that translated into greater social and legal responsibilities. According to the thinking of Renaissance Italians, younger children, while possessed of sufficient reason for primary learning, were still innocent. They lacked the judgment to discern good and evil in the world around them. Adolescents, in contrast, were acquiring that discretion and thus, incrementally, became liable for the consequences of their actions.

Teenage boys would start apprenticeships in the trades at around the age of 14. Shortly after this, a father could "emancipate" his son, that is, relinquish official authority over him and responsibility for his actions. The average age of emancipation was 20 years, though some merchants did it as early as 15. Female teenagers, by contrast, were watched over very carefully from the age of 12 until marriage to protect their chastity and the family honor. Where possible, the parents would restrict the young women's movements to the home and the circles of other female friends. Although plays such as *Romeo and Juliet* have fostered the idea that most people wed as teenagers, the average age was higher than that—in the early twenties for women, and the late twenties for men (Cohen and Cohen, 177–202).

FOR MORE INFORMATION

Bell, R. *How to Do It: Guides to Good Living for Renaissance Italians*. Chicago: University of Chicago Press, 1999.

Cohen, E. S., and T. V. Cohen. *Daily Life in Renaissance Italy*. Westport, Conn.: Greenwood, 2001.

Kapisch-Zuber, C. "Childhood in Tuscany at the Beginning of the Fifteenth Century." In *Women, Family and Ritual in Renaissance Italy*. Chicago: University of Chicago Press, 1985.

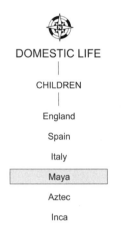

DOMESTIC LIFE

|

CHILDREN

|

England

Spain

Italy

Maya

Aztec

Inca

MAYA

The date of each person's birth in the 260-day almanac had different attributes—some good, some neutral, some bad. In this way each person's birth date controlled his or her temperament and destiny. To this day many highland peoples, such as the Cakchiquel Maya, are named after their date of birth in the 260-day almanac. In Yucatán at the time of the Spanish Conquest, each child's *paal kaba*, or given name, was determined by a divining ceremony conducted by a shaman. Like Americans and Europeans, the Maya are given multiple names. In Yucatán these are the *paal kaba*, the father's family name, the mother's family name, and an informal nickname.

Children are greatly desired and receive a great deal of love and affection by the Maya. At the time of the Conquest, women would ask the gods for children by giving offerings, reciting special prayers, and placing an image of Ix Chel, the goddess of childbirth, under their beds. Today, having many children is seen as beneficial and as security for the family. Sons assist their fathers in the fields, and older daughters assist their mothers in taking care of younger sisters and brothers. Children take care of their parents in their old age. These roles were probably little different in the past.

The Maya still perform ceremonies marking a child's acceptance into society. In Yucatán this ceremony is the *hetzmek*, performed when the baby is carried astride the mother's hip for the first time. For girls the *hetzmek* is held at three months; for boys it is held at four months. The girl's age of three months symbolizes the three stones of the Maya hearth, an important focus of a woman's life. The boy's age of four months symbolizes the four sides of the maize field, an important focus of a man's life. Participants in the ceremony, besides the infant, are the parents and another husband and wife who act as sponsors. The child is given nine objects symbolic of his or her life and is carried on the hip nine times by both sponsoring parents. The ceremony closes with offerings and a ritual feast.

In colonial Yucatán, and today, children are raised by their mothers until the age of three or four. At about age four, girls were given a red shell that was tied to a string around their waists. At the same age, boys received a small white bead that was fastened to their hair. Both symbols of childhood were worn until puberty, when another ceremony marked the transition to adulthood.

There is no evidence that the ancient Maya had formal schools. But it is certain that children selected on the basis of social status or aptitude were trained for specialized roles in society by an apprentice system. Scribes, priests, artists, masons, and other occupational groups recruited novices and trained them. Today, among some highland Maya peoples, shamans continue to recruit and train the future generation of specialists. In all Maya communities the girls learn women's roles from their mothers throughout childhood, doing household chores, buying and selling in the market, and assisting with specialized activities such as making pottery or weaving textiles. Boys are taught the skills of farming, hunting, fishing, and other male tasks by their fathers.

In colonial Yucatán the 260-day almanac was consulted to select an auspicious day for the community puberty ceremony marking the end of childhood and the beginning of adulthood. It was held every few years for all children deemed ready to take this step. The ceremony was conducted by a shaman; four assistant shamans, or *chacs* (after the Maya rain god); and a respected elder man of the community. The parents, children, and their sponsors assembled in the patio of the community elder's house, which was purified by a ritual conducted by the shaman. The patio was swept and covered by fresh leaves and mats.

After the *chacs* placed pieces of white cloth on the children's heads, the shaman said a prayer for the children and gave a bone to the elder, who used it to tap each child nine times on the forehead. The shaman used a scepter decorated with rattle-snake rattles to anoint the children with sacred water, after which he removed the white cloths from their heads. The children then presented offerings of feathers and cacao beans to the *chacs*. The shaman cut the white beads from the boys' hair, and the mothers removed the red shells from their daughters' waists. Pipes of tobacco were smoked, and a ritual feast of food and drink closed the ceremony. After this both the girls and boys were considered adults and eligible to marry.

In colonial times marriages were often arranged between families while the boy and girl were still very young. The wedding took place when they came of age, usually when the couple was around 20 years old. Today in most Maya communities the average age of men at marriage is about the same, and the average age of women at marriage is 16 or 17 years (Sharer, 117–19).

To read about children in 20th-century Latin America, see the Latin America entry in the section "Children" in chapter 2 ("Domestic Life") in volume 6 of this series.

FOR MORE INFORMATION

Sharer, R. *Daily Life in Maya Civilization*. Westport, Conn.: Greenwood, 1996.

Wilk, R. R., and W. Ashmore, eds. *Household and Community in the Mesoamerican Past*. Albuquerque: University of New Mexico Press, 1988.

AZTEC

From the moment of childbirth, Aztec parents were greatly concerned that their children avoid becoming "fruitless trees" and instead become productive citizens.

They believed that infants were exposed to the greatest dangers and that a child could be invaded by either natural or supernatural sources. In fact, very young children who had not yet eaten corn were considered pure, able to communicate with gods in direct ways. After children had eaten corn, which meant that they had begun to internalize the fruits of the earth and the cultivation of nature by human effort (and also to internalize the forces of death because something of the earth had been killed to feed them), education became the key to gaining strength and knowledge to one day become part of the economic and social community. Aztec children would receive both general and specialized instruction from parents, priests, teachers, and other members of the community through a variety of means and institutions.

The direction this education would take was determined early in the child's life, in fact only 20 days after birth. At this time, the parents chose what kind of education they wanted their child to have and then took the infant to the appropriate temple or school. The pact between the family, the gods, and the temple was sealed by incisions made in the body of the child. These physical marks were visible signs of a spiritual change. The lower lips of boys were cut open and a jewel was inserted. Girls were initiated when small cuts were made with obsidian blades in their breasts and hips. These incisions signified that they had been initiated into the lifelong educational process upon which their lives depended.

This ceremony reaffirmed what all Aztec parents knew and what all Aztec children were required to learn: their true parents were the gods, individuals were required to live in relation to the gods and the social group, and education was the key to bringing about the transformation from childhood to adult responsibility and becoming a "fruitful tree." Another passage says of the schools that "in the *calmecac* (a kind of school), people are corrected, people are instructed, it is the place of a chaste life, a place of reverence, a place of knowledge, of wisdom, of goodness, a place of virtues, a place without filth, without dust." One of the most effective strategies for ensuring that a child would be a "fruitful tree" was to engage in the various rituals, ritual instructions, and periodic rites of passage that individuals underwent throughout the Aztec life cycle. These rites of passage not only promoted the controlled development and maturation of Aztec children but also ensured that physical changes corresponded with spiritual changes and powers throughout their lives.

The first rite of passage came soon after birth. In a scene from the *Codex Mendoza* of how a child was treated and named soon after birth, a mother who has recently given birth is seated next to a cradle where her infant lies with four flower symbols above it. Four days after birth, the midwife, who played a major role in Aztec culture, took the naked child to the courtyard of the house, where a ritual cleansing took place. The midwife had prepared a mat of rushes or reeds with a small earthen tub of water, and she bathed the infant. She breathed upon the water, made the child taste it, touched the baby's chest and head with the water and said, "My youngest one, my beloved youth. . . . Enter, descend into the blue water, the yellow water. . . . Approach thy mother Chalchiuhtlicue, Chalchiuhtlatonac! May she receive thee. . . . May she cleanse thy heart; may she make it fine, good. May she give thee fine, good conduct!"

The bath scene has two sets of symbols, above and below the pan of water. The symbols below the bath scene are the female symbols, consisting of a distaff with a spindle, a basket, and a broom signifying the girl's future role as the keeper of the home. She will be educated into the labor and art of weaving, which was an invaluable part of Aztec life. The act of sweeping, to purify and to contribute to good health, was both a practical and a ritual activity associated with women. Aztec homes were extremely clean, as were the temples, where ritual sweeping was done in service to the gods. The spindle was also a fertility symbol associated with the capacity of females to bear children. For instance, two spindles attached to cotton fillets were part of the headdress of a fertility goddess. One Aztec riddle went, "What is that which becomes pregnant in only one day? The spindle." The symbols above the bath scene are the male objects used by the infant's father, which could be a shield and arrows if the father was a warrior, or wood, metal, or feathers if the father was a woodcarver, a metalworker, or a feather worker. There is also the symbol of the painter of books for boys whose fathers were scribes. A little shield with four arrows just above the rushes and pan of water, called *mitl chimalli* (shield and arrows), is an Aztec metaphor meaning war; each arrow represented one of the four cardinal directions of the universe.

> *Sweeping was both a practical and a ritual activity. Aztec homes were extremely clean.*

The Aztecs valued love and discipline. On the one hand, children were encouraged to express their feelings and attitudes openly, while on the other hand, they were watched carefully by their parents and given constant correction. When a child reached three years of age, the father began to instruct the boy, and the mother to instruct the girl, in how to be a helpful member of the family and the household. When a child was four years old, the parents became more specific in the tasks they wanted their children to carry out, and girls and boys began wearing different clothes appropriate to their gender. This was the year that children underwent a special growth ritual that was repeated every four years in the month of Izcalli (Growth). Children of both sexes born during the previous four years were purified by fire and had their earlobes pierced and earrings inserted. The ceremony was called Quinquechanaya (they stretch their necks) and the children were lifted by their foreheads and had their limbs stretched. Another ceremony held every 260 days, on the day 4 Movement, saw the children's noses, necks, ears, fingers, and legs pulled to encourage proper growth during the next 260-day cycle. These two rituals reflect one of the key ideas in Aztec education. The Aztec equivalent of the verb "to educate" was *tlacahuapahua* or *tlacazcaltia*, which meant "to strengthen persons" or "to make persons grow." This growing and strengthening was accomplished through a series of rituals that incorporated children into the work of the family and society. In these cases the children were introduced to the sacred numbers 4 and 260, which would continue to guide them even after death.

At the age of four, mothers began to teach girls the fundamentals of weaving, and fathers guided boys beyond the confines of the home and had them assist in water carrying. At five, boys helped in toting light loads of firewood and carrying light bundles of goods to the *tianquiztli*, or neighborhood marketplace. This allowed them to greet people, watch the process of exchanges in the market, and meet other children. Girls began to spin with their mothers, learning how to sit, use their hands, and manipulate the cotton.

Between the ages of 7 and 10, boys were given nets to fish with, while girls continued to learn how to spin and cook. Young girls were already proficient in their labor and art by this age and were supervised rather than instructed by their mothers. Apparently, it was during this period of growth that children began to act up and cause problems in the family. The *Codex Mendoza* presents these years as times when parents punished their children for a series of unacceptable behaviors, including laziness, disobedience, rudeness, and boastfulness. There are images of parents "putting before them [the children] the terror and fear of maguey thorns, so that being negligent and disobedient to their parents they would be punished with the said thorns." There are scenes of children weeping when presented with these thorns and admonished not to be deceitful. Girls' hands were pierced by their mothers, who used the thorns to punish them for idleness and negligence. Boys who really got out of line had their hands and feet bound, and maguey thorns were stuck into their shoulders, backs, and buttocks. Such was the price of rebellion by children. These punishments intensified between the ages of 10 and 14 and included being forced to inhale chili smoke or being tied by the hand and foot and forced to sleep on damp ground all night. If a girl was a sloppy spinner or clumsy in her work, she could be beaten by her mother for not paying attention or not concentrating on her work.

Parental Discipline. The Aztecs used physical discipline to keep their children in line. Both boys and girls suffered the same punishments, which differed in accordance with the age of the child. Nine-year-olds were pierced with maguey thorns, 10-year-olds were beaten with sticks, and 11-year-olds were exposed to chili smoke. From the *Codex Mendoza,* courtesy of Frances F. Berdan and Patricia Reiff Anawait.

Images in the *Codex Mendoza* show that the children got well into line during their 13th and 14th years. Boys were responsible for carrying firewood from the hills and are depicted transporting sedges, bulrushes, and other grasses for the household and fishing successfully in their canoes. Girls would grind maize and make tortillas for their parents and are seen weaving, cooking, and effectively handling the different foods, utensils, and life of the kitchen. In fact, a girl who could grind corn and make the *atole* drink was considered a maiden of marriageable age.

At the age of 15, children officially entered into their adult careers through joining one of the schools. These schools included the *cuicacalli*, which taught sacred song and dance; the *calmecac*, which instructed novice priests in religion, astrology, and fighting; and the *telpochcalli*, which trained warriors (Carrasco, 93–115).

To read about children in 20th-century Latin America, see the Latin America entry in the section "Children" in chapter 2 ("Domestic Life") in volume 6 of this series.

FOR MORE INFORMATION

Berdan, F. F., and P. Rieff Anawait, eds. *Codex Mendoza*. 4 vols. Berkeley: University of California Press, 1992.

Carrasco, D., with S. Sessions. *Daily Life of the Aztecs: People of the Sun and Earth*. Westport, Conn.: Greenwood, 1998.

León-Portilla, M., ed. and trans. *Native Mesoamerican Spirituality: Ancient Myths, Discourses, Stories, Doctrines, Hymns, Poems from the Aztec, Yucatec, Quiche-Maya and Other Sacred Traditions*. New York: Paulist, 1980.

INCA

No special event marked the birth of an Inca child. A woman simply went to the nearest stream and bathed herself and the newborn. She then resumed her duties around the household. After four days the baby was placed in a cradle, where it spent most of its time until it could walk. Garcilaso de la Vega, an Inca descendant, mentions that a woman never picked up her child, either to play with it or suckle it, lest the child become a crybaby.

It was an interesting custom of the Incas not to name a child until it was weaned from its mother's breast, around one year of age. This important event was associated with the child's first haircut. A great party was given for friends and relatives of the child's parents, with much drinking and dancing. At the end of the party the oldest male relative cut a small piece of the child's hair and its nails, and gave it a name. Then other relatives cut off a lock of hair, and each gave the child a gift. The nails and hair were carefully kept. The name given to the child at this ceremony was not his or her permanent name; he or she received a new one upon reaching maturity.

Childhood was spent learning the activities of the household. When boys were old enough and strong enough, they would help in the fields and with tending animals. Girls would help with the many household tasks of cooking, cleaning, making clothing, and probably taking care of younger brothers and sisters.

The end of childhood and the beginning of adulthood were marked differently for boys and girls. A girl became a woman at her first menstruation, and a ceremony was held to mark this notable transition. The girl was restricted to her house for three days, eating virtually nothing except a little raw corn on the third day. On the fourth day relatives assembled at her house, and she was bathed by her mother, who also braided her hair. She then put on new clothes and went out to serve her relatives food and drink. The most important uncle then gave her a permanent name and she received gifts from all involved.

A common puberty ritual was held for all boys reaching the age of 14, although the event only roughly coincided with the onset of puberty for the participants. For boys of the royal class living in the capital of Cuzco, the ritual took place in December at the same time as the Capac Raymi festival. The ceremony actually was a series of activities spread out over three weeks, with preparations lasting a good deal longer. Mothers had to prepare fine new garments to be worn at the different activities, a task that must have begun months in advance.

In November the boys made a pilgrimage to the sacred mountain of Huanacauri, located outside Cuzco. The purpose of the trip was to ask the spirit of the mountain for permission to perform the puberty ceremony. Each boy brought along a llama, which was sacrificed by slitting its throat. The llama's blood was smeared on the boy's face by a priest. Then each participant was given a sling to signify his new status as a warrior. Much dancing followed; and the boys had to do certain chores, such as collecting straw for their relatives to sit on and chewing the corn for preparing the *chicha* (an intoxicating drink) for the ceremonies to come.

Baby in a Cradle. This cradle was also a baby-carrier: it could be strapped to the mother's back as she went about her chores. Picture by Guaman Poma.

During the puberty ceremony the boys again made a pilgrimage to Huanacauri to make more sacrifices of llamas. The boys were whipped on their legs by relatives on the return home, as a means of making them strong and brave. The participants then performed a sacred dance, after which they drank some of the *chicha* they had helped to prepare previously. A week of rest was followed by another series of sacrifices, beatings, and dancing at the hill of Anahuarque, located near Huanacauri. The boys then participated in a race from the top of the hill to the bottom (the race often resulted in falls, some of them serious). At the end, each boy was given *chicha* by girls from the same royal class.

The final part of the puberty ceremony involved a trip to other hills near Cuzco where the boys were given loincloths, formally marking them as men. Then the boys traveled to a sacred spring called Callispuquio, where relatives gave them their weapons: the most important uncle gave a shield, a sling, and a mace. Other relatives gave gifts and advice on how to act as a man and as a proper Inca. The final activity was the piercing of the boys' ears for wearing the earplugs that were the hallmark of Inca nobility. This marked the participant as a warrior.

Similar rituals, although probably less elaborate, were conducted at the same time of year in provincial capitals—again, for boys of the noble class. The special ceremony for noble boys indicates the importance of becoming a warrior and a member in good standing of Inca society. No doubt the rituals also served to create special bonds between the participants (Malpass, 75–78).

To read about children in 20th-century Latin America, see the Latin America entry in the section "Children" in chapter 2 ("Domestic Life") in volume 6 of this series.

FOR MORE INFORMATION

Cobo, B. *History of the Inca Empire*. Ed. and trans. Roland Hamilton. 1653. Reprint, Austin: University of Texas Press, 1979.

Kendall, A. *Everyday Life of the Incas*. New York: Putnam, 1973.

Malpass, M. *Daily Life in the Inca Empire*. Westport, Conn.: Greenwood, 1996.

3

ECONOMIC LIFE

People work. The basic principle of economic life is that men and women must work to provide for themselves. Of course, throughout history it has always been that some have to work harder than others, but this does not violate the basic importance of work; it only reveals the complexities of economic life that includes everything from the production of income, to trade, to its unequal distribution throughout society.

At the basic level, people work on the land to produce their food and other items they need. However, even at this simplest level, people trade goods among themselves. Thus, economic life moves from the work that we do to the exchange of the products of our labor. This diversification contributes to increasing variety in society: some people work on the land and live in villages and farms, while others move to urban areas that grow ever larger throughout history. The patterns of farm, village, and urban life exist all over the world and help define the lives of the people who work within them.

Commerce, or the exchange of goods, is as central to human economic life as the production of goods. From the beginning of town life in Mesopotamia, the excitement generated within shops lining a street is palpable in the sources. Merchants hawking their wares and shoppers looking for the exotic, as well as the ordinary, form a core of human life. Merchants (and merchandise) have always ranged far beyond local markets as people moved their goods across large areas. Even during the prehistoric late Stone Age, domestic animals native to the Middle East moved down the Nile valley to sub-Saharan Africa, and plants native to the Euphrates valley moved as far east as China. Even today, the logical extension of the constant movement of people and things that goes on as people engage in their economic life is the basis of our global marketplace.

All societies have been in part defined by people at work. They have built societies with divisions of labor, of city and country, and of class, as some people grow richer than others. To study daily life through history is in large part to understand people at work.

The four articles of this section focus in turn on rural life, which formed the agricultural backbone of the economy; on city life, which was the environment of

ECONOMIC LIFE
|
RURAL LIFE
CITY LIFE
TIME
CALENDARS

merchants, skilled craftsmen, princes, and beggars; and on time and calendars, which regulated work life and punctuated the year with festivals and celebrations that lessened the stress caused by the demands of daily work life. During the 15th and 16th centuries, significant tensions were starting to develop between the people of the country and people in the city. In the mind of some rural people, the city dwellers were associated with wealth, power, and education, while the people of the countryside were associated with poverty, servitude, and ignorance. Moreover, the idea that city dwellers were ruthless businessmen that preyed upon the honest, innocent country dwellers was already in circulation. Cities, however, were also associated with dire poverty. People from the countryside would wander into the cities in search of a better life, drawn by the images of wealth. Without trade skills or learning, many of these immigrants would be reduced to begging on street corners, and faking injuries to draw more sympathy and money from passersby. With such tensions, it's clear that everyone needed holidays!

~*Joyce E. Salisbury and Lawrence Morris*

FOR MORE INFORMATION

Braudel, F. *The Wheels of Commerce*. New York: Harper and Row, 1979.
Wallerstein, I. M. *Historical Capitalism*. London: Verso, 1983.

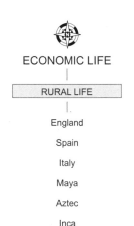

ECONOMIC LIFE
|
RURAL LIFE
|
England

Spain

Italy

Maya

Aztec

Inca

Rural Life

Food is necessary for life. The production of food, from plants and animals, is thus one of the most important concerns for any society, ancient or modern. Modern western societies frequently take food for granted. In the average American supermarket, one can buy at a reasonable price food products from around the world at any time of the year. This ready supply of food is largely due to technological advances, such as tractors, refrigerators, and long-haul trucks, that increase society's ability to produce, store, and transport food. People in the 15th and 16th centuries certainly did not have these technologies and never took their food supply for granted. A bad local harvest threatened the populace with poverty and frequently starvation. In the face of this threat, however, the rural population worked strenuously to cultivate fields, raise animals, and maximize the food production through hard work and what technology they had.

The peoples of Mesoamerica and South America inhabited some lands that were difficult to farm: for example, lakes and mountains. Yet they overcame these difficulties in a variety of clever and effective ways. The Aztecs, for example, lived among the lakes in the Basin of Mexico. Rather than allowing the surface covered by water to remain agriculturally unproductive, the Aztecs built a massive series of raised gardens up out of the lake bottoms. The Aztecs then farmed and lived upon these gardens. This land redeemed from the lake was exceptionally fertile, and mud from the lake bottom furnished a convenient supply of fertilizer. This system of agriculture is called the *chinampa* system, but the farms are sometimes called floating gardens. The Spaniards were especially impressed by this system upon their arrival in Mesoamerica.

The peoples of the Andes in modern-day Peru were also great innovators. These peoples lived in the Andes mountains and frequently had no level ground to plow. In reaction to this impediment, the Huari people, and later the Incas, developed a system of terraces, in which they built a series of walls on the mountainside and then filled in the area behind and uphill from each wall with soil, thereby creating a series of level fields ascending like steps up the mountainside. The Tiahuanaco culture, which lived in the highest reaches of the mountains near Lake Titicaca (which means the Lake on Top of the World), devised a series of raised fields and trenches to make arable and fertile terrain out of the marshy soil around the lake.

In Europe, by contrast, mountains were frequently given over to sheep and mostly the plains were farmed. Unlike the Americans, the Europeans had the advantage of plows pulled by oxen, mules, or sometimes horses. Each field would usually be divided into smaller strips, and any one family would farm particular strips in a large number of different fields. This layout was designed so that each family would have a share in both the more and less fertile fields. By the 15th century, farmers had also mastered a field rotation scheme through which they could maintain the fertility of their fields. By changing which crops they planted on a field and by leaving the field fallow (unplanted) once every three or four years, the farmers could maintain a decent level of soil fertility for their crops. This system of farming, inherited from the Middle Ages, was coming under increasing threat from domestic animals. The growth of the wool industry, especially in England, caused some landlords to switch their fields from agricultural use to grazing. Since sheep required much less care than fields, such an economic change could create a disaster for the peasants of the community, suddenly left without work and with no food. Frequently, the only choice was to go to the cities in search of work.

The system of land ownership was one of the main causes of such displacements. The overwhelming majority of land in Europe was controlled by a small number of people. Wealthy families could own all the land in a district and would lease out allotments to be worked by peasant families. The peasants would pay for this lease by working on the landlord's private fields and/or by giving the wealthy family a certain percentage of the produce of the fields the peasant leased. While this system could produce a stable and prosperous economy when it worked, the peasants were excluded from the decision-making process and had no redress against tyrannical or unsympathetic landlords. Some of them, at least, also saw an injustice in doing all the work, while having to relinquish most of the fruit of their labor.

Similar imbalances in wealth could exist also in South and Mesoamerica. In the Inca empire, for example, the king in the capital city, Cuzco, theoretically owned all the land. The produce of all the land was divided into three, with one portion going to religion, one portion to government, and one portion to the people who farmed the land. The local group or clan, however, seems to have had control over many decisions about land use throughout the great American civilizations. Thus, among the Inca, the *curaca* (local official) was drawn from the local community, while the *chinampas* in the Aztec empire were divided out amongst various *calpullis* (clans).

Despite the various differences between the European and Native American agricultural systems, the two societies had a fundamental similarity. The majority of their population lived in rural areas and spent long hours turning hard work into food.

~Lawrence Morris

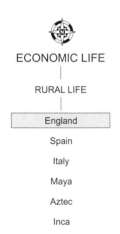

ECONOMIC LIFE
|
RURAL LIFE
|
England

Spain

Italy

Maya

Aztec

Inca

ENGLAND

England in the 15th and 16th centuries was still overwhelmingly rural, so for most people, work meant farm work. The production of food was a vital necessity and very labor-intensive, since hardly any machinery was involved. This meant that a substantial proportion of the population was engaged in the growing of staple foods, especially grains. Yet contrary to what is sometimes imagined, the English rural economy was already market oriented. Each household might produce some goods for its own use, notably foodstuffs, but it was not self-sufficient; people supported themselves by producing surpluses of agricultural goods for sale, rather than subsisting on their own produce.

Land productivity was improved by crop rotation, typically the three-field system. Over the centuries it had been discovered that constant farming of land exhausts its ability to produce crops. However, certain kinds of crops were found to help refortify the land for producing wheat. In the three-field system, the fields were divided into three parts. The agricultural year would begin in late September or October, when one part would be sown with a winter crop of rye and wheat (it was a winter crop because it was sown in the winter—all the crops were harvested in August–September). The second part would be sown with a spring crop of peas, beans, oats, and barley in February–March. The remaining land would lie fallow, or unused, and would be plowed and fertilized during the spring and summer to help restore its strength. The next year the fields were rotated: the fallow fields would be planted with the winter crop, the winter fields would be planted in the spring, and the spring fields would lie fallow.

There were two general forms of crop raising in Elizabethan England: champion (or open field) and woodland agriculture. In general, champion agriculture was most common in the central part of the country, and woodland was common around the edges.

In champion areas, all the fields around the village were open, without any hedges or divisions, and they belonged to the village as a whole. Each year the active fields were divided into a multitude of long, thin, half-acre strips. Each villager received a number of scattered strips according to the size of his landholding—the scattering of the strips ensured that no villager would receive all the inferior land. In champion lands, the villagers traditionally had the right to pasture their livestock on the village's pastures, on the fields and hay meadows after they were harvested, and on the fallows (where the manure helped refertilize the ground). There were also common rights over wastelands: forested areas were useful places for feeding pigs (they love acorns) and gathering firewood, and marshy lands could be used for pasturing livestock and gathering reeds. In a champion village, administration of agricultural matters would be subject to a court held by the landlord, or to a village meeting.

The mode of life in woodland areas was more individualistic and more efficient. There were no common lands, and each landholding was separate from the others. Since there were no commons, there was not the same need for the community to cooperate, and manorial courts and village meetings were not a part of woodland life. Woodland areas were not actually wooded: the borders of each holding were marked by tall hedges, which gave such regions a more wooded look.

During this period, landowners receiving fixed rents saw their real incomes decline, as the value of the rents was consumed by inflation. The inflation also hurt smaller landholders: only those with larger holdings produced enough surplus for their increased incomes to stay ahead of rising costs. This meant that smaller holdings were becoming less viable.

For many landowners and landholders, an obvious response to rising costs was to focus on raising sheep, which is much less labor-intensive than crop raising. Many landowners were finding means of ending tenancies and were enclosing open fields and commons for pasture. Contemporaries complained vociferously about this process of enclosure, which left increasing numbers of people without land or employment. They may have exaggerated the extent of the problem, but it was certainly a factor in the growing social displacement of the age.

Wool was England's principal source of wealth, its principal product, and its principal export. There were some ten to eleven million sheep in the country in 1558, or nearly four times the human population! Sheep raising provided little agricultural employment, but it did support a great deal of manufacturing work.

Once the sheep were shorn and the wool had been washed, it had to be carded. This involved stroking the wool between a pair of special brushes so that all the strands were running parallel, free of knots and tangles.

Agricultural Workers. The men have removed their outer garments in the heat; two women are also taking part. At bottom right are a basket and jug—harvest workers brought their food to the fields to save time. The wealthy landowner can be seen in the lower left-hand corner directing the work. From Raphael Holinshed, *The Chronicles of England, Scotlande and Icelande,* 1577.

The carded wool was then spun into thread. Spinning involved drawing out wool from the carded mass and spinning it so that it was tightly twisted. Wool fibers are covered with microscopic scales; when twisted in this way, the scaly strands cling to each other, making it possible for them to form thread. Woolen thread could be spun with a drop spindle (essentially a disk with a stick passing through the center). The spindle was suspended from the wool fibers and spun, causing the fibers to twist into thread. Alternatively, wool might be spun with a hand-cranked spinning wheel; the treadle wheel was used only for spinning flax into linen thread.

Carding and spinning could easily be done at home, and many, if not most, women practiced both daily as a means of supplementing the family income. Carding was also an easy job for children.

After spinning, the thread was woven into cloth on a horizontal loom. The cloth then had to be "fulled," or washed, to shrink and felt it. This made the fibers join more tightly with each other, so that the fabric was both stronger and denser, and therefore better at keeping out the English cold and rain. In fact, Elizabethan wools were so heavily felted that it was unnecessary even to hem them—they did not normally unravel. Sometimes the wool would be left its natural color, but often it would be dyed. This might happen as the very last stage, but sometimes it was done before the wool was even spun—hence the expression "dyed in the wool" (Singman, 27–29).

To read about rural life in Chaucer's England, see the Europe entry in the section "Rural Life" in chapter 3 ("Economic Life") in volume 2 of this series; for 18th-century England, see the entry in the section "Agriculture" in chapter 3 ("Economic Life") in volume 4 of this series; for Victorian England, see the section "Urban and Rural Environments" in chapter 3 ("Economic Life") in volume 5 of this series.

FOR MORE INFORMATION

Palliser, D. M. *The Age of Elizabeth*. New York: Longman, 1992.
Singman, J. L. *Daily Life in Elizabethan England*. Westport, Conn.: Greenwood, 1995.
Tawney, R. H., and E. Power. *Tudor Economic Documents*. London: Longmans, 1924.

ECONOMIC LIFE
|
RURAL LIFE
|
England

Spain

Italy

Maya

Aztec

Inca

SPAIN

In the 16th century, about 90 percent of the population of the country lived in rural villages and hamlets. Most were peasants who worked on the land. The landless day laborers (*jornaleros*) were the most unfortunate of the rural inhabitants and in some regions made up as much as half the population. They owned little or nothing and supported themselves by working for wages in other people's fields. They were often on the move in search of work, and lacking the means to save any money, they could never better their social condition. If there were seasonal labor shortages, they could demand higher wages, but often such boldness was quickly squashed. Laws were sometimes passed by local authorities that fixed the wages a *jornalero* could earn based on the price of food; the authorities were also the landowners who sold the food and paid the wages. Rural workers who became too vociferous in their demands were arrested and put in the pillory to be exposed to public ridicule.

Somewhat better off than the *jornaleros* were the independent peasant farmers who owned land. The *labradores*, who farmed their own fields, often possessed a pair of oxen and were self-employed. The oxen could be used to till the peasant's field, and they could also be rented out to neighbors.

Even the fairly well-to-do peasant lived on the edge of indigence, however, and could sink into the abyss of abject poverty at any time. The death of his beasts or a bad harvest could reduce him to the level of the day-wage laborer. But with good fortune such as a number of bountiful years, he could also acquire more wealth. He might buy more land to lease out to others and buy animals such as sheep and goats for meat, milk, and cheese, grazing them on common land. He could then live in a fine house and hire a few servants.

Rural villages usually also had public land that anyone could use. Communal ownership of property encompassed not only pastures and fields on the outskirts of town, but the village green and sometimes the public threshing and winnowing floor, the rubbish pile, and slaughter pen. The town also may have had ownership (or shared ownership with other towns) of nearby streams, lakes, and woodlands. There was also the community-owned, enclosed pasture for work animals such as oxen and mules.

Drinking water for residents and animals was considered public property and was generally controlled by the public officials. Another custom was the right of public gleaning for the benefit of the masses of rural poor. This allowed the collecting of apples, grapes, olives, and other fruit or vegetables that were overlooked during the harvest, or permitted the gathering of leftover grain when the regular harvest was finished. The old, the infirm, children, and women who could not support themselves from regular wages were entitled to participate in this practice. In regions where chestnuts and acorns grew, they were considered a common resource, along with uncultivated berries, fruits, or vegetables (such as wild asparagus, figs, and mushrooms). These could even be harvested on private lands, if not cultivated by the owner. In general, anything supplied by nature without being the product of man was common heritage. Such rights might include hunting and fishing and gathering firewood.

A little over half the land of Spain consisted of manor property, which was land owned by a wealthy individual (much of the rest was subject to the direct control of the king). The lord of the manor held nearly absolute power of life and death over his subject workers through his control of local justice and unrestricted authority over their possessions. He demanded and received allegiance from everyone, including the sheriff and the councilors of the towns in his jurisdiction. All knelt before him, swearing to pay the tributes and taxes he required in return for the safeguarding of the customs and usage that they enjoyed: such as the right, upon death, to be buried, the use of the oxen to plow the fields, and the mill to grind their wheat.

Wheat was the principal crop on the central plateau of Castile, and plowing the fields with oxen or mules, or hoeing the smaller patches of land in preparation for planting, was time-consuming and backbreaking work. Similarly, seeding the ground and tending the fields during the growing period, if vegetables or vines were involved, kept the farmer busy. The time of year and the phases of the moon dictated when planting and harvesting would take place. With the harvest finished in October, the peasant family worked in and around the house during the winter months, doing the odd jobs that required attention. Wine vats and irrigation ducts might need cleaning, the adobe walls of the house or the thatched roof might need repairing, farm implements and harnesses needed mending, cleaning, or sharpening, and animal manure needed collecting to fertilize the fields. Besides cooking, sewing, and tending the young children, the women usually looked after the domestic chickens or ducks (feeding them and gathering their eggs) and milked the goat or cow (making butter and cheese). They might also tend a vegetable patch near the house and sell some of the produce locally. Peasants' wives often spent the slack winter months engaged in artisan work such as spinning wool and making clothes, some of which might be sold at market.

Peasants paid about one-third to one-half of their harvests in rent if they did not own the land, another tenth or so to the lord of the manor for use of plowing oxen, and still more for the use of the threshing floor if it was not communally owned. They would then need enough of the harvest to feed the family and some to sell for cash to buy needed items, with still some left over for seed. Along with ecclesiastical and seigniorial taxes, and sometimes merchants' fees, it often happened that nothing was left over.

The councils of all cities, towns, and villages were endowed with the power to fix prices for agricultural products such as wine, oil, fruit, vegetables, grain, meat, and cheese. They granted monopoly rights to tavern keepers, butchers, and other dispensers of food and drink for the region. The official prices even applied to markets and were fixed to benefit the consumer, not the producer. Low prices drove some farmers out of business, for the councils attempted to regulate everything including working hours, milling procedures, and salaries. There were also prices fixed on the national level, where the crown dictated the maximum legal prices (the *tasa*) for grain, to ensure the poor could buy bread. The fact that there were no ceilings on the costs of farm tools, draft animals, seed, and other means of production, often drove the producer to cheat on the system, in spite of high penalties if caught, and to sell at black-market prices higher than those set by the government, to make ends meet.

There were some other occupations besides farming in the countryside, however. Often living at the subsistence level in the countryside were the shepherds who owned a few sheep or looked after the animals of a more affluent neighbor. Woodcutters and charcoal makers lived in the vast hinterland, often well away from civilization, and only came into towns to sell their products. Charcoal was always in demand in the winter months when families sat around the glowing brazier. Some peasants managed a living by hunting game in the forest or open table lands to sell at market.

A source of aggravation for the peasant of Castile was the destructive practice of the *Mesta*. This powerful corporation moved two to three million sheep to the south of the country for pasture in winter and back north again in summer. Guided by shepherds and protected by large, powerful dogs, the advancing flocks moved along the roads and through the fields, devouring everything in their path and raising vast dust clouds in their wake. Strings of mules and donkeys accompanied the flocks, carrying essential supplies, cooking pots, firewood, food for both shepherds and dogs, salt for the sheep, and even the lambs that were still too young to keep up. While crossing cultivated fields, certain marked-out paths (*cañadas*) were supposed to be followed, but the sheer number of animals made this difficult, and village crops would sometimes be devastated. The peasant had no recourse or compensation (Anderson, 147–58).

FOR MORE INFORMATION

Anderson, J. M. *Daily Life during the Spanish Inquisition*. Westport, Conn.: Greenwood, 2002.
Casey, J. *Early Modern Spain: A Social History*. London: Routledge, 1999.
Domínguez Ortiz, A. *The Golden Age of Spain, 1516–1659*. London: Weidenfeld and Nicolson, 1971.

ITALY

The economic base of rural society was agriculture, and land was its key resource. Many Italians owned land, but, in much of the countryside, most of it belonged to small numbers of large landholders. Typically, rural society divided sharply into those few who owned the bulk of the land and other productive resources, and the many who did the work.

Big landlords gathered their income from several sources. A major portion came from collecting rent or a share of the crop that their properties yielded. Many landowners also held the legal status of *signori* (lords), a feudal rank that entitled them to intervene in customary ways in the lives of their dependent peasants and to take compensation for those activities. As *signori* they administered justice; provided facilities such as mills, presses, and ovens; controlled hunting, fishing, and other uses of their domains, and commandeered labor for public projects. For revenue the *signore* (singular) collected fees and fines from those who brought suits or were convicted by his courts. He (or occasionally she) rented out the monopolies on the mill, the wine presses, the bakery, the inn, and the store. And if he did not want exclusive use of his woods and streams for himself, he sold licenses to others. Some lords also bought from the government the option to collect state taxes. Or the lord might encroach on the rights and revenues of the local churches and lay confraternities. Thus, the lords relied for their well-being on wealth exacted from the less advantaged rural majority. In theory, elite privileges entailed responsibility, and Christian duty urged charitable benevolence toward dependents and the needy. Lords and tenants on occasion did look out for one another's welfare. Yet the financial chasm between landlords and workers and the fundamental contradiction between their interests shaped more or less overtly antagonistic social relations in the countryside.

Peasants were the most numerous group of Renaissance Italians. In families they lived on and worked the land. Some peasants owned land, but mostly it belonged to landlords or, in rougher country, was commons. For access to land, peasants normally paid money rent or delivered a share of their yield to the owner. They might also enter contracts to secure livestock, tools, and equipment to work their farms. Furthermore, many of them owed various seigniorial dues in money, in kind, or in labor. They paid tithes to the church and, sometimes, taxes to the state. And, when times were hard, they often took on debt to pay their obligations. Feudal and economic dependency restricted peasants' options. Commonly, they had to piece together a livelihood from a medley of rural activities, in the home village or elsewhere. Theirs was not a closed world; economic necessity spurred much migration in search of income. Peasants consumed part of what they grew, but, for most, some of their produce, directly or via the landlord, made its way to market.

The organization of agriculture differed by locale, with varied patterns of family and residence. Peasant livelihood derived largely from family labor, supplemented where useful by hired workers. The most productive size and form of the residential group depended on the crops, holdings size, and tenure customs of a region. Thus, smaller nuclear families were better adapted to the less labor-intensive pastoralism of the mountain regions or to specialized farming with highly seasonal demands for workers. Larger, more extended family groups—whether built of three generations or of adult siblings—fitted well on the sharecropped, middle-sized farms of the arable north and center that could make use of a substantial supply of labor through much of the year. The lands a peasant household worked, especially in zones of mixed farming, were seldom contiguous and compact. Rather, the family might cultivate flax in one place, vegetables in another, and olives yet somewhere else.

Besides relying on family, peasants also used networks of assistance among their peers. Villagers enlisted one another's cooperation at the well and the washing place, in collective work, at religious festivals, in local government, and in collaborative lawsuits. These associations, though not always har-

Work on the Estate. Work in the countryside was very diverse—a true mixed economy. Here women milk the sheep and feed the chickens, while men work in the fields and at an oven. By Antonio Tempesta. Roma—Instituto Nazionale della Grafica. By gracious concession of the Ministero per i Beni e le Attività Culturali.

monious, extended peasants' capacity to cope. In dispersed settlements, such social exchanges, though probably scantier than in villages, were still crucial to sustaining peasant families.

Peasants' prosperity was unpredictable. Many factors shaped their fortune. It depended on the fertility of the land and on the weather. It shifted with the succession of good years, when prices favored the peasants, and bad years, when debts accumulated. When, in the later Renaissance, the population rose, the imbalance between scarce lands to work and many mouths to feed pressed on the peasantry as a whole. Yet some families fared better than others, whether through richer holdings, harder work, less greedy landlords, more fortunate timing of births and deaths, or just plain luck. Some peasants lived well, expanded their resources, and hired hands to boost their yield. Many others scraped by, improvising to keep the debt collector at bay and to hold on to their lands and goods.

Some rural people lacked access to land at all. Sharply disadvantaged, the landless were among the poorest in the community. There were, however, ways they—or surplus workers from landed peasant families—could earn a living. In some regions, instead of renting out parcels to families, landowners paid laborers to work their large estates. This pattern prevailed on the grain lands of the southeast and of Sicily. Elsewhere, harvesting and other labor-intensive seasonal tasks in agriculture provided at least temporary employment. And in many areas herding, woodcutting, and carting needed to be done. These activities often required workers to leave their home villages and move about the countryside. In some places, rural industry offered opportunities. Making bricks was country work. At a few sites workers extracted minerals: marble at the quarries near Carrara; iron in parts of Lombardy; and, from the 1460s, alum, used for fixing dyes in textiles, at the pope's mines at Tolfa. Elsewhere, the textile industries in wool, linen, and silk, though usually organized from cities, gave homework—spinning, weaving, fulling—to women and men in the countryside. Because such work was often only part-time, it often failed to provide a regular living. Especially in hard times, other options were to migrate or to seek work as a servant in the city, as a soldier abroad, or as a bandit in the hills. The sharp insecurities that the landless faced meant that families tended to fragment as they scrambled to survive (Cohen and Cohen, 21–26).

FOR MORE INFORMATION

Cherubini, G. *L'Italia rurale del Basso Medioevo*. Rome: Laterza, 1984.

Cohen, E. S., and T. V. Cohen. *Daily Life in Renaissance Italy*. Westport, Conn.: Greenwood, 2001.

McCardle, F. *Altopascio: A Study in Tuscan Rural Society, 1587–1784*. Cambridge: Cambridge University Press, 1978.

MAYA

The Maya economy was based on the production and distribution of food and a variety of goods, which were distributed throughout the Maya area and beyond. The development and growth of all civilizations require efficient means for producing food. The most important is usually agriculture; the harvesting of domesticated plants and, to a greater or lesser extent, the use of domesticated animals for food (animal husbandry). Today Maya men cultivate corn fields but also hunt and fish. Women often gather wild foods and maintain the gardens found next to most houses. The ancient Maya were probably no different, for in addition to hunting, fishing, and gathering wild foods, they relied on agriculture to produce many different crops and on several varieties of domesticated animals to produce an array of food sources. These methods were well adapted to the variety of environments found throughout the Maya area.

Over time, farmers perfected a variety of cultivation methods: nonintensive systems, in which fields were allowed to lie fallow between periods of cultivation; and intensive systems, in which fields were cultivated continuously.

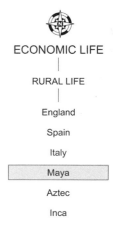

The most common form of nonintensive agriculture was swiddening. This involved clearing new fields from overgrowth or virgin forest, burning the debris, and planting for one or more years until the soil was depleted. In areas with better soils, the fallow periods may have lasted from one to three years for each year of cultivation. In areas with poorer soils, the fallow periods may have increased to three to six years for each year of cultivation. Large trees and species that provided wild foods or other useful products were probably left to grow with the stands of maize, beans, squashes, manioc, and other planted species. In most areas the fields could be planted and harvested for several successive seasons, depending on rainfall and soil fertility. When a field was depleted, it was abandoned to lie fallow and recover its fertility while other areas were cleared for fields.

Swiddening was probably among the oldest forms of agriculture used by the Maya. This method was undoubtedly used in the original colonization of forested areas. But it produced low yields while requiring large areas of land and therefore could only support small and scattered populations. As populations increased, fallow periods were shortened and more efficient methods were developed. Fallow periods were shortened by weeding and intercropping (growing several complementary species together, such as maize and beans). These techniques decreased competition for the food plants, reduced soil depletion, and even replenished nutrients in the soil.

Indirect evidence for the use of swiddening by the Maya comes from analyses of pollen samples in sediment cores from the beds of several southern lowland lakes. These show that the earliest settlers of that region grew maize. Remnants of ash fallout, possibly from field burning, indicate swiddening. Traces of ancient field systems are found mostly in the northern lowlands, consisting of stone boundary walls and water-flow deflectors; these could have been cultivated by swiddening.

Other relics of past agricultural uses have been found by archaeologists. Remnants of stone terraces have been identified in several areas of the lowlands. These were used to artificially level areas of sloped landscape and help retain water in the soil to increase productivity. Archaeological excavations indicate that these terraces were constructed during Middle Maya Civilization. Such agricultural features require a heavy investment of labor, which implies that they may have been used for intensive agricultural methods.

The Maya used several intensive agricultural methods, including continuous field cultivation, household gardens, arboriculture, and hydraulic modifications. Continuous field cultivation involves growing crops with little or no fallow periods, so that the fields never become overgrown. This requires constant weeding and maintenance. Continuous cultivation could have been used in areas with fertile soils and plentiful rainfall, such as the alluvial valleys in parts of the southern and coastal lowlands. Alluvial valleys provide especially fertile soils on natural river levees and bottom lands, where periodic flooding replenishes soil fertility by depositing new alluvial soils.

There is only indirect evidence to indicate that the Maya used continuous cultivation. It is likely that some Mayas constructed agricultural features, such as terraces, that were used for continuous cultivation. Estimates of peak sizes and densities of Maya populations in the southern lowlands suggest that continuous cultivation may have been a necessary part of the ancient system. The high potential yields from alluvial soils suggest that continuous cultivation could have transformed these areas into bread-baskets that supplied large amounts of maize, beans, and other staples to feed the great Maya cities.

Household gardens are a common form of intensive agriculture in Maya communities today. Gardens are cultivated in the open spaces adjacent to each house. These gardens usually provide a great variety of foods: annual root crops, maize, beans, and other field species, as well as perennial shrubs, vines, and trees. Because weeding and other maintenance is minimal and the rate of soil depletion is low, household gardens continuously supply large quantities of foods per unit of land. Soil depletion is minimized by intercropping; fertilization comes from plant residues and human and animal waste from the household.

The Maize Crop. Like the ancient Maya, this modern farmer feeds his family by growing large crops of maize despite difficult conditions. © David Alan Harvey/Magnum Photos.

In one extraordinary case, archaeologists have found portions of preserved household gardens buried by volcanic ash from a sudden eruption. These have been carefully excavated at Cerén, El Salvador. The ash preserved the casts of a variety of crops, some grown right next to the remains of houses. There were carefully tilled rows for cotton and several food plants, including maize and manioc, separated by furrows that facilitated drainage. The volcanic ash also preserved fences made of sticks that protected fields from pests, and storage facilities for the harvested food.

There are 16th-century Spanish descriptions of Maya household gardens. There is also indirect evidence for such gardens. Settlement studies show a nearly uniform spacing of residences throughout most sites. Spaces between the house remains, not large enough for agricultural fields, are just the right size for household gardens. At many lowland archaeological sites, there are unusually heavy stands of food-producing trees, especially ramon. They probably represent the descendants of stands grown around the houses of Tikal and other lowland cities. Some food trees—such as ramon, cacao (chocolate), and avocado—may also have been cultivated in extensive groves in areas of low population. Studies of the yields from ramon trees show that they produce ten times more food per unit of land than maize. Ramon is a starchy food that can be processed and used like maize to make tortillas. Tree crops require little labor, and the fruit or nuts of some species may be collected from the ground as they fall. By mingling different food tree species, the Maya would have discouraged pests or diseases that thrive on a single species.

Both archaeological evidence and ethnohistorical accounts indicate that tree crops were once important to the Maya. Cacao was a highly valued tree crop in lowland environments. In addition to its use as a beverage, cacao beans were used as money in economic exchanges (even counterfeit cacao beans made of clay have been found). Pottery images of cacao pods have been found at Copan, Quirigua, and other Maya sites, indicating these cities controlled important production areas for chocolate.

The Maya used hydraulic modifications to intensify food production. They dug extensive networks of ditches to irrigate crops and to drain excess water from saturated soils, thereby allowing better growth. Edzna, in the northern lowlands, has an impressive canal and reservoir system capable of irrigating at least 450 hectares of cultivated land. The Edzna hydraulic system was constructed during Early Maya Civilization (ca. 300–50 B.C.E.) and probably was used for several centuries thereafter.

Even more extensive are the remains of raised fields constructed in low-lying areas. These provided fertile and well-drained growing conditions for a variety of crops, including maize, cotton, and possibly cacao. Raised fields are built by digging narrow drainage canals in water-saturated soils and heaping the earth to both sides, forming raised plots for growing crops. By periodically dredging the muck from the drainage channels, farmers replenished the raised plots with fresh soil and organic debris, allowing continuous cultivation. The canals also may have been used to raise fish, mollusks, and other aquatic life.

Traces of raised fields have been detected by aerial photography in several areas of the Maya lowlands. Although more research is needed to verify the function of detected canal networks, it is obvious that hydraulic agriculture was a major source of food in the lowlands, beginning during Early Maya Civilization and, increasingly, during Middle Maya Civilization (Sharer, 95–110).

To read about rural life in 20th-century Latin America, see the Latin America entry in the section "Urban and Rural Experience" in chapter 3 ("Economic Life") in volume 6 of this series.

FOR MORE INFORMATION

Harrison, P. D., and B. L. Turner, eds. *Pre-Hispanic Maya Agriculture.* Austin: University of Texas Press, 1978.

Sharer, R. J. *Daily Life in Maya Civilization.* Westport, Conn.: Greenwood, 1996.

ECONOMIC LIFE

RURAL LIFE

England

Spain

Italy

Maya

Aztec

Inca

AZTEC

One of the most productive agricultural achievements in precontact New World history was the Aztec *chinampa* system, consisting of long, rectangular gardens made from reclaimed swampland within or connected to the lakes of the Basin of Mexico. The peoples who migrated into Central Mexico in the 13th century were expert farmers and learned that the success of the *chinampa* system depended in part on the remarkably fertile soils in and around the lakes. During their early years around Lake Tezcoco, the Aztecs developed their farming and military skills as they sought to attach themselves to the stronger city-states. They were eventually rejected by one of the most powerful communities and were driven off the mainland and forced to live on swamps. They responded by raising *chinampa* fields, which meant piling up vertical rows of mud and vegetation between pylons. Then they dug canals in between these raised gardens and planted willow trees on the margins of the fields so that the extensive roots of the willows would serve as effective walls to the earthen gardens. The Aztecs would dredge the mud out of the base of the canals and reapply it to the garden soils to rejuvenate them with nutrients. Thus, each *chinampa* was a slender, rectangular strip of garden land 10 to 25 feet wide by 50 to 300 feet long. Farming families lived on these earthen platforms in houses made of cane, wood, and reeds. The *Matrícula de Tributos*, a map of some of the *chinampa* system, shows several waterways separating *chinampas*, each with the figure and house of an owner, whose name appears as a hieroglyph and a Spanish annotation.

Eventually, this system of gardening required a sophisticated bureaucracy to manage the irrigation, planting, and harvesting of corn, amaranth, squash, and beans. It produced huge amounts of foodstuffs and flowers that contributed significantly to the rise and wealth of the city.

This system of farming was so productive that parts of the surfaces of three of the lakes (Chalco, Xochimilco, and Tezcoco) were reduced from open lakes into net-

works of *chinampas* and canals. This also meant that the produce could be easily loaded from the *chinampas* into canoes and taken directly to the urban markets along the lakes and to the markets in Tenochtitlan and Tlatelolco.

The *chinampa* lands were owned not by the individual farmer or his immediate family, but by the *calpulli*, or clan. On the one hand, the farmer and his family who worked the local *chinampa* could enlarge their holding if, for instance, the family increased in size and the *calpulli* owned vacant ground. On the other hand, failure to cultivate land under a farmer's control resulted, after two years, in a warning that one

> ### 📷 *Snapshot*
>
> **Sixteenth-Century Spanish Account of Aztec Gardens**
>
> We went to the orchard and garden, which was such a wonderful thing to see and walk in, that I was never tired of looking at the diversity of the trees, and noting the scent which each one had, and the paths full of roses and flowers, and the many fruit trees and native roses, and the pond of fresh water. There was another thing to observe, that great canoes were able to pass into the garden from the lake through an opening that had been made so that there was no need for their occupants to land. And all was cemented and very splendid with many kinds of stone [monuments] with pictures on them, which gave much to think about. (Carrasco, 66)

more year of neglect would mean loss of that land. These farmers paid taxes in the form of foodstuffs, flowers, and cloth woven by women. These taxes went to support local temple schools, governors, ministers, the military, and especially the nobles. When the Spaniards came, they called the *chinampas* floating gardens, a name that has persisted to this day. Visitors to Mexico City today can see and ride in small boats through an impressive remnant of the *chinampas* in the southern district of Xochimilco.

This combination of a raised earthen mound surrounded by water represents one of the most interesting archetypes or symbolic models of Aztec society. It reflects in miniature the image of Cemanahuac (or land surrounded by water) that expressed the general Aztec view of their world. A plot of land, especially a raised plot of land, was an *altepetl*, or water mountain, from the metaphorical phrase *in atl, in tepetl*, meaning the water(s), the mountain(s). But *altepetl*, or mountain of water, was the general term used throughout the Nahuatl-speaking world for an organization of people holding sway over a given territory, community, or city. It referred to the human and social need to organize life around two aspects of nature: a solid piece of ground and life-giving water, as well as human solidarity and agricultural resources. A great pyramid with a spring or nearby water resource was an *altepetl*, as was a social community of extended families and workers. The different *altepetl* were organized into larger units called *tlatocayotl,* small local states that were constantly forming alliances, trading, and fighting with one another. Each *tlatocayotl* organized the agricultural schedule, work, and products of its *altepetl* and regulated the work of the *chinampas.*

The *chinampas* surrounded most of the city of Tenochtitlan and were abundant along some of the lakeshores. A sizable portion of the plants grown there was shipped to the many city markets. Markets, called *tianquiztli,* were in every sizable neighborhood within the island community and in every town and most villages in the countryside. Villages had market days at five-day intervals, with inhabitants walking as many as 15 miles back and forth to meet friends and family, renew friendships, make deals, exchange information, and trade. As one scholar notes, "Certain towns were famous for their specialties: Acolman for edible dogs, Azcatpotzalco for birds and slaves, Cholula for featherwork, and Tezcoco for its textiles and painted gourds."

Due to the overwhelming importance of agriculture, the earth was considered a divine entity, a great sprawling god, and sometimes many different gods (or many different vessels), who provided food for humans and also consumed humans after they died. The people not only grew crops, but also believed that they were created by the spirits of the crops, especially the maize god. A general view of this human/agricultural relationship appears in this passage from the Maya creation story in the *Popul Vuh,* where human ancestors, "our first mother and father," were created: "Only yellow corn and white corn were their bodies. Only food were the legs and arms of man" (Carrasco, 93–115).

To read about rural life in 20th-century Latin America, see the Latin America entry in the section "Urban and Rural Experience" in chapter 3 ("Economic Life") in volume 6 of this series.

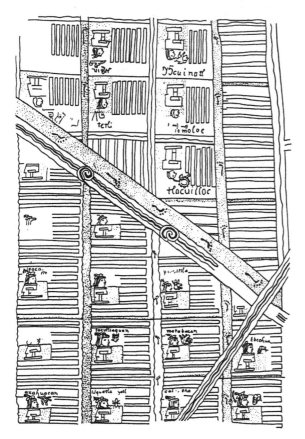

Matrícula de Tributos: A Map of *Chinampa* Plots. As this document makes clear, the *chinampas* (gardens built in the lake) were carefully laid out and organized. The *calpulli* (clan) that owned each plot is depicted as a head on top of a small house. Warwick Bray, *Everyday Life of the Ancient Aztecs.* London: B.T. Batsford, Chrysalis Books, 1968.

ECONOMIC LIFE
|
RURAL LIFE
|
England

Spain

Italy

Maya

Aztec

Inca

FOR MORE INFORMATION

Armillas, P. "Gardens on Swamps." *Science* 174 (1976): 653–61.

Carrasco, D., with S. Sessions. *Daily Life of the Aztecs: People of the Sun and Earth.* Westport, Conn.: Greenwood, 1998.

Sanders, W., J. Parsons, and R. Santley. *The Basin of Mexico: Ecological Processes in the Evolution of a Civilization.* New York: Academic Press, 1979.

INCA

For the Incas, the main means of subsistence was agriculture, the sowing and reaping of domesticated plants, and the breeding of domesticated animals. The Andes is one of several places in the world where many plants and animals were originally domesticated as people learned their cycles of reproduction. An entire range of plants was grown by Andean people in the different environmental zones. The most important crop grown was corn, also known as maize. Corn beer, called *chicha*, was consumed in large quantities as a dietary drink and during important ceremonies.

A wide variety of other crops were also grown, including potatoes, quinoa (a midaltitude grain with a high protein content), oca and *ullucu* (two high-altitude tubers, similar in use to potatoes but different in flavor and shape), many different kinds of beans and squash, sweet potatoes, manioc and yuca (both starchy, low-altitude tubers), tomatoes, chili peppers, avocados, and peanuts. Other inedible plants were also grown, such as coca (chewed with lime to withstand cold and fatigue), cotton, and gourds. The two main domesticated animals were llamas and alpacas; the former was used as a pack animal, and the latter's soft wool was used for clothing. Ducks and guinea pigs were raised for food as well.

These plants and animals were exploited in different combinations in different environmental zones in the Andes Mountains. The Incas used these zones very effectively, in terms of both the crops grown and the use of people to grow them. Farming implements were very simple: a foot plow, hoe, and clod breaker were used for preparing fields for planting. The foot plow turned up large chunks of earth, which were then crushed with the clod breaker, a clublike tool. The hoe, whose blade came straight out from the handle rather than at a 90-degree angle (like that of modern hoes), was used for weeding and breaking up clods as well. In the absence of draft animals, these were the only tools needed—and they were very effective. Even today it is common to see Andean people preparing fields with these same tools. Agriculture was done by both men and women, with men using the foot plow, and women the hoe. Harvesting was also done by both sexes working together, as it is today.

In addition to agriculture, the Incas used wild plants and animals to supplement their diet. Certain areas of each province were reserved as hunting grounds, although the inhabitants could request permission of the king to use them. Deer and guanaco, a wild relative of the llama, were the main prey. Vicuñas, another wild relative of the llama, were caught for their extremely soft wool; they were released after

---

 Snapshot

The Inca Messenger System

The Inca empire built a very effective road and communication system based around two major north-south highways that were roughly 3,000 kilometers long. One highway ran along the Pacific coast, one highway ran along the top of the Andes mountains, and there were numerous east-west roads connecting these two highways. There was a small hut called a *choza* approximately every two kilometers along all these roads. These huts were the bases for the *chasqui* (runners) who carried official government messages and reports. Between four and eight *chasqui* were stationed at each *choza*. When a message arrived, a *chasqui* would run quickly to the next *choza* and pass the message on to another *chasqui*, a system similar to the pony express in the western United States several centuries later. Because of the frequent change of runners and the short distances, the runners were always fresh and able to run at top speed.

The *chasqui* wore a white-feather headdress so that they could be seen a long way off from the next *choza*. They also blew a shell horn to announce their imminent arrival so that the next *chasqui* would be ready to meet them, run along with them in order to receive the message, and sprint off toward the next *choza*. This system was capable of transmitting messages and small parcels roughly 200 miles per day. Fresh fish from the Pacific was even delivered to the emperor at Cuzco, in the heart of the Andes, by means of this system! In contrast, it took the Spanish conquerors roughly one week to traverse 200 miles in this difficult terrain.

---

shearing. The wool was spun and woven into clothing. Birds were killed by snares, slings, or the bola, a series of leather strips with stones tied at the ends.

Because the Incas were a highland group originally, they did not make significant use of ocean and lake resources. However, Pacific coastal groups caught fish and shellfish, which were an important addition to the diet. There are reports that the Inca king had ocean fish brought to him as a delicacy, using the messenger service along the road system. Groups around Lake Titicaca fished the waters there as well and were allowed to pay tribute to the Incas in fish.

One of the Incas' less appreciated achievements was their development of significant agricultural systems throughout the Andes. The Incas reorganized conquered peoples to increase their production of agricultural crops, particularly corn. In the highland regions this was often done by constructing large groups of terraces and irrigation works. Today there are approximately one million hectares of terraced land in the Andes, and studies in different parts of the Andes indicate that many of the terraces were constructed during Inca times. Although the use of terracing preceded the Incas, they often expanded on existing systems and improved them by adding irrigation. The Inca engineers' effectiveness in planning terraces is indicated by the fact that many of them are still in use today, almost 500 years after their construction.

Remains of Terraces in the Colca Valley, Peru. These terraces were probably first built under the influence of the Huari people. When they were cultivated, the mountainside became valuable farmland. Photo by Michael A. Malpass.

Inca irrigation and water management systems also were impressive. Irrigation canals were often many kilometers long, and sometimes they were lined with stone and covered. The Incas also straightened entire river channels in the region of Cuzco; and it is reported that the bed of the Tullumayo River, where it flowed through Cuzco, was completely paved. Aqueducts, to bring water over gullies, and reservoirs, to store water during the dry season, were also notable features of Inca engineering.

The Huari people, who flourished 600–1000 C.E., were perhaps the first people to introduce the terracing system. These terraces were made by building a series of stone walls on the mountainside and filling the area behind and uphill from each wall with soil. Terraces provided flat area for planting; they were generally constructed one above another, like stairs going up the side of a mountain. In addition, irrigation canals were dug to bring water to the terraces.

The Huari were not the first agricultural innovators. Before them, the Tiahuanaco people, located on the Altiplano (high plateau) around Lake Titicaca in the puna zone (with an altitude above 11,500 feet), faced serious agricultural challenges. Because of the altitude, agriculture is exceedingly difficult and virtually all that grows are potatoes and other hardy plants of this zone. In addition, near Lake Titicaca the ground is flat and the water table is high, which makes farming difficult. The Tiahuanaco people used an ingenious method of raised fields for dealing with these problems. A raised field is built by digging a trench and piling the earth up to form a raised area above the trench. By building several of these together and connecting the ditches, one gets a system of low areas, the ditches, which fill up with water, and high areas, the fields, where crops can be planted. Two major advantages of raised fields are that they allow cold night air to run off the fields into the ditches, thus reducing frost damage, and they provide better drainage for the plants. Experiments done with modern fields constructed in the ancient manner indicate that they are much more productive than cultivation without raised fields. The rulers of Tiahuanaco developed a vast system of raised fields to increase the yields of crops, both to feed their population and for trade. Because many important crops—such as corn, beans, squash, and fruits—cannot be grown on the Altiplano, they must be obtained from regions lower down. To get these valuable foods, the people of Tiahuanaco had to develop a surplus that they could trade.

All the land of conquered people was said to belong to the Inca king. The conquered people then were required to work the land. The Incas divided the food produced by each conquered people into three parts: for support of the priests and priestesses of the Inca religion, for support of the large Inca political bureaucracy, and for use by the conquered people themselves. The Incas also claimed ownership of all animals and divided the conquered peoples' herds of llamas and alpacas by the same proportions. Apparently the relative sizes of the distributions were variable; in some regions the Inca religion received a larger part, and in others the state did. In these situations, it might appear that the Incas reduced the amount of food allotted to the conquered people by a substantial amount, which might have caused starvation. However, Spanish writers have noted that each household was given sufficient fields for its use and that each year the Incas evaluated whether a family's holdings were adequate. Furthermore, the Incas used the labor of conquered people to build new fields and irrigation systems to produce additional food. So people probably were not forced to give up most of their food; rather, they likely had to produce more to satisfy the Incas' tribute demands.

The Incas required all taxpaying individuals (i.e., the heads of households) to work a certain period of time each year for the empire. This labor was called *m'ita*. Each household, which was the unit of taxation, had to send a person for *m'ita* work. What they did depended on their skills. Many men were required to serve in the army. Others either transported food and goods from local fields to the Inca centers, or made crafts.

M'ita labor was organized in such a way as to minimize disruption in the lives of the worker and his family. When a person was called to do *m'ita* labor, other *ayllu* (family) members were required to do his other work for the community. Involving the *ayllu* was determined in such a way that enough men were left at home to tend the fields and crops. The principal job of the *curacas* (local governors) was to decide whose turn it was to work in the *m'ita* rotation (Malpass, 22–26, 42–44, 50–51, 65).

To read about rural life in 20th-century Latin America, see the Latin America entry in the section "Urban and Rural Experience" in chapter 3 ("Economic Life") in volume 6 of this series.

FOR MORE INFORMATION

Denevan, W., K. Matthewson, and G. Knapp, eds. *Pre-Hispanic Agricultural Fields in the Andean Region*. Oxford: British Archaeological Reports, International Series 359i, 1987.

Erickson, C. "Raised Field Agriculture in the Lake Titicaca Basin." *Expedition* 30, no. 3: 8–16.

Malpass, M. A. *Daily Life in the Inca Empire.* Westport, Conn.: Greenwood, 1996.

ECONOMIC LIFE

CITY LIFE

England

Spain

Italy

Ottoman Empire

Maya

Aztec

Inca

City Life

City is a very difficult term to define. Big cities today are associated with skyscrapers, subway systems, millions of inhabitants, and large immigrant communities. Obviously, cities of the 15th and 16th centuries were very different, though they often did have large numbers of immigrants. Population density alone does not offer an accurate definition of *city* since many villages were as densely populated as cities, even if they were ultimately smaller; size does not necessarily help either since major cities such as London had a population of only around fifty thousand, smaller than many large towns in the United States today. In fact, it may not be possible to give one definition that will fit all the various cases of cities.

While definition may ultimately fail, it is possible to list some traits that cities often possess. First of all, cities tend to be densely populated: houses are built in close proximity with little or no space between them. Secondly, cities tend to be governmental and organizational centers. For example, cities in Europe tend to be associated with the seat of a bishop, while the ruling nobility occupied the centers of cities in Mesoamerica and South America. Finally, and perhaps most importantly, the residents of cities tend to have occupations that do not directly involve agriculture. Cities are thus filled with shopkeepers, artisans, craftsmen, merchants, entertainers, sailors, servants, beggars, royalty, and the independently wealthy. Some of these may have contact with farm workers: they may ship agricultural goods or direct estates, but they do not actually work on the land itself. Densely populated centers where the residents farm tend to be called villages; if the occupants do other jobs, they tend to be called cities.

Life in European cities was exciting, but also hectic and dirty. In late 16th-century London, for example, people from many different social brackets could take the day off and watch a Shakespeare play. On the way to the theater, however, they would have to steer clear of pickpockets, beggars, and household refuse, including human waste, which was thrown out onto the street. On the way back, though, there was the opportunity to stop at an inn for a good meal, or to examine the work of the many cloth merchants and consider having a new garment made. In Seville, one could go down to the port and watch the ships coming and going to all parts of the known world, including the Americas.

Life in Mesoamerican and South American cities was also undoubtedly exciting. The Incas at Cuzco received merchandise from all over their empire. The king would even have fish delivered from the far away Pacific Ocean. At Tenochtitlan, one could watch the famous religious ceremonies and examine the new captives taken in the latest military campaign. Cities, moreover, were particularly tied to Native Americans' conception of self and the universe. Tenochtitlan, for example, reflected the Aztec notion of the world as divided into four quarters with one central section. Like the world, Tenochtitlan also had a central section, with a temple to the founder deity Huitzilpochtli, surrounded by four other districts. The founding myth of the Inca city of Cuzco, by comparison, highlighted the royal privileges of the Inca people due to their descent from the legendary original founder of the city, Manco Capac. Belonging to a city thus defined who you were and your place in the universe.

The cities of Europe, the Americas, and the Ottoman Empire were frequently segregated. In Europe, not only would immigrants, such as the Flemish in London, tend to live in the same district, but also members of the same profession would tend to live in the same area, even the same street. Artisans, craftsmen, and other skilled laborers all formed their own guilds, which were a kind of trade union that ensured both a certain standard of performance and a certain level of compensation. These guilds did not handle just economic matters, however, they also sponsored festivals, pageants, and charitable functions. Members of guilds often lived on the same street, went to the same church, and frequented the same inns. Many city streets in England and Spain are named after the various trades that used to dominate them. In the Americas, the segregation tended to take place on the lines of birth. If you were noble, you lived in the center of the town. If you were a particularly skilled craftsman, you might live in districts near the nobles, since they formed your main customers. Foreigners and commoners would live on the outskirts of the towns and in the surrounding villages. This segregation was sometimes very formally marked. In Cuzco, for example, the noble Incas that inhabited the center of the city were separated from the lower-status groups by a strip of arable land.

Cities, then, are densely populated organizational centers in which the residents are not agricultural workers. Especially in Mesoamerica and South America, cities were intimately connected with a nation's view of itself and its world. Cities served as centers of government and commerce, and also manifested the segregations in the life and work of their populace.

~Lawrence Morris

ENGLAND

In towns, the economy was dominated by crafts and trades. There was very little actual industry at this time; finished products were largely provided by craftsmen and tradesmen out of small specialty shops. Among the most common craftsmen and tradesmen were shoemakers, glovers, tailors, tanners, bakers, weavers, butchers, smiths, carpenters, and joiners. The independent craftsman combined the functions of employer, workman, merchant, and shopkeeper: he did his own work, and he marketed and sold his products from his own workshop. The craftsman or trades-man's shop was usually the front ground-floor room of his home; he would live upstairs with his family, servants, and apprentices, and might hire additional workers, called journeymen, who would assist him during the day but live elsewhere.

Crafts and trades were entered through the system of apprenticeship. An apprentice might have some hope of real economic and social advancement. He would live

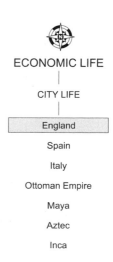

ECONOMIC LIFE
|
CITY LIFE
|
England

Spain

Italy

Ottoman Empire

Maya

Aztec

Inca

in the home of his master, receiving bed, board, and even some pocket money in exchange for his labor in the master's shop. The apprentice thereby would learn a marketable skill; in some cases instruction in reading, writing, and perhaps arithmetic would also be provided. Apprentices were supposed to be under their master's strict supervision, although in practice it seems that many found opportunity to roam about with their fellow apprentices. Apprenticeship lasted for seven years.

	Denomination	Value	Purchase Value	Equivalent
Silver Coins	halfpenny (ob.)	1/2 of a penny	1 quart of ale	$1
	penny (d.)		1 loaf of bread	$2
	twopenny (half-groat)	2d.		$4
	shilling (s.)	12d.	1 day's earnings for a craftsman	$25
Gold Coins	half-crown	2s. 6d.	1 day's earnings for a gentleman	$60
	quarter angel	2s. 6d.		$60
	angelet	5s.		$100
	crown	5s.	1 week's earnings for a craftsman	$100
	angel	10s.	1 lb. of spices	$250
	sovereign (new standard)	20s. (1 li.)		$500
	sovereign (old standard)	30s.		$750
	Dutch florin	2s.		$50
	French crown	6s. 4d.		$150
	Spanish ducat	6s. 8d.		$150
Moneys of Account	farthing (q.)	1/4 of a penny		$.50
	three-farthings	$3/4$d.		$1.50
	three-halfpenny	$1\frac{1}{2}$d.	1 lb. of cheese	$3
	threepenny	3d.	1 lb. of butter	$6
	groat	4d.	1 day's food	$8
	mark (marc.)	13s. 4d. (2/3 of 1 li.)		$350
	pound (li.)	20s.	1 carthorse	$500

Approximate Values of Elizabethan Money.

Another important form of work was service. Servants were very common in Renaissance England; they were particularly likely to be young people who would eventually leave service for a more advantageous position. Fewer in number but nonetheless significant were the sailors and soldiers who helped build England's incipient commercial and colonial empire. They were widely glorified for their exploits and achievements, yet they were also mistrusted by the population at large, as they integrated poorly into the fabric of civilian life.

Although the economy was organized around men, women played a crucial role in the economic life of the country. In fact, both husband and wife were expected to work, although she was normally engaged in labor that could be done at home. In towns, women engaged in a wide variety of work; they were especially likely to be employed as seamstresses, laundresses, and street vendors. The wife of a craftsman or tradesman often helped her husband in his work; and if he died, she might carry on the business herself. There were even a few instances of women plying crafts or trades in their own right in the city, but these were quite rare.

English money consisted of silver and gold coins; even the smallest, the halfpenny, was worth more than most coins today. There was a serious need for smaller denominations, but the halfpenny was already so tiny (about half an inch across) that a smaller coin would have been unusable. The problem was not solved until James I introduced brass coinage in the early 17th century. The typical 15th- and 16th-century coin bore the image of the monarch on one side and the royal coat of arms and a cross on the other. Its actual value was linked to the value of the gold or silver in it and was therefore susceptible to fluctuations in the prices of gold and silver, as well as to changes in the purity of the coins.

It is difficult to compare Renaissance English money with modern money, since the economy was very different from our own. Labor was relatively cheap—principally because it was widely accepted that commoners should expect a low standard of living. Manufactured goods, on the other hand, were comparatively expensive. There was almost no mechanization, so the vastly increased hours of labor more than negated the lower rate of pay. Moreover, prices could fluctuate enormously according to time and place. Prices today tend to be fairly constant because we have a well-developed system of transportation and storage. Renaissance people did not have the same opportunities to shop around, nor could they stock up on perishable goods when they were cheap and plentiful. Prices were therefore very sensitive to the supply and demand at a particular time and place. Naturally, wages and prices were higher in London than in the country.

Overall, the 16th century was a period of unprecedented inflation; prices rose during Elizabeth's reign by about 100–150 percent. This was good news for some, and bad for others. Substantial landholders whose production was considerably larger than their expenditures profited: higher prices meant they could sell their surplus for more money. Small landholders, producing little or no surplus, were more at risk, since their income barely kept pace with their expenditures. Above all, wage-earners suffered from inflation, as the real value of their wages was eaten up by rising costs. By the early 17th century, the real wages of agricultural laborers were only half of what they had been two centuries before.

Shepherd's Boy	2 1/2d./day with food
Shepherd	6d./week with food
Unskilled Rural Laborer	2-3d./day with food
Plowman	1s./week with food
Skilled Rural Laborer	6d./day
Laborer	9d./day 26s. 6d./year with food and drink
Craftsman	12d./day, 7d. with food and drink £4-10/year with food and drink
Yeoman	£2-6/year or more
Minor Parson	£10-30/year
Esquire	£500-1000/year
Knight	£1000-2000/year
Nobleman	£2500/year
30-acre landholding	£14, or a surplus of £3-5 after paying for foodstuffs
Soldier	5d./day
Sergeant, Drummer	$8^1/_2$d./day
Ensign	1s./day
Lieutenant	2s./day
Captain	4s./day

Sample Wages and Incomes.

Meal at an inn	4-6d.	Gentleman's meal in his room at an inn	2s.
Bed in an inn	1d.	Lodging a horse	12-18d.
Food for one day	4d.	Loaf of bread	1d.
Butter (1 lb.)	3d.	Cheese (1 lb.)	$1^1/_2$ d.
Eggs (3)	1d.	Fresh salmon	13s. 4d.
Beef (1 lb.)	3d.	Cherries (1 lb.)	3d.
Sugar (1 lb.)	20s.	Cloves (1 lb.)	11s.
Pepper (1 lb.)	4s.	Wine (1 qt.)	1s.
Ale (1 qt.)	$^1/_2$d.	Tobacco	3s./ounce
Officer's canvas doublet	14s. 5d.	Officer's cassock	27s. 7d.
Shoes	1s.	White silk hose	25s.
Candles (48)	3s. 3d.	Soap (1 lb.)	4d.
Knives (2)	8d.	Bed	4s.
Spectacles (2 pr.)	6d.	Scissors	6d.
Bible	£2	Broadside ballad	1d.
Small book	6d.-2s.	Theater admission	1, 2, or 3d.
Tooth pulled	2s.	Portraits	62s. to £6
Horse	£1-2		
Hiring a horse	12d./day or $2^1/_2$d./mile	Hiring a coach	10s./day

Sample Prices of Goods and Services.

In the 15th and 16th centuries, used goods played a much larger role in the economy than they do in today's economy. Crafted items such as furniture were quite expensive; clothing was especially costly, since so much labor went into producing the cloth. For this reason, many people bought such products secondhand from some sort of dealer, who might refurbish the goods to improve their resale value. The cost of materials likewise encouraged recycling, which was also a significant element in the economy: building materials, cloth, leather, and metal were all subject to reuse, and the paper industry relied wholly on recycled rags. See the tables given to gain an idea of the prices in English cities during the 15th and 16th centuries (Singman, 29–36).

To read about city life in Chaucer's England, see the Europe entry in the section "Urban Economic Life" in chapter 3 ("Economic Life") in volume 2 of this series and the London entry in the section "Great Cities" in chapter 3 ("Economic Life") in volume 2 of this series; for Victorian England, see the Victorian England entry in the section "Urban and Rural Environments" in chapter 3 ("Economic Life") in volume 5 of this series.

FOR MORE INFORMATION

Singman, J. L. *Daily Life in Elizabethan England.* Westport, Conn.: Greenwood, 1995.

ECONOMIC LIFE
|
CITY LIFE
|
England

Spain

Italy

Ottoman Empire

Maya

Aztec

Inca

SPAIN

There were two great cities in Spain: Madrid and Seville. Madrid, the capital, was inland and Seville, the great shipping port, was on the seacoast.

The position and growth of the capital posed problems in supply. Goods had to be transported overland on the backs of donkeys and mules, as few wagons were used due to the bad state of the roads, which were little more than rough trails. Long caravans of animals converged on the city from the vineyards of the river Duero in the north and the rolling wheat-growing hills of Salamanca. Fruits, vegetables, and olives from distant regions of the country found a place in Madrid markets. Congestion and long waits occurred at tax-collecting stations on the roads at the city's outskirts. The government struggled to keep necessities at an affordable level, but the threat of shortages and even famine was always a factor, and strict supervision was accorded the sale and price of wheat and bread.

Sheep, goats, and pigs were the principal source of meat and, along with cattle, could be grazed on the uncultivated lands near the city. On the many days of fasting, fish such as trout and carp from the local streams in the nearby mountains were in demand, but these could entail an all-day journey to market. On Fridays as the fish cart passed through certain residential districts to its place of sale, the residents complained to the authorities of the awful stench that forced them to close their doors.

Most of the working inhabitants of Madrid found some way to make a living from the activity generated by the court. Some were employed there or in the chancellery, and many found work in the transport of goods provisioning the city or in distribution and resale. Others engaged in the production of bread and pastries or the manufacture and sale of lingerie.

The city produced no products for export. Besides dealings in food, the economy also revolved around trade in the arts and crafts. Occupations such as embroidery, tailoring, and gilding transformed imported materials into finished luxury products for the aristocratic society at court and government officials. An underground economy also existed among hawkers who sold crucifixes, perfumes, toilet accessories, trinkets, and tawdry finery such as bracelets and necklaces. This trade was often in the hands of foreigners, especially the French, who were well represented in Madrid and who smuggled in much of the merchandise. Laws prohibiting the sale of objects originating in other countries had little effect on the trade.

The largest concentration of the poor was to be found in the southern sector of the city. Here life was lived in the narrow passageways, and loud squabbles between neighbors as well as tavern brawls were common. Street names stemmed from the occupations of the people living there, such as *Plateria*, or Goldsmith Street, and *Lenceria*, or Linen Street. There were streets of mostly halter makers and those of hatters, and here also was a street with the largest number of wet nurses in the city called *Comadre*, or Street of the Midwife. Their husbands and others of the poorer classes of society had occupations that included constables, masons, tanners, halter makers and shoemakers, coachmen, muleteers, bakers, soldiers, textile workers and leather workers, blacksmiths, tailors, barbers, wigmakers, bookbinders and sellers, servants, street porters, stall vendors and agricultural day laborers and other unskilled workers, lowly members of the staff in the royal palace, and beggars. These families barely scraped out a living.

Some other jobs not always associated with the poorer people were clerks, customs officials, teachers, barber-surgeons, and a few shopkeepers and innkeepers. The large number of unskilled in the workforce of the major municipalities can be in part explained by the many rural agricultural workers who came to the cities to seek employment or charity.

The poor dominated public places and could be seen on most streets slouching, squatting, and often begging. They would lie in wait outside the churches for the faithful to go in or come out and plead for a few pennies. They harassed servant girls buying goods at the market and housewives at the entrance to shops when they emerged with their parcels. Any conspicuous foreigner in town would be followed about by a gaggle of poor, hoping for a small handout.

Along with the genuinely unemployed cluttering the streets of the city was a rabble of beggars, purse snatchers, smugglers, confidence men, house breakers, military deserters, paid assassins, and an assortment of other disenchanted people. Many spent their days playing cards, waiting for the monasteries' soup kitchens to disgorge their watery broth, or making plans to ransack a promising house. The quartered remains of criminals displayed in various parts of the city and police efforts to patrol the town made little difference. Crimes increased with the growth of the city. Nighttime in many sections was particularly dangerous for the citizen out on some urgent errand, unless well guarded.

Seville grew steadily throughout the 16th century. The city was at the time the sole depot for all commerce with the West Indies. The inspectors of the *Casa de Contratación,* or House of Trade, had assumed for Castile the monopoly of all trade with the Americas since the time of Ferdinand and Isabella. They organized the merchant fleets that sailed to the New World, trained the captains and navigators, and formed a tribunal to handle all problems arising from commerce.

Toledo. Many cities, such as Toledo, had been built on hills for the sake of defense: attackers would have to run up the hill. El Greco, *View and Plan of Toledo.* © The Art Archive/Metropolitan Museum of Art New York/Album/Joseph Martin.

The streets of the city were replete with shopkeepers from Italy, France, England, Portugal, Greece, and nearly every other country in Europe. In one quarter of the city were the workshops of silversmiths, jewelers, wood-carvers, and silk and linen merchants. Here gold, silver, pearls, crystals, enamels, coral, brocades, and costly materials were to be found. Due to the influx of large numbers of merchants and traders, the population of the city doubled in the second half of the 16th century to become for a time larger than Madrid.

Trade with the Indies was a gamble, an adventure. It could bring 100 percent return on the value of merchandise going both to and from America, making millionaires in quick order, or it could bring sudden and shattering losses when ships were captured or sunk, resulting in immediate bankruptcy for those merchants who had pledged their capital to the enterprise.

The flashy, brilliant life of Seville had its darker side. Magistrates and the Municipal Council were generally in league with the rich speculators who controlled monopolies on certain goods. By the time food reached the common people of the city, for example, it had been through the hands of these speculators, resulting in high prices. The Municipal Council that controlled prices turned a blind eye to the higher costs since they received presents and kickbacks from the great merchants. If litigation arose, the magistrates protected the merchants for the same reasons.

In cities and towns throughout Spain, skilled workers organized into guilds that arose when a group of artisans who had similar interests, such as shoe menders or carpenters, united for mutual aid and protection. The members of a craft guild were divided into three classes: masters, apprentices, and journeymen. The master, who was a small-scale proprietor, owned the raw material and the tools and sold the goods manufactured in his shop for his own profit. The apprentices and journeymen often lived in the master's house. The apprentices, who were beginners in the trade and learned it under the direction of the master, usually received only their board in return for their work. After an apprentice had completed his training, he became a journeyman and was paid a fixed wage for his labor. In time a journeyman might become a master. Funds collected by the guilds from new memberships or dues often went to help widows or orphans of deceased members or charities.

Guilds had regulations concerning access to their trades, such as technical expertise and social acceptability. The carpenters, for example, wanted their members to be married and to have a house of their own. This was no doubt partly due to the fact that the guilds felt responsible for their members and helped them through hard times, such as sickness or accident. But money that could have been better spent, some members complained, was wasted on festive events celebrating the patron saint of the trade and other fiestas, instead of on charity and pensions. Many guilds ostracized minorities such as Jews and Muslims and insisted on racial purity (Anderson, 133–45).

FOR MORE INFORMATION

Anderson, J. M. *Daily Life during the Spanish Inquisition*. Westport, Conn.: Greenwood, 2002.

Crow, J. *Spain: The Root and the Flower*. 3rd ed. Berkeley: University of California Press, 1985.

Defourneaux, M. *Daily Life in the Golden Age*. Trans. Newton Branch. Stanford: Stanford University Press, 1979.

ITALY

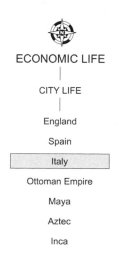

ECONOMIC LIFE
|
CITY LIFE
|
England

Spain

Italy

Ottoman Empire

Maya

Aztec

Inca

City life differed sharply from country life in scale and tempo. Density did not make the difference, for villages were, like cities, often closely packed. Rather, urban centers were big, teeming, and diverse in ways of life. Many cities owed their medieval origin or revival to commerce. The elite members of the city included a wealthy, politically active aristocracy and a stratum of affluent citizens, many of them large-scale merchants and entrepreneurs, plus a cohort of lettered professionals and bureaucrats. In the middle was a diverse assortment of skilled artisans. Further down the scale of workers came the semiskilled and unskilled, including, notably, servants. At the bottom struggled the deeply impoverished, many of them sick or physically or mentally disabled, probably disproportionately female, often capable only of begging and getting by at the whim of charity.

The aristocracies of Renaissance Italian cities varied in origins and evolution. Depending on the place, this class might include urban-dwelling members of the rural, feudal nobility. In the Middle Ages, some cities, such as Florence, greatly feared the power of these magnates and succeeded in excluding them from political office; elsewhere they made up part of the governing class. Even where these old-style nobles held power, they had to share it with a new, politically prominent group of rich families emerging out of international commerce, banking, and manufacturing. A new urban upper class that we call patricians emerged from the coalescence of these two groups: noble and mercantile. During the Renaissance, these patricians worked to consolidate their position, limiting political competition from other city constituencies and hindering social ascent into their caste.

In medieval and Renaissance Italy, the demand for literate public servants prompted the rise of a new elite group whose distinction derived from their education. The work demanded facility in reading and writing classical Latin, skills more accessible to those with some family means to pay for the schooling. Yet here was one avenue by which more modest men could rise.

Lettered professionals worked in several venues. Physicians and teachers belonged in this category, but their numbers were relatively few. High demand for literate employees came rather with the elaboration of government and associated public institutions. The tastes of the politically dominant groups favored those adept in the new culture of humanism. More and more, records needed keeping, negotiations with other bodies needed undertaking, speeches and letters of praise and persuasion needed writing. The appetite for lawyers, magistrates, administrators, secretaries, and notaries was sharp. Earlier in the Middle Ages, this kind of literacy and the work it led to belonged primarily to the church. Many Renaissance men who pursued careers in the expanding bureaucracies continued to find their way there by taking orders as celibate clerics. It became more common, however, for men to combine such work with marriage and family. In some cities, by the 16th century, the reproductive success of the lettered class contributed to its transformation into a closed, hereditary caste; only members' sons could apply to join.

The productive core of urban society was artisans and their families. The workers of this group made and sold goods for both local consumption and external markets. Typically artisans worked with considerable independence, acquiring raw materials, working them, and then selling directly to consumers. Some routine goods were produced for general sale, but many more specialized products were made on commission to a buyer's specifications. Artisans made things to fill the whole spectrum of Renaissance daily needs. Masons and carpenters carried on the skilled tasks of construction. Many artisans processed food, including bakers, cooks, and brewers. Others made hides into leather and leather into shoes, pouches, wall coverings, bookbinding, saddles, and harnesses. Woodworkers made barrels and furniture. Soap, candles, paper, baskets, bird cages, musical instruments, ceramic and metal containers, weapons, jewelry, playing cards, books, and countless other objects all were produced in artisan workshops. The manufacture of textiles occupied many workers, especially in a city like Florence, which specialized in high-end merchandise for international trade. There, some of the most complexly organized of Renaissance enterprises coordinated the efforts of carders, spinners, weavers, dyers, and fullers. The tight vertical integration of this major industry gave workers less autonomy than many other artisans exercised. The cutting and sewing of clothing and the confection of special decorations like gold thread and lace occupied numbers of hands. In some cities artisans produced specialties for luxury consumption throughout Europe, as did the glassworkers of the Venetian lagoon and the armorers of Milan and Brescia.

Renaissance cities depended on the efforts of workers who offered brawn and patience but only mediocre skills. To migrants from the countryside, such employment was the most accessible. Probably the most common form was domestic service. Where workplace and home merged, servants might participate in the economic activities of their masters as well

The Ca' d'Oro (Golden House) in Venice. Originally featuring a gilded façade, this is a prime example of a 15th-century urban mansion. © Library of Congress.

as keep their houses. Even very rich families seldom had more than one or two servants, although the numbers rose in the 16th century; the more aristocratic life-styles of the later Renaissance called for more domestic support. Servants typically worked on contract, receiving board, shelter, sometimes clothing, and either a salary paid periodically or a lump sum at the end. Sometimes, loyal servants, through long service, earned their master's lasting affection and protection. Nevertheless, rapid turnover was normal. Accordingly, in the literature of the period, old family retainers are less common figures than the tricky or deceitful servants who exploit their intimate knowledge of the household goings-on to please a grateful master or embarrass a resented one. Both males and females worked as domestic servants, with women increasingly outnumbering men later in the Renaissance. For both sexes, service was often work for the young—sometimes children from age seven, but mostly those in their teens and early twenties. Girls, in particular, hoped to lay up wages toward a dowry. Many left domestic work when they married, but some remained or returned. Married female servants had more status and security. Some servants were elderly; employers occasionally described keeping an aged servant as a work of charity.

Besides domestic service, the city offered other forms of semiskilled and unskilled work, usually at day or piece rates. Transport and haulage was one important area. Workers were needed to handle loads of goods entering and leaving the city, to shift earth and stone at building sites, and, in bigger cities, to deliver drinking water. Others had to remove garbage and sewage from the streets and latrines. Such jobs fell mostly to men, but women also worked in this nonprestigious and poorly paid sector of the urban workforce. Almost any female, for example, could nurse the sick, although particular experience or gifts might single some out (Cohen and Cohen, 26–33).

FOR MORE INFORMATION

Cohen, E. S., and T. V. Cohen. *Daily Life in Renaissance Italy*. Westport, Conn.: Greenwood, 2001.

Epstein, S. *Genoa and the Genoese, 958–1528*. Chapel Hill: University of North Carolina Press, 1996.

Romano, D. *Housecraft and Statecraft: Domestic Service in Renaissance Venice, 1400–1600*. Baltimore: Johns Hopkins University Press, 1996.

OTTOMAN EMPIRE

Ottoman cities played a crucial role in the trade and production of goods in addition to becoming crucial centers for the dissemination of imperial culture to the provinces. Although most cities in the Balkans and the Middle East had evolved in a number of different ways over the centuries, the Ottoman propensity for formal regimentation provided a new framework into which their previously random institutions became integrated. Guilds represented the most important of these institutions, as they both regulated the economic life of the city and provided a number of social services to their members. At the same time, the ruling elite's need for the

ECONOMIC LIFE

CITY LIFE

England
Spain
Italy
Ottoman Empire
Maya
Aztec
Inca

117

support and cooperation of city populations led local notables to play a significant role in government.

The layout of Ottoman cities varied greatly. Those in Greece, for example, had grown up around the acropolises of ancient city-states, while others focused on important geographical features or other monuments. Those in the Middle East often centered around a mosque. During Ottoman times, most cities generally came to have a mosque complex at the center, which included *madreses* (schools) and charitable foundations. Also in the city centers one found the central markets, baths, a square, and sometimes a fortress. The wealthiest citizens lived around the center, while the rest of the city was divided into boroughs generally consisting of twenty-five to fifty houses and separated from each other by ravines or other natural boundaries.

Ottoman cities had no formal government but were directed by a loose collection of notables consisting of the wealthiest merchants, guild representatives, and members of the ruling class, who lived there while administering their rural estates. There was also an official called the *kethuda* who served as the city representative to the capital. Each borough had its own headman, watchmen, and, frequently, places of worship and a small market. Usually a borough was occupied by people of the same religion, but this did not represent an enforced government policy.

Several classes made up the Ottoman subject population. The peasants of the rural areas formed one of these classes and made up a majority of the empire's overall population. The other four classes lived in the cities. The group with the highest status consisted of the long-distance merchants who handled trade across the empire and with foreign countries. Below them ranked the craftsmen, who made goods for both local use and export. Next in prestige came the small, local merchants. At the bottom of the social pile fell the Gypsies and others with no permanent home or occupation. Because this last group did not fit neatly into the Ottoman classification system, they were often pressured to leave or settle down.

Members of the highest class had a great deal of independence, and often gained influence even beyond their professional responsibilities. For example, their connections over a wide area led to their becoming an important news source. To broaden their reach, they formed partnerships with each other, creating trade networks over wide areas. Most lived in major trade centers such as Istanbul, Belgrade, and Edirne, but even the smallest cities had representatives for the large-scale commercial enterprises. The activities of these merchants involved exclusively liquid wealth, and they did not seek to acquire landed property beyond their own needs and luxuries. Despite their prestige, however, these merchants often earned the

Istanbul in 1422. The Hagia Sophia, a huge domed church built by the Emperor Justinian in the 5th century and turned into a mosque by the Ottomans, served as a symbol of Istanbul/Byzantium for many people, including this mapmaker. © The Art Archive/University Library Istanbul/Dagli Orti.

hatred of the rest of the population, who blamed their speculation and other business practices for food shortages.

The craftsmen and small merchants were organized into guilds that served both social and economic functions. Each guild had a narrowly defined specialty, such as coffin making or aquaduct digging, and the number of people in a given guild was fixed. Religion represented an important aspect of guild life, and new members joined via a mystic ceremony appropriate to the initiate's confessional community. Whereas a Muslim would take an Islamic oath, for example, Christians recited the Lord's Prayer while Jews repeated the Ten Commandments. Frequently non-Muslims had a Muslim craft father to ease their incorporation into group religious rituals.

Because it was formally linked with religion, the guild took on many aspects of benevolent societies and saw to the material needs of its members and their families, including widows and orphans. The highest official in an Ottoman guild was the *seyh*, whose task involved supervising religious and social programs. On the other hand, authority in economic matters rested with a *kethuda*, the same title as that of the city official, whom the masters elected to negotiate with other guilds and to represent the guild in matters affecting the entire city. Other officials included a buying agent, who obtained the raw materials with which all guild members worked, and another official, who supervised quality and price controls while mediating disputes among members.

The Gypsies and other drifters also lived in Ottoman cities, although they did not count as part of the population or fit into the administrative structure. They lived in housing they constructed themselves outside the city limits, and performed menial tasks such as carrying loads. Beggars also lived in cities, many of them with physical disabilities that rendered them unable to work. Sometimes people would buy blind slave girls and use them as begging agents, while at other times someone would take a sick relative and beg on their behalf. Frequently governors and city officials sought to prevent the able-bodied from begging and from using those with legitimate needs to enrich themselves. The rights of legitimate beggars, however, were generally protected.

Ottoman cities thus represented the heart of the Ottoman economy and civilization. Ottoman culture spread through the presence of far-flung trade networks and the houses and patronage of local elites. The city population remained diverse in terms of both religion and status. Life was highly regulated, but as long as the economy remained strong, people could expect a reasonable standard of living.

To read about city life in Medieval Islam, see the Islam and Baghdad entries in the section "Urban Economic Life" and "Great Cities" in chapter 3 ("Economic Life") in volume 2 of this series.

~Brian Ulrich

FOR MORE INFORMATION

Cicek, K., ed. *The Great Ottoman-Turkish Civilization 2: Economy and Society.* Ankara: Yeni Turkiye, 2000.

Sugar, P. F. *Southeastern Europe under Ottoman Rule, 1354–1804*. Seattle: University of Washington Press, 1977.

ECONOMIC LIFE
|
CITY LIFE
|
England

Spain

Italy

Ottoman Empire

Maya

Aztec

Inca

MAYA

Maya cities varied in size, arrangement, and style. The smallest covered less than a square mile; the largest, such as Tikal and Calakmul, extended over an area of some fifty square miles. The relative political and economic power held by these two cities was also evident in their elaborate buildings, their myriad monuments and hieroglyphic inscriptions, and the numerous times each was mentioned by other cities in historical texts.

Differences in size and complexity indicate that some Maya cities exerted political dominance over others. Economic, social, and political alliances provided varying degrees of control by more powerful cities over smaller centers. Dominant capitals such as Tikal sponsored the founding of colonial centers in outlying regions. Yet Calakmul used alliances with smaller cities to nearly surround and finally defeat Tikal. The kings of many cities waged raids and open warfare to defeat their neighbors, followed by the exaction of tribute to maintain their domination.

Downtown Tikal: The funerary shrine of Ah Cacau, the 26th king of Tikal, is on the left and the king's palace is on the right. Most large-scale Maya buildings were connected either with religion or with the king. © Painet.

The distribution of Maya road (*sacbe*) systems is evidence of the degree of political centralization of authority, as well as the extent of past political realms. The earliest example is the radiating causeway system that defines El Mirador's connections with its hinterland. Recent research at Caracol has discovered that this capital is connected to a series of satellite centers by causeways. The most extensive system is at Coba, where a network of roadways connects the site core with a series of outlying sites, including Yaxuna some sixty miles distant, clearly reflecting the extent of Coba's ancient centralized authority.

Reconstructing ancient population size from archaeological remains provides only approximations. Nonetheless, the results of settlement studies at lowland Maya sites gives a basis for comparing the numbers and densities of structures at these sites. Such studies reveal that lowland sites usually vary between 200 and 450 houses per square kilometer. Central Copan is outside of this range, having the greatest constructional density of any Maya site (1,450 structures/sq. km), due to the unusually close confinement of the Copan Valley. Mayapan shows the second highest density (996 structures/sq. km), in this case due to crowding within its defensive wall. At the low end of settlement density are both Quirigua (129 structures/sq. km) and Uaxactun (124 structures/sq. km).

To estimate population on the basis of house counts, we need to know the average number of people in a Maya family. Census figures from shortly after the conquest show that in several Maya communities the size of the family ranged from 5 to 10 people. Ethnographic studies show that average traditional Maya families today number between 4.9 and 6.1 people.

To arrive at population estimates for Maya cities for which settlement data are available, a reasonable average of 5.5 people per family can be used. These figures show that Tikal was the largest surveyed lowland city, with a Late Classic peak of some sixty-five thousand people within the site proper (defined by the 120 sq. km area bounded on the north and south by earthworks, and east and west by swamps, or *bajos*). The rural hinterland (an area within a 10 km radius of the site center) was occupied by about thirty thousand more people, giving greater Tikal a population of between ninety and one hundred thousand people during the Late Classic. For comparison, greater Copan was about one-quarter of the size of Tikal, with an estimated peak population of twenty to twenty-five thousand people during the same period. These are estimated population sizes for cities, not total polities. Because there is no way to gauge the size of political territories, the total number of people who were subjects of the kings of Tikal, Copan, or any other Classic Maya capital remains unknown.

In time, with continued population growth and social complexity, more groups emerged that reflected differences in wealth, authority, and status. By the time of Middle Maya Civilization, many Maya cities were populated by large numbers of nonagricultural specialists representing numerous occupational groups and divisions within the two social classes. The ruling elite was subdivided into many different ranks and specialties. The same process of differentiation took hold of the nonelite as well, although the basic producers of food, the farmers, probably were always the largest group within Maya society. The division between ruling elite and commoner classes was subsequently filled by an emerging middle class, defined by occupational groups derived from higher-ranking commoners and lower-ranking elite. The incipient middle class included full-time occupational groups such as administrators or bureaucrats, merchants, warriors, craftsmen, architects, and artists. They probably lived close to the core of the major cities and were clients of the kings and more powerful elite. Otherwise, the core of Classic Maya cities continued to be inhabited by the ruler, his family, and other members of allied elite lineages that held the major positions in the political, religious, and economic hierarchy of society.

Regardless of size, each of the independent Maya polities experienced growth and decline. A variety of events and circumstances contributed to the successes and failures of each kingdom. Some were internal and unique to each polity. For example, success might depend on the personal abilities and life spans of individual kings, the efficiency of the king's administrators, or the success of local farmers and merchants in providing essential food and goods for the population. Other factors were external and involved a much wider network of relationships with other states. These included social and economic exchanges, competition, and warfare. And these were not only social, political, or economic relationships; as with most aspects of Maya culture, they were also imbued with levels of religious motivation and meaning.

Maya lowland polities maintained many social and economic ties. For the most part these ties reflected the economic and social interactions between kingdoms, such as visitations and marriage arrangements between lineages, goods and services exchanged, or tribute extracted from one polity to another. It is likely that most social interaction, including visits and marriage alliances, occurred between people from the same or nearby communities, although some undoubtedly involved more distant regions. We know from inscriptions that Maya kings used royal visits and marriage exchanges between elite families to cement alliances between polities. At the time of the Spanish Conquest, there are records of reciprocal arrangements between Maya communities—some separated by several days' travel by foot—whereby each town provided female marriage partners for the men living in the other town (Sharer, 114–15, 133–40).

To read about city life in 20th-century Latin America, see the Latin America entry in the section "Urban and Rural Experience" in chapter 3 ("Economic Life") in volume 6 of this series.

FOR MORE INFORMATION

Fash, W. L. *Scribes, Warriors, and Kings: The City of Copan and the Ancient Maya*. New York: Thames and Hudson, 1991.

Hirth, K. G., ed. *Trade and Exchange in Early Mesoamerica*. Albuquerque: University of New Mexico Press, 1984.

Sharer, R. J. *Daily Life in Maya Civilization*. Westport, Conn.: Greenwood, 1996.

ECONOMIC LIFE
|
CITY LIFE
|
England

Spain

Italy

Ottoman Empire

Maya

Aztec

Inca

AZTEC

The great island city of Tenochtitlan was divided into five major sections with four great quarters surrounding the fifth and central section—the great ceremonial precinct. Each section had local markets, but the greatest marketplace was in the northwestern section of the capital at a site called Tlatelolco.

Everything that was grown or made in the empire could be found in this marketplace, which was under the control of the ruling class. Sellers had to pay a fee to the market superintendent, while supervisors scouted the scene, checking the quality of the goods and the conduct of merchants and customers. The complex exchanges that took place inevitably led to disputes, debates, and just decisions and rewards. To control the marketplace, the Aztecs built a courthouse at Tlatelolco " . . . where ten or twelve persons sit as judges. They preside over all that happens in the markets, and sentence criminals. There are in this square other persons who walk among the people to see what they are selling and the measures they are using." The marketplace was also the place for odd jobbers. People could hire singers, scribes, carpenters, carriers, and prostitutes.

Trade was generally carried out by barter, although some objects came to have generally fixed values. For example, mantles and copper ax blades were used to buy expensive items, while cocoa beans supplied small change. While these objects were commonly used as a form of money, the prices themselves fluctuated widely, with good quality native products becoming particularly more expensive after the Spanish Conquest.

The city was celebrated as a proud, invincible place, the foundation of the vertical structure of the cosmos. The city was constructed as an imitation, or at least an image, of the cosmos, ordered by the Giver of Life and located at the base of heaven as a kind of anchor that steadies the cosmos above it. The organization of the city is pictured in an image from the *Codex Mendoza* that shows the city at the moment of its foundation. Surrounding the island city is a series of 51 blue boxes, each containing a year sign. This calendar consists of four year signs—House, Rabbit, Reed, and Flint Knife—and 13 numbers depicted as dots. This combination results in a calendar round of 52 years, the number resulting from the four day signs—or, in this case, year signs—interacting with 13 numbers. Within this space are two types of activity: the foundation of the city and the early conquests of the Aztecs. The city is divided into four major sections, with canals crossing at the central

> **📷 Snapshot**
>
> **Comparison of Old and New World Urban Populations in the 16th Century**
>
> **Old World**
>
> | | |
> |---|---|
> | Tenochtitlan | 200,000 |
> | Cuzco | 40,000 |
>
> **New World**
>
> | | |
> |---|---|
> | London | 50,000 |
> | Seville | 60,000 |
> | Rome | 90,000 |
> | Paris | 300,000 |

area where the god, Huitzilopochtli, is perched on a blooming cactus growing from a stylized rock. Below the rock is a shield covered with seven eagle down feathers and attached to six arrows. The Aztec worldview emphasized, again and again, that the cosmos was a four-quartered structure organized around a center. That is the archetype. This image shows that the design of the city was a repetition of that exemplary pattern. The site of the eagle on the cactus was where the Aztecs constructed the first shrine to their god Huitzilopochtli (which means Southern Hummingbird or Hummingbird on the Left). It provided them with a center, an *axis mundi*, a place they could rely on, and it eventually became the greatest temple in the empire, a structure the Aztecs called Coatepec, which means Serpent Mountain. When the Mexica had arrived at the end of their long migration, Huitzilopochtli reappeared to the people and told them to build their " . . . city that is to be queen, that is to rule over all others in the country. There we shall receive other kings and nobles who will recognize Tenochtitlan as the supreme capital." According to Aztec myth, the god Huitzilopochtli ordered the people to divide the city into four main sections and also to build a central shrine in his honor.

Other elements in the image from the *Codex Mendoza* inform us about how the Mexica (Aztecs) viewed their city. Ten men are distributed throughout the four sections of the new settlement; each has his name glyph attached to his head with a thread. The leader of the group is immediately to the left of a giant cactus. He is distinguished by his elaborate hairstyle, the speech glyph in front of his mouth signifying that he is the chief speaker, and the woven mat he sits on, signifying political authority. This image stresses the importance of proper rule in the city and in each of its districts. Two important buildings are depicted: the skull rack upon which the decapitated heads of enemy warriors were hung, and the small house above the eagle, representing either the first shrine to Huitzilopochtli or the Men's House, the place of consultation and decision making. As the two buildings show,

the city stressed love of war, faithfulness to their god Huitzilopochtli, and proper government as the important ideologies of the city-state.

The importance of warfare can also be seen in the two scenes of battle and conquest below the central image. The buildings are temples that are tipped and burning, each attached to an image or place sign. The place sign on the left is Colhuacan (Curved Hill), whereas the one on the right is Tenayuca (Rampart Hill). The tipped and burning temples represent conquest. These are two of the first communities that the Aztecs conquered. It is interesting that a tipped and burning temple signifies the defeat of not just a religion or group of priests, but of an entire community. Two proportionally larger Aztec warriors are shown subduing enemy warriors from the two conquered towns by placing their shields on their heads. It is interesting to note that the shields rest on the part of the head where the *tonalli* or soul of the warrior resides. The idea is that the soul, power, or essence of the warrior has been conquered, just as the soul or essence of the town, with its temple in flames, has been destroyed. The *Codex Mendoza* tells us a lot about how Aztecs viewed their urban environment (Carrasco, 72–80).

To read about city life in 20th-century Latin America, see the Latin America entry in the section "Urban and Rural Experience" in chapter 3 ("Economic Life") in volume 6 of this series.

The Founding of Tenochtitlan. This picture shows the god Huitzilopochtli in the shape of a bird at the center of the four districts of Tenochtitlan. Depictions of two conquered cities can be seen in the bottom panel. From the *Codex Mendoza*. The Bodleian Library, University of Oxford. Ms. Arch. Selden A.1, fol. 2r.

FOR MORE INFORMATION

Broda, J., D. Carrasco, and E. Matos Moctezuma. *The Great Temple of Tenochtitlan: Center and Periphery in the Aztec World.* Berkeley: University of California Press, 1987.

Carrasco, D., with S. Sessions. *Daily Life of the Aztecs: People of the Sun and Earth.* Westport, Conn.: Greenwood, 1998.

ECONOMIC LIFE
|
CITY LIFE
|
England

Spain

Italy

Ottoman Empire

Maya

Aztec

Inca

INCA

Cuzco was the capital of the Inca empire and its major city. At the height of its power in the early 1500s, the valley of Cuzco might have had a population as high as one hundred thousand. Although it predates the ninth king, Inca accounts indicate that Pachacuti had designed the city in the layout that it had when the Spaniards arrived. The city had the form of a puma, or mountain lion, with the head being the fortress of Sacsahuaman located on a hill above the city to the north, and the tail being the section of the city that narrowed to the south between two rivers. Pachacuti ordered the two rivers straightened for this purpose.

Many Spanish writers have noted that the region around and including Cuzco was set up to be a small-scale model of the Inca empire itself. Therefore it consisted of Inca by blood, Inca by privilege, *mitimas* (forced laborers), and many representatives of conquered groups. People of various occupations resided there, fulfilling both permanent and temporary labor obligations to the Incas.

The city comprised several sectors that were occupied by these different groups. The central sector was the most important, being occupied by the Incas themselves. The focus of this sector was two plazas, one of which was covered to a depth of several inches with sand brought from the Pacific Ocean. Many important buildings were located around these plazas, including a workplace for Chosen Women, several *callancas* (large rectangular buildings), and the residences of Inca kings, other nobility, and royal *panacas* (lineages). Sacred shrines, storehouses, and temples were also located in the central part of Cuzco, including the Coricancha.

Surrounding the central sector was a zone reserved for agriculture. This area no doubt also separated the Inca nobility from lower-status groups living farther out from the center of town. Beyond the agricultural lands were several districts occupied by people who were not Inca: conquered leaders from the provinces, their sons and servants, and *mitimas* from all over the empire. The latter were often craftspeople who were there to serve the Incas. Farthest out from the center of town were the settlements of the Inca by privilege.

Thus the Inca capital was more an aggregation of small settlements separated from the central sector by field systems than a city of continuous streets, like modern ones. This very large area had a population of 100,000; the population of the central sector was no doubt much less.

Other Inca settlements were based on either a grid pattern, whereby streets crossed each other at 90-degree angles, much like in modern cities, or a radial pattern, like the spokes of a wheel. The grid pattern was less common and has been found mostly in regions around Cuzco. It appears to have existed on land that was relatively flat. Plazas have always been found in these patterns, but they were not in the center; rather, they were most often located at one end or side of the settlement. The central sector of Cuzco was laid out on a grid pattern, but the outlying settlements were organized on a radial pattern.

According to John Hyslop, a specialist in Inca architecture and settlement planning, the central sector of Cuzco may have had 20 different units defined by the intersection of the different streets. It is interesting to note that other Inca gridded settlements also have 20 or 40 units, suggesting they may have been modeled after the central sector of Cuzco. The fact that the grid pattern is found close to Cuzco also suggests that it may have been the earlier model, used before the beginning of the empire's major conquests.

Radial or spokelike patterns are more widespread than grid patterns, and most of the best examples are found far from Cuzco. Thus the pattern may have become more common as the empire expanded; it may have been the preferred later model. However, a radial pattern is also found in Cuzco itself, where the grid pattern becomes radial as one leaves the central sector for the outlying settlements.

Radial patterns are typical of Inca administrative centers in provincial areas. One of their key features is that they all radiate from a single point, typically an *ushnu*

Downtown Cuzco. This map shows the two main plazas used by the Inca nobility. The Huatanay River can be seen running through the middle of the picture. Map by Guaman Poma.

platform (a platform used for religious and political assemblies and ceremonies) in the center of a plaza. This suggests that the point of origin was highly symbolic; the presence of an *ushnu,* which was a ritual structure, supports this interpretation.

The use of a radial pattern suggests that the Incas used it as a formal model for settlements in conquered regions. It duplicated the royal capital at Cuzco and expressed some of the most important aspects of Inca society.

The Inca identity was bound up with the capital Cuzco, where the Inca people themselves dwelt. The founding father and first king of the Incas was Manco Capac, according to Guaman Poma. He came out of the earth from a cave at a place called Pacariqtambo, accompanied by three brothers and four sisters. Over a period of several years they traveled to Cuzco with a group of other people who were loyal to them, who also came from caves at Pacariqtambo. One brother became feared by the others for his exceptional strength and was sent back to Pacariqtambo, where he was sealed up in the original caves. Another brother stayed at the mountain of Huanacauri, where he originated the male puberty rites. He then turned to stone and subsequently became an important cult figure for the Incas. The two other brothers and the four sisters continued to Cuzco. Upon reaching the Cuzco valley the Incas drove a golden staff into the ground, which was the sign that this would be the place of their permanent settlement. A third brother turned himself into a stone field guardian. Under the direction of the remaining brother, Manco Capac, the Incas drove out the native occupants and founded the capital of Cuzco.

In another variation of this myth, Garcilaso de la Vega has Manco Capac and his sister (who was also his wife) travel to Pacariqtambo from Lake Titicaca, and then to Cuzco. After founding Cuzco, Manco traveled across the empire, organizing the ethnic groups and bringing them civilization.

The differences between these two versions are important, for they affected the social relations of the people who lived with the Incas in the Cuzco valley. In Guaman Poma's version, Manco Capac and his sister originated in Pacariqtambo and were accompanied from there by others; these others became the Incas by privilege. Because they accompanied the original ruler to Cuzco, they too are given the status of Inca. In Garcilaso's version, only Manco Capac and his sister came from Lake Titicaca; therefore the Incas by privilege were originally not Inca. They were given the title later. The differences between the two versions thus reflect a difference in whether the Incas by privilege were Incas from ancient times or only became Incas when the royal couple arrived in the Cuzco valley.

Garcilaso, however, was the great-grandson of Huayna Capac and hence a royal Inca. From Garcilaso's perspective, then, the Incas by privilege owed their Inca status to his ancestors having bestowed it on them. Guaman Poma, however, was from Huánuco and was therefore a non-Inca. He saw the difference between the Incas by blood and Incas by privilege as one of degree. Regardless, the clear implication of the origin myth is that the descendants of Manco Capac and the rulers of the Incas were the only noble Incas, and that others were subservient to them. It is interesting to note how closely this worldview was bound up with their capital city, Cuzco (Malpass, 62–64, 102).

To read about city life in 20th-century Latin America, see the Latin America entry in the section "Urban and Rural Experience" in chapter 3 ("Economic Life") in volume 6 of this series.

FOR MORE INFORMATION

Garcilaso de la Vega, El Inga. *Royal Commentaries of the Incas and General History of Peru, Parts 1 and 2.* Trans. H. Livermore. Austin: University of Texas Press, 1966 (1609).

Guaman Poma de Ayala, F. *Nueva Corónica y Buen Gobierno (Codex Péruvien illustré).* Vol. 23. Paris: Institut d'Ethnologie, Travaux et Mémoires, 1936.

Hyslop, J. *Inka Settlement Planning.* Austin: University of Texas Press, 1990.

Malpass, M. A. *Daily Life in the Inca Empire.* Westport, Conn.: Greenwood, 1996.

Time

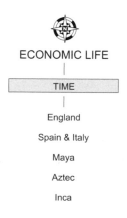

ECONOMIC LIFE
|
TIME
|
England

Spain & Italy

Maya

Aztec

Inca

Look at your wrist. There is a good chance that you are wearing a watch, or at the least that there is a clock or someone with a watch very near you. Look at the top of a newspaper—you will see the day, month, and year clearly emblazoned on the top. People in the modern Western world are surrounded by reminders of the current time. Schools, businesses, meetings, and television shows, they all start promptly, not only at a particular hour, but also at a particular minute, such as at 9:00 A.M. on the dot. If you arrive at 9:05 for a nine o'clock meeting, you are definitely late and may need to bear the antagonistic glances of both bosses and coworkers.

The ancient world had a very different relationship with time. While mechanical clocks and even watches existed in the 15th and 16th centuries, most people did not use them, and only a few people could afford them. At the start of the Renaissance, daily time was marked, not by mechanical devices, but by the passage of the sun across the sky, by the onset of hunger (and the resulting meal), and, when measuring small passages of time, by the time it took to say oral prayers. In European cities, especially toward the end of the 16th century, time was a bit more carefully marked, with church bells ringing at specific times according to city statutes and large town clocks built into the town hall. Nevertheless, few people marked the precise passage of time the way we do today.

The calendar has remained more stable over time. The 280-day sacred almanac calendar, used throughout the Mesoamerican world in the 16th century for prognostication and divination, is still used today by groups of Maya for purposes of naming and prediction. Likewise, the European calendar featured seven-day weeks and 12 months just as it does today, even if some things, such as when the new year begins, have changed: in the 16th century, some places celebrated the New Year on January 1, as today, while others celebrated it on March 25. As a result, a date such as February 2, 1586, might be referred to as February 2, 1585, in another part of Europe.

The European calendar, which has become the standard calendar in the United States as well, derived from the ancient Roman calendar. By the Middle Ages, the names of the months and the days had come to be the forms still in use today: January, February, Monday, Tuesday, and so on. Most of these names were derived ultimately from the Latin names that the Romans used. For example, Monday in the Latin was *lunae dies,* which became *lunedì* in Italian, *lundi* in French, etcetera. While the names in the Romance languages derived from a corruption of the Latin, the English terms generally derived from a translation. *Lunae dies* means day of the moon, which is exactly what Monday (from the Old English *monan-dæg* or moon's day) means. Similarly, Latin *veneris dies* (Italian *venerdì,* French *vendredi*) means day of Venus; Venus was the goddess of love. English Friday, in comparison, comes from Old English *Frige-dæg,* which means Freya's day. Like Venus, Freya was a goddess associated with love.

Both the European and Native American calendars had strong links with the divine. While the underpinnings of the European calendar derived from pagan Roman days, by the 15th century these associations had become names only and the calendar was more intimately connected with the Christian religion. Most days were associated with particular saints, and these associations affected working life. Every Sunday was at least nominally free from work and spent in worship and rest. Other major commemorative days were spent in similar fashion, and sometimes with much merrymaking. Christmas, celebrating the birth of Christ, and Easter, celebrating Christ's resurrection from the dead, were particular highlights in the year, and their celebration called for much feasting and rejoicing.

If anything, the Mesoamerican and South American calendars were even more strongly associated with the divine. The 260-day almanac calendar was used in Mesoamerica to name a child and to predict his future. Soon after birth, the new parents would invite the local shaman to their home. The shaman would inquire about the exact time of the birth, and then study the almanac to determine what that child's future might be. Some days were particularly auspicious. The Aztec day called 1 Deer, for example, was associated with nobility, fame, and success in war. If the child were born on a very ill-omened day, the calendar priest would recommend waiting to name the child until a more favorable day arrived.

Time was thus both more informal and also more closely linked with the divine in the 15th and 16th centuries. In the Americas and in Europe, time was dictated to most people by the course of the sun across the sky from its rising to its setting. The yearly calendar, moreover, laid out a pattern of festivals, and was sometimes considered to reveal the mysteries of the future. Even though its minute measure was not generally possible, time was very important.

~*Lawrence Morris*

ECONOMIC LIFE
|
TIME
|
England

Spain & Italy

Maya

Aztec

Inca

ENGLAND

For most English people the day began just before dawn, at cockcrow—or, strictly speaking, third cockcrow, since the cock would crow first at midnight and again about halfway to dawn. Artificial light was expensive and generally feeble, so it was vital to make the most of daylight. This meant, of course, that the daily schedule varied from season to season, dawn being at around 3:30 in the summer and 7:00 in the winter. According to law, from mid-September to mid-March laborers were supposed to begin work at dawn, and in other months at 5:00. Markets typically opened at dawn, and businesses at 7:00.

Portable clocks and watches were available to the Elizabethans, but they were expensive. Most people marked time by the hourly ringing of church and civic bells; there were also public sundials and clock towers. Time was invariably reckoned by the hour of the clock: normally only the hour, half hour, quarter hour, and sometimes the eighth hour were counted, rather than the hour and minute—in fact, clocks and watches had no minute hands. In the country, people were more likely to reckon time by natural phenomena—dawn, sunrise, midday, sunset, dusk, midnight, and the crowing of the cock.

After rising, people would wash their face and hands. As there was no hot water available until someone heated it on the fire, most people had to wash with cold water (those who had servants could be spared this hardship). After washing, one could get dressed—since people often slept in their shirts, this might just mean pulling on the overgarments. It was customary to say prayers before beginning the day, and children were expected to ask their parents' blessing: they knelt before their parents, who placed a hand on their heads and invoked God's favor.

Some people ate breakfast right away, while others did a bit of work first—a typical time for breakfast was around 6:30. The law allowed a half-hour breakfast break for laboring people, and perhaps half an hour for a drinking later in the morning. Work was interrupted at midday for dinner, which took place around eleven or noon. By law, laborers were allowed an hour's break for this meal, probably their main meal of the day.

After dinner, people returned to work. In the heat of the summer afternoon, between mid-May and mid-August, country folk might nap for an hour or two; the law provided for a half-hour break for sleep for laborers at the same time of year. It also allowed a possible half-hour drinking in the afternoon. Work would continue until supper; according to law, laborers were to work until sundown in winter (around 5 P.M. on the shortest day) and seven or eight o'clock in the summer. For commoners, supper was generally a light meal relative to dinner.

Bedtime was around 9 P.M. in the winter and 10 P.M. in the summer. As in the morning, people would say prayers and children would ask their parents' blessing before bed. Candles were extinguished at bedtime, although wealthy people sometimes left a single candle lit as a watch light (the hearth was a good place for this). Household fires were raked or covered enough to keep them from burning themselves out, without allowing them to die entirely. As a result, nighttime tended to be very cold and very dark—people often kept a chamber pot next to the bed to minimize the discomfort of attending to nighttime needs. The wealthy often had special nightshirts, but commoners probably just slept in their underwear—shirts and breeches for men, smocks for women. A woman might wear a coif to keep her head warm, and a man might wear a nightcap.

Bedtime more or less corresponded to the hour of curfew, after which people were not supposed to be out on the streets. Both town and country streets tended to be very dark at night, although some towns had laws requiring householders to put lanterns outside their doors. It was assumed that nobody who was outside at night had any honest business, and towns had watches, or patrols of civilian guards, who roamed the streets to keep an eye on matters and arrest anyone they found wandering after curfew.

Renaissance people generally worked from Monday to Saturday, although many had Saturday afternoon off. Markets took place on regular days of the week—

Night Watchman. Guards such as this one patrolled the streets with large dogs after curfew. Anyone caught outside was assumed to be up to no good and would be arrested. From Orie Latham Hatcher, *A Book for Shakespeare Plays and Pageants,* 1916.

Wednesday and Saturday mornings were the most common times. Wednesday, Friday, and Saturday were fasting days when no meat was to be eaten, except for fish.

Thursday afternoon was commonly a half holiday for schoolchildren. Thursday and Sunday were the big nights for food; they were often occasions for roasts. Saturday afternoon was often a half holiday for workers, and Saturday night was a favored time for carousing among common people, since they did not have to work the next day. Saturday, coming at the end of the work week, was the typical day for washing and laundry; if possible, people would wear clean clothes on Sunday morning for church.

Sunday was the Sabbath. Everyone in England was required by law to attend church services in the morning, under stiff penalties. On every second Sunday afternoon the parish priest was required to offer religious instruction for the young people of the parish. After church, people were customarily allowed to indulge in games and pastimes; Sunday was the principal occasion for diversion and entertainment. However, many people of Puritanical leanings felt that such activities violated the holiness of the Sabbath, so there was often vocal opposition to such entertainments.

The basic reckoning of the passage of the year was similar to ours today, with a few important differences. To begin with, the number of the year did not change on New Year's Day. The English calendar had come down from the Romans, for whom January 1 was the first day of the year. Accordingly this was called New Year's Day and was observed as an official holiday as the Feast of the Circumcision of Christ. However, the number of the year did not actually change until March 25, the Feast of the Annunciation. England differed from the Continent in this respect. The day that a 16th-century Frenchman (and a modern person) would consider January 1, 1589, would be called January 1, 1588, in 16th-century England. Educated Englishmen sometimes dealt with this problem by writing the date as 1 January 1588/9. On March 25 the year would be written as 1589, and England would be in line with the rest of Europe until January 1 came around again.

In addition to the cycle of the seasons, the year was shaped by the festive and religious calendar of holy days, also called feasts. Every official holiday was ostensibly religious, with the exception of Accession Day (November 17), commemorating Elizabeth's accession to the throne. Nonetheless, holidays had their secular side as well: like modern-day Christmas and Easter, religious holidays had accumulated secular elements that sometimes swallowed up their religious component. By law, everyone was to attend church on holy days as well as Sundays, and to take communion three times a year: generally on Easter, Whitsun, and Christmas. People did not necessarily observe this law rigidly, but most probably took communion at least at Easter. The observance of any holy day began on the evening before, which was called the eve of the holy day—the principal surviving example is Christmas Eve. The eve of a major holy day was supposed to be observed by the same fast that was held on Fridays and during Lent.

The Protestant reformation in England had done away with many of the traditional saints' days and other religious holidays observed by the Catholic Church, and there continued to be pressures from Protestant reformers in the Church of England to take the process even further. Reformers especially objected to holiday names ending with *-mas* (like Christmas), because these names alluded to the Catholic ceremony of the Mass. However, these traditional celebrations were firmly established in the popular mind—especially among country folk, for whom such festivals gave shape both to the year and to their lives. For a list of the major festivals in the English calendar, see the following section, "Calendars" (Singman, 55–60).

FOR MORE INFORMATION

Harrison, W. *Description of England*. 1587. Reprint, Ithaca: Cornell University Press, 1968.
Singman, J. L. *Daily Life in Elizabethan England*. Westport, Conn.: Greenwood, 1995.
Wilson, J. D. *Life in Shakespeare's England*. Harmondsworth, UK: Penguin, 1949.

SPAIN AND ITALY

Spain and Italy can be treated together because they had similar systems of time and celebrated many of the same festivals. The discussion that follows will focus on the Italian practices in particular.

Overall, for most Renaissance people, sharp temporal precision seldom mattered very much. Some technology existed for measuring time and announcing it to the public, but its capacity was limited and its availability was even scantier. People therefore often lacked a very exact notion of what time it was, nor did their way of life need one. Rather they lived with a set of general points of reference—dawn, dusk, the midday meal, in cities the communal and ecclesiastical bells—and with a sense of sequence. So, when they narrated events, they would say not, "It must have been a few minutes after ten, because I'd just watched the news," but rather, "I'd been with my friend, Ambrogio, and then I had supper, and then I wandered around for a while, and then it happened." When they did speak of units of time, they usually chose broad or approximate terms and often hedged those, as in, "It was around the fourth hour of the night." Their handling of days and weeks had a similar vagueness: "I met her on the street a week ago last Tuesday, if I remember rightly," or "I got to know him before Lent just past." When obliged, people had concepts

and terms to be more specific, but for the most part sequential and more general expressions of time were the practice.

When someone did want to designate a short interval, the usual phrasing drew on religious vocabulary, calling up the duration of common prayers: the Paternoster, the Ave Maria, and the Miserere. In examples that nicely illustrate the crossovers among the parallel times of nature, God, and state, these measures from the sacred realm were used to describe natural phenomena and the workings of the judiciary. In 1456, a Florentine wrote from Naples of experiencing an earthquake "that lasted the duration it would take to say a Miserere quite slowly and more specifically one and a half times." The correspondent picked this wording to make what he intended as a very precise empirical observation. With a similar commitment to exactitude, notaries for the criminal courts of 16th-century Rome and elsewhere also used the Miserere to record the carefully timed application of torture to witnesses.

In many circumstances, time telling was guesswork.

Through monasticism, the ancient Romans had bequeathed to late medieval Europe a system for dividing daylight. The Romans and then the monks numbered 12 hours of presumptively equal length, stressing groupings of three. Thus, Prime (first hour), Terce (third), Sext (sixth), and None (ninth) marked the significant segments. Several of these divisions corresponded to readily estimated heights of the Sun in the sky. By this scheme, the First Hour followed sunrise, the Sixth Hour came at midday, and the Twelfth Hour belonged to sunset. Between these reasonably fixed points, distinguishing one hour from the next was hard for several reasons. First, the duration of light shifted with the seasons, so that an hour, conceived as one-twelfth of the day, stretched or shrank. Second, the Sun itself was often an unreliable gauge. How many degrees of angle actually corresponded to an hour? And what to do when the Sun and the horizon were, as often, out of sight? With practice and the right conditions—in good weather, at sea, or elsewhere with an unimpeded view of the sky—a fair estimate of the hour should have been quite easy. Yet in many circumstances—at night, with cloudy skies—time telling was guesswork. While a sundial, properly positioned and read, could help give greater accuracy, such devices mostly belonged to institutions or the elite. At best, knowing the hour was a matter for specialists. It was seldom a possibility, or a need, for most medieval people.

Monks were those who most deliberately preserved the old system of Roman hours. Their lives had a sharper temporal ordering than those of most contemporaries. Central to their rule was a daily seven-part cycle of prayers, known as hours and named, in part, Prime, Terce, Sext, and None. Around these hours, the rest of the monks' regulated schedule was set. Yet the monastic hour was in fact conceptual and not technical. It denoted neither a measured length of time nor a particular moment in the Sun's passage. Rather, it was a step in a sequence, marked by a bell that called the brothers to prayer. Over the centuries, monasteries continued to observe the same rotation of hours, but their actual timing in the day shifted to fit the seasons and institutional convenience. Thus, although tradition associated the Sixth Hour with midday, houses varied in singing Sext; some chanted just before the Sun reached its height, while others did so as much as an hour and a half earlier.

By such a process, the None—the Ninth Hour—drifted from the middle of the afternoon toward the middle of the day and gave us our word *noon*.

During the Middle Ages, urban governments began to borrow the monastic system of sounded hours for secular uses. Thus, the church bells became the markers not only for sacred time, but also for administrative time. The patterns of ringing became more elaborate as they were put to ever more uses. Eventually, this proliferation of bongs and clanks threatened cacophony and confusion. A remedy came in a novel instrument: the public mechanical clock. This device first spread through northern and central Italy from the mid-14th century onward. As an emblem of civic pride, ambitious communes installed one in the tower of the city hall. But the clock was also functional, for it both counted out time regularly and, soon, with the incorporation of a second mechanism, struck the hours clearly and efficiently. The complicated codes of the church bells were no longer needed. They continued to sound for worship, but much less for other purposes. In the 15th century, a simplified round consisting of the Angelus (or Ave Maria) bell at dusk and at dawn marked the ends of the day. In 1456, Pope Calixtus III mandated that a third bell, at midday, signal a similar brief prayer, to ward off the Turkish threat.

While Italians of this era distinguished ordinary days from holidays, their week did not divide into five workdays followed by a weekend. Differences among days of the week came largely from religion. Wednesdays and Fridays were especially penitential, and the morally scrupulous might abstain from some foods and from sex; weddings were less often scheduled on these days. Sunday was for church, although in cities, where there were many occasions for worship, the faithful might attend services on other days of the week as well. Before, after, or instead of church, Sunday was also time for sociability. Moral reformers repeatedly had to denounce the taverns and ball games that competed with God for men's Sunday attention. Yet if Sunday was owed to God and was sometimes given to play, it was not a day of universal rest. The French visitor Montaigne noted that many Italians worked on Sunday; court testimony bears him out. Even some government officials regularly held meetings and conducted business then. For time out for worship and recreation, the annual Christian cycle of holidays set the schedule more strongly than the weekly rotation of days.

The traditional calendar provided a precise way to express dates, which became increasingly important to administrative time. Within the ever expanding compass of written culture—legal contracts, government orders, parish records, letters, and diaries—dates were noted carefully, because they had consequences. In communes it was important to keep track of officials' terms, which might rotate as often as three or six months. Debts came due on specific dates, and interest payments and other penalties were linked to them. Birth dates governed eligibility for government office, and times of death sometimes affected distributions of property. In addition, date sequence was one of the main devices for filing and retracing the ever-expanding volume of notarial documents.

At the same time, assorted vagaries up and down the peninsula vexed dating practices. For example, in different places the year began on different dates. The New Year fell on different days in different cities: January 1 in Rome, March 1 in

Venice, and March 25 (the day of the Annunciation) in Florence. Consequently, if two contracts were written on the same day, one in Rome and the other in Florence, the first would bear the date January 26, 1491, while the second would read January 26, 1490. Furthermore, because of 15 centuries of a little too much leap year, the movements of the sun and the nominal dates had parted company. By the 16th century, the equinox fell around the eleventh of March instead of the twenty-first. To haul things back into line, Pope Gregory XIII, in 1582, decreed calendrical reform and suppressed 10 days. His improved "Gregorian" calendar is the one we use today.

Mediterranean patterns of temperature and rainfall governed the agricultural rhythm and the movement of workers up and down the landscape. The winter, chilly and punctuated by rains, or by snow in the mountains, was a fairly quiet season for people on the land. It was a time to mend gear and practice home industry, to migrate to the lowlands for work, or just to rest. Then came spring, temperate and well watered, keeping peasants busy pruning vines and orchards, plowing and planting summer crops, and lambing. After lambing, shepherds moved their flocks from lowland winter pastures into the hills and began to make cheese. As summer arrived, bringing Mediterranean heat and dryness, farmers harvested winter grain and made hay. In the fall, as the temperature moderated, came another round of harvesting and processing, including grapes and olives. Before the heavy rains of late autumn, peasants planted the winter grain crop, and shepherds brought their flocks back down from the high country. The great diversity of Italian landscape and crops led to many variations in the timing and weight of these moments, but some pattern of this sort gave temporal form to most Renaissance lives. Important social and religious events fitted in among these yearly agricultural cycles.

September. Calendars frequently featured pictures of scenes associated with each month. Here, September is linked with the grape harvest and the making of wine. Civica Raccolta delle Stampe Achille Bertarelli–Milano.

The Christian calendar was an intricate roster of liturgical seasons. Only the clergy followed all the many lesser details, but major religious holidays punctuated the year for all Renaissance Italians and gave them reference points in time. The calendar not only recognized a crowded pantheon of saints, but also reenacted over the year's course the redeeming history of Jesus and his resurrection and, secondarily, the story of his mother. The religious year included two major sequences of observances, Christmas and Easter, each preceded by a long penitential preparation. Ascension Day, commemorating Christ's rising into heaven, occurred 40 days after Easter. Also, from the 13th century there developed a very popular, often elaborate celebration dedicated to the Corpus Christi, the body of Christ made visible as the eucharistic host; this feast, linked to the movable cycle of Easter, followed Pentecost in June. Interspersed through the year with these Christ-focused occasions were three important holidays honoring the Virgin Mary: February 2 marked her Purification after the birth of Jesus, March 25 recalled the angel's Annunciation of Mary's pregnancy, and August 15 celebrated her bodily Assumption into heaven.

Though distinctly lesser than Easter, Christmas, celebrating the birth of Jesus, was a principal religious feast. Based on the solar calendar of fixed dates, its cycle began with Advent, which lasted from December 1 until Christmas Eve. During this period for special penitence the devout could fast, abstain from sex, and listen to sermons. At its end, on the night of December 24, the vigil of the Nativity, people customarily went to church. Services were also held on Christmas Day; according to the traveler Montaigne, in Rome, the pope, assisted by several cardinals, performed an unusually grand mass at St. Peter's basilica. January 6, Epiphany, celebrating the biblical three kings with their rich presents for the infant Jesus, occasioned both pageantry and jollity. From the late 14th century, Florence enjoyed especially elaborate observances; a Company of the Magi staged mounted processions and enacted the tale of the kings' visit to Herod. St. Francis of Assisi is said to have first arranged a crib with a doll to represent the holy infant; such a dramatization is recorded in a Florentine friars' church in 1498. In imitation of the generosity of the magi, the Christmas season also brought forth gift giving and hospitality, though on a scale much more modest than in the early 21st century. Lords distributed coins to their dependents, and offerings of food circulated.

Easter, a movable feast in March or April linked to the Moon, anchored the longest and most important celebratory cycle of the year. It began soon after the 12 days of Christmas—in Venice, even overlapping them—with Carnival, a season of license that figured vividly in the popular temporal imagination. Echoing the ancient Roman year-end Saturnalia, Carnival was a time for parties, masquerades, theatrical performances, parades, athletic contests, street dances, jokes, egg throwing, flirtation, general high jinks, and bloody mayhem. Several weeks of festivities accelerated toward a culminating series of fat days. On *Giovedi Grasso* (Fat Thursday) Venetians crowded together to watch a bloody ritual during which a bull and 12 pigs were formally condemned to death, then chased around the piazza in front of the doge's palace and decapitated; the meat was then butchered and shared among the presiding dignitaries. Such rich foods were then penitentially renounced on the next Wednesday, the day of ashes, as Lent began. This period of renunciation and penance that prepared for Easter was known in Latin as the Forty Days, *Quadragesima*. Like Carnival, Lent was a temporal interval that Renaissance people linked to special behavior but was a stark inversion of what had gone on before. While in Carnival, people played and took moral chances, in Lent they tried harder than usual to live by the Christian rules: fasting, praying, hearing sermons, abstaining from meat and play, and shunning sex. Testimony in court alluded to Carnival as indeed a time for greater sexual indulgence, and seasonal declines in births suggest some restraint during Advent and Lent (Cohen and Cohen, 164–73).

FOR MORE INFORMATION

Cohen, E. S., and T. V. Cohen. *Daily Life in Renaissance Italy*. Westport, Conn.: Greenwood, 2001.

Dohrn-Van Rossum, G. *History of the Hour: Clocks and Modern Temporal Orders*. Trans. T. Dunlap. Chicago: University of Chicago Press, 1996.

Muir, E. *Ritual in Early Modern Europe*. Cambridge: Cambridge University Press, 1997.

ECONOMIC LIFE

TIME

England

Spain & Italy

Maya

Aztec

Inca

MAYA

The cycles of movements of the sky deities—Sun, Moon, and planets—were accurately recorded by the Maya through sophisticated arithmetical and writing systems. Of course, they had to rely on observations without the benefit of instruments of modern astronomy. A pair of crossed sticks or similar sighting devices was probably used from heights such as temple summits. With long lines of sight to the horizon, the Maya could fix positions for the rising or setting of the Sun, Moon, or planets to within less than a day's error. When any of these celestial bodies rose or set at the same point a second time, one cycle was completed.

Yet it must be noted that the Maya did not understand these movements as modern astronomy does. The movements were observed and recorded by the Maya to prophesy events the deities were believed to control. Like Babylonian and medieval sky watchers, the Maya used the results of their observations for both mystical and practical purposes. Indeed, they believed that numbers, time, and the entire universe were ruled by supernatural forces. By recording cycles of these forces, they created a series of calendars used to understand events and predict the future. The calendars were matched with the events of history, the reigns of rulers, their conquests and achievements, and the like. Each passing cycle produced the possibility of repeated destiny.

One of the oldest and most important calendars was an almanac of 260 days that operated without regard to the celestial cycles. There were several Maya calendars based on the recurring cycles of movement of the Sun, Moon, and planets. The first two form the basis of our modern 365-day calendar year and our 30-day (on average) month. The Maya marked the Sun's cycle with a solar calendar and the Moon's cycle with a lunar calendar, but they also recorded the cyclic movements of the visible planets such as Venus, Mars, and Jupiter. There was also a purely arbitrary count of 819 days associated with each of the four quadrants of the universe, each ruled over by one of the four color and directional aspects of the deity Kawil: red for the east, black for the west, white for the north, and yellow for the south.

Counts of days in these cycles were recorded by the bar and dot and the vigesimal positional notation discussed earlier in this chapter. To record the numbers 1 to 19 in calendrical texts, the Maya sometimes used alternative symbols known as head-variant numerals. The numbers 1 to 13 and 0 were represented by a series of unique deity head glyphs. The head-variant glyph for the number 10 is a skull. Head-variant numbers from 14 to 19 were formed by combining the appropriate head variant (numbers 4 to 9) with the skeletal lower jaw from the head variant for 10. For example, the number 17 is the number 7 head variant with a skeletal lower jaw.

The most common cyclic counts used by the ancient Maya—the 30-day lunar period, the 260-day almanac, the 365-day solar year, and the Calendar Round cycle of 52 years (discussed below)—were very old concepts shared by all Mesoamerican peoples. It is likely that most of the populace was familiar with these calendars, for they were believed to guide the daily lives and destinies of rich and poor alike. But the more complex calendars, such as those based on planetary cycles and the 819-day count, involved knowledge that must have been guarded by the ruling elite as a source of great power. Having knowledge of the sky deities and being able to predict their movements demonstrated to the common people that the kings and priests were in close communion with the supernatural forces that governed the universe.

The basis of prophecy and much of the pattern of daily life for all Maya people was governed by the count of days, a sacred almanac that repeated itself every 260 days. The origin and significance of the 260-day count are unclear but probably derive from the span of human gestation, which is about the same length of time. In fact, one of the prime uses of the sacred almanac was to determine the destiny of each person's life, which was established by the patron deities of birth dates. Many highland Maya people today continue to use the 260-day almanac for this and other means of divination, even assigning children's names based on the date of their birth.

Each day (*kin*) in the sacred almanac was designated by combining a number from 1 to 13 with one of 20 day names. Because the 13 numbers and 20 days were actually deities, the attributes of each day were determined by the characteristics of the particular combination of number and day. The names of the 20 day deities in Yucatec Mayan are: Imix, Ik, Akbal, Kan, Chicchan, Cimi, Manik, Lamat, Muluc, Oc, Chuen, Eb, Ben, Ix, Men, Cib, Caban, Etz'nab, Cauac, and Ahau.

A given day in the sacred almanac would be named 1 Akbal. This would be followed by 2 Kan, 3 Chicchan, 4 Cimi, and so on. After reaching the day 13 Men, the next day would be 1 Cib as the number cycle began again. This would be followed by 2 Caban, and so on. The next time the starting day deity in this example is reached, it would be associated with a new number deity (8 Akbal). One cycle of the sacred almanac cycle is completed when all 13 numbers have been combined in turn with all 20 day names (13 $\times$ 20 = 260).

The calendar based on the solar year of 365 days per year was the *haab*. The solar year was divided into 18 months of 20 days each (the *winal*) with an additional period of 5 days (the *Uayeb*). Each division began with a *kin* that was referred to as the seating of the month. The first day of the first *winal*, the seating of Pop, is usually written as 0 Pop, followed by the day 1 Pop, 2 Pop, and so on until the last day of the *winal*, 19 Pop, which is followed by the seating of Uo (0 Uo). The names of the *winals* in Yucatec are: Pop, Uo, Zip, Zotz, Tzec, Xul, Yaxkin, Mol, Chen, Yax, Zac, Ceh, Mac, Kankin, Muan, Pax, Kayab, Cumku, and Uayeb.

The complete designation of each *kin* referred to both the position in the sacred almanac and the *haab*, as in 1 Imix 4 Uayeb, followed the next day by 2 Ik 0 Pop, then by 3 Akbal 1 Pop, and so on. Any given day designation does not recur for 52 years. The 52-year cycle is the Calendar Round, which was used by most peoples of Mesoamerica even though their names for days and months varied according to their languages. The Mexica (Aztecs) saw time as an endless succession of 52-year cycles, which they called *xiuhmolpilli* (year bundles). But the Maya also conceived and used time periods longer than the Calendar Round.

The Maya were unique in Mesoamerica in recording a series of far longer cycles of time. Of these the Long Count, which had its heyday around 700 C.E., was the most prominent. The Long Count recorded Calendar Round dates within a larger cycle of 13 baktuns (1,872,000 days, or some 5,128 years). This anchored any given date within a great cycle of time that began in 3114 B.C.E. The beginning date probably refers to an important mythical event such as the creation of the current world. It precedes the earliest known use of the Long Count by some three thousand years. The great cycle will end on December 21, 2012.

Long Count dates record the number of days elapsed from the beginning date. To make this calculation, a modified vigesimal system was used to record (in reverse order) the number of elapsed *kins* (days), *winals* (20 *kins*), *tuns* (18 *winals*, or 360 days), *katuns* (20 *tuns*, or 7,200 days), and *baktuns* (20 *katuns*, or 144,000 days). In a pure vigesimal system, the third order would be 400 (20 × 20 × 1); but the Maya used 18 winals, or 360 (instead of 400) *kins*, to create a closer approximation to the length of the solar year (365 days). We now express Long Count dates in Arabic numerals—as in 9.15.10.0.0, referring to 9 *baktuns* (1,296,000 days), 15 *katuns* (108,000 days), 10 *tuns* (3,600 days), 0 *winals*, and 0 *kins* to reach the Calendar Round date of 3 Ahau 3 Mol (June 30, 741 C.E.).

As Middle Maya Civilization began to decline, the Long Count was often replaced by a less bulky count known as period-ending dating. This was used to record the day on which each *katun* fell—as in Katun 16, 2 Ahau 13 Tzec, equivalent to 9.16.0.0.0. Each of the 13 *katuns* had its patron deity, its prophecies, and its special ceremonies. Monuments and entire assemblages of buildings (such as Tikal's Twin Pyramid Groups) were erected for ceremonies to celebrate the end of the highly auspicious *katun* cycle. Once they were dedicated, period-ending notations were used as base dates for recording other dates and events, just like the Long Count.

During Late Maya Civilization, historical recording was abbreviated further. Dates were recorded in the *u kahlay katunob* (count of the *katuns*) of Yucatán (also known as the Short Count). This method referred only to the day of a *katun* ending in the sacred almanac; it did not give the number of the *katun* or the *haab* date. The period-ending date mentioned above—Katun 16, 2 Ahau 13 Tzec—would be recorded as Katun 2 Ahau in the *u kahlay katunob*. It was assumed the reader would know the critical information (the *katun* number) to understand the date.

Because every *katun* ended on a day Ahau, there were 13 differently designated *katuns* in this method of dating (1 Ahau, 2 Ahau, 3 Ahau, etc.). But the number of the day Ahau on each successive *katun* ending was two less than that of the previous *katun*, so the sequence was Katun 13 Ahau, Katun 11 Ahau, Katun 9 Ahau, and so on. After Katun 1 Ahau, the next ending date was Katun 12 Ahau, followed by Katun 10 Ahau, and so forth. The same Ahau day repeated every 260 *tuns* (256-1/4 solar years). One occurrence of the date Katun 13 Ahau ended in

771 C.E., another Katun 2 Ahau ended in 1027, another in 1283, and another in 1539, during the Spanish Conquest. The *u kahlay katunob* was an historical abstract that was useful as long as the sequence remained unbroken. By the time of the conquest, this record covered 62 *katuns* from 9.0.0.0.0 (435 C.E.), a span of 11 centuries (Sharer, 187–93).

FOR MORE INFORMATION

Sharer, R. J. *Daily Life in Maya Civilization*. Westport, Conn.: Greenwood, 1996.

AZTEC

According to the Aztecs, the universe passed through four great eras, each ending in a cataclysm but also giving way to a new cosmos. The Aztecs were also careful to mark their important memories with specific dates in the form of day signs. It is very important to know how all these spaces—the four quarters, the center of the world, the dualities, the 13 heavens, and the nine underworlds—revolved, changed, or experienced the passage of time.

The dynamics of the Aztec universe can first be understood in terms of the three kinds of time—the transcendent time of the gods, the active time of the gods, and the time of humans—which all flowed together. We will look at these three kinds of time and then outline the yearly and daily calendar that influenced every part of Aztec life.

Before there was human time or even the time of the creation myths, there was a transcendent time of the Dual God who dwelled quietly in the highest heavens. This supreme being existed in peace but provided the original energy and structure of the universe. This primordial time of the gods, when order first appeared out of chaos but did not exist as action, continued to exist in a celestial realm. This existence is reflected in the notion of Omeyocan, the Dual Heaven, where all was in balance and silence.

This peaceful time was broken by a second flow of time, the time when the gods acted out all kinds of events, including creations, abductions, violations, wars, deaths, games, and even the sacrifice and dismembering of other gods to make an existence in which humans could eventually dwell.

These creative/destructive actions gave way to a third kind of time, the time of humans, which flowed and developed in the middle of the universe—the Earth's surface—and the four lower heavens. It was during the second cosmic time, when the supernatural forces acted in all levels of the universe, that the calendar came into being, an invention of the gods to be used to govern and interact with the time of human beings. We know that the calendar was made during the second period, because the creation myths often tell of specific dates of creation. All humans and other significant beings created in the third era have sacred and magical names corresponding to the time of their birth.

What is fascinating and makes the story more complex is that neither the time of the transcendent gods nor the time of mythical action ceased after the birth of the time of human beings. In fact, supernatural beings were created who became intimately connected to daily life in human spaces on earth. Also, the forces from the time of the mythic events kept ruling the time of human life on earth through the cycles of nature and the Calendar Round. We can conceive of these three times as a wheel within a larger wheel within an even larger wheel, even though they don't always turn in the same direction or on the same plane. But each hour and day in earthly time is in touch with the particular forces of the time of the gods and the time of myth. In this way each human day coincided with a special moment in mythical time and received the imprint of the world of the gods. Each moment of human time was a kind of crossroad where a plurality of divine forces met to determine the kind of day that people lived.

The Aztec had a sacred almanac, a 260-day cycle called the *tonalpohualli*, or count of days. Twenty day signs ran consecutively from Alligator through Flower, repeating after the 20th day. These 20 signs interacted with the numbers 1 through 13, which also repeated. This meant that the 20 day signs and the 13 numbers, advancing side by side, yielded a 260-day cycle before starting over again.

Along with the 260-day cycle, there was also a 365-day cycle, or solar calendar, called the *xiuhpohualli*. This solar calendar was divided into 18 sections or months each containing 20 days, with five unlucky or empty days, called the *nemontemi*, situated after the 18th month at the end of the year. Each month had a major celebration. What is remarkable is that the 260-day *tonalpohualli* and the 365-day *xiuhpohualli* operated simultaneously, using the same day signs and counting system, and the interaction between these two calendars produced a larger cycle of 52 solar years. The ending and beginning of this cycle were vital moments of cosmic renewal in the Aztec world.

The calendars marked and regulated the passage of natural and supernatural influences into human life. The numbers and signs of the Aztec calendar, however, were much more than artistic combinations. They had to do with fate—human fate and the fate of all life—and they were used for naming individuals. For instance, as soon as a child was born, the parents invited a day-count reader to the home who was told the exact instant of the child's birth. These calendar priests would open up one of their divinatory books and study the paintings associated with the day signs and numbers surrounding the child's birth. A careful study ensued in which the priest identified the particular day sign of the child's birth, but also the other signs related to that major sign. Since each day sign had numerous powers and qualities, the family and the calendar priest looked for the most positive combinations. The numbers 3, 7, and 10 through 13 were fortunate, while 6, 8, and 9 brought bad luck. A combined reading could bring a positive interpretation into the naming of a child even if the basic number was negative. For instance, if a child was born on what was considered a negative day sign, the other associated signs could bring positive influences into the child's life. If the birth date were particularly gloomy, the day-count reader would urge the parents to wait for a favorable day sign and number, which would then become the child's name.

The person's life was forever shaped by the forces and influences of his or her calendar name. One of the most famous Aztecs, Nezahualcoyotl, the ruler of Tezcoco, had the calendar name 1 Deer, a day whose destiny included nobility, fame, and success in war. In fact, he was one of the great poet/warriors of Aztec history in spite of many obstacles. The day 4 Dog brought prosperity to a person, especially if he bred dogs for food. It was believed that his dogs would be healthy, breed well, and live long lives. "It was said: 'How can it be otherwise? The dogs share a day sign with him.'" An unfavorable day sign was 2 Rabbit, the day dedicated to the *pulque* gods; it meant that the child had the capacity to become a drunkard. Traders left and returned home on specific days. Wars were started only when the days had strong, positive signs. All events were regulated by this system (Carrasco, 59–62).

FOR MORE INFORMATION

Aveni, A. *Empires of Time: Calendars, Clocks, and Cultures.* New York: Basic Books, 1989.

Carrasco, D., with S. Sessions. *Daily Life of the Aztecs: People of the Sun and Earth.* Westport, Conn.: Greenwood, 1998.

INCA

ECONOMIC LIFE

TIME

England

Spain & Italy

Maya

Aztec

Inca

The Incas apparently used two different calendars, one for daytime and one for nighttime. The daytime calendar was based on the solar cycle and was approximately 365 days long. It was used for economic activities such as agriculture, mining, warfare, and construction. The movement of the Sun was particularly important to the Inca agricultural calendar, being used to fix the days of planting. Four towers were built on the horizons east and west of Cuzco to mark the rising and setting locations of the Sun in August and to determine the time to plant corn and potatoes. The point of view was the *ushnu*, the raised ceremonial platform in the main plaza of the city. When the Sun rose over the first tower on the eastern horizon and set over the corresponding tower on the western horizon, it marked when the early crops should be planted in August. When the Sun rose between two towers built close together farther south, it marked the time of general sowing in September.

The Incas' nighttime calendar was developed to mark important ceremonies to the Moon and stars, which were sacred deities to the Incas. It had only 328 days, or 12 months of 27.33 days each. These nighttime calendar months almost equal a lunar month, which has 28 days. There is an apparent problem with correlating the Inca daytime calendar, based on the Sun, and the Inca nighttime calendar, based on the Moon. The latter is 37 days shorter than the former. It is uncertain whether this correlation was important to the Incas.

Some scholars have argued that the Inca calendars could not have been based on such detailed, accurate observations, as there is no good evidence of either the accuracy of the measurements or the particular astronomical risings and settings needed. Part of this debate concerns whether the Incas recorded the solstices (the northernmost and southernmost points of the Sun), the equinoxes (the midpoint between the northernmost and southernmost positions), and the zeniths of the Sun and Moon (the highest points in their orbits overhead). Several recent scholars suggest they did, but they base their arguments on the presence of important ceremonies falling on or near the days of those events; others have argued that the observation lines are not sufficiently accurate to be sure that these ceremonies actually were celebrating the particular astronomical events.

What is clear about both Inca calendars is that they were used for determining when important ceremonies should be conducted, rather than simply for marking time. This relates to the Inca belief that nothing happened by accident but was always caused by a supernatural force. The agricultural activities and important ceremonies of the daytime calendar are listed in the next section, "Calendars," in terms of the modern months when they occurred. As stated previously, the Incas did not associate equal periods of time with each month; rather, they recorded the passage of the year in terms of the activities and ceremonies required of the gods at different times. Therefore the correlation of the Inca's calendars with the modern one is only approximate.

> *The Incas did not associate equal periods of time with each month.*

The nighttime calendar was more focused on nonagricultural ceremonies, although some months had rituals celebrating certain crops or related activities, such as irrigation. The importance of corn to the Incas is indicated by the significance of the month of May in both calendars, which celebrated the harvest. The nighttime calendar, based on the Moon's cycles, was important in setting the time of rituals. The Incas began their calendar in December with the Capac Raymi festival.

While calendars describe the flow of time on a yearly basis, the flow of time on a smaller, daily level can, perhaps, be best understood through a reconstruction of a day in the life of an Inca family living in Cuzco.

The day begins around sunrise with the principal wife rising from bed, leaving her husband and 14-year-old son to sleep, and going to wake the secondary wife at her adjacent house. The latter dresses and leaves to get water from the river, waking her 12-year-old daughter to accompany her. They leave their one-room house in the family's compound, cross the courtyard, and exit through the narrow, trapezoidal doorway into the street. They turn and walk down the street toward the river, pausing to talk with a friend from the next house who is already returning. It is a happy coincidence that this friend is from the same group as the secondary wife, although from a different village. At least they speak the same native language. The secondary wife wishes the Incas did not forbid them to speak it. It is amazing that they were both brought the month's walk to Cuzco from their native lands and are now neighbors!

Upon arriving at the river, she fills the one small and two large vessels she has brought with her, giving the smaller vessel to her daughter to carry. They return to the house, where the principal wife has stoked the fire from the embers of the previous night. The secondary wife begins preparing a meal of corn cooked with chili peppers under the watchful eye of the principal wife, who thinks to herself that this foreigner does not know the proper means for preparing food despite her training at the Inca center in her native land. Still, it is an honor for her husband to have been given this girl as a wife by the king in appreciation for his hard work for the empire. And she certainly makes life much easier.

Meanwhile, the husband and son have risen and are discussing the day's activities. Breakfast is served on silver plates placed on a fine cloth on the floor. The principal wife sits with her back to her husband, facing the small clay stove where the food simmers. The secondary wife sits to her side, with her daughter next to her. The son sits next to his father. Everyone eats with spoons of silver.

After the meal the secondary wife cleans the dishes and places them back in a niche in the wall. She and her daughter then leave to collect firewood, taking some toasted maize with them, because they expect to be gone for several hours. Both take their spinning tools and wool, from the family's alpacas, to make thread on their way to the fields. They go to look for wood in the hills to the east of the city, the closest place where public land for such purposes can be found.

The husband leaves to visit the family fields near Cuzco and speak with the servants who work the fields. The irrigation canal bringing water to the fields is in need of repair, and he must discuss what is required to repair it before damage is done to the corn crop. He too takes a portion of toasted maize with him, along with his usual bag of coca and lime. The son leaves the *cancha* (housing compound) to visit cousins in the next one up the street, to discuss the upcoming puberty rites. They plan to go out to the fields and practice running for the race down the Hill of Anahuarque, which will be part of their rite of passage into manhood. They also plan to check the family's alpaca herd in the pastures above the city.

The principal wife remains at home and works on preparing the costume her son will wear during the puberty rites. She carefully sews a new tunic, adding some gold disks to the top where they will catch the sun as he dances in the ceremonies. She also visits with her husband's brother's wife, who lives in the house across the courtyard from theirs in the *cancha*. They have become good friends since the brother's wife arrived several years earlier, even though she is six years younger than the principal wife. They have a second child on the way, their first having died two years ago. Both families suspect that the child died of sorcery, and they think it might have been caused by a neighbor that was jealous of the child. The principal wife stops abruptly—could the secondary wife have used a sorcerer to do it?

After midday, the two go to leave an offering at the Temple of the Moon, to improve the prospects of a successful childbirth. The priestess there seems confident that the offering of a guinea pig and wool from a white llama will ensure a successful outcome this time. On their way home they speak to the maker of pots to arrange for some new cooking vessels to be delivered to their houses, because two broke the day before. They pass by the *cancha* of the king's family, with its beautifully fitted stonework. How nice it would be to live in such a house, they say to each other. And to have so many *yanaconas* (servants) to do their bidding would be even better! Friends say the king's new country estate in the Urubamba valley is even more attractive, and that hundreds of conquered people were brought in from all over the empire to build it. The two women comment that although their lives are comparatively easy, they do not seem nearly as easy as the lives of the direct descendants of the Sun!

Returning home, they begin preparing the afternoon meal for their respective families. Slightly later, the secondary wife returns with the firewood. Told to prepare some more *chicha* (an alcoholic drink) for the festival coming up in three days, she goes to soak some corn in preparation. The principal wife prepares a stew of llama, potatoes, and quinoa for dinner, with corn dumplings on the side; *chicha* is served in wooden goblets.

After dinner the secondary wife cleans up and puts the dinnerware away while the principal wife talks with her husband and son about their day. Before sunset the husband goes to speak with his brother about their alpaca herds, which the son found had strayed away from their pasture. The brother agrees to bring the herd back in the morning, and the son says he will go along to help. The father has to return to the fields to coordinate the repair of the irrigation canal, along with several other relatives who all have fields along the same irrigation system. The principal wife prepares offerings to the deities of the water and earth, to ensure everything will go well. After sunset the families return to their respective houses and go to bed, each family sharing a bed covered with alpaca cloaks for warmth against the cool night air (Malpass, 96–99, 113–15).

FOR MORE INFORMATION

Malpass, M. A. *Daily Life in the Inca Empire*. Westport, Conn.: Greenwood, 1996.

Ziolkowski, M., and R. Sadowski, eds. *Time and Calendars in the Inca Empire*. Oxford: British Archeological Reports, International Series 479, 1989.

Zuidema, R. T. "The Sidereal Lunar Calendar of the Incas." In *Archaeoastronomy in the New World*, ed. A. Aveni, 59–107. Cambridge: Cambridge University Press, 1982.

ECONOMIC LIFE
|
CALENDARS
|
England

Aztec

Inca

Calendars

This section lists some of the important dates in the yearly cycles of the English, the Aztecs, and the Incas. For more general information about time and its measurement, including the passage of years, see the preceding section, "Time."

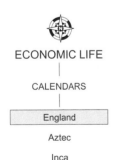

ECONOMIC LIFE
|
CALENDARS
|
England

Aztec

Inca

ENGLAND

January

In this month the ground was too frozen to be worked, so the husbandman would be busy with maintenance jobs around the holding, such as trimming woods and hedges, repairing fences, and clearing ditches.

1　*The Circumcision of Christ (New Year's Day)*. New Year's Day came in the midst of the Christmas season, which ran from Christmas Eve to Twelfth Day, and was generally a time for merrymaking and sociability. People often observed the day with an exchange of gifts: favored choices included apples, eggs, nutmegs, gloves, pins, and oranges studded with cloves. They would also drink wassail, a spiced ale traditionally served in a brown bowl; there were traditional wassail songs as part of the ritual.

6   *Epiphany (Twelfth Day)*. The Twelfth Day of Christmas (reckoned by counting Christmas itself as the first day) was the last day of the Christmas season. The evening before, called Twelfth Night, was traditionally the most riotous holiday of the year, an occasion for folk plays and merriment. One ritual was the serving of a spiced fruitcake with a dried bean and a dried pea inside. A man whose piece contained the bean would become the Lord of Misrule or King, and a woman who got the pea became the Queen; the two would preside together over the festivities. The wassail bowl was drunk, as at the New Year.

–   *Plow Monday (Rock Monday)*. This fell on the first Monday after Twelfth Night. On this day plows were blessed, and in parts of England the plowmen drew a plow from door to door soliciting gifts of money. The day also commemorated the work of women, under the name Rock Monday (rock is another word for a distaff).

8   *St. Lucian*

13 *St. Hilary*

18 *St. Prisca*

19 *St. Wolfstan*

20 *St. Fabian*

21 *St. Agnes*. According to tradition, a woman who went to bed without supper on the eve of St. Agnes would dream of her future husband.

22 *St. Vincent*

25 *The Conversion of St. Paul*. Elizabethan country folk believed that the weather on St. Paul's Day would reveal the future of the year: a fair day boded a fair year, a windy day presaged wars, and a cloudy day foretold plague.

February

This was considered the first month of spring. In February the snow would leave, the ground would thaw, and the husbandman could begin preparing the fields designated for the spring or Lenten crop. He would spread manure on the fields and plow them, and then begin to sow his peas, beans, and oats. Plowing was usually done with horses, but occasionally oxen were used in heavy soils.

2   *Feast of the Purification of Mary (Candlemas)*. The name Candlemas was derived from the tradition of bearing candles in a church procession on this day, although the custom was generally suppressed under the Protestant church.

3   *St. Blaise*. On this day the countrywomen traditionally visited each other and burned any distaffs they found in use.

5   *St. Agatha*

14 *St. Valentine*. In Elizabethan times (as today), this day was a celebration of love. Men and women drew one another's names by lot to determine who would be paired as valentines, pinning the lots on their bosom or sleeve and perhaps exchanging gifts.

24 *St. Matthias the Apostle*

–   *Shrove Tuesday (Shrovetide)*. Shrovetide was the day before Ash Wednesday, falling between February 3 and March 9. This holiday was the last day before the fasting season of Lent. On the Continent this day was celebrated with wild abandon, reflected in the modern Mardi Gras. The English version was more subdued but still involved ritual feasting and violence. On this day it was traditional to eat fritters and pancakes. It was also a day for playing football (a game much rougher than any of its modern namesakes), and for the sport of cock thrashing or cockshy. In cock thrashing, the participants tied a cock to a stake and threw sticks at it: they paid the owner of the cock a few pence for each try, and a person who could knock down the cock and pick it up before the cock regained its feet won the cock as a prize. In towns, this was often a day for the apprentices to riot; their violence was often aimed against those who transgressed sexual mores, especially prostitutes. The two days previous were sometimes called Shrove Sunday and Shrove Monday.

– *The First Day of Lent (Ash Wednesday).* Lent began on the Wednesday before the sixth Sunday before Easter (between February 4 and March 10). The medieval church had forbidden the eating of meat other than fish during Lent. Although the religious basis for this restriction was no longer a factor, Queen Elizabeth decided to keep the restriction in place as a means of boosting England's fishing industry. The name Ash Wednesday was officially disapproved, as it smacked of Catholicism, but it was still commonly used. Lent was sometimes observed by setting up an effigy called a Jack-a-Lent and pelting it with sticks and stones: as this season was a season for fasting, the Jack-a-Lent symbolized all the hardships in the life of a commoner.

March

In March the husbandman would sow his barley, the last of the Lenten crops. This was also the time to begin work on the garden, a task that generally fell to the woman of the house. She might also do the spring cleaning in this month.

1   *St. David.* David was the patron saint of Wales, and Welshmen traditionally wore leeks in their hats on this day.
2   *St. Chad*
7   *St. Perpetua*
12 *St. Gregory*
18 *St. Edward*
21 *St. Benedict*
25 *Feast of the Annunciation of Mary (Lady Day in Lent).* The number of the year changed on this day.
–   *Mid-Lent Sunday.* This was the Sunday three weeks before Easter (March 1 to April 4). This day was often called Mothering Sunday: it was traditional for people to visit their mothers on this day.

April

During this month the woman of the house would continue work on the garden, as well as begin work in the dairy.

3   *St. Richard*
4   *St. Ambrose*
19 *St. Alphege*
23 *St. George.* George was the patron saint of England.
25 *St. Mark the Evangelist*
–   *Palm Sunday.* This was one week before Easter Sunday, and it marked the beginning of the Easter Week. The ancient custom of bearing palm leaves or rushes into the church on this day had been suppressed by the Protestant church, although there may well have been conservative parishes where it was still observed.
–   *Wednesday before Easter*
–   *Thursday before Easter (Maundy Thursday).* This was traditionally a day for acts of charity.
–   *Good Friday*
–   *Easter Eve*
–   *Easter.* Like today, Easter was a movable feast. It was based on the lunar Jewish calendar, which is why it did not always fall on the same day in the solar calendar we inherited from the Romans. Easter was on the first Sunday after the first full moon on or after March 21; if the full moon was on a Sunday, Easter was on the next Sunday. This places

Easter between March 22 and April 25. Easter marked the end of Lent and was an occasion for great feasting, as it was once again permissible to eat meat.

- *Monday in Easter Week*
- *Tuesday in Easter Week*
- *Hocktide* (*Hock Monday* and *Hock Tuesday*). The second Monday and Tuesday after Easter. On Hock Monday the young women of the parish would go about the streets with ropes and capture passing men, who had to pay a small ransom to be released; the men would do the same on Hock Tuesday. The money raised would go to the parish funds.

May

May was the first month of summer. Now the hard work of spring eased somewhat: this was a prime season for festivals, before heavy work began again with haymaking at the end of June. In this month it was time to weed the winter crops and to plow the fallow fields in preparation for the next season. The woman of the house would sow flax and hemp.

1   *Sts. Philip and Jacob the Apostles (May Day)*. This day was often celebrated as the first day of summer. Both villagers and townsfolk might have traveled to the forests and fields to bring back flowers and branches as decorations—and this was notoriously an opportunity for young men and women to engage in illicit union in the woods. There might have even been a full-scale summer festival, such as was often celebrated on Whitsunday (see below).

3   *Feast of the Invention of the Cross (Crouchmass)*

6   *St. John the Evangelist*

10   *St. Gordian*

19   *St. Dunstan*

26   *St. Augustine of Canterbury*

-   *Rogation Sunday*. This fell five weeks after Easter (April 26 to May 30). This holiday was the time for beating the bounds: the parishioners would gather with the local curate to walk around the boundary of the parish, reciting prayers and psalms, and asking God for forgiveness of sins and a blessing on the crops, which had by now all been sown. This ceremony helped to identify the traditional borders of the parish.

-   *Ascension Day*. This was the Thursday after Rogation Sunday (April 30 to June 3). This was another popular occasion for summer festivals (see Whitsunday below).

-   *Whitsunday (Pentecost)*. Ten days after Ascension (May 10 to June 13). This was perhaps the favorite day for summer festivals, sometimes called ales, or mayings (even when they did not fall in May). Each locality had its own customs, but certain themes were common. There were often folk plays and dramatic rituals, especially ones involving Robin Hood or St. George. Another typical activity was morris dancing, a ritual dance in which the dancers, often just men, wore bells, ribbons, and outlandish attire. The dance sometimes involved other ritual figures: a hobby horse (a man dressed up with a false horse to make him look like a rider), a Maid Marian (typically a man dressed as a woman), and a fool (a jester figure). The occasion might also be marked by displays of banners and by military demonstrations. The celebrants often elected a man and woman to preside over the festival under such names as Summer King and Queen, May King and Queen, or Whitsun Lord and Lady. Many towns and villages erected a maypole, brightly painted and adorned with garlands or flags, around which there might be a maypole dance. Often a temporary hall or tent was erected where the parish would sell ale, the proceeds going to the parish church.

-   *Whitmonday*

-   *Whitsun Tuesday*. The two days after Whitsunday, as official holidays, often continued the Whitsun festival, and all three days together might be called Whitsuntide.

   —   *Trinity Sunday.* One week after Whitsunday (May 17 to June 20). This was another popular day for summer festivals, like that described for Whitsun.

June

June was the time to weed the Lenten crops and to wash and shear the sheep—sheep shearing was often an occasion for merrymaking. At about Midsummer began the mowing season: the men would go out to the meadows, where the grass had been allowed to grow long, and cut it down with scythes in preparation for hay-making.

  3   *St. Nichomede*
  5   *St. Boniface*
11   *St. Barnabas the Apostle*
17   *St. Botolph*
20   *The Translation of St. Edward*
24   *St. John the Baptist (Midsummer).* This festival was an important civic occasion, marked by a variety of festivities and displays of communal identity. There was often a huge bonfire on St. John's Eve, and it was common to stay up late that night. Midsummer was an occasion for parades featuring giants, dragons, explosions of gunpowder, drumming, military displays, and a march by the local watch and community officials.
29   *St. Peter the Apostle.* This holiday was sometimes observed with traditions similar to those on the feast of St. John.
30   *Commemoration of St. Paul*

July

During this month the mown grass was made into hay: it had to be laid out in the sun to dry, stacked, and then carted away for storage. It was crucial that the hay dry properly, as it would otherwise rot. Hay was very important to the rural economy, since it was fed to horses and cattle, especially during the winter, when they could not graze. July was also a time for a second plowing of the fallow fields and for gathering hemp, flax, and beans from the garden.

  1   *Visitation of Mary*
  3   *Translation of St. Martin*
15   *St. Swithun*
20   *St. Margaret*
22   *St. Magdalene*
25   *St. James the Apostle*
26   *St. Anne*

August

August began the hardest time of a husbandman's year, with the harvest of the main crops. There was a great deal of work to be done in a short time, so the entire family was involved and temporary workers were often hired. The men went into the fields with sickles to harvest the grain. Then the cut grain was bound into sheaves, often by the women and children. The sheaves were stacked and loaded onto carts to be taken away to shelter; as with the hay, it was very important to keep the grain dry lest it rot. The stalks of grain were cut toward the top, leaving the rest of the stalk to be harvested later with a scythe to make straw. The straw was sometimes fed to the livestock (although they did not generally care for it), and was especially useful for making baskets, stuffing beds, hatching roofs, and strewing on the floor.

 1 Lammas
 6 Transfiguration of Christ
 7 Name of Jesus
10 St. Laurence
24 St. Bartholomew the Apostle (Bartholomewtide)
28 St. Augustine of Hippo
29 The Beheading of St. John the Baptist

September

At the end of harvest, the harvesters celebrated harvest home, or hockey. The last sheaf of grain would be brought into the barn with great ceremony, and seed cake was distributed. After the harvest was done, and on rainy days when harvesting was impossible, the husbandman threshed and winnowed. In threshing, the grain was beaten with flails so that the husk would crack open, allowing the seed to come out. Then it was winnowed: the winnowers waved straw fans, blowing away the straw and the broken husks (called chaff). Chaff had uses of its own: it could be fed to livestock, or used for stuffing beds. After harvest was over, the husbandman began work on the winter crop: the winter fields had to be plowed, and the husbandman would begin to sow the rye. This was also the season for gathering fruit from the orchard.

 1 St. Giles
 7 St. Enurchus the Bishop
 8 Nativity of Mary (Lady Day in Harvest)
14 Holy Cross Day (Holy Rood Day). This was traditionally a day for nutting, or gathering nuts in the woods.
17 St. Lambert
21 St. Matthew the Apostle
26 St. Cyprian
29 St. Michael the Archangel (Michaelmas). This day marked the beginning of the agricultural year: all the harvests were in, and the annual accounts could be reckoned up. The day was often observed by eating a goose for dinner.
30 St. Jerome

October

October was the time to sow wheat, which had to be done by the end of the month. The end of the wheat sowing was often marked by a feast. This was also a good time to brew ale for the winter.

 1 St. Remigius
 6 St. Faith
 9 St. Dennis
13 Translation of St. Edward the Confessor
17 St. Ethelred
18 St. Luke the Evangelist
25 St. Crispin

28 *Sts. Simon and Jude the Apostles*
31 *All Saints' Eve*

November

The dairy season ended during this month, and the livestock were brought in from pasture and stalled for the winter. This was the time to slaughter any animals the household planned to eat during the winter, as a means of conserving winter fodder. As the weather began to become too cold for agricultural work, the farmer took time to cleanse the privies, burying the muck in the garden as fertilizer; he might also clean the chimney before the chill of winter set in.

1   *All Saints (All Hallows, Hallowmas, Hallontide)*
2   *All Souls*
6   *St. Leonard*
11 *St. Martin.* This day was traditionally associated with the slaughter of animals for the winter.
13 *St. Brice*
15 *St. Machutus*
16 *St. Edmund the Archbishop*
17 *Accession Day (Queen's Day, Coronation Day, St. Hugh).* This was the only truly secular holiday: it commemorated Queen Elizabeth's accession to the throne in 1558.
20 *St. Edmund King and Martyr*
22 *St. Cicely*
23 *St. Clement*
25 *St. Katharine*
30 *St. Andrew the Apostle*
–   The season of Advent began on the nearest Sunday to the feast of St. Andrew (i.e., between November 27 and December 3). People were supposed to observe the same fast as in Lent, although few actually did.

December

This was one of the least demanding times of the husbandman's year, and one of the principal seasons for merrymaking and sociability, especially around Christmas. Wood was split during this season; otherwise, relatively little outdoors work was suitable for this month, so it was a good time to sit at home, maintaining and repairing tools in preparation for the next year. The winter snows arrived sometime in December.

6   *St. Nicholas*
8   *Conception of Mary*
13 *St. Lucy*
21 *St. Thomas the Apostle*
25 *Christmas.* Christmas, along with Easter, was one of the two most important holidays of the year. The Christmas season lasted for the full 12 days of Christmas, from Christmas Eve to Twelfth Day (January 6); it was a time for dancing, gymnastics, indoor games (especially cards), and folk plays. Elizabethan Christmas rituals in many respects resembled some of the traditions still in use today. People decorated their homes with rosemary, bay, holly, ivy, and mistletoe; and they enjoyed a great dinner, sang songs, and exchanged gifts. People often chose a Christmas Lord, Prince, or King to preside over the festivities. Nuts were a traditional food for Christmas, in addition to festive pies and cakes and brawn, a type of pickled pork. Warmth and light were an important part of

the Christmas festivities, as observed in the burning of a Yule Log and the lighting of many candles. Christmas Eve was a highly festive occasion when people often drank the wassail (see its description under January 1).

26 *St. Stephen the Martyr*
27 *St. John the Evangelist*
28 *The Holy Innocents' Day (Childermas)*
29 *St. Thomas of Canterbury*
31 *St. Silvester the Bishop*

(Singman, 60–71)

FOR MORE INFORMATION

Singman, J. L. *Daily Life in Elizabethan England.* Westport, Conn.: Greenwood, 1995.

AZTEC

A schematized version of the 260-day almanac, as used by the Aztec, follows: all local and regional variations of the Mesoamerican calendar in use when the Spaniards arrived were based on a 260-day ritual cycle, referred to in Nahuatl as the *tonalpohualli*. The *tonalpohualli* was organized in 20 13-day periods, which the Spanish priests called *trecenas*. Each of the 260 days was uniquely named by combining 1 of 20 possible day signs with 1 of 13 possible numbers or numerical coefficients. The ritual calendar began with day 1 Alligator and ended with the day 13 Flower. The progression of days went: 1 Alligator, 2 Wind, 3 House, 4 Lizard, 5 Serpent, 6 Death, 7 Deer, 8 Rabbit, 9 Water, 10 Dog, 11 Monkey, 12 Grass, and 13 Reed. Upon reaching the coefficient 13, the first *trecena* was completed and the second *trecena* began using the coefficient 1 with the next day sign, Jaguar. Thus, the count continued with: 1 Jaguar, 2 Eagle, 3 Vulture, 4 Movement, 5 Flint, 6 Rain, and 7 Flower. After the 20th day sign (Flower), the count went back to the first day sign, Alligator. Thus, the count continued with: 8 Alligator, 9 Wind, 10 House, 11 Lizard, 12 Serpent, 13 Death, 1 Deer, 2 Rabbit, 3 Water, and so on, until all of the 260 combinations became exhausted on the day 13 Flower (Carrasco, 61).

FOR MORE INFORMATION

Carrasco, D., with S. Sessions. *Daily Life of the Aztecs: People of the Sun and Earth.* Westport, Conn.: Greenwood, 1998.

ECONOMIC LIFE
|
CALENDARS
|
England
Aztec
Inca

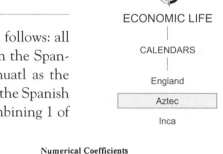

| Day-Signs | Numerical Coefficients | | | | | | | | | | | | |
Nahuatl English	1	2	3	4	5	6	7	8	9	10	11	12	13
Cipactli Alligator	1	41	81	121	161	201	241	21	61	101	141	181	221
Ehecatl Wind	222	2	42	82	122	162	202	242	22	62	102	142	182
Calli house	183	223	3	43	83	123	163	203	243	23	63	103	143
Cuetzpallin Lizard	144	184	224	4	44	84	124	164	204	244	24	64	104
Coatl Serpent	105	145	185	225	5	45	85	125	165	205	245	25	65
Miquiztli Death	66	106	146	186	226	6	46	86	126	166	206	246	26
Mazatl Deer	27	67	107	147	187	227	7	47	87	127	167	207	247
Tochtli Rabbit	248	28	68	108	148	188	228	8	48	88	128	168	208
Atl Water	209	249	29	69	109	149	189	229	9	49	89	129	169
Itzcuintli Dog	170	210	250	30	70	110	150	190	230	10	50	90	130
Ozomatli Monkey	131	171	211	251	31	71	111	151	191	231	11	51	91
Malinalli Grass	92	132	172	212	252	32	72	112	152	192	232	12	52
Acatl Reed	53	93	133	173	213	253	33	73	113	153	193	233	13
Ocelotl Jaguar	14	54	94	134	174	214	254	34	74	114	154	194	234
Cuauhtli Eagle	235	15	55	95	135	175	215	255	35	75	115	155	195
Cozcacuauhtli Vulture	196	236	16	56	96	136	176	216	256	36	76	116	156
Ollin Movement	157	197	237	17	57	97	137	177	217	257	37	77	117
Tecpatl Flint Knife	118	158	198	238	18	58	98	138	178	218	258	38	78
Quiahuitl Rain	79	119	159	199	239	19	59	99	139	179	219	259	39
Xochitl Flower	40	80	120	160	200	240	20	60	100	140	180	220	260

Aztec Nahuatl Calendar. Courtesy of Scott Sessions.

ECONOMIC LIFE
|
CALENDARS
|
England

Aztec

Inca

INCA

The Incas used two different calendars to keep track of time: one daytime calendar, which followed the rhythm of the Sun as it passed through the seasons, and the nighttime calendar, which tracked the cycles of the Moon and the stars. The daytime calendar was used to determine the proper dates for planting, while the nighttime calendar was more involved with rituals and worship.

Daytime calendar	Nighttime calendar
December. Coca planting.	Capac Raymi (December). The boys' puberty ceremony was an important part of Capac Raymi, as were other rituals concerning the Sun. Tribute for the Inca state and religion was brought to Cuzco from the provinces at this time.
January. Weeding of fields.	Camay quilla (January). A continuation of some of the puberty ceremonies from the previous month was conducted, along with others to Viracocha, the principal god.
February–March. Harvest of the potato and other root crops.	Hatun-pucuy (February). Ceremonies were conducted to increase the corn and other crops. Pacha-pucuy (March). More rituals were conducted to ensure that the crops ripened properly.
April. Protecting the corn fields from deer, foxes, and human theft.	Ayrihua (April). Ceremonies honoring the Inca king were held.
May. Corn harvest.	Aymoray quilla (May). Celebration of the corn harvest was held.
June. Large potatoes were harvested and other potatoes planted.	Inti Raymi (June). Important rituals were conducted to the Sun.
July. Storage of potatoes and other crops; cleaning of irrigation canals.	Chahua-huarquiz (July). Ceremonies for the irrigation systems were held.
August–September. Planting of the corn and potato crops.	Yapaquiz (August). Sacrifices were made to all the gods, especially those associated with the forces of nature. Coya Raymi (September). The city of Cuzco was purified, and the sacred idols of conquered people were brought to pay homage to the king. K'antaray (October). Ceremonies were conducted to ensure adequate rainfall.
November. Irrigation of the corn fields.	Ayamarca (November). The Festival of the Dead was conducted, with the bodies of dead kings brought out of their tombs to receive offerings and food.

(Malpass, 96–99)

FOR MORE INFORMATION

Malpass, M. A. *Daily Life in the Inca Empire*. Westport, Conn.: Greenwood, 1996.

ECONOMIC LIFE: WEB SITES

http://www.isourcecom.com/maya
http://www.britannia.com/history/londonhistory/tudlon.html
http://www.european-digest.com/ecd03/docs/digest15.htm
http://www.heritage.nf.ca/exploration/16fishery.html
http://www.blackstudies.ucsb.edu/antillians/trade2.html

4

INTELLECTUAL LIFE

The human mind is an amazing thing that allows people to reflect on ideas so abstract that we can imagine things we could never see or touch. We can think about things as complex as philosophical considerations of ethics, justice, and even thought itself. The study of ideas is called *intellectual history,* and it includes science, philosophy, medicine, technology, literature, and even the languages used to record the ideas.

At the basic level, the capacity for abstraction permits people to impose order (or to see order) in the astonishingly complex universe that surrounds us. As people in the Stone Age looked at the dark night sky dotted by millions of stars, they organized the view in patterns of constellations that allowed them to map and predict the movement of the heavens. They then echoed the heavenly order in such earthly monuments as Stonehenge in Britain and the Mayan pyramids in Mexico. Through time, this capacity to order extended from the heavens to the submicroscopic particles that dominate 21st-century physics, and the development of mathematics as the language to express these abstractions. An important part of intellectual life throughout history has been the growing evolution of science, but this is only one aspect of the accomplishments of the mind.

Some people have applied their creative capacity for abstract thought to technology, finding ways to make our lives easier. Technological innovations have spread more rapidly throughout the world than abstract scientific explanations. Horse collars from China, windmills from Persia, and Muslim medical advances transformed medieval Europe, as the Internet dominates world culture in the 21st century.

What makes these escalating advances possible is not an increase in human intelligence, but it is the ability to record abstract ideas in writing and preserve past accomplishments in education that allow human knowledge to progress. The medieval thinker John of Salisbury noted that if we can see further than the ancients, it is only because we build on their knowledge. We are as dwarfs on the shoulders of giants, and through our intellectual life, we can look forward to an even greater vision.

The articles that follow focus on four key aspects of intellectual life: language, education, literature, and health and science. Language is the hardwiring of the brain and thought; it affects the way we view the world and determines how we can express

INTELLECTUAL
LIFE
|
LANGUAGE
& WRITING SYSTEMS

EDUCATION

HEALTH & SCIENCE

LITERATURE

our emotions. A simple test can show how thoroughly language shapes our thought patterns. Say the following sentence out loud, filling in the blank without pausing.

The ship sailed across the _____.

If you used the word *sea* to fill in the blank, you are like most other English speakers. This simple tendency to choose the same word becomes more remarkable when one thinks of all the other words that would make sense within the context: ocean, deep, lake, channel, and so on. Linguistic hardwiring makes most people choose the very same word without thinking about it. Although remarkable, hardwiring can create problems among different cultures. For example, when early Spanish missionaries brought the Christian concept of God to Native Americans, they found it difficult to convert them because the Native American language did not have a word to express such a concept.

Education is a way society passes on information from generation to generation. While we normally associate the word *education* with official schools, education can refer more broadly to all kinds of learning, such as learning farming or learning domestic skills. The emphasis placed on formal education differed from culture to culture, but all cultures had well-developed systems of informal education.

Education lays the groundwork for both literature and science. Written literature depends, of course, upon the ability to read and write. However, there are other forms of literature, such as oral literature, which is learned by ear and passed down from generation to generation. Science likewise can exist on both literate and illiterate levels. While doctors of physics in Salamanca read and wrote learned treatises on the body and disease, local village healers in Maya society passed on their knowledge by word of mouth. In both cultures, specialized learning was highly regarded and sometimes closely guarded. Scientists today are still discovering useful medicines among the plants of Central and South America.

~*Joyce E. Salisbury and Lawrence Morris*

FOR MORE INFORMATION

Tarnas, R. *The Passion of the Western Mind: Understanding the Ideas That Have Shaped Our World View.* New York: Ballentine, 1991.

INTELLECTUAL
LIFE
|
LANGUAGE
& WRITING SYSTEMS
|
England

Spain

Italy

Ottoman Empire

Maya

Aztec

Inca

Language and Writing Systems

Language is essentially the way people communicate. Although there are many ways in which people communicate, such as with facial expressions and hand gestures, language is most often associated with vocal sounds and their written representation. By allowing communication, language often acts as a powerful force uniting peoples who speak the same language. At the same time, dialect, or the way a language is spoken in a particular area or by particular people, can set one group of people off against another group. For example, in Renaissance Italy, each city-state generally had its own dialect of Italian. While each separate political entity thus had its own dialect, the city-states of the Italian peninsula still shared a common bond and a sense of unity, despite the lack of political unity, due to their common language: Italian.

In Europe, in addition to dialects, there was also Latin. Latin was the language spoken and written by the ancient Romans. By the 15th century, Latin was no longer the native language—Latin had developed instead into various other languages called Romance languages (from the word *Roman*, the term did not have anything to do with love at the start), such as Italian, Spanish, and French. Although Latin was not spoken widely, it was still the language of education and learning. Most university courses in every subject, theology, law, biology, chemistry, were taught in Latin, and the textbooks were also written in Latin. Anyone contemplating higher education therefore needed a strong command of the language. In contrast, the vast majority of the peasant and laboring classes knew very little Latin, apart from a few prayers. These people were thus cut off from higher education and advanced learning. This linguistic situation was not entirely unique. In the Ottoman empire, while the many different ethnic groups all spoke their own native language, the Qur'an (Koran) was read only in Arabic, government business was conducted primarily in Turkish, and works of literature were frequently written in Persian. The average person from the Ottoman Empire would be able to understand only one of these languages at the most.

Before the arrival of the Spanish, Latin did not, of course, exist in the Native American cultures. Instead, the Native American cultures employed their own languages for education, rule, and everyday activities. The Mexica (Aztecs) spoke Nahuatl, the Maya spoke Mayan, and the Incas spoke Quechua. These languages were not intelligible to a person who spoke one of the different languages, and some languages, such as Mayan, had many different dialects. Depending on how close the dialects were to each other, the speakers might have had considerable difficulty in communicating. The Inca, by contrast, strove to teach everyone in their empire the Quechua that was spoken at Cuzco.

Many cultures have developed writing systems for their languages. For people who grew up in literate cultures, writing can seem like second nature, but it is in fact difficult to devise a successful writing system. To see how difficult it can be, try writing down the words of a person speaking Arabic, Chinese, or Swahili using the English alphabet. Most writing systems developed out of pictographs, which are pictures that symbolize the object or the thing the object represents. For example, a picture of a temple means *temple*. These pictographs frequently come to represent sounds and not just meanings. Thus, a picture of a temple might be used to indicate the sound *tem*. The Maya and Aztecs used this kind of writing system in which pictures represent either the item pictured or the sound of the item pictured. The Latin alphabet, from which the English and other European alphabets had derived, had gone one stage further. The letters, which had developed originally out of pictures, came to stand only for particular sounds. When the Spanish arrived in the Americas, they taught many natives how to use the Latin alphabet to write their own native languages, and several Nahuatl and Mayan texts written in the Latin alphabet survive from the 16th century.

While many Spanish religious authorities were happy to teach the natives how to write their language in the Latin alphabet, they were much less comfortable with writing in the original pictographic system developed by the Native Americans. The Europeans' discomfort with pictographs probably resulted in part due to misunderstanding: the Europeans were not able to read the pictographs. At the same time several prelates seemed to have believed that the pictographic writing was idolatrous—that it contained images of pagan gods that were supposed to be worshipped. As a result, many ancient pictographs by Native Americans were burned. It is impossible to estimate how much knowledge of early American culture and history we have lost as a result of these actions.

~*Lawrence Morris*

INTELLECTUAL
LIFE

LANGUAGE
& WRITING SYSTEMS

England

Spain

Italy

Ottoman Empire

Maya

Aztec

Inca

ENGLAND

Renaissance English was close enough to contemporary English that it would be comprehensible to us today. The main differences in pronunciation are in the vowels, especially *ea* which sounded like the modern-day long *a*. Thus, Renaissance English *weak* rhymes with modern English *brake*, but not with modern English *leek*. As in most modern North American accents in the Midwest, the sound *r* was always pronounced. Overall, Elizabethan English would most resemble a modern Irish or rural English accent; the pronunciation associated with Oxford and Cambridge, the BBC, and the royal family is a comparatively recent development. There was considerable difference in pronunciation from one place to another: the dialect of London was the most influential, but there was no official form of the language, and even a gentleman might still speak a local dialect.

In learning the language, a child would also learn the appropriate modes of address, which were more complex than they are today. For example, the word *thou* existed as an alternative to *you*. To us it sounds formal and archaic, but for the Elizabethans it was actually very informal, used to address a person of social inferiority or used to address close friends. You might call your son or daughter *thou*, but you would never use it to address strangers (*thee* stood in the same relationship to *thou* as *me* to *I*—"Thou art a fine fellow," but "I like thee well.").

The child would also have to learn the titles appropriate to people of different social status. As a rule, superiors were addressed by their title and surname, and inferiors were addressed by their Christian name. If you were to speak to a person of high rank or if you wished to address someone formally, you might say *sir* or *madam*; you would certainly use these terms for anyone at the rank of a knight or higher. As a title, *Sir* designated a knight (or sometimes a priest) and was used with the first name, as in *Sir John*.

More general terms of respect were *master* and *mistress*. These terms could simply be polite forms of address, but servants usually used them when speaking to their employers or commoners used them when speaking to gentlemen or gentlewomen.

The terms were also used as titles, *Master* Johnson being a name for a gentleman, *Master* William a polite way of referring to a commoner. Commoners might also be called *Goodman* or *Goodwife*, especially if they were at the head of a yeomanly household. Ordinary people, especially one's inferiors, might be called *man, fellow,* or *woman. Sirrah* was applied to inferiors and was sometimes used as an insult. A close friend might be called *friend, cousin,* or *coz.* Confidence tricksters often addressed their victims as if they were intimate friends, so that the term *to cozen* (i.e., cousin) came to mean "to cheat."

Most people had little formal training in English grammar, and Renaissance English, perhaps as a result, was a very flexible medium. Shakespeare, for example, freely used words as both nouns and verbs, for example "strangered with an oath." Indeed, the verb could have a variety of forms. During the 16th century, an author could choose from both the older, inherited Old English conjugation (pattern of changes in a verb) and the modern conjugation, for example, "it droppeth" (older system) or "it drops" (modern system). Another difference in verbs was the rarity of *do* and even *is* as auxiliaries (helping verbs). For example, questions usually just used the simple form of the verb, for example, "Goes the cow to market?" instead of "Is the cow going to market?" and "Went the king to London?" instead of "Did the king go to London?"

In the current era, where English is the dominant language of world communication, it can be hard to appreciate how relatively inconsequential and new English was during the Renaissance. As in the Middle Ages, most learned books were written in Latin during the Renaissance, and English therefore lacked a competent technical vocabulary. To make up for this deficiency, authors consciously borrowed many words from Latin and other languages. Even though some people objected to such borrowings, or inkhorn terms as their critics called them, many of them have become commonplace today. For example, words such as *democracy, encyclopedia, allusion, autograph, disability, impersonal, adapt, excavate, meditate,* and many others were first used in the English language during the Renaissance and were not understood by many contemporary readers. Such borrowing, however, strengthened the ability of the English language to express scientific and philosophical thought and helped ease the transition from Latin to English as the language of education and refinement.

The equipment used for writing at this time was typically a goose quill pen, an inkhorn, and paper. The quill was shaved of its feathers (contrary to our modern image), and a point, or nib, was cut into it. This was done with a small knife that folded into its own handle for safe transportation and was brought out when the nib needed sharpening—the origin of the modern penknife. The pen and its accessories were kept in a leather case called a *penner*. People who did a lot of calculating, such as shopkeepers, often used a slate, which could be written on and wiped clear afterward. Another form of temporary writing involved a wooden or metal stylus and a small thin board coated with wax called a wax tablet. The writer would inscribe the letters into the wax with the stylus, which might have a rounded top for rubbing out the letters afterward. Such tablets were typically bound in pairs (or even in books) to protect their faces, and were known as a *pair of tables*.

There were two principal types of handwriting used by the Elizabethans, known as secretary and italic. The secretary hand had evolved in the late Middle Ages as a quick and workaday form of writing. In the Elizabethan period it retained its workaday character, and was often used for correspondences, accounts, and other practical uses, although to the modern eye it seems very difficult to read. The italic hand, essentially the same style known as italic today, is much more clear and elegant by modern standards. Learned people in scholarly contexts especially used it.

The alphabet was essentially the same as we use today, with a few interesting exceptions. For a start, there were only 24 letters. The letters *i* and *j* were considered equivalent: *J* was often used as the capital form of *i*. The letters *u* and *v* were similarly equivalent, *u* commonly being used in the middle of a word and *v* at the beginning. So where we would write "I have an uncle," a person from the 16th century might write "J haue an vncle." Some Elizabethan letters have since dropped out of use. The normal form of *s* was the long form, resembling a modern *f*. The modern style of *s* was only used as a capital or at the end of a word. There was also a special character to represent *th*, which looked like a *y* but actually came from an ancient runic letter called *thorn*; when we see "Ye Olde Tea Shoppe," the *ye* should actually be pronounced *the*. Roman numerals were used more frequently than today, although reckoning was usually done with the more convenient Arabic numerals.

There were no dictionaries, so Renaissance spelling was largely a matter of custom, and often just a matter of writing the words by ear. Still, the normal spelling of words was for the most part very similar to the spelling known today. The most obvious difference is that the Elizabethans often added a final *e* in words where we do not: *school*, for example, was likely to be written as *schoole*.

In printed books, there were two principal typefaces: blackletter and Roman. Blackletter type, like the secretary hand, was derived from medieval writing; it resembled what is sometimes called Old English type today. Roman type, like the italic hand, was associated with the revival of classical learning during the Renaissance and eventually replaced the blackletter entirely: the standard type used today derives from Roman typeface. Italic type was also used, especially to set words apart from surrounding Roman text (Singman, 40–44).

To read about language and writing systems in Chaucer's England, see the Europe entry in the section "Language and Literature" in chapter 4 ("Intellectual Life") in volume 2 of this series; to read about 18th-century England, see the England entry in the section "Language and Literature" in chapter 4 ("Intellectual Life") in volume 4 of this series; for Victorian England, see the Victorian England entry in the section "Literature" in chapter 4 ("Intellectual Life") in volume 5 of this series.

~*Lawrence Morris*

FOR MORE INFORMATION

Baugh, A., and T. Cable. *History of the English Language*. 5th ed. Upper Saddle River, N.J.: Prentice Hall, 2002.

Singman, J. L. *Daily Life in Elizabethan England*. Westport, Conn.: Greenwood, 1995.

SPAIN

Spanish today comes from the dialect of Spanish spoken in and around the region of Castile in the center of the Iberian Peninsula. This language, called Castilian, was one of the many vulgar Latins spoken in Spain in the days of the Roman empire. About a quarter of all inhabitants, however, spoke languages other than Castilian during the Renaissance. Aragonese, in the north, with only dialectal differences, was close enough to Castilian to be mutually comprehensible. Similarly, Andaluz in the south was at the time becoming a dialect of Castilian as independent linguistic changes occurred in both Castile and Andalucía. On the other hand, Catalán, which was spoken by the majority of people in the east (for example Cataluña, Valencia, and Mallorca), was a separate language also developed from Latin but closer to Provençal, spoken in southern France (from which it evolved), than to Castilian. Galician was akin to Portuguese and not readily understood by Castilian speakers. Spoken in the western Pyrenees, Navarra, and west as far as Bilbao, the ancient Basque language was not related to any of the others and was entirely incomprehensible to all but Basque speakers. Another major language, employed especially in the south but with no relationship to the others, was Arabic, which was spoken by the Muslim population and remotely related to Hebrew; it was easier for Jewish scholars to learn than it was for speakers of the Hispano-Latin languages. Jews and their brethren converted to Christianity spoke the local languages and often acted as intermediaries and translators between Christian and Muslim cultures (Anderson, 7–8).

One of the most important linguistic events for the Iberian peninsula in the 15th and 16th centuries was the growth of Castilian as the preferred language throughout the Spanish kingdom. This trend had already started long before Madrid, located in the heartland of Castile, became the official capital in 1560. In the Middle Ages, the two main vernacular literary languages where Galician and Castilian. Each language was used for writing a particular kind of literature. Galician was used for lyrical poetry, while Castilian was used for epics. Regardless of their native dialect, a person would use Galician when writing poetry, but would use Castilian when writing epics. This tradition originated from the early histories of the genres: many early lyrics had been written in Galician, while the famous *Poema de mio Cid* had been written in Castilian, following a tradition already established by patriotic Castilian songs. This linguistic and literary division gradually changed however. When prose became a major genre, it was first written in Castilian. The addition of prose to the Castilian realm of influence increased the dialect's influence, and by the early 15th century, Castilian was the main language for lyrical poetry.

While Castilian had thus become the major literary language for the Spanish kingdoms by the mid-15th century, Castilian itself was not a standardized dialect. Instead, it represented a collection of mutually intelligible subdialects, and the language of most authors reflected the subdialect spoken in their own hometown. The 16th century, however, saw a strong move to standardize the language. Many of the early reformers, such as Fernando de Herrera, Antonio de Nebrija, and Juan de

Valdés, were united in admiration for the language and style of the influential author Garcilaso de la Vega, who died in 1536. While the theorists were frequently unable to agree with regard to details, a de facto standard emerged in the late 16th century, driven both by the language of the official capital Madrid and by the wildly popular theatrical *comedia,* which served as both entertainment and journalism. The pre-eminence of Castilian meant that the other dialects, even widely spoken ones such as Catalán, existed mainly as spoken and not as literary languages.

Different stylistic preferences also affected the Castilian language. During the 15th century, Castilian Spanish was heavily influenced by the Renaissance interest in Latin and the classics, and it incorporated many Latin words that had not survived into Spanish. Some authors, such as Santillana, even imitated Latin syntax by placing the main verb at the end of the sentence, in imitation of Latin, rather than at the start of the sentence (usually the second word) as is more common in the vernacular Romance languages. The favored style changed considerably in the 16th century, however. While the flowery Latinate style continued, a new style, drawing more upon Spanish's own resources and designed to be intelligible to everyone, not just to the learned, developed. Religious authors, such as St. Teresa and St. John of the Cross, were particularly influential in developing this style of written Spanish, but more secular authors, such as Garcilaso de la Vega and Boscán, also attempted to strike a balance between excessive Latinism and the speech of the uneducated.

One of the most important developments, however, was the importation of the Spanish language with the Spanish explorers and conquistadors into the Americas. These people brought the language spoken at the time, and Spanish in Latin America preserves some pronunciations, such as the *s* sound instead of the *th* sound for the letter ç, which more accurately reflect the pronunciation of Spanish in the 16th century than modern Castilian does. Moreover, the huge population in South and Central America that now speaks Spanish has given the language a global importance that cannot be ignored. During the 16th century, though, the Native American languages were still the most widely spoken by the inhabitants, and the true growth of Latin American Spanish into a major dialect belongs to a later period.

~*Lawrence Morris*

INTELLECTUAL
LIFE
|
LANGUAGE
& WRITING SYSTEMS
|
England

Spain

Italy

Ottoman Empire

Maya

Aztec

Inca

FOR MORE INFORMATION

Anderson, J. M. *Daily Life during the Spanish Inquisition.* Westport, Conn.: Greenwood, 2002.
Entwistle, W. *The Spanish Language, Together with Portuguese, Catalan and Basque.* 2nd ed. London: Faber and Faber, 1962.

ITALY

Italy used two main languages during the Renaissance: Latin and Italian. Italian itself had developed out of spoken Latin through a variety of changes, but it was still very similar to its parent language. Italian, however, was not really one language, but rather a collection of closely related and often mutually intelligible dialects. The presence of two languages, one with many dialects, gave Italy many kinds of language use, each with its own social geography. Latin itself had a double nature. In the millennium since the fall of Rome, the language had not died at all; like any living tongue, it had evolved to suit new uses. The Renaissance still used this practical Latin, which offered a rich, specialized vocabulary, for the technicalities of the law and intellectual arguments. It remained the language of learned treatises, much legislation, and legal record keeping. Notaries, lawyers, high churchmen, university professors, and many officials wrote this workaday Latin fluently and often spoke it readily. Debaters at a university and advocates before a judge could wrangle in it. At the same time, there was elevated Latin, used for writing letters, poetry, fine sermons, histories, and philosophical dialogues. The intellectual movement we call humanism had, from the beginnings of the Renaissance, rebelled against the working Latin of the universities and courts in the name of the elegant language of the classic authors of ancient Rome. It was this refined literary Latin that elite schools taught; the language had its practical uses, for a polished letter, a witty epigram, a handsome sermon, a refined funeral oration, which both gratified recipients and advanced the author. Polished Latin and a handsome fashionable handwriting were refinements very useful in both state and church careers. It is not clear how much Italians could actually converse in this literary Latin; at stricter boarding schools, pupils were supposed to use it. At some schools, student spies ferreted out backsliders. Certainly, when one tried to speak, one had to adapt a very ancient tongue to new circumstances.

Italian and spoken Latin leached into one another. Borrowing was all the easier because their close kinship gave them a similar grammar and a vast common vocabulary. The technical Latin of intellectual life and law was full of non-Latin terms transposed from the Italian: words for implements, articles of clothing, foods, and feudal tenures unknown to Cicero or Virgil. Meanwhile, spoken Italian, in educated mouths, was full of technical expressions from the Latin (for example *et cetera*, etc.), just as English today is full of foreign words. Nobles and merchants, if well schooled, might use them; men of the pen did so abundantly, but women, artisans, and peasants seldom did.

With its fixed grammar and spelling, Latin was more standardized than Italian, which had dozens of dialects and countless local variants. Some regional versions—Venetian, Lombard, Tuscan, and, to a lesser degree, Roman and Neapolitan—had written literary traditions in which there was a slowly evolving consensus about usage. In the absence of a hegemonic center of power, there was no agreed national language. To make themselves understood by strangers, Italians used a compromised form of the language, *cortegiano*, spoken in princely courts. When a tribunal's notary took down peasant testimony, for ease of use he transformed it into something more like *cortegiano*. In the 16th century, this written Italian gradually took on more and more Tuscan coloration.

Many Italians who knew little or no Latin were literate in some version of Italian. Just how many is hard to say; in general, few peasants and women could read or write, but many males in towns were fair readers, though fewer wrote. Good estimates from late 16th-century Venice suggest that one boy in three and one girl in eight at some point went to school. Rates would have been similar in other cities and lower in smaller places. In general, solid merchants wrote handily; further down the social scale there was a vast zone of artisanal semiliteracy. Unlike quirky English, Italian is phonetically simple; with the alphabet and a little patience one could sound out prose and even write sentences. Conventions for spelling were loose and variants tolerated. Without formal training, however, polished penmanship and composition were much harder. Those self-taught or skimpily instructed often wrote with an unsteady hand and a crude sense of where words stopped; their sprawled, uncertain block lettering betrays a valiant struggle to master an unfamiliar medium. By the 16th century, unschooled handwriting sometimes reflected the new letterforms featured on its model, the printed page (Cohen and Cohen, 135–36).

FOR MORE INFORMATION

Burke, P. "Languages and Anti-Languages." In *Historical Anthropology of Early Modern Italy*, 79–94. Cambridge: Cambridge University Press, 1987.

Cohen, E. S., and T. V. Cohen. *Daily Life in Renaissance Italy*. Westport, Conn.: Greenwood, 2001.

INTELLECTUAL
LIFE

LANGUAGE
& WRITING SYSTEMS

England

Spain

Italy

Ottoman Empire

Maya

Aztec

Inca

OTTOMAN EMPIRE

A person traveling through the Ottoman lands during the 16th century would likely have some difficulty mastering all the languages he would encounter along the way. Turkish, the language of government and the elites, would certainly take him a long way in most of the major cities, but the everyday speech in most towns and villages remained Greek, Arabic, Croatian, or whatever else it had been at the time of the Ottoman conquest. In addition, Arabic served as the language of religion and law for Muslims, while Orthodox Christians generally found themselves worshipping in Greek or in a literary language called Church Slavonic. Even Persian, the language of the Ottomans' rivals in the Safavid Empire, remained in vogue as the language of high culture and literature. In this way, different cultures were preserved within the Ottoman state as each language became the repository of different traditions and experiences.

Turkish, a language originally spoken by Central Asian nomads, served as the main administrative language of the Ottoman Empire. In order to increase its use, the government hired out to Turkish villagers at a low price many of the people taken as slaves for the military Janissary corps. At the same time, Arabic continued in use, both as a spoken language in North Africa and the Middle East, and as the language of law and Islamic theology throughout the empire. Enshrined in the untranslatable holy text of the Qur'an (Koran), a formal, scholarly Arabic served the needs of the educated for a universal language throughout the Islamic world, even as the spoken language evolved into a number of dialects sometimes difficult to understand even by other speakers of Arabic.

Because of the importance of Arabic in the Islamic world, its alphabet became the standard for both Turkish and Persian, the latter tongue acting as a language of high culture especially in Turkish-speaking areas. In addition, Persian and Arabic loanwords became part of other languages, especially in intellectual and religious vocabulary. Originally students learned these words during their studies and introduced them into their writing; however, during the 16th century, they began to enter the Turkish language itself as understood by native speakers. During the Ottoman period, Balkan languages also began to influence Turkish, especially in terms relating to trade and finance. Because of the opposition of religious scholars, the Ottoman Empire prohibited the use of printing presses to produce books in Turkish, Arabic, and Persian, though it was permitted for other languages.

People in the Balkans also continued to use the language spoken at the time of the Ottoman conquest, albeit with some Turkish influence. However, because the local bureaucrats wrote in Turkish for official government correspondence and because religious and literary figures wrote in an established scholarly language such as Church Slavonic, few samples of these languages—the ancestors of the modern Balkan tongues—have survived. One exception to this was Croatian. Because there was no formal Croatian literary language at the time, people simply wrote in their local dialect. The most important dialects were the Chakavian, spoken in Istria, the Kajkavian from the region around Zagreb, and two forms of the Shtokavian, spoken over a wide area from modern Bosnia into Hungary. The names of these dialects came from their different words for the interrogative pronoun *what*, and they differed mainly in the formation of new words, as well as in some elements of structure and syntax. They were written using the Latin alphabet, but with diacritical marks such as a small upside-down arrow above a *c* to indicate *ch*.

Greek also came to have a great influence on the Balkans during the Ottoman period, largely because the Ottoman system organized society by means of religious affiliation. All the national orthodox churches were placed under the authority of the Greek Orthodox, and so this influence spread throughout the peninsula. Thus, Greek gradually became the language of Orthodox religious services and books of Orthodox Christian theology. In addition, most major cities had a number of Greek-speaking Jews. During this period, Greek had both a high literary language used by learned monks and writers and several spoken vernacular dialects. The language also acquired a number of new words from western Mediterranean languages, especially Italian as well as Turkish. Turkish loanwords remaining in modern Greek include those for coin, celebration, coffee, shoes, and table.

The introduction of Greek as the liturgical language for Balkan Christians followed a common trend among Christians during this period. Many people worshipped in a language that was not their mother tongue. Just as Roman Catholics in Western Europe used Latin during mass, Coptic Christians in Egypt worshipped in Coptic, a language descended from ancient Egypt, while Jacobites in Syria and Nestorians in Iraq used Syriac, a language closely related to the Aramaic spoken by Jesus. The Coptic language was traditionally written using the Greek alphabet, while the Syriac used a Semitic alphabet similar to that of Arabic. All of these groups used Arabic in their everyday life. Before the spread of Greek, the Slavic Christians in the Balkans worshipped in Church Slavonic, the parent language of the modern Balkan languages which the Orthodox wrote in the Cyrillic alphabet of Russia and the Catholics in the Glagolitic alphabet. While the scripts of these alphabets were different, they had the same number of letters and the same sounds were represented.

The vast extent of the Ottoman Empire took in many peoples, each with their own linguistic heritage. In addition to those described above, our hypothetical traveler would encounter speakers of Albanian, Armenian, and several other tongues spoken over wide areas or in small isolated pockets. In addition, many people during the course of their daily lives encountered more than one language, whether they were a Turkish peasant who recited the Qur'an (Koran) in Arabic or a Serb deacon studying Church Slavonic and Greek as part of his studies. All of these languages enriched each other through new vocabulary and concepts, creating for the empire a sort of linguistic melting pot that remains today and continues the legacy of Ottoman multiculturalism.

To read about languages and writing systems in Medieval Islam, see the Islam entry in the section "Language and Literature" in chapter 4 ("Intellectual Life) in volume 2 of this series.

~Brian Ulrich

FOR MORE INFORMATION

Browning, R. *Medieval and Modern Greek.* Cambridge: Cambridge University Press, 1969.

Carlton, T. R. *Introduction to the Phonological History of the Slavic Languages.* Columbus, Ohio: Slavica, 1991.

Hadrovics, L. "The Status of the Croatian Regional Languages Immediately Before Gaj's Reform." In *The Formation of the Slavonic Literary Languages,* ed. Gerald Stone and Dean Worth, 133–45. Columbus, Ohio: Slavica, 1985.

Inalcik, H. *The Ottoman Empire: The Classical Age, 1300–1600.* London: Weidenfeld and Nicolson, 1973.

Sugar, P. F. *Southeastern Europe under Ottoman Rule, 1354–1804.* Seattle: University of Washington Press, 1977.

INTELLECTUAL
LIFE
|
LANGUAGE
& WRITING SYSTEMS
|
England

Spain

Italy

Ottoman Empire

Maya

Aztec

Inca

MAYA

In the Maya area today at least 4 million people speak one of the 28 closely related languages that make up the Mayan family of languages (the term *Mayan* is used to refer to the languages spoken by *Maya* people). Although most of these people also speak Spanish (the official language of Mexico, Guatemala, and Honduras) or English (the official language of Belize), their native language continues to define them as Maya people, holders of a proud cultural tradition.

The various Mayan languages are similar because they are descended from one ancestral language spoken thousands of years ago. Scholars who study the process of language divergence estimate that the ancestral Mayan language was spoken earlier than 2000 B.C.E., or around the time the Maya first settled into permanent communities. After this time the ancestral language began to separate into three major subgroups: Southern Mayan, Yucatecan, and Huastecan. These subgroups became distinct between 2000 B.C.E. and 100 C.E., during the era of Early Maya Civilization. Although the process of divergence has continued to the present, producing the many different dialects of today, most Mayan languages have remained in contact with each other and often blend into each other just like the environmental zones of the Maya area.

Using comparisons among languages today, scholars can reconstruct aspects of the ancestral language. In such cases the meanings of reconstructed words can tell us about early society and culture. For example, the ancestral Mayan language had a rich vocabulary for weaving and farming, indicating that these were important activities. Maize agriculture, in particular, had separate words for generic maize, the green ear, the mature ear, the cob, the three stages of maize flour, the maize dough, the tortilla, the maize drink, and the maize grinding stone.

Similar research has identified languages spoken in the southern lowlands during the era of Middle Maya Civilization. This has long been an issue of debate because the vast region—the central Peten and upper Usumacinta drainage—was largely depopulated by the time the Europeans arrived. Evidence from early texts excavated at southernmost sites such as Palenque, Dos Pilas, Aguateca, and Copan shows that closely related languages of the Southern Mayan subgroup, known as Cholan, were

spoken. But further north in the southern lowlands, texts at Tikal, Piedras Negras, Bonampak, Yaxchilan, Seibal, and Naranjo indicate that Yucatec Mayan, the primary member of the Yucatecan subgroup, was spoken in these cities. Thus it appears that the Maya lowlands were populated by speakers of several Mayan languages at the time of Middle Maya Civilization.

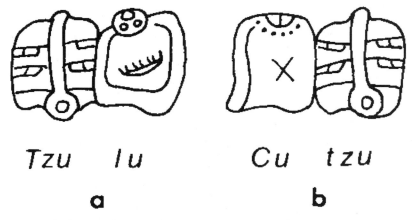

Maya Glyphs. Each Maya glyph represented the sound of one syllable. The two glyphs on the left, marked "a," spell *tzu lu* (= *tzul* for *dog*), while the two glyphs on the right, marked "b," spell *cu tzu* (= *cutz* for *turkey*). You should be able to recognize the glyph for *tzu* by comparing the two words. Created by Robert J. Sharer.

Before the Spanish Conquest, the Maya used glyphs (pictures) to record information. Each glyph represented either a whole word or a particular syllable within a word. Literacy, however, does not appear to have been widespread.

After the conquest the Spaniards taught Maya scribes to use the Spanish alphabet to write their own languages. This allowed the Maya to transcribe many of their own older documents, histories, prophecies, myths, rituals, and the like. Although only four pre-Columbian Maya books are known today, many additional colonial-period transcriptions have survived. These documents were often recopied over the years, but they provide an invaluable source of information about ancient Maya society.

These languages, and the remnants of Maya religion, have been more resistant to change than any other aspect of Maya civilization. This is because the Mayan language and religion reinforce the traditions of family and community life. Mayan languages persist because they are often the first learned language or the only language spoken in a traditional Maya family. Some knowledge of Spanish is necessary to interact with the non-Maya world, but even in today's world of instant electronic communication, at least four million people continue to speak the Mayan language. Some phrases in modern Yucatec Mayan: *Bix a belex!* (Hello, how are you?); *Maloob* (Fine); *Yum botic* (Thank you); *Mixba* (You're welcome) (Sharer, 6, 111–12).

FOR MORE INFORMATION

Bevington, G. *Maya for Travelers and Students: A Guide to Language and Culture in Yucatán*. Austin: University of Texas Press, 1995.

Sharer, R. J. *Daily Life in Maya Civilization*. Westport, Conn.: Greenwood, 1996.

AZTEC

The language of the Aztec empire is called Classical Nahuatl (pronounced *nahwatl* as two syllables). The language derived from this ancient Aztec language, modern Nahuatl, is spoken today by more than 1.5 million speakers in southern Mexico, stretching from Acapulco to Veracruz, and also in Ecuador. The Spanish conquerors, starting with Hernán Cortés, relied heavily on Nahuatl translators to help construct alliances with the native peoples and to administrate the districts effectively. Because of the language's importance from early on in the Spanish Conquest, many Nahuatl documents were preserved and protected. Nahuatl thus has a more richly documented history than many other Native American languages.

Before the arrival of the Spaniards, the Aztecs used a pictographic form of writing in which symbols were used to represent various objects. The symbols were used especially to keep track of the sacred calendar, but they were also used to record important historical events as well as other information. Moreover, the symbols could be combined to spell out the syllables of longer words. As in Europe, writing was confined to a relatively small percentage of the population.

The most famous Nahuatl translator was Doña Marina. She grew up as a Nahuatl-speaking daughter of a *cacique*, or chieftain, in the Gulf Coast region of the Aztec empire. When her royal mother remarried, it was decided to place a stepson in the line of royal succession rather than Marina, so she was sold into captivity among Maya peoples. She grew up in a Maya community near Cintla. After the Spaniards won a battle against the local natives, she was given, along with other native women, to Cortés. She became one of Cortés's mistresses and bore him a son, Martín, who appears to have been his favorite. Speaking at least two native languages, Chontal Maya (the language Aguilar, one of Cortés's team members, had learned) and Nahuatl, Doña Marina became Cortés's interpreter. She took information from the Nahuatl-speaking representatives of Motecuhzoma and translated it into Mayan for Aguilar, who then translated it into Spanish for Cortés. She accompanied the Spaniards during their march to the central plateau and was present during the initial meetings between Cortés and Motecuhzoma. It appears that Marina's real name was Malintzin, but both she and Cortés were popularly referred to by the name Malinche.

Today in Mexico she is known as La Malinche and has been the subject of both derisive books about her as a traitor to the natives and admiring books about her intelligent and shrewd tactics in bridging the cultures that made up Mexico (Carrasco, 214).

~Lawrence Morris

FOR MORE INFORMATION

Carrasco, D., with S. Sessions. *Daily Life of the Aztecs: People of the Sun and Earth*. Westport, Conn.: Greenwood, 1998.

INCA

INTELLECTUAL LIFE

|

LANGUAGE & WRITING SYSTEMS

|

England

Spain

Italy

Ottoman Empire

Maya

Aztec

Inca

The language spoken by the Incas is called Quechua. This language was originally spoken by several distinct ethnic groups who lived in the same area of the Andes as the Incas. The name actually comes from an ethnic group called the Quechua who lived to the north of the Incas but who were absorbed into the empire very early. One major problem that the Incas faced in trying to incorporate many conquered people into their empire was the language barrier. Probably dozens of different languages were spoken by people conquered by the Incas, and little is known about how communication was achieved between the Incas and them. The Incas required conquered leaders to learn Quechua, and their sons were taken to Cuzco for instructions that must have included learning the language. How people learned Quechua in the conquered areas is unknown, but it might have been through contact with Inca officials—either in their home villages or at the administrative centers where they worked. After the Spaniards arrived they found it convenient to continue using Quechua, because it was the most widely understood language in use. As a result, Quechua is still spoken by millions of people in areas from Ecuador to Chile, and it is the official second language of Peru.

The Incas had no written language. As a result, all that is known about Inca Quechua comes from early Spanish writers, none of whom used any fixed rules concerning how the language should be written. Thus it is not uncommon to see different spellings for the same word, for example *Quichua* or *Quechua*. In addition, Spanish writers often substituted letters

> **📷 Snapshot**
>
> **Some Words in Quechua**
>
> | *Quechua* | *English Meaning* |
> | --- | --- |
> | ajsu | clothing |
> | curaca | chief |
> | inca | emperor, warrior |
> | ipu | fine rain, cloud |
> | kaka | bastard, descendants |
> | raku | snow, clear color |
> | unu | water |

that were familiar from their own language. Thus *b* is often substituted for *p*, *g* for *k*, and *gu* or *hu* for *w*. For example, instead of the Quechua *pampa* or *waka*, the Spanish wrote *bamba* and *huaca* (Malpass, 35–36).

FOR MORE INFORMATION

Malpass, M. A. *Daily Life in the Inca Empire*. Westport, Conn.: Greenwood, 1996.

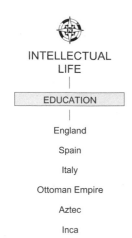

Education

Education today tends to refer to formal instruction in reading, writing, mathematics, and related disciplines. Education can also be used, however, to refer to all the different forms of instruction that prepare an individual for a productive life and role in society. During the 15th and 16th centuries, few individuals received any formal education in schools, yet everyone, from the wealthiest scholar to the poorest farmhand, learned a variety of skills to prepare them for their place in the world. The articles that follow will trace many of these different kinds of education.

Since men and women had fundamentally different roles in the societies under discussion, their education was correspondingly different. In both European and Native American cultures, boys would learn the skills that were necessary to the life of a man, such as hunting, fishing, farming, and hard physical labor, whereas girls would learn the skills expected of a grown woman, such as weaving, cooking, and housekeeping. Formal education also reflected gender differences: most women did not receive formal education, though there were many notable exceptions throughout the period. Nonetheless, while 20 percent of the men were able to read in England at the start of the 16th century, only 5 percent of women were able to read. But the Ottoman Empire was an exception, to some degree. There, although women were excluded from male establishments, villages frequently had separate primary schools for women, where the teachers themselves were women. However, social class played a decisive role; the wealthy were much more likely to attend formal schools and seek higher education, while sons of farmers would receive little or no education, and the sons of merchants might receive the equivalent of a grammar school education.

The ability to speak Latin was a major marker of superior formal education in western Europe. While the basics of reading and writing might be taught in the vernacular, all higher level education involved knowing Latin. Latin was originally the educated speech of the Roman Empire, but it had since disappeared and been replaced by other languages for most purposes. Most everyday life was conducted in the vernacular, and Latin was used only for education, church ritual, and diplomatic correspondence. Latin was very useful for all of these purposes. First of all, Latin was considered an international language; learned men from all over Europe were able to converse with each other in Latin regardless of what their own nation's language was. For diplomacy, Latin had the additional advantage of not being associated with any one country—it was a neutral language. Furthermore, there were many concepts easily expressed in Latin for which there were no corresponding terms in the vernacular languages. For example, Latin *homo* meant *human being*, while Latin *vir* meant *man* (human male). Neither Italian nor English contained this distinction and generally used one term to denote both males and human beings. The dominance of Latin affected some nations more than others. Italians and Spanish, who spoke languages closely related to Latin, could learn Latin more easily, while an English or German person, who spoke languages very different from Latin, might find learning Latin more of a chore. For example, the Latin expression *gratias Deo* is very similar to the Italian, *grazie a Dio,* or the Spanish, *gracias a Dios,* but very different from the English *Thanks be to God.* Nonetheless, regardless of nationality, a person attempting higher education would need to learn Latin thoroughly.

The Aztec educational system was somewhat more egalitarian than the European system. Anyone, whether a noble or a commoner, could attend the formal boarding schools to which a youth went at around the age of 15. The school a child would attend was determined at birth, with the guidance of a shaman. Some schools were dedicated to learning the sacred songs and dances of the Aztec, other schools were designed to produce strong warriors, and yet another kind of school trained future priests in the proper duties and skills, such as writing. Girls and boys attended separate schools, but the girls did not have the option of attending the *telpochcalli* (warriors' school).

A common feature between European and Native American education was the emphasis on strict discipline. The main method of enforcing proper conduct and ensuring learning in both Europe and America was physical punishment. In Europe punishment frequently involved smacking the student with a cane, particularly on the hands. The Aztecs had a more imaginative system, in which different punishments were assigned to delinquents depending on their age. For example, maguey thorns would be stuck into a disobedient 9-year-old child, whereas a disobedient 11-year-old child would be held over a fire into which chile had been thrown, producing a stinging smoke.

Another feature shared by Native American, European, and Ottoman education was the emphasis upon religion. One of the main aims of parents and schools was to teach their children the fundamentals of their religion so that they could live in harmony with their God or gods. In both Europe and the Americas, children learned the basic rituals and their meanings at a young age, as well as simple prayers. Formal education in Europe often combined learning to read with religion by instructing the students to read simple pious tracts. Similarly, reading and writing in the priestly schools of the Aztec focused on recording religious ritual and related history. Education, in all its forms, was designed to help the student fit in with the human and divine societies.

~Lawrence Morris

ENGLAND

In the early days of youth, all children, boy or girl, rich or poor, lived in similar ways until about the age of six. As the social differentiations of class and gender began to play a real role, girls entered into the world of women and boys entered into the world of men; and both began to be taught the skills appropriate to their rank in society.

For boys of privileged families, this meant going to school. Only a small minority of English children received formal schooling, although the number was growing. There was no national system of education, but a range of independent and semi-

INTELLECTUAL
LIFE

EDUCATION

England

Spain

Italy

Ottoman Empire

Aztec

Inca

independent educational institutions. Those children fortunate enough to have a formal education most often began at a petty school. Petty schools might be private enterprises or attached to a grammar school (a larger school offering more advanced levels of study), but in many localities, they were organized by the parish. Petty schools typically taught the fundamentals of reading and writing, and perhaps ciphering (basic arithmetic with Arabic numerals). The content of petty school education was strongly religious. After being introduced to the alphabet on a hornbook (a wooden tablet with the text pasted on it, covered with a thin layer of horn to protect the paper), the children would learn to read prayers and then move on to the catechism. Discipline was strict; schoolmasters had a free hand to use a birch rod to beat students for infraction of rules or for academic failures. Most of the students were boys, but girls occasionally attended the petty schools. Masters at these schools were of mixed origins. Some were men of only small learning; some were women, whose schools were sometimes known as dame schools; some were in fact well-educated men; and about one-third of licensed petty-school teachers may have been university graduates.

A Typical School Scene. One teacher taught all the levels of basic education. Pupils of the same level sat on the same bench, or *form*. The English school system still uses the word *form* instead of the American term *grade*. From F. J. Furnivall, *Phillip Stubbes Anatomy of Abuses,* 1879.

Basic literacy expanded significantly during Elizabeth's reign, although it was still the exception rather than the rule. Some 20 percent of men and 5 percent of women may have been literate at the time of Elizabeth's accession; by 1600 literacy may have risen to 30 percent for men and 10 percent for women. Literacy was generally higher among the privileged classes and townsfolk. Perhaps 60 percent of London's craftsmen and tradesmen were literate in the 1580s; and of a sample of London women in 1580, 16 percent could sign their names. Literacy was also more common among the more radical Protestants, and in the south and east. It tended to be lower among country folk and the poor, and in the north and west.

After petty school, if the family was wealthy or if the boy showed enough promise to earn a scholarship, he might go to a grammar school. This stage of schooling would last some 5 to 10 years—typically until age 14 or so. The grammar taught at a grammar school was Latin language and literature. The school might also teach a bit of French or Greek, but the emphasis was on Latin, the traditional language of learning. A boy who learned Latin could absorb the wisdom of ancient authors and read the works of the finest contemporary scholars, for Latin was still the international language of scholarship and science. Older students were expected to speak Latin at all times and were punished for speaking English. Grammar-school teachers were usually university graduates. It was rare for a girl to be admitted to a grammar school, and such an arrangement would only last from the age of seven to nine or thereabouts. However, there were also some special boarding schools for girls.

School hours were long. A typical school day would begin at six or seven o'clock in the morning, with a 15-minute break for breakfast at nine or so. There would be another break for dinner at eleven, with classes resuming at one; then a 30-minute break around three, with classes ending around five o'clock. Students generally had Thursday and Saturday afternoons off, as well as two-week holidays at Christmas and Easter. Some grammar schools boarded their students; others (particularly in the towns) were day schools from which the students would return home for their midday meal. Both petty and grammar schools were housed in single rooms. All the students at a particular level of schooling sat together on one bench, or *form*—to this day, the various grades in English schools are known as forms.

In addition to these publicly available forms of schooling, wealthy families sometimes hired tutors for their children. A tutor might provide the child's entire education, especially for girls; in other cases, a tutor might cover subjects not included in the school curriculum. For example, if you wanted your child to learn modern languages, you might have to hire a tutor (except in larger towns, where there were often specialized schools for such purposes). This was a very important matter, for the child of a privileged family was expected to learn French, and perhaps Spanish or Italian as well—these were the primary languages of international culture and communication. Tutors were often hired to teach dancing and music; a boy might also be taught fencing, riding, swimming, or archery. A girl's education was likely to focus on such skills and graces as would make her a desirable match, notably modern languages, needlework, and music. Book learning was not generally a high priority for girls, although plenty of parents ensured that their daughters had a good education—Queen Elizabeth herself was noted for her learning and was expert in both Greek and Latin.

In the Middle Ages, Latin and French had generally been the privileged languages in England. In the late 16th century, they still carried a great deal of social prestige. Anyone of advanced learning would know Latin, and perhaps even a little Greek; those of social pretensions would learn French as a matter of course. Nonetheless, the English were showing deep pride and interest in their native tongue. The same interest was not generally shared by other countries, however, and the English language in this period was not a significant international language.

After grammar school, a boy might pursue higher learning. University education in the Middle Ages had been almost exclusively the preserve of the clergy, but the 16th century witnessed a rising tide of secular students. Sons of the aristocracy would seek the sophistication required of a Renaissance gentleman, and bright young men of lesser status would seek an intellectual career. There were only two universities in England, Oxford and Cambridge, and each were subdivided into a number of semi-independent colleges. The usual age of matriculation was 15 to 17 years; all students were boys. The four-year course of study for a bachelor of arts included two terms of grammar (i.e., Latin grammar), four terms of rhetoric, five terms of logic, or dialectic, as well as three terms of arithmetic and two of music. Candidates for a master of arts degree studied astronomy, geometry, philosophy (including natural philosophy, which we call science), and metaphysics; the degree required three or four years of study. Doctorates, which took seven to twelve years, were available in divinity, law, and medicine. University teaching consisted primarily of lectures, and examinations took the form of oral disputations (Singman, 41–48).

To read about education in Chaucer's England, see the Europe entry in the section "Education" in chapter 4 ("Intellectual Life") in volume 2 of this series; for 18th-century England, see the England entry in the section "Education" in chapter 4 ("Intellectual Life") in volume 4 of this series; for Victorian England, see the Victorian England entry in the section "Education" in chapter 4 ("Intellectual Life") in volume 5 of this series.

FOR MORE INFORMATION

Byrne, M. St. Clare. *Elizabethan Life in Town and Country.* London: Methuen, 1950.

Sandys, J. "Education." In *Shakespeare's England: An Account of the Life and Manners of His Age.* Vol. 1: 224–50. Oxford: Clarendon, 1916.

Singman, L. J. *Daily Life in Elizabethan England.* Westport, Conn.: Greenwood, 1995.

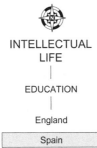

INTELLECTUAL
LIFE

EDUCATION

England

Spain

Italy

Ottoman Empire

Aztec

Inca

SPAIN

In contrast to the royal family whose education was, at least in theory, the best money could buy, church organizations and private individuals attended to the instruction of young commoners. Charitable endowments helped maintain primary and secondary schools run by the municipality or a patron. In small towns the parish priest or the sacristan often provided rudimentary education in reading, writing, and catechism. There were, to be sure, numerous young people from poor families or from orphanages, in the cities and countryside, who never saw the inside of a school. The state took no responsibility for educating youngsters and simply assumed the right of inspection and control. Some charitable endowments were available for the maintenance of primary or secondary schools run by individuals, the church, or the municipality, but many towns and hamlets did not bother at all with the education of children.

For those born into families of means, especially males, the situation was less forbidding. For example, a private instructor might be enlisted to teach young boys reading, writing, and the rudiments of Latin, a language that still enjoyed considerable prestige.

Alternatively, the male offspring of aristocratic or well-off families were sent away from their own homes to the household of some wealthy person, such as the house or palace of a nobleman, a bishop, or even the royal court, where they became pages or foster children. There they were expected to perform domestic service, such as waiting on his lordship, in exchange for instruction under the guidance of a tutor in reading and writing, Latin grammar, and classical authors such as Cicero or Caesar, Renaissance humanism, and aspects of basic mathematics. Horsemanship, etiquette, and the art of combat might also be included.

Bishops, or in some cases religious orders, provided a little elementary and secondary education. Bishops sometimes maintained a number of young nobles in their households and even a few orphans.

Secondary schooling was available for those who wanted to become priests or go to the university. A few academies established by individual entrepreneurs had good credentials, such as the Estudio de Madrid, which provided a humanist education, including instruction in poetry, and organized academic competitions. Other schools were operated by charlatans with little more education than the students or by poor rural clerics trying to supplement a meager stipend. The means of instruction was usually a generous use of the cane. Government measures were introduced to impede the proliferation of these institutions since it was thought they deprived the manual trades of conscripts.

In 1560 Jesuit schools began to appear. These were highly disciplined, the students learning through debates and lectures with more emphasis on reward than on punishment. The Jesuits, with a rapidly growing reputation for superior teaching, often succeeded in obtaining exclusive contracts with municipalities, alarming those who saw a monopoly on education in the making. The use of prefects and student fraternities gave aspiring pupils a sense of belonging and distinction.

With the advent of Jesuit schools, sons of the wealthy or nobility also sought a general grounding in history, mathematics, and science. Those students of promise were allowed to enroll in the university and further advance their studies.

At their peak in the 1580s, Castilian universities took in about 20,000 students a year, mostly from bourgeois city families and from the hidalgo class. Courses in the humanities gave way to career subjects in law, and the universities produced a homogeneous social group of *letrados*, or a corps of trained lawyers, who became prelates, councilors, magistrates, statesmen—the bureaucratic elite. In 1555 Latin grammar at Salamanca attracted 35 percent of the students and Greek 1 percent. Hebrew studies attracted only one student and the subject was cut that year. By 1595 only 9 percent studied Latin, and no one took Greek. In that year some 57 percent preferred canon law and another 16 percent studied civil law. In short, nearly three-fourths of all students took courses that would give them a career in the bureaucracy of state or church. Universities became training grounds for office seekers. They became dominated by professors who were generally *letrados*, not scholars. The graduates developed into dynasties that ruled through key posts over Spain and its empire.

Founded in 1243 the university at Salamanca, embedded in medieval origins, was the oldest and most prestigious in the country. In the 16th century the library contained about 38,000 books and manuscripts. The professor, who had to have a doctorate degree and wear his academic gown, delivered his lectures from a pulpit-like seat towering above the students. Sometimes a student just below this lofty position read from a book while the professor commented on the recitation. Some students took notes for everyone, and no one spoke in the classroom. Questions were relegated to the corridor following each lecture, the latter lasting up to about an hour and a half.

New rivals sprang up to challenge the authority of the University of Salamanca: In the middle of the 16th century, institutions of higher learning were begun at

A University Lecture. Students were expected to take careful notes and almost never asked questions. The distinctive robes of the lecturer indicate that he is a Dominican Friar. Martin de Cervera, *A University Lecture.* © Universidad de Salamanca.

Zaragoza, Valencia, Toledo, Seville, and even in a few smaller towns. There developed, however, only one serious rival to Salamanca, which was the University of Alcalá de Henares, about 25 miles east of Madrid. It was founded in 1508 by Cardinal Jiménez de Cisneros, archbishop of Toledo and Inquisitor General of Castile. When Madrid became the capital of the country in the mid-16th century, the university prospered. While at first it was concerned chiefly with theology and classical literature, it soon became a typical product of the new age. In the space of about half a century, the University of Alcalá became the symbol of Renaissance learning, breaking with the traditions of medieval scholasticism. The little town became a well-known center of scholarship throughout Spain and beyond. Nevertheless, the prestige of Salamanca attracted over three times as many students. The minor universities led a precarious existence and were often the butt of jokes regarding their academic qualities.

In 1492, the Catholic Kings Isabella and Ferdinand confirmed the immunity of students from ordinary civil law, making them subject only to the jurisdiction of the professor of theology, who at the time was nominated by the pope. His duties included the protection of the rights of students, which exempted them from military service and from all taxes affecting their person and their goods. Responsible for the welfare of the university community and its finances, the rector was elected by a committee made up half of students (selected by their peers) and half of professors. For prestige purposes the scion of one of the great families was generally chosen.

Women did not have nearly as many educational opportunities. The great majority of peasant girls of both country and town received not even a shred of the most rudimentary formal education, and only a very few learned to read and write. They acquired just what was necessary to perform domestic tasks.

Among aristocratic girls, the emphasis was less on physical labor and more on household management, needlework, social graces, and reading and writing. In the 17th century a few progressive thinkers took the position that women should not be restricted in what they might achieve through study and schooling, nor in any subjects they wished to pursue. But such views were propounded to make them better housewives. With some education they could teach their children, better contribute to the running of the house, and raise the cultural level of the family. However, these voices, with their albeit temperate views, were cries in the wilderness. Most men and certainly the powerful Church rejected even this modest assessment of women's capabilities. Some prelates hinged their opposition to female education on the basis that women were naturally intellectually inferior to men. Women were simply not suited to a study of science or to complicated business negotiations but were capable only of conducting simple transactions performed in the marketplace or in domestic affairs.

The education of many young ladies was often neglected because their fathers considered that any kind of intellectual edification would lead to loose behavior. Some parents felt that a well-educated daughter would never be able to find a husband. Given the general outlook of the times, this was undoubtedly close to the truth. It was considered sufficient that a woman's needs in the form of education could be obtained from sermons, religious books, and domestic instructions conveyed by their mothers.

A young girl from a noble or wealthy family learned to read and write from a private tutor, and perhaps she would study a little French, recite a few lines of poetry, embroider, play an instrument such as the harp, sing and dance, and practice her poise and posture among other social graces. She might even master some household chores. Even among the upper classes, there were fathers who thought any learning for a daughter was a bad thing.

Nevertheless, there were a few educated women who read Latin, knew the classics, and studied philosophy and current literature. They gathered in their homes small cultural groups of other women. But for their efforts they were often held in contempt (Anderson, 237–51).

FOR MORE INFORMATION

Anderson, J. M. *Daily Life during the Spanish Inquisition*. Westport, Conn.: Greenwood, 2002.

Domínguez Ortiz, A. *The Golden Age of Spain, 1516–1659*. London: Weidenfeld and Nicolson, 1971.

Kamen, H. *Spain 1469–1714: A Society of Conflict*. 2nd ed. London: Longman, 1991.

ITALY

Formal education was much less common in Renaissance Italy than in our days, for schooling was far from universal and lasted fewer years. Nevertheless, elite males studied long, and many others had at least some exposure. Teachers were many, in cities, villages, and the houses of the rich. Unlike teachers today, most of whom serve schools with staffs of dozens, most Renaissance instructors worked either on their own or in small groups. Some were private tutors to the rich, sometimes living with them. Many others were petty entrepreneurs, teaching from home some 20 to 40 pupils. Like artisans, they might keep a few assistants around the domestic shop to take extra classes or drill the students. Many such teachers were clerics. After 1550, the new religious orders set up bigger schools (similar to modern schools), where different teachers taught different grades. Like today, students who were promoted rose to a higher class and a better instructor.

Renaissance Italy had two educational streams matching its two languages. Latin schools taught skills desired by the governing classes; Italian schools taught skills for commerce. Some persons, such as Machiavelli, studied a little of both. The curriculum of Latin schools cultivated the eloquence of classical Rome; pupils concentrated on a few famous authors, in general the very same still taught in Latin classes today: Caesar, Cicero, Ovid, and Virgil. Cicero was especially useful, not only a masterful orator, but also the author of several works on rhetoric and of a mass of personal letters. Since most educated Italians were far likelier to use their Latin for official correspondence than for public speaking, Cicero's epistolary legacy was a precious model. Teachers drilled their students in the variety of sentence forms and made them write imaginary letters. This instruction taught imitation, not originality or discovery; it aimed to produce able readers, good orators, and fluent writers who adapted tone to a task at hand. Therefore, pupils kept notebooks in which they culled model sentences from the accepted works, in hopes of imitation. At the same time, this schooling paraded Roman models of the moral public life.

The Italian-language schools taught a different set of skills. They trained students in reading their mother tongue. The texts were often Christian: moral maxims, the lively stories of saints, and the pious *Imitation of Christ*. The material was medieval, easily accessible, colorful, and full of practical morality. Schools also used chivalrous romances, tales of knights, damsels, giants, and battles still vastly popular in the Renaissance. Alongside reading and writing, these schools taught a kind of mathematics called *abbaco*. The Florentines had separate *abbaco* schools for youngsters in their early teens. Other cities often taught math and language in tandem. *Abbaco* was the mathematics of commerce; it dealt with weights and measures, currency exchange, interest on investments, the estimation of volumes, and the calculation of costs. Textbooks set problems not very different from those we see in high school algebra textbooks; nevertheless, students did not use algebraic notation to solve them. Rather, to solve for the unknown answer, the preferred method was to find ratios among the terms. As with algebra today, the goal was nimble problem solving. Like today, Italians learned to recognize new problems as variants of a familiar model they could solve. Sometimes, with *abbaco*, there was also training in accounting.

Of the two kinds, only the Latin school led to university, which was also taught in Latin. The Italian school, furnishing too little Latin to support further study, led to trade. It is the mark of a deep division in culture that the Latin school taught no practical mathematics; what little they offered was tied to ancient Greek philosophy. The rise of the humanist Latin school coincided with the aristocratization of Italy; the processes that drove a wedge between merchants on the one hand and the governing classes on the other were reflected in the division of schooling into two zones, both pragmatic but very different.

Many students never went beyond lower school. This bottom level might feed both streams. Children started with their hornbooks, wooden boards holding a page printed with a model alphabet to trace and copy. Sometimes a transparent sheet of horn protected the paper underneath (whence the name). These single pages always started with the cross, followed by the alphabet. They might be in both gothic and Renaissance lettering. After Z, they often laid out all the syllables that made up Italian words; Italian and Latin are both easily phonetic; the whole-word approach sometimes used for quirky English was not needed. The hornbook might also have a Latin form of the Lord's Prayer. Beginners then went on to a primer, a little book of 20 or so pages, with more Latin prayers to learn by heart and simple readings in Italian. In the 16th century, charitable Sunday catechism schools taught the A-B-Cs by this system, alongside Christian doctrine.

Whether or not they could read them, Renaissance Italians took documents very seriously. Written records had great legal weight. Well before the Renaissance, there grew up a complex set of standards for validating them. The custodians of legal paper were the notaries, whose job it was to prepare them and to keep a reference copy in their own orderly registers. These men were at the bottom of the lettered ladder. Dozens worked in big cities, and others resided or circulated in small towns and villages. In drafting documents, notaries observed standard forms: a will, a record of sale, an inventory, a marriage contract, a rent, a loan, a hiring, a peace between enemies. Each had its habitual order and standard phrases. One began by setting out the date, those persons present, and those absent but represented by their agents, and then rolled through the essentials of the transaction, usually in Latin. The prose, like our modern legal language, was lumbered with redundancies—"to possess, to have, and to hold"—lest there be any doubt, and crammed with stock formulas, many of them concerning liabilities for not observing the terms. At the bottom, the notary recorded the place and the names of witnesses and often put his own elaborate sign. The elite notarized often. A strongbox in the master's bedroom or study held key papers. The rich often patronized a favorite notary, who might also serve as a family adviser. Artisans also used notaries, but far less often, to save on fees. Many of their contracts were unwritten—still binding but harder to prove in court.

Educated Italians were particularly interested in the past. Religion, lordship, civic identity, family pride, and legal and commercial imperatives all fostered records of the past. The Renaissance evolved in this area; far more than the Middle Ages, it wrote history. There were two distinct practices: retrieving the past to inform the present and recording the present to instruct the future. Historical writing had been a literary genre in ancient Greece and Rome. Educated Italians began, self-consciously, to imitate that model, composing histories of their cities and even, boldly, of Italy

> *Italian families hired genealogists to trace their remotest ancestors.*

itself. They also began to invent tools of scholarship to comment on the laws and customs of the ancient world. Such study very gradually helped build a sense of historical difference, of the cultural pastness of the past, a sense quite foreign to medieval thought, though we now take it for granted. The rise of historical thought probably inspired some of the family chronicles, meant not for publication but for domestic consumption. Marcello Alberini, a Roman nobleman who wrote just for family, for instance, set his own life, marked by the horrors of the Sack of 1527, in the context of the struggle between his class and the papal court to determine who ruled Rome. Other kinds of family history, however, lacked Alberini's sense of historical evolution. In the 16th century, noble families hired genealogists to trace their remotest ancestors, as if the reach were easy; with luck, effort, and self-delusion, one might thread one's way back to a Roman emperor or even a veteran of the Trojan War. There was another variety of domestic history writing. The hundreds of family record books (*ricordanze*) concentrated on domestic events and personal doings. Often such records smacked of ledger keeping: enter each wife and her dowry and the birth of each child; debit each of the many deaths. At the same time, the authors often took note of family memories, noted the doings of the extended kin, and laid down lessons in life useful to their posterity, for these writings aimed to instruct one's heirs. A closely related genre was the diary, strictly speaking a day-by-day record of events, though some works we call diaries in fact scooped several weeks into an entry. The merchants' habit of recording outgoing mail may have been one inspiration for the form. Most diaries were relatively impersonal; they focused on public events: wars, politics, portents, and natural calamities. Although they might note the writer's occasional amazement, distress, or indignation, they have none of the self-absorbed introspection of the modern diary (Cohen and Cohen, 138–44).

FOR MORE INFORMATION

Cohen, E. S., and T. V. Cohen. *Daily Life in Renaissance Italy.* Wesport, Conn.: Greenwood, 2001.

OTTOMAN EMPIRE

Although not compulsory, education represented the key to advancement in the Ottoman Empire. Only those with the appropriate academic credentials could become judges, ministers of state, or other officials. For that reason, the government took a keen interest in regulating the educational system. Islam served as the core of the curriculum, and all other subjects were related to it in some manner. Educational institutions were arranged in a hierarchy through which both students and teachers had to move before achieving the highest positions. Women also became educated, usually by other women within their homes, whereas palace servants had a separate school of their own.

The *medrese* served as the primary educational institution throughout the Islamic world. The sultan Orhan established the first in the Ottoman Empire in the 14th century, though when the Ottomans gained control of the Middle East in the 16th century, they also gained control of many that were far older. Most *medrese*s were established by means of a special permanent religious endowment by a person of elite status and were usually associated with a mosque. Their size varied greatly— some had only a single room and one or two students, while others had a number of rooms and dozens of students. The *medrese* itself, however, was not as important as the scholars who taught there, and at advanced levels students would travel great distances to find leading scholars in their area of interest.

During the Ottoman period, *medreses* came to be arranged in a sort of hierarchy based on the subjects they taught. The lowest level of *medrese* taught the basics of Arabic, logic, theology, geometry, astronomy, and rhetoric. These were commonly called *Medreses of Twenty*, as the teachers in them received a daily salary of 20 *akces*. The *Medreses of Thirty* taught more advanced rhetoric and literature, while the highest-ranking *medreses*, usually founded by members of the royal family in major cities, provided advanced training in such areas as Islamic law and theology. Major cities also had *medreses* dedicated to specific areas of knowledge.

Instead of taking courses that approached a body of knowledge from a number of perspectives, students in Ottoman *medreses* studied individual books considered critical to understanding a given topic. These books became standard throughout the Ottoman territories, though individual teachers often taught works beyond the established canon. The books almost invariably represented the great authorities of the Islamic past, leading to an adherence to tradition which proved difficult to overcome by anyone seeking to innovate.

Students in a *medrese* had four or five classes per day, each of which they attended in both the morning and afternoon. The afternoon sessions served as review or enrichment of what had been taught in the morning. Students sat in a semicircle, with the favored students in front. Teachers generally sought to engage students in discussion as a means of encouraging preparation and making sure they understood the material. During the first half of the 15th century, *medreses* had class five days a week, with Tuesdays and Fridays off. Later, students were also given Mondays off as a day to read and copy their lessons. In addition, classes were not held during religious festivals or the holy month of Ramadan. Students used Ramadan to visit their families or travel the countryside giving sermons, which increased their reputation.

Students went to a *medrese* after first gaining knowledge from a local imam (religious teacher), who then recommended them to the *medrese* instructors. Evaluation within the system focused solely on whether a student had mastered a particular book. Mastering a book was necessary to proceed to the next one, regardless of how long it took. Teachers would then grant students a certificate saying they had mastered the work. Students gradually progressed from lower- to higher-level *medreses* to achieve greater education on the basis of these certificates and personal connections.

A *Medrese*. The term *medrese* could be used for schools with students of any age. The school in this picture is aimed for older students. © The Art Archive/British Library/British Library.

Due to the informal nature of the educational system, personal connections in many cases came to outweigh academic achievement, and forming them always represented an important part of student life. Some students would progress through the education system, and the government passed laws to provide advantages to those from elite or scholarly families. Students who became certified at the highest level could become teachers themselves, which involved starting a career at the lowest level of *medrese* and working their way up. Those who advanced the furthest in their professional career could become judges or other officials.

Because women had no public role in the Ottoman Empire, they did not attend *medreses*, and only a few could independently achieve the highest levels of learning. These few were sometimes sought out by both male and female students and were sometimes cited as important authorities. Nonetheless, because Muslims believe that learning is incumbent on both men and women, countless women sought knowledge of theology and Islamic law. In addition, villages throughout Ottoman territories had separate primary schools for girls, where women provided the instruction.

Members of a sultan's household gained their education in a palace school, where they learned religion, high culture such as calligraphy and Persian, and military science. This education sought to make them cultured members of the elite rather than scholars. During their education, young boys could not leave the palace. The military and governing classes of the realm came from these schools.

Education thus played a vital role in the daily life of the Ottoman Empire and was highly regulated by the state. Despite this, academic life still depended upon personal knowledge, reputation, and relationships. Education provided chances for social advancement for men and opened the doors of culture and religious thought to both men and women. Because the core of the curriculum revolved around religion, the education system became the major means by which a standardized Sunni Islamic culture spread throughout the empire.

To read about education in Medieval Islam, see the Islam entry the section "Education" in chapter 4 ("Intellectual Life") in volume 2 of this series.

~Brian Ulrich

FOR MORE INFORMATION

Cicek, K., ed. *The Great Ottoman-Turkish Civilization 2: Economy and Society.* Ankara: Yeni Turkiye, 2000.

Dengler, I. C. "Turkish Women in the Ottoman Empire: The Classical Age." In *Women in the Muslim World,* ed. Lois Beck and Nikki Keddie, 229–44. Cambridge: Harvard University Press, 1978.

Imber, C. *The Ottoman Empire, 1300–1650.* New York: Palgrave, 2002.

Inalcik, H. *The Ottoman Empire: The Classical Age, 1300–1600.* Trans. Norman Itzkowitz and Colin Imber. London: Weidenfeld and Nicolson, 1973.

Roded, R., ed. *Women in Islam and the Middle East: A Reader.* London: Tauris, 1999.

INTELLECTUAL
LIFE
|
EDUCATION
|
England

Spain

Italy

Ottoman Empire

Aztec

Inca

AZTEC

From the moment of childbirth, Aztec parents were greatly concerned that their children avoid becoming "fruitless trees" and instead become productive citizens. Education was the key to gaining strength and knowledge to one day become part of the economic and social community. Aztec children would receive both general and specialized instruction from parents, priests, teachers, and other members of the community through a variety of means and institutions.

The direction of a child's education was determined very early, in fact 20 days after birth. At this time, the parents chose what kind of education they wanted their child to have and then took the infant to the appropriate temple or school. The pact between the family, the gods, and the temple was sealed by incisions made in the bodies of the children. These physical marks were visible signs of a spiritual change. The lower lips of boys were cut open and a jewel was inserted. Girls were initiated when small cuts were made with obsidian blades in their breasts and hips. These incisions signified that they had been initiated into the lifelong educational process upon which their lives depended.

The Aztecs valued love and discipline. On the one hand, children were encouraged to express their feelings and attitudes openly, while on the other hand, they were watched carefully by their parents and given constant correction. When a child reached three years of age, the father began to instruct the boy, and the mother, the girl, in how to be a helpful member of the family and the household. When a child was four years old, the parents were more specific about the tasks they wanted their children to carry out, and girls and boys began wearing different clothes appropriate to their gender.

At the age of four, mothers began teaching the girls the fundamentals of weaving; and fathers began guiding the boys beyond the confines of the home, having them assist in water carrying. At five, boys helped in toting light loads of firewood and carried light bundles of goods to the *tianquiztli,* or neighborhood marketplace. This allowed them to socialize with people, watch the process of exchanges in the market, and meet other children. Girls learned to spin with their mothers and learned how to sit, use their hands, and manipulate the cotton. A year later, the *Codex Mendoza* tells us, the parents:

. . . instructed and engaged them in personal services, from which the parents benefited, like, for boys, [collecting] maize that has been spilled in the marketplace, and beans and other miserable things that the traders left scattered. And they taught the girls to spin and to do other advantageous services. This was so that, by the way of the said services and activities, they did not spend their time in idleness, and to avoid the bad vices that idleness tends to bring.

Between the ages of seven and ten, boys were given nets to fish with, while girls continued to learn how to spin and cook. By this age, young girls were already proficient in their labor and art and were supervised rather than instructed by their mothers. Apparently, it was during this period of growth that children began to act up and cause problems in the family. The *Codex Mendoza* presents these years as times when parents punished their children for a series of unacceptable behaviors, including laziness, disobedience, rudeness, and boastfulness. There are images of parents "putting before them [the children] the terror and fear of *maguey* thorns, so that being negligent and disobedient to their parents they would be punished with the said thorns." There are scenes of children weeping when presented with these thorns and admonished not to be deceitful. Girls' hands were pierced by their mothers, who used the thorns to punish them for idleness and negligence. Boys who really got out of line had their hands and feet bound, and maguey thorns were stuck into their shoulder, back, and buttocks. These punishments intensified between the ages of 10 and 14 and included being forced to inhale chili smoke or being tied by the hands and feet and forced to sleep on damp ground all night.

Images in the *Codex Mendoza* show that the children got well into line at 13 or 14 years of age. Boys were responsible for carrying firewood from the hills and are depicted transporting sedges, bulrushes, and other grasses for the household, and fishing successfully in their canoes. Girls would grind maize and make tortillas for their parents and are seen weaving, cooking, and effectively handling the different foods, utensils, and life of the kitchen. In fact, a girl who could grind corn and make the *atole* drink was considered a maiden of marriageable age.

When Aztec children reached the age of 15, parents were required to bring their teenager to a neighborhood school (which they had selected shortly after the child's birth) and initiate the next stage of his or her educational process.

One kind of school to which parents chose to send their 15-year-old boys was the *cuicacalli* (house of song), although some historical sources suggest that all Aztec children—male and female, noble or commoner—began attending this school between the ages of 12 and 14. The *cuicacallis* were a kind of preparatory school found adjacent to temples throughout the city. They were also the residences of the priests and consisted of several large, elaborately decorated buildings arranged around a central patio with surrounding rooms. The courtyard was the scene of songs and dances. Instruction began an hour before sunset, when the boys and girls, under the guidance of the instructors, were taught to sing the sacred songs of the people and to dance the various ritual dances long into the night. These songs contained the most important mythological and historical information about the culture and its worldview. The songs praised the gods and told of their sacred history, the meaning of life and death, and the responsibilities humans had toward the deities. This was a powerful cohesive social experience for Aztec children and their families, who learned and relearned the sacred teachings, dance steps, and stories of their community.

The most rigorous school, however, was the *calmecac* (file of houses), a temple school run by a *tlamacazqui*, or head priest, who trained novice priests in a variety of subjects related to life in priesthood or in judicial and civil service. Regardless of the outcome, life in the temple schools was rich in content but rugged in style. Education in the school included little sleep, much labor, knowledge of the sacred history and forces of the universe, and ritual instruction on how to bleed oneself.

Education in the *calmecac* included military, mechanical, astrological, and religious training. Youths, both male and female (females had separate schools), were taught from large pictorial manuscripts painted in hieroglyphs telling of the genealogy, history, geography, mythology, laws, and arts of the society. As in the *cuicacalli*, songs and dances were a central part of *calmecac* life. Although this school was particularly attractive to noble families, it appears that common folk also dedicated their children to the rigors and riches of the *calmecac*. Key requirements for entering and remaining apparently included good morals, intelligence, discipline, and leading a pure life.

The *Codex Mendoza* shows the kinds of labor young men carried out during their training in the *calmecac*. Duties included the early-morning sweeping of temples, carrying boughs a long distance from the forest for temple decorations, bringing maguey thorns for sacrifice, and building fences. It is also clear that these youths were punished and disciplined frequently by piercing their ears, breast, thighs, and calves. One serious offense was leaving the school to sleep at home.

The education of the novice priests depended, in part, on effective service to the head priest, who

Training of Priests. The *calmecac,* the school for priests, emphasized both physical and mental exertion. This picture depicts some of the punishments for bad behavior that a young priest would undergo in the *calmecac*. From the *Codex Mendoza*. Courtesy of Francis F. Berdan and Patricia Reiff Anawait.

transmitted ritual, mythological, and astronomical information to the young students under his charge. This demanding and rigorous learning process included testing one's physical limits. These novices had to bleed themselves, fast for 5 to 10 days, limit their sleep in a ritual called "Staying Awake at Night," and go on pilgrimages to nearby mountains to do penance and carry out sacrifices. This involved learning how to incense a shrine with copal (a kind of incense), acknowledge the four directions of the universe, and use tobacco and magical instruments to communicate with the gods. One of the important nighttime rituals involved playing *teponaztli* drums and other musical instruments and singing to the gods to invite their favor and avoid their harmful powers.

It is also clear that Aztec priests taught their students a great deal about watching the sky. One of the most interesting images from the *Codex Mendoza* shows a head priest carefully observing the passage of stars to learn when certain ritual duties were to be carried out. The Aztec students learned the names, paths, and powers of numerous stars, constellations, and celestial events. Rigorous observation over many decades resulted in the transmission of star knowledge that had become precise and complex long before the Aztecs appeared in the Basin of Mexico.

Another important school where many parents sent their 15-year-old boys was the *telpochcalli* (young man's house). The *telpochcalli* was closely related to the *cuicacalli*, and a great majority of Aztec boys, mostly commoners, were trained for military life and warfare at this school. We know that many young men took to this kind of training easily, and the rewards were sometimes sumptuous. In the *telpochcalli*, a great deal of time was spent in physical labor, either in the school itself or in community projects, such as sweeping, hauling, cleaning, building walls, digging canals, and farming. Other exercises included training in martial arts and transporting large pieces of firewood and branches from the forests to the city for heating and decorating the school. Hauling firewood became a physical test as heavier and heavier piles of wood were loaded on a youth's back to see "whether perchance he would do well in war, when already indeed an untried youth they took him to war." These same youths would soon have to carry shields, food, military supplies, and weapons great distances into huge, open battlefields filled with enemy warriors. This training was designed to drain fear and arouse bravery from the youths and to shape them into reliable sentinels and scouts.

Since the training in the *telpochcalli* involved focused preparation for warfare, the school's instructors demanded from these youths total attention, great physical effort, bravery, and the ability to withstand intense pain. The entire society believed that its well-being depended on the training and courage of its warriors and put major demands on the *telpochcalli* to develop powerful warriors. Therefore, those who strayed from the training were severely punished.

Women also played a significant role in the priesthood. In some cases, an infant girl was taken to the temple by her mother a month or so after birth and dedicated to the priesthood. The mother would give the priest a censer and copal incense as a sign that the family hoped she would enter a religious vocation when she was older. When she was a mature teenager, she would become a *cihuatlamacazqui*, or woman priest. Priestesses had to be celibate and concentrate intensely on their temple duties and the yearly round of ceremonies they ministered. Some accounts of the sacrificial festivals make it clear that priestesses were essential to the rites. For example, Och-paniztli, the feast dedicated to the mother goddess Toci (Our Grandmother), was directed by a woman priest, while an assistant called Iztaccihuatl (White Woman—because she was painted white) was responsible for the preparation and decoration of the ritual area, such as sweeping the sacred site, and lighting and extinguishing the ritual fire (Carrasco, 93–116).

To read about education in 19th-century Latin America, see the Latin America entry in the section "Education" in chapter 4 ("Intellectual Life") in volume 5 of this series.

FOR MORE INFORMATION

Austin, A. L. *Educación mexica: antología de documentos sahaguntinos*. Mexico: Universidad Nacional Autónoma de México, 1985.

Carrasco, D., with S. Sessions. *Daily Life of the Aztecs: People of the Sun and Earth*. Westport, Conn.: Greenwood, 1998.

Soustelle, J. *Daily Life of the Aztecs: On the Eve of the Spanish Conquest*. Trans. Patrick O'Brien. Stanford: Stanford University Press, 1970.

INTELLECTUAL
LIFE
|
EDUCATION
|
England

Spain

Italy

Ottoman Empire

Aztec

Inca

INCA

There was little formal education in Andean societies: children learned from their parents and older siblings. Because there was no system of writing, knowledge was passed on orally. This could be done by anyone. An exception was the use of quipus, the specialized accounting system of the Incas.

A quipu is a set of strings with various knots tied at various lengths. The kind of knot used indicated the number, and its position along the string indicated whether it was a unit of 1, 10, 100, 1,000, or higher. The strings hung from a main cord, and their location along the cord probably indicated what category was being recorded, for example, people, llamas, or corn. Some quipus have been recovered with hundreds of strings. The *quipu* had the advantage of being portable, because it could easily be rolled up and stored.

As expected, there was a special tax-exempt class of accountants schooled in the use of quipus. These people went out among the *ayllus* (communities) and kept close records of the flow of goods and services throughout the empire's provinces. They must have worked closely with the *curacas* (local officials) to determine how many goods had been used or produced, and how many people were needed for certain tasks. Quipu officials also kept census data for the empire, although this information was not written down by the Spaniards and is thus lost to us today.

The only persons who received any formal training were the sons of the nobility and provincial rulers and the *acllyaconas* (Chosen Women). Boys received a four-year education at a school in Cuzco, where they learned Quechua (Inca language) in the first year, Inca religion in the second, quipu in the third, and Inca history in the fourth. Teachers were called *amautas*, or wise men. Training was by practice, repetition, and experience. The *amautas* maintained discipline through threats and beatings—although these were restricted to a single beating per day, and that only 10 blows to the soles of the feet!

The Chosen Women were selected from among conquered peoples in the provinces and from among noble families in Cuzco, and did a series of important jobs for the empire. They were selected for their physical attractiveness at around age 10, then they were sent to schools where they learned spinning and weaving, cooking, *chicha* (a kind of maize beer) making, and other domestic activities. This instruction lasted four years, after which they would be taken to Cuzco, where the Inca king would decide their fate. There was a hierarchy of these women based on their physical perfection and social rank. The most perfect were sacrificed to the Inca gods. Next were women, also of high beauty, who might have been daughters of local *curacas*. They were taken to Cuzco and made attendants at the most important temples or became secondary wives of the king. Many served as attendants to lesser Inca gods or were given as wives to lower-ranking *curacas*. Some became *mamaconas*, or teachers of other Chosen Women at Inca centers. Most Chosen Women probably remained in the provincial centers near their homelands. Daughters of the Cuzco nobility could also become Chosen Women and serve the same purposes: they became wives, priestesses in the temples, or *mamaconas*.

The Chosen Women apparently served a very important economic role, being in charge of producing the large quantities of cloth used by officials of the empire. They also prepared the food and *chicha* used at government installations for serving the workers, and perhaps they even provided entertainment. As a luxury commodity they were also given as favors by nobles to others, including conquered leaders, as a way of cementing alliances and social relationships. For these reasons the Chosen Women were very strictly controlled by the government. They were similar to slaves in the sense that they had no personal freedom, but they were more highly regarded in that their services were respected by the Incas (Malpass, 52–54, 81–82).

To read about education in 19th-century Latin America, see the Latin America entry in the section "Education" in chapter 4 ("Intellectual Life") in volume 5 of this series.

FOR MORE INFORMATION

Ascher, M., and R. Ascher. *Code of the Quipu*. Ann Arbor: University of Michigan Press, 1981.

Malpass, M. A. *Daily Life in the Inca Empire*. Westport, Conn.: Greenwood, 1996.

Silverblatt, I. *Moon, Sun, and Witches*. Princeton: Princeton University Press, 1987.

Health and Science

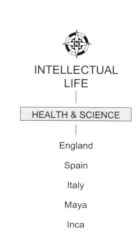

INTELLECTUAL
LIFE
|
HEALTH & SCIENCE
|
England

Spain

Italy

Maya

Inca

Health and science were frequently connected in the 15th and 16th centuries just as they are today. In fact, some sciences, such as astronomy, that are no longer associated with medicine today, were intimately involved in the treatment of disease during the 15th and 16th centuries; during that time it was widely believed that the movements of the planets and of the moon, which, after all, affected the tides, also affected the human body. Certain procedures were thought to be most beneficial if performed at certain times of the lunar month, but were thought to be dangerous if performed at other times. Bloodletting, for example, was best performed when only a quarter of the moon could be seen.

Despite such studies, disease was widespread and deadly in the 15th and 16th centuries. The main threats to public health in Europe were smallpox, malaria, stones, venereal diseases (especially syphilis), dysentery, influenza, measles, and the bubonic plague. The plague, which had been sweeping Europe periodically since the mid-14th century, was particularly feared, and cities would often close their main gates to travelers and refugees from plague-hit areas. While these diseases were dangerous enough in Europe, they were catastrophic when brought to the Americas. The Native American population had never been exposed to these diseases before and had no immunity to them. As a result, millions of Native Americans died from the rampant diseases, especially smallpox. At the start of the 16th century, there were approximately 25 million native inhabitants of Mesoamerica; by the end of the 16th century, only 1 million remained.

The cause of disease was not well understood by either Europeans or Native Americans in the 15th and 16th centuries. In Europe, the dominant theory involved the four humors. It was believed that the Earth was composed of four basic underlying elements: hot, cold, wet, and dry. These elements combined to produce the four humors: melancholy (cold and dry), phlegm (cold and moist), choler (hot and dry), and blood (hot and moist). If a person had too much of any one humor, they could become physically or mentally ill. Thus, a person with a cold might be thought to have too much phlegm, while a depressed person might have an excess of melancholy. Once a diagnosis was made, the basic treatment usually involved the application of elements opposite to the ones of which there was an excess in an attempt to regain equilibrium between the humors. Thus, someone suffering from too much melancholy might be advised to eat hot spicy foods, such as radish.

Other treatments besides the application of opposites were probably more effective. The anatomy of the body was somewhat better understood than the biology, so the setting of bones and joints fared somewhat better than the cure of serious diseases. The most important health measures, however, involved improved sanitation. Although faulty, a theory that bad smells caused disease resulted in significant improvements in the living environments in urban settings. During outbreaks of disease, city officials might order the streets to be washed and refuse collected regularly and dumped outside of the city. While such measures aimed at reducing bad smells, they had the beneficial side-effect of providing a cleaner living environment and reducing the number of vermin, who were one of the prime agents in spreading plague.

As in Europe, imbalance was also considered a cause of disease in Mesoamerica and South America, although the Native Americans did not employ any theories centered around the four humors. Many of the Native American cultures believed that it was important to maintain a cosmic order, and disease could result from upsetting that order. For example, if an Inca person fell ill, the local curer might diagnose that the person had offended a local *huaca* (spirit), and prescribe rituals designed to appease the *huaca*. The curer might also prepare some herbal medicines for the patient, and might perform a ritualized operation on the patient in which the curer appeared to remove various foreign objects, including things as extravagant as toads or snakes, from the person's body.

The Maya also believed that order must be returned for the sick to get better. As a result, in addition to applying herbal medicines and sometimes bleeding the patient (as was also done in Europe), the local shaman might also urge the patient to confess any wrongdoing that he or she had done to a neighbor, god, or animal. Part of the cure would involve making reparations for that wrongdoing. The Maya shaman thus oversaw both the physical and spiritual curing of the patient, roles that were divorced from each other in Europe and given over to the physician and the priest in turn.

Before leaving this discussion of health and science, some mention should be made of the famed astronomical observations of the Mesoamerican peoples. Like the Europeans, the Mesoamerican and South American peoples believed that the celestial bodies influenced the world on Earth. As a result, they were very interested in recording and studying movements of the Sun, the Moon, stars, and planets. The Maya and Aztecs developed a particularly accurate astronomical science. In addition to developing a 365-day calendar based upon the Sun, the Maya also developed a highly accurate lunar calendar, as well as recording cycles pertaining to other planets, such as Venus. These calendars were used not only to mark the passage of time, or to determine future events, but also to determine the best time for harvest and other such mundane but practical activities.

~Lawrence Morris

ENGLAND

Disease, aggravated by poor sanitary conditions, greatly impacted the lives of the Renaissance English. Health conditions were worsened by the omnipresence of vermin: rats were common, and lice a perennial source of discomfort. Common diseases included smallpox, malaria, stones, venereal diseases (especially syphilis), dysentery, influenza, and measles. Typhus was a frequent problem in crowded living conditions; it was rife in jails and among soldiers and sailors. Among sailors, scurvy was also common. A less serious but very common ailment was toothache: dentistry was even more primitive than medicine, and the means of tooth care were very poor.

Diseases often came and went in cycles. At the beginning of Queen Elizabeth's reign there was an epidemic of New Ague, perhaps a form of influenza, which lasted from 1557 to 1559. There was a particularly serious outbreak of smallpox in 1562, which, surprisingly, struck the upper classes hardest of all: Elizabeth herself almost died of the disease.

The most dreaded disease of all was the plague, or bubonic plague, which had first come to Europe in the 14th century and continued to be a problem in England until the late 17th century (and is still found in some parts of the world today). The plague is carried by the flea *Xenopsylla cheopis*, which normally lives on rats. If plague-carrying fleas transfer to a human host, there is a possibility they will communicate the disease and cause an outbreak of bubonic plague, with a mortality rate of about 50 percent. If the plague enters a person's pulmonary system, it can become pneumonic plague, an even more virulent and deadly form of the disease. Pneumonic plague can be transmitted directly from person to person, and its mortality rate is near 100 percent.

During the 16th and 17th centuries, the plague was largely an urban phenomenon and struck most severely in the summer. Epidemics commonly came from the Netherlands to London, whence they might spread to other towns, although occurrences in any given town were often independent of each other. London was visited by the plague in 1563, 1578–79, 1582, 1592–93, 1603, and other years, with particularly bad epidemics in 1563 and 1603, which may have had mortality rates of almost one in four; even worse was the outbreak in Norwich in 1578–79, which claimed nearly 30 percent of the town's population. Children and the poor were especially at risk.

The problem of disease was aggravated by the inability of medical science to treat it or even understand it. The medical profession in Renaissance England was largely shaped by structures inherited from the Middle Ages. At the top of the hierarchy of medical practitioners was the physician, a university-trained theorist who specialized in diagnosis and prescription of medicines. These medicines were provided by the apothecary, who was considered a tradesman and therefore far below the status of the physician, although he did belong to one of the most privileged and prestigious trades in England. Also ranking below the physician was the surgeon, who specialized in what we would call operations. Below the surgeon was the barber-surgeon, who performed similar procedures. Simple barbers also practiced basic forms of surgery, including cleaning teeth, and dentistry. In the latter part of Elizabeth's reign, there may have been one licensed medical practitioner for every 400 people in London. Outside of the formal medical hierarchy were the unlicensed practitioners, who typically practiced medicine only on a part-time basis. These included folk healers, midwives, and a fair number of outright quacks. Women often received some basic medical training as a part of their preparation for managing a household, and even an aristocratic lady might engage in charitable healing for her poorer neighbors.

If the structure of the medical profession was old-fashioned, its medical theories were even more so. By and large, there had been few major developments in medicine since the Middle Ages. Physiological theory was based on the ancient idea of the four humors, corresponding to the four elements: melancholy (cold and dry, like Earth), blood (hot and moist, like air), phlegm (cold and moist, like water), and choler (hot and dry, like fire). Physicians often attributed illness to an imbalance of these humors and treated it by prescribing foods and medicines whose properties were thought to be opposite to those of the excessive humor. Surgical practitioners may have been somewhat more effective, as the mechanics of the body were better understood than its biology. Yet surgery was also fairly primitive—one of the most common surgical procedures was bloodletting, whereby blood was removed from the patient either by an incision into a vein or by applying a leech (it was believed that this could help rid the patient of bad blood that might be causing illness).

The poor medicine, the resulting high rates of mortality, and the rapidly growing population dictated that the population of Elizabethan England was rather young. Still, a 40-year-old was not thought to be elderly. In fact, the 40s and 50s were considered the prime of a man's life. If any age marked the beginning of old age, it would be 60: laboring people were no longer required by law to work after that age, nor was one liable for

> *One of the most common surgical procedures was bloodletting.*

military service. It has been estimated that nearly 10 percent of the population were age 60 or older. Nonetheless, the prevalence of disease and the primitive level of medicine meant that illness could easily end a life long before its prime. Life expectancy at birth was only about 48 years, although anyone who made it through the first 30 years was likely to live for another 30. Life expectancy varied from place to place—it was particularly low in the cities, where crowded conditions and poor sanitation increased the dangers of disease.

English Renaissance learning tended to be theoretical and old-fashioned in general. The Renaissance was in many ways a time of broadening intellectual horizons, but science was still dominated by medieval traditions. Early in the 16th century, Copernicus had proposed the theory of a universe centered around the Sun rather than Earth; in the early 17th century, Galileo used a telescope to discover that Jupiter had moons of its own. Yet the predominant view of the universe remained that of the ancient astronomer Ptolemy, who had envisioned Earth at the center of the orbiting spheres of the heavens. Renaissance scholars also adhered to the ancient belief that all physical matter was made up of the four elements, each defined by two properties: fire (hot and dry), air (hot and moist), water (cold and moist), and Earth (cold and dry). There were some noteworthy scientific achievements during this period. In mathematics, for example, Robert Recorde invented the sign $=$. Thomas Hariot added the signs $<$ and $>$. However, the great scientific revolution was not to come until the 17th century.

In fact, a noteworthy feature of 15th- and 16th-century thought was that science and magic were not very distinct from each other. Elizabethan scholars adhered to the theory of signatures and correspondences: It was believed that different aspects of the physical world were in some way related to each other and that these relationships were indicated by physical resemblance. Such a theory was not fundamentally different from the principle of sympathetic magic. Many learned people still believed in alchemy, the mystical art of turning lead into gold. Indeed, even a noteworthy scholar like the mathematician John Dee believed deeply in the idea of magic, which he tried to pursue with scientific persistence and precision. Nevertheless, the desire to keep examining nature and testing theories laid the groundwork for the modern science and medicine of today (Singman, 48–53).

To read about health and science in Chaucer's England, see the Europe entry in the sections "Science" and "Health and Medicine" in chapter 4 ("Intellectual Life") in volume 2 of this series; for 18th-century England, see the entry on England in the sections "Science and Technology" and "Health and Medicine" in chapter 4

("Intellectual Life") in volume 4 of this series; for Victorian England, see the Victorian England entry in the sections "Science" and "Health and Medicine" in chapter 4 ("Intellectual Life") in volume 5 of this series.

FOR MORE INFORMATION

Palliser, D. M. *The Age of Elizabeth*. London: Longman, 1992.
Singman, J. L. *Daily Life in Elizabethan England*. Westport, Conn.: Greenwood, 1995.
Webster, C. *Health, Medicine, and Mortality in Sixteenth-Century England*. Cambridge: Cambridge University Press, 1979.

INTELLECTUAL
LIFE

HEALTH & SCIENCE

England

Spain

Italy

Maya

Inca

SPAIN

There was no royal council of public health equivalent to the councils of state, finance, or the Indies to oversee medical affairs, and the number of royal hospitals was small compared to those of religious organizations, confraternities, or even establishments financed and run by individuals. The vast majority of the king's subjects received no medical assistance from the crown, but in some towns the municipality administered public health through the town council, which set aside land for a building, fixed the fees, contracted a doctor, organized the medical provisions, and arranged for free treatment of the poor. Country people were attended by the local clergyman or itinerant healers whose knowledge and abilities were often of a doubtful nature.

There were many fraudulent medical practitioners and concomitant poor care. While the doctor might make a good living with high fees and few overheads, the sham doctor was always just around the corner, and many of the poor were forced to seek his services, which involved a good dose of superstitious ritual. Failed medical students with only a smattering of knowledge frequently passed themselves off as doctors, and others who could prove their qualifications sometimes had only mediocre training, having bought their degrees with gold. In 1563, the Cortes (a kind of parliament), meeting in Madrid to assess the situation, set some standards. Thereafter, the student was required to graduate in arts from an accredited university, then do another four years of study in medicine, to be followed by two years of training with an experienced physician.

The poor depended on the local barber-surgeons for certain medical treatment, however. These craftsmen were more common and widespread than physicians and less expensive. They treated trauma, set broken bones, cauterized bleeding wounds with the use of a red-hot iron, stitched up torn flesh, and bled ill patients. They also cut hair and shaved beards. Many moved around from village to village, tramping the country roads with their bag of instruments ready to bleed a sick cow, mule, or pig if no human patients required their services.

Physicians usually had a deep contempt for apothecaries and chemists and for barber-surgeons, who, they considered, were well beneath them in skill and class since they were once only barbers, pure and simple. These occupations involved manual labor, which was far beneath the dignity of the university-trained doctor. Bleeding and purging were the two most important measures used to cure almost everything, and repeated bleedings were even better, although they often cured the disease by killing the patient. The physician, of course, did not dirty his hands by bleeding the patient himself but left the job to the barber-surgeon.

Diagnosis, prognosis, and prescription constituted the domain of the surgeon's academically trained superior—the physician. Physicians did not often examine the patient bodily but took note of the symptoms as described by the person, sometimes examining the regurgitated food or urine to determine the remedy. Public confidence in the medical profession was not high in spite of the notion among doctors that they had reached the highest possible standards. Plays, cartoons, and satires of the times depict them as arrogant, greedy, money-grubbing villains whose only interest in the patient was focused on his purse.

The knowledge of theory and practice was still based on Hippocrates, the ancient father of Western medicine, and the Greek physician Galen (who died around 200 C.E.). Nevertheless, by bribing the hangman, some enterprising students were able to obtain corpses for anatomical research and to gain more understanding of bodily functions and disease. 16th-century medicine could have marked the beginning of a new epoch in medical science with the discovery of the pulmonary circulation of blood by the Catalan theologian and physician Miguel Servet working in France. His opposition to the doctrine of the Trinity and infant baptism resulted in his arrest by the papal Inquisition in Lyon, France, from which he escaped only to fall into the clutches of Calvin in Geneva, where he was burned at the stake as a heretic in 1553. Not until the English physician and anatomist William Harvey, who formally presented his findings in 1626 in which he rediscovered the circulation of the blood and the role of the heart in propelling it, were the theories of Galen laid to rest. This was a concept that eventually could not be denied by even the most conservative of the medical establishment.

Medical practitioners also needed a knowledge of astrology and often inquired into the patient's horoscope before prescribing. For example, treatment should not be taken when the Moon was in the sign of Saturn, as the humors would congeal; it was considered best to bleed the subject during the periods of the quarter Moon since the humors would then have retired to the center of the body; most illnesses began at the time of the new Moon when the heat of the Sun overpowered the watery Moon and left body functions feeble and susceptible; progress toward healing was best made between the new and full Moon.

Ingredient (element)	Humor	Temperament
air	blood	sanguine—hot, moist
fire	yellow bile	choleric—hot, dry
water	phlegm	phlegmatic—cool, moist
earth	black bile	melancholic—cool, dry

The Four Humors and Their Corresponding Elements.

The theory of the four humors, dating back to the ancient Greeks of the 5th century B.C.E., was still much in vogue in early modern Spain. The thesis was that human beings and the food they ate contained the same elements that constituted the universe—that is, air, fire, water, and earth. In human physiology these corresponded to certain humors, which in turn formed the basis of human health and temperament.

Some people contained an excess of one or the other ingredient that led to ill health, but good physical condition could be achieved by finding the proper balance. All disease fell under the four headings of hot, cool, moist, and dry. The theory of opposites prescribed that a person eat foods that possess qualities opposite to the problem they had. For example, a choleric or hot-tempered person would be advised to refrain from hot foods and partake of cool foods. Similarly, fevers were thought to originate from hot and dry causes, indicating excessive choler or yellow bile, and thus were treated with cooling medicines such as coriander or fresh roses. Diseases from cold causes, leading to lethargy and fatigue, could be treated with warming medicines including radish, garlic, saltpeter, and myrrh.

Herbal medicines for all kinds of illnesses were administered by nearly everyone with any knowledge of plants. From the lowest healer to the most prominent physician, herbs and spices such as cloves, china-root (for gout), sandalwood, ginger, pepper, and cinnamon, some grown at home, some imported, were used as the basic ingredients. The royal pharmacies were supplied with herbal remedies prepared by apothecaries from plants nurtured in the royal gardens. Philip II even sent his chief physician, Francisco Hernández, to the Spanish holding in the New World to investigate and collect medicinal herbs there; Hernández wrote back that he discovered over 1,000 medicinally useful new plants.

The common, often fatal diseases of the period were tuberculosis, influenza, dropsy or edema, dysentery, smallpox, diphtheria, syphilis, and typhus, which first appeared in Spain late in the 16th century. The latter was characterized by delirious fever and small purplish eruptions of the skin with symptoms much like the plague. Epidemics, especially of the bubonic plague, brought entire cities to a standstill as people panicked and left town for the hills or locked themselves away indoors. The heavy loss of life from this feared disease left towns and countryside decimated. In Valencia, for example, 300 people died daily between March and July during the outbreak of 1508. There were many other epidemics there and elsewhere in the country throughout the period. The plague of 1597 to 1602 affected the entire peninsula, causing half a million deaths.

Over time doctors began to learn that bleeding was a useless remedy against the plague. They were also starting to understand that a clean environment was beneficial. As a result, the sick were transferred to isolation hospitals outside the city, and the dead were collected by slaves and buried in lime pits well away from the town walls. The idea then prevalent that the airborne plague was spread through putrefaction led to some good results. For the first time, city officials sent carts around to collect refuse, and householders were instructed to keep the areas in front of their dwellings clean. Hospital floors were continuously scrubbed, and in some cities, such as Seville, rosemary and thyme, or juniper in Segovia, were burned in bonfires to help purify the air. These actions and the liberal use of vinegar spread around the streets were, of course, unhealthy for the infected carrier-flea and the rats that were host to it but more beneficial for the populace.

Some doctors had great faith in the curative powers of precious stones, which were thought to be useful against poison in the system. Ground-up pearls, rubies, and emeralds were particularly good; 9 grams of the latter were considered sufficient to resist all poisons.

Cities and towns maintained their pharmacies well stocked with medicines against the plagues such as bezoar (concretions of mineral salts formed in the gastrointestinal organs of humans and animals and believed by many to possess magical properties and to be a powerful antidote against poisons) and mithridate, an antidote extracted from the dogtooth violet. Another, theriaca, a pulverized concoction of some 70 drugs mixed with honey into a kind of medicinal paste or treacle (a recipe known to the ancient Greeks), was a further potion thought to counteract the poison inherent in the disease.

Oral hygiene was sorely neglected, as people were not in the habit of cleaning their teeth with any thoroughness. A woolen cloth or a finger wiped over them after eating, or a toothpick to extract debris from between them, generally sufficed. Tooth decay was rampant and often ignored until pain forced the victim to seek the help of a tooth-puller or the surgeon-dentist. The use of a file to remove decayed portions of a tooth was not unknown, and a visit to the surgeon-dentist was an experience not to be taken lightly. There were plenty of charlatans in this profession, too, and again, the poor were at their mercy. Bleeding was once more the primary remedy for toothache, while essence of cloves or spirit of nicotine might temporarily lessen the pain. Cotton soaked in oil of sage or poppy was also recommended for toothache. An actual extraction on a bench in the village square, often with dirty tools, by an itinerant dentist and clumsy assistant with a crowd looking on, was an adventure undergone only in dire circumstances (Anderson, 253–71).

FOR MORE INFORMATION

Anderson, J. M. *Daily Life during the Spanish Inquisition*. Westport, Conn.: Greenwood, 2002.

Goodman, D. *Power and Penury: Government, Technology and Science in Philip II's Spain*. Cambrige: Cambridge University Press, 1988.

ITALY

INTELLECTUAL
LIFE

HEALTH & SCIENCE

England

Spain

Italy

Maya

Inca

The Renaissance perception of disease had some elements in common with ours and some that were radically different. It is worth pausing to reflect on the raw experience of disease. Although our medicine is far from omnipotent, we trust its powers to shield us from many dangers and, above all, to dull or even banish pain. A fundamental fact: the Renaissance had no aspirin, or other pills, for pain. Headaches and toothaches—and they were common—simply had to be borne. Those with fever burned or shivered, and sweated, and waited for relief. And childbirth hurt a great deal more than it does today. Furthermore, without reliable antiseptic or anesthesia, internal surgery was extremely perilous. A condition like hernia, now cured by a simple operation, had no safe fix; its victims might go years or decades with their intestines, painfully bloated, sheathed in trusses outside their bellies. Italians, like other Europeans, learned to live with pain. They also lacked cures for infection. Thus, they went in fear of untimely death. They had their remedies, and their hopes in them, but they lacked our luxury of trusting one antibiotic or another to do its job. Hope therefore was shot through with an anxiety we can hardly comprehend.

The Renaissance conception of patterns of infection was unlike ours. Like us, Italians were aware of isolated illnesses and of epidemics, waves of sickness that swept through houses, towns, and districts. To them, as to us, these were manifestations of the natural world. However, for Christian reasons, they were also part of a larger divine plan—God's providence. Thus, one response to infection was prayer and ceremonies. There were other differences in response as well. Only late in the 19th century did medicine discover germs and work out a clear theory of contagion. Renaissance medicine, though aware of transmission, still hewed to ancient Greek theories that held that sickness commonly came from imbalances in the body: the four humors (body fluids: blood, phlegm, black and yellow bile) were out of healthy equilibrium. Each humor combined two factors: hot or cold, wet or dry. Thus, if sickness struck, the goal was to restore deficiencies and to remove excess: to warm the cold-wet sufferer and bleed the hot-wet one, and so on. To sustain health, one should aim, physicians said, for a temperate life, regulating diet and exercise, cultivating peace of mind, and calibrating the soul. Diseases, then, came from God, from the natural world, from the disorder of human souls and bodies. But they also proceeded by infection, and the vectors were not organisms but miasmas: vapors, smells, and malaria, which for instance means just "bad air." The bad air theory galvanized authorities. Ignorant of germs, they went after smells, and in doing so probably improved the general health. In the 16th century, the Grand Duchy of Tuscany had a vigorous body of health inspectors, who collected reports on the air of towns and villages. Their reports of manure piles, garbage-strewn streets, open sewers, and casual latrines remind us that the Renaissance had its smells, as well as colors, sounds, and textures. Where successful, the officials' efforts at hygiene probably curtailed water-borne diseases. They were, however, irrelevant to respiratory ailments and to the deadly sicknesses borne, as we now know, by insects: malaria, typhus, and bubonic plague.

The whole complex of Renaissance theories of infection called forth an elaborate program to defend public health. Authorities, with an eye to general welfare, developed a series of measures—some in fact appropriate, and others either irrelevant or even harmful—to hedge the spread of epidemics. Infected travelers could carry serious illnesses from one city to another. Thus, early on, cities learned that they could sometimes prevent an epidemic by excluding suspect travelers. The English word *quarantine* is of Italian origin, and it traces back to the common practice of making incoming ships from plague-ridden ports anchor in isolation for 40 (*quaranta*) days. The practice was often effective; the wait in fact was long enough to kill off the crew or prove a vessel clean. It was much harder to prevent contagions spread overland; terrestrial human traffic was both heavier and more diffuse. Nevertheless, since cities were walled, they could close their gates to travelers from infected zones. During epidemics, travelers had to show a certificate to prove they came from uninfested places. Although open to corruption and cheating, these measures did afford some protection.

By the same logic, when highly infectious diseases did strike, one response of the authorities was to isolate the victims. They often sequestered the poorer patients in a hospital. This measure, though it might help the populace as a whole, was often deadly to the sick. Renaissance hospitals, for all their good intentions, lacked efficacious medicines. Crowding and a plethora of diseases in cramped spaces made them deadly. A second recourse, often tried against bubonic plague, was to seal up a house if one resident fell sick, and not unseal it until the dying stopped. Due to the complex epidemiology of plague, this measure did little good and much harm, for houses were actually more contagious than their denizens. Unable to flee, imprisoned family members were thus at much greater risk. The experience of plague had taught Italians that flight was the most prudent remedy.

Disease attracted a variety of practitioners. Most Italians had little traffic with the university-trained physicians. These long-robed, bookish dignitaries did not deign to touch their patients. They peered intently, however, at glass vials of urine, for its color was a key diagnostic tool. The rich consulted these learned doctors, as did the big charitable hospitals, which employed them to tend their inmates. Other Italians generally turned for cures to other professionals, semiprofessionals, and amateurs. Wounds, broken bones, and skin problems were in the purview of the surgeons and barbers. Thus, the usual aftermath of a bloody fight was an urgent message to the surgeon to come clean up the havoc. Apothecaries prepared medicines from a smorgasbord of flowers, roots, gums, minerals, and other exotic materials, stored in labeled jars on their shelves; a guild usually regulated their work, as it did that of the empirics, narrow specialists low on the ladder of prestige. Other remedies, often with secret ingredients, came from itinerant medicine sellers. In many places, these men too fell under the supervision of the medical inspector's office. Some of these patent-remedy merchants were skilled hucksters, akin to the snake-oil salesmen of North American legend. Indeed, snakes and venom were part of the pitch and stock in trade. The showmen were called *ciarlatani*, a word derived from a verb meaning "to chatter." Our modern *charlatan* evokes the old suspicion that greeted their patter. Another name was *montebanchi*, for to make their sales they mounted a *banco*, a little stage. All these curers and sales folk belonged to the world of medical practice, as supervised by the public health authorities.

Still another sort of lay medical practitioner were men and very often women who prepared folk remedies. These were mostly people of modest means and scant literacy. Their concoctions typically combined herbs and other natural substances, gathered in the fields and woods or cultivated in gardens and then processed according to recipes passed through oral tradition. A body of venerable but uninstitutionalized knowledge guided these preparations, but their makers—often called *magare* (magic makers)—could also improvise, following their own intuitions and experiments. These lay healers were specialists within a larger domain of informal, do-it-

Montebanchi, or Mountebanks. These hawkers of false cures stood on top of benches in order to speak to a large crowd. These mountebanks have even hired a musician to draw people in. Civica Raccolta delle Stampe Achille Bertarelli–Milano.

yourself health care that likely included much of the female population. One consulted the wisewoman when the usual widely known home remedies did not avail. As an alternative, 16th-century printers began to offer literate women published household compendia with specialized recipes for treating many ills. By the later Renaissance, the wisewomen faced pressures from several directions. Not only had they to compete with these books and with other more prestigious medical practitioners, but they also became increasingly suspect as purveyors of not only healing cures but also harmful spells.

The difficulties of the wisewomen and men arose from the close ties between their preparations of herbal remedies and the practice of magic. Ointments to cool fever and salves to induce or banish love looked quite alike, and the underlying principles understood to do the job were often the same. Though medical in intent, cures might well call on supernatural as well as natural powers. Even the devil might be invoked, as when, for example, the healer deemed the illness to be brought on by a curse that could be countered only by a like force. Thus, sufferers might seek out magic itself to ease their pain or weakness.

Magic, as a shield against illness, was, unlike medicine and religion, an ethically ambiguous force, sometimes benign but often malevolent (or both at once). That which helped one person often hurt another. For example, almost everyone believed that love magic could bring on lovesickness, sometimes called the *martello* (the hammer), which enthralled the victim's emotions and weakened her or his body; this served the yearning lover but not necessarily the reluctant beloved. Such charms could also rattle proper gender hierarchy by taming a man, subjecting him to a woman's will. In the hands of a jealous woman, magic could cause impotence in a straying man. Similarly, a resentful competitor or a vengeful neighbor might buy from a sorcerer or witch a spell to cause bodily illness, diabolical possession, or death. Not all magic dealt harm, nor was human health its only domain. People also sought out workers of magic to solve problems of locating water, finding lost objects, or curing animals.

Magical beliefs belonged not just to commoners. Well-born and even educated Italians dabbled in magic, and among men accused of sorcery, some were priests. Learned churchmen and magistrates took such matters seriously, because to their eyes, magic was not mere silliness but possibly the work of the devil. The 16th-century movements of religious reform mounted increasingly sharp campaigns to suppress superstitious practices and witchcraft. Nonetheless, to bring Satan and his disciples to heel, the Italian authorities often adopted relatively mild tactics. While the Inquisitions prosecuted hundreds of women and men on various charges of illicit magic and witchcraft, unlike in some parts of Europe executions were few (Cohen and Cohen, 239–52).

FOR MORE INFORMATION

Arrizabalaga, J., J. Henderson, and R. French. *The Great Pox: The French Disease in Renaissance Europe*. New Haven: Yale University Press, 1997.

Carmichael, A. *Plague and the Poor in Renaissance Florence*. Cambridge: Cambridge University Press, 1985.

Cohen, E. S., and T. V. Cohen. *Daily Life in Renaissance Italy*. Westport, Conn.: Greenwood, 2001.

Park, K. "Medicine and Magic: The Healing Arts." In *Gender and Society in Renaissance Italy*, ed. J. Brown and R. Davis, 119–49. New York: Longman, 1998.

MAYA

Every member of Maya society—rulers, the elite, the common people (farmers and a variety of occupational specialists)—believed they had to keep the world an ordered place. If a person failed in his or her duties, he or she would be punished by accidents, illness, or death by the supernatural powers that governed the universe. These powers could be visible as celestial objects such as the Sun, the Moon, and the stars. Invisible power was inside all things: animals, mountains, and other places in the landscape such as caves (believed to be entries to the underworld). The Maya believed that knowledge of these things was revealed to religious specialists—shamans and priests—who held special powers to communicate with the supernatural.

The religious official most in touch with the people was the local *chilan* (shaman), who used divination to cure illnesses, foretell events, and communicate with the gods. This is the only ancient religious specialist to survive into modern times. Among the Maya of Yucatán the shaman (known today as *ahmen,* or "he who understands") conducts traditional rituals such as the *hetzmek* (a birth ritual) and treats illnesses through traditional medicines and divination.

Bishop Landa's colonial-era account describes Maya shamans "who cured with herbs and many superstitious rites. . . . The(se) . . . physicians performed their cures by bleedings of the parts which gave pain to the sick . . . (the Maya) believed that death, sickness and afflictions came to them for their wrong doing and their sin; they had a custom of confessing themselves, when they were already sick."

As in other matters, the Maya still believe their personal well-being depends on harmony with the world about them. Illness is a sign of disharmony. When a person is ill, a shaman is summoned. Shamans use a variety of techniques to reveal the cause of illness. The prescribed cure includes measures to correct the cause of the illness discovered by the shaman—usually some harm done to another person, animal, or deity. Curing rituals include praying and burning incense, along with taking medicines made from local plants. There are many medicinal herbs and plants in the Maya area, and shamans to this day preserve an extensive knowledge of these cures. Several colonial-period Maya manuscripts list a series of illnesses and their cures, and many of these remedies are considered effective today. Although the shamans were able to help their patients in some cases, there must nevertheless have been much more sickness and a higher mortality rate than is the case today. The Maya were particularly unprepared to fight diseases that the Spanish carried with them and against which the Maya peoples had built up no immunity, especially measles, chicken pox, and smallpox.

The Maya believed that all of nature and the world was connected with divinities. Much of their science thus involved divination rituals attempting to discover the causes and operation of the Maya universe. The Maya were particularly skilled in the sciences of mathematics and astronomy.

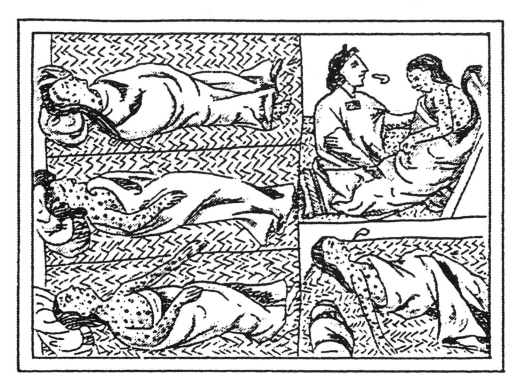

Native Americans Suffering from Smallpox. Before the arrival of the Spanish, smallpox had never existed in the Americas. As a result, the native population was very susceptible to this disease. Picture from the *Florentine Codex,* after Francisco Paso y Troncoso. Courtesy of the University of Utah Press and the School of American Research.

The Maya, like all Mesoamerican peoples, used a vigesimal (base twenty) numbering system, and their numeral expressions reflect this. Mayan languages use new words at the vigesimal multiples (20, 400, 8,000, etc.). The first 19 numerals were similar to our English terms, with unique numerals from 1 through 10, and the numerals 11 through 19 produced by combining 1 through 9 with 10.

The symbols used by the Maya to write numbers—bars and dots—were used throughout Mesoamerica.

The dot has a value of one, and the bar has a value of five. Very early on, the Maya also began to use a positional numeration system based on the mathematical concept of zero. Scholars believe this is the earliest known example of the concept anywhere in the world. Zero value, or completion, was symbolized by an elliptical shell. Bar and dot symbols were used for the numbers 1 to 19. Numbers above 19 were indicated by position.

In Maya calculations the values of the positions increase by powers of 20 in rows from bottom to top. The bottom row represents numbers from 1 to 19, the second row the 20s, third row the 400s, and so on. Thus a number such as 999 would be rendered by two dots in the third row ($2 \times 400 = 800$), a bar and four dots in the second row ($9 \times 20 = 180$), and three bars and four dots ($19 \times 1 = 19$) in the bottom row. The number 980 would be rendered in the same way, except a shell (zero) would replace the number 19 in the bottom row. Maya merchants used this system to record their transactions, and they used counters such as cacao beans to make computations on the ground or any available flat surface. Addition and subtraction was a straightforward process of adding or subtracting counters from the appropriate row. Modern studies have shown that more complex functions (multiplication and division) could also be done with this numerical system.

The Maya combined their numerical system with accurate and painstaking observation to record with great accuracy the cycles of movements of the sky deities—the Sun, the Moon, and planets. Of course, they had to rely on observations without benefit of the instruments of modern astronomy. A pair of crossed sticks or similar sighting devices was probably used from heights such as temple summits. With long lines of sight to the horizon, the Maya could fix positions for the rising or setting of the Sun, the Moon, or planets to within less than a day's error. When any of these celestial bodies rose or set at the same point a second time, one cycle was completed.

Yet it must be noted that the Maya did not understand these movements as modern astronomy does. The movements were observed and recorded by the Maya in order to prophesy events the deities were believed to control. Like Babylonian and medieval sky watchers, the Maya used the results of their observations for both mystical and practical purposes. Indeed, they believed that numbers, time, and the entire universe were ruled by supernatural forces. By recording cycles of these forces, they created a series of calendars used to understand events and predict the future. The calendars were matched with the events of history, the reigns of rulers, their conquests and achievements, and the like. Each passing cycle produced the possibility of repeated destiny.

One of the oldest and most important calendars was an almanac of 260 days that operated without regard to the celestial cycles. There were several Maya calendars based on the recurring cycles of move-

Astronomy. The Maya and Aztecs made careful measurements of the stars and used the constellations and other celestial patterns to predict the future. In this picture, an Aztec ruler examines a passing comet. From Diego Durán, *Códice Durán*. Mexico City: Arrendadora International 1990 (facsimile edition).

ments of the Sun, the Moon, and the planets. The first two form the basis of our modern 365-day calendar year and our 30-day (on average) month. The Maya marked the Sun's cycle with a solar calendar and the Moon's cycle with a lunar calendar, but they also recorded the cyclic movements of the visible planets such as Venus, Mars, and Jupiter. There was also a purely arbitrary count of 819 days associated with each of the four quadrants of the universe, each ruled over by one of the four color and directional aspects of the deity Kawil: red for the east, black for the west, white for the north, and yellow for the south.

Counts of days in these cycles were recorded by the bar and dot and the vigesimal positional notation discussed earlier in this section. To record the numbers 1 through 19 in calendrical texts, the Maya sometimes used alternative symbols known as head-variant numerals. The numbers 1 to 13 and 0 were represented by a series of unique deity head glyphs. The head-variant glyph for the number 10 is a skull. Head-variant numbers from 14 through 19 were formed by combining the appropriate head variant (numbers 4 through 9) with the skeletal lower jaw from the head variant for 10. For example, the number 17 is the number 7 head variant with a skeletal lower jaw.

The most common cyclic counts used by the ancient Maya—the 30-day lunar period, the 260-day almanac, the 365-day solar year, and the Calendar Round cycle of 52 years—were very old concepts shared by all Mesoamerican peoples. It is likely that most of the populace was familiar with these calendars, for they were believed to guide the daily lives and destinies of rich and poor alike. But the more complex calendars, such as those based on planetary cycles and the 819-day count, involved knowledge that must have been guarded by the ruling elite as a source of great power. Having knowledge of the sky deities and being able to predict their movements demonstrated to the common people that the kings and priests were in close communion with the supernatural forces that governed the universe.

The Maya particularly observed the phases of the Moon, which they believed helped control human destiny. By recording the length of the lunar cycle—the time span between new moons, for example—they soon realized this period is a little over 29.5 days. Because Maya arithmetic had no fractions or decimal points, they used another method to keep track of the lunar cycle. It is similar to the way in which we keep our own calendar year in harmony with the true year. Because the actual length of the solar year is between 365 and 366 days, we make a slight over-correction every four years by adding a day during leap year. This over-correction is compensated for by a slight under-correction once every century by skipping one leap year. The system of successive adjustments keeps our calendar in harmony with the Sun's annual cycle.

Initially the Maya seem to have alternated lunations (the period between successive new moons) of 29 and 30 days. Although the resulting average lunation is 29.5 days, the exact figure is a little longer. A lunar calendar based on a 29.5-day lunation would gain enough so that the error would reach an entire day every two and two-thirds years. To be more accurate, the Maya figured that 149 lunar cycles was equivalent to 4,400 days. This yields an average lunation of 29.53020 days, extremely close to the modern calculated period (Sharer, 127, 176–88).

To read about science in 19th-century Latin America, see the Latin America entry in the section "Science" in chapter 4 ("Intellectual Life") in volume 5 of this series.

FOR MORE INFORMATION

Marcus, J. *Mesoamerican Writing Systems: Propaganda, Myth, and History in Four Ancient Civilizations.* Princeton: Princeton University Press, 1992.

Sharer, R. J. *Daily Life in Maya Civilization.* Westport, Conn.: Greenwood, 1996.

Tedlock, B. *Time and the Highland Maya.* Albuquerque: University of New Mexico Press, 1982.

INTELLECTUAL
LIFE

HEALTH & SCIENCE

England

Spain

Italy

Maya

Inca

INCA

Curing involved a religious ceremony conducted by individual specialists. The Inca did not believe in natural causes of illness; all disease was thought to be caused by supernatural elements. Thus to get rid of a disease, one had to appease the spirit that was causing the illness. This usually involved some form of sacrifice to the offended spirit or *huaca* (a place or object with supernatural powers). People called curers specialized in this activity. Curers believed that they had been called by spirits to healing and that the spirits had given them special knowledge about how to cure ailments.

Curing could involve sacrifices and a variety of other activities. Many different plants were considered to have healing powers. In fact, some of these herbs have been tested for modern uses, and research is presently being conducted to determine whether any have commercial value.

The rituals involved with curing depended on what the cause of the disease was thought to be. If the illness was thought to be due to a failure to provide proper rituals for a *huaca*, then such was prescribed along with blowing the powder of corn and seashells toward the *huaca*. If the disease was thought to be caused by a foreign object in the person's body, the curer might simply massage the patient and suck on parts of the body where the pain was occurring. Usually the curer would produce an object that he claimed was the cause of the disease, such as a sharp object or some plant or animal material. If the disease was identified as sorcery-induced, then a sorcerer was needed to cure the patient. This might or might not be the same person, as there was no clear division between curing and sorcery.

Early Spanish sources mention very elaborate cures that were attempted for particularly grave illnesses. A small room was cleaned out completely; next, the walls and floor were scrubbed with black corn powder, which was then burned in it; then the procedure was repeated with white corn powder. After the room was thus purified, the patient was brought in and laid on his or her back in the middle of the room. He or she was then put to sleep or into a trance, possibly through hypnotism. The curer pretended to cut the patient open and produced exotic objects, such as toads and snakes, which were burned as the causes of the illness.

An interesting Inca medical practice, which was known to earlier Andean societies as well, is trepanation, or cutting open the skull to expose the brain. This was no doubt done to let evil spirits out, but it had the added factor of danger that comes with working on the nerve center of the body. It is a credit to the Inca curers that many of these operations were successful, because many excavated skulls show evidence of having healed prior to death. In other examples there are multiple holes, indicating that the operation was performed more than once. It seems likely that the patient was in a drunken or drug-induced stupor, because the operation would have been very painful.

It is uncertain whether the other sciences of the Incas were any more sophisticated than those elsewhere in the world during the 16th century. Certainly the Incas' astronomical observations and calendars were not as accurate as those of other groups, for example, the Maya of Mexico and Central America. Yet they evidently understood many scientific and mathematical principles, particularly those needed in engineering, because they built masterful buildings that still stand today.

A Curer. As in this picture, the Spanish often depicted the Native American shamans, including curers, as sorcerers in league with the devil. Nevertheless, the depiction (in the lower-right corner) of a curer sucking disease out of a patient gives an accurate impression of one of the rituals. Picture by Guaman Poma.

Regarding mathematics, it is known from the studies of quipus (knotted strings used to keep records) that the Incas used a decimal system of counting. They also understood the concept of zero, because there is a place for "no units" on the quipus. However, the quipu could not be used like an abacus for quickly adding, subtracting, or multiplying. For these purposes, the quipu accountant used pebbles, grains, or a tray with compartments similar to an abacus. Once the desired calculation had been made, the number could be recorded on the quipu.

The Incas must have utilized standardized units of measurement to plan their major construction works. For example, to be able to call up the proper number of *m'ita* workers (individuals from conquered people who had to supply a given number of work hours per year) for a project, Inca engineers must have had a system of determining the amount of work involved. Spanish writers differ on Spanish equivalents for Inca units of measurement, however, so it is uncertain how precise they truly were.

The Incas made astronomical observations, but only of the Sun, the Moon, and some constellations. Most astronomical bodies were considered to be deities, as they were to many ancient peoples. Hence the study of their movements was not as important as their veneration.

Which celestial bodies were actually charted by the Incas is unclear. Modern studies have confirmed that the Incas made astronomical observations of the constellation Pleiades from the Coricancha at Cuzco and a building at Machu Picchu; and there is evidence of an observation point for the summer and winter solstices at Machu Picchu as well. Other suggestions, including observations of the two main stars in the Southern Cross constellation, remain to be confirmed.

The Incas apparently used two different calendars, one for daytime and one for nighttime. The daytime calendar was based on the solar cycle and was approximately 365 days long. It was used for economic activities such as agriculture, mining, warfare, and construction. The movement of the Sun was particularly important to the Inca agricultural calendar, being used to fix the days of planting. Four towers were built on the horizons east and west of Cuzco to mark the rising and setting locations of the Sun in August, the time of planting corn and potatoes. The point of view was the *ushnu* (a central platform) in the main plaza of the city. When the Sun rose over the first tower on the eastern horizon and set over the corresponding tower on the western horizon, it marked when the early crops should be planted in August. When the Sun rose between two towers built close together farther south, it marked the time of general sowing in September.

The Incas' nighttime calendar may have been developed to mark important ceremonies to the Moon and stars, which were sacred deities of the Incas. It had only 328 days, which equals 12 months of 27.33 days each. The latter almost corresponds to a lunar month, which is 29 days long.

There is an apparent problem with correlating the daytime calendar, based on the Sun, and the nighttime calendar, based on the Moon. The latter is 37 days shorter than the former. It is uncertain whether this correlation was important to the Incas.

Most pre-Inca groups had little need for standardized units of measurement and probably did not have them. It is likely that many conquered people observed the movements of the Sun, the Moon, and the stars and marked the passage of time by them, as the Incas did. Whether they had detailed calendars is unknown (Malpass, 95–99, 107–12).

To read about science in 19th-century Latin America, see the Latin America entry in the section "Science" in chapter 4 ("Intellectual Life") in volume 5 of this series.

FOR MORE INFORMATION

Malpass, M. A. *Daily Life in the Inca Empire*. Westport, Conn.: Greenwood, 1996.

Ziolkowski, M., and R. Sadowski. *Time and Calendars in the Inca Empire*. Oxford: British Arcaeological Reports, International Series 479, 1989.

Zuidema, R. T. *Inca Civilization in Cuzco*. Trans. Jean-Jacques Decoster. Austin: University of Texas Press, 1990.

———. "The Sidereal Lunar Calendar of the Incas." In *Archaeoastronomy in the New World*, ed. A. Aveni, 59–107. Cambridge: Cambridge University Press, 1982.

Literature

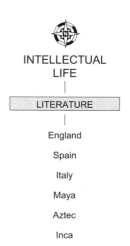

INTELLECTUAL
LIFE
|
LITERATURE
|
England

Spain

Italy

Maya

Aztec

Inca

Although separated by more than 5,000 miles of sea, the literature of medieval Europe and the 16th-century Native American empires shared a variety of similarities. Both Europeans and Mesoamericans entrusted important information to books in the form of manuscripts, and those manuscripts were copied laboriously by hand by succeeding generations to preserve and collect their society's knowledge. Both Europeans and Mesoamericans were interested in preserving especially religious, mythological, and historical material in these manuscripts: the vast majority of manuscripts on both continents was dedicated to religious subjects. While medieval Europe wrote about the saints that overcame the devil, the Maya wrote about the Hero Twins who overcame the death gods. In both Europe and the Americas, moreover, only a small percentage of the population could read, and a large number of stories and much information were passed down orally. Finally, in both cultures, ritual and drama, sometimes entrusted to manuscripts and sometimes passed on orally, played important parts in the cultural life of a community.

By the time of the Renaissance, however, European and Native American literature had begun to become significantly different in both audience and subject matter. The printing press, invented in the first half of the 1400s by Johann Gutenberg in Germany, caused many of the changes in European literature. For the first time, books were mass produced, rather than copied by hand with immense effort. The books thereby produced were also cheaper. As a result, more books were available to more people. At least as a partial result of the printing press, more people learned to read during the Renaissance than in the Middle Ages. The larger audience had diverse needs and interests, and the Renaissance printers responded by producing a larger variety of literature than had existed in the Middle Ages. First of all, the demand for literature in the vernacular languages, the languages the common people actually spoke, grew dramatically—most people with some education could read the phonetically spelled vernacular languages, but the ability to read Latin remained the privilege of scholars. The types of stories demanded also changed. While the medieval interest in religious literature continued into the Renaissance, the demand for tales of romance and adventure increased substantially. At the same time, political and religious agitators realized the potential of printed materials to reach large audiences, and treatises of all kinds poured forth from the presses.

The shift from the religious to the secular that took place in the Renaissance is one of the most important developments in the history of European literature. This shift can be easily seen in the dramatic arts. Before the Renaissance, most plays focused on religious events or taught moral themes and were staged during religious festivals. For example, the popular *Everyman* focused on the need to repent of evil deeds and to live a moral life, and Corpus Christi, a summertime festival celebrating the Body of Christ in the Eucharist, was usually celebrated with a pageant of religious dramas in England. These plays, such as *The Second Shepherd's Play*, focused on the birth of Christ or other biblical events. While the plays might be humorous and even slapstick, they also taught spiritual lessons.

By the time of Shakespeare in the 16th century, however, the subject matter had completely changed. A play like *Titus Andronicus* by Shakespeare, in which a pagan Roman father bloodily avenges the rape of his daughter, highlights how different drama had become. While such dramas sometimes convey a moral or speculate about the nature of human existence and the order of the cosmos, they do not present straightforward moral lessons like their medieval predecessors did. Other stories such as the *Morte d'Arthur* or the Italian *Orlando Furioso*, while set in a Christian world, are more interested in portraying the exploits of their knightly heroes in war and love than in increasing religious faith. While such stories, called romances, existed in the Middle Ages, their popularity increased tremendously in the Renaissance. Even the love song, a genre somewhat secular from the start, changed dramatically. Petrarch's love sonnets, written in the 14th century at the start of the Italian Renaissance, describe the poet's realization that only heavenly love, and not earthly love, is worth pursuing. Shakespeare's sonnets, written 200 years later, ignore heavenly love for the most part and describe the trials and tribulations involved in earthly love, of both the platonic and sexual kinds.

In addition to the shift to the secular, the Renaissance played an important role in establishing two important genres: the drama and the long narrative. Professional theater companies and permanent theaters first appeared during the 16th century. Before this time, plays were produced by amateur guilds only on special occasions or by traveling troupes of itinerant actors/entertainers. The growth of drama is probably due to the increasing urbanization of Renaissance Europe, which produced the critical mass of people and money necessary to support professional, permanent theaters. While theater commanded tremendous popularity, lengthy narratives were also starting to become popular. While works such as the Spanish *Don Quixote*, Italian *Orlando Innamorato*, and English *Faerie Queene* all developed out of the romance tradition that originated in the Middle Ages, they all were far longer than the average medieval romance and contained more twists and turns in their development. Their interest in a lengthy and cohesive narrative helped prepare the way for the eventual development, in the 18th century, of the novel.

Finally, as Marxist critics and others have proclaimed, all literature is political. Renaissance society was very aware of this fact, and authorities were keen to protect their positions by restricting the kind of literature allowed in their kingdoms. Most countries, both Protestant and Catholic, banned books that disagreed with the political and religious agenda of the current rulers. Banned books would be confiscated and destroyed, frequently by burning, if found. Spain was particularly vigorous in this activity. Since the Spanish burned many books by Spanish and other European authors, it is not surprising that they destroyed many of the Maya and Aztec codices that they found in Mesoamerica. Such destruction was a continuation of the policy that they practiced consistently in their homeland. Within this context, it is surprising that as many codices as we have today, describing the non-Christian mythology and religion of the Aztecs, survived. Clearly some of the Spanish priests, such as Bernardino de Sahagún, who collected encyclopedic records of Aztec culture and religion, were ahead of their time. The resiliency of the Native Americans themselves, however, takes most of the credit.

~Lawrence Morris

ENGLAND

Renaissance England witnessed the birth of a genuine entertainment industry, supported especially by the theater and by literature. In the Middle Ages and the early Renaissance, traveling troops of actors would travel the country, presenting plays in market squares or innyards. In 1576 London's first public theater was built—outside the city limits, to escape the stringent regulations imposed by hostile city authorities. This theater was not at first successful, but by the end of the 1580s such theaters had become a permanent fixture in London.

The early theaters resembled the innyards from which they had evolved. They were built around courtyards, with three-story galleries on three sides, facing a stage that projected out into the yard. People sat in the galleries, while the less privileged stood on the ground; a few ostentatious young gentlemen might sit on the stage itself. The plays were attended by all manner of people. Aristocrats were often to be found in the galleries, while standing room on the ground was certainly within the means of most people. General admission cost only a penny, the price of two quarts of beer—the price of going to the theater was analogous to going to the cinema today, although the low wages of working people meant they could not do it very often.

The plays had to be licensed, and authorities were always wary of the overcrowding, plague, and disorder associated with play-going. In fact, laws against vagrants were often used against actors and other performers, who lived wandering lives, unattached to any employer or household. In response, theatrical companies placed themselves under the patronage of the great noblemen of England, which allowed players to avoid punishment by becoming, technically, servants of the lord.

There was a constant and insatiable demand for plays, and actors became very popular figures—the first stars. The plays' action combined humor and violence along with musical interludes and dazzling special effects; in these respects they were very similar to modern popular films. Playwrights were typically university graduates, and their lives were often short and turbulent. Christopher Marlowe took Elizabethan audiences by storm. His *Tamburlaine the Great*, full of violence, ambition, and horror, was a true blockbuster. William Shakespeare began his theatrical career late in Queen Elizabeth's reign, in the late 1580s or early 1590s; Ben Jonson entered the scene later in the same decade.

William Shakespeare. Shakespeare was famous in his own day and is undoubtedly the most famous English author today, almost 400 years after his death. © Library of Congress.

In addition to the theaters in London, there were less formal settings for theatrical performances. The London companies occasionally brought their plays to the provinces, and there were plenty of minor performers, part-time folk players, puppeteers, acrobats, and other entertainers.

The other principal form of commercial public entertainment was literature. Elizabethan presses churned out all manner of texts: technical works, political and religious tracts (some of which were considered highly seditious by the authorities, who punished the authors severely if they were caught), ballads, almanacs, histories, and even news reports. These texts varied in format from lavish volumes richly illustrated with fine woodcuts or engravings—sometimes even colored by hand—down to cheap pamphlets and broadsides (single printed sheets) produced for the mass market and selling for just a penny. Reading was often a more public activity than it is today—people sometimes read out loud in groups.

Shakespeare is undoubtedly the most famous author from the Renaissance period. The son of a glove merchant from Stratford-on-Avon, Shakespeare became a literary sensation in his own time. Just like today, when popular music is pirated and sold in the streets of big cities months before its official release, unofficial copies of Shakespeare's plays were offered for sale long before the official versions. Some of these copies were produced by audience members who would write down the play as it went on before them—and they often made mistakes. Shakespeare himself wrote or helped to write 38 plays, covering all the main dramatic genres: comedy, history, tragedy, and romance. Comedies were stories that had happy endings, usually ending with a marriage of witty lovers. Tragedies were tales that had sad endings, and dealt with the fall of a noble personage, such as a king. The histories also dealt with kings, and usually with their demise: the main difference between Shakespearean history and tragedy was that history dealt with the kings of England while tragedy dealt with Roman or other ancient or legendary figures. The genre of romance contained stories of trials overcome to reunite families or to gain love; they were often set in magical lands. In addition to his plays, Shakespeare wrote a sonnet sequence, a series of short poems discussing love, eternity, and relationships. Some of the poems are addressed to a young male friend, while others are addressed to a brunette mistress; several of the poems have heavy sexual innuendo.

While Shakespeare may be the most famous now, Renaissance England produced many other skilled writers. At the start of the 15th century, the literature had much more in common with the preceding late medieval period than with the later Renaissance. Sir Thomas Malory's *Morte Darthur*, for example, described the adventures of the legendary knights of King Arthur's round table. The nature of literature changed dramatically, of course, when William Caxton brought the printing press to England around 1476. For the first time, books could be mass-produced and affordable to a much larger audience. The printing press allowed 16th-century authors to reach more people, and thus they became more popular than any of their predecessors.

In the mid-15th century, Sir Thomas Wyatt and Sir Philip Sidney both wrote famous sonnet sequences. Wyatt imported the 14-line sonnet and its themes of love and eternity from Italy, especially Petrarch, and Sidney further popularized the style in his *Astrophil and Stella*, which means "Star-lover and Star." Sidney also wrote an influential defense of creative literature entitled *The Defence of Poesy* (poesy simply meant creative literature or fiction during this time period), in which he argued that fiction was a better medium for expressing universal truths than either history or philosophy.

Edmund Spenser is best known today for his *The Faerie Queene*. This work resembles the old Arthurian tales insofar as it follows the adventures of various wandering knights. The book's main aim, however, is to satirize the perceived enemies of England, especially the Catholic Church, and to praise a militant Protestant ideal. Spenser also wrote the less strident *Amoretti* (love poems dedicated to his second wife), and *Epithalamion* (celebrating marriage). Shakespeare's main literary rival during his day was Christopher Marlowe. This popular playwright wrote many thrillers for the stage, one of the most famous being *Dr. Faustus*, which follows the demise of a scholar who sells his soul for knowledge and eventually despairs completely of salvation. The play was very controversial because it depicted devils on the stage. There were reports of actual devils appearing on stage and joining in the play!

Although Renaissance literature can be difficult for the modern student due to the differences in language, the literature is rich and well worth the effort (Singman, 150–51).

To read about literature in Chaucer's England, see the Europe entry in the section "Language and Literature" in chapter 4 ("Intellectual Life") in volume 2 of this series; for 18th-century England, see the England entry in the section "Language and Literature" in chapter 4 ("Intellectual Life") in volume 4 of this series; for Victorian England, see the Victorian England entry in the section "Literature" in chapter 4 ("Intellectual Life") in volume 5 of this series.

FOR MORE INFORMATION

Abrams, M. H., ed. *The Norton Anthology of English Literature*. New York: Norton, 2000.
Singman, J. L. *Daily Life in Elizabethan England*. Westport, Conn.: Greenwood, 1995.

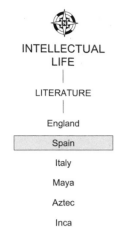

SPAIN

Literature in Spanish began to flourish, especially toward the end of the 16th century and into the 17th century, a period that is known as the *Siglo de Oro* (the Golden Age). Spain achieved this literary preeminence despite the vigorous workings of the Spanish Inquisition, which attempted to control the book trade to keep Spain free from heretical, blasphemous, or scandalous reading material. Although all countries, Catholic and Protestant, banned books and regulated the presses, Spain was more reactionary than most. Books that were allowed to be printed in France or Italy would often need to be smuggled into Spain.

The first ban on Lutheran books occurred in 1521, but by 1550 the Inquisition expanded to include all sorts of possibly heretical volumes, which included works by Protestants, heretics, or people condemned by the Inquisition, books in Hebrew or Arabic, unauthorized translations of the Bible, books on magic, and books showing disrespect to religion.

Some of the most well-known books were censored by the Inquisition. For example, the well-known *Lazarillo de Tormes,* written by an anonymous author, was banned. Lazarillo, a street urchin, lived by his wits and served many masters in his quest for survival. The miserly characteristics of a hypocritical clergyman portrayed in the book, and the unflattering remarks about an indulgence seller and about the pope, offended the church officials. Further editions of this highly popular picaresque (roguish) novel were prohibited. The book remained in demand, however, and pirated copies were plentiful. Philip II then ordered the novel purged of objectionable features since its sale was impossible to stop. The unreal world of heroes, chivalry, good deeds, saints, and miracles was the image the church and monarchy wished to convey, not the hunger, poverty, and struggle for survival of a good segment of the population.

The Inquisition also condemned the works of prominent churchmen if its suspicions were aroused. Luis de Granada's *Book of Prayer,* published in 1559, went through 23 editions before it was placed on the Index, the official list of banned books. Fray Luis appealed to the Council of Trent and the pope to have the ban lifted. Both approved the work, but the Inquisitors demanded and got corrections in the text before it was allowed to circulate freely. The duke of Gandía, Francisco Borja, a distinguished Jesuit, found his *Works of a Christian* on the Index. This threatened to bring disrepute to himself and the Society of Jesus. Fearing arrest, the future saint (canonized in 1671) fled to Rome and never returned to Spain. Even the *Spiritual Exercises* of Ignatius Loyola, founder of the Society of Jesus, which were used in manuscript form to train novices, were proscribed.

Despite this watchful concern, great works of literature were still produced. One of the most famous, *Don Quixote de la Mancha* by Miguel de Cervantes Saavedra, follows the adventures of a country gentlemen who has read too many romantic tales of adventure and sets out with his greedy page Sancho Panza in search of his own adventures. The foolish idealism of Don Quixote and the grasping nature of Sancho Panza in their journey through Spanish society provide a humorous and sometimes biting commentary on 16th-century Spain.

While Cervantes produced one of the most influential books in the history of the novel, Lope de Vega Cario was winning fame for himself as a prolific and skilled playwright. Lope produced plays in a wide variety of genres, including comedies, swashbuckling adventures, and religious plays. Many of Lope's dramas investigated the nature of honor, love, human nature, and tension between peasants and noblemen. Lope also wrote a treatise on play-writing, *Arte nuevo de hacer comedias*, in which he described some of his techniques. In general, Lope kept his plays short, written in a simple style, and with a surprise ending.

The lives of the Golden Age writers are almost as interesting as their literary works: some of them suffered great hardship while others seemed to lead carefree lives. Cervantes certainly had his share of suffering. He was born into a large family in Alcalá de Henares on September 29, 1547. His father was a barber-surgeon of little means. In 1568, when Cervantes was a student, a number of his poems appeared in a volume published in Madrid to commemorate the death of Queen Isabel de Valois, wife of Philip II.

To become a successful dramatist, his ambition, Cervantes needed to find a patron in Madrid, but the city teemed with other young men seeking sponsors. Restless and frustrated in his literary pretensions, he opted for one of three alternative paths open to youths with few ties and poor prospects: the king's service, emigration to the New World, or a career in the church. He chose the king's service and enlisted in the army. He was sent to Italy and in 1571 was engaged in the naval battle of Lepanto.

Back in Madrid at the age of 33, Cervantes turned out poems and plays at a prodigious rate between 1582 and 1585. But, still without a benefactor, he was always short of money and in search of employment. Some of his plays were accepted for the theater, but they fared poorly. At any rate, the paltry income from stage plays did not pay the bills.

With a crippled hand as a result of the war, options were limited. Through a petition to the king Cervantes secured a job as a messenger delivering dispatches and later took a post in Seville as commissary to the Armada, which was undergoing provisioning for the grand enterprise that, it was thought, would reduce England to the status of a Spanish province. Cervantes spent his time on the dusty dirt tracks of Castile, requisitioning supplies for the ships from the country towns and farms.

After the failure of the Armada, Cervantes continued with his job for the Council of War, collecting supplies for the Spanish forces in North Africa and Italy. Tired of the unrewarding and difficult work and with no pay coming his way, he tried to find employment in America for the government but was rejected. He gave up the unpleasant work after seven years and returned to Madrid.

Still impoverished, he landed a government job as a collector of overdue tax debts in Andalucía. With much of it collected, but reluctant to travel the dangerous road back to Madrid with so much money in his pocket, he turned the cash over to a merchant friend in Seville in exchange for a money order, to be cashed on his return to the capital. When time came in Madrid to cash the money order, the money was not there. The merchant had gone bankrupt and absconded, whereabouts unknown; but Cervantes was responsible to the royal treasury for the money. Cash raised from the departed merchant's estate by order of Philip II appeared 18 months later, and the royal treasury was satisfied, but the money that Cervantes's sister Magdalena had borrowed to pay some of her brother's debt to the royal treasury before the merchant's estate was settled was never returned by the government, nor was Cervantes's salary for his tax-collecting work ever paid to him. He gave up the ruinous job and joined the ranks of the unemployed.

Returning to Seville Cervantes continued to write, but in 1597 he received notice from the royal treasury that he was being held responsible for the taxes due in 1594 in Andalucía. There he had been able to collect only about half of the amount owed in back taxes, and the government now wanted the rest out of his own pocket. A subpoena was issued compelling him to go to Madrid with the money. He could not raise it, and a high court judge in Seville had him arrested and sent to the royal prison to languish for seven months in the filthy cells. Here, it is thought, he began to write *Don Quixote*, which soon became a best-seller. Spain's most celebrated writer died on April 23, 1616, the same day of the same year as William Shakespeare.

Lope de Vega Caprio, in contrast, seemed to have had a carefree life. The prolific author conducted a large number of illicit and adulterous affairs and had children with a number of different women. Lope even lived with a mistress after he became a priest in 1614. Such events show that many men entered the priesthood, not out of piety or religious vocation, but for the sake of a regular paycheck and for the chance to sell their religious services to the wealthy. Lope, nevertheless, would go on to be honored by Pope Urban VIII with the title of doctor of theology, mostly due to Lope's success in poetry. By contrast, Calderón de la Barca, who wrote in the 17th century, gave up writing the swashbuckling romances and wrote exclusively pious religious works after his ordination in 1651, after which time he lived a solitary and contemplative life (Anderson, 197–204).

FOR MORE INFORMATION

Anderson, J. M. *Daily Life during the Spanish Inquisition*. Westport, Conn.: Greenwood, 2002.
Díaz-Plaja, G. A *History of Spanish Literature*. Ed. Hugh Harter. New York: New York University Press, 1971.
Vega, L. de. *Four Plays*. Trans. J. G. Underhill. Westport, Conn.: Hyperion, 1978.

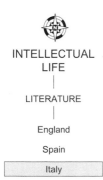

INTELLECTUAL
LIFE
|
LITERATURE
|
England

Spain

Italy

Maya

Aztec

Inca

ITALY

During the Renaissance, educated men studied a wide range of arts and sciences. The modern term *Renaissance man*, used to describe a well-rounded individual, derives from this tendency. Leon Battista Alberti, for example, was a skilled architect, painter, and author, while the famous Michelangelo sculpted, painted, and wrote poetry. When examining literature, then, we must remember that it did not exist in a vacuum.

Petrarch, or Francesco Petrarca, as he is known in Italian, is often credited with being the first major figure of the Renaissance, even though he lived in the 14th century. The term Renaissance itself means rebirth and refers to the rebirth of classical learning and literature that occurred at that time. Petrarch, along with Giovanni Boccaccio, was one of the first people since the fall of Rome to advocate studying classical Roman literature. Petrarch himself was a serious scholar and produced many books in Latin based on his study of the ancient literature, including philosophical treatises, biographies, and histories.

Petrarch's greatest fame today comes from his compositions in Italian, especially his *Canzoniere*. The *Canzoniere* uses a series of sonnets and other poems to describe the poet's relationship with the mysterious Laura, with whom he falls in love at first sight across a crowded room on Good Friday. During the course of the *Canzoniere*, the poet learns that earthly love is futile and that only heavenly love is worth pursuing. Although the *Canzoniere* was in a well-known style of Italian poetry called *dolce stil nuovo* (new sweet style), it had a tremendous impact on European poetry— it is a direct ancestor, for example, of the Shakespearean sonnet. As a result of such poetic and scholarly endeavors, Petrarch was crowned poet laureate of Italy in 1347.

In the 15th century, the prince-dictators of the Italian city-states actively supported the arts. One of the most famous, Lorenzo de' Medici was himself a capable poet, with an interest in nature. Artists flourished in such a climate, and some of the most notable include Angelo Poliziano and Matteo Boiardo. Poliziano wrote well-crafted lyrical poems, including the first major Italian drama, *Orfeo*, based upon the figure from classical mythology, Orpheus, who was able to tame animals with song. Boiardo, on the other hand, wrote *Orlando innamorato (Roland in Love)*, which describes the adventures of the love-sick warrior Roland in his quest to gain the hand of the beautiful Angelica. *Orlando innamorato* celebrated love, loyalty, and military exploits.

In the 16th century, Italian, as opposed to Latin, came into its own as an accepted literary language. Pietro Bembo, an influential intellectual in the first half of the 16th century, helped greatly to achieve this. In his *Le prose della vulgar lingua (The Prose of the Popular Tongue)*, he established Boccaccio's writings as the standard model for Italian prose.

The largest figures in the 16th century, however, were Machiavelli and Ariosto. Niccolò Machiavelli produced a variety of literary works, including poems, plays, histories, and treatises on war. His most famous and innovative work, however, is *Il principe (The Prince)*. In this work, which was part of a larger commentary on Livy's *History of Rome*, Machiavelli argued that the ruler should take any means necessary to ensure the preservation of his own state. In his recommendations, Machiavelli took into account only the effectiveness, and not the ethics, of any action. As a result, Machiavelli could advocate severe injustice and persecution for a short time if such actions made the state more stable. Such ideas were in direct contrast with other philosophies of statecraft, which were more concerned with the ruler's obligations to God.

Lodovico Ariosto's masterpiece was *Orlando furioso (The Mad Roland)*. In this continuation of Boiardo's *Orlando innamorato*, Ariosto focused on the wars between Charlemagne, under whom the hero Roland served, and the Muslim Saracens who had occupied Spain and were threatening to expand and capture all of Europe. The book is full of adventure, heroism, and romance, lightened with doses of tongue-in-cheek humor.

One of the most influential books throughout Europe during the European Renaissance period was *Il cortegiano (The Courtier)*, written in 1528 by Baldasar Castiglione. In this handbook, Castiglione described the behavior proper to a true gentleman. The book was widely read both on the European continent and in England.

The second half of the 16th century tended to be more serious than the first half, in part due to the religious and political disputes that were raging throughout Europe. Displeasing the local secular or religious authority could result in jail or execution. Toquato Tasso, however, produced one of the epic masterpieces of Italian literature: *Gerusalemme liberata (Jerusalem Delivered)*. This work follows the First Crusade and its quest to regain Jerusalem from Muslim control.

~*Lawrence Morris*

FOR MORE INFORMATION

Brand, P., and L. Pertile, eds. *The Cambridge History of Italian Literature*. Rev. ed. Cambridge: Cambridge University Press, 1999.
italy1.com. <http://italy1.com/literature/>

INTELLECTUAL
LIFE
|
LITERATURE
|
England

Spain

Italy

Maya

Aztec

Inca

MAYA

Many Mayan writings were destroyed by the Spaniards during their conquest because the Maya alphabet and pictures were considered to be pagan. Other writings decayed in the damp conditions of the Maya homeland. Most surviving records in Maya script are carved or painted on durable surfaces such as stone or pottery. But these are generally brief abstracts; the ancient Maya wrote much more detailed records on perishable materials, such as paper made from the soft inner bark of the amate tree (a tropical fig tree). Most important records were kept in books (or codices) like those destroyed by the Spaniards. These were long sheets of bark paper folded like a screen. Both sides of each page were coated with a smooth white surface made of fine lime plaster. Columns of texts were painted on the surfaces in black and red inks with a fine brush. The text was often illustrated with painted pictures. Not many of these codices survived. Three major pre-Columbian codices were saved, however, because they were sent back to Europe as mementos: the Dresden, Madrid, and Paris codices. A fourth major codex, the Grolier Codex, is named after the New York club where it was first publicly displayed. Many other codices, however, were copied from Maya glyphs into Spanish characters by Maya scribes soon after the conquest and have been preserved. Much valuable information, especially concerning religion, science, and history, comes from these codices. One of the most important codices is the *Popol Vuh*.

The *Popol Vuh*, the sacred book of the highland Quiche Maya, is the most complete and beautifully written record of Maya myth and history. It relates that there had been multiple creations before the present world and that the people of the present world were created out of maize. The central drama in the creation myth of the *Popol Vuh* is the saga of the first humans, the Maya Hero Twins. Their names in Quiche Mayan are Hunapu and Xbalanque (or Hun Ahau and Yax Balam in Yucatec). These names have contrasting associations, recalling both the Sun and Venus, and life and death. Hunapu (First Lord) is associated with Venus and celestial life. Xbalanque (Sacred Jaguar) is associated with the jaguar sun and death in the underworld.

The father of the Hero Twins was also a twin. He and his brother were ball players who had played ball in Xibalba and then were sacrificed by the gods of death. The brother was buried under the Xibalba ball court; the father was decapitated and his head hung in a calabash tree. From the tree his head impregnated one of the daughters of the death gods by spitting into her hand. Fleeing this angry death god, the pregnant girl came to the earthly realm. There she gave birth to the Hero Twins, who grew up and discovered their father's old ball game equipment. Realizing their heritage, they followed their father and uncle by becoming such famous ball players that they too were invited to play ball in Xibalba with the lords of the underworld.

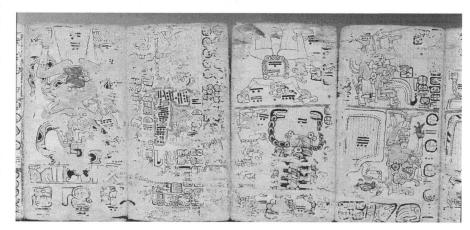

Manuscript Page. This page from the *Madrid Codex* is illustrated with pictures of gods. Few codices survive in the original Maya glyphs because the Spanish authorities viewed them as pagan artifacts and destroyed most of them. © The Art Archive/American Museum Madrid/Album/Joseph Martin.

In Xibalba the gods of death subjected the Hero Twins to a series of daily ball games and nightly trials, but they outwitted the death gods each time. However, the only way they could escape Xibalba was by jumping into a pit of fire. After the death gods ground up their bones and threw them into a river, the Hero Twins were reborn and returned to Xibalba seeking revenge. They succeeded by showing the death gods an amazing feat. One twin decapitated the other, then brought him back to life. The death gods were so amazed by this that they demanded the Hero Twins perform the trick on them. This is what the Hero Twins were waiting for, so they decapitated the gods of death but of course did not bring them back to life. Following their victory over death, the Hero Twins escaped from Xibalba and were transformed in the sky as the Sun and Venus, destined to reenact their descent into Xibalba and their escape and rebirth forevermore.

The central themes of the Maya creation myth were replicated in religious rituals and the lives of individuals. The account of the Hero Twins entering Xibalba, outwitting the gods of death, and returning to life was a metaphor for the Sun, the greatest power in the universe. It also showed that rebirth came through sacrifice. The rebirth of the Hero Twins after being sacrificed is a metaphor for human rebirth after death, a theme celebrated by the Maya ritual of human sacrifice. The ball court was the setting for the confrontation between the Hero Twins from this world and the death gods of Xibalba. In many Maya cities, the ball court symbolized the threshold between the earthly realm and Xibalba. The ritualized ball game played in this arena reenacted the original confrontation between the Hero Twins and the death gods. Maya kings had the closest associations with the Hero Twins. Kings had the power to enter Xibalba and confront the death gods, play the sacred ball game, and perform human sacrifice. When a Maya king was captured in a war, he was taken to the ball court to be defeated and sacrificed by decapitation. Thus he was sent to Xibalba to be born again in the sky in a ritual that reenacted the myth of the Hero Twins.

Dualistic symbolism is an important feature of Maya creation myth. Two sets of twins struggled with the lords of death. The struggle was between the forces of good (life) and evil (death). The Maya conceived of their world as an eternal replication of these two forces in conflict. For example, benevolent forces bring rain to make the fields grow to ensure that the people will have food. But evil forces cause drought, hurricanes, and plagues, which can destroy the crops and bring famine and death. Other dualistic themes reflected male-female and day-night contrasts. In fact, Maya deities had many contrasting sets of attributes (Sharer, 157–58, 179–82).

FOR MORE INFORMATION

Marcus, J. *Mesoamerican Writing Systems: Propaganda, Myth, and History in Four Ancient Civilizations*. Princeton: Princeton University Press, 1992.
Sharer, R. J. *Daily Life in Maya Civilization*. Westport, Conn.: Greenwood, 1996.
Tedlock, D. *Popol Vuh: The Mayan Book of the Dawn of Life*. New York: Simon and Schuster, 1985.

INTELLECTUAL
LIFE
|
LITERATURE
|
England

Spain

Italy

Maya

Aztec

Inca

AZTEC

Catholic churchmen played a large role both in destroying and in preserving Aztec literature. In 1535 the first Spanish bishop (and later, archbishop) of Mexico, Juan de Zumárraga, ordered the confiscation and collection of the pictorial manuscripts belonging to the Nahua cultural capital, Tezcoco. Zumárraga and other priests had long known that these painted histories, cosmologies, and calendars on animal skins and bark surfaces contained the vital indigenous worldviews and ritual formulas for the daily life of the native peoples. The screenfolds had become the target of intense suspicion, and Zumárraga, according to some reports, had hundreds of them collected in the marketplace of the town and burned them to ashes. It is sad to know that, of the hundreds of pictorial manuscripts extant in Mexico in 1521 carrying knowledge and symbols of traditions reaching back more than two thousand years, only 16 remain today. These pictorials, or storybooks, used a picture-writing system that served to communicate literal and metaphoric messages about all aspects of life. When these books were destroyed, the time-honored legacies of education and knowledge concerning medicine, astronomy, history, nature, and the cosmos were seriously damaged. One surviving passage describes the wisdom and educational importance of these manuscripts: "The wise man: a light, a torch, a stout torch that does not smoke. A perforated mirror, a mirror pierced on both sides. His are the red and black ink, his are the illustrated manuscripts, he studies the illustrated manuscripts." The phrase "the red and black ink" refers to the images painted on the illustrated books of bark paper or animal skins, which were folded like an accordion. Some images, for example, animals, plants, mountains, dances, battles, or sacrifices, were pictographs because they represented those persons, places, and things themselves. Other images were ideographs, or symbols of objects that stood for ideas associated with the image. For instance, in the first case, an image of a flower represented a flower, but as an ideograph, a flower could mean a poem or sacrificial blood, depending on the context. The image of a bundle of reeds likely signified a bundle of reeds as a pictograph, but a tied bundle of reeds appearing as an ideograph could refer to a 52-year cycle in the Aztec calendar.

While only a few of the surviving pictorial storybooks come from Aztec communities, many of the other manuscripts share the same symbol system with the Aztecs and can be used to study domestic life, the education of teenagers, courtship rules, time reckoning, the gods, genealogies, and other crucial aspects of life. And we are very fortunate that native peoples continued to produce these manuscripts after the conquest. Among the most relevant pictorials for the study of Aztec life are the *Codex Fejérváry-Mayer* (painted sometime before the Spanish Conquest), the *Codex Borbonicus* (painted about the same time as the Spanish Conquest), and the *Codex Mendoza* (painted a few years after the conquest). The first two are remarkable for their calendrical and ritual information, while the *Mendoza* gives us rich historical information about Mexica warfare, kingship, economics, and the life cycle of the people. Also, picture-writing in the native style appears on many surviving archaeological objects and structures, so that comparisons and contrasts can be made between the images carved in stone and those painted on screenfolds.

Throughout the 16th century, the descendants of the Aztecs, as well as Europeans and mestizos (people with both European and Native American parents), produced accounts written in Nahuatl (the native language spoken by many of the Indians of Central Mexico), Spanish, and even French about the cosmovision and ceremonial centers of the various Aztec communities. Among these important documents are the *Leyenda de los Soles* (Legend of the Suns), the *Anales de Cuauhtitlan* (Annals of Cuauhtitlan), and the *Histoyre du Mechique* (History of the Mexica). One of the greatest surprises and tools for learning is the 12-volume *Florentine Codex*, produced during the middle of the 16th century by a Spanish priest named Bernardino de Sahagún and his Aztec students. This document was modeled on time-honored European encyclopedias that organized knowledge in terms of (1) the gods and theology, (2) humans and society, and (3) the natural world.

Sahagún was a Franciscan priest who came to Mexico City in 1529 to participate in the great Spanish Catholic project of the evangelization and spiritual conversion of the natives. He was a very learned man with special abilities in language, and he planned to (1) learn as much as possible about the Indian religions, (2) create a Nahuatl vocabulary to assist in the effective preaching of the Holy Gospel, and

(3) create a documentary record of native culture so that it could be understood and transformed. How did he go about his work?

In 1536 the Spanish Crown, through the office, in part, of the book-burning Juan de Zumárraga, set up the Imperial College of the Holy Cross of Tlatelolco (Colegio Imperial de Santa Cruz de Tlatelolco), to be directed by a select group of Franciscan friars. This college, similar to the earlier *calmecac* (the most rigorous of the various pre-Hispanic Aztec schools), was designed to train native boys in the new educational traditions brought from Spain. Sahagún was one of the teachers and described some of its characteristics:

After we came to this land to implant the Faith, we assembled the boys in our houses, as is said. And we began to teach them to read, write, and sing. And, as they did well in all this, we then endeavored to put them to the study of grammar. For this training a college was formed in the city of Mexico, in the Santiago Tlatelolco section, in which were selected from all the neighboring villages and from all the provinces the most capable boys, best able to read and write. They slept and ate at the same college.

When the school first opened, other priests derided the Franciscans at Tlatelolco, claiming that the Indians would not be able to learn grammar and Latin and the other subjects taught at the school. But those who mocked them were soon proved wrong, as Sahagún reported that after a few years the Aztec teenagers "came to understand all the subjects of the grammar book and to speak Latin . . . and to write Latin, and even to compose hexametric verses." In spite of continued controversy, for some priests now objected that the Indians were learning too well and would discover in the Bible that the patriarchs had many wives (like some of the Aztecs) and would also discover in other books that the Spaniards had been conquered in the past, the school remained open and began to attract native *tlacuiloque*, or painters and scribes, who became important to the encyclopedia that was eventually produced.

Sahagún's teachings, along with those of the other priests, focused the native students on the trivium (grammar, rhetoric, and logic) and the quadrivium (arithmetic, geometry, astronomy, and music), along with Christian moral principles and the study of the Holy Scriptures. Painting and medical matters were also included, and the result was a select group of students whom Sahagún called trilingual because they spoke and read Nahuatl, Castilian, and Latin. These students and others who came to work with him helped Sahagún do important research on many aspects of Aztec life prior to and after the conquest. Sahagún organized a questionnaire and set up long-term interview sessions with groups of elders to learn about their gods, mythology, history, kings, medicine, astronomy, plants and animals, rhetoric, and omens, and even their experience of the conquest. It is important to emphasize that these elders, who talked with Sahagún 20, 30, or even 40 years after the arrival of the Spaniards, often used the surviving pictorial books we discussed earlier. Sahagún wrote about the elders: "They gave me all the matters we discussed in pictures, for that was the writing they employed in ancient times. And the grammarians [his trilingual students who listened to the elders' readings of the painted books] explained them in their language, writing the explanation at the bottom of the painting."

Sahagún may not have known that this oral recitation was exactly the way the Aztecs had taught their own children prior to the coming of Europeans. We know from surviving traditions that native youths were instructed by preceptors who used large and beautiful books with pictures and symbols in them. The key method of transmitting knowledge during the pre-Hispanic period, however, was the oral description or recitation of the knowledge on the pages.

Sahagún used this method—interviewing elders who recited or interpreted pictorial manuscripts to the trilingual students, who then wrote down their explanations—to develop the chapters that finally went into the *Florentine Codex*, which provides us with extraordinary insights into the daily life of Tenochtitlan and its citizens. One of the most extensive sections of the 12 volumes is Book VI, entitled *Rhetoric and Moral Philosophy*. We find page after page of eloquent speeches for different events and transitions in the life cycle of the community. Of particular importance are passages about the correct education of children and teenagers. Another priest noted, for instance, that "no people loved their children more" than the Aztecs. Consider this passage from one of the *huehuetlatolli* (ancient sayings) collected by Sahagún in which a ruler is speaking to his daughter when she reaches puberty: "Here you are, my little girl, my necklace of precious stones, my plumage, my human creation, born of me. You are my blood, my color, my image. . . . Listen, much do I want you to understand that you are noble. See that you are very precious, even while you are still only a little lady. You are a precious stone, you are a turquoise." A number of other important books produced under the guidance of or by Catholic priests, in spite of their goal of stamping out Aztec beliefs and ideas, can teach us a good deal about the ways these people thought and acted toward one another, nature, and their gods (Carrasco, 14–19).

FOR MORE INFORMATION

Carrasco, D., with S. Sessions. *Daily Life of the Aztecs: People of the Sun and Earth*. Westport, Conn.: Greenwood, 1998.

Sahagún, B. de. *Florentine Codex: General History of the Things of New Spain*. Ed. and trans. Arthur Anderson and Charles Dibble. 13 vols. Santa Fe: School of American Research and University of Utah, 1950–82.

INCA

All Inca literature was, of course, oral, since the Inca did not use a writing system. Inca literature consisted of stories, songs, and performance pieces that were passed down verbally and thus were subject to change and personal interpretation. There were at least four kinds of literature: prayers and hymns, dramatic pieces, narrative poems, and songs. Prayers and hymns gave elegant praise of the Inca deities, very

INTELLECTUAL
LIFE

LITERATURE

England

Spain

Italy

Maya

Aztec

Inca

similar to the hymns of the Old Testament. Only two examples of dramatic pieces survive, and these are poor translations.

The majority of Inca literature consisted of narrative poems dealing with religion, mythology, and history. Many of these myths were passed down as narrative poems. These stories were meant to be memorized and repeated at public gatherings. Dramatic pieces were presented as part of public dances, by one or two actors answered by a chorus. Myths and dramatic pieces probably emphasized religious themes.

Songs and poetry (indivisible in Andean terms, because most songs are but poems put to music) apparently are the least changed of all literary pieces. The subject most often is love—especially lost love—with many references to nature. One of the oldest is a poem remembered by Garcilaso, a 17th-century Inca, from his childhood:

In this place
Thou shalt sleep
Midnight
I will come

More would probably be known of Inca literature if the Spanish priests and officials had not so actively tried to stamp it out as reflecting pagan beliefs and customs. This is probably why poems are the least changed: they were the most likely to be passed on at the household level, and to be the least religious in nature (Malpass, 88–89).

FOR MORE INFORMATION

Garcilaso de la Vega, El Inga. *Royal Commentaries of the Incas and General History of Peru.* Pts. 1 and 2. Trans. H. Livermore. 1609. Reprint, Austin: University of Texas Press, 1966.

Malpass, M. A. *Daily Life in the Inca Empire.* Westport, Conn.: Greenwood, 1996.

Rowe, J. "Inca Culture at the Time of the Spanish Conquest." In *The Andean Civilizations.* Vol. 2 of *Handbook of South American Indians,* ed. Julian Steward. Washington, D.C.: Bureau of American Ethnology Bulletin 143, 1946.

INTELLECTUAL LIFE: WEB SITES

http://www.ai.mit.edu/people/montalvo/Hotlist/aztec.html
http://www.angelfire.com/ca/humanorigins/writing.html
http://www.history.ucla.edu/terraciano/images/PAGE2/pictures/codex_beker.htm
http://www.michielb.nl/maya/astro.html
http://www.history.hanover.edu/courses/350lit.html

5

MATERIAL LIFE

Material life describes all the things we use, from the houses that give us shelter to the food that sustains us, the clothes that protect us, and the items that amuse us. It also includes the luxury items that set us apart from others less fortunate than we. Studying material life is fascinating in its details: we learn that handkerchiefs were a luxury in 16th-century Europe designed to set the wealthy apart from the peasant who used a hat or sleeve, or that underwear was only widely adopted in Europe in the 18th century.

Aside from the delicious details that bring the past to life, the study of material life reveals much about society as a whole. For example, cultures that rely on rice as a major staple have to invest a great deal of labor into its cultivation, whereas societies that thrive on maize (corn), which is not labor-intensive, have ample spare time. People who had access to raw materials, such as iron ore, developed in ways different from those that did not and groups that had domesticated animals or large plows had different organizing principles from others. If we know what a culture uses, we know a great deal about those people's lives.

As we study material life, it is important to remember that humans want much more than the bare necessities of life. Indeed, we are creatures of desire rather than need, and this longing has fueled much of the progress in the world. We want spices to flavor our food, not just nourishment; we want gold to adorn us as much as we want clothing to cover us. Cultures, such as the Western culture, that have acquired a taste for change in fashion transform themselves in all areas much more rapidly than those, such as in Asia, who prefer a more conservative approach to clothing. All in all, the details of our daily life matter. From the Stone Age when humans adorned themselves with cowrie shells as they wielded stone tools to the modern world shaped by high technology, humans are defined by the things they use. Our material life reveals and shapes who we are.

The following sections examine in depth the food, clothing, and housing that defined the material life of the 15th and 16th centuries. This period saw particularly dramatic changes in the diet of both Europeans and Native Americans. Many of the most basic foods today were only found in the Americas prior to Columbus's trip, for example, potatoes, tomatoes, turkey, squash, and cranberries. While it took some

MATERIAL LIFE
|
CLOTHING & PERSONAL
APPEARANCE

FOOD & DRINK

HOUSES
& FURNITURE

time for these foods to catch on in Europe, some new imports were instant hits, especially cocoa and *bucara*, a kind of chewing gum. The Europeans in return introduced animals such as horses and chickens to the Americas.

The different cultures investigated here all had different kinds of clothing and housing. Nevertheless, all the cultures used clothing and housing to mark off social status. The wealthy generally lived in larger, more lavishly decorated homes, while the poor made do with one-room cottages or huts. Similarly, fashion and sumptuous dress could easily separate a noblewoman from a peasant. Clothing could also indicate a special status, such as that of priest or shaman. When examining the various aspects of material life, then, we should always keep in mind *why* people used what they did and not just *what* they used.

~*Joyce E. Salisbury and Lawrence Morris*

FOR MORE INFORMATION

Braudel, F. *The Structures of Everyday Life*. New York: Harper and Row, 1979.
Diamond, J. *Guns, Germs, and Steel*. New York: Norton, 1997.

MATERIAL LIFE
|
CLOTHING & PERSONAL
APPEARANCE
|
England

Spain

Italy

Maya

Aztec

Inca

Clothing and Personal Appearance

One of the prime purposes of clothing is to provide warmth. Anyone who has lived through a Boston winter or an English summer knows the value of a good sweater, indoors and out. While clothes are necessary to European climates due to the cold, the Maya, living in warm Mesoamerica, certainly did not need to worry about staying warm, yet they still used clothes. Clothes must therefore do more than just protect the wearer from the elements. Indeed, in most cultures, clothes are used to mark gender, rank, social status, and modesty, in addition to providing warmth and protection.

In all the cultures examined here, there were strong divisions between the sexes. Men and women had different occupations, roles, expectations, and rights within their societies. Clothing served as another way of marking the difference between the sexes. The differences in style were at least partly connected with the roles of women in their society. In most of the cultures discussed here, in both Europe and the Americas, the men wore garments, such as short trousers or loincloths, that left their legs unencumbered, while women wore garments, such as skirts and gowns, that tended to encumber their legs. The amount of motion restricted by such fashion could vary widely. Inca women, with their loose skirts, and English peasant women, with free-flowing kirtles, could easily help with planting and the harvest, though it would be somewhat harder for them to run than it would be for a man in a loincloth or in trunk hose. On the more extreme side, fashionable noblewomen in 16th-century Europe wore farthingales, hoops that widened out the skirts to sometimes as much as three times the woman's shoulder breadth, that could make even simple tasks, such as sitting down, difficult and certainly rendered strenuous activity almost impossible. In all of these situations, women's clothing restricted their vigorous movement, sometimes to a small degree, sometimes to a greater degree, while the men's clothes were much less encumbering. The implications are clear: women were not expected to be involved in vigorous activity while men were.

Clothing also revealed the social or economic status of the wearer. Noble and wealthier individuals could afford a level of ornamentation that was unattainable by less well-off families. Thus, in Europe, the upper classes would wear farthingales or the latest styles of trunk hose, while the peasants would wear free-flowing kirtles or canvas knee-length trousers. Not only were the wealthy able to afford the latest styles, but they could also afford more changes of clothes. While fashionable ladies might have many different dresses and gowns, the poorer people would make do with a few changes of clothes, which would be patched and resewn as needed to get as much use out of them as possible. Patching clothes was so important that the rag industry, which supplied the material for patches, was an important source of employment for many wandering salesmen. In South America and Mesoamerica, nobility was marked more by ornament than by clothing *per se*. For example, amongst the Inca, only noblemen were allowed to wear large earplugs, while the Maya kings wore special elaborate headdresses that set them off from others. Clothing as a marker of status was so important that it was often regulated by legislation. These laws, called sumptuary laws, were common in medieval Europe and prescribed the kind of clothes and wealth of ornament that each class could wear. Such formal prescriptions and prohibitions most likely also existed among the Native Americans. With regard to Europe, however, such formal legislation had mostly disappeared, and wealth, for example, the ability to purchase, along with other factors such as peer pressure, became the major means of determining who could wear what.

Clothing can also be used to reflect other kinds of rank besides socioeconomic status. As with modern military uniforms, for example, costume in the 15th and 16th centuries could be used to reflect military prowess and authority. The Aztecs developed a particularly rich system of military costume in which particular outfits were linked with having captured a particular number of captives in combat. A warrior that had captured one enemy was given a shield, a special oak club decked with obsidian blades, and special capes. A warrior that had captured two warriors was granted the right to wear sandals rather than bare feet into battle, and to wear a conical cap. The warrior who had made four captures became the feared jaguar warrior: he wore the skin of the ocelot in such a way that his head appeared between the jaws of the animal's skin. More experienced warriors wore even more sumptuous decoration with rich combinations of feather ornament.

One final purpose of clothing is modesty. In the warm-weather conditions of Mesoamerica, the loincloth universally worn by men did not provide warmth or even necessary protection—its main purpose seems to have been modesty. Most cultures around the world have a taboo that prohibits public nudity, though what counts as scandalous nudity differs from culture to culture. In 15th- and 16th-century

Spain and Italy, modesty demanded that a woman outdoors be covered almost completely from head to toe, a fashion similar to that seen in some Muslim countries today. While such fashions can seem restrictive to modern Westerners, it is interesting to note that the Spanish king Philip II banned such garments, not because they hampered women, but rather because it was believed that the garments allowed too much room for licentiousness; anyone could theoretically put on the long dark mantilla (shawl) and slip away unnoticed into the crowd. The mantilla could thus be a form of intense privacy. In contrast, English fashion in the 16th century allowed some unmarried women to wear dresses that exposed their bosom entirely. In this practice, the English women would have been joined by many of their Mesoamerican and South American counterparts, a practice which the Spanish authorities found abhorrent, however.

~Lawrence Morris

MATERIAL LIFE

CLOTHING & PERSONAL
APPEARANCE

England

Spain

Italy

Maya

Aztec

Inca

ENGLAND

English clothing may look hot and constrictive by today's standards, but it should be remembered that the Renaissance found England in a period of particularly cold weather known today as the Little Ice Age. English dress began with the shirt, which was an undergarment, usually made from linen. On men, the shirt reached to the thigh, while for women, the shirt, called a smock, came to below the knee.

Over the shirt, women might wear any of three general styles of attire, sometimes in combination with each other. The first was the kirtle, the second was a bodice and petticoat (skirt), and the third was a gown.

The kirtle was a long-fitted garment reaching down to the feet, resembling a long-fitted dress without any seam at the waist. It was a fairly simple style, closely related to medieval garments, and was not generally worn by itself among fashionable women, although it might be worn under another garment.

The bodice, or pair of bodies, was a close-fitting garment for the upper body, normally made of wool. It kept the torso warm and was stiffened to mold the body into the fashionable shape. This shape was rather severe and masculine: flat, broad in the shoulders, and narrow in the waist. In effect, the bodice combined the functions of bra, girdle, and vest all in one. Its waistline was pointed in front. The neckline reflected the trends of fashion: it was low toward the beginning and end of Queen Elizabeth's reign, high during the middle years. A low bodice might be worn with a high-neckline smock; the décolleté look was normal only with young unmarried women and in some fashionable circles.

The degree of stiffening in the bodice depended on the wearer's station in life. Upper-class women wore stiffly boned bodices, but ordinary women needed more freedom of movement to perform everyday tasks (such as churning butter, baking bread, or chasing children), so their garments had to be less constricting. Stiffening might be provided by baleen (whale bone), bundles of dried reeds, willowy wood, or even steel. A less fashionable bodice might be shaped with just a heavy fabric interlining. For extra stiffening in front, a rigid piece of wood, bone, or ivory, called a busk, might be inserted and held in place by a ribbon at the top; to this day women's undergarments often have a small ribbon bow just in the midpoint of the chest, the last trace of the busk.

Where the bodice served to flatten and narrow the upper body, Renaissance fashion called for volume in the lower body. This was generally achieved either with a farthingale or a roll or with a combination of the two. The farthingale had originated in Spain as a bell-shaped support for the skirts: it was essentially an underskirt with a series of wire, whalebone, or wooden hoops sewn into it. During the course of the 16th century, the wheel farthingale was introduced. This stuck directly out at the hips and fell straight down, giving the skirts a cylindrical shape. Sometimes the roll was worn by itself to give a somewhat softer version of the wheel farthingale look. This style was particularly common among ordinary people, for whom it served not only to imitate the fashionable shape but also to keep the skirts away from the legs for greater ease of movement.

The other main style of female garment was the gown, which was essentially a bodice and skirt sewn together, usually worn on top of a kirtle or petticoat. The gown was the richest form of garment, and it took many forms. The bodice was frequently adorned with false sleeves which hung down at the back, and often the skirt was open in front to reveal the contrasting skirts underneath.

Lower-body garments for men changed substantially during the course of the 16th century. In the early years some people still wore the old-fashioned long hose and codpiece, a style that had changed little since the late Middle Ages. The hose were roughly analogous to modern tights, but rather loose-fitting. The codpiece was a padded covering for the crotch, originally introduced for the sake of propriety. It also served the function of a modern trouser-fly: it could be unbuttoned or untied to allow the wearer to urinate.

This plain style of hose was already out of fashion by the time Elizabeth came to the throne. Well-dressed men had taken to wearing a trunk hose over their long hose. This was an onion-shaped, stuffed garment that extended from the waist to the tops of the thighs. It was often slashed vertically to reveal a contrasting fabric underneath, or even sewn together from a large number of separate panes.

Later in the Elizabethan reign, a new fashion arose of adding canions to these trunk hose. These were tight-fitting cylindrical extensions that reached from the bottom openings of the trunk hose to the top or bottom of the wearer's knees. At the same time, the trunk hose themselves became fuller and longer, reaching to mid-thigh, and were more likely to be of a solid fabric rather than slashed or paned. Such trunk hose were increasingly likely to have pockets and were worn with stockings rather than long hose.

Late Renaissance English Fashions. The man is wearing a doublet and trunk hose, and the woman sports a gown and petticoat. From Herbert Norris, *Costume and Fashion*, 1924.

Codpieces continued to be worn on the outside of trunk hose. They were sometimes quite elaborate, and often in a shape that strikes the modern eye as downright obscene. Fashionable gentlemen occasionally had them made as pockets in which they could store candy and other knickknacks! Codpieces became more subdued toward the latter part of the period and had fallen out of fashion by the end of the century.

During the latter part of the 16th century a new style of lower-body garment appeared, known as breeches. They were sometimes called Venetian breeches or just Venetians. Venetian breeches were essentially knee-length trousers, originally cut rather close to the body but more voluminous toward the end of the reign. The Venetians were not worn with codpieces; instead, they had a fly-opening that was either tied or buttoned. Like the later styles of trunk hose, they were worn with stockings instead of long hose.

Men's upper-body garments did not change nearly as much. The characteristic upper-body garment was the doublet, a short, fitted jacket with a narrow waste. It might be padded and quilted, or decorated with slashes. The doublet might have detachable sleeves that hooked or laced in. Early in the Elizabethan reign the doublet was cut straight around the bottom edge, but in time it became fashionable for the front to dip downward in a sharp V shape. In the latter half of the period, doublets were cut with a distinctive peascod belly, a padded, protruding flare at the front that imitated the design of military breastplates (on a breastplate this shape helped to deflect blows). An additional garment called a jerkin could be worn over the doublet when temperature or fashion demanded. The jerkin was essentially of the same design as the doublet, except that it might be sleeveless (Singman, 94–102).

To read about clothing and personal appearance in Chaucer's England, see the Europe entries in the sections "Clothing," "Fabrics," and "Appearance" in chapter 5 ("Material Life") in volume 2 of this series; for 18th-century England, see the entries on England in the sections "Male Clothing" and "Female Clothing" in chapter 5 ("Material Life") in volume 4 of this series; for Victorian England, see the Victorian England entry in the section "Fashion" in chapter 5 ("Material Life") in volume 5 of this series.

FOR MORE INFORMATION

Singman, J. L. *Daily Life in Elizabethan England*. Westport, Conn.: Greenwood, 1995.

Willet, C., and P. Cunnington. *Handbook of English Costume in the Sixteenth Century*. London: Faber and Faber, 1954.

MATERIAL LIFE

CLOTHING & PERSONAL
APPEARANCE

England

Spain

Italy

Maya

Aztec

Inca

SPAIN

During the 16th century, the royal Spanish court at Madrid set the fashion trends for not only Spain but also for much of western Europe. As Spain's political power decreased, however, so did its influence on fashion. Courtly fashion favored the colors red, yellow, green, and especially black, perhaps due to the lengthy mourning for the death of Philip II. Blue was uncommon since it came from the tropical, and expensive, Asian indigo plant.

The most distinctive feature of women's fashion was the farthingale, called *guardinfante* in Spanish. The *guardinfante*, introduced in the middle of the 16th century, consisted of a padded framework of whale bone or cane hoops under the petticoat and skirt that became progressively larger as they went from waist to hem. The upper skirts were flared and distended over the hoops. The first hoop, at the waist, could be as large as three times the shoulder-span of the woman wearing the gown. In these exaggerated garments a woman walked gracefully as if floating over the ground; but trying to enter the narrow portal of the church or even sitting down presented a major undertaking.

On top, stiff, high bodices were the trend, with corsets worn underneath to emphasize a long, thin waist. In the mid-16th century, ruffs with high collars came into fashion. As time went on, the collars became more and more voluminous, and more and more stiff, often held up with pasteboard frames and wires. Numerous servants were employed in ironing and preparing these ruffs. The expensiveness of the ruff led to its banning in 1623 by Philip IV, who wished to restrain the perceived excesses in costly fashion.

The *Guardinfante*. The *guardinfante,* or farthingale, was a series of hoops that caused the dress to poof out. Although painted in the 17th century, this picture shows a fashion that was also common in the 16th century. Velasquez, *The Infanta Margarita* from Las Meninas. Madrid: Prado.

It was considered immodest to see a lady's feet, and as a result the dresses were designed to cover the feet. When outside, however, tall chopines (clogs) with cork heels were worn so as to keep the dusty or muddy streets of the town away from the garments and the lady herself.

All formal occasions required gloves, but one of the most indispensable items for a lady's wardrobe was the fan. The fan was used in a variety of ways to communicate thoughts and emotions from a distance. As Leucadio Doblado indicated in *Letters from Spain:*

A dear friend at the farthest end of the public walk, is greeted and cheered up by a quick, tremulous motion of the fan, accompanied with several significant nods. An object of indifference is dismissed with a slow formal inclination of the fan, which makes his blood run cold. . . . A gentle tap of the fan commands the attention of the careless; a waving motion calls the distant. A certain twirl between the fingers betrays doubt or anxiety—a quick closing and displaying the folds, indicated eagerness or joy.

Perhaps the most common garment in Renaissance Spain, however, was the mantilla, a black headdress worn by all classes of women, especially outdoors. The length of the mantilla depended on the wearer's marital status: a widow's mantilla reached to the ground, while a young woman's was much shorter. Unmarried women, especially in the south, would hold the mantilla in such a way that the garment covered their face except for one eye. While such customs, similar to some modern Muslim customs, may be thought of as restrictive, Philip II proscribed its use due to concerns that it allowed too much freedom: anyone could don a veil and slip off wherever they wanted, unknown and unnoticed.

Wealthy men's fashions were also sumptuous. On top, men wore a padded doublet designed to imitate plate armor, with a strong central line coming to a point below the waist. As with women, tall stiff collars were worn. Men wore short, wide pantaloons, with stockings covering the rest of the legs. A hooded cape generally completed the outfit.

The lower economic classes obviously wore less expensive clothing. Men wore brown shirts and knee-length trousers made from wool or canvas, and woolen hose, while women wore loose skirts that fell in natural folds instead of the farthingale (Anderson, 169–82).

FOR MORE INFORMATION

Anderson, J. M. *Daily Life during the Spanish Inquisition*. Westport, Conn.: Greenwood, 2002.
Doblado, L. *Letters from Spain*. London: Henry Colburn, 1822.

MATERIAL LIFE
|
CLOTHING & PERSONAL
APPEARANCE
|
England

Spain

Italy

Maya

Aztec

Inca

ITALY

Basic male attire was a shirt and tunic with hose. The shirt, a loosely fitted linen garment worn against the skin, was the item of clothing most often changed and washed. Over it, men usually wore some form of tunic or jacket that extended partway down the legs and cinched at the waist or hips. With the belt, length could be adjusted to accommodate the needs of work. Lacking zippers or elastic and with only a few buttons, Renaissance men kept their close-fitting hose up by tying laces through holes in the upper and lower garments. Early on, a hose consisted of two separate legs not seamed together. This drafty arrangement, while convenient for excretion, depended on the overhanging tunic for modesty. As the Renaissance progressed, the two columns of fabric came to be joined at least partway around. Short breeches also filled the gap; in the 16th century, for fashion-conscious men, these became quite puffy and might be accessorized with a codpiece at the front. Hose tended to wear through at the knees. So, for warmth and protection, working men sometimes wore extra leggings bound around the lower leg and over the knee. A cloth cape—sometimes trimmed or lined with fur for the wealthy—usually completed the ensemble. Such were the standard components of the male *short* costume. For reasons of age, civic office, or membership in a profession or the clergy, other men wore *long* garb, which replaced or covered the thigh-length tunic with a straight or flowing robe that ended near the ankles. Caps and hats came in a variety of colors and silhouettes: some of cloth fitting snugly to the head or rising to high, even bulbous crowns; others of felt or straw with broad, flat brims. Gracing a prime site of bodily honor, headgear served tastes from the soberly functional to the fashionably flamboyant. Footwear ranged from wooden clogs to thin-soled leather shoes.

Although women's clothing distinguished them from men, breeches aside, it had many elements in common with the male garb. Under it all went the shirt, sometimes cut wider at the neck. Over it went a one-piece dress, with fitted waist, from which fell a long, fairly full skirt. Its folds fell close enough to the body, especially when layered over the tails of a long shirt, to provide warmth and modesty. Italian women wore stockings but only rarely leggings rising to the waist. Nor were they needed before the arrival of the Spanish fashion for bell-shaped hoopskirts that stood out from the body, exposing it to drafts. For much of the Renaissance, the often square-cut neckline was quite open, allowing the shirt underneath to show. Sleeves often came separately and attached to the armholes of the dress with laces; one relatively cheap way to refresh a wardrobe was to get a new pair. When needing another layer of clothing or for sheer display, women wore a flowing overgown that sometimes trailed on the ground. Urban women shod their feet in slippers sometimes made with colored fabrics; the soles were firm enough, however, that they sometimes served as weapons. To rise above mud and water in the streets, in Venice especially, there were high-heeled shoes or pattens of wood and cork that lifted the wearer even a foot above the ground; these caused women to hobble precariously, and some critics claimed they led to miscarriages. On their heads, atop often elaborate hairstyles, women generally wore veils. Although those in mourning and nuns shrouded the body and sometimes the face with long and somber folds of fabric, Italian ladies are often depicted with light, sheer veils spread over their backs that more enhanced than hid their looks.

During the Renaissance, fashion came into its own. For the wealthy, clothing became more elaborately shaped and decorated. Courtiers and their rich imitators began to distinguish cuts and ornaments and to define themselves by wearing what was novel and prestigious. Competitors for status sought not only lavishness but style. The cut of sleeves, for example, became a focus. For both men and women, they grew bigger and layered; from some, arms emerged through slits while the rest of the ample sleeve drooped almost to the ground. Others puffed out at the shoulder but fit snugly to the forearm. Eye-catching sleeves, like other items of apparel, might be trimmed in gold thread, embroidered with flowers and leaves, or strewn with pearls. Another decorative fad was slashing: cutting across the fabric to allow the underlay, in white or a contrasting color, to show through. This fashion much reduced the possibility of reuse and drew criticism as wasteful. Indeed, the pursuit of fashion in general was frequently condemned as expensive, inconvenient, vain, and immoral. Sermons and sumptuary laws, however, never quenched the appetite to spend and flaunt. While many reproaches targeted women, portraits show that men too invested heavily in an impressive, modish look. In these and other fashions, during much of the Renaissance, Italy was Europe's trend-setter. Even the king of France, François I, requested from Isabella d'Este, countess of Mantua, a doll dressed in courtly style as a model to take back for the ladies of Paris. Costume books published from the middle of the 17th century show the growing awareness of fashion. With pictures and text, Cesare Vecellio's book, for example, highlighted variations in dress both over time and among regions even within Italy. By then, however, clothing in general was shifting to a more sober tone. With the emerging Spanish mode, paralleling Spain's sway in the peninsula, black replaced the old vibrant

Modest Dress in Southern Italy. In many parts of Italy, women were expected to cover up from head to toe, leaving just a small opening for the face, when traveling outside. Notice the platform shoes used to keep the feet away from the dust and dirt of the street. P. Bertelli, *Diversarum Nationum Habitus Padua* 1594 (KK7. 11). By concession of del Ministero per i Beni e le Attività Culturali. Reproduction or ulterior duplication for any purpose is prohibited.

colors and women's décolletage gave way to high collars and ruffs (Cohen and Cohen, 232–34).

FOR MORE INFORMATION

Cohen, E. S., and T. V. Cohen. *Daily Life in Renaissance Italy.* Westport, Conn.: Greenwood, 2001.
Newton, S. M. *The Dress of the Venetians, 1495–1525.* Aldershot: Scolar, 1988.
Vecellio, C. *Vecellio's Renaissance Costume Book.* New York: Dover, 1977.

MATERIAL LIFE

CLOTHING & PERSONAL
APPEARANCE

England

Spain

Italy

Maya

Aztec

Inca

MAYA

As in other cultures, the Maya used personal appearance, clothing, and adornments to mark social status. One way of doing this was to alter their physical appearance. For example, crossed eyes were considered a mark of beauty for the ancient Maya. In colonial times mothers induced crossed eyes by tying little balls of resin to their children's hairs so they would hang between their eyes. Other marks of beauty included piercing the ears, lips, and septum of the nose to hold a variety of ornaments that indicated the individual's status. Flattened foreheads were also considered a mark of beauty and status. This was done by binding babies' heads between a pair of boards, one at the back of the head, the other against the forehead. These boards were left in place for several days. Once the cranial bones had set, the desired flattened appearance remained for life. Carved and painted representations of profile heads show that this practice was often used in the past to indicate elite status.

The Maya cultivated cotton and wove beautifully decorated textiles for clothing and other uses. Since only a few specimens of ancient Maya weaving have survived, the best evidence for this well-developed craft are the representations of textiles in Maya art. Clothing depicted on sculptures indicates that the cotton fabrics of the period were of complicated weaves that were elaborately embroidered. Woven cotton cloaks of fixed size were used as articles of trade in ancient times, and after the conquest they became the principal form of tribute exacted by the Spaniards.

The traditional patterns and color symbolism used in highland textile designs today derive from ancient times. Black represents weapons because it is the color of obsidian; yellow symbolizes food because it is the color of corn; red represents blood; blue represents sacrifice. Green remains the royal color because it is the color of quetzal feathers, once reserved for the headdresses of Maya kings. The most highly prized traditional dye was a deep purple obtained from a Pacific mollusk (*Purpura patula*). Modern Maya women still decorate handwoven clothing with cross-stitch embroidery, known in Yucatec Mayan as *xoc bil chui* (threads that are counted).

Clothing marked gender and status differences among the ancient Maya. Men wore a loincloth, called an *ex*, a band of cotton cloth that went between the legs and was wrapped around the waist. The *ex* is represented in Maya art, ranging from elaborately decorated examples worn by kings and other elite men, to simple, undecorated versions worn by commoners. Elite men often wore a large square cotton cloth, called a *pati*, around the shoulders, elaborately decorated with different patterns, colors, and featherwork depending on the wearer's status. Simple versions of the *pati* were worn by commoners and also served as a bed covering at night.

Men wore sandals made of untanned deer hide that were bound to the feet by two thongs, one passing between the first and second toes, the other between the third and fourth toes. The sandals worn by kings and elite men seen on carved monuments were very elaborate. Many Maya men today still wear sandals similar to the ancient examples (except they are tied by a single thong).

Ancient Maya men wore their hair long, usually braided and wound around the head except for a queue that hung down behind. Body paint was often used to mark special groups. Priests were painted blue, the color usually associated with sacrifice; warriors painted themselves

Royal Maya Fashion. In addition to the flattened foreheads and noses, note the *ex* (loincloth), *pati* (cloak), and the elaborate headdresses. © University of Pennsylvania Museum.

black and red. War captives are sometimes shown painted black and white. Paint was also used in tattooing, the painted designs being cut into the skin with an obsidian knife. This was done only after marriage.

The principal garment worn by Maya women was a woven cotton skirt, called a manta. According to Bishop Landa's colonial-era account, "The women of the coast and of the Provinces of Bacalar and of Campeche are more modest in their dress, for, besides the (skirt) which they wore from the waist down, they covered their breasts, tying a folded manta underneath their armpits." Another popular garment was a loose-fitting gown, called a *huipil*. Women also covered their head and shoulders with a cotton shawl called a *booch*.

As they still do today, Maya women and girls wore their hair long, arranged in various ways. Married and unmarried women each had distinctive hairstyles. Both women and men anointed themselves with a sweet-smelling red ointment, an odor that lasted for many days. Like men, married women also tattooed themselves—except for their breasts—with delicate designs.

Clothing reflected status. The costumes worn by men of the highest status in a society, such as Maya kings, were the most elaborate and were decorated with the symbols of supernatural power. Portraits of classic period kings show them wearing beautifully decorated loincloths, capes, sandals, and huge headdresses. The belt holding the *ex* was adorned with jade masks (probably derived from earlier versions that used real human trophy heads) from which jade celts (an ax-like tool) were suspended. Earlier belts often included a chain dangling a small image of a god. A large jade god mask was often worn on the chest, along with necklaces of jade beads. Jewelry of jade, shell, and other materials was formed into beads, pendants, and mosaics; these were worn in the ears, nose, and lips and around the neck, arms, wrists, and ankles. The king's *pati* was a magnificent cape of embroidered cotton, accompanied by jaguar pelts and featherwork. On his feet the king wore elaborately decorated sandals.

Completing the royal display was a huge headdress adorned with an array of iridescent tail feathers from the sacred quetzal bird. The headdress framework was probably made of wood, including a front piece carved to represent one or more heads of Maya gods. The headdress was also adorned with mosaics and carved jades. Specialized head-dresses were used by kings for special events, including one associated with warfare. On early representations the ruler wore a headband with a tri-lobed element, sometimes per-sonified by three heads of the so-called jester god. At Copan, each ruler of the royal dynasty is often shown wearing a distinctive textile headdress wound like a turban.

Noblewomen's Clothing. This scene from the Bonampak Mu-rals shows a collection of well-born Maya women adorning themselves with the aid of a male (probably castrated) servant. The women are wearing the *huipil,* the loose-fitting gown characteristic of Maya communities. © Charles & Josette Lenars/CORBIS.

Even commoners wore jewelry—usually simple nose plugs, lip plugs, and earrings of bone, wood, shell, or stone. Adornments worn by the elite were much more elaborate and were made of jade, stone, obsidian, coral, and shell. The most precious were delicately made mosaics and inlays. The elite also wore collars, necklaces, wristlets, anklets, and knee bands made of feathers, jade beads, shells, jaguar teeth and claws, crocodile teeth, or, in later times, gold and copper (Sharer, 121–25, 210–11).

FOR MORE INFORMATION

Sharer, R. J. *Daily Life in Maya Civilization.* Westport, Conn.: Greenwood, 1996.

Tozzer, A. M. *Landa's Relación de las cosas de Yucatán.* Cambridge, Mass.: Peabody Museum, 1941.

MATERIAL LIFE

CLOTHING & PERSONAL APPEARANCE

England

Spain

Italy

Maya

Aztec

Inca

AZTEC

Men's clothes, especially those of warriors, reflected experience and valor in the field. But the common man wore a loincloth that was wound around his waist and between his legs, and knotted so that one end hung down from behind and the other from the front. Nobles wore elaborate cotton cloths with colorful embroidered designs. While some poorer workers were limited to these loincloths, most men wore cloaks that were knotted on their shoulders. The clothing of a ruler was astonishing in its color, beauty, and symbolism.

Women wore skirts that reached to their ankles and were tied to their bodies by embroidered belts. Upper-class women wore a blouse over their skirts decorated with certain designs, according to their class or hometown. As Warwick Bray notes, the Aztecs greatly enjoyed ornamenting their bodies and clothes whenever they could:

The Mexicans loved display and were uninhibited in their use of jewelry and such accessories as fans, fly-whisks, and head-dresses made of green or red feathers. Beads were made of rare stones or of gold cast into the form of crabs, scorpions, birds, or sea shells, and necklaces were hung with bells which tinkled when the wearer moved. The same materials were used for pendants and chest ornaments and the limbs of rich young men were adorned with leather or gold bands set with jade and turquoise mosaic. Poorer folk wore ornaments of a similar kind, but substituted shells or less expensive stones for the precious materials used by the aristocracy.

Clothing was particularly important in showing a warrior's rank, which was determined by how many captives a warrior had taken. A one-captive warrior carried a *maquahuitl*, or club made of well-finished oak. Grooves were cut along both sides, and obsidian or flint stone blades were inserted with turtle dung to make them stick. The warrior was also given a *chimalli*, or shield, without decorations. This feat of taking a captive meant that the warrior had truly embarked on a warrior's career, and he was rewarded with a manta, or cloak, decorated with flowers. He also received an orange cape with a striped border, a carmine-colored loincloth, and a scorpion-knotted design cape. The wearing of designs was a valued addition to one's attire.

A two-captive warrior was given the highly valued right to wear sandals onto the battlefield as well as a pointed, cone-shaped cap and a feathered warrior suit with parallel black lines. This is the costume that appears most often in the *Codex Mendoza*'s pictorial program of warrior outfits. In fact, more than 19 culturally diverse provinces sent this kind of costume to the Aztec capital as tribute payment.

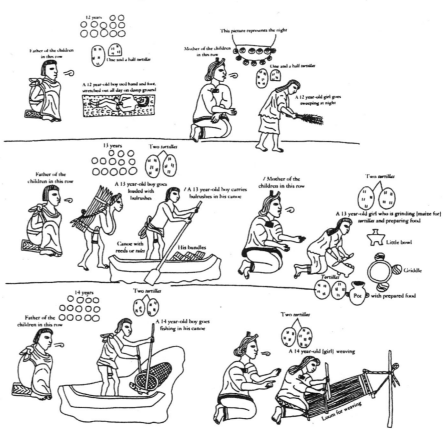

Typical Aztec Clothing. On the men, note the loincloth and the cloak tied at the shoulder. On the women, note the decorative blouse worn over the skirt. These pictures come from a treatise about raising children. From the *Codex Mendoza*. Courtesy of Frances F. Berdan and Patricia Reiff Anawalt.

One of the most impressive costumes was the four-captive warrior's *ocelotl*, or jaguar, outfit. Ocelots were powerful, stocky animals with great hunting and attacking skills. The body of a warrior was enclosed within an ocelot skin and his head emerged from the mouth of the animal. These warriors constituted a special unit within the army. Warriors of extreme distinction were made into generals and were decorated with lavish quetzal-feathered hair ornaments and long, yellow lip plugs made of amber. Their capes were called the jewels of Ehecatl (the wind god), and they had awesome titles such as Keeper of the Mirrored Snake, Keeper of the Bowl of Fatigue, Keeper of the House of Darts, or Raining Blood.

The Aztecs were careful to groom their appearance with baths and cosmetics. Aztec peoples enjoyed bathing and personal cleanliness, and they used the fruit of a soap tree and the roots of certain plants for soap. They took cold baths but were especially committed to steam baths. Many homes had steam bathhouses, some of which have been excavated in the Basin of Mexico. These steam baths were used for ritual purification, for sicknesses, and for helping pregnant women, but they were also used for daily hygiene.

Aztec women, especially the more well-to-do, shaded their brown complexions with a yellow color extracted from insects and cooking oils. Men appear to have painted their bodies only for certain ceremonies. If women colored their faces too much or before they were old enough, their parents admonished them. Women also used perfumes extracted from plants and used a kind of chewing gum to sweeten their breath. It appears that obsidian mirrors were used in homes so that people could evaluate their personal appearance before going out into the community (Carrasco, 121–22, 145–47).

FOR MORE INFORMATION

Bray, W. *Everyday Life of the Aztecs*. London: Batsford, 1968.

Carrasco, D., with S. Sessions. *Daily Life of the Aztecs: People of the Sun and Earth*. Westport, Conn.: Greenwood, 1998.

MATERIAL LIFE
|
CLOTHING & PERSONAL
APPEARANCE
|
England

Spain

Italy

Maya

Aztec

Inca

INCA

Clothing for both men and women was very simple. Women wore a large piece of cloth wrapped around their bodies, tied at the waist with a belt, and pinned at the shoulder. Another piece of cloth, a mantle, was worn over the shoulders and fastened in front with a large pin, or *tupu*. *Tupus* were made most often of copper, but higher-class individuals might also have ones of silver or gold. Men wore a tunic over a loincloth wrapped around the waist and groin. Very similar to modern ponchos, the tunic was a large piece of cloth doubled over and sewn along the sides, with slits left for the arms and head. Men also wore woolen or cotton fringes below their knees and around their ankles. In cold weather, men wore a cloak over their garments.

Both men and women wore simple sandals made of woven wild plant, cotton, or camelid fibers with an untanned leather sole. They were held to the feet with woolen straps, which often were elaborately tied. Gold ornaments were sometimes attached as well. Both men and women wore headdresses, one of the main indicators of ethnic identity. In fact, each ethnic group had unique headdresses. The Inca nobility also wore crowns of silver and gold.

Even though the Incas' basic clothing was simple, it was often elaborately decorated with brightly colored patterns that conveyed symbolic information. The designs on Inca men's tunics were highly standardized, reflecting symbols of membership in a particular group (e.g., membership in a royal *panaca*, or household).

Fine tunics worn only on special occasions might have designs from top to bottom, but the day-to-day dress tunic had a single band of square design around the waist, a band at the lower edge, and an inverted triangle at the neck.

Especially prized by the Incas was clothing decorated with feathers from brightly colored tropical birds. Sometimes an entire tunic or mantle was covered, at other times only a portion. Plaques of gold and other metals were also attached to the clothing of Inca nobility as an additional emblem of status.

Inca men wore their hair short. The women wore it long, parted in the middle. Women cut their hair only in mourning or as a sign of disgrace. Men's hair was bound up in a specially woven band or a sling. The king's band was wrapped several times around his head and included a fringe, or series of tassels, that hung off the headband over the forehead. His band also had a small pompom on a stick worn above it. The fringe and pompom were emblems of the kingship: no one else was allowed to wear such articles. Women also bound their hair in a band of cloth, covered with a piece of fine cloth.

Jewelry was worn by both Inca women and men. Women apparently only wore *tupu* pins and necklaces. The main piece of men's jewelry was the large earplugs that were the insignia of nobility. These had a shaft that went through the holes in the earlobes, and a round head with a diameter of about 2 inches. They were made of gold, silver, or other materials. Men also wore bracelets. For bravery in war, soldiers were awarded metal disks that hung around their necks, and they also wore necklaces of human teeth taken from their defeated enemies.

Little else is known about Inca ideals of fashion or beauty. Martín de Morúa, an early Spanish writer, states that Inca women tied strings above and below their knees to thicken the flesh of their thighs and shins, which was considered a particular mark of beauty. The Incas also apparently painted their faces, not for aesthetic purposes, but for war and mourning (Malpass, 83–86).

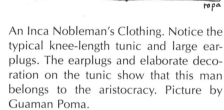

An Inca Nobleman's Clothing. Notice the typical knee-length tunic and large earplugs. The earplugs and elaborate decoration on the tunic show that this man belongs to the aristocracy. Picture by Guaman Poma.

FOR MORE INFORMATION

Malpass, M. A. *Daily Life in the Inca Empire*. Westport, Conn.: Greenwood, 1996.

Morris, C., and A. von Hagen. *The Inka Empire and Its Andean Origins*. New York: American Museum of Natural History and Abbeville Press, 1993.

Rowe, J. H. "Inca Culture at the Time of the Spanish Conquest." In *Handbook of South American Indians*. Vol. 2., *The Andean Civilizations*, ed. Julian H. Steward. Washington, D.C.: Bureau of American Ethnology Bulletin 143, 1946. 183–330.

Food and Drink

Think of Italian food—what comes to mind? Probably bowls of spaghetti, adorned with a rich tomato sauce. What comes to mind if you think of Irish food? Probably potatoes. And if you think of Belgium, there's a good chance that their world-famous

MATERIAL LIFE

FOOD & DRINK

England

Spain

Italy

Ottoman Empire

Maya

Aztec

Inca

chocolates will come to mind. These modern images of traditional European cuisine are all actually of fairly recent origin, mostly of the 17th and 18th centuries. During the vast majority of the 15th and 16th centuries, none of the above foods mentioned were to be seen in Europe. Why? Because the main ingredients (tomatoes, potatoes, and chocolate) all are foods native only to the Americas. In fact, many of the foods that people in Western societies take for granted today, for example, tomatoes, potatoes, chocolate, pumpkins, cranberries, turkeys, and squash, all came originally from the Americas. If European cuisine has been much enlivened by contact with the culinary treasures of the Native Americans, modern American cuisine also changed dramatically. For example, Mexican food today is associated with rice (*arroyo*), but the Aztecs had no rice—it was brought by the Europeans. Likewise, chickens and pigs, both staples in Mesoamerican and South American diets today, were brought by the Europeans.

As seen by the previous images of national cuisine, food can be used to create a sense of identity and community and also emphasizes how different communities can be. Making Italian food can be a way of affirming a link with a geographical or ethnic community. If you travel through Europe, you travel not only from place to place, but from language to language, and from cuisine to cuisine. While food can thus mark geographic and ethnic boundaries, it can also mark off boundaries of social or economic class. For example, in the United States, people in lower income brackets eat fast food more regularly than people in higher income brackets. Such differences were even greater in the 15th and 16th centuries. The Inca king, for example, is said to have dined on fresh seafood brought many miles inland from the ocean to the capital of Cuzco by special runners, while the rest of the population would have to rely on dried ocean fish at best. In Italy, pork was the main meat that a laborer might be able to afford, while the wealthy dined on such exotic foods as wild boar and cormorant. Not only what was eaten varied in relation to wealth, but also how it was eaten. Wealthy Europeans could afford not only the money but also the time to spend long hours over the dinner table, sampling a variety of courses and wines, discussing matters with friends and families. Peasants and laborers had less time due to their many work obligations, and they certainly had less money. Inca noblemen similarly would eat and drink out of golden vessels whereas their poorer subjects would use plates and cups made out of pottery.

Food, however, is much more than a way of identifying a person's community or social class. First and foremost, food is a necessity of life, even more necessary than shelter during many months of the year. As such, farming and the other means of producing food are the foundation of the state's welfare and its economy. For our investigation here, it is worth remembering that in the 15th and 16th centuries food was not a luxury item, nor was it an item that was constantly supplied; instead, food was the very means of life itself, and its value, monetarily and psychologically, should not be underestimated.

Both in Europe and in the Americas, one main crop, such as grain or corn, formed the staple of most people's diet. In Europe, rice, wheat, and barley, as well as other grains, were made into bread. Bread was usually made with a thick crust to help it remain fresh longer. A meal for many families might consist mostly of some bread with perhaps some cheese or butter and a little roast meat. In the Americas, maize was the chief crop and formed the largest part of most people's diet. Maize could be made into tortillas or sometimes used in tamales or soups. Tortillas could form the base of any kind of meal, accompanying beans or roast turkey for example.

Finally, we should discuss alcoholic drinks such as beer and wine, as well as unfamiliar drinks such as *chicha*, an Andean beverage made from fermented corn and other plants. In modern Western societies, alcoholic drinks are viewed as unnecessary beverages that can bring a festive touch to a meal or social event. In the 15th and 16th centuries, however, beer, wine, and *chicha* were important ways of preserving the harvest. For example, when grapes became ripe, there were far too many of them to be consumed by the populace during that week or even that month. As a result, various methods were devised long ago to preserve the caloric value of the crop. In Europe, fermenting the grapes with water was the main method of preserving the grapes. The wine produced as a result could be used throughout the year. Producing beer was a similar way of preserving the grain crop, and *chicha* preserved the maize crop. The caloric value of such beverages can be surprisingly high, and can produce things today such as beer bellies! In the 15th and 16th centuries, when most people consumed too few calories, beer and wine was an essential part of any diet. Avoiding alcoholic drinks, as the Muslims in the Ottoman Empire did, for example, was therefore a greater sacrifice than one might think at first. Finally, it should also be noted that 15th- and 16th-century wines and beers were generally much lower in alcoholic content. It would not be a good idea today to have wine for breakfast the way some Europeans did, or to fast by eating no food but drinking beer, as some monks did!

~Lawrence Morris

ENGLAND

The first meal of the day was breakfast, which was generally an informal bite on the run rather than a sit-down meal. Many people did not take breakfast at all but waited until dinner in the late morning. Those who did have breakfast might eat right after rising or several hours later. A simple breakfast might consist of porridge or pottage (stew), or even scraps and leftovers. A more hearty breakfast could include bread with butter or cheese, ale or wine, fruit, and some sort of meat—beef, mutton, or chickens.

The real meals were dinner, served around eleven o'clock or noon, and supper in the evening, somewhere from six to nine o'clock. For ordinary people, the midday dinner was probably the larger meal of the two, but those of the privileged classes may have had their principal meal in the evening. A simple meal might be served all at once, but in wealthy households—or on special occasions like holy days—a meal might consist of many courses, each containing several dishes, with cheese and fruits at the end of the meal. Sweet dishes would be included in each course, rather than served only at the end. One contemporary cookbook offers the following sample menu:

MATERIAL LIFE
|
FOOD & DRINK
|
England

Spain

Italy

Ottoman Empire

Maya

Aztec

Inca

The First Course: Pottage or stewed broth; boiled meat or stewed meat, chickens and bacon, powdered [salted] beef, pies, goose, pig, roasted beef, roasted veal, custard.
The Second Course: Roasted lamb, roasted capons, roasted conies [rabbits], chickens, peahens, baked venison, tart.

These formal meals were not the only times people ate. Those who felt hungry during the day might have a bit of bread or cold food, and perhaps a bit of ale. During haymaking and harvesting seasons, rural folk took their food into the fields; common harvesting fare included bottled beer, apple pasties (a sturdy, hand-sized pastry), bread, cheese, and butter. At the other end of the social scale, an aristocratic hunting party might bring along cold meats, pies, and sausages.

A Family Dinner. Note that the father and mother sit in the positions of importance at each end of the table. The small child uses a step stool to reach her plate. From Charles Hindley, ed., *The Roxburghe Ballads*, 1837–74.

Bread, a prominent feature of everyone's diet, was always present at meals. Wheat was the favored grain for bread, and whiter breads were preferred to dark ones, although even the whitest Renaissance bread was almost as brown as a modern whole-wheat loaf. Poorer people often made do with rye, barley, or mixed-grain bread; beans, peas, and oats were used in times of dearth. Breads were not baked in pans, so they were low and round rather than tall. Although bread would go stale after a few days, nothing was wasted: stale bread could be used to make bread puddings, and bread crumbs served to thicken soups, stews, and sauces.

England was particularly noted for the quality of its roast meats. A greater variety of meat was consumed in the 16th century than is common today. Red meats included beef, mutton, veal, lamb, kid, and pork. For poultry there were chickens, ducks, geese, and even pigeons. Game meats included deer, rabbit, and an enormous variety of wildfowl—for example, larks, sparrows, pheasants, partridge, quail, crane, plovers, and woodcocks. Another distinctive feature of Renaissance cuisine was that very little of the animal went to waste: cookbooks for prosperous households include recipes for pigs' and calves' feet, lamb's head, and tripe.

Seafood was another important source of protein—in fact, fish were a large part of the diet. English fishermen exported a great deal of cod and herring, the coasts abounded in oysters and mussels, and the rivers supplied freshwater fish and eels. Popular seafood included flounder, mackerel, carp, pike, salmon, trout, shrimp, crab, and even the occasional porpoise or seal. During the season of Lent people were supposed to abstain from eating meat, relying on fish instead: this was no longer a religious requirement, as England was a Protestant country, but the ban was reinstated by Queen Elizabeth as a means of supporting English fisheries (and thereby English sea power in general). The same rule applied on Wednesdays, Fridays, and Saturdays, as well as throughout Advent and on the eves of certain holy days; in total, it accounted for more than one-third of the year. This fasting was not vigorously observed by English subjects; nevertheless, seafood was a handy staple: it was relatively cheap, it was available fresh in much of the country, and it could be preserved by salting, drying, or pickling.

Vegetables probably had a larger part in the Renaissance diet than is sometimes supposed today. It was common for houses to have gardens, even in the middle of London; such gardens provided a variety of vegetables for the household, including artichokes, asparagus, cucumbers, endive, radish, spinach, lettuce, beans, cabbage, carrots, leeks, parsnips, peas, and turnips. Fruits were also a regular part of the diet: they were used to flavor dishes, and were often served at the end of a meal. They too were likely to be grown in the garden. Domestically produced fruit included apricots, grapes, figs, strawberries, raspberries, apples, pears, plums, currants, mulberries, and cherries. England also imported certain fruits, especially oranges from the Mediterranean.

The content of a meal depended very much on the season, since fresh food did not keep or transport well. The meats were preserved by smoking or salting; bacon, ham, and sausage were all familiar winter fare. Fish were likewise smoked, dried, or salted. Salted meats were soaked before cooking to remove some of the excess salt, but they tended to be fairly salty nonetheless. Another means of preservation was pickling, especially for seafood and vegetables. Fruits, peas, and beans could be preserved by drying; fruits were also made into preserves.

There were three principal ways of cooking a main dish: boiling, roasting, or baking. Of these, boiling was the easiest and probably the most common. It involved placing the food in a pot over hot coals or an open flame. Once the food was set to boil it needed relatively little attention, so boiled soups, pottages (stews), and meats were convenient dishes.

Since the water quality was low in much of England, most drinks were fermented. The traditional English beverage was ale, made of water, malted barley, herbs and spices; it lacked hops, so it tasted little like what we call ale today, and its shelf-life was short. Already, beer—similar to ale but brewed with hops—had come to be favored in the cities. Beer was lighter and clearer than ale; it also kept longer, and was therefore cheaper. Ale varied greatly in strength, from the watery small ales to "double ale," or even the rather expensive "double-double," often known by such evocative names as Mad Dog and Dragons' Milk. As a daily staple, ale was generally consumed in forms with very low alcohol content; children drank it as well as adults, and people would drink it when they breakfasted and throughout the working day. A gallon a day seems to have been a normal ration for a grown man.

> *Snapshot*
>
> **Recipe for Elizabethan Spiced Beer**
>
> Take three pints of beer, put five yolks of eggs to it, strain them together, and set it in a pewter pot to the fire, and put to it half a pound of sugar, one pennyworth of nutmegs beaten, one pennyworth of cloves beaten, and a halfpennyworth of ginger beaten, and when it is all in, take another pewter pot and draw them together, and set it to the fire again, and when it is ready to boil, take it from the fire, and put a dish of sweet butter into it, and brew them together out of one pot into another.

English grapes were not suitable for wine, so wine was generally imported from the continent. Due to the cost of importing, only the wealthy had wine regularly. The English preferred their wines sweet and would often sugar them heavily. Wine was also made from English fruit, such as gooseberries and cherries. Both wine and beer could be seasoned with herbs and spices, or served mixed, somewhat similar to eggnog (Singman, 131–37).

To read about food and drink in Chaucer's England, see the Europe entries in the sections "Food" and "Drink" in chapter 5 ("Material Life") in volume 2 of this series; for 18th-century England, see the entries on England in the sections "Food" and "Drink" in chapter 5 ("Material Life") in volume 4 of this series; for Victorian England, see the Victorian England entry in the section "Food" in chapter 5 ("Material Life") in volume 5 of this series.

FOR MORE INFORMATION

Peachey, S., ed. *The Good Huswifes Handmaide for the Kitchin*. Bristol: Stuart, 1992.

Singman, J. L. *Daily Life in Elizabethan England*. Westport, Conn.: Greenwood, 1995.

MATERIAL LIFE
|
FOOD & DRINK
|
England

Spain

Italy

Ottoman Empire

Maya

Aztec

Inca

SPAIN

The Spanish rose early and often skipped breakfast. If eaten, breakfast often consisted of a little bread, perhaps a mouthful of sheep's cheese, and a drink or two of wine or a cup of chocolate. A rasher of bacon, roasted not fried, was served in every eating house for breakfast and was inexpensive. For many, though, a swallow of brandy was breakfast, especially on cold winter mornings. It was often taken with a little dose of thick jam, honey, or marmalade. A drink in the morning to fend off the cold was not looked upon by the authorities as a good thing, and many attempts were made to prohibit it, but the tradition persisted.

For most people, the midday meal, the main repast of the day, coincided with the high point of the sun, about one o'clock, although some put it off until the meat markets reopened. Butchers generally did their business between six and ten in the morning, opening again at two or three. With the exception of a few grandees who had a larder, no one kept food in the house, and for every meal, people went out and bought the necessary ingredients. With the lack of refrigeration, food, especially meat and seafood, did not last long, especially in the sweltering summer months. A siesta (nap) was usually taken after the midday meal.

Venders were not permitted to sell their products at any price they chose. The government set the prices, and the municipal authority was always on the lookout for elevated prices or fraud in the weighing of merchandise.

The wealthy had professional cooks that also did the shopping. A great deal of animal meat was consumed, and several different kinds were devoured at one meal. Meat was often served as a *cocido* (stew) or marinated. Spices and condiments usually consisted of pepper, garlic, and saffron. Certain dishes were very common, including olla podrida (literally, rotten pot), a pork-based stew, and *blancmange*, a kind of hash incorporating a base of thin slices of chicken simmered in a milk sauce with rice flour and sugar. Ordinary food could be much enhanced by sauces of which there were many different varieties. For example, with peacock, a sauce might be composed of bacon and onion, chicken broth, minced almonds, lemon juice, bitter oranges, sugar and honey, walnuts, cinnamon, cloves, and ginger, all mixed with the fat from the roasted bird. A typical sauce, common since Roman times, was composed of toasted bread soaked in vinegar, pepper, cloves, and ginger mixed with beef broth, saffron, almond milk, and some minced meat of the bird or animal being cooked. To conclude the meal there were desserts that consisted of fruit, olives, and cheese. More sweet dishes included fruit pies, egg yolks preserved in sugar, sugared almonds, and a nougat called *turrone* that was especially popular around Christmas.

The poorer classes consumed much less meat. While the wealthy consumed roughly 350 grams of meat per person per day, the poor consumed around 50 grams. The diet consisted mostly of vegetables, including artichokes, beans, garlic, onions, olives, eggs, and perhaps a bit of goat's or sheep's cheese. Most important of all, however, was bread. Rises in the cost of bread could lead to large riots, and the government tried to carefully regulate the trade as a result. The poorer peasants ate almost exclusively turnip stew, a few vegetables, rye bread, onions, cheese, and olives. In the central provinces, a grain porridge, made of boiled rye, millet, or barley, was consumed instead of bread.

Wine was the most common drink. The wines were classified as good and expensive or as ordinary and cheap, and a tavern could not sell both kinds at the same time, presumably to prevent diluting. Ever since its introduction into Spain around 1521, chocolate, gained from the Aztecs of Mesoamerica, was one of the most popular drinks at breakfast and throughout the day. In the summer, cool drinks such as orange or strawberry juice, or almond-flavored syrup, were popular. To cool the drinks, large quantities of snow and ice were transported during the winter from the mountains 40 miles away to huge pits especially dug in Madrid. During the summer, tall thin glasses designed to cool their contents quickly were placed in containers of snow.

One of the unique aspects of Spanish cooking was its religious implications. In Spain's politicized religious climate, people were often anxious to display their Christianity. For example, the olla podrida was inherited from a Jewish recipe called *adafina*, but with the addition of conspicuous amounts of pork, the meat forbidden to Jews by Mosaic law. Converted Jews or Muslims made it a practice to eat pork in a public area at least once a day to show off their new beliefs. While the olla podrida had Jewish origins, the famous gazpacho, a cold tomato and garlic soup, came from the Muslim areas of Spain (Anderson, 183–95).

📷 *Snapshot*

Recipe for Spanish Gazpacho

4 large tomatoes
1 cucumber, peeled and chopped
1 green pepper, seeded and chopped
2 garlic cloves, mashed
2 cups bread, crumbled
2 cups cold water
4 tbsp. wine vinegar
4 tbsp. olive oil
1 1/2 cups tomato juice

Dip the tomatoes in boiling water and remove the skin. Take out the seeds and chop. Puree the tomatoes, cucumber, pepper, garlic, and bread. Mix in the water, vinegar, olive oil, and tomato juice. Cover and chill for several hours. Stir to recombine the ingredients before serving. In separate dishes, place cucumber, green or red peppers, hard-boiled egg, olives, and green onions for each diner to add as desired.

FOR MORE INFORMATION

Anderson, J. M. *Daily Life during the Spanish Inquisition*. Westport, Conn.: Greenwood, 2002.

ITALY

The Renaissance diet lacked many foods central to Italian eating today: tomatoes, corn, potatoes, chili pepper, chocolate, and coffee, and gelato had yet to be invented. Pizza was a simple flat bread, not ubiquitous and never red. Pasta was no staple, but an occasional treat. Most of the missing ingredients were products of the New World, whose culinary gifts first infiltrated Europe in the mid-16th century. Then they were only for occasional or special uses. Tomatoes, for example, served first as medicine and aphrodisiac, then enlivened salads, but routinely sauced spaghetti only in the 1800s. Some new foods reached Italy from the East rather than the West. Coffee, for instance, found its way from Arabia via Egypt; it arrived in Italy, at Venice, only late in the 16th century and diffused rapidly from there. Italians probably also owed the Arabs for pasta, made from particular hard-grained wheat. Pasta was known in the Middle Ages, but during the Renaissance it cost three times more than bread and usually appeared for special events, not for everyday nutrition. Not until the 17th century, in Naples, and later in other zones, did pasta become ordinary people's daily fare.

Renaissance Italians ate well, in quantity, and in variety and balance. Between 1400 and 1600 there were few critical shortages, and the government stepped in quickly to prevent price gouging. Indeed, in this period, Italians were on average bigger and more robust than they would be during the much more impoverished centuries to follow; even 1900 was less healthy than 1500.

Carbohydrates were central to Renaissance nutrition, growing more so as the population rose. Because land yielded five times as many calories per acre from grain as from meat, it fed more people on bread. In cities and villages, specialized artisans made most bread. Typically it was dense, perhaps lumpy, and wrapped in a thick crust; such loaves kept longer but required serious chewing, even when fresh. Rather than making sandwiches with thick fillings and dressings, ordinary Italians often ate their bread plain, in hunks, perhaps seasoned in peasant fashion with a bit of raw garlic or onion. As a moister alternative, bread might serve as a plate under a helping of meat or cooked vegetable or as a sop dipped in an individual bowl or in a common pot in the middle of the table. Wheat was the preferred grain for bread, and white bread commanded more prestige and higher price. In southern Italy and in northern cities, everybody, even the poor, ate wheat bread. Elsewhere, peasants often had to eat loaves made at least partly with lesser grains, cheaper and easier to grow but harder to digest. Depending on the region, these included millet, oats, rye, barley and spelt. In addition to bread, Italians consumed much carbohydrate in the form of boiled grain, as mush (thick), porridge (thinner), or *minestra* (thinnest).

At the high end of the scale, more costly grain foods included rice and pasta. Rice production from the 15th century spread rapidly in the Po Valley, but supplied a luxury trade for soups and medicines. Renaissance Italy knew pasta in a variety of shapes and names. It was served usually for a special event, or as a Sunday treat, not with the savory tomato sauces of today, but either plain with meat or fish, or dressed with cheese and sweet spices such as cinnamon.

Meat and other animal proteins were reasonably plentiful in the diet. The 15th century marked a high point of consumption, after which a rising population needed grain that competed for productive acreage. Cooks prepared meat for the table by boiling or roasting, sometimes in combination. Long cooking, which helped destroy dangerous microbes, left meat soft, bland, and, if affordable, ready for a sweet or tangy sauce. Nuts, fruits, and sweet spices, such as cinnamon, cloves, nutmeg, and ginger, were welcome components, yielding a flavor akin to our mincemeat for pie, which derives from medieval cookery and originally had meat in it. Saffron, another favorite seasoning, besides adding taste, gave the dish a glamorous golden color that suggested well-being. The meat consumed varied with the season and the eater's wealth. The poorer classes ate pork, killed in early winter and preserved as ham and sausages, until Lent, ate fish during Lent, and then lamb, born in the spring and symbolically tied to Easter, in the months following that holiday. For variety, there were chicken and rabbit, as well as game. Aristocratic banquets, in contrast, featured a stunning display of exotic meats, prepared to delight the eye as well as the taste buds: boar, venison, peacock, swan, crane, and cormorant. During the Renaissance, the elite increasingly preferred the lighter flesh of fowl and fish to the heavier flavors of big game.

A Wealthy Kitchen. Servants roast the meat on spits over a fire. Picture by Antonio Tempesta. Roma—Instituto Nazionale della Grafica. By gracious concession of the Ministero per i Beni e le Attività Culturali.

Other foods included eggs and cheese. Fresh milk was generally unsafe to drink and did not keep. As cheese, however, it could be processed during the summer and then, especially in hard and dry forms, saved for eating year long. For cooking, much of Italy relied on olive oil, though Lombardy in northern Italy adopted butter, which was used by its transalpine neighbors. Italians made good use also of protein-rich pulses such as beans and chickpeas. They ate cabbage, squashes, artichokes, spinach, and other greens as well as garlic, onions, and leeks. Vegetables were served both stewed and raw; salads—dressed amply with oil, moderately with salt, and lightly with vinegar—were very popular. Fruits, including apples, grapes, peaches, pears, and oranges, were more of a treat.

For drink, almost everyone drank wine, either straight or watered, as their principal beverage. Estimates vary upward from two-thirds of a liter per person per day. Wine was a big source of calories. Most people drank cheaper local wines, but for the affluent there was also a lively trade in prized vintages such as the sweeter ones from Naples, or whites from Chianti (Cohen and Cohen, 225–30).

FOR MORE INFORMATION

Capatti, A., and M. Montanari. *La cucina italiana*. Rome: Laterza, 2000.
Cohen E. S., and T. V. Cohen. *Daily Life in Renaissance Italy*. Westport, Conn.: Greenwood, 2001.

OTTOMAN EMPIRE

Food formed an important part of social life in the Ottoman Empire. Evening entertainment for the wealthy featured food that was as much a part of the overall

experience as singing or poetry reciting. Important festivals—both holidays such as the end of Ramadan and personal transitions such as marriage and circumcision—became occasions for feasting. Coffeehouses became centers of socialization, and any guest in an Ottoman home would stand little chance of escaping unstuffed. Staples of the Ottoman diet included bread, fruit, and vegetables, with meat on certain special occasions.

People in the Ottoman Empire ate four meals each day. The two largest were breakfast, which took place between the morning and noon calls to prayer when people went to work for the day, and dinner, when the entire family gathered just after the evening prayer for the main meal of the day. Lunch was small and usually consisted simply of leftovers from the previous day's dinner. In some areas, a fourth meal was eaten at the end of the evening. This was called the "go to bed and drop dead" meal, and consisted of fruit, sweetened pastries, or other breakfast foods.

Ottoman houses did not have a separate dining room, and people ate meals wherever they happened to be at mealtime. Women or servants laid out the food on a mat known as a *sofra* which was usually made of leather. The most common dishes were copper bowls and pots, and in order to prevent poisoning, they were lined with tin. Special traveling craftsmen came to villages and towns to renew the tin linings. In the 15th century, dishes decorated with abstract designs became fashionable, whereas in the 16th century floral patterns predominated. Spoons were provided with desert; otherwise, people ate with their hands.

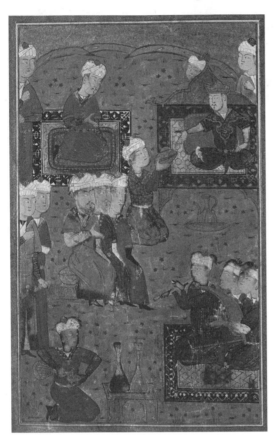

Banquet Scene. Most Turkish meals had several courses, and elaborate dinner parties like the one pictured here would feature a large variety of dishes for each course. © The Art Archive/ Biblioteca Nazionale Marciana Venice/Dagli Orti.

Women prepared all the food, and were considered rulers of the kitchen. At the start of a meal, one of the family elders would invoke God. If someone left the *sofra* or got a drink of water, everyone stopped and waited for them. Soup made up the first course, followed by pilaf and other dishes. People drank between the courses, which were served separately. After the meal, someone read a prayer, and then everyone took a final mouthful from whichever dish lay furthest away. People then went to wash their hands in order of seniority, after which they took coffee.

Records from the 17th century tell us much about the Ottoman diet. Grain products, especially bread, represented the most important of staples. Almost all bread was made from wheat and in rural areas baked once a week. In homes without baking ovens, women made a flat, unleavened loaf in fireplace ashes. One popular pastry was *borek*, which consisted of sheets of dough filled with meat and vegetables and either baked or cooked in fat. Wheat and millet gruel were put into soups. Rice was considered a luxury and often stretched by cooking it into soups and desserts.

Most meals were enlivened by fruits and, when possible, meats. The preferred types of fruits and vegetables depended on the trade and agriculture of a given area. Olives, apples, peaches, grenadines, and grapes were among the possibilities, as were plums, cherries, apricots, melons, and almonds, among others. Meat served as an expensive luxury, though one most people had at one time or another. *Pastirma* was meat preserved with garlic and spices in the sun and eaten in thin slices. Mutton represented the most common meat. Lambs were slaughtered at the youngest possible age and the skin was roasted to crackling. Beef, poultry, and fish were also consumed. Although Muslims did not eat pork for religious reasons, Christians in the Balkans did.

Desserts also formed an important part of the Ottoman diet. Among the most popular was baklava, made with dough and a sweet mixture of nuts or almonds. People also made unjellied jams called *recel* from fruits and sugar. Honey and grape syrup ranked as important sweeteners. *Helva,* a dish made in a variety of ways featuring such ingredients as dates, grape syrup, and milk was also popular and, in cities, served in the names of deceased persons as a final good deed.

Not all meals were eaten in the home. People in the cities could go to cookshops, which prepared food and in many cases had tables where people could eat it on the premises. Coffee became popular in the mid-16th century, when coffeehouses spread throughout the empire. Yemen was the only place coffee was grown during that period, and merchants in Egypt generally functioned as middlemen shipping it to the Balkans and Anatolia. Intellectuals and others also congregated in coffeehouses, where they would read, play games, and discuss the issues of the day. Generally, however, only men could gather at such public places, and women entertained each other in homes.

Despite its popularity, some conservative religious scholars objected to coffee, not only because it had not existed in the time of the Prophet, but because it seemed to have effects on the body similar to those of alcohol. Alcohol itself was forbidden for Muslims, and even Jews and Christians had great difficulty in obtaining it. Popular drinks in the Ottoman Empire included *boza*, made from fermented millet, and *salep*, often consumed with breakfast during the winter.

The Ottoman Empire thus had a very rich culinary culture based on traditional Turkish foods yet influenced by the many other cultures the realm encompassed. Locally grown vegetables were staples, and prepared in a variety of ways. Meats were more of a luxury, and often used only for festive occasions. Those with a sweet tooth could find something to sate it among the variety of available desserts, while between meals and in the evenings, people could gather with their fellows and discuss the news of the day. Turkish food thus not only represented a necessary part of daily life, but lay in the quiet corners decorating the entire culture from the court to a village circumcision ceremony.

To read about food and drink in Medieval Islam, see the Islam entries in the sections "Food" and "Drink" in chapter 5 ("Material Life") in volume 2 of this series.

~Brian Ulrich

FOR MORE INFORMATION

Cicek, K., ed. *The Great Ottoman-Turkish Civilisation 4: Culture and Arts*. Ankara: Yeni Turkiye, 2000.

Faroqhi, S. *Subjects of the Sultans: Culture and Everyday Life in the Ottoman Empire from the Middle Ages until the Beginning of the Twentieth Century*. Trans. Martin Bott. London: Tauris, 2000.

Goodwin, G. *The Private World of Ottoman Women*. London: Saqi Books, 1997.

MATERIAL LIFE
|
FOOD & DRINK
|
England

Spain

Italy

Ottoman Empire

Maya

Aztec

Inca

MAYA

Foods consumed by the ancient Maya are similar to the traditional diet of Maya peoples of today. The major differences include domesticated plants and animals introduced after the Spanish Conquest (such as rice, wheat, chickens, and pigs). The core of the Maya diet—past and present—is maize, beans, and squashes. Maize is usually dried, removed from the cob, and soaked in water and lime to remove the casing around each kernel. The process releases amino acids that would otherwise not be utilized when maize is consumed; this boosts its nutritional value. After being dried and ground on a metate (grinding stone), the maize flour is mixed with water to form a dough that is formed into flat tortillas and baked over a fire on a *comal* (pottery griddle) or wrapped in leaves and steamed in a clay pot to make tamales. Traces of hearths are sometimes found inside the remains of ancient Maya houses. In some cases the Maya may have cooked inside special kitchen structures next to their houses. On the basis of present practices, we can assume that food was prepared and cooked by women.

A variety of beans is still grown, but among the most favored are the black beans of the Maya highlands. A major source of protein, beans are cooked and served whole, or mashed and refried. In fact, the combination of either tortillas or tamales with beans provides most of the protein essential to human nutrition. A variety of squashes is also part of the traditional diet. Both the flesh and the seeds (often dried and roasted and used in sauces) are consumed. Several kinds of chilies were used fresh, roasted, or sun-dried as a condiment. A variety of root crops, such as cassava (manioc), were also grown. The diet was further supplemented by fruits that were either domesticated or collected wild from the forest, including avocados, papayas, guavas, and *ramon* (breadnut).

The major sources of animal protein were from domesticated turkeys, supplemented by other birds and animals. A rich and spicy turkey soup remains an especially important festive dish among the Maya today. Because the Maya kept no other fully domesticated animals except for the dog, a great variety of wild animals were hunted or trapped. The most important food animals included deer, rabbits, peccaries, tapirs, agoutis, armadillos, and monkeys. They could be roasted or stewed with chilies and other condiments. Rivers, lakes, and the sea were harvested for snails, shellfish, and fish, which were roasted or cooked in soups.

The Maya stingless bees were kept in hives, particularly in Yucatán, and the honey they produced was used for sweetening. Cacao (chocolate) was prepared as a beverage, mixed with honey (and sometimes chili). Other beverages, such as *atole*, were made from maize, water, and similar mixtures. One ceremonial drink was made from ground beans and squash seeds. A potent, intoxicating beverage was made from the bark of the *balche* tree; other fermented drinks were made from maize, honey, and fruits.

Honey, cacao, and salt were the most commonly traded dietary items, but almost any food product could be dried and transported. Salt was produced by evaporating sea water or water from salt springs. In Yucatán, extensive salt pans were constructed along the northern coast to harness the sun to evaporate sea water. Saltwater collected from the highlands (where there are several areas with salt springs) and along the Pacific coast were boiled in large pots to produce salt.

All pre-Columbian peoples relied in part on the wild for food. After all, there were far fewer species adaptable for domestication in the Americas than in the Old World. Thus the Maya supplemented their protein diet by fishing and hunting. Hunting was done with bow and arrow, spear, and blowgun, as well as traps and snares. The most desirable food animals were deer, tapirs, agoutis, rabbits, monkeys, and birds. The use of snares to trap deer is depicted in an ancient Maya book. The blowgun was used to hunt birds, monkeys, and other arboreal animals. Not all hunted or trapped animals were eaten; some, especially the carnivores, were used for their pelts, teeth, claws, and other products.

Aquatic species were very important to the ancient Maya diet. Fired clay net weights and bone fishhooks are often found at Maya sites. The Maya used dugout canoes, which are depicted on murals and artifacts. Fish and shellfish were a major source of food for people living along the coasts. It is likely that dried fish were traded far inland, just as is done today throughout the Maya area. Freshwater lakes and rivers throughout the highlands and southern lowlands provided a variety of fish and freshwater mollusks. The importance of both fish and shellfish is indicated by their frequent representations in Maya art.

A variety of useful wild plants are found throughout the Maya area. Today many are still collected for food, fibers, medicines, and other uses, and doubtless, the same was true in the past as well. Among the common forest plants used by the Maya are papaya, *annona*, sapodilla, cherimoya, *coyol*, allspice, vanilla, and oregano. Some of these trees and plants were also tended and cultivated in household gardens.

Although the Maya did not rely on domesticated animals for food, they did raise a few species. The most important was the turkey, although doves and Muscovy ducks may have been raised for food as well. (The Muscovy duck was domesticated in South America but was probably known to the Maya before the Spanish Conquest.) As in many societies, dogs were the most important domestic animal. They were used as household guardians and hunting companions. Special species of dog may have been fattened and eaten, as was the custom elsewhere in Mesoamerica. The Maya also probably raised captured wild animals, such as deer, in pens for food. In addition, the drainage canals in raised field systems could have been used to raise fish and mollusks (Sharer, 96–99).

 Snapshot

Bishop Diego de Landa's Account of Domesticated Deer among the Maya

[Women] raise other domestic animals, and let the deer suck their breasts, by which means they raise them and make them so tame that they never will go into the woods, although they take them and carry them through the woods and raise them there. (Sharer, 99)

FOR MORE INFORMATION

Harrison P. D., and B. L. Turner, eds. *Pre-Hispanic Maya Agriculture*. Austin: University of Texas Press, 1978.

Sharer, R. J. *Daily Life in Maya Civilization*. Westport, Conn.: Greenwood, 1996.

Tozzer, A. M. *Landa's Relación de las cosas de Yucatán*. Cambridge, Mass.: Peabody Museum, Harvard University, 1941.

MATERIAL LIFE

|

FOOD & DRINK

|

England

Spain

Italy

Ottoman Empire

Maya

Aztec

Inca

AZTEC

One of the most significant and creative cultural events in the development of pre-Aztec life, and one that was essential to the daily existence of Mexica families, was the control of food energy contained in plants. The domestication of several agricultural plants began before 6500 B.C.E. and was flourishing by 2000 B.C.E. in numerous areas within and beyond the Basin of Mexico. During this period, ancient Mesoamericans came to rely upon three important crops: corn, squash, and beans. This important group of vegetables, when consumed together, provided native Mesoamericans with the proper combination of proteins necessary for a complete diet. But for several millennia prior to the emergence of the Aztecs, the central crop of Mesoamerica was (as it continues to be) corn—white, black, red, and yellow maize. The most productive strands take six months to mature, though some types can take as little as four months. The problem facing the Aztecs was that maize, originally developed at altitudes lower than the Basin, had little resistance to frost. This meant that a late rainy season or early frosts could disrupt the growing season and cause havoc with the economic well-being of the Aztecs. In fact, surviving records tell us of devastating droughts and famines in the 1450s during the reign of the first Motecuhzoma (Motecuhzoma Ilhuicamina). In one report, some Aztecs sold themselves to the Totonacs: 400 cobs of maize for a young woman and 500 for a working male. During these periods some families had to sell their children into servitude or periods of slavery, later to buy them back when abundance returned. In times of regular harvests, the agricultural system was a model of order and productivity.

For further details of the Aztec diet, see the description of Maya diet in the entry above. Aztec food was very similar to that of their Mesoamerican cousins (Carrasco, 9–11).

FOR MORE INFORMATION

Bray, W. *Everyday Life of the Aztecs*. London: Batsford, 1968.

Carrasco, D., with S. Sessions. *Daily Life of the Aztecs: People of the Sun and Earth*. Westport, Conn.: Greenwood, 1998.

MATERIAL LIFE

|

FOOD & DRINK

|

England

Spain

Italy

Ottoman Empire

Maya

Aztec

Inca

INCA

A wide variety of foods were eaten by the Incas and their subjects. Most of their food was domesticated. The Incas grew corn, potatoes, coca, *ullucu*, quinoa, *tarwi* (a kind of grain), and squashes of several varieties. The main sources of meat were guinea pigs and ducks, although llamas were also eaten. Wild plants and animals were relatively minor contributors to the food supply. Fish was consumed along the coast and near Lake Titicaca.

Food was either boiled in a pot or roasted over an open flame. Soups and stews were the main dishes, and a wide variety was eaten. The recipe for one of these, called *motepatasca*, consisted of corn cooked with herbs and chili peppers until the kernels split open. Another, called *locro*, was a stew made of meat, potatoes, *chuño* (freeze-dried potatoes), other vegetables, and chili peppers. As in the Andes today, chili peppers and other spices were often used to make food more flavorful. A kind of corn bread was also made, either by boiling it or baking it in the ashes of a fire. Corn was toasted for eating while traveling. Popcorn was considered a delicacy.

The main drink was *chicha*, a mildly fermented beverage made from any of several plants, predominantly corn. To prepare it, women chewed the kernels, seeds, or fruit and spit the pulp into a large jar filled with warm water. Enzymes in the saliva broke down the sugars in the pulp, allowing it to ferment over the course of several days. The longer the fermentation process went on, the stronger the alcohol content became. *Chicha* was the staple drink of natives throughout the Andes, but it also had enormous religious importance for the Incas, being used in all religious ceremonies. Bernabé Cobo mentions in his book that water was never drunk unless there was no *chicha* or other drink.

The Incas ate only two meals a day, one in the morning at eight or nine o'clock and one in the afternoon at four or five o'clock. Whether certain foods were preferred for these meals is not known. The Incas ate sitting on the ground. Women ate back to back with the men, facing the cooking pots. Cooking was done in ceramic pots with pedestals or tripods placed directly in the fire. The Incas ate from flat plates, sometimes decorated with animal-head handles, and drank from tall cups made of wood or pottery. The only difference between nobles and others was that nobles used plates and cups made of gold and silver, rather than pottery.

For special occasions people sat in two lines. They sat on the ground, facing each other, with the most important person sitting on a stool at the head of the lines. The food was the same as at any other meal, and each family brought its own food.

Food and drink were stored in large pots or jars, typically with pointed bases. Household storage was done in bins of cornstalks plastered with mud, attic or rafter space, and mud-lined pits in the floor. Outside storage structures were made of adobe and were typically larger. Food from the harvest was stored in outside structures, then brought inside when its use was imminent.

Meat and fish were preserved by freeze-drying, a process also used to make *chuño* from potatoes. This procedure was commonly done in the winter, when it is cold and dry in the highlands. Potatoes were softened in water, then ground up and left to freeze at night. During the day when temperatures rose, the potatoes thawed and the water evaporated, drying the pulp. This was repeated until the potatoes were dried and would not spoil. Meat was cut into thin strips, pounded, then left to freeze at night and dry in the hot midday sun. This meat was called *charqui* (whence comes the term *jerky*). Freeze-drying enabled the Incas to store large quantities of food for imperial uses. Dried food also had the advantage of being easier to transport from its place of production to its place of storage.

The Incas used no intoxicants other than *chicha,* although they did use two drugs—coca and wild tobacco—as mild narcotics. Coca, from which the modern narcotic cocaine is derived, is a small bush that grows in the eastern foothills. The leaves were chewed with a small amount of lime to release the active ingredient, an alkaloid that mildly numbs the senses. Its use was restricted to the nobility and the religious elite. Tobacco, which was not cultivated but collected wild, was taken as a snuff and was used as a charm against poisonous animals (Malpass, 82–83).

FOR MORE INFORMATION

Cobo, B. *Historia del Nuevo Mundo.* 4 vols. 1653. Reprint, Seville: Sociedad de Biliófilos, 1890–5.

———. *History of the Inca Empire.* Ed. and trans. Roland Hamilton. 1653. Reprint, Austin: University of Texas Press, 1979.

Malpass, M. A. *Daily Life in the Inca Empire.* Westport, Conn.: Greenwood, 1996.

Rowe, J. "Inca Culture at the Time of the Spanish Conquest." In *Handbook of South American Indians.* Vol. 2, *The Andean Civilizations,* ed. Julian Steward. Washington, D.C.: Bureau of American Ethnology Bulletin 143, 1946. 183–330.

MATERIAL LIFE

HOUSES
& FURNITURE

England

Spain

Italy

Ottoman Empire

Maya

Inca

Houses and Furniture

Houses today are frequently homes and just homes—they are places to which the busy family retires after a hard day at school, work, or the shopping mall. The home is a place of retreat and privacy. These images and functions of modern houses have their roots in the 15th and 16th centuries, yet are not accurate representations of the role of the house in Renaissance life. The typical house during the 15th and 16th centuries was more crowded, and it was often the place of work as well. A typical English urban house, for example, consisted of a workshop and store on the ground level, with living space on the second floor for the family. Excavations of the Maya village at Cerén, El Salvador, which was destroyed suddenly by a volcanic eruption, show that houses from the middle Maya period contained workshops for such industries as weaving, pottery, and the manufacture of chipped-stone tools. Homes in the 15th and 16th centuries were places both for family life and for business life. Such integration of home and work is particularly true for women in both Europe and the Americas. While men might be engaged in business outside of the home, women were generally expected to stay at home, engaged in weaving and other activities. In the Ottoman Empire, many women had an area especially reserved for them, where male visitors were not allowed to enter. This area was known as a harem. Harem does not literally mean a band of wives of the same husband, but rather an area reserved for women and family.

Differences in the style of house reflect a range of influences, including taste, wealth, and environment. The environment could play a particularly interesting role, as houses in different regions adapted to meet the unique conditions of that region. For example, in the Quadix region of Granada, Spain, the inhabitants took advantage of the local soft and eroded tufa-stone hills and carved their homes into the sides of the hills, putting chimneys at the top and using the gullies between hills as streets. In the Inca empire, houses along the seacoast, where it seldom rains, were built out of adobe (dried mud) and had flat roofs, while in the rainy highlands, the houses were built of fieldstone, which would not deteriorate in the rain like adobe would, and featured steep roofs for the rain to run off.

Some styles of house have become strongly associated with particular regions, and are worth highlighting here. These housing styles are the English Tudor house, the Italian villa, and the Inca stonework building. The Tudor house, which gets its name from the Tudor kings of England in the 15th and 16th centuries (Henry VII, Henry VIII, and successors) is distinguished today by the dark timber frame that divides the outside walls into small squares of white plaster. In the Renaissance, these walls were constructed of wattle and daub. Wattle refers to wooden sticks that are interwoven between poles to form the base of the wall between two timber posts. This wattle is then covered over with daub, a thick paste made from clay and dung combined with straw or horsehair that hardens into a kind of durable plaster. The daub would then be painted. Many 15th- and 16th-century Tudor homes still survive to this day and are still in use as homes and shops.

The Italian villa is properly a large home in the Italian countryside, but we shall use the term to refer to larger Italian homes in general. One of the main features of such houses is a central atrium: a small courtyard open to the sky that is placed in the middle of the home, with the house surrounding it on all four sides. This atrium would frequently be made into a sumptuous garden, with special plants, some statues, and a central fountain or pond. Surrounding the atrium, there might be a covered walkway, called a loggia, where one could stroll or sit and enjoy the outside air while getting protection from the rain or the sun. Such areas were particularly valuable during the hot Mediterranean summers when the hot air trapped indoors could be stifling.

Perhaps the most impressive buildings of this period are the large stone structures built by the Incas. These buildings, in the shape of large rectangles like most Inca houses, were built with a dry-stone technique, in which stones are laid one on top of the other without mortar or other adhesive. Despite the lack of mortar, many of these buildings still stand and are in use today. The durability of these edifices reflects the tremendous skill and craftsmanship of the stonemasons. These professionals would carefully shape each stone with hard stone and metal tools until the stones fit perfectly together. The stones are so well matched that you cannot fit a knife blade between them! It is doubtful that any of the chipboard homes built today in the United States will last nearly as long, though perhaps the steel skyscrapers, our own form of monumental architecture, may.

~Lawrence Morris

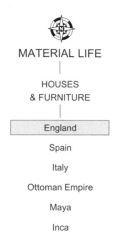

MATERIAL LIFE

HOUSES
& FURNITURE

England

Spain

Italy

Ottoman Empire

Maya

Inca

ENGLAND

"A man's house is his castle," wrote the jurist Sir Edward Coke in the early 17th century. The sentiment still resonates today, yet the meaning of one's house for people in Coke's day was not the same as it is for us. Today the house is a place of refuge, the place for private life. Although these trends had roots in the Renaissance period, the distinction between a person's private and public life was much less obvious then than it is today. For the Renaissance Englishman, the home was not just a private space: it was the focus of all aspects of life. People were born in their homes, they died in their homes, and often they worked in their homes too.

Then as now, the nature of one's dwelling varied between the city and the country, as well as between social classes. There were also distinctive building traditions in each area of the country, as well as differences of design between any one house and another. For the sake of simplicity, we will concentrate on three primary types: the rural cottage, the gentleman's manor house, and the town house.

The houses of the country folk were based on jointed frames of oak: instead of nails, which would be too weak, the timbers were carved with tongues (tenons) and slots (mortices) so that the whole frame fit together, with the tenons secured in their mortices by thick wooden pegs. Ideally the frame would rest on a stone foundation, since prolonged contact with moisture in the ground would eventually cause the timbers to rot. However, the cheapest sorts of structures simply had their main posts sunk into the ground.

The basic frame carried the weight of the house, and it had to be filled in to make the walls. The typical means of filling was a technique known as "wattle and daub." Wattling consisted of upright wooden stakes fixed at the top and bottom into the horizontal timbers of the house, with pliant sticks woven between them. The wattling created a rough base for the wall, which was then covered with daub—a mixture of clay and dung with straw or horsehair added for strength. The walls could be plastered on the inside and outside; sometimes the outside was whitewashed with a lime solution to prevent rain from washing away the clay too quickly. This style of home is frequently called a Tudor house today.

The commonest form of roofing was thatch, a very thick covering made with straw or reeds. A thatch roof was the best for keeping a house warm, as the thickly layered stalks provided good insulation and kept the rising heat from escaping through the top of the house. Unfortunately, it could also be a haven for vermin, and it posed a serious fire risk as well. Alternatives were clay tiles, slate, or shingles, depending on the circumstances—tiles were expensive, as was slate, while shingles were only readily available in regions with plenty of trees. Some wooden roofs were covered with lead to reduce the risk of fire, though again this increased the cost.

The peasant house was commonly just a two-room cottage. The front door led into an all-purpose hall, used for cooking, eating, and working. An inner door in

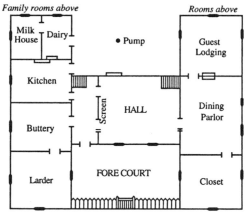

Floor Plan of a Manor House. Note the layout in the shape of the letter *E*. The closet was a private room, the larder was used for storing food, and the buttery stored drinks. The screen was a wooden partition separating the hall from the main passageways to cut down on drafts. Created by Jeffrey L. Singman.

the hall gave access to a parlor or chamber, which was typically the sleeping room for the householder and his wife; young children slept there too. Slightly more prosperous households had an additional workroom for food preparation and similar tasks; this was separated from the hall by a narrow passage running between the front and back doors.

The doors were made of wood and might be secured with bolts, although it was not uncommon even for ordinary people to have locks. An especially prosperous householder might even have glass windows, made of many small panes held together with lead. Most homes probably had wooden shutters, although thin layers of horn or oiled linen were alternatives that let in light while keeping out the wind.

The simplest form of cottage had an open hearth in the center of the room, with the smoke escaping through a hole in the roof. However, chimneys were becoming increasingly common. The chimney was sometimes made of wattle and daub, sometimes of brick to reduce the fire hazard. Most homes probably had just one floor with perhaps some planking laid on the overhead beams to create a bit of additional space. Cellars were rare; in the simplest cottages the floor might be no more than packed dirt, although those who could afford them had wooden floors. Access to upper levels was provided by ladders in simpler cottages, or by permanent stairs in better cottages.

A Tudor House. The timber frame is clearly visible. The space between the dark wood is filled in with wattle and daub and painted white. From Francis Gentleman, *Prolegomena to the Dramatick Writings of Will,* 1804.

During this period the gap between the houses of the rich and the poor was increasing. The compact medieval manor house, designed for defensibility, had given way in the 16th century to a more expansive and luxurious style that combined traditional medieval elements with new influences from Renaissance Italy. The stately 16th-century home was typically based on an E or a H shape. The middle section was a large hall, the principal public space of the house. It was flanked on one side by the family wing, which included the various private chambers of the family, and on the other by the service wing, which housed the kitchens, stores, and other working areas. Manor houses might be built on a timber frame filled in with brick, or of solid brick or stone.

These homes were distinguished from their medieval predecessors by their open design. Aristocratic feuding and civil wars during the Middle Ages required a manor home surrounded by a stout wall, with the exterior walls of the house itself built to resist assault. By Queen Elizabeth's time only a light wall enclosed the grounds, and the building itself abounded in windows.

Townhouses were similar in construction to those of country folk, save that they tended to be taller and closer together; they might even be built several in a row, since space was scarce in urban areas. Instead of wattle and daub, the walls were of wooden lathes covered with plaster; the best houses were of brick or stone. Two, three, or even four stories were typical; the upper floors might be built to jut out into the street over the lower ones, creating additional space. There was likely a proper floor and a cellar; however, there were still many simple cottage-type townhouses. The larger towns generally tried to forbid thatched roofs in favor of tile or wood covered with lead: a fire in the country might destroy only one house, but in the crowded conditions of a town, it could lead to a major public disaster.

If the owner was a tradesman or craftsman, the front of the ground floor might serve as a shop. The window shutter might swing downward into the street to create a kind of shop counter, with a canopy overhead to protect against rain. The family slept above the main floor. Additional space in the upper floors might be occupied by servants or apprentices, or rented to laboring folk too poor to have a house of their own—then as now, taking on boarders was a common way for a family to supplement its income. Boarders, like servants and apprentices, were likely to eat with the family, as there were probably no separate kitchen arrangements. Individual rooms were rather small, often as little as 10 to 15 feet on a side. The townhouse often had a garden in back.

The floor of a room in a commoner's house might be covered with straw or rushes; better houses sometimes had rush mats, which would be patterned and quite attractive. Loose straw or rushes might be mixed with sweet-smelling herbs; herbs and flowers were sometimes strewn upon the floors in fine houses too. Carpets were used as coverings for furniture rather than the floor, and only in well-to-do households. The walls might be plain or plastered; the wealthy would have them covered with wooden paneling, which was sometimes brightly painted. For decoration and extra warmth, the walls were often adorned with tapestries (for the wealthy) or with painted cloths (for the rest). These might depict biblical or legendary scenes; a painted cloth might even reflect folkloric themes such as the tale of Robin Hood.

The homes of the wealthy, lavishly endowed with windows, were airy and bright; but in poorer houses, where glass would have been too expensive, window openings had to be few and small to conserve heat; such houses were rather dark even in the daytime. After dark, light was provided by beeswax or tallow candles.

Houses were drafty and poorly insulated. There was no central heating, although prosperous houses sometimes had tile stoves. Otherwise heating was provided by open fires, either on open hearths or in proper fireplaces. Wood or coal served as fuel, but wood was preferred since coal produced a foul smoke. Naturally, the best houses had fireplaces in as many rooms as possible, but ordinary people were unlikely to have more than one hearth. Hot coals from the fire might be placed in an earthen vessel to provide warmth in other parts of the house.

The Renaissance home was sparsely furnished by modern standards. Furniture was wooden—mostly of oak and other hardwoods. Softwoods such as pine are cheaper nowadays, but pine was rare in England. Furniture was quite durable, since old oak becomes almost as hard as metal. The wood might be brightly painted, carved, inlaid, or simply coated with a linseed oil finish. Drawers were still quite rare in furniture at this time; doors, lids, and shelves were used instead.

The sparseness of furniture is illustrated by the inventory of a tanner in 1592, whose hall was furnished with a table, five joint stools, a chair, a bench, and painted cloths to hang on the walls. As indicated by the inventory, most people sat on stools or benches. Chairs (distinguished by having a back) were relatively rare: as in this tanner's hall, there was often just one, reserved for the head of the household (for this reason the term *chair* is sometimes used today to designate a position of authority, as in *chairman*). The nicest chairs were upholstered, but this was a luxury seen only in wealthy homes; cushions were the more usual means of making a seat comfortable. In the Middle Ages, chairs always had arms as well as backs, but the 16th century saw the emergence of the farthingale chair: fashionable women wore large hoopskirts (farthingales) that were too big to fit between the arms of a chair, so the farthingale chair was made without arms. There were also benches with backs, called settles (Singman, 73–82).

To read about houses and furniture in Chaucer's England, see the Europe entries in the sections "Housing" and "Furnishings" in chapter 5 ("Material Life") in volume 2 of this series; for 18th-century England, see the entry on England in the section "Housing" and "Furnishings" in chapter 5 ("Material Life") in volume 4 of this series; for Victorian England, see the Victorian England entry in the section "Housing" in chapter 5 ("Material Life") in volume 5 of this series.

FOR MORE INFORMATION

MacQuoid, P. "The Home." In *Shakespeare's England*. Vol. 2: 119–52. 1916.
Singman, J. L. *Daily Life in Elizabethan England*. Westport, Conn.: Greenwood, 1995.

SPAIN

Houses in Madrid were seldom aligned in rows along a street but were scattered helter-skelter. They were generally constructed of brick or adobe. A façade of stone might indicate the dwelling of a nobleman or a rich bourgeois. Small windows, many without glass, let in only a dim shaft of light through the paper or greased parchment that covered them, which was replaced by lattice screens in the summer. Windows had grilles to deter housebreakers. Gallants that came to serenade a señorita behind them pressed their faces against the bars to be nearer to the girl of their dreams; the contemporary metaphor for courting, *comer hierro* (to eat iron), was derived from this act.

If a house had more than one story, the warmest months of the year would be spent on the ground floor in the cooler rooms. Ladies stayed inside in the unbearable heat of summer in Madrid and other towns of the high plateau, wearing only short sleeveless shifts covering them from the neck down. Not until after sundown did the hot paving stones of the city begin to cool down. In the winter the warmer upstairs rooms were more comfortable.

The interior walls of the house would be decorated with tapestries and mirrors, whereas the floors were flagged or tiled. In the houses of the well-to-do, thick carpets were laid down in the winter months. If the family were rich, there would be a room for receptions and ceremonies where family treasures and beautiful furniture were

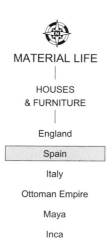

displayed. Pictures, mostly of religious themes, hung on the walls above ponderous carved wooden chests inlaid with mother-of-pearl or ivory, standing next to sideboards with shelves displaying silver plates.

Such a room might be partitioned, separating men and women, the former sitting on chairs or stools, the latter on silk or velvet cushions or squatting on the floor in Moorish style. Heat for the rooms was generated by large metal braziers mounted on wooden stands. Olive stones were often burned as fuel, as they gave off little odor; coal was more effective but more expensive. In wealthy households a person was paid to maintain the braziers throughout the cold winter months. The fumes often caused headaches and, on occasion, fatalities in the closed rooms. In poor houses sulfurous dung was burned, emitting a bad stench.

Lighting came from oil lamps or candelabra. Ostentatious display, characteristic of the age, led to competition in home furnishings and decoration, sometimes reducing a modest family to penury trying to keep up with more affluent segments of society. The private sections of the house that visitors did not see were often uncomfortable and lacking light. There were no toilets, and the chamber pots were kept under the beds.

The type of construction of peasant houses depended on the region: stone and wood were used where available, but often the soil itself was all there was to erect a dwelling. Village and farmhouses on the plateau north of Madrid were made of sun-dried mud bricks or blocks of clay about three feet square, studded with pebbles. One-story farm buildings were easy to build but disintegrated in heavy rain or under a hot sun. In La Mancha, south of Madrid, village houses were similarly constructed but had tiled roofs. A roughly hewn table and a few wooden benches made up the furniture, whereas the beds, in small dark rooms leading off the central living space, were often a single plank or a woolen mattress on the floor. The ample fireplace in a corner of the main room served to cook food (usually stew) and sometimes contained a brushfire when the temperature dipped low. In the poverty-stricken area far north of the country the entire house was a single round room shared by humans, pigs, and cattle. If there was an upper story, then the lower floor was used for the livestock.

The villages of Extremadura and Andalucía had sharp contrasts between the widely separated large manorial houses, sometimes displaying a coat of arms, and the lowly mud-brick quarters of the laborers clustered around them. In some hilly regions such as the town of Quadix in Granada where the porous tufa rock was soft and eroded, peasants hollowed out their homes in the sides of the cliffs, creating comfortable rooms that were cool in summer and easily heated in winter, with chimneys protruding from the tops of the hills and the gullies between the dwellings serving as streets. In the more prosperous regions of Cataluña, peasant estates flourished around the *masía*, a solidly built farmhouse of stone with a roof built from wooden beams. A peasant farmer here might have a number of workers on his land living in comfortable conditions (Anderson, 133–34, 150).

FOR MORE INFORMATION

Anderson, J. *Daily Life during the Spanish Inquisition*. Westport, Conn.: Greenwood, 2002.

ITALY

Houses varied hugely in structure, shape, and size. Since every region had its own architecture, general remarks are hard, but some distinctions made a great difference: urban versus rural, rich versus poor, and new versus old. Urban houses were often suited to trade, rural ones to farming. The former often had shops, workshops, storage rooms, and an open front for street-side commerce, while the latter often housed livestock and stored tools and supplies. In some zones, country houses were solid and spacious, in others often mean and squalid. Urban houses, protected by the city walls, less often built safeguards against attack than did isolated farmsteads. As for wealth, the houses of the very rich in the Renaissance were proper palaces, with a sumptuous architecture that made dramatic use of space to delight and to impress. Those of the well-to-do shared some of the same features, especially the desire for convenience and comfort. The urban poor, meanwhile, dwelled in one room or two alongside other households, or shared a bed in a room in a building neither grand nor solid nor agreeable. Older buildings in the Renaissance, and they were many, still had medieval lineaments: military trim, tight windows randomly placed, bits of structure jutting up or out. Newer ones took on the traits of a rapidly evolving architecture that prized grandeur, symmetry, light, and comfort.

Whether grand or humble, Renaissance buildings had some common spatial traits. An important one was the courtyard. Almost all palaces had at least one great central space and often several minor ones. One entered through an imposing central door, passing down a vaulted corridor, and entered a shapely central yard, paved and lined on all or most sides by columns and porticoes. They were utilitarian expanses, convenient and fairly secure. There might be a well and doors to storerooms; sometimes tradesmen arrived with donkeys to unload gear. A second common spatial configuration was the loggia, an arcaded porch or balcony. In the Mediterranean, a covered place to take the air sheltered from sun or rain made excellent sense. The colonnaded walks around courtyards fitted this architectural pattern, as did the covered walks of many cities. Some loggias were on the public street; palaces offered them magnanimously to passers-by or used them to hold showy dinners under the envious public gaze. As the Renaissance progressed, this last custom fell from favor; a move toward privacy, and toward class segregation, encouraged indoor loggias, facing the back garden. More modest houses also might have such upstairs galleries. From an upstairs loggia, women might hang washing, observe the men's activities, or flirt from a discreet distance.

The ground floor of a house was used less for living and more for work and storage. Above this utilitarian level, there might be a modest mezzanine that housed the proprietors of the shops below. Above that, in a palace, came the *piano nobile* (the noble floor). It was there that a wealthy resident would receive guests of honor, entertain, and live; higher floors would house lesser members of the household. Simpler houses were no grander on one floor than on another.

Indoors, all houses had two basic rooms: the *sala* and the *camera*. The *sala*, the bigger of the two, accommodated the more public gatherings, while the more common *camera* almost always served for sleeping. Nevertheless, our customary division of the living room and the bedroom, the former public, the latter private, does not altogether fit the Renaissance. In Italy, the distinction was far less sharp. People often slept in the *sala*; moreover, not rarely, they entertained guests and did business on or by the bed, in the *camera*. The *sala*, being big, was the room most likely to have a fireplace. In simpler homes lacking a kitchen, people often cooked in the *sala*, and in dwellings of all sizes, they ate there.

The urban palace was not only big but symmetrical, harmonious, and almost always ornamented with motifs from ancient architecture. Owners sometimes bought up nearby houses, knocking them down to make a square out front, the better to overawe the neighborhood. Although the ideal palace had the kind of internal symmetry that delighted architects, in fact, many real palaces were an internal jumble behind a deceptively regular facade. For palaces and houses often grew haphazardly, swallowing older dwellings and reusing their spaces and their internal stress-bearing walls. As families grew, they annexed neighbors or built upward. And, when brothers split an inherited building, they might partition it. Because walls were often thick and sturdy, a wealthy family's city house might rise five or six stories.

The urban palace interposed between the very public *sala* and the master's bedroom a suite of rooms: perhaps a *saletta* for more intimate meals, and an *anticamera* (antechamber). Behind the bedroom were spaces even more private, including, very often, a studio for books, important papers, and art treasures. There were no corridors; in general, guests passed from room to room, penetrating deeper into private space the more the host wished to pay them honor or take them into confidence. The whole series of the master's rooms came in the Renaissance to be called an *appartamento*.

To a modern eye, the furniture in even a wealthy Renaissance house would have looked sparse, bulky, and unvaried. Carpenters built solidly and simply in wood. During the 15th and especially the 16th centuries, the rich purchased more and more fancy, decorated pieces—embellished with carving and inlay and upholstered with tassels, scallops, and fringes. Yet basic types and designs of furniture remained few: beds, tables, seats, and chests. A mix of these, often only a few per chamber, lined walls throughout the house. These pieces were heavy, but one would move them as occasion required.

The bed was, both symbolically and functionally, at the center of the house. When a newly married couple set up their home, the bed was their principal acquisition. In this bed the next generation would be conceived; the women would later gather to congratulate the new mother and her child. Suitably, the bedroom was often better furnished, decorated, and warmed than other parts of the dwelling.

The simplest bed frames consisted of planks or rough boxes set on low trestles. At the high end of the spectrum were substantial wooden structures built tall and flanked by low, flat-topped chests, on which guests might sit or servants sleep. In 15th-century Florence, where luxury furniture making flourished, a wealthy consumer might pay a skilled worker's annual wage for a highly decorated bed or chest. From the 1490s, good beds boasted columns at the corners to support hangings. Even before four-poster beds came in, curtains suspended variously from walls and ceilings were an important aid to sleep. Draperies in winter held warmth in and in summer kept bugs out.

Though less central than beds, tables and places to sit counted among the most common kinds of furniture. Like beds, tables ran a gamut from simple, easily dismantled rigs of boards and trestles to broad, heavy edifices of carpentry, of the sort now seen in museums and historic castles. An ordinary household might well have only one table used for meals, but also for work, recreation, and sleep, as needs arose. When people sat—at the table, near the fire, or elsewhere—what few seats there were may have been uncomfortable. Sometimes they sat directly on the ground or floor or cross-legged on flat platforms, as tailors did for work; even patrician women might be painted sitting with only a cushion for support. But there was also furniture. Pictures of peasant houses feature wooden stools and benches. For the grand, who bought more ease and prestige, there were armchairs, sometimes upholstered in leather or gold-embroidered velvet.

Chests of various kinds made up the last great sort of furniture for the home. Storage—of food, dishes, clothing, and so on—was an essential house function. For clothes in frequent use, pegs attached to the wall were handy. Foodstuffs could be kept away from vermin by suspension from ceiling hooks. Much of a household's worth, however, lay stowed in chests of many sizes. Some small ones enclosed valuables, while others, for clothing, were large enough to hide a person. Elegant inlay decoration or narrative painting from a premier workshop could turn even a wooden box into a luxury item. Fancy chests bore high honor; they served as potent markers of status when transporting the trousseau at a patrician wedding or when given as a gift to a foreign potentate (Cohen and Cohen, 158–61, 221–23).

FOR MORE INFORMATION

Coffin, D. *The Villa in the Life of Renaissance Rome*. Princeton: Princeton University Press, 1979.

Cohen, E. S., and T. V. Cohen. *Daily Life in Renaissance Italy*. Westport, Conn.: Greenwood, 2001.

OTTOMAN EMPIRE

Much of daily life in the Ottoman Empire revolved around the family, and the life of the family revolved around the home. The form taken by housing varied greatly throughout the empire, based on such factors as climate, wealth, and cultural models sometimes going back thousands of years. Most homes were small; however, the fact that textiles represented the most important furnishings meant that a small area could serve a variety of functions. The most important architectural function was the seclusion of a private living area that male guests could not enter. Although housing itself was often bland, the interiors of homes featured comfortable cushions and carpets woven in a variety of designs and colors.

MATERIAL LIFE

HOUSES
& FURNITURE

England

Spain

Italy

Ottoman Empire

Maya

Inca

Despite the many elaborate mosques and palaces found in the major cities, most people in the Ottoman Empire lived in simple houses with minimal furnishings. Most Anatolian houses had only one or two rooms, enough space for a single nuclear family. The husband and father of the family usually had ownership of the building, and when he died he passed it to his children. The children then sold shares of the house to each other, so that each house generally had a single owner, though sometimes a married couple would assume joint ownership. Fortunately, the low cost of housing meant that most people found another dwelling after they sold their share to a sibling.

Larger Anatolian houses traditionally consisted of a stone ground level with any upper stories being made of wood or earthen materials in a wooden frame. Many huts, however, were simply wooden or brick. Materials for building houses could come from such places as ruins of older buildings or riverbeds. Some homes were simply made of mud with wooden roofs. Dwellings typically had an open fireplace in one room to provide heat with chests or cupboards built into the wall as storage areas. In some areas, people had terraced roofs that they used as the living quarters during the warm summer months. Sometimes more well-to-do families had an upper story for that purpose. Rooms did not open onto each other directly, but were instead separated by a hall or veranda which served as the setting for much family life.

Most houses in Ottoman Anatolia did not have separate spaces for most activities. Bedding, for example, was kept in cupboards or chests during the day and taken out when it was time to sleep. Although wealthy families may have had a kitchen, most people cooked food either outside or in the main room, depending on weather conditions. However, people did keep separate areas for family living and the reception of visitors. This family area, often called the harem, was forbidden to male guests so as to preserve privacy. This practice led to many fanciful tales by European travelers about wealthy Muslims keeping hordes of wives and concubines behind closed doors.

During the day, people set out cushions and carpets as furniture. There were two main types of cushions, one for sitting on, the other for reclining against. People did not enter homes in their street shoes in order to protect the carpets inside. Despite this, the carpets often wore out and had to be replaced. Ottoman carpets were usually decorated with abstract geometric designs. Often the designs on carpets carried symbolism related to folklore, and the carpets could thus convey certain messages. A daughter, for example, could select a certain set of motifs to indicate a desire to marry. Prayer rugs represented a final important fabric item central to the Ottoman Muslim religious life.

Houses of the wealthy often had a courtyard in front featuring a well, pond, trees, and on rare occasions a flower garden. A stairway from the courtyard led to the second floor, if there was one. The kitchen, washroom, and storerooms were typically found on the ground floor, while the family lived upstairs. Family members gathered in the *hayat*, a large balcony-like area in the center of the second floor. Many houses of the wealthy also included the *selamlik*, an area reserved for male guests so they could be entertained without violating the sanctity of the harem. Sometimes the *selamlik* was even a separate building near the stables or servants' quarters. Many of the wealthy townspeople would also own another home in the countryside where they lived during the summer.

Other parts of the empire had different architectural styles. In Cairo, for example, people lived in large family units consisting of a number of smaller apartments, each consisting of a large, central room with side rooms for purposes such as cooking or sleeping. These apartments did not have separate harems, and men were received simply by assigning them their own apartment. In Cairo, most houses had windows overlooking the street, while in Aleppo they overlooked a central courtyard, with the streets running between blank walls. Under no circumstances could a window provide a view of the inside of a neighboring house. Because the Ottomans taxed houses in some districts based on the number of doors each had, in the Balkans many dwellings would open onto a central courtyard with only one door opening onto the street for all of them. Christians and Jews generally had to live in houses smaller than those of Muslims.

In reality, Ottoman living spaces varied as much as Ottoman subjects. People from Hungary to Arabia lived in housing similar to what they had since before the Ottoman dynasty arose. People in the rural areas continued to build simple dwellings from whatever materials were locally available, while the wealthy developed more ornate forms which served both to increase their own luxury and to display their status for all to see. Yet in all of these types of houses, we see an insight into the most personal lives of the people who lived there, their sense of family intimacy and hospitality which represents an important aspect of the Ottoman experience.

To read about houses and furniture in Medieval Islam, see the Islam entries in the sections "Housing" and "Furnishings" in chapter 5 ("Material Life") in volume 2 of this series.

~Brian Ulrich

FOR MORE INFORMATION

Cicek, K., ed. *The Great Ottoman-Turkish Civilisation 2: Economy and Society.* Ankara: Yeni Turkiye, 2000.

————. *The Great Ottoman-Turkish Civilisation 4: Culture and Arts.* Ankara: Yeni Turkiye, 2000.

Faroqhi, S. *Subjects of the Sultans: Culture and Everyday Life in the Ottoman Empire from the Middle Ages until the Beginning of the Twentieth Century.* Trans. Martin Bott. London: Tauris, 2000.

Goodwin, G. *The Private World of Ottoman Women.* London: Saqi Books, 1997.

Sugar, P. F. *Southeastern Europe under Ottoman Rule, 1354–1804.* Seattle: University of Washington Press, 1977.

MAYA

Low mounds can usually be recognized as the remains of ancient Maya houses. These are the remnants of low earthen or rubble platforms that once supported oblong or rectangular houses of one or more rooms. The ancient Maya house (*na*)

MATERIAL LIFE
|
HOUSES
& FURNITURE
|
England

Spain

Italy

Ottoman Empire

Maya

Inca

was very much like those in use today. Some were built with stone or adobe (mud) walls roofed with pole and thatch; others were built entirely of perishable pole and thatch. They were about the same size as modern Maya houses; like today, they undoubtedly sheltered a nuclear family—wife, husband, and children.

In the past there was more variation in house materials and size based on status. Houses of the Maya elite were much larger than those of the common people and were often built completely of masonry blocks, had vaulted roofs, and were supported by higher masonry platforms. The houses of Maya kings were so large and elaborate that they are usually referred to as palaces.

Ruins of a Royal Palace. This complex at Caracol, Belize, was the home of the ruler and his family and once stood at the center of a village. The huge structure must have thoroughly impressed the subjects of the king. © Macduff Everton/CORBIS.

The remains of ancient Maya houses often reflect the range of past household activities. These include food storage, preparation, and cooking. Houses were also used for craft manufacturing, with workshop areas where textiles were woven, pottery was made, and stone tools and a variety of other products were produced. When family members died, they were usually buried beneath the house. The sudden volcanic eruption that buried a middle Maya civilization village at Cerén, El Salvador, provides a rare view of the buildings, tools, and activities within a rural Maya community as they were at the moment of the disaster. Careful excavation of the buried areas at Cerén have exposed several adobe houses and even the charred remains of their pole-and-thatch roofs, outbuildings, workshops, storage areas, household articles, and adjacent fields where maize and a variety of crops were grown.

Maya houses are seldom found in isolation. Most often they are in clusters (*nalil*) of two to six units arranged around a central patio. Based on similar situations in modern Maya communities, we can assume these *nalil* were occupied by an extended family, that is, two or more related nuclear families. The extended family groupings are often composed of grandparents, parents, and married children living in separate but adjacent houses. The head of the extended family may be indicated by the largest or most elaborate house in the group. Ancillary buildings—used for storage, workshops, or other purposes—may be included. A repeated pattern in the *nalil* clusters at Tikal consists of a central patio bordered on three sides by houses and a smaller but higher building on a platform on the east side. This was probably the extended family's household shrine, where the founder of the residential group was buried and which served as the focus of rituals to venerate the important ancestor.

Clusters of *nalil* often form wards or barrios (*china*). These may have been occupied by larger kin groups, such as lineages. But not all residents of the typical *china* may have belonged to the lineage. Some houses may have been occupied by retainers, servants, and other clients of lineage members.

Although they could be organized in various ways, the sum total of people living together in one place defined the *cah*, or Maya community. The *cah* could be of any size, from the smallest agricultural village (*chan cah*) to the largest political capital (*noh cah*). Yet even the largest Maya cities included the same residential components—some much larger and more complex than others, of course. At the heart of a capital such as Tikal was the *noh nalil* (palace complex) of the royal family, along with those of the other elite extended families. The larger Maya cities also included many more public buildings and facilities than the smaller communities. Regardless of its size, the *cah* was the setting for the organizations that gave society its basic structure. Many were based on kinship: nuclear family, extended family, and lineage bonds.

Normal Maya furnishings included baskets and mats, which were important for both practical and symbolic uses. The natural fibers from which they were made are found throughout the area. Baskets and mats represent ancient crafts now known mostly by depictions in carved or painted art. A variety of decorated baskets are represented on painted Maya vases. Maya baskets made today are less elaborate. Those used to carry corn and other rough tasks are woven from thin, tough vines. Smaller and more carefully woven baskets made of split cane are for household uses.

A related craft was the weaving of mats, which are still used in many Maya households for sleeping. Mats played an important practical and symbolic role in ancient Maya life. Sitting on a mat was a mark of authority, as indicated by the royal title *ahpop*, "lord of the mat," used by Maya kings. Depictions of Maya rulers often show the king seated on a mat. The hieroglyph for the first month of the Maya solar year, Pop, was a piece of matting combined with the sun symbol, also associated with royalty. Few pieces of ancient matting have survived, but impressions have been found on pottery and plaster. At Copan several burials have been excavated with impressions of matting still in place. In one case the body was placed in a seated position on a mat, indicating his high status. In another, the corpse of a sacrificed warrior was wrapped in a mat before burial. The weaves of these mats are identical to those made and used in the Copan area today (Sharer, 116–17, 211–12).

To read about housing in nineteenth-century Latin America, see the Latin America entry in the section "Housing" in chapter 5 ("Material Life") in volume 5 of this series.

FOR MORE INFORMATION

Sharer, R. J. *Daily Life in Maya Civilization*. Westport, Conn.: Greenwood, 1996.

INCA

The Incas are probably most famous for their method of fitting building stones so closely together that one cannot slip even a knife blade between them. This technique was only one of several used by the Incas, and was reserved for the most important buildings, such as temples, administrative structures, and kings' residences. More common techniques were used for most other buildings, and these are often much less recognizable as Inca in origin. Yet Inca architecture, be it of high or low quality, has common features that do make it identifiable.

Inca constructions were most often made of stones collected from fields and then laid in mortar. Adobe, or mud brick, was also used, although in the rainy highlands

MATERIAL LIFE
|
HOUSES
& FURNITURE
|
England

Spain

Italy

Ottoman Empire

Maya

Inca

this material is less well preserved. To cover the rough appearance of either fieldstone or adobe, a layer of mud or clay was put on the walls and then painted.

The best-known Inca buildings are made of fine masonry, that is, of carefully shaped stones that fit snugly against their neighbors. To achieve walls of exceptionally smooth and uniform appearance, the Inca stoneworkers used tools of other harder stones and bronze chisels. Sometimes the stones were shaped into roughly square or rectangular forms, then used much like bricks. This method appears to have been reserved for the most important buildings. Sometimes the stones were left in irregular shapes but were worked along the edges to fit together tightly. This technique was used more often when very large stones were needed, as in terrace walls or riverbank constructions.

Quality Inca Stonework. Note how the stones are carefully cut to fit securely together without the use of mortar or cement. Photo by Michael A. Malpass.

All forms of fine masonry involved enormous effort, because the fitting was accomplished by pounding and grinding the edges with harder stones or bronze chisels until they fit. Although there is no mystery about how Inca stonework was done, it is not generally appreciated how tedious and slow the work must have been. Very likely the fine stonework was a craft done by specialists, as were pottery and weaving. However, a large number of unskilled workers must have helped quarry the rocks, move them, and raise them into position. Earthen ramps were used to raise the large stones if more than one row was needed. This activity indicates how enormous a labor force the Incas were able to mobilize.

Although it might be very large or very small, the fundamental Inca structure was a rectangular building with a single room. Usually there was one door in the middle of a long wall, although there might be more than one if the room was very long. Most Inca buildings contained a single floor. If the building was on a very steep hillside, a second floor might be added and entered from the rear and above. In the area around Cuzco, two- and even three-story buildings were also built, although the latter are very rare. The roofs were made of thatch. Highland structures almost always had steeply sloping roofs, which allowed rain to run off. Most Inca buildings were rectangular, but other shapes were sometimes used, including round and U-shaped.

Rectangular structures were typically grouped together into a *cancha*, a compound of three or more buildings surrounding an open patio. The compound was enclosed by a wall. Like the basic rectangular building, the *canchas* could be small, with few buildings and a small patio or very large, with more and much bigger structures enclosing a much larger space.

The *canchas* apparently served a variety of purposes. Many were living quarters, but others might have been used for temples or craft production areas. The buildings within the *cancha* may have served different purposes. It is suggested that when a *cancha* was used as a residence, the group occupying it was probably an extended family.

Another distinctive Inca building was the *callanca* (great hall). As the name implies, it was a long rectangular building—but like most Inca structures, it had no interior walls. *Callancas* often had multiple doors. These buildings are usually found around Inca plazas, with doors opening onto the plazas. It is uncertain what these structures were used for, although excavations in them typically uncover little trash of any kind. They may have been used as temporary residences for people in the Inca centers outside of Cuzco, although the ones in Cuzco itself were probably used for ceremonies.

An interesting multipurpose structure found in Inca settlements is the *ushnu*, or central platform. This is usually found in the center of important state institutions, either in the middle of the main plaza or off to one side. It was used in rituals, as a review stand, and as a place where the Inca king could meet conquered leaders. *Ushnus* are only found at Inca centers built to administer conquered provinces and in Cuzco. Thus, like other Inca public buildings, they were symbols of Inca dominance over conquered people.

The second most noted feature of Inca architecture is its use of trapezoids. In the vicinity of Cuzco, most openings to buildings, doors, windows, even interior niches are trapezoidal, with the widest part at the bottom. The significance of this shape is unknown. In areas south of Cuzco, rectangular forms appear. The trapezoid disappears in the regions of the Inca Empire south of Lake Titicaca.

Stonemasons at Work. Stonemasons were very skilled engineers. Contrary to the illustration, however, most of the stones were too large to be picked up easily by just one person. Picture by Guaman Poma.

The typical house of the Incas around Cuzco was a rectangular, single-roomed building with one door and no windows. It was built of rough fieldstone, then plastered and painted. The roof was steeply sloped and had a thatch covering. Three or more of these buildings were grouped into a *cancha*, which was occupied by an extended family. Both royalty and commoners lived in such structures, although those of the royalty were no doubt considerably larger and made of finer masonry.

Outside of Cuzco in the conquered areas, houses tended to be different. Because it was the Inca custom to leave a conquered people as unchanged as possible, most continued occupying the kinds of houses they had prior to their subjugation. Thus in the provinces houses might have been round or rectangular. The Wanka, a group living in the central highlands due east of modern Lima, had compounds of round houses, as did groups of the Huánuco area. Construction techniques might also be different. On the coast, where rock is not as abundant as in the highlands, adobe was a more common building material; and because rain seldom fell, roofs were flat and made of woven reeds.

In fact, it is sometimes difficult to identify a settlement as belonging to the Inca Empire, because its houses and tools might be the same kind as were used prior to the Inca conquest. Sometimes the only way one can identify the presence of an Inca official is by the presence of a rectangular house among round ones or by the presence of Inca pottery (Malpass, 56–60).

To read about housing in 19th-century Latin America, see the Latin America entry in the section "Housing" in chapter 5 ("Material Life") in volume 5 of this series.

FOR MORE INFORMATION

Gasparini, G., and L. Margolis. *Inca Architecture*. Bloomington, Ind.: Indiana University Press, 1980.

Hyslop, J. *Inka Settlement Planning*. Austin: University of Texas Press, 1990.

Malpass, M. A. *Daily Life in the Inca Empire*. Westport, Conn.: Greenwood, 1996.

MATERIAL LIFE: WEB SITES

http://www.lib.virginia.edu/dic/colls/arh102/index.html
http://www.flmnh.ufl.edu/maya/maya4.htm
http://www.smm.org/sln/ma/duty.html
http://www.isourcecom.com/maya/themaya/architecture.htm
http://www.pbm.com/~lindahl/food.html
http://www.geocities.com/napavalley/6454/history2.html

6

POLITICAL LIFE

The ancient Greek philosopher Aristotle (384–322 B.C.E.) claimed that humans are by definition political animals, and by this he meant that an essential part of human life involves interacting in the public sphere with people who are not our intimate family members. It is these relationships—along with their complex negotiations—that permit the development of cities, kingdoms, nations, and civilization itself. Throughout history different cultures have developed different political systems to organize their lives, and all political systems are in constant states of change as they accommodate the changing needs and interests of the populace. Political life involves two different spheres of influence: organizing the relationship among those within a political unit and negotiating the relations between different political entities (countries or tribes or kingdoms). However, at its basic level, politics is about power—finding out who has it and who does not.

People create a political system first of all to ensure internal peace and security for themselves. As the political theorist Thomas Hobbes (1588–1679 C.E.) noted, without a strong authority, people's incessant struggle for power would result in a life that is "nasty, brutish, and short." This is why we want our power structures clear. Our political systems also clarify and solidify our loyalties and allegiances—nationalism has served as a sentiment that can unify people with diverse interests and backgrounds.

As people interact in ever-widening circles, our political life must negotiate the often-difficult relations with other kingdoms, countries, or empires. Diplomacy is the tool of our political life that is used to smooth these interactions, and war is the breakdown of these negotiations. In war—which has unfortunately dominated so much of human history—we can often see both the noblest and worst expressions of our human spirit. In war we can also definitively see the struggle for power that marks our political life.

The entries in this section will focus on three interrelated aspects of political life: hierarchy, government, and justice. *Hierarchy* originally meant "rule by the holy," but it has come to refer to any system, such as social class or education, that creates different levels of authority. In a hierarchical system, every individual has a specific position in the chain of command. In both Europe and the Americas, the most

POLITICAL LIFE

HIERARCHY

GOVERNMENT

JUSTICE
& LEGAL SYSTEMS

fundamental hierarchies were those of birth and class. People who were born into noble families, such as the king, were at the very top of the hierarchy, while those born to peasant parents were at the bottom. The accumulation of wealth, however, enabled people to climb upward in the hierarchy and to give their own children a better start in the climb toward the top.

Hierarchy has clear ramifications on government. Many governments of the 15th and 16th centuries were simply hierarchies invested with legal authority. In monarchies, for example, the most noble-born person, the king, ruled the realm. Some governments, however, modified the monarchy and developed aristocracies, a form of government in which a collection of nobles or wealthy individuals jointly directed the city. While aristocracies were sometimes more democratic than monarchies, nothing like our modern democracy existed. Government, however, is a more inclusive term than hierarchy. Government does not simply describe *who* was in charge of whom; it also investigates *how* those peoples managed their set of responsibilities and duties.

One of the fundamental duties of government was justice. Without some form of official legal system, society was threatened by the prospect of circular and never-ending blood feuds. The peace of the realm depended upon the functioning of a trustworthy and authoritative system of justice. The justice system, however, was frequently threatened by the hierarchy, the very people who controlled the government. Wealthy individuals and petty nobles might have used bribes or other enticements to gain favorable decisions against litigants who were less well off. Indeed, since a peasant's landlord was also frequently the judge at court, the peasant could not effectively enter into a legal dispute with the lord. Although there are many exceptions, in practice, people were therefore willing to go to court only against people of the same social class.

~*Joyce E. Salisbury and Lawrence Morris*

FOR MORE INFORMATION

Van Evera, S. *Causes of War: Power and the Roots of Conflict*. Ithaca, N.Y.: Cornell University Press, 1999.

POLITICAL LIFE

HIERARCHY

England

Spain

Italy

Maya

Aztec

Inca

Hierarchy

Hierarchy, which originally meant in Greek "rule by the holy," has come to mean in modern speech simply the social stratification of a society, for example, the various social ranks from king through duke to commoner. Such stratification is common not only among humans but also among many mammals. Many species of fowl, for example, have a pecking order that determines who must give way to whom. A group of chickens can have a complex chain in which any given chicken must yield to certain other chickens in the group, and these chickens must in turn yield to other chickens. Similar chains of dominance can be seen among wolf packs or groups of apes. While some of the chain of dominance among animals is linked to physical strength and personality, human hierarchies have tended in the past to be linked more usually with lineage, that is, who your parents were. Thus, kingship in the Americas and Europe frequently passed from father to son or sometimes from brother to brother or a more distant relation, but it almost inevitably stayed within the family. As a result, while the heads of wolf packs are always strong, daring animals, there have been many kings that lacked any ability in war or management.

The most basic division recognized in Europe and Mesoamerica and South America was between the nobility and the commoners. The Yucatec Maya, for example, split the people into either *almehenob* (elite) or *ah chembal uinicob* (commoners). In Spain, the main dividing line was the payment of taxes: those who paid taxes were commoners while those who were exempt were nobility. Throughout Europe, the word *gentleman* and its various forms in the other languages (such as *gentilhuomo* in Italian), while theoretically referring to a refined, virtuous person of any rank, in practice was a designation of a nobleman who had inherited a life of prestige, luxury, and leisure from his father.

Although this two-fold distinction was central to society, there were many different ranks within each section. Most European systems recognized ranks of nobility that started with an emperor and descended through king, prince, grand duke, duke, count, marquis, and down to knight. For the most part, all of these positions were inherited and did not depend on wealth; it was conceivable that a knight might be wealthier than a marquis, though in practice the wealthy applied pressure to the king to be granted more and more prestigious titles. Ranks of commoners were a bit more fluid, with the prime distinctions resulting from wealth, not birth. A farmer who ran a large estate was more greatly esteemed than a small farmer who also had to work the local lord's land, and both were more esteemed than a hired hand that had no land of his own. Of course, most land was also inherited, so wealth itself was a system of inherited prestige. Merchants sometimes occupied a middle class between commoner and nobility. Many wealthy merchants, who were not infrequently self-made men, mimicked the customs of the nobility and sought to buy their way into their ranks.

While the nobility controlled the vast majority of land and wealth and dominated the government offices, they were also the least numerous. Perhaps 2 percent of the population of 16th-century England was composed of recognized members of the nobility. In Inca society, nobility was limited to those who were related to the king or one of the previous kings, and vast numbers of non-Inca people were therefore excluded from the ranks of the nobility. There are some exceptions to this trend, however. In northern Castile, a region in Spain, a large part of the population claimed to have hidalgo status, the lowest rank of nobility within the Spanish system. The economic advantages, principally freedom from taxation, as well as the societal esteem, must have encouraged many families to make such claims regardless of their true background.

For the most part, however, the nobility was a small group that controlled the economic and political resources of the state. The upper classes also jealously guarded their privileges and sometimes took positive measures to prevent social climbing in the hope of thereby keeping a larger slice of the pie for themselves. Such restrictions were particularly prevalent in Italy, where coteries of established families attempted to dominate political life and various professions. By 1600, entry into colleges for notaries, lawyers, or physicians was often only open to members of particular families and was not connected with merit. Similarly, government office in some cities, such as Venice, could only be held by certain families. In such systems of exclusion, it is no wonder that there was frequent social unrest, with the threat of riots and other disturbances. It is no wonder that the right to bear arms was generally limited to the nobility.

~Lawrence Morris

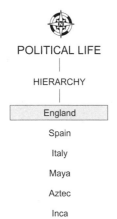

POLITICAL LIFE

HIERARCHY

England

Spain

Italy

Maya

Aztec

Inca

ENGLAND

Renaissance society was in many ways still dominated by the feudal and manorial system inherited from the Middle Ages. During the Middle Ages, society and the economy had focused on people's relationship to land—a relationship of *holding* rather than *owning*. A landholder inherited the right to occupy and use a certain allotment of land—the landholding—under certain terms. Theoretically, all land actually belonged to the monarch and was passed downward in a hierarchical chain, each landholder providing service or payment to a landlord in exchange for the landholding.

The upper ranks of society were supposed to pay for their land with military service. When their lord called upon them, they were expected to come to him fully equipped as mounted knights with a following of soldiers. Those who owed military service were considered to be of *gentle*, that is, noble, birth, as was everyone in their families, during the Middle Ages and Renaissance. *Gentle* meant primarily *noble*—it acquired the connotations of peaceful or refined only later. Gentle status went hand in hand with political influence, social privilege, and cultural prestige. A gentleman's landholding would be large—a hundred acres or so was the lower end of the scale.

Part of a gentleman's landholding was demesne land, that is, land that he himself administered, hiring workers to cultivate it. The rest was rented out as landholdings to tenants (a word that means holders). This rental was likewise determined by inheritance: a landlord's tenants inherited the right to their landholdings and paid for them according to the custom associated with the holding, typically a combination of labor service and rents in kind. The labor service was usually an obligation to spend a certain amount of time doing work for the landlord. The rents in kind were produce from the land—especially grain and livestock. Tenants who paid in labor or material rents were considered commoners. In fact, the label "commoner" applied to everyone who did not belong to the gentle class (except the clergy, who in the Middle Ages were considered a class by themselves).

While this was the principle, things had changed somewhat by the Renaissance. For example, most tenants paid with money rather than with labor or agricultural products, and the noblemen were generally replaced by professional soldiers on the battlefield. Still, the privileges of gentle birth persisted. The gentlemen of Renaissance England still dominated government and society, and they were the effective owners of most of the land in the country. Whereas the medieval aristocrat had been defined by his military activities, Renaissance society laid more emphasis on the other aspects of gentle birth. The classic definition of the gentleman was the formulation offered by Sir Thomas Smith in his treatise on English society, *De Republica Anglorum* (The English State):

Who can live idly and without manual labor and will bear the port, charge, and countenance of a gentleman, he shall be called "master," for that is the title which men give to esquires and other gentlemen, and shall be taken for a gentleman.

As Smith suggests, the principal characteristic of the gentleman was that he could live handsomely without labor, which generally meant having enough land to live off the rents. There were alternatives, however, for gentlemen with little or no land. Government service was considered an acceptable occupation for a gentleman, who might also supplement his income through commercial speculation. In addition, anyone with a university education or working in a profession (i.e., as a physician, lawyer, priest, etc.) was considered a gentleman.

The gentlemanly class was subdivided into its own hierarchy. At the top was the titled nobility, comprising around 50 noblemen and their families. Titles of nobility were inherited: the eldest son would receive the title of his father, and his siblings would be lords or gentlemen, ladies or gentlewomen, depending upon their father's actual rank. The 16th-century titles of nobility were, in descending order, duke, marquis, earl, viscount, and baron; the female equivalents were duchess, marchioness, countess, viscountess, and baroness. Below these was the title of knight, which was never inherited; it had to be received from the monarch or a designated military leader. Knighthood in the Middle Ages was supposed to be a military status, but by the Renaissance period it had become a general mark of honor. There were probably about 300 to 500 knights in England at any given time.

At the bottom of the gentlemanly hierarchy were esquires (also called squires) and simple gentlemen. The distinction between the two was not always clear. In theory, an esquire was a gentleman who had knights in his ancestry, but he might also be a gentleman of especially prominent standing. Esquires and gentlemen together may have numbered some 16,000 at the end of the 16th century. Seventeenth-century estimates suggest that lords, knights, and esquires accounted for well less than 1 percent of the population, and simple gentlemen accounted for about 1 percent.

Below the gentlemen in the manorial hierarchy were the landholding commoners. The most privileged, called freeholders, held their lands in perpetuity: their holdings were passed on from generation to generation with no change in terms. The rent charged for freehold lands had generally been fixed in the Middle Ages, and inflation had rendered the real cost of these holdings minimal. A freeholder was therefore in a very strong financial position and was almost the effective owner of his landholding. Freeholders may have numbered around 100,000 in all.

Less fortunate than the freeholders were the leaseholders. Their tenancies were for fixed periods, sometimes as much as a lifetime, sometimes as little as a year. At the very bottom among landholders were the copyholders, also called customary tenants or tenants at will. Their holdings were simply by custom, and the rent could be altered or the tenancy terminated at any time.

Freeholders whose lands yielded revenues of at least 40 shillings a year were considered to have the rank of yeomen, a very respectable title for a commoner that not only implied a fairly high degree of economic prosperity but also entitled the holder to vote in Parliamentary elections. A 17th-century estimate suggests that yeomen constituted about 15 percent of the total population of England; a 16th-century estimate numbers yeomen at around 10,000. A large landholding for a commoner would be some 50 to 100 acres. Lesser landholders were known as husbandmen—a term that might also be applied generally to anyone who worked his own landholding. The smallest landholders were called cottagers: these people held only the cottage they lived in and perhaps a few acres of land. Their holdings were too small to support them, so they had to supplement their income by hiring themselves out as laborers.

The rural hierarchy was the most prominent in the Renaissance worldview, but there also existed a fully developed and independent social structure in the towns. Towns were independent of the feudal hierarchy, owing allegiance directly to the monarch. Citizenship in a town was a privilege restricted to male householders who were not dependent on others for their wages, typically craftsmen and tradesmen who had their own shops. Citizens may have numbered as many as a quarter to a half of the adult male population in any given town; a 17th-century estimate suggests that citizens constituted roughly 5 percent of the overall population.

At the base of both the rural and urban hierarchies were the laborers and servants. In the country, there was need of shepherds, milkmaids, harvesters, and other hired hands; the towns required porters, water carriers, and other unskilled workers. In the country, paid labor sometimes went to cottagers, but increasingly it fell to a growing class of mobile and rootless laborers who followed the market in search of employment. Unskilled laborers in the city and hired workers in the country made up the bulk of the population—agricultural laborers alone represented a quarter to a third of the rural population. Such people were always at risk of slipping into the ranks of the vagrants and chronically unemployed.

At the very base of the social hierarchy was a substantial and growing number of unemployed poor. The number of poor people unable to sustain themselves may have been 10 percent in the country and 20 percent in towns. The poor particularly included children, widows, abandoned wives, the elderly, and the infirm; but their ranks were increased by growing numbers of unemployed but able-bodied men displaced by economic transformations or returning home from service in the army or navy. There was also a significant community of permanent beggars and vagabonds who may have numbered as many as 20,000.

In principle, Renaissance society was a rigid and orderly hierarchy. Social and economic advancement of the individual were not priorities. People were expected to live within the social class of their parents. In practice things were not always so straightforward. Sometimes it was difficult to be entirely certain of a person's social status. Actual titles were easy to verify, as in the case of a nobleman, a knight, or a master craftsman. However, the distinction between an esquire and a gentleman, for example, or between a gentleman and a yeoman, was not always so clear. William Shakespeare is one good example of Renaissance social mobility: born the son of a glover in Stratford-upon-Avon, he returned from his successful theatrical career in London to live as a gentleman, the proud possessor of a coat of arms and the largest house in town. Conversely, a gentleman who acquired excessive debts might slide down the social scale, and we have already discussed how landholders and laborers could sometimes find themselves without a livelihood (Singman, 9–19).

To read about the social hierarchy in Chaucer's England, see the Europe entries in the sections "Social Structure," "Aristocracy," "Peasants, Serfs, and Slaves," and "Urban Social Structure" in chapter 6 ("Political Life") in volume 2 of this series; for 18th-century England, see the entry on England in the section "Social Structure" in chapter 6 ("Political Life") in volume 4 of this series; for Victorian England, see the Victorian England entry in the section "Class and Caste Experience" in chapter 3 ("Economic Life") in volume 5 of this series.

FOR MORE INFORMATION

Singman, J. L. *Daily Life in Elizabethan England.* Westport, Conn.: Greenwood, 1995.

Smith, Sir Thomas. *The State of England, AD 1600.* Vol. 3 of *Camden Miscellany,* ed. F. J. Fisher, 52. London: Camden Society, 1936.

Trevelyan, G. M. *Illustrated English Social History.* Harmondsworth, UK: Penguin, 1942.

SPAIN

Renaissance Spain was chiefly an agricultural society, and the vast majority of the people were peasants who worked the land. The upper class (the nobility) monopolized land, education, and public offices but was itself a diverse institution of privilege ranging from the extremely wealthy grandees at the highest level down to the poor hidalgo, with the lowest aristocratic standing. The impoverished hidalgo might scrape a living in a rural village from a petty estate or cultivation of a patch of ground. But poor or not, he invariably felt himself far above the demeaning, vile class of taxpayers, namely, the artisans, bourgeoisie, and the peasants.

Some hidalgos went off to conquer new lands in the Americas, but most remained at home where they kept locked away their precious testaments to their noble rank that ensured their privileges. Some came to the large cities in search of an occupation suitable to their station and found employment as squires or chaperons of high-class ladies; others just wandered the streets. Contempt for manual labor, considered degrading by the upper classes, often kept them idle and hungry. Disdain of manual

POLITICAL LIFE

HIERARCHY

England

Spain

Italy

Maya

Aztec

Inca

work was not confined to the aristocratic class, however, but was widespread throughout society, as many people aspired to noble rank and adopted a noble attitude even if they did not have the credentials. In northern Castile much of the population claimed hidalgo status, legitimately or not.

Hidalgos with money, who usually resided in the cities, preferred to be called caballeros and were there considered middle-rank aristocracy. They lived in town houses and drew income from their estates, supplemented by investments. From the rank of caballero, they attempted to enter the ranks of the *titulados*, or titled nobility, and rise to the status of viscount, count, marquis, or even duke. For this significant leap in status, which had to be granted by the king, money, land, vassals, a life of ostentatious spending, and enough cash to make loans to the royal treasury were generally required. Those in possession of great wealth might move up to the level of grandee, the highest rank short of the royal family. Grandees were addressed as cousin by the king and allowed to keep their hats on in his presence. In 1520, when they were legally defined by Charles I, only 25 families held this lofty position, many of whom were lords of hundreds of villages from which they received taxes, rents, and other revenue. By 1600 there were 41 families of this elevated rank.

Below the nobility were the guild masters, merchants, manufacturers, shipowners, modest property owners, and proprietors of mills. Having money and imitating the aristocracy with fine clothes and houses was not enough for many of them, however. Such people squandered their wealth in pursuit of noble rank to the detriment of expanding their businesses or initiating new enterprises. The use of profits to buy estates, to supply a dowry for a daughter, or to acquire securities deprived industry of investment.

To achieve noble status involved proving that the family lineage was free from Jewish ancestry. This entailed expensive litigation, as the claim could be contested by enemies. Jewish (*converso*) or Muslim (*morisco*) ancestry was a bar to societal advancement in general. The struggle and expense involved to obtain some kind of noble status were worth the effort for many families for several reasons, the most important, apart from the honor of the title, being exemption from direct taxation and access to the best jobs in public office. Other rights included the privilege of bearing arms; immunity from debtors' prison; release from jail for petty crimes, from torture if accused, or from the galleys if convicted; and in the event of a capital crime, avoiding the dishonor of the gallows—decapitation being considered the aristocratic punishment. Noble status also exempted the family from the billeting of troops in their private houses.

Aristocratic rulers of the towns often tried to thwart this upward pretension by keeping commoners from important positions—for example, by passing laws that only noblemen could serve as aldermen or in other official capacities with the self-justifying argument that nobles were above the petty self-interest of trade and presumably more impartial. But wealthy merchants founded entailed estates (by which the inheritance of property was restricted to the owner's lineal descendants) that continued to grow until the family's voice had to be heard and its demands met. Another way to advance socially was to buy a title from the king, who always needed more income. Thus a man could become a hidalgo with the same privileges as those who were so by birth. Many claims of noble lineage were made and rejected, often on the basis that granting noble status deprived the crown of tax money.

There was little prospect for improvement of the living conditions for the vast majority of peasants in the fields and for laborers in the towns. That they might slide lower on the scale of social values into the world of beggars, thieves, and vagabonds was a definite possibility that was aggravated by a fiscal policy that weighed most heavily on the poor. The *alcabala,* a Castilian sales tax levied at about 10 percent for most of the period, and the *millones,* a special tax on consumer items such as meat, wine, and oil, hit hardest those who could least afford them. In addition, many of the lower classes could find jobs only at certain times of the year such as during periods of planting and harvesting on the farms around the towns. The remainder of the time they had little to do. Numerous people, mostly young, standing around idle in the marketplace or cathedral squares was a common sight.

The lowest person in the hierarchy of the dispossessed was the beggar. This occupation, for those who could not work, was recognized as a right under the law, but the beggar was obliged to obtain a license furnished by the local priest that allowed soliciting alms in the immediate locality. Among the legal beggars was a privileged subgroup of the blind that held a monopoly on the recitation of prayers intended to protect individuals and the community from all manner of evil. In some cities the blind formed brotherhoods whose statutes, recognized by the municipal authorities, guaranteed their privileges. In Madrid the statutes assured members of the right to sell gazettes, that is, gossip sheets, and almanacs.

However, the cities abounded with bogus blind and crippled people who crowded around the church doors and the public market and squares, assailing the populace with groans and entreaties. During the reign of Philip III, a discourse was written on the protection of the genuine poor and the lessening of pretenders in which the figure of those living on charity was given at 150,000, the majority of them frauds. Reported also were the stratagems used by the pretenders to deceive the public, such as covering the body with false scars, feigning to have only one arm, or faking a death scene while companions passed the hat for money to bury the poor fellow.

Finally, there were a number of slaves in Renaissance Italy. Originally, most of the slaves were Muslims captured during the frequent warfare within the Iberian Peninsula, but black African slaves began to be imported toward the end of the period, and most wealthy families owned one or two slaves (Anderson, 32–34, 41–45).

FOR MORE INFORMATION

Anderson, J. *Daily Life during the Spanish Inquisition.* Westport, Conn.: Greenwood, 2002.

Defourneaux, M. *Daily Life in Golden Age.* Trans. Newton Branch. Stanford: Stanford University Press, 1979.

Elliott, J. H. *Spain and Its World, 1500–1700.* New Haven: Yale University Press, 1989.

ITALY

Especially for the upper classes, by far the paramount determinant of rank was family. Families cohered, owned property, waged politics, and advanced the welfare

POLITICAL LIFE
|
HIERARCHY
|
England

Spain

Italy

Maya

Aztec

Inca

of their members; they also had reputations, which they proclaimed, cultivated, and defended. Everyone could name the better and the best. In many cities, family membership increasingly conferred the right to election to high public office. Venice had had such a rule since 1323 when it closed admission to its ruling councils. Such arrangements, still rare in 1400, by 1600 had spread to many cities. Increasingly, elites turned inward for sociability, working alliances, and marriages. As this aristocratization spread, the same closure infected the professions. Thus, in many cities, genealogy rather than merit governed entry into the ruling colleges of notaries, lawyers, or physicians. The hierarchy of families and that of professions increasingly aligned. Even village elites often had a sense of caste. The working classes and the poor, however, whose families lacked material and political resources, looked elsewhere in assigning local rank. There, personal attributes usually weighed more.

Closely allied with the hierarchy of families was that of noble titles. Italians revered the labels that traced back to old feudal powers of jurisdiction and military command. Emperor (*imperatore*) came first, then (in descending order) king (*re*), prince (*principe*), grand duke (*granduca*), duke (*duca*, or in Venice *doge*), count (*conte*), marquis (*marchese*), down to knight (*cavagliere*). Many knights belonged to one of the military orders, such as the Knights of Saint John in Malta, that specialized in anti-Muslim piracy, or the less-often bellicose Order of Santo Stefano of late 16th-century Tuscany. There was only one emperor, the so-called Holy Roman Emperor, who actually was the elected ruler of Germany. His prestige was immense. In Italy, there was only one king, in Naples, until the 1490s, and then there was none. From then on, foreign royalty took precedence over all native Italian nobles. Tuscany had a grand duke, by papal grant, from 1569 on. Dukes were fairly common; some of them were independent rulers, others not. Some of these noble titles were centuries old, and others were recent confections bestowed by grateful rulers as rewards for political or financial support or even sold by penurious monarchs for ready cash. Latter-day titles lacked the prestige of older ones, no matter how venal these once had been. Nevertheless, a new duke could lord it over a *marchese* of great antiquity, for title denoted rank, not reputation. Family and title were closely linked because all such honorific labels, like the powers and privileges that went with them, passed down the male line by in-

Clues to Social Rank. Many features set the servant in this picture apart from the nobles. For example, the servant is on foot, while the nobles ride; the servant is wearing simple clothes, while the nobles have richly ornamented clothing; and the servant is doing work (holding horses and dogs), while the nobles chat. Picture by Antonio Tempesta. Roma—Instituto Nazionale della Grafica. By gracious concession of the Ministero per i Beni e le Attività Culturali.

heritance. Usually they went to the firstborn male, for they did not easily divide, though a father with several titles might spread them among his sons. An heiress, lacking brothers, could carry a title with her and pass it on to her descendants. Wives, as consorts, carried female analogues to their husband's titles (for example, *duchessa, contessa*) and commensurate prestige.

Alongside formal titles, Italians reveled in a rich vocabulary for distinguishing grades in the social hierarchy. A man of the titled class was a *gentilhuomo* and a woman a *gentildonna*. These were descriptive terms, not titles. The meaning was imprecise; anyone who lived nobly, titled or not, could share the glow. One could also call such persons a *signore* and a *signora*. Villagers, speaking to one another, would simply call their masters *i signori* (the lords) or *i padroni* (the masters). In Italy today, modern values have democratized these terms of address, as they have *sir* and *madam* in the English-speaking world. In the Renaissance, however, all these words of feudal origin still denoted real prestige. Indeed, God was addressed as "Signore," as in the English "Lord." In Venice, where titles of nobility were not in use, one called the patricians *clarissimi* or *magnifici*. The Italian middling ranks lacked generic terms but had titles of address. Below *signore* came *messer,* a title that was restricted to lawyers and notaries in the 15th century but was extended to other prosperous urban men in the 16th century. The upper and lower boundaries of *messer* were fluid. The same holds true for the feminine *madonna,* a term less grandiose than *signora. Madonna* had a huge range; it attached easily to the mother of God, to nobles' wives and daughters, to those of burghers, and even to the wives of prosperous artisans and to courtesans. Among males, an independent artisan who was a master of a shop was called *maestro.* A few professions carried special titles: *dottore* for a holder of a university degree, *colonello* and *capitano* for commanders of troops, *monsignore* for high clergymen, *padre* or *don* for priests, *fra* for friars, *suor* for nuns. The poor lacked titles of address.

Another source of rank, closely allied with social station, was eligibility for public office. In cities, towns, and villages, there was a political class from which, by nomination, election, and lottery, one picked those who served. Since terms of office were generally short, many had a chance to take their turn. Guilds, professional colleges, confraternities, and learned academies often chose their leaders by these means. Corporations and ruling circles also had internal hierarchies. Eligibility marked social standing, but often it came in degrees; only some could stand for the higher offices. Thus, older men usually ran things. Wealth, reputation, and, not rarely, family might also count. Sometimes only membership in one elite body granted admission to the ballot in another. Thus, the pinnacles of society readily became an interlocking directorate of the privileged.

The clergy too had an acute sense of precedence tied to office. While many preferments came by appointment rather than election, the ambitious politicked hard for posts. Not only were there hierarchies of titles to consider, but also great variations in the wealth and power that came with each specific office. Better to be bishop of a rich see than archbishop of a poor one. Sometimes a high prelate might trade a better title for a better income, though, in general, before the reforms decreed by the mid-16th-century Council of Trent, the aim was to snap up plural benefices by the handful. A man, in such a case, was addressed by his best title and esteemed for the whole collection.

Public office itself was a powerful status marker. Italians strove for election not only for pay and power but also for glory. Both state and church reveled in splendid pomp. In many cities, each post had its magnificent robes of office. Officeholders, both lay and clerical, paraded on the many solemn occasions on which a polity deployed its majesty for the glory of God and the awe of citizens and visitors.

The many rules did not lock Italians in; rather they gave them all sorts of avenues for nuanced self-expression. Hierarchy, although a social system, left room for agency. In the face of many rules and even more ways to break them, men and women invested endless energy in jockeying for position (Cohen and Cohen, 76–87).

FOR MORE INFORMATION

Cohen, E. S., and T. V. Cohen. *Daily Life in Renaissance Italy*. Westport, Conn.: Greenwood, 2001.

Jardine, L. *Worldly Goods: A New History of the Renaissance*. New York: Doubleday, 1996.

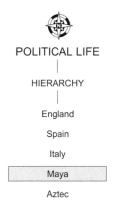

POLITICAL LIFE

|

HIERARCHY

|

England

Spain

Italy

Maya

Aztec

Inca

MAYA

Before the Europeans' arrival, Maya society was stratified into two classes: elite and nonelite. In Yucatán these were known as the *almehenob* (elite) and the *ah chembal uinicob* (commoners). Among the Quiche Maya of the highlands, the elite class was called the *ahawab* and the nonelite was called the *al c'ahol*. Social stratification means that the two groups had different rights, roles, and obligations. The most obvious distinction is based on wealth and power. In ancient Maya society, as in other stratified societies, the elite had a monopoly on wealth and power. The nonelite had little of either.

Stratified societies often define gradations of status within each class. In Maya society we are certain that the elite class was divided into positions of higher and lower status. Obviously the king held the highest position within the elite class. Of course, not all kings and their kingdoms were equal. At any point in time there were wealthy and powerful kings and polities, and there were less wealthy and powerful kings and polities.

Below the king and the royal lineage were a variety of other elite positions. Some probably were determined by lineage membership; a member of the elite class might have inherited his or her status and position in society from his or her father. Some classes were determined by profession. Bishop Landa reports that the title for priests who were members of the elite class was *ahkinob*. The Quiche Maya distinguished several occupational groups, such as merchants (*ahbeyom*), professional warriors (*achij*), and estate managers (*uytzam chinamital*).

In ancient times, social and political offices were probably transmitted within patrilineal descent groups from father to son, brother to brother, or uncle to nephew.

During the Classic period, the succession of kings is sometimes specified as from father to son. There are also examples of younger brothers succeeding older brothers as king. But succession in even the highest offices was not according to a single inflexible rule. At some sites historical texts stress descent through both the male and female lines, as at Palenque; other sites emphasized the male line, as at Tikal and Copan. There are prominent portraits of elite women associated with kings at Piedras Negras, Yaxchilan, and several other sites, and paired male and female portraits are found at both Calakmul and El Peru. There are accounts of women rulers at Palenque.

The nonelite class was less formally ranked. Gradations in their burials and houses suggest that there were internal divisions of wealth and status. Some distinctions probably derived from occupations—for example, skilled craftsmen may have been held in higher regard than unskilled laborers. The largest occupational group was the farmers, whose toil supported both themselves and the king. Most Maya farmers worked their own land, which was held in common by their lineage. In some areas there was also a group of landless peasants (known as the *nimak achi* among the Quiche Maya) who worked estates owned by the elite and were inherited along with the land.

Commoners lived outside the central areas of the towns and cities; the core areas were reserved for the elite. Generally speaking, the greater the distance a family lived from the central plaza, the lower its position on the social scale.

The lowest status was that of slaves or captives owned by the elite. These were known as *p'entacob* in Yucatán or *munib* among the Quiche Maya. They included commoners captured in war, sentenced criminals, and impoverished individuals sold into slavery by their families. Elite captives were usually ritually sacrificed. Nonelite captives were either enslaved for labor or adopted by families to replace members lost to war or disease. Thieves were sentenced to be enslaved by their victims until they could pay for what they had stolen. Children of slaves were not considered slaves but were free to make their way into society based on their abilities. But unwanted orphans were often sacrificed, especially if they were the children of slave women. Slaves were usually sacrificed when their masters died so they could continue in their service after death.

All commoners had obligations to pay tribute to their rulers, their local elite lords, and the gods by offerings made through the priests. Tribute consisted of all kinds of agricultural produce, including woven cotton cloth, domesticated fowl, salt, dried fish, and hunted game. The most valuable offerings were cacao, *pom* (copal) incense, honey, beeswax, jade, coral, and shells. Each commoner lineage also had an annual labor obligation, which went toward building the great temples, palaces, and other buildings as well as the causeways (*sacbeob*) that connected the principal Maya cities. Bishop Landa wrote: "The common people at their own expense made the houses of the lords (and) did their sowing for the lord, cared for his fields and harvested what was necessary for him and his household; and when there was hunting or fishing, or when it was time to get their salt, they always gave the lord his share" (Sharer, 129–32).

FOR MORE INFORMATION

Sharer, R. J. *Daily Life in Maya Civilization*. Westport, Conn.: Greenwood, 1996.

Tozzer, A. M. *Landa's Relación de las cosas de Yucatán*. Cambridge, Mass.: Peabody Museum, 1941.

POLITICAL LIFE

|

HIERARCHY

|

England

Spain

Italy

Maya

Aztec

Inca

AZTEC

Aztec society recognized two main social classes, nobles and commoners, though there were several grades within each rank. Nobles made up about 7 percent of Aztec society, but most of the contemporary sources are dedicated to noble life—thus we know much more about the nobles than about the commoners. At the top of the social order was the *tlatoani*, the king of the city-state. The *tlatoani* technically owned all the lands of the city-state (*altepetl*), but granted estates to various lords. Beneath the *tlatoani*, but still noble, were the *tecuhtin* (singular: *tecuhtli*), who occupied large estates that they passed down to their heirs. Below the *tecuhtin* were the regular nobles, called *pipiltin* (singular: *pilli*). These lords were generally in the service of the *tecuhtin* or *tlatoani* and did not run their own large estates.

Nobles were those who were descended, in theory, from either Quetzalcoatl, the Plumed Serpent man-god of the ancient Toltec kingdom, or from Xiuhtecuhtli, the fire god, who was the mother and father of all the gods and therefore the patron god of the rulers and nobles. This meant that the nobility carried enormous magical powers that were embedded in their families, bodies, and actions. A noble lineage meant that a person inherited—at least in theory—a name, clothes, traditions, and a moral purity superior to those of a commoner. The themes of moral purity and upright behavior were preached to children, especially those of the nobility, throughout their upbringing. One common theme was that if you acted immorally, which meant everything from walking wildly in the street to sexual misconduct, you were infecting the reputation of your family and its members, both living *and* dead! On the other hand, knowledge gained through education and the experience of commanding workshops, schools, and courts resulted in the heightened reputation and power of the lineage, which was then considered to be morally uplifted. When a noble was particularly successful in leadership or artistic expression, his or her lineage acquired extraordinary magical fire in the heart of the kinship system. The term for this kind of achievement was *yollopiltic*, or "one who has an ennobled heart."

The nobles had superior privileges. Their homes, clothes, food, and access to opportunity were of the highest quality, especially in times of abundance and political stability. They had access to the most valuable goods, including capes, mantles, jewelry, flowers, cacao, musical instruments, and even human flesh. Everything was capable of having *tonalli*, the animistic power that resided mainly in the human brain. Nobles had the most direct access to limited forms of human flesh from sacrificial victims, which was considered the flesh of the gods. This flesh contained the vital force of the god's power, which passed to the person who ingested it. Nobles periodically enjoyed small amounts of human flesh in ritual meals. Another way that nobles and *macehualtin*, who were elevated to noble status as a result of extraordinary feats on the battlefield, acquired magical power was through the ingestion of cacao, the inhaling of burning incense, and the taking of psychotropic drugs such as peyote or hallucinogenic mushrooms. The visionary state that resulted from ingesting these plants was believed to be a direct communication with gods and goddesses who entered into human awareness during these times. It was thought that the nobles became stronger and more effective in their public duties when they ate peyote, cacao, mushrooms, or human flesh. This was a privilege of the noble class, but it must be remembered that the main purpose was to enable them to carry out their responsibilities more effectively.

Commoners were called *macehualtin* (singular: *macehualli*). Commoners generally were obliged to pay tribute to a particular lord. This tribute took the form of both labor and goods. The *macehualli* was obligated to spend several weeks per year working on the lands of his lord and was also obliged to provide the lord with a certain quantity of agricultural goods. The amount of the tribute demanded could vary widely from family to family. In wartime the *macehualli* was also expected to fight for the lord.

Commoners could elevate their positions in a variety of ways. Warriors gained prestige and official position through capturing the enemy—a specific rank was attached to a specific number of captured enemies. The most successful warriors could even gain some of the advantages and privileges of the nobles. Another avenue for advancement was trade. The *pochteca* (merchants) commanded a large amount of wealth in the cities. The *pochteca* seem to have formed an unrecognized middle class, with more wealth than the vast majority of *macehualtin*, but without the lineage and privileges of the *pipiltin*.

At the very bottom of the social system were *tlacotin* (singular: *tlacotli*), or slaves. Most people became slaves through debt—to pay off their debts they had to sell themselves into slavery. Slavery was not hereditary, however, and the children of slaves were considered to be free. Most slaves worked as servants in the palaces of the nobility (Carrasco, 132–34).

FOR MORE INFORMATION

Carrasco, D., with S. Sessions. *Daily Life of the Aztecs: People of the Sun and Earth*. Westport, Conn.: Greenwood, 1998.

Hicks, F. "Prehispanic Background of Colonial Political and Economic Organization in Central Mexico." In *Ethnohistory*, supplement 4 to *Handbook of Middle American Indians*, ed. Ronald Spores. Austin: University of Texas Press, 1986.

Lockart, J. *The Nahuas After the Conquest: A Social and Cultural History of the Indians of Central Mexico, Sixteenth through Eighteenth Centuries*. Stanford: Stanford University Press, 1992.

Smith, M. *The Aztecs*. Oxford: Blackwell, 1996.

INCA

There were several kinds of citizens in the Inca empire. The social status of each was defined by kinship and occupation rather than income. The highest-status mem-

POLITICAL LIFE
|
HIERARCHY
|
England

Spain

Italy

Maya

Aztec

Inca

bers of the empire were the Incas who were members of the royal and nonroyal *ayllus* (households). The Incas are often called "Inca-by-blood" in the literature. The social organization of Inca society at the upper level was based on the relative closeness of one's family to the Inca king. The Incas of royal blood were directly related to the Inca kings and were therefore ultimately related to the founding ancestor of all Incas, Manco Capac. By the time of the European conquest, there were 11 royal households, each descended from a previous or reigning Inca king.

In addition to the royal *ayllus*, there were 10 households of nonroyal Incas. These were Inca people who were not related to the kings but lived in or near Cuzco. In the Inca origin myth, these people descended from the groups recruited by the eight original Incas who emerged from the cave at Pacariqtambo. Their *ayllus* were somewhat lower in status and were lumped into one of two moieties (i.e., divisions of a society into two parts). For the Inca there was an Upper (Hanansaya) and Lower (Hurinsaya) moiety. These moieties chiefly functioned to divide ritual activities among the *ayllus* of each. The Incas imposed the moiety system on their subjects, although it is possible that a similar division may have been present prior to the Inca conquests.

The Inca status also included another larger group called "Inca-by-privilege." These were people who also spoke Quechua and lived near the valley of Cuzco. The Incas-by-privilege were especially important during the period of imperial expansion. The ruling elite used the Incas-by-privilege as the empire's administrators and colonists. Because the empire expanded so rapidly, there were apparently not enough members of the Inca-by-blood *ayllus* to fill all the government posts. It was necessary to extend the concept of nobility (i.e., "being Inca") to another group so there would be enough Inca-class people to fill the posts. The Inca-by-privilege groups were also used extensively as colonists, being extremely loyal to the empire and knowledgeable about its policies.

Below the Incas in the social order came the non-Inca peoples who had become subjects of the Inca empire. The highest rank achievable by these people was *curaca*, or lower nobility. This was the group of government officials who were part of the administrative hierarchy—the *curacas* of 5,000 or 100 taxpayers, for example, plus their descendants. These people were either leaders of conquered groups or other individuals with administrative capabilities.

Below the *curacas* there must have been a labor class: the conquered people who were not leaders and therefore not *curacas*. This class carried out the day-to-day activities that allowed the empire to function. They provided food and labor for the construction of the cities and monuments for which the Incas are famous.

In the Inca empire, the *mitimas* had a special status. *Mitimas* were people living away from their place of birth, people who had been moved to another area. There

---

📷 *Snapshot*

Inca Social Hierarchy

Listed from highest ranking (top) to lowest ranking (bottom):

Inca	Inca-by-blood
	11 royal *panacas* (royal households)
	10 nonroyal *ayllus* (households)
	Inca-by-privilege
Curaca	*curacas* (officials)
Laborer class	conquered people

were two kinds of *mitima*, defined by their role in the empire. One kind allowed the Incas to gain access to certain zones. For example, if all of a conquered people were living in the Puna zone (above 11,500 feet, where corn cannot grow), the Inca might move *mitimas* into the Quechua zone (5,000–11,500 feet, where major food crops can be grown) of that area to increase the amount of crops grown there. As corn was the most important crop to the Incas, very often the Incas moved *mitimas* into the Quechua zones to increase its production there.

The second kind of *mitima* was political; it afforded control over rebellious people. Groups who were difficult to conquer, or who rebelled after their initial conquest, might be moved from their native homeland to another part of the empire. Typically they were moved into an area among more loyal groups, so they would be less likely to cause additional problems. Loyal *mitimas*, often Inca-by-privilege, would then be moved into the vacated lands to continue producing food there. This must have been a very effective means of control: imagine how psychologically devastating it would be to be removed from the lands where your ancestors had lived to a new region that was totally foreign and to be forced to live among people whom you neither knew nor trusted (Malpass, 37–40).

FOR MORE INFORMATION

Bauer, B. *The Development of the Inca State*. Austin: University of Texas Press, 1992.

Malpass, M. A. *Daily Life in the Inca Empire*. Westport, Conn.: Greenwood, 1996.

Rowe, J. "Inca Culture at the Time of the Spanish Conquest." In *The Andean Civilizations*. Vol. 2 of *Handbook of South American Indians*, ed. Julian Steward. Washington, D.C.: Bureau of American Ethnology, 1946.

Government

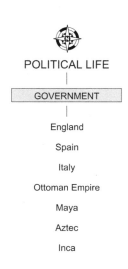

POLITICAL LIFE

GOVERNMENT

England

Spain

Italy

Ottoman Empire

Maya

Aztec

Inca

Governments in the 15th and 16th centuries took a multiplicity of forms, ranging from monarchies to republics (states without monarchs) and numerous systems in between. The size of the nation governed also differed tremendously. Charles I of Spain was the head not only of Spain, but, as head of the Holy Roman Empire, also of modern-day Belgium, Holland, Austria, Germany, Czech Republic, Slovakia, Hungary, Italy, and the Americas; by 1570 even lands in the far Pacific such as the Philippines had been added. Similarly, the Inca empire extended from its highland center at Cuzco in all directions for hundreds of miles. In contrast, Italy and the Maya territory were not unified nations but rather a collection of independent states with their own armies and domestic and foreign policies that nevertheless shared a common ethnic identity due to the closeness of their languages and their shared political and cultural history.

Monarchy is one of the earliest forms of government. In a monarchy, one individual, the king (or sometimes the queen), acts as the supreme head of the government and makes the laws that bind the nation. The monarch is linked with the divine in many cultures. Among the Aztec, the king was thought to be related to the god Huitzilopochtli and served as intermediary between the gods and human-kind, while Early Maya chieftains similarly were called *k'ul ahaw* (divine ruler). There was also a tradition of linking the king with the divine in Europe. In the ancient Roman Empire, for example, the emperor was thought to be a god and people were forced to offer sacrifices to the emperor as a god. While no one believed that monarchs were actually gods in Renaissance Europe, the monarchs were thought to have some connection with a divinely ordered universe. According to a belief called the "divine right of kings," the monarch was believed to have been entrusted by God with the rule of the kingdom. In other words, God himself had given the kingdom to the king. As a result, to rebel against the king or to disobey the king also meant to disobey God to some degree. The divine right, however, did not necessitate that the king would be a just or good ruler, but rather only that he had been granted his position by God. The faithful subject would patiently suffer under a bad king and accept his suffering as an act of God's will. Of course, people were obliged to go against the king if the king ordered them to do something immoral or against what they thought was right—thus many people died resisting the Reformation and the Counter Reformation. But in the everyday running of the government, one was expected to obey. This system of acceptance is not as unusual as it may sound today. A similar code of conduct is to be found in the army and other branches of the military. In these armed forces, one is expected to obey his or her commanding officer without question. In both the modern armed forces and in the Renaissance such obedience was thought to be the only way of maintaining an orderly and prosperous society.

While kings were still very powerful during the 15th and 16th centuries, their power had started to be curbed by parliaments (elected assemblies that advised the king) and other councils. In England, the *Magna Carta*, signed by King John in 1215, granted noblemen the right to advise the king. By the 16th century, this advisory council had grown into a parliament with elected representatives from all over the country. It is important to note that this parliament was not a democratic body as we understand democracy today—there was no principle such as one man, one vote. Instead, only the wealthy and middle classes were eligible to vote in the elections. Parliament's main power lay in its ability to control taxation. The king was not allowed to impose any tax without the approval of Parliament. Thus if the king needed more funds to run the country or to prepare for a foreign war, it was necessary to convene a session of Parliament. Once Parliament was convened, the elected members would attempt to trade agreement to the new taxation for legal, political, or economic concessions to their district or social class. The king was thus often forced to create laws that he would not otherwise wish to do. The most successful English monarchs during this time, such as Elizabeth I during the start of her reign, were able to manage their own immense wealth so as to avoid new taxes and the need to call Parliament.

Spain had a similar system: for the king to levy new taxes, the regional Cortes (parliaments) had to agree to the measures. In return for their agreement, they expected the king to grant them additional legal, political, and economic advantages. While Parliament grew stronger and stronger in England, for the most part, the Spanish Cortes entered a period of decline during this period. The Spanish kings developed a method in which they would pass over the Cortes and ask for funds directly from particular towns. By applying intense pressure on one town at a time, the king was able to gain funds without calling the Cortes. Among the Maya, however, the power of the king had been lessened considerably to allow a council of nobles, called a *multepal,* a greater role in the running of the government. This change may have come about due to the disadvantages of the dependence of the kingdom's welfare upon the personal success of the king. If the king was a charismatic leader and a clever warrior, the kingdom would do well, but if the king was a poor strategician and diplomat, the kingdom could even lose its own autonomy. Having a *multepal* allowed the talents of more people to be involved in the running of the kingdom and increased the state's stability.

While kings and councils formed the highest level of the state, the average people, especially the peasants, had very little contact with either. For the most part, the peasant's life was controlled and ruled by the local lord. In Italy, for example, the *signore* (lord) controlled most aspects of peasant life. The *signore* dictated what work the peasant would do, oversaw the prices of the local mill, and sat as judge in the local court, collecting the fines himself for legal infractions. A similar system was in place among the conquered people in the Inca empire. An official, called a *curaca,* administered Inca law in his region and ensured that the group under his supervision sent the requisite tribute and worked the prescribed number of hours for the Incas. Throughout Europe and the Americas, these forms of local government are what controlled the everyday aspects of most people's lives, though the king and council might be at the top of the government.

~Lawrence Morris

ENGLAND

The government of England centered on the figure of the monarch, who relied heavily on the Privy Council for the day-to-day running of the country. The monarch and the Council acting in the monarch's name had some power to issue decrees enforceable as law, but the exact extent of these powers was ill defined. This constitutional ambiguity led to bloody results in the 1640s when King Charles and his Parliament came to civil war over the issue of the king's authority.

Renaissance kingship was still rooted in the "divine right of kings." According to this belief, kings had been granted the right to rule by God himself; as a result, insurrection of any kind could be viewed as a sin against God, and not just as treason against the king. Divine right did not ensure that the king himself was a just man, but his subjects were to accept his authority nevertheless as an act of submission and humility.

While the monarch theoretically held appointment from God, the monarch's right to rule was consistently reduced over time, especially after 1215 when King John signed the *Magna Carta* (Great Charter), in which he limited his rights in

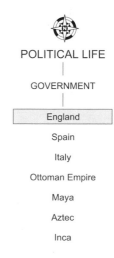

POLITICAL LIFE
|
GOVERNMENT
|

certain ways. One of the most important results of the *Magna Carta* was that the king could not levy taxes without first consulting a Great Council composed of noblemen. This council had developed into the English Parliament by the time of the Renaissance. During the Renaissance, as before, the monarch could rule with almost absolute power provided he or she had sufficient funds from private estates. When the king needed more money, however, he or she would have to call a session of Parliament, and Parliament then had the opportunity to start dictating both domestic and foreign policy.

Queen Elizabeth. This queen was one of the strongest rulers of England during the Renaissance. © The Art Archive/Miramare Palace Trieste/Dagli Orti (A).

As a result, the most comprehensively powerful organ of government was the monarch sitting in Parliament: a bill passed by Parliament and assented to by the monarch was the highest legal authority in the land. Parliament was divided into two houses: the House of Lords and the House of Commons. The House of Lords consisted of approximately 65 lay peers, 22 bishops, and the country's 2 archbishops (Canterbury and York). Members of the House of Lords were not elected by the people, rather they inherited their positions either from their fathers, in the case of lay peers, or from their ecclesiastical position, in the case of bishops. The House of Commons consisted of 2 representatives chosen from each of England's 39 shires, 2 from each of about 65 English cities and towns (with some exceptions, including London, which sent 4), as well as a single representative from each of 12 Welsh shires and 1 each from 12 Welsh towns, for a total of about 450 representatives. The exact means by which the representatives were chosen depended on the shire or town, but in the shires any holder of lands worth 40 shillings a year was entitled to vote. The landless thus did not have a right to vote.

In general, the institutions of Renaissance English government seem haphazard by modern standards. The basic unit of governmental organization in both town and country was the parish. Each parish had its own officials, such as a constable who was responsible for basic law enforcement, ale-conners who ensured that the laws regulating the quality of ale were observed, and churchwardens who were responsible for the state of the parish church. In towns there were also scavengers who oversaw public sanitation.

The actual bureaucracy was small and woefully underfunded. This meant that the governmental apparatus required extensive participation by the citizenry. Great lords might serve in the Privy Council or in major offices of the state, army, or navy; local gentlemen were vital in administrating the individual shires; and even ordinary craftsmen, yeomen, and husbandmen might be called upon to serve in minor local offices of the village, town, or parish. At the same time, this kind of unpaid work was a cause of governmental corruption; men who had to spend considerable time and money on an unsalaried government office would frequently find other ways to make the post profitable (Singman, 20).

To read about government in 18th-century England, see the entry on England in the section "Government" in chapter 6 ("Political Life") in volume 4 of this series; for Victorian England, see the Victorian England entry in the section "Government and Politics" in chapter 6 ("Political Life") in volume 5 of this series.

~*Lawrence Morris*

FOR MORE INFORMATION

Palliser, D. M. *The Age of Elizabeth*. New York: Longman, 1992.

Singman, J. L. *Daily Life in Elizabethan England*. Westport, Conn.: Greenwood, 1995.

SPAIN

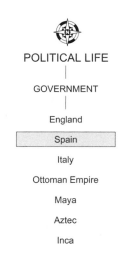

POLITICAL LIFE

GOVERNMENT

England

Spain

Italy

Ottoman Empire

Maya

Aztec

Inca

During the Renaissance, Spain was one of the largest and most diverse empires. At the start of the 15th century, Spain was divided into independent Muslim and Christian states. The famous monarchs Isabella and Ferdinand unified Spain when they defeated Granada, the last Muslim state on the Iberian Peninsula, in 1492— the same year in which they sent Christopher Columbus on his quest for the Indies. Charles I, grandson to Isabella, came to the throne in 1516. In addition to Spain, he inherited, from the other side of the family, the throne of the Holy Roman Empire. By 1519, Charles I controlled not only Spain but also lands in modern-day Belgium, Holland, Austria, Germany, Czech Republic, Slovakia, Hungary, Italy, and the Americas. By 1570, lands in the Pacific, such as the Philippines, had been added. Governing Spain involved much more than just the Iberian Peninsula.

Although the monarch had great power, Spanish cities had some independence. Early modern municipalities were not unlike small city-states, an outgrowth of earlier times when concessions and liberties were granted to them by the monarchs or nobility in order to attract settlers to the frontier areas under their control, where Muslims and Christians confronted each other. The inhabitants were authorized to surround their towns with defensive ramparts, to carry out their own internal administration, to maintain a militia, and in whole or in part to elect their own magistrates. The community was often given the right to tax itself to pay for local improvements, with only a light tribute destined for the monarch. Sometimes freedom from persecution of the town officials was guaranteed by the crown against charges brought by royal agents.

Thus personal liberty and fiscal and administrative autonomy were the primary features inscribed in the municipal charters, or *fueros,* which differed somewhat from town to town depending on the historical circumstances. In 1025 Barcelona obtained a charter of privileges from Count Ramón Berenguer, and Zaragoza was given extensive privileges in 1125 by Alfonso the Battler. Toledo, Córdoba, Seville, and other towns all received their *fueros* from the reigning monarch as they were reconquered from the Muslims.

Some communities were designated cities and had jurisdiction over larger territories or several parishes that might include neighboring villages and hamlets. Towns, on the other hand, were usually limited to the areas encompassed by their walls and immediate surroundings. Those magistrates charged with communal affairs formed the *ayuntamiento,* or municipal council. There were also many other officials such as the *alcaldes,* responsible for civil and criminal justice; the *regidores,* who administered the affairs of the city; and the *alguacil mayor* (principal peace officer), who commanded the militia. Other officials controlled the building crafts and communal property. Cities sent representatives or deputies (*procuradores*) chosen by the municipal council to the Cortes, the body that looked after the interests of all the subjects of the kingdom but that was summoned to meet only at the will of the king. As guardian of the local *fueros,* the Cortes could refuse to obey orders from the crown if the demands jeopardized the interests of the region.

While the Cortes advised the monarch on numerous matters including royal marriages and foreign alliances, its real power lay in controlling financial matters. The king could not levy new taxes or raise old ones without its consent.

As *procuradores* left their towns for meetings of the Cortes, they took with them detailed instructions. They were entrusted with the mandate to present complaints to the king from their constituents. Although they had no power to legislate while in Castile, their suggestions were sometimes made into law by royal edicts. Some remote areas of the two kingdoms of Castile and Aragón were underrepresented or not represented at all, such as Galicia and Extremadura, which were areas with no important cities.

In Castile the Cortes consisted of the three estates: the nobility, the church, and the commoners. Since it only had real authority over taxes and the first two groups paid none, nobles and clergy often absented themselves from the meetings. In time they were not summoned, and the king went directly to the cities and towns for his requirements. Unable to withstand the pressure exerted by the sovereign, the towns gave him what he wanted, and the Cortes gradually became a useless body. In the reign of Charles II, the last Habsburg king, it was never called to session, and the money required for the crown treasury was solicited directly from the town councils.

The Cortes of Aragón, Valencia, and Cataluña were not so compliant, and various kings were often frustrated by their refusal to grant them money, to levy troops for wars, or to house soldiers in their territory without considerable concessions. In these realms the Cortes shared legislative power with the king and approved or denied royal edicts. Here the nobility did not shun the sessions and scrupulously watched over their own interests. The Cortes was often more interested in submitting complaints than listening to the king's pleas for money. Always finding obstacles to put in the way of the king's demands, they were seldom called.

The administration of each region was overseen by the Council of Castile. This royal body was designed by Isabella and Ferdinand in 1480 to be the central governing body of the kingdom. It was the supreme court of justice and supervised the workings of local governments. Under Charles I, it had about 12 members, all university-trained lawyers, since the king preferred them to the grandees (the high landowning nobility). Early in the 16th century, other councils were formed to deal with Aragón, finance, the Indies, war, and foreign policy. The Council of the Supreme Inquisition, known as the Suprema, was founded in 1488. There were others of lesser importance, such as the Council of Military Orders, but none had much authority except the Suprema and the Council of Castile. The latter appointed *corregidores,* or civil governors, who served as representatives of the crown at the local level throughout the kingdoms. Their seats were in the larger cities where

Philip II. This king oversaw the vast Spanish Empire during the last half of the 16th century, and he launched the Spanish Armada in an attempt to capture England. Sanchez Coello, *Felipe II.* Madrid: Prado.

they presided over the town council and maintained vigilance over the area under their jurisdiction. By the end of the 16th century, there were 68 *corregidores*; this number increased to 86 over the next century (Anderson, 19–21).

FOR MORE INFORMATION

Anderson, J. *The Spanish Inquisition*. Westport, Conn.: Greenwood, 2002.

Mariéjol, J. H. *The Spain of Ferdinand and Isabella*. Trans. Benjamin Keen. New Brunswick, N.J.: Rutgers University Press, 1961.

ITALY

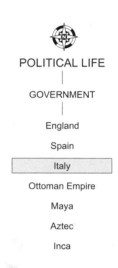

During the Renaissance, there was no centralized government that controlled all of the Italian peninsula. Instead, there was a large variety of states and city-states. The political map was so complex that, especially in the North, a traveler met borders everywhere. The many states varied in size and in form of government. Ranging from monarchies to republics, Italian regimes had countless roads to power, from inheritance to election to assassination and stealthy coup d'état. Some states were fairly big, and others were mere sovereign fingernails of territory. The smallest were autonomous feudal lordships, nominally parts of the Holy Roman Empire. This body, despite its name, was an elective monarchy of the Germans that still asserted residual claims to northern Italy. Though legally subordinate to the emperor, these functionally independent lords might rule a clutch of villages, presiding over their own courts of justice and collecting fines and taxes. Somewhat larger were the self-governing cities, some, like Lucca, with modest territories a few dozen miles across, and others, like Florence, Ferrara, and Venice, capitals of fair-sized states with their own subject towns and cities. Some of these city-states were democratic, though suffrage was limited to elites, while others had fallen under the power of *signori*, lords who ruled in an autocratic spirit. Midway down the peninsula was a principality like none other, the State of the Church, centered on Rome and ruling a wide band that cut across the middle of the peninsula. The pope was therefore not only the head of Latin Christendom but also an elected temporal monarch, with his army and navy, his foreign policies and diplomats, his local governors, judges, and taxmen. The southern third of mainland Italy, down to the heel and toe of the boot, and Sicily belonged to Italy's only kingdom, Naples.

The political institutions of so richly mixed a scene do not summarize easily. Nevertheless, a few typical features are discernible. First comes sophistication. Renaissance Italy pioneered in statecraft. The origins of modern diplomacy and espionage, seldom far apart, owe much to Italian ingenuity. The medieval visiting emissary gradually evolved into the resident ambassador, with his chancery and his diplomatic immunities. The brilliant reports from Italy and beyond by the ambassadors of Milan, Florence, and Venice, or by the papal nuncios, with their sharp eye for local detail, were precious sources of data for both the regimes that paid their wages and modern historians. Italian regimes were precociously literate and, by continental standards, complex and ambitious. States and cities devised various clever ways of financing their operations—military, judicial, and administrative. They legislated with an eye to regulating the economy, the environment, urban spaces, public health, and private morality. On the other hand, one should not overstate their modernity, for many states' ambitions outran their powers of coercion. Early modern statecraft was a dialogue between an ambitious center and a recalcitrant periphery. Subject territories, remote districts, and privileged groups and persons all strove, sometimes successfully, to balk the will of governments. A mark of weakness was that governments compromised, granting and selling exemptions from the rules, to the point that it sometimes seemed that Italian states ruled as much by exceptions as by decrees and laws.

Participation in power varied greatly. Some regimes were tightly held, while others were surprisingly open. In general, in states and towns of all shapes and sizes, political participation was much sought after, by both elites and those of middling station. This desire held as true for villagers as for city dwellers. Some positions came by appointment, others by ballot. Wherever elected councils sat, there were complex routines of nomination, election, and choice by lottery for offices of surprisingly short duration—perhaps three months, perhaps a year, seldom longer. The rapid circulation of council members was meant to spread the fruits of power and block anyone from becoming overly mighty; the subtle electoral machinery, with its element of chance, was designed to forestall alliances, connivance, influence peddling, and party factions. Alongside local councils, there were independent judges, almost always from some other place—for locals were thought to play favorites—and a corps of secretaries, notaries, and other lettered functionaries. In all regimes, from autocratic to democratic, power was unevenly distributed. Women, the young, the poor, and even the less wealthy working classes had no formal role. In general, even in democratic regimes, the rich amassed the lion's share of seats, thanks either to the rules, often made by them, or to their social influence. As the Renaissance went on, in many places the base of power narrowed in a process of aristocratization of elites.

Princely regimes increasingly developed courts. A court is a social world gathered around a monarch, where his friends and friends of friends battened off his wealth and power. There the ruler exchanged patronage for the submission and loyalty of his more privileged subjects. The richer the state, the more lucrative, though dangerous, courtly life could be. Courtiers, brokers of news and influence, traded in secrets, gifts, commissions, appointments, introductions, invitations, privileges, and other perquisites of power to build their own careers and to advance their kinsmen and friends. The court favored those who possessed tact, subtlety, and an exquisite sense of timing. It was a competitive, sometimes cutthroat place where the mastery of appearances, self-control, and smooth social graces were prize assets. There was little in common between the blunt public discussions of a republic's elected council and the veiled innuendo of much courtly talk.

In the countryside, the peasants were generally ruled by the landlord, who frequently held the legal status of *signore* (lord). The *signore* admin-

Lorenzo de Medici. The powerful Medici family controlled Florence for most of the Renaissance. Lorenzo de Medici, often called Lorenzo the Magnificent, was one of these dictators. Portrait by Vasari. © The Art Archive/Galleria degli Uffizi Florence/Dagli Orti (A).

istered justice; provided facilities such as mills, presses, and ovens; controlled hunting, fishing, and other uses of his domains; and commandeered labor for public projects. For revenue the *signore* collected fees and fines from those who brought suits or were convicted by his courts. He (or occasionally she) rented out the monopolies on the mill, the winepresses, the bakery, the inn, and the store. Some lords also bought from the government the option to collect state taxes. The *signori* (lords) might even wage private wars against each other.

Running estates and villages, especially where landlords were routinely absent, fell to a local elite who mediated between the residents and the larger outside world. Agents, employed by the owners, managed the land, oversaw work on the lord's personal domains, and collected rents and dues. These deputies juggled contradictory sets of demands: to serve their employer's interests, make their own way, and live among the often impoverished or resentful tenants who had to pay out. The village elite also included professionals who came from elsewhere or had ties to external institutional networks. Among these, priests, though often not highly educated, were men of influence. A council of senior villagers, a small version of the communal assemblies in the cities, formed part of local government. But the central official, often called the *podestà* or *vicario*, was an outsider appointed by the feudal lord or the rulers of the state. Commonly assisting these administrators, even in the country, were notaries who wrote and preserved contracts and other documents. Their outside origins, professional ties, and official power tended to separate them from the rest of the rural community. Certainly local officials could demand and punish in the name of external authority. At the same time, they mediated conflicts between the village and the larger world and between contentious locals (Cohen and Cohen, 10–13, 21–24).

FOR MORE INFORMATION

Cohen, E. S., and T. V. Cohen. *Daily Life in Renaissance Italy*. Westport, Conn.: Greenwood, 2001.

Lane, F. *Venice, a Maritime Republic*. Ann Arbor: University of Michigan Press, 1997.

OTTOMAN EMPIRE

The Ottoman Empire, together with the Safavid and Mughal states, formed one of the Islamic world's three "Gunpowder Empires" and was founded by nomadic warriors of Central Asian ancestry and based on military conquest. The state was viewed as the indivisible patrimony of the Ottoman family, which became the longest-ruling dynasty in Islamic history with a reign of over 600 years. In Ottoman political theory, society was made up of the *askeri*, or rulers, and the *reaya*, or ruled (literally "flock"). Government officials were considered members of the sultan's household, the locus of all authority, which had the absolute right to exploit those under its rule.

According to Turkish political traditions, political sovereignty rested with the family itself rather than a particular member of it, though one male member of the

family ruled as sultan khan, who is usually referred to today as just "sultan." Both men and women of the Ottoman family were addressed with the title sultan. Hence Suleyman the Magnificient was called Sultan Suleyman Khan, his son was Sultan Mehmed, and his daughter Mihrimah Sultan. The position of the Ottoman dynasty was paramount, and after a certain point males ceased to marry because under Islamic law women become their husbands' equals, and the Ottoman rulers wanted no equals.

Suleyman the Magnificent. Under this sultan, who ruled from 1520–1556, the Ottoman Empire reached its zenith of culture and power. © Giraudon/Art Resource, NY.

Because any male could accede to the highest power, princes often became the favorites of different parties at court and in society, which used them to foment rebellion against the ruler. For example, after the death of Bayezit II in 1512, several of his sons claimed the throne. Ahmed was considered an able administrator and favored by the people, but the military opposed him in favor of his brother Selim because of several occasions on which he had led them to defeat. The religious scholars favored Korkut, who was learned and pious. Selim prevailed and proceeded to execute all of his brothers, nephews, and all except one of his sons to prevent further challenges to his authority.

In addition to blood relatives and concubines, the ruling household included the sultan's slaves. This did not mean that they became the sultan's property, but rather that their personalities and ambitions had been subsumed beneath those of the ruler. They included recruits from noble families, Christian conscripts from the provinces who were converted to Islam, and individuals purchased from the Caucasus. Such people became the army commanders, bureaucrats, and sometimes provincial governors of the empire.

The official in charge of the day-to-day running of government was the *sadr-i azam*, under whom served a number of *vazirs* who had charge of various departments. Through much of Ottoman history, the *sadr-i azam* also presided over the *divan*, a council made up of the civilian and military leaders that made key decisions of state policy, dispensed justice, and received foreign ambassadors. During the 16th century, this group met in the Second Chamber in the Second Courtyard of the New Palace, next to the Hagia Sophia in Istanbul. If the *sadr-i azam* accompanied a military campaign, they met in his tent. Sometimes a sultan would present a member of the council with a black cloak. This meant that councilor was scheduled for execution and showed the power the ruler had even over his highest officials.

Within this structure Ottoman government remained highly informal. Many important decisions came through unrecorded conversations of the rulers with whichever officials held their ears at a given time. Even in meetings of the *divan*, petitions came from a variety of sources. Sometimes a provincial judge would forward a difficult legal case or a petitioner would appear in person with a complaint. Decrees usually contained the means through which the matter came to the *divan*'s attention: "The governor of Menteshe, Ahmed—may his glory endure—has sent a man to make it known that soldiers are necessary for the galleys, which were given to the aforenamed for the defense of the sea-shore."

The "men of the pen" formed another important element of the Ottoman ruling class. They were divided into two branches, the Imperial Treasury, which was in charge of financial matters, and the Imperial Council, which dealt with administrative matters. The Imperial Council kept the records of the *divan*, drawing up its decrees and storing them, and dealt with personnel matters and diplomacy throughout the empire. The Imperial Treasury kept track of the revenue of the provinces and government expenditures.

The basic structure of this central government was reproduced in the provinces. Provincial governors appointed by the sultan had their own households and in theory held absolute authority over the provinces, though in practice they had to take into account the concerns of local citizens. The extent of Ottoman control also varied from region to region. Tribal chieftains continued to show independence in the mountains of eastern Anatolia, while in sensitive areas such as Egypt, governors were rotated frequently to prevent them from gaining independence.

The *reaya* were divided into a number of different groups based on both residence and religion. City dwellers, farmers, and nomads all had a particular social status and duties to the state. In addition, under Islamic law, Jews and Christians were allowed to practice their religion freely under Muslim protection. In the Ottoman Empire, each religious group formed a *millet*, with the religious leaders serving as intermediaries between the people and the state. *Millets* recognized by the Ottomans included the Muslims, Orthodox Jews, and non-Orthodox Christians. Each community lived according to its own law, save where it conflicted with the decrees of the sultans.

The Ottoman family thus headed a highly centralized state in which all decisions theoretically went back to their own authority. Members of the Ottoman household formed the imperial elite, and the sultan's slaves were of greater importance than a provincial city's leading citizens. Bureaucracies oversaw the daily administration and record-keeping that kept this administration running. Nonetheless, politics as such remained highly informal, with personal connections among the elites and between elites and notables representing different factions that determined both personnel decisions and state policies.

To read about government in Medieval Islam, see the Islam entries in the section "Social Structure" in chapter 6 ("Political Life") in volume 2 of this series; for Islam in the 19th century, see the Islamic World entry in the section "Empire" in chapter 6 ("Political Life") in volume 5 of this series; for Islam in the 20th century, see the Islamic World entries in chapter 6 ("Political Life") in volume 6 of this series.

~Brian Ulrich

FOR MORE INFORMATION

Hourani, A. *A History of the Arab Peoples*. New York: MJF Books, 1991.

Imber, C. *The Ottoman Empire*. New York: Palgrave, 2002.

Peirce, L. *The Imperial Harem: Women and Sovereignty in the Ottoman Empire*. New York: Oxford University Press, 1993.

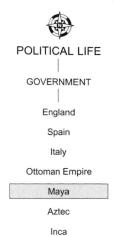

POLITICAL LIFE
|
GOVERNMENT
|
England

Spain

Italy

Ottoman Empire

Maya

Aztec

Inca

MAYA

The Maya were never politically unified, always being divided into numerous independent polities. The earliest monuments and texts indicate that rule by powerful individual kings (*ahaw*) began during the era of Early Maya Civilization in the southern area. By the beginning of Middle Maya Civilization, the kings were also in power throughout the lowlands, where they took on the title of *k'ul Ahaw*, or "divine (or supreme) ruler." In the royal inscriptions, later kings often referred to the earliest ruler in each polity as a founder and counted the line of succession from this hallowed individual. Especially successful kings accumulated additional titles honoring their achievements in battle ("captor of. . . . "), their age ("four katun lord"), and their identification with supernatural powers ("sun lord" or "sun-faced lord"). The elite class and the various secondary offices held by elite men grew in numbers. The hierarchy of authority continued to expand, and in some Maya states the king designated subordinates with formal titles such as *Cahal* or *Sahal* (subordinate ruler).

An overriding feature of Maya state organization was the reliance on kinship ties for lines of authority that radiated out from the king and his elite council to the hinterlands. These lines were enforced by economic and religious factors. The ruler and his elite officials provided security and protection for their subjects, but people were also motivated to be obedient because they received economic and religious benefits as a result. From the king on down, officials rewarded good deeds with gifts of food and goods. Religious belief reinforced the system by holding that everyone's success and health depended on staying in harmony with the Maya universe, an important part of which meant obeying the king and his officials. Sanctions for disobedience would be loss of economic benefits and the wrath of the gods, bringing misfortune and even death.

In Maya government there was less authority based on true political power than is common in today's world. Maya kings had less ability to do physical harm to those who disobeyed than is found in modern industrial states. Political power in most modern states is based on the threat or use of coercive force through laws, courts, and police dedicated to the enforcement of authority. The Maya state relied instead on economic and religious sanctions—although we can be sure that when all else failed severe punishments were given to individuals who displeased the king.

Each polity had a capital where the king, his court, and the advisory council lived. A loose hierarchy of subordinate centers surrounded the capital. The size of the kingdom and the number of subordinate centers shifted over time according to the personal success of each king in promoting his followers' loyalty or defeating his neighbors in war. At the same time, some of the more self-sufficient subordinate centers attempted to break free of the control of the capital or shift their alliances to other centers, especially when a weak king was on the throne. Aggressive and powerful kings attempted to expand or centralize their power, which often created further instability in the system. For example, Calakmul used a network of alliances to defeat Tikal, its chief rival. Tikal's fortunes were at low ebb until an especially effective and powerful king took power and defeated its former enemies.

In a government where the power and success of each polity was dependent on the personal performance of its king, a Maya ruler had to be a successful war leader, a successful diplomat to organize alliances, and a successful religious leader to conduct successful ceremonies. He also had to personally control his subordinates, especially in the collection of tribute in goods and labor. Thus it was the charismatic leadership qualities of the king more than anything else that allowed a Maya polity to expand and prosper.

When an ever-increasing number of Maya kings failed to solve the problems of overpopulation, degradation of the environment, and escalating violence, their prestige and power rapidly evaporated. By the end of Middle Maya Civilization, the problems in many areas of the southern lowlands were severe beyond recovery. Even in less-devastated regions, such as Yucatán and the highlands, the old system of divine kings was discredited and a new political order emerged. The new political order relied less on the personal achievements and charisma of the king and more on the collective wisdom of the *multepal,* or elite council. The *multepal* proved to be far more flexible and responsive than the former royal system.

At the time of the Spaniards' arrival, the 18 independent Maya states in Yucatán had three forms of political organization. In fact, there were a great deal of shared features between these systems. All but a few were ruled from a capital city (*cah*) with a ruling lord and a council of elite-lineage leaders. The elite council met in the *popolna* (house of the mat) and functioned as (1) an advisory body to the ruling lord or (2) in the absence of a single ruler, as supreme authority within the state. In addition, several polities without a central capital relied on a loose confederation of allied cities, each controlled by elite lineages.

Nine of the 18 polities were ruled by a single lord, called either *ahaw* or *halach uinic* (true man). Although this system was the descendent of the old royal political system, it differed in important respects. The later ruling lords did not advertise their achievements and prestige on monuments or in texts as their predecessors during Middle Maya Civilization had done. In fact, they possessed less personal power, shared more authority with their advisory councils, and did not link their personal prestige with the fate of the kingdom. In these ways the lords of Late Maya Civilization avoided the central weakness of the more powerful but vulnerable kings of Middle Maya Civilization.

Landa reports that both civil and religious offices were hereditary and were derived from the elite class. However, there were important exceptions. The ruling lords of Yucatán were *usually* succeeded by their oldest sons, although Landa himself says that a brother or the best-qualified candidate could become king if there was no qualified son.

The power of each *halach uinic* was far from absolute. He formulated foreign and domestic policies only after consulting his council. He received annual tribute in goods and labor from his subjects. He appointed his subordinates, the town and village overseers (*batabob*), who were usually his close kin, and governed the major provinces of his kingdom. In addition, the *halach uinic* was the highest religious authority in his kingdom.

There were several other important officials in the small Yucatecan states. The *holpop* (he at the head of the mat) was an ancient and important title among the Maya. In most polities of Yucatán groups of these officials (*holpopob*) formed the council that met in the *popolna* and advised the *halach uinic* on foreign and domestic policy. They also served as intermediaries for subjects who wished to approach the ruling lord. In at least two cases the *holpop* was the title of the ruler of the town.

A subordinate elite official, or *batab,* oversaw each subdivision within the state and reported to the ruling lord. The glyph for *batab* has been identified in texts from the southern lowlands, so this official probably served a similar role in some polities of Middle Maya Civilization. In any case, during Late Maya Civilization these officials were usually based in an outlying town where they held administrative, judicial, and military authority. Each *batab* saw to it that the subjects under his control paid their tribute in goods and labor to the *halach uinic*. The *batab* ensured that his town was kept clean, its buildings kept in repair, and that the farmers cut and burned their fields at the proper time. As a judge he sentenced criminals and decided civil suits, always consulting the *halach uinic* in serious cases before passing judgment. Each *batab* commanded his own warriors, although in times of war all *batabob* served under a single military commander.

Each *batab* presided over a local council composed of town councilors, the *ah cuch cabob*. These councilors were the heads of the next level in the government hierarchy, the *nalil,* or subdivisions, within each town. The *batab* also had two or three assistants, the *ah kulelob,* who accompanied him wherever he went and carried out his orders. Finally, each town had constables, the *tupiles,* charged with keeping the peace. Forms of government in the highlands were similar to those in Yucatán (Sharer, 142–47).

To read about government in 19th-century Latin America, see the Latin America entry in the section "Government and Politics" in chapter 6 ("Political Life") in volume 5 of this series; for 20th-century Latin America, see the Latin America entry in the section "Government" in chapter 6 ("Political Life") in volume 6 of this series.

FOR MORE INFORMATION

Schele, L., and D. A. Freidel. *A Forest of Kings.* New York: Morrow, 1990.

Sharer, R. J. *Daily Life in Maya Civilization.* Westport, Conn.: Greenwood, 1996.

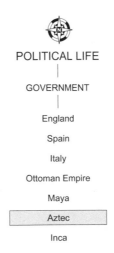

POLITICAL LIFE

|

GOVERNMENT

|

England

Spain

Italy

Ottoman Empire

Maya

Aztec

Inca

AZTEC

Although the Aztecs commanded a vast empire, the city-state was the center of most government. While the capital cities of Tenochtitlan, Texcoco, and Tlacopan received large amounts of tribute, most government was carried out on the local, not imperial, level. The Aztec city-states maintained their own identity, society, and government. When the Spanish arrived, there were about 50 Aztec *altepetl,* and almost 500 non-Aztec city-states that were subject to various Aztec *altepetl.*

The *altepetl* (city-state) was a community with its own town center, boundaries, laws, farmland, and *tlatoani* (pl. *tlatoque*), which means king. The most important buildings and the symbolic heart of the *altepetl* were the royal palace, the pyramid-shaped temple, and the marketplace. The royal palace served not only as a home for the *tlatoani* but also as the administrative and social center of the *altepetl*.

Tlatoque were chosen by a council of noblemen who were related to the recently deceased king. The new *tlatoani* was usually a son or brother of the previous king, but more distant relations, such as grandson or nephew, were sometimes selected. After selection, the new *tlatoani* underwent an elaborate initiation: the *tlatoani* pierced himself to offer blood to the god Huitzilopochtli, underwent four days of fasting, and a crown of green stones and gold was placed on his head by a *tlatoani* from a different region. The inauguration was accompanied by speeches, gifts, dance, music, and human sacrifices. By the end, the *tlatoani* was intimately linked with the gods. One of the *tlatoani*'s chief duties was to wage war, and the new *tlatoani* would undertake a new war very soon into his reign. A successful campaign showed that he was the true king, while a failure could result in the end of his authority.

We can get the clearest picture of the power and authority of an Aztec ruler such as Motecuhzoma Xocoyotzin, the *tlatoani* who greeted Cortés, by studying the great coronation rituals that taught him and everyone who witnessed them his place in the world. The coronation ceremony for the new ruler involved his social lowering, followed by a social elevation. The ruler-to-be was stripped of his noble clothes, dressed humbly in a loin-cloth, and taken to the base of the pyramid of Huitzilopochtli. Other nobles accompanied him, and he was led by the *tlatoque* of the allied cities of Tezcoco and Tacuba up the steps of the temple. There he was painted black by the chief priests before being adorned with a sleeveless green jacket, a tobacco gourd, and a green cotton incense bag decorated with bones. He was taken by the priests, or "keepers of the gods," before Huitzilopochtli's statue, which he perfumed with incense. The text reads, "All common folks stood looking up at him. Trumpets were sounded and shell trumpets were blown." Then, four nobles dressed in a similar manner with veiled faces, fasting capes, and the bone design led him down the temple steps into the house of fasting, which was a military headquarters. There, the nobles and the ruler-to-be underwent four days of fasting and penance. Each day they would silently ascend the temple of Huitzilopochtli to carry out autosacrifices, bleeding themselves to nourish the god. They bathed to purify themselves each day. On the fifth day, the ruler was escorted to his royal palace and the nobles returned to their homes. The *tlatoani* announced a royal feast, and rulers from all over the realm, including enemy rulers, were invited to receive gifts and food, to dance, and to join in procession with the Aztec nobles.

Motecuhzoma Xocoyotzin. Motecuhzoma was the ruler of Tenochtitlan and the effective head of the Aztec empire when the Spanish arrived. Motecuhzoma is featured sitting in the center of the painting surrounded by images of 16 of his 44 conquests. From the *Codex Mendoza*. Courtesy of Frances F. Berdan and Patricia Reiff Anawait.

In this first stage of the coronation ceremony the ruler learned his place in the world. He was taken *out* of society and magically transformed before reentering society for the second stage of the coronation. He was stripped of his clothes, painted the color of the priesthood, turned into the servant of Huitzilopochtli, whom he fed with incense, and then he was displayed from above to the populace, and taken down into a military monastery, where he meditated before ascending the temple four times to give blood and purify himself. His place was a sacred place, and his being was turned into a sacred being, above and below the rest of humanity, greater than humans, *other* than humans, but also among humans, as displayed in the feast. But in this feast, he proclaimed himself ruler of the world, for all the other nobles were required to come and receive his gifts and foods and participate in his dances and processions.

The second phase of the coronation began when the *tlatoani* of Tenochtitlan appeared, now more than a man, before the ruler of the sister city of Tezcoco. For only another sacred king could crown a sacred king. A crown of green stones and gold was placed on the new ruler's head, and his nose was pierced through the septum, where an emerald was inserted. The king was then led to the "eagle seat," where he was seated to hear a series of speeches instructing him on his new responsibilities. A sampling of these speeches tells us some surprising things about how Aztecs valued and depended on their rulers.

Following these speeches, the new ruler was transported to the eagle and ocelot thrones in Huitzilopochtli's temple, where he was given a jaguar claw to pierce periodically his ears and legs. In this moment, he again ascended upward to the temple of Huitzilopochtli, the sun and war god. Then he was taken to the Coate-coalli, the House of Foreign Gods, where more rites were carried out. In this moment he visited the temple containing the gods of other peoples who have been conquered by the Aztecs and who have been carried by Aztec priests from the enemy town into the capital city and symbolically imprisoned. In a sense, he visited the horizontal landscape of the four quarters, the earthly level of social and religious conquest now integrated in the House of Foreign Gods. Then, he was taken to the temple-cave of Yopico, where he communicated with the gods of the earth. In this moment, he symbolically descended into the earth, where he offered blood, quail, and incense.

Following this symbolic journey to the above, the below, and the four quarters, the new ruler was taken back to the palace for more speeches by other rulers and nobles; he was reminded of his lineage with Quetzalcoatl, Tezcatlipoca, and Huitzilopochtli. Then, in his first act of generosity, he distributed gifts to friends and allies. After the gift giving he was ready for his first war as *tlatoani*.

The *tlatoani* owned the land of the city-state and received tribute from the people. He was ultimately responsible for waging war, overseeing religious festivals, and resolving disputes. Helping the king were a council of nobles and lower-level administrators who probably conducted most of the day-to-day requirements of the city. The *tlatoani*, however, was ultimately responsible.

The *tlatoani* was also in charge of overseeing the city-states subject to his own *altepetl*. The *tlatoani* most likely did not interfere with the daily affairs of these subject states, but rather ensured that they sent the required tribute and maintained any stipulations imposed upon them. If the subject state failed in these regards, the *tlatoani* frequently chose war as the preferred political instrument (Carrasco, 134–37).

To read about government in 19th-century Latin America, see the Latin America entry in the section "Government and Politics" in chapter 6 ("Political Life") in volume 5 of this series; for 20th-century Latin America, see the Latin America entry in the section "Government" in chapter 6 ("Political Life") in volume 6 of this series.

FOR MORE INFORMATION

Carrasco, D., with S. Sessions. *Daily Life of the Aztecs: People of the Sun and Earth*. Westport, Conn.: Greenwood, 1998.

Smith, M. *The Aztecs*. Oxford: Blackwell, 1996.

INCA

POLITICAL LIFE
|
GOVERNMENT
|
England

Spain

Italy

Ottoman Empire

Maya

Aztec

Inca

The Incas built their empire in less than a century. This in itself was an extraordinary achievement, but other empires have expanded as rapidly or even more so. For example, Alexander the Great's conquests of the Middle East occurred in less than 30 years. Conquering people is a relatively straightforward thing to do; all one needs is many well-armed soldiers and effective military leaders. However, to integrate conquered peoples into a single empire that functions as a unit with central control is much more difficult. This is especially so when the conquered societies are spread out over a broad area of very rugged terrain, such as the Andes mountains. Perhaps the greatest achievement of the Incas is that they appear to have successfully organized all the groups they conquered into an empire that did function as a unit. This is not to say the empire ran smoothly; quite to the contrary, the history of the Inca empire is one of rebellions and conflict. It is also apparent that the Incas did not use a single policy of incorporation for every conquered group; rather, they tailored their policies to the particular circumstances of each group.

One of the reasons for the Incas' success was their use of the existing political and social structures of conquered people for ruling them. Instead of trying to change the people's lives, they tried to maintain continuity so the subjects' lives were disrupted as little as possible. The Incas saw their relationship to conquered peoples as one of institutionalized reciprocity. This means that the Incas expected the conquered people to work for them, but in return they provided them with services and goods, food and clothing, beer, coca, and even entertainment. They assigned conquered leaders positions of authority in the government, gave them high-status gifts, and honored their religious beliefs and practices. In return the Incas expected the conquered people to work hard for them; to produce, among other things, food, cloth, pottery, buildings, and other large and small items; and to be obedient and loyal subjects.

Another key to the Incas' success in forming a unified empire was their organization of conquered peoples. Pachacuti, the ninth king, is credited with setting up the empire and making it run effectively, although it is possible that the process began earlier. The empire was divided into four *suyus,* or divisions: Chinchaysuyu (north), Collasuyu (south), Antisuyu (east), and Cuntisuyu (west), which radiated from the capital city of Cuzco. The *suyus* were not equal in size; the north and south divisions were large, and the east and west quarters were small.

Each quarter was made up of several provinces. A province usually corresponded to the area occupied by a conquered people. If the conquered group was small, it might be added to other small ones to make a single province. If a conquered group was large, like the Chimu, it might be divided into more than one province. The ideal was to have approximately 20,000 households in a province. Households were the basic unit in most Andean societies, and they generally corresponded to a family. However, unlike the concept of family in U.S. society (a mother and father and their children), Andean families might also include grandparents, grandchildren, aunts, or uncles.

The Inca empire was administered by a well-developed bureaucracy that collected tribute and distributed it. At the top was the king, who was the ultimate authority on all matters. Below the king were four officials, called *apos,* each in charge of one of the quarters. These officials were close advisors of the king and probably relatives as well. Each province had a governor who was responsible for its affairs. There were more than 80 provinces in the Inca empire, so this added 80 or more individuals to the bureaucracy. Each governor was under the orders of the *apo* of the quarter in which his province lay.

King on an *Ushnu.* The *ushnu* was a platform at the center of an Inca city and was reserved for the king or the local representative of the king. Picture by Guaman Poma.

The 20,000-household province was set up so it could be most effectively ruled. The system was hierarchical in that officials lower down were responsible to ones higher up, and it was based on a decimal system of counting, like that of most modern countries. Below each provincial governor were two government officials called *curacas,* who were in charge of 10,000 households each. These *curacas* were each in charge of two other *curacas* of 5,000 households. These *curacas* in turn directed the activities of five *curacas* who managed 1,000 households each. The lowest-level administrators were two *curacas* who had responsibility for 500 households and five *curacas* who handled 100 households each.

What did all the *curacas* do? Their chief responsibilities were to make sure the proper number of people showed up to work for the Incas and to distribute the workload among the households for which each was responsible. It was also the *curaca's* duty to ensure that the correct amount of tribute was produced and transported to the nearest Inca center and to allocate to each household adequate land to support itself. If a *curaca* did a good job, he was rewarded by his superiors; if not, he was punished. Punishments ranged from public rebuke to death, depending on whether the individual was merely being lazy or actually dishonest (Malpass, *The Inca Empire,* 31–35).

To read about government in 19th-century Latin America, see the Latin America entry in the section "Government and Politics" in chapter 6 ("Political Life") in volume 5 of this series; for 20th-century Latin America, see the Latin America entry in the section "Government" in chapter 6 ("Political Life") in volume 6 of this series.

FOR MORE INFORMATION

Bauer, B. *The Development of the Inca State*. Austin: University of Texas Press, 1992.

Malpass, M. A. *The Inca Empire*. Westport, Conn.: Greenwood, 1996.

———, ed. *Provincial Inca*. Iowa City: University of Iowa Press, 1993.

Justice and Legal Systems

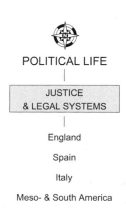

POLITICAL LIFE

JUSTICE
& LEGAL SYSTEMS

England

Spain

Italy

Meso- & South America

Legal systems are intended to maintain the peace and order of the society by establishing rules for behavior, business, and ethics. When these rules are broken, the legal system prescribes various punishments for the guilty to deter the guilty one and other individuals from committing crime. The role of the state as the arbiter is what distinguishes a legal system from simple retribution. In many premodern societies, blood feud was the only system of justice practiced. In blood feud, a victim and his or her family would seek retribution upon the person that had hurt them. For example, if a neighbor stole some cows and killed the owner, the owner's relations would come together and plot to assassinate the thief and murderer. Such systems of retribution and vengeance have a tendency to grow completely out of hand. Thus, in the above example, once the murderer/thief had been killed, the relatives of the thief might decide that they were obliged to avenge his death on those who had killed him. Such blood feuds risked giving rise to a perpetual circle of violence that could utterly destroy the community.

The appointing of a nonpartial arbiter was the first step in establishing a legal system that was not based upon vengeance alone. This arbiter could be a group of men, such as a jury, but in most cases consisted of a single individual, the judge, who had been appointed by the king or other ruling body. For the arbiter to be successful in bringing peace to the community, he must have the trust and faith of the parties involved, and/or he must have the means of enforcing his decisions. Obviously, the best case scenario is when all the parties affected by and implicated in a crime accept the authority of the judge and his decision; in practice, however, the judge needed to rely on armed force, or the threat of armed force, to ensure that everyone would accept his decision.

An amazing diversity of legal systems existed in the 15th and 16th centuries, ranging from the well organized to the haphazard. The Incas had one of the most well-organized systems. The Inca government in general had created an extremely efficient bureaucracy based upon a system of minor officials called *curacas* who ruled over small segments of the society. At the lowest administrative level, a *curaca* oversaw 100 households. If a dispute arose between members of the community overseen by the *curaca* then he would hear the case and pass judgment. If a dispute arose between a member of his community and a member of a community overseen by a different low-level *curaca*, then one of the higher-level *curacas*, who oversaw both communities, would hear the case. There would thus be an appropriate official familiar with the local communities judging most cases.

By contrast, the Italian legal system could be frustratingly haphazard. In part, the inefficiency of this system was created by the plethora of small city-states, each with its own independent territories, laws, legal systems, and concerns. A criminal could use these divisions to great advantage: if a criminal was wanted by the authorities in one city-state, he or she could flee to another city-state. Many criminals found a kind of patronage from wealthy lords, who gave protection to brigands from government prosecution provided that the brigands were loyal to their patrons. Despite such complications, Italian states and courts did make earnest attempts to create and uphold the law. Most Italian states issued regulations about an astonishing array of subjects, including things such as the permitted width of sleeves, and had active court systems in which all manner of civil and criminal proceedings were heard by a judge.

Most premodern legal systems seem harsh by today's standards. Very striking is the reliance upon torture to exact evidence and confessions. Most suspected criminals were tortured as part of the interrogation process, and many convictions were the result of confessions given under torture or under the threat of torture. The penalties handed out to those found guilty were also severe. The death penalty was a common punishment and could even be assigned for crimes such as robbery. Many of these punishments were intentionally spectacular, to impress the event upon the memory of those witnessing it and to deter them from crime. In Europe, those condemned to die might be left hanging from the gallows for months to serve as an example to others that they should not embark upon a criminal career. In the Inca empire, those convicted of treason were thrust into an underground prison filled with snakes and dangerous animals. Few people emerged alive.

~*Lawrence Morris*

POLITICAL LIFE

JUSTICE
& LEGAL SYSTEMS

England

Spain

Italy

Meso- & South America

ENGLAND

The mechanisms for legal enforcement in Renaissance England were quite complex. There were several legal institutions for trying a criminal case. It might be tried in one of several royal courts; it might fall under the jurisdiction of ecclesiastical courts; a minor matter might be handled summarily by a gentleman commissioned as a justice of the peace. Professional law enforcement did not exist—there was no actual police force, which meant that the various tasks associated with police work had to be done by other sorts of officers or not at all. At the local level, two important institutions were the town watch, responsible for patrolling the streets of the town at night, and the constable, the closest thing to a local policeman, although this was always a temporary and part-time office.

Capital offenses were treason, murder, and felony, of which the last included manslaughter, rape, sodomy, arson, witchcraft, burglary, robbery, and grand larceny (stealing of goods worth at least 12 pence). All these offenses carried a mandatory death sentence, for which reason juries were sometimes reluctant to convict. A man convicted of a capital crime might be pardoned by the crown, or in the case of a felony might pray "benefit of clergy." In the Middle Ages the clergy had been exempted from secular punishment for felony, an exemption that extended to any man who could prove he was literate. The custom was still in use in the late 16th century, but in slightly altered form: benefit of clergy could only be exercised once, at which time the convict would be branded on the thumb to mark that he had exercised this privilege. Benefit of clergy was not available to those convicted of the most serious felonies, such as burglary and robbery. In some instances, serious crimes might be punished by branding or loss of a body part such as a hand or an ear.

In addition, there were diverse lesser crimes of the sort that would now be called misdemeanors. Punishments for such crimes might include fines, whipping, or imprisonment. In some cases the punishment might be confinement in the stocks or the pillory. The pillory was more unpleasant, as it confined both the head and hands, leaving the convict vulnerable to the abuse of passersby. The stocks confined only the legs, and most of the time only one leg was confined.

A Court Scene. Two men plead their case before a chief judge and his assistants. Note the gestures of humility and imprecation such as removing one's hat and kneeling before the judge. From F. J. Furnivall, *Phillip Stubbes' Anatomy of Abuses,* 1879.

Ecclesiastical courts might impose public penance, which would involve some form of public ritual in which the wrongdoer would publicly acknowledge his or her offense. It was difficult for the church courts to enforce their punishments against the truly recalcitrant. The ultimate sanction was excommunication, or exclusion from church services. This punishment theoretically excluded the wrongdoer from society, but in practice many people defied such sanctions—in fact, as many as 5 percent of the population may have lived as excommunicates (Singman, 20–22).

To read about justice and legal systems in Chaucer's England, see the Europe entry in the section "Law" in chapter 6 ("Political Life") in volume 2 of this series; for 18th-century England, see the entry on England in the section "Law, Crime, and Punishment" in chapter 6 ("Political Life") in volume 4 of this series; for Victorian England, see the Victorian England entry in the section "Law and Crime" in chapter 6 ("Political Life") in volume 5 of this series.

FOR MORE INFORMATION

Singman, J. L. *Daily Life in Elizabethan England.* Westport, Conn.: Greenwood, 1995.
Underhill, A. "Law." In *Shakespeare's England,* vol. 1, 381–412. Oxford: Clarendon, 1916.

SPAIN

Renaissance Spanish literature often made allusions to corrupt officials. The police of the Santa Hermandad (Holy Brotherhood), responsible for law and order in the

POLITICAL LIFE
|
JUSTICE
& LEGAL SYSTEMS
|
England

Spain

Italy

Meso- & South America

countryside, had a despicable reputation for corruption. Royal edicts of 1610 and 1613 illustrate the lack of confidence the government had in its own judicial officials and police by ordering that these officers were not to frequent taverns and that tavern owners, innkeepers, and wine merchants were not to advance them any money.

The fact that some criminals met an untimely end on the gallows suggests that not all officials were scoundrels, however. Punishment intended to set an example was severe for those who were sentenced. The condemned prisoner, wearing a blue hat and a white tunic (the uniform was supposed to give the wearer some heavenly indulgences), made the journey from the prison to the scaffold riding a donkey or mule, his hands tied to a crucifix, a halter fastened around his neck. He was flanked by two monks saying prayers and exhorting the condemned man to die bravely. In front of this little group, the town crier marched along loudly heralding the crimes of the prisoner, and on horseback behind the condemned came the constable who had captured him and the judge who had sentenced him. The procession halted at each shrine or church along the way while prayers were recited, then moved on toward the rendezvous with death. The execution was generally by hanging unless the malefactor was a nobleman, in which case he had the right to be decapitated.

Sometimes there was a general call-up of citizens to chase outlaws—a kind of posse system. At other times soldiers were employed to hunt down criminals. These soldiers were paid for by the royal treasury or by the municipalities. Robberies and banditry were such problems that some towns adopted draconian methods to deal with them: friends or relatives who sheltered criminals were themselves subject to the galleys, for example.

The Death Penalty. The death penalty was a frequent punishment during the Renaissance. In this picture, several condemned heretics are being burned. As the picture shows, large crowds would gather around these public executions. Bernard Picart, *Burning of the Condemned after an Auto de Fe in Lisbon*. Madrid: Biblioteca Nacional.

A refuge for criminals was sometimes found on the estates of the upper nobility over which the king had little jurisdiction. Most high-ranking aristocracy resented royal authority and wanted to maintain their independence from the crown. But the immunity from the law that the nobles had long enjoyed began to slip away. During the 16th century, the government gradually brought the grandees to its point of view by threatening to confiscate their lands unless they were more active against bandits; eventually the feudal lords agreed to turn over to the law thieves or highwaymen found on their properties.

Sanctuary for criminals was a discordant issue between government and clergy. Anyone, cleric or layman, could claim immunity from the law by entering the sacred space of a church. Here in its inner recesses the law had no authority. Sometimes, as a result, the church was turned into a meeting place of brigands where they planned their exploits, but such matters differed from town to town. In Valencia, for example, only the main church could be used as a sanctuary, but even then, someone who had murdered with intent or was engaged in brigandage on the roads was excluded. The conflict between Church and state was part of a broader struggle between the conservatives who wished to maintain the old order, the status quo, fearing arbitrary government rule, and the new proponents of strong government who felt the safety of the nation, backed up by wide-ranging laws, was the best way forward.

Aragón had, among its special privileges, limitations or prohibition on torture and habeas corpus, but these safeguards were often denounced by the authorities as making their work more difficult. Such conflicts and debates were, in a general way, searching for the limits of government. For the greater good of public order, the state gained more and more adherents to its point of view in the wake of widespread criminal activity. Social attitudes were clearly changing toward more judicial absolutism, and the old nobility who had always marched to a different drummer gradually bowed to new legal constraints.

To enforce state authority, a fairly steady stream of men went to the scaffold, after which in some places the bodies remained strung up in the market square. Bandits received special treatment and were dragged through the streets before being hanged, drawn, and quartered. Various confraternities were dedicated to the assistance of fallen humanity: the Valencian Brotherhood of Our Lady of the Forsaken, every 24 February, Saint Mathias' Day, gathered up the bones of those executed during the year and whose bodies had been left dangling from the gallows in the center of town or, in more enlightened communities, a mile or so outside the gates. The remains were solemnly interred in the common ground of the General Hospital. Other cities also had their confraternities to retrieve the corpses of the executed and bury them, even picking up the pieces of those who had been drawn and quartered. Penal reform began only slowly in the 18th century. Sentences to the galleys, where a man might spend a lifetime at the oar, ended in 1748; torture was abolished in 1814.

In addition to the legal system, though, there was also the more personal system of honor, which might call for private revenge. Personal honor stemmed from the centuries of the reconquest of the country from the Moors. The proud knight often possessed little more than his horse and sword, but he had a high sense of his own self-worth sustained by his courage, trusted name, and reputation. A man's honor was a sensitive issue that, by extension, applied to all members of the household. For example, a woman's virtue had to be maintained inviolate; but if blemished, the affront had to be avenged.

Dishonor could arise from malicious slurs on the virtue of a wife or daughter. To protect their reputation, all male members of a wronged family—father, sons, and uncles—would seek revenge as their duty. Dishonor might arise from the infidelity of a wife or from the promiscuity of a daughter in which case a husband might kill an unfaithful wife and her lover or a brother might kill his sister if she brought shame to the name of the family. Courts took a lenient view of crimes of passion involving honor, but acts of vengeance often brought on prolonged and bloody feuds between families.

A challenge to a duel could not be ignored. To face death bravely and to die unruffled was the pinnacle of honor. Even the convict who died on the scaffold commanded great esteem when he showed disdain for his fate.

The French countess Madame d'Aulnoy found that the major defect of the Spaniard was his unchristian passion for revenge and the means by which he accomplished it. According to her, when a Spaniard received an affront, he assassinated the offender.

For example, if one gave another a box o' the ear, or strikes him on the face with his hat, his handkerchief, or his glove, or has wronged him in calling him a *drunkard,* or lets drop any words that reflect on the virtue of his wife, these things I say must be no otherwise revenged than by assassination.

Carried to extreme degrees the concept of honor brought on a reaction in which antihonor became fashionable among society's outcasts, as seen in various novels of the time where the cynical protagonist rejects and mocks such noble values by rejecting public opinion and exalting actions such as cowardice and deceit (Anderson, 37–41).

FOR MORE INFORMATION

Anderson, J. *Daily Life during the Spanish Inquisition.* Westport, Conn.: Greenwood, 2002.
Defourneaux, M. *Daily Life in the Golden Age.* Trans. Newton Branch. Stanford: Stanford University Press, 1979.

POLITICAL LIFE
|
JUSTICE
& LEGAL SYSTEMS
|
England

Spain

Italy

Meso- & South America

ITALY

Italians had a welter of legislation. There was no overarching code but rather a vast mass of ancient Roman compilations, learned medieval commentaries, and case law. Judges heeded this body of *ius commune* (common law). On top of this were local statutes. These rambling collections of coherent legislation and occasional decrees set procedures of governance and established rules about many things, from inheritance rights to commerce, garbage, and stray beasts in streets and gardens. Statutes were conservative; they brimmed with archaic bans on things no longer done and rehashed ancient rules, for they evolved slowly. Meanwhile, governing bodies legislated fast, spewing out decrees on lanterns after curfew, the width of sleeves, distinguishing clothing for Jews and prostitutes, the duty of hue and cry, gambling, swearing, and how to keep the holy days. Legislation waxed and waned with the ups and downs of regulatory zeal. New decrees were posted in "the usual places"—on the doors of major churches, by government buildings, in the marketplace, on the city gates—and read aloud by official criers on foot or horseback, often to the blare of trumpets. By the 16th century, they often appeared in print, under the bold woodblock insignia of their official authors.

In this vast swarm of legislation, certain thematic concerns stand out. One was health; decrees sought to free the town of garbage and dung, confine and cure the sick, and quarantine travelers from suspect places. A second charge was the good order of public space: zoning issues like the lay of buildings and the freedom of the public way from private encroachment and also the upkeep and operation of public facilities like walls and gates, markets, and fountains. A third issue was public safety. Legislation not only curbed violent acts and insulting gestures but also regulated the carrying of arms and strove to ban the occasions for fighting. A fourth concern was warding off offense to God. The masters of Venice, keen to fend off divine ire, instituted a special magistracy against blasphemy. Likewise, rules to ensure respect for holy times and to shield churches from ribaldry courted providence. Social regulation also sought to control beggars and the idle poor, who might be banished or, toward 1600, confined to a zone or a workhouse, supposedly for their own benefit.

Almost always, in Renaissance Italy wherever there was a law exceptions abounded. Many regulations aimed as much at raising money as at squelching behavior; again and again, the authorities sold exemption licenses. Thus, although massive, Italian legislation had uncertain reach, for wealth, power, and privilege knocked enforcement full of holes. Not all exceptions to the law were sold; police jurisdiction had other vacuums. Churches were sanctuaries; he who ran inside ducked arrest. Embassies and their precincts had extraterritoriality. Police who made an arrest in their shadow risked indignant drubbing by the ambassador's servants. Nobles in the city and countryside sheltered protégés in their palaces; not rarely, the authorities hesitated to take a magnate on. Many rural outlaws therefore huddled under the protection of the great.

To enforce its will, the government needed a constabulary. Larger cities had several competing troops, each under its captain. The countryside made do with small local detachments, plus squadrons out on missions from the city. Nowhere were the police reliable. Recruited from the poorest classes, they had no prestige, little discipline, and a healthy appetite for loot. The police roughed up prisoners and grabbed their belongings. Often they broke into houses without a warrant, snooping for stolen goods and breaches of the sexual code. In general they bullied the weak and cowered before the strong. Paid for each successful arrest, they had a greedy zeal that blackened their repute.

Central to governmental control of society were the courts. Tribunals came in many kinds; some were criminal, others civil, ecclesiastical, or administrative in scope; not rarely, one magistrate combined several functions. In general, courts were sticklers for procedure; they loved paper, keeping complicated records, often in Latin. To uneducated Italians, courts seemed imposing, with their obscure formulas in a learned tongue, their rituals, robes of office, harsh methods, and heavy punishments. Yet far more than most of us today, Italians knew the insides of courtrooms from rich firsthand experience, for they often took part in proceedings, as plaintiffs, witnesses, guarantors, suspects, or victims of a civil suit. Their testimonies show that they usually understood the rules and rituals and knew how to use them.

Of all state organs, the criminal courts tried hardest to control society. There the rules tilted sharply against the suspect. Examined in a closed room, without friends, counsel, or public observers and unaware of the charges, accusers, and evidence, the accused was on his guard. The magistrates questioned him cagily, first circling around the issue looking for clues and inconsistencies and only gradually tipping their hand as they closed in on the suspected crime. When stories clashed, they could at their discretion call in another witness for a face-to-face confrontation. By theories of proof, a conviction required strong evidence from at least two credible witnesses or a confession. Often, lacking good witnesses and detectives to seek them out, the judges tortured the suspects. They usually targeted suspects of low estate. They also sometimes tortured witnesses and even the victims of a crime.

There were several methods of torture. Commonest was the rope; the court's men stripped the suspect to the waist, tied his hands behind his back, put a rope to his wrists, and hoisted him. If he did not confess, they might give the cord a jerk, a *strappado*. Other devices in the repertoire varied in severity. On the milder end were sundry instruments to squeeze feet or fingers, sometimes applied to women. More dire were long sessions spent standing in painful postures or fire to the feet, an ordeal so hideous some jurists condemned it. Whatever the torment, all the while the notary wrote down each piteous moan and imprecation; his transcripts prove that the procedures caused a great deal of pain. While torture was not infrequent, it was restricted somewhat. For example, it could not maim or leave a lasting mark. Moreover, excessive torture could cause the prosecution's case to be thrown out of court, and confessions gained under torture would have to be ratified by the suspect also on the day after the torture.

Most criminals escaped justice, however, due to the inefficient police and the ability to flee across a border easily. If one had the bad luck to be caught, hard times often loomed. Not only were courtroom rules stacked against the accused, so too was sentencing. Condemnation was likely and the penalty often harsh. Weak states with inefficient organs of repression used the few criminals they caught to set a horrible example for the many who got away, for justice was meant to teach a lesson. Punishment therefore often employed public spectacle. For lesser crimes, the state used public shame. Malefactors were put in the stocks, and explanatory placards were displayed while bells were rung. Those who had spoken ill of state or church might have their tongues in bridles. Other middling offenses earned a public whipping through the streets or *strappado* hoists on a high pole in the market or at the gate. For graver misdeeds, sometimes the authorities adorned the body of the condemned with a lasting shameful testimony to their power and judgment; they cut off the nose or tongue, an ear, hand, or foot, or gouged out an eye or two. When they put a person to death, they lacked modern bashfulness. An execution was a major drama for both state and church; they put on a spectacle that drew a crowd. The convicted would be hung, if a commoner, or decapitated, if a nobleman, and the corpse was frequently simply left hanging on display. Prior to the hanging, churchmen and faithful would ask the convict to repent and offer urgent prayers for the soul of the prisoner. An execution would not soon be forgotten by the crowds in attendance.

Such executions were special events; they occurred as a part of life but were hardly daily events. In general, courts preferred cash to blood. Most murderers, if convicted, suffered only confiscation and banishment. Many other crimes too were fined. Unlike us, Renaissance Italians eschewed prisons; they were expensive and unproductive. Jail was mostly for holding debtors and persons awaiting trial, not for punishment. The galleys were far more useful; a few years spent rowing, chained to a naval bench, was a common 16th-century penalty. Jail itself, for Italians of lower station, was a frequent experience. A villager could spend a few weeks in the castle tower while raising money to pay a fine; poor townsmen might be locked up as suspects or even as important witnesses. Until testifying, one might be kept in isolation. Jail cost money; inmates paid their own keep, and the rich bought what comforts they could. One of the most common punishments was banishment. It was cheap and, given all the borders, easily done. Without much income, however, the banished man (*bandito*) often fell back on banditry; our English word shows the old linkage between *banishment* and brigandage. Thus, as a device for social control, banishment often only exacerbated things, putting rural lives and goods at risk (Cohen and Cohen, 116–22).

FOR MORE INFORMATION

Cohen, E. S., and T. V. Cohen. *Daily Life in Renaissance Italy*. Westport, Conn.: Greenwood, 2001.

Edgerton, S. *Pictures and Punishment: Art and Criminal Prosecution during the Florentine Renaissance*. Ithaca: Cornell University Press, 1985.

Hughes, S. "Fear and Loathing in Rome and Bologna: The Royal Police in Perspective." *Journal of Social History* 21 (1987): 97–116.

Langbein, J. *Torture and the Law of Proof: Europe and England in the Ancient Regime*. Chicago: University of Chicago Press, 1976.

OTTOMAN EMPIRE

When the Turks adopted the religion of Islam, they also adopted Islamic Law (or *Sharia*). Their rulers—called sultans—believed themselves the successors of Muhammad, and therefore empowered to interpret Muslim law. In this way, Islamic law was reinvigorated in the empire of the Ottoman Turks. For the origins of Islamic law see the section "Law" in chapter 6 ("Political Life") in volume 2 of this series; for the continuation of this legal tradition into the 20th century see the section "Law and Crime" in chapter 6 ("Political Life") in volume 6 of this series.

POLITICAL LIFE
|
JUSTICE
& LEGAL SYSTEMS
|
England

Spain

Italy

Meso- & South America

MESOAMERICA AND SOUTH AMERICA (MAYA, AZTEC, AND INCA)

Relatively little is known about the legal systems of the great empires of Mesoamerica and South America, since these systems were destroyed entirely by the Spanish conquistadors. The evidence does show, however, that the Native Americans had effective institutional ways of dispensing justice and maintaining peace in their communities.

Political power in most modern states is based on the threat or use of coercive force through laws, courts, and police dedicated to the enforcement of authority. The Maya state relied instead on economic and religious sanctions—although we can be sure that when all else failed, severe punishments were given to individuals who displeased the king.

The *batab* official generally oversaw ordinary disputes. The *batab* was based in an outlying town and held administrative, judicial, and military authority. Each *batab* saw to it that the subjects under his control paid their tribute in goods and labor to the *halach uinic* (the ruler of the Maya city-state). The *batab* ensured that his town was kept clean, its buildings kept in repair, and that the farmers cut and burned their fields at the proper time. As a judge he sentenced criminals and decided civil suits, always consulting the *halach uinic* in serious cases before passing judgment (Sharer, 146–47).

Like the Maya, Aztec society was not bound by codified law to the same degree that much of Renaissance Europe was. Nonetheless, there was a series of lower-ranking officials that heard disputes and passed sentence. According to the Spanish governor Alonso de Zorita,

The Indian judges of whom I spoke would seat themselves at day-break on their mat dais, and immediately begin to hear pleas. The judges' meals were brought to them at an early hour from the royal palace. After eating, they rested for a while, then returned to hear the remaining suitors, staying until two hours before sundown. Appeals from these judges were heard by twelve superior judges, who passed sentence in consultation with the ruler. (Zorita, 126)

Aztec law seems to have contained two strains, that of "the reasonable man" and that of "legalism." In practice, the two strains were intermingled. In the "reasonable man" tradition, the judge based his decision on what the society generally decided was reasonable and just. In the legalist strain, judgments were based upon codified systems of law. For example, the king Netzahualcoyotl created a system in which certain punishments were prescribed for certain crimes, regardless of any mitigating circumstances. Manuscripts survive in which captioned pictures illustrate the prescribed penalties for various crimes.

While many legal cases undoubtedly involved squabbles amongst peers of the lower social ranks, some of the cases may have resulted from attempts by commoners to raise themselves above their station. A flavor for Aztec legal priorities can be gleaned from the legal code proclaimed by Motecuhzoma I (15th century)—here is a selection of the statutes:

1. The king must never appear in public except when the occasion is extremely important and unavoidable. . . .
3. Only the king and the prime minister Tlacaelel may wear sandals within the palace. . . .
5. The great lords, who are twelve, may wear special mantles of certain make and design, and the minor lords, according to their valor and accomplishments, may wear others. . . .

7. The commoners will not be allowed to wear cotton clothing under pain of death, but can use only garments of maguey fiber. . . .

8. Only the great noblemen and valiant warriors are given license to build a house with a second story; for disobeying this law a person receives the death penalty.

13. All the barrios (*calpolli*) will possess schools or monasteries for young men where they will learn religion and correct comportment.

14. There is to be a rigorous law regarding adulterers. They are to be stoned and thrown into the rivers or to the buzzards.

15. Thieves will be sold for the price of their theft, unless the theft be grave, having been committed many times. Such thieves will be punished by death.

Aztec law thus theoretically kept one safe not only from thieves but also from social climbers.

Inca law applied to many activities such as tribal rights, division of land, policy of rotation for work, and even support of the elderly and disabled. Inca law was quite severe, laying out strict punishments for many offenses. The higher the status of the individual, the more severe the punishment for a crime. For example, adultery among commoners was punishable by torture; but if the woman was a noble, both parties were executed. Crimes against the government were treated with special severity. Stealing from the fields of the state was punishable by death. If a *curaca* (local official) put a person to death without permission of his superior, a stone was dropped on his back from a height of three feet. If he did it again, he was killed. Treason was punished by imprisoning the person in an underground prison in Cuzco that was filled with snakes and dangerous animals. The person rarely survived the imprisonment.

The judicial system was based on the administrative one, with the appropriate *curaca* presiding over the proceedings. For example, if a case involved grievances of one individual against another but both were within the same unit of 100 households, then the *curaca* of that unit officiated. However, if the case was against an individual from another unit of 100, then the *curaca* of 500 who was in charge of both would be the official. Crimes punishable by death, such as those mentioned above, were taken to the provincial governor or king (Malpass, 35).

To read about justice and legal systems in 19th-century Latin America, see the Latin America entry in the section "Law and Crime" in chapter 6 ("Political Life") in volume 5 of this series.

FOR MORE INFORMATION

Kendall, A. *Everyday Life of the Incas*. New York: Putname, 1973.

Malpass, M. A. *Daily Life in the Inca Empire*. Westport, Conn.: Greenwood, 1996.

Sabloff, J. A., and E. W. Andrews, eds. *Late Lowland Maya Civilization: Classic to Postclassic*. Albuquerque: University of New Mexico Press, 1986.

Sharer, R. J. *Daily Life in Maya Civilization*. Westport, Conn.: Greenwood, 1996.

Smith, Michael. *The Aztecs*. Oxford: Blackwell, 1996.

Townsend, R. F. *The Aztecs*. London: Thames and Hudson, 1992.

Zorita, Alonso de. *Life and Labor in Ancient Mexico: The Brief and Summary Relation of the Lords of New Spain*. Ed. and Trans. Benjamin Keen. New Brunswick, NJ: Rutgers University Press, 1963.

POLITICAL LIFE: WEB SITES

http://www.geocities.com/Athens/4903/mexica2.html.
http://www.civilization.ca/civil/maya/mmc12eng.html.
http://www.chronique.com/Library/Fighting/vadi_translation.html.
http://www.law.utexas.edu/rare/aztec.html.
http://www.evergreen.loyola.edu/~cmitchell/.

7

RECREATIONAL LIFE

Play is serious business. All mammals play, but humans have cultivated recreation to a high art. After family and work, most of our energies and time are devoted to recreational activities, and as any modern sports enthusiast knows, we play with as much passion as we work. What are recreational activities? There are several characteristics that all play shares: first, it is voluntary—one cannot be forced to play. As such, it is in fact the very essence of freedom, and even slaves and prisoners treat themselves to games, music, or dance for the sheer voluntary quality of the activities. Second, recreation is outside of real life, limited in time, duration, and space. Thus, playtime by contrast almost defines work time; recess at school not only offers a break from study, it marks the serious times when one is to learn. Third, recreation has its own rules that are more rigorous and predictable than anything we can encounter in our complex real lives. At the end of the game—and there is a definitive end—there is a winner and loser, and the rules are clear. Of course, cheating is always a possibility (archaeologists have even found loaded dice in Anglo-Saxon settlements), but even unsportsmanlike conduct is recognizable. It may be that we love games precisely for the clarity of the rules. Fourth, recreational life builds a group identity among the players, and this is true even of individual sports such as archery or bicycling, for archers and cyclists see themselves as linked with others who share the pastime.

While recreational activities throughout history share these general characteristics, the particular forms of play we choose shed light on who we are and what we value. In play, we prepare ourselves for the rest of our lives. For examples, games ranging from the Olympics to chess hone our skills for war, while music and art stimulate our creativity. Violent sports such as dogfights and boxing steel us to face violence in life, and team sports like American football prepare us to work together in an economy of separation of skills. In studying the games people play, we can more fully understand the society they are creating.

In the entries that follow, we will look at three overlapping fields of recreation: games (including sports), outdoor pursuits, and the arts. Games are perhaps the most fundamental leisure activity. Children spend much of their early years playing in the house or creating havoc outside. Adults also played lots of games in the 15th and

RECREATIONAL
LIFE

GAMES & SPORTS

OUTDOOR PURSUITS

THE ARTS

16th centuries. While sometimes the games could be deadly serious, such as the Mesoamerican ballgame, many of them, such as the English hot cockles, were decidedly lighthearted. In hot cockles, one person hid their head in the lap of another person and was slapped on the behind. If he or she could guess who had given the slap, they changed places.

There is no firm dividing line between games, sports, and outdoor recreations. The outdoors has a special place in European culture, however, especially in connection with hunting. Since the late Middle Ages, hunting had become a pastime rather than a means of survival. The upper classes were particularly fond of it. The Mesoamerican and South Americans did not have the same cult of hunting, however, and therefore do not appear in the Outdoor Pursuits section. While Europeans hunted for fun, the Native Americans hunted for food, and descriptions of their hunting are thus found in the section "Rural Life" in chapter 3 ("Economic Life"). Some other pastimes, such as Spanish theater, were more like outdoor festivals than modern drama, and have therefore also been discussed in the section on outdoor recreation.

Theater is often also considered to be one of the arts, however, and that is where we have placed English theater because Shakespeare has played such a central role in the development of the Western artistic canon. Speaking more generally, the arts refer to all kinds of creative activity that do not always serve an entirely practical purpose. Some of the most common arts are music, painting, feather work, and sculpture. We will look especially at some aspects of European music and at characteristically American arts, such as feather working. While we may need work to live, we need the arts to live well.

~*Joyce E. Salisbury and Lawrence Morris*

FOR MORE INFORMATION

Huizinga, J. *Homo Ludens: A Study of the Play Element in Culture*. Boston: Beacon Press, 1964.

Towner, J. *An Historical Geography of Recreation and Tourism in the Western World 1540–1940*. Chichester, UK: Wiley, 1996.

RECREATIONAL
LIFE
|
GAMES & SPORTS
|
England

Spain

Italy

Maya

Aztec

Inca

Games and Sports

Games and sports are valuable forms of recreation. Sports help train the body and maintain physical condition, while games, which differ from sports primarily in the level of physical exertion, are structured ways of breaking the ice—both forms of entertainment, of course, help to pass the time.

Sports and games were also frequently the object of betting, often of large amounts. In both Europe and the Americas in the 15th and 16th centuries, people of all social classes bet on the outcome of games and sports. Inca noblemen would wager whole estates on the game of *allyoscas*, while Europeans were known to lose fortunes over dice or cards. In Europe, such gambling was viewed as a serious evil, and with good cause: excessive gambling could leave a family destitute, hungry, and homeless, and even low-level gambling frequently resulted in arguments and fistfights during this period. As a result, preachers frequently denounced gambling from the pulpits, not so much because of the gambling itself, but rather because of the many bad consequences that generally followed wagering. Governments even occasionally attempted to curtail certain kinds of gambling. Spain, for example, outlawed the manufacture and use of dice, and anyone found guilty of breaking this ban was subject to harsh penalties, such as two years' exile for the manufacture of dice.

The most popular indoor betting games in Europe were dice and cards. While the card games of Renaissance Spain or Italy would appear somewhat different to us today, many of the English games have similarities to games still played today. For example, the English played a card game called one-and-thirty, which is very similar to twenty-one, though played to a higher number. Likewise, some of their dice games are similar to the modern craps.

Other games were less associated with gambling, though they could sometimes border on the indecent! In the English game of hot cockles, one player hid his or her head in the lap of another and the other players slapped his or her bottom. If the player being slapped could identify who had just slapped him or her, the two would change places. Blindman's buff was similarly physical; a blindfolded player would attempt to catch the other players who approached stealthily to give a buffet (a blow) to the blindfolded player.

Many modern outdoor sports were played in some form in 15th- and 16th-century Europe. Tennis, using a less lively ball than today, was played throughout western Europe and several games similar to American football, such as rugby and soccer, were played in England and Italy. English stoolball, in which a player attempted to throw a ball past a batter against a stool placed on its side, is an ancestor of modern baseball and cricket. A particularly common game was bowls (Italian bocce) in which players attempted to toss their own large balls as close as possible to a smaller target ball. There was even a version of the modern 10-pin bowling in which sticks or ox bones were knocked down by a rolled ball.

The Italians and Spanish particularly enjoyed martial games. Rival parishes in Italy would frequently meet on the boundary between two districts and engage in large fights with clubs and fists. In Venice, these matches frequently took place on bridges, and many combatants would be thrown over the bridge into the canal. Casualties and even mortalities frequently resulted from these competitions. Both the Spanish and Italians relished tournaments, in which noblemen displayed their prowess in horsemanship and engaged in jousting and javelin throwing. The tips of the weapons were blunted or made of cane to make these activities safer for the participants.

Unfortunately, not as much is known about Native American games and sports of Mesoamerica and South America. There was most likely a wide range of pastimes employed when there was no farm work to be done. While there are tantalizing references to betting games such as the Inca *aylloscas,* by far the most prominent and famous game from the Americas was the Mesoamerican ballgame, played by both the Maya and the Aztec. This ballgame, called *ollamaliztli* by the Aztecs, appears to have been played at first with a large basketball-sized rubber ball. The two sides (the game was sometimes played by individuals and sometimes by teams) hit the ball back and forth between them, using primarily their thighs and rears—it was illegal to use either feet or hands. A point was scored by getting the ball past the other side. As time went on, the ball became smaller and a hoop was added to both side walls of the court; if a team managed to put the ball through a hoop, they won the game immediately. Amongst the 16th-century Aztecs, the team that managed to put the ball through the hoop was entitled to seize the clothing of the opposing team, and the supporters of the winning team were entitled to seize the clothing of the supporters of the losing team. It must have been quite a scramble when a ball was hooped: one side fleeing from being denuded and the other side right on their heels! While the ballgame was a central form of sport and spectacle, it also had religious importance. The ballgame reenacted the victory of the Maya Hero Twins over the death gods. As a result ballgames were occasionally played against war prisoners, who were sacrificed after the match to commemorate the victory of the Hero Twins. Sport could be fun, but also deadly serious.

~Lawrence Morris

RECREATIONAL
LIFE
|
GAMES & SPORTS
|
England
Spain
Italy
Maya
Aztec
Inca

ENGLAND

The English enjoyed a wide variety of games, some of them surprisingly physical. In hot cockles, for example, one player hid his or her head in another's lap while the others slapped him or her on the rear—if he or she could guess who had slapped last, the two traded places. Blindman's buff, also known as hoodman blind, was a similar game in which a blindfolded player tried to catch the others while they dealt him buffs, or blows. If he could identify the person he caught, they would trade places. In both of these games, men and women might play together, although they were more commonly played by boys and girls.

One piece of equipment most people carried at all times was a knife, and these were used in several games. In penny prick, a peg was set in the ground with a penny on top; players would throw their knives at it, trying either to knock the penny off or to lodge their knife in the ground closest to the peg.

Similar to football in concept, if not equipment, was the game of bandy-ball, the ancestor of modern field hockey. The object of the game was to drive a small, hard ball through the opponents' goal with hooked clubs (almost identical to field hockey sticks).

Stoolball was an ancestor of cricket and baseball in which a stool was set on its side and players tried to hit the seat with a ball. In this game, women were expected to hike up their skirts and play with the men. In the game of trap, or trapball, the ball was placed on a device for casting it up in the air to be hit with a stick.

Tennis, a game introduced from France during the Middle Ages, called for expensive equipment and an equally expensive court, so it was popular only among the rich. The tennis ball was made of fabric scraps tightly wrapped in packing thread and encased in white fabric; the rackets were made of wood and gut. Tennis was perhaps the most athletic game played by the upper classes, and it was only played by men. The plebeian version of this game was handball: as the name suggests, the ball was hit with the hands rather than with a racket. A similar game was shuttlecock, comparable to modern badminton. The shuttlecock was a cylinder of cork rounded at one end with feathers stuck in it; it was batted back and forth with wooden paddles known as *battledores*.

A less demanding outdoor game was bowls, similar to the modern English game of that name, or to Italian bocce. Bowls involved casting balls at a target with the goal of having your ball end up closest to the target. It was a very popular pastime. There were even commercial bowling alleys; as played in such settings, bowls could be quite sophisticated, involving different shapes of balls, an elaborate terminology for describing the lay of the ground and the course of the ball, and a formalized system of betting. Moralists often criticized the game, yet when betting was not involved it was played by even the most respectable men and women.

A slightly more dangerous form of this game was quoits, in which a stake or spike was driven into the ground and players tossed stones or heavy metal disks at it. The game seems to have been played with vigor rather than finesse, and serious injury was known to result. The modern game of horseshoes is a variant of this game.

Similar to modern American bowling was the game known by such names as nine-pegs, ten-pins, skittle pins, skittles, or kittles. Nine conical pins were set up on the ground, and players would try to knock them down with a wooden ball. In a related game called kayles or loggats, the pins were knocked down with a stick instead of a ball. Country folk sometimes used the leg bones of oxen for pins.

Some games involved a great deal of running and little or no equipment. The game known in modern schoolyards as prisoner's base was played under the name base or prison bars. A particular favorite in this period was barley break, a chasing game in which two mixed-sex couples tried to avoid being caught by a third couple, with the couples changing partners each time. Footraces were also a popular entertainment.

Other athletic sports included leaping and vaulting, swimming, and throwing weights. Riding was a favorite sport among the wealthy, and wrestling was popular among common folk. People also liked simply to take walks for exercise; members of the upper classes were especially fond of strolling in their gardens after a meal.

Many games were specifically geared for indoor recreation. Among table games, chess was the most prestigious. Its rules were essentially the same as they are today. Chess was unusual among table games in that it did not normally involve betting. For those who wanted a simpler game, the chessboard could be combined with table men (backgammon pieces) for the game of draughts (now known in North America as checkers), again with essentially the same rules as today.

Cards were widely popular throughout society, and inexpensive block-printed decks were readily available. 15th- and 16th-century playing cards were not waxed, and the custom had not yet evolved of printing a pattern on the back to prevent marking. The cards were divided according to the French system, essentially the same one used in English-speaking countries today. The French suits were the same as in a modern deck, and each suit contained the same range of cards. The first three were called the *ace*, *deuce*, and *tray*, and the face cards were called *king*, *queen*, and *knave* (there was no *joker*). The cards had only images on them, no letters or numbers. The images on the face cards were very similar to modern ones, save that they were full body portraits (without the mirror image of modern cards).

Many Renaissance card games have disappeared from use, but some still have modern equivalents. One-and-thirty was the equivalent of the modern twenty-one, except that it was played to a higher number. Noddy was an earlier variant of cribbage (which first appeared in the early 17th century). Ruff and trump were ancestors of modern whist, and primero was an early version of poker.

There were several games in the family known as tables, played with the equipment used in modern backgammon. Backgammon itself was not invented until the early 17th century, but the game of Irish was almost identical to it. Games at tables varied enormously. The childish game of doublets involved only one side of the board: each player stacked his pieces on the points of their side, then rolled dice first to unstack them, then to bear them off the board. Perhaps the most complex game was ticktack, in which the general idea was to move all of one's pieces from one end of the board to the other, with several alternative ways of winning the game at single or double stakes en route.

Dice were the classic pastime of the lower orders of society—they were cheap, highly portable, and very effective at whiling away idle time (for which reason they were particularly favored by soldiers). Dice games were played by the aristocracy also; Queen Elizabeth herself was known to indulge in them. The dice were typically made of bone, and the spots, from 1 to 6, were called the *ace*, *deuce*, *tray*, *cater*, *sink*, and *sise*—thus a roll of 6 and 1 was called *sise-ace*.

Shovelboard or shove-groat was an indoor game in which metal discs (often groats—4d. pieces) were pushed across a table to land as close as possible to the other end without falling off. Various horizontal lines were laid out on the board, and points were scored according to which set of lines the piece stopped between. Wealthy households sometimes had special tables built for this game. Another coin game was cross and pile, identical to heads or tails—the *cross* was the cross on the back of English coins, the *pile* the face of the king or queen on the front.

Fox and geese and nine men's morris were two simple board games in which each player moved pieces about on a geometric board, trying to capture or pin his opponent's pieces. Boards for these games could be made by cutting lines into a wooden surface or by writing on it with chalk or charcoal.

📷 *Snapshot*

Put: An English Renaissance Drinking Game

This game had a particularly low reputation as an alehouse pastime. All cards are used, of which the three ranks highest, the two next, and then the ace, king, queen, and so on. Suits are irrelevant to this game. This game is usually played with two players but can be played with more. Each player is dealt one more card than there are players. The eldest leads a card, and the other players play cards to it until all players have laid down a card. Whoever plays the highest card takes the trick. Ties go to nobody. Each round consists of as many tricks as the players have cards, and whoever wins two of the tricks scores one point. If nobody wins two tricks, nobody scores a point. Once the round is played, the next player deals. Play is normally to either five or seven, as agreed on by the players before the game. At any point a player may knock on the table and say "Put!" If the other says, "I see it," whoever wins that round wins the game, regardless of the score, and takes the stakes. If the other does not see, the first player automatically wins the round and scores the point.

One of the simplest of games involved the tee-totum, a kind of top, used exactly like a Hannukah dreidel. It had four sides, each bearing a letter: *T* for take, *N* for nothing, *P* for put, and *H* for half. Depending on which side came up, the player would take everything, get nothing, put another stake into the pot, or take half the stakes out of the pot.

A few new table games appeared during Queen Elizabeth's reign. Billiards appears to have been introduced to England during this period. The game of goose came to England from the Continent in 1597. This was the earliest ancestor of many of today's commercial board games. The game of goose was a commercially printed sheet bearing a track of squares spiraling toward the center. Players rolled dice to move their pieces along the track. Some of the squares bore special symbols: the player who landed on such a square might get an extra roll or be sent back a certain number of squares. The first player to reach the end won.

Some entertainments involved nothing more than words. Jokes were as popular then as they are now—there were even printed joke books. Riddles were another common word game. In general, English people greatly enjoyed conversation and were especially fond of sharing news: in a world without mass or electronic media, people were always eager for word of what was going on in the world around them.

As in modern times, the custom of game playing began in childhood. Children played many of the games described above; other children's pastimes included tag (called tick), leap-frog, hide-and-seek (called all hid), hobby-horses, whiptops, see-saw, blowing bubbles, swings, mock drilling with drums, banners, stick pikes, muskets and swords, and cup-and-ball. In the autumn when nuts began to harden, children would play at cob-nut: nuts on strings were struck against each other, the one whose nut broke first being the loser. However, where modern-day people tend to lay aside much of their childhood game playing when they enter adulthood, games remained an integral part of the life of 15th- and 16th-century adults.

Games were often segregated by gender. Women did not engage in martial, dangerous, or extremely vigorous sports such as fencing, football, or tennis. However, they might take part in lighter physical games such as blindman's buff or barley break. Games with minimal physical activity such as bowls and card games were especially common pastimes for women; and they often participated as spectators at sports that they did not play themselves, even violent sports like bearbaiting.

Most Renaissance games were less rule-oriented and standardized than is true today. Rules were often minimal and might vary from one locality to the next. This was especially true of children's games and folk games, less true of table games and games of the upper classes, which were generally more elaborate and formalized.

One last distinctive feature of 15th- and 16th-century games was the prevalence of gambling, which pervaded English culture. A wager might be laid on almost any game, and in many cases betting was an integral part of the game itself. Even children gambled, playing for lacing points, pins, cherry stones, or various sorts of counters (Singman, 156–60).

To read about games and sports in Chaucer's England, see the Europe entry in the section "Sports and Games" in chapter 7 ("Recreational Life") in volume 2 of this series; for 18th-century England, see the entry on England in the section "Games" in chapter 7 ("Recreational Life") in volume 4 of this series; for Victorian England, see the Victorian England entry in the section "Sports" in chapter 7 ("Recreational Life") in volume 5 of this series.

FOR MORE INFORMATION

Hartmann, C. H., ed. *Games and Gamesters of the Restoration*. London: Routledge, 1930.

Parlett, D. *The Oxford Guide to Card Games*. Oxford: Oxford University Press, 1990.

Singman, J. L. *Daily Life in Elizabethan England*. Westport, Conn.: Greenwood, 1995.

RECREATIONAL
LIFE
|
GAMES & SPORTS
|

England

Spain

Italy

Maya

Aztec

Inca

SPAIN

The Spanish enjoyed a wide range of card and board games, in addition to mock combat. A good deal of activity was generated by mock battles between men dressed as Christians and others dressed as Moors. The reenacting of dramatic battles gave each person in the town or village a part to play, and everyone was kept busy in their spare time making or repairing the costumes and weapons and rehearsing their roles. Most young men preferred the role of the Moor, with his dashing and colorful clothes, often creating an imbalance between numbers of Moors and Christians. The former were generally armed with crossbows and the latter with firearms. Christians always won, and the defeated Moors were then led through the streets of the town in chains, while the conquering heroes fired off their arquebuses and waved their swords.

Contests of skill and bravery performed by the nobles in jousting tournaments of the Middle Ages continued into the reign of the Habsburgs, but the contests gave way to less dangerous encounters than knocking a heavily armored knight out of the saddle with a stout iron-tipped lance at the speed of two galloping horses. Displays of prowess and horsemanship were demonstrated in cane tilting in which the aristocratic participants, richly attired, formed into opposing groups and rode into an enclosure, where the battle took place, on highly caparisoned horses, displaying wooden or leather shields decorated in the colors of their houses or those of their ladies. To the rattle of drums, the blast of trumpets, and the delight of the crowds, they paraded around the arena. Their colorfully dressed squires then came forward and presented their masters with the cane (bamboo) javelin they would use in the forthcoming combat. All retired then to opposite ends of the field or plaza and formed into squadrons of three or four riders. On the signal of the judge, a squadron broke forth, launching an attack, crossing the arena at full gallop. Once in range, they hurled their javelins at their mounted opponents, who deflected the missiles with their shields. Then it was the turn of the other side to charge forward and release their shafts. The battle continued until all the riders had thrown their javelins. A general but nonlethal charge by all participants concluded the tournament. These resplendent and vibrant spectacles of horsemanship constituted a sporting occasion for the aristocrats and an entertaining afternoon for the plebeians seated on the wooden stands around the enclosure. Often the tournament took place in the Plaza Mayor in Madrid, where the high-ranking nobility could observe it from the balconies of the surrounding apartments. The very competitive ring game in which horsemen took turns charging a small ring at full gallop in an attempt to place their javelin through the hole was also a contest of great skill and showmanship and attracted large crowds.

Games in which a ball was hit back and forth between two opponents with rackets, a primitive form of tennis, and a kind of bowling were common indoor and outdoor activities played by both children and adults, especially at court. Popular among the children were puppetry, hoops, tops, kites, and skipping ropes.

A favorite indoor game of the nobility was chess. Spaniards dominated the chessboard in the 16th and 17th centuries until their supremacy was taken away by the Italians.

A major preoccupation from the king down to the peasant was card games. Philip III was a passionate player. In Castile, decks of cards were controlled and sold under license held by the king, and it was illegal to play with a deck of cards not authorized and stamped by the government. To use any other, such as French or Catalan cards, was to defraud the royal treasury and carried a heavy penalty. There was a large variety of different card games, some legal and some not, played in establishments referred to euphemistically as Houses of Conversation, which were located throughout the cities and attended by nobles and wealthy bourgeois. The lower classes also had their own less ostentatious places to get together and play cards. After clothes, horses, and women, more money was spent on gambling than anything else.

Dice games were prohibited, and it was illegal to manufacture dice or sell them. Penalties included two years' exile for the manufacturer and heavy fines for the players. However, many clandestine establishments existed in big cities such as Madrid and Seville where professional card sharks fleeced the unsuspecting novice, and dice were rolled in the back rooms. In the gaming houses gambling continued 24 hours a day. Food and toilets in such places were provided so that the players might not be inconvenienced. Games of cards and dice were, along with guitar music, supplied by the brothels and attracted all segments of the population from the high-ranking nobleman to the lowliest pickpocket (Anderson, 216–17).

FOR MORE INFORMATION

Anderson, J. M. *Daily Life during the Spanish Inquisition*. Westport, Conn.: Greenwood, 2002.
Defourneaux, M. *Daily Life in the Golden Age*. Trans. Newton Branch. Stanford: Stanford University Press, 1979.

ITALY

Unlike us, who curb the violence of our sports—boxing and North American hockey excepted—Renaissance Italians relished violent play. They watched it and massively took zestful part. Their real warfare often had its playful side, and much of their play was warlike. The Middle Ages had imparted a tradition of fighting for

RECREATIONAL
LIFE
|
GAMES & SPORTS
|
England

Spain

Italy

Maya

Aztec

Inca

fun. In many Italian towns of the early Renaissance, teams of young men, marshaled by their captains, would march on the chosen day to the field, square, or bridge appointed for battle. Their adversaries were often fellow townsmen, from another parish or quarter, ancestral enemies against whom they sang insulting songs and shouted slogans, or there might have been a provocative sally, when a few made a mad armed dash into hostile territory. Then, the notion was to storm in, often mounted, to taunt adversaries or cow them with a show of force, and then to scoot back home before the defenders fielded a response. On the big day itself, fighters came armed with swords and clubs of hardened wood and with wicker shields and helmets. A clash, with its single combats and grand melee, could go on for hours. Almost always, there were wounded and, not rarely, several corpses.

This violence provoked opposition but was only slowly tamed. The usual preachers preached their usual sermons, and town councils passed countless futile ordinances. Yet Renaissance sportive brawling throve during Carnival (the days immediately before Lent) and burst readily forth whenever neighborhoods or parishes skirmished for place, as when marshaling a procession. Only very gradually did the mayhem lose its cutting edge. Swords and clubs yielded to stones and fists, but those remained in plenty. In Venice, against the general trend, fistfighting throve well into the 18th century, much applauded by the elite, who backed champion pugilists and flocked to see the bridge-top fist wars from their gondolas, keeping just a little back to avoid the knots of brawling men who tumbled still grappling into the canal.

The sons of the Renaissance elite gradually deserted street fighting for safer, more elegant forms of combat. Patricians increasingly turned to expensive formal competitions, based on revived rites of chivalry. Drawing on the mythology laid out in medieval romance, they played at a world of knights in shining armor who undertook military contests to win honor and the hand of a ladylove. Well-born sponsors of ritual fighting wrapped the whole occasion in fancy rhetoric, writing pompous challenges and evoking allegories of love, youth, fidelity, and other overblown virtues. The elaborate ceremonies and play combats enacted by Renaissance lordlings partook more of nostalgic fantasy than of the robust crudity of real medieval warfare. The tourney, for example, was a set-piece mock battle, with field combat and perhaps a siege or naval fight. The joust pitched riders, lance in arm, one on one, against one another, or ran them at a target, perhaps a dummy or a hanging ring. Lance splitting set riders noisily ramming their weapons against a wall or other barrier. All three sports featured gorgeous costumes and fancy horsemanship. Helmet plumes stood up to six feet tall. Riders wore costly armor, exquisitely wrought

Pallone. The game shown here is an ancestor of both soccer and American football. The object of the game was to carry the ball through the house-shaped goal posts. From P. Bertelli, *Diversarum Nationum Habitus Padua* 1594 (KK 7. 11). By concession of del Ministero per i Beni e le Attivatà Culturali. Reproduction or ulterior duplication for any purpose is prohibited.

and flashing with gems, and rode fine horses mantled in brocaded coats and rigged with jingling bells and sparkling trim. Alongside the splendid fighters were troops of retainers on foot, adorned at their leader's expense in his colors and devices. The whole spectacle had undertones of courtship; the ladies were part of the show. It fell to them to praise riders and accept dedicated prizes. Mounting a tourney was costly. Besides the equipment of the combatants, there were jousting barriers to rig and seats and judges' booths to install. In addition, sponsors paid for the floats and other decorations, a lavish banquet, and, from the 15th century on, sometimes a finale with fireworks. While both these spectacles and the neighborhood street battles had their rituals, the expense and the feudal trappings set the former apart. The chivalric nostalgia fit the aristocratic ambitions of elite Renaissance families and prettified the autocracy of regimes. Ironically, the resuscitated medievalism coincided with the rise to supremacy in real warfare of gunnery, grisly nemesis of the mounted knight.

Children and adults alike played a multitude of less warlike games. They ranged from cards, dice, and chess to more athletic stick-throwing and jumping contests. There was also an array of more or less orderly ball games. There was a form of indoor tennis, with leather, down-filled balls, and a raucous kind of wall-ball, where one struggled to catch the rebound. Renaissance Italians already had a game like modern bocce, an outdoor form of bowling. A very popular pastime was *palla maglia* (mallet ball), a robust ancestor of croquet. They also played *pallone*, a rough-and-tumble kind of football with shielded arms in play. These sports were male. Girls were more confined; we see them less in outdoor pictures and know less about their games. They certainly played, but more often in the house, courtyard, and garden than in the street.

Dice and cards were among the most common games. Playing cards were already on the scene from the 1370s on, but only in the 16th century did cheap decks spread. By the 17th century, they were ubiquitous; ragged card players perched on wagons, walls, or handy lumps of ruin became a painter's emblem of the daily life of commoners. As for the dice games, there were several variants. In one, a player called out the total of three dice before the throw. In another, called *zara*, contestants moved colored pieces—squares, circles, and stars—on a checkered board, taking turns. If one threw a seven or less, or a fourteen or more, one lost one's turn. Players, when blocked, shouted *"Zara!"* A good moment to add an oath or two! Another favorite sedentary game, *morra*, required no equipment. Much like our rock, paper, and scissors, it required the players to guess how many fingers would be extended. At the inn, drinkers played *morra* to see who had to pay for the next round.

Men and women of all ages and classes were addicted to betting. They wagered on dice and cards and *morra*, and also on future events: who would be elected pope or what sex an unborn child would have. Some operators made a living off this appetite, making book, renting out dice and tables, or, like the Florentine diplomat Buonaccorso Pitti, playing for high stakes. This

 Snapshot

A Crooked Gambler in 16th-Century Italy

The following testimony in a 16th-century trial was given by a nobleman against Ascanio Giustini:

Your Lordship, yes, I have seen him cheat. For once he was playing with me, and I had a 49. Ascanio showed me a 51. He had a card, slipped under another, so you could not see it. But Asdrubale Sanguigni made me a sign that he [Ascanio] had another card hidden underneath, so I pulled out the cards that he had in his hand and discovered the other card, and found that there were five of them. I got furious, and he returned my money. Another time, I saw him do the same thing when he was playing with messer Pier Nicola, that when the cards came into his hand, and he was dealing, sometimes he took five, but in such a way that Vincenzo and the others weren't aware of it, but I, who was watching, saw it. And I am sure he did this on purpose, for he never showed his cards [at the hand's end].

love of gambling horrified moralists, both clerical and lay. To them, betting was the ruin of fortunes, the calamity of heirs; it gave rise to fights and provoked blasphemy. At the same time, gambling appealed to the taste for risk and to the sense of strategy and calculation so central to Italian culture. Furthermore, although it made for quarreling, it also sometimes bolstered alliances. There can be solidarity in sustained rivalry; in many societies, internal foes often lock ranks swiftly against outside enemies. This fact could hold for partners at dice, as it did for the squalling fistfight factions of Pisa, Venice, and Siena, fierce patriots all. Gambling also spun webs of debt, and debt, though fractious, also sustained solidarities.

As with prostitution, rather than strive in vain to banish vice, regimes often sought to curtail and channel gambling. Campaigns to abolish betting met dogged popular resistance. The captain of a Maltese privateer, according to the memoirs of the Spanish buccaneer Contreras, to avoid the usual ructions tossed overboard all dice and cards. Undaunted, the crew of many nations carved concentric circles on the deck; then each man rummaged in hair and clothes, caught his racing louse, placed it in the center, and, at the signal, cheered its progress to the finish line. Winner took all. The captain just gave up. Unlike the thwarted captain, many governments tried compromise. Some authorities permitted gambling only on certain days or in certain places. They preferred to keep the danger out in the open. Others, to profit from what they could not quench, auctioned off the rights to run a gaming house (Cohen and Cohen, 285–92).

FOR MORE INFORMATION

Coffin, D. R. *Gardens and Gardening in Papal Rome*. Princeton: Princeton University Press, 1991.

Cohen, E. S., and T. V. Cohen. *Daily Life in Renaissance Italy*. Westport, Conn.: Greenwood, 2001.

Davis, R. *The War of the Fists: Popular Culture and Public Violence in Late Renaissance Venice*. New York: Oxford University Press, 1994.

RECREATIONAL
LIFE

GAMES & SPORTS

England

Spain

Italy

Maya

Aztec

Inca

MAYA

In Maya society each person's time and labor was critical to ensure that the daily needs of life were maintained. Once each family's needs were met, adults had obligations to fulfill for their king or kingdom: surplus food and other goods were given as tribute, and labor was given to build and maintain the great temples and palaces. Thus there was little leisure time for most of the Maya population, and recreation as we know it today was almost nonexistent. Even children, as soon as they were old enough to help their parents, had to put work before play.

Nothing is known about the games children played in the past; but we can assume that at least some games made use of balls made from the elastic gum of the rubber tree, cultivated and widely traded by the Maya. We can also assume that people found time between their labors to relax and enjoy themselves. Certainly the great religious feasts and festivals held periodically throughout the year broke the difficult routine of daily life. We can also assume that both children and men (when they could find free time) played various ball games.

This Maya ball game is known from both archaeological evidence and carved representations, although these tell mostly about a formal version played in the major capitals of Maya kingdoms. We speculate that an everyday version of the game was played by nonelite people in their communities.

The formal version was played in a specially constructed ball court. One or more of these are found at most larger Maya cities, usually near the center. The ball courts have a level paved surface between two masonry platforms and an open end zone at both ends of the playing alley. In most cases there are no provisions for large crowds, although at both Copan and Quirigua the ball courts are placed near extensive stepped terraces that could have accommodated several thousand spectators. The size of the playing alley varied from court to court but was generally smaller than a baseball infield (the playing alley of the Great Ball Court at Chichen Itza, the largest known, was about the size of a football field). Most Classic period ball courts have sloping side walls, whereas most postclassical ball courts have vertical side walls with a single vertically set stone ring placed high up at the center point of each wall.

The game was played between two teams with a hard rubber ball that could be struck with the body but not the hands or feet. For protection, ball players wore special padded garb around the waist and on the head. There were at least two versions of the game.

The Classic-era game was played with a large heavy ball, larger than a basketball. The rules are unknown, but it seems that the objective was to keep the ball moving back and forth between the two teams, each defending one end zone. Points were probably scored on the opposing team if they failed to properly strike the ball or if the ball landed in their end zone. The postclassical version was played with a smaller rubber ball. The rules are also unknown, but the objective was probably similar to the Classic-era game. We do know from Bishop Landa's description that the game would be instantly won by the team that managed to direct the ball through one of the stone rings. This was a rare event, so much so that the winning team and its spectators could seize the clothing and possessions from the losing team and its spectators—provided they could catch them!

A Ball Court. Ball courts, like this one at Chichen Itza, were shaped like a capital *I*. The object was for a player to get the ball past his opponent and into the wide end-zone area. © The Art Archive/ Dagli Orti.

We also know that the Maya ball game was closely associated with religious belief and ritual. The Hero Twins of Maya myth were expert ball players who defeated the death gods in a game. Because of this religious association, a ritual version of the ball game was played out to dramatize military victories. We can be certain that the ritual had no recreational value for the losing side. In such rituals the defeated captives, including kings on those rare occasions when a Maya ruler was captured in battle, were forced to play a ball game with the victors. The result of the contest was preordained, and after the defeated captives lost the game they were sacrificed. Defeated kings were decapitated, just as the Hero Twins decapitated the defeated death gods in the Maya myth. We actually know more about this ritualized aspect of the ball game than we know about the game itself. We assume that the original ball game played in every Maya community was a far less fatal contest (Sharer, 125–27).

To read about games and sports in 19th-century Latin America, see the Latin America entry in the section "Sports" in chapter 7 ("Recreational Life") in volume 5 of this series.

FOR MORE INFORMATION

Sharer, R. J. *Daily Life in Maya Civilization*. Westport, Conn.: Greenwood, 1996.
Whitlock, R. *Everyday Life of the Maya*. New York: Putnam, 1976.

RECREATIONAL
LIFE
|
GAMES & SPORTS
|
England

Spain

Italy

Maya

Aztec

Inca

AZTEC

The games of *patolli* and *ollamaliztli*, the ballgame, demanded both skill and luck. Let us look at the ballgame first. Archaeologists have found *tlachtli* ball courts all over Mesoamerica, and this game was also enjoyed by the Aztecs. The Mexica rulers and nobles supported these games, and they became sites for gambling by the noble classes. The ruler who played "caused the ball to enter . . . the ball court rings. . . . Then he won all the costly goods, and he won everything from all who watched there in the ballcourt."

The court was shaped like a thick capital *I* turned on its side and was surrounded by tall walls. On each side, a stone ring was set in the wall. A player scored by sending a hard rubber ball through a small opening in the opposing team's ring. Hands could not be used, nor could a player use his feet, calves, or arms. He could strike the ball with his knees, thighs, and buttocks. According to Diego Durán, who witnessed some of these ballgames after the Spaniards arrived, the ball was extremely lively: "Jumping and bouncing are its qualities, upward and downward, to and fro. It can exhaust the pursuer running after it before he can catch up with it." According to Durán, some players were so skillful that they could play for an hour and the ball would never touch the ground!

Finally, the game of *patolli* was used to win valuable pieces of jewelry and other expressions of value and beauty. In this game, beans were placed on a board divided into squares, the object being to be the first to move six beans through the entire course. There were moments of high tension and excitement in *patolli*, for if a player threw the dice beans so that one landed and stood up on its side, it

Ollamaliztli. This ball game was the most popular sport in Mesoamerica. Warick Bray, *Everyday Life of the Ancient Aztecs.* London: B.T. Batsford, Chrysalis Books, 1968.

was regarded as a triumphant moment and the thrower was in a winner-take-all position. The game has been compared to parcheesi or backgammon. Here is a succinct contemporary description of how it was played on a mat painted with a big X made out of liquid rubber:

Within the arms of the X, lines were drawn so as to form squares. Twelve pebbles—red and blue—were used in these compartments. Bets were made on the player who could best handle the dice, which were five or six black beans, each of which had a number painted on it. The game invariably drew a large crowd. Onlookers and gamblers pressed each other around the mat, some waiting to play, others to place bets.

> ### 📷 *Snapshot*
>
> **Diego Durán's Description of the Dangers of the Aztec Game of *Ollamaliztli***
>
> On seeing the ball come at them, at the moment that it was about to touch the floor, they [the players] were so quick in turning their knees or buttocks to the ball that they returned it with an extraordinary swiftness. With this bounding back and forth they suffered terrible injuries on their knees or thighs so that the haunches of those who made use of these tricks were frequently so bruised that those spots had to be opened with a small blade, whereupon the blood which had clotted there because of the blows of the ball was squeezed out. (Carrasco, 180)

The winner won some of the precious objects examined in the section "The Arts" below, showing the importance of art in Aztec life. Art was not only decorative, but a valuable commodity for which people wagered in games of chance and skill. As Bernardino de Sahagún noted,

He who won in playing *patolli* won all the costly goods: golden necklaces, green stone, fine turquoise, bracelets on which were round, green stones or fine turquoise, quetzal feathers, slaves, houses, fields, precious capes, mats, large capes, green stone lip plugs, golden ear plugs, duck feather capes. But even here, in the gambling dens of the Aztecs, the spirits of the gods could be present and pushing themselves through the thin, permeable membrane that divided the seen from the unseen world. For we are told, "And he who played *patolli*, who cast the beans, if then he made one of them stand, if the bean stood up there on its thicker end, it was taken as a great omen; it was regarded [as] a great marvel." (Carrasco, 179–82)

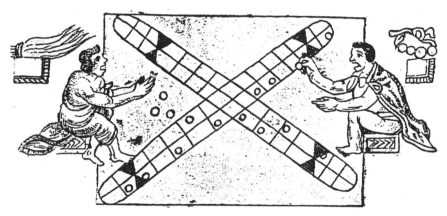

Patolli. People frequently bet large amounts of wealth on this game that was played with beans on a rubber mat and is somewhat similar to backgammon. From Diego Durán, *Códice Durán*. Mexico City: Arrendadora International, 1990 (facsimile edition).

To read about games and sports in nineteenth-century Latin America, see the Latin America entry in the section "Sports" in chapter 7 ("Recreational Life") in volume 5 of this series.

FOR MORE INFORMATION

Berdan, F., and P. Anawalt. *Codex Mendoza.* 4 vols. Berkeley: University of California Press, 1992.

Carrasco, D., with S. Sessions. *Daily Life of the Aztecs: People of the Sun and Earth.* Westport, Conn.: Greenwood, 1998.

Durán, D. *The History of the Indies of New Spain*. Trans. Doris Heyden. Norman: University of Oklahoma Press, 1995.

Sahagún, B. de. *Florentine Codex: General History of the Things of New Spain*. Ed. and trans. Arthur Anderson and Charles Dibble. 13 vols. Santa Fe: School of American Research, and University of Utah, 1950–82.

RECREATIONAL
LIFE
|
GAMES & SPORTS
|
England

Spain

Italy

Maya

Aztec

Inca

INCA

Little is known about the recreational activities of the Incas, perhaps because there were few times when people were not involved with the day-to-day activities of making a living. This was as true for children as for adults. For conquered peoples, it would have been doubly true.

Inca children played with tops, balls, and round pieces of pottery that were ground down to use as gaming pieces. Adults played games involving dice that had five numbers on them, not six. They also played games with a board and beans as counters, but exactly how the games were played is unknown.

The Incas also gambled. Although most games appear to have been played more for fun than to win, there is one game called *aylloscas* played by royalty (and perhaps by others as well) that involved wagering entire estates. This suggests that among the nobility, at least, some betting had high stakes.

Games of skill were also important in boys' training for the puberty rites and adulthood. Races and mock battles were undertaken to evaluate the youths' abilities to become warriors. Because participating in warfare was an important part of being a man, there is little doubt these games were conducted with serious intentions and the level of competitiveness was high. Reports of grave injuries to some participants point to this conclusion. Such games prepared the young men for the more serious activities of warfare (Malpass, 86–87).

To read about games and sports in 19th-century Latin America, see the Latin America entry in the section "Sports" in chapter 7 ("Recreational Life") in volume 5 of this series.

FOR MORE INFORMATION

Julien, C. "Finding a Fit: Archaeology and Ethnohistory of the Incas." In *Provincial Inca*, ed. Michael A. Malpass, 177–233. Iowa City: University of Iowa Press, 1993.

Malpass, M. A. *Daily Life in the Inca Empire*. Westport, Conn.: Greenwood, 1996.

Rowe, J. "Inca Culture at the Time of the Spanish Conquest." In *Handbook of South American Indians*. Vol. 2, *The Andean Civilizations*, ed. Julian Steward. Washington, D.C.: Bureau of American Ethnology Bulletin 143, 1946. 183–330.

RECREATIONAL
LIFE
|
OUTDOOR PURSUITS
|
England

Spain

Italy

Outdoor Pursuits

Renaissance culture in Europe was developing a special interest in outdoor life, perhaps because their culture was becoming more and more urban. As a result of this increasing urbanization, the countryside was a recognizably different sphere of life, and one that offered escape from the daily grind. At all events, cultures that were more rural, such as in the Americas, do not seem to have had a concept of the great outdoors as distinct from regular life. The Native American cultures viewed the outdoors as an integral part of their daily life, and not as a separate sphere for recreation. Since the Native Americans did not view being outdoors as a kind of recreation, this section on outdoor recreational pursuits focuses on the European phenomenon.

It can be difficult to distinguish between games and outdoor pursuits. For example, should the rough form of soccer played in England be grouped with games such as blindman's buff or with pursuits such as hunting? In this case, English soccer has been placed with outdoor pursuits in order to distinguish it from the popular English parlor games, such as blindman's buff. However, the Italian *pallone*, another form of football, has been discussed in the section on games and sports, in part to distinguish *pallone* from the garden entertainments popular in Italy. Since the decision on what to consider an outdoor recreation has been based upon the factors of each individual culture, the reader is encouraged to read the section on games and sports along with this section in order to develop a more complete picture of such activities.

Some pastimes, such as hunting and hiking, are clearly outdoor activities for all of Europe. By the 15th century, hunting had largely become dominated by the aristocrats. The landed gentry frequently refused hunting rights to anyone but themselves on their own estates, and since the landed gentry owned most of the land in Europe, hunting effectively became restricted to the aristocracy. This movement happened earlier in England than other countries, but it spread quickly during the Renaissance.

Related to hunting, and accessible to everyone regardless of wealth or social class, was bearbaiting and other animal blood sports. In these spectacles, a wild animal would be pitted against another animal in a fight to the death. For example, in bearbaiting, dogs were set upon a bear. While the bear might maim or kill a couple dogs, the pack would eventually wear the bear down and kill the animal. Other contests more directly involved humans, for example the bullfighting in Spain, which is still practiced today. In these popular entertainments, the crowd was more interested in the fight than in the death of the animal, and we should remember that people in the 15th and 16th centuries had much more first-hand experience with farm animals, abattoirs, and butchers.

Somewhat similar to the martial flavor of bullfighting was the practice of military drills. These drills were particularly popular in England, where the Trained Bands, a kind of National Guard, would go through their exercises and march in formation. These drills provided exercise for the participants, and entertainment for onlookers, while also building the military backbone of the nation.

The Italians were particularly interested in wandering about the countryside. It was very common in the summertime for city-dwellers to take long walks after work along the grassy banks of the river, greeting their friends and neighbors as they strolled. The wealthy constructed large intricate gardens that were carefully landscaped and filled with chosen animals. The gardens would usually sport elaborate fountains, and some, such as the garden at Tivoli, would include various practical jokes, such as flagstones that caused a fountain to drench the unfortunate person who stepped on that particular paving slab. While some of these gardens were private, many of their owners opened them up to everyone, and the poor thus had a chance to relax under the cool shade of a tree and listen to the tinkle of fountains and the songs of birds.

Finally, some entertainments, such as theater, have become indoor activities although they were originally outdoor activities. The Spanish theater, for example, more closely resembled a modern American football match than the hushed theaters of broadway. The spectators, most of whom stood in an open-air field, mingled around, shouted praise and insults, and got into occasional brawls. Theater shows how difficult it can be to peg down some leisure activities—see the entry in the section "The Arts" below and the entry in the section "Literature" in chapter 4 ("Intellectual Life") for information on the literary and other aspects of the theater.

~*Lawrence Morris*

RECREATIONAL
LIFE

OUTDOOR PURSUITS

England

Spain

Italy

ENGLAND

15th- and 16th-century pastimes were not all as gentle as music and dance. One of the preferred sports of gentlemen was hunting—particularly for deer, sometimes for foxes or hares. Birds were also hunted, in two different ways. One was the ancient and difficult sport of falconry in which trained falcons were sent after the prey. However, guns were used increasingly instead. Rather more sedate was the sport of fishing, enjoyed by many who found hunting too barbarous or expensive. All these sports might be enjoyed by women as well as men. Ordinary people did not generally hunt or fish for sport. Indeed, they were not allowed to do so. The rights of hunting and fishing were normally reserved for landowners, although poaching was still common as a means of obtaining extra food.

Hunting was a relatively mild pastime in comparison with some Renaissance sports, especially bullbaiting, bearbaiting, and cockfighting. Cockfighting involved pitting roosters against each other in a cockpit, a small round arena surrounded by benches—sometimes a permanent structure was built for the purpose. In bullbaiting, a bull was chained in the middle of a large arena with one or more bulldogs or bull mastiffs. The dogs were trained to clamp their jaws closed on the bull's nose or ears and hang on until the bull fell down exhausted; the bull meanwhile tried to shake the dogs free and gore them to death. Bearbaiting was very similar, with the bull replaced by a bear. In all of these sports the onlookers would place wagers on the outcome of the combat.

While some sports pitted animals against each other, others involved human combatants. The aristocracy sometimes practiced the medieval sport of jousting; jousts were sometimes the centerpiece of major public festivals. Fencing was popular both as a spectator entertainment and a participatory sport. Fencing weapons had blunted edges and rounded ends but the sport was dangerous nonetheless. The rapier used in fencing was a great deal heavier than a modern fencing weapon; the only protective gear was a padded jacket, and occasionally a large rounded button placed over the tip of the blade to reduce the risk of putting out an eye. The rapier was sometimes supplemented by a small round shield, called a buckler, or by a larger one, either round or square, called a target. Alternatively the fencer might use a rapier in one hand and a dagger in the other, or even two rapiers at once.

The rapier was considered an Italian weapon; those who preferred English traditions might fight with a sword instead. The sword was a slightly heavier weapon with a thicker blade, designed to deliver cutting blows instead of thrusts with the point. Sometimes the fencers used wooden swords called wasters. Combat with the quarterstaff was another popular sport.

These martial arts had some practical application. There was a certain amount of lawlessness in 15th- and 16th-century England: even in London, street fights and brawls were known to break out in broad daylight. For many people, the ability to defend oneself was an important life-or-death skill.

Other martial sports were geared toward military rather than civilian purposes. By law, every English commoner was to practice archery regularly. The law was originally introduced in the 14th century, when archery was still very important on the battlefield. By Queen Elizabeth's time archery had declined in importance, but Elizabeth encouraged it nonetheless (she sometimes engaged in the sport herself, as did many English aristocrats). There were archers in the militia, and some military theorists still preferred the bow to the gun. Laws promoting archery were not strictly observed, but the sport remained popular among all classes and was widely seen as an especially patriotic pastime.

More useful for the national defense was the practice of military drill with pike and shot. Elizabeth's government made a concerted effort to improve England's defenses by training a national militia known as the Trained Bands. Sixteenth-century warfare required more training of the ordinary soldier than had once been the case. The matchlock musket required less physical strength and skill than the bow, but it was a fairly complex weapon to fire, requiring 20 to 30 seconds for each shot and some two dozen distinct motions—all of this while holding a slowly burning piece of treated rope (called the match) and charging the weapon with gunpowder. An error could be fatal.

The pike, a 16- to 24-foot spear designed to ward off cavalry, was less dangerous but even more demanding. There were about a dozen positions in which the pike might be held, and the pikemen had to learn to move from each position to all the others in precise formation with the rest of the pikemen or else the pikes would strike each other and become hopelessly tangled. The government's efforts to pro-

A Hunting Party. Hunting was a favorite pastime among the upper class. As you can see from this picture, much of its attraction was due to the elaborate picnics that were held in the woods. A hunting dog and a horse can be seen at the top of the picture, however. From Emily Jessie Ashdown, *British Costume,* 1910.

mote military training met with extraordinary success, for military drill actually became a fashionable pastime, as well as a popular spectator entertainment.

Even games that were not martial could be quite perilous. The most characteristic English outdoor game of the period was football, especially favored by the lower classes. Football was traditionally violent, loud, and dangerous to bystanders as well as players. As described by the Puritan social critic Phillip Stubbes, "Football playing . . . may rather be called a friendly kind of fight, than a play, or recreation; A bloody and murdering practice, then a fellowly sport or pastime." Football was roughly the same as modern European football (called soccer in America), but with fewer rules. Two teams would try to kick a ball through their opponents' goal. The ball was made of a farm animal's bladder, inflated and tied up and sewn into a leather covering. A major part of the game was the subtle art of tripping up one's opponents on the run. Even more violent were the versions known as camp-ball in England, hurling in Cornwall, or *cnapan* in Wales. In these games, a ball (or other object) was conveyed over open country to opposing goals by any means possible—even horsemen might be involved. These games frequently led to serious injuries (Singman, 163–66).

Fencers. Military sports of all kinds were common in England. The small dagger for parrying is called a *main gauche,* or "left hand," because that's where it was carried. From Egerton Castle, *Schools and Masters of Fence.*

To read about outdoor pursuits in Chaucer's England, see the Europe entry in the section "Hunting" in chapter 7 ("Recreational Life") in volume 2 of this series.

FOR MORE INFORMATION

Holme, R. *The Academy of Armory.* 1688. Reprint, Menston: Scolar, 1972.

Singman, J. L. *Daily Life in Elizabethan England.* Westport, Conn.: Greenwood, 1995.

Vale, M. *The Gentleman's Recreations: Accomplishments and Pastimes of the English Gentleman, 1580–1630.* Cambridge: Brewer, 1977.

RECREATIONAL
LIFE
|
OUTDOOR PURSUITS
|
England

Spain

Italy

SPAIN

Most Spanish pastimes, especially male sports, were conducted outdoors. Since homes tended to be small, there was no space for sports, or often even for large groups of people. In the long hot summer days, people were particularly happy to seek out a breezy and shady area to stroll or engage in pastimes. Many of the smaller-scale outdoor pursuits are described under the section "Games and Sports." In this section, the focus will be directed on two of the most passionate pastimes in the 15th and 16th centuries: bullfighting and the theater.

Bullfighting events were attended by all classes, even the clergy who had been forbidden to witness it by Pius V in 1572. The king, guilds, local authorities, and aristocracy all organized bullfighting events, and they were performed on all festive days, religious or secular. The spectacle, an exercise in which the nobility could show off their prowess and skill to the public, took place in the public square of the towns. In the Plaza Mayor in Madrid the commoners crowded onto grandstands, while the high nobility, which often included the king, watched from the surrounding colorful, richly draped balconies.

The event began with an introduction of the noble champions armed with a sword and daggers and clad in short capes and multiplumed hats, attended by their squires. This was followed by a salute to the king, if present, and the local dignitaries. Eventually the bulls were released from their pens, and the toreadors or noble horsemen rode in for the attack, which consisted of planting a wooden iron-tipped spear in the side of the animal. The shaft then was designed to break off, leaving it in the hands of the horseman while the tip remained in the bull. The winner was the one with the largest number of broken spears. Numerous horses were fatally injured on each occasion, gored by the desperate bull.

When the bull was seen to be exhausted from the struggle, trumpets sounded the final stage of the performance. The toreadors left the ring, leaving the peons, whose role up to then had been to tire the bull by harassing it with their capes and banderillas, to finish off the wretched animal. The bull was then hamstrung and, once immobilized, slashed to pieces.

In the villages, where the ritual slaughter of the bull was organized by local authority, nobles were generally not involved. Local amateurs or professional matadors (bull killers), hired for the event, fought on foot and were the prototypes of the modern bull-slayer of the corrida (bullfight) who finishes the wounded and exhausted animal off after it has undergone teasing, torture, and futile charges at an elusive cape.

It may seem strange to regard the theater as an outdoor pursuit, but we must remember that the modern indoor theater is a recent invention. Most Spanish acting groups gave their performances in the open air. These troupes traveled from town to town and would put on their productions in the village square atop their wagon, or in the central courtyard of the local inn. Even those theaters that were permanent were mostly open air. Only the wealthy and ladies were able to sit in sections that were covered from the weather; most theatergoers milled around in a central pit area in front of the stage. On the way in, there was often considerable jostling and buffeting, and performances could be brought to an end with a barrage of rotten vegetables. Attending the theater in the 15th and 16th centuries was thus more like attending a modern sports event instead of the hushed and restrained modern theater.

The Spanish theater appealed to everyone from nobleman to peasant. The only subjects that were prohibited on the stage were criticism of the monarchy, the church, and the Inquisition. The two theaters in Madrid, the Correl del Príncipe and the Correl de la Cruz, were rectangular areas with the stage at one end and a wooden balcony at the other, reserved for women. In this section, the *cazuela* (stewing pot), men were not allowed. Here the women talked incessantly, argued, fought, ate snacks, and watched the play. In front of them was the pit, a kind of promenade where people remained standing during the performance and often moved about. Between the pit and the stage were benches for the merchants and artisans who could afford the better position. Lateral balconies along the sides of the theater were reserved for gentry. Only the *cazuela* and the gentry sections had a wooden roof, while a canopy stretched overhead protected the audience in the pit and on the benches from the sun; but the show stopped if heavy rain began.

The performances generally played to a full house, and a given drama rarely ran for more than a few days. Only the expensive boxes could be reserved in advance of the play, which commenced between two and four o'clock in the afternoon, depending on the season. The doors nevertheless opened at noon as crowds milled around, hoping to get in early. Since there were no tickets, and seats were first come, first served, there were frequent quarrels over who sat where. On occasion a serious fight erupted, knives were drawn, and one of the patrons would lose his seat and sometimes his life.

Attendants tried to collect the price of admission as the crowd rushed in. Many would attempt to enter without paying, claiming they were officials who paid nothing or playwrights themselves, who had the privilege of attending free of charge the works of their colleagues. Some claimed to be friends of the actor or actress and demanded free seats. A free seat was a status symbol, and those who got them often brought in their friends to occupy more free space.

When the crowd finally settled down to only a mild commotion, the spectators passed the time before the show purchasing food and drinks from vendors carrying trays of assorted items. This was the time when those in the pit directed loud comments toward the women who occupied the balcony above and who in turn shouted to the men below, made rude gestures, and threw candies, limes extracted from their drinks, small cakes, orange peelings, nuts and shells, or other missiles that came to hand on the milling mob below.

All kinds of people went to the theater, including cobblers, grocers, shop assistants, and workmen who went truant from their jobs to attend. The men arrived with cape, sword, and dagger and called each other by the title *caballero*. It was common for the audience to throw turnips, tomatoes, or rotten fruit at the actors if the play did not suit its fancy. The most troublesome were the *mosqueteros* who stood in the promenade section of the pit, like the soldiers from whom they took their name, and maintained a constant applause or noises of disdain throughout the performance. Most carried concealed vegetables. Many claimed to be great critics of the theater; their applause, jeers, or whistling could make or break a play on opening day.

It was known that during a particularly bad play or poor performance the audience rioted and tore the theater to pieces, breaking up the benches and tearing the curtains and decorations to shreds.

The *doctos*, or learned and cultured people, who sat in the boxes along the sides of the theater were the most feared by the playwright, for, less disturbing than the *mosqueteros*, their sarcastic pronouncements on the play would be the talk of the town the following day. Playwrights sometimes tried to assure support in advance of the performance by bribing the most notorious of the critics.

The theater gave to the people in popular form the things they were proud of and never grew tired of hearing about: the virtues of their kings and of the church, patriotism, honor, and the privilege of having been born in a country of *caballeros*, heroes, and saints—a country superior to all others.

While large cities supported professional theatrical companies and smaller towns had their own theater in which amateurs organized the performances, villages relied on strolling players to give their inhabitants the opportunity to enjoy plays. Traveling from one town to the next over bumpy and dusty roads in uncomfortable wagons loaded with stage sets, costumes, musical instruments, and makeup boxes, along with paraphernalia for cooking and sleeping, itinerant performers generally led a hard life.

Not all rambling theatrical troops possessed ample costumes and stage props. Some traveled with only the bare rudiments of stage scenery, a few clothes, false beards, and wigs. A well-worn blanket with cords attached served as the stage curtain. They set up their performances in the town square or in a closed street, where the stage consisted of a few planks laid out on top of some benches. A colored canvas behind the makeshift stage served as the backdrop. The windows and balconies of surrounding houses became the theater boxes. The actresses, when not on stage, were often besieged by men in the audience, but they tried to maintain some decorum, lest the more obnoxious males booed or heckled and ruined the performance. For a small town audience the stage became for a little while their entire universe, taking their minds off the daily drudgery of village life.

Members of the clergy were apt to be critical of the theater. Many actors and actresses did not lead exemplary lives—far from it. Their dissolute lifestyle shocked some churchmen, yet these same people played religious roles as saints and even the Virgin Mary. Plays of intrigue and passion solely designed to excite human emotions also annoyed some clergy. Taking a dim view of these matters, the church sometimes withheld the sacraments from performers even though it was often the religious organizations in the large towns that owned the theaters and leased them out to managers of the stage companies.

In addition to being outdoors, bullfighting and theater had one thing in common—spectacle. And the Spanish loved it (Anderson, 211–16).

FOR MORE INFORMATION

Anderson, J. M. *Daily Life during the Spanish Inquisition.* Westport, Conn.: Greenwood, 2002.

Defourneaux, M. *Daily Life in the Golden Age.* Trans. Newton Branch. Stanford: Stanford University Press, 1979.

ITALY

Perhaps because their civilization was urban, Renaissance Italians loved taking leisure amid space, light, good air, and greenery. So they often fled their domestic haunts and workplaces in search of natural settings that soothed and stimulated town-worn senses. Riverbanks were popular for strolling and fishing. Rivers and lakes welcomed swimmers and boaters, and, on the rare occasion when they froze solid, invited games, races, and even an impromptu market. But the sea was not to toy

RECREATIONAL
LIFE
|
OUTDOOR PURSUITS
|
England

Spain

Italy

with; beaches were for working fishermen, not for play. Other natural sites for recreation were the hot springs scattered across volcanic western Italy. People believed in the curative powers of these mineral waters. Some of these attracted so many patients that a spa life sprang up, with hostelry and social gatherings. Montaigne devoted much of his Italian voyage to long cures for his kidney stones. He soaked at length in hot and tepid pools, drank prodigious quantities of smelly water, and chronicled his belly's every stirring. Between aquatic moments, he attended dances, exchanged gifts and courtesies, and enjoyed the company of well-born seekers after health.

A convenient green space for urban play was a *vigna*. Literally, the term means vineyard, but the typical *vigna* also sported fruit trees and vegetables and might house rabbits, chickens, or pigeons. Many such small farming plots lay close at hand, on cities' outskirts. Their owners often lived in town, hired a *vignerolo* to work them in exchange for part of the crop, and used them for outings in good weather. Roman court records are full of *vigna* matters—not only squabbles over boundary ditches and fences or over thefts of fruit and water but also troubles arising from play gone awry: raucous parties, seductions, and brawls. A trial in July 1563 shows a police official, Captain Ottavio, riding back at dusk one Sunday from his vineyard to the pleasant sound of a lute and a woman singing. Returning with the captain from his picnic were a band of friends, kinsmen, and servants, some with swords and halberds and others with musical instruments. The party included two clergymen, a prosecutor and his wife, a butcher, the captain's own son and daughter, several serving men and women, and five Jews wearing the yellow hats required of them by law. One of these, elderly, paunchy, bearded, and bent, was Mastro Abraham, strumming his lute as he rode. To avoid nonkosher meat, the Jewish guests, said Abraham, dined at a small table of their own, off bread and cucumber salad. In the growing gloom, as the captain's party descended a steep, narrow road toward town, a pack train, outward bound, forced the women's horses against a looming wall. "The street is plenty large! No need to crowd the ladies," the captain said. Harsh words ricocheted, and soon the captain's servants, taking up another common recreation, hurled stones on top of insults at the departing drivers. Had his men but known that the drivers were the pope's own grooms carrying in their baskets a fragile gift of wine from their master to a great lord, they would have been more discreet, the flustered captain later told the judge. Note how mixed the excursion's company had been; clergy, laity, men, women, Christians, Jews, parents and their offspring, masters and their servants had, on a summer afternoon, enjoyed food and music together amid suburban greenery.

Renaissance Italians not only took pleasure from the working landscape; they also loved to reshape it—as garden and villa—into artful forms. Lacking the modern cult of nature as raw wilderness, they preferred a pleasant, safe, and ordered domain stocked with flora and fauna of their choosing. This appetite and the building projects that it fed had a long pedigree. The ancient Romans had been great builders of villas and gardens. Cicero, among others, had praised such retreats for fostering a civilized life of leisure and contemplation. Later the walled medieval garden and monastic cloister hearkened back to Near Eastern images of paradise (the word, in old Persian, meant garden). Renaissance landscape architects and their wealthy patrons, steeped in humanistic admiration of classical ways, transformed the simple medieval close, with its modest geometric plots of herbs and flowers, into a far more ambitious space, traversed by tunneled arbors and well-laid lanes and ornamented by intricately patterned beds, fountains, pools, ancient and modern statuary, and artificial grottoes. Sometimes peacocks pecked and strutted under the orange, lemon, pear, and laurel trees. Grander gardens had wide lanes for running horses and for jousting, and paths for bowling and mallet ball.

The gardens of the rich figured in Renaissance intellectual and cultural life, both sober and playful. Circles of learned men met under the trees to discuss politics, religion, and literature, to declaim poems and orations, or to hear music. These gatherings also punned and joked; participants might take on fancy, mock-serious Latin or Greek names and celebrate a literary hero or debate an outlandish proposition. Many gardens were also open to the public; some posted Latin inscriptions citing ancient Roman customs of inviting strollers to enjoy them. Montaigne reports his uninvited visits to those in Rome and remarks that not only could one enjoy the birds, fish, and art, one could even take a nap.

Some elegant Renaissance gardens were built in or near the city, while others attached to pretty rural mansions called villas. These were a Renaissance development, as the more violent Middle Ages had discouraged country building for sheer pleasure. Like the ancient Romans they admired, urban elites retreated to a villa to relax with rural pastimes—strolling, riding, and hunting—and to delight and awe their guests. Many Renaissance villas thus grew out of earlier farms or forts, but transformed them with elegant, classicizing pavilions and grounds. While owners did often oversee leisured agriculture, many villas put beauty and entertainment well ahead of function. Fanciful waterworks, a clever marriage of art and engineering, were a favorite showpiece. Many of the famous 16th-century fountains of the Cardinal d'Este at Tivoli still spout and spray. In their heyday, these great set-pieces featured a water-driven musical organ and singing birds of bronze that fell

A Wealthy Garden. In addition to offering a tranquil spot of repose, gardens also employed large numbers of people. Note the ladder in the background and the numerous gardeners attending the shrubs and flower beds. The men on the right are playing bocce. By Antonio Tempesta. Roma—Instituto Nazionale della Grafica. By gracious concession of the Ministero per i Beni e le Attività Culturali.

silent at the approach of the statue of an owl. There were also practical jokes, hidden nozzles, triggered by trick paving stones, to douse the unsuspecting guest, and oozing benches with tiny pores, to soak unwary bottoms.

Hunting and fishing that long had supplemented commoners' diet, though akin to work, also had their pleasures. A judge once asked a witness, "Are you and the suspect friends?" He answered, "At times we fished together, and he told me one thing and another." Thus, like commensality, a shared riverbank, rod in hand, signaled alliance. Bird catching too was companionable; it was a beloved subject of 16th-century and later art, a cloying image of rustic sociability. Italians ate birds of every size and shape. They had ingenious devices for catching them: gooey limed twigs, hidden nets, caged songbirds to call the wild ones down, dummy birds of prey, and insidious baited traps.

Bullbaiting. In bullbaiting, dogs attacked a bull until it was dead. The area of the baiting was usually more enclosed for the sake of safety. P. Bertelli, *Diversarum Nationum Habitus Padua* 1594 (KK 7. 11). By concession of del Ministero per i Beni e le Attività Culturali. Reproduction or ulterior duplication for any purpose is prohibited.

In the later Middle Ages, lords increasingly shouldered ordinary folk out of hunting, and even fishing. They laid claim to communal woodlands and river rights, selling fishing privileges for money and grabbing for themselves the meatier, more prestigious big game: boar and deer. Princes built great hunting lodges, with stables and kennels, to support lavish expeditions for dozens, even hundreds of participants. Nonetheless, by the Renaissance period, rising population and shrinking habitat had in many regions reduced the nobles' hunt. Pockets survived in the valley of the Po and the empty landscape near Rome. There, hunting continued as a grand affair, a fancy picnic crossed with butchery. Popes, cardinals, and princes did not chase their victims but camped at a suitable spot. Then they waited while a horde of dogs, mounted huntsmen, and beaters traversed the woodland, barking, shouting, thrashing the underbrush, and applying smoke to drive the wild animals toward cloth enclosures and nets, where the patrons could slaughter them at leisure.

Our notion that animals may have rights or feelings worth respecting never crossed the Renaissance mind. Alongside the hunt were other cruelties. An animal's death struggle was a common entertainment, not only during carnival but also at other times. There were still bears enough to furnish an occasional bearbaiting. Many cities staged bullfights; Naples had a *corrida*, with cape and sword on the classic Spanish model, but elsewhere the fight was more a crazy melee, as at Pamplona now, but bloodier, as men with swords and spears dodged and thrust among the animals. In 1584, a Roman duke, to show his wealth, staged a three-way fight, pitting a lion against a bull and dogs. To spectators' chagrin, the lion, terrified of the bull, wasted his ferocity on the dogs. To make sense of entertainments such as this, remember that Italians saw death, animal and human, all the time. What amused them here was not agony, but the unpredictable fight and the ticklish confusion of the boundary between beasts and men locked in struggle.

Cruelty to some animals did not prevent kindness to others. Renaissance Italians, both nobles and commoners, kept pets. Some people had favorite horses or hunting dogs or beloved smaller canines. The duke of Mantua had painted into the famous family portrait in the Camera degli Sposi some of his beloved dogs, including a woolly-coated spinoni and a huge red-brown beast snuggled under the ducal throne. In the city, many a quarrel flared over a dog stolen, borrowed overlong, or hurt. Women sometimes fondly nursed puppies, like children, at the breast. Cats were another matter, good for catching mice but usually beneath respect or love. Still, since courtesy books warned against letting them onto the table at meals, they must have prowled the palace (Cohen and Cohen, 278–89).

FOR MORE INFORMATION

Coffin, D. R. *Gardens and Gardening in Papal Rome*. Princeton: Princeton University Press, 1991.

———. *The Villa in the Life of Renaissance Rome*. Princeton: Princeton University Press, 1979.

Cohen, E. S., and T. V. Cohen. *Daily Life in Renaissance Italy*. Westport, Conn.: Greenwood, 2001.

The Arts

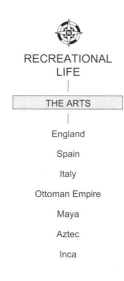

RECREATIONAL
LIFE

THE ARTS

England

Spain

Italy

Ottoman Empire

Maya

Aztec

Inca

The cave paintings in the Ardèche region of France, made around 30,000 B.C.E., suggest that human beings have always been interested in the arts. Around the world, different cultures have developed their own forms of painting, sculpture, pottery, music, dance, and literature. Because literature has been treated in chapter 4 ("Intellectual Life"), the following entries will focus on other forms of artistic expression.

Although some people today view artistic endeavors as unconnected with the real world, perhaps due to the expression *art for art's sake*, art in the 15th and 16th centuries, as today, performed a variety of useful and even essential functions. Music and dance, for example, served as a healthy Sunday break for European peasants that had spent the week from dawn to dusk in back-breaking farm work. Dance, especially for the aristocratic classes of Europe, also offered a way for young men and women of nubile age to meet each other under carefully supervised and controlled conditions, though some Puritans suggested that even these rather tame dances by modern standards had a tendency to get out of control! In Mesoamerica and South America, dance and music were especially associated with ceremonies performed in the worship of the gods, and were viewed as necessary for the continued well-being of the state and the people.

Painting and sculpture, meanwhile, were used as propagandistic tools to further religious or political goals. The eight-foot, snake-headed statue of the Aztec goddess Coatlicue must have inspired awe and fear in all who saw this image; it was portrayed wearing a necklace made from the body parts of sacrificed mortals. In a somewhat similar vein, Spanish painters like El Greco were encouraged by the Catholic Church to make vivid depictions of Christ, including His suffering, so that people could relate more readily and more emotionally with their God. Ottoman calligraphers, meanwhile, turned the Qur'an (Koran) into a work of art.

While the arts are thus similar in their intimate connection with the world, different cultures employ different arts in different ways. For example, while dance was not generally used in religious worship in Europe, dance was almost exclusively sacred in the Americas. Artistic media could also differ dramatically. Most fine painting in Europe was done on canvas in the 15th and 16th centuries, while painting in Mesoamerica and South America was principally applied directly to walls and vases. Similarly, fine jade carving was plentiful in the Americas, but very rare in Europe. The entries that follow will focus on the arts most important to the daily life of the cultures. Thus in Europe, most people regularly sang and danced, while only the fairly wealthy had access to fine paintings and sculpture, since museums had not yet come into existence (though churches and civic sculpture gave some exposure to these arts); in Mesoamerica and South America, unfortunately, little is known about the native traditions of song and dance—sculpture and other material arts survived the Spanish conquest much better. Nonetheless, an urban Native American may indeed have had more daily contact with the jade sculptures of the marketplace and the monumental statues of the deities than with troops of dancers.

European music and dance can be roughly divided into two large categories: popular and aristocratic. While these two traditions overlapped somewhat and influenced each other, they differed substantially with regard to the instruments employed or the liveliness of the action. The instrument perhaps most associated with popular music is the bagpipe. Although most Americans think of Scotland or Ireland today when they think of the bagpipe, this instrument was popular throughout western Europe in the 15th and 16th century, and is still played in several parts of France and Italy; *zampognari* (Italian bagpipe players) still come down into Rome from the surrounding hills during Christmastime and enliven the city with their playing. Today, as in the Renaissance, the bagpipes are associated especially with rural folk. Amongst the aristocrats, mellower sounding instruments with a greater range, such as the lute or the viol, were more popular. Some instruments, such as the violin, gradually came to be used in different ways, depending upon the audience. Thus, the violin today can be used to play classical music, fast-moving Irish reels, or the quick, sawing tunes of country music. Dance, likewise, could range from the more slow and graceful aristocratic allemande, to the quick-tempoed, and ultimately banned for obscenity, saraband.

One final European art form that developed significantly during the Renaissance, especially in England and Spain, was drama. At the start of the 15th century, drama generally consisted of moral tales featuring allegorical characters such as Mankind and Good Works. By the end of the 16th century, there were permanent theaters that enjoyed large crowds and that performed plays about a wide range of subjects, from the lives of kings to bloody tales of revenge. In such drama, we can see the origins of the modern entertainment industries of television and motion pictures.

The major pieces of art that have survived from the Native American empires were created by highly trained and skilled craftsmen under the patronage of the king and other wealthy members of society. A Maya peasant family generally would not have the means to produce or purchase one of the delicately drawn multicolored vases associated with the king and wealthy merchants. Such a farming family, however, might be able to collect some small jade carvings, and would improvise their own more minor decoration on pots they made themselves.

Native American artists were believed to have a close relationship with the divine, indeed to share in the gods' ability to create. This connection between artist and god is seen most clearly in the Aztec culture. The Aztecs believed that human beings and all the created world were images in a book painted by the god Ometeotl, who would eventually erase them. The *tlacuilo* (a person skilled in Aztec picture writing) was thought to engage to some degree in this same activity of creation. According to an early Aztec poem about the *tlacuilo*, "God is in his heart. / He puts divinity into things."

One particularly distinctive Mesoamerican art form was feather working. The Maya and Aztecs elaborately decorated many objects with feathers, especially headdresses and shields. These feathers came from all over Central America and were frequently imported at great cost. One of the most prized was the feather of the quetzal, a bird that lived in the rain forests of Guatemala. Elaborate feather headdresses and shields were the exclusive right of noblemen, and were considered spectacular gifts; Moctecuhzoma gave a beautiful feathered headdress to the Spanish conquistador Cortés as a token of friendship when they first met. Unfortunately, friendship between the Spanish and Aztecs did not last long—art could only do so much.

~*Lawrence Morris*

ENGLAND

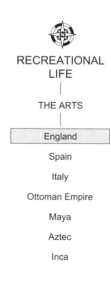

Leisure, no less than work, played an important part in the lives of the Renaissance English. The landowning classes were not obliged to work at all. Many of them did work quite hard, whether in government, estate management, or some other aristocratic calling; but all of them had plentiful opportunity to pursue leisure activities. Ordinary people had much harder schedules, laboring from dawn to dusk most days of the week, yet they eagerly pursued entertainments in such free time as was allowed them. For such people, the principal leisure time was after church on Sundays and holidays, although religious reformers increasingly objected to Sunday games as a violation of the Sabbath.

The Elizabethan period witnessed the first emergence of a genuine entertainment industry, especially in the theaters of London. At the beginning of Elizabeth's reign, theatrical performances took place in the courtyards of large inns. In 1576 London's first public theater was built outside the city limits, to escape the stringent regulations imposed by hostile city authorities. This theater was not at first successful, but by the end of the 1580s such theaters had become a permanent fixture in London.

The early theaters resembled the inn yards from which they had evolved. They were built around courtyards, with three-story galleries on three sides, facing a stage that projected out into the yard. People sat in the galleries, while the less privileged stood on the ground; a few ostentatious young gentlemen might sit on the stage itself. The plays were attended by all manner of people. Aristocrats were often to be found in the galleries, while standing room on the ground was certainly within the means of most people. General admission cost only a penny, the price of two quarts of beer—the price of going to the theater was analogous to going to the cinema today, although the low wages of working people meant they could not do it very often.

The plays had to be licensed, and authorities were always wary of the overcrowding, plague, and disorder associated with playgoing. In fact, laws against vagrants were often used against actors and other performers, who lived wandering lives, unattached to any employer or household. In response, theatrical companies placed themselves under the patronage of the great noblemen of England, which allowed players to avoid punishment by becoming, technically, servants of the lord.

There was a constant and insatiable demand for plays, and actors became very popular figures—the first stars. The plays' action combined humor and violence along with musical interludes and dazzling special effects; in these respects they were very similar to modern popular films. Playwrights were typically university graduates, and their lives were often short and turbulent. Christopher Marlowe took Elizabethan audiences by storm. His *Tamburlaine the Great,* full of violence, ambition, and horror, was a true blockbuster. William Shakespeare began his theatrical career late in Elizabeth's reign, in the early 1590s; Ben Jonson entered the scene later in the same decade.

In addition to the theaters in London, there were less formal settings for theatrical performances. The London companies occasionally brought their plays to the provinces, and there were plenty of minor performers, part-time folk players, puppeteers, acrobats, and other entertainers.

The other principal form of commercial public entertainment was literature. Sixteenth-century presses churned out all manner of texts: technical works, political and religious tracts (some of which were considered highly seditious by the authorities, who punished the authors severely if they were caught), ballads, almanacs, histories, and even news reports. These texts varied in format from lavish volumes richly

SELLENGER'S ROUND

(The Beginning of the World)

This dance is first mentioned in 1593 but was probably popular for some time before that; the melody is recorded in sixteenth-century collections. Any number of couples stand in a circle facing inwards, with each man on his partner's left.

This tune was extremely popular during the 16th century. It sounds particularly good on a recorder.

illustrated with fine woodcuts or engravings—sometimes even colored by hand—down to cheap pamphlets and broadsides (single printed sheets) produced for the mass market and selling for just a penny. Reading was often a more public activity than it is today—people sometimes read aloud in groups. See the section called "Literature" in chapter 4, ("Intellectual Life") for more information on English literary activity.

If theater and literature were predominantly consumer entertainments, most other Renaissance pastimes involved people as producers as well as consumers. Perhaps the most prominent example is music. The people of the 15th and 16th centuries, like people today, enjoyed listening to music. Unlike people today, they had no access to recording technology: all music had to be performed live. To some degree, people made use of professional musicians to satisfy their desire for music. A wealthy householder might hire musicians to play during dinner, and major towns had official musicians known as waits who sometimes gave free public concerts—such as those that took place at the Royal Exchange in London after 7 P.M. on Sundays and holidays.

Musicians. Here a fiddler and a viol player are welcomed by a wealthy landowner. A feast can be seen going on in the background. Music frequently accompanied the dinner parties of the wealthy. From Charles Hindley, *The Roxburghe Ballads,* 1837–74.

For the most part, people made their own music. Laborers and craftsmen often sang while working; gentlefolk and respectable townspeople frequently sang part-songs or played consort music after a meal. The ability to hold one's own in a part-song or a round (known to the Elizabethans as a catch) was a basic social skill. In fact, musical literacy was expected in polite society, and well-bred people could often play or sing a piece on sight. Even those of Puritanical leanings who frowned on most forms of music found pleasure in singing psalms.

Favored instruments among the upper classes included the lute, the virginals (a keyboard instrument in which the strings are plucked rather than struck), the viol (resembling a modern viola or cello), and the recorder. Among common folk the bagpipe was popular, especially in the country; other common instruments were the fiddle and the pipe and tabor (a combination of a three-hole recorder, played with the left hand, and a drum, played with the right). Public music was most often performed on loud instruments such as the shawm (a powerful double reeded instrument) and sackbut (a simple trombone). In the countryside, the ringing of church bells was a popular form of entertainment.

Dancing was also a popular activity. It was considered a vital skill for an aristocrat (Queen Elizabeth was said to look favorably on a man who could dance well), but was equally important to ordinary people: it was not merely a pleasant diversion, but one of the best opportunities for interaction between unmarried people. The Puritan moralist Phillip Stubbes complained in his *Anatomy of Abuses,*

What clipping and culling, what kissing and bussing, what smooching and slavering one of another, what filthie groping and uncleane handling is not practised in those dancings?

The preferred type of dancing varied between social classes. Those of social pretensions favored the courtly dances imported from the Continent, especially Italy.

These dances were mostly performed by couples, sometimes by a set of two couples; they often involved intricate and subtle footwork. Ordinary people were more likely to do the traditional country dances of England, which were danced by couples in round, square, or rectangular sets, and were much simpler in form and footwork. The division was not absolute: ordinary people sometimes danced *almains*, which were originally a courtly dance from France, while Elizabeth herself encouraged the cultivation of country dances among the aristocracy. In addition to social dances, there were performance and ritual dances. Foremost among these was morris dancing, characterized by the wearing of bells, and often performed as a part of summer festivals (Singman, 149–53).

To read about the arts in Chaucer's England, see the Europe entry in the section "Entertainment" in chapter 7 ("Recreational Life") in volume 2 of this series; for 18th-century England, see the entry on England in the section "Arts and Hobbies" in chapter 7 ("Recreational Life") in volume 4 of this series; for Victorian England, see the Victorian England entries in the sections "Music" and "Leisure Time" in chapter 7 ("Recreational Life") in volume 5 of this series.

FOR MORE INFORMATION

Cunningham, J. *Dancing in the Inns of Court.* London: Jordan, 1965.

Greenberg, N., W. H. Auden, and C. Kallman. *An Elizabethan Song Book.* London: Faber and Faber, 1957.

Singman, J. L. *Daily Life in Elizabethan England.* Westport, Conn.: Greenwood, 1995.

Vale, M. *The Gentleman's Recreations: Accomplishments and Pastimes of the English Gentleman, 1580–1630.* Cambridge: Brewer, 1977.

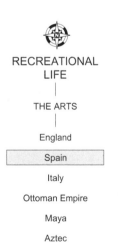

RECREATIONAL
LIFE
|
THE ARTS
|
England

Spain

Italy

Ottoman Empire

Maya

Aztec

Inca

SPAIN

In Renaissance Spain, painters and sculptors fought for recognition, since most of society viewed them as mere artisans and they were subject to rules laid down by their guilds and set by clients who were particular about what they wanted. While great painters of the period were only names to the common people, the grandees and the wealthy merchants, along with the church, who employed their services were often on intimate terms with them. The Roman Catholic Church was a highly influential patron, and its Counter Reformation, to combat the spread of Protestantism, demanded emotional, realistic, and dramatic art as a means of preserving the faith. Intense spirituality was often present in works of Spanish art, which included scenes of ecstasies, martyrdom, or miraculous apparitions. In 1586, El Greco (the Greek), born on the island of Crete, whose real name was Domenikos Theotokopoulos, painted his masterpiece, *The Burial of Count Orgaz* for the Church of Santo Tomé in Toledo. The painting portrays a 14th-century nobleman laid in his grave by Saints Stephen and Augustine. Above, the count's soul rises to a heaven densely populated with angels, saints, and contemporary political figures.

The wealthy aristocracy of Castile and Aragón had their own resident musicians who performed at festive events. When soft music was required at weddings, string players often performed. In contrast, bagpipes were commonly used to vigorously celebrate the birth of a child. Other instruments included drums, trumpets, tambourines, and woodwind.

Members of the royal family were often trained in music. The *vihuela* (Spanish guitar) was a favorite instrument of Isabella and her son Juan. The *vihuela* was considered indispensable as an accompaniment to songs and dances and was employed as much by the general populace as it was by the nobility. This practical instrument was easily portable and used inside or outdoors. There were several different kinds in use throughout the period with a varying number of strings, usually plucked with the fingers although a plectrum was sometimes used. Seville was the first center of instrument making, as it was for the publication of printed music.

El Greco, Master of Spanish Painting. In this masterpiece, painted in 1586, the soul of Count Orgasz appears as a child-shaped object being led up to heaven by an angel. El Greco, *The Burial of Count Orgasz.* © Giraudon/Art Resource, NY.

One of the most distinguished of the poet-musicians during the reign of the Catholic kings was the priest Juan del Encina, who composed some of the best poetry and music of the 15th century. During the closing decades of the 15th century and the beginning of the 16th, the *cancioneros* (songs) were written. Their themes concerned chivalry, politics, history, religion, love, and humor and were composed for three or four voices. Those concerning rustic life were known as *villancicos*, in which the music followed closely the form of the verse, enhancing and emphasizing the meaning of the words. They were usually accompanied by a dance. The *villancico* was to Spain what the madrigal was to the rest of Europe.

Next to the *villancico*, the ballad was the most widely used song form of the time. It was originally derived from earlier versified epic tales of chivalry. Ballads recounted the adventures of all manner of people and were enormously popular with all classes of society. The short epic-lyric poetry represented the traditional spirit of Spain and was originally intended to be sung to the accompaniment of a single instrument such as the guitar. Simple, direct, and highly condensed, the ballads dealt with the Reconquest, the heroic deeds of the Cid, treachery and heroism, and the attributes of beautiful women.

Some ballads dealt with peasant life. A ballad concerning the *Mesta* (the sheep migration) went:

Ya se van los pastores
Ya se van marchando
Más de quatro Zagales
Quedan llorando

Ya se van los pastores
a la Extremadura;
ya se queda la sierra
triste y oscura

Now the shepherds are going
Now they are going away
More than four women
Remain weeping

Now the shepherds are going
to Extremadura
the hills remain
sad and dark.

Dancing amounted to a national passion. The aristocrats enjoyed the *paván*, a 16th-century court dance of Italian origin, which consisted of a majestic procession performed by a column of couples in ceremonial dress accompanied by woodwind instruments. It went out of fashion near the end of the century.

The 16th- and 17th-century courtly dance, the *allemande*, of German origin, consisted of gliding steps and also involved a line of couples (in moderate 2/4 or 4/4 time). In certain processions, professional dancers performed various kinds of allegorical ballet and sometimes went into the churches and performed before the high altar.

Popular dancing among the lower classes was very different from the measured and formal steps of the aristocracy. In villages and city streets, dancing was vigorous and even frenzied, executed to the strumming of guitars, to the sound of tambourines and the snapping of fingers. (Castanets began to make their appearance in Spain in the 17th century.) The notorious but popular saraband was banned in 1583 for its suggestive movements and obscene lyrics sung to its rhythms.

Two dances for which Spain is now famous, the bolero and the flamenco, had not yet come into existence in the 16th century. The bolero, now the national dance of Spain, involved abrupt turns and stamping feet in syncopated rhythm. The dancers, solo or in couples, were accompanied by a guitar, and the performers sometimes sang and used castanets. The bolero came into being in the late 18th century. Similarly, the intense and emotional Gypsy song and dance known as flamenco was just beginning to make an appearance at the end of the 18th century (Anderson, 205–11).

FOR MORE INFORMATION

Anderson, J. M. *Daily Life in the Spanish Inquisition*. Westport, Conn.: Greenwood, 2002.

Kamen, H. *The Spanish Inquisition: An Historical Revision*. London: Weidenfeld and Nicolson, 1998.

Livermore, A. *A Short History of Spanish Music*. London: Duckworth, 1972.

Starkie, W. *Spain: A Musician's Journey through Time and Space*. Geneva: Edisli, Editions Rene Kister, 1958.

RECREATIONAL
LIFE
|
THE ARTS
|
England

Spain

Italy

Ottoman Empire

Maya

Aztec

Inca

ITALY

Renaissance people produced and consumed music prodigiously. Many slipped readily between performing and listening. The streets were full of song. Some artisans, if we can believe novelle, sang Dante's poetry while working. Idlers in the evening sat on steps, picking on the lute-like stringed *chitarra*. Gypsies played in search of coin. Revelers, on a shaming expedition, attacked their victims with a nocturnal serenade of insult songs, strumming and caterwauling below the windows. Groups too had their street music: soldiers marched to drums and trumpets; clergy and devout laity processed to psalms and *laudes*, songs of praise to God. Not only religious liturgy, but secular events—pageants, jousts, and banquets—came with music. For courts, composers developed new polyphonic musical forms, combining multiple voices and instruments in motets and madrigals. Performers, such as Laura Peverara and the women singers at Ferrara, helped shape these innovations. Many Italians studied with music masters to learn to play the clavichord, a protoharpsichord, and other instruments and to sing sophisticated harmonies to amuse themselves and friends.

One job of music was to animate the dance, a pastime central to Renaissance festivity, fun for both participants and spectators. At court and elsewhere, dance marked special occasions. Weddings, May Day, and Carnival were prime occasions. Jews danced for Purim, their early spring holiday, much like Carnival, full of wine, masks, and mischief. The rather formal dances of the court we know fairly well from paintings, written accounts of celebrations, and manuals by dancing masters. Elite dance both fed off and fed a vital popular tradition, one we can see far less well. At its most flamboyant, court dance produced great allegorical or mythological pageants, splendid with costumes and stage machinery, where the prince inevitably danced Hercules or Zeus, while the squires and maids-in-waiting played mere centaurs, nymphs, and shepherdesses. Other court performances featured couples, who took turns showing off their steps. On less formal occasions, sometimes in the women's quarters, courtiers danced for their own delight.

Renaissance dance, in its rhythms and movements, was unlike modern. On the beat, dancers rose, not fell. They held their upper bodies gracefully upright, keeping their hands mostly low. The lively movement was in the legs, where complicated steps, kicks, hops, and stamps showed style and virtuosity. Improvisation was prized. Men, in their hose and short tunics, had more room—and encouragement—to show off. Images of dancing usually show them kicking merrily, while their female partners, demure in long gowns, lift a hem to reveal not feet, but a fancy undergown. Though encumbered by skirts and proprieties, women dancers were still much admired for skill and elegance. Sometimes a girl soloed with her teacher to entertain the court. Images also often feature women dancing in circles, holding hands. The elite danced to small bands of a drum, pipes, and several shawms (like oboes); peasants often resorted to bagpipes. Tempos varied from the slow *bassa dansa* to the quick *saltarello* and *piva*.

Choreography was richly varied. Group dances shared much with modern country or square dancing, forms descended from Renaissance court dance. For example, couples held one another by the hand, waist, or shoulder; in facing rows or circles, they reverenced or honored one another and moved through symmetrical patterns. While many dances enacted courtship, only a few featured close embraces. Some dances were games, and some for men mimed combat. Dancing masters recorded, invented, and published steps, carrying court forms far and wide. Their skills were in great demand; dance figured in the curriculum of schools for nobles and aspiring bourgeois, for whom good footwork was a social grace. Masters even gave lessons in villages. Commoners, schooled or self-taught, danced for their own pleasure, but sometimes also entertained the public. One Roman carnival company, led by a stocking maker and including a weaver, a slipper maker, a saddler, and a shoemaker, turns up practicing their *moresca* in a cardinal's garden before performing in the city (Cohen and Cohen, 282–84).

FOR MORE INFORMATION

Cohen, E. S., and T. V. Cohen. *Daily Life in Renaissance Italy*. Westport, Conn.: Greenwood, 2001.

Sutton, J., ed. "Rules for Dancing." In *Nobilità di Dame*. *Fabritio Caroso*. New York: Oxford University Press.

RECREATIONAL
LIFE

THE ARTS

England

Spain

Italy

Ottoman Empire

Maya

Aztec

Inca

OTTOMAN EMPIRE

The Ottoman Empire at its height produced a vibrant artistic culture in the Islamic tradition. Mosques formed important centers of religious and community life, from the capital of Istanbul to smaller provincial towns throughout the empire. The Qur'an (Koran) and other texts became visual art through their calligraphy, gilding, and illustrations. Craftsmen created forms of decoration such as the Iznik tile to adorn elite homes and other buildings. Finally, music and other types of performance, influenced by both Sufi religious ritual and regional folk traditions, entertained people of all classes.

Most Muslim religious scholars in the Ottoman Empire believed that Islamic law forbade the representation of living things. Thus, traditional Islamic art came to display a number of unique qualities, as devout Muslims strove to express their religious sensibilities along with their artistic visions. Geometric designs made of simple line patterns or vegetal forms adorned everything from major monuments to small household items. Words themselves became artwork in the manner in which people formally recited the Qur'an and in the elaborate calligraphy with which they were written.

Although a mosque is simply any space dedicated to the worship of God, over time they had come to have a number of distinct features, which became the basis for Islamic architecture. Traditionally, mosques consisted of a series of prayer halls around a central courtyard. During the Ottoman period, architects added a dome and vaulted room with one side open to the court, features which spread to other important buildings such as tombs and *medreses* (schools). During the 15th and 16th centuries, Ottoman mosques featured one main dome supported by a half dome on the side facing Mecca. Many mosques, as well as other buildings, were decorated with tiles from the Anatolian city of Iznik. These ceramic tiles, which could be rectangular, triangular, or hexagonal, covered the walls and floors with sometimes intricate geometric patterns.

One can trace many of the most important developments in Ottoman architecture to the work of Sinan, who lived during the 16th century. The son of Greek Orthodox parents, the Ottomans took him as part of the *devshirme* (forced education program), and after being converted to Islam and receiving an education he became an architect within the sultan's household and produced 79 mosques, 34 palaces, 33 public baths, 19 tombs, 55 schools, 16 poorhouses, 12 caravansarais, 9 *medreses,* plus a number of other urban improvements such as fountains and hospitals. Among these works was Istanbul's Suleymaniye Mosque, the largest ever constructed in the Ottoman Empire, the central dome of which featured 32 openings through which light illuminated the interior.

Sinan also took advantage of a city's existing layout, considering how a building would appear against the silhouette as seen from different vantage points. Hence in the Selimye Mosque in Edrine, which features four minarets emphasizing the dome rising to the sky, a caravan coming along the road from Istanbul toward Europe would see only two of the minarets from a great distance.

Pages from a Qur'an illuminated in the mid-16th century. Sacred texts such as the Qur'an were particularly decorated in order to give honor to God. Calligraphy was a particularly prized art form since the Qur'an forbade pictures of material objects. © The Art Archive/Bodleian Library Oxford/The Bodleian Library.

Calligraphers ranked among the most important artists in the Ottoman Empire. Artists used calligraphy as decoration on everything from mosques and other monuments to household items such as bowls and plates. Calligraphic inscriptions included verses from the Qur'an and proverbs, as well as anything else deemed appropriate in a given context. Frequently books were published entirely in calligraphy as a means of enhancing their artistry. Calligraphers passed down their trade from master to disciple, and used different colors of handmade polished paper, as well as different colors of special ink. They also had special tools with which to sharpen their pens. One means of producing different styles of calligraphy was by varying the size of the pen tip. During the Ottoman centuries, many calligraphers worked with reed pen tips, which were curved instead of straight. During the late 15th century, Seyh Hamdullah developed a variation on this style based on his own artistic taste.

Ottoman books became works of art not only for their calligraphy, but for their decoration as well. *Tezhip* was the art of manuscript gilding. Usually the artist took gold leaf crushed into a powder and used a brush known as the hair pen to apply it to the paper. The use of other colors led to a variety of decorative motifs designed to highlight the text while creating an atmosphere appropriate to its meaning. In addition, miniature paintings among the pages of a text served as illustrations of important incidents. Because of people's religious concerns about painting humans, artists portrayed Muhammad with fire or a veil covering his face. Using these means, artists produced elaborate books coveted as much for display as for their contents.

People in the Ottoman Empire also expressed themselves through the performing arts. Musicians entertained all classes of society, and played an important part in some Sufi rituals. *Meddah* was the art of performative storytelling—practitioners would tell a story not simply through words, but also through using various objects to make noise, such as a walking stick, and techniques, such as a handkerchief, to alter their voices to represent different characters. Other types of dramatic performance were the *karagoz*, or shadow play, the *ortaoyunu*, or a play performed on a definite topic but without a fixed text, and the *kukla*, or puppet show.

People in the Ottoman Empire thus took part in a rich artistic culture expressed in a variety of ways. The mosques in which people prayed stemmed from an old tradition of Islamic architecture, one which in some cases came to involve even the total outline of the cities in which they lived. Works of literature became expressions of visual art in their miniature paintings and brightly colored illumination. In the performing arts, both cities and villages were the scenes of different musical and dramatic performances. In all of these ways, the traditions and values of the society were passed down in a pleasurable manner that has left monuments to this very day.

To read about the arts in Medieval Islam, see the Islam entries in the sections "Music and Dance" and "Entertainment" in chapter 7 ("Recreational Life") in volume 2 of this series.

~*Brian Ulrich*

FOR MORE INFORMATION

Cicek, K., ed. *The Great Ottoman-Turkish Civilisation 4: Culture and Arts*. Ankara: Yeni Turkiye, 2000.

Irwin, R. *Islamic Art in Context*. New York: Harry N. Abrams, 1997.

RECREATIONAL
LIFE
|
THE ARTS
|
England

Spain

Italy

Ottoman Empire

Maya

Aztec

Inca

MAYA

The ancient Maya were heavily involved in the arts. In addition to singing and dancing, which were often parts of festivals, the Maya were interested in several forms of sculpting and painting. This entry will focus on these plastic (tangible) arts.

The Maya carved in both stone and wood. Only a few wooden examples have survived, so most of the sculpture that remains today is of stone. Much surviving Maya sculpture is of limestone, the most available resource. Sandstone was used at a few sites, including Quirigua, and a volcanic tuff was used at Copan. Limestone is relatively soft so it is easy to quarry and carve, but it hardens over time with exposure to the air. Quarrying limestone blocks involved cutting along their sides and ends, then prying them loose from the bedrock. They were moved by water (on rafts) and overland (on log rollers) by laborers. Maya sculptors were specialists and artists. They used tools of harder stone, along with wooden mallets and wedges, to work the stone. Large chisels and hammer stones were used to quarry and roughly dress the stone, and the final shaping was done by chisels. For the actual carving, Maya sculptors used small chisels two to six inches in length and then finished the stone by abrasion and painting.

Maya sculpture covered all the exposed stone surface, leaving little free space. Carving ranged from low to high relief. Motifs usually combined natural forms (human and animal) and supernatural symbolism. The natural forms are more recognizable to modern eyes, whereas the supernatural elements are less familiar. It is likely, however, that the distinctions we see between natural and supernatural forms did not have the same meaning to the Maya, given what we know about Maya religion.

Indeed, Maya buildings and sculpture were imbued with deep and complex meanings. Monuments were also imbued with supernatural qualities. The Maya named stelae stone trees, perhaps because the earliest monuments were carved from trees. Altars were called throne stones, indicating that the flat stones were not altars but the seats used by kings during public ceremonies.

The Maya also fashioned ornaments from jade, a very hard semiprecious stone. It was the most precious substance known to the Maya, who considered it sacred because its *yax* (blue-green) color symbolized the abodes of the gods: the sky and the watery underworld (*yax* also means precious and first). Jade accompanied the dead into Xibalba (the underworld)—even the most humble Maya burial often has a simple jade bead placed in the mouth. Jade was obtained from outcrops, boulders, and waterworn pebbles in the streams of the Middle Motagua Valley of Guatemala, and probably other areas as well. Maya jades are usually made from jadeite, which differs in chemical composition from Chinese jade, or nephrite. It is slightly harder and less translucent than nephrite. The colors of jadeite may be mottled, usually dark green to light blue-green, or gray-green. Sometimes jadeite is nearly black or almost white.

Because it is such a hard stone, jade working was a specialized skill. Some jade objects were fashioned from naturally shaped cobbles. Otherwise jade was cut into pieces used for mosaics, pendants, plaques, and similar objects. Cut marks on a waterworn boulder of solid jade, weighing some 200 pounds, show that many pieces were sawed from it before it was ceremonially cached under a platform at Kaminaljuyu, where it was found by archaeologists. To cut jade, tough cords, embedded with fine stone abrasives, were drawn back and forth over it and continuously rinsed with water. Jade was perforated with drills of bone or hardwood, again using abrasives and water as the cutting agents. After the shaping and drilling was complete (probably done by an apprentice), a master artisan carved the delicate portraits and other scenes found on the finest examples. The Maya also carved other, softer green stones not easily distinguished from jadeite.

There are many notable examples of Maya jade work, although far too many have been found by looters rather than archaeologists. Perhaps the most famous is the Leyden Plaque, with a portrait incision of a Maya king from Tikal and text that dates back to 320 C.E. A carved jade head found at Chichen Itza was originally from Piedras Negras, because the historical date it presents (equivalent to 674 C.E.) pertains to the royal succession of that Usumacinta city. The largest Maya jadeite sculpture was discovered in a tomb at Altun Ha, Belize. It is carved in the round and portrays the Maya sun god, Kinich Ahau.

The Maya used brightly colored paints to decorate buildings and monuments. Specialists did this finishing work, and skilled artists created the most intricate painted decorations and murals. Red was the most common color for buildings and carved monuments. Several shades of dark red were made from hematite, an oxide of iron found throughout the Maya area. A brighter red was made from a rarer substance, mercuric sulfide (cinnabar). Yellows could be made from hematite. Blues and greens were also important, usually derived from clays and other minerals. Carbon-based black was used for outlining and other details.

Although the multicolored decorations on monuments and buildings were visible to all, the painted decorations inside most buildings were intended only for the elite residents and were never seen by commoners. The murals at Bonampak are the most spectacular example. Bonampak is significant because it is so unique; most other buildings have long since lost their painted decorations. In most cases only traces of the original paint remain on buildings and some monuments. Painting was also used on portable objects such as ceramics and in illustrating books. The pigments were applied with a variety of brushes. Some were as fine as a single hair; coarser brushes filled in backgrounds and broad spaces.

In Yucatán, wall paintings have been found at Chichen Itza, Tancah, Tulum, and several other sites. The best known are frescos from the Temple of the Warriors, the Temple of the Jaguars, and the Monjas at Chichen Itza. These are of a cosmopolitan Mesoamerican style, in keeping with their probable Putun Maya heritage. There are two scenes of human sacrifice and another two of attacks on a village. In contrast, a tranquil coastal village scene from the Temple of the Warriors shows a temple with a feathered serpent rising from its inner chamber. People go about their daily tasks among the thatched houses interspersed with trees; the sea swarms with a variety of marine life, and on its surface are fishermen in canoes.

Most everyday pottery was made in households. Women in many farming families produced vessels for domestic needs; any excess was probably exchanged in markets for other goods. Households that did not make their own pottery exchanged other goods for the vessels needed for cooking, storage, and other uses. In time some households began to specialize in pottery forms or types that were in greater demand;

Polychrome Vase. King Ah Cacau is shown here sitting on his throne. This vessel was found inside the king's tomb. © University of Pennsylvania Museum.

they produced pottery more for external distribution than for local household use. Such specialized production may have occurred in households where pottery making was the primary economic activity, with one or more family members as artisans. In these households farming probably became secondary or ceased. Vessels were produced for artists who decorated them with intricately painted scenes that mark the finest Maya polychromes. A few kinds of pottery were made in more specialized facilities, often using pottery molds and other mass-production methods.

By these means the Maya developed a remarkable ceramic tradition, one of the most varied and diverse in the world. They produced a great variety of pottery types, forms, and decorative techniques over a span of some 3,500 years. Among their outstanding achievements are lustrous, polished monochromes (red, orange, brown, and black), elaborate modeling, mass-produced mold-made vessels, including the only glazed wares in the Americas, and beautiful polychromes, including the famous portrait vases of the Late Classic period.

Polychrome decoration is a hallmark of Middle Maya Civilization. The tradition of nonfired polychrome painting (or stuccoed vessels) had its origins almost a thousand years earlier but reached its peak with the multicolored stuccoed vessels of the Early Classic era. The more durable polychrome painting that was fired onto vessels was also developed by this time (these are typically red and black painted designs on an orange or cream base). By the Late Classic era the art of fired polychrome pottery reached its peak, with skillfully and delicately rendered painted scenes. Motifs include both naturalistic and geometric designs, glyphic texts, and portraits of gods, kings, and their entourages. The most famous examples come from the southern lowlands, but other centers for this art were in the northern Maya highlands and along the southeastern periphery. Unfortunately, far more examples of these beautiful vases have been looted and sold to private collections than have been excavated and documented by archaeologists.

Many finely painted vessels have been excavated from burials and tombs at many lowland sites. The tombs of Ah Cacau and other kings of Tikal contained a variety of polychrome vessels, including ones that portray the kings receiving tribute, conducting rituals, and participating in similar royal activities. The scenes on several famous polychrome vessels from the adjacent northern Maya highlands depict elite merchants rather than kings.

Maya music and dance was generally associated with religious worship and was not a secular pastime. Maya music was dominated by percussion instruments: wooden drums, two-toned *tunkul* drums (made from hollowed-out logs), turtle-shell drums, bone raspers, and gourd rattles. Wind instruments included trumpets made from conch shells, and whistles, ocarinas, and flutes made from fired clay or wood. We can assume that music was believed to be pleasing to the gods and thus facilitated the success of religious ceremonies. Music undoubtedly (1) accompanied the impressive processions of priests that opened most public ceremonies, (2) punctuated the steps in each important ritual, and (3) enhanced the general celebration that closed most ceremonies. With regard to dancing, there were separate dances for men and women, and only rarely did they dance together. Many dances required great skill and would have been performed by professional dancers (Sharer, 166, 171–73, 200–208).

FOR MORE INFORMATION

Kubler, G. *The Art and Architecture of Ancient America: The Mexican, Maya, and Andean Peoples*. Baltimore: Pelican History of Art, 1962.

Miller, M. E. *The Art of Mesoamerica from Olmec to Aztec*. New York: Thames and Hudson, 1986.

Osborne, L. de Jongh. *Indian Crafts of Guatemala and El Salvador*. Norman: University of Oklahoma Press, 1965.

Sharer, R. J. *Daily Life in Maya Civilization*. Westport, Conn.: Greenwood, 1996.

AZTEC

For the Aztecs, art was a temporary expression, a technique to (1) open the artist and the audience to divine truth, (2) imitate and approximate the cosmic beauty and pattern of the gods, and (3) communicate and celebrate the gods so that life on

earth would be better for humankind. This art was sometimes used in trade and was also part of domestic and political life, royal display, and ritual sacrifice. But the power of the best art came from its ability to reflect and communicate with gods. In what follows we will study the *tlacuilo* (the painter of the red and black), the sculptor, and the feather worker.

The *tlacuilo*, that is, a person skilled in the pictorial writing system of the Aztecs, shared a gift in common with the gods, as seen in the following poem.

With flowers you write,
Giver of Life;
With songs you give color,
With songs you shade
those who live here on the earth.
Later You will erase eagles and tigers,
We live only in Your book of paintings,
here, on the earth. (León-Portilla, *Native Mesomerican Spirituality*, 244)

This poem depicts Ometeotl, the Dual God, as a writer, a singer, and a painter. The Giver of Life is the divine artist who sings and paints human life into existence in his/her divine book. The message is also that those who live here on the earth are perishable, existing for only a short time. The world is created by the flowers and songs of the gods. As we shall see, humans created their own flowers and songs as ways of imitating the divine and communicating with the gods. If gods painted the world in a book, then the human painter, the *tlacuilo*, "he who paints in the red and black ink," was the artist closest to the gods. We see this tie between painting and the gods in this poem about the ideal painter:

The good painter is a Toltec, an artist:
he creates with red and black ink,
with black water. . . .
The good painter is wise,
God is in his heart.
He puts divinity into things;
he converses with his own heart.
He knows the colors, he applies them and shades them;
he draws feet and faces,
he puts in the shadows, he achieves perfection.
He paints the colors of all the flowers,
as if he were a Toltec. (León-Portilla, *Aztec Thought*, 172–73)

These painters, trained in the priestly schools, were profound stores of knowledge about the mythology, genealogy, and history of the community. The pictorial books of the Aztecs recorded calendars, festivals, mythology, history, conduct of wars, omens, astronomy, coronation ceremonies, and many other aspects of social life. But all these events and patterns were understood to be infused with divine purpose and meaning. To be a true painter, a person had to develop an inward sense of feeling and understanding about the nature and intention of the god. This was called "conversing with one's heart," which resulted in the painter becoming a *yolteotl*, or "a heart rooted in god." A person who had taken a god into his or her heart could then transfer the images and purpose of the divine reality into the paintings, codices, and murals that were so important to the Aztecs.

We gain a sense of the creative power of these artists when we gaze at images from the surviving codices and vase paintings. The color, fluidity of line, composition of pages, and the frozen drama of the stories painted on the pages are inspirational even to those who do not understand well the messages being conveyed. On the one hand, they look something like our cartoons, while on the other, they dazzle us with combinations of color and drama. The surviving books are full of images of gods, goddesses, sacred hills, calendar signs, rituals, and the cosmos. We see the Tlaloc gods dwelling in heaven, the four quarters of the universe balanced around a warrior god, rituals of sacrifice, and brilliant calendar signs associated with gods, all with elaborate and symbolic costumes. The bright procession of garments decorating the gestures, gazes, and postures of gods, goddesses, rulers, and animals is full of signs and meanings that are only now becoming clearer to scholars, who for centuries have tried to decipher these scenes. The problem, in part, goes back to the phrase "He puts divinity into things." It is very difficult for 20th-century people to grasp the Aztec concept of divinity or to understand how an artist puts gods, magic, and spirit into paint, wood, stone, feathers, and other kinds of artistic work.

Mexica sculptors were guided by certain principles of carving that required a magical act of illuminating, for those who had eyes to see, the sacred forces hidden in nature: "What is carved should be like the original, and have life, for whatever may be the subject which is to be made, the form of it should resemble the original and the life of the original. . . . Take great care to penetrate what the animal you wish to imitate is like, and how its character and appearance can best be shown" (Clendinnen, 226). In fact, Aztec stonework, both monumental and miniature, reveals that the natural world of squash, grasshoppers, snakes, butterflies, monkeys, frogs, fleas, and birds was observed in minute detail, and that such objects were viewed as passageways for the sacred forces of the gods into the world. The representations of these animals and insects appear in obsidian, basalt, shells, amaranth dough, and other natural mediums. Sometimes there are impressive combinations of the natural and the supernatural, as in the two magnificent stone images known to us as the Calendar Stone and the statue of Coatlicue (Lady of the Serpent Skirt).

The Aztec artists were as fascinated with perishable, vulnerable natural elements as they were with permanent, invulnerable stones. Nowhere is this commitment to the fragile more evident than in the florid feather work that adorned rulers, warriors, gods, and people at all levels of the Aztec empire.

The art of feather work was immediately evident to the Spaniards when they met the ruler Motecuhzoma Xocoyotzin in 1519. Not only was he wearing a magnificent headdress, but he gave one to Cortés, which today resides in the Museum für Volkerkunde in Vienna. This gift consisted of 500 green and gold quetzal tail plumes and blue and red feathers, fastened with gold

Monumental Statue of Coatlicue from the National Museum of Anthropology, Mexico City. This statue of Coatlicue (Lady of the Serpent Skirt) stands over 8 feet tall and must have dominated the space around it. The statue exhibits the emphasis upon duality and unity associated with many Aztec deities. For example, the head is at one and the same time a snake facing the audience, showing its fangs and sticking out its tongue, and also two snake heads seen from the side facing each other. Courtesy of Salvador Guil'liem Arroyo, INAH.

disks and clasps. The quetzal feathers originated in faraway Guatemala and had to be imported into the Basin of Mexico and brought to the royal market. The blue feathers came from what the Aztecs called the *xiuhtototl* (turquoise bird), which lived in the hot lowlands of the eastern and southern regions. Parrots and scarlet macaws provided the red feathers, all of which were tied together by maguey thread to a coarse-meshed fabric onto a wicker frame to appear and be enduring. The Aztecs were careful observers of birds, and we have a number of detailed accounts of how birds looked, flew, nested, ate, and sang. The transformation from the bird to the headdress or other objects depended on the skills of the feather worker, described as "accomplished, ingenious."

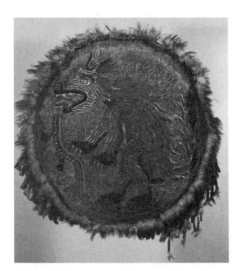

Feather working. Feather working was a popular art form throughout Mesoamerica and South America. The feather from the quetzal bird was highly prized. Here, feathers decorate a warrior's shield. © The Art Archive/Museum für Völkerkunde Vienna/Dagli Orti.

The feather worker was a craftsperson skilled in measurements, sensitive to the relations of color, light, and the texture of feathers, and no doubt trained in the theory of symbolism, that is, the overall meaning of colors, shadows, and arrangements of both. The feather workers depended on the scribes for help, because the designs of the feather devices of the rulers, especially for important ceremonial occasions and dances, showed evidence of their skill. One text says: "They who first drew [the pattern] were the scribes. When [the feather workers] had seen how it was designed, that it was well done, that the painting was sufficiently detailed, then on a *maguey* leaf they reinforced cotton; they strengthened it with glue" (Sahagún, vol. 9, 89). The feathers were not only valuable, but were understood to carry the power and beauty of the bird into the very object, whether a headdress or a shield. And it is significant that the Aztecs had a law forbidding the wearing of certain feather articles called the "Shadow of the Lords and Kings" unless the ruler granted permission. Feather work was a highly valued art, and many nobles took up the honorable career of feather worker. This work was considered a protection during hard times. One father instructs his sons and daughters to pay attention to "the art of feather working" so that in the time of "suffering, when hardship dominates, the artisanship will be a support, a buttress." Several feather shields have survived, indicating that in battle warriors were not only meant to appear intense and dangerous, but beautiful and florid (Carrasco, 161–79).

FOR MORE INFORMATION

Carrasco, D., with S. Sessions. *Daily Life of the Aztecs: People of the Sun and Earth*. Westport, Conn.: Greenwood, 1998.

Clendinnen, I. *Aztecs: An Interpretation*. Cambridge: Cambridge University Press, 1991.

León-Portilla, M. *Aztec Thought and Culture*. Norman: University of Oklahoma Press, 1963.

———, ed. and trans. *Native Mesoamerican Spirituality: Ancient Myths, Discourses, Stories, Doctrines, Hymns, Poems from the Aztec, Yucatec, Quiche-Maya and Other Sacred Traditions*. New York: Paulist, 1980.

Pasztory, E. *Aztec Art*. New York: Henry N. Abrams, 1983.

Sahagún, B. de. *Florentine Codex: General History of the Things of New Spain*. Ed. and trans. A.J.O. Anderson and C. E. Dibble. 13 vols. Santa Fe, N.M.: School of American Research and University of Utah, 1950–82.

INCA

The Incas did not have a special medium that could be defined as art in the way that modern paintings or sculptures are considered art. What art existed is found on pottery, wooden cups, and cloth. There can be little doubt that art took a back seat to function. Inca art did not attain the levels of beauty that are attributed to the earlier Moche or Nasca cultures, but it is well made and attractive. This is probably due in part to the Incas' practice of bringing the finest craftspeople from conquered regions to make their artwork for them.

A common criticism of Inca art is that it is repetitive and lacks imagination with regard to subject matter. The Incas used a relatively small number of decorative elements, especially triangles, feather patterns, and squares. Plants, flowers, llamas, pumas, and human figures were also used, although very often in a stylized and geometric manner. This is partly because Inca art was mass-produced and partly because the purpose of the art was to convey symbolic messages about the Incas' power. The variety of forms and color combinations is certainly less than in earlier societies.

Some aspects of Inca art have not survived for modern appreciation. There were reports that the walls of the Coricancha were sheathed in gold and that the Inca king had a garden consisting of gold and silver models of plants and animals. It is also likely that houses were plastered and painted. The probable medium of choice for artistic expression was cloth, little of which survived either the Spanish Conquest or the ravages of time.

One can find an aesthetic quality in Inca stoneworking, in the way that the massive supporting stones were fitted with their edges recessed. The play of light and shadows over walls constructed in this fashion is pleasing. Different styles were prominent at different times. Many of the fitted-stone buildings for which the Incas are famous were constructed by Pachacuti, and they reflect his personal perspective on the world; later kings had different architectural styles. This suggests that certain other artistic features associated with the Incas might be due to particular kings and their personal tastes.

Andean music today is enjoying wide popularity owing to its pleasing combination of instruments such as the Andean panpipe, harp, and guitar. The distinctive rhythms of the music, too, are very different from modern pop music. Yet it is uncertain how ancient this kind of music is. Certainly the guitar is post-Inca, having been introduced to the Andes by the Spaniards. But panpipes (made of pieces of cane cut to different lengths to produce different tones) have an ancient history in this area, so they may reflect a continuity of sorts between the past and present. It is not known if the music played on these instruments is as old as the instruments themselves.

Other instruments that the Incas likely used (known either through chroniclers' reports or archaeological specimens) include simple flutes, drums, seashell trumpets, tambourines, bells, and rattles. Music was apparently important in the entertainment of laborers who came to work for the Incas, in festivals, and in war. Musicians were trained to perform at the royal court and several flutes were played together to extend the range of the music. This flute was somewhat similar to the modern recorder. It was used for love songs and was the only instrument in general use throughout the Andes.

Dance was restricted to festivals or rituals; the modern idea of a dance as a purely social function did not exist. Sometimes dances were limited to men or women; sometimes both sexes were involved. As with dances at the royal courts of Europe during the 17th and 18th centuries, Inca dances were very formalized, with each participant essentially duplicating what the others did.

It is likely that there was little difference in recreational activities between conquered peoples and the Incas. If anything, conquered people had less leisure time for socializing and playing: the additional labor requirements of the Incas would have taken up much of their spare time. Even today, subsistence farmers work from morning to night and have little time for leisurely activities.

Information from Guaman Poma suggests that dancers from the provinces often wore very elaborate costumes and masks, but little else is known about these customs. The artistic activities of a conquered people, manifest in their ceramics and other objects, might have been distinctive enough to be recognized in different regions (Malpass, 87–88).

FOR MORE INFORMATION

Guaman Poma de Ayala, F. *El Primer Nueva Corónica y Buen Gobierno [1584–1615]*. Ed. John Murra and Rolena Adorno. Trans. Jorge Urioste. 3 vols. Mexico City: Siglo Ventiuno, 1980.
Kendall, A. *Everyday Life of the Incas*. New York: Putnam, 1973.
Malpass, M. A. *Daily Life in the Inca Empire*. Westport, Conn.: Greenwood, 1996.

RECREATIONAL LIFE: WEB SITES

http://www.ballgame.org/main.asp.
http://athena.english.vt.edu/~jmooney/renmats/drama.htm
http://renaissance.dm.net/compendium/45.html.
http://www.bodley.ox.ac.uk/dept/scwmss/wmss/medieval/mss/buchanan/e/003.a.htm

8

RELIGIOUS LIFE

RELIGIOUS LIFE
|
DEITIES
& DOCTRINES

PRIESTS & RITUALS

SACRED STORY:
BEGINNINGS & ENDINGS

The human world is made up of more than the material and social environments that surround us. Throughout history, people have left records of their recognition of and longing for something larger than themselves, and this desire to transcend daily life forms the basis for people's religious faith. Religions have two intertwined components—belief and rituals, and the latter derives from and preserves the former. Thus, through careful enactment of rituals, the faithful believe they can rise above the mundane realities of day-to-day life, and historians find the study of religious practice offers a window into people's spiritual beliefs.

Religious beliefs have served to help people make sense of the natural world— from its beauties to its disasters. For example, an ancient Egyptian pharaoh (Akhenaton) and a medieval Christian saint (Francis) both wrote magnificent poetry praising the blessings of this world. In addition, the Buddha and the Hebrew Scriptures' Book of Job both talk about the deep suffering in this life. In these ways, religion has always helped people make sense of the world that surrounds them.

At the same time, religious rituals serve the needs of society. The faithful reinforce their social ties by worshiping together, and sociologists of religion argue that religion is the symbolic worship of society itself. Sacred songs, dances, and feasts have always served to bind communities closer together, and in these ways the religious and secular lives of the people mingle. This intimate relationship between religious beliefs, rituals, and societies make the study of religious life a fruitful one. The complex nature of societies also yields complexities in religious beliefs and practices. Throughout history, we can follow the reforms and revolutions in religious ideas that have profoundly shaped our past.

Through the study of religious life, we can thus learn about how people viewed the natural and supernatural, how rituals organized people's daily lives, and how beliefs brought out the best (and the worst) in people. At the same time, we can see a glimpse of the deep longing in the human souls that has generated some of people's noblest thoughts.

In the following entries, we will look at deities, doctrines, rituals, and myths. All these fields are clearly interwoven. For example, most of our knowledge about the deities of various religions comes from their myths. Myths likewise are the source of many doctrines (religious teachings). Rituals in turn often derive from various doctrines. While interconnected, these aspects of religion still form cohesive categories and can be studied and described on their own.

The 15th and 16th centuries are particularly interesting with regard to religion. Great events were underway. The Protestant Reformation (see "Deities and Doctrines" below for more information) was underway, causing tremendous and sometimes bloody controversy. While the religious landscape of Europe was thus changing dramatically, Europeans were also meeting completely new religious traditions in the Americas. It is clear from the number of detailed accounts of Native American religion, left by Spanish Catholic priests, that the Spanish were very interested in the beliefs, rituals, and myths of the inhabitants of the Americas. These accounts were supposed to help in the process of converting the Native Americans to Christianity, but they also served other purposes. For example, similarities between Native American religion and Christianity were used as evidence that God had given some revelation, even if imperfect, to the Native Americans. Such evidence was used to defend the Americans from Spanish atrocities, though the conquistadors ultimately proved to be uninterested in defending the native population.

Finally, the human sacrifices in the Americas, and the many people who died for their religious beliefs in Europe, give testimony to a shared fundamental understanding that faith is ultimately worth more than life itself.

~*Joyce E. Salisbury and Lawrence Morris*

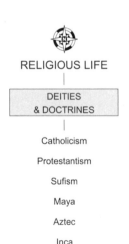

RELIGIOUS LIFE
|
DEITIES
& DOCTRINES
|
Catholicism

Protestantism

Sufism

Maya

Aztec

Inca

Deities and Doctrines

Belief in a god is a near universal trait among cultures around the world. From the mountains of Tibet to the rainforests of the Amazon, an amazing variety of different belief systems exist, but most of them share a belief in a god or some kind of supernatural being. Humankind seems to believe in the supernatural automatically.

There are many theories about why this belief is so universal. Some people claim that the widespread belief in a god is a sign that the supernatural is constantly calling to human beings, wanting to make itself known to them. Other people argue that belief in the supernatural stems from ignorance about the scientific rules that govern the universe—since premodern people were unable to understand the workings of the universe, they thought that some other being must be controlling everything and making it work. Other people follow Freud, who claimed that human beings create an imaginary father figure that will take care of them and give them comfort, because the human consciousness cannot face up to the harsh realities of the world. Still other people, like Marx, claim that systems of religious belief are mainly used simply to keep poor people happy with empty promises of heaven, while the wealthy dominate the resources of this world. Regardless of how religious beliefs developed, however, it is clear that most people believe in a god.

Belief in the supernatural is frequently divided into *polytheism* and *monotheism*. In polytheism, people believe that there are many different gods, while in monotheism, people believe that there is only one god. In polytheistic religions, such as the religions practiced by the Native Americans in Mesoamerica and South America, different gods are often linked with different aspects of the earth. For example, in Maya religion, Kichi Ahau was the god of the sun, while Chac was the rain god. If someone wanted rain to come to help the crops, he or she would pray to Chac. The sun god, however, was ultimately viewed as keeping the whole universe together, so it was particularly important to venerate Kichi Ahau and to provide the god with anything he might want. In monotheism, one god is responsible for everything. Christianity, Judaism, and Islam are all monotheistic religions, and all believe in the same God. Christians, however, believe that this one God consists of three persons: the Father, the Son, and the Holy Spirit, who are all distinct from one another and are all equally God, but are also all just one God. This teaching is called the Trinity, and is termed a mystery, since it is difficult to grasp how the Trinity functions—it may help to imagine an infinite ocean that is divided into three infinite sections.

Doctrine means official teaching, and has always played a large part in the Judaeo-Christian and Islamic traditions. Long before the birth of Christ, Jewish people enjoyed debating religious issues and highly valued correct belief. Disagreements could be fierce and sometimes bloody. Christianity continued this tradition. Different branches of Christianity, such as Catholic or Lutheran, had well-defined beliefs and a person was expected to hold all those beliefs. Those who didn't agree with the doctrine risked being thrown out of the church and possibly being executed. Similarly, not every Muslim shared the same beliefs, and there were many branches and movements of Islam, including Sufism, examined in this section. The Native American religions did not have such well-developed doctrines. There was no list of beliefs that a person was expected to hold. This lack of doctrine could result in great flexibility, and differences in belief. While Mesoamerican and South American religions did not have doctrine, they did have faith communities somewhat similar to the different denominations of Christianity found in Europe. These communities were not so much created by united belief as by locality; that is to say that all the people in one area worshipped the same deities. These deities were frequently the symbol of the collective identity of the people. For example, when the Aztec captured a city-state, they would destroy the temples and take the statues of the gods back to their own state, where they would be held with respect, but in captivity. This captivity of the enemy city's gods symbolized the captivity of the city-state itself.

One teaching common in many religions is the resurrection from the dead. The Aztecs, for example, believed that the Hero Twins had come back to life and had defeated the death gods. Christianity similarly believed that Jesus had risen from the dead and had made eternal life possible for others. There are similar stories about other people returning from the dead, such as Persephone among the ancient Greeks. One major difference between these accounts, however, is that the resurrection event in Christianity happened in historical times (i.e., when writing was widespread) and was witnessed by many people, while the other resurrection events discussed above are set in the far distant past. Some Christians believed that the resurrection stories among the Native Americans had been God's way of preparing them to hear the story of Jesus. Other people believe that humankind has a common fantasy about being able to live forever. Either way, the number of shared beliefs, such as god and life after death, among world cultures can be startling, but we should never lose sight of the very many differences.

~Lawrence Morris

RELIGIOUS LIFE

|

DEITIES
& DOCTRINES

|

Catholicism

Protestantism

Sufism

Maya

Aztec

Inca

CATHOLICISM (SPAIN, ITALY, ENGLAND)

The word catholic means universal. The idea that the church was Catholic meant first of all that its believers, wherever they were located geographically, were members of the same church. It also meant that everyone should believe the same things. The head of the Catholic Church was the Bishop of Rome, who, in consultation with theologians and high-ranking church officials, made decisions regarding correct belief and practice.

The Catholic Church, like all Christian churches, believed that Jesus, a Jewish carpenter from a remote town in Israel, was the son of God. This belief was based upon Jesus's controversial teachings and the many miracles he performed. The main source of information about Jesus's teachings and miracles was the New Testament, a collection of books by different authors that described Jesus's birth, ministry, death, and the religious movement that he left behind. The core beliefs of Christianity are bound up with the person and background of Jesus.

The writers of the New Testament believed that Jesus was the Christ, which means Anointed One, and is the Greek translation of the Hebrew-derived term Messiah. The Jewish nation was mostly expecting a Messiah that would free them from the Roman Empire, but Jesus preached that the Messiah would start a new spiritual, not political, kingdom. In his teaching, Christ focused attention on spiritual matters and away from physical appearances. For example, Christ taught that it was wrong not just to kill, but also to nourish anger against one's neighbor. Similarly, Jesus taught that the purity laws concerning food, which forbade certain foods such as pork and shellfish and commanded that other foods be prepared in very specific ways (foods prepared in that way are called kosher), were not as important as nurturing a pure soul, free from greed and hatred.

As a result of some of his teaching, and the growing number of people who viewed Jesus as the Messiah, Jesus came into conflict with the Jewish and secular authorities in Israel, and was sentenced to death by crucifixion. The death of Jesus threw his disciples into despair and they feared that they too would be hunted down by the authorities. Three days after the crucifixion, however, some of Christ's followers went to Jesus's tomb to pay respects to the body, and found the tomb empty, with the massive gravestone rolled away. They were amazed at this, and then had a series of visions or mystical encounters with an angel that said that Jesus had risen from the dead and was alive once more. Jesus appeared to the disciples many times after this, and some of those who hadn't believed the resurrection story, told at first by the visitors at the tomb, came to believe through these mystical encounters. Fifty days after the resurrection, which is celebrated as the feast of Pentecost today, Jesus ascended in glory to heaven, leaving behind the Holy Spirit to guide the Church, and promising to come in person once more.

As a result of all these events, the early Church came to interpret Christ's death as a kind of sacrifice. Sacrifice was an important part of Jewish religion, and was used to worship God and to seek forgiveness of sins. Christ's sacrifice was understood to be a kind of sin offering; through his death, humankind was granted forgiveness for their sins. All that was needed for salvation was belief and trust in Christ, which also entailed turning away from sin, living a charitable, truthful, and honest life, and participating in the sacraments (sacred rituals) established by Christ.

The above were the core beliefs of Christianity, but Jesus, the early Church, and later theologians had further defined aspects of their belief. With regard to God, it was believed that there was only one true God, though there were many lesser spiritual beings, such as angels and devils who could influence the world but who were all infinitely weaker and less important than God, even if they were more powerful than human beings. God himself was thought to have three persons: the Father, the Son (Jesus), and the Holy Spirit. The three persons together were often referred to as the Trinity. It was not clearly defined or understood how these three persons interacted within the one godhead.

While God was uncreated, angels and devils, and everything in the world for that matter, had been created by God. Devils were thought to be angels that had attempted to revolt against God and seize control of the universe. Their basic sin was pride, believing that they were better than everyone else: this sin is often called hubris today. All of creation was viewed as a kind of hierarchy. Below the several kinds of angels were human beings, and below human beings were animals, below whom were plants, and then inanimate objects.

Some human beings, who were believed to have lived particularly holy lives, were called saints (which means holy) and were paid particular reverence. It was believed that the saints were given special powers for good by God, and that these saints could wield this power both in life and in death. Many people traveled hundreds and sometimes thousands of miles to visit a living saint or the tomb of a dead saint. Tombs were often decorated with abandoned crutches and other tokens, giving witness to miraculous cures that had been received through the prayers of the saints. The reverence paid to saints was ultimately supposed to give glory to God, from whom their power came, but sometimes unlearned people treated the saints as miniature gods in their own right.

The Holy Trinity. The three persons in God (Father, Son, and Holy Spirit) are depicted in this painting. Christ, the Son, is shown with wounds from his crucifixion; the Father is portrayed as an older man with a bishop's hat; and the Holy Spirit is depicted in the form of a dove. © The Art Archive/Museo del Prado Madrid/Dagli Orti (A).

The structure of the church itself reflected the notion of heavenly hierarchy and had a well-defined line of command. At the top of the chain was the Bishop of Rome, called the pope. The pope was ultimately responsible for deciding any disagreements about belief. Advising and assisting the pope were a group of men called cardinals. These cardinals also elected the next pope when the current pope died. It was necessary for two-thirds of the cardinals to agree on the same candidate in order to elect a new pope, and this process could sometimes take weeks of deliberation. Waiting crowds would sometimes attempt to speed the process up by trying to cut off the food supply into the building where the cardinals were debating! Underneath the pope were bishops. The bishops were responsible for managing a particular diocese, which is a geographical area that includes several hundred churches. Below the bishops were the priests, who worked in one particular church or parish (small community based on a geographic area such as a village). There were many gradations, such as archbishops, within the hierarchy listed above, but the basic outline stands.

The lifestyle of a Christian could vary widely. Many people, particularly people who joined religious orders, such as the Franciscans and Dominicans, gave away all their possessions and pledged to lead a simple life of generosity and prayer. Other people, including many bishops and some priests, lived lives of considerable luxury and enjoyed a lifestyle comparable to that of a prince. While the life of poverty and contemplation was considered to be far superior, the princely life was not expressly forbidden.

To read about religion in Medieval Europe, see the Europe entries in the section "Religious Beliefs," "Monasticism," and "Religious Buildings" in chapter 8 ("Religious Life") in volume 2 of this series.

~Lawrence Morris

Snapshot

The Pater Noster

Most Catholics said some of their prayers in Latin. One of the most popular was the Lord's Prayer, also called Our Father or Pater Noster after the prayer's first words in English and Latin. Below is the text of the Latin prayer with its usual English translation.

Pater noster qui es in caelis sanctificetur nomen tuum.	Our Father who art in heaven hallowed be thy name.
Adveniat regnum tuum fiat voluntas tua sicut in caelo et in terra.	Thy kingdom come, thy will be done on earth as it is in heaven.
Panem nostrum cotidianum da nobis hodie, et dimitte nobis debita nostra sicut et nos dimittimus debitoribus nostris et ne inducas nos in temptationem sed libera nos a malo. Amen.	Give us this day our daily bread, and forgive us our trespasses, as we forgive those who have trespassed against us, and lead us not into temptation, but deliver us from evil. Amen.

RELIGIOUS LIFE

|

DEITIES
& DOCTRINES

|

Catholicism

Protestantism

Sufism

Maya

Aztec

Inca

FOR MORE INFORMATION

Catechism of the Catholic Church. Dublin: Veritas, 1994.

Johnson, K. *Why Do Catholics Do That? A Guide to the Teachings and Practices of the Catholic Church.* New York: Ballantine, 1995.

New Advent. <http://www.newadvent.org>.

PROTESTANTISM (ENGLAND)

Protestantism refers to a range of Christian churches that do not recognize the authority of the pope of the Catholic Church. The name Protestantism derives from

Religious Life | Deities and Doctrines

the protests that the various religious leaders made against the Catholic Church. As a well-organized movement, Protestantism dates to the Reformation, a period and movement of intense zealous religious debate that started in the 16th century. The Reform movement had many precursors, such as the Wycliffite movement in 14th- and 15th-century England, but none of these movements succeeded in creating long-lasting congregations independent of the Catholic Church.

The two men most associated with the Protestant Reformation are Martin Luther and John Calvin. Martin Luther was born in 1483 in Germany. Luther had stern parents, and Martin Luther became a monk in part to escape the stress of his domestic life. Luther was a serious and very engaged student, and wrestled particularly with the notion of guilt. Luther felt that humankind was heavily burdened with sin and he could not see how a person could possibly reach heaven as a result. Luther's career as a public reformer began in earnest in 1517, when he nailed the 95 Theses to the castle door that served as the announcement board of the university at Wittenberg. The 95 Theses argued against the current practice of indulgences, which were thought to lessen the divine punishment due sin. The selling of indulgences, in which people simply paid money for the indulgence instead of undertaking some form of prayer, was particularly hated by Luther and others. Many people view the 95 Theses as Luther's official break with the Catholic Church, though his separation occurred, in fact, more gradually.

The most distinctive teaching of Lutheranism, as the movement started by Luther came to be called, concerns how man is saved. Luther believed that human beings were incapable of any good; therefore, they could never deserve to go to heaven. Yet Luther did not believe that they all went to hell. Rather, he taught that God applied the merits of Jesus to sinful human beings, and that people were thus saved through Christ's goodness. To have Christ's merits applied to oneself, one simply had to believe and trust in Jesus. This doctrine is sometimes given the catchy phrase of "Salvation by faith alone." The phrase faith alone is meant to exclude good works. Since Luther believed that no one was capable of doing sufficient good works to merit salvation, they played no role in his scheme of salvation. It didn't matter if a person helped the poor—they would be damned to hell unless they believed in Christ. Similarly, a flagrant sinner could go to heaven if they believed in Christ.

While justification by faith alone was Luther's most important and influential teaching, Luther made many other changes to the Catholic faith. For example, Luther contradicted the doctrine of transubstantiation, which held that the substance, or underlying nature of the bread and wine, was changed into the body and blood of Christ during the Mass (the Christian celebration of Jesus's last supper with his disciples). Luther, instead, believed in consubstantiation, which meant that both the substance of the bread and wine and the substance of Christ's body and blood were truly present. In addition, Luther also believed in the sacrament of baptism. Luther did not believe that the other five sacraments of the Catholic Church (see the following section "Priests and Rituals") gave any supernatural benefit, but he did keep many of the rituals associated with the sacraments, such as confirmation, confession, and holy orders.

John Calvin was born in 1509 and was exposed to the ideas of the early Reformers while he was still growing up. His book *Institutes of the Christian Religion* contains the basic system of his religious thinking and is considered a masterpiece of theological argument. Like Luther, Calvin was very interested in the question of salvation. Calvin had a separate answer to the question of how a person could be saved. While Luther emphasized faith, Calvin emphasized God's predestination. Calvin argued that since God was ultimately in control of everything, God must also be ultimately responsible for a person's salvation or damnation. A person's fate in the afterlife had been determined before the beginning of time, according to Calvin. It did not matter whether the person thought that they believed in Jesus, or whether they performed good works; they would go to heaven or hell regardless in accordance with the destiny that God had laid out for them.

While Calvin's emphasis on predestination is very striking, he changed many other aspects of Catholicism. For example, Calvin kept only baptism and Eucharist out of the seven sacraments in Catholicism. Even for these two sacraments, Calvin denied that they provided any real supernatural benefits, since salvation did not depend on them, but rather upon predestination. Calvin and many other Reformers were also very opposed to the reverence paid to saints in Catholicism. For these Reformers, one should pray only to God, and Calvinist churches were usually stripped of all statues of saints and other ornamentation associated with Catholicism.

St. Paul's Cathedral, London. This view of London demonstrates how the church dominated not only philosophy but also the architecture of Renaissance England. More radical Protestants objected to such elaborate buildings, which were left over from Catholicism. From Orie Latham Hatcher, *A Book for Shakespeare Plays and Pageants,* 1916.

While Calvinists and Lutherans, and the followers of various other Reformers, are generally called Protestants, it is worth noting that these Reformers frequently did not agree with each other and did not form a united front against the Catholic Church. The Calvinists in Geneva, for example, burned a variety of dissenters from the Catholic Church because the dissenters did not subscribe to Calvin's teachings. As with the Spanish Inquisition, religious dissent was considered a crime like theft or murder, and was punished severely as a result. As a result of the Reformers' work, Europe, which had been more or less unified in belief in the year 1400, by 1600, had been broken up into different communities that believed very different things and that often punished people who didn't hold the same beliefs.

This division is seen particularly clearly in England. Catholicism was very strong in England until the reign of Henry VIII. When the pope wouldn't allow Henry VIII to put aside his wife Katherine of Aragon, Henry VIII eventually declared, in the Act of Supremacy of 1534, that he, the king, and not the pope, was the head of the church in England. At first, the Anglican Church, as the church in England came to be called, did not differ dramatically from the Catholic Church, and most people probably did not notice profound differences. Gradually, however, more and more changes were introduced. One of the major changes was the use of English, instead of Latin, in the liturgy. There was considerable complaint, and even a few attempted rebellions, when some of these bigger changes were put in place. During Elizabeth's reign, the Anglican Church became a generally tolerant institution that accepted a range of religious beliefs, provided that the person be willing to worship according to the Common Book of Prayer. Anglican theology was influenced significantly by both Lutheran and Calvinist teachings. Many Anglicans, for example, share the Lutheran belief that Christ is present in the Eucharist, even if they do not believe in transubstantiation. Other Anglicans remained sympathetic to the teachings of the Catholic Church and attempted to retain the old methods of worship as much as possible. The wide range of religious opinion, ranging from extreme Calvinist to crypto-Catholic formed a mix that proved to be highly explosive, especially in the English Civil War of the 17th century.

To read about religion in Chaucer's England, see the Europe entries in the sections "Religious Beliefs" and "Monasticism" in chapter 8 ("Religious Life") in volume 2 of this series; for 18th-century England, see the entry on England in the section "Religious Beliefs" in chapter 8 ("Religious Life") in volume 4 of this series; for Victorian England, see the Victorian England entries in the section "Religion" in chapter 8 ("Religious Life") in volume 5 of this series.

~Lawrence Morris

FOR MORE INFORMATION

Calvin, J. *Institutes of Christian Religion*. Trans. Henry Beveridge. 2nd ed. Chicago: Encyclopaedia Britannica, 1990.

Fernández-Armesto, F., and D. Wilson. *Reformations: A Radical Interpretation of Christianity and the World (1500–2000)*. New York: Scribner, 1996.

Luther, M. *Martin Luther's Basic Theological Writings*. Ed. Timothy Lull. Minneapolis: Fortress, 1989.

SUFISM (OTTOMAN EMPIRE)

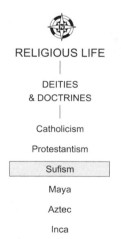

RELIGIOUS LIFE

DEITIES & DOCTRINES

Catholicism

Protestantism

Sufism

Maya

Aztec

Inca

Sunni Islam represented the dominant religion in the Ottoman Empire. Like the Shi'ite sect, which came to prominence in the Safavid Empire of Iran during the 16th century, Sunnis believe in a strict monotheism grounded in the mission of Muhammad as the seal of the prophets and the infallibility of the Qur'an (Koran) as God's word. However, while the Shi'ites developed a belief in the Imam, or an infallible figure given by God to guide the community, the highest Sunni authority was the religious scholars who studied the Qur'an and the Sunna, or Tradition of the Prophet. While such activities as praying five times per day and fasting during the holy month of Ramadan represented the core of Muslim religious practice, many people also looked to Sufism, or Islamic mysticism, for a deeper religious experience. Islamic mysticism, which began with the quest of individuals to draw closer in their personal relationship with God, developed over time into a new form of religion organized into *tariqas*, or orders, each with its own history and practices. During Ottoman times, many types of Sufi orders came to play a critical role in people's spiritual and social lives.

The word Sufi comes from the Arabic word for wool, a reference to the wool garments worn by early mystics who renounced the comforts of medieval Islamic society. Sufis sought to draw closer to God through the repetition of his names and constant prayer. They placed great emphasis on the internal state of the soul, while sometimes downplaying external forms of worship. In order for individuals to properly follow a Sufi path, they required a master into whose hands they placed their spiritual quest.

Over time, this way of doing things became formalized in the *tariqa* system. The word *tariqa* literally meant path, and each order took a unique path to attain union with the divine. These groups were not exclusive, and people often belonged to several at once. Some, for example, emphasized the use of music, while others found images helpful in concentrating on God. Some people lived in lodges with other members of their order, while most continued as regular members of their communities with varying degrees of devotion to their chosen *tariqas*. In the countryside, where important Sufis were buried, people simply venerated their tombs as *walis*, or friends of God, who had miraculous powers to intervene in the everyday world.

The Qalandars formed one important order of Sufis in the Ottoman Empire, and distinguished themselves physically by shaving off all of their hair, including beards, moustaches, and eyebrows. According to legend, Jamal ad-Din Savi, the order's founder, was being pursued by a beautiful woman. In one of his attempts to escape, he shaved off his hair, with the result that she became disgusted and threw him out of her home. Qalandars wore felt cloaks, which allowed them to freeze in winter, gold or black woolen mantles, and conical hair hats. They sang joyful songs and chanted prayers accompanied by drums and tambourines while carrying banners. Qalandars believed in wandering so as to avoid becoming attached to a particular place, which caused many to believe them mischievous thieves.

The Mevlevis, descended from the followers of the 13th-century poet Jalal ad-Din Rumi, were more in the mainstream of Ottoman life, placing a greater emphasis on social conformity and adherence to Islamic law. However, they also did not believe in controlling religious ecstasy once achieved. Because of the importance of music and dance in their rituals, people came to call members of the Mevlevi *tariqa* whirling dervishes. Their leader, a descendant of Rumi, lived in the Turkish city of Konya, where Ottoman governors relied on their acquiescence in governing the city. In the cities, Mevlevi lodges became important cultural centers where people studied dance, music, and Persian, and Mevlevi themes thus had a great impact on the development of Ottoman high culture. Many members of the elite, including the royal family, belonged to this order.

Another order of Sufis common in Ottoman times was the Haydari, who believed that the human face was a mirror of the Prophetic Spirit. The Haydaris, who represented an extreme form of Sufism that rejected worldly norms as well as temptations, believed they were exempt from all rules, including the five pillars of Islam, and hence they did not pray or fast. They shaved their beards to avoid the possibility of dust interfering with the illumination their faces provided the world. At the same time, they wore extremely long moustaches so as to follow the example of the caliph Ali, whom they believed never trimmed his moustache. Locks of twisted hair and earrings symbolized their repression of the animal soul. Earrings symbolized the fact that they ignored unworthy speech, collars symbolized their subjugation to Ali, girdles showed freedom from debasement, and bracelets and anklets represented the avoidance of touching that which is illicit or of walking on sinful paths. They also wore iron bells to keep themselves together.

One order that developed during Ottoman times was the Baktashi, which began in the Balkans where it played an important role in the conversion of Christians to Islam and the integration of non-Muslims into Ottoman society. The Bektashis believed that official religious practices represented merely an external form that could be shed in the quest for true spiritual experience, and hence tolerated non-Muslim beliefs. Many Bektashi rituals stemmed from shamanism and popular religion, and included singing and dancing, as well as a communal meal. Christian influences were seen in the celibacy of those who lived in lodges, the confession of sins, and the belief that God, Muhammad, and Ali represent one single being. Many holy places became assimilated to the Bektashi tradition, with Muslim associations replacing the earlier Christian or pagan ones. The Bektashis became highly influential among the Janissaries, who revered their patron, Haci Bektash.

Over time, the Ottomans began to crack down on the more deviant groups, and orders such as the Qalandars and Haydaris ceased to have much importance during the course of the 16th century. However, it was through Sufism that the largely Christian territories that represented the core of the Ottoman Empire became Islamized, and it was through Sufi orders and rituals that people throughout the empire made important social and cultural connections and sought deeper religious experiences. In addition, whether through folktales of thieving dervishes drawn from the stereotypes of the mendicants or the music and literature of the elites, these groups left a vital stamp on centuries of Ottoman and Turkish culture.

To read about Medieval Islam, see the Islam entry in the section "Religious Beliefs" in chapter 8 ("Religious Life") in volume 2 of this series; for the 19th century, see the Islamic World entries in the sections "Morality" and "Religion" in chapter 8 ("Religious Life") in volume 5 of this series; for the 20th century, see the Islamic World entry in the section "Religion" in chapter 8 ("Religious Life") in volume 6 of this series.

~Brian Ulrich

FOR MORE INFORMATION

Inalcik, H. *The Ottoman Empire: The Classical Age, 1300–1600.* Trans. Norman Itzkowitz and Colin Imber. London: Weidenfeld and Nicolson, 1973.

Karamustafa, A. T. *God's Unruly Friends: Dervish Groups in the Islamic Later Middle Period, 1200–1550.* Salt Lake City: University of Utah Press, 1994.

MAYA

Maya religion was based on a body of beliefs about supernatural powers that explained life and the universe. These concepts reinforced the social and political order

RELIGIOUS LIFE

DEITIES
& DOCTRINES

Catholicism

Protestantism

Sufism

Maya

Aztec

Inca

and were used by kings and the elite to maintain their power and control. Indeed, the political system included priests who oversaw rituals and knowledge that allowed them to both communicate with the supernatural and, through the keeping of historical chronicles, interpret events. Maya religious beliefs were held by all levels of society: commoner, king, elite, and priest.

Information about ancient Maya religion comes from a variety of sources, including ancient Maya texts and accounts written by the Spanish immigrants. While much of Maya religion disappeared when the Spanish brought Christianity, some native groups preserved elements either as part of a syncretistic Christianity or as an independent religion. One such group is the Lacandon Maya in the southern lowlands of the state of Chiapas, Mexico. Many vestiges of ancient Maya religion have survived in their beliefs and rituals. For example, they continue to make and use pottery *incensarios* (incense burners) that are similar in form and use to those of the pre-Columbian era. Lacandon rituals are still held in sacred caves and, until recently, in the ruined temples of several lowland Maya cities.

According to Maya belief, the most powerful supernatural beings controlled aspects of the universe. The Maya referred to these beings as *k'u*, best translated as sacred or divine entity (*k'u* is the root of the word *k'ul*, referring to the sacred quality or essence in all things). The Maya saw the beings we call gods as the most powerful embodiments of this sacred quality in the universe, but it would be a mistake to assume they had distinct or anthropomorphic (human-like) qualities like the gods of ancient Greece or Rome.

Maya deities were not finite. They were complex and contradictory beings. They possessed multiple aspects that blended together, often making precise identification difficult. Some aspects were visible, like the sun god seen in the sky each day. But other aspects of the same deity were invisible, like the sun after being transformed when it entered Xibalba at night. In this aspect the sun took on the attributes of the most powerful nocturnal animal of the tropical forest and became the jaguar sun of the underworld. Any Maya representation of the sun god, whether carved on a stone monument or painted on a vessel, might emphasize any one of these multiple aspects, so that each depiction may appear to us as being very different. Moreover, the portraits of Maya rulers often show them wearing costumes, masks, and head-dresses with attributes of one or more of the gods. This makes it difficult to identify who is actually being depicted.

Any Maya deity could take on a multitude of other aspects and be transformed as a result. There were different aspects based on sex (male or female), direction (east, west, north, south, and center), age (old or youthful), color, and so forth. Direction and color were usually linked, so that one aspect of the rain god (Chac) was referred to as Chac Xib Chac, or the Red Chac of the East. Gods also could possess one or more inner essences, or *wayob*, adding even more variability. Because of these diffuse qualities, there is general agreement about the identity of some Maya deities, but disagreement about the remainder and the total number of such deities. However, we can briefly describe several of the most important Maya deities.

Itzamna (Reptilian House) may have been the central deity of ancient Maya religion. One famous Maya scholar, Sir Eric Thompson, proposed that all other deities were but aspects of Itzamna, making Maya religion in a sense monotheistic. At least two aspects of Itzamna are often defined as gods in their own right: *Hunab K'u* (*hun*, first; *ab*, living; *k'u*, god), creator of the universe; and *Kukulcan* (*kukul*, feathered; *can*, serpent), patron of writing and learning. In his various aspects Itzamna was lord over the most fundamental opposing forces in the universe: life and death, day and night, and sky and earth. As lord of the celestial realm he was the Milky Way, which the Maya usually depicted as a two-headed reptile or serpent. There his body represented the sky, from which other sky deities (stars) were suspended. His front head faced east, symbolizing the rising sun (day), the morning star (Venus), and life. His rear head faced west, symbolizing the setting sun (night), the evening star (Venus), and death. The two-headed ceremonial bar held by kings on many Classic Maya portraits represents Itzamna as this manifestation of the celestial realm.

Kinich Ahau was the sun god, one of the Hero Twins, who possessed several aspects corresponding to phases of the sun's daily journey. During the day the face of Kinich Ahau was represented with crossed eyes and a distinctive curl at the corners of his mouth. At dusk he was the dying sun. In his night aspect he became *Yax Balam* (or *Xbalanque*, his Hero Twin name), the jaguar sun of the underworld in his journey through Xibalba. At dawn he was the sun reborn. These aspects were closely associated with concepts of life, death, and rebirth. Maya kings associated themselves with Kinich Ahau and his power; in fact, his name often appears in the titles and names of rulers, and representations of him are frequently found on the headdresses and shields borne by kings in their carved portraits.

Hunahpu was the Venus deity, the other Hero Twin, and closely linked to his brother, the sun god. This link was visible in the sky because Venus, as morning star, precedes the sun at dawn, pulling the sun out of Xibalba. As evening star Venus follows the sun at dusk, pushing the sun into Xibalba. The Venus deity was closely associated with warfare. In addition, a calendar based on its cyclic movements was used to fix important events in the history of kingdoms such as Copan.

Bolon Tzacab, He of Nine (Many) Generations, was a reptilian deity also known in the Classic Period by the name of Kawil. Bolon Tzacab was usually

Maya Gods as Depicted in Manuscripts. (a) Itzamna, god of the sky; (b) Chac, god of rain; (c) Bolon Tza'cab, patron god of ruling family; (d) Yum Kaax, god of maize; (e) Yum Cimil, god of death; (f) Ah Chicum Ek, god of the North Star; (g) Ek Chuach, patron god of merchants; (h) Buluc Chabtan, god of war and human sacrifice; (i) Ix Chel, god of the rainbow; (j) Ixtab, god of suicide. Note how some of the gods have attributes that match their roles. For example, Ixtab, the god of suicide, is depicted as a hanged corpse, while Yum Cimil, a death god, is depicted as a skeleton. © Perry Casteneda Library.

shown with an upturned snout and a smoking ax in his forehead. He was a special patron of Maya kings. The image portrayed on the so-called manikin scepter, often held as a symbol of office by kings, is that of Bolon Tzacab. In fact, the ritual of acquiring or presenting the manikin scepter was essentially the inauguration ceremony for Maya rulers. Bolon Tzacab's name often appears in the titles or names of kings.

Chac, the rain deity, is also represented with reptilian features—including a downward curling snout and two downward projecting fangs—indicating that he may also be an aspect of Itzamna. Many aspects of Chac have been identified, including four associated with colors and directions: Chac Xib Chac (Red Chac of the East), Ek Xib Chac (Black Chac of the West), Sac Xib Chac (White Chac of the North), and Kan Xib Chac (Yellow Chac of the South). An image of Chac Xib Chac was often shown dangling from the belt of Maya kings. The benevolent aspect of Chac was associated with creation and life. For Maya farmers, Chac was an all-important deity who nourished the fields and made life possible.

Yum Ka'x, as he is known in Yucatán, was an agricultural deity whose most important aspect may have been the maize god, represented as a youth with an artificially elongated head (a mark of beauty), sometimes with a headdress formed of an ear of corn. He was benevolent, representing life, prosperity, and fertility. Occasionally Maya kings were depicted impersonating the maize deity scattering grains of maize (or drops of blood).

Yum Cimil is the name in Yucatán for the primary god of death. He was depicted either as a skeleton or as a bloated and marked figure with black circles, suggesting decomposition. He was often adorned with bells fastened in his hair, arms, legs, and collar. He had several aspects: one associated with human sacrifice and another presided over Mitnal, the lowest of the nine underworlds. To this day the Yucatán Maya believe that Yum Cimil prowls around the houses of the sick, looking for victims.

Buluc Chabtan, Eleven Faster, was a god of war and human sacrifice and was probably closely related to Yum Cimil. Buluc Chabtan's face was adorned with black lines encircling his eyes and extending down his cheeks. In the codices he was shown burning houses with a torch in one hand and a spear in the other.

Ah Chicum Ek, The Guiding Star, was the benevolent god of the North Star. He was shown with a snub-nosed face and black markings on his head. The North Star was the guide of merchants, who offered *pom* (copal) incense to him at roadside altars.

Ek Chuah, Black Scorpion, was the patron of merchants. He was usually shown painted black with a large, drooping underlip and carrying a bundle of merchandise on his back, like an itinerant merchant. Ek Chuah was also the patron of cacao, one of the most important crops produced and traded by Maya merchants.

Ix Chel, She of the Rainbow, was a rainbow deity who probably had both malevolent and benevolent aspects. Her benevolent aspects were associated with healing, childbirth, and divination. At the time of the conquest, Cozumel Island (off the eastern coast of Yucatán) was a major place of veneration for Ix Chel.

Ixtab was a suicide deity, depicted in the Maya codices in a gruesome manner: hanging by a rope around her neck, her eyes closed in death, with a black circle representing decomposition on her cheek. Suicide was considered an honorable death by the Maya, and a qualification for residing in the place of rest in Xibalba.

There were a multitude of other deities, including the Oxlahuntik'u, gods of the 13 levels of the sky, and the Bolontik'u, gods of the 9 levels of the underworld. Each number and unit of time that made up the various calendrical counts used by the Maya was also considered a god (Sharer, 151–63).

To read about religion in 19th-century Latin America, see the Latin America entry in the section "Religion" in chapter 8 ("Religious Life") in volume 5 of this series.

FOR MORE INFORMATION

Sharer, R. J. *Daily Life in Maya Civilization.* Westport, Conn.: Greenwood, 1996.

Tedlock, B. *Time and the Highland Maya.* Albuquerque: University of New Mexico Press, 1982.

AZTEC

The Aztecs had what can be called a pantheon—a world with many gods. There was a supreme creator deity, Ometeotl, or the Giver of Life, who was a dual god consisting of the pair Ometecuhtli and Omecihuatl. This god was celestial and androgynous (both male and female) and was the primordial creator of the universe. Like the God of certain Western traditions, this god was omnipotent, omniscient, and omnipresent—all-powerful, all knowing, and present everywhere. The male aspect was especially found in fire, in the sun, and in all the corn gods, who ensured the growth of corn. The female aspect was in the plants, the water, and the earth and ensured regeneration. A song that reflects the many presences and powers of this dual god goes like this:

He is the Lord and Lady of Duality
He is Lord and Lady of our maintenance
He is mother and father of the gods, the old god
He is at the same time the god of fire, who dwells in the navel of fire
He is the mirror of day and night
He is the star which illumines all things, and he is the Lady of the shining skirt of stars
He is our mother, our father
Above all, he is Ometeotl who dwells in the place of duality, Omeyocan. (León-Portilla, 90)

Before we get deeper into the pantheon, it is important to realize that there were scores of gods associated with all aspects of existence. This was because all of life was considered inherently sacred and literally filled with the potency of divine beings. These gods were expressions of the sacred powers that permeated the world. References to these numinous forces were expressed in the Nahuatl term *teotl*, which the Spaniards translated as god, saint, or demon. But to the Aztecs, *teotl* signified a sacred power manifested in natural forms (such as a tree, a mountain, or a rainstorm), in persons of high distinction (such as a king, an ancestor, or a warrior), or in mysterious and chaotic places (such as caves, whirlpools, or storms). What the Spanish translated as god really referred to a broader spectrum of sacred powers and forces that animated the world.

The deities were represented in story, pictorially, and in sculpture as anthropomorphic beings. Even when gods took an animal form, as in the case of Xolotl, the divine dog, or the form of a ritual object, as in the case of Iztli, the knife god, they often had human features like arms, legs, a torso, a face, and so on. Certain gods were associated with certain activities; Xipe Totec, for example, was linked with human sacrifice, while Yacatecuhtli was linked with trade. Many of these gods dwelt in the different levels of the 13-layered celestial sphere or the 9-layered underworld. In many cases there were quadruple or quintuple groups of gods. For instance, in one of the remaining storybooks, the *Codex Borgia*, Tlaloc (the rain god) inhabits the central region of heaven, while four other Tlaloque (rain gods) inhabit the four regions of the sky, each dispensing a different kind of rain. Perhaps the two most central groups of gods were the creator gods and the fertility gods.

Xipe Totec. This god was called "The Flayed One," and was depicted wearing the skin of a captured warrior. Impersonators of this deity would put on the skin removed from war captives sacrificed to the sun. From *Codex Borgia*. Courtesy of Siglo Veintiuno Editiores, Mexico.

Besides Ometeotl, the Lord of Duality, who was the Supreme Creator God, there was a series of creator gods who did the work of organizing the universe. Each was revered by the general populace, from ruler to commoner. The four main creator gods, Quetzalcoatl, Tezcatlipoca, Xiuhtecuhtli, and Tlaloc, received widespread representations carved in wood and stone or painted in murals and manuscripts. These were the gods who struggled for ascendancy during the four suns that preceeded the Fifth Sun. There are widespread images of these deities as well as myths about their powers, adventures, and influences.

One of the most powerful creator gods was Tezcatlipoca, the Lord of the Smoking Mirror. He was lavishly decorated with feathers and mirrors. On the social level of the local community, he was the great sorcerer whose smoking obsidian mirror revealed the powers of darkness, night, jaguars, and shamanic magic. He was active, involved, intimidating, and overbearing. Consider this list of alternative names for this god: he was also called Yohualli Ehecatl, Night Wind (or invisible wind); Moyocoyatzin, Capricious One; Monenequi, Tyrannical One; Yaotl, The Enemy; or Necoc Yaotl, The Enemy on Both Sides. In other words, he was awesome. In fact, he was capable of being everywhere. One prayer to Tezcatlipoca went like this: "O master, O our lord . . . O night, O wind; thou seest, thou knowest the things within the trees, the rocks. And behold now, it is true that thou knowest of things within us; thou hearest us from within, what we say, what we think; our minds, our hearts. It is as if smoke, mist arose before thee."

Another creative power was Xiuhtecuhtli, the ancient fire god who influenced every level of society and the cosmos. Xiuhtecuhtli was the fire of existence that was kept lighted in certain temples at all times. He was also the fire in each family's home, providing warmth, light, and power for cooking. Xiuhtecuhtli was especially present in the various new fire ceremonies that accompanied the inauguration of new temples, ball courts, and palaces, and he was especially important during the great New Fire Ceremony that took place once every 52 years at the end of the Aztec Calendar Round.

Daily life in the Aztec world revolved in large part around farming and the powers of fertility and agricultural regeneration. Every family depended on various forms of intensive agriculture that required organized labor schedules of planting, nurturing, and harvesting. The gods of agriculture were all around and part of everyday existence. People carried out rituals for burning fields, preparing the ground for seed, planting, observing the stages of growth, sowing the maize, storing the food, and eating it. Like young children, the fields needed constant attention, care, and nurture. While many female deities inspired worship and the regeneration of plants, the most ancient and honored fertility-rain god was Tlaloc, who lived on mountain peaks where clouds were thought to emerge from caves to fertilize the land with rain. One mountain in particular, Mt. Tlaloc, was worshipped as the original source of the waters and vegetation. As you would expect, Tlaloc was accompanied by a female counterpart, sometimes known as Chalchiuhtlicue, the goddess of the lake and running water; she was represented in various forms, including precious greenstone effigies.

One of the most fascinating aspects of Tlaloc was his paradise, Tlalocan. It was one of the desired places of afterlife, a kind of earth paradise setting. The Aztecs who spoke to Father Bernardino de Sahagún about their worldview told him that in Tlalocan "there is great prosperity . . . and great wealth. There is no suffering. There is no lack of maize, squash, tomatoes, beans, or marigolds. The *tlaloque* live there, who are like priests, like the priests who offer fire." People struck by lightning and those who drowned were assured of a place in Tlalocan. Dying in these ways meant that Tlaloc had chosen them as a reward or as a way of demonstrating his power. Most of all, Tlalocan was conceived of as a great storehouse of water and fertilizing energy. The Tlaloque, or Tlalocs, gave and took the treasured forces of new life.

There was an ensemble of mother goddesses, and some were thought of as earth-mother figures that represented the abundant powers of the earth, women, and fertility. These were the deities of earth, water, the moon, drunkenness, sex, the birth of life, fertilization, illness, and healing of diseases. The underlying concept was of the Mother who could provide comfort or harm, love or terror, and life or death. One of the most important mother goddesses was Tonantzin, Our Venerable Mother, who was revered far and wide in Aztec times. When the Spaniards came, the Virgin of Guadalupe appeared on the same hill that was dedicated to the worship of Tonantzin. Other earth goddesses who present the opposing, life-giving elements of the earth include Xochiquetzal, or Precious Flowery Feather, who was the goddess of romance, love, and sexual desire and was associated with flowers, feasting, and pleasure. There was

Yacatecuhtli. This god was the patron deity of merchants. The cross-like object with footprints represents the four directions of the world to which the merchants travel. From *Codex Fejervdry-Mayer.* Courtesy of Akademische Druck-und Verlagsantalt, Graz, Austria, 1971 (facsimile edition).

also Tlazolteotl, the Goddess of Filth, who was the goddess of sexual sin, and Mayahuel, Circle of Arms, who was the goddess of drinking. Following the pattern of duality seen earlier, these goddesses could also appear in masculine forms (Carrasco, 47–53).

To read about religion in 19th-century Latin America, see the Latin America entry in the section "Religion" in chapter 8 ("Religious Life") in volume 5 of this series.

FOR MORE INFORMATION

Carrasco, D., with S. Sessions. *Daily Life of the Aztecs: People of the Sun and Earth*. Westport, Conn.: Greenwood, 1998.

Durán, D. *Book of the Gods and Rites and the Ancient Calendar*. Ed. and trans. Fernando Horcasitas and Doris Heyden. 2nd ed. Norman: University of Oklahoma Press, 1977.

León-Portilla, M. *Aztec Thought and Culture*. Norman: University of Oklahoma Press, 1963.

RELIGIOUS LIFE
|
DEITIES
& DOCTRINES
|
Catholicism

Protestantism

Sufism

Maya

Aztec

Inca

INCA

The Incas had many deities, or gods, each with a particular area of influence and power. The most powerful was Viracocha, the Creator. This deity was neither male nor female. The Spaniards saw several statues of this being in various temples. One such statue, of solid gold, was in Cuzco; it stood about four feet high. The figure's right arm was raised and its fist was clenched, except for the thumb and forefinger. Viracocha gave the other gods their authority. For this reason Viracocha was seen as a more distant power in the world, and the other gods had more immediate influence and control over the actions of humans. Thus individuals were more preoccupied with rituals for the other gods.

The three principal gods under Viracocha were Inti, the Sun; Illapa, the Thunder or Weather god; and Mama-Quilla, the Moon. Inti, the most powerful, was the god of agriculture. This god was represented as a golden disk with rays and a human face in the center. Illapa, the next most powerful, was associated with rain. He was usually depicted as a man in the sky wearing radiant clothing, holding a war club in one hand and a sling in the other. Mama-Quilla was a woman and the wife of the Sun. The Moon did not appear to have any particular functions, but the lunar cycle was the basis for the Inca nighttime calendar.

The gods of the sky, Inti and Illapa, were important to the Incas, no doubt because the sky was the source of both sun and rain for sustaining the crops. However, of equal importance were the god of the earth, Pacha-Mama, and the god of the sea, Mama-Cocha, both of which were regarded as female. Pacha-Mama was important to the Incas as agriculturalists, whereas Mama-Cocha was important to fishing groups residing near the ocean. Mama-Cocha was also the ultimate source of all water, including rivers, streams, and irrigation water. Hence she was important even to the Incas in Cuzco. Below these deities were various gods associated with stars or constellations that served different functions. For example, some stars watched over flocks of llamas, others over wild animals, and still others over plants and seeds.

All major deities of the Incas constituted an official cult. Although the cult religious structures were called Sun Temples by the Spaniards (suggesting that they were used exclusively by the priests of Inti), they also housed the other deities and the priests who served them. Only the most important deities, such as Viracocha, Inti, and Illapa, were represented by images. Mama-Quilla, Pacha-Mama, and Mama-Cocha apparently had no images, and neither did the lesser deities.

In addition to the deities just discussed, the Incas had a host of other beliefs in the supernatural. A pervasive part of Inca religious life involved the belief that many places and objects were imbued with supernatural powers. These supernatural features were called *huacas*. It is unclear whether the objects and places were spirits themselves or simply the locations where spirits resided. Most *huacas* were local features of a settlement, significant to its residents only. Apparently the most common were springs and rocks. The Incas also had amulets that they believed held supernatural powers and that functioned like portable *huacas*.

Particular reverence was also given to the bodies of the dead, who were regarded as *huacas*. The Inca kings' bodies were mummified after death and placed in temples, to be brought out during festivals and worshipped. Moreover, the dead Inca kings were considered to be active participants in the activities of their *panacas*, so their mummies were provided food and drink.

An unusual element of Inca religion was the *ceque* system. This was a series of straight lines that radiated out from the Coricancha (the Temple of the Sun) in Cuzco, extending to the horizon and possibly beyond. Along the *ceques* were a series of 385 *huacas*. The *ceque* system served two purposes: to organize the geographic space around Cuzco, and to order the *huacas* according to the days of the year. For each *huaca* there was a special day when rituals were observed, and different social groups in Cuzco were responsible for the rituals of each *huaca*. The royal *panacas* were responsible for some of the *huacas*, and the nonroyal *ayllus* and Incas-by-privilege were responsible for others. The system reinforced social distinctions between these groups.

The Incas believed in both evil and good powers that could be manipulated for the good or detriment of humans. Evil spirits were dreaded by the Incas. Unlike the deities and *huacas* discussed above, who were generally considered helpful to humans unless proper rituals were not observed, spirits were always considered to be evil and intent on harming humans (Malpass, 103–6).

To read about religion in 19th-century Latin America, see the Latin America entry in the section "Religion" in chapter 8 ("Religious Life") in volume 5 of this series.

FOR MORE INFORMATION

Cobo, B. *Inca Religion and Customs*. Ed. and trans. Roland Hamilton. Austin: University of Texas Press, 1990.

Conrad, G., and A. Demarest. *Religion and Empire: The Dynamics of Aztec and Inca Expansion.* New York: Cambridge University Press, 1984.

Malpass, M. A. *Daily Life in the Inca Empire.* Westport, Conn.: Greenwood, 1996.

Rowe, J. "Inca Culture at the Time of the Spanish Conquest." In *Handbook of South American Indians.* Vol. 2, *The Andean Civilizations,* ed. Julian Steward. Washington, D.C.: Bureau of American Ethnology Bulletin 143, 1946. 183–330.

Zuidema, R. T. *The Ceque System of Cuzco: The Social Organization of the Capital of the Inca.* Leiden: Brill, 1964.

OTTOMAN TURKS

When the Ottoman Turks migrated westward from the Asiatic steppes in the 14th century, they converted to Islam and brought a new vigor to Muslim expansion. For a detailed explanation of the beliefs of Islam that were shared by the Turks, see the Muslim World entry in the section "Religious Beliefs" in chapter 8 ("Religious Life") in volume 2 of this series.

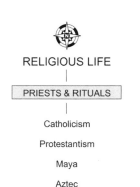

RELIGIOUS LIFE

PRIESTS & RITUALS

Catholicism

Protestantism

Maya

Aztec

Inca

Priests and Rituals

A ritual is a prescribed series of actions used in the worship of a deity. Rituals are a feature of most religions in the world, and can consist of simple actions, such as lighting a candle before a statue, or complicated routines, involving detailed knowledge of special languages and phrases, the movements of the stars, astrology, and so on. Some religions, such as many denominations of Protestantism, however, strive to cut out as much ritual as possible from their worship. One of the most important rituals in the premodern world, and still in many religions today, involved offering sacrifices to the gods.

Sacrifice comes from Latin words that together mean to make holy. In practice, sacrifices are gifts that are offered to the gods. The gifts can range from plants, such as wheat, to animals, such as sheep, and even to human beings. The physical destruction of the gift is often a part of the sacrificial rituals. For example, grain may be burnt, a lamb may have its neck slit, or a human may be thrown from the top of a cliff. There is often an emphasis on the quality of the gift offered. The gift should be as perfect as possible, free from any physical blemishes. There is often an emphasis also on how the sacrifice should be performed. For example, the ritual may demand that the grain be cooked in a particular way or that an animal be slaughtered in a particular place. Many of the ritual demands make clear rational sense within the system of belief. For example, offerings to Chac, the Maya god of rain and water, were thrown into deep lakes. The sacrifice of human beings, widely practiced in 15th- and 16th-century Mesoamerica and South America, can be abhorrent to modern westerners, but it should be remembered that human sacrifices taught two lessons that were important to the communities that practiced them: first that the gods were more important than human beings, and second that the community, which benefited from the sacrifice, was more important than the individual.

Most modern Western societies no longer have an instinctive understanding of sacrifice, even though Christianity was based upon the notion of human sacrifice. Christianity viewed Jesus's death on a cross to be a kind of sacrifice that saved his people from their sins. Thus, the central act in salvation history involved human sacrifice, and, since Jesus was considered to be God as well as a man, involved god-sacrifice. It should not be thought from this that Christianity or Judaism advocated human sacrifice. It was important that Jesus had been put to death by other people, by unbelievers. A strange and beautiful paradox arose from contemplating this sacrificial death: a sin (killing Jesus) ended up saving mankind from sin. In a way, the devil was viewed as defeating himself with his own weapons! The closest modern parallel might be found on a battlefield, where a soldier jumps on a grenade to save his platoon, and his action ultimately ends up winning the war.

One importance of rituals, sacrifices included, is the demarcation of sacred space. Most rituals create a separate space or community that is considered to be particularly holy. In ancient religions, this sacred space was often the temple, which was considered to be the home of the god. Like temples, rituals were frequently designed to make a person, place, or thing different from its profane (nonsacred) surroundings. For example, a candle that had been blessed was treated with more respect than ordinary candles. The separate treatment of such objects reinforced the notion of the sacred, and also brought the sacred into contact with everyday life. A peasant in Europe or South America might bring home a blessed object and feel closer to the divine.

While most religions embrace rituals, many forms of Protestantism were strongly against rituals. Reformers such as Martin Luther and John Calvin felt that the mainstream Church had become obsessed about material things, such as blessed candles, and had forgotten about spiritual things, which were the only important things. As a result, many Protestant congregations attempted to rid their churches and worship services of the trappings of Christian ritual: bells, candles, statues, luxurious clothing, holy water, and stained glass windows. Protestant churches were thus much more simply furnished inside than most Catholic churches. While the buildings were different, the service was even more different. The main weekly worship service in Catholic churches consisted of two parts. In the first part, the priest gave a simple lesson based upon the Bible; in the second part, the priest celebrated the Eucharist, a ritualistic recreation of Christ's Last Supper. Moreover, most of the church service, outside of the sermon (simple lesson) was conducted in Latin, a language that most people could not speak, though those people who spoke a language derived from Latin, such as Spanish or Italian, could understand bits and pieces. Most Protestant congregations changed the language from Latin into the vernacular, the speech of the common people. They also reduced the frequency of the Eucharist, celebrating it perhaps once a month and sometimes even less frequently. Instead of the Eucharist, with its many connections with rituals, Protestant congregations, especially Calvinist ones, substituted much longer sermons and more in-depth lessons on the Bible. The Protestants hoped that these changes would focus the people more immediately on spiritual lessons, and less on the physical aspects of ritual. Ritual is hard to escape, however, and the weekly practice of a group of people gathering in the same place, at the same time, to engage in the same worship of God, can certainly be called its own kind of ritual.

Finally, a word should be said about priests. Priests are the people who perform rituals. Like temples, they are often set apart from the world around them, and may, like Catholic priests and the Native American priests, wear special clothing to mark their status. The priest's main role is to help the people and the divine to come together. Priests from different religions do this by advising the people and especially by performing rituals designed to bring divine blessing upon the community as a whole. The word priest itself comes from a Greek word, meaning elder, and is connected with the elders mentioned in the New Testament. As such, priest is not the best term for Native American and other religious experts, who have no connection with the New Testament. Another word for priest, which survives in various Romance languages in different forms, is *sacerdos*. This word means performer of holy things and more accurately describes the performers of rituals in non-Christian religions. Priest, however, is the most common word used today, and it has been kept for this volume. Most Protestant congregations, in their desire to avoid the connotations of Catholic ritual, generally call their religious leaders ministers and not priests.

~*Lawrence Morris*

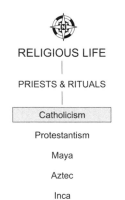

RELIGIOUS LIFE
|
PRIESTS & RITUALS
|
Catholicism

Protestantism

Maya

Aztec

Inca

CATHOLICISM (SPAIN, ITALY, ENGLAND)

The Catholic Church had very many rituals, ranging from processions around a town's borders, to all-night vigils spent in prayer and worship before the Eucharist. The most important of these rituals were called sacraments and it was believed that the sacraments gave the participant special graces from God. The Catholic Church believed that there were seven sacraments: baptism, confirmation, Eucharist, matrimony, holy orders, confession, and last rites.

Baptism was the sacrament through which one entered into the Church. Most people were baptized shortly after birth, though those who converted to Christianity, from Judaism, Islam or any other religion, as adults were baptized when they converted. During baptism, the soon-to-be-member of the Church was sprinkled with water or dipped into a pool of water. The water was a symbol of many things. First of all, it was a symbol of purification. The word baptism itself comes from a Greek word meaning to wash. During baptism, a person was cleansed of their previous sins, including the basic sin of disobedience that they inherited from their ancestors Adam and Eve. Water was also a common symbol of the Holy Spirit, who was believed to be the person of the Trinity that created faith and helped belief. Going down into the water was also a symbol for dying with Christ, while coming out of the water was linked to rising with Christ. In baptism, a person became linked to the saving actions of Christ. After baptism, the person was considered a member of the Church.

Confirmation was a sacrament of initiation, like baptism. Confirmation marked the mature decision to believe in Christ. Adult converts were confirmed at the same time that they were baptized. Those who were baptized as children were confirmed at a later time, once they were believed to be able to make their own decisions rationally. The age of confirmation varied massively from place to place. In some districts, confirmation could be received as early as seven years old; in other localities, a person might wait until the teenage years to be confirmed. The basic ritual was the same: a bishop anointed the head with oil and urged the believer to be ready to suffer for the faith, if persecution came. The sacrament was believed to complete baptism and the Holy Spirit dwelt more fully in the recipient.

Matrimony was also considered a sacrament. The ritual of the sacrament could be very simple: a man and woman promised to live as husband and wife until the death of the other person. Jesus had taught that it was God's will that husbands and wives should not divorce one another. As a result, the Church forbade divorce. If a couple did not get along in serious ways, a separation, in which the woman went back to her parents, might occur, but the partners were still considered married and were not allowed to remarry. On rare occasions, people received annulments. An annulment was a certification that a valid marriage never existed. Few things invalidated a marriage, but they included being forced to marry against one's will, being more closely related than allowed by the Church, and being too young.

The Eucharist was the central sacrament of Catholic life. The Eucharist was the repetition of the last supper that Jesus shared with his disciples. At this meal, which occurred during the festival of Passover which celebrated the Jewish people escaping their Egyptian captors, Jesus took bread and wine and gave it to his disciples to eat saying that these were his body and blood, which would be offered up for the forgiveness of sins. Jesus commanded his disciples to perform this same ritual in remembrance of him. At the Eucharist, a priest similarly took special bread and wine, repeated Jesus's words, and gave them to the faithful. The Catholic Church believed that the bread and wine mystically became the true body and blood of Christ, and that eating the consecrated host (wafer of bread) and drinking from the chalice (cup for the wine) allowed the faithful to participate in and benefit from Christ's sacrifice on the cross. This ritual was firmly rooted in the notion of sacrifice as practiced in Judaism and other religions.

Holy orders was the sacrament through which one became a priest in the Catholic Church. The word priest comes from the Greek word *presbyter,* which means elder. In the early church, the elders administered the local community of believers. Likewise, priests were charged with managing particular churches and serving the local community. Priests were particularly important because only they could perform the Eucharistic ritual. While baptism and marriage could be performed by anyone, although usually performed by a priest, the Eucharist could only be performed by a priest. Today, many people view priests as holy people or people particularly interested in religion. It is important to note that in the 15th and 16th centuries, being a priest was frequently looked upon as a profession like any other. The vast majority of people in Renaissance society believed deeply in Christianity, so priests were not different in that respect. Rather, priests were more like government employees in today's world. While most people are patriotic and interested in serving their country, only some people choose it as a profession. Similarly, priests were those who chose the Church as their profession. In the same way that we might not expect a government employee to be more patriotic than a shopkeeper, Renaissance people did not expect a priest to be necessarily more pious than a merchant. It was generally believed, however, that priests should try extra hard to provide a good example to those around them.

Confession was a sacrament that gave forgiveness for sins. One of the main parts of Jesus's teachings was the claim that he could forgive sins. Before Jesus went to heaven, he passed on this power to the Church. During confession, the priest, as representative of the Church, forgave the sins of a person. To receive confession, a person would tell the sins that he had committed to a priest and express his sorrow for those sins, and promise to try to avoid them in the future. Without sorrow, a confession was not valid. The priest would advise the penitent (person who was confessing) on ways of trying to avoid those particular sins, and would usually assign a small punishment, such as fasting or saying particular prayers, to the penitent as a means of encouraging the penitent to do better in the future.

Last rites, also called extreme unction or the anointing of the sick, was a sacrament designed to give comfort to the ill. If a person were in danger of death, he or she would send for the priest and ask for this sacrament. During the ritual, the priest would anoint the sick person with oil and pray for their spiritual and physical well-being. Many miraculous cures were linked to last rites, but its major effect was usually the spiritual and emotional comforting of the dying person.

To read about religious ritual in Medieval Europe, see the Europe entries in the sections "Religious Beliefs," "Monasticism," and "Festivals and Holidays" in chapter 8 ("Religious Life") in volume 2 of this series.

~*Lawrence Morris*

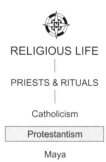

RELIGIOUS LIFE

|

PRIESTS & RITUALS

|

Catholicism

Protestantism

Maya

Aztec

Inca

PROTESTANTISM (ENGLAND)

Out of the seven sacraments practiced by the Catholic Church (see above), most Protestant denominations recognized at most two sacraments: baptism and the Eucharist. Most Protestants accepted these sacraments because they were well attested in the Bible, whereas the other rituals appear only a few times. While most Protestants kept some form of baptism and Eucharist, different denominations understood these rituals in different ways. Anglicans and Lutherans believed that these rituals imparted some spiritual benefit, while extreme Calvinists tended to view such rituals mostly as symbols. While Lutherans didn't recognize them as sacraments (special instances of divine grace), they did preserve rituals that functioned in similar ways to confirmation, confession, and holy orders. For example, confession in a Lutheran church was not considered to remove sin, but the sorrow of the repentant was thought to remove the sin; thus, the ritual did not actually achieve anything—instead, everything depended on the faith of the individual believer.

Most Protestant churches not only reduced the number of sacraments, they also reduced the amount of ritual in general. The Catholic Church had many religious festivals that included such rituals as long processions, the use of incense and bells, sumptuous clothing, and long prayers to saints. The Protestant churches got rid of most of these practices, since they felt that these practices removed attention from God and focused it excessively on physical things. Many Protestant churches, especially those influenced heavily by Calvin, removed all statues from their churches. While Catholic churches were usually filled with statues of saints, many Protestants felt that statues were a form of idolatry. The Protestants feared that people were worshipping the statues, or the saints represented by the statues, instead of directing all their worship to God. Protestant church buildings therefore tended to be simple buildings lacking rich ornament. A pulpit (a raised platform for giving sermons and speeches) often replaced an altar (where the ritual of the Eucharist was performed) as the main focus of the congregation in Protestant church buildings. While a Catholic service usually focused on the Eucharist, Protestant church services generally involved reading from the Bible, followed by long sermons and many hymns. These meetings, while not as elaborate as Catholic practices, can be considered a kind of ritual.

To read about religious ritual in Chaucer's England, see the Europe entries in the sections "Religious Beliefs," "Monasticism," and "Festivals and Holidays" in chapter 8 ("Religious Life") in volume 2 of this series; for 18th-century England, see the entry on England in the section "Religious Practices" in chapter 8 ("Religious Life") in volume 4 of this series; for Victorian England, see the Victorian England entries in the sections "Morality" and "Religion" in chapter 8 ("Religious Life") in volume 5 of this series.

~*Lawrence Morris*

MAYA

Maya religion was guided and controlled by two kinds of specialists: shamans and priests. They had powers to communicate with the deities and thereby understand the universe.

Shamans undoubtedly represent a tradition with origins long before the development of Maya civilization. Most were commoners who looked after people's well-being in local communities throughout the Maya area. Shamans provided medicines based on their knowledge of illness, and they used divination rituals to determine the meanings of events, to foretell the future, and to cure the sick. These skills gave them prestige and a measure of power over other members of society. Shamans undoubtedly helped establish the basics of the Maya calendar and were considered essential to the world order because they knew how to track the cycles of time reckoned by the movements of the sky wanderers. With this knowledge the annual coming of the rains could be predicted and the proper time to plant the crops could be chosen. This boosted the shamans' prestige and power in farming communities.

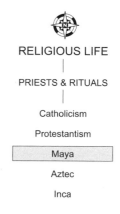

RELIGIOUS LIFE

PRIESTS & RITUALS

Catholicism

Protestantism

Maya

Aztec

Inca

As Maya society became larger and more complex, priests who were full-time specialists in religious matters emerged. The Maya priesthood undoubtedly evolved from the older tradition of shamanism, which was primarily associated with the nonelite farming population. But because the management of religious matters was a fundamental concern of the ruling elite, Maya priests were associated with the elite class. By managing religion, the elite could reinforce and support their own elevated status and ensure their prosperity. Thus aspects of Maya religion that involved social and political concerns beyond the local level were taken over by elite-class priests. They managed the calendar, divination, books of history and prophecy, and public ceremonies—all of which ensured success and prosperity for the king and his polity.

Blood Offerings. The Maya, like most Mesoamerican and South American societies, believed it was important to offer human blood as a sacrifice to the gods. Here, the wife of the king draws blood from her tongue. The king, Shield Jaguar, stands guard over his wife. *Corpus of Maya Hieroglyphic Inscriptions,* by Ian Graham and Eric von Euwr, 1979, by permission of the President and Fellows of Harvard College.

The Maya priesthood was a self-contained group of specialists that was perpetuated through the recruitment and training of acolytes. Because there were not enough political offices for every member of the elite class, the priesthood served an important function as an alternative occupation for the increasing number of younger sons of elite families, including the many children of the royal families.

Over time Maya priests developed a considerable amount of esoteric knowledge that was codified and recorded in books. This body of knowledge—records of myth, history, prophecy, ritual, and astronomical observations—had both practical and religious purposes. Some of the information was used to develop an increasingly complex calendrical system to record events and cycles of time. The calendrical cycles were used for astrological purposes, that is, to predict events and determine the destiny of the king, his polity, and ultimately the entire Maya world.

Elaborately costumed Maya priests conducted spectacular public ceremonies calculated to inspire awe and obedience on the part of the king's subjects. These religious ceremonies included music, processions, dancing, incense burning, and making offerings to the gods. Offerings were made of food and drink, sacrificed birds and animals, and the blood of priests and even the king, drawn by sharp bloodletting tools made for the occasion. On especially important occasions, human sacrifices were made. Maya kings often served as the chief priest for their subjects, conducting rituals to protect them from disease and misfortune, divining the future and the gods' will to ensure the success of the state, and maintaining the harmony of the Maya universe through their own blood sacrifices.

To keep the universe harmonious and to prevent disasters or the end of the world, deities had to be placated by rituals and offerings. The Maya concept for this was feeding the gods. Nourishment came directly from offerings, or indirectly from devoting time and energy to the deities. When something did go wrong, it was thought to be due to the anger of gods who had not been properly nourished. Thus a drought was explained as the anger of an offended rain god.

The Maya conducted a variety of private rituals and public ceremonies to secure individual and collective success. Religious rituals were a part of everyday life: a mother might offer a bit of tortilla to Ixchel for the health of her child, or a farmer might make a quick prayer to Chac to begin his day in the fields. In contrast, the larger public ceremonies sponsored by king and state often extended over several days and nights. Whether small or large, most ceremonies included offerings to the gods. The most potent offering was life itself, or the *k'ul* (divine or sacred) essence represented by blood.

Sacrifices varied according to the urgency of the occasion. They included offerings of food, small birds, animals, and precious substances—even human blood. Sacrifices to cure illness or solve a minor problem might require offerings of food, birds, or small animals. Larger ceremonies might require the sacrifice of a deer, which also contributed to the feast that followed. The dedication of Altar Q by the 16th king of Copan included the sacrifice of 15 jaguars, each symbolizing the powerful spirit essences (*wayob*) of the 15 predecessors of Yax Pac. For especially important ceremonies—such as those conducted to bring rain or to end a drought for the common good—one or more human sacrifices might be required.

The sacred essence, or *k'ul*, was in the blood of living things. Blood from animals was—and still is—one of the most important offerings used by the Maya. In the past, human blood drawn with sharp obsidian blades was the most important personal offering that could be made to the gods. Several scenes carved on monuments show the wives of kings and other elite women drawing blood, often from the tongue. Maya kings offered sacrifices of their own blood to ensure the continuity of the cosmos. Rulers were sometimes depicted holding implements used for bloodletting, made from stingray spines, that were used to draw blood from the penis, a ritual of symbolic meaning for human fertility. Drawn blood was absorbed by strips of bark paper in pottery vessels and then burned as an offering to the gods. In later times in Yucatán, the Spaniards recorded that blood was sprinkled over idols of gods inside temples. An offering found at the base of the Hieroglyphic Stairway at Copan included a spondylus shell containing a residue identified by chemical tests as human blood.

The ultimate offering of the sacred *k'ul* essence came from human sacrifices. This was the practice that most horrified the Spaniards. It was used not only by the Maya, but also by many other peoples of the Americas in their most crucial ceremonies; ironically, in their claims of horror the Spaniards overlooked their own practice of burning people alive in the name of religious orthodoxy.

Among the Maya, human sacrifice was not an everyday event but was considered essential to sanctify major rituals, such as the inauguration of a new ruler, the designation of a new heir to the throne, or the dedication of an important new temple or ball court. Warfare usually provided the victims. After all, taking captives was a major goal of warfare; whereas those of low status might be adopted or enslaved, those of elite status were sacrificed. The heads of decapitated captives were worn as trophies by Maya kings or were buried with dead rulers in their tombs, beginning during Early Maya Civilization. The most prized of all sacrifices was another king. Although relatively rare, the sacrifice of a Maya ruler by another king required a special ceremony and ritual decapitation. The decapitation event apparently was performed at the climax of a ritual ball game, seen as a re-enactment of, first, the victory and capture of the defeated king, and, second, the Hero Twins' defeat and decapitation of the lords of Xibalba in Maya mythology.

Other than in the ritual ball court, sacrifices usually took place at the summit of a temple platform or in a courtyard in front of a temple. Human sacrifices were performed in several different ways, as illustrated in painted and sculptured scenes or on ancient graffiti found on abandoned building walls. One famous graffiti at Tikal depicts the ritual of scaffold sacrifice in which the victim was tied to a wooden framework and shot through by a cluster of arrows. In the excavations of Group G at Tikal, a graffiti vividly depicts a disemboweled captive, his hands tied to a post behind his back. An example of the self-sacrifice of a young woman by throat cutting is depicted on a famous ceramic vessel excavated at Altar de Sacrificios.

One of the most famous places for sacrificial rituals was the Well of Sacrifice at Chichen Itza, sacred to the gods of rain. When there was drought or famine, the Maya made pilgrimages from all over the lowlands to attend sacrifices to appease the angry rain gods. Human sacrifices were thrown from the rim of this great cenote into the water some 65 feet below. Some victims were used to divine the will of the gods. For example, children were thrown into the cenote at daybreak; those who survived the plunge were pulled out at midday to be asked by the priests about messages from the gods they might have heard while in the cenote. Offerings of jade, gold, and other precious materials were also hurled into the well by those witnessing the ceremony. At the end of the 19th century the cenote was dredged, bringing to the surface about 50 human skulls and numerous human bones. Also found were sacrificial knives made of flint; masks, bells, jewelry, cups, and plates made of gold and copper; and pendants and beads made of jade and shell. The most numerous items were blue-painted cakes of *pom* incense, many still inside pottery *incensarios*.

By the time of the Spanish Conquest, the custom of removing the victim's heart (probably acquired from central Mexico) had become prevalent in sacrifices of men, women, and children. The victim was painted blue (the sacrificial color), wore a special peaked headdress, and was led to a stone altar. There, after ritual purifications, four *chacs* or assistant priests (also painted blue) grasped the victim by the arms and legs and held him on his back on the altar. The *nacom* priest plunged the sacrificial flint knife into the victim's ribs just below the left breast, thrust his hand into the opening, and pulled out the still-beating heart. The heart was handed to the *chilan* priest, who smeared the blood on the idol to whom the sacrifice was being made. If the sacrificial victim had been a valiant and brave warrior, parts of his body might be prepared and eaten by elite warriors to gain his strength. Later, some of his bones would be worn by his captor as a mark of prowess (Sharer, 163–71).

FOR MORE INFORMATION

Benson, H. P., and E. H. Boone, eds. *Ritual Human Sacrifice in Mesoamerica*. Washington, D.C.: Dumbarton Oaks, 1984.

Sharer, R. J. *Daily Life in Maya Civilization*. Westport, Conn.: Greenwood, 1996.

Vogt, E. Z. *Zinacantan: A Maya Community in the Highlands of Chiapas*. Cambridge, Mass.: Harvard University Press, 1969.

AZTEC

The Aztecs are most famous, perhaps, for their practice of human sacrifice. Indeed, human sacrifice was a central and essential element of Aztec religion. To understand human sacrifice among the Aztecs, we must investigate the larger, more complex ceremonial system in which a tremendous amount of energy, wealth, and time was spent in a variety of ritual festivals dedicated to a crowded and hungry pantheon of divine entities. This dedication is reflected in the many metaphors and symbols related to war and sacrifice. Human hearts were likened to fine burnished turquoise, and war was referred to as *teoatltlachinolli*, meaning divine liquid and burnt things. War was the place "where the jaguars roar," where "feathered war bonnets heave about like foam in the waves." And death on the battlefield was called *xochimiquiztli*, meaning flowery death. This may be similar to one of the claims made about death in 20th-century wars: that it was "good and noble to die for one's country."

This crowded ceremonial schedule was acted out in the many ceremonial centers of the city and empire. The greatest ceremonial precinct formed the axis of Tenochtitlan and measured 440 meters on four sides. It contained, according to some accounts, over 80 ritual temples, skull racks, schools, and other ceremonial structures. Book II of Sahagún's *Florentine Codex* contains a valuable list with descriptions of most of these buildings, including the Great Temple, which stood "in the middle of the square . . . very large, very tall . . . and . . . faced toward the setting of the sun." We also read of a temple where "Motecuhzoma did penances . . . there was dying there; captives died there." Also, there was the main high school of the city, called "Mexico Calmecac: there dwelt the penitents who offered incense at the summit of the pyramid Temple of Tlaloc. This they did quite daily." There was a temple from which men were thrown into fires and burned to death. Nearby stood the Great Skull Rack, where the heads of sacrificial victims were hung up for display. Another temple was dedicated to the corn goddess, where a young woman impersonating the goddess 7 Snake was sacrificed at night. "And when she died, then they flayed her . . . the fire priest put on the skin." There were also cooking temples, such as the one where they "cooked the amaranth seed dough for the image of Huitzilopochtli." Another temple related to cooking and eating human flesh was described where "they gathered together the sacrificial victims called Tlalocs . . . when they had slain them, they cut them to pieces there and cooked them. They put squash blossoms with their flesh . . . then the noblemen ate them, all the high judges; but not the common folk—only the rulers."

These place names and short descriptions show us that Aztec sacrifice was a special kind of violence carried out in specific ceremonial centers to help the Aztecs communicate with particular deities, forces, and sacred beings. These sacred places served to limit the action to a certain ritual space and also provided mental and emotional focus to the practitioners carrying out the sacrifice.

Though important variations of ritual activity were carried out at these temples, schools, skull racks, and bathhouses, the general pattern of human sacrifice was as follows. Most Aztec rituals began with *nezahualiztli,* a preparatory period of priestly

fasting, usually lasting four (or a multiple of four) days. An important exception was the year-long partial fast by a group of priests and priestesses known as the *teocuaque* (god eaters) or the greatly feared *in iachhuan Huitzilopochtli in mocexiuhzauhque* (the elder brothers of Huitzilopochtli who fasted for a year). This preparatory period also involved *tozohualiztli* (nocturnal vigils) and offerings of flowers, food, cloth, rubber, paper, poles with streamers, as well as *copaltemaliztli* (incensing), the pouring of libations, and the embowering of temples, statues, and ritual participants. Dramatic processions of elaborately costumed participants, moving to music ensembles and playing sacred songs, passed through the ceremonial precinct before arriving at the specific temple of sacrifice. The major ritual participants were called *teteo ixiptla,* or deity impersonators. All important rituals involved a death sacrifice of either animals or human beings.

Sacrifice to the Sun. The Aztecs believed that sacrifice was necessary to keep the sun moving in its path and to keep the world in existence. In the most famous ritual, the heart was removed from a still-living war captive. From *Florentine Codex.* Courtesy of the University of Utah Press and the School of American Research.

The most common sacrifice was autosacrifice, or the sacrifice of oneself. This involved the use of maguey thorns or other sharp instruments to pierce one's earlobes, thighs, arms, tongue, or, in the case of sinners and priests, genitals to offer blood to the gods. The most common type of killing was the beheading of animals like the quail. But the most dramatic and valued sacrifices were those of captured warriors and slaves. These victims were ritually bathed, carefully costumed, often taught to dance special dances, and sometimes either fattened or slimmed down during the preparation period. They were elaborately dressed to impersonate specific deities to whom they were sacrificed.

The different primary sources reveal a wide range of sacrificial techniques, including decapitation, shooting with darts or arrows, drowning, burning, hurling from heights, strangulation, entombment, starvation, and gladiatorial combat. The ceremony, which often lasted as long as 20 days, usually peaked when splendidly attired captors and captives sang and danced in procession to the temple, where they were escorted (often unwillingly) up the stairway to the *techcatl,* or sacrificial stone. Victims were quickly thrust onto the stone, where a temple priest cut through their chest wall with a *tecpatl,* or ritual flint knife. The priest grasped the still-beating heart, called precious eagle cactus fruit, tore it from the victim's chest, offered it to the sun for vitality and nourishment, and placed it in a carved circular vessel called the *cuauhxicalli,* or eagle vessel. In many cases, the body, now called eagle man, was rolled, flailing, down the temple steps to the bottom, where it was dismembered. The head was cut off and the brains taken out. After being skinned, the skull was placed on the *tzompantli,* or skull rack, consisting of long poles laid horizontally and loaded with skulls. In some cases, the captor was decorated, for instance, with chalk and bird down, and given gifts. Then, together with his relatives, he celebrated a ritual meal consisting of "a bowl of stew of dried maize called *tlacatlaolli* . . . on each went a piece of the flesh of the captive."

One of the most distinctive sacrificial festivals was in honor of the god Xipe Totec (Our Lord the Flayed One). During this ceremony, captive warriors were first purified and adorned as living images of Xipe Totec, some 40 days before the actual feast itself. When the feast day came, however, the captive's leg was tied by rope to a round pillar stone and the captive was given a shield and a club adorned with feathers. A jaguar (experienced) warrior armed with shield and a sharp obsidian-bladed club would then attack the captive. Sometimes multiple warriors were required to overcome the captive. Once the captive was killed, and the offering of the heart was made to the sun, the captive's body was flayed. The flesh formed part of a ritual meal consumed by the relatives of the captor, but not by the captor himself, who was viewed almost as having a kind of father-son relationship with the captive. The skin, however, was worn by the friends of the captor, who would parade through the districts going from door to door asking for food, somewhat similarly to Halloween today. The men in the flayed skins were believed to bring a blessing to the households at which they stopped, especially to children. The young men of the district, however, would attempt to snatch some of the dead man's skin from the warriors, who would use rattle sticks to drive off the assailants.

While such rituals can be difficult for modern westerners to understand, it is clear that for the Aztecs, sacrifice in general, and human sacrifice in particular, was believed to be essential for the continued welfare of society and the world. Death would come to all mortals eventually—the Aztec priests attempted to use some deaths to benefit the whole society (Carrasco, 187–205).

FOR MORE INFORMATION

Carrasco, D., with S. Sessions. *Daily Life of the Aztecs: People of the Sun and Earth.* Westport, Conn.: Greenwood, 1998.

———. "Give Me Some Skin: The Charisma and Sacrifice of the Aztec Warrior." *History of Religions* 35 (1995): 1–26.

Read, K. "Human Sacrifice." In *Encyclopedia of Religion.* Vol. 6: 515–18. New York: Macmillan, 1986.

Sahagún, B. de. *Florentine Codex: General History of the Things of New Spain.* Ed. and trans. A.J.O. Anderson and C. E. Dibble. 13 vols. Santa Fe, N.M.: School of American Research and University of Utah, 1950–1982.

Sanday, P. Reeves. *Divine Hunger: Cannibalism as a Cultural System.* New York: Cambridge University Press, 1986.

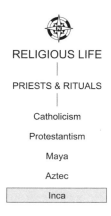

RELIGIOUS LIFE

PRIESTS & RITUALS

Catholicism

Protestantism

Maya

Aztec

Inca

INCA

Priests and priestesses associated with the official shrines and deities were full-time specialists, supported by the tribute paid by conquered people. The fact that a third of the tribute went to the support of formal Inca religion indicates how many people were involved. There was a hierarchy of priests roughly paralleling the administrative hierarchy of the state. The priests were graded according to the rank of the shrine in which they worked. The highest ranking priests were those who worked for the Sun. At the very top was a high priest, who was a close relative of the king and therefore related to the Sun. There was also a hierarchy of the individuals at each shrine: the attendants were subservient to the priests in charge of ceremonies.

The most important ceremonies involved sacrifices of humans.

All the major deities of the Incas were worshipped in the same temples, each with its own shrine. The shrines of the major deities—the Sun, Viracocha, the Thunder, and so on—had attendants; the more important the shrine, the more attendants were present. Different attendants had different functions: for example, some were in charge of divination, others of sacrifices, still others of day-to-day activities. The temples of the official Inca cult had their own group of consecrated women, the *mamaconas*, who were selected from the Chosen Women. These women did the same tasks as other Chosen Women, making *chicha* (maize beer) and textiles for the temples, but could not marry or be given as wives to officials. A woman of highest nobility was in charge of them. It is apparent that the *mamacona* for a temple served all the different deities at that temple; they were not exclusively for the use of the Sun.

To the Incas, the ritual, or practice of religious beliefs, was an essential aspect of life. One conducted rituals to ensure that one's life and well-being were not jeopardized, or to ward off evil spirits. If rituals were conducted properly, misfortunes could be avoided.

Almost all rituals were accompanied by some kind of sacrifice, most often of guinea pigs or llamas but occasionally of children. Most *huacas* were given llamas or guinea pigs. The main deities—Viracocha (the Creator), Inti (the Sun), and Illapa (the Thunder)—always had distinctive colored llamas sacrificed to them: brown to Viracocha, white to Inti, and mixed color to Illapa. The animal was sacrificed by having its throat cut. Food, *chicha*, and coca were also given to *huacas* as sacrifices. The food and coca were usually burned, whereas the *chicha* was poured on the ground. *Cumbi* cloth was also an important sacrificial item, especially to the Sun. Seashells, gold, silver, and corn flour were used as offerings as well.

The most important ceremonies, natural catastrophes, war, and the coronation of new kings, involved sacrifices of humans—always children between the ages of 10 and 15. The children, always non-Incas, had to be physically perfect. The procedure involved a feast for the child so he or she would not go to Viracocha hungry. Following the feast the child would be strangled, its throat cut, or its heart cut out and offered to the deity still beating. Sometimes children were sacrificed to mountain *huacas* by bringing them to the summit, getting them drunk, and then killing them.

The practice of child sacrifice might appear cruel to the reader, but one must remember that the sacrifice only occurred for the most important religious reasons. Humans were sacrificed for these events because they were considered the most worthy thing that could be offered to the gods. Children, rather than adults, were offered presumably because they were more pure in spirit than adults. Although it was no doubt a painful emotional experience for the families of the sacrificed children, to be selected was considered a great honor by both the child and his or her family.

Numerous public ceremonies were associated with the calendars and with special events. Some ceremonies were held on a daily basis, such as the sacrifice of wood, food, and cloth to Inti. More elaborate ceremonies—including making sacrifices, dancing, feasting, and perhaps recounting important historical events—were held during times of crisis, at the coronation or death of a king, and during the various months of the calendar.

The three most important ceremonial months were Capac Raymi (December), Aymoray (May), and Inti Raymi (June). Capac Raymi celebrated the beginning of the rainy season and included the summer solstice, marking the longest day of the year. The most important rituals conducted were the male puberty rites (for more information, see the section "Life Cycles" in chapter 2, "Domestic Life"). Ceremonies to other deities, especially Inti, were also conducted during this month. To emphasize the importance of the rituals, all non-Inca residents of Cuzco had to leave the center of town for the three weeks of the rites. They stayed in special areas near the main roads leading to their place of origin. When they returned at the end of the ceremony, they were fed lumps of corn flour mixed with the blood of sacrificed llamas. The lumps were said to be gifts from Inti to them, but ones that would inform the deity if the person spoke badly of it or the king. Several days of dancing and drinking *chicha* followed the return of the provincial residents of Cuzco, and the month closed with a special sacrifice on the last day. To celebrate the end of the puberty rites, and therefore the entrance into manhood of a new group of boys, food tribute from the provinces was delivered to Cuzco at this time.

Aymoray took place in the modern month of May, to celebrate the corn harvest. People brought the corn from the fields, dancing and singing songs that asked that the corn not run out before the next harvest. Still singing and dancing, the people joined together in the city, where a large number of llamas were sacrificed. The raw meat from the llamas was distributed to all Incas, young and old, who ate some of it with toasted corn. Thirty other llamas were sacrificed and the meat burned at all the *huacas* in Cuzco, the most important ones receiving more meat, the less important ones receiving less meat.

Later in the month, more offerings of llamas were made to Inti in thanks for the corn harvest. Then the people assembled in a sacred field near Cuzco, where the boys who had received their emblems of manhood in the previous initiation ceremonies brought small sacks of the field's harvest into the city. Then everyone returned and plowed the field as a symbol of the importance of the corn harvest. Rituals to the corn deity, *mamazara*, were also conducted in each family's home to ensure an adequate supply of this grain.

Inti Raymi, celebrated in June, was the most important festival for the sun god, Inti. The entire festival was conducted on a hill near Cuzco called Manturcalla, and only Inca males of royal blood were allowed to attend. On the first day, 100 brown llamas were sacrificed. On the following days more llamas were sacrificed, not only to Inti, but also to Viracocha and Illapa. Many statues were carved of wood, dressed in fine *cumbi* cloth, and burned at the end of the festival. A special dance was performed four times a day, with much drinking of *chicha*. After the sacrifices were made on Manturcalla, half the participants went to nearby hills to make further sacrifices, while the rest stayed and danced. Llama figurines of gold, silver, and seashells were buried on the three nearby hills. The climax of the festival involved the sacrifice of special young llamas to Viracocha, whose image had been brought to Manturcalla on litters carried by important individuals. After this, all the charcoal and burned bones from the sacrifices were collected and deposited in a place near the hill, and everyone returned to Cuzco to continue singing and dancing for the rest of the day.

Every other month had associated rituals as well, making a full calendar of ceremonial events. In addition, there were public ceremonies for special events such as war or natural catastrophe. Although the event might vary, the ceremony was the same. As with the initiation rites, all nonnoble residents were sent away from Cuzco and all residents avoided eating salt, chili peppers, and *chicha* (corn beer) and refrained from sexual activity. The images of Viracocha, Inti, and Illapa were brought into the main square, along with the kings' mummies (which were also gods), and sacrifices—including children—were performed. Then boys under 20 years of age put on special costumes and walked around the square eight times, followed by a nobleman who scattered coca on the ground. The boys spent the night in the square praying to Viracocha and the Sun to end the particular problem that warranted the ceremony. In the morning, everyone broke fast with a great feast and much *chicha* drinking, which lasted two days.

In addition to the ceremonies conducted according to the calendar and for the good of the empire, there were ceremonies for other purposes. These fall into three general categories: divination, curing, and sorcery. Divination was the attempt to foretell events in the future. This was widely practiced by the Incas, who rarely did anything without trying to divine the outcome. Oracles were supernatural figures that could answer questions about the future. They were the most powerful form of divination and were consulted only for important reasons, such as when to attack an enemy or if disease had struck a king. They might be human images or other figures. The Oracle of Pachacamac, on the central coast south of Lima, was described by Cobo as a wooden image carved into a "fierce and frightening figure." An important oracle near Cuzco was a post decorated with a golden band to which two golden breasts were attached. It was dressed in fine women's clothing, with a row of smaller figures on each side.

An individual would approach the oracle and ask it a question. The oracle was said to answer in a voice that could be understood only by the priests or attendants of the oracle. There were four main oracles: the one near Cuzco, two on the coast near modern-day Lima, and one in the central highlands. At least one of these, the Oracle of Pachacamac south of Lima, predated the Incas, having been founded during the Middle Horizon (600–1000 C.E.).

For less serious divinations, the priests sacrificed a llama, took out a lung, and blew into a vein. The markings on the vein as it was distended indicated to the priest if the outcome would be positive or negative. The same ceremony could be conducted with guinea pigs, although these were used for less important divinations.

Even simpler forms involved counting whether a group of pebbles had an even or odd number; chewing coca, spitting the juice on the hand, and seeing how it ran down the fingers; observing the movement of spiders or snakes; and burning llama fat or coca leaves and inspecting the way the fire burned. It is obvious that the priests in charge of interpreting these signs had a great deal of influence in deciding what the outcome should be.

Sorcerers also could be consulted to foretell the future by speaking to evil spirits. Often they did this by drinking themselves into a stupor, which allowed them to see and speak to the spirits. This kind of divination was used by individuals for personal reasons. Sorcery was performed for the purpose of bringing misfortune or even death on another person. This was often done in a manner akin to modern voodoo, by making a figure of the person and piercing it with sharp objects or burning it. Another means was to obtain some part of the victim—such as hair, nails, skin, or teeth—and injure or harm it as a means of passing on that treatment to the victim. Sorcery was forbidden. Not only would a sorcerer be put to death if discovered, but also his entire family.

Unusual events could be interpreted as omens of good or evil, usually the latter. Eclipses and shooting stars were considered particularly bad luck. Rainbows, the hooting of an owl, or the howling of a dog, were also signs of bad things to come. Dreams were important portents of good or evil, although the individual who had the dream interpreted its significance; there were no special interpreters of dreams.

In contrast to the priests and priestesses in service to the official Inca religious shrines, both curers and sorcerers were part-time practitioners, doing the supernatural work in addition to their other jobs, such as farming or making pottery (Malpass, 106–12).

FOR MORE INFORMATION

Cobo, B. *Inca Religion and Customs*. Ed. and trans. Roland Hamilton. Austin: University of Texas Press, 1990.

Malpass, M. A. *Daily Life in the Inca Empire*. Westport, Conn.: Greenwood, 1996.

Reinhard, J. "Sacred Peaks of the Andes." *National Geographic Magazine* 181, 3 (1992): 86–111.

Rowe, J. "Inca Culture at the Time of the Spanish Conquest." In *Handbook of South American Indians*. Vol. 2, *The Andean Civilizations*, ed. Julian H. Steward, 183–330. Washington, D.C.: Bureau of American Ethnology Bulletin 143, 1946.

Sacred Story: Beginnings and Endings

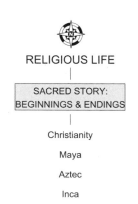

RELIGIOUS LIFE
|
SACRED STORY:
BEGINNINGS & ENDINGS
|
Christianity

Maya

Aztec

Inca

Although the word *myth* is frequently used in everyday language to mean an untrue, but widely believed statement, scholars of religion use the word *myth* to refer to sacred stories that teach important lessons about the world. In this sense of the word, myths are stories that explain how the world works, how things came to be, what man's role in the world is, and what things may happen in the future. Sometimes myths are believed to be literally true and sometimes they are viewed more as fables that are fiction, but teach a lesson. Myths are frequently set in a time period long ago, or in the future. Myths are different from historical accounts, because historical accounts rely on verifiable sources of information, such as eye-witness accounts or archaeological remains. Myths, rather, are handed down from generation to generation and are not concerned greatly with the trivia of history. While myths are not historical accounts, that does not mean that they may not contain historical, as well as allegorical and spiritual, truths. An interesting connection between myth and history appears in the Aztec and Inca origin myths. The Mexica (Aztecs) believed that they first appeared out of seven caves. Similarly, the Inca believed that their ancestors appeared first in a cave, and then left to found the city of Cuzco. These stories may perhaps reflect a time period when the ancestors of these tribes were living as hunter-gatherers and would take refuge in caves, rather than building permanent dwellings.

Creation myths are found in very many religions. These stories answer some of the most basic questions of human self-reflection: how did I come to be here, and why am I here? The answers to these questions directly affect the lives of individual people. For example, in the Christian story of creation, human beings are created by God and are made in God's image. As a result, human life is treated as something sacred, and acts such as murder are outlawed. In Aztec creation myths, the Sun, and the world with it, was brought about by sacrifice. The Aztecs believed that the Sun still needed sacrifice to maintain its regular course across the sky, creating the days, nights, and seasons. As a result, human sacrifice was an important part of Aztec religious life. Even nonreligious creation myths have strong impacts. For example, the Darwinian creation myth, that holds that life is essentially an accident and that only the strong survive, was influential in forming the laissez-faire ethics of the late-19th and early-20th century. Laissez-faire essentially taught that people should look out primarily for themselves alone and that it was fine to cause other people suffering. It is clear that beliefs about where we came from and why we are here can dramatically affect how we act and behave.

Stories about the end of the world or about life after death can also have a great impact on how humans live their lives in the present. Very many religions believe that the soul will go either to a place of reward or to a place of suffering upon death. Most people in the Western world are familiar with the Christian concepts of heaven and hell. Depending on the Christian denomination, one goes to heaven either because of good works, or because of faith, or because of God's predestination. Hell is reserved for those who don't go to heaven. The religious systems in the Americas had many similarities. For example, the Aztecs believed that a person's souls could go to a variety of places after death, some pleasant and some not. For example, warriors killed in the battlefield, women who died in childbirth, and people sacrificed to the Sun would go to the sky of the Sun after death and would live a pleasant life of leisure there. On the other hand, ordinary people who led an undistinguished life and died of disease would go to Mictlan, a foul-smelling place full of torments. As seen in these examples, the criteria for determining where one's souls went was frequently related to the manner of death; while a woman who died in childbirth would join the Sun, a woman who bore several children but died of disease in old age would go to Mictlan. Yet these criteria do interact somewhat with the qualities of leading a distinguished life. A warrior was more likely to be killed if he was at the forefront of the fighting, than if he was hanging back in the rear lines and constantly shunning battle. An Aztec was thus encouraged to live a daring and intrepid life, while a Catholic was urged to live a charitable life toward others. In all cases, myths and the sacred stories about the beginning and end of the world taught lessons that changed lives.

~Lawrence Morris

CHRISTIANITY (ENGLAND, SPAIN, ITALY)

RELIGIOUS LIFE

SACRED STORY:
BEGINNINGS & ENDINGS

Christianity

Maya

Aztec

Inca

The Christian story about the creation of the world was the same as the Jewish story, since Christianity accepted the Jewish account of the history of God's action up until the coming of Christ. According to the Book of Genesis, God had created the world. There are actually two creation stories in Genesis. The first one delineates the various things that God created on each day. The whole of creation took God six days to make, and on the seventh day God rested. This creation story reflected the Jewish week, which has come to be the standard work unit in Western countries. Jewish communities would work six days, but would set aside the seventh day as free from work and dedicated to the worship of God in commemoration that God himself rested on the seventh day. The Christian community transferred the day of rest from Saturday, which was the Jewish day of rest, to Sunday, in honor of Jesus's resurrection, which occurred on a Sunday. According to Genesis, at the end of each day's work of creation, the story repeated the words, "God looked at what he had created, and it was good." These words had a strong impact on Christianity. While certain religions in the Middle East, Zoroastrianism for example, viewed the material world as evil, the Jewish and Christian communities viewed the material world as essentially good, even if inferior to the spiritual realm.

The second story of creation in Genesis, which immediately follows the first story, goes into greater detail about how God created human beings. In this story, God fashioned Adam, the first man, out of clay and breathed life into him. God then created various animals and brought them to Adam, who gave them names. None of the animals, however, were suitable companions for Adam, so God put Adam into a deep sleep, removed one of his ribs, and made a new creature, a woman, out of the rib and clay. When Adam saw Eve, the first woman, he said, "This is bone of my bone and flesh of my flesh." And the two were united and became one. This story taught several lessons. First of all, that man had a special relationship with God and had been filled with God's breath. Secondly, man was in charge of the animals. And finally, that man and woman were natural partners and designed to live together as man and wife.

Christianity had a well-developed notion of what the end of the world would be like. Jesus gave several descriptions of the end of the world, to which the early Church added further details, and the end was generally very frightening. Before the end, there would be great wars and the world would be consumed with fire. Jesus would return on the clouds, and the dead would rise up from their graves. All the living and the dead would be brought to one place and would be judged by Jesus. Those who had helped the poor and disadvantaged in this life would be led to heaven, while those who had led selfish lives would be brought to everlasting pain and suffering.

While the full judgment would come at the end of the world, it was believed that those who had died would undergo some form of immediate judgment at the moment of their death. The very holy would go to heaven directly, while unrepentant sinners would go to hell. Those who were repentant but not very holy would go to a place called purgatory, where they would be purified of their attachment to sinful things and made ready for heaven. Purgatory was often viewed as a place of suffering and punishment, since those were the usual associations of sin. Many people's view of heaven and hell was affected by Dante's vivid descriptions in his *Divine Comedy*, written in the 14th century. In this story, based upon earlier descriptions of the afterlife, Dante imagines himself taking a tour of hell, purgatory, and heaven. These places are divided into different sections. Those who are guilty of the most serious sins, for example, are condemned to lower levels of hell where the torments are greatest, while those who are guilty of less serious sins are in the upper levels where the suffering is less. The punishments and rewards were carefully balanced so that the punishment would fit the crime. For example, those who were easily persuaded in this life to follow the whims of lust are pictured being blown around by a perpetual breeze in hell.

Another realm in the afterlife was limbo. This realm was reserved for children that had died before being baptized. Since they had not yet become united with God through baptism, they were not deemed capable of entering heaven, but since they had not committed any sins themselves, they would not be thrust into hell. Instead, they were brought to limbo, a place of pleasant contentment devoid of the great happiness of heaven and the great suffering of hell.

While Christian churches of all denominations believed in heaven and hell, most Protestant denominations did not believe in purgatory, and especially not in limbo, because there were no clear references to them in the Bible. Regardless of denomination, the vivid descriptions of heaven and hell to be found in the Bible, sermons, and popular literature, created a fear of hell and a hope for heaven that served as powerful motivations to live a just life.

To read about the view of death and the afterlife in Medieval Europe, see the Europe entry in the section "Death and the Afterlife" in chapter 8 ("Religious Life") in volume 2 of this series.

~Lawrence Morris

FOR MORE INFORMATION

The Catholic Study Bible. Ed. D. Senior. Oxford: Oxford University Press, 1990.

Dante. *The Divine Comedy.* Trans. J. D. Sinclair. 3 vols. New York: Oxford University Press, 1939.

New Bible Commentary: 21st Century Edition. Ed. D. A. Carson, R. T. France, J. A. Motyer, and G. J. Wenham. Leicester, UK: Inter-varsity Press, 1994.

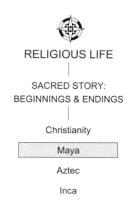

RELIGIOUS LIFE

SACRED STORY:
BEGINNINGS & ENDINGS

Christianity

Maya

Aztec

Inca

MAYA

The most complete and beautifully written record of Maya myth and history is preserved in the *Popol Vuh,* the sacred book of the highland Quiche Maya. It relates that there had been multiple creations before the present world and that the people of the present world were created out of maize. The central drama in the creation myth of the *Popol Vuh* is the saga of the first humans, the Maya Hero Twins. Their names in Quiche Mayan are Hunapu and Xbalanque (or Hun Ahau and Yax Balam in Yucatec). These names have contrasting associations, recalling both sun and Venus, and life and death. Hunapu (First Lord) is associated with Venus and celestial life. Xbalanque (Sacred Jaguar) is associated with the jaguar sun and death in the underworld.

The father of the Hero Twins was also a twin. He and his brother were ball players who had played ball in Xibalba and then were sacrificed by the gods of death. The brother was buried under the Xibalba ball court; the father was decapitated and his head hung in a calabash tree. From the tree his head impregnated one of the daughters of the death gods by spitting into her hand. Fleeing this angry death god, the pregnant girl came to the earthly realm. There she gave birth to the Hero Twins, who grew up and discovered their father's old ball game equipment. Realizing their heritage, they followed their father and uncle by becoming such famous ball players that they too were invited to play ball in Xibalba with the lords of the underworld.

In Xibalba the gods of death subjected the Hero Twins to a series of daily ball games and nightly trials, but they outwitted the death gods each time. However, the only way they could escape Xibalba was by jumping into a pit of fire. After the death gods ground up their bones and threw them into a river, the Hero Twins were reborn and returned to Xibalba seeking revenge. They succeeded by showing the death gods an amazing feat. One twin decapitated the other, then brought him back to life. The death gods were so amazed by this that they demanded the Hero Twins perform the trick on them. This is what the Hero Twins were waiting for, so they decapitated the gods of death, but of course did not bring them back to life. Following their victory over death, the Hero Twins escaped from Xibalba and were transformed in the sky as the Sun and Venus, destined to re-enact their descent into Xibalba and their escape and rebirth forevermore.

The central themes of the Maya creation myth were replicated in religious rituals and the lives of individuals. The account of the Hero Twins entering Xibalba, outwitting the gods of death, and returning to life was a metaphor for the Sun, the greatest power in the universe. It also showed that rebirth came through sacrifice.

The rebirth of the Hero Twins after being sacrificed was a metaphor for human rebirth after death, a theme celebrated by the Maya ritual of human sacrifice. The ball court was the setting for the confrontation between the Hero Twins from this world and the death gods of Xibalba. In many Maya cities, the ball court symbolized the threshold between the earthly realm and Xibalba. The ritualized ball game played in this arena re-enacted the original confrontation between the Hero Twins and the death gods. Maya kings had the closest associations with the Hero Twins. Kings had the power to enter Xibalba and confront the death gods, play the sacred ball game, and perform human sacrifice. When a Maya king was captured by another in war, he was taken to the ball court to be defeated and sacrificed by decapitation. Thus he was sent to Xibalba to be born again in the sky in a ritual that re-enacted the myth of the Hero Twins. For more information on the ball game, see the section "Games and Sports" in chapter 7, "Recreational Life."

Dualistic symbolism is an important feature of Maya creation myth. Two sets of twins struggled with the lords of death. The struggle was between the forces of good (life) and evil (death). The Maya conceived of their world as an eternal replication of these two forces in conflict. For example, benevolent forces bring rain to make the fields grow to ensure that the people will have food. But evil forces cause drought, hurricanes, and plagues, which can destroy the crops and bring famine and death. Other dualistic themes reflected male-female and day-night contrasts. In fact, Maya deities had many contrasting sets of attributes.

Xibalba, the underworld, was the dwelling place of the dead. Its nine levels may have been associated with differences in life. After the Conquest, Bishop Landa reported that the Maya believed the underworld was divided into places of rest and places of suffering, although there may be European influence in this account. Priests and kings were said to go to the place of rest after death. Women who died in childbirth, warriors killed in battle, and suicides also went there. All who went to the place of rest could dwell in the shade and be free from labor. There was an abundance of food and drink, and no pain or suffering. Those who led evil lives went to the place of suffering in the ninth and lowest underworld, Mitnal.

The *Popul Vuh* creation myth also relates a Maya concept of rebirth after death. Evidence from inscriptions and excavations of royal tombs at Palenque, Tikal, and other cities suggests that after death and journeying to Xibalba, Maya kings were believed to be transformed into deities. This royal apotheosis replicated the myth of the rebirth of the Hero Twins and the daily rebirth of the sun rising out of the underworld. Apparently after their rebirth, the Maya kings were believed to dwell in the sky. But there is no evidence that any other people were believed to escape Xibalba after death (Sharer, 157–59).

FOR MORE INFORMATION

Sharer, R. J. *Daily Life in Maya Civilization.* Westport, Conn.: Greenwood, 1996.

Tedlock, D. *Popul Vuh: The Mayan Book of the Dawn of Life.* New York: Simon and Schuster, 1985.

AZTEC

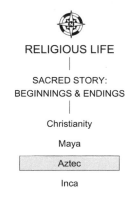

The Aztecs believed that there had been four ages, each with its own sun, before the present age. The First Age, or First Sun, had its beginning over three thousand years ago and was called 4 Jaguar. That age lasted 676 years, during which the different gods did battle to gain ascendancy, and then ocelots descended on the people and devoured them in a ravenous battle. The First Sun was destroyed and the cosmos was in darkness. Then the Second Sun, called 4 Wind, was created, and it lasted 364 years. The gods battled again before huge winds came and destroyed the homes, trees, and everything, and the sun was even carried away by the storm. Then the Third Sun was created and called 4 Rain, which really meant rain of fire. Again there was a dramatic confrontation among the gods, and the people were destroyed again, this time by fire, which rained for a whole day. The sun was also burned up and the cosmos was in darkness once again. Then the Fourth Sun, called 4 Water, was created; it lasted for 52 years before the heavens collapsed and the waters swallowed up everything, including the mountains. Finally, the Fifth Sun, the age in which the Aztecs dwelled, was created. It was called 4 Movement, which meant two things. On the one hand, it meant that the sun would move in an orderly fashion across the heavens. On the other hand, it meant that the age would end when the earth moved violently. It was feared in Aztec times that their age would be destroyed by colossal earthquakes. We can feel the tension of Aztec worry when we look at the details of the following story of how their age, the Fifth Sun, was created.

The world was dark and without movement at the end of the Fourth Sun when the gods gathered in a place called Teotihuacan, the Abode of the Gods. The gods gathered around a fire that gave them warmth, and they contemplated how to re-create the sun, the world, and life. It was decided that one of the gods must sacrifice himself by hurling himself into the fire, out of which the sun would be born. The gods debated among themselves about who would make the ultimate sacrifice.

Then the gods spoke: they said to Tecuciztecatl, "Now, Tecuciztecatl, enter the fire!" Then he prepared to throw himself into the enormous fire. He felt the great heat and he was afraid. Being afraid, he dared not hurl himself in, but turned back instead. . . . Four times he tried, four times he failed. After these failures, the gods then spoke to Nanahuatzin, and they said to him: "You Nanahuatzin, you try!" And as the gods had spoken, he braced himself, closed his eyes, stepped forward, and hurled himself into the fire. The sound of roasting was heard, his body crackled noisily. Seeing him burn thus in the blazing fire, Tecuciztecatl also leaped into the fire. (León-Portilla, 44)

Then the "gods sat waiting to see where Nanahuatzin would come to rise—he who fell first into the fire—in order that he might shine as the sun. In order that dawn might break." The gods sat for a long time looking in all directions, and a reddening of dawn appeared in all directions. But there was confusion because the gods did not know from which direction the sun would rise. "They expected that he might rise in all directions, because the light was everywhere." This confusion about the direction of the sunrise is solved by one of the gods, Quetzalcoatl (Feathered Serpent), who faced east and was imitated by other gods, including the Red Tezcatlipoca. And the sun rose in the east. "When it appeared, it was flaming red . . . no one was able to look at it: its light was brilliant and blinding, its rays were magnificently diffused in all directions."

But there was a problem. The sun did not move across the sky but rather "kept swaying from side to side." Faced with this partial sunrise and the crisis of no heavenly movement, the gods decided to sacrifice themselves. "Let this be, that through us the sun may be revived. Let all of us die." They cast themselves into the fire, but still the sun did not move, and the age or sun named 4 Movement did not begin. Only Ehecatl, the wind god, was left, so he "exerted himself fiercely and violently as he blew" the sun into motion across the sky. The dawn had truly come, and the orderly universe was created!

What do you make of this amazing story? First, it is important to note that, as with the other four ages of the world, it is very hard to get stability and order in the universe. The orderly flow of the sun is achieved only after extreme efforts. Second, this long struggle to bring the world into order and motion depends on sacrifices, real sacrifices of the gods, who give their lives so that the sun will move across the heavens. This involves violence, which, paradoxically, according to the believers in these myths, results in creation. The sun is created out of death, and even that is not quite enough. The last god, Ehecatl, must exert himself to the fullest. Finally, and this is a key point to understanding the expectations that Aztec peoples carried around during their days and nights, the universe was filled with a pessimistic tone. The myth of the four suns ends, "And as the elders continue to say, under this sun there will be earthquakes and hunger, and then our end shall come." The worldview was of a universe that was dynamic, unstable, and one day doomed to collapse.

One of the most profound and revealing ritual processes in Aztec society focused on death and the destiny of human beings after death. Every aspect of the passage from life to death and the destiny of the individual's souls (for the Aztecs believed that each human being had not one but three souls) was marked by rites that assisted in the dangerous and powerful passage.

One key to understanding the Aztec view of death is found in the lines of a poem recited by contemporary descendants of the Aztecs who live in the state of Puebla:

We live here on this earth
We are all fruits of the earth
the earth sustains us
we grow here, on the earth and lower
and when we die we wither in the earth
we are all fruits of the earth
We eat of the earth
because the earth eats us. (Carrasco, 122)

The point is this: humans need to eat to live. To eat, humans are forced to kill other beings, including plants and animals. Therefore, when they eat they ingest death into their bodies, and therefore carry death inside them, which also gives them life.

Death in the Aztec worldview is intimately tied up with this image of the earth from which and to which everyone, in part, comes, and on which everyone depends.

The earth was also thought of as a hungry mouth with cosmic jaws that demanded to be fed by humans. The lords of the underworld, Mictlantecuhtli and Cuezalli, it was said, "thirst and hunger for us, they pant after us, on our heels." All human bodies would suffer death, which was a destruction and fragmentation, but also an entrance into another world where another kind of life existed and was regulated by rituals.

The Aztecs believed that an individual had three kinds of soul: the *tonalli*, located in the head, which was the soul of will and intelligence; the *teyolia*, located in the heart, which was the soul of fondness and vitality; and the *ihiyotl*, located in the liver, which was the soul of passion, luminous gas, and aggression. All three were gifts from the gods deposited in the human body, but they were also found in animals, plants, and objects. At the time of death, these three souls in the human body dispersed into different regions of the universe. They could go to one of four places: Mictlan, which was in the underworld, for those who died an ordinary death; the sun in the sky, for warriors who died in combat, people sacrificed to the sun, and women who died while giving birth for the first time; Tlalocan, the rain god's mountain paradise, for those whose death was caused by water or water-related forces like frost or cold sicknesses; or Chichihualcuauhco, which was exclusively reserved for infants who died while still nursing from their mothers, that is, who had not yet eaten from the earth.

It appears that at least one of the souls, the *teyolia*, which resided in the heart, did not leave the body until one was cremated. This was especially true of a dead ruler, who could still be in communication, through the *teyolia*, with his ministers until his body was burned. At this point, rituals were important because relatives made offerings, shed tears, and said prayers at the fire's hearth. These ritual actions protected the soul and gave it strength during its dangerous journey. In the case of some rulers, the servants were sacrificed and cremated on a nearby pyre, but their hearts were extracted and burned on the same pyre as the dead *tlatoani*. These hearts, the *teyolia* of the servants, vessels of invigorating drinks, and clothes accompanied the soul of the ruler and protected it on its journey after death. The fires of cremation were also believed to call down a divine dog that would help the *teyolia* soul on its journey.

> *The Aztecs believed that an individual had three kinds of soul.*

After the death of the body, it took extended periods of time for the souls to reach their destination. It took four years to reach Mictlan, which was the lowest of the nine levels, but only 80 days to reach the Sky of the Sun, where the souls of warriors accompanied the solar god on his daily journey. During this time, the mourners carried out ritual offerings to assist the souls. Once the warrior's soul arrived in the Sky of the Sun, or Tonatiuh Ilhuicatl, the mourners could bathe and groom themselves for the first time in 80 days.

A special destiny awaited the souls of women who died in childbirth. These women were considered equal to warriors who died in battle or on the sacrificial stone. They too had made a sacrifice of their own lives so that a new life could come into the world. Their souls ascended into the female side of heaven, where they dwelt together and accompanied the sun from its zenith to its setting. On certain dates these spirits would come to earth and haunt the living.

It is also important to note that the souls of all human beings could become part of lesser gods and divine forces after death. Those who died without distinction from a common disease traveled along the icy paths of the underworld for four years until they arrived at the land of Mictlantecuhtli, where they would become part of his realm. This was a foul-smelling place of torment, to be avoided by living a life of distinction. By living a morally admirable life, a person would be selected by one of the gods who dwelled in another realm of the afterlife. It is also true that accidental deaths not related to human conduct could result in a more favorable afterlife (Carrasco, 37–41, 122–26).

FOR MORE INFORMATION

Carrasco, D., with S. Sessions. *Daily Life of the Aztecs: People of the Sun and Earth.* Westport, Conn.: Greenwood, 1998.

Durán, D. *The History of the Indies of New Spain.* Trans. Doris Heyden. Norman: University of Oklahoma Press, 1995.

Knab, T. "Tlalocan Talmanic: Supernatural Beings of the Sierra de Puebla." *Actes du XLIIe Congrés International des Américanistes, Congrés du Centenaire, Paris, 2–9 Septembre 1976.* Vol. 6: 127–36. Paris: Société des Américanistes, 1979.

León-Portilla, M. *Aztec Thought and Culture* Norman: University of Oklahoma Press, 1963.

López Austin, A. *The Human Body and Ideology: Concepts of the Ancient Nahuas.* Trans. Thelma Ortiz de Montellano and Bernardo Ortiz de Montellano. Salt Lake City: University of Utah Press, 1988.

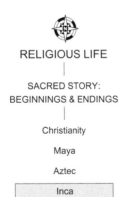

RELIGIOUS LIFE
|
SACRED STORY:
BEGINNINGS & ENDINGS
|
Christianity

Maya

Aztec

Inca

INCA

Myths are stories or legends concerning people and events in the past, especially ones that attempt to explain why the world or a people came to be. Myths of many societies, such as those of the Greeks, are mostly fanciful and have little basis in fact. Others may have some basis in fact, yet through countless years of telling and retelling, they have become more story than fact. Inca mythology contains examples of both. Also, myths concerning the origins of the world have been used by political leaders in many societies to justify the world order as they see it, especially in cases where there were marked inequalities between people. The Inca leadership certainly used their mythology for such purposes. All the Inca myths recorded by the Spaniards either explained where the Incas came from (origin myths) or described historical events. Whether or not other kinds of myths were held by the Incas is not known.

The origin myth of the Incas justified their elevated social standing over other people. The founding father and first king of the Incas was Manco Capac, according to Guaman Poma. He came out of the earth from a cave at a place called Pacariqtambo, accompanied by three brothers and four sisters. Over a period of several years they traveled to Cuzco with a group of other people who were loyal to them, who also came from caves at Pacariqtambo. One brother became feared by the others for his exceptional strength and was sent back to Pacariqtambo, where he was sealed up in the original caves. Another brother stayed at the mountain of Huanacauri, where he originated the male puberty rites. He then turned to stone and subsequently became an important cult figure of the Incas. The two other brothers and the four sisters continued to Cuzco. Upon reaching the Cuzco valley the Incas drove a golden staff into the ground, which was the sign that this would be the place of their permanent settlement. A third brother turned himself into a stone field guardian. Under the direction of the remaining brother, Manco Capac, the Incas drove out the native occupants and founded the capital of Cuzco.

In another variation of this myth, the author Garcilaso has Manco Capac and his sister (who was also his wife) travel to Pacariqtambo from Lake Titicaca, and then to Cuzco. After founding Cuzco, Manco traveled across the empire, organizing the ethnic groups and bringing them civilization.

The differences between these two versions are important, for they affected the social relations of the people who lived with the Incas in the Cuzco valley. In Guaman Poma's version, Manco Capac and his sister originate in Pacariqtambo and are accompanied from there by others; these others become the Incas-by-privilege. Because they accompanied the original ruler to Cuzco, they too are given the status of Inca. In Garcilaso's version, only Manco Capac and his sister come from Lake Titicaca; therefore the Incas-by-privilege were originally not Inca. They were given the title later. The differences between the two versions thus reflect a difference in whether the Incas-by-privilege were Incas from ancient times or only became Incas when the royal couple arrived in the Cuzco valley.

An interesting perspective is provided by Brian Bauer. He notes that Garcilaso was the great-grandson of Huayna Capac and hence a royal Inca. From Garcilaso's perspective, then, the Incas-by-privilege owed their Inca status to his ancestors having bestowed it on them. Guaman Poma, however, was from Huánuco and was therefore non-Inca. He saw the difference between the Incas-by-blood and Incas-by-privilege as one of degree.

Regardless, the clear implication of the origin myth is that the descendants of Manco Capac and the rulers of the Incas were the only noble Incas, and that others were subservient to them. The myth also justifies the Inca royal tradition of the king marrying his full sister (because Manco Capac did). In addition, it explains the existence of some of the shrines near Cuzco (where the two brothers were turned to stone) and the importance of the male puberty rites, because they were given to the Incas by one of the original brothers before he turned to stone.

Another important myth describes how the Earth began. The Incas believed in Viracocha, who was both the god who created the world and also a man who traveled the earth doing great deeds. Viracocha created the world and the sky with all its stars, and he brought the Sun and Moon out of an island in Lake Titicaca to light it. He then went to Tiahuanaco and formed people and animals out of clay. He painted each tribe's clothing differently. He gave them distinctive cultures and sent them into the earth, to emerge from it in their homelands. He then traveled throughout the world to see if everyone was behaving properly. Upon reaching Ecuador, he said farewell and walked out across the Pacific Ocean. Garcilaso's version of the Inca origin myth seems to combine the myth of Viracocha and that of Manco Capac.

The myth of Viracocha explains in simple terms how the Earth, stars, and people were all created by a divine being. In this respect it is similar to the version of God's creation of the world in the Bible. In general, the Incas used parts of the origin myths of other people—both of their own area and others, especially the Lake Titicaca region—to come up with one that explained the world as they had re-designed it.

The Incas' beliefs in an afterlife were akin to beliefs in a heaven and hell. Good people went to live with the sun, where life was the same as on earth but there was always plenty of food and drink. Bad people went to live beneath the earth, where they were perpetually cold and had only stones to eat. The Inca nobility went to heaven regardless of character. The Incas believed that the soul of a dead person protected its descendants from evil and liked its body to be brought out during festivals to be given food and *chicha* (maize beer) (Malpass, 101–6).

FOR MORE INFORMATION

Bauer, B. *The Development of the Inca State*. Austin: University of Texas Press, 1992.

Cobo, B. *Inca Religion and Customs*. Ed. and trans. Roland Hamilton. Austin: University of Texas Press, 1990.

Garcilaso de la Vega, El Inga. *Royal Commentaries of the Incas and General History of Peru*. Pts. 1 and 2. Trans. Harold Livermore. 1609. Reprint, Austin: University of Texas Press, 1966.

Guaman Poma de Ayala, F. *El Primer Nueva Corónica y Buen Gobierno [1584–1615]*. Ed. John Murra and Rolena Adorno. Trans. Jorge Urioste. 2 vols. Mexico City: Siglo Ventiuno, 1980.

Malpass, M. A. *Daily Life in the Inca Empire*. Westport, Conn.: Greenwood, 1996.

Rowe, J. "Inca Culture at the Time of the Spanish Conquest." In *Handbook of South American Indians*. Vol. 2, *The Andean Civilizations*, ed. Julian H. Steward. Washington, D.C.: Bureau of American Ethnology Bulletin 143, 1946. 183–330.

RELIGIOUS LIFE: WEB SITES

http://www.acoyauh.com/dioses.html.
http://www.jaguar-sun.com/gods.html.
http://www.ship.edu/~cgboeree/judaism.html.
http://www.islamfortoday.com/c15.htm.

PRIMARY SOURCES

AN ENGLISH BUSINESSWOMAN: THE AUTOBIOGRAPHY OF MARGERY KEMPE (CA. 1435)

Margery Kempe, a controversial mystic who lived in the early 15th century, left behind a valuable autobiography. This passage gives a glimpse of the opportunities that were available to women in her time, even though society was still largely run by males.

And then, out of pure covetousness, and in order to maintain her pride, she took up brewing, and was one of the greatest brewers in the town of N. for three or four years until she lost a great deal of money, for she had never had any experience in that business. For however good her servants were and however knowledgeable in brewing, things would never go successfully for them. For when the ale had as fine a head of froth on it as anyone might see, suddenly the froth would go flat, and all the ale was lost in one brewing after another, so that her servants were ashamed and would not stay with her. Then this creature thought how God had punished her before—and she would not take heed—and now again by the loss of her goods; and then she left off and did no more brewing.

And then she asked her husband's pardon because she would not follow his advice previously, and she said that her pride and sin were the cause of all her punishing, and that she would willingly put right all her wrongdoing. But yet she did not entirely give up the world, for she thought up a new enterprise for herself. She had a horse-mill. She got herself two good horses and a man to grind people's corn, and thus she was confident of making her living. This business venture did not last long, for shortly afterwards, on the eve of Corpus Christi, the following marvel happened. The man was in good health, and his two horses were strong and in good condition and had drawn well in the mill previously, but now, when he took one of those horses and put him in the mill as he had done before, this horse would not pull in the mill in spite of anything the man might do. The man was sorry, and tried everything he could think of to make his horse pull. Sometimes he led him by the head, sometimes he beat him, and sometimes he made a fuss of him, but nothing did any good, for the horse would rather go backwards than forwards. Then this man set a pair of sharp spurs on his heels and rode on the horse's back to make him pull, but it was no better. When this man saw it was no use, he put the horse back in his stable, and gave him food, and the horse ate well and freshly. And afterwards he took the other horse and put him in the mill. And just as his fellow had done so did he, for he would not pull for anything the man might do. And then this man gave up his job and would not stay any longer with the said creature.

Then it was noised about in the town of N. that neither man nor beast would serve the said creature, and some said she was accursed; some said God openly took vengeance on her; some said one thing and some said another. And some wise men, whose minds were more grounded in the love of our Lord, said it was the high mercy of our Lord Jesus Christ that called her from the pride and vanity of this wretched world.

And then this creature, seeing all these adversities coming on every side, thought they were the scourges of our Lord that would chastise her for her sin. Then she asked God for mercy, and forsook her pride and her covetousness, and the desire that she had for worldly dignity, and did great bodily penance, and began to enter the way of everlasting life as shall be told hereafter.

Margery Kempe, *The Book of Margery Kempe*, trans. B. A. Windeatt (London: Penguin, 1994).

ECONOMIC THEORIES FROM WILLIAM HARRISON'S *DESCRIPTION OF ENGLAND* (1587)

As coauthor of a history of Britain, William Harrison set out to give a description of the countryside and the current customs of its inhabitants. In the section below, Harrison blames middlemen, called *bodgers* or *loders*, for raising the market prices above what the poor country people could afford.

There are (as I take it) few great towns in England that have not their weekly markets, one or more granted from the prince, in which all manner of provision for household is to be bought and sold for ease and benefit of the country round about. Whereby, as it cometh to pass that no buyer shall make any great journey in the purveyance of his necessities, so no occupier shall have occasion to travel far off with his commodities, except it be to seek for the highest prices, which commonly are near unto great cities, where round and speediest utterance is always to be had. And as these have been in times past erected for the benefit of the realm, so are they in many places too-too much abused, for the relief and ease of the buyer is not so much intended in them as the benefit of the seller. Neither are the magistrates for the most part (as men loath to displease their neighbors for their one year's dignity) so careful in their offices as of right and duty they should be. For in most of these markets neither assizes of bread nor orders for goodness and sweetness of grain and other commodities that are brought thither to be sold are any whit looked unto but each one suffered to sell or set up what and how himself listeth, and this is one evident cause of dearth and scarcity in time of great abundance.

I could (if I would) exemplify in many, but I will touch no one particularly, sith it is rare to see in any country town (as I said) the assize of bread well kept according to the statute. And yet if any country baker happen to come in among them on the market day with bread of better quantity, they find fault by and by with one thing or another in his stuff; whereby the honest poor man, whom the law of nations do commend that he endeavoreth to live by any lawful means, is driven away and no more to come there upon some round penalty by virtue of their privileges. Howbeit, though they are so nice in the proportion of their bread, yet in lieu of the same there is such heady ale and beer in most of them as for the mightiness thereof among such as seek it out is commonly called huffcap, the mad-dog, father-whoreson, angels'-food, dragons'-milk, go-by-the-wall, stride-wide, and lift-leg, etc. And this is more to be noted, that when one of late fell by God's providence into a troubled conscience after he had considered well of his rechless life and dangerous estate, another, thinking belike to change his color and not his mind, carried him straightway to the strongest ale as to the next physician. It is incredible to say how our maltbugs lug [suck] at this liquor, even as pigs should lie in a row lugging at their dam's teats till they lie still again and be not able to wag. Neither did Romulus and Remus suck their she-wolf, or shepherd's wife, Lupa, with such eager and sharp devotion as these men hale at huffcap till they be red as cocks and little wiser than their combs. But how am I fallen from the market into the ale-house? In returning, therefore, unto my purpose, I find that in corn great abuse is daily suffered, to the great prejudice of the town and country, especially the poor artificer and householder which tilleth no land but, laboring all the week to buy a bushel or two of grain on the market day, can there have none for his money, because bodgers, loders, and common carriers of corn do not only buy up all but give above the price to be served of great quantities. Shall I go any further? Well, I will say yet a little more and somewhat by mine own experience. . . .

It is a world, also, to see how most places of the realm are pestered with purveyors, who take up eggs, butter, cheese, pigs, capons, hens, chickens, hogs, bacon, etc., in one market under pretense of their commissions and suffer their wives to sell the same in another or to poulterers of London. If these chapmen be absent but two or three market days, then we may perfectly see these wares to be more reasonably sold and thereunto the crosses sufficiently furnished of all things. In like sort, since the number of buttermen have so much increased and since they travel in such wise that they come to men's houses for their butter faster than they can make it, it is almost incredible to see how the price of butter is augmented; whereas, when the owners were enforced to bring it to the market towns and fewer of these butter buyers were stirring, our butter was scarcely worth 18*d.* the gallon that is now worth 3*s.* 4*d.* and perhaps 5*s.* Whereby also I gather that the maintenance of a superfluous number of dealers in most trades, tillage always excepted, is one of the greatest causes why the prices of things become excessive, for one of them do commonly use to outbid another. And whilst our country commodities are commonly bought and sold at our private houses, I never look to see this enormity redressed or markets well furnished.

William Harrison, *The Description of England,* ed. Georges Edelen (Ithaca, N.Y.: Cornell University Press, 1968).

THE MARRIAGE OF MARGERY PASTON (1469)

The letters and papers of the Pastons, an English land-owning family, comprise the largest and best-known archive of private correspondence to survive from the 15th century. The documents provide much insight into the social and political history of England during the period of civil strife known as the Wars of the Roses. In this passage, one of the most poignant in the collection, Margaret Paston explains to her son John her decision to disown John's youngest sister Margery, who had outraged the family by pledging herself in marriage to Richard Calle, the Pastons' bailiff—a man significantly below Margery in social rank.

On Friday the bishop he sent for her [Margery] by Ashfield and other[s] that are right sorry of her demeaning. And the bishop said to her plainly, and put her in remembrance how she was born, what kin and friends that she had, and should have more if she were ruled and guided after them; and if she did not, what rebuke, and shame, and loss should be to her, if she were not guided by them, and cause of forsaking of her for any good, or help, or comfort that she should have of them; and said that he had heard say that she loved such one [Calle] that her friends were not pleased with that she should have, and therefore he had her be right well advised how she did, and said that he would understand the words that she had said to him, whether it made matrimony or not. And she rehearsed what she had said [in promising marriage to Calle], and said if those words made it not sure, she said boldly that she would make it surer ere than she went thence, for she said she thought in her conscience she was bound, whatsoever the words were. These lewd words grieve me and her grandam as much as all the remnant. And then the bishop and the chancellor both said that there was neither I nor no friend of her would receive her. . . . I was with my mother at her place when she [Margery] was examined, and when I heard say what her demeaning was, I charged my servants that she should not be received in my house. I had given her warning, she might have been aware afore, if she had been gracious; and I sent to one or two more that they should not receive her if she came. She was brought again to my place for to have been received, and Sir James [Gloys] told them that brought her that I had charged them all and she should not be received; and so [the bishop has sent her to] Roger Best's . . . I am sorry that [Best and his wife] are cumbered with her, but yet am I better paid that she is there for the while than she had been in other place, because of the sadness [i.e., seriousness] and good disposition of himself and his wife, for she shall not be suffered there to play the brethel [i.e., whore]. I pray you and require you that you take it not pensily [i.e., heavily] for I wot [i.e., know] well it goes right near your heart, and so does it to mine and to other[s]. But remember you, and so do I, that we have lost of her but a brethel, and set it the less to heart, for, an' she had been good, wheresoever she had been, it should not have been as it is, for, an' he [Calle] were dead at this hour, she would never be at mine heart as she was. . . . For wot it well, she shall full sore repent her lewdness hereafter, and I pray God she might so.

John Warrington, ed., *The Paston Letters*, rev. ed., 2 vols. (London, J. M. Dent and Sons, Ltd, 1956).

THE BURNING OF BISHOPS LATIMER AND RIDLEY (1555)

Hugh Latimer and Nicholas Ridley, Protestants who had served as bishops of the English Church under Henry VIII and Edward VI, were burned to death for heresy in 1555 under Henry VIII's Catholic daughter Mary I. Like others of the so-called Marian martyrs, their story was later told by John Foxe in his popularly named *Book of Martyrs*, one of the most popular and widely read literary works of Elizabethan England. Foxe's work kept green the memory of those English men and women who died for their Protestant faith and helped fuel centuries of English hatred and distrust of Roman Catholicism.

The place of death was on the north side of the town [i.e., Oxford], opposite Baliol College. Dr. Ridley was dressed in a black gown furred, and Mr. Latimer had a long shroud on, hanging down to his feet. . . . When they came to the stake, Mr. Ridley embraced Latimer fervently, and bid him: "Be of good heart, brother, for God will either assuage the fury of the flame, or else strengthen us to abide it." He then knelt by the stake, and after earnestly praying together, they had a short private conversation. Dr. Smith then preached a short sermon against the martyrs, who would have answered him, but were prevented by Dr. Marshal, the vice-chancellor. Dr. Ridley then took off his gown and tippet, and gave them to his brother-in-law, Mr. Shipside. He gave away also many trifles to his weeping friends, and the populace were anxious to get even a fragment of his garments. Mr. Latimer gave nothing, and from the poverty of his garb, was soon stripped to his shroud, and stood venerable and erect, fearless of death.

Dr. Ridley being unclothed to his shirt, the smith placed an iron chain about their waists, and Dr. Ridley bid him fasten it securely; his brother having tied a bag of gunpowder about his neck, gave some also to Mr. Latimer.

Dr. Ridley then requested of Lord Williams . . . to advocate with the queen the cause of some poor men to whom he had, when bishop, granted leases, but which now the present bishop refused to confirm. A lighted fagot was now laid at Dr. Ridley's feet, which caused Mr. Latimer to say: "Be of good cheer, Ridley; and ply the man. We shall this day, by God's grace, light such a candle in England, as I trust, will never be put out."

When Dr. Ridley saw the fire flaming up towards him, he cried with a wonderful loud voice, "Lord, Lord, receive my spirit." Master Latimer, crying as vehemently on the other side, "O Father of heaven, receive my soul!" received the flame as it were embracing of it. After that he had stroked his face with his hands, and as it were, bathed them a little in the fire, he soon died (as it appeared) with very little pain or none.

William Byron Forbush, ed., *Foxe's Book of Martyrs* (Grand Rapids, Mich.: Zondervan Publishing House, 1967).

THE RESULT OF READING TOO MUCH, FROM MIGUEL DE CERVANTES'S *DON QUIXOTE* (1604–15)

Don Quixote, in which Miguel de Cervantes makes fun of the many stories of adventure that circulated in Spain at the time, is a masterpiece of Spanish Golden Age literature. While the book is fundamentally humorous, it also made serious statements about contemporaneous society and the role of fiction in shaping the perception of reality.

Writers there are who say the first adventure he met with was that of Puerto Lapice; others say it was that of the windmills; but what I have ascertained on this point, and what I have found written in the annals of La Mancha, is that he was on the road all day, and towards nightfall his hack and he found themselves dead tired and hungry, when, looking all around to see if he could discover any castle or shepherd's shanty where he might refresh himself and relieve his sore wants, he perceived not far out of his road an inn, which was as welcome as a star guiding him to the portals, if not the palaces, of his redemption; and quickening his pace he reached it just as night was setting in.

At the door were standing two young women, girls of the district as they call them, on their way to Seville with some carriers who had chanced to halt that night at the inn; and as, happen what might to our adventurer, everything he saw or imaged seemed to him to be and to happen after the fashion of what he read of, the moment he saw the inn he pictured it to himself as a castle with its four turrets and pinnacles of shining silver, not forgetting the drawbridge and moat and all the belongings usually ascribed to castles of the sort. To this inn, which to him seemed a castle, he advanced, and at a short distance from it he checked Rocinante, hoping that some dwarf would show himself upon the battlements, and by sound of trumpet give notice that a knight was approaching the castle. But seeing that they were slow about it, and that Rocinante was in a hurry to reach the stable, he made for the inn door, and perceived the two gay damsels who were standing there, and who seemed to him to be two fair maidens or lovely ladies taking their ease at the castle gate.

At this moment it so happened that a swineherd who was going through the stubbles collecting a drove of pigs (for, without any apology, that is what they are called) gave a blast of his horn to bring them together, and forthwith it seemed to Don Quixote to be what he was expecting, the signal of some dwarf announcing his arrival; and so with prodigious satisfaction he rode up to the inn and to the ladies, who, seeing a man of this sort approaching in full armour and with lance and buckler, were turning in dismay into the inn, when Don Quixote, guessing their fear by their flight, raising his pasteboard visor, disclosed his dry dusty visage, and with courteous bearing and gentle voice addressed them, "Your ladyships need not fly or fear any rudeness, for that it belongs not to the order of knighthood which I profess to offer offense to anyone, much less to highborn maidens as your appearance proclaims you to be." The girls were looking at him and straining their eyes to make out the features which the clumsy visor obscured, but when they heard themselves called maidens, a thing so much out of their line, they could not restrain their laughter, which made Don Quixote wax indignant, and say, "Modesty becomes the fair, and moreover laughter that has little cause is great silliness; this, however, I say not to pain or anger you, for my desire is none other than to serve you."

The incomprehensible language and the unpromising looks of our cavalier only increased the ladies' laughter, and that increased his irritation, and matters might have gone farther if at that moment the landlord had not come out, who, being a very fat man, was a very peaceful one. He, seeing this grotesque figure clad in armour that did not match any more than his saddle, bridle, lance, buckler, or corselet, was not at all indisposed to join the damsels in their manifestations of amusement; but, in truth, standing in awe of such a complicated armament, he thought it best to speak him fairly, so he said, "Senor Caballero, if your worship wants lodging, bating the bed (for there is not one in the inn) there is plenty of everything else here." Don Quixote, observing the respectful bearing of the Alcaide of the fortress (for so innkeeper and inn seemed in his eyes), made answer, "Sir Castellan, for me anything will suffice, for 'My armour is my only wear, My only rest the fray.'" The host fancied he called him Castellan because he took him for a "worthy of Castile," though he was in fact an Andalusian, and one from the strand of San Lucar, as crafty a thief as Cacus and as full of tricks as a student or a page. "In that case," said he, " 'Your bed is on the flinty rock, Your sleep to watch alway;' and if so, you may dismount and safely reckon upon any quantity of sleeplessness under this roof for a twelve-month, not to say for a single night."

Miguel de Cervantes Saavedra, *The Ingenious Gentleman Don Quixote of La Mancha*, trans. John Ormsby (London: Smith, Elder & Co., 1885).

EXCERPTS FROM THE DIARY OF FLORENTINE APOTHECARY LUCA LANDUCCI (1507, 1514)

Luca Landucci ran a small shop as an apothecary in Florence and kept a diary that relates intimate details of aspects of daily life. The passage regarding the animal fight gives some insight into what shocked the sensibilities of Renaissance Italians. Apparently, the sight of mating horses proved more shocking than that of a dying man.

A Personal Tragedy, August 2, 1507

As it pleased God, the house in which I lived, next to the shop (the shop being in the middle of a house), was burnt down, and I lost my rooms, in which were all my things, worth more than 250 gold ducats. I had to buy all my household goods, clothes and furniture afresh, three rooms completely stocked; my son Maestro Antonio alone losing more than 50 or 60 ducats' worth: a red-cloth cloak, a purple tunic, both new, and all his other clothes and silk waistcoats, with all his books which were worth more than 25 ducats. I and my three other sons had nothing left but our shirts; and what was worse, Battista's bed had caught fire whilst he was asleep, and he escaped perfectly naked, and went to borrow a shirt in the neighbourhood. Nothing was saved except what the women had with them in the country, and Messer Antonio who was with them; so that they were not here to see the grief we suffered. But I accept adversity like prosperity, and thus give thanks to the Lord for the one as for the other; and I pray Him to pardon my sins and to send me all which tends to His glory. May God always be praised by all His creatures; every infirmity and pain can be comforted by such a thought, and we may learn from the saintly Job, who said: "The same Lord who gave them me has taken them away, praise be to God!"

An Animal Fight, June 25, 1514

There was a hunt in the *Piazza de' Signori*: two lions, and bears, leopards, bulls, buffaloes, stags, and many other wild animals of various kinds, and horses; the lions were brought in after the rest, and chiefly the one that came first did nothing, on account of the great tumult of the crowd; except that certain big dogs approaching him, he seized one with his paw and dropped it dead on the ground, and a second the same, without taking any notice of the other wild beasts; when he was not molested, he stood quite still, and then went away further on. They had made a tortoise and a porcupine, inside of which were men who made them move along on wheels all over the Piazza, and kept thrusting at the animals with their lances. This hunt was thought so much of, that the number of wooden platforms and enclosures made in the Piazza was a thing never before seen, the cost of bringing the timber and of erecting these stands being very great; it seemed incredible that any city in the world could have such a mass of timber. One carpenter paid 40 gold florins for the permission to put up a platform against one of these houses, and there were people who paid three or four *grossoni* for a place on the stands. All the stands and enclosures were crowded, as also the windows and the roofs, such a concourse of people never having been known, for numbers of strangers had come from many different parts. Four cardinals had come from Rome disguised, and many Romans accompanied by a quantity of horsemen. At the end of the evening it was found that many men had been injured and about three killed in fighting with the wild beasts; one had been killed by a buffalo. They had made a beautiful large fountain in the middle of the Piazza, which threw the water up in four jets, and round this fountain was a wood of verdure, with certain dens very convenient for the animals to hide in, and low troughs full of water round the fountain, for them to be able to drink. Everything had been very well arranged, except that someone without the fear of God did an abominable thing in this Piazza, in the presence of 40 thousand women and girls, putting a mare into an enclosure together with the horses; which much displeased decent and well-behaved people, and I believe that it displeased even the ill-behaved people. Finally the lions made no more attacks, becoming cowed by the immense tumult of the people. I remember another time when the same sort of hunt was made, more than 60 years ago, two lions also being brought in; and in the first attack one of them threw himself upon a horse, and caught hold of him in the soft part of his body, and the powerful horse, being terrified, dragged him from the *Mercatantia* to the middle of the Piazza; the lion got nothing but the mouthful of skin that was torn off; and this fact caused such a tumult, that the said lion was frightened and went and sat in a corner, and neither he nor the second one would make another attack. Which shows that there cannot be a display amidst the tumult of the people. That earlier hunt had been held on the occasion of the Duke of Milan coming to Florence.

Luca Landucci, *A Florentine Diary from 1450 to 1516*, trans. Alice de Rosen Jervice (London: Dent, 1927).

BALDESAR CASTIGLIONE ON GENTLEMANLY SPORT IN ITALY (1527)

> *The Book of the Courtier* by Baldesar Castiglione defined what it meant to be a gentleman for centuries after its publication in 1527. It set the standard of behavior for anyone interested in achieving a significant social position. This passage also highlights the importance of class in Renaissance Italy.

There be some other exercises that may be done both openly and privately, as dancing: and in this I believe the Courtier ought to have a respect, for if he dances in the presence of many and in a place full of people, he must (in my mind) keep a certain dignity, tempered notwithstanding with a handsome and sightly sweetness of gestures, and for all he feels himself very nimble and to have time and measure at will, yet let him not enter into that swiftness of feet and doubled footings, that we see are very comely in our Barletta, and peradventure were unseemly for a Gentleman, although privately in a chamber together as we be now, I will not say but he may do both that, and also dance the morsico and braulles, yet not openly unless he were in a mask. And though it were so that all men knew him, it skills not, for there is no way to that, if a man will show himself in open sight about such matters, whether it be in arms, or out of arms. Because to be in a mask brings with it a certain liberty and license, that a man may among other things take upon him the form of that he hath best skill in, and use study and preciseness about the principal drift of the matter wherein he will show himself, and a certain Recklessness about that is not of importance, which augments the grace of the thing, as it were to disguise a young man in an old man's attire, but so that his garments be not a hindrance to him to show his nimbleness of person. And a man at arms in form of a wild shepherd, or some other such kind of disguising, but with an excellent horse and well trimmed for the purpose. Because the mind of the lookers on runs forthwith to imagine the thing that is offered unto the eyes at the first show, and when they behold afterward a far greater matter to come of it then they looked for under that attire, it delights them and they take pleasure at it.

Therefore it were not meet in such pastimes and open shows, where they take up counterfeiting of false visages, a prince should take upon him to be like a prince in deed, because in so doing, the pleasure that the lookers on receive at the novelty of the matter should want a great deal, for it is no novelty at all to any man for a prince to be a prince. And when it is perceived that beside his being a prince, he will also bear the shape of a prince, he loses the liberty to do all those things that are out of the dignity of a prince. And in case there should any contention happen especially with weapon in these pastimes, he might easily make men believe that he keeps the person of a prince because he will not be beaten but spared of the rest: beside that, doing in sport the very same he should do in good earnest when need required, it would take away his authority in deed and would appear in like case to be play also. But in this point the prince stripping himself of the person of a prince, and mingling himself equally with his underlings (yet in such wise that he may be known) while refusing superiority, let him challenge a greater superiority, namely, to pass other men, not in authority, but in virtue, and declare that his prowess is not increased by his being a prince.

Therefore I say that the Courtier ought in these open sights of arms to have the self same respect according to his degree. But in vaulting, wrestling, running and leaping, I am well pleased he flee the multitude of people, or at least be seen very seldom times. For there is nothing so excellent in the world, that the ignorant people have not their fill of, and smally regard in often beholding it. The like judgment I have in music: but I would not our Courtier should do as many do, that as soon as they come to any place, and also in the presence of great men with whom they have no acquaintance at all, without much entreating set out themselves to show as much as they know, yea and many times that they know not, so that a man would ween they came purposely to show themselves for that, and that it is their principal profession. Therefore let our Courtier come to show his music as a thing to pass the time withal, and as he were enforced to do it, and not in the presence of noble men, nor of any great multitude. And for all he be skillful and does well understand it, yet will I have him to dissemble the study and pains that a man must needs take in all things that are well done. And let him make semblance that he esteems but little in himself that quality, but in doing it excellently well make it much esteemed of other men.

Baldesar Castiglione, *The Book of the Courtier*, trans. Sir Thomas Hoby (London: David Nutt, 1900). The spelling has been modernized.

NICCOLÒ MACHIAVELLI ON THE TRUE QUALITIES OF PRINCES (1532)

Machiavelli's *The Prince* created a stir throughout Europe. Written in 1513 and published in 1532, the book was banned by the Catholic Church in 1559. Machiavelli caused controversy by attempting to write a book that was based upon the real methods of obtaining and maintaining power and that was not concerned primarily with moral instruction about ruling justly.

All the States and Governments by which men are or ever have been ruled, have been and are either Republics or Princedoms. Princedoms are either hereditary, in which the sovereignty is derived through an ancient line of ancestors, or they are new. New Princedoms are either wholly new, as that of Milan to Francesco Sforza; or they are like limbs joined on to the heredity possessions of the Prince who acquires them, as the Kingdom of Naples to the dominions of the King of Spain. The States thus acquired have either been used to life under a Prince or have been free; and he who acquires them does so either by his own arms or by the arms of others, and either by good fortune or by merit. . . .

And the manner in which we live, and that in which we ought to live, are things so wide asunder, that he who quits the one to betake himself to the other is more likely to destroy than to save himself; since any one who would act up to a perfect standard of goodness in everything, must be ruined among so many who are not good. It is essential, therefore, for a Prince who desires to maintain his position, to have learned how to be other than good, and to use or not to use his goodness as necessity requires.

Leaving aside, therefore, all fanciful notions concerning a Prince, and considering those only that are true, I saw that all men when they are spoken of, and Princes more than others from their being set so high, are characterized by some one of those qualities which attach either praise or blame. Thus one is accounted liberal, another miserly (which word I use, rather than *avaricious*, to denote the man who is too sparing of what is his own, *avarice* being the disposition to take wrongfully what is another's); one is generous, another greedy; one cruel, another tender-hearted; one is faithless, another true to his word, one effeminate and cowardly, another high-spirited and courageous; one is courteous, another haughty; one impure, another chaste; one simple, another crafty; one firm, another facile; one grave, another frivolous; one devout, another unbelieving; and the like. Every one, I know, will admit that it would be most laudable for a Prince to be endowed with all of the above qualities that are reckoned good; but since it is impossible for him to possess or constantly practice them all, the conditions of human nature not allowing it, he must be discreet enough to know how to avoid the infamy of those vices that would deprive him of his government, and, if possible, be on his guard also against those which might not deprive him of it; though if he cannot wholly restrain himself, he may with less scruple indulge in the latter. He need never hesitate, however, to incur the reproach of those vices without which his authority can hardly be preserved; for if he well consider the whole matter, he will find that there may be a line of conduct having the appearance of virtue, to follow which would be his ruin, and that there may be another course having the appearance of vice, by following which his safety and well-being are secured. . . .

And here comes in the question whether it is better to be loved rather than feared, or feared rather than loved. It might perhaps be answered that we should wish to be both; but since love and fear can hardly exist together, if we must choose between them, it is far safer to be feared than loved. For of men it may generally be affirmed that they are thankless, fickle, false, studious to avoid danger, greedy of gain, devoted to you while you are able to confer benefits upon them, and ready, as I said before, while danger is distant, to shed their blood, and sacrifice their property, their lives, and their children for you, but in the hour of need they turn against you. The Prince, therefore, who without otherwise securing himself builds wholly on their professions is undone. For the friendships which we buy with a price, and do not gain by greatness and nobility of character, though they be fairly earned are not made good, but fail us when we have occasion to use them.

Moreover, men are less careful how they offend him who makes himself loved than him who makes himself feared. For love is held by the tie of obligation, which, because men are a sorry breed, is broken on every whisper of private interest; but fear is bound by the apprehension of punishment which never relaxes its grasp.

Nevertheless a Prince should inspire fear in such a fashion that if he do not win love he may escape hate. For a man may very well be feared and yet not hated, and this will be the case so long as he does not meddle with the property or with the women of his citizens and subjects. And if constrained to put any to death, he should do so only when there is manifest cause or reasonable justification. But, above all, he must abstain from the property of others. For men will sooner forget the death of their father than the loss of the patrimony. Moreover, pretexts for confiscation are never to seek, and he who has once begun to live by rapine always finds reasons for taking what is not his; whereas reasons for shedding blood are fewer, and sooner exhausted.

But when a Prince is with his army, and has many soldiers under his command, he must needs disregard the reproach of cruelty, for without such a reputation in its Captain, no army can be held together or kept under any kind of control.

Niccolò Machiavelli, *The Prince,* trans. N. H. Thomson (New York: P. F. Collier & Son, 1910).

EXCERPTS FROM THE *POPUL VUH,* THE BOOK OF MAYAN MYTHOLOGY (CA. 1550)

The *Popul Vuh* (Council Book) is the great book of Maya mythology. In it the Maya accounts of such events as the creation of the world and the victory of the

Hero Twins over the gods of death have been preserved. This central myth of the victory of the Hero Twins encapsulates the victory of the sun and life over the powers that sought to destroy them.

And on the fifth day they reappeared. They were seen in the water by the people. The two of them looked like catfish when their faces were seen by Xibalba. And having germinated in the waters, they appeared the day after that as two vagabonds, with rags before and rags behind, and rags all over too. They seemed unrefined when they were examined by Xibalba; they acted differently now.

It was only the Dance of the Poorwill, the Dance of the Weasel, only Armadillos they danced.

Only Swallowing Swords, only Walking on Stilts now they danced.

They performed many miracles now. They would set fire to a house, as if they were really burning it, and suddenly bring it back again. Now Xibalba was full of admiration.

Next they would sacrifice themselves, one of them dying for the other, stretched out as if in death. First they would kill themselves, but then they would suddenly look alive again. The Xibalbans could only admire what they did. Everything they did now was already the groundwork for their defeat of Xibalba.

And after that, news of their dances came to the ears of the lords, One and Seven Death. When they heard it they said:

"Who are these two vagabonds? Are they really such a delight? And is their dancing really that pretty? They do everything!" they said. An account of them had reached the lords. It sounded delightful, so then they entreated their messengers to notify them that they must come:

" 'If only they'd come make a show for us, we'd wonder at them and marvel at them,' say the lords, you will say," the messengers were told. So they came to the dancers, then spoke the words of the lords to them.

"But we don't want to, because we're really ashamed. Just plain no. Wouldn't we be afraid to go inside there, into a lordly house? Because we'd really look bad. Wouldn't we just be wide-eyed? Take pity on us! Wouldn't we look like mere dancers to them? What would we say to our fellow vagabonds? There are others who also want us to dance today, to liven things up with us, so we can't do likewise for the lords, and likewise is not what we want, messengers," said Hunahpu and Xbalanque. Even so, they were prevailed upon: through troubles, through torments, they went on their tortuous way. They didn't want to walk fast. Many times they had to be forced; the messengers went ahead of them as guides but had to keep coming back. And so they went to the lords.

And they came to the lords. Feigning great humility, they bowed their heads all the way to the ground when they arrived. They brought themselves low, doubled over, flattened out, down to the rags, to the tatters. They really looked like vagabonds when they arrived. So then they were asked what their mountain and tribe were, and they were also asked about their mother and father:

"Where do you come from?" they were asked.

"We've never known, lord. We don't know the identity of our mother and father. We must've been small when they died," was all they said. They didn't give any names.

"Very well. Please entertain us, then. What do you want us to give you in payment?" they were asked.

"Well, we don't want anything. To tell the truth, we're afraid," they told the lord.

"Don't be afraid. Don't be ashamed. Just dance this way: first you'll dance to sacrifice yourselves, you'll set fire to my house after that, you'll act out all the things you know. We want to be entertained. This is our heart's desire, the reason you had to be sent for, dear vagabonds. We'll give you payment," they were told.

So then they began their songs and dances, and then all the Xibalbans arrived, the spectators crowded the floor, and they danced everything: they danced the Weasel, they danced the Poorwill, they danced the Armadillo. Then the lord said to them:

"Sacrifice my dog, then bring him back to life again," they were told.
"Yes," they said.
When they sacrificed the dog
he then came back to life.
And that dog was really happy
when he came back to life.
Back and forth he wagged his tail
when he came back to life.

And the lord said to them:
"Well, you have yet to set my home on fire," they were told next, so then they set fire to the home of the lord. The house was packed with all the lords, but they were not burned. They quickly fixed it back again, lest the house of One Death be consumed all at once, and all the lords were amazed, and they went on dancing this way. They were overjoyed.

And then they were asked by the lord:

"You have yet to kill a person! Make a sacrifice without death!" they were told.
"Very well," they said.
And then they took hold of a human sacrifice.
And they held up a human heart on high.
And they showed its roundness to the lords.

And now One and Seven Death admired it, and now that person was brought right back to life. His heart was overjoyed when he came back to life, and the lords were amazed:

"Sacrifice yet again, even do it to yourselves! Let's see it! At heart, that's the dance we really want from you," the lords said now.
"Very well, lord," they replied, and then they sacrificed themselves.

And this is the sacrifice of little Hunahpu by Xbalanque. One by one his legs, his arms were spread wide. His head came off, rolled far away outside. His heart, dug out, was smothered in a leaf, and all the Xibalbans went crazy at the sight.

So now, only one of them was dancing there: Xbalanque.

"Get up!" he said, and Hunahpu came back to life. The two of them were overjoyed at this—and likewise the lords rejoiced, as if they were doing it themselves. One and Seven Death were as glad at heart as if they themselves were actually doing the dance.

And then the hearts of the lords were filled with longing, with yearning for the dance of little Hunahpu and Xbalanque, so then came these words from One and Seven Death:

"Do it to us! Sacrifice us!" they said. "Sacrifice both of us!" said One and Seven Death to little Hunahpu and Xbalanque.

"Very well. You ought to come back to life. What is death to you? And aren't we making you happy, along with the vassals of your domain?" they told the lords.

And this one was the first to be sacrificed: the lord at the very top, the one whose name is One Death, the ruler of Xibalba.

And with One Death dead, the next to be taken was Seven Death. They did not come back to life. . . .

Such was the defeat of the rulers of Xibalba. The boys accomplished it only through wonders, only through self-transformation.

Dennis Tedlock, *Popul Vuh: The Mayan Book of the Dawn of Life*, rev. ed. (London: Touchstone, 1996).

BISHOP DIEGO DE LANDA'S ACCOUNT OF CONFESSION AND SUFFERING IN THE AMERICAS (CA. 1566)

As the second bishop of the Yucatán, Diego de Landa had extensive dealings with the native population. Typical of many of the Spanish missionaries, he stridently suppressed the native religion, but he strove to protect them from the cruelties imposed by Spanish businessmen and adventurers.

CONFESSION AMONG THE MAYA

The Yucatecans knew by nature when they had committed an evil deed, and they believed that death, disease, and suffering came as a result of evil and sin. As a result, they practiced a kind of confession, as follows. Whenever as a result of sickness or other cause they were in danger of death, they confessed their sins, and if perhaps they forgot to do this, their close relatives or their friends reminded them of it. They then publicly announced their sins to the priest, or if he was not available, to their fathers and mothers, or a wife might confess to her husband, and a husband to his wife.

The most common sins of which they accused themselves were theft, murder, lust, and false witness. After they had done this, they believed that they were saved. It sometimes happened that, though they managed to escape death, that arguments arose between man and wife as a result of the infidelities that they had committed, and arguments also with those men or women who had caused the infidelities.

The men confessed their weaknesses, except those which they committed with their slaves, since they said that it was permitted to use those things that belonged to them. Nor did they confess sinful thoughts, though they believed them to be harmful, and in their gatherings and sermons they advised people to avoid such thoughts. The most common fast was to restrain from salt and spice in their meals, which they thought to be very difficult. During the celebration of all their festivals, they also abstained from sexual relations.

Those who were widowed would not remarry until a year after the death of their spouse, in order to remain chaste for that year. Those who broke this custom were thought to have little self-control and it was believed that they would suffer some evil as a result.

THE SUFFERING OF THE INDIANS

The Indians resented the yoke of slavery, but the Spanish had split them up in various areas. Nevertheless, there were some Indians who revolted against them, to which the Spanish responded with some very cruel measures that caused the population to decrease. Some of the chief men from the district of Kupul were burnt alive and others were hanged. They also prosecuted the people of Yobain, in the district of the Chels: they seized some prominent men, chained them, and placed them in a house to which they then set fire. They were burnt alive with unimaginable cruelty. And Diego de Landa said that he had seen a large tree near this area where a captain had hanged a great number of Indian women, and had hanged small children from the feet of their mothers. In this same area, and in another area called Verey two miles from there, they hanged two Indian women, one a virgin and one recently married for no other reason except that they were beautiful. This happened when there was fear of an uprising in the Spanish camp on account of these women and they decided to kill these women in order to make the Indians believe that the Spanish did not care about their women. The beauty of these two and the cruelty of those who killed them is still much remembered by the Indians and the Spanish.

The Indians of the provinces of Cochuah and Chectemal revolted, and the Spanish put them down in such a manner that these two provinces, which had been the most populous and full of people, became the most desolate in the whole country. The Spanish committed cruelties never before heard of, cutting off noses, hands, arms, legs. They cut off women's breasts and threw the women into deep lakes with gourds attached as weights to their feet, and they stabbed the children because they did not march as quickly as their mothers. And if those who wore the neck-ring fell ill or didn't travel as fast as the others, they cut off their heads in front of the others so as not to stop and lose time in untying them. They used similar methods to drag along a great number of captives, men and women, destined for slavery. But it is confirmed that Don Francisco de Montejo never committed any of these cruelties, and that they were never done in his presence; instead, he always condemned them but was not able to stop them.

The Spanish attempted to defend such barbarity by saying that since there were only few Spanish in the country, they were unable to conquer so many people without subjecting them to terrible punishments, and they cited the example of the Hebrew people when they came to the promised land and how such great cruelties were committed at God's own command. On the other hand, the Indians were right to defend their liberty, and to place their trust in the brave captains among them in the hope of ridding themselves of the Spanish.

Diego de Landa, *Relation des choses de Yucatán*, ed. and trans. (into French) Jean Genet (Paris: Genet, 1928). These selections translated into English by Lawrence Morris.

BERNAL DIAZ DEL CASTILLO'S DESCRIPTION OF THE AZTEC RULER MOTECUHZOMA (1517)

In search of adventure and wealth, the twenty-four-year-old Bernal Diaz del Castillo set off for the Americas in 1517. After several disastrous expeditions, Bernal joined the forces under Cortés and was a first-hand witness to many parts of Cortés's campaign to subdue the Aztec empire. In this excerpt, the young Spaniard describes the person and court of the Aztec ruler Motecuhzoma (Montezuma).

The Great Montezuma was about forty years old, of good height and well proportioned, slender and spare of flesh, not very swarthy, but of the natural colour and shade of an Indian. He did not wear his hair long, but so as just to cover his ears, his scanty black beard was well shaped and thin. His face was somewhat long, but cheerful, and he had good eyes and showed in his appearance and manner both tenderness and, when necessary, gravity. He was very neat and clean and bathed once every day in the afternoon. He had many women as mistresses, daughters of Chieftains, and he had two great Cacicas as his legitimate wives. He was free from unnatural offences. The clothes that he wore one day, he did not put on again until four days later. He had over two hundred chieftains in his guard, in other rooms close to his own, not that all were meant to converse with him, but only one or another, and when they went to speak to him they were obliged to take off their rich mantles and put on others of little worth, but they had to be clean, and they had to enter barefoot with their eyes lowered to the ground, and not to look up in his face. And they made him three obeisances, and said: "Lord, my Lord, my Great Lord," before they came up to him, and then they made their report and with a few words he dismissed them, and on taking leave they did not turn their backs, but kept their faces towards him with their eyes to the ground, and they did not turn their backs until they left the room. I noticed another thing, that when other great chiefs came from distant lands about disputes or business, when they reached the apartments of the Great Montezuma, they had to come barefoot and with poor mantles, and they might not enter directly into the Palace, but had to loiter about a little on one side of the Palace door, for to enter hurriedly was considered to be disrespectful.

For each meal, over thirty different dishes were prepared by his cooks according to their ways and usage, and they placed small pottery braziers beneath the dishes so that they should not get cold. They prepared more than three hundred plates of the food that Montezuma was going to eat, and more than a thousand for the guard. When he was going to eat, Montezuma would sometimes go out with his chiefs and stewards, and they would point out to him which dish was best, and of what birds and other things it was composed, and as they advised him, so he would eat, but it was not often that he would go out to see the food, and then merely as a pastime.

I have heard it said that they were wont to cook for him the flesh of young boys, but as he had such a variety of dishes, made of so many things, we could not succeed in seeing if they were of human flesh or of other things, for they daily cooked fowls, turkeys, pheasants, native partridges, quail, tame and wild ducks, venison, wild boar, reed birds, pigeons, hares and rabbits, and many sorts of birds and other things which are bred in this country, and they are so numerous that I cannot finish naming them in a hurry; so we had no insight into it, but I know for certain that after our Captain censured the sacrifice of human beings, and the eating of their flesh, he ordered that such food should be prepared for him thenceforth.

Let us cease speaking of this and return to the way things were served to him at meal times. It was in this way: if it was cold they made up a large fire of live coals of a firewood made from the bark of trees which did not give off any smoke, and the scent of the bark from which the fire was made was very fragrant, and so that it should not give off more heat than is required, they placed in front of it a sort of screen adorned with figures of idols worked in gold. He was seated on a low stool, soft and richly worked, and the table, which was also low, was made in the same style as the seats, and on it they placed the table cloths of white cloth and some rather long napkins of the same material. Four very beautiful cleanly women brought water for his hands in a sort of deep basin which they call *xicales*, and they held others like plates below to catch the water, and they brought him towels. And two other women brought him tortilla bread, and as soon as he began to eat they placed before him a sort of wooden screen painted over with gold, so that no one should watch him eating. Then the four women stood aside, and the four great chieftains who were old men came and stood beside them, and with these Montezuma now and then conversed, and asked them questions, and as a great favour he would give to each of these elders a dish of what to him tasted best. They say that these elders were his near relations, and were his counsellors and judges of law suits, and the dishes and food which Montezuma gave them they ate standing up with much reverence and without looking at his face. He was served on Cholula earthenware either red or black. While he was at his meal the men of his guard who were in the rooms near to that of Montezuma, never dreamed of making any noise or speaking aloud.

Bernal Diaz del Castillo, *The Discovery and Conquest of Mexico, 1517–1521*, trans. A. Maudslay (London: Routledge, 1928).

BERNARDINO DE SAHAGÚN ON AZTEC SOCIETY: HUMAN SACRIFICE AND WOMEN'S DUTIES (1570)

The Franciscan priest, Bernardino de Sahagún, arrived in New Spain, as Spain's American possessions were then called, in 1529, shortly after the conquest of the Aztec empire. The first selection offers a description of the rituals leading up to the sacrifice of a captured warrior, while the second selection categorizes the various kinds of women in Aztec society and their potential vices and virtues.

SACRIFICE RITUALS

Tlacaxipeualiztli. This feast came and was thus celebrated; [it was] when all the captives died, all those taken in war—the men, the women, the children.

Those who had taken captives, when, on the morrow, their prisoners were to die, then began the captives' dance, when the sun had passed noon. And they held an all-night vigil for their prisoners there in the tribal temple. And they placed [the captives] before the fire and took hair from the top of the captives' heads, when half the night had passed and when they made offerings of blood from the ear.

And when the dawn came, then they made them leave, that they might go to die, they who were to die appropriately to this feast day. For during the entire festival they were all flayed. . . .

And the captives were called *xipeme* and *tototecti*. Those who slew them were the priests. Those who had taken them captive did not kill them; they only brought them as tribute, only delivered them as offerings; [the priests] went laying hold of their heads, and seizing [the hair of] their heads. Thus they went leading them up to the top of the temple.

And when some captive faltered, fainted, or went throwing himself upon the ground, they dragged him. . . .

And so they were brought up [the pyramid temple steps] before [the sanctuary of] Uitzilopochtli.

Thereupon they stretched them, one at a time, down on the sacrificial stone; then they delivered them into the hands of six priests, who threw them upon their backs, and cut open their breasts with a wide-bladed flint knife.

And they named the hearts of the captives "precious eagle-cactus fruit." They lifted them up to the sun, the turquoise prince, the soaring eagle. They offered it to him; they nourished him with it.

And when it had been offered, they placed it in the eagle-vessel. And these captives who had died they called "eagle men."

Afterwards they rolled them over; they bounced them down; they came tumbling down head over heels, and end over end, rolling over and over; thus they reached the terrace at the base of the pyramid.

And here they took them up.

And the old men, the *quaquacuilti,* the old men of the tribal temples, carried them there to their tribal temples, where the captor had promised, undertaken, and vowed [to take a captive].

There they took [the slain captive] up, in order to carry him to the house [of the captor], so that they might eat him. There they portioned him out, cutting him to pieces and dividing him up. First of all they reserved for Moctezuma a thigh, and set forth to take it to him.

DIFFERENT KINDS OF WOMEN

The Mature Woman

The mature woman [is] candid.

The good mature woman [is] resolute, firm of heart; constant—not to be dismayed; brave, like a man; vigorous, resolute; persevering—not one to falter; a steadfast, resolute worker. She is long-suffering; she accepts reprimands calmly—endures things like a man. She becomes firm—takes courage. She is intent. She gives of herself. She goes in humility. She exerts herself.

The bad mature woman [is] thin, tottering, weak—an inconstant companion, unfriendly. She annoys others, chagrins them, embarrasses, shames, oppresses once. Extremely feeble, impatient, chagrined, exhausted, fretful, she becomes impatient, loses hope, becomes embarrassed—chagrined. She goes about in shame; she persists in evil. Evil is her life. She lives in vice.

The Weaver of Designs

The weaver of designs is one who concerns herself with using thread, who works with thread.

The good weaver of designs is skilled—a maker of varicolored capes, an outliner of designs, a blender of colors, a joiner of pieces, a matcher of pieces, a person of good memory. She does things dexterously. She weaves designs. She selects. She weaves tightly. She forms borders. She forms the neck. She uses an uncompressed weave. She makes capes with the ballcourt and tree design. She weaves loosely—a loose, thick thread. She provides a metal weft. She forms the design with the sun on it.

The bad weaver of designs is untrained—silly, foolish, unobservant, unskilled of hand, ignorant, stupid. She tangles [the thread]; she harms [her work]—she spoils it. She ruins things scandalously; she scandalously ruins the surface of things. . . .

The Physician

The physician [is] a knower of herbs, of roots, of trees, of stones; she is experienced in these. [She is] one who has [the results of] examinations; she is a woman of experience, of trust, of professional skill: a counselor.

The good physician is a restorer, a provider of health, a reviver, a relaxer—one who makes people feel well, who envelopes one in ashes. She cures people; she provides them health; she lances them, she bleeds them—bleeds them in various places, pierces them with an obsidian lancet. She gives them potions, purges them, gives them medicine. She cures disorders of the anus. She anoints them; she rubs, she massages them. She provides them splints; she sets their bones—she sets a number of bones. She makes incisions, treats one's festering, one's gout, one's eyes. She cuts [growths from] one's eyes.

The bad physician [pretends to be] a counselor, advised, a person of trust, of professional knowledge. She has a vulva, a crushed vulva, a friction-loving vulva. [She is] a doer of evil. She bewitches—a sorceress, a person of sorcery, a possessed one. She makes one drink potions, kills people with medications, causes them to worsen, endangers them, increases sickness, makes them sick, kills them. She deceives people, ridicules them, blows [evil] upon them, removes an object from them, sees their fate in water, reads their fate with cords, casts lots with grains of maize, draws worms from their teeth. She draws paper—flint—obsidian—worms from them; she removes these from them. She deceives them, makes them believe.

Bernardino de Sahagún, *Florentine Codex: General History of the Things of New Spain*, trans. and ed. Arthur J. O. Anderson and Charles E. Dibble, 13 vols. (Santa Fe, N.M.: School of American Research and University of Utah, 1950–1982).

GARCILASO DE LA VEGA ON THE INCAS OF PERU (1609)

Born in 1539 to a Spanish father and an Inca mother, Garcilaso de la Vega grew up learning the stories and history of the Inca. Throughout his work, *The Royal Commentaries of the Incas*, which was published in two parts in 1609 and 1616, de la Vega is concerned to paint the Incas in a favorable light. He contends that Inca society was just and honest before it was corrupted by the Spanish.

For the better understanding of the idolatry, mode of life, and customs of the Indians of Peru it will be necessary for us to divide those times into two epochs. We shall narrate how they lived before the time of the Incas, and afterwards we shall give an account of the government of those kingdoms by the Incas, that the one may not be confounded with the other, and that neither the customs nor the gods of the period before the Incas may be attributed to the Inca period. It must be understood, then, that in the first epoch some of the Indians were little better than tame beasts, and others much worse than wild beasts. To begin with their gods, we must relate that they were in unison with the other signs of their folly and dullness, both as regards their number and the vileness of the things they adored. For each province, each nation, each house had its gods, different one from another; for they thought that a stranger's god, occupied with some one else, could not attend to them, but only their own. Thus it was that they came to have such a variety of gods, and so many that they could not be counted. And as they did not understand, like the gentile Romans, how to make ideal gods, as Hope, Victory, Peace, and such like, because they did not raise their thoughts to invisible things, they adored what they saw. The one desired to have a god different from the other, without thinking whether the objects of adoration were worthy or not, and without self-respect in considering whether the things they adored were not inferior to themselves. They only thought of making one differ from another, and each from all. Thus they worshipped herbs, plants, flowers, all kinds of trees, high hills, great rocks, and the chinks in them, hollow caves, pebbles, and small stones of different colours found in rivers and brooks, such as jasper. They adored the emerald, particularly in a province which is now called Puerto Viejo; but they did not worship rubies and diamonds because there are none in that country. In place of them they worshipped different animals, some for their fierceness, such as the tiger, lion, and bear; and as they looked upon them as gods, they did not fly from them, if they crossed their path, but went down on the ground to worship them, and these Indians allowed themselves to be killed and eaten, without attempting flight, or making any defense. They also adored other animals for their cunning, such as foxes and monkeys. They worshipped the dog for his faithfulness and noble character, the cat for its agility, the bird which they call *cuntur* for its size, and some nations adored the eagle because they thought they were descended from it, as well as the *cuntur*. Other nations worshipped falcons for their swiftness, and for their industry for procuring food. They worshipped the owl for the beauty of his eyes and head, and the bat for his quickness of sight, which caused much wonder that he could see at night. They also adored many other birds according to their caprices. They venerated the great serpents, that are met with in the Antis, twenty-five to thirty feet in length, more or less, and thicker than a man's thigh, for their monstrous size and fierceness. They also looked upon other smaller snakes as gods, in places where they are not so large as in the Antis, as well as lizards, toads, and frogs. In fine, there was not an animal, how vile and filthy soever, that they did not look upon as a god; merely differing one from the other in their gods, without adoring any real God, nor being able to hope for anything from them. They were indeed most foolish in all these things, like sheep without a shepherd. But we should not wonder that a people without letters or any instruction should fall into these follies; for it is notorious that the Greeks and Romans, who prided themselves so much on their science, had, when their empire was most flourishing, 30,000 gods. . . .

The Indians living to the south and west of Cuzco, in the provinces called *Colla-suyu* and *Cunti-suyu*, give another account of the origin of the Incas. They say that this great event happened after the deluge . . . Their account is that, after the flood subsided, a man appeared in Tiahuacanu, to the southward of Cuzco who was so powerful that he divided the world into four parts, and gave them to four men who were called kings. The first was called Manco Ccapac, the second Colla, the third Tocay, and the fourth Pinahua. They say that he gave the northern part to Manco Ccapac, the southern to Colla (from whose name they afterwards called the great province Colla), the eastern to Tocay, and the western to Pinahua. He ordered each to repair to his district, to conquer it, and to govern the people he might find there.

But they do not say whether the deluge had drowned the people, or whether they had been brought to life again, in order to be conquered and instructed; and so it is with respect to all that they relate touching those times. They say that from this division of the world afterwards arose that which the Incas made of their kingdom, called Ttahuantin-suyu. They declare that Manco Ccapac went towards the north, and arrived in the valley of Cuzco, where he founded a city, subdued the surrounding inhabitants, and instructed them . . . But they do not know what became of the other three kings.

Garcilaso de la Vega, *The Royal Commentaries of the Incas*, ed. and trans. Clement R. Markham, vol. 1 (London: Hakluyt Society, 1871).

CUMULATIVE INDEX

Boldface numbers refer to volume numbers. A key appears on all verso pages.

1: Ancient World	**4:** 17th and 18th C.
2: Medieval World	**5:** 19th C.
3: 15th and 16th C.	**6:** Modern World

Bowls (game): England (15th & 16th Centuries), 3:315, 317, 319; Europe (Middle Ages), 2:371

Bows and arrows: ancient world, 1:369; Byzantium, 2:360; Greece (ancient), 1:396; Japan (17th & 18th Centuries), 4:409; Mesopotamia, 1:393–94; Mongols, 2:362; Nubia, 1:387–88; Vikings, 2:353. See also Archers

Boxer Rebellion, 5:13, 178

Boxing: England (17th & 18th Centuries), 4:421; England (Victorian era), 5:403; Greece (ancient), 1:413; Japan (20th Century), 6:509; Mesopotamia, 1:405; United States (19th Century), 5:398, 399, 400; United States (1960–90), 6:497, 504, 505

Boxing Day, 5:413–14

Box making, 5:95

Boycotts: Japan (20th Century), 6:453; Olympic Games during Cold War, 6:499; United States (1960–90), 6:310

Boyle, Kay, 6:221

Boy Scouts, 6:54

Boza, 3:245

Bracey, Bertha, 6:91

Bradbury, Ray, 6:216, 224

Braddon, Mary Elizabeth, 5:191

Bradford, William, 4:515–16

Bradlaugh, Charles, 5:320

Bradstreet, Anne, 4:215

Brady, Matthew, 5:186

Brahman (Indian god), 5:466

Brahmanas (Brahmins): India (ancient), 1:11, 38, 206–7, 338; India (19th Century), 5:42, 52, 99; India (20th Century), 6:136

Braiel, 2:237

Braies, 2:237

Brain death, 6:292

Brain surgery, 1:286

Branch, Taylor, 6:442

Branding as punishment: England (17th and 18th Centuries), 4:393; England (15th & 16th Centuries), 3:303; New England, colonial, 4:385, 397

Branding of cows on American frontier, 5:88–90

Branding of slaves: Greece (ancient), 1:113; Mesopotamia, 1:489; Rome (ancient), 1:116

Brandy, 2:213, 215

Brants, 5:228

Brasidas, 1:333

Brassieres: Europe (Middle Ages), 2:238; Greece (ancient), 1:310

Braudel, Fernand, 2:222, 268

Bravo of Venice, The (Lewis), 5:184

Bray, Warwick, 3:232–33

Brazil: coffee, 5:97; gold, 5:132; government, 6:385, 387; independence, 5:17; Jesuits, 5:471; law and crime, 6:421. See also Latin America entries; Slaves in Latin America (19th Century)

Bread: Australia, colonial, 4:242; Byzantium, 2:208; England (15th & 16th Centuries), 3:238; England (1914–18), 6:304; England (17th & 18th Centuries), 4:246; England (Victorian era), 5:218, 219, 237, 241; Europe (15th & 16th Centuries), 3:236; Europe (Middle Ages), 2:97, 198, 199; France (1914–18), 6:303, 304; Germany (1914–18), 6:303; Greece (ancient), 1:254; Inca, 3:249; India

(19th Century), 5:243; India (20th Century), 6:316; Italy (15th & 16th Centuries), 3:242; Mesopotamia, 1:246; Ottoman Empire, 3:244; Spain (15th & 16th Centuries), 3:112, 241; United States (Civil War era), 5:220, 222, 223, 224–25; United States (1920–39), 6:306; United States (Western Frontier), 5:230; Vikings, 2:203

Breadfruit, 2:211

Breadlines during Great Depression, 6:165

Breakfast: England (15th & 16th Centuries), 3:237; England (Middle Ages), 2:201; England (17th & 18th Centuries), 4:247; England (Victorian era), 5:219, 240; Latin America (20th Century), 6:314–15; New England, colonial, 4:252; Ottoman Empire, 3:244; Polynesia, 2:210; Spain (15th & 16th Centuries), 3:240; United States (Western Frontier), 5:233, 234. See also Meals

Breast feeding: England (17th & 18th Centuries), 4:70–71; France (17th & 18th Centuries), 4:72; Inuit, 6:321, 322; North American colonial frontier, 4:69; Spain (15th & 16th Centuries), 3:60; United States (1960–90), 6:312. See also Wet nurses

Brecht, Bertolt, 6:219

Breckinridge, John C., 5:57, 312–13, 316

Breeches: England (15th & 16th Centuries), 3:226; England (17th & 18th Centuries), 4:290–91

Breechloaders: United States (Civil War era), 5:293; United States (Western Frontier), 5:366

Brescia, 3:116

Breton, Nicholas, 3:57

Brezhnev, Leonid, 6:554

Bribery. See Corruption

Bricks: Greece (ancient), 1:277; Mesopotamia, 1:270; North American colonial frontier, 4:273; Rome (ancient), 1:279

Bride-price: India (19th Century), 5:39; Islamic World (Middle Ages), 2:47, 62; Mesopotamia, 1:40–41; Rome (ancient), 1:48–49; Vikings, 2:43

Bridger, Jim, 5:46, 48

Bridges: Baghdad (Middle Ages), 2:118; Changan in Tang dynasty, 2:115; China (Tang Dynasty), 2:281; England (Middle Ages), 2:110; Europe (Middle Ages), 2:134; Japan (17th & 18th Centuries), 4:321; London (17th & 18th Centuries), 4:334; Paris (Middle Ages), 2:112–13

Brigands, 2:346, 348

Bright, Bill, 6:582

Britain. See England entries

Britain, Battle of, 6:466

British Admiralty, 4:362, 364

British and Foreign School Society, 5:173

British colonies in North America: agriculture, 4:12; government, 4:12, 350–51; immigration, 4:12; names, 4:350; Proclamation Line of 1763, map, 4:11; royal charters, 4:350

British East India Company, 5:14, 16, 375–76; 6:229

British invasion of American music, 6:543

British Museum Library, 5:141

British Royal Navy (17th & 18th Centuries): able seamen, 4:365; administrative bodies, 4:362, 363–65; admirals, 4:365; admiralty, 4:364; aging and death of sailors, 4:81; battle tactics, 4:413–15; boatswains, 4:364; captains, 4:365, 383; chanties, 4:383; conscription, 4:399; death penalty, 4:399–400; ethnicity, 4:382; food, 4:254; gunners, 4:364; impressment,

4:399; lashes, 4:400; loot, 4:407; marines, 4:365; meals, 4:382; midshipmen, 4:364; officers, 4:199–200, 363–65, 382–83, 407; organizational structure, 4:345; petty officers, 4:365; pursers, 4:364; ratings, 4:365; seamen, 4:363, 382–83; social structure, 4:381–84; wardrooms, 4:382; warrant officers, 4:364; warships, 4:413–14; widows of seamen, 4:91; wives at sea, 4:64; women as seamen, 4:65

British Supplemental Treaty of the Bogue, 5:13

Brittain, Vera, 6:62

Briyani, 5:243

Brodsky, Joseph, 6:235

Broken Commandment, The (Touson), 6:236

Brontë, Charlotte, 5:181, 191

Brontë, Patrick, 5:461

Bronze: Mesopotamia, 1:232, 272, 318; Rome (ancient), 1:239; Vikings, 2:100

Bronze Statue, The (Reynolds), 5:190

Brooches: Vikings, 2:261. See also Jewelry

Brooks, Preston, 5:4

Brooms, 2:269

Brothels: Greece (ancient), 1:67; Japan during World War II, 6:494; Rome (ancient), 1:72; Spain (15th & 16th Centuries), 3:321. See also Prostitution

Brother-sister marriage: Egypt (ancient), 1:24; Polynesia, 2:301, 308

Brown, John, 5:57, 311, 313, 315, 346

Brown v. Board of Education (1954), 6:17, 206, 441, 446

Browne, H.K., 5:183

Browning, E.B., 5:382

Bruce, Robert V., 5:153

Bruff, J. Goldsborough, 5:332

Brumalia, 2:303

Brumberg, Joan, 6:273

Bryan, William Jennings, 6:571

Bryant, Samuel, 4:382

Bubonic plague: Byzantium, 2:190; England (15th & 16th Centuries), 3:189–90; Europe (Middle Ages), 2:183; France (17th Century), 4:226–27; Islamic World (Middle Ages), 2:85; Italy (15th & 16th Centuries), 3:196; Jews blamed for, 6:143; Middle Ages, 2:4, 22; Spain (15th & 16th Centuries), 3:194; Valencia, 3:194

Búcaro, 3:60

Buchanan, James, 5:310, 311

Buck, Franklin A., 5:60

Buckskins, 5:280

Budd, William, 5:209

Buddha: All Souls' Feast, creation as holiday, 2:456; finger bone of, 2:271, 445; holidays dedicated to, 5:416; life of, 2:417; 5:464–65; religious life (15th & 16th Centuries), 3:359

Buddha Jayanti, 5:416

Buddhism: afterlife, 2:466; China (19th Century), 5:463, 464–65; China (Tang Dynasty), 2:12, 147, 153, 408; death, 2:459; Eightfold Path, 2:417; ethical behavior as part of, 2:409; founding of, 1:11, 465; 2:417; 6:8, 588; fraudulent ordinations, China (Tang Dynasty), 2:59; India (19th Century), 5:14, 466; India's caste system and, 1:338; Japan (17th & 18th Centuries), 4:74, 193–94, 456, 477, 494; Japan (20th Century), 6:567, 599; monasteries, 2:432, 441, 444; Mongols and, 2:22, 429; monks, 2:417, 432, 433, 438–40; 4:410; original teachings, 1:207; practice of, 2:417; vegetarianism, 1:258

Buddhist holidays: India (19th Century), 5:416; Japan (17th & 18th Centuries), 4:438

Buffalo, 5:228, 229, 230–31

Centuries), 3:241; United States (Western Frontier), 5:234

Deus ex machina, 1:427

Devi, Phoolan, 6:79–80

Devil in Catholicism, 3:363

DeVoto, Bernard, 5:46–48, 231

Devshirme, 2:318; 3:349

Dewey, John, 5:177, 452; 6:199, 200, 204

Dharma, 1:206, 352–53, 466; 5:466

Dhotis, 5:286

Dial-a-prayer, 6:573

Dialects: Europe (Middle Ages), 2:168; Greece (ancient), 1:176, 334; India (ancient), 1:431; Italy (15th & 16th Centuries), 3:163; Japan (17th & 18th Centuries), 4:212; Rome (ancient), 1:189; Spain (15th & 16th Centuries), 3:161–62; Sumerian, 1:194. *See also* Language

Diamonds in Latin America, 5:132

Diapers: life at sea (17th & 18th Centuries), 4:79; United States (1960–90), 6:361

Diarrhea, 5:199, 204

Díaz, Porfirio, 5:159, 179

Dice: England (15th & 16th Centuries), 3:318; Europe (Middle Ages), 2:367, 369, 372; India (ancient), 1:449; Italy (15th & 16th Centuries), 3:323; Mesopotamia, 1:406; Rome (ancient), 1:415–16; Spain (15th & 16th Centuries), 3:315, 321; United States (Civil War era), 5:429; Vikings, 2:375

Dickens, Charles: Christmas, writings on, 5:406; Lao She, influence on, 5:195; magazines, stories published in, 5:189–90; popularity in U.S., 5:181, 184–85; white collar workers, writings on, 5:83, 110

Dickstein, Morris, 6:222

Dictators of ancient Rome, 1:351

Diderot, Denis, 4:210

Diet: Africa (17th & 18th Centuries), 4:240–42, 430; Australia, colonial, 4:49, 51, 242–43; Australian Aboriginals, 1:260, 261; Aztec, 3:248; Byzantium, 2:190, 197, 208–10; changes after European conquest of Americas, 3:221–22, 236; China (19th Century), 5:248; China (Tang Dynasty), 2:128, 187, 197, 204–6, 455; Civil War soldiers, 5:219–27; as cure (Middle Ages), 2:179; England (15th & 16th Centuries), 3:238–39; England (1914–18), 6:303; England (17th & 18th Centuries), 4:140, 245–48; England (Victorian era), 5:218, 237–42; Europe (Middle Ages), 2:124, 197, 198–201, 277; France (1914–18), 6:303; Germany (1914–18), 6:303, 304; Greece (ancient), 1:256; Inca, 3:105, 106; India (19th Century), 5:219, 242–44; India (20th Century), 6:315–17; Inuit, 6:320–21; Islamic World (Middle Ages), 2:282; Islamic World (19th Century), 5:247, 468–69; Italy (15th & 16th Centuries), 3:242; Japan (17th & 18th Centuries), 4:114, 146, 229, 248–50; Japan (20th Century), 6:319–20; Latin America (19th Century), 5:219, 244–47; Latin America (20th Century), 6:314–15; Maya, 3:246–47; Mesopotamia, 1:246, 263; Native Americans (colonial New England), 4:250–51; Native Americans (New England, colonial), 4:61–62; New England, colonial, 4:117–18, 250–53; 19th Century, 5:218–48;

North American colonial frontier, 4:244–45; Nubia, 1:259; Ottoman, 3:244–45; Polynesia, 2:210–12; Rome (ancient), 1:256; seamen, 4:253–55; 17th & 18th Centuries, 4:238–55; United States (1920–39), 6:306–9; United States (Western Frontier), 5:218, 227–37; Vikings, 2:202–3. *See also* Food; *specific types of food and drink*

Diet (Japan governmental body), 6:399–400

Diet plans, 6:280, 302, 310

Digest of Roman Law, 1:365

Dillinger, John, 6:416

Dining rooms in Victorian England, 5:263

Dinner: England (15th & 16th Centuries), 3:237; England (17th & 18th Centuries), 4:247; England (Victorian era), 5:219, 238, 240–42; Europe (Middle Ages), 2:201; Latin America (20th Century), 6:315; life at sea (17th & 18th Centuries), 4:254; New England, colonial, 4:252; North American colonial frontier, 4:244; Ottoman Empire, 3:244; 17th & 18th Centuries, 4:239; United States (Western Frontier), 5:234. *See also* Meals

Dinner parties. *See* Banquets

Diocletian, 1:389

Dionysius, 1:480, 492

Dioscorides, 2:181, 188

Diphtheria: England (Victorian era), 5:209; Spain (15th & 16th Centuries), 3:194

Diplomats (Mesopotamia), 1:139, 155, 343

"Dirty wars" (Latin America 20th Century): deaths in, 6:8, 33, 44; historical overview of, 6:480–81; Honduras, 6:370; women's role in protests, 6:61, 77

Disciples of Christ, 5:458

Disco, 6:547

Discovery, 6:189

Discovery and Conquest of Mexico, The (Castillo), 3:421–22

Discrimination: Africa (20th Century), 6:193; Catholic Church condemnation of, 6:577; China (Tang Dynasty), 2:324; England (17th & 18th Centuries), 4:492–93; India (20th Century), 6:110, 140, 154–56; India (20th Century), 6:161; Japan (20th Century), 6:140, 159–61; Jews (17th & 18th Centuries), 4:483; Latin America (20th Century), 6:134; Title IX of Education Amendments of 1972, 6:618–19; 20th Century, 6:139–61; United States (1920–39), 6:145–49, 516; United States (1940–59), 6:16, 150–51, 375–76; United States (1960–90), 6:110, 129, 151–54. *See also* Anti-Semitism; Civil rights movement

Diseases: Africa (17th & 18th Centuries), 4:220–21; Africa (20th Century), 6:293–95; China (Tang Dynasty), 2:185–86; England (17th & 18th Centuries), 4:224; England (Victorian era), 5:451; Europe (Middle Ages), 2:181; 15th & 16th Centuries, 3:188–90, 194, 196, 199; Greece (ancient), 1:294–98; India (ancient), 1:301–2; Inuit, 6:295–96; Japan (20th Century), 6:291; Mesopotamia, 1:284–88; Native Americans (colonial New England), 4:88, 231; 19th Century working-class people, 5:217; North American colonial frontier, 4:223; Paris (Middle Ages), 2:114–15; Puritans, religious doctrine, 4:233; Rome (ancient), 1:298–301; Soviet Union, 6:288; Spain (15th & 16th Centuries), 3:194; United States (Civil War era), 5:137; United States (1960–90), 6:278; Vikings, 2:164. *See also specific diseases*

Disney, Walt, 6:98, 521

Disneyland, 6:98–99

Dispensaries, 4:225

Disraeli, Benjamin, 5:10

Dissection: Greece (ancient), 1:296; Mesopotamia, 1:287; Rome (ancient), 1:301

Dissenters, 4:471–73, 491–92

Distilleries in colonial New England, 4:265–66

Ditches, 4:333

Divination: Inca, 3:392–93; Japan (17th & 18th Centuries), 4:423

Divine Comedy (Dante), 2:461; 3:396

Divine right of kings, 3:284

Divine River judgments in Mesopotamia, 1:359, 362, 526

Diviners: Greece (ancient), 1:379; Mesopotamia, 1:370, 527; Rome (ancient), 1:495, 496. *See also* Entrails, reading of

Divorce: ancient world, 1:39–40; Byzantium, 2:63; Catholic Church views on (1960–90), 6:577; China (Tang Dynasty), 2:41, 46–47; England (17th & 18th Centuries), 4:37–38; Europe (Middle Ages), 2:41, 42; Greece (ancient), 1:45, 47, 68; India (19th Century), 5:41; Islamic World (Middle Ages), 2:40, 49; Islamic World (19th Century), 5:38; Japan (17th & 18th Centuries), 4:40; Jesus Christ on, 3:381; Maya, 3:46; Mesopotamia, 1:39, 41, 42; New England, colonial, 4:42; Polynesia, 2:68; Rome (ancient), 1:37, 50; 17th & 18th Centuries, 4:29; Spain (15th & 16th Centuries), 3:35, 59; 20th Century, 6:33; United States (1920–39), 6:35–36; United States (1940–59), 6:38; United States (1960–90), 6:42; United States (Western Frontier), 5:60; Vikings, 2:44–45, 57

Diwali, 5:396, 406, 414–15

Dix, Dorothea, 5:199

Dixie Primer for Little Folks, 5:160, 167

Dixie Speller, 5:160, 167

Dixon, James, 4:487

Dixon, Thomas, 6:140, 146

Dobiwallas, 5:52

Doblado, Leucadio, 3:227

Dockers (China), 5:94, 115

Doctorow, E.L., 6:379

Doctors. *See* Healers and healing; Physicians

Doctors' Plot (Soviet Union), 6:158

Doctor Zhivago (Pasternak), 6:614–16

Dodge, Richard I., 5:280, 369

Doenitz, Karl, 6:412

Doges: Italy (15th & 16th Centuries), 3:276; Venice, 3:277

Dogfighting: 15th & 16th Centuries, 3:313; Middle Ages, 2:369

Dogs: England (Victorian era), 5:440; Mesopotamia, 1:78, 93; Paris (Middle Ages), 2:114; Polynesia, 2:212; United States (Western Frontier), 5:229; Vikings, 2:462. *See also* Hunting dogs

Dog shooting, 4:424

Dog tents, 5:254, 258

Dokia Makrembolitissa, 2:63

Dolabra, 1:386

Dom Casmurro (Machado de Assis), 5:197

Domestic life: ancient world, 1:19–72; defined, 1:19; 2:29; 6:31; 15th & 16th Centuries, 3:29–88; Middle Ages, 2:29–92; 19th Century, 5:25–79; 17th & 18th Centuries, 4:27–100; 20th Century, 6:31–108. *See also* Children; Family life; Marriage; Sexuality

Domestic Revolutions (Mintz & Kellogg), 6:39

Domestic violence: Africa (17th & 18th Centuries), 4:47; China (Tang Dynasty), 2:333; Europe (Middle Ages), 2:43; Islamic World (Middle Ages), 2:48; Latin America (20th Century),

India (19th Century), **5:**244; Islamic World (Middle Ages), **2:**273; Japan (17th & 18th Centuries), **4:**146; life at sea, **4:**255; New England, colonial, **4:**252; Rome (ancient), **1:**256; United States (Western Frontier), **5:**234

Ebla, **1:**140

Ecclesiastical courts in England, **3:**303

Eclipses: Greece (ancient), **1:**225; India (ancient), **1:**216

Eco, Umberto, **6:**227

Economic life: Africa (20th Century), **6:**86, 124–25; ancient cities, **1:**101–8; ancient world, **1:**73–167; 15th & 16th Centuries, **3:**89–154; India (20th Century), **6:**9, 388; Japan (20th Century), **6:**24; Latin America (20th Century), **6:**387; meaning of "economy," **1:**74; Middle Ages, **2:**93–144; 19th Century, **5:**81–148; 17th & 18th Centuries, **4:**101–66; 20th Century, **6:**109–79, 434; United States (1960–90), **6:**40. *See also* Accounting; Money; Rural life and agriculture; Trade; Travel and transportation; Urban life; Work; *specific city and civilization*

Ecuador: language, **3:**168; Peru, border wars with, **6:**479. *See also* Latin America *entries*

Ecumenism (20th Century), **6:**568, 575–78

Eddic poems, **2:**172

Edelin, Kenneth C., **6:**74

Edema, **3:**194

Edict of Nantes (1598), **4:**355, 474

Edict of Toleration, **2:**410

Edicts. *See* Royal decrees and edicts

Edirne, **3:**118, 349

Edison, Thomas Alva, **5:**142; **6:**183–84, 360, 513

Edo (17th & 18th Centuries), **4:**328, 336–37, 358; **6:**160

Education: Africa (17th & 18th Centuries), **4:**181, 183–86; Africa (20th Century), **6:**124, 194, 196, 212–14; ancient world, **1:**182–92; Australian Aboriginals, **1:**28–29, 191–93; Aztec, **3:**47–48, 84–85, 182–86; China (19th Century), **5:**176–78; China (Tang Dynasty), **2:**84, 147, 153–55; England (15th & 16th Centuries), **3:**32–33, 171–74; England (17th & 18th Centuries), **4:**71, 188–90; England (Victorian era), **5:**50, 111, 114, 171–76, 373, 480–81; Europe (Middle Ages), **2:**148–52, 159; Europe (1914–18), **6:**89–90; Florence, **3:**178; France (17th & 18th Centuries), **4:**72, 73, 182, 190–93; Greece (ancient), **1:**187–89, 424; Inca, **3:**186–87; India (19th Century), **5:**67, 77–78; India (20th Century), **6:**104, 105; integration in United States, **6:**17, 153, 154, 195, 206–8; Inuit, **6:**196, 214–15; Islamic World (Middle Ages), **2:**85, 147, 155–57; Islamic World (19th Century), **5:**181; Italy (15th & 16th Centuries), **3:**81, 177–80; Japan (17th & 18th Centuries), **4:**193–95, 512–15; Japan (20th Century), **6:**106, 192, 196, 210–12, 400; Jews in Europe pre-World War II, **6:**143, 144; Latin America (19th Century), **5:**69–70, 178–80; Latin America (20th Century), **6:**88, 101–2; life at sea (17th & 18th Centuries), **4:**79–80, 198–200; Maya, **3:**82–83; Mesopotamia, **1:**54, 183–86; Middle Ages, **2:**146–57; Native Americans (colonial frontier of North

America), **4:**187–88; Native Americans (colonial New England), **4:**195–96; New England, colonial, **4:**182, 195–98, 380; 19th Century, **5:**160–81; North American colonial frontier, **4:**155–56, 182, 186–88; Ottoman Empire, **3:**118, 180–82; Polynesia, **2:**177; Rome (ancient), **1:**189–91; separation of religion and education in U.S., **6:**200, 208, 578, 587; 17th & 18th Centuries, **4:**181–200; Soviet Union, **6:**195, 196, 208–10; Spain (15th & 16th Centuries), **3:**35, 77, 174–77; 20th Century, **6:**195–215; United States (Civil War era), **5:**161–68; United States (1920–39), **6:**195, 196–99; United States (1940–59), **6:**18, 88, 199–205; United States (1960–90), **6:**205–8, 381, 382; United States (Western Frontier), **5:**168–71; Vikings, **2:**152–53. *See also* Curriculum; Schools; *specific subject of teaching*

Education Act of 1870 (England), **5:**10

Educational reforms in Europe, **2:**148

Education Amendments of 1972, Title IX, **6:**618–19

Education of priests: Europe (Middle Ages), **2:**149, 150; Latin America (19th Century), **5:**471; Polynesia, **2:**431

Education of women: Africa (20th Century), **6:**86; Australian Aboriginals, **1:**191–92; England (Victorian era), **5:**485; Europe (Middle Ages), **2:**149; France (17th & 18th Centuries), **4:**58; Greece (ancient), **1:**188; India (20th Century), **6:**78; Islamic World (Middle Ages), **2:**157; Mesopotamia, **1:**184; Rome (ancient), **1:**36; Title IX of Education Amendments of 1972, **6:**618–19; United States (1920–39), **6:**195; United States (1940–59), **6:**202–5; United States (1960–90), **6:**205; Vikings, **2:**153

Edward, Duke of York, **2:**483–85

Edward III (king of England), **3:**12

Edward IV (king of England), **3:**13

Edward VII (king of England), **5:**11

Edward VI (king of England), **3:**16, 409

Edward V (king of England), **3:**13

Edward the Confessor, **2:**109

Edwin Smith Surgical Paprus, **1:**290–92

Edzna, **3:**102

Eels: Australian Aboriginals, **1:**419; Greece (ancient), **1:**255; Rome (ancient), **1:**256–57

Eggs: Byzantium, **2:**209; England (15th & 16th Centuries), **3:**57; England (1914–18), **6:**303; England (Victorian era), **5:**219, 238, 240; Italy (15th & 16th Centuries), **3:**243; Spain (15th & 16th Centuries), **3:**96; Vikings, **2:**202

Egil's Saga (Skallagrimsson), **2:**89, 398

Egypt, **3:**20, 165; British control of, **6:**11, 230; Byzantine Empire, **2:**19; European control, free from, **6:**483; food variety (Middle Ages), **2:**207; French invasion of, **6:**230; legal system of, **6:**423; Muslim conquest of, **2:**15; Napoleonic invasion, **5:**353–54. *See also* Islamic World *entries*

Egypt (ancient): accounting, **1:**186–87, 197; alimony, **1:**40; alphabet, **1:**175; amulets, **1:**124, 319–21, 514, 524, 531–32, 533; anatomy, **1:**292; animal games, **1:**409–10; appearance, **1:**56, 235, 319–24; apprenticeships, **1:**123; archers, **1:**375, 376, 391, 393–94; architecture, **1:**274; art, **1:**232–37; astronomy, **1:**211; autopsies, **1:**292; axes, **1:**394; bad breath, **1:**289; banks and banking, **1:**135; banquets, **1:**252–53, 423; bas-reliefs, **1:**234, 236; battering rams, **1:**375; battle

casualties, **1:**292, 374; beards, **1:**322; bedrooms, **1:**274; beds, **1:**276; beer, **1:**249, 264; bees, **1:**252; birds, **1:**82, 236, 250; block statues, **1:**234; board games, **1:**408, 409; bows and arrows, **1:**376; brains, **1:**513; bread, **1:**249; breath mints, **1:**289; bricks, **1:**275; bronze, **1:**234–35, 310; bullfighting, **1:**410; cabinetry, **1:**232; calendar and time, **1:**209–11; captives as slaves, **1:**110, 111, 491; carpentry, **1:**125, 395; carvings, **1:**364, 503, 516–17; cataloguing and classifying, **1:**222; cattle, **1:**81; cellars, **1:**275; chariots, **1:**391, 395–96; checkers, **1:**409; cheese, **1:**264; childbirth, **1:**24, 293, 457; childless couples, **1:**24; children, **1:**24, 55–56; circumcisions, **1:**291; clothing, **1:**235, 305–8; clothing manufacturing, **1:**305; colors, **1:**236, 276, 305, 322, 516; combs, **1:**324; cooking methods, **1:**249; cooking utensils, **1:**249; copper used as currency, **1:**134; corpses, care of, **1:**506; cosmetics, **1:**322–23; courts and judges, **1:**362–63; craftsmen, **1:**122–26; creation stories, **1:**475–76; crowns, **1:**308; curses, **1:**533; dance, **1:**253, 422–24; day of rest, **1:**210, 437; death, burial, and the afterlife, **1:**23, 33, 233–34, 249–52, 265, 422, 457, 459, 477, 511–17; debt slavery, **1:**111; deities, **1:**457–58, 474–77; dental care and problems, **1:**253, 289, 293; diet, **1:**250–51; diplomats and ambassadors, **1:**347; diseases, **1:**288–93; divorce, **1:**24, 40, 43–44; dogs, **1:**251, 410; donkeys, **1:**160; doors, **1:**275; dreams and dream interpretation, **1:**293, 491–92; drink, **1:**264–66; drinking methods, **1:**264; drinking water, **1:**375; eating habits, **1:**249, 252–53; education, **1:**56, 186–87; elixers of life, **1:**291; entertainment, **1:**253, 347; epidemics, **1:**291; exile, **1:**363; family life, **1:**23–24; fictional literature, **1:**198; fireplaces, **1:**276; fish, **1:**250; fishing, **1:**82, 409; floods, **1:**3, 75, 80; floorplans, **1:**274, 275; floors and floor coverings, **1:**276; food, **1:**249–53; footwear, **1:**308; fortifications, **1:**375; fowl, **1:**250; fruit, **1:**250; furniture, **1:**125, 276; games, **1:**408–10; gilding, **1:**236; glass, **1:**124–25; gold jewelry, **1:**319–20; gold works of art, **1:**123; government, **1:**344–48; government workers, **1:**122, 143, 345, 347; grains, **1:**250; gymnastics, **1:**408; hair removal, **1:**323; hairstyles, **1:**321; harems, **1:**347; health and medicine, **1:**222, 288–94; hearts, **1:**513; henna, **1:**323; herbs and spices, **1:**249, 251; hieroglyphics, **1:**175, 186, 223, 235, 250, 292, 293; history of, **1:**3–6; holidays, festivals, and spectacles, **1:**210, 437–38; honey, **1:**252; horses, **1:**160, 396; hospitals, **1:**292; houses, multistoried, **1:**275; housing, **1:**274–76; housing materials, **1:**275; hunting, **1:**251–52, 408–10; incense, **1:**323; infant mortality, **1:**56; jewelry, **1:**319; juggling, **1:**408; lamps, **1:**274, 276; landowners, **1:**331, 345; language and writing, **1:**175–76, 186–87, 197; latrines, **1:**274; law, **1:**128, 362–63; leather, **1:**305–6; linen, **1:**305–6; literature, **1:**197–200; litters, **1:**160; love poetry, **1:**199; mace, **1:**394; magic and superstition, **1:**289–300, 531–32; malaria, **1:**289; mansions, **1:**275; map of, **1:**5; marriage, **1:**23–24, 43–44; marriage of slaves, **1:**111; mathematics, **1:**222–24; meat, **1:**249, 251; men's clothing, **1:**305–8, 310; metal artwork, **1:**234; military games, **1:**408; milk and dairy products, **1:**249, 264; mining, **1:**123; mirrors, **1:**323; moat, **1:**375; money,

United States (Western Frontier), **5:**254, 259–61; Vikings, **2:**222, 226–29

Housing and Urban Development Act of 1965, **6:**382

Housing cost: Greece (ancient), **1:**276; Latin America (19th Century), **5:**268

Housing materials: Australian Aboriginals, **1:**281; China (Tang Dynasty), **2:**230–31; Europe (Middle Ages), **2:**222, 223–24; Greece (ancient), **1:**277; India (19th Century), **5:**264, 265, 266; India (20th Century), **6:**334, 343; Inuit, **6:**335, 346–47; Islamic World (Middle Ages), **2:**222, 232; Japan (20th Century), **6:**346; Mesopotamia, **1:**270; Middle Ages, **2:**222; Polynesia, **2:**222–23, 233–35; Rome (ancient), **1:**279; United States (Western Frontier), **5:**254, 260; Vikings, **2:**222, 226. *See also specific type of material (e.g., concrete, bricks)*

Housing projects, federally subsidized, **6:**342–43

Houston, Jeanne Wakatsuki, **6:**525

Howard, Catherine, **3:**15

Hreppar, **2:**295

Hrotswitha of Gandersheim, **2:**396, 397

Hsia Dynasty, **5:**11

HUAC. *See* House Un-American Activities Committee

Huacas, **3:**203, 377, 390, 391

Huanacauri, **3:**52–53, 88

Huánuco, **3:**126

Huari people: agriculture, **3:**91, 106; history of, **3:**5

Huascar, **3:**22

Huaso, **5:**289

Huastecan language, **3:**167

Huayna Capac, **3:**7, 22–23, 126

Hubal, **2:**418

Hubbard, John, **5:**420

Hubble space telescope, **6:**189

Hudson River, **4:**317

Hudson's Bay Company, **5:**123

Huey tecuilhuitl, **3:**69

Hughes, Langston, **6:**223

Hughes, Thomas, **5:**484

Huguenots: France (17th & 18th Centuries), **4:**474; North American colonial frontier, **4:**373, 470

Huipil, **3:**231; **5:**288

Huipilli, **3:**50

Huitzilopochtli, **3:**5, 109, 123, 284, 297–98

Hukkas, **5:**53

Hula dances, **2:**394

Hulbert, William A., **5:**399

Hülegü, **2:**22, 38, 429

Hulls, **4:**323–24

Humanism, development of, **3:**8, 116, 163

Human rights: Islamic World (20th Century), **6:**592; Latin America Catholic Church and (20th Century), **6:**592; standards of, **6:**7. *See also* Morality

Human sacrifices: Aztec, **3:**387–89, 423–24; Inca, **3:**390–93; Maya, **3:**385–86; Mesopotamia, **1:**486; Polynesia, **2:**364, 365, 366

Human waste disposal: Changan in Tang dynasty, **2:**116; England (Victorian era), **5:**141, 264; Europe (Middle Ages), **2:**123; Greece (ancient), **1:**298; India (19th Century), **5:**265; Islamic World (Middle Ages), **2:**232; London (15th & 16th Centuries), **3:**108; London (Middle Ages), **2:**111; Mesopotamia,

1:92, 272; Middle Ages, **2:**95, 108; Paris (Middle Ages), **2:**114; Rome (ancient), **1:**100, 280; Spain (15th & 16th Centuries), **3:**256; United States (1960–90), **6:**361. *See also* Waste disposal

Humor and satire: *Aucassin and Nicolett*, **2:**485–88; Japan (17th & 18th Centuries), **4:**213. *See also* Jokes

Humors of the body: Galenic science, **4:**227; India (ancient), **1:**301–2; India (20th Century), **6:**286; Rome (ancient), **1:**298–300

Hunab, **3:**371

Hun Ahau, **3:**215, 397

Hunahpu, **3:**215, 371, 397, 417–19

Hundred Years' War, **2:**4, 346–47; **3:**12

Hungary: houses, **3:**261; Magyars, **2:**2; as part of Holy Roman Empire, **3:**18, 283, 287; as part of Ottoman Empire, **3:**20; Shtokavian spoken in, **3:**165; war against Ottoman Empire, **3:**12

Hung Chao, **2:**11

Hunger in America (TV documentary), **6:**313

Hung Hsiu-Ch'üan, **5:**13

Hungress Days Congress, **6:**436

Huni, **1:**514–15

Huns, Chinese wars with, **2:**354

Hunter, Jim "Catfish," **6:**506

Hunthausen, Raymond G., **6:**586

Hunting: Africa (17th & 18th Centuries), **4:**47, 105, 240–41; ancient world, **1:**404–19; Australian Aboriginals, **1:**418–19; China (Tang Dynasty), **2:**315, 381–82; England (15th & 16th Centuries), **3:**330; England (17th & 18th Centuries), **4:**420; Europe (Middle Ages), **2:**198, 379–80; Greece (ancient), **1:**410–14; India (19th Century), **5:**397, 404; Islamic World (Middle Ages), **2:**382–84; Italy (15th & 16th Centuries), **3:**338; *Master of Game* (Edward, Duke of York), **2:**483–85; Maya, **3:**99, 247; Mesopotamia, **1:**392, 405–8; Middle Ages, **2:**368, 377–86; Mongols, **2:**363, 377, 384–86; North American colonial frontier, **4:**137–39; Nubia, **1:**259, 416–18; Rome (ancient), **1:**414–16, 445–46; United States (19th Century), **5:**398; United States (1920–39), **6:**500; United States (Western Frontier), **5:**47, 229, 230–31; Vikings, **2:**202, 374, 380–81. *See also* Fishing; Trappers and trapping

Hunting dogs: Europe (Middle Ages), **2:**379–80; Middle Ages, **2:**378

Hunyadi, John, **3:**12

Hurinsaya, **3:**282

Hurons (17th & 18th Centuries): social structure, **4:**372; tattoos, **4:**448

Husayn, **2:**457–58

Husband's role. *See* Family life; Marriage

Hu Shi, **5:**195

Hutchins, Robert, **6:**200–201

Hutchinson, Anne, **4:**396

Hyde, Henry, **6:**74

Hyde Amendment, **6:**74

Hydraulic mining, **5:**299

Hydraulic (water) organ, **1:**430

Hydrogen bomb. *See* Nuclear weapons

Hydropathy, **5:**211

Hygiene: England (17th & 18th Centuries), **4:**225; England (Victorian era), **5:**451; Greece (ancient), **1:**278; India (ancient), **1:**259; India (20th Century), **6:**589; Japan (17th & 18th Centuries), **4:**229; Mesopotamia, **1:**248; 17th & 18th Centuries, **4:**219; United States (1920–39), **6:**272; Vikings, **2:**260–61

Hyksos, **1:**395

Hymns: England (Victorian era), **5:**422; Greece (ancient), **1:**424, 438; India (ancient), **1:**206; Mesopotamia, **1:**194–95

Hyslop, John, **3:**125

IBM, **6:**119, 252

Ibn Abd al-Wahhab, **6:**423

Ibn 'Asakir, **2:**157

Ibn Fadlan, **2:**137–38, 260–61, 463, 478–79

Ibn Hanbal, Ahmad, **6:**423

Ibn Miskawayh, **2:**138

Ibn Sa'udi, **6:**451

Ibn Sina (Avicenna), **2:**166–67, 179, 192

Ibn Taymiya, Ahmad B., **6:**450–51

Ibrahim b. Ya'qub al-Turtushi, **2:**57

Icarus, **1:**448

Ice cream, **5:**245

Iceland: historical overview, **2:**7; poor persons (Middle Ages), **2:**295. *See also* Vikings

Ice skating, **4:**420

Ichikawa Kon, **6:**535

I Ching (Book of Changes), **2:**164; **4:**423

Icons, **2:**426, 433, 441; Ethiopia (17th & 18th Centuries), **4:**447

Ideograms, **1:**172

Idlers on merchant vessels (17th & 18th Centuries), **4:**363

Idli, **5:**243

Idolatry and Protestantism, **3:**382

"Idol singers" (Japan), **6:**556

Id-ul-Fitr, **5:**416

Ie, **4:**379; **6:**48–49

Ieharu, **4:**18

Ienobu, **4:**17

Ife Kingdom, **4:**14

Igbo (17th & 18th Centuries), **4:**369

Iglu, **6:**346

Ihiyotl, **3:**51, 401

I Ho Ch'uan, **5:**13

Ihram, **2:**423–24

Ikki, **4:**394–95

Île de la Cité (Paris), **2:**112, 113

Iliad (Homer): Achilles, **1:**369, 378; depicting Greek Mythology, **1:**478, 479, 481; description of, **1:**200; educational role, **1:**188; excerpt from, **1:**547–50; on racial prejudice, **1:**335

Il-khan Ghazan, **2:**22

Il-khanid dynasty, **2:**38

Ilkum, **1:**371

Illapa, **3:**376–77, 391–92

Illegitimate children: England (17th & 18th Centuries), **4:**93–94; Europe (Middle Ages), **2:**292; Latin America (20th Century), **6:**43, 45; North American colonial frontier, **4:**35

Illnesses. *See* Diseases; *specific disease*

Illness of Central America, The (Mendieta), **5:**158

Ill People, An (Arguedas), **5:**158

Illustrated London News, **5:**192

Illustrious August (Xuanzong): dance performance by and for, **2:**390, 392; economic policies of, **2:**253, 306; elderly, treatment of, **2:**91; harem of, **2:**316; officials of, **2:**71; reign of, **2:**10; sports as favorite of, **2:**376

I Love Lucy (TV show), **6:**247–48, 566

Imams, **2:**457; **3:**42; **5:**468

Imhotep, **1:**476

Immigration: British colonies, **4:**12; Chinese quota to U.S., **6:**526; Jewish quota to U.S., **6:**143; Jews from Soviet Union to Israel, **6:**159; Latin America (19th Century), **5:**19–20, 98, 117, 267, 326; Latin America (20th Century), **6:**44; New England, colonial,

6:316; hospitals, **6:**287; housing, **6:**300, 334, 343–45; humors of the body, **6:**286; hygiene, **6:**589; independence, **6:**371; infant mortality, **6:**45–46; language, **6:**388–89; literature, **6:**228–30; malaria, **6:**287; marriage, **6:**32, 33, 46, 78, 104, 156, 590; meat, **6:**316; men, **6:**57–59; menstruation, **6:**104; mosques, **6:**343; mythology, **6:**79, 228; old age, **6:**47, 58; patriarchy, **6:**57–59, 78; patrilineages, **6:**46–47; political life, **6:**10, 78; poultry, **6:**316; poverty, **6:**388; railroads, **6:**255, 389; rape, **6:**79; religious beliefs, **6:**568, 588–91; religious purification, **6:**316; religious rituals, **6:**46–47, 58, 104, 316; rice, **6:**301, 315–16; riots, **6:**389; rural life and agriculture, **6:**334; schools, **6:**344; shrines, **6:**345; slums, **6:**344; social structure, **6:**135–37; sons, **6:**45, 47, 58, 103–4; sports, **6:**509; tea, **6:**301, 316; technology, **6:**254–55; temples, **6:**343, 589; urban life, **6:**334, 344–45; vegetarianism, **6:**316; wells, **6:**344; wheat, **6:**301, 316; widows, **6:**79, 156; women, **6:**78–80, 156, 611–12

Indigo, **5:**132

Indra, **1:**352

Industrial Revolution in England, **5:**8

Industry: Africa (17th & 18th Centuries), **4:**120–21; China (19th Century), **5:**115, 156; England (17th & 18th Centuries), **4:**2, 123–26, 124; England (Victorian era), **5:**92–93, 109, 300; Great Depression, **6:**164; India (19th Century), **5:**77, 291, 301; Japan (17th & 18th Centuries), **4:**126–28; Latin America (20th Century), **6:**170–71; life at sea (17th & 18th Centuries), **4:**130–32; New England, colonial, **4:**13, 128–30; North American colonial frontier, **4:**121–23; 17th & 18th Centuries, **4:**118–32; United States (Civil War era), **5:**2–3; United States (20th Century), **6:**110, 114–16

Indus Valley civilization. See India (ancient)

Infant care: England (Victorian era), **5:**239–40; Europe (Middle Ages), **2:**80; Middle Ages, **2:**78. See also Child care; Wet nurses

Infanticide: Egypt (ancient), **1:**56; Greek and Roman, **1:**57, 58; **6:**141; Japan (17th & 18th Centuries), **4:**74–75; Mesopotamia, **2:**64; Polynesia, **2:**68; Vikings, **2:**81–82

Infant mortality: England (15th & 16th Centuries), **3:**33, 75; Europe (Middle Ages), **2:**79; Greece (ancient), **1:**46, 59, 295; India (19th Century), **5:**77; India (20th Century), **6:**45–46; Islamic World (Middle Ages), **2:**85, 318; Latin America (20th Century), **6:**314; Mesopotamia, **1:**52; Spain (15th & 16th Centuries), **3:**77; 20th Century, **6:**88; United States (Civil War era), **5:**29; United States (1920–39), **6:**67; Vikings, **2:**34, 81

Infections. See Diseases

Infertility. See Childless couples

Infidels in Islamic World (19th Century), **5:**447

Infirmaries, **5:**390. See also Hospitals

Inflation: England (15th & 16th Centuries), **3:**93, 111, 271; United States (1920–39), **6:**436; United States (Western Frontier), **5:**61

Influenza: England (15th & 16th Centuries), **3:**189; England (Victorian era), **5:**209; Europe (20th Century), **6:**62–63; Spain (15th & 16th

Centuries), **3:**194; United States (1920–39), **6:**272

Inheritance. See Estates and inheritances

In-line skates, **6:**505

Inns: Greece (ancient), **1:**162; Rome (ancient), **1:**164

Inoculation. See Vaccination

Inquisition, **2:**326, 411. See also Spanish Inquisition

Insanity. See Mental illness and treatment

Insecticides, **6:**260, 275

Insects: China (Tang Dynasty), **2:**205, 206; United States (Western Frontier), **5:**105, 254. See also specific insects

Insider trading (Japan), **6:**400–401

Institutes of the Christian Religion (Calvin), **3:**366

Insulae, **1:**280

Insurance: England (Victorian era), **5:**350–51; long-term care insurance (Japan), **6:**292. See also Health insurance

Integration. See Civil rights movement; School desegregation

Intellectual life: ancient world, **1:**169–241; China (Tang Dynasty), **2:**11; 15th & 16th Centuries, **3:**155–220; France (17th & 18th Centuries), **4:**56–58; Middle Ages, **2:**4, 145–94; 19th Century, **5:**149–216; 17th & 18th Centuries, **4:**167–236; 20th Century, **6:**181–298. See also Art; Literature

Intercalary month: India (ancient), **1:**216; Mesopotamia, **1:**209; Rome (ancient), **1:**214

Intercourse. See Sexuality

Internal Security Act of 1950, **6:**376

International Workers of the World, preamble, **6:**619–20

Internet, **3:**155; Japan (20th Century), **6:**259

Interstate Highway Act of 1956, **6:**362

Inti, **3:**53, 376–77, 391–92

Intifada, **6:**483

Inti Raymi, **3:**391

Inuit: breast feeding, **6:**321, 322; cancer, **6:**322; childbirth, **6:**296; children, **6:**50–51, 107; Christianity, **6:**603; colonial rule, **6:**402; cooking methods, **6:**367; discrimination, **6:**161; diseases, **6:**295–96; education, **6:**196, 214–15; environment, **6:**296, 321–22; family life, **6:**33, 50–51; food, **6:**302, 320–22; fur trade, **6:**347; government, **6:**401–4; health and medicine, **6:**261, 295–96, 295–98; historical overview, **6:**26–27; housing, **6:**51, 346–48; hunting, **6:**321; kinship, **6:**402; language, **6:**214–15; life expectancy, **6:**296; literature, **6:**239–41; mercury and, **6:**302; missionaries, **6:**603; music, **6:**557–58; names, **6:**50; newspapers, **6:**239; Nunavut land claims agreement (1993), **6:**620–22; old age, **6:**51; patrilineages, **6:**50; poetry, **6:**239; pollution, **6:**296, 321–22; religion, **6:**603–4; shaman, **6:**295; social activism, **6:**604; technology, **6:**349, 367–68; tuberculosis, **6:**296; writing, **6:**239–40

Inuit Circumpolar Conference, **6:**403

Inuktitut language, **6:**214–15, 239, 240–41, 403

Inupiat Ilitqusiat, **6:**604

Inventions: England (17th & 18th Centuries), **4:**176–77. See also Science; Technology

Investiture Controversy, **2:**328

Invisible Man (Ellison), **6:**441

Invitation to an Inquest: A New Look at the Rosenberg and Sobell Case (Schneir), **6:**380

Ionian Rationalism, **1:**225

Ionians, **1:**225, 333; vs. Dorians, **1:**333. See also Greece (ancient)

Ionic architecture, **1:**504–5

Iormungand, **2:**412

Iowa cattle drives, **5:**106

Iqbal, Muhammad, **6:**229

Iran, **3:**20; European colonialism in, **5:**353; government, **6:**390–91; language, **6:**390; revolution, **6:**11; war with Iraq, **6:**11; women's roles, **5:**37

Iran hostage crisis, **6:**392

Iraq, **3:**20, 164; European control, free from, **6:**483; invasion of Kuwait, **6:**478; war with Iran, **6:**11. See also Islamic World (Middle Ages)

Ireland, **3:**235, 340; Dublin, founded by Vikings, **2:**99; towns founded by Vikings, **2:**99

Iron: China (Tang Dynasty), **2:**275, 280; England (17th & 18th Centuries), **4:**176; England (Victorian era), **5:**300; Europe (Middle Ages), **2:**124, 275, 276; Islamic World (Middle Ages), **2:**275; Italy (15th & 16th Centuries), **3:**99; Maya, **3:**351; New England, colonial, **4:**129; Vikings, **2:**100, 126

Iron Age, **1:**122, 371. See also Mesopotamia

Irons, electric, **6:**335

Ironworkers (Japan), **4:**409

Iroquois: confederation of tribes, **4:**348; New France, **4:**10; religious beliefs, **4:**469; social structure, **4:**372; tribal government, **4:**349; villages, **4:**332

Irrigation: Byzantium, **2:**130, 284; China (Tang Dynasty), **2:**127, 197; Inca, **3:**106; India (19th Century), **5:**14, 302; Islamic World (Middle Ages), **2:**282–83; Maya, **3:**102; Mesopotamia, **1:**75, 78, 79; Nubia, **1:**87

Irving, Washington, **5:**348

Isaac, Jorge, **5:**196

Isabel de Valois, **3:**211

Isabella, **3:**10, 176, 287, 288, 345

Isadore of Seville, **2:**169

Isherwood, Christopher, **6:**219

Ishmael, **2:**418, 424

Ishtar, **1:**471, 488, 510

Isidore of Seville, **2:**180–81

Isidoros of Miletus, **2:**285, 447

Isis, **1:**289, 430, 475, 476, 477

Isla Cerritos, **3:**7

Islam: Africa (20th Century), **6:**433, 601, 602; alcoholic beverages and, **3:**237, 245; **5:**252; charity, **6:**595; Christianity, relationship with, **6:**11; death, burial, and the afterlife, **3:**43; ethical behavior as part of, **2:**409; fasting, **6:**595; founding of, **2:**12, 417–25; **5:**16, 467–68; **6:**10; guilds, **3:**119; Hindu vs. Muslim feud in India, **6:**9, 10; India, Muslim conquest of, **6:**8–9; India (19th Century), **5:**466; Jews, relationship with, **2:**421; **6:**11; life cycles, **3:**30–31; Mongols and, **2:**429; monotheism, **3:**361; Ottoman Empire, **3:**65; pork and food restrictions, **2:**207–8; **3:**241, 245; **6:**316; prayers, **5:**454, 456, 468, 469; **6:**595; prophets and prophecy, **6:**594; rituals, exclusion from, **3:**30–31; Soviet Union, **6:**23, 597; views on women, religion, slaves, and war, **5:**494–96; women's dress, **5:**287. See also Five Pillars of Islam; *Hajj;* Muhammad; Qur'an (Koran); Sharia; Shi'ites

Islamic World (Middle Ages): abandonment of spouse, **2:**49–50; age of marriage, **2:**85–86; alcoholic beverages, **2:**283; archers, **2:**358; astronomy, **2:**147, 166; banks and banking, **2:**143–44; banquets, **2:**85; bathhouses, **2:**232; beds, **2:**273; board games, **2:**401; bride-price, **2:**47, 62; bubonic plague, **2:**85; camels, **2:**129, 142; carpentry, **2:**273; chairs, **2:**267, 273; chess, **2:**369; childbirth, **2:**423; children, **2:**84–86; circumcision, **2:**85; civil wars, **2:**357; clothing, **2:**243–45; coffee, **2:**219;

4:229; beans, 4:248; birth, social status, 4:366; blacksmiths, 4:127; blockhouses, 4:278; books, 4:213–14; bowing by women, 4:60; bows and arrows, 4:409, 424; boys' clothing, 4:294; bridges, 4:321; cards, 4:424; castles, 4:408; charcoal production, 4:127; childbirth, 4:230; child labor, 4:75, 126; children, 4:74–76, 423; chopsticks, 4:250; city commoners, 4:60–61, 75, 194, 249, 295, 378, 395; city life, 4:328–29, 336–38, 378; cleanliness, 4:219, 229; clothing, 4:495; contraception, 4:95–96; cooking methods, 4:248–50; coopers, 4:127; cosmetics, 4:312; cottage industries, 4:126; craftsmen, 4:60, 126–27, 377, 408–9; crickets, 4:423; crimes, 4:394–96; crops, 4:113–15; daimyo, 4:295, 322, 336–37, 357–59, 395–96; death, burial, and the afterlife, 4:86–88; death penalty, 4:395–96; dialects, 4:212; divination, 4:423; divorce, 4:40; dog shooting, 4:424; dowry, 4:39–40; drink, 4:263–65; drums, 4:455; education, 4:193–95, 512–15; elders, 4:359; emperors, 4:17–19; ethnic areas of cities, 4:328; family life, 4:379; ferries, 4:321; field hockey, 4:424; finance, 4:133; firemen, 4:152, 159–60; fish, 4:249; fishing, 4:126; flower festival, 4:439; food, 4:114, 146, 229, 248–50; footwear, 4:311; furnishings, 4:270–71; furniture, 4:278; futures commodity trading, 4:144; gambling, 4:422–23; games, 4:422–25; gardening, 4:278; geisha, 4:153, 160–61; girls' clothing, 4:310; government, 4:17, 96, 144–46, 345, 357–59; guilds, 4:146; guns, 4:409; hairstyles, 4:295, 296, 311–12; harvest festivals, 4:439; harvest of rice, 4:114–15; head of household, 4:86; health and medicine, 4:229–31; historical overview, 4:17–19; holidays and festivals, 4:437–40; homosexuality, 4:92–93, 96; horses, 4:321; hostages, daimyo "alternate attendance" system, 4:322–23, 336–37, 358; hot springs baths, 4:229; housing, 4:276–79, 378; humor, 4:213; industry, 4:126–28; infanticide, 4:74–75; jewelry, 4:311; Kansei Reforms, 4:19; kitchens, 4:278; Kyoho reforms, 4:17–18; lacquer, 4:127–28; language, 4:211–13; law, 4:378, 394; law enforcement, 4:385, 395; legumes, 4:248; literacy, 4:193–94; literature, 4:213–14; longbows, 4:409; magic and superstition, 4:423; map of Tokugawa Japan (1550–1853), 4:18; marriage, 4:38–40; martial arts, 4:410; material life, 4:237–38; meals, 4:249; men, 4:59–61; men's clothing, 4:294–96; merchants, 4:75, 145–46, 366–67; miso, 4:249; money, 4:144–45; morality, 4:456; mourning conventions, 4:87; moving restrictions, 4:322; music, 4:455; names of children, 4:75; new year's celebration, 4:438; oils, 4:249; old age, 4:86; outcasts, 4:378–79; paintings and drawings, 4:455–56; palanquins, 4:321; papermaking, 4:126–27; pawnbroking, 4:423; pets, 4:423; pharmacists, 4:230; philosophy, 4:59, 194–95, 377–78; physicians, 4:230; pilgrimages, 4:494–95; plays, 4:456–57; population, 4:336, 338, 377; pornography, 4:213; postal systems, 4:322; post stations, 4:322–23; pottery, 4:127; premarital sex, 4:38; preservation of food,

4:249; privy, 4:278; professions, 4:159–61; prostitution, 4:96–97; punishment, 4:385–86, 394–96; puppets, 4:457; regional governments, 4:357–59; religion, 4:419, 464–65, 476–79, 493–95; restaurants, 4:249; rice, 4:113–15, 248; rice festivals, 4:438; rice trade, 4:144–45; roads, 4:316, 322–23; roofs, 4:276–77; rural life and agriculture, 4:60, 377–78, 437–38; sake, 4:263–64; samurai, 4:61, 92, 193–95, 295–96, 310–11, 359, 377–78, 394–96, 408–9; sanctuaries, 4:493–94; "sending-back," 4:74; sentence structure, 4:212; servants, 4:153; sexuality, 4:92, 95–97; shamans, 4:478, 494; shoguns, 4:17–19, 357–58; shrines, 4:482, 493; silk production, 4:126; sleeping quarters, 4:277; social behavior of women, 4:60; social structure, 4:337, 377–79; soy sauce, 4:264; spies, 4:358; spring ritual, 4:438; star festival, 4:439; sumo wrestling, 4:424; superstitions, 4:87; sweet potatoes, 4:248; sword pulling, 4:410; swords, 4:408–10; tattoos, 4:152, 160; taxes, 4:17, 145, 394–95; tea, 4:256, 263; technology, 4:177–78; theater, 4:444, 456–57; thumb wrestling, 4:423; tofu, 4:248; toys, 4:76; trade, 4:144–46; travel and transportation, 4:315–16, 320–23; typhoon season, 4:439; undergarments, 4:311; upper class women, 4:61; uprisings, 4:394–95; urban life, 4:60; vegetables, 4:248; vernal equinox, 4:438; villages, 4:378, 394; walls of houses, 4:277; warfare, 4:408–10; waterwheels, 4:177; wealth, social status, 4:366; weapons, 4:408–10; wedding ceremony, 4:39; widows, 4:40; women, 4:59–61, 86; women's clothing, 4:302, 310–12; woodblock prints, 4:456; wrestling, 4:423. *See also* Peasants of Japan (17th & 18th Centuries)

Japan Socialist Party, 6:84

Japan (20th Century): acupuncture, 6:291; alcoholic beverages, 6:324, 330; Allied Occupation of, 6:494; apartments, 6:345; arranged marriages, 6:49; assassinations, 6:493, 600; attorneys, 6:431; automobile production and sales in U.S., 6:362, 363; banks and banking, 6:453; battle casualties, 6:493; beer, 6:330; bottled water, 6:330; censorship, 6:237; charity, 6:600; child care, 6:106; children, 6:88, 105–6, 430; communication, 6:258–59; Constitution, 6:399, 494, 567, 600; cooking methods, 2:205; 6:319–20; copyrights, 6:366; courts and judges, 6:400, 430–31; cremation, 6:600; crimes, 6:429–30; dating, 6:49; death, burial, and the afterlife, 6:599, 600; death penalty, 6:431; desserts, 6:320; discrimination, 6:140, 159–61; diseases, 6:291; drink, 6:324, 330–31; earthquakes, 6:345; economic life, 6:24; education, 6:106, 192, 196, 210–12, 400; energy drinks, 6:330; entertainment, 6:106; environment, 6:453; family life, 6:33, 48–50; feminism, 6:84; film, 6:512, 533–35; food, 6:319–20; furniture and furnishings, 6:346; golf, 6:508; government, 6:399–401; government workers, 6:83; health and medicine, 6:59, 290–93; Hiroshima, bombing of, 6:469, 493; historical overview, 6:24–25; hospitals, 6:291; housing, 6:345–46; insider trading, 6:400–401; Internet, 6:259; juvenile delinquency, 6:106; kinship, 6:401; law, 6:401, 429–31; life expectancy, 6:59, 291; lifetime employment, 6:123; literacy, 6:211; literature, 6:216, 236–39; long-term care insurance, 6:292; mail service, 6:259;

marriage, 6:49; mathematics, 6:192; men, 6:59–60; mobile telephones, 6:259; morality, 6:566–67; music, 6:554–57; Nagasaki, bombing of, 6:469, 493; newspapers, 6:259; old age, 6:292; parents, care of, 6:49; patents, 6:366; patrilineages, 6:48–49; Pearl Harbor, attack on, 6:468; poetry, 6:238–39; population, 6:49; prisons and prisoners, 6:431; public officials, 6:400; radio, 6:259; reform, 6:452–54; religion, 6:599–601; religious rituals, 6:600; religious shrines, 6:599; restaurants, 6:320; rice, 6:319; rural life and agriculture, 6:162, 176; salt, 6:320; science, 6:191–93; sex discrimination, 6:84; sexual harassment, 6:453; social structure, 6:48; soft drinks, 6:330; soup, 6:319, 320; space exploration, 6:192; sports, 6:508–9; suicide, 6:59, 60, 106, 211, 237; sumo, 6:508; Supreme Court, 6:430–31; technology, 6:349, 365–66; telephones, 6:259; television, 6:259; toys, 6:106; trials, 6:401; unemployment, 6:123; universities, 6:211; urban life, 6:162, 176–77; war, 6:492–94; windows, 6:346; women, 6:60, 83–85, 493, 494; women, work of, 6:49, 83–84, 453; work, 6:59, 111, 122–23

Jati, 1:86, 339

Javelins: Italy (15th & 16th Centuries), 3:315; Mesopotamia, 1:394; Spain (15th & 16th Centuries), 3:315, 320

Jaws (film), 6:528

Jazz Singer, The (film), 6:519

Jean, Bishop of Quebec, 4:503–4

Jean de Joinville, 2:479–81

Jefferson, Thomas, 5:6, 150, 151, 228, 343, 347–48; 6:564

Jefferson Airplane, 6:545

Jehovah's Witnesses in Holocaust, 6:406

Jemison, Mary, 4:434, 435

Jerkins, 3:226

Jerusalem, 3:65, 214; 5:146. *See also* Crusades (Middle Ages)

Jesuits: Brazil, 5:471; France (17th & 18th Centuries), 4:474; Latin America (19th Century), 5:470, 471; North American colonial frontier, 4:489; Spain (15th & 16th Centuries), 3:175, 210

Jesus Christ: art featuring, 3:340; death of, 3:379; divorce, views on, 3:381; Eucharist, 3:381; Puritanism, 4:480–81; Qur'an on, 2:468; Resurrection, 3:361–62, 395–96

Jesus Christ Superstar (musical), 6:580

Jesus movement (United States), 6:580

Jewelry: Australian Aboriginals, 1:315; Greece (ancient), 1:324; Inca, 3:234–35; India (19th Century), 5:286; Japan (17th & 18th Centuries), 4:311; Latin America (19th Century), 5:288, 289; Maya, 3:232, 351; Mesopotamia, 1:317; Native Americans (colonial frontier of North America), 4:449; Nubia, 1:312, 313; Rome (ancient), 1:326; Spain (15th & 16th Centuries), 3:114; Vikings, 2:100, 261. *See also* Gold jewelry

Jews: aid from Eleanor Roosevelt, 6:16; alcoholic beverages, 3:245; as American authors, 6:216, 223; Australia, colonial, 4:488; dance, 3:347; ecumenism and, 6:577–78; England (17th & 18th Centuries), 4:492; Evian Conference prior to World War II, 6:561–62; exclusion from rituals, 3:30–31; expulsion from European countries, 6:142–43; food, 3:241, 362; food restrictions, 2:207; ghetto life, 6:142; Greek spoken by, 3:165; guilds, 3:115, 119; Islam and, 6:11; Italy (15th &

Japan (17th & 18th Centuries), 4:322; Japan (20th Century), 6:259; seamen, 4:217

Mailer, Norman, 6:220–21

Mair, 5:37, 39

Maize: Australia, colonial, 4:106–7; Aztec, 3:104, 221, 237, 248; Inca, 3:2, 221, 237, 248–49; Latin America (19th Century), 5:133, 245, 246, 247; Maya, 3:100–102, 221, 237, 246; United States (Western Frontier), 5:230; Vikings, 2:126

Makar Sankranti, 5:415

Makeup. See Cosmetics

Makioka Sisters, The (Jun'ichirou), 6:237

Malaeska, the Indian Wife of the White Hunter (Stephens), 5:187

Malaria: England (15th & 16th Centuries), 3:189; Europe (15th & 16th Centuries), 3:166; India (19th Century), 5:253; India (20th Century), 6:287; Italy (15th & 16th Centuries), 3:196; New England, colonial, 4:88; United States (1940–59), 6:275

Malatesta family, 3:8

Malcolm X, 6:152, 448, 595

Male prostitution, 1:67–68

Malaria, 1:295

Maliki, 3:65

Malil, 3:262

Malintzin, 3:168

Mallorca, 3:161

Malls, shopping, 6:169–70

Malnutrition: England (17th & 18th Centuries), 4:225; Latin America (20th Century), 6:314; seamen, 4:234; United States (1920–39), 6:307; United States (1960–90), 6:313

Malpractice. See Medical malpractice

Malta Knights of Saint John, 3:276

Mama-Cocha, 3:376

Mamaconas, 3:72, 187, 390

Māui, 2:177–78, 469

Mama Ocllo, 5:417

Mama-Quilla, 3:376

Mamluks, 2:317–18, 319

Manahuatzin, 3:399

Manchu Dynasty, 5:453

Manco Capac, 3:109, 126, 282, 402–4; 5:417

Manco Inca, 3:23

Mandal Commission Report (India), 6:156

Mandamiento, 5:134

Mandarins, 2:296, 454

Mandel, Yelena, 6:159

Mandela, Nelson, 6:433

Mandelshtam, Osip, 6:233

Mande (17th & 18th Centuries), 4:153–54

Mandeville, Bernard, 4:143–44

Mandulis, 1:468

Manhattan Project, 6:184, 185, 469

Manic depression, 6:281

Manioc: Inca, 3:105; Maya, 3:246

Mannes, Marya, 6:97, 565

Man Nobody Knows, The (Barton), 6:572

Manorialism, 2:290, 291, 311

Manors and manor houses: England (15th & 16th Centuries), 3:253; Europe (Middle Ages), 2:123–24, 290, 291; Middle Ages, 2:301; Spain (15th & 16th Centuries), 3:95

Manslaughter, 3:302. See also Homicide

Mansour, 2:117, 118

Mantas: Aztec, 3:233; Maya, 3:231

Mantillas, 3:223, 227

Mantle, Mickey, 6:503

Mantua: Countess of, 3:229; Duke of, 3:339

Manturcalla, 3:391–92

Manductio Ad Ministerium (Mather), 4:214

Manufacturing industry: England (17th & 18th Centuries), 4:123–24; Europe (Middle Ages), 2:276; North American colonial frontier, 4:121–22

Manumission, 1:115

Manus marriage in Roman Empire, 1:48–49, 50

Manu Smriti, 1:338

Manzikert defeat of Byzantium (1071), 2:356

Mappa mundi, 1:220–21

Maps: Africa (18th Century), 4:15; Australia (1606–1818), 4:20; Aztec Empire, 3:12; Byzantine Empire, 2:18; China (19th Century), 5:12; China (Tang Dynasty) divided into three kingdoms (Wei, Shu, and Wu), 2:9; China under Tang dynasty, 2:8; Crusades, 2:14, 16; England and Wales (16th Century), 3:4; England (1789), 4:3; England (Victorian era), 5:9; Europe and Mediterranean (Middle Ages), 2:3; France (1789), 4:3; Greece (ancient), 1:7, 225; Inca Empire, 3:17; India (ancient), 1:12; India (19th Century), 5:15; Islamic World (Middle Ages), 2:13; Japan (1550–1853), 4:18; Latin America (19th Century), 5:18; Maya, 3:13; Mesopotamia, 1:2, 155, 220; Mongol conquests, 2:21; Oceania (Middle Ages), 2:24; oceanic trading routes (17th Century), 4:8; Ottoman Empire, 3:19; Paris (Middle Ages), 2:113; Proclamation Line of 1763, 4:11; Renaissance Italy, 3:9; Rome (ancient), 1:9; Spain (16th Century), 3:7; United States (19th Century), 5:5; United States (Western Frontier), 5:5; Vikings in the North, 2:6. See also Cartography

Maqlû, 1:525

Maquahuitl, 3:233

Marable, Manning, 6:153

Marabouts (17th & 18th Centuries), 4:347, 467

Maracatú, 5:416

Marathon, Battle of, 1:379

Marble, 3:99

Marcheses, 3:276

March on Washington, 1963, 6:447

Marcian (Byzantine emperor), 2:426

Marconi, Guglielmo, 6:241, 243

Marco Polo: on Mongols drinking koumiss, 2:221; trading journey to Mongols, 2:22, 94, 133, 140, 363; *Travels of Marco Polo*, 2:481–83

Marcus, Greil, 6:540–41

Marcy, Randolph, 5:488–90

Marduk, 1:456, 471, 472, 474

Mare Mount settlement, 4:441

Margaret (queen of England), 3:13

Mari, 1:140

María (Isaac), 5:196

Marianismo, 6:55, 75, 77

Marine Corps, 6:64

Marines (British Royal Navy), 4:365

Maris, Roger, 6:503

Marjoram, 4:223

Marketplaces: Byzantium, 2:106; China (Tang Dynasty), 2:101–3; Europe (Middle Ages), 2:98, 133; Greece (ancient), 1:97; Islamic World (Middle Ages), 2:104–5; Mesopotamia, 1:91

Marling, Karal Ann, 6:340

Marlowe, Christopher, 3:206, 208, 209, 342

Mármol, José, 5:197

Marquess of Queensberry, 5:403

Marquis and marchinesses: England (15th & 16th Centuries), 3:271; Italy (15th & 16th Centuries), 3:276; Spain (15th & 16th Centuries), 3:274

Marriage: Africa (17th & 18th Centuries), 4:30–32, 46–47; ancient world, 1:39–50; Australia, colonial, 4:32–33; Australian Aboriginals, 1:28; Aztec, 3:32, 49–51; Catholicism (Spain, Italy, England), 3:31, 380–81; China (19th Century), 5:447; China (Tang Dynasty), 2:45–47; England (15th & 16th Centuries), 3:33; England (17th & 18th Centuries), 4:35–38, 55; England (Victorian era), 5:27, 34, 64–65, 110, 352, 373, 462; Europe (Middle Ages), 2:41–43, 434; Greece (ancient), 1:44–47; Hindu, 6:590; Inca, 3:32, 53–54; India (ancient), 1:38; India (19th Century), 5:27, 39, 53, 286; India (20th Century), 6:32, 33, 46, 78, 104, 156, 590; Islamic World (Middle Ages), 2:39, 47–50; Islamic World (19th Century), 5:27, 37, 447; Italy (15th & 16th Centuries), 3:39–40, 61, 347; Japan (17th & 18th Centuries), 4:38–40; Japan (20th Century), 6:49; Latin America (20th Century), 6:43; love and (17th & 18th Centuries), 4:28; Maya, 3:45–46; Mesopotamia, 1:21, 22, 40–43; Middle Ages, 2:30, 39–50; Native Americans (colonial frontier of North America), 4:34; New England, colonial, 4:40–43, 62; New South Wales, 4:32; North American colonial frontier, 4:33–35; Ottoman Empire, 3:42–43, 65; Protestantism (England), 3:31; Rome (ancient), 1:36, 47–50, 69, 385; seamen, 4:43–45; 17th & 18th Centuries, 4:27–45; slavery, 5:27; slaves in colonial America, 4:42; Spain (15th & 16th Centuries), 3:35, 59; United States (1920–39), 6:35; United States (1960–90), 6:39; United States (Western Frontier), 5:27; Vikings, 2:43–45. See also Annulment of marriage; Brother-sister marriage; Dowry

Marriage contracts: China (Tang Dynasty), 2:45; Europe (Middle Ages), 2:41; Middle Ages, 2:40

Marriage of slaves: Mesopotamia, 1:110, 489; New Orleans, 5:28

Mars, 1:483

Marsden, Samuel, 4:486–87

Marshall, John, 5:366

Marshall, Thurgood, 6:442

Marshall Plan, 6:469

Martens, 5:122

Martial arts in Japan, 4:410

Martial games: England (15th & 16th Centuries), 3:331; Inca, 3:328; Italy (15th & 16th Centuries), 3:315, 321–22; Spain (15th & 16th Centuries), 3:315, 320

Martial sports in Europe (Middle Ages), 2:370

Martine, Arthur, 5:274

Martineau, Harriet, 5:63

Martín Fiero (Hernández), 5:196

Martín Rivas (Blest Gana), 5:197

Martyrs, Muslim, 2:457

Marx, Karl, 3:207, 360; 5:485–87

Marxism, 6:137

Mary (queen of Netherlands), 4:2

Mary I (queen of England), 3:15, 409

Marye, Etienne-Jules, 6:512

Maryland: government (17th & 18th Centuries), 4:350–51; slavery in, 5:86, 121

Mashkan-shapir, 1:91

Masia, 3:256

356, 387–89; wild animals, hunting of, **1:**259, 405, 416; wine, **1:**87, 259; women's clothing, **1:**312–13

Nuclear energy: Japan, **6:**192; United States (1960–90), **6:**364–65

Nuclear family, defined, **1:**21

Nuclear threat, **6:**40, 183. *See also* Cold War

Nuclear weapons: invention of, **6:**183, 184; United States (1939–45), **6:**468–69, 493

Nudity: 15th & 16th Centuries, **3:**223; Greek art, **1:**237–38. *See also* Sexuality

Nullification crisis (United States), **5:**313–14, 316

Numbers: Arabic numerals, **2:**165; Aztec, **3:**85, 140, 151; England (15th & 16th Centuries), **3:**160; Maya, **3:**136–37, 200–202; Mesopotamia, **1:**173, 218; Roman numerals, **2:**165

Numina, **1:**454–55

Nun, **1:**475

Nunavut Territory: creation and government of, **6:**403; land claims agreement (1993), **6:**620–22

Nuncheon, **2:**201

Núñez, Rafael, **5:**341

Nuns: Buddhism, **2:**432; Civil War hospitals, **5:**201; convents (Byzantium), **2:**64; Europe (Middle Ages), **2:**53–54, 258, 434–35; Latin America (20th Century), **6:**591–92; Middle Ages, **2:**51

Nur al-Din, **2:**359

Nuremberg Trials, **6:**404, 410–12

Nurses: England (Victorian era), **5:**110; Soviet Union, **6:**290; World War I, **6:**61–62

Nursing homes, **6:**383

Nut (Egyptian goddess), **1:**475, 476

Nutrition: development of field of, **6:**302–3; United States (1920–39), **6:**307–8; United States (1960–90), **6:**310–11, 312

Nuts: Africa (17th & 18th Centuries), **4:**240; Byzantium, **2:**209; China (Tang Dynasty), **2:**204, 206; Greece (ancient), **1:**255; India (19th Century), **5:**53–54, 244; Vikings, **2:**203

Nuzi: women's role, **1:**30–31. *See also* Mesopotamia

Nyamakala, **4:**154

Nye, David E., **6:**358–59

Oath of the Horatii, The (David), **4:**454

Oaxaca, Valley of, **3:**3

Oaxacan Civilization, **3:**3

Obelisks (Mesopotamia), **1:**231

Observation and experimentation: Australian Aboriginals, **1:**229; China (Tang Dynasty), **2:**164; Europe in Middle ages, **2:**161; Holocaust victims, **6:**409, 410; Islamic World (Middle Ages), **2:**167

Obstetrics. *See* Childbirth

Oca, **3:**105

Occupations. *See* Professions and occupations

Oceanic exploration and travel: England (17th & 18th Centuries), **4:**7–9; map (17th Century), **4:**8; 17th & 18th Centuries, **4:**1–2, 7, 315

Ocelotl, **3:**233

Ochpaniztli, **3:**69, 186

O'Connor, Flannery, **6:**221

O'Connor, Sandra Day, **6:**74

Ocopa, **5:**245

Octavian, **1:**10. *See also* Augustus Caesar

Odin, **2:**399, 412, 413–14

Odoric of Pordenone, Friar, **2:**266

Odyssey: on death, burial, and the afterlife, **1:**520; educational role of, **1:**188; on magic, **1:**533; on money, **1:**134; on slavery, **1:**111, 112; stories of, **1:**200, 481; on travel and transportation, **1:**161; on women, **1:**33–34

Oedipus the King (Sophocles), **1:**200

Office of Economic Opportunity, **6:**381

Officers. *See* Military officers; Naval officers

Office work, **6:**117

Ogden, Peter Skene, **5:**47, 49

Oghul Qaimish, **2:**65, 246

Ögödei, **2:**221, 246, 343, 363, 428

OGPU (Unified State Political Administration), **6:**426

Oil: Japan (17th & 18th Centuries), **4:**249; lighting in Spain (15th & 16th Centuries), **3:**256; Nubia, **1:**259. *See also* Olive trees and olive oil

Okitsuga, Tanuma, **4:**18

Olaf Sigurdson (Viking king), **2:**7

Olaf Skotkonung (Viking king), **2:**137, 415

Olaf Tryggvason (Viking king), **2:**137, 279, 374, 397, 415

Old age: China (Tang Dynasty), **2:**87, 90–92; England (17th & 18th Centuries), **4:**84; Europe (Middle Ages), **2:**87, 88–89, 183; Greece (ancient), **1:**297; India (20th Century), **6:**47, 58; Inuit, **6:**51; Japan (17th & 18th Centuries), **4:**86, 359; Japan (20th Century), **6:**292; life at sea (17th & 18th Centuries), **4:**89–92; medical care (United States 1960–90), **6:**382–83; Mesopotamia, **1:**287; Middle Ages, **2:**86–92; New England, colonial, **4:**88–89; North American colonial frontier, **4:**82–83; Rome (ancient), **1:**297; 17th & 18th Centuries, **4:**80–92; Vikings, **2:**87, 89–90

Old Bailey, **5:**336

Old English, **3:**159

Old Jules (Sandoz), **5:**31–32

Oligarchy in India, **1:**353

Oliphant, Margaret, **5:**191

Oliver Twist (Dickens), **5:**181, 185, 190

Olive trees and olive oil: Byzantium, **2:**130, 208, 284; Greece (ancient), **1:**83, 144, 255, 440; Islamic World (Middle Ages), **2:**206; Italy (15th & 16th Centuries), **3:**243; Rome (ancient), **1:**85, 99, 256

Ollamaliztli, **3:**315–16, 326

Ollo podrida, **3:**241

Olluca, **5:**246

Olmec Civilization, **3:**3

Olmstead, Frederick Law, **5:**421

Olmstead v. U.S. (1927), **6:**416

Olympic Games: Africa (20th Century), **6:**510; England (Victorian era), **5:**402–3; Europe (20th Century), **6:**499; Greece (ancient), **1:**6, 63, 66, 211, 381, 411–13, 479; reinitiated in 1896, **6:**498; South Africa ban, **6:**511; 20th Century, **6:**498; United States (1960–90), **6:**506–7

Omecihuatl, **3:**373

Omens: ancient world, **1:**524–25; Aztec, **3:**218, 354; China (Tang Dynasty), **2:**164; Greece (ancient), **1:**379; Inca, **3:**393; Mesopotamia, **1:**272, 285, 436, 526–28; Polynesia, **2:**364, 365. *See also* Diviners; Entrails, reading of

Ometecuhtli, **3:**373

Ometeotl, **3:**341, 354, 373–74

Omeyocan, **3:**139, 373

"On Being Brought from Africa to America" (Wheatley), **4:**215

One Day in the Life of Ivan Denisovich (Solzhenitsyn), **6:**234

One Flew over the Cuckoo's Nest (film), **6:**281, 528

One Hundred Days of Reform of 1898 (China), **5:**324

Ongghot, **2:**428

Only Yesterday (Lewis), **6:**12

On the Origin of Species by Means of Natural Selection (Darwin), **5:**154

Opera: Latin America (19th Century), **5:**426; New York Opera Association, **6:**547

Opium: China (19th Century), **5:**131, 375–76; England (Victorian era), **5:**207; India (19th Century), **5:**54, 442; Latin America (19th Century), **5:**246

Opium War: causes of, **5:**375; Chinese defeat in, **5:**323; effects of, **5:**130; foreign influence resulting from, **5:**176; historical overview, **5:**13; start of, **5:**132, 355; Taiping Rebellion resulting from, **5:**452

Oppenheimer, J. Robert, **6:**184, 185–86

Oracle of Pachacamac, **3:**392

Oracles: ancient world, **1:**485; Greece (ancient), **1:**493–94; Mesopotamia, **1:**530

Oral tradition: Australian Aboriginals, **1:**192; Europe (Middle Ages), **2:**169; Middle Ages, **2:**145–46, 167; Polynesia, **2:**23, 25, 176; Vikings, **2:**172

Oratory (ancient Rome), **1:**191, 203, 205

Orchestras: Latin America (19th Century), **5:**427; United States (1920–39), **6:**245

Ordeal by Slander (Lattimore), **6:**376

Ordeals to determine innocence/guilt: Europe (Middle Ages), **2:**327; Vikings, **2:**330

Order of Santo Stefano, **3:**276

Ordinary seamen on merchant vessels (17th & 18th Centuries), **4:**363

Oregon Trail, **5:**6, 487–88

Oresme, Nicole, **2:**161

Oresteia, **1:**200–201

Orfeo, **3:**213

Organically grown food, **6:**312

Organized crime (Soviet Union), **6:**430

Organized labor: Latin America (19th Century), **5:**326. *See also* Labor unions

Organ transplants, **6:**277

Orhan, **3:**180

Oriental Acquaintance (DeForest), **5:**188

Origen, **2:**70, 76

Orisha, **4:**466

Orlando furioso (Ariosto), **3:**206, 213

Orlando inamorato (Boiardo), **3:**206, 213

Orphanages (England), **5:**35, 389

Orphics, **1:**520

Ortaoyuno, **3:**350

Ortega, Aniceto, **5:**426

Ortenberg, David, **6:**158

Orthodox Church. *See* Greek Orthodox Church; Russian Orthodox Church

Osaka (17th & 18th Centuries), **4:**144–45, 337

Osamu, Dazai, **6:**237

Oshogatsu, **4:**438

Osiris: death of, **1:**289; description of, **1:**476; family of, **1:**475; as god of the dead, **1:**476, 507, 512; Set's feud with, **1:**471

Osman, **3:**10

Ostia, **1:**147–48

Ostraka, **1:**178–79, 188

Ostrogothic kingdom, **2:**2

Other America, The (Harrington), **6:**120, 129, 380

Otogi-zoshi, **4:**213

Otomies, **3:**5

Otranto, **3:**12

United States (1850–65)

ABOUT THE
CONTRIBUTORS

General Editor

Joyce E. Salisbury is Frankenthal Professor of History at University of Wisconsin–Green Bay. She has a doctorate in medieval history from Rutgers University. Professor Salisbury is an award-winning teacher: she was named CASE (Council for Advancement and Support of Education) Professor of the Year for Wisconsin in 1991 and has brought her concern for pedagogy to this encyclopedia. Professor Salisbury has written or edited more than 10 books, including the award-winning *Perpetua's Passion: Death and Memory of a Young Roman Woman*, *The Beast Within: Animals in the Middle Ages*, and *The West in the World*, a textbook on western civilization.

Volume Editor

Lawrence Morris received his Ph.D. from Harvard University in 2002 and has taught English literature and history at a variety of institutions, including Harvard, University of Wisconsin–Green Bay, and Fitzwilliam College (Cambridge University). He has received a number of academic awards and fellowships, including a Packard Fellowship and a Frank Knox Memorial Traveling Fellowship. Dr. Morris is currently writing about the relationship between truth and literary fiction in the religious writing of the medieval British Isles.

Additional Contributors

Brian Ulrich, University of Wisconsin–Madison
Paula Rentmeester, University of Wisconsin–Green Bay

We also acknowledge the following authors of Greenwood Publishing's "Daily Life through History" series, whose books contributed much to entries in the current volume:

James M. Anderson, *Daily Life during the Spanish Inquisition*, 2002.
Davíd Carrasco, with Scott Sessions, *Daily Life of the Aztecs: People of the Sun and Earth*, 1998.
Elizabeth S. Cohen and Thomas V. Cohen, *Daily Life in Renaissance Italy*, 2001.
Michael A. Malpass, *Daily Life in the Inca Empire*, 1996.
Robert J. Sharer, *Daily Life in Maya Civilization*, 1996.
Jeffrey L. Singman, *Daily Life in Elizabethan England*, 1995.